The Palgrave Handbook of Ethnicity

Steven Ratuva
Editor

The Palgrave Handbook of Ethnicity

Volume 2

With 46 Figures and 57 Tables

Editor
Steven Ratuva
Department of Anthropology and Sociology
University of Canterbury
Christchurch, New Zealand

Macmillan Brown Centre for Pacific Studies
University of Canterbury
Christchurch, New Zealand

ISBN 978-981-13-2897-8   ISBN 978-981-13-2898-5 (eBook)
ISBN 978-981-13-2899-2 (print and electronic bundle)
https://doi.org/10.1007/978-981-13-2898-5

© Springer Nature Singapore Pte Ltd. 2019, corrected publication 2020
This work is subject to copyright. All rights are solely and exclusively licensed by the Publisher, whether the whole or part of the material is concerned, specifically the rights of translation, reprinting, reuse of illustrations, recitation, broadcasting, reproduction on microfilms or in any other physical way, and transmission or information storage and retrieval, electronic adaptation, computer software, or by similar or dissimilar methodology now known or hereafter developed.
The use of general descriptive names, registered names, trademarks, service marks, etc. in this publication does not imply, even in the absence of a specific statement, that such names are exempt from the relevant protective laws and regulations and therefore free for general use.
The publisher, the authors, and the editors are safe to assume that the advice and information in this book are believed to be true and accurate at the date of publication. Neither the publisher nor the authors or the editors give a warranty, express or implied, with respect to the material contained herein or for any errors or omissions that may have been made. The publisher remains neutral with regard to jurisdictional claims in published maps and institutional affiliations.

This Palgrave Macmillan imprint is published by the registered company Springer Nature Singapore Pte Ltd.
The registered company address is: 152 Beach Road, #21-01/04 Gateway East, Singapore 189721, Singapore

Preface

Since the end of the cold war, the world has seen an unprecedented multimodal transformation involving the complex interplay of various forces such as globalization and nationalism; the resurgence of extreme right and the unrelenting response from the left; the consolidation of neoliberal hegemony and creation of conditions for its own crisis; the rise of authoritarian leadership and the widespread democratic reactions; the popularization of the social media and the declaration of cyber wars; and the rise of China and how this poses a threat to US hegemony. A salient feature of many of these is the multiple expressions of ethnicity as a factor in shaping geopolitical, socioeconomic, and sociocultural relations. The explosion of ethno-nationalist conflicts and religious tension; the resurgence and electoral mainstreaming of ultra-right political groups with racial supremacist ideals; the widespread expressions of extremist Islamic groups; the anti-immigration policies of President Trump and various European states; the use of the cyberspace as an arena for racial vilification; the rise of extremist and terroristic violence; and the fluid nature of ethnic relations are just some of the manifestations of the new transformation. These have justifiably inspired a surge in interest in research and discourses around ethnicity.

Commissioned by Palgrave Macmillan, this comprehensive work on global ethnicity – which spans diverse national, political, cultural, and ideological boundaries, schools of thought, and methodological approaches – is a result of an exhaustive international search for the right experts, mobilization of a wide range of resources, writing, editing, reviewing, and production over 3 years. With 102 chapters (and more than 90 authors from around the world), this was a mammoth task, which involved the collective synergies of the editor-in-chief, section editors, chapter authors, the Palgrave editorial team, and the production team. It is a great example of transnational cooperation, innovative communication, systematic networking, and durable patience. At a time when academia is obsessed with the fetishization of individual output, as a result of the pervading audit and metric culture wrought by neoliberal reforms, a collaborative interdisciplinary and transnational effort of this scope and magnitude is a rarity. This is why all those involved in this mega project deserve whole-hearted congratulations.

The different parts and individual themes of the chapters are connected in a complex web of historical, intellectual, sociocultural, and political narratives and are meant to converse with each other using different contextual yet familiar discourses. Ostensibly, while they encapsulate different schools of thought and disciplinary traditions, they share a common thread of optimism and hope of expanding the horizons of knowledge of humanity and contributing to debates and discussions about creating a better world.

Ethnicity is not an easy subject to deal with because of its intersectional relationship with a host of factors including identity, inequality, conflict, religion, economic distribution, class, politics, and other aspects of everyday life. History is littered with the residues of ethnicity's connection with wars, mass killings, terrorism, poverty, and discrimination. History is also blessed with moments of interethnic embracement, multicultural engagements, and collective voices of humanity crying for justice and yearning for equality against the forces of discrimination, abuse, and oppression. These three volumes echo the multiple sentiments of history and capture some of the moments of human frailty and strength, human fiasco and fortitude, human retardation and progress, manifested in the different corners of the globe.

Some chapters are theoretical and some are based on empirical case studies and cover more than 70 countries around the world. Due to the massive size of the undertaking and the limited time available for its completion, the volumes are not able to cover all the countries in the world. Nevertheless, the existing chapters provide a wealth of discourses, experiences, reflections, and analysis, which would no doubt enrich our understanding of ethnicity as complex developments in our contemporary world unfold over time. The volumes are meant to inspire further debate and research and not meant to provide the panacea for global ethnic utopia. They are meant for a wide range of interests including scholars and researchers, policy makers, political leaders, corporate personnel, international agencies, peacebuilders, educators, security community, civil society organizations, and the public at large. This diversity reflects the underlying normative sentiments of inclusivity, accessibility, (in)formativeness, and enrichment.

Some chapters provide practical solutions to problems, while some provide abstract analyses of complex dynamics to unpack deeper and latent manifestations of social realities. While some are concerned with the global context, some revolve around geopolitical and geocultural regions, and some are focused on national and even local situation. These multiple layers of narratives are interconnected and provide intellectual enrichment for each other. The volumes do not pretend to provide definitive and conclusive analysis of ethnic issues that enshroud our times, but rather speak to them and raise important issues that need closer and serious scrutiny with the ambitious goal and sincere hope of making the world a better place for humanity.

Department of Anthropology and Sociology Steven Ratuva
University of Canterbury Editor
Christchurch, New Zealand

Macmillan Brown Centre for Pacific Studies
University of Canterbury
Christchurch, New Zealand

Contents

Volume 1

1   Exploring Global Ethnicity: A Broad Sociological Synopsis   1
Steven Ratuva

Part I   Nexus Between Ethnicity and Identity   27

2   Ethno-cultural Symbolism and Group Identity   29
Elya Tzaneva

3   Cultural Socialization and Ethnic Consciousness   49
Sara N. Amin

4   Historical Memory and Ethnic Myths   65
Cindy Zeiher

5   Indian Identity in South Africa   77
Kathryn Pillay

6   The State and Minority Nationalities (Ethnic Groups) in
China   93
Roland Boer

7   Ethnic Blindness in Ethnically Divided Society: Implications
for Ethnic Relations in Fiji   109
Romitesh Kant

8   Post-Arab Spring: The Arab World Between the Dilemma of
the Nation-State and the Rise of Identity Conflicts   131
Hassanein Ali

Part II   The State, Society, and Ethnopolitics   147

9   The Significance of Ethno-politics in Modern States
and Society   149
Joseph R. Rudolph

10	**Religion and Political Mobilization** Jóhanna K. Birnir and Henry D. Overos	169
11	**Foreign Military Occupations and Ethnicity** Radomir Compel	187
12	**Ethnic Politics and Global Justice** Geoff Pfeifer	209
13	**Shared Citizenship and Sovereignty: The Case of the Cook Islands' and Niue's Relationship with New Zealand** Zbigniew Dumieński	221
14	**State Hegemony and Ethnicity: Fiji's Problematic Colonial Past** Sanjay Ramesh	247
15	**Ethnicity and Politics in Kenya** Jacob Mwathi Mati	265
16	**Ethno-politics in the People's Republic of China** Matthew Hoddie	283
17	**Ethnicity and Cultural Rights in Tibet** Jianxia Lin	301
18	**Volga Tatars: Continuing Resilience in the Age of Uncertainty** Renat Shaykhutdinov	315
19	**Identity and Conflict in Northern Ireland** Cathal McManus	331
20	**Immigration Policy and Left-Right Politics in Western Europe** Trevor J. Allen and Misty Knight-Finley	347
21	**Lost in Europe: Roma and the Search for Political Legitimacy** Neil Cruickshank	363
Part III	**Stereotypes and Prejudices**	**381**
22	**Race and Racism: Some Salient Issues** Vijay Naidu	383
23	**Media and Stereotypes** Tara Ross	397
24	**Japanese Representation in Philippine Media** Karl Ian Uy Cheng Chua	415

| 25 | Racism in Colonial Zimbabwe | 429 |

Alois S. Mlambo

| 26 | Ethnic Riots in United Kingdom in 2001 | 447 |

Paul Bagguley and Yasmin Hussain

| 27 | Racialized Identity Under Apartheid in South Africa | 463 |

Suryakanthie Chetty

| 28 | Racism and Stereotypes | 483 |

Paul Spoonley

| 29 | Discussing Contemporary Racial Justice in Academic Spaces: Minimizing Epistemic Exploitation While Neutralizing White Fragility | 499 |

Adele Norris

| 30 | Ethnicity, Race, and Black People in Europe | 513 |

Stephen Small

Volume 2

| Part IV | Ethno-nationalism and Power | 535 |

| 31 | Contemporary Ethnic Politics and Violence | 539 |

Adis Maksic

| 32 | Ethnic Conflict and Militias | 559 |

Andrew Thomson

| 33 | Evolution of Palestinian Civil Society and the Role of Nationalism, Occupation, and Religion | 577 |

Yaser Alashqar

| 34 | Ethno-nationalism and Political Conflict in Bosnia (Europe) | 595 |

Aleksandra Zdeb

| 35 | Ethnic Conflicts and Peace-Building | 613 |

Sergio Luiz Cruz Aguilar

| 36 | Ethnicity and Violence in Sri Lanka: An Ethnohistorical Narrative | 633 |

Premakumara de Silva, Farzana Haniffa, and Rohan Bastin

| 37 | Ethno-communal Conflict in Sudan and South Sudan | 655 |

Johan Brosché

| 38 | Patterns and Drivers of Communal Conflict in Kenya | 675 |

Emma Elfversson

39	Elites in Between Ethnic Mongolians and the Han in China Chelegeer	695
40	Ethnicity and Cultural Wounding: Ethnic Conflict, Loss of Home, and the Drive to Return Amanda Kearney	715
41	Constitutional Features of Presidential Elections and the Failure of Cross-ethnic Coalitions to Institutionalize M. Bashir Mobasher	735
42	The Making of a Mobile Caliphate State in the African Sahel Hamdy Hassan	755
43	Consequences of Globalization for the Middle East Political Geography Mostafa Entezarulmahdy	773
44	National Imaginary, Ethnic Plurality, and State Formation in Indonesia Paul J. Carnegie	791
45	Ethno-nationalism and Ethnic Dynamics in Trinidad and Tobago: Toward Designing an Inclusivist Form of Governance Ralph Premdas	809
46	Islam in Trinidad Nasser Mustapha	825

Part V Indigeneity, Gender, and Sexuality **847**

47	Indigenous Rights and Neoliberalism in Latin America Jeffrey A. Gardner and Patricia Richards	849
48	Settler Colonialism and Biculturalism in Aotearoa/New Zealand Jessica Terruhn	867
49	Nuclear Testing and Racism in the Pacific Islands Nic Maclellan	885
50	Nagas Identity and Nationalism: Indigenous Movement of the Zeliangrong Nagas in the North East India Aphun Kamei	907
51	Reclaiming Hawaiian Sovereignty Keakaokawai Varner Hemi	927

52	**Perpetual Exclusion and Second-Order Minorities in Theaters of Civil Wars** Jovanie Camacho Espesor	967
53	**Indigenous Australian Identity in Colonial and Postcolonial Contexts** Michael Davis	993
54	**China: Modernization, Development, and Ethnic Unrest in Xinjiang** Kate Hannan	1011
55	**Ethnicity and Class Nexus: A Philosophical Approach** Rodrigo Luiz Cunha Gonsalves	1033
56	**Islamic Identity and Sexuality in Indonesia** Sharyn Graham Davies	1063
57	**LGBT and Ethnicity** Arjun Rajkhowa	1077
58	**Migration and Managing Manhood: Congolese Migrant Men in South Africa** Joseph Rudigi Rukema and Beatrice Umubyeyi	1111
59	**Race and Sexuality: Colonial Ghosts and Contemporary Orientalisms** Monique Mulholland	1129

Part VI Globalization and Diaspora **1147**

60	**Diaspora as Transnational Actors: Globalization and the Role of Ethnic Memory** Masaki Kataoka	1149
61	**Global Chinese Diaspora** Zhifang Song	1167
62	**Greek Identity in Australia** Rebecca Fanany and Maria-Irini Avgoulas	1185
63	**Italian Identity in the United States** Stefano Luconi	1203
64	**Faamatai: A Globalized Pacific Identity** Melani Anae	1223
65	**Migrant Illegalization and Minoritized Populations** Paloma E. Villegas and Francisco J. Villegas	1247

66	Indian Diaspora in New Zealand .... 1265 Todd Nachowitz
67	Ethnic Migrants and Casinos in Singapore and Macau .... 1313 Juan Zhang
68	Ethnic Minorities and Criminalization of Immigration Policies in the United States .... 1331 Felicia Arriaga
69	Diaspora and Ethnic Contestation in Guyana .... 1351 Ralph Premdas and Bishnu Ragoonath

Volume 3

Part VII Ethnic Relations and Policy Responses 1363

70	Role of Crown Health Policy in Entrenched Health Inequities in Aotearoa, New Zealand .... 1365 Sarah Herbert, Heather Came, Tim McCreanor, and Emmanuel Badu
71	Aboriginal and Torres Strait Islander Secondary Students' Experiences of Racism .... 1383 Gawaian Bodkin-Andrews, Treena Clark, and Shannon Foster
72	Stereotypes of Minorities and Education .... 1407 Jean M. Allen and Melinda Webber
73	Rural Farmer Empowerment Through Organic Food Exports: Lessons from Uganda and Ghana .... 1427 Kristen Lyons
74	Local Peacebuilding After Communal Violence .... 1445 Birgit Bräuchler
75	Cultural Identity and Textbooks in Japan: Japanese Ethnic and Cultural Nationalism in Middle-School History Textbooks ..... 1465 Ryota Nishino
76	Asian Americans and the Affirmative Action Debate in the United States .... 1483 Mitchell James Chang
77	Affirmative Action: Its Nature and Dynamics .... 1501 Ralph Premdas
78	Negotiating Ethnic Conflict in Deeply Divided Societies: Political Bargaining and Power Sharing as Institutional Strategies ...... 1515 Madhushree Sekher, Mansi Awasthi, Allen Thomas, Rajesh Kumar, and Subhankar Nayak

Part VIII Ethnic Cleansing and Genocide 1537

79 The Threat of Genocide: Understanding and Preventing the
    "Crime of Crimes" 1539
    Eyal Mayroz

80 Separation Versus Reunification: Institutional Stagnation and
    Conflict Between Iraq and Kurdistan Region 1555
    Nyaz N. Noori

81 Ethnic Cleansing of the Rohingya People 1575
    Nasir Uddin

82 Displaced Minorities: The Wayuu and Miskito People 1593
    Christian Cwik

83 Ethnic Conflict and Genocide in Rwanda 1611
    Wendy Lambourne

Part IX Ethnicity, Migration, and Labor 1643

84 Policing Ethnic Minorities: Disentangling a Landscape of
    Conceptual and Practice Tensions 1647
    Isabelle Bartkowiak-Théron and Nicole L. Asquith

85 Romanian Identity and Immigration in Europe 1671
    Remus Gabriel Anghel, Stefánia Toma, and László Fosztó

86 Refugee Protection and Settlement Policy in New Zealand 1689
    Louise Humpage

87 Indian Indentured Laborers in the Caribbean 1711
    Sherry-Ann Singh

88 New Middle-Class Labor Migrants 1729
    Sam Scott

89 Slavery, Health, and Epidemics in Mauritius 1721–1860 1749
    Sadasivam Jaganada Reddi and Sheetal Sheena Sookrajowa

90 The Legacy of Indentured Labor 1767
    Kathleen Harrington-Watt

91 Global Capitalism and Cheap Labor: The Case of Indenture ... 1795
    Brinsley Samaroo

92 United Nations Migrant Workers Convention 1813
    Sheetal Sheena Sookrajowa and Antoine Pécoud

93	The Rhetoric of Hungarian Premier Victor Orban: Inside X Outside in the Context of Immigration Crisis .... Bruno Mendelski	1829
94	Different Legacies, Common Pressures, and Converging Institutions: The Politics of Muslim Integration in Austria and Germany .... Ryosuke Amiya-Nakada	1853
95	Intended Illegal Infiltration or Compelled Migration: Debates on Settlements of Rohingya Muslims in India .... Sangit Kumar Ragi	1877
96	Indonesia and ASEAN Responses on Rohingya Refugees ...... Badrus Sholeh	1891

Part X Cultural Celebration and Resistance **1907**

97	Rewriting the World: Pacific People, Media, and Cultural Resistance .... Sereana Naepi and Sam Manuela	1909
98	Kava and Ethno-cultural Identity in Oceania .... S. Apo Aporosa	1923
99	Museums and Identity: Celebrating Diversity in an Ethnically Diverse World .... Tarisi Vunidilo	1939
100	Artistic Expressions and Ethno-cultural Identity: A Case Study of Acehnese Body Percussion in Indonesia .... Murtala Murtala, Alfira O'Sullivan, and Paul H. Mason	1957
101	Ethnic Film in South Africa: History, Meaning, and Change ... Gairoonisa Paleker	1977
102	Multiculturalism and Citizenship in the Netherlands .... Igor Boog	1993

Correction to: Diaspora and Ethnic Contestation in Guyana C1

Index 2015

About the Editor

Steven Ratuva
Department of Anthropology and Sociology
University of Canterbury
Christchurch, New Zealand

Macmillan Brown Centre for Pacific Studies
University of Canterbury
Christchurch, New Zealand

Steven Ratuva is Director of the Macmillan Brown Center for Pacific Studies and Professor in the Department of Anthropology and Sociology at the University of Canterbury. He was Fulbright Professor at UCLA, Duke University, and Georgetown University and currently Chair of the International Political Science Association Research Committee on Security, Conflict, and Democratization. With a Ph.D. from the Institute of Development Studies at the University of Sussex, Ratuva is an interdisciplinary scholar who has written or edited a number of books and published numerous papers on a range of issues including ethnicity, security, affirmative action, indigenous intellectual property, geopolitical strategies, social protection, militarization, ethno-nationalism, development, peace, and neoliberalism. He has been a consultant and advisor for a number of international organizations such as the UNDP, International Labour Organization, International Institute for Democracy and Electoral Assistance, Commonwealth Secretariat, and the Asian Development Bank, and has worked in a number of universities around the world including in Australia, USA, New Zealand, Fiji, and UK.

About the Section Editors

Steven Ratuva
Department of Anthropology and Sociology
University of Canterbury
Christchurch, New Zealand

Macmillan Brown Centre for Pacific Studies
University of Canterbury
Christchurch, New Zealand

Steven Ratuva is Director of the Macmillan Brown Center for Pacific Studies and Professor in the Department of Anthropology and Sociology at the University of Canterbury. He was Fulbright Professor at UCLA, Duke University, and Georgetown University and currently Chair of the International Political Science Association Research Committee on Security, Conflict, and Democratization. With a Ph.D. from the Institute of Development Studies at the University of Sussex, Ratuva is an interdisciplinary scholar who has written or edited a number of books and published numerous papers on a range of issues including ethnicity, security, affirmative action, indigenous intellectual property, geopolitical strategies, social protection, militarization, ethno-nationalism, development, peace, and neoliberalism. He has been a consultant and advisor for a number of international organizations such as the UNDP, International Labour Organization, International Institute for Democracy and Electoral Assistance, Commonwealth Secretariat, and the Asian Development Bank, and has worked in a number of universities around the world including in Australia, USA, New Zealand, Fiji, and UK.

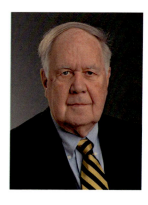

Joseph R. Rudolph
Department of Political Science
Towson University
Baltimore, MA, USA

Joseph R. Rudolph, Jr. received his Ph.D. from the University of Virginia and is currently a Professor in the Department of Political Science at Towson University (Baltimore, Maryland, USA). He has served as a Fulbright appointee to Czechoslovakia (1991–1992) and Kosovo (2011–2012), and has published in the field of ethnic and nationalist politics for more than 30 years. Since 1997, he has also frequently been a part of the democratization operations of the Organization for Security and Cooperation in Europe (OSCE) in areas of the former Yugoslavia and former Soviet Union. His Palgrave publication *Politics and Ethnicity: A Comparative* Study (2006) is now in its second printing. More recent work includes compiling and contributing to *The Encyclopedia of Modern Ethnic Conflicts* (editor, 2nd edition, 2015), and *From Mediation to Nation Building: Third Parties and the Management of Communal Conflict* (coeditor, 2013).

Vijay Naidu
University of the South Pacific
Suva, Fiji

Vijay Naidu completed his undergraduate and M.A. studies at the University of the South Pacific in Fiji, and his doctoral degree at the University of Sussex in the UK. He has been Professor and Director of Development Studies in the School of Government, Development, and International Affairs at the University of the South Pacific (USP), and the School of Geography, Environment, and Earth Sciences at the Victoria University of Wellington. He is a Pacific development scholar and has written on aid, electoral politics, ethnicity, higher education, land tenure, migration, urbanization, social exclusion, the state, poverty and social protection, informal settlements, human security, and MDGs.

About the Section Editors

Paul J. Carnegie
Institute of Asian Studies
Universiti Brunei Darussalam
Bandar Seri Begawan, Brunei Darussalam

Paul J. Carnegie is Associate Professor of Politics and International Relations at the Institute of Asian Studies, Universiti Brunei Darussalam and the former Director of the Postgraduate Governance Program at the University of the South Pacific. He has research specializations in comparative democratization, human security, and localized responses to militant extremism in Southeast Asia, MENA, and the Asia Pacific with a particular focus on Indonesia. Paul has published widely in his fields including the monograph *The Road from Authoritarianism to Democratization in Indonesia* (Palgrave Macmillan) and the coedited volume *Human Insecurities in Southeast Asia* (Springer). He has been awarded multiple research grants with related output in leading international journals including *Pacific Affairs*, *Australian Journal of Politics and History*, the *Middle East Quarterly*, and the *Australian Journal of International Affairs*. Paul has extensive applied research experience and networks having lived and worked previously in Australia, Brunei Darussalam, Egypt, Fiji, and the United Arab Emirates.

Airini
Faculty of Education and Social Work
Thompson Rivers University
Kamloops, BC, Canada

Professor Airini is Dean of the Faculty of Education and Social Work at Thompson Rivers University, British Columbia, Canada (https://www.tru.ca/), and previously at the University of Auckland, Aotearoa New Zealand. Airini's research looks at how to build world-class education systems where success for all means all. Her current focus is on closing education achievement gaps experienced by Indigenous school and university students in Canada and internationally. Airini is the recipient of national research and teaching awards in New Zealand (*Success for All: What university teaching practices help/hinder Maori and Pasifika student success*) and Canada (*Knowledge Makers: Indigenous undergraduate and graduate student research mentoring*). To identify how we can influence better outcomes for all, Airini went to Washington DC as a Fulbright Scholar and investigated how to convert tertiary education policy into better results for underserved students (E-mail: airini@tru.ca; Twitter: @truAirini; LinkedIn: https://ca.linkedin.come/in/airini).

Melani Anae
Pacific Studies|School of Māori Studies
and Pacific Studies,
Te Wānanga o Waipapa
University of Auckland
Auckland, New Zealand

Lupematasila, Misatauveve Dr. Melani Anae, is Senior Lecturer in Pacific Studies, Te Wānanga o Waipapa, at the University of Auckland. Anae has been a former Director of the Centre for Pacific Studies (2002–2007), a recipient of the Fulbright New Zealand Senior Scholar Award (2007), and was awarded the Companion to the Queen's Service Order for services to Pacific communities in New Zealand (2008). In 2014, she was awarded the prestigious Marsden Grant from the Royal Society of New Zealand for her project "Samoan transnational matai (chiefs): ancestor god avatars or merely titleholders?" Focusing on her research interests of ethnic identity for first-/second-generation Pacific peoples born in the diaspora, social justice and Pacific activism, and the development of her teu le va paradigm in relational ethics, her transformational work has successfully developed strategies for policy formation, service delivery, and optimal research outcomes for Pacific peoples/families and communities across the sectors of education, health, and well-being for Pacific peoples, families, and communities in New Zealand. She has taught, researched, and published extensively in these specialty areas and is currently focused on transnational identity construction of Pacific peoples and communities in the diaspora. She carries two Samoan chiefly titles from the villages of Siumu and Falelatai in Samoa, is part of a large transnational Samoan aiga, and is a grandmother and mother of three children.

About the Section Editors

Radomir Compel
School of Global Humanities and Social Sciences
Nagasaki University
Nagasaki, Japan

Radomir Compel is Associate Professor of comparative politics at the Global School of Humanities and Social Sciences of Nagasaki University in Japan. He has edited or coauthored several books, including *Guns and Roses: Comparative Civil-Military Relations in the Changing Security Environment* (2019), *Hito to Kaiyo no Kyosei wo Mezashite VI* (2013), and *Ashida Hitoshi Nikki 1905–1945 V* (2012), and has published articles in Japanese and English on Okinawa, Japan, East Asia, Middle East, and maritime issues. He obtained a Ph.D. from Yokohama National University, and taught at Hosei University, Yokohama National University, Nihon University, University of Oulu, and other educational institutions in Japan and Europe.

Sergio Luiz Cruz Aguilar
Sao Paulo State University (UNESP)
Marilia, São Paulo, Brazil

Sergio Luiz Cruz Aguilar holds a Ph.D. in History (UNESP), and is Associate Professor at the Sao Paulo State University (UNESP), Brazil, where he coordinates the Group of Studies and Research of International Conflicts and the International Conflicts Observatory. He is also Professor of the postgraduation programs San Tiago Dantas Program on International Relations (UNESP/UNICAMP/PUC-SP) and Social Sciences (UNESP – Campus of Marilia/SP). He was visiting researcher at the Department of Politics and International Relations – University of Oxford, UK. He was military observer on the United Nations Peace Force (UNPF) and on United Nations Transitional Administration for Eastern Slavonia (UNTAES), during the civil war in the former Yugoslavia. Sergio was also Director of the Brazilian Defense Studies Association (ABED) and wrote four books, edited five books, and published many journal articles in Portuguese, English, and Spanish languages.

Lyndon Fraser
Department of Sociology and Anthropology
University of Canterbury
Christchurch, New Zealand

Historian **Lyndon Fraser** is currently the Head of Department (Sociology and Anthropology) at the University of Canterbury, Christchurch, New Zealand, and Research Fellow in Human History at the Canterbury Museum. He is coeditor (with Linda Bryder) of the *New Zealand Journal of History*, and his recent publications include *Rushing for Gold: Life and Commerce on the Goldfields of Australia and New Zealand* (Otago University Press, 2016, with Lloyd Carpenter) and *History Making a Difference: New Approaches from Aotearoa* (Cambridge Scholars Publishing, 2017, coedited with Katie Pickles, Marguerite Hill, Sarah Murray, and Greg Ryan).

Contributors

Sergio Luiz Cruz Aguilar Sao Paulo State University (UNESP), Marilia, São Paulo, Brazil

Yaser Alashqar Trinity College Dublin (the University of Dublin), Dublin, Ireland

Hassanein Ali Department of International Studies, College of Humanities and Social Sciences, Zayed University, Dubai, United Arab Emirates

Jean M. Allen Faculty of Education and Social Work, The University of Auckland, Auckland, New Zealand

Trevor J. Allen Department of Political Science, Central Connecticut State University, New Britain, CT, USA

Sara N. Amin School of Social Sciences, Faculty of Arts, Law and Education, The University of the South Pacific, Suva, Fiji Islands

Ryosuke Amiya-Nakada Tsuda University, Kodaira, Japan

Melani Anae Pacific Studies|School of Māori Studies and Pacific Studies, Te Wānanga o Waipapa, University of Auckland, Auckland, New Zealand

Remus Gabriel Anghel The Romanian Institute for Research on National Minorities, Cluj Napoca, Romania

S. Apo Aporosa Te Huataki Waiora: Faculty of Health, Sport and Human Performance, University of Waikato, Hamilton, Waikato, New Zealand

Felicia Arriaga Sociology Department, Appalachian State University, Boone, NC, USA

Nicole L. Asquith Western Sydney University, Kingswood, NSW, Australia

Maria-Irini Avgoulas School of Psychology and Public Health, College of Science, Health and Engineering, La Trobe University, Bundoora, VIC, Australia

Mansi Awasthi Tata Institute of Social Sciences (TISS), Mumbai, India

Emmanuel Badu Faculty of Health and Environmental Studies, Auckland University of Technology, Auckland, New Zealand

Paul Bagguley School of Sociology and Social Policy, University of Leeds, Leeds, UK

Isabelle Bartkowiak-Théron Tasmanian Institute of Law Enforcement Studies, University of Tasmania, Hobart, TAS, Australia

Rohan Bastin School of Humanities and Social Sciences, Deakin University, Geelong, VIC, Australia

Jóhanna K. Birnir Government and Politics, University of Maryland, College Park, MD, USA

Gawaian Bodkin-Andrews Centre for the Advancement of Indigenous Knowledges, University of Technology Sydney, Broadway, NSW, Australia

Roland Boer School of Liberal Arts, Renmin University of China, Beijing, People's Republic of China

Igor Boog Institute of Cultural Anthropology and Development Sociology, Leiden University, Leiden, The Netherlands

Birgit Bräuchler Monash University, Melbourne, VIC, Australia

Johan Brosché Department of Peace- and Conflict Research, Uppsala University, Uppsala, Sweden

Heather Came Faculty of Health and Environmental Studies, Auckland University of Technology, Auckland, New Zealand

Paul J. Carnegie Institute of Asian Studies, Universiti Brunei Darussalam, Bandar Seri Begawan, Brunei Darussalam

Mitchell James Chang University of California, Los Angeles, Los Angeles, CA, USA

Chelegeer University of Leeds, Leeds, UK

Karl Ian Uy Cheng Chua History Department, Ateneo de Manila University, Quezon City, Philippines

Suryakanthie Chetty University of South Africa, Pretoria, South Africa

Treena Clark Centre for the Advancement of Indigenous Knowledges, University of Technology Sydney, Broadway, NSW, Australia

Radomir Compel School of Global Humanities and Social Sciences, Nagasaki University, Nagasaki, Japan

Neil Cruickshank Political Scientist and Dean of the Faculty of Arts, Science, and Technology, North Island College, Courtenay, BC, Canada

Faculty Associate, Centre for European Studies, Carleton University, Ottawa, ON, Canada

Christian Cwik Department of History, The University of the West Indies, St Augustine, Trinidad and Tobago

Sharyn Graham Davies Auckland University of Technology, Aotearoa, New Zealand

Michael Davis Department of Sociology and Social Policy, The University of Sydney, Sydney, NSW, Australia

Premakumara de Silva Department of Sociology, University of Colombo, Colombo, Sri Lanka

Zbigniew Dumieński Auckland University of Technology, Auckland, New Zealand

Emma Elfversson Department of Peace and Conflict Research, Uppsala University, Uppsala, Sweden

Mostafa Entezarulmahdy Political Science Department, Robat Karim Branch, Islamic Azad University, Tehran, Iran

Jovanie Camacho Espesor Department of Political Science and International Relations, University of Canterbury, Christchurch, New Zealand

Department of Political Science, Mindanao State University, General Santos City, Philippines

Center for Middle East and Global Peace Studies, Universitas Islam Negeri Syarif Hidayatullah Jakarta, Tangerang, Indonesia

Rebecca Fanany School of Health, Medical and Applied Sciences, Central Queensland University, Melbourne, VIC, Australia

Shannon Foster Centre for the Advancement of Indigenous Knowledges, University of Technology Sydney, Broadway, NSW, Australia

László Fosztó The Romanian Institute for Research on National Minorities, Cluj Napoca, Romania

Jeffrey A. Gardner Department of Sociology, Sam Houston State University, Huntsville, TX, USA

Rodrigo Luiz Cunha Gonsalves European Graduate School (EGS), Saas fee, Switzerland

University of Sao Paulo (IPUSP), Sao Paulo, Brazil

Farzana Haniffa Department of Sociology, University of Colombo, Colombo, Sri Lanka

Kate Hannan Department of History and Politics, University of Wollongong, Wollongong, NSW, Australia

Kathleen Harrington-Watt Anthropology, Canterbury University, Christchurch, New Zealand

Hamdy Hassan College of Humanities and Social Sciences, Zayed University, Dubai, UAE

Keakaokawai Varner Hemi University of Waikato, Hamilton, New Zealand

Sarah Herbert Faculty of Health and Environmental Studies, Auckland University of Technology, Auckland, New Zealand

Matthew Hoddie Department of Political Science, Towson University, Towson, MD, USA

Louise Humpage Sociology, Faculty of Arts, University of Auckland, Auckland, New Zealand

Yasmin Hussain School of Sociology and Social Policy, University of Leeds, Leeds, UK

Aphun Kamei Department of Sociology, Delhi School of Economics, University of Delhi, Delhi, India

Romitesh Kant Institute for Human Security and Social Change (IHSSC), College of Arts and Social Sciences, La Trobe University, Melbourne, VIC, Australia

Masaki Kataoka University of Canterbury, Christchurch, New Zealand

Institute of Developing Economies, Japan External Trade Organization, Chiba, Japan

Amanda Kearney College of Humanities, Arts and Social Sciences, Flinders University, Bedford Park, SA, Australia

Misty Knight-Finley Department of Political Science and Economics, Rowan University, Glassboro, NJ, USA

Rajesh Kumar Tata Institute of Social Sciences (TISS), Mumbai, India

Wendy Lambourne Department of Peace and Conflict Studies, University of Sydney, Sydney, NSW, Australia

Jianxia Lin University of Leeds, Leeds, UK

Stefano Luconi Department of Education (DISFOR), University of Genoa, Genoa, Italy

Kristen Lyons School of Social Science, University of Queensland, Brisbane, QLD, Australia

Nic Maclellan Melbourne, Australia

Adis Maksic International Burch University, Sarajevo, Bosnia and Herzegovina

Sam Manuela University of Auckland, Auckland, New Zealand

Paul H. Mason School of Social Sciences, Monash University, Clayton, VIC, Australia

Department of Anthropology, Macquarie University, North Ryde, NSW, Australia

Jacob Mwathi Mati School of Social Sciences, Faculty of Arts, Law and Education (FALE), The University of the South Pacific, Suva, Fiji Islands

Society, Work and Politics (SWOP) Institute, The University of the Witwatersrand, Johannesburg, South Africa

Eyal Mayroz University of Sydney, Sydney, NSW, Australia

Tim McCreanor Te Rōpū Whāriki, Massey University, Auckland, New Zealand

Cathal McManus School of Social Sciences, Education and Social Work, Queen's University Belfast, Belfast, Northern Ireland

Bruno Mendelski Institute of International Relations (IREL), University of Brasilia, Brasilia, Brazil

International Relations at Department of Economics, University of Santa Cruz do Sul, Santa Cruz do Sul, Viamão, Brazil

Alois S. Mlambo University of Pretoria, Pretoria, South Africa

M. Bashir Mobasher Department of Political Science, American University of Afghanistan, Kabul, Afghanistan

Monique Mulholland College of Humanities, Arts and Social Sciences, The Flinders University of South Australia, Adelaide, Australia

Murtala Murtala Suara Indonesia Dance Troupe, Sydney, NSW, Australia

Nasser Mustapha Department of Behavioural Sciences, University of the West Indies, St Augustine, Trinidad and Tobago

Todd Nachowitz University of Waikato, Hamilton, New Zealand

Sereana Naepi Thompson Rivers University, Kamloops, Canada

Vijay Naidu University of the South Pacific, Suva, Fiji

Subhankar Nayak Tata Institute of Social Sciences (TISS), Mumbai, India

Ryota Nishino University of the South Pacific, Suva, Fiji

International Research Center for Japanese Studies (Nichibunken), Kyoto, Japan

Nyaz N. Noori Department of Economic History, Uppsala University, Uppsala, Sweden

Lecturer, Department of Economics, University of Sulaymaniyah, Sulaimaniyah, Kurdistan Region, Iraq

Adele Norris School of Social Sciences, Sociology and Sociology Program, The University of Waikato, Hamilton, New Zealand

Alfira O'Sullivan Suara Indonesia Dance Troupe, Sydney, NSW, Australia

Henry D. Overos Government and Politics, University of Maryland, College Park, MD, USA

Gairoonisa Paleker Department of Historical and Heritage Studies, University of Pretoria, Pretoria, South Africa

Antoine Pécoud University of Paris 13, Paris, France

Geoff Pfeifer Worcester Polytechnic Institute, Worcester, MA, USA

Kathryn Pillay University of KwaZulu-Natal, Durban, South Africa

Ralph Premdas University of the West Indies, St. Augustine, Trinidad and Tobago

Sangit Kumar Ragi Department of Political Science, Social Science Building, North Campus, University of Delhi, Delhi, India

Bishnu Ragoonath Department of Political Science, University of the West Indies Trinidad, St. Augustine, Trinidad and Tobago

Arjun Rajkhowa University of Melbourne, Melbourne, Australia

Sanjay Ramesh Department of Peace and Conflict Studies, University of Sydney, Camperdown, NSW, Australia

Steven Ratuva Department of Anthropology and Sociology, University of Canterbury, Christchurch, New Zealand

Macmillan Brown Centre for Pacific Studies, University of Canterbury, Christchurch, New Zealand

Sadasivam Jaganada Reddi Réduit, Mauritius

Patricia Richards Department of Sociology, University of Georgia, Athens, GA, USA

Tara Ross University of Canterbury, Christchurch, New Zealand

Joseph R. Rudolph Department of Political Science, Towson University, Baltimore, MA, USA

Joseph Rudigi Rukema School of Social Sciences, University of KwaZulu-Natal, Durban, South Africa

Brinsley Samaroo History Department, University of the West Indies, St. Augustine, Trinidad and Tobago

Sam Scott University of Gloucestershire, Cheltenham, UK

Madhushree Sekher Centre for Study of Social Exclusion and Inclusive Policies (CSSEIP), Tata Institute of Social Sciences (TISS), Mumbai, India

Renat Shaykhutdinov Florida Atlantic University, Boca Raton, FL, USA

Badrus Sholeh Department of International Relations, Faculty of Social and Political Sciences, Syarif Hidayatullah State Islamic University, Jakarta, Indonesia

Sherry-Ann Singh The University of the West Indies, St. Augustine, Trinidad and Tobago

Stephen Small Department of African American Studies, University of California, Berkeley, Berkeley, CA, USA

Zhifang Song University of Canterbury, Canterbury, New Zealand

Sheetal Sheena Sookrajowa Department of History and Political Science, Faculty of Social Sciences and Humanities, University of Mauritius, Réduit, Mauritius

Paul Spoonley College of Humanities and Social Sciences, Massey University, Auckland, New Zealand

Jessica Terruhn Massey University, Auckland, New Zealand

Allen Thomas Tata Institute of Social Sciences (TISS), Mumbai, India

Andrew Thomson Queens University of Belfast, Belfast, UK

Stefánia Toma The Romanian Institute for Research on National Minorities, Cluj Napoca, Romania

Elya Tzaneva Institute of Ethnology and Folklore Studies with Ethnographic Museum, Bulgarian Academy of sciences, Sofia, Bulgaria

Nasir Uddin Department of Anthropology, University of Chittagong, Chittagong, Bangladesh

Beatrice Umubyeyi School of Built and Environmental Studies, University of KwaZulu-Natal, Durban, South Africa

Francisco J. Villegas Department of Anthropology and Sociology, Kalamazoo College, Kalamazoo, MI, USA

Paloma E. Villegas Sociology, California State University, San Bernardino, CA, USA

Tarisi Vunidilo Department of Anthropology, University of Hawaii-Hilo, Hilo, HI, USA

Melinda Webber Faculty of Education and Social Work, The University of Auckland, Auckland, New Zealand

Aleksandra Zdeb Centre for Southeast European Studies of the University of Graz, University of Graz, Graz, Austria

Cindy Zeiher University of Canterbury, Christchurch, New Zealand

Juan Zhang Department of Anthropology and Archaeology, University of Bristol, Bristol, UK

Part IV

Ethno-nationalism and Power

Part Introduction

We live on an increasingly globalized and interdependent planet, but sovereign nation-states still operate as the primary units of territorial rule in world affairs. They function as essential constituents of socioeconomic and cultural development. In fact, it is a world of nation-states. And for better or worse, nationalism has been one of the major forces of change in the twentieth century and beyond. The nationalist aspiration certainly hasn't dimmed. In 1945, there were 51 United Nations member states, today there are 193.

We could say that when enough members of a "nation" display sufficient collective awareness to start calling for their political self-determination, they are making a demand for statehood. Of course, that leaves us with the question of what is a "nation." And there the problems begin. To borrow an Ernest Gellner truism, nationalists can agree on the belief that the nation and state should be congruent but little else. Ideas of "nationhood" can include a wide variety of both distinct and imprecise markers that a group might "imagine" themselves to have in common, i.e., race, ethnicity, culture, language, religion, territory, and sentiment, etc., and not necessarily in that order. It is worth pointing out that using the word "imagine" is not to infer illusory but rather to indicate the power of subjective perception in the construction of collective identities. In other words, people who perceive themselves as part of a national community ultimately imagine it. They cannot meet or know everyone in that community, but they do believe that they have things in common that bind them.

That said, nationalism is disconcertingly Janus faced. It has two distinct but sometimes overlapping aspects, namely ethnic and civic. The ethno-national impulse speaks to a shared inheritance based on ethnicity, language, culture, or religion that is closely associated with exclusive forms of national identity believed to be in some ways "natural" or "ineluctable." Countries with deep ethno-national traditions tend to produce *jus sanguinis* (law of blood) types of exclusive citizenship. While countries shaped by more civic traditions are assumed to embrace "people" who accept and are loyal to the state and its institutions, regardless of their origins. They in turn are usually associated with *jus soli* (law of soil) types of inclusive citizenship.

Civic underpinnings are often held up (with some justification) as a "good" form of nationalism devoid of the toxicity of its "evil" twin.

But does the ethnic/civic distinction sufficiently explain why some nation-state formations descend into deadly chauvinistic irredentism and others do not? Digging a little deeper, we find that the relationship between ethno-nationalism and political order is not a simple one. In the twentieth century, the postcolonial world "breech-birthed" newly independent nation-states into convulsions of ethnic disaggregation with the exchange, expulsion, and "cleansing" of local minorities. Evidently, notions of history, nation, and ethnicity have constitutive power with potentially harmful consequences. Messy congruences of political community, ethnic group, and territory produced powerful "othering" based on the belief in a common "us." Groupings also diverged along elite or mass-led vectors. In fact, conflict over how to define postcolonial identities and resolve past exclusionary injustices still trouble the present.

But what roles do economics and politics play in stoking ethno-national consciousness in multiethnic societies? It is a consideration that takes on ever worrying dimensions in an age of rapacious economic globalization and identity politics. Many livelihoods are becoming more uncertain and precarious. It could be argued that increasingly disruptive inequalities and conflict are perpetuating poverty, emboldening criminality, and deepening shadow economies in many countries. In such circumstances, although sometimes frail, bonds of cultural identity, connection with the past, celebration of tradition, and the mutual support, which underpins these claims for continuity, are sometimes all that can be mustered to counter feelings of deepening frustration and insecurity. Identities and ethnic allegiances can often forge and harden in the face of perceived threats and material insecurity, and the domination of minorities by others. In extremis, cultural expressions of such interethnic identity formations can result in violence.

The extent and frequency of economic, environmental, and conflict-related disruption to forms of sociopolitical organization and the migration of people of one culture to places with very different traditions should give us pause for thought. It complicates matters considerably. Large numbers of the global precariat do not have ready access to alternative livelihoods and forms of support nor do they have receptive channels of communication to voice their concerns. For our febrile times, the internal structures and borders of established civic nation-states may not be as impervious to the ethno-national siren call as might at first appear. It is telling how ubiquitous and pernicious more or less subtle forms of ethno-nationalism have become in the immigration policies of different countries around the world. The processes and impulses that led to the formation and the dominance of the forms of ethno-nationalism in the twentieth century are likely to reproduce in the twenty-first century but not necessarily in quite the same ways.

The chapters in this part explore the power and consequences of ethno-nationalism in its various guises. They range from analyses of ethno-communal conflict in Bosnia by both Adis Maksić and Aleksandra Zdeb, Kenya by Emma Elfversson, Sri Lanka by Premakumara de Silva, Farzana Haniffa, and Rohan Bastin, and Sudan by Johan Brosché to reflections on ethnic dynamics in Trinidad and

Tobago by Ralph Premdas and explorations of ethnicity in relation to cultural wounding and healing in Yanyuwa communities, northern Australia by Amanda Kearney. These chapters and the others in this part provide key insight on the ways in which certain group identities crystallize and communal tensions and conflicts emerge, while offering possible resolutions to such struggles and contestations.

Paul J. Carnegie

Contemporary Ethnic Politics and Violence

31

Adis Maksic

Contents

Introduction	540
Discourse, Ethnicity, and Violence	541
Toward a Discursive-Affective Analytics of "Ethnic Violence"	543
Ethnic Nationalism, Affect, and Descent into War in Bosnia-Herzegovina	545
Contemporary Nonwar in Bosnia-Herzegovina	549
Conclusion	555
Cross-References	555
References	556

Abstract

This chapter offers a perspective on the relationship between ethnic politics and violence that applies lessons from discourse theory and the recent findings on the role of emotions in human cognition. It proceeds by discussing the intersection between discourse theory and the literature on affective cognition, outlining a discursive-affective analytical framework, and applying it toward an understanding of ethnic politics in Bosnia and Herzegovina. The first part of the chapter analyzes the processes that led to the Bosnian War by exposing the role of nationalist parties in producing emotional polarization that culminated into armed mobilization. It then argues that the War's emotional legacy decisively shaped contemporary politics in Bosnia and Herzegovina, maintaining deep ethnic cleavages and potential for future violence. By emphasizing the role of nationalist agents and discursively mobilized emotions in producing homogenized ethnic groups primed for armed mobilization, the discussion challenges groupist and rationalist approaches to ethnically framed conflicts.

A. Maksic (✉)
International Burch University, Sarajevo, Bosnia and Herzegovina
e-mail: adis.maksic@ibu.edu.ba

© The Author(s), under exclusive license to Springer Nature Singapore Pte Ltd. 2019
S. Ratuva (ed.), *The Palgrave Handbook of Ethnicity*,
https://doi.org/10.1007/978-981-13-2898-5_38

Keywords

Discourse · Affect · Ethnic nationalism · Ethnic violence · Bosnia-Herzegovina · Bosnian War

Introduction

> It was genetically deformed material that embraced Islam. And now, of course, with each successive generation this gene simply becomes concentrated. It gets worse and worse, it simply expresses itself and dictates their style of thinking and behaving, which is rooted in their genes. (Popovic 1993)

The above statement was made in 1993 at the peak of the Bosnian War by Biljana Plavsic, a leading figure in ethno-political mobilization of Bosnian Serbs during the 1990s and one of the most prominent politicians convicted for war crimes by the International Tribunal for the Former Yugoslavia. The statement is notable not only for its depiction of the genetic inferiority of Bosnian Muslims coming from an influential ethno-national leader but also for being spoken from the position of scientific authority, as Plavsic was a distinguished professor of biology at the University of Sarajevo (Halimovic 2009).

Plavsic's depiction of the Bosnian Muslims exemplified a larger theme of biological determinism in Serb nationalist discourse that served to legitimize violence perpetrated against the Muslim ethnic "other." Yet, its most important lesson for understanding ethnically motivated conflicts emerges only after situating it into a temporal context of Plavsic's previous statements that date back to her emergence as a leading politician in mid-1990. With only a cursory glance, the contrast becomes obvious. Prior to the November 1990 elections, Plavsic's Serb Democratic Party (SDS) was in a partnership with Muslim ethno-national Party for Democratic Action (SDA), with the two having joined forces to defeat the incumbent Bosnian communists. At that time, Plavsic and other SDS leaders had only praise for Muslims, depicting them as "good neighbors" and promising a "genuine peace" between the two imagined ethnic nations (Maksic 2017, p.203). While the two parties began to engage into a bitter ethno-political conflict after their joint electoral victory, there is no evidence of a single instance of SDS leaders describing Muslims as a lower race until the onset of the Bosnian War in the spring of 1992. Considering the Bosnian tradition of "common life" between Serbs, Croats, and Muslims that routinely blurred and transgressed ethnic boundaries, such language was socially unacceptable and politically costly at the time.

The events would show that the tradition could not indefinitely serve as a bulwark against polarizing ethnic politics, as it eventually gave way to brutal violence between the people who once shared a "common life." Yet, when it comes to understanding ethnically motivated violence, peacetime traditions are no less important than the wartime rivalries. They invite us to depart not from an account of fixed preferences and long-standing animosities, but from an examination of the political processes that transform peacetime sensibilities into polarizing hostilities conductive for armed mobilization. In the Bosnian case, this involves an understanding of how the sensibilities of Serb masses evolved in a span of a year and a half to allow Biljana Plavsic to publicly describe former "good neighbors" as a despised lower race. For it is the emergence of a social environment in which the branding of an ethnic category as morally inferior is permitted that usually precedes armed mobilization. This environment is not an enduring feature of any social field, but is constituted through political dynamics that are shaped more by leading politicians than the pre-existing sentiments of the popular masses.

The following pages offer a perspective about how such an environment is created, ethnicity elevated into the politically most relevant social cleavage, and people belonging to different ethnic categories primed for violence against one another. The perspective is developed by applying the lessons from discourse theory and the recent findings about human cognition toward enriching our understandings of ethnically motivated conflicts. The focus is on the developments that culminated in the 1992–1995 Bosnian War, as well as the dynamics of postwar ethnic rivalries. The case of Bosnia-Herzegovina (BiH) will illustrate the ways through which conflicts may leave a durable legacy of ethnic polarization and the potential for future violence, thus offering wider lessons for understanding contemporary post-conflict ethnic politics.

Discourse, Ethnicity, and Violence

In recent years, a considerable wealth of literature has challenged commonplace understandings of ethnic violence as clashes of well-bounded ethnic groups with incompatible political interests. This challenge is motivated in part by indicators that only relatively small segments of "ethnic masses" actually participate in criminal violence and sometimes with motives that may have little to do with ethnic politics. Mueller (2000) thus finds that, during the Yugoslav Wars, the murderous core was not made up of ordinary citizens, but of thugs and hooligans that politicians recruited for the job. In the case of Rwandan genocide, the same author observes that many Hutus hid and protected their Tutsi neighbors and that 98% of male Hutus over the age of 13 were not among the killers. The groupist framework is also challenged by the data from the case of Northern Ireland that points to high levels of "intergroup killings." Fearon and Latin (2000) estimate that 22% of the killings committed by Ulster loyalists were against other Protestants, either in feuds or because the victims were accused of being informers.

These and similar findings invite us to trace the emergence of an environment in which small minorities engage in crimes and atrocities in the name of ethnicity unopposed by majorities. This involves shifts and lurches in the dominant modes of understandings that at specific times and places produce widespread toleration of violence as an instrument in dealing with the ethnic other. The question becomes not why or how Serbs engaged in the genocidal slaughter of Bosnia's Muslims, or why the Hutus sought to exterminate the Tutsis, but how the majority of Serbs and Hutus came to either legitimize or remain silent amid the atrocities committed in the name of their ethnic nations by murderous gangs, military units, and violence-prone individuals.

One perspective is offered by institutionalists, who emphasize the role of institutions in reifying ethnic differentiation. Autonomously from the pre-existing social cleavages, such reification serves as a resource for leaders to "create a competitive dynamic that increases the likelihood of spiraling aggression" (Lieberman and Singh 2012). In BiH, for instance, career and employment prospects have been tied to an individual's ethnic background through the so-called "ethnic key" policy designed to maintain equal ethno-national balance in governmental bureaucracies. At a time when the Yugoslav state began to disintegrate in the 1990s amid ethno-political rivalries, ethnicity acquired added significance and commanded loyalties. As Ignatieff (1993, p.42) puts it, the institutional collapse raised new, existential questions not directly linked to one's actual ethnic sentiments: "will the local Croat policeman protect me if I am a Serb? Will I keep my job in the soap factory if my new boss is a Serb or a Muslim?"

Other scholars focus on the sociological dimension. Bhavani (2006) thus examines the emergence of violence-promoting "ethnic norms." Bhavani observes that in Cambodia the Khmer Rouge made use of the pre-existing norm of "honor" to shame those who refused to be involved in the killings. In the Rwandan case, the Hutu *génocidaires* made appeals for Hutu unity against the Tutsi threat, imparting a moral and social obligation to eliminate the Tutsi "cockroaches." In both cases, those who sympathized with the ethnic other or who were reluctant to participate would put their own lives in danger, leading to a progressively higher level of compliance and, consequently, greater overlap between an ethnic category and murderous behavior.

Obershall (2000) examines the question from the cognitive side and speaks of "cognitive frames" or mental structures that connect events, people, and groups into narratives that make sense of the social world and can be shared with others. In the Yugoslav case, he observes the transformation from a normal frame to a crisis frame. The latter was grounded in the memories of historical suffering at the hands of the ethnic other, most notably the atrocities that occurred during World War II. While the Yugoslav communist regime sought to eliminate this crisis frame during "normal times," it continued to simmer in the memories of those who lived through the events, the families of victims, and among some religious and intellectual leaders. During the ethnopolitical rivalries in the early 1990s, this cognitive disposition was activated and amplified by ethno-nationalist leaders to produce fears and animosities able to override the "normal frame" and legitimize aggression.

Beyond this, some scholars have sought to identify psychological factors at the individual level. Kreadie and Monroe (2002), for instance, have conducted interviews with perpetrators of violence against civilians during the Lebanese Civil War. While the specific motives varied between interviewees, all felt that they had been forced into violent acts by the threatening "other." The fighters on both sides identified their ethno-religious group as a victim of unfair political arrangements, which was an indicator of both an existential threat to their group and moral bankruptcy of the other. As the authors point out, for some interviewees "genocide and ethnic violence were akin to a process of extermination of vermin, and killing human beings became analogous to killing cockroaches that infest a home" (p.32). For many others who shared such an interpretation but did not directly participate in criminal violence, removal of the "infection" would not feel very criminal at all.

While institutional factors, psychological approaches, and sociological concepts such as "ethnic norms" all offer avenues for advancing our understandings of ethnically motivated violence, an approach chosen here argues that their most valuable lessons can be unified under a framework of critical discourse analysis. The framework departs from an understanding of language as an intersubjective field that assigns meanings to the world and generates social realities autonomously from any external, objective realities. When it comes to ethnicity, this approach recognizes that no ethnic identity exists independent of discourses on ethnicity that differentiate people according to the particular criteria of decent. Beyond this, particular understandings of ethnic "self" and "other" are produced through discourses that narrate ethnic histories and assign moral virtues to differentiated ethnic groups. When narrated by ethno-nationalists, these discourses typically open up into descriptions of friendly nations with whom the self should ally and the threatening and morally profane foes against whom one has obligation to mobilize in defense. Applied to the discussion above, such discourses served to legitimize atrocities committed during the Lebanese Civil War, produce violence-promoting "ethnic norms" in Rwanda, and activate and amplify cognitive "crisis frames" in the former Yugoslavia.

Moreover, a discursive approach recognizes that official ethnic categorizations, density of social ties, or cultural commonalities may not be reflected in the actual self-understandings of the people who fall into a single ethnic category. Rather than assuming the existence of a self-conscious group, a discursive analytical approach seeks to explain the power of nationalist discourse to generate such consciousness, increase levels of group solidarity, or "groupness" and create correspondence between an ethnic category and a palpable group (Brubaker and Cooper 2000). It is also well-suited to expose nuances of the relationship between political rivalries and violence by recognizing the "ethnic" attribute in "ethnic violence" as an interpretative frame and an inherently political action, rather than an objective description. What this approach brings to light are the heterogeneous dynamics and motives involved in the making of diverse cases of violence that are often casually given a common, "ethnic" attribute.

Toward a Discursive-Affective Analytics of "Ethnic Violence"

The above section has illuminated the power of discourse to generate modes of understanding conductive for violence waged in the name of ethnic nations. It has also raised new questions about the cognitive mechanisms through which such understandings are produced at particular times and places. Do people rationally asses competing discourse, only to conclude that it is in their interest to follow calls for mobilization against the ethnic "other"? How does discourse generate motivations to commit savagery against former friends and neighbors, even in the absence of an obvious material gain? Do nationalist discourses merely mobilize fear and hatred of the ethnic other that has been lurking underneath in times of the peacetime pleasantries, waiting for a "right" moment to erupt, or do they invent such emotions? Have many Bosnian Serbs approved of Biljana Plavsic's 1993 statement because they always believed at some level that Muslims were biologically flawed?

A search for answers takes us to the recent advances in the studies of human cognition that challenge commonplace image of a unified, stable, and rational subject. One such challenge is offered by psychologist Drew Westen (2007), whose study of political partisans has problematized the distinction between reason and emotions. Westen's team asked the partisans to comment on a series of slides displaying contradictory statements, while the functional magnetic imaging technology (fMRI) measured their brain activity. The partisans had a hard time finding contradictions made by their favored candidate but quickly identified those made by rival politicians. The findings suggested that positive emotional associations toward favorite candidates shaped the perceptions of the statements by overriding the rational distress of logical contradictions. Westen concludes that when reason and emotions collide in politics, emotions carry the day.

A study by neuroscientist Antonio Damasio (2005) arrives at a similar conclusion. He argues that emotions and gut feelings participate even in those activities that seem exclusively rational, such as the cost-benefit analyses. It appears that instinctive sensibilities and bodily feelings associated with particular situations through experience, which Damasio terms "somatic markers," operate subconsciously in any cost-benefit deliberations. These sensibilities first highlight some options and eliminate others before deliberative reasoning takes over. A related argument is made by psychologist Daniel Kahneman (2011) who thinks of two systems involved in human cognition. System 1 refers to fast, split-second impulsive thinking, while system 2 is that of conscious, analytical deliberations. The affective reaction of system 1 has the effect of shaping, or "priming," the rationality of system 2.

In what specific ways is this research relevant for our attempts to understand ethnic nationalism and violence? Most generally, it invites us to explore the generative powers of nationalist discourse by going beyond the level of a conscious subject. The analysis of meaning-making shifts from a search for some objectivized "common sense" meanings to an interpretative exploration of emotions and sensibilities that create many diverse perceptions and interpretations of a single predicament. The task, then, is not so much to identify objective political conditions that compel a rational individual or group to mobilize for ethnic violence, but to develop a rigorous interpretative insight into the discursively engineered affective experiences that legitimize and drive violent acts.

When it comes to the diachronic discourse analysis, its task shifts to exploring how discourses generate affective sensibilities of new types and intensities across time. This requires that we drop the assumption of a fixed ethnic subject with a stable cognitive-affective makeup in favor of a departure point that sees the generation of subjectivities as fluid and situational. The approach recognizes the constitution of affects in relation to discursive action as a difference maker between peace and war. When Serb nationalists spoke of Muslims as "good neighbors" prior to the Bosnian

War, for example, the interpretative frame corresponded to popular sentiments formed during nearly half a century of common Yugoslav experience. While these sentiments gradually weakened as ethno-political rivalries escalated, it was the ethnically framed destruction and bloodshed of the Bosnian War that created angers and animosities of such intensities that could make Biljana Plavsic's racist statement resonate as a scientific fact.

What roles does this entanglement of discourse and affect leave for historical factors, which are so frequently emphasized in mainstream understandings? Historical events matter not as sources of deterministic structures that compel future behavior, but as discursive resources for assembling emotionally resonant narratives. Sectarian violence in Lebanon during the nineteenth century, intercommunal atrocities in BiH during World War II, or long-standing land distribution issues between the Tutsi and the Hutu did not cause wars in the late twentieth century. Yet, they left emotionally salient collective memories that nationalist agents could discursively map onto contemporary political developments, reinforce popular dictums of "history repeating itself," and produce disturbing perceptions of existential threat.

The analytical focus on multidirectional discursive-affective processes outlined in this section can help us understand not only past violence but also cognitive and social machinations of contemporary ethno-political rivalries. In postwar BiH, for example, the polarizing affective intensities have subsided to make genetic racism, such as that of Biljana Plavsic, once again unacceptable in mainstream political discourse. Yet, the war has left a legacy of deep ethnic cleavages, institutionally reified through complicated consociational arrangements, which provide resources for ethno-nationalists to continuously revive wartime sentiments and ambitions and, hence, maintain high levels of ethnic groupness. The rest of the chapter applies the discursive-affective approach to give an account of both the path to the Bosnian War and its legacy in the country's contemporary ethnic politics.

Ethnic Nationalism, Affect, and Descent into War in Bosnia-Herzegovina

In present-day BiH, ethnicity seems to represent a natural axis of belonging. Ethnic lines are deep, territorially enshrined, and easily visible in daily practices. Considering the ubiquitous presence of ethnic markers, one could easily reduce the causes of the Bosnian War to a simple clash of its ethnic groups. Yet, a closer look reveals that, as late as the first half of 1990, 2 years prior to the War, the social landscape looked quite different. Yugoslav national sentiments were widespread, social ties routinely and densely transgressed ethnic boundaries, and there were few signs of ethnic dissent and no ethnically motivated unrest on any collective scale.

All too often, commonplace analyses disregard this evidence as having no sustenance beyond the repressive power of Yugoslav communist authoritarianism. Such exclusion maintains historical continuity required for explaining the conflict in terms of long-standing ethnic animosities. Yet, a more nuanced approach tells a different story, the one with indicators that the Yugoslav era not only repressed pre-existing ethnic self-expressions but also generated new, genuinely felt national self-understandings on a socially significant scale. The opinion polls, for instance, indicate that different modes of understandings reigned in early 1990. A March 1990 found that only 16% believed that ethnic parties would have a significant influence on future developments (Sarac 1990). Another poll conducted a month later found that only 23.6% of Muslims and 19.8% of Serbs believed that religion was important when choosing a marriage partner (Carić 1990). A census conducted a year later, in April 1991, showed that 5.54% Bosnians, or a quarter of a million people, wrote in "Yugoslav" as their nation despite it not being offered as one of the acknowledged categories ("Stanovnistvo Bosne i Herzegovine po popisima 1879–1991"). Moreover, at a time of ethnopolitical rivalry that pushed BiH to the brink of violence, the largest public gatherings were peace rallies that expressed desires for survival of Yugoslavia or preservation of "common life" in BiH.

Rather than selectively searching for long-standing animosities, these observations beg a different question – how did social and political environment *change* to produce mass sentiments of new types and intensities? The processes in need of explanation are those that resulted in nationalist messages acquiring such emotional resonance to overpower Yugoslav sentiments and delegitimize meanings Bosnians had been internalizing for nearly half a century of communist rule. This did not come automatically with the end of the single-party regime that came in the spring of 1990. What did flow directly from the transition, however, was the emergence of three ethno-national political parties, SDA, SDS, and Croatian Democratic Union (HDZ), that would actively work on transforming the society. The hallmarks of this agency have been visible in the dominant modes of understandings of Bosnians ever since and, as such, deserve analytical attention.

Looking back from the perspective of contemporary BiH, it may seem surprising that in 1990 a Muslim, Serb, and Croat ethnic party recognized each other as political partners, rather than rivals. As SDA, SDS, and HDZ launched their campaign for the November 1990 elections, their discourses merged into an echo of messages that would jointly serve to intensify ethnic sentiments and create palpable ethnic groups. In recognition to the presence of powerful alternative solidarities, the three parties focused on defeating their common rivals that stood in the way of ethnic homogenization – the incumbent communist and the nonethnic but widely popular reformist party. The first step was the creation of sharper cultural differentiations. The parties organized new social practices through which Bosnians could be sensitized to cultural differentiation, such as numerous ethnic literature and poetry nights, celebrations of ethnic holidays, and observances of religious traditions. In the words of the party leader Radovan Karadzic, SDS was "teaching Serbs to be Serbs" (Toal and Maksic 2014). SDA and HDZ only applauded this pedagogy, as it created the "other" in opposition to which they could promote a Muslim and Croat cultural self.

Yet, there was also a duality in the three campaign discourses, driven by developments outside of BiH. By mid-1990, Yugoslav constitutional order came into jeopardy amid nationalist rivalries between the governments of neighboring Croatia and Serbia. In the summer of 1990, first instances of disorder were occurring in Serb-majority areas of Croatia, as local officials unilaterally declared Serb autonomous regions, and armed loyalists placed barricades on roads to prevent the nationalist Croatian government from imposing its writ (Flegar and Rebac 2010). Considering that BiH was a site of most atrocities in World War II, the previous time the two nationalisms led to mass violence, these developments were generating a spillover of anxiety into BiH. For the 1990 nationalists, the availability of this emotional resource was a major framing opportunity. Hence, each of the three revisited historical suffering at the hands of the ethnic other, drew parallels between the political moment of 1990 and that of half a century earlier, and portrayed itself as the only guardian that could prevent past tragedies from repeating. Somewhat paradoxically, this threat discourse coexisted with the portrayal of national parties as the only genuine representatives of the three ethnic groups and as harbingers of a more genuine peace than that experienced in communist Yugoslavia.

BiH's nationalist discourses, then, were originally structured to simultaneously generate pride in ethnic cultures, intensify anxieties of existential danger, and promise peaceful resolutions. Despite logical tensions, this structure found affective correspondence in BiH's social realities at a time, marked by a diversity of sensibilities and solidarities. While SDA, SDS, and HDZ adjusted to these realities to achieve a convincing victory in the November 1990 elections, once in power the three parties began to use newfound institutional capabilities to transform them. The three worked together to naturalize and enshrine ethnicity by changing names of towns and streets, building monuments to ethnic heroes, and officially institutionalizing ethno-religious holidays.

Beyond this, however, it was becoming apparent that there was little about which the parties could agree. The dangerous incompatibility of their ethno-national agendas, which had been obscured by cultural revivals, now came to the forefront. The primary line of confrontation was the future of BiH amid the accelerating processes of Yugoslav disintegration. SDA and HDZ took a firm stance that, in case of Croatian secession, the Bosnian republic would not remain in what was left of Yugoslavia. According to SDS, remaining in any Yugoslavia, and consequently in state union with Serbia, was a national imperative of Bosnian Serbs. With Croatia declaring independence in the summer of 1991, and full-scale war in Croatia erupting in the aftermath, these conflicting definitions of ethno-national interest were set on a collision course.

In the discourses of the three parties, "national interests" were part of wider, affectively intense narratives that portrayed the political moment as a matter of national survival. While the cultural revival of pre-election period increased the visibility of boundaries between the ethnic self and other, these narratives inscribed the binaries with moralizing descriptions. For each, existential threats and ill intent lied behind the agenda of the other. In SDA's interpretation, SDS desired to split up or absorb BiH into greater Serbia, in order to establish domination over non-Serbs. This malicious intent had a long tradition, as evidenced in World War II-era atrocities that Serb Chetniks committed against Muslims. In SDS's narration, Muslims pursued integrity of BiH only to cover up the true intent of establishing an Islamic state in which Serbs would be second-class citizens, in the same manner as they were when subjugated to Islamic rule during the five-century-old Ottoman occupation of Serbia (Maksic 2017, p.181).

As Yugoslav disintegration progressed throughout 1991, the threat discourses would become progressively more frequent. By the fall of 1991, the increasingly polarizing discursive-affective environment allowed SDS to mobilize many ethnic Serbs for the activities that began fragmenting the Bosnian institutional framework. SDS began to unilaterally join adjacent Serb-majority municipalities and other Serb-majority areas into Serb autonomous regions and form a Serb-only parliament that it declared superior to the parliament of BiH. Along with the affective imperative that produced mass commitments, this was made possible by access to superior weaponry of the Yugoslav People's Army (JNA), which had sided behind a Serb nationalist cause. On January 9, 1992, SDS leadership declared these areas as belonging to the nascent Serb Republic of Bosnia-Herzegovina, a predecessor of today's Republika Srpska, and there was little the official BiH government could do to stop it.

While SDS had territorial control in much of the Republic, the BiH government emerged on the winning side of the battle for international recognition. In late November 1991, the Badinter Arbitration Committee, set up by the European Economic Community, declared Yugoslavia in the process of dissolution and internal boundaries between its republics as boundaries subject to international law (Pellet 1992). The BiH declaration of independence would be recognized, provided that it happened after a successful independence referendum. The BiH government, minus its SDS members, met this condition by holding a successful independence referendum on February 29 and March 1, 1992. The results showed that 62% of the electorate voted for independence, despite the referendum being boycotted by most Bosnian Serbs (Shoup 1992, p.28). Consistent with its ethnicized understanding, SDS framed the referendum as merely a plebiscite of the Croat and Muslim ethnic nations.

In the meanwhile, the Party's leaders adjusted to the new situation by leaving open the possibility that an independent BiH could be acceptable as a loose union of ethnic cantons and engaged in internationally mediated negotiations on internal restructuring of the state. It was the failure of these negotiations and recognition of independent BiH by major international actors that triggered the Bosnian War. With the European Community and the United States recognizing BiH on April 6 and 7, 1992, the only instrument left at SDS's disposal was armed mobilization of the Serb population that had been primed for an existential fight and equipped with superior weaponry (Binder 1992). Indeed, the consistent and widespread violence that characterized the Bosnian War would begin amid the international recognition of BiH, as Serb nationalist forces began a campaign to capture contested, ethnically mixed areas and cleanse them of non-Serbs. These activities would ensure that independent BiH was a state without most of its population and territory.

The Bosnian War, then, came not as a spontaneous clash of ethnic masses, but as continuation of politics by other, violent means. The preconditions were set over the previous 2 years through nationalist activism that would create new perceptions, self-understandings, and, ultimately, palpable ethnic groups primed for armed mobilization. This initially took form of cultural revival and the "good neighbors" frame, which signaled a nonantagonistic but essential difference between Bosnians of different ethnic backgrounds, and later evolved into antagonistic narratives of existential threat. These narratives contextually acquired affective momentum that the political leaders would channel toward armed mobilization. The Bosnian War came at cost of nearly 100,000 lives, hundreds of thousands were displaced, and the country's infrastructure was thoroughly destroyed (Sito-Susic and Robinson 2013). This mass suffering, most often interpreted to be at the hands of the ethnic other, also served to legitimize the prewar threat narratives of the three national parties and take the associated affective intensities to new peaks. With animosities intensifying into hatreds, and anxieties into fears, Plavsic's statement of racial superiority would find emotional affirmation.

Contemporary Nonwar in Bosnia-Herzegovina

In the fall of 1995, after 3.5-year-long bloodshed, the warring parties ended the Bosnian War by signing the Dayton Peace Accords. The compromise deal internally restructured the country by establishing two ethno-territorial autonomous entities, the Serb-majority Republika Srpska and the Bosniak-Croat Federation of Bosnia-Herzegovina (FBiH). Beyond the territorial solutions, the Dayton Accords also created complex consociational institutions designed to ensure that none of the three constituent ethnicities could make decisions without the consent of the other two. Hence, the collective Head of State is a three-member presidency that makes decisions by consensus, while the decisions of a bicameral parliament must receive consent of the House of the People, a chamber that has an equal number of Bosniak, Serb, and Croat members (The Europa World Year Book 2003).

At first glance, the Bosnian example appears to show that consociational/federal arrangements are able to reverse ethnic antagonisms and produce a functional state. In the years since the signing of the Dayton Accords, the country has shown signs of undoing the results of ethno-political rivalries that began in 1990 and culminated in the War. The guns have fallen silent, refugees allowed to return to their homes, and the infrastructure largely rebuilt. State institutions were able to make decisions that brought the country closer to NATO membership and integration into the European Union. Indeed, many analysts have declared BiH as a success story, which it appears to be when compared with some other post-Communist conflicts that have been frozen or simmering without a peace deal, such as those in Nagorno-Karabakh, the Republic of Georgia, and Transnistria.

Yet, in many ways, Bosnia's society has not moved beyond the conflict years of the 1990s. The Dayton Accords were able to stop the War only with the force of the 60,000-strong NATO-led Implementation Force (Baumann et al. 2012). Much of the country's progress in establishing a relatively stable institutional framework came not from domestic actors but through coercive measures passed by the Office High Representative, an international body established at Dayton to oversee the civilian implementation of the Accords (Szewcyzk 2010). Most importantly, the structure of political discourse has not been transformed to generate affective commonalities that would unify the former warring parties into a single social field. To be sure, ethnic animosities have been reduced with the silencing of guns and the development of economic and cultural ties. However, one thing that the Dayton Accords have not been able to create is common narratives that would bridge the discursive polarization of the 1990s. The divisive nationalist discourses have not only survived the War, but are now invested with its powerful emotional legacy.

Indeed, ethnic nationalism has continued to dominate Bosnian public discourse to the present day. Its generative power is different today, however, from that of the prewar rivalry involving SDA, SDS, and HDZ. The nationalisms of 1991 and 1992 were situated within the transformative context marked by the collapse of the Yugoslav order and institutional fluidities. In contrast, the postwar ethnic nationalisms are occurring within the internationally protected security and institutional framework. The force of Bosnia's international overseers serves as an assurance that the spiral of political rivalry would be held back before it reaches collective mobilization and threatens the Dayton order. No such assurances existed in 1992.

In what ways, then, do the competing postwar nationalist discourses create realities so crucial for Bosnia's current predicament? Most generally, they mobilize divisive emotional memories, revive unachieved wartime ambitions, and generate perceptions that the country remains contested despite the Dayton compromise. When mobilized, the affectively salient memories of the War produce experiences on different sides of wartime divides that are of similarly high intensities but opposing types. Since there is a significant overlap between these lines and ethnic categories, such mobilization amplifies the affective ties that elevate levels of ethnic solidarity. Moreover, considering the role of affect in human cognition, it has power to sideline other issues that may be more pressing for everyday life but appeal more to rational than emotional parts of the brain. The painful memories of a lost loved one, of a childhood spent in refugee camps, and of cold winter days spent in trenches, the stories of heroism, and savage brutality all serve to create affective distraction away from contemporary daily struggles with low wages, corrupt officials, and other social injustices.

While the protagonists of these discourses are well aware of the mechanisms in place to ensure against action that would unravel the established order, the postwar nationalist engineering is useful for a different purpose. Nearly a quarter of a century after the War, the discursive mobilization of wartime emotions still wins elections. This is not for the lack of pressing issues affecting the livelihoods of Bosnians of all ethnic backgrounds. BiH is near the bottom of the list of European countries in terms of the GDP per capita, adjusted for purchasing power parity (GDP per capita, current prices 2018). At the same time, it has one of the highest rates of corruption (Transparency International 2017). Nonetheless, the successful reproduction of ethnic animosities has incentivized political parties to offer emotional outlets in the form of a bold response to the other side and revival of wartime objectives that the Dayton deal has left unfulfilled. This structure has prevented the Bosnian political discourse from normalizing into the debates between the positions on the left-right political spectrum typical of stable democracies.

It is not surprising that the ethno-national parties formed in 1990, and for whom identity politics is raison d'etre, have been among the main beneficiaries of postwar discursive antagonisms. They have helped SDA and HDZ remain in power in FBiH for the vast majority of the postwar period. SDS kept its dominant position in Republika Srpska until 2006, losing it to the Union of Independent Social Democrats (SNSD) only after the latter outbid SDS's nationalism by launching the idea of Republika Srpska independence referendum (Maksic 2009).

What, then, is the performative structure of these rival discourses? An answer to this question can help us better understand the current Bosnian predicament and possibilities for future violence, as well as offer lessons exportable to other cases of post-conflict state-building. The discourses are structured around two related areas of contested meaning. One refers to the competing narratives about the character of the 1992–1995 War, while the other addresses the current situation and future prospects. While both mobilize the polarizing emotional resources of the War, the dangers of the latter appear to be more direct insofar as it disputes the legitimacy of the institutional order that brought peace to BiH in 1995.

Some of the conflicting narratives are a continuation of those established by nationalist parties in the early 1990s. While the Dayton Accords created a mutually agreed institutional framework, they testify that the modes of understanding that led to the War have remained to the present day. This continuity is particularly evident in the opposing narratives between major parties in Republika Srpska and those performed by Bosniak and civic-oriented parties. The latter have continued the romanticized description of the Bosnian homeland, while the former seek to empty it of meaning beyond that of a toponym artificially turned into a state. In contrast to the prewar period, the contemporary frames are now invested with powerful emotions stemming from the War. The evidence of suffering at the hands of the other is no longer only in the narrated collective memory, but is also present in living memory of most Bosnians. The struggle for BiH is now much more than about protecting the republic from menacing neighbors, as it also preserves the legacy of the thousands who have fought and died for it.

The new geopolitical unit created during the War, Republika Srpska, has become a new rhetorical commonplace invested with polarizing emotions. The Bosniak and civic-oriented parties occasionally depict Republika Srpska as a "genocidal creation," having been created on multiethnic territory from which non-Serbs have been expelled (SDP: Vladajuća koalicija je slagala građane da je mehanizam koordinacije usaglašen 2016). For SDS, SNSD, and other major Serb parties, Republika Srpska is a homeland created by the will of the Serb people in order to ensure national survival. Much like BiH is for the Bosniaks, Republika Srpska is built on lives of thousands of soldiers, and its preservation ensures that their sacrifice would not be in vain.

It is no surprise that the current leader of Republika Srpska and SNSD, Milorad Dodik, owes his political ascent to rhetoric that placed him into the slot of a champion of Serb nationalist cause, rather than any policy decisions. Dodik has occupied this slot since 2006, a year when he became the first leading politician to openly advocate the idea of Republika Srpska independence referendum. During the 2006 election campaign, Dodik's rhetorical escalation found legitimization in the discourse of a rival Bosniak politician. The then-candidate for a Bosniak member of BiH presidency, Haris Silajdzic, campaigned under the slogan 100% BiH, which insinuated BiH without entities. Despite inability by either to fulfill the fantasies they vividly depicted, the dynamic of rival but mutually reinforcing discourses, not unlike that of the prewar nationalist rivalries, propelled both to electoral victory. Since then, Milorad Dodik has regularly revisited the theme of Republika Srpska's independence, while portraying BiH as a "rotten" country bound for eventual collapse (Dodik: BiH se raspada 2012). As this invited reciprocal response from the Bosniak and civic parties, the space was reduced for themes that focused not on the violent past or future fantasies, but on the present-day livelihoods.

Indeed, the discursive space of post-Dayton BiH is inundated with contestation over the meaning of BiH and Republika Srpska and conflicting narratives about the character of the Bosnian War. These discourses branch out into numerous conflicting story lines about individual events, political personalities, and the role of international actors and organizations. They also open up to renewed flirtation with unachieved wartime aims. Some of the major structures of this contention are outlined in the two tables below (Tables 1 and 2).

How, then, have the Bosnians from different sides of the wartime divides managed to peacefully interact for over two decades, sharing workplaces, developing friendship, and forming other social and economic ties? Indeed, the lived experiences speak of the relations quite different than the nationalist imaginaries and large-scale depictions of the menacing collective other. This tension has been addressed with differentiation between ethnic nations as a collective imaginary and their individual members. While many Serbs think of the Bosniak politics in terms of an existential threat and vice versa, this does not stop individual Bosniaks or Serbs to be commendable people of virtuous character. In everyday exchange, Bosnians have coped with the apparent contradiction by avoiding the divisive topics, adding humor to wartime memories, and framing the divisions as a product of self-interested politicians or outside agitators who had set ordinary people at odds. Dodik himself has occasionally echoed these frames by calling Bosniaks good people victimized by their own leaders and national politics (Dodik Bez dijaloga BiH je neodrziva 2017).

Indeed, this discursive compensation has created ruptures in the wartime divides, stabilizing daily interactions and creating cooperation necessary for the functioning of common institutions. BiH seems to have made strides from the time when Biljana Plavsic depicted the Bosnian Muslims as genetically inferior. Yet, at the same time, the elections are won by politicians who most effectively mobilize the emotional legacy of that time and offer promises that would unravel the existing order. Despite

Table 1 Narratives about character of the Bosnian War

Topic	Frames by Bosniak and civic parties	Frames by major Serb parties
General description of the war	External aggression by Serbia and Montenegro to ethically partition a democratic and civic sovereign Bosnian state, aided by collaborating Serb nationalists from within BiH. The project was to create "greater Serbia" in which non-Serbs would be second-rate citizens	Classic civil war between historically incompatible ethnic groups whom the international community attempted to force within a single state. Serbs were defending themselves from attempt by Muslims to create an Islamic republic
Srebrenica massacre	Genocide, evidence that Republika Srpska is a genocidal creation	Atrocities happened, but not genocide. Revenge attack for previous atrocities against Serbs. Numbers grossly exaggerated and events fabricated in order to demonize Serbs
Roles of Radovan Karadzic and Ratko Mladic	Despised war criminals directly responsible for genocide, ethnic cleansing, and loss of tens of thousands of innocent lives	Defenders of Serb nation unjustly accused by the enemies. Mladic is seen as hero general. Karadzic is seen as hero leader by some, but a corrupt politician by others
Siege of Sarajevo	Urbicide by a savage Serb army that killed thousands of innocent Sarajevans and destroyed much of the cosmopolitan city	Not even a siege. Serbs only defended their neighborhoods and suburbs. The destruction and casualties grossly exaggerated. Some massacres committed by Bosniaks against their own people in order to blame Serbs
Presence of Islamist fighters	Islamist fighters brought foreign, non-Bosniak traditions but were accepted as assistance in stopping the genocide. There were only a few hundreds of them, and they had no impact on the character of the war	Proof of religious character of the War. Serbs were fighting against the jihadists, just as Israel and Western powers had been doing in the Middle East. Thousands of fighters came, with full blessings of Bosniak leaders
Role of the Hague Tribunal	Made necessary verdicts that helped discover truth about the war. Yet, politics corrupted the court. Sentences were too lenient, especially on officials from Serbia. The charge of genocide should have applied to more places than only to Srebrenica	Political court set up by Western powers to demonize Serbs. Crimes against Serbs left unpunished. Court promoted new divisions, rather than reconciliation

the ruptures, the war aims continue to command mobilizational power. In the current configuration of political opportunities and constraints, this is mobilization to the ballot boxes. Should new configuration arise, armed mobilization remains a real possibility. Rather than peace, perhaps a more accurate depiction of this predicament may be nonwar.

Table 2 The current predicament and actions to be taken

Topic	Frames by Bosniak and civic parties	Frames by major Serb parties
Bosnia-Herzegovina as created in the Dayton peace accords	Internal divisions into entities cemented ethnic cleansing. Yet, the state is accepted and embraced as another instantiation of a thousand-year-old continuity of Bosnia, this time with independence and international subjectivity	Serbs do not desire any form of Bosnia. Yet, the Dayton Accords recognized Republika Srpska as an entity without which no decisions could be made. Bosnia is nothing else than a union of its entities. As such, it is acceptable as a compromise solution
What is BiH?	Dear homeland with a long and rich heritage. All its ethnic groups are also at the same time Bosnians, with their common way of life. BiH has historically exemplified coexistence and tolerance between different ethnicities and religions, but Serbia and Croatia have stirred chaos in order to divide it among themselves	BiH is an artificial creation, while its three ethnic communities are national. As such, it is doomed to dysfunction and eventual collapse along ethnic lines. Serbs are forced into the framework of BiH against their national will
What is Republika Srpska?	Despised genocidal creation. In contrast to the long and rich history of BiH, Republika Srpska created in the 1990s through ethnic cleansing of non-Serbs	Dear homeland. Expression of the will of the Serb people who created it to defend themselves. Republika Srpska assures survival of Serbs within a threatening environment
Description of the "other"	Serb politics are aggressive and barbarous, desiring to establish domination against non-Serbs. This has historical roots, as seen in both the Bosnian War and Cetnik atrocities against Muslims during World War II	Bosniak politics aim to impose an Islamic way of life and relegate Serbs to second-rate citizens. This has deep historical roots, as seen in the treatment of Christians during the Ottoman rule
Institutions formed by high representative	The Dayton accords provide a legal basis for the Office of High Representative. All decisions and institutions made by high representatives are binding	High representatives have been abusing their powers. The institutions they created are illegitimate, and BiH should revert only to those explicitly provided at Dayton. The Court of BiH and the BiH Prosecutor's Office have been particularly anti-Serb, and as such RS is under no obligation to obey them
Referendum as a political instrument	BiH is a state, and any referendum affecting the whole country could only occur at the level of BiH. Entities have no right to secession	Referendums demonstrate "will of the people." BiH is not a single nation but a union of three ethnic nations. Therefore, Serbs will 1 day exercise their national right to self-determination by means of an independence referendum in Republika Srpska

(*continued*)

Table 2 (continued)

Topic	Frames by Bosniak and civic parties	Frames by major Serb parties
Desired scenario	BiH without entities	Independent Republika Srpska
Possibility of a new war	Attempt at secession of RS would lead to bloodshed. Bosnian integrity will be defended. The idea of RS independence is warmongering	BiH will fall apart naturally, and separation will happen peacefully. Bosniaks desire to destroy RS, but RS has capacities to defend itself

Conclusion

The previous pages have offered a path toward advancing our understanding of the relationship between ethnic nationalism and violence by outlining a discursive-affective analytical framework and applying it to the Bosnian case. The discussion has departed from recognition that discourses produce subjectivities, emotional predispositions, and behavioral imperatives. It has brought together historical, cultural, and contingent situational factors and traced the interaction of both structure and agency. The case was made that violence happens not as some automatic consequence of objective conditions, but with the emergence of dominant modes of understandings that see ethnicity as a primary axis of identification and violence as a permissible instrument for dealing with the threatening other.

The chapter has also argued that once these understandings are in place, they do not produce murderous masses. Rather, they desensitize ethnic majorities to the suffering of the perceived other, creating conditions in which small minorities commit ethnically framed crimes with impunity. In one such condition, a survivor of one of the massacres against Bosniaks in the Prijedor area interviewed for this chapter lost a father. As he recalled, one person from the armed unit that entered his village was committing murders, another one seemed indifferent, while the face of the third was red in shame (Music 2018). It was not an enduring historical condition that drove one to murder, another one to stand by unconcerned, and the dissenter to remain silent. Rather, the condition emerged with evolution of sensibilities, itself driven by a radical change in the dominant portrayals of the other from "good neighbors" to the genetically malformed race. Indeed, the Bosnian case teaches us that talking is doing.

Cross-References

▶ Ethno-nationalism and Political Conflict in Bosnia (Europe)
▶ Ethno-Cultural Symbolism and Group Identity
▶ Ethno-nationalism and Political Conflict in Bosnia (Europe)
▶ Historical Memory and Ethnic Myths

References

Baumann R, Gawrych G, Kretchik W (2012) Armed peacekeepers in Bosnia. CreateSpace Publishing, p 120

Bhavnani R (2006) Ethnic norms and interethnic violence: accounting for mass participation in the Rwandan genocide. J Peace Res 43:651–669

Binder D (1992) US tecognizes three Yugoslav Republics as independent. The New York Times

Brubaker R, Cooper F (2000) Beyond "identity". Theory Soc 29:1

Carić M (1990). Moral, pa nacija. NIN. p 2

Damasio A (2005) Descartes' error. Penguin Books, London

Dodik Bez dijaloga BiH je neodrziva (2017) Glas Srpske. Retrieved from http://www.glassrpske.com/novosti/vijesti_dana/Dodik-Bez-dijaloga-BiH-neodrziva-VIDEO/lat/232242.html

Dodik: BiH se Raspada (2012) Radio and television of Serbia. Retrieved from http://www.rts.rs/page/stories/sr/story/11/region/1183306/dodik-bih-se-raspada.html

Fearon and Latin (2000) Violence and the social construction of ethnic identity. Int Organ 54(4) p.868

Flegar S, Rebac I (2010) Na ovaj dan prije 20 god. je pocelo. 24sata.hr Retrieved from https://www.24sata.hr/news/balvan-revolucija-na-ovaj-dan-prije-20-god-je-pocelo-186759

GDP per capita, current prices (2018) International monetary fund. Retrieved from http://www.imf.org/external/datamapper/PPPPC@WEO/THA/BIH/EUQ

Halimovic DZ (2009) Plavsic povukla priznanje krivnje. Radio Slobodna Evropa. Retrieved from https://mail.google.com/mail/u/0/#search/paul.carnegie%40usp.ac.fj/1642573d7517. 0896?projector=1&messagePartId=0.2

Ignatieff M (1993) Blood and belonging: journey into the new nationalism. Farrar Strauss, New York

Kahneman D (2011) Thinking fast and slow. Farrar, Straus and Giroux, New York

Kredie LH, Monroe KR (2002) Psychological boundaries and ethnic conflict: how identity constrained choice and worked to turn ordinary people into perpetrators of ethnic violence during the Lebanese civil war. Int J Polit Cult Soc 16:1

Lieberman E, Singh P (2012) The institutional origins of ethnic violence. Comp Polit 45:1

Maksic A (2009) Referendum discourse in Republika Srpska politics: an analysis of its emergence and performative structure. Unpublished Master's Thesis

Maksic A (2017) Ethnic mobilization, violence and the politics of affect: Serb democratic party and the Bosnian War. Palgrave Macmillan, Cham

Mueller J (2000) The banality of 'ethnic war'. Int Secur 25(1):42–70

Music S (2018) Personal Interview

Obershall A (2000) The manipulation of ethnicity: from ethnic cooperation to violence and war in Yugoslavia. Ethn Racial Stud 23:6

Pellet A (1992) The opinions of the Badinter arbitration committee: a second breath for the self-determination of peoples. Eur J Int Law 3(1):178–185

Popović V (1993) Even if we get 70% of the territory, there can be no peace with the Muslims. Svet. Retrieved from http://icr.icty.org/LegalRef/CMSDocStore/Public/English/Exhibit/NotIndexable/IT-00-39/. ACE35199R0000152382.tif

Šarac A (1990) Jenjava strah od višestranaštva. Oslobođenje. p 2

SDP: Vladajuća koalicija je slagala građane da je mehanizam koordinacije usaglašen (2016) Patria News Agency. Retrieved from http://www.nap.ba/new/vijest.php?id=22681

Shoup P (1992) The Bosnian crisis of 1992. The National Council for Soviet and East Europan Research

Sito-Susic D, Robinson M (2013) After years of toil, book names Bosnian war dead. Reuters. Retrieved from https://www.reuters.com/article/us-bosnia-dead/after-years-of-toil-book-names-bosnian-war-dead-idUSBRE91E0J220130215

Szewcyzk B (2010) The EU in Bosnia and Herzegovina: powers, decisions and legitimacy. European Union Institute for Security Studies, Brussels

The Europa World Year Book (2003) Taylor and Francis Group. p 814

Toal G, Maksic A (2014) Serbs, you are allowed to be Serbs! Radovan Karadžić and the 1990 Election Campaign in Bosnia-Herzegovina. Ethnopolitics

Transparency International (2017) Corruption perceptions index. Retrieved from: https://www.transparency.org/news/feature/corruption_perceptions_index_2017

Westen D (2007) The political brain: the role of emotion in deciding the fate of the nation. Public Affairs, New York

Ethnic Conflict and Militias

32

Andrew Thomson

Contents

Introduction	560
Militias and Pro-government Militias	561
Ethnicity, Ethnic Conflict, and Militias	563
Defector PGMs	565
Rival PGMs	566
Ethnic PGMs and Their Effects on Conflict Dynamics	568
Conclusions	572
References	573

Abstract

Militias of various kinds, such as pro-government militias, paramilitaries, vigilantes, death squads, and civil defense forces, are common features of many civil conflicts around the world. They are also prevalent in "ethnic conflicts." Ethnic mobilization into militias, where recruitment into such armed groups takes place across ethnic divides, constitutes an important facet of many ethnic conflicts. From Serbian pro-state militia forces during the breakup of Yugoslavia, to the "Arab" Janjaweed fighters in Sudan, to Pashtun Achekvai militias in Afghanistan, and to Kurdish Village Guards in Turkey, pro-government militias mobilized and recruited along ethnic lines are common. This chapter provides an overview of some of the literature on militias in ethnic conflict. It highlights and draws distinctions between specific conceptualizations and categories of militia forces, such as "ethnic militias" and "ethnic pro-government militias" as well as subcategories of the latter, such as "ethnic defectors" and "rival militias." It highlights some common approaches to theorizing the mobilization of ethnic militias. It then covers some empirical research into their impact on conflict dynamics.

A. Thomson (✉)
Queens University of Belfast, Belfast, UK
e-mail: a.f.thomson@qub.ac.uk

Keywords
Ethnic conflict · Ethnic militia · Pro-government militia · Ethnic mobilization

Introduction

Until relatively recently most studies on civil wars have focused on governments and insurgent groups, largely leaving out analysis of extra-dyadic actors such as pro-government militias, civil militias, vigilante forces, and paramilitary groups (Ferguson 2017; Carey et al. 2013). In a similar fashion, most empirical studies have tended to conceptualize "ethnic conflict" in relation to the ethnic characteristics of warring parties such as the government or rebel forces (Cederman et al. 2013). For example, Wucherpfennig and colleagues (2012) identify conflicts as "ethnic" based on ethnic cleavages and insurgent recruitment from ethnic groups vis-à-vis the government. Wimmer et al. (2009) also theorize the relationship between ethnicity and violent conflict with reference to ethnically exclusionary politics and ethno-political configurations of power between those ethnic groups in control of the incumbent government and the mobilization of excluded groups into insurgent factions. Moreover, many studies have analyzed how the ethnic composition of both states and insurgent groups affects dynamics such as recruitment, intensity of violence, and the duration of conflict (Eck 2009; Montalvo and Reynal-Querol 2005; Wucherpfennig et al. 2012). Until recently, less attention has been paid to the role of militias, pro-state armed forces, and similar vigilante groups in ethnic disputes.

However, ethnic nationalism, the politicization and polarization of identities, and ethnic mobilization have contributed to the emergence of armed militia groups within many conflicts. Ethnic militias and ethnic pro-government militias have arisen as extra-dyadic or third actors in many civil wars around the world. Such actors have taken on various roles or functions such as counterinsurgent forces, protecting ethnic minorities, community policing, defending the interests of ethnic groups and/or political parties, among others. From Serbian pro-state militia forces during the breakup of Yugoslavia, "Arab" Janjaweed and Murahaleen fighters in Sudan, Pashtun Achekvai militias in Afghanistan, Kurdish Peshmerga in Iraq, Mende Kamajor civilian defense forces in Sierra Leone, to Rwandan Hutu Interahamwe militias, ethnic militias and ethnic pro-government militias are a common feature of civil conflicts. In addition, according to Raleigh (2016) and Francis (2005), within civil conflicts across Africa, such actors have become increasingly prevalent and violent phenomena over the last few decades.

This chapter understands "ethnic conflict" as civil war characterized by the ethnic composition of warring parties and the extent to which those warring parties' objectives represent ethnic group interests. In so doing, this chapter largely avoids debates over whether or not (and how) ethnicity is linked to civil war onset as well central debates on whether or not "ethnic conflict" is an appropriate description of certain intrastate wars (e.g., Eck 2009; Kaufmann 1996; Gilley 2004). It focuses primarily on political violence in civil war rather than low-intensity forms of inter-ethnic violence in which militias might play a role, such as in riots or violence and intimidation during elections. This chapter reviews some of the existing research into militias in ethnic conflict. It highlights specific conceptualizations and categories of militia forces, such as "ethnic militias" and "ethnic pro-government militias." It further points to subcategories of the latter that recent scholarship has identified, such as "ethnic defectors" and "rival militias." It starts by examining militia forces more generally or those not necessarily affiliated with one or more ethnic groupings. It very briefly highlights some prominent theories of the mobilization of militias. It then turns to the ethnic composition and mobilization of militia forces. Looking more in-depth at a few examples of "ethnic militias" and "ethnic pro-government militias" helps describe these types of ethnic militia actors, their relation to the state and insurgents, and their activities within ethnic conflict. In other words, this chapter will cover what ethnic militias are, some different types of militias, why they emerge, and what they do. It then moves on to some of the theorized effects of the presence of such actors in ethnic conflicts. Finally, it identifies some areas for future research in the conclusion.

Militias and Pro-government Militias

There has been a plethora of terms used for a vast array of militia-type actors, including "civil militia," "vigilantes," "paramilitaries," "civil defense forces," "death squads," and "irregular forces," among many others, both inside and outside of civil war. Most terms correspond to very specific types of actors, and definitions emphasize differences in the roles they undertake, their recruitment base, modes of organization, targets, and their relationship to the state and relations with insurgents. Circumnavigating the wide variety of actors and associated terms can also be difficult because the contexts in which these forces operate, and therefore some of their fundamental features, vary significantly (Raleigh 2016; Schuberth 2015; Mazzei 2009; Campbell 2002). In addition, the "politics of naming" has obstructed agreement over different categories and their definitions. The term "warlord," for example, conjures negative connotations (MacKinlay 2000).

Many authors have settled on the term "civil militias" to encapsulate a variety of non-state armed organizations in civil wars with a diverse range of functions, activities, and objectives (Francis 2005; Bertrand 2004; Tar 2005; Raleigh 2016). Civil militias may have various possible relationships with the state and corresponding activities, ranging from waging insurgency or a separatist movement against the state, to conducting vigilante community defense, to operating as predatory criminal enterprises, to reinforcing state counterinsurgent efforts. However, a large body of recent research has concentrated more specifically on "pro-government militias" (PGMs). In their introduction of the first comprehensive database on such actors, Carey et al. (2013) defined PGMs as organized armed groups with some level of organization that are aligned with the incumbent government or subregional government institutions, but not identified as being part of the "official" armed forces. PGMs are distinct from civil militias in that the PGMs are specifically pro-state or pro-government actors and usually anti-insurgent in nature. Yet, a review of the PGM database reveals that PGM is also a heterogeneous category. For example, civilian defense forces, death squads, and paramilitaries often differ in whether they have a direct (semi-official) or an indirect (unofficial) relationship with the state, the strength of that relationship, their area of operation, their targets, and operational parameters (see Carey and Mitchell 2017; Carey et al. 2013; Böhmelt and Clayton 2018; Clayton and Thomson 2016).

Many studies have linked the emergence of both civil militias and PGMs in civil wars to state weakness. For instance, many analysts place weak state control or governance as a necessary precondition for the emergence of civil militias (Francis 2005; Meagher 2012; Allen 1999). In the absence of strong state institutions, militia forces fill in the gaps serving as local vigilante security forces, counterinsurgents, or armed groups in defense of local interests and often operate as opportunistic predators conducting extortionate roadblocks or looting local resources. Similarly, others argue that governments often have little choice in delegating violence to PGMs where government presence is limited and where PGM forces offer a cheaper, more readily available fighting force compared to the official armed forces. The state weakness thesis, however, falls short in explaining the emergence of militias and PGMs in the context of strong states, among other areas. Often juxtaposed against this explanation of what states *cannot* do are approaches that emphasize what the state *won't* do. Many scholars posit that states mobilize or support PGMs, and death squad actors in particular, as a plausibly deniable mechanism to disavow responsibility for targeting civilians or other "dirty war" tactics (Campbell 2002; Carey et al. 2015). Both these sets of explanations reside on a state-militia relational perspective.

Others have provided more long-term structural explanations for the emergence of militia forces. Ahram (2011), for example, has traced militia actors to the historical development of states and military institutions. In a similar fashion, Mason and Krane (1989) adopt a political economy approach, linking death squad actors and repressive tendencies to broader global and local political-economic trends. Other authors understand PGMs as emerging within the contexts of capitalist expansion and development, connecting these actors to large business interests (Sprague-Silgado 2018; Hristov 2014; Sprague 2012; Lasslett 2014). Hristov (2009, 2014), for example, analyzes the emergence and role of paramilitary groups in Colombia within systems of violent capital accumulation.

Finally, some commentators argue in favor of actor-centric explanations emphasizing the autonomous mobilization of militia forces and their interaction with insurgent groups. For example, many have examined how local communities and/or powerful leaders mobilize armed organizations for opportunistic and predatory reasons, such as "warlords," and often develop local vigilante governance structures in pursuit of power and legitimacy (e.g., Reno 1998; Hills 1997; Jackson 2003; MacKinlay 2000). Others, such as Barter (2013) and Fumerton and Remijnse (2004), focus on local or community mobilization of civilian self-defense militias (a type of PGM) in response to insurgent violence. Communities faced with violent rebel groups may organize themselves for the protection of their own villages or towns. For example, in Peru some towns mobilized *Comites de Autodefensa* to protect themselves from predatory attacks by the Sendero Luminoso insurgency. Similarly, in Banda Aceh, in Indonesia, many ethnic minority enclaves formed militia groups in response to separatist insurgent forces. In these cases, both "warlord" mobilization and community formation of civilian defense forces and militia organizations formed from the "bottom-up," rather than in "top-down" state-led initiatives.

This very brief overview of some prominent theories explaining the rise of militias and PGMs has not yet included, more specifically, why militias often recruit along ethnic lines nor on how militias operate in the context of ethnic conflict. While the politicization of ethnic divisions or identity-based grievances is often a devise used for militia mobilization (see below), this occurs within broader complex and shifting ideological, political, and economic contexts. The above contexts and factors may play a significant role in the emergence of militia groups, regardless of whether such forces were recruited along ethnic divisions or not.

Ethnicity, Ethnic Conflict, and Militias

How the saliency of ethnicity and ethnic mobilization aid in the formation of militias and pro-government militias specifically (rather than insurgents) has been explored in various contexts. For instance, the literature on ethnic conflict has sought to provide better understandings of ethnic mobilization into armed groups more generally, which does offer significant insight into the emergence of ethnic militias and PGMs. Ethnicity and other shared forms of identity have provided the basis for recruitment into armed organizations. Ethnicity has often formed a powerful marker of identification between in-groups and out-groups, and, under certain circumstances, ethnic politicization can lead to polarization (Sambanis and Shayo 2013; Horowitz 1985). Within emerging inter-ethnic security dilemmas, armed group mobilization across ethnic divisions can accelerate (Rose 2000; Posen 1993). In incipient conflict, ethnicity can provide a stronger or more powerful basis for recruitment into armed organizations than others, such as ideology (Eck 2009; Cederman et al. 2010, 2013). Recruitment along ethnic lines helps to overcome collective action problems, lowers potential coordination costs, and can help more easily identify common interests or goals (Eck 2009). Insurgents and militias alike often use identity-based cleavages or politicize ethnicity for recruitment, tactical, and political purposes. While much research on ethnic mobilization into armed groups has focused primarily on insurgents, many scholars point to how this applies to recruitment into militia forces as much as it does to anti-state rebels (e.g., Magid and Schon 2018; Alden et al. 2011; Ikelegbe 2005).

Some analysts have referred to "ethnic militia" (sometimes "community militias") to identify civil militia forces mobilized along ethnic lines and that uphold specific ethnic group goals in ethno-political struggles. Ethnic militia are irregular or non-state armed actors composed of primarily one ethnic grouping that defend the security and interests of their kin against multiple competing ethnic factions in the context of weak, factionalized, or indifferent state representation (Guichaoua 2010; Agbu 2004). In other words, ethnic militias recruit exclusively from within a single ethnic group, are comprised of members from certain villages or areas, provide security for their co-ethnics, and contend for power and resources among other competing ethnic groups. Such groups are often compared to "warlords" or local power brokers who exert a modicum of control over territory, people, and/or resources (e.g., Reno 1998; Hills 1997). These militias usually provide vigilante policing functions and alternative government structures either within their own ethnic enclaves or externally to protect their interests against rival criminal bands. Crucially, in this conception, ethnic militias are not necessarily identified as pro-state or anti-state but instead often have a contentious relationship to the state in the pursuit of ethnic group objectives (Ikelegbe 2005).

The term "ethnic militia" is usually, but not exclusively, used to refer to militia factions in countries in Africa experiencing ethnic fractionalization and polarization. Guichaoa (2010), for example, argues that such groups are "idiosyncratic" to some countries across Africa and constitute "hybrid creatures made of culturally-based reformist insurgencies, armed wings of political parties, but also...extra-legal governance agencies." One example includes the Oduduwa People's Congress (OPC) in Nigeria, a Yoruba nationalist association that emerged within the context of weak state presence and spiraling intergroup struggles for political domination, resources, and representation (Guichaoua 2010; Ikelegbe 2005; Agbu 2004; Akinyele 2001). Similar organizations in Nigeria include Ijaw Youth Council or the Arewa People's Council. The OPC constituted an ethnic movement at the forefront of the Nigerian ethno-political landscape representing Yoruba peoples in the southwest of the country, claiming a huge membership of 4.2 million people with various factions and youth wings (Ikelegbe 2005). From its beginnings in the 1990s, it has had a nationalist orientation and militant approach in the promotion of Yoruba collective interests, intragroup policing, defense against other ethnic group militants, and in its assertion of Yoruba rights. Its militarized wing has primarily been involved in clashes and retaliatory actions with other ethnic militias or groups in the defense or advancement of Yoruba interests. However, the OPC also had nationalist goals of self-determination, leading to violent conflict with the Nigerian government, which has only just stopped short of insurgency. The Nigerian government, in turn, has outlawed the group. Thus, the OPC, as an "ethnic militia," has had multiple functions in the representation of Yoruba ethnic minorities in fractionalized and polarized ethno-politic struggles in Nigeria. Its status as a "militia" refers to its militant characteristics and autonomous nature whereupon it has not necessarily been identified as strictly anti-state or pro-state.

In contrast to research into ethnic militias, with its broad focus on various ethnically mobilized armed formations including insurgent separatist groups, recent empirically oriented scholarship has begun to examine the ethnic composition and ties of pro-government militias (PGMs). Magid and Schon (2018) have recently coded PGM databases according to PGM ethnic composition and their relations to the state and insurgent factions. Carey et al.'s (2013) PGM database also codes for "ethnic" membership, identifying 95 PGM groups with an identity-based recruitment platform. An ethnic PGM can be defined as a non-state armed group that is pro-government in some fashion, but that is not identified as a part of the official armed forces, and is recruited along ethnic lines in order to uphold ethnic goals. Ethnic PGMs recruit exclusively from a single ethnic group or from a collection of ethnic groups that have some shared identity. Recruiting from specific ethnic groupings into pro-state militia forces is common across the world. For example, the Uzbek Junbesh-e-Milli in Afghanistan is composed almost entirely of recruits from the Uzbek community. Ethnic PGMs often include recruits from transnational ethnic diaspora or ethnic kin from neighboring states. They can also link with armed factions from other countries. For instance, the Army for the Liberation of Rwanda often crosses the border into the DRC in cooperation with fellow Hutu Congolese. Ethnic PGMs uphold certain ethnic goals or objectives. These objectives vary across groups but might include defending ethnic group access to resources, maintaining a dominant position in a political or economic hierarchy, or defending certain sections of the civilian population.

Building on existing literature, empirical research on ethnic pro-state militias tend to divide ethnic PGMs into "defector PGMs" and "rival PGMs." This provides a theoretically informed categorization of ethnic PGMs. These categories based on PGMs' relationship to both the state and insurgent groups with respect to ethnic mobilization and ethnic bonds form the basis for theorizing some of the effects of particular types of ethnic PGM in civil war. After briefly outlining these distinct sets of ethnic PGM, this chapter then touches on some of the short-term and long-term effects on conflict dynamics that these types of ethnic PGMs can have.

Defector PGMs

Defector PGMs "share an ethnic tie with the anti-government local population" (Magid and Schon 2018). They are composed of defected individuals from an excluded or anti-government ethnic civilian population or from an ethnic insurgent group. According to Kalyvas (2008, 1045), ethnic defection is a process whereby individuals or groups turn against their co-ethnic insurgent population that ostensibly represent the interests of their ethnic group and end up fighting alongside the government against their own ethnic kin. In essence, ethnic defectors "switch sides" against their own ethnic cohort to collaborate with the government, usually in a counterinsurgent role. This helps to demonstrate that ethnic allegiances, and in some cases identities, are not primordial or static but can change during the course of conflict (see Kalyvas 2008).

Ethnic defectors may have multiple incentives to collaborate with the government against their ethnic brethren. This can include gaining patronage and access to resources, aligning with a more powerful group or "winning side," or to gain security from insurgent groups that prey on civilian populations. The process of ethnic defection can occur from the "top-down" whereby the state encourages defection into anti-insurgent militias. The mobilization or co-optation of ethnic defectors is a common counterinsurgency strategy designed to use the local knowledge, language and cultural skills, and ethnic ties in order to overcome the "identification problem"

(Kalyvas 2008; Lyall 2010; Staniland 2012). States seek to gain tactical advantages by promoting ethnic defection to further their counterinsurgent cause. For example, the Russian military actively encouraged defection of Chechen rebels and civilians from Chechen communities into counterinsurgent paramilitary forces known as *Kadyrovsky* in order to identify, denounce, arrest, or issue threats against those who had joined or supported Chechen rebel groups (Lyall 2010; Staniland 2012). On other occasions this process can occur from the "bottom-up" whereby segments of a community, ethnic faction, or tribal group defect autonomously from an insurgency, often in response to security concerns or unfavorable power relations, which governments then later support (e.g., Barter 2013). For example, the Sunni Awakening in Iraq involved a series of Sunni tribal groups' defection due to rifts with foreign elements of the anti-occupation insurgency and Al-Qaeda. Once defection caught momentum, the US Army capitalized to create a "Sons of Iraq" militia program (Clayton and Thomson 2014). In these cases, ethnic or other identity-based affiliations facilitated defection through kinship networks such as tribes or clan-based shifting of allegiances.

One prominent example of such ethnic defector PGMs includes the Kurdish Village Guards and their collaboration with the Turkish government against the Kurdish ethno-nationalist insurgent PKK (Kurdish Worker's Party). The Turkish government systematically encouraged Kurdish civilian collaboration, often by appealing to labels such as "loyal Kurds" as an identity, and established a Kurdish village guard militia system in 1985 to "defend" their communities from the Kurdish PKK (Belge 2011; Gurcan 2015; Biberman 2018). The Turkish government provided salaries, weapons, and other materials to willing conscripts. Rather than individual applicants, however, recruitment usually occurred through informal deals between state authorities and clan leaders, enticed by higher-than-average salaries and joining a stronger side (see Belge 2011). The Turkish government and armed forces aimed at utilizing ethnic defectors' local knowledge to identify PKK insurgent members living in or around their communities. The Turkish government also used ethnic defection as a method to tie the Kurdish identity to the Turkish state, thereby limiting the PKK's appeal to the Kurdish identity as a platform for ethno-nationalist mobilization or recruitment into the PKK. Other examples of ethnic defector militias include Kashmiri Muslim fighters joining the Indian armed forces in their campaign to control and suppress Muslim separatists in Kashmir. Another example includes how French colonial authorities managed to garner loyalty of Muslim Algerians, organized into Harkis militias, to fight on their side against an anti-colonial ethno-nationalist FLN (*Front de Liberation Nationale*) which appealed to a native Muslim Algerian ethnic identity against non-Muslims as the basis of its insurgency.

Rival PGMs

Rival PGMs, on the other hand, constitute ethnic PGMs that defend governments dominated by certain ethnic group(s) against other rival ethnic groups. Rival PGMs are usually comprised of individuals or groups that hail from the same or similar ethnic grouping as the government. They are usually co-ethnics with those in power. They also operate in the context of ethno-political power imbalances in aiding the incumbent government to preserve ethnically exclusionary power where one or more ethnic groups dominate the government. As part of a broader strategy and "logic of ethno-political exclusion" (Cederman et al. 2013; Wucherpfennig et al. 2012; Roessler 2011), ruling factions often turn to loyal co-ethnic militia forces to defend their dominant positions or to provide for "coup-proofing." Similarly, ethnically based political parties often turn to tribal leaders or "big men" (possibly "warlords") from their own or similar ethnic groupings as a way to mobilize support for the regime and to defend against other rival ethnic groups, ultimately to ensure their group's grip on power and mitigate power challenges (see Roessler 2011). Alternatively, in the context of the presence of multiple warring ethnic groups, rival PGMs can be members of ethnic groups that simply share similar goals to that of the government. The process of ethnic mobilization into rival PGMs can be a "top-down" state-led initiative whereby states seek to exploit existing divisions and co-opt certain ethnic factions that are loyal to the state, or a "bottom-up" process in response to inter-ethnic security dilemma, or some combination of both. Rival PGMs, and especially those that share ethnicity or ethnic grouping with the government, often have incentives to defend the government and these ethno-political imbalances as they benefit in the associated power, prestige, and spoils of the remaining loyal to the regime. Systems of patronage and other benefits help solidify rival PGM commitment to defending the government and favorable configurations of ethno-political power.

One example of rival PGM mobilization includes how the "Arab"-dominated Sudanese government in the north of the country relied on a variety of rival PGMs in its overlapping counterinsurgency campaigns against "African" ethnic insurgents. Examples include the Popular People's Front and Murahaleen, which fought against the Sudan People's Liberation Army/Movement (SPLA/M) during the second Sudanese civil war (1983–2005), as well as the Janjaweed which combatted the Sudan Liberation Movement (SLA) and Justice and Equality Movement (JEM) in the Darfur conflict (2003–2011). After the 1989 coup that brought the National Islamic Front party to power, the government leveraged Arab-Muslim militias by appealing to common Arab-Muslim identity among "Arab" peoples primarily in the northern half of Sudan, such as the Baggara, as well as via Islamist political and popular mobilization platforms (e.g., Jihad) (Idris 2005). Many rival militias mobilized autonomously in response to perceived threats to their ethnic group and access to resources and to defend their status as an in-group within an "Arab"-dominated state. "Arab" militias such as the Murahaleen and Popular Defense Forces in the second Sudanese civil war and the Janjaweed in Darfur became militia forces fighting on behalf of the "Arab"-dominated government of Sudan and simultaneously defending their own ethnic groups' interests (Tar 2005). They operated along exclusionary ethnic lines, violently attacking "African" civilians and those believed to be sympathetic to the insurgent SPLA/M causes, and participated in the displacement of opposing groups as well as engaged in looting, slave driving, and burning down entire villages.

The Sudanese government supported these co-ethnic rival PGMs for a variety of reasons. State weakness in hard-to-reach contested areas was significant (Tar 2005). In order to protect the interests and security of co-ethnic "Arab" tribes and to counter the advances of "African" insurgent groups, the government of Sudan has long supported Arab tribal militias in order to extend influence into rural areas and the contested boundaries between the northern and southern territories of the country. For example, the government supported Murahaleen incursions into Dinka-held territory in order to maintain or advance control of remote regions of Sudan and to jockey for access to resources (Johnson 2003, 44–49, 83). Another major rationale for creating and/or supporting rival PGMs was that the Sudanese Armed Forces were composed of conscripts from a variety of ethnic groups and tribal affiliations who were often reluctant to commit violence against their perceived ethnic kin in the insurgent southern regions (Idris 2005, 88; Tar 2005, 150). Rival PGMs that comprised of groups co-ethnic to the government were seen as more loyal to the state and more willing to exercise violence on its behalf than the official military armed forces.

Other examples of rival PGMs include the Filipino government support for various Christian militias, such as the Ilagas, to fight against Muslim separatist insurgent groups in Mindanao in the 1970s. More recently, in the early 2000s, with the Ivory Coast (Côte d'Ivoire) divided between an insurgent Muslim majority in the north and a government led by majority Christians in the south, "death squad" style actors mobilized among the President Laurent Gbagbo's ethnic Bede (sometimes "Bete") group targeted Muslim northerners and other minority ethnic groups deemed a threat to Bede (or Christian) rule. In addition, in Syria, the Assad regime has deployed co-ethnic Alawite militias to protect the regime against growing civil unrest and opposition to the state.

Ethnic PGMs and Their Effects on Conflict Dynamics

While recent research has made significant headway in understanding ethnic mobilization into militias and their roles in ethnic conflicts, much less has yet investigated the effects of ethnic militias and PGMs on conflict dynamics. Researchers have sought to investigate how militias and PGMs more generally, or those not necessarily mobilized along ethnic lines, affect conflict dynamics such as the intensity of violence, targets, and types of violence. For example, some have argued that PGMs that are unofficially or informally linked to the state tend to exhibit higher levels of violence against civilians (Carey et al. 2015; Mitchell et al. 2014; Ferguson 2017). This research has so far largely excluded how ethnicity or ethnic relationships impact these dynamics. On the other hand, research into ethnic conflicts tends to focus on how ethnic mobilization affects the onset of conflict (Cederman and Girardin 2007; Montalvo and Reynal-Querol 2010; Cederman et al. 2010). Select few have begun to focus on how ethnic mobilization affects dynamics of violence. For example, Eck (2009) argued that the ethnic mobilization of warring parties can lead to quicker escalation and more intense fighting than non-ethnically based mobilization. Fewer studies have addressed how the ethnic makeup of militia forces influences such processes in conflict. It is worth keeping in mind, though, that the contexts in which militias operate are influenced by a variety of shifting political, economic, and ideological factors. It is difficult to isolate exactly how ethnicity, ethnic recruitment, or ethnic relationships play a role in militia violence outside of a broader understanding of the complex conditions in which they are operating. However, among the few studies that do exist in this area point to the potential powerful effects that ethnic mobilization into both defector PGMs and rival PGMs might have, but more research is needed.

Defector PGMs, for example, can offer states certain tactical advantages in counterinsurgency settings, affecting government targeting of its enemies and civilians. States often harness ethnic defection in efforts to undermine insurgencies by making use of the defectors' knowledge of the local people and terrain, their language, and their extended ethnic ties in order to more effectively overcome the "identification problem" (Staniland 2012; Lyall 2010). Since ethnic defectors hail from insurgent populations, they are privy to and can tap into local information better than state forces (who are not co-ethnic to the insurgent population). This is particularly the case when defectors are turned insurgents. Lyall (2010), for example, highlighted how Chechen defector PGMs, *Kadyrovsky*, many of which had previously operated for the insurgency, provided Russian counterinsurgents distinct advantages in identifying and locating Chechen rebels. Harnessing ethnic defection can aid in reducing the propensity for state indiscriminate or collective ethnic targeting, which is more likely where the government is unable to identify who the insurgents are (Kalyvas 2006; Fjelde and Hultman 2014). Defector PGMs can therefore help improve the selectivity of state violence and thereby facilitate lower collective ethnic civilian targeting. Some studies have argued that harnessing defector PGMs has aided in the reduction of state violence against civilians and certain ethnic groups in this manner and/or can help improve state capacities, especially in occasions of mass defection (Peic 2014). For example, the US military use of turned Sunni insurgents in the Sons of Iraq militia program had an effect on the US military ability to identify and target insurgents as well as drive a wedge between the insurgents and local civilian populations in Anbar province (Clayton and Thomson 2014, 2016). In addition to this, militia forces themselves recruited from the same ethnic group as the insurgents or excluded minority populations might be less apt to indiscriminately target co-ethnic civilians. Defector PGMs are not likely to challenge their own ethnic kin with extreme violence (Stanton 2015).

However, insurgents may respond to ethnic defectors with force, prompting intra-ethnic violence and insurgent civilian targeting. The mobilization of a PGM force from ethnic populations that are traditionally associated with or supportive of insurgents threatens insurgents in a number of ways. The formation of defector PGMs can undermine intra-ethnic cohesion, challenge the "legitimacy" of ethnically mobilized insurgents as the main representative of excluded ethnic groups, threaten insurgent access to a co-ethnic recruitment pool, and help undermine support for the insurgents among local populations (Lyall 2010; Souleimanov et al. 2018). Insurgents therefore often seek to deter defection, to punish those that have defected, and to re-establish their control and dominance within their own ethnic enclaves (Kalyvas 1999; Staniland 2012; Lyall 2010). Where ethnic defection takes place, insurgents often target their own ethnic brethren for their "betrayal" against their groups' objectives. For example, Lilja and Hultman (2011) observed that insurgent intra-ethnic violence and violence against co-ethnic civilian groups in Sri Lanka were often associated with targeting defectors. The emergence of Tamil militia forces such as the Eelam People's Democratic Party and other "citizen volunteer forces" among the Tamil population represented a challenge to the insurgent groups' (such as Liberation Tigers of Tamil Eelam LTTE) control over the co-ethnic (i.e., Tamil) civilian population, prompting insurgent retaliation against them and civilian groups that supported the defector PGMs.

This set of dynamics of insurgent reactions can apply to both ethnic mobilization of defector PGMs and the non-ethnic defection of civilian groups or insurgent factions against an insurgency. For example, Clayton and Thomson (2016) show that insurgents often react violently to such challenges among civilian populations and the formation of anti-insurgent civilian defense forces (see also Kalyvas 1999). Further research might better and more systematically address how the saliency of ethnicity and strength of ethnic bonds could either reinforce insurgent violent punishment of ethnic defection or weaken it (see Kalyvas 2008; Souleimanov et al. 2018). For instance, as suggested above, insurgents may not want to violently clash with their co-ethnics and seek different mechanisms to avoid defection (Stanton 2015). Indeed, Lyall (2010) demonstrates that ethnic ties between insurgents and defectors actually helped produce lower levels of insurgent violence overall in Chechnya. This finding is at odds with those looking at similar dynamics in non-ethnic conflict settings, a difference that the ethnic dimension might help to explain (e.g., Clayton and Thomson 2016). Other research has shown that ethnic defection can carry with it more significant implications for those "defecting." For example, the PKK labeled Kurdish Village Guard members in Turkey as "traitors" to Kurdish nationalism for their cooperation with Turkish counterinsurgency efforts and they were subsequently reluctant to publicly identify as members of the Village Guard (Gurcan 2015; Belge 2011). More research is needed to explore exactly how ethnicity plays a role in these dynamics.

Rival PGMs, on the other hand, tend to be associated with higher levels of violence and higher levels of indiscriminate civilian targeting and human rights violations. For example, Magid and Schon (2018) find that, in countries in Africa at least, rival ethnic militias that are highly committed to the defense of a particular regime tend to exhibit higher levels of civilian abuse than other types of ethnically mobilized PGMs. There are many reasons why rival PGMs might be more apt to target civilians. Firstly, in distinction to defector PGMs, since rival PGMs are not from the same ethnic group(s) or communities as insurgent forces, rival PGMs do not possess intimate knowledge of their "enemies." This can lead to higher chances of indiscriminate targeting of civilians by both state patrons and the PGM itself (Kalyvas 2006). Secondly, targeting enemy civilians is often understood as a way to weaken opposition and therefore is much more likely where actors use ethnic affiliations to identify potential targets (Fjelde and Hultman 2014). Thirdly, since rival PGMs are mobilized or co-opted to defend the incumbent regime and maintain ethno-political power hierarchies, the mobilization of rival PGMs can serve to further polarize ethnic divisions, intensifying cleavages and inter-ethnic violent conflict (Roessler 2016; Sambanis and Shayo 2013). For example, the Sudanese government's support for "Arab" militias against neighboring "African" groups was fundamental to the polarization of ethnic division between the "Arab" north and the "African" south as well as the escalation of violence and civilian victimization on both sides.

Similarly, while not necessarily positing a causal relationship between the rise of rival militias and genocidal violence, it is clear that Hutu militias, such as the Interahamwe, played a major role in the Rwandan government-backed genocide of Tutsi minorities in 1994. The emergence of the Interahamwe Hutu militias was part of the defense of Hutu dominance in the government of Rwanda. Originating from the youth wing of the then ruling political party, the MRND, Interahamwe Hutu militias, and other party militias, such as the Impuzamugambi, were prominent in maintaining ethno-exclusionary power configurations and pivotal in the increasing inter-ethnic tensions between Hutu and Tutsi in the buildup to genocide. Following the RPF invasion of Kigali in 1990 from Uganda, and the initiation of the Rwandan civil war, the Interahamwe organization accelerated pro-Hutu and anti-Tutsi propaganda via the RTLM radio stations. This aided in the increasing politicization of ethnic identities and inter-ethnic polarization between Hutu and Tutsi. When President Habyarimana was killed (his plane was shot down), the Rwandan Army, the organized bands of Interahamwe militias and other party militias, and civilian collaborators quickly set about the extermination of Tutsis and political moderates, killing an estimated 900,000 people in 100 days. Sections of the government directly supported militia forces in the perpetuation and perpetration of inter-ethnic violence, and militia groups were noted to have actively collaborated with the official armed forces in the genocide. The militias, in turn, encouraged and enforced civilian participation in the mass killings.

While some of these short-term effects of ethnic militias and PGMs are relatively clear, empirical research is only beginning to focus on how the presence of ethnic PGMs could have long-term effects such as on the intractability of conflict, conflict duration, and on peace negotiations. Recent research suggests that, again, the use of PGMs generally (i.e., non-ethnic militias) can contribute to longer-lasting civil conflict (Aliyev 2017, 2019). The presence of extra-dyadic actors can complicate negotiations by adding veto players (e.g., Cunningham 2006), serve as the basis for continued rivalries between the PGMs and insurgents, since PGMs are usually anti-insurgent (Phillips 2015), and where excluded from negotiations, they can potentially give way to spoiler problems or conditions of "partial peace" (Nilsson 2008). Similarly, significant research has gone into showing that ethnic conflicts tend to be more intractable and durable than non-ethnic violence, primarily due to hardening of ethno-political identities and polarization between groups and the ways in which ethnic mobilization enables the continuation of ethnic exclusion from power (Kaufmann 1996; Montalvo and Reynal-Querol 2010; Wucherpfennig et al. 2012). There are therefore good reasons to think that the rise of ethnic PGMs could significantly affect long-term conflict outcomes. However, further research is needed to demonstrate how the ethnic composition or affiliations of PGMs might have such specific effects.

Abbs et al. (forthcoming) find evidence that rival PGMs serve to extend conflicts. This is due to a number of factors. They argue that in the long-run rival PGMs entrench ethnic divisions and polarization (also see Montalvo and Reynal-Querol 2010). Spiraling inter-ethnic competition can harden ethnic identities and enhance intragroup cohesion on both sides of a conflict (Kaufmann 1996). Alden et al. (2011) also note the particular difficulties in demobilizing militias in the context of the "politicization of ethnic cleavages" owing to strengthened identity-based grievances and group interests. Similarly, while militia mobilization along ethnic lines helps to solidify ethnic divisions, it also improves insurgent's ability to recruit from those ethnic groups excluded from power (Cederman et al. 2010), making peaceful resolutions more difficult to reach and harder for the conflict to dissipate. For example, in Sudan the continued presence and state support for "Arab" militias helped intensify and harden ethnic divisions between the north and the south, which has, in turn, sustained conflict (Idris 2005).

In addition to this, if a state is unable to control rival militias, continued militia violence might exacerbate inter-ethnic security tensions and credible commitment problems during government-rebel peace processes. Continued insurgent-militia rivalries and violence may send a signal that neither the government nor the militias are fully committed to finding a peaceful solution to conflict (see Phillips 2015; Young 2003). For instance, continued "Arab" militia violence in Sudan served to undermine various ceasefires and peace agreements between the government of Sudan and rebel groups (Barltrop 2011, 55; Abbs et al. forthcoming). In one case, on 8 April 2004, continued Janjaweed violence in Darfur led to United Nations Security Council Resolution 1564 aimed at punishing the Sudanese government for non-compliance with a ceasefire between the government and rebels.

Finally, rival PGMs, because they receive state patronage and share in the benefits of ethno-political power, are most likely going to be resistant to changes that undermine or alter their privileged positions (Cederman et al. 2013). More generally, peace can pose an existential threat to PGMs and their member's access to more secure livelihoods, lucrative sources of income, and power. Ethnic PGMs, much like non-ethnic groups, may have incentives to "spoil" peace processes (e.g., Pearlman 2009; Staniland 2012). In summary, preliminary theoretical and empirical evidence points to some of the potential long-term consequences of rival PGMs on conflict duration. Further research could delve much deeper into how the ethnic composition and ties of militias could have consequences for various other long-term conflict dynamics and outcomes.

Conclusions

This chapter has only begun to scratch the surface of the collection of existing work on ethnic conflict and militias. It has pointed to how most researchers have focused on militia-type forces without examining how ethnicity or inter-ethnic tensions form the basis for their mobilization or alternatively how scholars have analyzed ethnic mobilization and ethnic conflict more broadly, primarily analyzing the ethnic composition and goals of states and insurgents. It then turned to recent scholarship that has already begun to systematically examine ethnic militias and ethnic pro-state forces, theorize how ethnicity is linked to the formation of such groups, and address some of their possible effects on conflict dynamics. There also exists a very rich and diverse case-study literature on various conflicts around the world that emphasize the central role that ethnic militias and PGMs play. For example, many analyses focus on ethnic militias and ethnic PGMs in African states. Collectively this literature has pointed to the diverse roles that militias have played in ethnic conflicts; their historical development; why people join such forces; their activities and relations to the government, rebels, and other ethnic groups; and some of their effects on human rights violations, intensity of violence, and their targets, among other central conflict dynamics.

Yet, much more research is needed into various areas of how ethnic mobilization into militia groups is connected to conflict dynamics and outcomes, as well as to the prospects for peace. For example, while the presence of militias more generally have been demonstrated to affect conflict duration and cessation, and ethnic mobilization has been argued to argued to affect similar conflict outcomes, empirically inclined research has yet to pinpoint the long-term effects of ethnic mobilization into PGMs. Does ethnic mobilization into militias and ethnic relationships affect the course of violence or peace, or is it primarily other aspects of conflict? What role might ethnically motivated armed pro-state groups, or their individual members, have in conflict transformation and overcoming violence? There are many unanswered questions about militias in ethnic conflict.

References

Abbs L, Clayton G, Thomson A (forthcoming) Ethnicity, pro-government militias, and the duration of conflict. Working paper under review as of November 2018
Agbu O (2004) Ethnic militias and the threat to democracy in post-transition Nigeria, No 127. Nordic Africa Institute, Uppsala
Ahram AI (2011) Proxy warriors: the rise and fall of state-sponsored militias. Stanford Security Studies, Stanford
Akinyele RT (2001) Ethnic militancy and national stability in Nigeria: a case study of the Oodua People's Congress. Afr Aff 100(401):623–640
Alden C, Thakur M, Arnold MW (2011) Militias and the challenges of post-conflict peace: silencing the guns. Chicago University Press, Chicago
Aliyev H (2017) Pro-regime militias and civil war duration. Terrorism Polit Violence. 29 November, Online First: 1–21
Aliyev H (2019) 'No peace, no war' proponents? How pro-regime militias affect civil war termination and outcomes. Cooperation Confl. 54(1):64–82
Allen C (1999) Warfare, endemic violence and state collapse in Africa. Rev Afr Polit Econ 26(81):367–384
Barltrop R (2011) Darfur and the international community: the challenges of conflict resolution in Sudan. IB Tauris, London

Barter SJ (2013) State proxy or security dilemma? Understanding anti-rebel militias in civil war. Asian Secur 9(2):75–92

Belge C (2011) State building and the limits of legibility: kinship networks and Kurdish resistance in Turkey. Int J Middle East Stud 43(1):95–114

Bertrand R (2004) "Behave like enraged lions": civil militias, the army and the criminalisation of politics in Indonesia. Global Crime 6(3–4):325–344

Biberman Y (2018) Self-defense militias, death squads, and state outsourcing of violence in India and Turkey. J Strateg Stud 41(5):751–781

Böhmelt T, Clayton G (2018) Auxiliary force structure: paramilitary forces and pro-government militias. Comp Pol Stud 51(2):197–237

Campbell BB (2002) Death squads: definition, problems, and historical context. In: Campbel BB (ed) Death squads in global perspective. Palgrave Macmillan, New York, pp 1–26

Carey SC, Mitchell NJ (2017) Pro-government militias. Annu Rev Polit Sci 20:127–147

Carey SC, Mitchell NJ, Lowe W (2013) States, the security sector, and the monopoly of violence: a new database on pro-government militias. J Peace Res 50(2):249–258

Carey SC, Colaresi MP, Mitchell NJ (2015) Governments, informal links to militias, and accountability. J Confl Resolut 59(5):850–876

Cederman LE, Girardin L (2007) Beyond fractionalization: mapping ethnicity onto nationalist insurgencies. Am Polit Sci Rev 101(1):173–185

Cederman LE, Wimmer A, Min B (2010) Why do ethnic groups rebel? New data and analysis. World Polit 62(1):87–119

Cederman L-E, Gleditsch KS, Buhaug H (2013) Inequality, grievances and civil war. Cambridge University Press, Cambridge, UK

Clayton G, Thomson A (2014) The enemy of my enemy is my friend... the dynamics of self-defense forces in irregular war: the case of the sons of Iraq. Stud Confl Terrorism 37(11):920–935

Clayton G, Thomson A (2016) Civilianizing civil conflict: civilian defense militias and the logic of violence in intrastate conflict. Int Stud Quart 60(3):499–510

Cunningham DE (2006) Veto players and civil war duration. Am J Polit Sci 50(4):875–892

Eck K (2009) From armed conflict to war: ethnic mobilization and conflict intensification. Int Stud Q 53(2):369–388

Ferguson NT (2017) Just the two of us? Civil conflicts, pro-state militants, and the violence premium. Terrorism Political Violence 29(2):296–322

Fjelde H, Hultman L (2014) Weakening the enemy: a disaggregated study of violence against civilians in Africa. J Confl Resolut 58(7):1230–1257

Francis D (2005) Introduction. In: Francis D (ed) Civil militia: Africa's intractable security menace? Routledge, London, pp 1–30

Fumerton M, Remijnse S (2004) Civil Defense Forces: Peru's Comite de Autodefensa Civil and Guatemala's Patrullas de Autodefensa Civil in comparative perspective. In: Koonings K, Kruijt D (eds) Armed actors. Zed Books, London, pp 52–72

Gilley B (2004) Against the concept of ethnic conflict. Third World Q 25(6):1155–1166

Guichaoua Y (2010) How do ethnic militias perpetuate in Nigeria? A micro-level perspective on the Oodua People's Congress. World Dev 38(11):1657–1666

Gurcan M (2015) Arming civilians as a counterterror strategy: the case of the village guard system in Turkey. Dyn Asymmetric Confl 8(1):1–22

Hills A (1997) Warlords, militia and conflict in contemporary Africa: a re-examination of terms. Small Wars Insurgencies 8(1):35–51

Horowitz D (1985) Ethnic groups in conflict: theories, patterns, and policies. University of California Press, Berkeley

Hristov J (2009) Blood and capital: the paramilitarization of Colombia. Ohio University Press, Athens

Hristov J (2014) Paramilitarism and neoliberalism: violent systems of capital accumulation in Colombia and beyond. Pluto Press, London

Idris A (2005) Conflict and politics of identity in Sudan. Springer, New York
Ikelegbe A (2005) State, ethnic militias, and conflict in Nigeria. Can J Afr Stud/La Rev Can Etudes Afr 39(3):490–516
Jackson P (2003) Warlords as alternative forms of governance. Small Wars Insurgencies 14(2):131–150
Johnson DH (2003) The root causes of Sudan's civil wars, vol 601. Indiana University Press, Bloomington
Kalyvas SN (1999) Wanton and senseless? The logic of massacres in Algeria. Ration Soc 11(3):243–285
Kalyvas SN (2006) The logic of violence in civil war. Cambridge University Press, Cambridge, UK
Kalyvas SN (2008) Ethnic defection in civil war. Comp Pol Stud 41(8):1043–1068
Kaufmann C (1996) Possible and impossible solutions to ethnic civil wars. Int Secur 20(4):136–175
Lasslett K (2014) State crime on the margins of empire: Rio Tinto, the war on Bougainville and resistance to mining. Pluto Press, London
Lilja J, Hultman L (2011) Intraethnic dominance and control: violence against co-ethnics in the early Sri Lankan civil war. Secur Stud 20(2):171–197
Lyall J (2010) Are coethnics more effective counterinsurgents? Evidence from the second Chechen war. Am Polit Sci Rev 104(1):1–20
MacKinlay J (2000) Defining warlords. Int Peacekeeping 7(1):48–62
Magid Y, Schon J (2018) Introducing the African Relational Pro-Government Militia Dataset (RPGMD). Int Interactions 44(4):801–832
Mason TD, Krane DA (1989) The political economy of death squads: toward a theory of the impact of state-sanctioned terror. Int Stud Q 33(2):175–198
Mazzei J (2009) Death squads or self-defense forces?: How paramilitary groups emerge and challenge democracy in Latin America. Univ of North Carolina Press, Chapel Hill
Meagher K (2012) The strength of weak states? Non-state security forces and hybrid governance in Africa. Dev Chang 43(5):1073–1101
Mitchell NJ, Carey SC, Butler CK (2014) The impact of pro-government militias on human rights violations. Int Interactions 40(5):812–836
Montalvo JG, Reynal-Querol M (2005) Ethnic polarization, potential conflict, and civil wars. Am Econ Rev 95(3):796–816
Montalvo JG, Reynal-Querol M (2010) Ethnic polarization and the duration of civil wars. Econ Gov 11(2):123–143
Nilsson D (2008) Partial peace: rebel groups inside and outside of civil war settlements. J Peace Res 45(4):479–495
Pearlman W (2009) Spoiling inside and out: internal political contestation and the Middle East peace process. Int Secur 33(3):79–109
Peic G (2014) Civilian defense forces, state capacity, and government victory in counterinsurgency wars. Stud Confl Terrorism 37(2):162–184
Phillips BJ (2015) Enemies with benefits? Violent rivalry and terrorist group longevity. J Peace Res 52(1):62–75
Posen BR (1993) The security dilemma and ethnic conflict. Survival 35(1):27–47
Raleigh C (2016) Pragmatic and promiscuous: explaining the rise of competitive political militias across Africa. J Confl Resolut 60(2):283–310
Reno W (1998) Warlord politics and African states. Lynne Rienner Publishers, Boulder
Roessler P (2011) The enemy within: personal rule, coups, and civil war in Africa. World Polit 63(2):300–346
Roessler P (2016) Ethnic politics and state power in Africa: the logic of the coup-civil war trap. Cambridge University Press, New York
Rose W (2000) The security dilemma and ethnic conflict: some new hypotheses. Secur Stud 9(4):1–51
Sambanis N, Shayo M (2013) Social identification and ethnic conflict. Am Polit Sci Rev 107(2):294–325

Schuberth M (2015) The challenge of community-based armed groups: towards a conceptualization of militias, gangs, and vigilantes. Contemp Secur Policy 36(2):296–320

Souleimanov EA, Aliyev H, Ratelle JF (2018) Defected and loyal? A case study of counter-defection mechanisms inside Chechen paramilitaries. Terrorism Polit Violence 30(4):616–636

Sprague J (2012) Paramilitarism and the assault on democracy in Haiti. NYU Press, New York

Sprague-Silgado J (2018) Global capitalism, Haiti, and the flexibilisation of paramilitarism. Third World Q 39(4):747–768

Staniland P (2012) Between a rock and a hard place: insurgent fratricide, ethnic defection, and the rise of pro-state paramilitaries. J Confl Resolut 56(1):16–40

Stanton JA (2015) Regulating militias: governments, militias, and civilian targeting in civil war. J Confl Resolut 59(5):899–923

Tar UA (2005) The perverse manifestations of civil militias in Africa: evidence from Western Sudan. Peace Confl Dev Interdiscip J 7:135–173

Wimmer A, Cederman L-E, Min B (2009) Ethnic politics and armed conflict: a configurational analysis of a new global data set. Am Sociol Rev 74(2):316–337

Wucherpfennig J, Metternich NW, Cederman L-E, Gleditsch KS (2012) Ethnicity, the state, and the duration of civil war. World Polit 64(1):79–115

Young J (2003) Sudan: liberation movements, regional armies, ethnic militias & peace. Rev Afr Polit Econ 30(97):423–434

Evolution of Palestinian Civil Society and the Role of Nationalism, Occupation, and Religion

33

Yaser Alashqar

Contents

Introduction	578
Phase 1: Civil Society Prior to 1948	579
Phase 2: Civil Society and National Structures Under Israeli Occupation (1970s–1980s)	581
Changing Political Framework and Institutional Growth	582
Inside and Outside Conflictual Relations	583
Social Organizations: Alternative Power and Political Representations	584
Civil Society: Islamist Framework	585
Phase 3: Intifada Struggle and Civil Society Engagement (1987–1993)	586
Popular Committees: Civil Society and National Initiative	587
Deeper Understanding of Popular Committees	589
Critical Reflections	590
Conclusion	591
References	592

Abstract

This chapter examines the development of Palestinian civil society and its relationship to nationalism, occupation and religion in the wider Israeli-Palestinian context. The study identifies and analyzes the three phases of Palestinian society development which are social formations prior to the creation of the State of Israel in Palestine in 1948, the emergence of civil society structures in the 1970s and 1980s including nationalist and Islamist grassroots organizations, and the engagement of nationalist civil society with the Palestinian national movement during the first Palestinian Intifada (uprising of 1987–1993).

Y. Alashqar (✉)
Trinity College Dublin (the University of Dublin), Dublin, Ireland
e-mail: alashqay@tcd.ie

© The Author(s), under exclusive license to Springer Nature Singapore Pte Ltd. 2019
S. Ratuva (ed.), *The Palgrave Handbook of Ethnicity*,
https://doi.org/10.1007/978-981-13-2898-5_42

The main argument in this chapter is that the Palestinian social structures emerged historically in the three key phases and have been influenced in recent history by critical realities and forces including nationalism, occupation and the role of religion in society. The examination of this central argument is informed by research and secondary sources. The main analytical findings suggest that the defining characteristics of the three development phases of Palestinian civil society include elitism, conflict with Zionism, revival of Palestinian nationalism, emergence of an Islamization agenda in the civil society sphere, and the conflicting nature of the social formation process in the 1970s and 1980s in the Palestinian territories under Israeli occupation. For clarity, it is important to point out that this chapter does not address the transformation of Palestinian civil society post-Oslo peace process in 1993 as previous research has covered this transformational process.

Keywords

Palestine · Civil society · Zionism · Conflict · Nationalism · Occupation · Religion

Introduction

This chapter focuses on the development of Palestinian civil society and examines its relationship to nationalism, occupation and religion in the context of the wider struggle for Palestine. In particular, three key phases of Palestinian civil society formation and engagement are identified and discussed, namely: phase 1 concerning the emergence of Palestinian social structures prior to the creation of Israel in 1948 in response to Zionism and its attempts to create a Jewish state in Palestine, phase 2 concerning service provision and alternative structures under Israeli military rule in the 1970s and early 1980s including the formation of secular and nationalist local organizations and Islamist social structures, phase 3 concerning the engagement of secular and nationalist grassroots organizations in supporting the political struggle for self-determination in the first Palestinian Intifada. This study does not focus on Palestinian civil society transformations post Oslo peace process in 1993 since this particular aspect has been extensively addressed in previous studies and research (Alashqar 2018).

The overall argument in this chapter is that formal social structures in the Palestinian case emerged historically in three key phases and have been influenced in recent history by key realities and forces including nationalism, occupation and the role of religion in society. In the following sections, the three key phases of the development of Palestinian civil society are explored and examined. The chapter ends with an analysis of the defining characteristics of these phases. The first phase concerning the nature and development of Palestinian civil society during Ottoman and British rule and before the creation of the State of Israel in Palestine in 1948 is discussed in the next section.

Phase 1: Civil Society Prior to 1948

Social activities and structures existed in Palestine during the historical Ottoman period and British rule of the country from 1917 until the establishment of the State of Israel in 1948.

During that time, the rural nature of Palestinian society and prominent clans dominated the social structures in Gaza and the West Bank, especially in Jerusalem where these elite families and their politics came into the national scene during the era of British control of Palestine. These influential families included, for example, the Husseinis, the Nashashibis, and the Khaldis in Jerusalem and the Shawas in Gaza. Palestinian communities were rural and 80% of the population depended on farming and agriculture for their income and livelihood (Rigby 2010, 13). Therefore, as Sara Roy argues, institutional development in Palestine at that time was mainly in response to immediate needs and not a "strategy of social development" (Roy 2001, 229).

As a result, the powerful families acted on behalf of the population and their needs and they, in the process, represented the Palestinian community. Moreover, based on their status and power, not only did they see themselves as the rightful and legitimate representatives of the Palestinian indigenous populations but also as "natural intermediaries between local society and the dominant external authority" during both Ottoman and British periods in Palestine, as Rashid Khalidi points out (Khalidi 2001, 22). This combined role of civil society and political representation, assumed by the notable families as the main components of Palestinian traditional and social structures prior to 1948, derived its power and legitimacy from deeper roots in Palestinian society beyond issues of access and influence. According to Yehoshua Porath,

> This elite drew its authority from traditional prestige factors such as religious status (filling religious posts, belonging to the *Ashraf* [i.e. notables], possession of landed property and long-standing family claims to positions in the Ottoman administration, along with a consciousness of noble origin....It thus needed no popular democratic confirmation of its status. (Porath 1974, 283)

These urban social actors and their local rural clients constituted the main features of the Palestinian social life before 1917 and during the Ottoman era in Palestine. However, with the arrival of massive numbers of Jewish immigrants from Europe between the 1920s and the 1940s and the advancement of the Jewish Zionist project during British rule of Palestine, these influential social players entered into the national framework and contributed to the early formation of the Palestinian national movement. Following the Balfour Declaration in 1917 and the stated British commitment to facilitating the goal of the Jewish Zionist movement in establishing a Jewish state in Palestine, the sense of nationalism increased among the Palestinian elites and they voiced their opposition to Zionism. Hence, a significant section of the Palestinian leadership worked to preserve Christian and Muslim unity among the Palestinian population and established joint organizations to support the national movement and strengthen its social foundations. Therefore, the process of creating associational infrastructures had been closely linked to the threat of Zionism and its quest of colonizing Palestine with British support. In his focused study of that particular period, Porath elaborates further:

> The resurgence of nationalist feeling throughout the country in the wake of the 1929 riots led to the awakening of the various associations previously dormant. Several attempts were also made at that time to widen the organizational framework. In both Ramallah and Ramleh-two towns in which the leaders of opposition (Bulus Shihadah and Sheikh Sulayman al-Taji Al-Faruqi) had considerable influence- Muslim-Christian Associations were set up, and the one in Ramleh even began to show signs of activity....[Nonetheless] this organizational character suited the traditional social structure and the accepted status of the local elite. (Porath 1974, 280–282)

Though it played an important role in national and social revival, the dividing politics of notables and their differences over power issues and effective approaches to address Britain and influence its support for Zionism proved destructive and undermined any real possibility of building strong social and national institutions. For example, some of the notables wanted to engage Britain and convince it through diplomacy and dialogue of the Palestinian demands for self-determination, and still some others sought to fight British and Zionist forces and achieve national liberation through armed struggles. Discussing this polarized state of affairs, Khalidi provides a critical account:

> Although the Palestinians were able to present a united front to their foes and for many years after World War I, the internal divisions among the elite eventually surfaced, ably exploited by the British, with their vast experience of dividing colonized societies in order to rule them more effectively. They were exploited as well by the Zionists, whose intelligence services presumably engaged in undercover activities among the [Palestinian] Arabs in these years that have yet to be fully elucidated. (Khalidi 2001, 24)

In *Popular Resistance in Palestine*, Mazin Qumsiyeh reflects further on the negative impact of these divisions and differences among the social and political elites on the entire Palestinian project of statehood and independence. The national struggle for freedom and self-determination, points out Qumsiyeh, was "hampered by quarrels between the Husseini and Nashashibi factions and the elites' isolation from the interest of most Palestinians" (Qumsiyeh 2011, 229).

This, in fact, was the historical context in which Palestinian social players and structures had existed and evolved in political and national terms until 1948 and the establishment of Israel.

In 1948, the Palestinians people were shattered by the *Nakba* (i.e., Catastrophe) and its disastrous consequences on their lives, existence, and society. The Nakba refers to the destruction of hundreds of Palestinian towns and villages and the expulsion of 700,000 Palestinians in 1948 as a result of the creation of the State of Israel in Palestine, and Zionist massacres during that time. In the period between 1948 and the mid-1960s, the Palestinians seemed to have "disappeared from the political map as an independent actor, and indeed as a people" (Khalidi 1997, 178). Also, a new system of foreign rule was imposed on them by their Arab neighboring states. The Egyptian authorities took control of Gaza and the West bank came under Jordanian rule following the 1948 tragedy. In Gaza, the Egyptian government banned any political organizations and restricted associational activities, stressing the temporary political status of the Gaza Strip (Roy 2001, 229).

The Nakba, however, reinforced and sustained preexisting elements of the Palestinian identity. "The shared events of 1948 thus brought the Palestinians closer together in terms of their collective consciousness, even as they were physically dispersed all over the Middle East and beyond" (Khalidi 1997, 22). It was this collective identity and consciousness as an oppressed people with a national and just cause that led to the re-emergence of Palestinian nationalism in the mid-1960s. These developments put the Palestinians back on the "political map" of the Middle East and beyond. The reformation of the national movement had been enhanced by a new middle class leadership in exile, which organized political structures like Fatah and the Palestine Liberation Organization (PLO) and excluded the elitist leaders who had failed during British rule and the 1948 Nakba (Khalidi 1997, 27). The PLO represented different nationalist factions and Fatah became the largest and leading faction in this political structure. In the context of liberation and nationalist politics, the PLO-Fatah became the major Palestinian political force in exile from the mid-1960s onwards. It also gained a vast popular support and allegiance from the Palestinian diaspora and refugees inside and outside Palestine.

The subsequent two major phases of Palestinian civil society development in the context of Israeli occupation, revival of Palestinian nationalism, and the role of religion from the 1970s to the early 1990s are examined in the next section.

Phase 2: Civil Society and National Structures Under Israeli Occupation (1970s–1980s)

The creation of the State of Israel resulted in the annexation of approximately 78% of historical Palestine and the displacement of more than three quarters of a million people who fled to the West Bank and Gaza. Also, seeking safety from the Israeli atrocities of 1948 and the subsequent 1967 War, thousands of Palestinian people crossed the borders into Jordan, Lebanon, and Syria and have stayed in these countries as refugees until this present time. The United Nations Works and Relief Agency (UNWRA) has been providing humanitarian services to Palestinian displaced persons and refugees outside Palestine and in particular inside the Gaza Strip and the West Bank including East Jerusalem. These areas are also recognized by the UN as the "occupied Palestinian territories" since Israel expanded its state and occupied them illegally during the 1967 War. The UN Security Council responded by issuing 242 Resolution that called for the Israeli occupying power to respect international law and for the "withdrawal of Israeli armed forces from territories occupied in the recent conflict." Furthermore, it called for "achieving a just settlement of the refugee problem" (UN 1967).

At the Palestinian level, the relationship between the PLO and Palestinian grassroots organizations developed in significant terms following the Arab-Israeli

War of 1967 and Israeli military occupation of Gaza and the West Bank. Since the re-emergence of the national movement in the early 1960s, Palestinian nationalist leaders focused on achieving the liberation of Palestine through Arab power and nationalism, and the creation of a democratic secular state in all of Palestine. However, the 1967 War and the military victory of Israel over the Egyptian, Syrian and Jordanian joint forces, and Israeli occupation of the remainder of Palestine (i.e., Gaza and the West Bank including East Jerusalem), led the Palestinians to lose confidence in the ability of the neighboring Arab countries to deliver national liberation. The 1967 War forced the Palestinian people and their national leadership to realize that Arab leaders were unable to bring about change and that the time had come for the Palestinian leadership to make their own strategy and begin to build their own independent structures (Qumsiyeh 2011, 130).

Changing Political Framework and Institutional Growth

By the early 1970s, the goal was no longer concerned with the achievement of the total liberation of Palestine through Arab nationalism and the creation of a secular democratic state in all of Palestine. Instead, the national movement, led by the PLO, was willing now to build a national authority and Palestinian entity on any part of Palestine that Israel might withdraw from. The occupied territories of Gaza and the West Bank represented the overall base and foundation for the possibility of creating a Palestinian self-rule government on the homeland soil as an initial step on the way of gradual and complete independence. The key objective was to build a Palestinian independent state alongside the State of Israel. This represented the emerging and new political framework from the early 1970s onwards. As a result, most of these existing and newly formed local organizations inside the territories supported the PLO project of state-building in Gaza and the West Bank during this critical phase.

In his study and examination of the Palestinian national movement from 1949 to 1993, Yezid Sayigh remarks that the PLO had wanted to create a "'revolutionary authority' with a defined territory and international relations" based on the Chinese and Vietnamese experiences of national liberation. The long-term goal was about achieving statehood (Sayigh 1997, 152). Examining further the relationship between this nationalist thinking and, in his own words, the emerging "statist framework" and how it had contributed to the growth of associational life in Gaza and the West Bank in the 1970s, Sayigh argues:

> Increasingly, the institutional initiative was being taken at grassroots level and by a new generation of activists.... A key element in their emergence as a distinct force was the establishment of three universities in the West Bank in 1972–1975.... The social and economic transformations in the occupied territories were not uniform in their impact, nor led to similar political results. Yet, they were sufficient to allow the PLO to redirect the political engagement and nationalist identification of significant sectors of the population towards its own, statist framework.... It was within this context that all the guerrilla groups sought allies and constituencies in the occupied territories, determinedly retaining political and operational control in their own hands all the while. (Sayigh 1997, 468–470)

Israeli military control, the banning of political parties inside Gaza and the West Bank, and the exile status of the PLO, represented major factors for the nationalist groups to penetrate the institutional sphere in the territories and use it as a platform for political expression during this historical phase. In this context, given their inability to organize openly, various political factions had employed the trade unions, social and professional organizations, student unions, and other grassroots organizations as key arenas for political competition, mobilization and recruitment (Rigby 2010, 49). The usefulness and significance of these social networks extended beyond political influence and competition. They would "shield the military apparatus" of factions, gather intelligence about the enemy, analyze the intelligence, and send their assessment to the "appropriate bodies" in political organizations (Sayigh 1997, 474). Therefore, not only did grassroots groups provide social services to the local population in the occupied territories, but they also represented a means of political resistance (Roy 2001, 229).

Inside and Outside Conflictual Relations

During this key phase of civil society development, tensions at times developed between local associations and the leadership of the PLO outside the territories as Fatah worked to seek and fund allies within particular social circles such as women and the trade union and student groupings and excluded other social players from political and financial support inside Gaza and the West Bank. This included the Palestinian Communist Party and their popular grassroots organizations which Fatah distrusted and viewed with suspicion. In this context, the PLO/Fatah leadership on the outside created, for instance, a division in the trade union movement in 1981, channeling the *Sumud* (steadfastness and resilience) funds to its own supporters and client associations (Rigby 2010, 49).

Another notable example of such conflictual relations between the national leadership on the outside and social forces on the inside is that the PLO/Fatah ranks in exile focused mainly on sustaining their political "statist framework" through popular organizations as a vehicle for Palestinian self-determination and also as a challenge to Israeli power in the occupied territories. However, some social groups and their young professional leaders who were educated in the West and enjoyed independent sources of funding, disagreed with the PLO statist strategy in the institutional sphere, and saw it as an organizational tool to co-opt, and not to mobilize the wider social base. In this context, they argued that the PLO viewed the local population as passive and target audience to be co-opted through the *Sumud* funds and service provision. Therefore, these professional and social representatives sought active participation from all sectors of society as a form of both political action and collective empowerment. This represented a sharp contrast with the PLO statist approach and the role of the local constituencies in implementing political strategies as they perceived it, and caused further tensions between these popular organizations on the inside and the mainstream leadership outside the occupied territories (Sayigh 1997, 611–612).

Social Organizations: Alternative Power and Political Representations

By aligning generally with the national movement and the PLO as the main political and powerful actor within the Palestinian situation (albeit in exile), the Palestinian nationalist local organizations found themselves in a very delicate and unique position. On the one hand, their declared goal was to support the Palestinian people through social and community services, but, on the other hand, they willingly entered into the core politics of the conflict by being part of the Palestinian struggle and the national movement. This required these grassroots groups to provide leadership in the occupied territories, given that the PLO was operating from outside Palestine. Local leaders, therefore, had no alternative but to embark on this combined socio-political role in the complexities of the conflict. In other words, removing themselves from the political struggle would have meant a fundamental disconnection with the community and the context in which they existed, and perhaps a loss of legitimacy.

Moreover, because of the lack of Palestinian government structures in occupied Palestinian territories and Israeli unwillingness to address the needs of the occupied population, Palestinian grassroots and nationalist organizations were determined during this phase to fill the organizational and institutional gap that the Israeli government had ironically created in the occupied territories. Building social and economic infrastructures in Gaza and the West Bank was not a priority from the perspective of the Israeli policy for reasons relating to the prevention of both Palestinian economic development, which may compete with Israel, and national independence (Sayigh 1997, 608). Through academic research and personal observation in the region, Andrew Rigby provides an analysis of this situation:

> In a somewhat paradoxical manner, the absence of certain state services created the institutional space for the development of alternative Palestinian "quasi-state" organizations and agencies. Through the provision of much needed services and facilities, such grass-roots organizations gained the allegiance of the majority of the Palestinian population, and as such constituted the nucleus of an alternative structure of authority and power to rival that of Israeli military government. (Rigby 1991, 6)

Therefore, not only did the social and popular movement with its nationalist component become coherent during this period of civil society development, but it also emerged as a legitimate representative for Palestinian alternative social and political infrastructures outside of Israeli domination throughout the 1970s and the 1980s. However, with the outbreak of the popular Intifada in 1987, these powerful grassroots organizations embarked on a direct resistance role in support of the broader Palestinian struggle for national independence. Furthermore, boosting the PLO statist framework of the early 1970s and their goal of creating a national authority in Gaza and the West Bank as discussed earlier, the Intifada established further "the inside," the occupied territories, as the center of gravity of Palestinian politics, rather than "the outside," the Palestinian diaspora, where it had been located

33 Evolution of Palestinian Civil Society and the Role of Nationalism... 585

for many decades (Khalidi 1997, 200). However, before examining the third phase of civil society development during the Intifada, the following section examines the emergence of Islamist grassroots organizations in the 1980s in the occupied Palestinian territories. This helps to analyze the second phase of Palestinian civil society development in a more comprehensive and critical manner.

Civil Society: Islamist Framework

The formation of Islamist informal institutions in the occupied territories was connected to two ideological and political forces: the Muslim Brotherhood (MB) and later the Islamist Resistance Movement (Hamas). As the MB expanded in Egypt in the 1940s, they turned their attention to Palestine as an essential cause for Muslims and also because of its prominent religious status as a holy land in Islam. Their aim was to extend their presence and influence in their neighboring and significant Palestinian constituency. Since it was founded in the late 1920s, and especially between the 1950s and 1980s, the MB had been mainly concerned with the *Nahada* (renaissance) of Muslim societies by returning them to the true path of Islam as a precondition for liberation from colonialism and oppression. In other words, liberating the "soul" was an essential prerequisite for freeing the "homeland" from the point of view of the MB. Therefore, as Sara Roy points out, the MB chose to focus on preparing the "liberation generation through proselytizing and religious education" towards achieving renaissance (Roy 2011, 22). Hence, nationalism and politics of national liberation contradicted their reformation strategy.

It was within this ideological framework and philosophy that members of the MB and a small number of Palestinian individuals who joined them during their study in Egypt began to arrive in Gaza and the West Bank in the 1970s and put this religious revival strategy into practice. As discussed before, this was a time when Palestinian nationalist grassroots groups and secular politics had been dominant. Ahmed Yassin, who was a Palestinian refugee and a member of the MB and later became the leader of Hamas, played a key role in establishing the institutional framework for the Islamic transformation in Palestinian territories, and particularly in Gaza where he enjoyed greater freedom to organize. In order to achieve their goal and in line with the MB thinking, Yassin decided not to engage in any resistance or nationalist activities against Israeli military occupation. Instead, he and his supporters directed their attention and efforts towards grassroots communities and services to secure a social base and win public support for their Islamic revivalism project. Israel, on the other hand, was pleased to see an alternative and a challenger for the PLO emerging in the Palestinian territories and believed it would weaken its Palestinian nationalist and secular enemy. Studying the early formation of Hamas, Beverley Milton-Edwards and Stephen Farrell point out:

> Throughout the 1970s and 1980s Yassin and his followers assiduously set about building ever expanding networks of mosques, charitable institutions, schools, kindergartens and other social welfare projects-seeds planted early with a view to later harvesting hearts and

minds and souls. It was not until the eruption of the first Palestinian Intifada in December 1987 that Yassin formed Hamas, to capitalize on the spontaneous outburst of street-level protest against Israeli occupation (Milton-Edwards and Farrell 2010, 10).

The overall coordinating body of these newly established local networks and organizations in Gaza was Al-Mujamma' Al-Islami (Islamic Centre), which Yassin built with Israeli permission in 1978. The leaders of the Mujamma' saw secular nationalists as a threat to their reformation agendas and Islamization of Palestinian society. Hence, professional associations and other local institutions that traditionally aligned with the PLO became battlegrounds between the followers of the Mujamma' and the supporters of the national movement (Milton-Edwards and Farrell 2010, 44). Nonetheless, in the overall context of Israeli military occupation and oppression, the Islamic movement and its effective grassroots networks, proved their vitality to the Palestinian community by providing essential services to local people and addressing their immediate needs with a good degree of coherence and organization.

The Mujamma' and its civilian structures throughout the Gaza Strip provided free medical care and employed social workers who provided loans and financial assistance for students to pursue their education in school and university and allocated welfare assistance to thousands of poor families and their children (Milton-Edwards and Farrell 2010, 10). In this context, the Islamist associations in Gaza "provided islands of normality and stability" in a socio-political situation of chaos, dispossession, trauma, dislocation, and pain (Roy 2011, 5). This was the overall context in which Hamas and their grassroots networks emerged and came to play a significant role in the Palestinian situation in later years and especially after the year 2000 and the collapse of the Oslo peace process between Israel and the Palestinians.

The third phase of Palestinian civil society development concerning the engagement of the secular and nationalist social structures in the Palestinian national struggle, represented now by the Intifada, against Israeli military occupation is examined in the following section.

Phase 3: Intifada Struggle and Civil Society Engagement (1987–1993)

The popular Intifada came about as a response to Israeli military control of Palestinian land and people. International peace plans to resolve the conflict had failed as they continue to do so today. This is largely because Israel has consistently refused to allow Palestinians to have complete independence and full national rights. In *Palestinian Children and Israeli State Violence*, James Graff and Mohamed Abdolell point out that the Intifada was aimed at "breaking Palestinian dependence on Israel and securing the national and individual rights of Palestinians." Therefore, according to Graff and Abdolell, "Palestinian children who are old enough to understand what military occupation means, want the Israelis to leave." Hence, they had been active in confronting and harassing Israeli soldiers and settlers. They were also major targets for the Israeli army and settler attacks (Graff and Abdolell 1991). Israeli settlers are armed and living illegally, contrary to international law, in settlements and houses built on Palestinian land in the occupied territories.

The Palestinian human rights organization Al-Haq presents a critical account of the root causes of the Intifada:

> The popular uprising by the Palestinians in the Occupied Territories should have come as a surprise to no one. The uprising has primarily been an act of collective anger, a reaction to twenty years of expropriation, disenfranchisement, oppression and frustration. In the light of the continued failure on the part of the international community to protect the population living under the occupation and to safeguard their rights, it also reflects a loss of confidence in the political will and ability in other states to carry out their responsibilities under international law. (Al-Haq 1988, 4)

Furthermore, in *The Politics of Dispossession: The Struggle for Palestinian Self-Determination*, Edward Said remarks that what made the Intifada unusual is that the adversaries have unusual histories and what they dispute is "perhaps the most unusual piece of territory in history: Palestine, a land drenched in historical, religious, political and cultural significance" (Said 1994).

Popular Committees: Civil Society and National Initiative

As discussed earlier, because of the external presence of the PLO and the existence of the Israeli armed forces inside the Palestinian territories, civil society groups and activists became an important part of the national leadership which sought to protect the Palestinian population and maintain the Intifada. Therefore, a stronger and more combined structure of local civil society and nationalist movement was formed during the uprising. This consisted mainly of what was called the "popular committees." The committees were responsible for supporting the Intifada struggle and maintaining the evolving infrastructure for Palestinian independence. The overall political objective was to achieve a Palestinian independent state alongside the State of Israel.

The popular committees and their nationalist role consisted of the following (Rigby 1991, 22–23):

1. Strike Forces: Their main function was to defend the Intifada activities especially in intense situations involving Israeli troops and settlers. They also ensured that the instructions of the Intifada leaders for public protests and strikes were implemented and Israeli spies were punished.
2. Women's Committees: The female members of these committees were responsible for specific areas in the struggle. They promoted, for instance, local economy by producing home-made products and clothes, selling them in small shops they themselves managed. They also held regular meetings with women coming from different neighborhoods to discuss the progress of the Intifada and related developments. They paid regular visits to villages and small

towns, offering basic healthcare and adult literacy classes. Their activities also included demonstrating solidarity with bereaved families and the injured and newly released political prisoners. In certain circumstances, according to Andrew Rigby, the women organized themselves into "snatch squads" to rescue youths from the hands of Israeli soldiers through chaos and confusion set up for the soldiers (Rigby 1991, 22).

3. Guard Committees: The Guard committees were formed to protect Palestinian property and growing institutions from armed settlers and street criminals. Their main function was to create a degree of local security and protection for communities living through the Intifada.
4. Popular Education Committees: Because of the regular Israeli closure of Palestinian schools in the Intifada, the task of these committees was to provide "home-based education" for young boys and girls (Rigby 1991, 23). Teachers and tutors were the driving force behind this education campaign.
5. Food and Supply Committees: Their responsibility was to identify the humanitarian needs of the local population and deliver food supplies especially to areas and residents who were under curfew and severely lacked foods.
6. Medical Committees: Providing medical treatment to the injured resulting from confrontations with the Israeli army and supplying general medical services to people was the core of their assigned role.
7. Committees for Self-sufficiency: Members of these committees worked to ensure that the local community was not a consuming market for Israeli goods. As Rigby noticed, they suggested local methods that encouraged families to do home-economy and showed people how to achieve self-sufficiency by growing their own vegetables, food, and rearing chickens (Rigby 1991, 23).
8. Social Reform Committees: The primary function of these committees was to design and facilitate a "community-based conflict resolution service" for resolving disputes at both community and individual levels. Rigby indicated that the reason for these activities was to "replace the Israeli courts" in the occupied territories, which many Palestinians refused to recognize during the Intifada (Rigby 1991, 23).
9. Committees to Confront the Tax: The aim of these committees was to expel Israeli tax collectors who came with the Israeli troops during their invasions of towns and villages.
10. Merchants' Committees: Recognizing the strength of the business sector, the Merchants' committees focused on engaging local shop-owners and small businesses in the national initiatives of the Intifada. This included participating in public and general strikes.
11. Information Committees: The Information Committees coordinated media sources in Gaza and the West Bank. They had worked with local journalists and international news agencies to report the Intifada events and their political purpose. In addition, supporting and substituting Palestinian journalists who were illegally arrested by the Israeli army constituted an important part of their role.

Deeper Understanding of Popular Committees

The previous section provides a clear idea about the functions and the joint structures of civil society and political leadership, which had developed during this critical phase of the Intifada. The experience of the popular committees suggests that it had connected well with the various sectors in Palestinian society. Most importantly, the committees responded effectively to immediate community needs and offered tangible solidarity to bereaved families, the injured, political prisoners, and those in refugee camps among others. This initiative was very effective because the popular committees had been, above all, made up of and driven by local civil society groups and political activists. They drew on both people's experiences and skills and their unshakable commitment to the Palestinian cause.

Also, the presence of political organizations in the committees had certainly granted them further credibility and support but, overall, relying on the human resources and expertise available in the indigenous community had contributed to a greater sense of unity and cooperation between all sections of Palestinian society. In effect, by joining the popular committees and playing a significant leading role in their activities, local organizations had to deal with two challenges: supporting the Intifada and the struggle for liberation as well as sustaining the culture of service provision which they initiated in phase 2. Discussing these crucial challenges and subsequent outcomes, Uda Olabarria Walker points out:

> From 1987–1990, the [nationalist and secular] grassroots organizations served as the driving and organizing force behind the popular committees of the intifada while continuing to provide services for the Palestinian community. Throughout this period, many organizations became more formalized and moved into professional civil society spheres including research centres, human rights organizations and advocacy groups. (Walker 2005)

However, some key challenges emerged in this important phase of civil society development. Firstly, while there is credible evidence that indicates the popular committees proved to be of importance to the community and offered valuable support to groups and families involved in the political struggle of the Intifada, the degree of coordination between these socio-political structures was not always effective. For example, at times when the Strike Forces in Gaza declared a public strike throughout Gaza and the West Bank, the strike would only be observed in certain places and not in all Palestinian areas. Rigby also observes that "consistency and standardization" were difficult to achieve within the structure of the popular committees (Rigby 1991, 23).

Secondly, narrow political affiliation to factions also constituted a problematic issue that occasionally presented challenges to the popular committees and left them vulnerable to factional loyalty and divisions. Nonetheless, there was an advantage to dual membership of factions and local popular committees. Available information indicates that the committees flourished and grew bigger in size and effort in areas where a political faction operated prior to the Intifada and a pre-existing system of grassroots networks was active (Rigby 1991, 23).

Thirdly, the military response of the Israeli government to the 1987 Intifada and to political and civil society developments in the Palestinian territories resulted in further intimidation and repressive measures including deportations and long prison sentences without trial for many members of the popular committees and nationalist grassroots organizations (Al-Haq 1988, 145). However, with the signing of the Oslo Peace Agreement between Palestinian and Israeli leaders in 1993, secular and nationalist civil society organizations experienced significant transformations and organizational changes. Moreover, their direct and active role in the Palestinian national movement and the political struggle against Israeli military occupation came to an end. Nonetheless, the three key phases of civil society development in the Palestinian case have defined the historical and present foundations of the Palestinian social sector, and this evolution has been influenced by the key realities and forces of nationalism, occupation, and religion. The following section analyzes the key characteristics of these phases.

Critical Reflections

Firstly, Palestinian social formation prior to 1948 was influenced by the role of the elites and their dominance over social and political life in Palestinian society. As discussed earlier, their power in civil society was derived from family status, land ownership, positions of power in the Ottoman administration, patronage, and client dealings. The divisions among the elite representatives and their factions within a wider dangerous conflict involving the British and Zionist forces, and the Palestinians, reflected negatively on social and political transformations in Palestine and contributed to the Palestinian Nakba and failure in 1948. Moreover, the local elites focused on protecting their power and position during that period and did not possess a vision for building representative institutions and effective social structures. Therefore, elitism and conflict with Zionism represent the key characteristics in the first phase of Palestinian civil society development prior to 1948 and the creation of Israel in Palestine.

Secondly, the reformation and development of nationalist social structures during the second phase in the 1970s and early 1980s came about to revive Palestinian nationalism following the shattering effects of the 1948 Nakba and to respond to Israeli occupation of Gaza and the West Bank in 1967 by means of service provision and institutional development. The nationalist grassroots organizations acted not only as service providers but also as engaged actors of institutional and political resistance towards Israeli military occupation throughout the 1970s and the 1980s. Therefore, the politicization of the nationalist social sphere and its alliance with the national movement became one of the major defining characteristics of the third phase of civil society development in the Palestinian case.

Thirdly, the emergence of Islamist social structures in the second phase of Palestinian civil society development was closely linked to the Islamization agenda and promoting the role of religion in the occupied territories. Similar to Palestinian nationalists who saw civil society as an important arena for political mobilization and nationalism in the context of challenging Israeli military occupation and seeking statehood, Palestinian Islamists equally perceived local associations and the broader field of civil society as a major area for Islamization campaigns and the achievement of religious revival in Palestinian society in the 1980s. Islamist forces historically, and until the beginning of the first Intifada, believed that secularism and nationalism represented corrupt influences. Therefore, religious reforms constituted the main priority for their social and civil society engagement.

Fourthly, as a community-based national liberation process, the Intifada provided means and channels of civil society empowerment and collective participation among people inside Gaza and the West Bank. Moreover, it created a significant degree of legitimacy and acceptance in society for social structure representations and their leading position in the national movement and wider society during the third phase of civil society development. This, for example, explains the goal of Israeli policy which focused on banning nationalist local organizations and arresting its leaders during the Intifada as discussed previously, in an attempt to break the close relationship between civil society forces and Palestinian nationalism.

Finally, civil society transformation in the second and third phases from the 1970s to the early 1990s was neither coherent nor unified. It experienced internal conflicts and power struggles among Palestinian nationalist forces and between the nationalist and religious actors. The emergence of Islamist civil society rivals and subsequent fighting between Islamist and nationalist forces in the occupied territories during the 1980s are examples in point. These social and political divisions are still affecting Palestinian society and weakening the Palestinian national struggle against Israeli occupation. Since the late 1980s, Hamas has based its political philosophy on Islamic revival and the use of armed struggle against the State of Israel as an occupying power. In other words, Hamas strategically combines nationalism with religion. Unlike Hamas, the PLO-Fatah signed the Oslo Peace Agreement with Israel in 1993 and its political programme has accepted negotiations with Israel and diplomatic engagement as a formula to end the conflict and achieve Palestinian statehood. Fatah, therefore, continues to combine politics with nationalism. These ideological and political differences, which have strong roots in civil society foundations in previous decades, continue to define the Palestinian social and political arenas in the present situation in Gaza and the West Bank.

Conclusion

This chapter focused on Palestinian civil society formations and examined its relationship to nationalism, occupation and religion in the wider struggle for Palestine. The overall argument is that formal social structures in the Palestinian case emerged historically in three critical phases and have been influenced by key realities and forces involving nationalism, occupation, and the role of religion in society.

To examine this argument, the analysis identified the three key phases in Palestinian civil society development and engagement. The examination of the first phase focused on the emergence of social structures before the creation of Israel in 1948 in response to Zionism and its attempts to create a Jewish state in Palestine. The analysis of the second phase addressed Israeli occupation of Gaza and the West Bank since 1967 and the revival of Palestinian nationalism, and its impact on the development of nationalist civil society structures under Israeli military rule in the 1970s and 1980s. The analysis of the second phase also examined the emergence of Islamist social structures and their relationship to the religious revival agenda in the occupied Palestinian territories. The examination of the third phase focused on the role of secular and nationalist civil society formations and the engagement in political struggle for self-determination in the first Palestinian Intifada (1987–1993). Supporting examples included the formation of popular committees and the participation of nationalist grassroots organizations in the Palestinian struggle for self-determination and statehood in Gaza and the West Bank.

The chapter concluded by examining some of the key and defining characteristics in the three phases of civil society development in the Palestinian context. These characteristics have included (a) the elitist nature of civil society representations during the Ottoman and British era, and the conflict with Zionism in Palestine; (b) the formation of nationalist social structures in the occupied territories as a reflection of nationalist revival in the Palestinian political arena and in response to Israeli occupation; (c) the emergence of Islamist local associations as a result of an Islamization agenda; (d) the active engagement of nationalist grassroots organizations and their strong alliance with the Palestinian national movement during the Intifada; and (e) the conflictual nature of social formation processes in the Palestinian context and under Israeli occupation including the continuing divisions between Islamist and nationalist approaches in the Palestinian political and social arenas.

References

Alashqar Y (2018) The politics of social structures in the Palestinian case: from national resistance to depoliticization and liberalization. Soc Sci J 7(4):69

Al-Haq (1988) Punishing a nation: human rights violations during the Palestinian uprising, December 1987–1988. Al-Haq Organisation, Ramallah

Graff J, Abdolell M (1991) Palestinian children and Israeli state violence. The Near East Cultural and Educational Foundation of Canada, Toronto

Khalidi R (1997) Palestinian identity: the construction of modern national consciousness. Columbia University Press, New York

Khalidi R (2001) The Palestinians and 1948: the underlying causes of failure. In: Rogan E, Shlaim A (eds) The war for Palestine: rewriting the history of 1948. Cambridge University Press, Cambridge, p 22

Milton-Edwards B, Farrell S (2010) Hamas (trans: Milton-Edwards B, Farrell S). Polity Press, Cambridge

Porath Y (1974) The emergence of the Palestinian- Arab National Movement 1918–1929. Frank Cass, London

Qumsiyeh M (2011) Popular resistance in Palestine: a history of hope and empowerment. Pluto Press, London

Rigby A (1991) Living the intifada. Zed Books, London

Rigby A (2010) Palestinian resistance and nonviolence. PASSIA, Jerusalem

Roy S (2001) Civil society in Gaza strip: obstacles to social reconstruction. In: Norton AR (ed) Civil society in the Middle East. Brill, Leiden, p 229

Roy S (2011) Civil society and Hamas in Gaza: engaging the Islamist social sector. Princeton University Press, Princeton

Said E (1994) The politics of dispossession: the struggle for Palestinian self-determination 1969–1994. Vintage, London

Sayigh Y (1997) Armed struggle and the search for state: the Palestinian National Movement 1949–1993. Oxford University Press, Oxford

UN (1967) UN security resolution 242. Retrieved from United Nations: https://unispal.un.org/DPA/DPR/unispal.nsf/0/7D35E1F729DF491C85256EE700686136

Walker UO (2005) NGOs and Palestine. Retrieved from Leftturn: http://www.leftturn.org/ngos-and-palestine

Ethno-nationalism and Political Conflict in Bosnia (Europe)

34

Aleksandra Zdeb

Contents

Introduction 596
Ethnicized History of BiH 597
Power-Sharing Institutions of BiH 601
Fragmented Political Elites of BiH 605
Conclusions 609
References 610

Abstract

Already in the medieval period, Bosnia and Herzegovina took on a specific multicultural and multiethnic shape that has been formed and strengthened throughout the following centuries. The unique composition of the country that consists of three groups, Bošniaks, Croats, and Serbs, should not only be enumerated among the elements that influenced the 1992–1995 war but also defined the post-conflict processes of state and peace building. This means that ethnicity and nationalism remain the main elements that define Bosnian politics, its political arena, and, inevitably, political conflict. This chapter aims at showing the ethnicized reality of the Bosnian state from three interconnected perspectives: historical, institutional, and, last but not least, cultural one oriented toward political parties. Consequently, the first one briefly introduces formation of the groups and relations between them; the subsequent two focus on the postwar politics and explain the specifics of power-sharing institutions and political parties. It shows that, in Bosnia and Herzegovina, the ethnicity versus political conflict equation comprises another variable – power-sharing (or, in other words, classical consociationalism) which should be seen not only as a conflict management tool but also a building block of the post-conflict system.

A. Zdeb (✉)
Centre for Southeast European Studies of the University of Graz, University of Graz, Graz, Austria
e-mail: aleksandra.zdeb@edu.uni-graz.at; ola.zdeb@gmail.com

© The Author(s), under exclusive license to Springer Nature Singapore Pte Ltd. 2019
S. Ratuva (ed.), *The Palgrave Handbook of Ethnicity*,
https://doi.org/10.1007/978-981-13-2898-5_43

Keywords

Bosnia and Herzegovina · Consociationalism · Political parties in Bosnia and Herzegovina · Political system of Bosnia and Herzegovina · Situational definition of ethnicity

Introduction

Ethno-nationalism and conflict can be merged together in one specific term – ethnic conflict. Leaving aside the question whether either ethnicity itself or special configurations of ethnic groups trigger ethnic conflicts, one can without a doubt define some conflicts as ethnic, and it should be emphasized that they are a very specific kind. It is enough to look at an extreme form of them – armed conflicts: wars concentrated on national liberation or ethnic autonomy constituted only one-fifth of the conflicts which took place between the Congress of Vienna and the Treaty of Versailles. In the twentieth century, their share increased to 45%, with a peak of 75% since the end of the Cold War (Wimmer et al. 2009: 316). However, as Ted Gurr observes (2000: 275–276), the eruption of ethnic problems in the early 1990s was in fact the culmination of a long-term general trend of increasing communal-based protests and rebellion that began in the 1950s and simply peaked after the end of the Cold War.

Yet, conflict does not have to be violent. The most reliable definition of an ethnic conflict was provided by Stefan Wolff (2013:11) who describes them as "a form of group conflict in which at least one of the parties involved interprets the conflict, its causes, and potential remedies along an actually existing or perceived discriminating ethno-national divide; it involves at least one party that is organized around the distinct ethno-national identity of its members." In this spirit, Judith Nagata (1974) offers a situational definition of ethnicity: circumstances define the way in which a particular person would present themselves. Especially in multiethnic states, people may perceive their place of birth, lineage, aspects of their tradition, and culture as fundamental for their existence.

Thus, they assign "primordial" meanings to these features – perceiving them as fundamental or even organic – similar in their nature to kinship ties. When cultural features are perceived in this way, they are "primordialized" – so the "primordialism" of ethnicity depends on the situation (relations) and is not rooted in its nature – what actors see as primordial, scholars should define as constructed (Fenton 2007: 104–106). This "situational ethnicity" model is based on actors' perception of ethnic identity, which has its own meaning for social actions of the people concerned, but clearly is contained in the social situation in which the interaction is taking place (Mitchell 1974: 21). It is then obvious that ethnic identity, once mobilized, may become a powerful source of activity – for an individual human being, but also for the whole group, it is potentially a "total identity" which may be involved in all aspects of social life (Fenton 2007: 135) and be used as a convenient tool for political movement to press claims on government (Horowitz 2000: 81) and politicians to gain as well as preserve power.

Hence, once woken up, ethnicity is not easily forgotten, and it becomes an important part of everyday politics as a source of suspicion instead of trust, polarization instead of accommodation, and repressions instead of tolerance (Diamond and Plattner 1994: xix). Bosnia and Herzegovina (terms Bosnia and Herzegovina, Bosnia, and BiH will be used interchangeably), in a historical as well as contemporary perspective, exemplify all the main aspects in which situationally understood ethnicity could be seen throughout the history of social relations where ethnicity was rather a tool chosen to shape them, the institutional structure of the state created to settle the conflict, as well as its political arena and politics founded on the idea of ethno-nationalism. The chapter shows what does ethnicity and divisions mean for a society and its development when it becomes the dominant point of reference and is inextricably linked to politics.

Ethnicized History of BiH

Already in the medieval period, Bosnia took on a specific cultural and spiritual profile among the South Slavs as it was positioned between two blocks: the East and West Roman Empires. Lying on the periphery of each, neither had a sufficiently intense influence upon it to achieve its radical assimilation; thus, the whole spiritual and material culture of medieval Bosnia had a bifocal development – it was also at the basis of the multiform cultural parallelism that has characterized BiH throughout history – in the Middle Ages the cultures of Western and Eastern Christendom coexisted, enriched each other, and were themselves enriched by the relics of autochthonous tradition, Catholic, Orthodox and Bosnian Churches, Cyrilic, Greek, Latin, Glagolitic scripts, and Bosancica (Lovrenović 2001:45–6).

With time, BiH became a classic example of a borderland, a space where cultures, traditions, and religions have merged, forcing its inhabitants to constantly define their identity and its boundaries in contact with the "important" others (Dąbrowska-Partyka 2004: 63). In consequence, medieval Bosnia triggered development of multiple confessions on its territory: the Catholic Church in the North, West and, since the 1340s, in central Bosnia as well as, the Orthodox Church in the South and East from the beginning of the fifteenth century. Yet, its mountainous character made it also a natural breeding ground for heretical religious practices like a schismatic Bosnian Church which gradually gained an important position in political life, while with the Ottoman conquest, the confessional map of BiH changed, and Islam began to gain a foothold (Hoare 2007: 41; Lovrenović 2001: 49; Donia and Fine 2011: 37).

Nevertheless, it was only in the context of the Ottoman all-embracing confessionalism that complex cultural identities emerged: Muslim-Bošniak in which Turkish-Islamic culture dominated; Serbian-Orthodox linked to the Byzantine religious tradition; Catholic-Croatian shaped by Western Christian traditions, and later the Sephardic-Jewish of the communities exiled from Spain at the end of the fifteenth century (Lovrenović 2001: 108). Ethnically and religiously diverse population of BiH has not always been divided into three separate and rigid categories of Muslims

(Bošniaks), Serbs, and Croats. Rather, successive generations have interpreted their identities according to their own geographic, political, social, and cultural circumstances, while BiH's contemporary social structure is a product of its medieval statehood and the Ottoman, Austro-Hungarian, and Yugoslav periods of rule (Hoare 2007: 28, 33) during which particular communities had more privileged position than others.

Moreover, the process of nation-state consolidation that took place throughout Europe in the nineteenth and early twentieth centuries, to some extent, bypassed BiH. Since the fourteenth century, the region passed from under the control of one multinational empire to another, retaining many social and economic traces of its Ottoman origins until the Communists entirely eliminated the old social order – prior to this, BiH was never an independent state yet retained its identity and boundaries (Burg and Shoup 1999: 18). As a consequence of all these circumstances and developments, instead of one dominant nation, three ethnic groups, described by the 1995 Constitution as constituent peoples – Bošniaks, Croats, and Serbs – evolved on the basis of a strong confessional cleavage which had triggered subsequent cultural differences. According to the 1948 figures, there were 44,7% Serbs, 23,9% Croats, and 30,9% Muslims (Ramet 1992: 177); according to the census in 1991, 43,7% Muslims, 31,3% Serbs, and 17,3% Croats (Ramet 1992: 259); and according to the last, 2013 census, 50,11% Bošniaks (Muslims), 30,78% Serbs, and 15,43% Croats (Al Jazeera 2016). Yet, a serious ethnic rivalry between them started only after 1918 (Donia and Fine 2011: 20), and the earliest moment when it is possible to identify hatred based on ethnicity is with the raise of romantic nationalism in the nineteenth century (Andjelić 2003: 8–9).

Despite the dominant discourse, the three main ethnic groups of BiH have never constituted homogenous entities. There have been other powerful cross-cutting cleavages beside ethnicity: class, education, and geographic location which were mixed with the ethnic one but also remained significant factors in producing antagonistic relations. For example, during the 1992–1995 war, additional divisions emerged inside groups since some people did not follow the mainstream politics (Donia and Fine 2011: 17). Through the ages, there were two crucial dichotomies that defined social relations on the territory of contemporary BiH: between landowners and dependent peasants (the first ones were mostly Muslims and the second ones mostly Christians) and between urban and rural worlds. Until the nineteenth century, cities were predominantly Muslim, with the percentage of other communities increasing with the beginning of the nineteenth century (McCarthy 1994: 60–2). Then cities became centers of mixed ethnic and religious structures, but still each religious community lived in a separate segment of the city (mahala) with limited mutual contact (Bataković 2001: 67).

Nevertheless, between the World War II and 1991, roughly 40% of urban marriages were mixed, and over 20% of urban Bosnians declared themselves "Yugoslav" or "other" in censuses, refusing to define themselves in ethnic terms. Also, six of Bosnia's ten largest urban centers in 1991 had no majority ethnicity, and the four that did (Tuzla, Bihać, Brčko, and Bijeljina) had Muslim majorities under 60%, which made the ethno-national categories hybrid and fluid. Villages, on the other hand, tended to be more conservative and mostly made up of people who all belonged to a single ethnicity (Fine 2002: 13). With the urbanization of the whole country, bigger villages and cities became "Bosnian pots," while the rural areas, despite the modernization that took place in BiH, remained the same (Grandits 2009: 34). While urban centers created multiethnic, civic communities that cut across religious differences with a shared sense of urban belonging, it was the pure ethno-religious character of the villages that imposed its stamp on the national movements, ensuring they would be unable to bridge the religious divide (Hoare 2007: 57; Lovrenović 2001: 52–3).

The semi-exclusiveness of each religious community coexisted with interreligious good neighborliness in urban centers, but rural society was characterized neither by hostility nor by true multiethnicity (Lovrenović 2001: 56). In 1989, as Neven Andjelić writes, images of a unified BiH were present only in Sarajevo and in other larger centers; the countryside and smaller communities were on their way to support the ethnic leaders and had become the basis for ethnic politics and nationalism (Andjelić 2003: 105). According to Robert Donia and John Fine (2011: 35), a military ethos, which created a fertile ground for the nationalist propaganda and recruitment, was deeply rooted among the rural inhabitants, especially in East Herzegovina. In consequence, when in the 1990s the war broke out in Yugoslavia, it was commonly seen as a problem created by "papci," people from rural backgrounds with "peasant mentalities." In fact, the whole conflict was seen as the legacy of the past – many of the areas that saw severe ethnic cleansing in 1991 were the sites of similar massacres during WWII – Bosnian politicians spoke of Četniks and Ustaša villages and regions as if place and political identity were coterminous and predetermined. Yet, Bosnian nationalist parties were led by urban professionals, not rural leaders, so the division rural-urban itself is not enough to explain the level of hostility between all groups (Toal and Dahlman 2011: 14–15).

As Noel Malcolm argues, it is true that during the course of Bosnian history, there had been hatred and hostility, but these were largely based on economy, not ethnicity or religion, as the relations between local Christian peasantry and Muslim landowners are usually described. Also, while there was substantial intra-BiH violence during the World War II, two major cases of religious or ethnic hatred in the more distant Bosnian history – during the First and Second World Wars – were triggered from *outside* the country (Malcolm 2011: 39–40). This point has been underlined by John Fine, who claims "toleration has marked Bosnia's entire history, except when foreigners or locals stirred up by foreign governments have incited the Bosnians to other paths" (Toal and Dahlman 2011: 48). Neven Andjelić (2003: 6–7) is also clear when he says "one cannot completely dismiss the existence of animosity between different ethnic communities, but there was far more coexistence, mutual understanding and tolerance than suppressed hatred or open confrontations. [...] two worlds existed: one was a world of hatred toward others, while the other was of love, or tolerance at least, towards the rest of the society."

This image was also confirmed by Ivan Lovrenović (1999: 99–100), who claims that "the Bosnian paradigm of unity in diversity" has created a situation in which mutual differences between cultures led to cultural isolation on the one hand but acceptance of those differences on the other. Dealing with cultural differences was part of people's most immediate experience of social life outside the confines of their home, and it was therefore an essential part of their identity (Bringa 1993: 87) in both a positive and a negative sense. Consequently, two terms – neighboring relations (komšijski odnosi) and common life (zajednički život) – both meaning ways of recognizing, respecting, and accommodating differences for further harmonious coexistence, instead of a transcendence of ethnic or cultural differences, have been developed throughout centuries. For the post-WWII Bosnian, it meant growing up in a multicultural and multireligious environment where cultural pluralism was intrinsic to the social order, while the terms komšiluk and došluk, of which there are many examples in folk memory, should be perceived as a ground-roots negation of division and particularization (Lovrenović 2001: 100).

Yet, it was not enough to prevent Bosnia and Herzegovina from falling into a violent, armed conflict in the 1990s. By the end of the 1980s, the Bosnian Communist regime, as the Yugoslav one, was crumbling. It started with intra-party tensions that resulted in the differentiation and democratization of its structures with no ethnic dimensions, but by the end of the decade, after a long period of destabilization, the explosion of nationalism in Serbia and Croatia triggered events in BiH. In effect, the republic became a "political battleground," but as Andjelić observes: "as long as the highest institutions of the system remained undivided on ethnic issues, inter-ethnic relations were secured" (Andjelić 2003: 69–72; Hoare 2007: 341–2). In result of the armed conflict, the country was largely destroyed, hundred thousand people were killed, and half of the citizens of the country were forced to leave their homes (Ramet 2002: 206–8). As Burg and Shoup (1999: 17) say, the horror of the 1992–1995 war shows that Bosnian society was deliberately destroyed and replaced by a war of all against all. The ease with which this was accomplished was the product of the interaction between external forces, the breakup of Yugoslavia, Bosnian society itself with its deep ethnic, regional, and class cleavages, and Bosnian history (Toal and Dahlman 2011: 75).

The war has had a dominant effect on the structure of the postwar country, the importance of group identity and its goals. Despite the fact that for centuries the Bosnian "identity" question took the shape of both extremes – ethnic hatred and peaceful coexistence – and local identities were more or less flexible, they have become more rigid in the post-conflict environment with groups separating themselves from each other (Nation-building BiH 2011) and presenting somehow contrasting attitudes toward the common state. In BiH, differences were constantly encountered and negotiated in public spaces, and out of this mixing came distinctive habits of tolerance, a culture of borrowing and hybridity that was distinctively Bosnian. Nevertheless, the last war reflected contradictory traditions of conflict and accommodation that have characterized intergroup relations in the state for centuries. For most of its history, Bosnian society had been deeply segmented, with Muslims, Serbs, and Croats organized into distinct communities, where the balance between conflict and cooperation depended heavily on external factors (Burg and Shoup 1999: 16). Nowadays, after more than 20 years since the end of the armed conflict, BiH remains a deeply divided society with three groups divided along a dominant ethnic cleavage, and a clearly weaker, re-crystallizing fourth group, rooted in pan-ethnic Bosnian identity and situated on the left side of the political scene.

Power-Sharing Institutions of BiH

In consequence of the 1992–1995 war, Bosnia and Herzegovina arose as a territorially, politically, and socially segregated country – a deeply divided society, with Bošniaks, Serbs, and Croats as its main groups, and only a brief experience of independence before 1992. The armed conflict itself ended with the signing of the General Framework Agreement for Peace in Bosnia and Herzegovina – better known as the Dayton Peace Agreement (DPA) – on November 21, 1995, at the Dayton air force base in Ohio, which formalized a process that had its roots in earlier initiatives attempting to mediate between the parties (Chandler 2000: 39). Yet, it was hardly a blueprint for a sustainable state. The predominant subject of negotiations was an agreement on the map (Toal and Dahlman 2011: 155, 157), while its implementation offered the parties the opportunity to continue their conflict by other means (Daalder 2000: 161).

Territorially, it attempted to bridge the divergent interests of the three ethnic communities, with strict facts on the ground and the principle of the "Contact Group plan" for the 51–49% division between the Croats and the Bošniaks, on the one hand, and the Serbs, on the other. Politically, the agreement endeavored to reconcile Serb and Croat demands for Bosnia's partition along ethnic lines with the Bosnian Muslim demand for the preservation of Bosnia's integrity and the restoration of its ethnic balance; thus, the product of the negotiations was a delicate compromise which affirmed Bosnia's unity but also foresaw the country's division into two legal entities, the Croat-Muslim Federation of BiH and Republika Srpska (Tzifakis 2007: 87).

The Accord was to be something more than cessation of hostilities; among its goals were also sustainable peace, reversal of ethnic cleansing, and the development of a Constitution – "not just a peace treaty but a sort of operation manual for the entire post-conflict reconstruction process" (Haynes 2008: 4–5). It contained provisions dealing with military aspects of the peace settlements, regional stabilization, elections, human rights, refugee and displaced persons, and the new constitutional order and defined the role and responsibility of international military and civilian agencies to assist in its implementation (Daalder 2000: 137–8) – it was a document designed to create a new country (Lyon 2006: 50), while the majority of annexes to the DPA were related to the political project of democratizing Bosnia and of "reconstructing a society" (Chandler 2000: 43). Despite the fact that it represented an effective instrument for bringing the Bosnian conflict to an end (Morrison 2009: 9) and establishing at least a negative peace in a war-torn country, it has been criticized for not being capable of restoring a political system which would allow for the establishment of a functioning democratic state, lasting peace, and stability (Mansfield 2003: 2055; Koneska 2017: 37).

The two predominant features of the post-Dayton state building and political system imposed in BiH have been a consociational arrangement (Lijphart 1969, 1977) at the level of the joint state institutions and an asymmetric multinational federalism which can be considered to be a supplement or even an aspect of the consociational structure (Bieber 2006b: 46). In this manner power sharing (or rather a classic corporate consociationalism which places primary importance on ethnicity) has become the essence of the postwar constitution (Chandler 2000: 67; Bose 2002: 216). In fact, one might argue the DPA represents plural consociational settlements within the boundaries of a single state – the sovereign consociation of the state of BiH, and the regional consociations of the entities (Weller and Wolff 2006: 4), while also taking into consideration cantons and some municipalities. The implementation of consociational arrangements has been justified for three reasons: first, it is a paradigmatically divided society; secondly, even before the war, the religious and ethnic divisions of the society were recognized and institutionalized in different guises similar to consociational mechanisms (as the previous part shows); and thirdly, during and after the war, the ethnic cleavages among the social segments not only widened but have been territorialized and politically institutionalized (Kasapović 2005: 7–8).

The institutional setup created in BiH after the 1992–1995 was not a novelty to this region. As noted by Soeren Keil (2013: 129): "although Bosnian history is characterized by change, there are also important continuities," also Sumantra Bose (2002: 68) claims that the institutional framework of BiH and one of its entities, the Federation of BiH, were copied from the confederational, consociational model of the last 20 years of Yugoslavia. In the same spirit, Florian Bieber underlines that "much of the institutional development since Dayton does not constitute an abrogation from the institutional legacy of Bosnia and Herzegovina," e.g., the concepts of reserved seats or ethnic key (Bieber 2006: 23; Seizović 2005: 257) linked to the concepts of ethnicity and consensus developed throughout the centuries (Banović 2008: 70). On the other hand, it is also fully justified to claim that the postwar power-sharing structures had also reproduced the mechanisms that fostered political deadlock, collapse of the constitutional systems, and war on the territory of Yugoslavia (Hayden 2005: 252).

Given the consociational and federal nature of the Bosnian state, it is difficult to classify its political system as either parliamentary or presidential – yet it is usually defined as a mixed system with presidential elements (direct election of the president who can also dissolve the Parliament but, on the other hand, with both legislative and executive branches of government cooperating in a manner typical for parliamentary systems) (Sahadžić 2011: 24). Nevertheless, almost all aspects of BiH's governing scheme are to be perceived through the lenses of its ethnicized power-sharing model, and this includes the classic division of powers into legislative, executive, and judiciary branches represented by a bicameral Parliamentary Assembly, dual executive, and the Constitutional Court.

According to Art. IV of the constitution, the legislative branch is represented by a bicameral Parliamentary Assembly (Parlamentarna skupština) which consists of a 42-member House of Peoples (Dom naroda) and a 15-member House of

Representatives (Predstavnički dom) elected for a 4-year term (2-year till 2002) and based on two principles: of ethno-territorial representation and equality (legislative powers) of the chambers (Saračević 2011: 236). The executive branch is divided between two institutions: the Presidency of BiH (Predsjedništvo Bosne i Hercegovine) and Council of Ministers (Vijeće ministara) (Constitution BiH: Art. V), with more important functions envisaged for the first one, defined as the head of the state. Last but not least, there is also an independent judiciary, which is not really regulated by the federal constitution, with an exception for an institution crucial in federal states – the Constitutional Court of BiH (Constitution BiH: Art. VI). Initially, the judiciary system, with an exception for the federal Constitutional Court, was located at the level of entities – only after the reforms in 2000 were the Court of BiH and the Prosecutor's Office of BiH created at the federal level (Smailagić and Keranović 2011: 301).

Beside those regular elements of a modern political system, the DPA's annex IV established in BiH a constitutional system that includes all four consociational elements at various levels of governance: a grand coalition government in the form of a presidency and a council of ministers, both composed following a strict quota; group autonomy in the form of two federal units called entities, the Serb-dominated Republika Srpska and the Federation of Bosnia and Herzegovina; a system of representation that at times exceeds the needs of proportionality by prescribing parity; and a complex system of veto powers that allows each group to halt legislation in the national parliament (Merdzanovic 2016: 7).

According to Nina Caspersen (2004: 572) the DPA introduced into BiH elements of both consociational (visibly prevailing) and integrative models of conflict management, as the Accord was filled with elements of both, partition and reintegration. Yet, although some of the provisions of the DPA could be read as attempts to introduce integrative elements (e.g., the importance of the return of refugees in order to restore the multiethnic composition of certain regions), generally the Accords opted for consociationalism (Touquet and Vermeersch 2008: 269). More significant examples of integrative measures were introduced in Bosnia later, in the form of an election law focused on creating incentives for cross-ethnic appeals and voting, while the peace mission experimented with introducing integrative power sharing in the RS and FBiH (2000). In order to increase the chances of Milorad Dodik (SNSD), it prescribed preferential voting for electing the president of the RS, but, given the demographic data, there was no incentive to campaign for votes from members of other ethnic groups, and the more radical candidate won. It could be even said that the preferential voting system was counterproductive because voters understood that this new procedure would support moderate candidates and weaken the ethno-nationalist ones, so they closed ranks behind SDS.

In the second attempt, the Provisional Election Commission, dominated by the OSCE mission, introduced new rules for delegating Croat representatives in the House of Peoples in the Federation. Until then, the members of the Cantonal Assemblies could vote only for delegates from their own ethnic group, but according to the new rules, all members of the Cantonal Assemblies could decide on the complete candidate list. Consequently, due to the demographic balance in the

FBiH, Bošniaks as well as "others" would elect the Croat delegates, making Croat candidates dependent on support by non-Croat representatives and only hardening the already flame-raking pre-election campaign of the HDZ. Thus, the attempts to introduce integrative power sharing did not reduce but rather heightened the tensions (Gromes 2006: 26) while the system has remained almost purely consociational.

Between 1995 and 2002, power-sharing existed at the state level between all three constituent nations – i.e., Serbs, Bošniaks, and Croats – and in the FBiH between Croats and Bošniaks, but the system was fundamentally changed in 2002 when the OHR imposed far-reaching constitutional amendments in both entities, guaranteeing legal equality to all constituent peoples throughout the Bosnian territory (Belloni and Deane 2005: 235–6). Even though the "constituent peoples" decision marked a significant step forward in recognizing the equal constitutional position of all constituent peoples, it did nothing to improve the position of the non-constituent population of BiH (ICG 2002; Mujkić et al. 2008:13; Sahadziić 2011: 35). Since then, the primary focus of the constitutional reform in BiH has been the discriminatory status of the "others" – the political rights of the non-constituent population (e.g., ethnic and national minorities) (Banović and Gavrić 2010: 163) and, in consequence, implementation of the European Court of Human Rights' (ECtHR) decision in the case Sejdić and Finci v. Bosnia and Herzegovina from 2009 (and Azra Zornic in 2014 as well as Ilijaz Pilav in 2016). The BiH Constitution labels Bošniaks, Croats, and Serbs as "constituent peoples," meaning they, solely, have the right to run for the Presidency and be appointed to the House of Peoples of the Parliamentary Assembly of BiH. The "others," or the people who do not identify with these three groups (but also a Serb from the FBiH or Bošniak/Croat from the RS), do not have the right to run for either of these posts (Hodžić and Stojanović 2011a: 8, b: 23).

Twenty years after the signing of the DPA, the Bosnian political system is criticized for a number of shortcomings. Political decision-making is described as being in a deadlock (Trnka 2009); also, the pattern of elections where hard-line nationalists of each side have been elected into office has largely survived (Belloni 2007). Much of the criticism is also directed at institutional matters: several state institutions appear to be ethnically discriminatory (Bochsler 2012: 66); there is a predetermination of positions for the three constituent peoples and enforcement of ethnic identity along with the tension between the weak institutions at the state level and the extensive autonomy of the entities (McEvoy 2015: 114). The federal level remains handicapped by a weak executive, a parliamentary decision-making process in which there are multiple veto points, limited competencies that are often shared with other levels of government with no clear hierarchy of functions or enforcement capacity at state-level, an inadequate public administration in terms of both quality and quantity, and continued reliance on international intervention in day-to-day governance (FPI 2007: 27–8). In fact, the DPA not only failed to remedy the deep ethnic divides but to some extent intensified them (Guss and Siroky 2012: 310).

Yet, the DPA created also a complex political structure composed of 1 state, 2 entities, 3 peoples, 4 million citizens, and 5 layers of governance led by 14 prime ministers and governments, making Bosnia the state with the highest number of presidents, prime ministers, and ministers in the entire world (Belloni 2007: 44; Tzifakis 2007: 85). Moreover, Brendan O'Leary describes Bosnia as a "complex consociation" where, in addition to the four elements of consociation originally set out by Lijphart, the settlement includes an important role for international actors as well as cross-border or confederal relationships (and sometimes institutions) for the groups with their kin in other states (McEvoy 2015: 114). What is more, by continuously intervening in the political system, the external actors affected its internal and long-term dynamics – how the different consociational institutions relate to and interact with each other. These interventions altered the incentive structures for political behavior and created a new kind of consociational system, identified as an "imposed consociation" (Merdzanovic 2016: 3). This situation has been also redefined by political actors who are to use those ethnicity-based institutions.

Fragmented Political Elites of BiH

The classic left-right approach to understanding politics and political parties fails to adequately grasp the reality of Bosnian party system (Pugh and Cobble 2001: 45–46). Since it is extremely fragmented, with only few parties having a base in both entities or in more than one community, it has been described as a complex party system with three subsystems dominated by "ethnic parties" of which representation of ethnic interests is a central feature (Kapidžić 2015: 40, 46). It is also defined more by electoral competition among parties that represent a single ethnic group rather than explicit electoral competition between parties representing different ethnic groups. In result they have no incentive to create party programs that can appeal beyond their own ethnic bloc and may, in fact, be punished for doing so. Despite having similar programs, parties are able to compete with each other due to their strong personalization and orientation around strong leaders – in the end they almost do not realize their political programs. Also the tendency to split is both cause and effect of personalization – relatively low barriers to entry in elections mean that intra-party challengers have a good chance of gaining representation and therefore power by creating a new party. Thus, emerging party leaders who might push for a less leader-based structure instead leave to form their own parties on a similar model (Hulsey 2015: 521).

Consequently, the party system has been divided into four groups of parties, which are further split between three communities. On the one end are "extremely national parties" that advocate a change of the status quo, usually secession, threaten other nations, and endorse the use of force and then the "established national parties" that have engaged in a higher degree of cooperation with each other and largely operate within the status quo, even if they might favor fundamental changes to the existing system. The next category groups together "moderate parties" and includes parties that have a stronger commitment to cross-national cooperation and emphasizes a not exclusively identity-based political agenda. At the same time, these parties have a well-defined commitment to only one community with at best token inclusion of others. The final category includes "nonnational parties" which do not have a group-specific program and potentially appeal to more than one group (Bieber 2006b: 103–4).

Even though the segmentation of politics along ethnic lines remains its main characteristic, the parties themselves went through some changes. What the first ruling parties, SDA (Stranka demokratske akcije, Party of Democratic Action), HDZ (Hrvatska demokratska zajednica BiH, Croatian democratic union of BiH), and SDS (Srpska demokratska stranka, Serbian Democratic Party), had in common was that the respective ruling ethno-nationalist party controlled almost all spheres of society during and right after the war: the armed forces, militias, police, secret services, courts, the most important media, the distribution of humanitarian aid and flats, and the economy, including the payment system (through "payment bureaus") and the black market (Gromes 2006: 6). Despite the continuing influence of the national parties and their attempts to constrain political pluralism and consolidate respective ethnic groups by underlying the need for political unity, their monopolistic hold on the electorate has declined around the years 2004–2006 due to changes in their policy and leadership (Bieber 2006b: 105–6), as well as strong international pressure and control. The resurgence of two challenging parties, SNSD (Savez nezavisnih socijaldemokrata, Alliance of Independent Social Democrats) and SBiH (Stranka za Bosnu i Hercegovinu, Party for Bosnia and Herzegovina), coincide with a nationalist turn in both of them. Reacting to international pressures, SDS and SDA moderated their stances, which created opportunities for SNSD and SBiH to take over their position and electorate, but it was possible only through their radicalization (Hulsey 2010: 1136–7).

Yet, after the collapse of the 2006 constitutional reform package, the challenger parties have been strengthening their position. In a way that reminds the worst, postwar days, the post-2006 era was characterized by the conscious usage of noncooperation as a strategic device, directed at the internationals and the domestic audience alike. The 2014 state level elections revealed not only a victory of nationalist parties but to some extent a massive return to the voting patterns from the 1990s. Thus, for the party system, there is a visible continuity from the 1990 and fist elections (Sedo 2010: 89), but the main feature of the ethnic blocks has become their fragmentation and growing visibility of intra-ethnic outbidding.

In the Serb block, the dominance of SDS established before the war was broken by the combination of international efforts to cut financing for the party and ban party leaders and the emergency of new party – SNSD and its charismatic leader Dodik who was held up as a moderate Serb politician. The 2006 attempted constitutional reforms provided a political opening for Dodik to shift to the radical right and took over SDS position. In the Bošniak camp, SDA has been the main actor with strong SBiH as the main challenger, but SDA was never as suppressed by the OHR as SDS was, so SBiH has not supplanted SDA in the way that SNSD has supplanted SDS. The bipolar situation was changed in 2010 when SBB (Savez za bolju budućnost, Union for a Better Future of BiH) joined the race and ultimately the governing coalition. The more important split within the Bošniak electoral corpus is however the one between the traditional Bošniak parties SDA and SBiH and SDP

(Socijaldemokratska Partija Bosne i Hercegovine, Social Democratic Party of Bosnia) – the main nonethnic party.

Because of the role played by HDZ in Croatia, its financial dominance in the block, and the size of the Croat population in Bosnia, Croats have been the most "stable" and coherent group. Only few viable parties emerged after the war, and most have been splinter parties from the dominant HDZ, advocating a stronger support for the Bosnian state and seeking votes among Bosnian Croats, who had been marginalized in the HDZ by the dominant Herzegovinian stream (Bieber 2006b: 42). The main split happened in 2006 inside HDZ BiH and resulted in creation of HDZ 1990 – the change was triggered by a personal rivalry inside the party. Thus, even though smaller parties existed since the end of the war, the real intra-ethnic division happened only in 2006. Interestingly enough, it was at the same time that Željko Komšić of the multinational SDP won the Croat seat in BiH's presidency (Merdzanovic 2016: 8). Nevertheless, being aware of their fragile situation of the smallest constituent nation, Croatian parties from time to time try to build all-Croat agreements in an attempt to constrain the intra-ethnic competition: the Fojnica Declaration (Fojnicka deklaracija), the Kreševo Declaration (Kreševska deklaracija), but also the 2010 Mostar Agreement (Mostarski sporazum) between HDZ and HDZ1990.

Beside the three ethnic blocks, a nonnational (or multinational) block has also continued to exist since the prewar period. Among those parties, SDP has had a unique position – it combines broad electoral success with serious efforts to field candidates of more than one ethnicity – that's why it might be considered as a major nonethnic party, but it should be underlined that it receives a vast majority of votes from Bošniaks who has become its major target. By contrast, the Socialist Party of Republika Srpska (SPRS) is not easily categorized. It was one of the main parties to evolve out of the League of Communists of Yugoslavia; its policies are more ideological in their left-wing content (on pensions, education, and health services) and relatively moderate on the nationalist issue (Pugh and Cobble 2001: 33–4). John Hulsey (2010: 1133, 1135) adds here also People's Party for Work and Betterment (Naša stranka radom za boljitak, NSRzB) and Liberal Democratic Party (Liberalno Demokratska Stranka, LDS); recent elections brought into light two new ones: Demokratic Front (Demokratska fronta, DF) and Our Party (Naša stranka, NS). Some explanations of the poor support for multiethnic parties blame consociational aspects of Bosnia's system, particularly the proportionality principle, and the monoethnic constituencies carved out by Bosnia's consociational system show greater support for multiethnic parties. Thus, it looks like while the long-term effect of consociationalism may be to solidify the role of ethnicity in politics, in Bosnia today the presence of ethnically homogenous electoral contexts is creating space for less nationalist parties.

The experience of war only strengthened the division into homogenous sub-electorates and position of the national parties – their dominance during the post-conflict period has been primarily explained by, first, territorial homogenization and the constitutional system that effectively segmented the electorates of the different communities. Second, with two exceptions of SDP and DF, no significant cross-ethnic campaigning has taken place in the postwar electoral races. In spite of the fact that for more than 20 years that have passed since the end of the war, the actors' constellation has not really changed – the system is still dominated by the same national parties: SDA, HDZ, and the only successful challenger – SNSD that replaced, in 2006, SDS.

There is a differentiation over time in regard to parties' orientations and their fluctuation between the moderate and national identifications visible in the cases of SDS, HDZ BiH, SNSD, or SBiH. Nevertheless, the Serb political elite has been consequently focused on weakening the federal level and preserving their position and power on the territory of the RS without sharing it with other groups. This is why it is against the transfers of competences to the state level, and territorial rearrangement of BiH is of their biggest concerns seen as violation of the "Dayton order" (Banović and Gavrić 2010: 170). Both, SNSD since 2006 and SDS, reject the demands to weaken the federal consociational democracy to the benefit of the majority, since, from their perspective, realization of such a program would lead to unitarization and majoritization by the Bošniaks (Gromes 2010: 369). The pro-autonomy behavior is a common trait shared in BiH by Serbs and Croats. The policies of the HDZ (while HDZ 1990 is not far from this picture) center on lobbying for more autonomy for Croats, but among Croats different politics has always been represented by Croats from Posavina – here, Croats never fought with Bošniaks and have felt abandoned by the Croats from the rest of the country and by their kin state, but first and foremost by HDZ. It was in West Herzegovina where Croats have always been a radicalized ethnic majority oriented toward Dalmatia and Croatia – a policy best represented by HDZ that dominated the contemporary Croat discourse in BiH (Pejanović 2002: 118). The Bosniak block has always been the most diverse when it comes to the popular support for political parties, but SDA, SBiH, and SDP share the same view on Bosnia and have similar ideas for its improvements – they have continued to seek the building of a state without the entities agreeing that BiH should become a regionalized country, but they offer different solutions on how to reach that point though (Banović and Gavrić 2010: 1690). While SDA and SDP argue for gradual centralization and abolition of entities, SBiH wants a completely new constitutional negotiations under the US-American leadership, the so-called Dayton II (Keil 2013: 148).

The post-Dayton era has been characterized by a continuing friction between politicians from the three main ethnic groups who have "used the DPA not to build peace, but to continue the pursuit of their war aims" (Morrison 2009: 8). Personal rivalry has become a more frequent reason for party splits than program conflicts with a highly limited intra-party democracy (Sedo 2010: 88), nontransparent methods of funding, and absence of clear policies regarding fundamental problems of the country. As education of "professional politicians" and experts does not really exist (Friedrich-Ebert-Stiftung 2005: 21) and power remains personalized and based on informal connections, political legitimacy is derived from political actors' ability to nourish the clientele on which their power rests – everything in the country is patronage-based (Ornert ansd Hewitt 2006: 8). Political parties operate and are organized more like Mafia than like modern political parties, but all these elements could be treated as examples of patriarchal values transferred into politics from the sacral sphere (Fejzić-Čengić 2009: 197).

Yet, this situation on the political scene does not come out of nowhere. The armed conflict emphasized also one of the crucial problems of the region: lack of the culture of political compromise that dominated the political arena after the conflict. Since the first democratic elections in Bosnia and Herzegovina in 1991, politics has been characterized by ethno-politics rather than interest-based politics. The result is that political competition for voters has been warped with the role of voters reduced to cyphers in an ethnic census. While the specific leaders and parties change from time to time, the content of the rhetoric employed by victorious politicians has not changed (Hulsey and Mujkić 2010: 144).

Conclusions

As the previous sections show, history of Bosnia and Herzegovina has been marked by periods of hatred and conflict, as well as cooperation and peaceful coexistence between its groups. Also, it is difficult to determine if the fact that the three constituent nations still live together is to be blamed for the instability and fragility of the country nowadays. Nevertheless, there are two elements that, in the postwar period, have been dominated by ethnicity – political institutions and political parties – so the whole political process. While, in the case of institutions, it was difficult to avoid given the fact that Bosnia is a post-conflict, divided society, the corporate character of the consociational model further enhanced the omnipotence of ethnicity in everyday life. Yet, it was the choice of political elites (only to some extent constrained by the institutional system in which they operate), leaders, and their parties that eventually combined ethnicity with politics and, in effect, political conflict.

The DPA brought about a measure of peace between the three warring parties but at the same time left in power the same political groups and parties that had started the war – it was a compromise, but it had its costs. The ethnic leaders who had manipulated ethnic tensions beforehand continued to maintain the divisions afterward, exploiting the recovery process for their own interests. Not only they took over economic resources but also merged party interests with those of "their" nations. As a result of their stay in power, three problems could be indicated that plague BiH today: political party patronage networks, corruption, and lack of transparency.

Federal values of equality, justice, and diversity have not yet become a part of Bosnian political culture (Keil 2013: 134), and consociationalism is understood more as a mechanism that provides autonomy than shared responsibilities. While in the prewar years the parties engaged in a flawed attempt of "power sharing," the cooperation after the Dayton Peace Accords amounted largely to a division of power. Each main party largely respected the "right" of the other nationalist parties to govern their respective nation, and cooperation, if required by the institutions, was limited to a division of access to state assets and resources (Bieber 2001: 5). It is then understandable that political parties are cited as the most corrupt segment of society in the majority of opinion polls – in 2010 that was the answer of 75% respondents (Blagovcanin 2012: 82–3).

References

Al Jazeera (2016) Rezultati popisa: U BiH zivi 3.531.159 stanovnika. 2.10.2016. http://balkans. aljazeera.net/vijesti/bih-danas-rezultati-popisa-iz-2013-godine

Andjelić N (2003) Bosnia-Herzegovina. The end of legacy. Frank Cass Publishers, London

Banović D (2008) Neki aspekti utjecaja politike na pravo. In: Godišnjak Pravnog fakulteta u Sarajevu. pp 63–78

Banović D, Gavrić S (2010) Ustavna reforma u Bosni i Hercegovini. Politička Misao 2:159–180

Bataković DT (2001) Etnički i nacjonalni identitet u Bosni i Hercegovini (XIX–XX vek.). Jezik, vera, identitet. Dijalog Povesničara-Istoričara 3

Belloni R (2007) State building and international intervention in Bosnia. Routledge, New York

Belloni R, Deane S (2005) From Belfast to Bosnia: piecemeal peacemaking and the role of institutional learning. Civil Wars 7(3):219–243

Bieber F (2001) Croat self-government in Bosnia – a challenge for Dayton? ECMI Brief #5 May

Bieber F (2006) After Dayton, Dayton? The evolution of an unpopular peace. Ethnopolitics 5(1):15–31

Bieber F (2006b) Post-war Bosnia. Ethnicity, inequality and public sector governance. Palgrave Macmillan, Basingstoke

Blagovčanin S (2012) BiH: captured state. In: Dzihić V, Hamilton D (eds) Unfinished business. The Western Balkans and the international community. Center fir Transatlantic Relations, Washington, DC

Bochsler D (2012) Non-discriminatory rules and ethnic representation: the election of the Bosnian state presidency. Ethnopolitics 11(1):66–84

Bose S (2002) Bosnia after Dayton. Nationalist partition and international intervention. Oxford University Press, New York

Bringa T (1993) National categories, national identification and identity formation in 'Multinational' Bosnia. Anthropol East Eur Rev 11(1–2):100–108

Burg SL, Shoup PS (1999) The war in Bosnia-Herzegovina: ethnic conflict and international intervention. M. E. Sharpe, New York

Caspersen N (2004) Good Fences Make Good Neighbours? A Comparison of Conflict-Regulation Strategies in Postwar Bosnia. Journal of Peace Research 41(5):569–588

Chandler D (2000) Bosnia. Faking democracy after Dayton. Pluto Press, London/Sterling

Daalder H (2000) Getting to Dayton. The making of America's Bosnia policy. Brookings Institution Press, Washington, DC

Dąbrowska-Partyka M (2004) Literatura pogranicza, pogranicza literatury. WUJ, Kraków

Diamond L, Plattner MF (1994) Introduction. In: Diamond L, Plattner MF (eds) Nationalism, ethnic conflict, and democracy. J. Hopkins University Press, London

Donia RJ, Fine JVA (2011) Bosna i Hercegovina: iznevjerena tradicija. Institut za istoriju, Sarajevo

FBiH - Vital National Interes Decisions – listing. (2000) https://www.parlament.ba/Content/Read/ 39?title=Vitalninacionalniinteres&lang=bs

Fejzić-Čengić F (2009) Patrijarhalne vrijednosti političkih elita u Bosni i Hercegovini i njihov utjecaj na formiranje vrijednosnih stavova prema Bosni i Hercegovini i Evropskoj uniji. In: Ćurak N (ed) Politička elita u BiH i EU: Odnos vrijednosti. FPN, Sarajevo

Fenton S (2007) Indifference to National Identity. What Young Adults Think about Being English and British. Nations and Nationalism 13(2):321–339

Fine JVA (2002) The various faiths in the history of Bosnia: middle ages to the present. In: Shatzmiller M (ed) Islam and Bosnia. Conflict resolution and foreign policy in multi-ethnic states. McGill-Queen's University Press, Montreal

Friedrich Ebert Stiftung (2005) Analiza rezultata općih izbora u Bosni i Hercegovini. Sarajevo oktobar, 2005

Grandits H (2009) Ambivalentnosti u socijalističkoj nacionalnoj politici Bosne i Hercegovine u kasnim 1960-im i u 1970-im: perspektive odozgo i odozdo. In: Rasprave o nacionalnom identitetu Bosnjaka: zbornik radova. Institut za istoriju, Sarajevo

Gromes T (2006) Containing the dangers of democratization: a record of peacebuilding in Bosnia and Herzegovina. Cornell University Peace Studies Program Occasional Paper 30-2

Gromes T (2010) Federalism as a means of peace-building: the case of postwar Bosnia and Herzegovina. Nationalism Ethn Polit 16:354–374

Gurr TR (2000) Peoples versus states: minorities at risk in the new century. US Institute of Peace Press, Washington, DC

Guss J, Siroky DS (2012) Living with heterogeneity bridging the ethnic divide in Bosnia. Comp Sociol 11:304–324

Hayden RM (2005) "Democracy" without a demos? The Bosnian constitutional experiment and the intentional construction of nonfunctioning states. East Eur Polit Soc 19(2):226–259

Haynes DF (2008) The Deus ex Machina descends: the laws, priorities and players central to the International Administration of post-conflict Bosnia and Herzegovina. In: Haynes DF (ed) Deconstructing the reconstruction. Human rights and rule of law in postwar BiH. Ashgate, Aldershot/Burlington

Hoare MA (2007) The history of Bosnia. From the middle ages to the present day. Saqi, London/Berkeley

Hodžić E, Stojanović N (2011a) Izazovi izvršenja presude u predmetu Sejdić i Finci protiv BiH. Analitika, Sarajevo

Hodžić E, Stojanović N (2011b) Novi-stari ustavni inženjering? Izazovi i implikacije presude Evropskog Suda za Ljudska Prava u predmetu Sejdić i Finci protiv BiH. Analitika, Sarajevo

Horowitz DL (2000) Ethnic groups in conflict. University of California Press, Berkeley

Hulsey J (2010) 'Why did they vote for those guys again?' Challenges and contradictions in the promotion of political moderation in post-war Bosnia and Herzegovina. Democratization 17(6):1132–1152

Hulsey J (2015) Electoral accountability in Bosnia and Herzegovina under the Dayton framework agreement. Int Peacekeeping 22(5):511–525

Hulsey J, Mujkić A (2010) Explaining the success of nationalist parties in Bosnia and Herzegovina. Politička Misao 2:143–158

ICG (2002) Implementing Equality: the Constituent Peoples Decision in Bosnia & Herzegovina. ICG Balkans Report No. 128

Kapidžić D (2015) Party system of Bosnia and Herzegovina. In: Arnautović S, Mujagić N, Kapidžić D, Osmić A, Huruz E (eds) Political pluralism and internal party democracy. Centar za monitoring i istraživanje, Podgorica, pp 35–56

Kasapović M (2005) Bosnia and Herzegovina: consociational or liberal democracy? Politička Misao XLII(5):3–30

Keil S (2013) Multinational federalism in Bosnia and Herzegovina. Ashgate, Surrey

Koneska C (2017) On peace negotiations and institutional design in Macedonia: social learning and lessons learned from Bosnia and Herzegovina. Peacebuilding 5(1):36–50

Lijphart A (1969) Consociational Democracy. World Polit 21(2):207–225

Lijphart A (1977) Democracy in plural societies: a comparative exploration. Yale University Press, Yale

Lovrenović I (1999) Unutarnja Zemlja. Kratki pregled kulturne povijesti Bosne i Hercegovine. Zagreb: Durieux

Lovrenović I (2001) Bosnia: a cultural history. Saqi Books, London

Lyon J (2006) Overcoming ethnic politics in Bosnia? Achievements and obstacles to European integration. In: Fischer M (ed) Peacebuilding and civil society in BiH. Berghof Forschungszentrum für konstruktive Konfliktbearbeitung, Munster

Malcolm N (2011) Bosnia. Kratka povijest. Buybook, Sarajevo

Mansfield AM (2003) Ethnic but equal: the quest for a new democratic order in Bosnia and Herzegovina. Columbia Law Rev 103(8):2052–2093

McCarthy J (1994) Ottoman Bosnia, 1800 to 1878. In: Pinson M (ed) The Muslims of Bosnia-Herzegovina. Their historic development from the middle ages to the dissolution of Yugoslavia. Harvard University Press, Harvard

McEvoy J (2015) Governing in Bosnia, Macedonia, and Northern Ireland. University of Pennsylvania Press, Philadelphia

Merdžanović A (2016) 'Imposed consociationalism': external intervention and power sharing in Bosnia and Herzegovina. Peacebuilding 5(1):22–35

Mitchell JC (1974) Perceptions of ethnicity and ethnic behaviour: an empirical exploration. In: Cohen A (ed) Urban ethnicity. Tavistock, London

Morrison K (2009) Dayton, divisions and constitutional revisions: Bosnia & Herzegovina at the Crossroads. Balkan Series 09/11

Mujkić A, Seizović Z, Abazović D (2008) The role of human and minority rights in the process of reconstruction and reconciliation for state and nation-building: Bosnia and Herzegovina, MIRICO: Human and Minority Rights in the Life Cycle of Ethnic Conflicts. Bozen – Bolzano

Nagata JA (1974) What is a Malay? Situational selection of ethnic identity in a plural society. Am Ethnol 1(2):331–350

Nation-building BiH (2011) In strategies of symbolic nation-building in West Balkan states: intents and results. http://www.hf.uio.no/ilos/english/research/projects/nation-w-balkan/

Orrnert A, Hewitt T (2006) Elites and institutions – literature review. University of Birmingham: GSD RC Report http://gsdrc.ids.ac.uk/docs/open/hd293.pdf

Pejanović M (2002) Through Bosnian eyes. The political memoirs of a Bosnian Serb. Sahinpasić, Sarajevo

Pugh M, Cobble M (2001) Non-nationalist voting in Bosnian municipal elections: implications for democracy and peacebuilding. J Peace Res 38(1):27–47

Ramet SP (1992) Nationalism and federalism in Yugoslavia 1962–1991. Indiana University Press, Indianapolis

Ramet SP (2002) Balkan babel: the disintegration of Yugoslavia from the death of Tito to the fall of Milosević. Westview, Colorado

Sahadžić M (2011) Priroda politickog sistema u Bosni i Hercegovini. In: Banović D, Gavrić S (eds) Drzava, politika i drustvo i Bosni i Hercegovini. Analiza postdejtonskog politickog sistema. University Press – Magistrat izdanja, Sarajevo

Saračević N (2011) Parlamentarna Skupština Bosne i Hercegovine. In: Banović D, Gavrić S (eds) Drzava, politika i drustvo i Bosni i Hercegovini. Analiza postdejtonskog politickog sistema. University Press – Magistrat izdanja, Sarajevo

Sedo J (2010) The party system of Bosnia and Herzegovina. In: Stojarova V, Emerson P (eds) Party politics in the Western Balkans. Routledge, New York/Abingdon

Seizović Z (2005) Bosnia and Herzegovina: concord of diversity – compilation of legal essays. Studio Flas, Zenica

Smailagić N, Keranović N (2011) Pravosudni sistem Bosne i Hercegovine. In: Banović D, Gavrić S (eds) Drzava, politika i drustvo i Bosni i Hercegovini. Analiza postdejtonskog politickog sistema. University Press – Magistrat izdanja, Sarajevo

Toal G, Dahlman CT (2011) Bosna remade. Ethnic cleansing and its reversal. Oxford University Press, Oxford

Touquet H, Vermeersch P (2008) Bosnia and Herzegovina: thinking beyond institution-building. Nationalism Ethn Polit 14(2):266–288

Trnka K (2009) Proces odlučivanja u Parlamentarnoj Skupštini Bosne i Hercegovine. Stanje – komparativna rješenja – prijedlozi. Fondacija Konrad Adenauer Stuftung, Sarajevo

Tzifakis N (2007) The Bosnian peace process: the power-sharing approach revisited, perspectives. Cent Eur Rev Int Aff 28:85–101

Weller M, Wolff S (2006) Bosnia and Herzegovina ten years after Dayton: lessons for internationalized state building. Ethnopolitics 5(1):1–13

Wimmer A, Cederman L-E, Min B (2009) Ethnic politics and armed conflict: a configurational analysis of a new global data set. Am Sociol Rev 74(2):316–337

Wolff S (2013) Managing ethno-national conflict: towards an analytical framework. In: Woods ET, Schertzer RS, Kaufman E (eds) Nationalism and conflict management. Routledge, London

Ethnic Conflicts and Peace-Building

35

Sergio Luiz Cruz Aguilar

Contents

Introduction 613
Concepts 615
Ethnicity and Civil Wars 618
Ethnic Conflicts and Peacebuilding 624
Conclusion 627
Cross-References 628
References 628

Abstract

The chapter highlights the challenges to resolve and/or transform ethnic conflicts and bring peace to ethnically divided societies through peacebuilding activities. Using examples of ethnic civil wars in Africa, the chapter discusses some of the more common ways used in the attempts to resolve or transform these types of armed conflicts, focusing on consociational democracy and regional autonomy formulas.

Keywords

Ethnic conflicts · Civil war · Conflict resolution · Peacebuilding · Power sharing

---

This chapter is part of a research project funded by the São Paulo Research Foundation (FAPESP) – Grant 2016/21211-8.

S. L. C. Aguilar (✉)
Sao Paulo State University (UNESP), Marilia, São Paulo, Brazil
e-mail: sergio.aguilar@unesp.br

© The Author(s), under exclusive license to Springer Nature Singapore Pte Ltd. 2019
S. Ratuva (ed.), *The Palgrave Handbook of Ethnicity*,
https://doi.org/10.1007/978-981-13-2898-5_46

Introduction

Conflicts are seen as a complex phenomenon. Contemporary conflicts involve a multiplicity of actors (both state and private) in large conflict structures where the scope of public authority is limited. In numerous intrastate conflicts, ethnic components are central to these dynamics, especially (but not exclusively) in Africa, some of which extend over a long period of time and are considered intractable. When transnational actors are present and interlinked through ethnic groups, a conflict within one country can potentially spread to its neighbors and, in some cases, develop into a regional conflict system.

The presence of diverse ethnic groups in a specific country or region is a secular characteristic of Africa that intensifies social divisions and tensions. An ethnic division of power is the result of colonial practices that favored one ethnic group over another, for example, in Rwanda and Uganda. Overlapping ethnic populations remain as a potential source of conflict either through covert support for rebel groups or direct military intervention, such as in the Democratic Republic of Congo (DRC) (see Horowitz 1985).

Numerous conflicts are connected through ethnic manipulation, since it is a fundamental requirement to achieve and/or maintain power. Policies that exacerbate ethnic categories inflate and politicize the significance of ethnicity and "serve to disguise the struggle over the more fundamental matters of power and resources." In Central Africa, Belgian administrations introduced ethnic identity cards, dividing population into Hutu, Tutsi, or Twa, politicizing ethnicity (Taras and Ganguly 2016, p. 214).

Deeply rooted historical violence and animosity between ethnic groups generate fear, distrust, and violence at all levels. Fear of extermination by adversaries has led to the formation of armed groups, some of which conduct preemptive attacks in the name of self-defense, including against government forces when deemed necessary. Therefore, the nature of conflicts has both ethnic and military dimensions.

According to Denny and Walter (2014, p. 200), "almost half of the remaining civil wars (all of which are fought for control of government) are started by rebel groups with a different ethnicity from the government (33 of 73 cases, or 45%)."

The diffusion of military violence by regional identity and ethnic factors is a common feature of conflicts in African regions and takes place in variety of ways, such as feelings of insecurity provoked by conflict in a neighboring country; solidarity with a similar ethnic group in a neighboring country; grievances between ethnic majorities and minorities within one country or region, often linked to a political inability to manage multiethnic societies; struggles for secession; and mobilization of ethnic or identity groups by charismatic leaders, among others. Furthermore, ethnic civil wars normally take longer to resolve than nonethnic civil wars (see Lake and Rothchild 1996; Weiner 1992; Salehyan and Gleditsch 2006).

This chapter aims to present a range of considerations regarding ethnic conflicts, using examples in Africa. Beginning with the most important concepts, it describes the various characteristics of ethnicity in civil wars. It then moves on to discuss some of the more common ways these types of conflicts are resolved or transformed within the scope of peacebuilding activities.

Concepts

Ethnicity is defined in various ways. Cederman et al. (2010, p. 98) define it as "any subjectively experienced sense of commonality based on the belief in common ancestry and shared culture." Thus, it is tied to culture. The literature generally agrees that ethnicity involves individuals identifying with one another based on shared characteristics such as appearance, language, religion, or traditions (Nagel 1994; Horowitz 1985).

Conflict and violence often occur together. There is conflict without violence when its causes are addressed in an appropriate and timely manner. However, this chapter refers to conflict in the sense of violent (armed) conflict, which appears when inconsistencies between the goals of different groups or individuals lead to violent behavior and hatred or when hatred already exists between groups due to historical factors, in which case even the smallest contradiction can generate violence.

Cederman et al. (2010, p. 102) consider rebel groups to have strong ties with an ethnic group if it articulates ethno-nationalist objectives and recruits on the "basis of ethnic affiliation."

Ethnic wars are classified as "conflicts over ethno-national self-determination, the ethnic balance of power in government, ethno regional autonomy, ethnic and racial discrimination (whether alleged or real), and language and other cultural rights'; all other aims are defined as nonethnic" (Denny and Walter 2014, p. 201).

Ethnic wars engage "non-state actors, singled minded groups lacking the full panoply of interests and linkages that often moderate the behavior of governments" (Wedgwood 2001, p. 5). Ethnic divisions are condition for mass violence; however alone they do not furnish an adequate explanation for armed violence, i.e., it is necessary their connection with other factors.

Transborder ethnic groups are those whose fractions are indigenous to more than one state. Transborder ethnic groups are abundant in Africa and arose from the colonial partition of the continent. According to Onah (2015, p. 86), "it is now an acknowledged fact that this partition was arbitrary, with the frontiers of the new African territories neither reflecting the limits of natural regions, nor the regions of separate ethnic groups." Consequently, "many ethnic groups were divided in such a way that fractions of the same ethnic group fell into the territorial possessions of different colonizing powers, each part subsequently being administered separately from the other."

On these areas, conflicts normally lie in the overlapping of ethnic and religious as well as porous borders.

Taras and Ganguly (2016, p. 223) highlighted that "the northeastern border of the DRC with Uganda and Sudan has represented an ethnic powder keg." Civil conflict in one country inevitably to spill over into another and "one country's confrontation between government and rebel armies swiftly becomes the entire region's dispute."

Conflicts also lie in the inflammation of ethnic tensions by political, military, and economic networks (AI 2005). When ethnic transborder groups are barred from the commanding heights of the economy and politics of the countries in which they live, "the tendency is always for them to see the larger ethnic group as the alternative, hence their increased attachment to the group and solidarity with other fractions in the other countries" (Onah 2015, p. 90). This type of exclusion led the Tauregs to fight for their own country, the Azawad. In the Great Lakes, Tutsis and Hutus have been seeking power for decades. Moreover, in the absence of a credible political process and in an environment of political uncertainty, ethnic communities turn to armed groups as local guarantors of security. This is the characteristic feature of the Mayi-Mayi groups in the DRC. Thereto, in some cases, national and provincial political leaders deliberately incited local conflicts in order to obtain or demonstrate power for personal gains (IPI 2017).

According to Onah (2015), there are different ways in which intrastate conflicts arise and develop. For example, one way that intrastate conflicts can arise is through hostile relations between the state and transborder peoples, including fractions of transborder ethnic groups falling within its borders. This form of conflict can emanate from either the state or from the ethnic group. In Mali, the long-standing problem of the Tuareg, an ethnic group partitioned across borders, has led to numerous revolts emanating from the group itself, including the present conflict. The conflict in Cote d'Ivoire put the Dioula transborder ethnic group at the center of its war, involving ethnic and identity issues.

The concept of *Ivoirité*, referring to the purported intrinsic characteristics of an indigenous Ivorian, became part of the political and social lexicon of the country. It was promoted by President Bedie to restrict the rights of foreign workers in the country, further exacerbating ethnic and regional divisions in Cote D'Ivoire (Woods 2003). When the concept was drummed up to discredit Alassane Ouattara, a northern politician and a Dioula, preventing him from running for elections, the New Forces, a Dioula rebel group, took up arms in 2002 (Onah 2015). In the DRC, the Tutsi ethnic group (*Banyamulenge*) formed the Alliance of Democratic Forces for the Liberation of Congo-Zaire (ADFL-CZ) to confront President Mobutu and, later, would also form the Rally for Democracy (RCD) that confronted President Kabila (Onah 2015).

Intrastate conflicts can also arise from hostilities between a fraction of transborder ethnic groups and other ethnic groups living in the country, such as the fight between Hutus and Tutsis within the DRC. Moreover, hostility can also lead to conflicts between two states, where one has ties to transborder ethnic groups on the land of the other. In Liberia, throughout the period of the second Liberian civil war, "the Liberian government continued threatening to take the war back to Guinea, which it accused of sponsoring the rebels" (Onah 2015, p. 89). In the DRC, the hostility between Tutsi and Hutu ethnic groups led to Rwanda and Uganda invading Congolese territory in 1996 and 1998 to fight Hutu armed groups, who were allegedly being sheltered by the DRC government. After withdrawing at the end of 2002, Rwanda and Uganda continued to assist rebel proxies in eastern DRC (Onah 2015).

The problems between Sudan and Chad can be directly traced to the Zaghawa ethnic group, people who live in Sudan, Chad, and the Central African Republic

(CAR) and share a common border in the Darfur region. After Idriss Déby, a Zaghawa, took power in Chad (in December 1990), some dynamics began to operate around Zaghawa ethnicity such as a mixture of political intrigue, active support of his kin beyond the borders, political support in neighboring countries (Sudanese support to Déby, Déby support to Bozize in the CAR, etc.), and demands of "equality and justice." There is also evidence that violence in the CAR in May 2013 was carried out by Zaghawa rebels from the CAR and Chad (Onah 2015).

Empirical analyses have found that rebel victory is less likely to occur in identity-based civil wars fought along ethnic and religious lines (De Rouen and Sobek 2004; Mason et al. 1999) and that conflicts between different ethnic groups are more violent than others (Denny and Walter 2014). Conflicts founded on ethnic divisions may lead to dehumanization, entailing ethnic cleansing or symbolic violence intended to terrorize unwanted residents. In these contexts, ethnic cleansing can be used by political actors as a strategy to make certain geographic areas more defensible or to shore up their control during conflict.

Although some authors separate the concepts of conflict management, containment, and settlement (Ramsbotham et al. 2011), this chapter uses the term "management" to cover a wide range of conflict handling mechanisms, including preventive action, peacekeeping activity (containment/alleviation of intensity), and agreements (settlement/peace-making). Conflict resolution implies that a conflict is solvable and highlights a comprehensive sense that all its deep-rooted sources are treated (Azar 1991). Conflict transformation, on the other hand, goes beyond resolution and implies "a deep transformation in the institutions and discourses that reproduce violence, as well as in the conflict parties themselves and their relationships" (Azar 1991, pp. 31–32). Consequently, transformation applies a comprehensive and long-term approach to social change in situations of violence and necessitates the involvement of all actors present in the conflict.

In these terms, peacekeeping deals with ethnicity in the short term, while peacebuilding aims for conflict transformation instead. As such the latter addresses more long-term activities. This is because the main aim of conflict transformation is to deeply alter conflicting parties' relationships in order to avoid the reoccurrence of violence. It highlights constructive and destructive agents of change (at the global, regional, and state levels, as well as in the context of conflicting parties, elites, or individuals) and in doing so can be used as a theoretical framework, showing external actors how to move on from the conflict (see Lederach 2003). Transforming conflict means putting an end to structural violence and achieving long-lasting peace or positive in the Galtung (1996) sense that the mere absence of violence is negative peace and positive peace means a stable social equilibrium in which the surfacing of new disputes does not escalate into violence and war.

Thus, the main objective of conflict transformation is comprehensive analysis that results in appropriate intervention by outside mediators, peacekeepers, peacebuilders, etc., to rebuild and transform structures and social relationships. If a conflict runs along ethnic lines, this issue should be prioritized during peacekeeping/peacebuilding activities.

Ethnicity and Civil Wars

There are states that face power struggles between ethnically and ideologically diverse groups. The existing literature on civil war addresses ethnic groups and attempts to explain whether a state's ethnic characteristics make a country more or less likely to experience civil war and why some ethnic groups are motivated to launch rebel movements while others are not (Horowitz 1985; Fearon and Laitin 2003; Cederman et al. 2010). Thus, numerous arguments connecting ethnicity and rebel movements have been raised, among them: common language and cultural ties favor cohesion; the geographic concentration of ethnic groups makes it easier for rebel movements to extract resources and evade repression; and ethnic cross-border movements can offer financing and support to rebel groups, such as recruits, popular support, and a safe haven (Gates 2002; Humphreys 2005).

In the CAR, poor leadership and governance, and neglect, led to ethnicity and religion becoming a point of leverage during both the 1980s and the crisis of 2013–2014. The conflict is also connected to successive governments' irresponsible and unaccountable administration of extensive mineral deposits in the country. In South Sudan, the violence in 2013 was linked to societal polarization along ethnic lines. The new country was made up of 64 tribes with no national vision, cohesion, or identity. The government, including the army – the Sudan People's Liberation Army (SPLA) – remained separated by ethnicity (UN A/69/968–S/2015/490 2015). When a political crisis occurred at the head of the government in 2013, violence quickly spread throughout the country.

According to Denny and Walter (2014, p. 202), "collective violence – such as rebellion – requires motivation and opportunity." Moreover, "civil wars so often separate along ethnic lines because grievances, opportunity, and bargaining problems tend to fall disproportionately along ethnic lines, making mobilization easier and more probable."

Ethnic groups' grievances are more likely to be a conflict driver when political power has historically been divided along ethnic lines (Denny and Walter 2014). Politics of exclusion provide a related set of conflict drivers. When one set of ethnic interests dominates power to the exclusion of others, minorities that are oppressed, scapegoated, violently targeted, or politically exploited by elites are more incentivized to organize a rebellion (UN. A/69/968–S/2015/490 2015). Ethnic conflict is particularly likely when ethnic groups suffer from (perceived) relative deprivation (Gurr 2000) or horizontal inequalities (see Stewart 2002; Cederman et al. 2011). According to Cederman et al. (2011, p. 482), "the perception of injustice generates grievances that serve as a formidable tool of recruitment."

The ethnic distribution of Hutus and Tutsis has been manipulated by Rwandan, Burundian, Ugandan, and Congolese elites for their own ends since independence. In former Zaire, President Mobutu earned the loyalty of the *Banyamulenge* (the name given to the ethnic Tutsi concentrated on the DRC High Plateau of South Kivu, close to the Burundi-Congo-Rwanda border) by alternating between threatening to deport them and allowing them participation in political and economic life (Thom 1999).

The *Banyarwandas* – Rwandan colonials or nationals who emigrated to the DRC between the end of World War I and 1960 acquired Congolese citizenship at independence from Belgium in 1960, which was revoked in 1981 (Nest et al. 2006). In Uganda, *Banyarwanda* refugees were deprived of social independence and faced great internal prejudice even after they had allied with elements of the National Resistance Army (NRA) against President Obote (Golooba-Mutebi 2008). In Rwanda, the massacre of Tutsi politicians and civilians carried out by the Rwandan Army between December 1963 and January 1964 was repeated in 1994. The denial of citizenship to the *Banyarwanda* community is one of the sources of conflict in the DRC. The Tutsi-speaking groups (*Banyamulenge*) of the DRC-Kivu region have never had their position within Congolese society recognized (Rukundwa 2004).

In Burundi, between 1962 and 1966, conflicts were mainly due to political competition for power on the basis of ethnicity between the Tutsi and the Hutu. During the next period (1966–1993), conflicts revolved around monopolized state power control and oppression of the majority Hutu and minority Twa by minority Tutsi. This ethnic division led to massacres in 1972 and 1973, during which nearly 300,000 people lost their lives, and a protracted civil war (1993–2004) (Berahino 2011).

Motivations arise in various ways. In ethnically divided countries, natural resources can provide an additional motive and opportunity to help groups collectively overcome their problems by providing the necessary financial means for them to do so. Thus, besides generating grievances, natural resources may provide incentives – immediate material benefits or promises of future rewards – that encourage collective action to overcome common problems and facilitating the mobilization of ethnic groups (Wegenast and Basedau 2014). Furthermore, "ethnic groups may use commodities concentrated in their territory as a means by which to seek secession" (Wegenast and Basedau 2014, p. 438). Conflict is also likely to last longer when a group has access to natural resources (Buhaug et al. 2009). Conflicts in the CAR, the DRC, and South Sudan all involve natural resources, despite also being described as ethnic conflicts.

Ethnic groups are also more likely to be able to rebel because they are more accustomed to living in concentrated or geographically peripheral areas (Denny and Walter 2014). Country borders reflect how far leaders have extended their domestic powers in terms of providing goods and services to the people. However, in reality, leaders in some countries such as the DRC, the CAR, and South Sudan only genuinely extend power into certain specific areas of the territory. In some cases, such as Somalia, governments do not extend their control beyond the capital.

Vulnerability to conflict in peripheral areas can also increase in response to localized factors, such as when the local population interacts with ethnic minorities that are excluded from the political process (Buhaug et al. 2008). In Uganda, armed groups were created according to ethnic lines. The Allied Democratic Forces (ADF) were formed in the late 1990s by Muslim Ugandans who merged with the remnants of the National Army for the Liberation of Uganda (NALU) and received support from the Sudanese government and Ugandan ethnic groups that were hostile to the local government (West 2015). In the DRC, the hesitant approach of the government "to extending effective state authority to deal with the ethnic tensions and economic rivalries among ethnic communities still puts large numbers of civilians at risk in the eastern Congo" (Doss 2011, p. 21).

Ethnic groups are likely to display more grievances against the state, have an easier time organizing support and mobilizing a movement, and face more difficult-to-resolve bargaining problems than groups organized along other lines. According to the bargaining theory, parties choose to resolve their disputes through violence when the core of the dispute is not mutually perceived to be divisible; agreements on the groups' relative strength and the likely outcome of war do not exist; and parties are not able to enforce the terms of a settlement, if it exists (Denny and Walter 2014). According to the authors, it is due to three factors: "the ways in which political power has historically been divided; leaders' ease of mobilizing support to demand change; and the relatively non-fluid nature of ethnic identity." Consequently, "members of ethnic groups will have greater incentives and opportunities to fight the government than members of other types of groups" (Denny and Walter 2014, p. 207).

In ethnically divided states, a trigger (also called a precipitant, facilitating or igniting factor) is seen as the immediate cause of violence. A trigger could be an economic or political crisis with ethnic undertones, the real or imagined fears of an ethnic group regarding its security and even survival, or a specific event. The assassination of Rwandan President Habyarimana and Burundian President Ntaryamira, in April 1994, triggered genocide in Rwanda, which in turn triggered a regional conflict system in the Great Lakes. Regional conflict systems are characterized "by their complexity of actors, causes, structural conditions and dynamics" (Ansorg 2011, p. 175), and are formed of "sets of violent conflicts – each originating in a particular state or sub-region – that form mutually reinforcing linkages with each other throughout a broader region" (idem, p. 179).

The first consequence of the Rwandan genocide was a large refugee flow which added new dynamics and increased old ones present in the region. However, whether such flows always result in regional conflict systems is associated with other factors, such as changes to ethnic and social structures, and the growth of instability impacting states, governments, and other ethnic communities (Lischer 2005; Weiner 1992).

When groups migrate along ethnic lines or when political power in a state is divided along ethnic lines, they are more likely to present grievances against that state (Cederman et al. 2013; Cederman et al. 2010). Oppositional groups of a given country usually utilize their ethnic links on the other side of the international border to obtain sanctuary, base of operations, and support (Suhrke and Noble 1977; Salehyan 2007). When refugees share ethnic kinship with a politically marginalized group or a rebel organization of the host country and the influx is large, the spread of conflict is more likely (Lischer 2005; Salehyan and Gleditsch 2006; Salehyan 2007).

In the Great Lakes, refugees from Burundi, the DRC, Rwanda, and Uganda sought shelter within similar ethnic groups in neighboring countries. Rwandan

Hutu refugees upset the precarious balance of power in the DRC-South Kivu province populated by *Banyamulenge*. When Ugandan troops withdrew from the DRC-Ituri region, in 2003, refugees from the DRC, mainly Hema and Lendu people who have close relationships with the Ugandan ethnic groups, fled to Uganda (Nest et al. 2006). In South Sudan, it is common that the movement of internally displaced peoples (IDPs) takes place according to their ethnic groups gaining or losing control of certain areas, according to an UNMISS former official interviewed by the author in June 2018.

IDPs also affect ethnic conflicts. IDPs may harbor strong grievances and experience traumatic situations, which increases the salience of ethnic identities and encourages engagement in violence as a way of changing their situation. Consequently, they are particularly likely to provide support, recruits, and logistical bases to rebels from the same ethnic groups (Cederman et al. 2010).

Both IDPs and refugees are more willing to engage with rebels when they share a common history, e.g., Tutsi and Hutu in the Great Lakes region. Ethnicity facilitates IDPs' and refugees' mobilization of rebel groups by generating shared loyalties and obligations among co-ethnics (Bohnet et al. 2016). Movements and settlements established according to ethnicities provide the context in which interactions fuel ethnic conflicts (see Weidmann 2009).

Despite the process of conflict regionalization being historically rooted, the present regional conflict system in the Great Lakes was catalyzed by the 1994 genocide in Rwanda. The subsequent flow of refugees into different countries caused tensions and changed dynamics in an entire region. Within this process, groups were formed and later disappeared, transborder activities of armed groups increased, and alliances were both established and broken over the following decades.

During and after the 1994 genocide in Rwanda, Hutus fled to the DRC provinces of North Kivu and South Kivu and formed alliances with the DRC-Hutus and Mayi-Mayi groups against the DRC-Tutsis. Rwandan armed groups *Ex-Forces Armées Rwandaises* (ex-FAR) and *Interahamwe* – a Hutu paramilitary organization and wing of the ruling party of Rwanda – became collectively known as the *Armée pour la Libération du Rwanda* (ALIR), the main group composed of Hutus operating in the DRC. The group received support from the DRC government and operated in close cooperation with the *Forces Armées Congolaises* (FAC) and Burundian *Forces pour la Défense de la Démocratie* (FDD), armed wing of the Conseil National pour la Défense de la Démocratie (CNDD). The Burundian armed groups Forces for the Defence of Democracy (FDD) and *Forces Nationales pour la Libération* (FNL) also extended their presence in the DRC. The FDD – an armed wing of the *Conseil National pour la Défense de la Démocratie* (CNDD) – fought alongside the Congolese armed forces in the province of Katanga and undertook joint operations with ALIR and Mayi-Mayi groups in South Kivu (UN, S/2002/341 2002) and became a political party in 2005 (Alusala 2005). The FNL was a "Rwasa faction" of the *Parti pour la Libération du Peuple Hutu* (PALIPEHUTU), which established bases in east DRC and alliances with *Interahamwe* and Mayi-Mayi groups. In 2008, PALIPEHUTU leaders signed an agreement and changed its name to FNL, deleting the ethnic element (Mulamula 2011).

The Alliance of Democratic Forces for the Liberation of Congo-Zaire (AFDL) was formed by a coalition of Rwandan, Ugandan, Burundian, and Congolese dissidents who toppled President Mobutu and brought Laurent Kabila to power in the First Congo War (1996–1997) (AI 1998). In August 1998, the Rally for Congolese Democracy (RCD) was formed by Uganda and Rwanda, composed of former ADFL members, including many *Banyamulenge*. The group continued to be the primary Tutsi force that also aligned with Burundi (SAIIA 1999).

In the Ituri region, a branch of the RCD split into the *Union des Patriotes Congolaises* (UPC), a Hema militia, and the *Front Nationalise et Intégratif* (FNI), a Lendu armed group. The growing hegemony of the UPC in the town of Bunia and part of Ituri led the Ugandan government to support the formation of the Front for Integration and Peace in Ituri (FIPI), a coalition between three ethnically based political parties created in December 2002, which shared the objective of dismantling the UPC (AI 2005). New tensions within the UPC and the FNI resulted in the formation of the *Force de Résistance Patriotique en Ituri* (FRPI), a Southern Lendu group, and the *Parti pour l'Unité et la Sauvegarde de l'Intégrité du Congo* (PUSIC), a Southern Hema group (Oga 2009).

The FDLR, the primary remnant of a Rwandan Hutu rebel group in the eastern DRC, was formed in September 2000 to oppose Tutsi rule and influence in the region. The group was composed of former members of the *Interahamwe* and backed by President Kabila, who used the group as a proxy force against the Rwandan army which was operating within the DRC. In 2002, FDLR units moved into the Kivus and continuously attacked Tutsi forces in both eastern DRC and Rwandan territory (ICG 2003).

The *Congrès National pour la Défense du Peuple* (CNDP), a Tutsi political armed militia established in the Kivu region in December 2006, also engaged in the armed conflict against the DRC government (HRW 2007). In 2012, former CNDP soldiers formed the March 23 Movement, also known as the Congolese Revolutionary Army, sponsored by the Rwandan government. The group faced the FAC and Intervention Brigade of UN Organization Stabilization Mission in the DRC (MONUSCO) and surrendered in November 2013.

Flows of refugees and IDPs can affect land-related issues, including water, pastoral areas, etc. When people move from their homes and cross borders due to conflict, they often alter patterns of land access where they resettle. If these movements are associated with ethnic groups, land disputes can become the heart of conflicts at community, state, and regional levels. The question is worsened when it is manipulated by elites for political purposes.

In the Congo, Hema and Lendu claims to land and grazing rights were not the main source of conflict. However, Belgian colonial rule had favored the Hema, and after the fall of Mobutu's regime, "Lendu began to fear that their land rights would be eroded by increased Hema ambitions" (Taras and Ganguly 2016, p. 223). In Rwanda, unequal access to land was one of the causes of the 1994 genocide. The complex process of interactions between different types of environmental scarcities, demographic pressure, inequitable access to and shortage of land resources, resource depletion or degradation, and distribution of ranches and fields in productive wet valleys to men of influence or to rural relatives of the elites resulted in a cycle of poverty and dissatisfaction with the state. During the process, the rhetoric of the rich (*abakire, in Kinyarwanda language*) versus the poor (*abakene, in Kinyarwanda language*) developed in the 1980s shifted to Hutu versus Tutsi in the 1990s (Gasana 2002).

In the Sahel region, several structural conditions shape a large number of conflicts related to land use. A mix of "agricultural encroachment on productive key resources for pastoralism and on livestock corridors, obstructing the necessary mobility of herders and animals," "political vacuum that led rural actors to follow opportunistic strategies to claim ownership of land and natural resources," and lack of trust in government institutions (Benjaminsen et al. 2012, p. 109), combined with the nomadic nature of ethnic groups and climatic or environmental conditions, led to numerous land-use conflicts in that region.

In South Sudan, it is the Bari-Mundari groups who dispute land rights (and authority). The presently contested border between Sudan and South Sudan is the same border that the two communities have been disputing since 2009 (Justin and Vries 2017).

In the Sudan-CAR borderland, large groups of heavily armed poachers enter from the former to plunder wildlife resources of the latter. The Sudan/South Sudan borders have not been completely demarcated and have therefore become the scene of military campaigns against Nubba people, as well as cross-border cattle theft (Angsthelm et al. 2013). In the DRC-CAR-South Sudan borderland, armed bands of cattle herders cross the borders to pasture their herds. These cases often result in clashes with the local population, e.g., in the South Sudan Western Equatoria province, the Arrow Boys groups fight against cattle keepers (ICG 2016).

Moreover, security dynamics closely connected to ethnicity commonly led to the eruption of violence in areas that the conflict had not previously reached. In the DRC,

> South of the city of Beni in North Kivu, tensions between the Nande and Hutu ethnic groups have given rise to an alliance of Mai Mai groups that have committed violence against the population and attacked government forces. Ethnic violence between the Twa and Luba populations has reignited, with violence on the border of South Kivu and Tanganyika provinces. (IPI 2017, p. 2)

Numerous ethnic conflicts present the following common characteristics:

1. Ethnic interests that dominate national interests in politics.
2. Ethnic interests crossing borders and generating dynamics of loyalty and adherence (or not) to state rules.
3. Use of citizenship as a claim for rights.
4. Political-social alienation between capitals and the periphery where sociopolitical disintegration is present.
5. Ethnic communities employing security and economic survival tactics/strategies.

6. Economic factors fueling the war, involving both internal and external actors' own interests.
7. Involvement of leaders (government and armed groups) in trade and resource exploitation or their support and provision of security on an ethnic basis.
8. Manipulation of ethnic rivalries for particular interests (mainly economic and political).
9. The practice of numerous illegal activities and crimes such as occupation of lucrative locations, extortion, parallel administrative structures, forced labor, sexual exploitation, etc.
10. Government providing benefits to ethnic kins or partisans in order to guarantee loyalties.
11. State security forces structured along ethnic lines.
12. Use of insurrection by armed groups' leaders as a way of accessing posts and privileges.
13. Transnationalization of ethnic conflict due to the perceived insecurity of ethnic groups.
14. Elements of a group's historical memory or fear of physical insecurity.
15. Real or perceived discrimination, inequalities, or inequities.
16. Forced migration.
17. Loss of land rights.

If ethnicity is at the center of conflict, it must also be at the center of any peace effort, i.e., ethnical impact on the conflict must have priority when addressing ethnic wars.

Ethnic Conflicts and Peacebuilding

Johan Galtung (1978) proposed a conflict analysis model in which a conflict can be viewed as a triangle whose sides are represented by A (attitudes), B (behaviors), and C (contradictions). In ethnic conflicts, contradiction would be defined by the parties' negative relationship, i.e., incompatibilities. Attitude includes the parties' perception and non-perception of themselves and each other. In violent conflicts, strongly negative perceptions developed by the parties often include humiliating stereotypes of each other. Behavior in violent conflicts involves threats, coercion, and/or destructive attacks.

Conflict resolution belongs to the field of behavior and contradiction. When a conflict is settled, the behavior of parties turn to nonviolent actions and incompatibility is eliminated. Transformation belongs to the attitudinal side of the triangle, in the sense that it changes perceptions in the long term. It involves reconciliation, public policies, and programs that permit constituent ethnic groups to live together. Such efforts are usually connected to strong governance in building trust between ethnic groups, engendering a sense of respect of rights in general, and to political leaders' commitment to social justice, among others, all leading to the establishment of a political system operating according to the principles of democracy and the Rule of Law.

The concept of peacebuilding presented in the Boutros Galhi' Agenda for Peace was related to "the construction of a new environment should be viewed as the counterpart of preventive diplomacy, which seeks to avoid the breakdown of peaceful conditions" (UN 1992, para 57). Thus, the aim of peacebuilding is to promote positive peace. To these ends it must address the "root causes" of a conflict, which are frequently complex and hard to identify and understand. If peacebuilding activities intend to remove the root causes of a conflict, its aim is to transform the conflict and not just to find ways to resolve disputes. In this sense, peacebuilding entails a broad gamut of activities in security, humanitarian, economic, political, and societal areas and must be programmed as medium- to long-term arrangements. Whether it is implemented in countries facing ongoing armed conflict or in the aftermath of civil war, activities should be carried out (and normally are carried out) by external actors in conjunction with local actors (state officials and civil society) in a process encompassing concrete efforts on all parts (projects and programs).

However, ethnic conflicts have shown that permanent solutions are difficult and nearly impossible. Thus, prevailing idea is that success is most likely through prevention. Notwithstanding, in practice it has been shown that international community intervention is more likely to occur once an armed conflict has already been initiated, rather than through preventive diplomacy or preventive deployment. It leads to the management of deep violent ethnic conflict, which is commonly conducted through peacekeeping operations (PKOs). These operations prioritize the protection of civilians within its mandates including the use of all necessary means to prevent or halt civilian victimization and widespread abuses.

Nevertheless, in African examples, some PKOs that were intended as short-term interventions have become long-term, some of which present minor results that indicate a possible resolution of conflict. In the DRC, the deployment of PKOs has been ongoing for almost 20 years, since the creation of MONUC in 1999. In the CAR, international interventions are approaching 20 years, encompassing the UN Mission in the CAR (MINURCA) (1998–2000), the United Nations Mission in the CAR and Chad (MINURCAT) (2007–2010), and the UN Multidimensional Integrated Stabilization Mission in the CAR (MINUSCA), from September 2014 to date. These were interspersed by other missions such as the UN Integrated Peacebuilding Office in the Central African Republic (BINUCA) and the African-led International Support Mission in the Central African Republic (MISCA) (see UN, DPKO 2018). Despite the long presence of PKOs, these conflicts (among others) have not yet been "resolved," which would create the right conditions to actually implement transformative activities. Nevertheless, peacebuilding is being carried out in conjunction with peacekeeping and peacemaking activities.

When ethnicity in deeply divided societies is at the heart of conflict, it cannot be separated from politics. Existing literature and practices present various strategies for managing or eliminating ethnic differences. Any negotiated solution to disputes between a dissatisfied ethnic group and the government often requires political reform.

In civil wars fought between ethnic factions, the partition of the state into ethnically homogenous regions and the installation of a government system according to the model of consociational democracy, a governmental type of power sharing overlaps with the concept of consociationalism developed by Lijphart (1969), is one way of building a new country.

Power sharing was tested in numerous countries in Africa, such as Burundi, Djibouti, the DRC, and South Africa, where the main focus was to assure ethnic groups' representation at all levels of government.

Institutional structures that are typically set on consociational democracies in ethnically divided societies include segmental (regional) autonomy, a government formed by a coalition of political elites, proportional representation in government, and the "mutual minority veto" allowing each group to block legislation they deem "threatening" to its ethnicity (Rice 2017; Merdzanovic 2015).

Agreements that impose a structural form of consociational democracy can end ethnic war by offering power sharing to rebels, if and when parties' leaders can convince each other that they will honor the terms of the agreement. Indeed, power sharing formulas can be viewed as a healthy tool to "resolve" this type of conflict.

Lijphart (1969) determined several factors that were favorable to creating a successful consociational democracy in a divided society, such as the presence of an external threat, a tradition of elite accommodation, geographical concentration of factions of equal size, and overarching and crosscutting loyalties to the state. Accordingo to Rice (2017), when these preconditions are absent, it increases the chance of the failure.

Thus, the consociational formula can be ineffective in the long term as it can perpetuate ethnic differences. Due to a lack of overarching state loyalties and the absence of cooperation among political elites, combined with geographical divisions in the state and the legitimization of ethnic homogeneity as consequence of movements during civil war, ethnic nationalism and secessionist politics are rooted and legitimized within the state (Rice 2017). A pattern of voting for candidates and parties according to ethnic divisions in conjunction with the consociational model can practically paralyze central institutions and prevent the state from advancing economically and politically (Merdzanovic 2015).

Regional autonomy is another approach used to build multiethnic societies and bring together groups that formerly fought. It is a less restrictive form of power sharing in which ethnic groups have autonomy in regions they have predominantly settled themselves. These arrangements can come from federal arrangements and grant access to executive power without "veto power."

Scholars have different visions regarding the formulas and effects of "resolving" conflicts in deeply divided societies. While some argue that regional autonomy reduces the likelihood of recurring conflict (Lijphart 1985; Gurr 2000), others view this model as an ineffective model of conflict resolution (Snyder 2000; Roeder 2007), and that decentralization along ethnic lines can reinforce divisive ethnic identities and pressure on the state and increase secessionist groups' mobilization (e.g., Brancati 2009).

Both formulas, power sharing and regional autonomy, also rely on the commitment of leaders (government and ethnic groups) to respect all rights for all citizens and not institutionalize ethnic divisions (Cederman et al. 2013). Notwithstanding, in ethnically divided countries, where ethnic politics are in place and where groups gather around ethnic identity, commitment is commonly problematic. In the short term, this happens because of distrust, and in the long term because of the high possibility of groups establishing patterns of behavior in accordance with their ethnicity, e.g., voting for ethnicity-based parties or perpetuating ethnical divisions (Rice 2017; Merdzanovic 2015).

Simonsen (2005) argues that peace processes in ethnic conflicts have to build legitimate institutions that lead to social stability through a "transformative movement," addressing the sensitivity of conflict patterns. This implies attempts to reduce the salience of ethnic divisions by creating institutions that provide proportional ethnic representation in the aftermath of war without accentuating ethnicity in politics, i.e., not institutionalizing ethnic divisions as usually occurs in the power sharing model.

Thereby, transformation should be based on reconciliation and ethnic inclusion, as part of long-term peacebuilding strategies. Simonsen (2005) highlights that inclusive policies, whether based on group rights, autonomy, inclusion, or democracy, constitute the safest path to peace and that reducing the prominence of ethnicity is possible when integrated into mechanisms employed for peacebuilding in a post-conflict situation. The author presents two main entry points for reducing the political salience of ethnicity in post-conflict societies: the promotion of cleavages that crosscut ethnic ones, in which conflicting interests are recognized and shared by someone of a different ethnicity, and the behavior of political elites competing for political support, focusing on ways to encourage elites to transcend ethnic boundaries.

Damaged relationships between ethnic groups can be difficult to remedy due to the memories of what occurred during war, which can negatively affect attempts to build a consociational system (Rice 2017). It can lead nations to construct a "nation identity" instead of "ethnic identities." The case of Tanzania demonstrates that fostering a national identity in a country with many ethnic groups can dismantle the strength of these groups' political identity and can prevent elites from manipulating ethnic interest. Consequently, no group is strong enough to significantly impact the policy and politics of the government (Erickson 2012).

Conclusion

Ethnicity is the center of many armed conflicts around the world. Contemporary conflicts are often composed of various interacting actors and relationships, which give them complex characteristics and, in some cases, a protracted and intractable nature. Ethnic conflicts often are part of complex dynamics that link invasions, plunder of resources, politicized ethnic cleavages with high political tensions, refugee and IDP flows, political instability, territorial ambitions (normally due to land scarcity and population pressure), support of rebel groups, and transborder movements. Such conflicts underline key actors' lack of desire for peace, in a context in which ordinary people are both the targets and the main victims.

In Africa, transborder ethnic groups have often been involved in many of the conflicts. However, conflicts are more deeply connected to failed state systems than to these groups, e.g., lack of democracy in the sense of good governance and justice.

Ethnic lines of division and exclusion and lack of services and facilities, among many other factors, have led to ethnic groups becoming more prone to subversion. Competition between ethnic groups for the control of state power coupled with scarce resources has generated a cycle of violence that has been proven to be complex and difficult to resolve.

Thus, the state must change in order to take care of collective interests above individual ones. Thereby, ethnic conflicts' transformation encompasses a wide variety of activities, which range from political and economic to societal and security reforms to improve civil society. Such transformation should be carried out based on policies that permit reconciliation, inclusiveness, respect of rights, and that have a direct impact on ethnic groups and their regions. However, when violence is protracted, it can lead to an impossible coexistence. Ethnical identity overlaps with any attempt to build a national identity and also undermines attempts to transform the state and its society.

Peacebuilding aims to transform conflicts and its activities should be thought of long-term activities. Under the attempts to "transform" ethnic conflicts, consociationalism and regional autonomy are more likely to be accepted by ethnical leaders as it gives to them guarantees of power and autonomy. However, these formulas are normally challenged by ethnical patterns, which can perpetuate divisions and paralyze states.

In sum, ethnic identities are dynamic identities which become exacerbated during times of conflict, when mobilization along ethnic lines increases. While resolution tools attempt to alleviate the causes of ethnic conflicts, transformation processes need to address root causes in order to diminish the salience of ethnicity. However, ethnic conflicts are often complex and so are attempts to solve them. Thus, the challenges are enormous to really transform such conflicts and create the conditions for people of different ethnicities to live peacefully.

Cross-References

▶ Ethnicity and Cultural Rights in Tibet
▶ Identity and Conflict in Northern Ireland
▶ Patterns and Drivers of Communal Conflict in Kenya

References

AI – Amnesty International (1998) Democratic Republic of Congo. A long-standing crisis spinning out of control. 3 September. https://www.amnesty.org/download/.../afr620331998en.pdf. Accessed 31 Nov 2016

AI. Amnesty International (2005) Democratic Republic of Congo: arming the east. 5 July, AFR 62/006/2005. http://www.refworld.org/docid/439453011.html. Accessed 19 Dec 2017

Alusala N (2005) Disarmament and the transition in Burundi: how soon? ISS Paper, n. 97, January

Angsthelm B, Dupont V, Zuriel S, Sultane S (eds) (2013) Societies caught in the conflict trap regional research findings Chad, Central African Republic, Sudan, South Sudan. Accord/CCFD-Terre Solidaire, Nairobi/Paris, October. http://www.acordinternational.org/silo/files/conflict-research-chad-car-sudan-south-sudan.pdf. Accessed 25 Oct 2016

Ansorg N (2011) How does militant violence diffuse in regions? Regional conflict systems in international relations and peace and conflict studies. Int J Confl Violence 5(1):173–187

Azar E (1991) The analysis and management of protracted social conflict. In: Volkan J (ed) The psychodynamics of international relationships, vol 2. S.C. Heath, Lexington, pp 93–120

Benjaminsen TA et al (2012) Does climate change drive land-use conflicts in the Sahel? J Peace Res 49(1):97–111

Berahino C (2011) Understanding obstacles to peace in Burundi: actors, interests and strategies politics of ethnicity. In: Baregu M (ed) Understanding obstacles to peace actors, interests, and strategies in Africa's Great Lakes region. Fountain Publishers, Kampala

Bohnet H, Cottier F, Hug S (2016) Conflict-induced IDPs and the spread of conflict. J Confl Resolut 62(4):691–716

Brancati D (2009) Design over conflict. Managing ethnic conflict and secessionism through decentralization. Oxford University Press, Oxford

Buhaug H, Cederman L-E, Rød JK (2008) Disaggregating ethno-nationalist civil wars: a dyadic test of exclusion theory. Int Organ 62(3):531–551

Buhaug H, Gates S, Lujala P (2009) Geography, rebel capability, and the duration of civil conflict. J Confl Resolut 53(4):544–569

Cederman L-E, Wimmer A, Min B (2010) Why do ethnic groups rebel? New data and analysis. World Polit 62(1):87–119

Cederman L-E, Weidmann NB, Gleditsch KS (2011) Horizontal inequalities and ethnonationalist civil war: a global comparison. Am Polit Sci Rev 105(3):478–495

Cederman L-E, Gleditsch K, Buhaug H (2013) Inequality, grievances, and civil war. Cambridge University Press, Cambridge, UK

De Rouen KR Jr, Sobek D (2004) The dynamics of civil war duration and outcome. J Peace Res 41(3):303–320

Denny EK, Walter BF (2014) Ethnicity and civil war. J Peace Res 51(2):199–212

Doss, A (2011) Great expectations: UN peacekeeping, civilian protection, and the use of force. GCSP Geneva Papers. Research Series 4, Dec

Erickson A (2012) Peace in Tanzania, an Island of stability in sub Saharan Africa. Jackson Sch J 3(1):18–31

Fearon JD, Laitin DD (2003) Ethnicity, insurgency, and civil war. Am Polit Sci Rev 97:75–90

Galtung J (1978) Conflict as a way of life. Essays in Peace Research. Peace and Social Structure, vol 3. Christian Ejlers, Copenhagen

Galtung J (1996) Peace by peaceful means: peace and conflict, development and civilization. IPRI/Sage Publications, Oslo

Gasana JK (2002) Natural resource scarcity and violence in Rwanda. In: Matthew R, Halle M, Switzer J (eds) Conserving the peace: resources, livelihoods and security. IISD, Winnipeg, pp 199–246

Gates S (2002) Recruitment and allegiance: the microfoundations of rebellion. J Confl Resolut 46(1):111–130

Golooba-Mutebi F (2008) Collapse, war and reconstruction. In: Uganda an analytical narrative on state-making. Working Paper 27. Crisis States Working Papers Series 2. Crisis States Research Centre, LSE, London, January

Gurr TR (2000) Ethnic warfare on the wane. Foreign Aff 79(3):52–65

Horowitz DL (1985) Ethnic groups in conflict. University of California Press, Berkeley

HRW – Human Rights Watch (2007) Renewed crisis in North Kivu. 19(17). 22 October. https://www.hrw.org/report/2007/10/23/renewed-crisis-north-kivu. Accessed 12 Dec 2016

Humphreys M (2005) Natural resources, conflict, and conflict resolution: uncovering the mechanisms. J Confl Resolut 49:4

ICG – International Crisis Group (2003) Rwandan Hutu rebels in the Congo – a new approach to disarmament and reintegration. Africa Report 63, 23 May
ICG – International Crisis Group (2016) South Sudan's South: conflict in the Equatorias. Africa Report 236, Bruxelas, 25 May
IPI – International Peace Institute (2017) Applying the HIPPO recommendations to the DRC: toward strategic, prioritized, and sequenced Mandates, July
Justin PH, De Vries L (2017) Governing unclear lines: local boundaries as a (re)source of conflict in South Sudan. J Borderl Stud. https://doi.org/10.1080/08865655.2017.1294497
Lake DA, Rothchild D (1996) Containing fear: the origins and management of ethnic conflict. Int Secur 21(2):41–75
Lederach JP (2003) The little book of conflict transformation. Good Books, Intercourse
Lijphart A (1969) Consociational democracy. World Polit Xxi(2):207–225
Lijphart A (1985) Non-majoritarian democracy: a comparison of federal and consociational theories. Publius J Federalism 15(2):3–15
Lischer SK (2005) Dangerous sanctuaries: refugee camps, civil war, and the dilemmas of humanitarian aid. Cornell University Press, Ithaca
Mason TD, Weingarten JP, Fett PJ (1999) Win, lose, or draw: predicting the outcome of civil wars. Polit Res Q 52(2):239–268
Merdzanovic A (2015) Democracy by decree: prospects and limits of imposed consociational democracy in Bosnia and Herzegovina. Ibidem-Verlag, Stutgart
Mulamula L (2011) DRC and its neighbours: policy options for the Great Lakes region and the international community. In: Baregu M (ed) Understanding obstacles to peace actors, interests, and strategies in Africa's Great Lakes region. Fountain Publishers, Kampala
Nagel J (1994) Constructing ethnicity: creating and recreating ethnic identity and culture. Soc Probl 41(1):152–176
Nest M, Grignon F, Kisangani EF (2006) The Democratic Republic of Congo: economic dimensions of war and peace. Lynne Rienner, London
Oga J (2009) Impasse en Ituri. Operation Artemis. DDR. Et Apres? L'Harmattan, Paris
Onah EI (2015) The role of trans-border ethnic groups in intra-state and inter-state conflict in Africa. J Borderl Stud 30(1):85–95
Ramsbotham O, Woodhouse T, Miall H (2011) Contemporary conflict resolution. Polity Press, Cambridge, UK
Rice ME (2017) Building a state from a broken nation: the case of Bosnia-Herzegovina. Towson Univ J Int Aff 2:1–15
Roeder PG (2007) Where nation-states come from. Princeton University Press, Princeton
Rukundwa SL (2004) The Banyamulenge of the Democratic Republic of Congo: a cultural community in the making. Department of New Testament Studies University of Pretoria. HTS 60(1–2):369–383
SAIIA – South African Institute of International Affairs (1999) Intelligence update: guerrillas in their midst: shifting alliances in the DRC 13. http://dspace.africaportal.org/jspui/bitstream/123456789/31610/1/Guerrillas%20In%20Their%20Midst.pdf. Accessed 12 Dec 2016
Salehyan I (2007) Transnational rebels: neighboring states as sanctuary for rebel groups. World Polit 59:217–242
Salehyan I, Gleditsch KS (2006) Refugees and the spread of civil war. Int Organ 60:334–366
Simonsen SG (2005) Addressing ethnic divisions in post-conflict institution-building: lessons from recent cases. Secur Dialogue 36(3):297–318
Snyder J (2000) From voting to violence: democratization and nationalist conflict. Norton, New York
Stewart F (2002) Horizontal inequalities: a neglected dimension of development. QEH Working Paper Series 81. Queen Elizabeth House, University of Oxford, Oxford
Suhrke A, Noble LG (1977) Ethnic conflict in international relations. Praeger Publishers, New York

Taras R, Ganguly R (2016) Weak states and ethnic conflict: state collapse and reconstruction in Africa. In: Taras R, Ganguly R (eds) Understanding ethnic conflict, 4th edn. Routledge, New York, pp 210–242, cap. 8

Thom WG (1999) Congo-Zaire's 1996–97 civil war in the context of evolving patterns of military conflict in Africa in the era of independence. J Confl Stud XIX(2), [S.l.], September. https://journals.lib.unb.ca/index.php/JCS/article/view/4358/5015. Accessed 15 Apr 2017

UN (1992) A/47/277 – S/24111. An Agenda for Peace Preventive diplomacy, peacemaking and peace-keeping. United Nations, New York. 17 June

UN (2002) S/2002/341. Letter dated 1 April 2002 from the Secretary-General addressed to the President of Security-Council. United Nations, New York. 5 April

UN (2015) A/69/968–S/2015/490. Challenge of sustaining peace Report of the Advisory Group of Experts on the review of the peacebuilding architecture. United Nations, New York. 30 June

UN. DPKO. United Nations Peacekeeping (2018) https://peacekeeping.un.org/en/where-we-operate. Accessed 21 Ago 2018

Wedgwood R (2001) United Nations peacekeeping operations and the use of force. Wash Univ J Law Policy 069. https://openscholarship.wustl.edu/cgi/viewcontent.cgi?article=1552&context=law_journal_law_policy. Accessed 12 Jul 2016

Wegenast TC, Basedau M (2014) Ethnic fractionalization, natural resources and armed conflict. Confl Manag Peace Sci 31(4):432–457

Weidmann N (2009) Geography as motivation and opportunity group concentration and ethnic conflict. J Confl Resolut 53(4):526–543

Weiner M (1992) Peoples and states in a new ethnic order? Third World Q 13:317–333

West S (2015) The rise of ADF-NALU in Central Africa and its connections with al-Shabaab. Terrorism Monit 13(1). 9 January. https://jamestown.org/program/the-rise-of-adf-nalu-in-central-africa-and-its-connections-with-al-shabaab/#.VTk5J5NHaJc. Accessed 31 Nov 2016

Woods D (2003) The tragedy of the cocoa pod: rent-seeking, land and ethnic conflict in Ivory Coast. J Mod Afr Stud 41:641–655. https://doi.org/10.1017/S0022278X03004427

Ethnicity and Violence in Sri Lanka: An Ethnohistorical Narrative

36

Premakumara de Silva, Farzana Haniffa, and Rohan Bastin

Contents

Introduction	634
Historical Emergence of Ethnic Identities	635
Ethnicization of the Sri Lankan State and the Emergence of the Ethnic War: Colonial Impact	636
The "Ethnic Riot" as a Political Instrument of Majoritarianism	639
The Ethnic Riot in Contemporary Sri Lankan History	640
Postwar Violence: Ethnicity and Violence in Sri Lanka Today	650
Conclusion	652
References	653

Abstract

The ethnicity and violence in Sri Lanka have many root causes and consequences that are closely interconnected. Given the nature and the complexity of root causes and consequences of these highly contested concepts, it should not be treated as a part of linear historical processes where one event led to another. Sri Lanka presents case of how intersecting not only ethnicity and violence but also religion, caste, class, linguistic, and cultural mosaics have been and might be billeted within the borders of a nation-state. However, state building in Sri Lanka has been riddled with paradoxes. The curious notion of numerically dominant ethnic group, Sinhala manifesting a "minority complex" or anxieties about minority groups, Tamil and Muslims, is evident in the rise of Sinhala Buddhist nationalism during the nineteenth and the twentieth century of the country. Since state building has often meant

P. de Silva (✉) · F. Haniffa
Department of Sociology, University of Colombo, Colombo, Sri Lanka
e-mail: prema@soc.cmb.ac.lk; prema112@hotmail.com; ffhaniffa@gmail.com

R. Bastin
School of Humanities and Social Sciences, Deakin University, Geelong, VIC, Australia
e-mail: rohan.bastin@deakin.edu.au

centralization and a single ethnic group dominating the symbolic framework of the nation, there has been the tendency by minority groups such as Tamil and Muslims who have felt marginalized by the process to reinvent new collective ethnic identities. Moreover, cultural-religious minorities have responded to such hegemonic state-building process through mobilization of both non-violence and violent means. A complicated coming together of anti-minority sentiment at the level of the state, permissive politics that made violence a possibility, and the utilizing of this permissive violent politics for working out various class and caste enmities resulted in an extremely difficult political time for Sri Lanka in the 1980s. However, the central narrative through which the prevalence of violence was understood was the ethnic conflict. This paper too shall lay out the important historical moments where disadvantages toward minorities were institutionalized at state level while calling attention to ways in which ethnic politics were utilized for a multiplicity of ends.

Keywords
Sri Lanka · Ethnicity · Violence · War and Peace

Introduction

Ethnicity and violence in Sri Lanka are understood in Sri Lanka using two primary frameworks. In the first instance, given that Sri Lanka experienced a violent conflict primarily based on the politicization of ethnic difference and the claim for a separate state on the basis of ethnicity, we have retraced the historical antecedents to the ethnic conflict to the manner in which first Sinhala nationalism and later sustained minority marginalization were institutionalized into the state. Secondly we have traced the manner in which the cultivated nationalism of the state and majoritarian politics created the possibility for mobilizing violence within communities based on ethnic difference for different political and economic needs. This second form of violence often played out along class cleavages as well and was instrumentalized in the service of a variety of political interests that were not merely ethnic.

In the early 1980s, Sri Lankan scholarship shifted to the study of the nature of violence in Sri Lankan society. Understanding communal violence was considered a matter of increasing urgency as outbreaks of violence between ethnic minority groups and the majority Sinhala became more and more frequent. Concomitantly the insurgent activity in the north of the Island also became more prominent. The violence provoked several anthropologists into analyses of the underlying political, economic, and ideological factors of ethno-religious violence (e.g., Obeyesekere 1984; Gunasinghe 1986; Tambiah 1986, 1992; Kapferer 1988; Rogers 1987; Spencer 1990; Roberts 1994; Abeysekara 2002; Ismail 2005, and more recently Udalagama and de Silva 2014; Haniffa 2016; Nagaraj and Haniffa 2018; Venugopal 2018). Further, given the escalation of the conflict since 1983, the question of ethno-religious nationalism and violence has informed most anthropological and sociological work on Sri Lanka. Today the emphasis has shifted to understanding processes of postwar reconciliation and, to an extent, the reemergence of violence targeting minority communities – this time Evangelical Christians and Muslim communities in the country.

Historical Emergence of Ethnic Identities

Though Sri Lanka entered its period of political independence from Britain with a strong pluralist orientation, ethnic thinking had been developed through colonial experiments with ethnic representation in the early 1900s, and with increasing state centralization, ethnicity became a dominant category in the postcolonial period. In response to the majoritarian politics and violence, the Tamil minority responded by demands for self-determination either within or outside the existing bounds of the nation-state. Since state building has often meant centralization and a single ethnic group dominating the symbolic framework of the nation, there has been a tendency by minority groups such as Tamil and Muslims who have felt marginalized by the process to reinvent new collective ethnic identities. Moreover, cultural-religious minorities have responded to such hegemonic state-building process through mobilization of both non-violence and violent means. For example, segments of the moderate Tamil elites dug their heels in for a political battle that culminated in a demand for a separate state in the north and east of Sri Lanka, where Tamils constitute a majority and the less privileged Tamil youth minority groups and castes were mobilized into armed factions such as the Liberation Tigers of Tamil Eelam (LTTE). In relation to the Muslims, Haniffa has argued that the success of the religious reform movements can also be traced to Muslims' feeling of marginalization within the majoritarian polity and, more specifically, to the wartime polarization of the Sinhala and Tamil communities (Haniffa 2013). Research into the internal politics within Sri Lanka's minoritized communities was sometimes submerged in the overarching narrative of Sinhala state enmity toward the Tamil ethnic group as a whole. Brian Pfaffenberger points out the manner in which the northern politicians themselves overemphasized Sinhala Tamil enmity to detract from the prevalence of caste politics in their own communities in Jaffna (Pfaffenberger 1990). A complicated coming together of anti-minority sentiment at the level of the state, permissive politics that made violence a possibility, and the utilizing of this permissive violent politics for working out various class and caste enmities resulted in an extremely difficult political time for Sri Lanka in the 1980s. However, the central narrative through which the prevalence of violence was understood was the ethnic conflict. This paper too shall lay out the important historical moments where disadvantages toward minorities were institutionalized at state level while calling attention to ways in which ethnic politics were utilized for a multiplicity of ends. Further, the war – the most sustained period of ethnic violence in the country since independence – requires its own framing.

From independence in 1948 to the beginning of the civil war in 1983, Tamil demands changed from peaceful attempts to gain language equality to violent demands for a distinct Tamil nation and complete secession from Sri Lanka. Arguably, it is the cultivation of the cultural and political hegemony of the Sinhala Buddhists in an increasingly centralized nation-state that has been the greatest irritant to the ethnic minorities including Muslim. The failure of the Tamil leadership's attempts to work through government institutions and the Sinhala majority governments' repeated failure to respect attempts at non-violent protest have led to the violent means eventually used by the Liberation Tigers of Tamil Eelam.

Ethnicization of the Sri Lankan State and the Emergence of the Ethnic War: Colonial Impact

The efforts of the colonial rulers to manage the problem of ethnicity and pluralism in the colony fall roughly into two phases. In the first phase, they were influenced by their own objectives as the imperial power ruling the country. In this phase the governing institutions that were established beginning with the Legislative Council in 1833 following the Colebrook Commission cautiously provided for the participation of the Ceylonese in stages and in a very limited way and introduction of 'new game of politics' (see Scott 1999, 2000). The British colonial government nominated Ceylonese members to represent their communities. Among other British colonial officials and Burgher community (descendent from Portuguese and Dutch), the first Legislative Council contained three Ceylonese members one from each of the three communities Sinhala, Tamil, and Muslim who were nominated by colonial government to represent their "Communities." In 1889 with the increase in the number of members in the Legislative Council, there were three colonial officials, a "Low country" Sinhalese, a "Kandyan" Sinhalese, a Tamil, a Muslim, and a Burgher.

The colonial government therefore recognized the principle which came to be described as "communal representation." This form of communal representation paid little regard to the size of each community, and the representatives did not enjoy any effective decision-making power and performed only the limited function of debating official policies and actions, agitating for reforms and in the process speaking for their communities. But this regime of communal representation created its own political environment. The colonial rulers were defining the roles for the different communities in a manner that gave them a sense of equality in their relations with each other.

This perception contributed to the approach that was taken later in drafting the Donoughmore Constitution (1928) and the Soulbury Constitution (1945). It was an approach which favored a unitary state. Both constitutions designed by the British constitution makers placed their faith in the "orthodox" forms of democratic, territorial representation with universal adult franchise and hoped that this would produce the social and economic changes that will achieve the desired outcomes. Meanwhile some weightage to the minorities in the demarcation of electorates and the executive committee system was expected to ensure adequate participation by the minorities in the tasks of government. The political discourse and the search for constitutional solutions in the period 1923–1945 took place within this ideological framework.

The political question for the period was posed in terms of how "minorities" could gain a fair share of political power in a state which from the beginning was conceived in unitary terms. The arrangements had to accommodate the demands of the minorities without violating the basic principle of democracy, that of majority rule. The framework of a unitary state and majority rule in a democratic polity narrowed the options that were available. The Kandyan Sinhalese advocated a federal type of government as the answer to their problems and made proposals to the Donoughmore Commission in 1928. The party which proposed a federal solution, although an influential group, was not the sole representative of the Kandyans. There were many Kandyans who were in the mainstream of politics with the "low-country" Sinhalese who did not subscribe to these proposals. Over a brief period of time, the Kandyan federalist discourse faded away from the political scene even as the Tamils moved toward federalism. For a variety of reasons, ethnicity-, religion-, and language-related issues dominated the debate. Federal demand began to appear at the time as the Sinhala ethnocultural identity was beginning to assert itself from the 1930s onward, and the system was failing to work for the Tamils.

The experience under the Donoughmore Constitution during the period preceding independence provided lessons which went unheeded. The democratic representation with a unitary state would not suffice to prevent a Sinhala majority from emerging and acting unilaterally without reference to the minorities. Notwithstanding the lessons of the Donoughmore Constitution, the Tamils continued to place reliance on constitutional arrangements that would increase their representation such as the fifty-fifty formula. The fifty-fifty formula proposed by the Tamil Congress to the Soulbury Commission in 1945 sought to increase representation in a manner which prevented the Sinhalese from being in a clear majority in the democratically elected legislature. This demand was seen by the British constitution makers as an unacceptable perversion of democracy. Eventually there was to be no compromise on the basic tenets of the British ideology of parliamentary democracy and the concept of a secular nation-state which should rise above ethnicity, religion, and caste. The constitution recommended by the Soulbury Commission embodied these principles while providing one fundamental safeguard for the minorities by adding the section that denied Parliament the power to make any laws "rendering persons of any community or religion liable to disabilities or restrictions to which persons of other communities are not liable or confer upon any persons of any community or religion any privileges or advantages which are not conferred on persons of other communities or religions" (Soulbury Commission Report, 52).

During this entire period preceding independence, the agitations of the Tamil and the responses of the Sinhala majority were essentially contained within this ideology of British democracy and that too within one part of it. Tamils were content as yet to adopt a pragmatic approach to the problems they faced and to eschew any new ideological positions which went beyond the political paradigm which had evolved during colonial rule. The few voices that spoke of the federal system as appropriate to the Sri Lankan situation, such as that of S.W.R.D. Bandaranaike during the early part of his political career in the 1920s, were too far outside the mainstream to carry any serious weight. The Tamils themselves were critical of the federal idea; particularly the Jaffna Youth Congress was critical of the federal idea.

What then were the forces that made them abandon their pragmatic position and what led to the rise of the new Tamil ideologies which replaced it? To answer it, we need to examine some of the turning points or historical conjunctures in the relations between the political leadership of the two communities and the turning points or conjunctures which drove them apart and hardened the ethnonationalist ideologies of each. One such early turning point came with the constitutional reforms of 1923. The reforms enlarged the elected representation in the Legislative Council. The main political disagreements between the Sinhalese and Tamils centered on the issues of sharing this representation. The Tamil demanded an arrangement whereby one Tamil representative would be elected for the Western Province, a demand that was opposed by the Sinhala politicians. Up to this time, the Ceylon National Congress had been the organization in which both Tamil and Sinhala politicians acted together in campaigning for constitutional reforms. It was a partnership in which the Tamils participated as one of the two major communities in the country. These developments following the 1923, reforms led to the split in the Ceylon National Congress and the formation of a separate political organization to represent the Tamils. The response of the Tamil party was to suggest the fifty-fifty formula, a remedy that was worse than the disease and only served to outrage the majority. Nevertheless, as the tensions between the two communities grew, the inequities of untrammeled majority rule in a society which contained a mix of ethnic groups, some of whom were small minorities, were slowly becoming evident. The term "tyranny of the majority" was freely used by the Tamil spokesmen to pinpoint this flaw which was inherent in the system. But the problems of "majoritarian" democracy were not clearly conceptualized, and the options that were available had not yet been identified and clearly articulated.

However, at the time Sri Lanka became independent, a somewhat fragile and uneasy compromise had been reached within the framework of the constitution that had been inspired by the ideology of British democracy. The "Sinhala Only" ideology and Tamil federalism had still not entered the political arena in its uncompromising form. Maintaining this fragile balance and building on it was a formidable challenge to both the Sinhala and Tamil leadership. The acceptance of a new balance required continuous attention and adjustment on the part of both Sinhalese and Tamils to each other's sensitivities that had developed over a long history of coexistence and conflict and that could react sharply to the latent implications of words and actions. There were two ideological responses to this situation. The Sinhala Buddhist ideology became increasingly exclusive and began to attack the pluralistic elements in the Sri Lankan society that had developed during the colonial period (see Sivathamby 1987; Spencer 1990; Tambiah 1992; Obeyesekere 1995; Robert 1994; Jeganathan and Ismail 1995; Jayawardene 1984; Robert 2010; Spencer et al. 2015; Tambiah 1996; Seneviratne 1999; de Silva 2013). It perceived these elements as obstructions on the path of the Sinhala Buddhist revival (see Bond 1988; Gombrich and Obeyesekere 1988). It veered more explicitly toward a Sinhala Only position.

The second was the Tamil response. Tamil politicians who broke away from the Tamil Congress made a decisive break with the mainstream Tamil politics that had prevailed up to that time. The breakaway group established the Federal Party which sought a federal solution to the problem with regional autonomy for the Tamil speaking Northern and Eastern Provinces. These two ideological developments, the "Sinhala Only" and the Federal idea were independent of each other. The "Sinhala Only" stance was not a reaction at this stage to the formation of the Federal Party nor was the establishment of the Federal Party a response specifically to the rising of Sinhala Buddhist nationalism. The Federal Party came in the wake of disagreements within the Tamil congress on the policy of collaboration with the government. The breakaway was precipitated by the disenfranchisement of the Indian Tamils who were brought to the country under the British plantation economy. The three objectives of the FP were regional autonomy for the Northern and

Eastern provinces, restoration of the franchise for the Indian Tamils, and action to stop colonization in the north and east. It was taken for granted that Tamil and Sinhala were the official languages of the country. The immediate objectives in the Sinhala Buddhist agenda were action to make Sinhala the only official language of the state. The take-over of denominational schools and employment in the public service on the basis of religion and ethnicity and key appointments in the public service to be reserved for Sinhala Buddhists were considered necessary to redress the historical imbalances and remove the disadvantages suffered by the Buddhists in the Colonial govermentalities.

The later development and strategies adopted by the Federal Party to find some form of accommodation with the Sinhala majority, from the Bandaranaike-Chelvanayagam pact to the Senanayake-Chelvanayagam pact and the District Councils under the Jayawardene government, are also fully consistent with the interpretation that Tamil were seeking some form of regional autonomy. The FP's attempts to project an economically viable and self-reliant Tamil region in their election propaganda did not seem to be convincing to the large majority of Tamils. What dramatically transformed this situation were the action of the Sinhala majority in the 1953–1956 period and the ideology which inspired these actions. The shift of Tamil support from Tamil Congress to the Federal Party occurred swiftly within this time span and coincides clearly with the events during that period. To declare Sinhala the sole official language and burst out in widespread ethnic violence in 1958 against Tamil who were residing outside of the north and east. The lesson that the Tamil did learn from the violence of 1958 was that Sri Lanka state essentially functioned as a Sinhala state and did not or could not act impartially to protect the life and property of the Tamils in areas where the Sinhalese were in a majority.

As the twentieth century progressed and more of the population became enfranchised, the Tamils began to see their political dominance fade. However, they remained dominant in the universities and the business sector. The Tamil domination would later be used as a major justification for the Sinhalese preferential policies, which attempted to reverse these positions. Therefore, the colonial circumstance laid the groundwork for the eventual Sinhalese domination and cannot be ignored as one of the preconditions leading to the secessionist movement.

The "Ethnic Riot" as a Political Instrument of Majoritarianism

Today Sri Lanka is considered a country emerging from a long protracted ethnic conflict. The conflict between the state and Tamil militants fighting for a separate political unit – first a federal state and then a full nation-state, based on ethnic identity – defined life in Sri Lanka for three decades. In many ways ethnic animosity and violence are widely understood in the literature – and as outlined above – as drawing from the newly formed Ceylonese state's assertion of a Sinhala Buddhist national identity and resistance posed to it principally by minority Tamils.

Ethnic identity politics in the country needs to be understood as undergirding the entire political system that Sri Lanka inherited from its Colonial years.

Animosity against ethnic others have long defined ethnic relations in Sri Lanka. However, their deterioration to the level of perpetrating violence in the name of ethnic difference happens almost always through the sophisticated coordination of and coming together of various political and economic interests. Also, as stated earlier, the politicization of ethnic difference is also something that has been endemic to the Sinhalization of the Sri Lankan nation-state.

The ethnic "riot" where organized violence was perpetrated against a community identified as an ethnic religious or political minority, where the attackers were generally identified as Sinhalese and mobilized by the idea of their ethnic group being under threat, was almost always carried out in a highly organized manner. While there are documented outbreaks of ethnic violence in Chilaw in 1897 and countrywide in 1915, this paper will deal principally with the violence that takes place in the aftermath of independence and the Sinhala and later Tamil nationalism that is produced as a result of the consolidation of the postcolonial nation-state. The incidents that were carried out against the members of the Tamil community in various locales are well documented. The violence in the aftermath of the passing of Sinhala Only legislation in 1956 in Galoya, the countrywide violence against Tamils in 1958 that saw retaliation in the north and east, the postelection violence of 1977 where upcountry Tamils were targeted in large numbers, and the violence of July 1983 now known as the Black July Pogrom have all been understood as moments in a trajectory of intensifying ethnic violence against Tamils that ultimately led to the emergence of the Liberation Tigers of Tamil Eelam. That particular narrative of the emergence of Tamil nationalism can perhaps be questioned. However, targeting minority communities for organized violence has been possible due to the ethnicized nature of postindependence electoral political mobilization in the country. Further the manner in which politicians and others with vested interests have consistently placed at a slow boil the ethnic animosities inevitable in a plural polity has made the ethnic "riot" into a political tool that can and has been brought out at different moments in the country's history. The violence was generally against Tamil communities in different parts of the country with violence in 1977 and 1983 taking place throughout the country. When the war was ongoing, there were few such conflagrations in the south. However, in the aftermath of the war, there have now been three such events against Muslims.

The Ethnic Riot in Contemporary Sri Lankan History

This section will take a closer look at the manner in which ethnic violence manifested itself on the ground at different political moments in Sri Lanka after independence from British rule. As outlined in the earlier sections, struggles about political representation language use and citizenship defined Sri Lanka's postcolonial political landscape. From 1958 onward, these struggles were accompanied by periodic outbreaks of violence. These violent events eventually culminated in the countrywide riots of 1983 sometimes referred to as Black July or the anti-Tamil pogrom (see Gunasinghe 1986).

Each of the violent events that have been called "riots," the countrywide violence of 1977 and 1983, and the more localized violence against Tamils in 1956 in Gal Oya and in 1981 and Muslims in 1976, 1982, and 2001 can also be characterized in those terms. There have been numerous other smaller conflagrations including the new round of violence against Muslims that takes on a similar hue – the violence in Aluthgama and Beruwela in 2014 and the violence in Kandy (Digana and Theldeniya in 2018). In these events there is an instrumentalization of the country's politics and the ideologies cultivated by such politics at the ground level by ground level actors for very specific ground level advantages. The ethnic riot then always was and continues to be mobilized not just in relation to national level political preoccupations but to give expression to local level hostilities and ethnic competitiveness in business trade and politics. Additionally there has been a constant spate of violence against Christian communities during the war years and after. For instance, there is violence against Evangelical Christian churches, and the very presence of Evangelicals engaged in what has long been perceived as "unethical conversions" in the local discourse has resulted in community endorsed attacks at which monks, village elders, and the police are seen to be colluding (Mahadev 2018).

The following are some of the pivotal moments of anti-minority violence in independent Ceylon and Sri Lanka.

1958

Tarzie Vittachchi, a veteran journalist took it upon himself to document what he called "Emergency 58, the story of the Ceylon race riots."

In a small book which earned him the wrath of the then government, Vittachchi outlines the manner in which the "ethnic riot" arguably the first of its kind with a national reach in postindependence Sri Lanka, inflamed the Island for close to one month. In his recounting of the violence, Vittachchi stresses economic issues, the cultivation of ethnic animosity for political ends, local political leaders mobilizing their supporters – usually local thugs – to gain favor, and minor political advantage utilizing prevailing tensions as inciting the local manifestation of violence. Vittachchi also points to the prevailing demoralization of the police in the face of the violence due to the lack of political support for maintaining law and order (Vittachchi 1958).

The 1958 riots broke out in May that year and were most intense in the districts of Colombo, Jaffna, Anuradhapura, Polonnaruwa, Batticaloa, and Kurunegala. Vittachchi provides a detailed account of the outbreak of violence against Tamils in Polonnaruwa, Anuradhapura, and Colombo and the retaliations by Tamil mobs against Sinhalese in Jaffna and Batticaloa.

This violence was the result of the increasing political tensions that were unleashed by the passing of legislation in 1956 to make Sinhala the country's sole national language. The legislation was passed despite the fact that a significant segment of the country's population had no knowledge of this language and entire sections of the country had not been speaking this language. The passing of the legislation was a very active assertion of the fact that one section of the population had a greater entitlement to the largess of the state than did the section of the population that did not speak this language. As Vittachchi describes, the cultivation of ethnic sentiment for political ends that was carried out without any clear appreciation of the consequences came to roost in the violence that was unleashed. There was also a deterioration in the government's control of law and order – many illegal acts, in the form of the obstruction of peaceful protests through thuggery and damage of property by mobs, were not responded to. The retaliations in the south to the Sri protests in the north – where a Sinhala letter was assigned for vehicle registration numbers amidst prevailing tensions over language – were permitted to take place through the government taking no action to stop or halt the protestors. These circumstances were understood by Vittachchi as setting the stage for the violence.

The Tamil Federal Party organized a countrywide protest in response to the passing of "Sinhala Only." Subsequently Prime Minister Bandaranaike entered into a pact with S.J.V. Chelvanayagam the leader of the Federal Party. The pact called for greater autonomy and recognition for Tamils in the country. There was also recognition for the need to use Tamil as the administrative language in the north and east. However, in the face of countrywide protests against the Bandaranaike-Chelvanayakam pact (the BC pact as it continues to be known) and the presence of 200 Buddhist Monks protesting on his lawn, Bandaranaike reneged on his agreement.

The passing of Sinhala Only resulted in increased ethnic tensions throughout the country and breakout of violence in the Gal Oya area of the eastern province where new Sinhala settlements had been formed. In the following 2 years, there were several other related occurrences signaling ethnic animosity and a deteriorating law and order situation. For instance, the settlement of Tamil families displaced from Trincomalee due to the expansion of the harbor were planned in Padaviya a place thought by its people to be predominantly Sinhala. The settlement of persons was stopped repeatedly by local political actors with no significant response from the authorities. Additionally, as stated above there was protest against the implementation of the Sinhala language "Sri" symbol on car licence plates in the north. The imposition of the Sinhala letter was seen by many as incendiary in a context where there was such tension related to language and there were protests in the north. The protestors would paint over the Sinhala letter Sri with tar and replace it with the Tamil letter. Retaliatory attacks in the south took the form of tarring any and all signage containing Tamil lettering causing substantial damage to businesses.

There was also trade union action and meetings that deteriorated into outbreaks of violence that were not handled with adequate seriousness by the authorities. The context of ethnic tensions and the selective response of the law and order mechanisms laid the groundwork according to Vittachchi that brought about the violence of 1958.

Vittachchi alludes to the organized nature of the violence of 1958 particularly in the Polonnaruwa district in the following way. He connects it to the resistance to Tamil settlements in the area of Padaviya where community members whom he describes as Sinhalese laborers led by a monk and a gang of Sinhalese squatters go and camp out on the areas allocated for the settlement of Tamils. According to Vittachchi:

> The ministry could or would do nothing to counter this forcible occupation. Once again, the government by inaction gave its tacit sanction to a fait accompli carried out deliberately and openly by people who seemed to be confident of being able to flout authority with impunity.. … Their political bosses now decided to use these shock troops to stage demonstrations against the Tamils bound for the Vavuniya convention. (Vittachchi, 34–35)

Violence breaks out in Polonnaruwa through thugs attacking the train that brought in those traveling to attend the annual Federal Party convention in Vavuniya. The violence in Polonnaruwa continues to escalate and spread and wreaks havoc on the country for several weeks. The prime minister is late to react in any meaningful way and avoids declaring an emergency until nearly 7 days have passed after the outbreak of violence. The violence continues even while the emergency is in place and many people are killed by the rioters and the military that were deployed to control them. Vittachchi documents the events in several areas and points to the role played by rumor in the attacks. Vittachchi describes them as tit for tat attacks based on rumors that were rarely verified. Even after the military brings the situation under control, ethnic or racial tensions (in Vittachchi's words) persist, and sporadic violence continues for some time. Vittachchi also describes the manner in which the Prime Minister (of whom he is very critical) mishandled the situation at every level and permitted the deterioration of civil liberties to a dangerous extent. Not only did the law and order officials feel compelled to neglect their duties the government muzzled the press and under emergency regulations permitted the burial of bodies without an inquiry. Vittachchi laments not just the deterioration of ethnic relations but also the suspension of democratic norms. It is also telling that Vittachchi concludes his documentation of 58 by asking the question "Have the Sinhalese and the Tamils reached the parting of the ways?"

The next large-scale event of communal violence occurs in 1976 and, interestingly, takes place not against the Tamils but against Muslims in the context of prevailing tensions between the Muslim trading communities and landowners in the Puttalam district and the less economically privileged Sinhala communities in the areas surrounding Puttalam town.

Puttalam in 1976

The political economic context of the 1970s was heavily shaped by the UF government – a coalition between the SLFP and the Left parties that soundly defeated the UNP in the general elections of 1970. The UF won on the promise of establishing socialist economic policies in the long term and a commitment to reinstating the food subsidy dismantled by the previous government. However, a mere 8 months into power, compelled to confront serious balance of payment issues that had haunted the previous government, it resorted to unwelcome economic measures. The UF was unable to sustain the belief of the electorate and had to face a violent youth insurrection spearheaded by some sections that had supported the regime's electoral victory.

The insurrection, which was controlled through very repressive measures by the state, institutionalized police and armed-force aggression. Further, the state of emergency that was declared to deal with the uprising was maintained virtually for the entire duration of the regime's time in power. When Puttalam happened 5 years later, the shooting orders for the massacre in the mosque as well as the declaration of curfew until 10 February were done under emergency regulations.

Sri Lanka's first autochthonous constitution (1972) rendered Buddhism the state religion, enshrined Sinhala as the official language and Tamil as a language requiring translation, and did away with minority rights provisions through section 29 of the 1947–1948 constitution (Wilson 1975, 115).

Ethnic tensions were heightened by the new constitution. SJV Chelvanayagam leader of the TULF resigned from his seat compelling the government to hold an election for which he campaigned on a rejection of the republican constitution. The government delayed the election by 2 years, but Chelvanayagam nevertheless won a resounding victory which he understood as the Tamil electorate rejecting the Sinhala government's ethnic politics. The government's increasingly authoritarian and anti-democratic actions included taking over of newspapers, and the extension of its term in office by 2 additional years by utilizing its overwhelming majority in the constituent assembly eroded public confidence but also entrenched executive power (De Silva 1981, 546). De Silva also claims that the institutionalization of unicameral legislature, a powerful executive with insufficient checks on the exercise of its powers, and the doing away with of judicial review of legislation were measures that would institutionalize the authoritarianism of Sri Lanka's state for the long term. The National State Assembly as the vehicle of the sovereignty of the people was entrenched through the rejection of judicial review (De Silva 1981, 546). The above is the background within which the violence in Puttalam in 1976 and the country-wide anti-Tamil postelection violence occurred.

In Puttalam in 1976 there were sustained Sinhala Muslim tensions, and episodes of violence took place over a period of 2 months. The incident is seen as significant to the UNP election victory of 1977. Sinhala Muslim relations in Puttalam in the 1970s deteriorated with the influx of Sinhalese settlers from the south and Sinhala factory workers from Colombo (Brun 2008).

In early January 1976, an altercation between a *nattami* and a Sinhalese bus conductor whom he brushed against when unloading goods led to a general fracas with the Muslim *nattamis*. The staff at the bus depot, virtually all Sinhalese, went on a flash strike demanding the bus stand be moved away from the Muslim-dominated town center, a demand the government agent promptly conceded to.

The moving of the bus stand, which came while the NCGE Grade Ten O level exams were on going, led to tensions that appear to have persisted until the outbreak of massive violence on 2 February 1976.

The violence in Puttalam town included the police opening fire into the Puttalam Jumma mosque and killing 8 persons and the burning of over 225 houses and businesses, with 6 deaths (all Muslim). The groups of persons who attacked the shops were guided by a local Buddhist monk. When tensions were high, rumors were rampant of Sinhalese attacking Muslims and Muslims attacking Sinhalese.

Muslims also felt victimized by the police (who claimed that Muslims had fired from the mosque and compelled the police to fire in turn.) and later by the state response to the event. There have been two attempts at documenting the violence (Scott (unpublished n.d.); Nagaraj and Haniffa 2018). The findings of both sets of investigations outline the many ethnic fault lines that existed in Puttalam at the time and point to the possibility that economic enmity, ethnic animosity, and political expediency were paramount in terms of what occurred. Commentators have also documented the fact that the UNP capitalized on the violence in Puttalam for the1977 election and managed to redirect the vote that Muslim politician Badiuddeen Mahmood had managed to direct toward the Sri Lanka Freedom party back to the UNP (Nagaraj and Haniffa 2018).

According to De Silva, the regime's handling of the insurgency of 1971 entrenched the powers of the police and armed forces and set the stage for the increasing authoritarianism of the regime in the face of eroding public legitimacy. The violent suppression of the rebellion was made possible by bringing in emergency regulations. De Silva claims that the emergency regulations were in place for far longer than was warranted by the incidents of 1971. They seem to have been used to control perceived Tamil opposition against the State in 1975 and then early the next year to quell what seems to have been perceived as opposition by Muslim groups in Puttalam.

There has so far not been an attempt to substantially integrate the investigations into the anti-Tamil violence and the anti-Muslim incidents into one narrative regarding the political use of ethnic violence. It is essential that this is done.

The continuing mobilization of hate sentiment against the Tamils by the Sinhala political elites and the cultivation of a victim mentality among the Tamils by their own politicians speaking against the problematic politics of the Sinhala politicians lead to further violence in the future. By 1977 for instance, the perpetration of violence and the locations of violence based on ethnicity were of a more intense and protracted order than that of 1958.

The UNP had won the general elections of 1977 by a landslide. Following the election victory, there was widespread violence in the country originating in postelection violence in Jaffna. The almost 1-month-long period of violence that followed, to which the state response was minimal, mainly targeted upcountry Tamils. It was a time that was seen by many –mainly Tamil minority politicians speaking in parliament – as a time where anti-minority sentiment intensified in the country. In the north, militancy by young Tamils directed against the state was growing, and significant violent incidents began to be reported. Pivotal moments in the escalation of Tamil militancy, such as the murder of Alfred Duraiappah and the killing of Inspector Bastiampillai, the first act of violence for which the rebel group the Liberation Tigers of Tamil Eelam (LTTE) claimed responsibility, occurred during the mid-1970s.

While the UNP won the elections on a platform accepting that the Tamils had legitimate grievances, it was soon clear that the UNP leader J.R. Jayawardena lacked the foresight to anticipate what measures may be required to resolve the issue. J.R. did not anticipate the escalation of Tamil nationalist militancy and was not in any way interested in accommodating what he saw as Tamil recalcitrance. The anti-Tamil violence after the elections of 1977 lasted over a month and was a further reflection of the state's chosen mode of engagement with and management of ethnic tensions and minority demands.

Jayawardena's speech in parliament 2 days after violence broke out in Jaffna called attention to the fact that it was the language of the Tamil leadership and the actions of unruly Tamils that brought about the violence.

Jayawardena was attributing the violence to the rhetoric of the Tamil leadership and its anticipation of violent action against the state. "If you want a fight let there be a fight." This treatment of the issue by Jayawardena is a further reflection of the lack of responsibility taken by the government to address the law and order situation and the manner in which the state had not only ethnicised its own response to post election violence but in fact utilized such violence to make a political point or "to teach the Tamils a lesson." There were many such "uses" for ethnic political violence in Sri Lanka.

At the insistence of the leader of the opposition A. Amirthalingam, M.C. Sansoni a former chief justice was appointed to a one-man commission to investigate the violence of 1977. The Sansoni commission report recounts that the state did little to halt the violence – by not immediately declaring an emergency for instance – and that there was evidence of the police colluding in carrying out the violence. Although the postelection violence of 1977 erupted in Jaffna, it spread throughout the country, and as already stated, many of its victims were upcountry Tamils. Echoing Jayawardena's words referenced above, the Sansoni report faults of Tamil politicians for their "duplicity" of asking for a peaceful settlement while threatening the dawn of militant violence in the pursuit of separation attributes the breaking out of violence to their rhetoric.

1975 to 1983 saw significant political conflagrations in Sri Lanka targeting both the Muslim and Tamil minorities. Researchers have mainly looked at the anti-Tamil violence as part of the narrative of the ethnic conflict, but it is important that the origin of attacks on Muslims too is looked into as part of this same narrative.

The Violence of 1981

The nature of anti-minority sentiment in the country in the late 1970s and early 1980s must be clearly understood in order to appreciate the background to the violence in Galle in 1982. The manner in which such outbreaks of violence against minorities were normalized by various representatives of the state is an especially important factor.

The UNP proposed the District Development Councils as a way of addressing the grievances of the Tamil people. In June 1981, local elections were held in the north to elect members of the newly established district development councils. The Tamil United Liberation Front TULF had decided to participate and work in the councils. In doing so, TULF continued to work toward autonomy for the Tamil areas. The militant groups, however, opposed working within the existing political framework. They viewed participation in the elections as compromising the objective of a separate state. Shortly before the elections, the leading candidate of the

UNP, Dr. Thiagarajah, was assassinated as he left a political rally. Violence broke out immediately after. When elections were held a few days later, concomitant charges of voting irregularities and mishandling of ballots created the nation's first election scandal since the introduction of universal suffrage 50 years earlier.

This was also the time of increasing militant activity that the Jayawardena government was determined to quell. Emergency rule was imposed on Jaffna after the murder of Police Inspector Guruswamy in 1979. In July 1979 the draconian prevention of Terrorism Act is introduced. On 4 June 1981 on the eve of the DDC elections, the militants killed four policemen. The police went on a rampage of retaliation in Jaffna destroying property. Bandarage sees the destruction of the Jaffna public library and the burning of its 95,000 volumes as part of this retaliatory wave. In August 1981, ethnic violence erupts in the Ampara District, the south-western towns, and hill country and upcountry Tamils again, as in 1977, become the targets of Sinhala thugs' "anger." Many have seen these violent events as leading up to the conflagration of July 1983 as episodes in the continuous narrative of the deterioration of ethnic relations between Sinhalese and Tamils. This narrativization has tended to miss ethnic violence that has targeted Muslims. Current research reveals at least two such events as having occurred during the difficult years from the mid-1970s that culminate in July 1983.

1982 in Galle: Violence erupted in Galle in July 1982. The violence – between Sinhalese and Muslims – began on July 26 and continued till the 31st. The 6 days of violence resulted in two deaths and millions of rupees in property damage. The rioting spread from Galle town to suburban areas with small Muslim concentrations and had eventually to be controlled with the intervention of the military. The government declared an island-wide emergency, and curfew was imposed within the limits of the Galle municipality. There were limits imposed on news coverage of the incident at the national level by the government "in an effort to prevent the incident from spreading to other parts of the country" (Daily Mirror, Thursday, August 5. "Curfew in Galle Lifted").

There was a one person commission appointed to look into the violence. However, this report that the Muslim community representatives considered to be biased was never released. The Alles report was accessed and commented upon by George Scott. The Alles report refers to the incident as a confrontation between two rival gangs. It suggests some commensurability between the organized actions of the Sinhala and Muslim groups (Scott 1989).

Scott's narrative traces the underlying cause of the riots to economic rivalry between the Muslim traders and the up and coming Vahumpura business people in the Galle Bazaar who Scott identifies as having possibly instigated and provided the (costly) petrol for the arson to the Sinhala thugs. Scott states that while the Sinhala higher caste Goyigama and Karawa traders were arguably in greater economic ascendency in Galle at the time, and were as powerful a set of competitors, the Muslims were an easier target. Muslim "difference" as well as what was seen as Muslim's manipulation of local authorities and power structures through bribes and other modes of informal patronage/exchange according to Scott may have motivated such anger. While all business engagements regardless of ethnicity probably entailed some amount of similar patronage, Muslims were considered much more adept at this and were thought to wield greater influence due to their wealth. To this date stereotypes regarding Muslims-using-bribery-to-get-things-done abound.

Both Alles as referenced in Scott and Scott's own narrative reference the fact that the Muslims were the landowners and that it was also a property dispute. In a manner similar to the case of Justice Sansoni, Alles too reports the incidents of police failure but blames the Muslim leadership for instigating the violence through their own poor judgment (Scott 1989).

In both state-sponsored narratives – by Sansoni and by Alles (as reported in Scott) – the "anger of the Sinhalese" through which the violence occurred is rendered legitimate through calling attention to the recalcitrant and irresponsible behavior of the Tamil and Muslim minority leadership. This way of holding all those with a similar ethnic identity responsible for the political (and in the case of Galle economic) actions of a few enables state support for ethnic violence. These victim-blaming narratives appear in relation to most "riots" that have been documented.

With regard to state culpability, Scott references the following in the Alles report. "Alles cites as secondary immediate causes the corrupt collusion of some of the higher police officers in this attempt, their incompetence in dealing with the initial stages of the conflict, and the depleted state of police and army personnel and equipment prior to the outbreak"(Scott, 26).

A report on the violence produced by Muslims of Galle vehemently opposed the violence being framed as sparked off by personal animosities. They consistently stressed the targeting of Muslims by widespread groups of armed and equipped Sinhalese. They also drew attention to the fact that the trigger event that was being talked of occurred 1 month prior to the outbreak of widespread violence. They state that this time lag seems to indicate that the attacks were planned. They accused the police and prominent local Sinhala business interests of colluding in the attacks. (The report asked, if this was indeed the result of a personal animosity, "why were people in other areas attacked? Why were mosques attacked? Why were unconnected people's property robbed?")

1983 July

The ethnic violence of July 1983 while arguably the culmination of a long trajectory of events by which the Sri Lankan leadership has managed ethnic tensions has become emblematic in the Social Science literature as the defining moment of the ethnic conflict and of Sri Lanka descending into violence (Jeganathan 1997). It has been used as a marker of the moment when the Sri Lankan government's conflict with the separatist Liberation Tigers of Tamil Eelam (LTTE) was born. The event was of great significance. Countrywide violence lasted several weeks and saw hundreds of deaths and thousands displaced and set in motion the exodus of large numbers of Tamils from the island and fed the burgeoning militant movements. Arguably the extent of the violence and the hate displayed against Tamils by Sinhala mobs was similar to that which happened in 1958–1977. One element that was different was that there was a disappearance of class privilege. In earlier instances those who were attacked were poorer persons and small businesses. But in 1983 no such distinction was maintained. The government response followed an established pattern of blaming the victims for the violence. "The Sinhalese lost their patience" or there was a "Naxalit plot." In fact, the government's response in the aftermath of violence was to proscribe the Marxist political party the Janatha Vimukthi Peramuna.

The militancy grew in the aftermath of 1983 with high numbers of recruitment and substantial attacks. The country saw 30 plus years of brutal conflict. The conflict led to the further marginalization of minority ethnic groups with Tamils being especially targeted at checkpoints in the larger town at times when the violence in the theater of war in the north and east was at its height. The war years also saw the LTTE targeting civilians outside the war zone through suicide bombings of nonmilitary targets. The LTTE also carried out specially targeted assassinations of both Sinhala leaders and Tamil leaders with a political orientation that was different from theirs. They also assassinated members of other militant groups that had differing ideologies. The manner in which the choices of Tamil nationalist politicians and the militancy devastated the Sri Lankan Tamil community remains to be written. Currently the discourse of Tamil nationalism is understood chiefly as emerging from the harassment of Tamils by the Sinhala identified state. The work of Sumathy and Thiranagama and the reports produced by UTHR(J) are exceptions to this narrative (Sumathy 2016; Thiranagama 2011, Reports by UTHR(J)).

The institutionalization of the draconian prevention of terrorism act (PTA) in 1981 and the 6th amendment to the constitution where propagating the idea of a separate state was considered a criminal offence were also set in place further marginalizing Tamil political activity and polarizing the ethnic groups in the country. The polarization that saw its beginnings with the Sinhala Only legislation of the 1950s culminated in a gruesome war based on ethnicity that lasted over 30 years. The LTTE asserted themselves to be the sole representatives of the Tamil people and developed into one of the most feared and sophisticated armed groups in the world. They developed the suicide bomber as a major weapon and wrought a fearsome war throughout the north and east for several decades.

In the south, the state was compelled to invest heavily in the military, and joining was seen as a lucrative career move for many from depressed and marginalized Sinhala communities. The figure of the Sinhala war hero or Ranaviruwa was popularized as a means of ensuring recruits for the military and maintaining morale in a context where over the years the government troops suffered heavy casualties.

Demonizing and dehumanizing of the other became standard practice within the country with Tamil visibility becoming less and less. Tamil festivals were no longer celebrated in the south with the same pomp and pageantry as prior to 1983, and Tamil artists and musicians virtually disappeared (Jeganathan 2000). Checkpoint culture became the norm with the cities of Colombo and Kandy and larger towns everywhere marked by the ubiquitous presence of the military. Harassment of ethnic Tamils at checkpoints was common practice, and people were compelled to carry identification documents wherever they went. Being Tamil in the south of Sri Lanka became dangerous for many. There was a time during the Rajapaksa regime when Tamils traveling in to Colombo from out of town were required to report at police stations.

Postwar Violence: Ethnicity and Violence in Sri Lanka Today

This section will look at the manner in which ethnic polarization operates in Sri Lanka's postwar climate. Sri Lanka's ethnic war ended rather brutally in May 2009. The armed forces of the government of Sri Lanka forged an all-out attack on LTTE positions, and the war ended with an enormous civilian death toll. The LTTE's own using of civilians as cover for their military activities and the government's refusal to respect civilian presence in the areas that it attacked have marked the end of the war. The government of Sri Lanka and the Sri Lankan military are under international scrutiny for alleged human rights violations and the perpetration of war crimes for what happened during the final weeks of the war (International Crisis Group 2010). Given this polarization and the sanitized coverage that the last weeks of the war received in the south through the Sinhala language media, there was little awareness or opposition among Sinhalese to the horrendous loss of life during the final months (Haniffa and Samuel 2016). The cultivation of a postwar Sinhala supremacist ideology of the government in power having liberated the country from terrorism has had some longevity in the country and still informs political platforms of a set of political actors with dynastic ambitions.

Ethnic relations at the end of the war were unprecedented in the country's history (see Bastin & de Silva 2017). The Rajapaksa regime that prided itself on winning the war exploited the victory for political purposes cultivating a particular Sinhala supremacy that supported the longevity of the regime. The Rajapaksas capitalized on the war victory and thereby cultivated a narrative of ethnic superiority that understood the Tamils as a community as vanquished and as having been taught a lesson. In the aftermath of the war, when the LTTE was no longer the principle enemy against whom Sinhala nationalism could define and explain itself, there emerged a Buddhist monk-led movement that was at pains to create and consolidate a new enemy around whom popular ethnic sentiment might again be mobilized (Haniffa 2016).

Anti-Muslim sentiment was cultivated in postwar Sri Lanka principally through the Bodu Bala Sena (BBS) organization and later by many others that adopted sections of its model including the Ravana Balakaya, Sinhala Ravaya, Sinha Le, and the Mahason Balakaya. As already well documented, the BBS's activities were unprecedented in the history of the island, and their discourse created a wider conversation among Sinhala society in the south about Muslims in which Muslims themselves could play no part (Haniffa 2016). The cultivation of the anti-Muslim sentiment was such that by 2018 when the 2nd large event of anti-Muslim violence took place in the Kandy district, the populace was primed for an attack of this nature. The first event took place in Aluthgama and Beruwela in 2014 (Haniffa et al. 2014). Ethnic violence in this event had taken on an added religious dimension as well.

In the aftermath of the war, especially in 2012, the BBS appeared as significant actor on the Sri Lankan political landscape. Housed initially in a multistory high-rise building owned by the Buddhist Cultural Center and with their mode of transportation being large SUVs that were similar to those used by government ministers, the

BBS looked as if it was well funded and had friends in high places. They also seemed to operate with impunity, and there was no opposition to the new mode in which they engaged with the public – large public meetings with thousands of devotees where the order was to speak about how the Muslims were the country's latest threat.

The cultivation of hate sentiment against Muslims was done by the Bodu Bala Sena with such planning and precisions, and with sophisticated use of social media by the second or third year of their activity, the spread of the ideology had lost some of its urgency and had sedimented. Today anti-Muslim sentiment operates at the level of truisms among the Sinhala population across geographical areas and is available for mobilization at very short notice.

The mobilization of anti-Muslim sentiment toward the perpetration of violence occurred in two major incidents in the country in June 2014 and in March 2018. There were slightly less widespread incidents in November 2017 in Gintota and in February 2018 in Ampara. In most of these incidents, in addition to the sedimented anti-Muslim sentiment, there is a trigger event or immediate cause. In the case of Aluthgama, it was an altercation between the driver of a van in which a Buddhist monk was traveling and three Muslims. Muslims were accused of beating up the van driver – sometimes the story was spun to indicate that it was the monk that was assaulted. In the Kandy event, the altercation was between a speeding Sinhala van driver and three drunken Muslim youths in a three-wheeler. They were in competition, and the three-wheeler drivers were angry that they were not permitted to overtake the van. There is a fight at a petrol station, and one of the Muslim young men hits the Sinhala man on the head with a chair. They leave shortly. However, later, the young Sinhala man who is hit on the head collapses and dies of his injuries several days later. Violence breaks out the day of his funeral. In both instances, there is a presence of monks and other actors well known to spearhead anti-Muslim agitation at the location.

Documentation of the events reveal that there is an element of organizing that is evident in and around the event as well as the mobilization through roumer of local interlocutors. There is also a careful avoidance of physical violence against individuals, and the ire is directed at property. There is a provision of makeshift weaponry, information regarding the location of houses businesses, and mosques, and the clear targeting of those to attack. Those who benefitted from the attack include competing businesses, minor politicians in the area, as well as national level politicians who can benefit from distractions. The Muslim community as a whole is thereby held back in terms of their economic development due to the destruction of the property. In the case of Kandy, many of the attackers who were mobilized locally were youth and seemed to be under the age of 30.

Muslim businesses and homes are attacked systematically. Some retaliatory attacks against Sinhala businesses are recorded as well, but these are scattered. While there was evidence of government collusion in the attacks in 2014, it is less apparent in 2018. However, what seems clear is that there are many that reap advantages from the violence, and funding is being provided to various individuals and groups to maintain offices and a social media presence to sustain the spread of anti-Muslim sentiment.

Moreover, the Easter Sunday terrorist attacks by a local extremist Islamist group called National Thowheed Jamath (NTJ) have drastically changed Sri Lanka's social and political spheres. Muslim community of the country came under surveillance as well as virulent hate speech. Islamophobic propaganda reached a new height and communal tensions swayed the Island in the period following Easter Attacks. The key issues Sri Lanka is facing in the aftermath of Easter Attacks are the continued threat of global terrorism and the increasingly influential ultra-nationalist Sinhala Buddhist forces and ideology – Islamophobia and polarization on ethnic and religious lines.

Our sense of both ethnicity and ethnic relations in Sri Lankan history is one where a principle of dynamic relations is paramount, especially as these relate to the Sinhala Buddhist polity and to Tamil-speaking minorities. To that end, Sri Lanka's Muslim communities are not a single community descended from Arabs or any other specific group. They are not Tamils simply because they speak Tamil any more than the Sinhalese are Sinhalese simply because they speak Sinhala. Instead, they reflect in their diversity the richness of the island's history in the commerce and associated movement and upheaval of Indian Ocean trade over the last couple of millennia. The starting point for accommodation must not, therefore, be the roots of Muslim ethnicity but the fact of Muslim ethnicity in all of its historical richness (see Bastin and de Silva 2019; McGilvray 2008).

Conclusion

This chapter has attempted to closely look at the manner in which ethnic violence manifested itself on the ground at different political moments in Sri Lanka after independence from British rule. As outlined in the chapter, struggles about political representation language use and citizenship defined Sri Lanka's postcolonial political landscape. From 1958 onward, these struggles were accompanied by periodic outbreaks of violence. These violent events eventually culminated in the country-wide riots of 1983 sometimes referred to as Black July or the anti-Tamil pogrom. It is a critical moment in a trajectory of intensifying ethnic violence against Tamils and badly mishandled political moments by both the Sinhala and Tamil leadership that ultimately led to the emergence of the Liberation Tigers of Tamil Eelam. Sri Lanka's ethnic war ended rather brutally in May 2009. The armed forces of the government of Sri Lanka forged an all-out attack on LTTE positions, and the war ended with an enormous civilian death toll. In the aftermath of the war, when the LTTE was no longer the principle enemy against whom Sinhala nationalism could define and explain itself, there emerged a Buddhist monk-led movement that was at pains to create and consolidate a new enemy around whom popular ethnic sentiment might again be mobilized.

Failure to arrive at a collective identity common to all ethnicities can be seen as one main reason for the outbreak of violence in Sri Lanka. Tensions are inevitable, especially in a country where rich ethnic diversity is present that cerates minority and majority groups. The establishment of ethno-nationalists organizations before, during, and after the ethnic war itself illustrates the failure to arrive at a collective national identity even 10 years after the end of brutal violence. It is also clear that the end of the war has not given rise to any positive repercussions in terms of addressing root causes of the ethnic tensions in Sri Lanka.

References

Abeysekara A (2002) Colors of the robe: religion, identity and difference. University of South Carolina Press, Columbia
Bastin R (2001) Globalisation and conflict. In: A history of ethnic conflict in Sri Lanka. Marga monograph series on ethnic reconciliation, no. 23. MARGA Institute, Colombo
Bastin R, de Silva P (2017) Military Tourism as State-Effect in the Sri Lankan Civil War. In: John Eade and Mario Kati (eds) Military Pilgrimage and the Battelfield Tourism. Routledge, London.
Bastin R, de Silva P (2019) Historical Threads in Buddhist-Muslim Relations in Sri Lanka. In Michael Jerryson and Iselin Frydenlund (eds) Buddhist-Muslim Encounters in South and Southeast Asia, Palgrave Macmillan (in press)
Bond G (1988) The Buddhist revival in Sri Lanka: religious tradition, reinterpretation, and response. Comparison studies in religion series. University of South Carolina Press, Columbia
Brun C (2008) Finding a place. Local integration and protracted displacement in Sri Lanka. Social Scientists' Association, Colombo
De Silva KM (1981) A history of Sri Lanka. University of California Press, Berkeley/Los Angeles
de Silva P (2013) (Re)ordering of Postcolonial Sri Pada in Sri Lanka: Buddhism, State, and Nationalism, History and Sociology of South Asia, 7(2):155–176
Gombrich R, Obeyesekere G (1988) Buddhism transformed: religious change in Sri Lanka. Princeton University Press, Princeton
Gunasinghe N (1986) Ethnic conflict in Sri Lanka: perceptions and solutions. Comp Stud South Asia Afr Middle East 6(2):34–37
Haniffa F (2013) Piety as politics amongst Muslim women in contemporary Sri Lanka. In: Osella F, Osella C (eds) Islamic reform in South Asia. Cambridge University Press, New York
Haniffa F (2016) Stories in the aftermath of Aluthgama: religious conflict in contemporary Sri Lanka. In: Buddhist extremists and Muslim minorities. Oxford University Press, Oxford. pp 164–193
Haniffa F, Samuel K (2016) Men women and war talk: the gendered nature of references to war in parliamentary debates. In: Parliament's representation of women, a selective review of Sri Lanka's Hansards from 2005–2015. Women and Media Collective, Colombo
Haniffa F, Amarasuriya H, Wijenaike V (2014) Where have all the neighbors gone? Aluthgama riots and the aftermath. Law and Society Trust, Colombo
International Crisis Group (2010) War crimes in Sri Lanka. International Crisis Group. https://www.crisisgroup.org/asia/south-asia/sri-lanka/war-crimes-sri-lanka
Ismail Q (2005) Abiding by Sri Lanka: on peace, place, and postcoloniality. University of Minnesota Press, Minneapolis
Jayawardene VK (1984) Ethnic consciousness in Sri Lanka: continuity and change. In: Committee for Rational Development (ed) Sri Lanka, the ethnic conflict: myths, realities, and perspectives. Navrang, New Delhi, pp 115–173
Jeganathan P (1997) All the Lord's Men: recollecting a riot in an urban Sri Lankan community. In: Roberts M (ed) Collective identities revisited. Marga Institute, Colombo
Jeganathan P (2000) On the anticipation of violence. In: Anthropology, development, and modernities: exploring discourses, counter-tendencies, and violence. Routledge, London
Kapferer B (1988) Legends of people, myths of state: violence, intolerance and political culture in Sri Lanka and Australia. Smithsonian Institution Press, Washington, DC

Mahadev N (2018) Economies of conversion and ontologies of religious difference: Buddhism, Christianity, and adversarial political perception in Sri Lanka. Curr Anthropol 59:665. in press

McGilvray, Dennis B. (2008) Crucible of Conflict: Tamil and Muslim Society on the East Coast of Sri Lanka. Duke University Press, Durham and London

Nagaraj VK, Haniffa F (2018) Towards recovering histories of anti-Muslim violence in the context of Sinhala–Muslim tensions in Sri Lanka. International Center for Ethnic Studies, Colombo

Obeyesekere G (1984) The origins and institutionalization of political violence. In: Manor J (ed) Sri Lanka in change and crisis. Croom Helm, London, pp 153–174

Pfaffenberger B (1990) The political construction of defensive nationalism: the 1968 temple-entry crisis in Northern Sri Lanka. J Asian Stud 49(1):78–96. https://doi.org/10.2307/2058434

Robert RI (2010) Creating peace in Sri Lanka: civil war and reconciliation. Brookings Institution Press/World Peace Foundation

Roberts M (1994) Exploring confrontation, Sri Lanka: politics culture and history. Harwood Academic Publisher, Switzerland

Rogers DJ (1987) Social mobility, popular ideology, and collective violence in modern Sri Lanka. J Asian Stud 16(03):583–607

Scott D (1999) Refashioning Future: Criticism after Postcoloniality. Princeton: Princeton University Press

Scott D (2000) Toleration and Historical Traditions of Difference. In: Chatterjee P. & Jeganathan P. (eds) Community, Gender and Violence. Subaltern Studies XI Delhi: Permanent Black

Scott GM Jr (1989) The economic bases of Sinhala Muslim ethnic conflict in 20th century Sri Lanka. International Center for Ethnic Studies, Colombo

Scott GM Jr (n.d.) Violence in Puttalam: the basis for the 1976 incidents of Sinhalese- Moor ethnic conflict and its means of resolution. Unpublished manuscript

Sivathamby K (1987) The Sri Lanka Ethnic Crisis and Muslim Tamil Relationships: A Socio-Political Review. In: Charles Abeysekera and Newton Gunasinghe (ed) Facets of Ethnicity in Sri Lanka, 192–225. Social Scientists' Association, Colombo

Spencer J (ed) (1990) Sri Lanka: history and the roots of conflict. Routledge, London

Spencer J et al (2015) Checkpoint, temple, church and mosque: a collaborative ethnography of war and peace. Pluto Press, London

Sumathy S (2016) Territorial Claims, Home, Land and Movement: Women's History of Violence and Resistance. In: Jayawardena, Kumari, Pinto-Jayawardena, Kishali, (eds) The search for justice: The Sri Lanka papers. Zubaan series on sexual violence and impunity in South Asia. Zuban, New Delhi

Tambiah SJ (1986) Sri Lanka: ethnic fratricide and the dismantling of democracy. University of Chicago Press, Chicago

Tambiah SJ (1992) Buddhism betrayed: religion, politics and violence in Sri Lanka. University of Chicago Press, Chicago/London

Tambiah SJ (1996) Leveling crowds: ethnonationalist conflicts and collective violence in South Asia. Berkeley University Press, California, pp 36–100

Thiranagama S (2011) In my mother's house: civil war in Sri Lanka. University of Pennsylvania Press, Philadelphia

Udalagama T, de Silva P (2014) Formation of group-violence against state: the hindsight story of the thirty-year war in Sri Lanka. In: Hawdon J, Ryan J, Lucht M (eds) Bullies to terrorists: the courses and consequence of groups violence. Lexington Book, New York, pp 91–107

Venugopal R (2018) Nationalism, development and ethnic conflict in Sri Lanka. Cambridge University Press, Cambridge

Vittachchi T (1958) Emergency '58: the story of the Ceylon race riots. Andre Deutsch, London

Wilson AJ (1975) Electoral politics in an emergent state. The general elections of 1970. Cambridge University Press, Cambridge

Ethno-communal Conflict in Sudan and South Sudan

37

Johan Brosché

Contents

Introduction	656
Center-Periphery Dynamics and Civil Wars in Sudan	657
Darfur: An Intricate Web of Ethno-communal Conflicts	659
Land and Identity in Darfur	660
Communal Conflicts in Darfur	661
From Communal Conflicts to Civil War and Ethnic Cleansing	663
South Sudan: Ethno-communal Conflicts in The World's Newest Nation	666
The Painful Path to Independence	666
The Interim Period (2005–2011)	667
From Peaceful Independence to Full-Fledged Civil War	669
Conclusions	670
References	671

Abstract

This chapter analyzes ethno-communal conflicts in Sudan and South Sudan, which gained independence in 2011. In these two countries, ethno-communal rivalries have primarily manifested in three different types of violent conflicts: communal conflicts, rebel-rebel fighting, and civil wars. The study consists of three core parts. First, the chapter provides some empirical information about center-periphery relations (in both Sudan and South Sudan, elites in the center enjoy outmost political and economic power, while other regions are severely marginalized) and the major violent conflicts in the two countries. Second, the chapter focuses on ethno-communal conflicts in Sudan's westernmost region, Darfur. This section illustrates that an intricate web of ethno-communal conflicts exist in Darfur. It also emphasizes the importance of land and examines the government's role in these different conflicts. Third, the chapter studies the

J. Brosché (✉)
Department of Peace- and Conflict Research, Uppsala University, Uppsala, Sweden
e-mail: Johan.Brosche@pcr.uu.se

civil war that has devastated South Sudan since December 2013. It shows that legacies from Sudan's North-South war (particularly the Sudanese government's strategy of divide-and-rule) are important for how the war in South Sudan has manifested.

Keywords

Sudan · South Sudan · Darfur · Conflict complexity · Communal conflict · Civil war · Conflict interlinkages

Introduction

Located in northeast Africa, separated from the Arabian Peninsula by the Red Sea, and split in half by the Nile River, Sudan occupies a particularly conflict-torn region of the world. Although all parts of Sudan are ethnically heterogeneous, Muslims with an Arab culture primarily inhabit the north, while an African identification is more common in the south, and its inhabitants generally follow Christianity or animist religions. Yet, this simplified dichotomy disguises a wide variety of ethnic groups living in both the north and the south (Johnson 2006). On 9 July 2011, Sudan split, and South Sudan became independent after Africa's longest war, and this chapter analyzes ethno-communal conflicts in both Sudan and South Sudan (Fig. 1). In this chapter, Sudan generally refers to the united country before it split, and the text will clearly indicate when referring to Sudan after the division. Furthermore, South Sudan refers to the independent country and Southern Sudan to this part of Sudan before the split.

Ethno-communal rivalries have been a central part of Sudan's history for a long time and resulted in different violent, and non-violent, conflicts. This chapter focuses on violent conflicts. Violent ethno-communal conflicts in Sudan have manifested in primarily three different types of conflict:

Fig. 1 Map of Sudan and South Sudan

First, *communal conflicts*, which here means conflicts between non-formally organized non-state groups organized along a shared communal identification that engage in fighting over issues like scarce resources and political influence. In Sudan, these conflicts, typically, pit farmer against herders or take place between various pastoralist groups. Both Darfur (Sudan's westernmost region) and South Sudan have experienced numerous violent conflicts of this type.

Second, *rebel-rebel conflicts*, comprising fighting between rebel groups with different ethno-communal support bases. Many opposition movements have split along ethnic lines, and this category captures violence between such factions.

Third, ethno-communal rivalries can also constitute a central part of *civil wars* where rebel groups fight against the government.

These different types of conflicts are intertwined, and this chapter elucidates different interlinkages between these conflicts. While this chapter emphasizes the ethno-communal component of these various conflicts, it is important to remember that all these types of conflicts are complex and caused by a multiple set of political, economic, and environmental (to name just a few) factors.

The analysis consists of three sections. First, to situate the ethno-communal conflicts, the chapter provides some empirical information focusing on center-periphery relations and violent conflicts in Sudan and South Sudan. Second, the focus is on Darfur and probing how different types of ethno-communal conflicts have combined into the disastrous situation that has shattered Darfur for the last 15 years. Third, the chapter focuses on the civil war that has devastated South Sudan since December 2013. This part starts with analyzing some of the roots to this war, and thereafter it examines how the war has manifested (often along ethno-communal lines). The chapter ends with some conclusions.

Center-Periphery Dynamics and Civil Wars in Sudan

Sudan is very heterogeneous when it comes to ethnicity, language, and religion. This diversity is, however, not reflected in the leadership of the country (Thomas 2009). Instead, Sudan is characterized by unequal power relations where the elites at the center retain a privileged position and people living in peripheral areas are marginalized (El-Tom 2009). These elites have ruled Sudan in ways that have reinforced the existing power inequities between the center and the disparate ethnic communities at the margin. Elites originating from the Nile Valley, north of Khartoum, have controlled the reigns of political power since Sudan's independence in 1956. At times, unstable parliamentary governments have ruled Sudan, and at other times, military regimes have governed the country. Yet, regardless of the type of government, the elites from the Nile Valley have been at the country's helm, controlling the channels of power, blocking access to power for other groups, and strongly dominating the national political scene (el-Din 2007; Hassan 2009). The central elites in Khartoum also dominate Sudan's economy, and resources from peripheral areas are taken to Khartoum (de Waal 2007).

The elites utterly dominating Sudanese politics do not constitute a united group but contain different factions that compete for power (de Waal 2007). While often fighting each other fiercely, the various elites in Khartoum have since independence endorsed efforts to create a national Sudanese identity around Islam and Arabism (Sørbø and Ahmed 2013). While these elites attempt to endorse an Arab-Islamic project that portrays Sudan as an outright Islamic and Arabic country, it often excludes both Muslims and people with legitimate claims to an Arab identity. The prime purpose of this ideology is thus to promote the interest of the riverine elites (El-Tom 2009). Nevertheless, this project has strongly favored the Arab religion, ethnicity, and culture that dominate in northern Sudan over the African religious and cultural identity more prevalent in the south (Deng 1995). Since 1989, the National Congress Party (NCP), until 1998 called the National Islamic Front (NIF), has dominated the center. In a key historical event, this party took power in Sudan through a military coup on 30 June 1989. The coup placed Omar al-Bashir as Sudan's President, a position that he still holds 30 years later. As head of state, President Bashir oversees a cadre of elite officials, and his political power is primarily derived from close ties with the military (Temin and Murphy 2011).

For the marginalized peripheral groups, the paralyzing domination enjoyed by the center of Sudan has had devastating effects. Not only have these groups been the prime victims for Sudan's wars, they have also been subject to hardships due to the inadequate distribution of essential services and resources, such as roads, education, healthcare, food, and housing. The political and economic domination of the center has caused frustration among the people in the marginalized areas. This resentment is evident among resistance movements in various regions of Sudan that all have redistribution of power from the center to the regions as a fundamental part of their political agenda (Mohamed 2007).

Sudan's unequal center-periphery relations have been a key driver for the numerous civil wars that have shattered Sudan for decades. The antagonism against the regime in Khartoum has been particularly strong in Southern Sudan. The North-South tensions partly originate from the colonial period. Between 1821 and 1885, Sudan was part of the Ottoman Empire and called Turco-Egyptian Sudan. During this period, the colonialists used Southern Sudan (one third of Sudan) only to collect slaves. Under British colonial rule (1898–1956), Sudan was called Anglo-Egyptian Sudan, and despite being part of the same country, the south and the north were ruled as different entities, which created an intricate situation. Since independence, consecutive governments in Khartoum have exacerbated north-south divisions (Jok 2007). Sudan has been embroiled in a north-south war for long periods since its independence. The initial period of conflict was from 1962 to 1972 and then again from 1983 when Sudan People's Liberation Movement/Army (SPLM/A) took up arms against the regime in Khartoum. In January 2005, this war ended after 22 years of fighting – and an estimated two million casualties – through the signing of the Comprehensive Peace Agreement (CPA). The CPA stipulated that Southern Sudan should be an autonomous part of Sudan until a referendum in 2011 should decide the region's final status (Johnson 2006). In January 2011, close to 99% voted for independence, and the world's newest nation was born 6 months later (Rolandsen and Daly 2016). In relation to South Sudan's secession, a new rebel group called SPLM/A-North launched an insurgency in South Kordofan and Blue Nile, two states located in Sudan but close to the border with South Sudan. Besides these intrastate conflicts, Sudan and South Sudan also fought each other in a relatively brief interstate conflict over oil resources and demarcation of the contested border in 2012 (UCDP 2018).

The Government of South Sudan, which has ruled South Sudan since 2005, shares several characteristics with its counterpart in Sudan. The regime in Juba (the capital of South Sudan) is primarily made up of former SPLM/A rebels, which means that both governments largely consist of military men (Brosché and Höglund 2016). A core aspect of SPLM/A's political program was ending marginalization. Yet, even though SPLM/A has been in power for over a decade, South Sudan remains characterized by an imbalanced periphery-center relation where most of the resources are allocated to Juba, leaving other parts of South Sudan deprived. Hence, both Sudan and South Sudan are deeply unequal where elites at the center have a privileged position, while people on the peripheries suffer from enduring poverty and prevailing violence (Thomas 2015).

Since its independence, the Republic of South Sudan has experienced numerous rebellions where different insurgent groups have challenged the government. These rebellions were relatively minor during the first 2.5 years after independence. In December 2013, however, a full-fledged civil war emerged in South Sudan (Brosché and Höglund 2016). The intense fighting has caused tens of thousands of fatalities, and more than four million – over a third of South Sudan's population – have been displaced. Around two million have fled to bordering countries, and about two million remains internally displaced in South Sudan. In August 2015, the warring parties signed a peace agreement, but this did not stop the fighting. The belligerents signed a new peace deal in the end of July 2018 (UN News 2018). However, at the time of writing, August 2018, it remains unclear if this agreement will succeed to bring peace to South Sudan. The third section elaborates on the history and dynamics of ethno-communal conflict in South Sudan. First, the next section will cover developments in Darfur, which in some regards have intertwined with the development of the North-South divide.

Darfur: An Intricate Web of Ethno-communal Conflicts

In 2003, as negotiations to end the North-South war were ongoing, a new civil war started in Sudan when Darfurian insurgents launched a rebellion against the regime in Khartoum. After more than 15 years of fighting, this conflict is still active, and the United Nations estimates that it has killed more than 300,000. Darfur came on the international radar after the Sudanese government answered to the rebellion with a counterinsurgency that involved extensive human rights violations. However, Darfur has experienced violent conflicts, primarily over scarce resources such as land, for several decades. The pages below illustrate some of the core dynamics of Darfur's different ethno-communal conflicts and some of their inherent intricacy.

Land and Identity in Darfur

Media often portrays the conflict in Darfur as a conflict between Africans and Arabs. Such a description is unsophisticated. There are around 40–90 ethnic groups in Darfur (Flint and de Waal 2008), and dividing them along an Arab-African line constitutes an oversimplification. In fact, the division between Arabs and Africans (or non-Arabs) is not based on language, skin color, religion (all Darfur's communities are Muslim), culture, or way of life. Instead, its basis is claims to an Arab identity, which is vital for those who adhere to it (Tubiana 2007). The distinction between Arab and Africans is also fairly new. In fact, Darfurians customarily referred to people by using their tribal identity, such as Zaghawa or Misseria. However, in the 1970s, the Fur – the largest community in Darfur that has given the region its name Dar Fur (homeland of the Fur) and one of several "African" groups – increasingly started to refer to themselves as Africans, which contributed to create the highly polarized and political Arab-African dichotomy (Mamdani 2009). Hence, although concealing the complexity of the situation, the distinction is important for some of the dynamics in Darfur.

An essential element of Darfur's various conflicts is land. Not only is land crucial for livelihood; it is also vital for identity, collective action, and political representation. In fact, land is so important that it often is inseparable from political power (Unruh and Abdul-Jalil 2014). The traditional tenure system in Darfur divides the region in different *Dars* (homelands), and each Dar consists of smaller land units called *Hawakir* (*Hakura* in singular). This system – created during the Fur sultanate that ruled the region from the seventeenth century until the British destroyed it in 1916 – remains important until today. Each *Dar* is normally associated with a major ethnic group but also includes groups from smaller communities. This system favors larger communities over smaller. For example, while the large cattle-herding (*Baggara*) Arab groups in Southern Darfur had their own *Dar*, the smaller camel-herding (*Abbala*) Arab groups (mainly from North and Western Darfur) were left without any *Dar* (Tubiana 2007; Unruh and Abdul-Jalil 2014). This had grave consequences for Darfur's future. In fact, landless Abbala Arab communities largely see their involvement in the war in Darfur as part of a 250-year-old quest for land (Flint and de Waal 2008).

In Darfur, there exist two principal competing narratives over land. The Arab/pastoralist narrative accentuates injustices regarding land that dates back to the Fur sultanate but is ongoing today. The rival sedentary narrative emphasizes that the system of *Dar* and *Hakura* is crucial for the administration of land in Darfur. Furthermore, *Dars* and *Hawakir* constitute crucial parts of the communal memory. This narrative also holds that Arab pastoralists, and the government, attempt to conquer their historical land (Unruh and Abdul-Jalil 2014). When reflecting on these narratives, one should keep in mind that they disguise a lot of complexity. For instance, not all Arab communities are pastoralists, and it exists important non-Arab groups (like the Zaghawa) that primarily are herders. Moreover, some pastoralists see herding as a crucial component of their identity (and perceive their nomadic culture being under threat), but other pastoralists prefer settlement as it would increase opportunities for their children to access education. Land remains critical for both positions, as pastoralism requires grazing pastures and settlement land for cultivation (Flint 2010).

Communal Conflicts in Darfur

During the last decades, Darfur's communities have fought each other fiercely. This constitutes a sharp contrast to a long tradition of relatively tranquil inter-communal relations. In fact, an effective system to settle disputes between Darfur's communities had resulted in a situation where nomads and farmers had managed to coexist in relative peace for centuries (Burr and Collins 2008). In the mid-1980s, however, both farming and herding activities were gradually expanding. At the time, Darfur had experienced significant population growth, and many traditional migratory routes for herders had disappeared. This caused the interactions between pastoralists and agriculturalists to become increasingly contentious (Abdul-Jalil and Unruh 2013; Unruh and Abdul-Jalil 2014).

Furthermore, the Sudanese government introduced policies that manipulated ethnicity in their (and their regional allies) interest (ICG 2004). As part of this strategy, the government took an increasingly partial position in Darfur and favored some groups over others. This bias contributed to intensifying communal conflicts in Darfur. Not only did this partiality increase the grievances among non-favored groups; it also undermined local institutions, most importantly the *Judiya* (a customary system for traditional justice and reconciliation). Traditionally, the government has a facilitator role in *Judiya*, but the current regime has interfered extensively with this system to promote its own interests. The government's intrusion has undermined this crucial institution (Tubiana et al. 2012; Brosché 2014). Together, the increased herder-farmer tensions and the government's exceedingly partial policies deteriorated inter-communal relations in Darfur. Previously, communal conflicts in Darfur had been sporadic and at a low level of violence, but the conflicts that emerged in the late 1980s were persistent and extraordinarily fierce (ICG 2004).

To get an overview of these conflicts, this chapter uses the Uppsala Conflict Data Program's (UCDP) non-state conflict dataset (Sundberg et al. 2012). The table below summaries the violent communal conflicts recorded by UCDP for the 1989–2017 period. The table shows ethnic identification, main livelihood, and active years (for UCDP a conflict is active if it has caused at least 25 fatalities in a calendar year). When interpreting this data, it is important to remember that ethnicity is fluid, livelihood often mixed, and data on number of deaths are often hard to confirm. Hence, the table constitutes a summary, rather than a complete delineation, of violent communal conflicts in Darfur (Table 1).

The table shows that UCDP has recorded 21 communal conflicts in Darfur, causing between 7,300 and 8,500 fatalities, from 1989 to 2017. Given estimations of 300,000 killed in Darfur since 2003, this seems like a low figure. Much of the violence in Darfur, however, are part of other UCDP categories like one-sided violence (deliberate targeting of civilians) and state-based violence (UCDP 2018). In addition, while UCDP only includes direct deaths, i.e., people killed in combat, the 300,000 estimation includes both direct and indirect deaths (such as fatalities from conflict-related diseases and starvation). Two thirds of the conflicts stood between pastoralists group, while one third pitted farmers against herders. Regarding the Arab-African dichotomy, 13 of the 21 conflicts stood between groups that both

Table 1 Violent Communal Conflicts in Darfur, 1989–2017 (coded by UCDP)

Communities	Ethnicity	Main livelihood	Active years	Estimated deaths
Salamat/Beni Halba-Fur	Arab-African	Cattle herders and farmers-farmers	1989	1500
Baggara Arabs-Fur	Arab-African	Cattle herders-farmers	1989, 1990	500–900
Reizegat Abbala-Zaghawa	Arab-African	Camel herders-camel herders	1996, 2017	191
Reizegat, Awlad Rashid, Beni Halba-Masalit	Arab-African	Camel herders-farmers	1995, 1998, 1999	340
Awlad Zeid Arabs-Zaghawa	Arab-African	Camel herders-camel herders	2001	70
Rizeigat Baggara-Maaliya	Arab-Arab	Cattle herders-cattle herders	2002, 2004, 2013, 2014, 2015, 2016, 2017	1093–1214
Hotiya Baggara-Newiba, Mahariba, and Mahamid	Arab-Arab	Cattle herders-camel herders	2005	210–260
Reizegat Baggara-Habbaniya	Arab-Arab	Cattle herders-cattle herders	2006, 2015	348
Reizegat Abbala-Tarjem	Arab-Arab	Camel herders-cattle herders	2007	380
Misseria-Reizegat Abbala	Arab-Arab	Camel herders-camel herders	2008, 2009, 2010, 2012, 2015	760
Maaliya-Zaghawa	Arab-African	Cattle herders-camel herders	2008	40–50
Habbaniya-Falata (and Salamat)	Arab-Arab	Cattle herders-cattle herders	2007, 2008, 2009	230
Beni Halba-Gimir	Arab-Arab	Cattle herders-cattle herders	2013	164–221
Beni Hussein-Reizegat Abbala	Arab-Arab	Cattle herders-camel herders	2013, 2014	387–915
Hamar-Ma'aliya	Arab-Arab	Farmers-cattle herders	2013, 2014	90–94
Misseria-Salamat Baggara	Arab-Arab	Camel herders-cattle herders	2013, 2014, 2017	516–811
Falata-Salamat Baggara	Arab-Arab	Cattle herders-cattle herders	2015, 2016	290
Al-Zayadia-Berti	Arab-African	Camel herders-farmers	2015	127
Masalit-Reizegat Baggara	African-Arab	Farmers-cattle herders	2016	39
Habbaniya-Salamat Baggara	Arab-Arab	Cattle herders-cattle herders	2017	41
Mahadi-Reizegat Abbala	Arab-Arab	Farmers-camel herders	2016	26

identify as Arabs, while 8 conflicts pitted Arabs against Africans. While the data does not include any conflict between two non-Arab groups, there exist tensions also between non-Arab communities, such as between the Fur and the Zaghawa. The Fur alleges that the Zaghawa desires a "Greater Zaghawa" that would oust other groups from vast areas. In contrast, the Zaghawa argues that the Fur unfairly denies their legitimate right to settle on new land (Unruh and Abdul-Jalil 2014). The table also reveals an important shift in regard to whom fighting whom. Before the 2003 rebellion, a clear majority of the conflicts were Arab-African, while most of the conflicts thereafter have stood between Arab groups. The chapter returns to the reason for this shift below.

From Communal Conflicts to Civil War and Ethnic Cleansing

Darfur's first major conflict in modern times was the "Arab-Fur war" of 1987–1989 that pitted the Fur community against numerous Arab groups and killed at least 2,500 Fur and 500 Arabs (Harir 1994; de Waal 2005). While being referred to as a war, it was an exceedingly intense communal conflict in the terminology used in this chapter. The Sudanese government was not neutral in this conflict but strongly favored the Arabs. This partiality caused Daud Bolad, an Islamist from the Fur community that had worked close to the government, to leave the regime and join the SPLM/A rebellion. In December 1991, Daud Bolad led a unit of SPLM/A when it attacked government positions in Darfur. A combined force of regular army and Beni Halba Arabs annihilated the unit and killed Bolad. Following this attack, the government came to perceive the Fur as their main enemy in Darfur and therefore sought to cement its alliances with various Arab tribes (Flint 2007).

A prime example of the government's anti-Fur policy was its decision to split Darfur (that traditionally had been one state) in three states in 1994. The administrative change was politically motivated and sought to weaken the power of the Fur community by dividing their traditional stronghold into three new states (ICG 2004). Previously, the Fur had been a majority group in Darfur, but the government designed the partition, so this community became minorities in all three new states: South Darfur, West Darfur, and North Darfur (Leonardi and Abdul-Jalil 2011). In addition to weaken the Fur's power, the split was motivated by an agenda to promote Arabization, and it empowered Arab groups but decreased the power of non-Arabs. The division of Darfur into three states had grave consequences for Darfur and was "perhaps the most crucial decision" (Burr and Collins 2008: 287) for the disastrous developments that followed. The government's partiality against the Fur and support for the Arabs in several conflicts incited the Fur to start targeting government positions rather than its rival communities (Flint and de Waal 2008).

During the 1990s, two other significant non-Arab groups, Zaghawa and Masalit, also fought fierce conflicts against various Arab communities. The Sudanese government favored the Arab groups also in these conflicts. As a result, also the Zaghawa and Masalit communities came increasingly to perceive the regime in Khartoum as their prime enemy (Tubiana 2007). An illustrative case of such dynamics is the conflict between the Zaghawa and the Awlad Zeid Arabs over an important waterhole in 2001. When the fighting ceased, the Zaghawa discovered that the government had armed their enemies. The Zaghawa's resentment against the government increased further when government soldiers prohibited them from using the waterhole. Following this incident, the Zaghawa came to perceive the government as the main threat to their security. The Masalit community fought a conflict against several Arab groups in mid-1990s. The conflict started when Arab raiders attacked a group of villages around Mejmerie, east of al-Genina in Western Darfur. Although these attacks destroyed numerous villages and the attackers killed many people, the government did nothing to punish the raiders because it sided strongly with these communities. This enraged the Masalit and intensified the conflict (Flint and de Waal 2008). The government's bias was also evident in an administrative adjustment of West Darfur in 1995. This change divided the Masalit's customary homeland in 13 domains, and the government allocated 5 of these to Arabs. This partition is widely perceived as the main trigger for the Masalit-Arab conflict (ICG 2004).

To increase its protection from attacks from various Arab groups, and to strengthen their position against the government that they increasingly saw as the main enemy, the Fur, Zaghawa, and Masalit all formed self-defense forces. In 2001, the Fur and Zaghawa groups joined forces in their struggle against the government and rivaling communities. After being defeated by different Arab communities, the Masalit joined the Fur-Zaghawa alliance. By the early 2000s, this alliance (which first took the name Darfur Liberation Front) constituted a serious military threat to the government. In February 2003, after an attack in which this group had overrun an army outpost, the group declared that it had changed its name to Sudan Liberation Movement/Army (SLM/A). Soon, another Darfurian rebel group, Justice and Equality Movement (JEM), launched a rebellion against the Sudanese government. The roots of the two Darfurian rebel groups were different. While the origin of SLM/A is in the peripheries, JEM came more from the center, and most JEM leaders had held significant positions in Khartoum. In addition, while Khalil Ibrahim (a Zaghawa from Darfur) was the official leader, Hassan al-Turabi (who had been the architect behind the 1989 coup that put al-Bashir in power) was, allegedly, the real founder and leader. The former alliance between al-Bashir and al-Turabi had dissolved, and it is widely believed that al-Turabi, in order to decrease al-Bashir's power, contributed significantly to the creation of JEM (Prunier 2007; Burr and Collins 2008).

The Darfurian rebel groups were, partly due their knowledge about the local terrain, successful on the battlefield in the initial phase of the war. As a response, the regime in Khartoum recruited militias (primarily from landless Arab groups from northern Darfur) that came to be known as *Janjaweed*. To entice recruits, the Sudanese government promised to provide land to the groups that joined the militias. The strong desire for land among these groups meant that such assurances were a fundamental reason for joining these militias (Prunier 2007). In fact, while defeating the rebels was the prime aim of the government, controlling land was the prime purpose of the war for these militias (Flint 2009). Forceful displacement of certain communities was thus not just a consequence of the war but a prime purpose for some of the armed actors (Tubiana 2007). Hence, while non-Arabs in possession of a

Dar constitute the backbone of the resistance movements, landless Arab communities contributed largely to the government's militias. The two main belligerents in the communal conflicts that preceded the war, thus, stood on opposing side in the civil war. Together, the army and the militias implemented a scorched-earth campaign that primarily targeted the Fur, Zaghawa, and Masalit communities and included human rights violations, such as killing of civilians and ethnic cleansing (Brosché and Sundberg 2019). This chapter does not thoroughly assess these atrocities because other studies cover them in detail (c.f. Daly 2007; Prunier 2007).

In 2005, Minni Minawi (chief of staff of SLM/A from the Zaghawa community) challenged Abdul Wahid (SLM/A's chairman from the Fur community) over leadership of SLM/A, and the movement split in two factions (SLM/A-Wahid and SLM/A-Minawi). The two factions fought each other for the first time in November 2005, a battle that caused at least 45 fatalities (Prunier 2007). Six months later, Minni Minawi and the Sudanese government signed a peace agreement called Darfur Peace Agreement (DPA). However, the leaders of the other two main rebel movements, Abdul Wahid (SLM/A-Wahid) and Khalil Ibrahim (JEM), refused to sign the agreement (Brosché and Rothbart, 2013). The focus of DPA was to terminate fighting between Minawi and the government, but the agreement did not address many of the prime problems in Darfur (such as land). Thereby, the agreement failed to acknowledge the complexity of the war and recognizing that the situation in Darfur composed of several interlinked types of conflicts. As a result, rather than leading to peace, the DPA intensified fighting and led to further fragmentation of the opposition movements (Mohammed 2007).

A few years into the government's counterinsurgency, it had resulted in the displacement of millions of Darfurians, primarily from non-Arab communities like the Fur, Zaghawa, and Masalit. This left large areas of fertile land abandoned, and several Arab communities started to fight each other over who should control these areas (ICG 2007, 2015). Control over land is hence the main driver of the shift (indicated in the table above) from communal conflicts primarily standing between Africans and Arabs to mainly be fought between various Arab communities (Brosché and Rothbart 2013). Not only had the relation between various Arab communities shifted starkly; many Arab communities had also changed its relation to the Sudanese government. Although some Arabs remained neutral, and others joined the resistance movements, the regime in Khartoum had good relations with many Arab communities when the Darfurian rebellion started in 2003 (Flint 2010). The government, however, did not keep its promises to allocate land to the communities that had contributed to the militias, which caused extensive bitterness among these groups. Tensions mounted when the rulers in Khartoum, as part of the DPA, declared that they would disarm the Janjaweed. The communities contributing to the militias felt that the government who wanted to scapegoat the Janjaweed to escape its own responsibility (de Waal 2007) had betrayed them. Quite ironically, Musa Hilal – the most notorious *Janjaweed* leader who had receive extensive support from the regime in Khartoum – launched a new rebel group (Sudanese Awakening Revolutionary Council, SARC) in 2014 to fight the Sudanese government (UCDP 2018).

As illustrated in the pages above, Darfur has experienced an intricate web of ethno-communal conflicts for the last decades. In the mid-1980s, communal conflicts, primarily over land and largely pitting Arab groups against non-Arabs, started to become increasingly intense. In these conflicts, the Sudanese government took a partial stance, favoring Arabs over non-Arabs, which was a key motivation for the Darfurian rebellion launched in 2003. The government responded by recruiting the notorious Janjaweed militia, which (together with the army) evicted millions of non-Arabs. Thereafter, various Arab communities started to fight each other to control this land, and later some of these organized in insurgent movements to fight the government because of unmet promises of land. Thus, while some factors (such as the importance of land) remain constant in Darfur's ethno-communal conflicts, who is fighting whom is constantly shifting. This has generated a situation with a plurality of grievances and extensive resentments between many groups, where a peaceful resolution seems elusive.

South Sudan: Ethno-communal Conflicts in The World's Newest Nation

Since December 2013, South Sudan has been shattered by a civil war that has caused tens of thousands of deaths, displaced a third of the population, and created starvation in parts of the country. This war has clear ethno-communal manifestations and sometimes described as a Dinka-Nuer conflict. As in Darfur, however, the crisis in South Sudan is complex and consists of several types of conflicts that together create an intricate situation. Below, this chapter analyzes this devastating situation by probing some of the roots to war and some of its manifestations.

The Painful Path to Independence

In 1983, SPLM/A launched a rebellion in Southern Sudan. The political goal for the movement's leader, John Garang, was "to establish a united socialist democratic Sudan" (Garang 1987) while other elements within the movement sought independence for South Sudan. The SPLM/A took control over several towns in the late 1980s, and the government started to recruit militias, primarily from the Misseriya and Reizegat communities in Darfur and Kordofan, to increase its military power. Promises to land, similar to tactics later used in Darfur, was essential to entice these militias (HRW 2003; Johnson 2006). To counter the SPLM/A insurgency, the Sudanese government extensively used a Machiavellian divide-and-rule tactic, resurrecting the logic of "the enemy of my enemy is my friend," and used ethnic tensions to increase divisions in Southern Sudan (Brosché and Rothbart 2013). John Garang came from Southern Sudan's largest ethnic group, the Dinka, and people from other communities sometimes perceived the SPLM/A as a Dinka movement (Young 2006).

In 1991, two SPLM/A commanders – Riek Machar and Lam Akol, from the Nuer and Shilluk community, respectively – instigated a coup against Garang who they accused of being a dictator of the movement. The coup failed and Machar and Akol launched a new rebel group called SPLM/A-Nasir, which had session of South Sudan as its prime political goal. The Sudanese government saw the mainstream SPLM/A as their main threat and therefore heavily supported the Nasir faction both militarily and economically. While stating that it fought for independence, the SPLM/A-Nasir never clashed against the Sudanese government (UCDP 2018). Instead, the rival SPLM/A factions fought each other fiercely. Actually, in the first half of the 1990s, fighting between these groups killed more people than the war between insurgencies and the government. Both factions carried out human rights violations, including burning of villages, killing of civilians, and forced displacement. While SPLM/A was predominantly a Dinka movement, the Nasir faction recruited primarily from non-Dinka groups, particularly the Nuer. The leaders of these factions fueled the flames of ethnic hatred and intensified civil unrest for their own political ambitions. This accentuated the ethnic dimension of the struggle, and the fighting (as well as atrocities) largely pitted various communities against each other. Although numerous communities were involved in this rebel-rebel fighting, most violence pitted Southern Sudan's two largest ethnic groups, Dinka and Nuer, against each other (Young 2006; LeRiche and Arnold 2012).

In 2002, the two factions reconciled and Machar returned to SPLM/A. This strengthens the movement's military power and changed power balance between the rebels and the regime. At the same time, efforts to end the North-South war had been ongoing for many years without finding a solution. In 2005, however, conditions at the local, national, and international level were more conducive, and the antagonists reached an agreement. A key reason for the Sudanese government to sign the Comprehensive Peace Agreement (CPA) was the enhanced military threat that the united SPLM/A composed (Brosché and Duursma 2018).

The Interim Period (2005–2011)

The CPA meant that Southern Sudan should be an autonomous part of Sudan between 2005 and 2011. The Government of South Sudan ruled this area, and John Garang became the first President of Southern Sudan. After fighting a war for 22 years, however, John Garang died in a helicopter crash only 6 months after signing the CPA. Salva Kiir, a commander in SPLM/A who had fought alongside Garang throughout the war, and been his deputy since 1997, replaced him (LeRiche and Arnold 2012). While Kiir became President, Riek Machar became Vice President. However, this arrangement was not an indication of genuine friendship between the two; instead, Kiir and Machar were wary about each other and competed for influence. In essence, this was a power-sharing agreement that gave the highest position to a Dinka (the largest community) and the second highest position to a Nuer (the second largest community).

At times of its installment, the government of South Sudan faced severe threat from numerous armed groups. Former militias that previously had fought for the regime in Khartoum constituted the strongest challenge. Salva Kiir took on a drastically different strategy than his predecessor to deal with such contenders. While Garang usually fought against his competitor, Kiir tried to incorporate them into the SPLM/A. In this "big tent" policy, leaders of different armed groups received prominent positions in the military (and sometimes government), and the rank and file of these groups were included in the army. On 8 January 2006, many former militias integrated in the SPLM/A structures, when Kiir and Paulino Matip (who controlled many of the former militias) signed the Juba Declaration. Analysts saw this agreement as crucial for the security situation in Southern Sudan (some even held it as more important than the CPA) and hailed it as a big diplomatic victory for Kiir (Young 2007).

Yet, soon it became evident that Kiir's integration strategy also prompted many problems. A core part of this procedure was to give amnesties to leaders and soldiers in the insurgency groups that challenged the regime in Juba. As a result, violence and threat of violence constituted powerful methods for gaining influence and concessions, in the political landscape that followed the signing of the CPA (LeRiche 2014). Sudan and South Sudan expert Alex de Waal has illustratively labeled these insurgencies as "rent-seeking rebellions" in which:

> A commander or a provincial leader can lay claim to a stake of state resources (rents) through a mutiny or rebellion. The government then attacks the leader and his constituency to press him to accept a lower price. After a number of people have been killed, raped, and displaced, and their property looted or destroyed, as an exercise in ascertaining the relative bargaining strengths of the two parties, a deal will be reached. In South Sudan, these cycles have become known as "rent-seeking rebellions". Such conflicts follow a material logic but have ethnic manifestations. (de Waal 2014; De Waal 2014: 350)

Therefore, while the "big tent" policy successfully dealt with some of the government's threats, this policy also encouraged armed rebellion as the government regularly rewarded, rather than punished, people who revolted against the regime. In addition, this policy was exceedingly expensive and created a deeply divided army (Brosché and Höglund 2016).

When the CPA was signed, it was widely believed that fighting between Juba and Khartoum would soon restart. Yet, while there were some clashes between the former belligerents close to the contested border, the north-south war did not restart. This, however, did not mean that armed conflict ended in Southern Sudan. Instead, a few, relatively limited, insurgencies challenged the regime in Juba, and numerous communal conflicts caused severe problems in the region. Various cattle-herding communities (like the Dinka, Nuer, Shilluk, and Murle) primarily inhabit the northern part of Southern Sudan, and communal conflicts largely stood between different pastoralist groups. Some of the conflicts were very intense. The Lou Nuer-Murle conflict, for example, resulted in more than 1,000 fatalities in 2009 alone (UCDP 2018). Competition over land and cattle constitutes important components of these conflicts. Another crucial aspect of these conflicts is politics. Indeed, both local and central elites have fanned inter-ethnic violence to increase their influence. These communal conflicts are furthermore often highly influenced by governmental decision. Uneven disarmament, where the regime prioritizes to take the weapons from the communities seen as most anti-government, has, for instance, spurred several of Southern Sudan's communal conflicts (Brosché 2014).

From Peaceful Independence to Full-Fledged Civil War

As stipulated in the CPA, Southern Sudan held a referendum on 9 January 2011. Close to 99% voted for independence, and the Republic of South Sudan was born 6 months later, 9 July 2011. The transition to independence was relatively peaceful, especially in relation to what many analysts anticipated at the time, and armed conflicts during South Sudan's two and a half first years as an independent nation resembled the situation during the interim period. Thus, insurgents challenged the regime and some intense communal conflicts occurred. While these various conflicts caused death and devastation, the magnitude of these conflicts was relatively minor in relation to what should follow in December 2013 (UCDP 2018).

When John Garang died, his vision of a "New Sudan" also died, and almost all South Sudanese aspired independence. This shared desire for independence created some unity, and the rivalry between various elites was less strong until independence was secured. In fact, a "remarkable display of unity by southern Sudanese of all tribes and political persuasions" characterized the period preceding the referendum (Young 2012: 291). Yet, with independence secured, long-standing power struggles between different political leaders intensified. Positioning within the SPLM ahead of elections scheduled for 2015 (later postponed) was particularly important as this party completely dominates South Sudanese politics. In fact, SPLM's position means that the leader of the party is almost certain to win elections. In March 2013, Riek Machar declared that he intended to challenge Salva Kiir over the leadership of SPLM at a convention supposed to take place 2 months later. Yet, Kiir canceled this gathering and many other important meetings (ICG 2014).

To maintain his power, Kiir took a drastic move in July 2013 and sacked the entire government. When Kiir reinstalled the government, he had replaced people who he perceived as threats with persons he perceived as more loyal. Yet, the challenges against Kiir continued and intensified. On 6 December 2013, many of the people who had been fired from the government held a press conference in Juba where they accused Kiir of "dictatorial tendencies" and outlined a political program that challenged the incumbent President (Sudan Tribune 6 December 2013). The group took the name SPLM/A-In Opposition (SPLM/A-IO). While Riek Machar led this group, it also included prominent politicians from numerous other communities (including Dinka), and this broad coalition constituted an extensive threat to Kiir. To curtail this threat, Kiir removed some of his critics at a SPLM/A meeting on 14 December. Several officials boycott the second day of the meeting in protest to Kiir's actions (ICG 2014; Small Arms Survey 2014).

On the evening of 15 December 2013, fighting erupted within the South Sudan's Presidential Guard where one faction (primarily Dinka) which supported President Kiir fought against another faction (primarily Nuer) that supported Vice President Machar.

The following day, Kiir announced on state television that he successfully had put down a coup attempt, led by Riek Machar (Johnson 2014). Machar denied these accusations, and it is widely believed that there was no coup attempt but that efforts by Dinka presidential guards to disarm their Nuer counterpart sparked the fighting (ICG 2014). More important than the details about what generated the combat is to understand that the tensions between Kiir and Machar had, during the preceding 9 months, escalated to a level where largely any hostile event could ignite clashes. The fighting spread quickly, first to different parts of Juba but later to other areas of South Sudan, and were very intense. A core reason for how quickly things spiraled out of control was that the South Sudanese army split, with about half of it (primarily Nuer) joining the SPLM/A-IO and the rest staying with the government. In fact, "within two days the whole edifice of government, party, and army was blown apart. The 2006 Juba Agreement, the basis of internal stability in South Sudan, was dead" (de Waal 2014: 366).

In the days that followed the alleged coup, government soldiers killed hundreds of Nuer civilians in Juba (HRW 2016). This sparked outrage in the Nuer community, and many Dinka were killed in revenge attacks. The government's atrocities also became a core motivation for Nuer to join the anti-government forces. For the Nuer, the "Juba Massacre" constitutes a significant trauma, and many felt targeted by genocidal tactics (Young 2016). Hence, much of the fighting clearly had an ethnic dimension, with Dinka-Nuer being the main dividing line, and many people were targeted because of their ethnicity.

Yet, to label this as a Dinka-Nuer war leaves out crucial dimensions of the conflict. First, rather than being driven by ethnic animosities, the 2013 war followed the logic of rent-seeking rebellions described above. Second, such description omits an institutional perspective. Not only was weak institutionalization of important organizations (like the army, government, and party) pivotal for the dynamics in the war; South Sudan's institutional structures were also too weak to handle political struggles peacefully. Third, throughout the war, there have been Dinka elements fighting with the opposition and Nuer elements battling on the government's side. Fourth, some of the most intense fighting in the war has pitted Nuer against other Nuer. Fifth, the war has taken place in almost all parts of South Sudan and thereby influenced all the country's communities. Not only have other communities been victimized; they have also fought on both sides of the war and in some cases formed their own insurgencies.

Hence, the war in South Sudan resembles the one in Darfur with numerous, intertwined types of conflict taking place at the same time. This creates a complex situation that becomes exceedingly difficult to resolve. If one type of conflict is ripe for resolution, another might not be, and since the conflict types influence each other, this might derail the potentials for solving also the conflict that was ripe.

Conclusions

This chapter deals with ethno-communal conflicts in Sudan and South Sudan. A core finding from the chapter is that such conflicts can manifest in various forms and that the different types of conflict are intertwined. This has ramifications for policy.

If connections between different types of collective violence are overlooked, efforts to manage and prevent conflicts might be futile. The Darfur Peace Agreement (DPA) exemplifies how a focus on one type of conflict – instead of acknowledging that the situation consisted of several parallel but interlinked types of conflict – can intensify fighting rather than be a path to peace. In order to grasp this complexity, outside actors need to make greater efforts to increase the understanding of the local dynamics in general and the effects of international interventions on this dynamics in particular. If not, there is a risk that such efforts do more harm than good.

Another central finding revealed by this study is the key role various elites often play in fermenting ethno-communal conflicts. Hence, while conflicts in Sudan and South Sudan often have ethnic manifestations, they are often spurred by various elites' that – in their aspiration to increase their political and economic power –use ethnic divisions. South Sudan's most recent civil war constitute as a prime example. Although much of the fighting has followed ethnic lines, the prime causes to the war were a deepening crisis of governance in South Sudan and an escalating power struggle between Salva Kiir and Riek Machar.

References

Abdul-Jalil M, Unruh JD (2013) Land rights under stress in Darfur: a volatile dynamic of the conflict. War Soc 32:156–181

Brosché J (2014) Masters of war – the role of elites in Sudan's communal conflicts. Uppsala University Press, Uppsala

Brosché J, Höglund K (2016) Crisis of governance in South Sudan: electoral politics in the World's newest nation. J Mod Afr Stud 54:67–90

Brosché J, Duursma A (2018) Hurdles to peace: a level-of-analysis approach to resolving Sudan's civil wars. Third World Q 39:560–576

Brosché J, Rothbart D (2013) Violent conflict and peacebuilding: the continuing crises in Darfur. Routledge, London

Brosché J, Sundberg R (2019) This land is whose land? ? 'Sons of the soil' conflicts in Darfur. In: Côté I, Mitchell M, Toft M (eds) People changing places: new perspectives on demography, conflict and the state. Routledge, New York

Burr MJ, Robert Collins O (2008) Darfur: the long road to disaster. Markus Wiener Publisher, Princeton

Daly MW (2007) Darfur's sorrow a history of destruction and genocide. Cambridge University Press, Cambridge

de Waal A (2007) Sudan: the turbulent state. In: De Waal A (ed) War in Darfur and the search for peace. Global Equity Initiative, Harvard University and Justice Africa, Cambridge, MA

Deng FM (1995) War of visions conflicts of identities in the Sudan. The Brookings Institution, Harrisonburg

el-Din K (2007) Islam and Islamism in Darfur. In: De Waal A (ed) War in Darfur and the search for peace. Global Equity Initiative Harvard University and Justice Africa, Cambridge, MA

El-Tom OA (2009) Darfur people: too black for the Arab-Islamic project of Sudan. In: Hassan SM, Ray CE (eds) Darfur and the Crisis of governance in Sudan: a critical reader. Cornell University Press, Ithaca

Flint J (2007) Darfur'S armed movements. In: De Waal A (ed) War in Darfur and the search for peace. Global Equity Initiative Harvard University and Justice Africa, Cambridge, MA

Flint J (2009) Beyond 'Janjaweed': understanding the militias of Darfur. Small Arms Survey, Geneva

Flint J (2010) The other war: inter-Arab conflict in Darfur. Small Arms Survey, Geneva
Flint J, de Waal A (2008) Darfur – a new history of a long war. International African Institute, the Royal African Society and Social Science Research Council, London
Garang J (1987) John Garang speaks. KPI Limited, London
Harir S (1994) "Arab Belt" versus "African Belt" ethno-political conflict in Dar Fur and the regional cultural factors. In: Harir S, Tvedt T (eds) Short-cut to decay the case of the Sudan. Nordic Africa Institute, Uppsala
Hassan SM (2009) Naming the conflict: Darfur and the crisis of governance in Sudan. In: Hassan SM, Ray CE (eds) Darfur and the crisis of governance in Sudan: a critical reader. Cornell University, Ithaca
HRW, (Human Rights Watch) (2003) Sudan, oil, and human rights. Human Rights Watch, New York
HRW, (Human Rights Watch) (2016) South Sudan: ethnic targeting, widespread killings. Human Rights Watch, New York
ICG, (International Crisis Group) (2004) Darfur rising: Sudan's new crisis. International Crisis Group, Brussels
ICG, (International Crisis Group) (2007) Darfur'S new security reality. International Crisis Group, Brussels
ICG, (International Crisis Group) (2014) South Sudan: a civil war by any other name. International Crisis Group, Brussels
ICG, (International Crisis Group) (2015) The chaos in Darfur. International Crisis Group, Brussels
Johnson DH (2006) The root causes of Sudan's civil war, African Issues. Indiana University Press, Bloomington
Johnson DH (2014) Briefing: the crisis in South Sudan. Afr Aff 113:300–309
Jok MJ (2007) Sudan: race, religion and violence. Oneworld, Oxford
Leonardi C, Abdul-Jalil M (2011) Traditional authority, local government & justice. In: Ryle J, Willis J, Baldo S, Jok MJ (eds) The Sudan handbook. James Currey, Suffolk
LeRiche M (2014) South Sudan: not just another war and another peace in Africa. https://africanarguments.org/2014/01/28/south-sudan-not-just-another-war-and-another-peace-in-africa-by-matthew-le-riche/. Accessed 13 Sept 2018
LeRiche M, Arnold M (2012) South Sudan from revolution to independence. Hurst, London
Mamdani M (2009) Saviors and survivors: darfur, politics, and the war on terror. Pantheon Books, New York
Mohamed AA (2007) The comprehensive peace agreement and Darfur. In: De Waal A (ed) War in Darfur and the search for peace. Global Equity Initiative Harvard University and Justice Africa, Cambridge, MA
Prunier G (2007) Darfur the ambiguous genocide. Cornell University Press, Ithaca
Rolandsen HØ, Daly MW (2016) A history of south Sudan: from slavery to independence. Cambridge University Press, Cambridge, UK
Small Arms Survey (2014) The Splm-in-opposition. Small Arms Survey, Geneva
Sørbø GM, Ahmed AGM (2013) Introduction. In: Sørbø GM, Ahmed AGM (eds) Sudan divided continuing conflict in a contested state. Palgrave Macmillan, New York
Sundberg R, Eck K, Kreutz J (2012) Fighting without the state: introducing the Ucdp non-state conflict dataset. J Peace Res 49:503–516
Temin J, Murphy T (2011) Toward a new republic of Sudan. United States Institute of Peace, Washington, DC
Thomas E (2009) Against the gathering storm – securing Sudan's comprehensive peace agreement. Royal Institute of International Affairs Chatham House, London
Thomas E (2015) South Sudan: a slow liberation. Zed Books, London
Tubiana J (2007) Darfur; a war for land? In: De Waal A (ed) War in Darfur and the search for peace. Global Equity Initiative Harvard University and Justice Africa, Cambridge, MA
Tubiana J, Tanner V, Abdul-Jalil M (2012) Traditional Authorities' peacemaking role in Darfur. United States Institute of Peace, Washington, DC

UCDP (2018) Ucdp conflict encyclopedia. Uppsala University, Department of Peace and Conflict Research

UN News (2018) South Sudan peace deal a 'big step forward': Un Mission Chief. https://news.un.org/en/story/2018/08/1016422. Accessed 3 Sept 2018

Unruh JD, Abdul-Jalil M (2014) Constituencies of conflict and opportunity: land rights, narratives and collective action in Darfur. Polit Geogr 24:104–116

Waal d (2005) Who are the Darfurians? Arab and African identities, violence and external engagement. Afr Aff 104:181–205

Waal d (2014) When Kleptocracy becomes insolvent: brute causes of the civil war in south Sudan. Afr Aff 113:347–369

Young J (2006) The South Sudan Defence forces in the wake of the juba declaration. Small Arms Survey, Geneva

Young J (2007) Emerging North–South tensions and prospects for a return to war. Small Arms Survey, Geneva

Young J (2012) The fate of sudan: the origins and consequences of a flawed peace process, zed books, London

Young J (2016) Popular struggles and Elite Co-optation: the nuer white army in South Sudan's civil war, Small Arms Survey, Geneva

Patterns and Drivers of Communal Conflict in Kenya

38

Emma Elfversson

Contents

Introduction 676
Dynamics and Drivers of Communal Conflict in Kenya 678
  Electoral Politics 680
  Cattle Raiding 683
  Local Resources 685
  Boundaries and Local Authority 686
Addressing Communal Conflicts: Responses by State and Non-state Actors 687
Devolution: Diffusing Macro-conflict but Intensifying Local Conflict? 689
Conclusion 691
Cross-References 691
References 691

Abstract

This chapter analyzes patterns of communal conflict – i.e., violent conflicts between non-state groups which are organized based on communal identities – in Kenya. The politicized nature of ethnicity in Kenya, and the fact that both elections and land tenure are closely associated with ethnic identity, are highlighted as key factors explaining the prevalence of violent communal conflict. After discussing the main patterns of conflict since 1989, the chapter goes on to identify four main drivers of conflict: electoral politics, cattle raiding, local resources, and boundaries and local authority. The specific dynamics at play in different conflicts vary, and empirical examples illustrate how the precise way that different conflict drivers interact is different from case to case. The chapter also discusses different strategies by state and non-state actors to address and resolve communal conflicts and how devolution – the decentralization of significant power to the local level under the 2010 constitution – has affected communal conflicts. As the discussion of devolution

E. Elfversson (✉)
Department of Peace and Conflict Research, Uppsala University, Uppsala, Sweden
e-mail: emma.elfversson@pcr.uu.se

© The Author(s), under exclusive license to Springer Nature Singapore Pte Ltd. 2019   675
S. Ratuva (ed.), *The Palgrave Handbook of Ethnicity*,
https://doi.org/10.1007/978-981-13-2898-5_50

illustrates, a major point is that while communal conflicts in general should be seen against the background of a state and a political culture where ethnicity is strongly politicized, the impact of national-level political dynamics on communal conflicts will vary from case to case.

Keywords
Communal conflict · Kenya · Electoral violence · Land conflict · Pastoralist conflict · Ethnic politics · Conflict management · Devolution

Introduction

Unlike most of its East African neighbors, Kenya has since independence not experienced large-scale rebellion or civil war. However, it has experienced a high number of more localized ethnic conflicts which at times have resulted in high death tolls (UCDP 2018; Kimenyi and Ndung'u 2005). Since 1989, by very conservative estimates, such conflicts have directly killed over 4000 Kenyan citizens. They have also caused the internal displacement of thousands of people and large-scale disruptions to local livelihoods. For example, in Tana River County in eastern Kenya, two waves of violence – in 2001 and 2012 – between the Pokomo and the Orma and Wardei led to hundreds of deaths, the destruction of homes and villages, the displacement of thousands of people, and large-scale disruption of education and economic activities (Kirchner 2013; Martin 2012). The conflict is situated in a largely arid area, where the communities – who are mainly sedentary farmers, and pastoralists, respectively – are dependent on the river for their livelihoods. In Mount Elgon, which is located in western Kenya near the border of Uganda, conflict between local communities over the legitimate claim to local land and authority has pitted Sabaot against Luhya and more recently Sabaot subgroups against each other following controversy over government resettlement schemes. The latter wave of conflict gave rise to the militia Sabaot Land Defense Force (SLDF) which terrorized local citizens and was eventually quashed by a heavy-handed military intervention (Lynch 2011b).

This chapter deals specifically with this subcategory of ethnic violence which is termed communal conflicts and where the government and state apparatus are not directly (but often indirectly) involved. There is a large body of research on how the Kenyan state has, under different regimes, engaged in violence and repression against its citizens (see, for instance, Hassan 2017; Boone 2011; Klopp and Zuern 2007; Murunga 2004). In contrast, in the case of communal conflict, the primary conflict stands between two non-state groups which are organized based on communal identities and which use lethal violence to gain control over some disputed and perceived indivisible resource, such as a piece of land or local political power. The fact that the primary parties in the conflict are non-state groups implies that neither side controls the state and armed forces. In turn, state actors and agencies may actively or passively support one side in the conflict and/or intervene to end the violence and assist in promoting a negotiated solution.

A communal conflict is distinguished by the fact that mobilization, and the lines of confrontation, are based on communal identification, often ethnic identities. While rebel groups and state militias often organize along similar identity lines, the groups involved in communal conflicts are not formally organized in the same way as rebel groups – which have standing armies and a hierarchical command structure – and also tend to feature more sporadic outbursts of violence as compared to civil wars or conflicts between rivalling rebel groups. Communal identity is here understood as subjective group identification based on, for instance, a common history, culture, or core values. Although identities are fluid and constructed and not inherently conflictual, under certain circumstances, they become more salient and can be activated for conflict mobilization (Klaus and Mitchell 2015; Svensson 2013). Because communal identity is socially constructed, it may change over time, and the dimension of identity that is emphasized for mobilization depends on the context. For instance, it may be ethnicity, religious affiliation, length of residence (i.e., "indigenes vs. settlers"), or livelihood (Brosché and Elfversson 2012).

In Kenya, political developments during colonial rule and following independence have meant that ethnic identity is often activated and mobilized in conflict over resources and political power (Branch et al. 2010; Lynch 2011a; Oucho 2002; see also Mati in this volume). Importantly, land tenure has remained closely connected to communal identity, and political parties have largely formed and mobilized along ethnic lines (Elischer 2010; Kimenyi and Ndung'u 2005; Omolo 2002). This form of ethnic politics may contribute to different forms of organized violence, including civil war, secessionism, and ethnic cleansing, but in Kenya, the main violent manifestations have been in the form of communal conflict. Under colonial rule, the British favored certain ethnic communities and deliberately sought to prevent the emergence of broad-based political movements (Branch et al. 2010). After independence in 1963, Jomo Kenyatta, the country's first president, took steps to centralize power in the hands of himself and a small elite, mainly from his own ethnic group, the Kikuyu. Kenyatta and his allies were also able to claim much of the best land around the country, a fact that still underlies bitter conflicts in the country. Subsequent political elites have continued to favor mainly their own ethnic community; land and resources have remained heavily concentrated in the hands of a few, and politics continues to be a very ethnic affair. Kenya has – depending on who you ask – 42–44 ethnic groups or "tribes," many of which comprise culturally distinct subgroups, and none of these groups makes up more than around 20% of the country's population. This has been noted as one potential explanation that ethnic politics has not resulted in a broad-based rebellion against the state (Kimenyi and Ndung'u 2005). Meanwhile, it has also meant that election politics have often been strongly characterized by a "game of numbers" whereby elite politicians enter short-lived alliances to create a sufficient electoral support (Lynch 2006; Elischer 2010).

This chapter begins by giving an overview of patterns of violent communal conflict in Kenya since 1989. It proceeds to discuss the main drivers of conflict and illustrates these by discussing a few specific conflicts in more depth. Next, different strategies by state and non-state actors to address and resolve conflicts are discussed. Finally, the chapter discusses how devolution – the decentralization of significant power to the local level, introduced under Kenya's 2010 constitution – affects communal conflicts.

Dynamics and Drivers of Communal Conflict in Kenya

Due to the politicized nature of ethnicity in Kenya, communal conflicts have tended to be particularly frequent and intense in connection to national elections. Figure 1 below illustrates overall patterns of violence since 1989, using the data from the Uppsala Conflict Data Program (UCDP), which systematically collects information about different forms of organized violence, including communal conflict. The figure gives an overview of the number of conflicts each year that reached an intensity level of at least 25 deaths (left-hand axis/gray line) and the total number of fatalities resulting from these conflicts (right-hand axis/dotted line), over time. In addition to these high-intensity conflicts, there are many conflicts each year that turn violent but result in fewer casualties. In Fig. 1, there are three notable peaks in terms of fatalities, and these coincide with the 1992, 1997, and 2007 elections. There are several reasons that election times often become particularly violent. First, politicians may call on ethnic identities and land-related grievances to mobilize support and often whip up animosities against other communities (Boone 2011; Klaus and Mitchell 2015; Kurgat 2012). Furthermore, the outcome of elections at the local level often has implications for which community has access to local resources and patrimonial networks (Omotola 2010; Mieth 2012). This means that in addition to conflicts that are directly election related (i.e., where violence is directed at affecting the election outcome (Höglund 2009)), conflicts

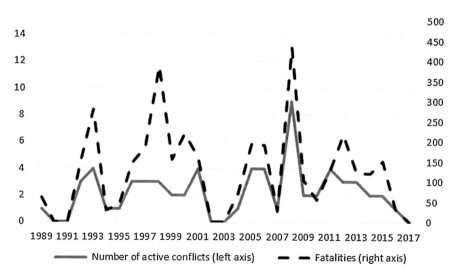

Fig. 1 Active communal conflicts and fatalities in Kenya, 1989–2017. (Based on UCDP Non-State Conflict Dataset v 18.1 Sundberg et al. 2012)

revolving around other issues may also become intensified by the electoral dynamics. A peak in the number of active conflicts (as well as in total fatalities) can be seen in 2008 (in the aftermath of the 2007 elections): that year, there were nine conflicts that resulted in at least 25 deaths. It can also be noted that there were no conflicts of this intensity in 2002–2003, coinciding with the rise and electoral triumph of the National Alliance of Rainbow Coalition (NARC) which, at least at that point, brought together key representatives from all major ethnic groups in Kenya (Elischer 2010).

Communal conflict has affected most regions of Kenya, but since 1989, the most intense conflicts have particularly been concentrated in the Rift Valley and in the northeast and on the coast. Figure 2 below illustrates the locations of major communal violence events – that is, incidents of lethal violence that form part of a violent communal conflict – since 1989. It should be noted that the figure only includes

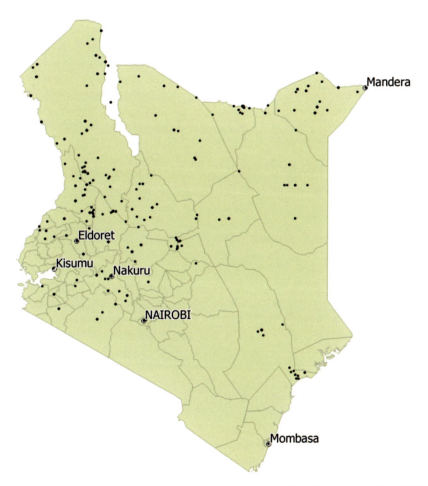

Fig. 2 Locations of major communal violence events, Kenya, 1989–2017. Map made in QGIS. (Based on UCDP Georeferenced Events Dataset v 18.1 (Sundberg and Melander 2013))

events in conflicts which at some point crossed the threshold of 25 deaths in a year. As the map illustrates, communal violence has also taken place in the major cities, including the capital Nairobi.

On a general level, most communal conflicts in Kenya can be understood against the background of a political history that has rendered ethnic identity politically salient and important in relation to access to resources and opportunities. Other prominent underlying causes include socioeconomic inequality, marginalization, resource scarcity, and the weakening of customary institutions that used to manage conflicts between neighboring communities. However, there is also a lot of variation in terms of the specific issues that communities fight over, and different regions and localities face different combinations of factors contributing to conflict. For instance, in the Rift Valley, many conflicts are related to long-standing grievances over land and oftentimes overlapping land claims. Much of this violence has pitted groups with claims to indigeneity – notably, Kalenjin and Maasai – against ethnic groups who have more recently settled in the area, partly aided by political favoritism – notably Kikuyu and Kisii (Lynch 2011a; Anderson and Lochery 2008). Whereas active state orchestration has fueled communal violence in this region (cf. Boone 2011), in other areas, conflict has erupted partly due to an absence of state governance and security provision. In the north rift and northeast Kenya, poor security provision in conjunction with porous borders and conflict in neighboring states have created a security vacuum wherein conflicts relating to cattle raids and territorial control have escalated to high levels (Mkutu 2008; Kumssa et al. 2009; Eaton 2012). Table 1 presents an overview of all communal conflicts in Kenya that have been recorded by the UCDP since 1989. Again, it should be noted that the figures are conservative and that the table does not capture the totality of intercommunal violence in Kenya but only the most intense conflicts.

Given the different underlying and proximate causes of communal conflicts, they are fought over different issues, which in turn affect the type of strategies needed to manage and resolve them. Broadly, four main drivers of communal conflict can be observed in Kenya: electoral politics, cattle raiding, local resources, and boundaries and local authority. Oftentimes, several different drivers overlap; for instance, pastoralist conflicts often feature cattle raiding but also revolve around natural resources and local boundaries. In turn, while these drivers – as well as the overall political dimension emphasized above – often overlap, there is variation in which drivers coexist and how. Consequently, the precise dynamics in each case of communal conflict are distinct and require locally well-anchored solutions.

Electoral Politics

Many of Kenya's communal conflicts have been directly related to national and local elections. In particular, election-related communal violence became prominent under President Daniel arap Moi. Ascending to power after Kenyatta's death, Moi, who belongs to the Kalenjin community, continued to centralize power and turned Kenya into an authoritarian and corrupt one-party state. In the 1990s, Moi was under intense

Table 1 List of communal conflicts in Kenya, 1989–2017

Communities	Main locations of violence	Active years (with at least 25 fatalities)	Estimated total deaths
Dassanetch – Nyangatom, Toposa	North rift	1989	60
Kalenjin – Kikuyu	Rift Valley, Nyanza	1992–1994, 1998, 2008	327
Kalenjin – Luhya	Uasin Gishu, Bungoma	1992–1993	96
Kalenjin – Kisii, Luo	Rift Valley, Nyanza	1992	40
Kikuyu – Maasai	Nakuru, Narok	1993	102
Nyangatom – Turkana	Turkana; South Omo (Ethiopia)	1993	246
Pokot – Turkana	Turkana, West Pokot, Baringo	1995, 1999, 2005–2006, 2008, 2010, 2013–2015	630
Pokot, Samburu – Turkana	Samburu	1996	51
Samburu – Turkana	Samburu, Laikipia, Isiolo	1996, 2015	211
Samburu – Somali	Isiolo	1996	49
Dassanetch – Gabra	Marsabit; South Omo (Ethiopia)	1997	112
Kisii – Maasai	Trans Mara, Kisii	1997	77
Dassanetch – Turkana	Turkana, South Omo (Ethiopia)	1997, 2000, 2005, 2009, 2011	413
Nandi – Pokot	Trans Nzoia	1998	35
Borana – Degodia	Wajir; Somali state (Ethiopia)	1998	357
Jie – Turkana	Turkana; Jie (Uganda)	1999, 2008	101
Ajuran – Garre	Wajir, Moyale	2000	78
Borana – Samburu	Isiolo	2001	70
Marakwet – Pokot	Kerio valley	2001, 2016	115
Orma, Wardei – Pokomo	Tana Delta	2001	66
Rer Ahmad – Hawarsame Rer Hasan and Habar Ya'qub	Mandera; Belet Hawa (Somalia)	2004	69
Borana – Gabra	Marsabit, Moyale; Oromiya (Ethiopia)	2005–2007, 2012	244
Garre – Murule	Mandera	2005, 2008	94
Nyangatom, Toposa – Turkana	Turkana	2006	58
Pokot – Samburu	Samburu, Laikipia	2006, 2009	76
Kalenjin – Kisii	Rift Valley	2008	81
Kikuyu – Luo	Nairobi, Kisumu, Nakuru	2008	61

(continued)

Table 1 (continued)

Communities	Main locations of violence	Active years (with at least 25 fatalities)	Estimated total deaths
Toposa – Turkana	Turkana; Equatoria (Sudan)	2008. 2011	339
Borana – Turkana	Isiolo	2011	31
Orma – Pokomo	Tana Delta	2012	194
Degodia – Garre	Mandera, Wajir	2012–2014	216
Borana – Burji, Gabra	Moyale	2013	55

Based on UCDP Non-State Conflict Dataset v 18.1 (Sundberg et al. 2012) and UCDP Georeferenced Events Dataset v 18.1 (Sundberg and Melander 2013)

international and domestic pressure to liberalize and democratize the country, and opposition movements became stronger (Murunga and Nasong'o 2007). Moi tried to prevent these developments by fueling ethnic violence, both as a way to repress the opposition and to underline his claim that democracy would plunge Kenya into ethnic civil war (Klopp 2001). Around the first multiparty elections, held in 1992, there were clashes mainly in the Rift Valley between Kalenjin and Maasai militias and other politically relevant ethnic groups – Kikuyu, Kisii, Luo, and Luhya. Another wave of election-related communal violence followed in connection to the 1997 elections, this time also including clashes between "indigenous" groups and "newcomers" on the coast (Kimenyi and Ndung'u 2005).

The election-related communal conflicts in the 1990s were fueled by a political history and rhetoric that created a perception of ethnic voting as the way to ensure a stake in national and local resources and more directly by political agents orchestrating ethnic violence (Kimenyi and Ndung'u 2005; Klopp 2001; Elischer 2010; Omolo 2002). For instance, Moi and his allies convinced the Kalenjin community – which is in turn made up by a number of culturally distinct subgroups with varying interests in relation to the then-ruling elite – that an opposition victory would threaten Kalenjin interests including access to land and would lead to domination by other ethnic communities. In this context, politicians manipulated grievances related to land which can be traced back to colonial times and to perceived unjust land allocations under Kenyatta, and calls for *majimboism* – strengthened regionalism, commonly understood to correlate with ethnic "homelands" – were commonly heard at political rallies in the Rift Valley (Lynch 2011a).

Large-scale election-related communal violence also broke out in the aftermath of the 2007 elections. At this point, the presidential race stood between incumbent Mwai Kibaki (a Kikuyu) and opposition leader Raila Odinga (a Luo). Again, the Rift Valley was one of the main arenas of violence, but there were also intense clashes in Nairobi and sporadic violence in western Kenya and on the coast. The violence was preceded by rumors of electoral malpractices, and when the election results were announced on 29 December – with a victory for the incumbent – opposition supporters around the country believed the results were fraudulent and that they had been cheated of "their turn to eat" (a phrase referring to the notion that only those in power get a share of the country's resources). Importantly, the Luo are one of Kenya's largest ethnic groups but have largely been excluded from the top echelons of power (de Smedt 2009; Lynch 2006). At the same time, many Kalenjin in the Rift Valley hoped that an opposition victory would decrease the influence of the Kikuyu in their region and that their access to land would increase (Anderson and Lochery 2008).

When the results from the election started to circle, Kalenjin and Luo militias in Rift Valley and western Kenya started to attack Kikuyu, seeking to drive them away from local areas and to take over land and businesses by force. Kikuyu groups in turn also organized themselves and fought back. These patterns were also seen in the informal settlements in Nairobi, prominently Kibera, which was Odinga's main political base and where Luo "tenants" turned against "landlords" from Kikuyu and other communities (for an in-depth account of the dynamics in Kibera, see de Smedt 2009). Both in the Rift Valley and in Nairobi, ethnic militias involved in the violence were paid and organized by different local politicians as well as different local businessmen (Waki 2008). Waves of violence continued for several weeks, ending only after a national-level power sharing arrangement was negotiated under high international pressure, whereby Odinga was given a post as prime minister and a process to reform the constitution was set in motion (cf. Mati 2013).

Cattle Raiding

Some of the most violent communal conflicts in Kenya in recent decades have involved pastoralist communities that have attacked each other and raided cattle. Such conflicts have a long history and are rooted in pastoralist customs, where cattle raids have filled a dual function as a rite of passage as well as restocking herds or acquiring bridewealth. However, a focus only on the cattle-raiding dynamics underplays the political dimension of these conflicts, and a portrayal of violence as "tribal" and "traditional" has at times been an active strategy by authorities to downplay its importance and its connection to local and national politics (Greiner 2013; Okumu et al. 2017; Schilling et al. 2015). By implying that pastoralist livelihoods are inherently violent and conflictual, state authorities can simultaneously downplay their own failure to prevent or address these conflicts and further underline the general marginalization and lack of accommodation of groups whose livelihoods do not easily fall in line with national agendas for development. Generally speaking, the development of the Kenyan state has weakened customary pastoralist institutions and decreased the availability of pastoral land but has to a very limited degree provided strong state institutions and alternative livelihood opportunities.

When taking a historical view of these conflicts, there is broad consensus that cattle raids have become increasingly violent over the past half century and that the high level of armament among the involved communities have generated an arm race dynamic that further compounds insecurity (Mkutu 2008; Okumu et al. 2017). These conflicts take place in areas where the state's presence is very limited and security poorly enforced, leading to self-defensive armament and preemptive violence; these dynamics in turn have been fueled by the inflow of small arms and light weapons (SALW) from war-affected neighboring countries (Mkutu 2008; Eaton 2012).

A further factor contributing to intensified violence is the fact that raiding has become "commercialized"; whereas cattle were traditionally only raided for family or community needs, they are now quickly transported out of the area and sold on the black market. Finally, while raiding for a long time was largely detached from conflicts over land and boundaries – a function of the imposition of fixed local borders during colonial rule – more recently these conflicts have also gained a territorial dimension, and as such also become more politicized, as local political elites may use the violence to seek to renegotiate administrative boundaries (Greiner 2013).

One notable example where cattle raiding has played a major part is the conflict between the Pokot and Turkana, two communities that inhabit neighboring areas in northwest Kenya (the Pokot, who are a Kalenjin subgroup, mainly inhabit Baringo and West Pokot Counties, and the Turkana dominate Turkana County). Both are pastoralist, seminomadic groups and move around with their cattle across vast arid lands, which have for long been at the periphery of the Kenyan state-building project and largely neglected in terms of development and infrastructure. Security provision is sparse and largely made up of the paramilitary General Service Unit (GSU) and police reservists or "home guards" (Mkutu 2008). The relative weakness and inefficiency of state security provision have contributed to create a local security dilemma and concomitant arm race, whereby the groups have an incentive to arm themselves for defensive purposes and at times to make preemptive attacks when the enemy is relatively weak. At times, the government has sought to disarm raiders in order to decrease violence, but when such campaigns have been conducted in an uneven fashion, it has instead contributed to more violence by upsetting the local power balance (Lind 2018).

The Pokot-Turkana conflict has experienced violent and peaceful phases over a very long time, with the most recent wave of conflict beginning in the mid-1990s. At that point, the conflict gained a territorial dimension as the Turkana tried to occupy a piece of territory belonging to the Pokot (Greiner 2013). Subsequent raids have at times laid siege to villages or been aimed at capturing water holes, in addition to cattle raiding. Since 1995, violent clashes between the Pokot and Turkana have been recurring (see also Table 1 above) and have, by conservative estimates, caused more than 600 deaths. Both sides have heavily armed and well-organized militias, and large-scale raids often involve several hundred raiders most of whom are armed with AK47s or similar weapons. The level of armament is evidenced by the fact that the groups involved have also at times overpowered security forces sent to the region to halt the violence. In one highly publicized event, more than 20 police officers were ambushed and killed by Pokot raiders in Kapedo (on the border between Turkana and West Pokot) in November 2014, prompting President Kenyatta to deploy the military in the region (Lind 2018).

The conflict has intertwined with politics in several ways, further fueling the violence. Firstly, as in other communal conflicts in Kenya, violent displacement and the renegotiation of boundaries can affect electoral outcomes. More directly, political elites have benefited financially from the raiding "industry" and have in turn allegedly provided weapons to raiders from their community (Greiner 2013; Okumu et al. 2017). Border revisions by the central state have further fueled tensions; for instance, ahead of the 2013 elections, local borders were redrawn so that the aforementioned Kapedo was "moved" from Turkana to Baringo County. The conflict gained a further dimension, adding to its intensity and complexity, as oil was discovered in Turkana in 2012. This has increased the value of the land and has further heightened the local political stakes (Schilling et al. 2015; Greiner 2013). It also led to the entry of new actors – notably, the Anglo-Irish oil company Tullow Oil – in the region, ostensibly representing a promise for more local development and improved infrastructure but so far mainly serving to underline the marginalized nature of pastoralist livelihoods in relation to the Kenyan state. For instance, while many hoped that oil exploration and extraction would create much-needed local jobs and development, few locals have been hired by Tullow, and when they have, the question of who gets hired or not has been manipulated by local politicians appealing to ethnic support bases (Lind 2018).

Local Resources

As the discussion of the Pokot-Turkana conflict illustrates, one prominent driver of communal conflict relates to the control over, or access to, local natural resources such as grazing land or water. Oftentimes, this conflict driver is connected to group livelihoods – such as competition over the use of land between two pastoralist communities or between sedentary farmers and nomadic herders. This form of conflicts, which revolve around scarce natural resources, is often understood in relation to a broader context of natural degradation and climate change. They are also often fueled by unclear or overlapping rights and tenure provision. For instance, resource conflict in the Kajiado district in southern Kenya has been described as relating to population growth, changes to land tenure regulations, and international and national policies incentivizing changes in land use (Campbell et al. 2000). However, while a shrinking resource base and unclear rules about access may contribute to conflict, it is usually not enough for conflict to escalate into large-scale violence (Brosché 2014; Adano et al. 2012); to understand patterns of violence, local and national political dynamics must also be taken into account.

One example where local resources are at the heart of the conflict is found in the Tana Delta in the coastal region. Here there has been repeated violent conflict over resources between the Pokomo, who to a large degree pursue sedentary farming livelihood, and the pastoralist communities Orma and Wardei. Both sides depend on the river Tana for their livelihoods – the farmers grow their crops along the river, and the pastoralists move in with their animals during dry spells so they can drink from the river (Martin 2012). When violent conflict has erupted, it has often been triggered by incidents where cattle have destroyed farms or where farmers have denied pastoralists access to the river. The communities have different traditions concerning communal and private land tenure and have taken different positions in relation to irrigation projects and other state policies affecting land use. In 2001, a proposed land adjudication program increased tensions between the communities. The pastoralists interpreted the program as potentially excluding them from access to the river.

These tensions coincided with the fact that a drought in 2000–2001 had caused the pastoralist communities to move closer to the river, increasing the pressure on local resources. In this context, clashes between the communities took place on several occasions during 2001, resulting in over 100 deaths (Kagwanja 2003; Martin 2012).

While differences in livelihood, land tenure systems and culture are often emphasized in analyses of the conflict, it is also clear that escalations and de-escalations have been driven by political dynamics. While the central government has arguably not been directly involved in the same way as in election-related conflicts in Rift Valley, both sides in the Tana Delta conflict have at times perceived that the government was biased against them. The Pokomo have accused the government of failing to disarm the pastoralists; there have been claims that many of the cattle held by the pastoralists belonged to powerful government officials, who wished to keep those who guarded their property well-armed. On the other hand, land adjudication was perceived as mainly benefiting the farmers, and there have been strong and persistent fears among the pastoralists that together, the Pokomo, the government, and the foreign companies are trying to displace them from the area (Kirchner 2013). A history of arbitrary displacement of people due to dam construction and irrigation projects in the area lends credence to such fears. Local political aspirants have also played a more direct role in fueling the conflict (Kagwanja 2003). In connection to the 2013 elections, the conflict became violent again, partly because local politicians fueled ethnic tensions to gain votes; this time almost 200 people were killed (Kirchner 2013).

Boundaries and Local Authority

Another key driver of communal conflict, closely connected to the control over local resources as well as to electoral dynamics, concerns boundaries and local authority. As noted previously, land and the notion of "ethnic homelands" play a crucial role in Kenyan politics. Holding land is a source of security and power for individuals, and at the group level, being associated with a piece of territory provides an important component of being perceived as genuine Kenyan citizens with a legitimate claim on a stake in national power (Kurgat 2012; Lynch 2011a). The strong political salience of land and territory, together with the fact that much of the land in rural areas is communal land rather than privately owned, implies that land conflict often takes on an ethnic dimension. In many locations, exact border demarcations are unclear or there are overlapping claims, and de facto settlement patterns and displacement can often affect formalizations of land claims. The question of local borders and which group has a legitimate claim to a certain territory also affects local political power and authority.

A conflict between the Garre and Murule, two Somali sub-clans, in Mandera in northeast Kenya illustrates these dynamics. The two groups, which are both traditionally pastoralist communities, have a long history of conflict and clashes over pasture and water (Menkhaus 2015). They have also been fighting about local power – which group should excert authority over Mandera district (now Mandera County).

Local border demarcations were a core issue in the conflict and became strongly politicized during Moi's rule. In 1988, administrative borders were redrawn so as to create separate political constituencies for the two clans in Mandera district, but these measures had the unintended consequence of intensifying clan-based competition and animosity and resulted in ethnic cleansing of the respective constituencies. The redrawing of constituency borders became so strongly contested because it affected control over resources as well as electoral outcomes, and local elites used ties to the president and other national elites to acquire "their own" constituencies (Ojielo 2010).

Aside from this form of political maneuvering, the conflict was further exacerbated by overall insecurity in the region, which borders Somalia and Ethiopia. The conflict also has cross-border dynamics, with both communities building alliances with their kin in Somalia and Ethiopia and accusing each other of harboring foreign militants. Like other pastoralist areas, Mandera has suffered from a high degree of marginalization, and there is a lingering distrust against the state, particularly the security forces, from the time of the Somali secessionist struggle in the 1960s when severe and indiscriminate force was employed (Ojielo 2010; Menkhaus 2015). The most recent waves of fighting between Garre and Murule began in 2004 (UCDP 2018). The trigger was a dispute over land, as the Garre attempted to use pasture that they had access to in the past but which now belonged to the Murule constituency. Initially, isolated killings became a spiral of revenge attacks, resulting in more than 60 deaths, with many thousands fleeing the violence-affected areas. The worst single incident took place on 16 March 2005 when Murule raiders attacked El Golicha village, leaving 22 dead, with many children among the victims. This event, which gained significant news attention, prompted strong action from the government, and an arbitration committee was appointed to resolve the conflict. However, the agreement that was reached mainly addressed issues of compensation and other direct outcomes of the violence, leaving the core issues unaddressed, and violence re-erupted in 2008.

Addressing Communal Conflicts: Responses by State and Non-state Actors

When lethal intergroup violence breaks out, it represents a challenge to the state's claim to have a monopoly over violence and its ability to ensure the safety of its citizens. Consequently, even in those cases where violence was more or less instigated by the state (most notably the "ethnic clashes" under Moi), the Kenyan government has generally intervened when communal conflicts have broken out. Oftentimes, such interventions have entailed the deployment of security forces to halt violence and restore order. In turn, peace enforcement has in many cases been followed by campaigns to disarm local communities and efforts to facilitate negotiated agreements. In the case of Mandera, mentioned above, the Kibaki government appointed an arbitration committee consisting of recognized local clan and religious leaders. In other cases, broad peace conferences have been arranged to address a broader set of conflicts. For instance, a state-led peace process among pastoralist groups in northern Kenya culminated in the 2001 Modogashe Declaration which formalized an acceptance of customary conflict regulation mechanisms in addressing pastoralist conflicts (Odendaal 2013). In addition to central and local government actors, a broad range of non-state actors have also been prominent on conflict management. For instance, local community-based organizations (CBOs), non-government organizations (NGOs), and faith-based organizations have to a large extent been involved in activities such as mediation and facilitation. In many cases, several different actors – state and non-state – have been involved in responding to a specific conflict, at times working in parallel and at times actively coordinating their activities. Because the government tends to be viewed with suspicion due to the connections between communal conflict and macro politics, non-state actors are often better able to promote trust between the conflict parties and to serve in a credible mediator role. A peace process in the Kerio Valley in the early 2000s exemplifies this: After steadily escalating violent conflict over local land and cattle raiding but also heavily influenced by local and national politics, leaders from the two groups involved – Marakwet and Pokot – began dialogue to resolve the conflict (Elfversson 2016). They turned to the Catholic Justice and Peace Commission (CJPC), a faith-based organization that had long been engaged in providing local services such as education and health care, to facilitate their negotiations. Consequently, church officials acted as mediators, with a focus on convening and facilitating meetings, until the two sides were able to reach a peace agreement known as the Kolowa Declaration. Government representatives were present at the declaration and endorsed the agreement, with local government officials playing a key role in its implementation.

One outcome of the Kerio Valley peace process was the establishment of local bodies to regulate and manage minor disputes and prevent their escalation into violent conflict. Such District Peace Committees (DPCs) are of high relevance throughout conflict-affected regions of Kenya. DPCs, which can be described as hybrid bodies (encompassing both formal and informal structures), have played a major role in many local peace processes. These conflict management bodies have been of growing importance in Kenya since the 1990s, drawing upon the success of such a body in addressing long-standing conflict in Wajir in northeast Kenya. District Peace Committees are hybrid bodies that incorporate local customary conflict resolution while also drawing on formal structures and connecting to government institutions (Odendaal 2013). Membership of the peace committees is made up of locally elected elders as well as women, youth, civil society organizations, and government representatives. Their main purpose is to resolve conflicts and promote peace among the different communities in a district and its neighboring area. In 2001, a National Steering Committee (NSC) was established to coordinate the work of DPCs and other peace building bodies in Kenya and link these formally with government and development activities (Odendaal 2013). This move effectively formalized the role of DPCs, granting them additional power and legitimacy by way of having official authority; at the same time, in some cases, their customary legitimacy has been eroded by their formalization. Furthermore, many have criticized the official recognition of bodies and mechanisms that encompass customary practices such as blood compensation and oftentimes the de facto exclusion of women from formal negotiations.

Devolution: Diffusing Macro-conflict but Intensifying Local Conflict?

Since independence, the gradual centralization of power in the hands of the president has been challenged by opposition movements and civil society. One of the reasons has been that the very high stakes in the national political contest have helped fuel election-related communal violence. By devolving and diffusing power, it was argued, the notion that only the groups represented at the center are able to "eat" can be overcome. The struggle for constitutional reform picked up during the last years of Moi's rule, culminating in a referendum in 2005 where the final draft – which contained significantly less radical reforms than those promised during the campaign that got Kibaki and NARC elected – was defeated (Lynch 2006; Ghai 2008). However, after the intense election-related violence in 2008, and under significant international pressure, a new constitution was drafted which includes strong checks on executive power and a progressive bill of rights. The constitution was adopted in a referendum held on August 4, 2010, where 67% voted in its favor, and promulgated later the same month. While the constitution has been acclaimed for its far-reaching and progressive content, it should be noted that implementation of many provisions has been obstructed or ignored by elites with an interest in maintaining the old order (Murunga et al. 2014).

A cornerstone of the constitutional reform was the devolution of power to 47 counties. These became operational after the 2013 elections, in which local governors and county assemblies were elected for the first time. The new county governments were given significant power over fiscal resources and legislation, prompting concerns from several analysts that while devolution might diffuse the contest over national power, it also had the potential to intensify communal conflicts at the local level. Indeed, rather than resulting in "everyone's turn to eat," devolution in many cases produced locally excluded minorities (D'Arcy and Cornell 2016). From the perspective of ethnic violence, such situations were particularly concerning when local minorities were powerful at the national level or had strong cross-border networks, suggesting the capacity to mobilize for violence against the community in power at the local level. In line with such concerns, Lind (2018) points out that "in recent years levels of conflict have been greatest in counties with pointed majority-minority group divisions, notably Moyale, Marsabit, Mandera, Isiolo and Tana River." To prevent communal violence during the 2013 elections, the National Cohesion and Integration Commission (NCIC) – a government body which was created after the 2008 election-related violence and tasked with promoting peace and national unity – in several locations promoted pre-election agreements between communities on how to distribute elected posts. Essentially, such power-sharing agreements were negotiated among community "elders" – a term commonly encompassing leaders with a customary or moral authority as well as influential businessmen and other "big men" – together with party representatives, and then anchored within the broader community. This form of "negotiated democracy" in several locations was credited with the avoidance of violence in the 2013 elections (Mitullah 2017; Lind 2018).

In Migori County, for instance, a deal was made whereby the positions as deputy governor and senator were promised to the second largest community (Mitullah 2017). Migori is ethnically heterogenous and has experienced communal violence between Luo (the numerically largest group in the county) and Kuria. The Kuria are the second largest group numerically and ahead of the 2013 elections feared exclusion from power and that they would not have a stake in the distribution of county resources. The Kuria elite were able to leverage their community's presidential vote – promising to support the Luo candidate Odinga only if they were promised a seat at the table in Migori (Mitullah 2017). A similar negotiated deal was reached in Nakuru, which had been one of the hotbeds of previous waves of election-related violence between Kalenjin and Kikuyu (Elfversson and Sjögren 2019). Kikuyu are the largest community in Nakuru County, and Kalenjin the second largest. Among local and national elites, there were strong fears that the 2013 elections would cause renewed violence, and a pact was negotiated whereby the Kalenjin (or, more formally, the Kalenjin-dominated URP party) were promised the deputy governor post. The pact should be seen against the backdrop of the national level deal between the Kikuyu presidential candidate Uhuru Kenyatta and his Kalenjin running mate William Ruto, and the pair also pushed strongly for the local Nakuru deal. The local and national pacts, in conjunction, played a major role in preventing communal violence in Nakuru in the 2013 and 2017 elections (Elfversson and Sjögren 2019; Mitullah 2017).

The idea of negotiated democracy, and whether it is a useful tool to overcome communal conflicts or rather serves to reinforce ethnic politics, has been a topic of intense debates in Kenyan media. While this form of agreements may diffuse intercommunal tension, they may also generate new disputes, and they may be seen as disenfranchising ordinary voters. Local power sharing can also entail exclusion: in both Migori and Nakuru, there were other sizeable communities that were excluded from the negotiated electoral pacts. More broadly, cases such as Nakuru and Migori illustrate that while devolution has increased the stakes at the local level, whether or not this exacerbates communal conflict is conditional on broader political dynamics. Aside from power sharing, local leaders do have the opportunity to improve local service provision and accountability vis-à-vis all local citizens and have done so in some cases, which arguably can contribute to decrease the risk of communal conflict. Returning to Fig. 1 above, there is not any visible support for the notion that violent communal conflicts have increased following devolution – if anything, the period since 2013 has seen a decrease both in the number of active conflicts per year and in the number of fatalities. Still, there is cause for caution, given increased tensions in some locations (Lind 2018). In Nakuru in particular, the national-level deal between Kalenjin and Kikuyu elite politicians has restrained local elites, but future developments in the national political dynamic may well open up for renewed election-related violence here and elsewhere in the Rift Valley (Elfversson and Sjögren 2019).

Conclusion

This chapter has presented an overview of the patterns of communal conflict in Kenya and highlighted key drivers. The politicized nature of ethnicity in Kenya, and the fact that elections and land tenure are closely associated with ethnic identity, has been highlighted as key factors explaining the prevalence of violent communal conflict. In addition to national political dynamics, four main drivers of conflict were discussed: electoral politics, cattle raiding, local resources, and boundaries and local authority. The chapter has also emphasized that specific dynamics are at play in different conflicts: The precise way that different conflict drivers interact is different from case to case, suggesting that actors seeking to manage and resolve conflicts need to conduct careful analysis of the conflict at hand. This also implies that although all conflicts should be seen against the background of a state and a political culture where ethnicity is strongly politicized, the impact of national-level political dynamics on communal conflicts will vary from case to case.

Cross-References

► Ethnicity and Politics in Kenya
► Ethno-communal Conflict in Sudan and South Sudan

References

Adano WR, Dietz T, Witsenburg K, Zaal F (2012) Climate change, violent conflict and local institutions in Kenya's drylands. J Peace Res 49(1):65–80
Anderson D, Lochery E (2008) Violence and Exodus in Kenya's Rift Valley, 2008: predictable and preventable? J East Afr Stud 2(2):328–343
Boone C (2011) Politically allocated land rights and the geography of electoral violence: the case of Kenya in the 1990s. Comp Pol Stud 44(10):1311–1342
Branch B, Cheeseman N, Gardner L (eds) (2010) Our turn to eat: politics in Kenya since 1950. Lit Verlag, Münster
Brosché J (2014) Masters of war: the role of elites in Sudan's communal conflicts. Uppsala University, Uppsala
Brosché J, Elfversson E (2012) Communal conflict, civil war, and the state: complexities, connections, and the case of Sudan. Afr J Confl Resolut 12(1):33–60
Campbell DJ, Gichohi H, Mwangi A, Chege L (2000) Land use conflict in Kajiado District, Kenya. Land Use Policy 17:337–348
D'Arcy M, Cornell A (2016) Devolution and corruption in Kenya: everyone's turn to eat? Afr Aff 115(459):246–273
de Smedt J (2009) 'No raila, no peace!' Big man politics and election violence at the Kibera grassroots. Afr Aff 108(433):581–598

Eaton D (2012) Revenge, ethnicity and cattle raiding in north-western Kenya. In: Witsenburg K, Zaal F (eds) Spaces of insecurity: human agency in violent conflicts in Kenya. African Studies Centre, Leiden, pp 48–62

Elfversson E (2016) Peace from below: governance and peacebuilding in Kerio Valley, Kenya. J Mod Afr Stud 54(3):469–493

Elfversson E, Sjögren A (2019) Do local power-sharing deals reduce ethnopolitical hostility? The effects of 'negotiated democracy' in a devolved Kenya. Ethnopolitics (forthcoming)

Elischer S (2010) Political parties, elections and ethnicity in Kenya. In: Branch D, Cheeseman N, Gardner L (eds) Our turn to eat: politics in Kenya since 1950. Lit Verlag, Münster

Ghai Y (2008) Devolution: restructuring the Kenyan state. J East Afr Stud 2(2):211–226

Greiner C (2013) Guns, land, and votes: cattle rustling and the politics of boundary (re)making in Northern Kenya. Afr Aff 122(447):216–237

Hassan M (2017) The strategic shuffle: ethnic geography, the internal security apparatus, and elections in Kenya. Am J Polit Sci 61(2):382–395

Höglund K (2009) Electoral violence in conflict-ridden societies: concepts, causes, and consequences. Terror Polit Violence 21(3):412–427

Kagwanja PM (2003) Globalizing ethnicity, localizing citizenship: globalization, identity politics and violence in Kenya's Tana River Region. Afr Dev 28(1–2):112–152

Kimenyi MS, Ndung'u NS (2005) Sporadic ethnic violence: why has Kenya not experienced a full-blown civil war? In: Collier P, Sambanis N (eds) Understanding civil war: evidence and analysis. World Bank, Washington, DC, pp 123–156

Kirchner K (2013) Conflicts and politics in the Tana Delta, Kenya: an analysis of the 2012–2013 clashes and the general and presidential elections 2013. Leiden University, Leiden

Klaus K, Mitchell MI (2015) Land grievances and the mobilization of electoral violence: evidence from Côte d'Ivoire and Kenya. J Peace Res 52(5):622–635. https://doi.org/10.1177/0022343315580145

Klopp JM (2001) "Ethnic clashes" and winning elections: the case of Kenya's electoral despotism. Can J Afr Stud 35(3):473–517

Klopp JM, Zuern E (2007) The politics of violence in democratization: lessons from Kenya and South Africa. Comp Polit 39(2):127–146

Kumssa A, Jones JF, Williams JH (2009) Conflict and human security in the North Rift and North Eastern Kenya. Int J Soc Econ 36(10):1008–1020

Kurgat AJ (2012) The ethnicization of territory: identity and space among the Nandi in Turbo Division. In: Witsenburg K, Zaal F (eds) Spaces of insecurity: human agency in violent conflicts in Kenya. African Studies Centre, Leiden, pp 20–47

Lind J (2018) Devolution, shifting centre-periphery relationships and conflict in northern Kenya. Polit Geogr 63:135–147

Lynch G (2006) The fruits of perception: 'ethnic politics' and the case of Kenya's constitutional referendum. Afr Stud 65(2):233–270

Lynch G (2011a) I say to you: ethnic politics and the Kalenjin in Kenya. University of Chicago Press, Chicago

Lynch G (2011b) The wars of who belongs where: the unstable politics of autochthony on Kenya's Mt Elgon. Ethnopolitics 10(3–4):391–410. https://doi.org/10.1080/17449057.2011.596671

Martin P (2012) Conflict between pastoralists and farmers in Tana River District. In: Witsenburg K, Zaal F (eds) Spaces of insecurity: human agency in violent conflicts in Kenya. African Studies Centre, Leiden, pp 167–193

Mati JM (2013) Antinomies in the struggle for the transformation of the Kenyan constitution (1990–2010). J Contemp Afr Stud 31(2):235–254

Menkhaus K (2015) Conflict assessment: Northern Kenya and Somaliland. Danish Demining Group, Copenhagen

Mieth F (2012) In between cattle raids and peace meetings: voices from the Kenya/Ugandan border region. In: Witsenburg K, Zaal F (eds) Spaces of insecurity: human agency in violent conflicts in Kenya. African Studies Centre, Leiden, pp 63–87

Mitullah W (2017) Negotiated democracy: a double-barrelled sword. In: Njogu K, Wekesa PW (eds) Kenya's 2013 general election: stakes, practices and outcome. Nairobi: Twaweza Communications

Mkutu K (2008) Guns & governance in the Rift Valley: pastoralist conflict & small arms. James Currey, Oxford

Murunga G (2004) The state, its reform and the question of legitimacy in Kenya. Identity, Cult Polit 5(1&2):179–206

Murunga G, Nasong'o SW (2007) Kenya: the struggle for democracy. Zed Books, London

Murunga G, Okello D, Sjögren A (eds) (2014) Kenya: the struggle for a new constitutional order. Zed Books, London

Odendaal A (2013) A crucial link: local peace committees and national peacebuilding. United States Institute of Peace Press, Washington, DC

Ojielo O (2010) Dynamics and trends of conflict in greater Mandera. Amani papers. UNDP Kenya, Nairobi

Okumu W, Bukari KN, Sow P, Onyiego E (2017) The role of elite rivalry and ethnic politics in livestock raids in northern Kenya. J Mod Afr Stud 55(3):479–509

Omolo K (2002) Political ethnicity in the democratisation process in Kenya. Afr Stud 61(2):209–221

Omotola S (2010) Explaining electoral violence in Africa's 'new' democracies. Afr J Confl Resolut 10(3):51–73

Oucho JO (2002) Undercurrents of ethnic conflicts in Kenya. African social studies series. Brill, Leiden

Schilling J, Locham R, Weinzierl T, Vivekananda J, Scheffran J (2015) The nexus of oil, conflict, and climate change vulnerability of pastoral communities in northwest Kenya. Earth Syst Dynam 6(2):703–717

Sundberg R, Melander E (2013) Introducing the UCDP georeferenced event dataset. J Peace Res 50(4):523–532. https://doi.org/10.1177/0022343313484347

Sundberg R, Eck K, Kreutz J (2012) Introducing the UCDP non-state conflict dataset. J Peace Res 49(2):351–362

Svensson I (2013) One god, many wars: religious dimensions of armed conflict in the Middle East and North Africa. Civil Wars 15(4):411–430. https://doi.org/10.1080/13698249.2013.853409

UCDP Conflict Encyclopedia (2018) Uppsala conflict data program (UCDP). Uppsala University, Uppsala. www.ucdp.uu.se

Waki PN (2008) Report of the commission of inquiry into post-election violence. Government Printer, Nairobi

Elites in Between Ethnic Mongolians and the Han in China

39

Chelegeer

Contents

Introduction	696
MINZU in China at a Glance	696
Mongolian Elites Before 1949	699
The Old Nobility	700
From Old House to New Elite	702
Mongol MINZU from 1949 to 1979	704
Economic and Cultural Reforming	705
MINZU as Social Transformation	707
Ongoing Generations from the 1980s	709
Conclusion	711
References	712

Abstract

Whether an ethnicity or a nationality is a natural and historical entity with clear self-consciousness, or a constructed identity as one of the consequences of modernity, there are always academic debates in sociology. By concerning Mongolian elites, this chapter argues their essential role in interacting with Han, the dominant population of China, through history and informing their modern concept of MINZU. Indeed, this research is not taking Mongol as a group-in-itself but as a dynamic identity with constant changing.

Keywords

Mongolian elites · Inner Mongolia · MINZU · China · Ethnic identity

Chelegeer (✉)
University of Leeds, Leeds, UK
e-mail: sscch@leeds.ac.uk

© The Author(s), under exclusive license to Springer Nature Singapore Pte Ltd. 2019
S. Ratuva (ed.), *The Palgrave Handbook of Ethnicity*,
https://doi.org/10.1007/978-981-13-2898-5_51

Introduction

The intention of this chapter is to sketch how Mongolian elites had been and are now interacting with the majority Han of China through the history and in the context of today's Chinese sovereignty. Mongol was once a federal community with conflicting clans, who were widely believed as barbarians and invaders to the Confucian culture. However, the recent elite politics reformed the pan-Mongol society into two major regimes: one republic state while the other one a province in China. Thereafter, the "Mongolians in China" had been constructed as an official notion of the Chinese MINZU category whose ethnic identity was classified and inherited restrict to law, and their history was a part of the history of China for its own sake. Scholars like Bulag (2002) believed the Mongolians in China could be a subject of postcolonial criticism, while this chapter would take a more neutral view to see the changes of Mongolian elites. Indeed, the departure point of this research is not taking Mongolians in China as a consistent group-in-itself but as choices made by certain people in the view of Brubaker (2006) and Song (2003), which may touch the debate on nationality being a historical and cultural entity or a modern creation.

Dillon (2016) introduces that a popular stereotype in the West is that China is a single monoculture, populated entirely by a homogeneous Chinese population who all speak the same Chinese language and have a more or less uniform Chinese culture. The fact is that the People's Republic of China today is founded by combining Inner Mongolia, Tibet, Xinjiang, and other ethnic areas together. Indeed, there are 55 national minorities with state-certificated communities of people and distinct languages, customs, economic lives, and psychological makeups in culture, whose autonomous habitats account for 64% of the country's total land territory (Yi 2008). In other words, China is not and had never been a monoculture society. The various peoples of the MINZU category are believed that have been weaving intricate networks of conflict, interconnection, and influence over the entire Chinese history (Dreyer 1976; Heberer 1989). They are considered important for China, and studies on them could also be enlightening to the more general sociology on ethnic relationships around the world.

MINZU in China at a Glance

One may feel confused about studies on Chinese Mongolians or other minorities in China for there is even no consensus on what "China" means (Ge 2011; Bo 2007). In fact, the Chinese language makes no difference between nation, nationality, minority, ethnicity, and ethnos. A liquid situation of Chinese identity has explained that whoever believes in Confucianism and relative ethics could be considered as belonging to the Chinese cultural community, and this cosmopolitan ideology of "TianXia" has shaped the basic structure of Chinese worldviews throughout the history (Xu 2017).

The modern concept of "nationality" was firstly introduced by Liang Qichao into the Chinese literature in 1899 (Huang 1995). Borrowed the term "MINZU" (民族)

from Japanese, he initially called for protecting the Zhonghua MINZU and fighting against colonialism from the western powers. Soon afterward, the term was applied in complicated ways and referred to different entities. Sun Yat-sen considered Zhonghua MINZU a racial concept and expressed his ambition to found a pure nation-state with only the Han population in his Three People's Principles, by saying "Qu Chu Da Lu" (驱除鞑虏). Here, "Qu Chu" meant "swiping out" and "Da Lu" mainly referred to Manchu and Mongol, who were not only the ruling ethnicities in Qing Dynasty but also the ones considered really different from Han and Zhonghua population. Soon after the successful revolt, he replaced the nationalism principle into "Wu Zu Gong He" (五族共和) which meant ruling a republic China with the cooperation of Manchu, Mongol, Tibetan, and Muslims for political purpose. Furthermore, Sun's successor, Chiang Kai-shek, went opposite to classify minorities to avoid ethnic nationalism. Being backed by scholars like Fu Sinian and Gu Jiegang, he argued a theory of "Jie Yi Lei Shi de Hun Yin" (结以累世的婚姻) which stressed that even Mongolians, Manchu, and Tibetans were offspring of Chinese ancestors and their kinships, so that there should be a consensus of Zhonghua Unity for all of them.

On the contrary, the Chinese Communist Party recognized the importance of identifying minorities and committing them with privileges. Chairman Mao stressed a "Political Model of Soviet Ethnicities" as the way to go against colonialism and hegemonism and the way to call for support from marginal areas of Han's culture in his strategy of "encircling the cities." The leader of the new sovereignty also tried to stop controversial discussions on the term "MINZU" by politically defining it as a description of various ethnicities of people came into being on a certain territory. In specific, all citizens in the People's Republic of China were described as belonging to the *Zhonghua MINZU Family* under a common destiny, while the dominant population was named as "Han-MINZU" or just "Han" for short, and non-Hans were identified as "Shaoshu-MINZU" no matter they could be "minorities" to sociological and historical studies or "races" under the discourse of conflicts. Even "nationalism" in the worldwide had been translated into MINZUism (民族主义). Indeed, the wildly used Chinese term "MINZU" is a concept concealing complicated situations of ethnic groups in both academic and daily practice.

At the beginning of the twentieth century, it was an uncertain task to count how many MINZUs with how big populations were living in China. The census of 1953 focused on the question of MINZU as a fill-in-the-blank query wherein a registrant dictated survey objects' MINZU name to the census taker, who then transcribed it into Chinese characters (Huang 1995). The census turned out more than 400 entries, which challenged the government for allocating seats of deputies for the National People's Congress (Mullaney 2010). Since then, more than 200 historians and anthropologists of the China Academy of Sciences, associated with professors and students from the MINZU University and other institutes, and experts on music, art, and literature all worked together for recognizing and classifying ethnic minorities. Led by professors like Xiaotong Fei, Guangxue Huang, and Yaohua Lin, they were trying to convince whether some ethnic minorities could be branches of another one.

While Qin (2013) argued the classification process was not a formal mission released by the United Front Work Department, it was also not a simple scientific project for understanding the new state's population. Quoted by Yaohua Lin, the research "must unite with politics, particularly with the problem of national security." For example, in Leyao, local cadre Pan Demao stressed that the mass peasants there had no idea whether they belonged to Han, Zhuang, or others; however, they would be pleased to be identified as Yao for certain privileges, and so they did.

Indeed, a willing principal was widely applied. In 1953, Deng Xiaoping and Liu Shaoqi confirmed that the government would respect personal rights that the process shall consult individual's own pleasure whether he or she hoped to be identified as an ethnic or a Han; however, officials and scholars taken charge of the registration should not emphasize this principle (Qin 2013).

Later in 1987, the classification project closed. At that time, prof. Huang Guangxue made a completion report confirming 55 ethnic minorities had been recognized, which could be regarded as the basic population structure of China. Not only numerous articles and statistics were published based on this category explaining their internal history and cultural heritage as well as their external challenges. Inspired by the Inner Mongolia autonomous region founded in 1947, the central government also extended the autonomy system to most MINZU of the category to establish their autonomous regions. While there were uproar debates on the territorial entitlements of almost every autonomous region, an overwhelmingly strong stereotype emerged, assuming these MINZU as natural entities with fixed living spheres, continuity histories, everlasting cultures, and strong self-determined integrations (Ge 2005). The population census 2010 further indicated that the population of Shaoshu-MINZU reached 112 million, whose distribution was known as showed in the figure below (Fig. 1).

Although Kaup (2000) argues that unified minority nations *did not exist* in southern and southwestern areas of China, she also suggests the biggest three Shaoshu-MINZU – Tibetans, Xinjiang Uygurs, and Mongolians – are those who could be in real sense nations. However, according to Rossabi (2017), the last one continues to be downplayed and unappreciated in recent discussions. In historical reviews, Tibetans and Han people had never been a jointed society until 1276 when Mongols conquered both of their capitals and reunified with Uyghurs' ancestors for the first time since the fall of the Tang dynasty. Analysts like Wang Lixiong and Takasugi even argues that the Yuan dynasty is a history of China being invaded so that Han had not exercised sovereignty over those areas. Birge (2017) concludes it is Mongolians that matters all aspects like the consolidation of territory, which became what we think of as "China" proper the authority and agenda of the central government; penal law; and the development of a national Confucian intelligentsia.

At the turn of the twenty-first century, Bulag (2002) noticed Mongols or rather their history and their quintessential heroes had fought for the Chinese "wholeheartedly." There are numerous books and movies sanctificated Chinggis Khan, once the leader of northern barbarians, as "the only Chinese to defeat the Europeans in our Chinese glorious era." Indeed, the Mongolian history has weaved so deeply with Chinese history that every textbook in the mainland reads that the Yuan dynasty with

Fig. 1 Distribution of MINZU . (Adapted from UNICEF's online open resource)

Mongolian emperors is a history of China's own and any questions on this consent may challenge the legitimacy of the territory of the nation-state today. Furthermore, different from Tibetan and Xinjiang Uyghur, Mongolians play a much better role in cooperating with the central government and has established a much easier political and economic atmosphere compared with other ethnic areas.

All the situation mentioned above raises the significance of Chinese Mongolians as the most important MINZU in understanding the state's ethnic policies and its ethnic relationship. How Mongolians have been weaving their history with Han and, along with generational changes, how young Mongolians will react to the central government today as well as to their intricate identity of being a Mongolian as well as being a Chinese citizen are crucial questions to the Chinese government and may serve solutions for Trilemma with Han, Xinjiang Uyghur, and Tibetans. It may also favor more general debates on the study of China and the sociology of ethnicity.

Mongolian Elites Before 1949

The following part would trace the pan-Mongol society with a federal system centered on Chinggis Khan and his royal family in a long history and would indicate the Mongolian identity being constructed by allegiance in between nobilities, kinships, and subsequent religious. Clans and tribes occupied most significant positions until the twentieth century when great social changes introduced new elites of young modernizers.

The Old Nobility

Scholars like Lattimore (1962) explains that nomadic tribes came into being in central Asia since the third century BC and formed their professional confederacy for military and civil affairs 1500 years thereafter to compete with agricultural people on the other side of the Great Wall in Qin and Han dynasty, when the term "Han" occurred as the name to distinguish the majority Chinese population with "outsiders." "Mongol" was one of those Han's strangers or nomadic barbarians, whose tribes could be traced back to early ninth century according to archaeology evidence and literature in the Chinese language.

In 1206, a powerful state *Mongol Uls* was established under the leadership of Chinggis Khan, who integrated most tribal alliances in Mongolia Plateau, the central Asia grassland, and gradually unified a pan-Mongol community with national consciousness and a created language in standardization (Huang 1995). That regime was initially an alliance of 95 units, *Myangad*s, with small administrative rulers and militaries; however, the emperor enjoyed such a superiority that he could take whatever he wanted from his people and remain as a cultural and spiritual icon (Hsiao and Sung 1978).

Nobilities were principally composed of those considered to be members of the Borjigin clan of Chinggis Khan and their spouses, who would be named as the leaders of those *Myangad*s and new territories obtained into the Mongolian empire. In other words, the Mongolian society could be forthright in describing as "truly feudal" because the social order was clearly stratified and hierarchically organized (Sneath 2000). Even Khubilai, the founder of Yuan, did not inherit the unified empire as a whole. Based on his princedom in the north part of today's Chinese territory, he swept the Song dynasty, expanded a strong controlling power all over China with support from most of the pan-Mongol societies and the Tibetans, whose religious master identified him as a figure in the Buddhist pantheon. But there were still some lords like Qaidu, the ruler of today's Xinjiang and certain parts of Middle East Asia, went against him and struggled to support his little brother.

The risk of noble politics grew gradually. In the late of the fourteenth century, Qaidu's descendant princess married to an Islamic Amir Timur. While the new couple failed to revive the great Mongolian empire, their domain, Chagatai, had serendipitously been turned to a center of Muslim culture. To their east, Khubilai's great-grandson, emperor Temur retreated to the far end of his territory as Northern Yuan after his being defeated by uprising troops of Han. Once again, the mainland of China was under control of its dominant population and came into the new dynasty of Ming. So far, one could tell that, along with the struggling against each other among Mongol rulers of the different sections of the vast empire, their relative military superiority declined.

After 20 years, the parallel history of Northern Yuan dynasty and Ming dynasty came into the end as the Mongolian capital being sacked. Since then, the pan-Mongolian alliance had collapsed into three major regimes and lost their power upon Chinese society. Besides the Muslim Chagatai, an Oriad Mongol community with created lords not belonging to the Chinggisid line grew rapidly, who were treated as another big threat to the old nobilities.

Historian Yao Dali (2016) introduced a model of periodically expansion and collapse of the nomadic society for the wealth disparity. As the pastoral production based on elaborate usage and adoption of severe natural resources, tribes far apart from each other could hardly develop themselves without making alliances (Wang 2008). However, not only the dualistic opposition of elites and the common could be troublesome but those lords ruling more south forward areas would also quarrel with their northern kinships, for they would more likely to plunder or treat for rich productions with agricultural Han. This division was not simply a problem of economics; in fact, northern lords would criticize southern families being influenced by the farming culture and Confucianism. To a certain extent, it seemed like a betrayal to their common identity, and this was the other reason why old nobilities could hardly maintain the glory of the Borjigin clan while staying in their southeastern appanages for years. Till the seventeenth century, Ligdan Khan became so unpopular that most lords of northern and western Mongolian tribes, like those leading Horchin, Harchin, and Halh all refused to protect him. They left Lindan died far west in exile in 1634 after being defeated by the Manchu Khan.

Manchus was a promising power with strong militaries and sophisticated political skills, grown from affiliated and independent tribes in the east end of the pan-Mongol area (Bai 1990). After Ligdan's death, the Manchu's leader, Abahai khan, married three princesses from the Borjigin clan and rewarded Lindan's son a diplomatic marriage with his own daughter. Till 1636 most of Chinggis Khan's lineage from the southeast part of Mongolia submitted to Abahai. These nobilities worked as Abahai's vassals and handed him the authority to rule directly through the Court of Dependencies in Beijing. With their support, this Manchu Khan swept Ming dynasty and took control of China as the start of Qing dynasty. In 1691 the Halh Mongol, along with other subdivided administrative units in the northern part of Mongolia, also swore fealty to the new king. But they were ruled indirectly via the military governors of Urga, Uliasutai, and Hovd thousands miles away from the Qing's capital. According to the different administrative practices, Qing emperors introduced terms of "Inner Mongolia" and "Outer Mongolia" to distinct their fields.

Over the next 60 years, Qing destroyed the created power of the Oriad Mongol and returned their land to the traditional Borjigin family. For a further ruling purpose, Qing's emperors served them high status and privileges and, at the same time, strengthened their division by intermarriages and supporting Mongolian princes and princesses to form small competitive councils in their league. The measurements were so successful that the pan-Mongolism could no longer gain popularity, especially not in the aristocrat house.

From Old House to New Elite

Mongolian nobilities kept their loyalty to Manchu empires for two centuries. Till the twentieth century when Qing weakened and started to reclaim land in Inner Mongolia, which broke its former prohibition on immigrating agricultural population. As a result, the proportion of Mongols dropped from an estimated 50–34.5% in 1912 (Bureau of Statistics 1997). Mongolian independence movements also emerged then, drawing upon the political and financial interests of the elite and the anti-Chinese sentiment among the commoners. A few months before the Qing Dynasty's collapse, the *8th Jabzandamba Khutagt* lama proclaimed the Outer Mongolia's sovereignty and purified themselves from China in 1911 with support from more than 30 noble leaders of competitive clans in the northwest of the vast territory of Mongolian habitat.

Tibetan Lamaism revived the alliance with Mongol nobility in 1578 when Sodnamjamsu lama of the Ge-luk-pa was seeking for support to rival with the old school of Nyingma. In 1642 the new faith became the dominant one and, in return, invested the title of Jebtsundamba Khutagt, the "Living Buddha," to certain Mongolian Khan's relatives. At the beginning, it was the Shamanism and other rural-localism norms that rooted in the pan-Mongol society, but being central oriented with the noble family gave the chance to Buddhism to extend influence all over the Mongolia plateau. Qing emperors, who made even stronger connections with Tibetan leaders, also supported the religion power in both Inner and Outer Mongolia as another way to fragment noble's ruling power (Yu 2005). By the early twentieth century, there were over a thousand monasteries and at least 135,000 lamas, who usually owned large herds of livestock, land, Han Chinese tenant farmers, and a considerable income from trading and transportation activities (Heissig 2000).

The Tibetan Buddhism had grown so influential that after Outer Mongolia proclaimed its independence, nobilities in Inner Mongolia found it impossible to wave popularity without a religious leader (Jagchid 1999). That was why when the Panchen Lama escaped from Tibet in the 1920s, Prince Demchugdongrub welcomed him overwhelmingly to Bat-haalag monastery, where he launched a conference for Inner Mongolia autonomous right later in 1933. The conference was known in the history as Bailingmiao Movement, which, besides Prince De and some other noble leaders, had also attracted many young modernizers who concerned the future of Inner Mongolia.

Qing was dragged to modernity by wars in the late nineteenth century and was flooded by opium and other international products along with new technologies and fresh ideas. After 1900 when an international military of British, America, France, Austria, Germany, Japan, Italia, and Russia broke the siege of Boxer Rebellion and occupied Peking for days, the Qing emperors had almost no controlling power upon both Inner and Outer Mongolia anymore. As the conservative state who kept the Shut-Door policy collapsed soon afterward, China and its people were facing uncertainties and dramatic changes.

Mongolians' future was also ambiguous. The declaration of independence of the Outer Mongol was not real for sovereignty. At that time, the Russians signed a secret treaty with the Japanese that divided Mongolia into two spheres of influence: Outer Mongolia was allocated to the Russians, while Inner Mongolia was considered to be part of the Japanese sphere (Rossabi 1975). As the de facto ruler, Russians increased their interests and economic activities in the county at the expense of the Chinese, who were increasingly excluded in 1912. The Soviet Union, later on, kept a standoff with conflicts and more treaties with the Japanese along the border of the Hulun Buir district for more than 20 years, until the Yalta Conference when the international landscape being rearranged. The Outer Mongol then became a republic nation-state, the Mongolian People's Republic (MPR), after the unanimous vote in 1945. The situation for Inner Mongolia was even more complicated for its struggling with more political and military forces from the Russians, the Japanese, local warlords, and the administrative powers from mainland China.

In 1934, the Nanjing government accepted the Bailingmiao Movement and President Chiang Kai-shek visited Prince De in Inner Mongolia; however, the Kuoming Dang had no power to restrict Japanese from pressing its influence upon this area. In 1936, Prince De was somehow controlled by the Japanese, which led to attacks from Han warlord Fu Zuoyi who invalided the autonomous government next year. More autonomous movements happened with the leadership of Prince De and his relatives and trusted subordinates, but none of them existed long enough to gain popularity. Indeed, the history had indicated times and times again that although some old nobilities and the religious icons remain beloved, these elites could no long reunify the Mongolian alliance or pointed out the future of Inner Mongolia.

It was Ulanhu, or Yun Ze as his real name, who made the administrative system similar to today's Inner Mongolia. In 1922, the 16-year-old boy was sent to Mongolian-Tibetan Academy in Beijing by Prince Gungsangnorbu as a part of the modernization movement for the common Inner Mongolian people and became a communist while furthering his study in the Soviet Union (Bartke and Schier 1985). During the period of the 1930s, he undertook an information job for the Chinese Communist Party and also worked as a small leader in a security team of the Bathaalag monastery under the Prince De's autonomous government. Later on, he joined the rebellion against Prince De and went to Yan'an for serving MINZU issues in the heart of the communist base area. Supported by most Mongolian young modernizers, he replaced the head of the Eastern Mongolian Autonomous Government, which was a Japanese client, and started his pro-communist movement in 1946. Ulanhu's diplomatic efforts were under two frameworks of autonomy and communist. Till 1954, the man born from nothing became the President of Inner Mongolian Autonomous Region and the Vice-Premier of the People's Republic of China.

Different from traditional elites, Ulanhu was born in a peasant family and had nothing related to the aristocratic house or a religious center. There even had controversial arguments about his identity whether he was a Mongolian person or a Han. His real name Yun Ze was a typical Chinese one, and his name in the Mongolian language was, in fact, the translation of "a red son of the communism."

While being doubted by many Mongolian commoners, his education backgrounds in the Tibetan-Mongolian Academy and in Moscow from 1925 to 1929 were extremely helpful for his career. During those periods, he made friends with activists like Wang Ruofei, Chou Enlai, Wu Xiuquan, and so on (Bulag 2002). In short, his success was partly rooted in coincidences and opportunities in that changing era. As concluded by Sneath (2000), the early twentieth century had seen the emergence of a new political elite of young, educated, Inner Mongolian intellectuals, with experience of Japanese, nationalist, and communist administrations.

Throughout the Mongolian history, we can tell that an elite politics had worked for hundreds of years with the Borjigin family containing most accesses to the administrative system. Noble leaders' same ancestral assumption kept the vast area concentered with the historical memory of Mongol Uls and the pan-Mongol identity. However, there were always conflicting of competitive identities of clans and struggles from created powers as well as contradictions caused by the interactions with Han. Indeed, the pan-Mongol society had never been a real united monocultural one and had separated into different regimes for times until the twentieth century when great changes embraced new elites concerning the future of Inner Mongolia and bringing new ideas about the identity.

Mongol MINZU from 1949 to 1979

Inner Mongolia Province, the well-known first communist autonomous region and the habitat of Mongolian people, had changed its administrative division for times. When Ulanhu established the autonomous government, the district mainly contained five leagues of clans with a 538,000 km^2 land and two million population. In 1949, besides the Shilingol, Higgan, Chahar, Noni-Muren, and Hulun Buir, two further leagues –Jirem and Juu – joined. Even after the new state confirmed the legal status of Inner Mongolian, the autonomous region was reformed thrice more according to orders from the central government. In 1954, Premier Chou Enlai stressed to reunify Suiyuan as it was historically a part of the pan-Mongol area while leaving regions like Alashan and Bayangol to Gansu and Xinjiang provinces. Later in 1956, the Alashan was replaced into the Inner Mongolia province. The Hulun Buir district, however, had been enforced out of the Inner Mongolia province in 1969 to Heilongjiang province as a Han district and then moved back to be an ethnic area in 1980. Since then, the province of 1,183,000 km^2 had been written and believed as the constant hometown for the Mongolian population of China.

Indeed, the reform of the administrative districts of Inner Mongolia represented a new power taking control of the old noble conflicts and indicated the historical and cultural entities being an object to a modern ideology and its creations. The following parts will focus on how Inner Mongolia being reformed and modernized as a trustworthy borderland of China, and how mainstreaming ideology came into being and will discuss the consequences of the MINZU category in the socialist transformation of the Inner Mongolian people (Fig. 2).

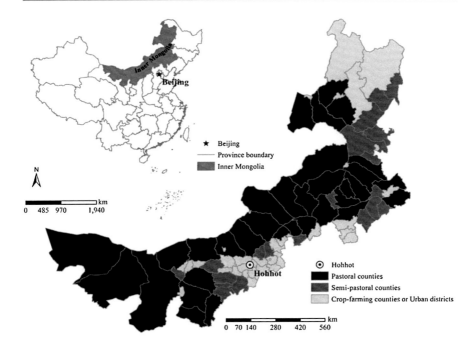

Fig. 2 Inner Mongolia and its 102 counties in P.R.C. (Online open resource)

Economic and Cultural Reforming

After the communists won the civil war, a land reform campaign began all over China. In the Inner Mongolia province, the reform had been to eliminate feudal privileges, to open the pasture to unrestricted private grazing, and, more seriously, to wipe out considered "enemies" from the Party. In some places, the old elites were dispossessed of their power and wealth but retained a measure of high status among locals; however, in other areas, the campaign was more sustained that many were killed or forced to flee (Sneath 2000).

Buddhists and lamas were also reviewed superstitious and suspectable, who had supported the feudal order and the Kuoming Dang. Since 1951, radical people in Hulun Buir started to attack monasteries. More and more lamas were sent to special schools for education and were "encouraged" to be transferred into productive labors. At the end of the 1950s, 80% of lamas had been eradicated from this area (Sneath 2000).

Noble leaders especially those in pastoral regions, on the other hand, were not being abused that much. Some studies indicated that upheavals were mainly led by Han peasants in most semi-pastoral and crop-farming counties, who were immigrated in as "slaves" to Mongolians, who, as a whole, were believed in a higher position. The class struggle was aroused by Chairman Mao, while Ulanhu tried different ways to control the situation and improve social justice to keep the autonomous region secure.

The Ulanhu's effort was soon interrupted in the 1960s when Mao's class struggle line emboldened the second land reform to differentiate Han and Mongols. The Sino-Soviet split even caused suspect of Mongolians being in separatism, which started new "revolutionary" organizations to exclude Mongols (Bulag 2002). The Vice-Premier himself was being under house arrest in Beijing since 1966. Later in 1968, General Teng Haiqing from Beijing associated with other local Maoists exaggerated the Movement in Inner Mongolia by further ransacking monasteries, arresting lamas, and "dragging out" senior Mongolians who might be evil to the Cultural Revolution, which led to 22,900 people being killed and 120,000 permanently injured (Woody and Schoenhals 1993). After all, the old nobilities, religious leaders, and growing modernizers of Mongolian intellectuals had all been wiped out off the social bureaucracy in Inner Mongolia, left only new "lords" of Maoists taking charge.

The growing of this Maoist could be seen as a result of intra-conflicts between loyal natives and dubious Mongolians, while in another aspect, the inter-provincial connections between Inner Mongolians and Han from southward China were strengthened. During the period from 1959 to 1962, many agricultural areas in southern parts of China suffered from a serious lack of food. The central government made a decision to move thousands of abandoned babies and orphans to Inner Mongolian ordinary families to keep them alive. An approximated 50,000 children had flooded into the ethnic area then and founded strong interethnic connections. Inner Mongolian families could feed these extra-mouths for their distinct nomadic production system, excess land reclamation, and the relatively stable scale of livestock, which was another main subject for the socialist transformation.

According to the government work report in 1958, establishing Peoples Communes were the main way in forming cooperative economics and had experienced great success. At the end of that year, there were 2292 communes including 96.29% of households, which increased the level of state planning and control of the economy to climax. Before the 1950s, grasslands were owned by nobilities, lamaseries, or clans and remained in common use by herders, while in the collectivist period, grasslands, as well as livestock on them, were transferred their ownership to communes and were used communally by all local herders under the supervisions of both the central and local institutions (Hua and Squires 2015). As the consumption of livestock was strictly limited, a total calculation of economics increased seemingly. In fact, not only the forced collectivization frustrated Inner Mongolians productivity but also the central government's policy to protect "farming oxen" decreased the price of beef and inhibited the market consumption demand. After all, the benefits of pastoral families in Inner Mongolia shrank more than a third (Rinqin and Li 2011; Sneath 2003).

While not clearly regulated, other policies reforming the socioeconomic structure of Inner Mongolia at this period were introduced as the campaign to settle down the nomads and to step up Han immigration in the hope of developing agricultural productions (Humphrey and Sneath 1999). Since the late 1950s, a movement for building mud-brick houses swept the pastoral area and nomadic families who enjoyed great mobility in the grassland before were encouraged to stay in fixed houses with limited "moving herding" for "enjoying" government furnished equipment like schools (Liu and Guangzhi 1979). As pastoral Mongolian people had no skills in building and farming crops, the movement was mostly initiated by migrant Han labors whose population doubled by 1960. Till 1963, the proportion of Mongols to the total population in the Inner Mongolia autonomous region dropped to 10.2%.

As Bulag (1998) concerned, all these changes had made original Inner Mongolians feeling of diaspora and hybridity, which was a story of natives becoming strangers in their own homelands. Although, as accused by Ulanhu, those Inner Mongolian Maoists should also be blamed for they were the latest elites who directly responsible for the miscarriage of justice and contradictions between party and intelligentsia and between ethnicities.

MINZU as Social Transformation

The cultural and economic transformation during this period also raised a crucial question that what would being a Mongolian mean when the natives were being marginalized and disconnected with the pastoral producing lifestyle for the socialist transformation. As Ulanhu himself was charged in the dark period as both a Mongolian nationalist and the one not fighting for the rights of ethnic compatriots, there were contradictions about his own background as a Han or a Mongol. Indeed, the boundary of Mongolians and Han was not that clear. Ulanhu could be a Han but he behaved like a Mongol, while, as recorded by Wang (2016), there were also many Han pretended to be among the Mongolian MINZU.

In the census of 1953, there were five questions being asked including the most basic ones on name, gender, age, the relationship between the head of household, and the fill-in-blank MINZU category. This census brought the newly established state some basic knowledge about its population and its ethnic distribution while applying the original HUKOU system. In fact, the later on classification process of MINZU category was related to this national household registration system.

The first formal regulation on HUKOU was released in 1958, and since then, it had been the most basic legal document with a certification page where a citizen's MINZU category and other identifying information such as his or her residence, name, spouse, and date of birth had to be confirmed. It had been widely used in people's daily practices for migration, registering a school and applying for social insurance, with the purpose of maintaining social security, restricting and guiding population mobility, distribution of welfares, and ethnic management (Wang and Fang 2008).

Different from white ethnics from Europe continent in America who can report their ancestral backgrounds freely, as ethnicity is not something that influences their lives unless they *want* it to (Waters 1990), the categories of MINZU in China are restricted political entities not allowed changing optionally. Furthermore, the ethnic identity in China is heritable through the HUKOU system as the *Measures for Administration of the Ethnic Composition* stipulates that an individual's ethnic identity shall be recorded the same as the identity of either his or her father or mother, including step- and foster-parent relationship. For those who are younger than 18 years old, changes can be made according to the different ethnic identities between the father-in-law and mother-in-law.

As shown in Fig. 3, after being classified, each Chinese citizen had been certificated with a certain ethnic identity. Take a Mongolian as an example, when he or she got married with a Han or another one with another ethnic identity, their child could be recorded as either a Mongolian or a Han/other according to the decision made by this couple. If they divorced or the child got a new foster relationship with other Mongolian parents, he or she could also change the record to be a Mongol before his or her 18-year-old birthday based on the family's choice. Indeed, the identification of Mongolians in China had been reformed from expressing consanguinity and cultural relations with the Borjigin clan to the formal certification.

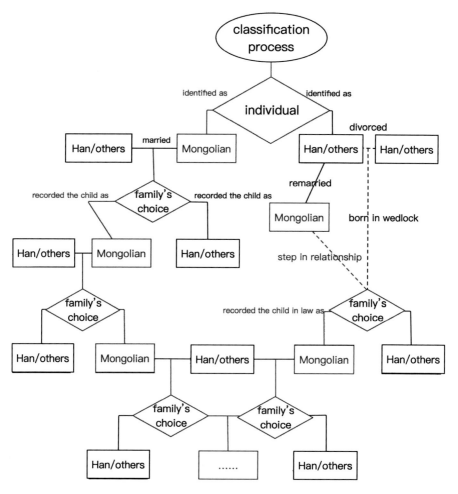

Fig. 3 Chinese ethnic identities are heritable through the ID card and HUKOU system. (Drawn by the author)

While it is still often simply asserted as obvious that the MINZU identified in China today are simply new names for natural social categories (Caffrey 2004), they are now politically oriented as modern creations. Furthermore, being an ethnic person means getting extra marks in the national college entrance examination, getting financial subsidies and immunity rights of the One-Child Policy, and accessing to other special treatments in occupation, education, landing, and criminal sanctions. No statistics data is available on how many newborns were "mistakenly" recorded; news reports on changing ethnic identity illegally can be seen every now and then. In fact, the situation is so serious that the State Ethnic Affairs Commission cooperated with the Ministry of Public Security has released a regulation, which empowers related departments at all levels to investigate and to give an administrative penalty or even a *criminal sanction* to those who changed their ethnic identities for purposes.

In 1960s a lot of the adopted orphans and children from southern China were recorded as Mongolian MINZU legally, while other migrants flooded in this area had too considered it more carefully. However, Wang (2016) concluded that changing ethnic identification record to Shaoshu-MINZU was actually a common way for Han migrants to interact with natives and the government for benefits in Inner Mongolia. It was possible when the willing principal was applied in the classification process, and the following generations could make family choices, or even break the law, in recording their children for privileges. In fact, no matter how hard it has been for Han to change their ethnic certification, there will always be ways as long as MINZU category can be seen as a social resource and let alone in that period of chaos.

Ongoing Generations from the 1980s

Till now we have seen great changes in Mongolian society. In history, the Mongolian identity was identified and maintained by the noble families who strengthened their connection with Chinggis Khan and influence upon the commoners. But nobilities were not always in solidarity, on the contrary, they competed with each other seriously which rooted the risk of fragmentation. Since the nineteenth century, the pan-Mongol area was dragged into the new world with uncertainties. Represented by Ulanhu, the new political elite of young, educated, Inner Mongolian intellectuals, with experience of Japanese, nationalist, and communist administrations finally lead the Inner Mongolian area into the People's Republic of China. However, they were quickly replaced by Maoist cadres. The socialist transformation from 1949 fundamentally challenged the pastoral culture and producing measurements, and the classification and registration process further disconnected the modern MINZU category with the historical community, while more uproars about assimilation and confliction were just around the corner of the new era.

The modernization of Inner Mongolia started from the 1980s when the whole county began to correct its class struggle line to economic development. Since the Opening-Up, the gross regional product (GRP) of Inner Mongolia increased from 5.8 billion Yuan in 1978 to 100 billion in 1996, while the rate kept high and the number reached 1863.2 billion at the end of 2016, almost ten times higher than in Tibetan or Xinjiang. Urbanization is one of the most influential progresses to the human world. Durkheim (1984) argued an emergence of *organic solidarity*, where relationships of economic reciprocity and mutual dependency had replaced beliefs in creating social consensus. In Inner Mongolia, the proportion of "illiterate population" dropped so quickly from 17.82% to 3.3% at the beginning of 1990s that almost every school-age children could join either a mandarin or a bilingual one to study compulsory courses on Chinese characters and national MINZU policies. The proportion of interethnic marriage further jumped to 38.137%. The Han-Mongol family count to 37.49%, while another 64.7% are with ethnic minorities like Manchu, Hui, and Daur. The studies of Naran Bilik (1985) and Wang Minjun (2001) introduced a marrying up mechanism in the ethnic region for economic benefits, improving social status and more sources for social mobility.

According to the tabulation of population census of 1990, 2000, and 2010, as shown in Table 1, there is an ever-growing trend for Inner Mongolians to go to urban areas to make a living as a salesperson, dining and entertainment server, and owner of an enterprise. While being leaders in administrative departments or public institutions are shrinking even through preferential policies are seemingly in favor of their needs.

All in all, what had been changed in the 1960s had been intensified along with the urbanization process. As more and more rural families moving to urban areas and some settlements of nomad becoming modern cities, the ethnic identity of Mongolian people was kept on *disembedding* with their traditional cultural and pastoral way of life. Being mixed with Han, as well as those "fake Mongols" who would have been Han but finally certificated as a Mongolian, challenged the existence of the Mongol community in China. Bulag (1998) along with other scholars noticed that there was a burning desire for many Chinese Mongolians to communicate with Mongols in Mongolian People's Republic for cultural and kinship until 1990, while the more general context represented the intense between the orthodox writing of the Great Mongol Uls and the modern created category of Mongolian MINZU.

While along with generational changes, a new nationalism and a different attitude toward outer kinships occurred. In the biggest question-and-answer website ZHIHU. COM, there is a discussion section on how Mongolian MINZU thinks of their relationship with Mongols outside China. Most young users express their paying no attention to them; while others believe that Inner Mongolia could be the real center of Mongolian history and culture.

Table 1 The occupation structure of Chinese Mongolians

	Leaders	Intellectuals	Serving staff	Business professionals	Workers	Rural labors	Others
1990	2.7%	9.4%	2.9%	2.7%	9.6%	70.3%	0.1%
2000	2.22%	8.29%	3.66%	6.77%	8.26%	70.75%	0.05%
2010	1.63%	9.09%	5.05%	11.06%	9.82%	63.25%	0.1%

Adapted by the author

In Hulun Buir the biggest lamasery, Ganzhuermiao, which ruined in the 1960s began to rebuild in 2001 and started to hold seasonally dharma assembly since 2003. While in Hohhot, 23 more bilingual schools were built in 2010 which would serve more than 8000 pupils to learn how to write and read the Mongolian language with the old Uyghur alphabet, which had been replaced by Cyrillic characters in the Mongolian People's Republic as a result of being colonized. An interviewee described that:

> The biggest difference between Chinese Mongolians and Outer Mongolians is we are being Sinicized while they are being Europeanized. Sinicization is, somehow, a good thing to combine our culture with an efficient economic entity. Thanks to the donations and intensive investments, we developed much faster and had been more capable to protect our tradition and heritages than people in the PRM could. While they are living with the Mongolian language and Mongolian citizenship, it is we that kept the writing system created by Genghis Khan alive.

Tamir (1993) stressed that individuals should have the right to choose their national identities and the right to keep the ethno-culture they embraced. However those Mongolian MINZU in higher classes and with more social resources are people who stick to their national identity record on one hand, and have to react with the ethno-culture unfamiliar to them on the other. To certain extent, they have been pragmatists. On one hand, they avoid arguing Mongolian MINZU being a modern creation but still an identity shared by the historical entity with specific habitat and culture; while, on the other hand, they are trying to express this identity under the social policies and economic frameworks of China.

A survey conducted by the author indicates a pilgrim system for Mongols from Inner Mongolia toward Beijing for education and social resources. Some interviewees simply stressed to make a living in the cosmopolitan for better opportunities, while others expressed their willingness to access the resources in the center of China to their marginal hometown. In the pilgrim, new images of Mongols as modern components of Chinese citizens and a language of development have been created.

Conclusion

Tamir (1993) could be right that ethnic identity and nationalism are mainly the contexts of culture. But it is not a simple question on how to leave ethnic movements under a liberal atmosphere of protecting and developing their own culture. There are indeed more subtle factors like how the ethnic elites are generating and spreading their knowledge and how territorial relationship comes across to biological myths. In the history, Mongolian people seemed to be connected by bloodlines with the Borjigin family, while the new political elite of young and Maoist finally transformed the community into a modern MINZU category with official constructed certification of identity. Along with the urbanization process which even disconnected the traditional way of life to this identity, the ongoing generations have to react to their MINZU identification accordingly. A desire for communicating kinships with Outer Mongols happened until the 1990s, while more recent young urban born intellectuals are moving their Mecca to Beijing.

Indeed, this research challenges the idea of Mongolians being a clear ethnicity in itself but favors the idea that ethnicity is an everlasting process where elites negotiate the language describing the identity with their commoners and others.

References

Bai F (1990) Shi xi Ming mo Qing chu Man Zu, Menggu Zu guan xi li shi shang de yin guo xing. Manchu Minor Res 1:17–28
Bartke W, Schier P (1985) China's new party leadership: biographies and analysis of the twelfth central committee of the Chinese communist party. Macmillan, London
Bilik N (1985) On Mongol-Han Intermarriages in Hohhot (Doctoral dissertation, Masters thesis, Central University for Minority Nationalities, Beijing. 1998. "Language Education, Intellectuals, and Symbolic Representation: Being an Urban Mongolian in a New Configuration of Social Evolution." Nationalism and Ethnic Politics 4, 1: 2)
Birge B (2017) "How the Mongols Mattered: A Perspective from Law". In How Mongolia Matters: War, Law, and Society, Leiden, The Netherlands: BRILL. Available From: brill
Bo Z (2007) China's elite politics: political transition and power balancing. World Scientific, London
Brubaker R (2006) Ethnicity without groups. Reviewed by Sinisa Malesevi. Nations Nationalism 12(4):699
Bulag UE (1998) Nationalism and hybridity in Mongolia. Clarendon Press, Oxford
Bulag UE (2002) The Mongols at China's edge: history and the politics of national unity. Rowman & Littlefield, Oxford
Bureau of Statistics (1997). From: http://data.stats.gov.cn/
Caffrey K (2004) Who "who" is, and other local poetics of National Policy: Yunnan MINZU Shibie and Hui in the process. China Inf 18(2):243–274
Dillon M (2016) Majorities and minorities in China: an introduction. Ethn Racial Stud 39(12):2079–2090
Dreyer JT (1976) China's forty millions: minority nationalities and national integration in the People's Republic of China. Harvard University Press, Cambridge, MA
Durkheim E (1984) The division oflaborin society. (WD Hall trans., New York: FreePress) Essig, Mark (2003) Edison & The Electric Chair: A Story of Light and Death, pp.23–24
Ge J (2005) Zhong Guo Yi Min Shi. Wu Nan Tu Shu Chu Ban Ltd
Ge Z (2011) Zai Zi Zhongguo. Zhonghua shu ju, Beijing
Heberer T (1989) China and its National Minorities: autonomy or assimilation? M.E. Sharpe, New York
Heissig W (2000) The religions of Mongolia. Kegan Paul, London
Hsiao C-C, Sung L (1978) The military establishment of the Yuan dynasty. Council on East Asian Studies, Harvard University, Cambridge, MA
Hua L, Squires VR (2015) Managing China's pastoral lands: current problems and future prospects. Land Use Policy 43:129–137
Huang G (1995) Zhong Guo de MINZU Shi Bie. MINZU Chu Ban she, Beijing
Humphrey C, Sneath D (1999) The end of nomadism. Society, state and the environment in inner Asia. Duke University Press, Durham
Jagchid S (1999) Report. The Last Mongol prince: the life and times of Demchugdongrub, 1902–1966. Center for East Asian Studies, Western Washington University, Bellingham
Kaup KP (2000) Creating the Zhuang: ethnic politics in China. Lynne Rienner Publishers
Lattimore O (1962) Inner Asian frontiers of China. Beacon Press, Boston

Liu J, Guangzhi Z (1979) Neimenggu Zizhiqu Jingji Fazhan Gaikuang. People's Press of Inner Mongolia, Hohhot

Mullaney TS (2010) Coming to terms with the nation: ethnic classification in modern China. University of California Press, Berkeley

Qin H (2013) "The origin of the fifty six nationalities"does not derive from the nationality classification project – understandings and reflections on the nationality classification project. J Ethnol 05:17–29

Rinqin, Li Y (2011) The animal husbandry socialist transformation in Inner Mongolia. Meng Gu Xue Ji Kan 2:1–13

Rossabi M (1975) China and inner Asia: from 1368 to the present day. Thames and Hudson, London

Rossabi M (2017) How Mongolia matters: war, law, and society. Brill, Boston

Sneath D (2000) Changing Inner Mongolia: pastoral Mongolian society and the Chinese state. Oxford University Press, Oxford

Sneath D (2003) Land use, the environment and development in post-socialist Mongolia. Oxf Dev Stud 31(4):441–459

Song M (2003) Choosing ethnic identity. Polity, Cambridge, UK

Tamir Y (1993) Liberal nationalism. Princeton University Press, Princeton

Wang M (2008) The Nomad's choice: the first encounter between northern nomads and imperial China. Guang Xi Shi Fan Da Xue Chu Ban She, Guilin

Wang J (2001) Qing Cheng MINZU: yi ge bian jiang cheng shi minzu guan xi de li shi yan bian. Tian Jin Ren Min Chu Ban She

Wang J (2016) Mu Qu de Xuan Ze. China Social Science Press, Beijing

Wang MC, Fang (2008) Hu Ji Zhi Du de Gai Ge yu Fa Zhan. Soc Sci Guangdong 06:19–26

Waters MC (1990) Report. Ethnic options: choosing identities in America. University of California Press, Berkeley

Woody W, Schoenhals M (1993) The cultural revolution in Inner Mongolia: extracts from an unpublished history. Center for Pacific Asia Studies, Stockholm University, Stockholm

Xu J (2017) Jia Guo Tian Xia: Xian Dai Zhong Guo De Ge Ren Guo Jia Yu Shi Jie Ren Tong. Shang Hai Ren Min Chu Ban She, Shanghai

Yao D (2016) Du Shi De Zhi Hui. Fu Dan Da Xue Chu Ban She, Shanghai

Yi L (2008) Cultural exclusion in China: state education, social mobility and cultural difference. Routledge, London

Yu Z (2005) Lun Qing chao de MINZU zheng ce. Manchu Minor Res 03:41–51

Ethnicity and Cultural Wounding: Ethnic Conflict, Loss of Home, and the Drive to Return

40

Amanda Kearney

Contents

Introduction	716
Ethnicity and Cultural Wounding	718
Loss of Home amid Ethnic Conflict and Violence	720
Yanyuwa Families and 42 Years of Seeking Land Rights	722
Healing and Return	727
Concluding Remarks	730
Cross-References	731
References	731

Abstract

This chapter presents a discussion of ethnicity in relation to cultural wounding and healing. Cultural wounding is the violation of persons and their cultural lives through insult and injury, motivated by the desire to destroy or significantly harm this culture and its bearers. This is understood as a process of attacking human groups, in particular those bound by an ethnic distinction and declaration. What binds human groups and ultimately locates them in the path of "ethnic violence" is the perception of an "ethnic distinction" and a cultural orientation that is determined "other." This chapter aims to take stock of the meanings and expressions of ethnicity available to people in a prevailingly tense world, where tensions are born of ethnic conflict and culturally prescribed violence and shaped by the dynamic ethnic configurations that survive such encounters. Committed to better understanding the experiences of cultural wounding that precipitate a need for healing, for Indigenous families in northern Australia, a case study of the Yanyuwa community experiences with legislative land rights is presented. This grounds the discussion of ethnicity and cultural wounding, revealing the ways in

A. Kearney (✉)
College of Humanities, Arts and Social Sciences, Flinders University, Bedford Park, SA, Australia
e-mail: Amanda.Kearney@flinders.edu.au

© The Author(s), under exclusive license to Springer Nature Singapore Pte Ltd. 2019
S. Ratuva (ed.), *The Palgrave Handbook of Ethnicity*,
https://doi.org/10.1007/978-981-13-2898-5_52

which groups heal and retain a sense of belonging through distinctive pathways of return and restitution.

> **Keywords**
> Cultural wounding · Ethnic conflict · Healing · Indigenous Australia · Place · Land rights

Introduction

This chapter presents a discussion of ethnicity in relation to cultural wounding and healing. Cultural wounding is the result of attempts to rupture and assault a people's culture and cultural habit in physical, emotional, spiritual, and ideological terms. Inspired by Cook et al. (2003: 18) and developed further through an ethnographically informed discourse of wounding and healing (see Kearney 2014), cultural wounding is the violation of persons and their cultural lives through insult and injury, motivated by the desire to destroy or significantly harm this culture and its bearers. This is understood as a process of attacking human groups, in particular those bound by an ethnic distinction and declaration that collectively share meaning through cultural expressions and subjective loyalties to one another and a social universe of meaning. The motivations behind the violent acts – as consisting of both physical and epistemological violence – that precipitate cultural wounding are vast and, in the field of ethnic studies, emerge out from experiences of colonialism, racism and oppression, discrimination and prejudice, territorial conflict, and political suppression. Epistemological violence is emerging an ever-expanding field of inquiry in anthropology, Indigenous, ethnic, and critical race studies. For the purpose of this research, epistemological violence is defined as a practice of knowledge habits, which negatively impact upon marginalized populations, due, in large fact, to the importation of bias, assumptions of power and powerlessness, and representative authority without consideration of the epistemic habits called upon and reinforced through certain ways of knowing. For Teo (2010) operating within the empirical social sciences, it is "closer to personal than to structural violence in that it has a subject, an object, and an action, even if the violence is indirect and nonphysical: the subject of violence is the researcher, the object is the *Other*, and the action is the interpretation of data that is presented as knowledge."

What binds human groups and ultimately locates them in the pathway of "ethnic violence" is the perception of an "ethnic distinction" and a cultural orientation that is determined "other." This cultural orientation is evidenced in explicit and implicit action and performance and becomes a declared site of contention for incoming human agents or other ethnic groups. Out of these contexts, culture becomes the identifiable object associated with an ethnic group. Yet the culture that binds an ethnic group through such encounters with violence, prejudice, and intentional harm is ultimately more sophisticated, nuanced, and complex than simply being reducible to an object of hateful attack in times of conflict. Culture, by nature, does not easily disappear, and in turn the capacity for ethnicity to reinvent, emerge, and reform, in the aftermath of cultural wounding, is significant. This is because healing and ethnic survivals are so profoundly interwoven with the experience of cultural wounding, as ethnic groups grapple with the effects of harm, knowing that the process of finding strength and cultural resilience is one of "urgent patience;" that is, a task that must begin immediately, but in the knowledge that to culturally thrive once again, in the aftermath of ethnically targeted violence, may take some time (Gordon 2008, 2011: 16).

Ethnicity, cultural wounding, and healing are the key themes guiding this chapter's discussion of human distinctiveness, conflict, and survival. In a commitment to enriching the field of global ethnic studies, this chapter aims to take stock of the meanings and expressions of ethnicity available to people in a prevailingly tense world, where tensions are born of ethnic conflict and culturally prescribed violence and shaped by the dynamic ethnic configurations that emerge from and survive such encounters. The types of ethnic conflict to which I refer throughout this chapter are not conflict in the form of a "battle," an interactive, multisided happening in which two or more ethnic groups expressly agitate and fight one another for their ethnic group's dominance and position within society. The forms of ethnic conflict which precipitate cultural wounding, as defined here, are often more one-sided and unilateral, involving disproportionate amounts of violence being enacted by one group upon another and, in turn, suffering disproportionately experienced by that other group. Such a view does not suggest passivity among those who experience ethnic violence; instead it seeks to highlight the overwhelming assumption and execution of dominance on behalf of some ethnic groups and their pursuit of power and authority. These are the hallmarks of colonization and distinguish the experience of settler colonial invasion, which began in Australia in 1788, with the arrival of the British. This view of conflict has been shaped by my ethnographic training and professional life as an anthropologist in Australia, working with Indigenous families and histories of settler colonial violence and frontier conflict and enduring hardship for Indigenous peoples within the context of the nation state.

It is in midst and aftermath of ethnic conflict, violence, and cultural wounding that targeted groups strive to find pathways home, that is, a return to some sense of belonging and security. "Finding a way home" is on the one hand, a reference to locating and securing the healing pathways that close the loop around an ethnic or cultural group asserting a self-determined universe for survival and future health. On the other hand, "finding a way home" can be an actual and committed exercise in seeking a return to home, as a geographical homeland, or the pursuing of land and sea rights, or asserting a diasporic identity and claiming a site of refuge into which a memory of origins and sense of belonging may be projected. This chapter is committed to better understanding the experiences of cultural wounding that precipitate a need for return as contained in the action of "finding a way home," for Indigenous families in northern Australia. This example works to ground the discussion of ethnicity and cultural wounding and reveal the powerful ways in which groups heal and retain a sense of belonging through distinctive pathways of return and restitution.

Ethnicity and Cultural Wounding

Methodologically, this work is born of my experiences as an anthropologist and ethnographer, working with Indigenous families in northern Australia for the last 18 years. In both instances, I have witnessed cultural wounding, as the lasting impact of histories distinguished by forced child removal, theft of homelands, waters and resources, and entrenched racism and poverty through imposed powerlessness. I have listened to the form cultural wounding takes in narratives of personal and group experiences, across generations. Yet I would be remiss if I failed to mention the remarkable and creative ways in which people enact their own capacity to "get on with things," to continue to live life while attesting to the importance of their ethnic identity and gathering around ethnic distinctions as markers of self-esteem and worth. Much of this effort is directed at ensuring a place in the world for the ethnic group and being able to enact the cultural orientations that distinguish the group. Thus, place and context for cultural distinctiveness to take hold and be performed are enduring qualities of ethnic belonging, even in the aftermath of cultural wounding. Before moving into an ethnographically informed reading of cultural wounding in the context of Indigenous Australia, specifically, Yanyuwa country in northern Australia, I must first dedicate some time to discussing the very nature of ethnicity and ethnic belonging, relative to place and also the lived experience of cultural wounding.

Simply stating one's ethnic identity as "X" is only part of the process of ethnically aligning and establishing subjective loyalties. To be fully subsumed into an ethnic group requires recognition; such is the relative nature of ethnicity. The desire to belong is measured alongside group willingness to include as well as the extent to which individuals are capable of performing the identity as one made up of agreed-to terms (Kearney 2014: 17). "Agreed-to" is a nod to the formal and informal sanctioning of knowledge and processes for articulating this knowledge. This knowledge can express itself through ancestral narratives and social memory and requires a context or setting for action. This is the relational dependency between human life, ethnic belonging, and place. Place need not be "set or fixed" in relation to ethnicity, and in equal parts, ethnic identities can be located within a known and ancestrally derived place world, or they may move beyond a singular site of origin or performance, moving through an ever-expanding world of place possibilities, as with the experience of diaspora.

The highly relational bond between ethnicity and place reveals a logic of "connectivity and fit" between people and their place world, configured as they may be, as either ecologies, cities, villages, nations, journeys, or memoryscapes. A memoryscape is described as a "complex and vibrant plane upon which memories emerge, are contested, transform, encounter other memories, mutate and multiply" (Phillips and Mitchell Reyes 2011: 14), and a portal through which groups remember. A memoryscape may be a place that no longer exists in real time, or in the reachable world of physical presence, but may be one of memory, of the past. Writing specifically of this connectivity and fit (Rose 2014) outlines how humans pattern their social, ecological, and cultural relations in the Simpson Desert of

Central Australia. This is partly a relationship of response to water in a desert setting, whereby the arrival of rain, the forming of water holes, or the impermanence of water is a sign of life to which people respond. Desert water expresses connectivity through the lives of every living creature, whereby the ancestral actions, weather patterns, species fecundity, and human response are woven together through a form of poetry, that is, according to Rose (2014) contained in Indigenous song and narrative, expressive hallmarks of ethnic identity. It reveals the manner in which "human culture" and ethnic distinctiveness pulse and flow within the patterns of surrounding life, as rains come, people sing of species fecundity and respond to a dynamically changing landscape (see also Toussaint et al. 2005). For others this fit derives from the nexus between people, place, embodied practices of cultural law, social memory, and all the elements that constitute the ethnic group.

Ecologies that fit are imagined as ones in which humans are situated within the communicative world and thus within a myriad passionate calls for response and connection (Rose 2014: 441). A poetics of fit resonates through the contexts in which ethnic groups find their places of hold and belonging. This is found across the Indigenous homelands of Yanyuwa families in northern Australian where, through ethnographic encounters, I have witnessed the very way in which calls for response and connection are extended to the everyday practices of living with and among a community that defines itself ethnically through a shared history, contemporary strengths and hardships, and motivations to heal and culturally thrive in terms not wholly given or accepted by the majority.

As a statement of social relativism, an ethnic identity is constituted by group participation, group recognition, a context for action, and the ability to apprehend and subscribe to a set of social memories. Being conscious of these conditions for belonging, a person may assert an ethnic loyalty through literal declaration, knowing that this takes force once the individual is subsumed by the group, through affiliations and the adoption of group ideology, behaviors, or affirmation of symbols in everyday life. In this moment, the individual performs their ethnicity in immediate life while sustaining and projecting the presence of the group. This view of ethnicity requires both individual and collective presences to exist. An ethnic identity can be understood as a "person's self" as well as a "collective's delimits." Whether an individual imagines their selfhood as separate from the collective depends on the context in which this ethnic identity has come to exist and how the wider social universe receives it. Evidently, claims of belonging are not without their complexities.

Ethnicity plays a vital role in the substantiating of a person, community, or entire population and provides a context for identifying with social, historical, and political frameworks, whereby groups of individuals perceive themselves in relation to others (Scott 2008: 175; see also Karner 2007). Place is an essential part of this social becoming and movement. Within any cultural context, it is what mediates, constrains, delimits, or even allows performance and celebration of certain ways of being. By constituting and reinforcing particular human presences or by being the site of human life, place also renders people distinct. A homeland can justify a people, or a journey through place might distinguish a cultural and ethnic group's narrative. In turn, place can determine the extent to which a person or entire ethnic group is existentially inside place or existentially outside of place (Relph 1976; Seamon 1996; Seamon and Sowers 2008). The former resonates with the principle of a "poetics of fit," whereby life "makes sense" in the context of place, while the latter can bring deep anxieties around belonging and emplacement. To be existentially outside of place is to live with the experience of alienation, to feel a powerful loss of home, or an inability to locate home (Relph 1976: 51–55). In what follows, I examine why it is that "home" as both a context for belonging and setting for cultural and ethnic distinctiveness becomes a target in times of conflict and violence and why alienation, expulsion, and place erasure become weapons to harm an ethnic group. Yet the prevailing narrative of home endures beyond that of cultural wounding and is often a central theme in healing projects and narrations aimed at ethnic survival and endurance.

Loss of Home amid Ethnic Conflict and Violence

A classic and defining feature of ethnicity is affiliation with place, either configured as a homeland, a region, nation, site of commemoration, memorial, or, even more locally, a community organization. These become contexts for sharing in an ethnically prescribed experience of life, ensuring that identities are able to form, and then perform the requisite patterns that assert them as something and someone distinctive. Whether this is a homeland claimed through primordial and ancestral connections or a new place into which an identity is projected, following diaspora, there is a foundational importance in having a place to enact the patterns that allow us to find and assert belonging and security. Given the centrality of a spatial universe (of contracting or expanding size) for ethnic identities to come into being and to survive and also thrive, then what does it mean when violence is aimed at place or is by design enacted to ensure the pathways home can no longer be found or retraced?

Ethnic conflict and cultural wounding often target the contexts in which ethnic groups make their home or enact the specificities of their identities (through economic, political, spiritual, and social life). Attacks on place and alienation from home are proven strategies designed to bring about violent effects, which map onto social depression, ill health, declining birth rates, early death, addictive behaviors, and domestic violence (Fullilove 2004). The loss of home and/or forced removal of ethnic constituents from their place or origin is shown to induce cultural trauma by uprooting place-based identities and thus interrupting the relationships and practices that ensure the lived experience of ethnic belonging (see, e.g., Davis 2005; Fullilove 2004; Windsor and McVey 2005). Another form of violence in times of ethnic conflict might also be the precipitation of ecological decline and toxicity (poisoned water sources, drought through river diversions, introduction of feral species) by incoming ethnic presences with disregard to ecological order which is aligned with existing laws of interaction. This kind of violence can compel widespread evacuation of ethnic groups and turn homelands into unviable contexts for everyday life (see Eriksen 2011; Shkilnyk 1985). These involve the disregard of existing order, and delivery of harm to place's constitutive parts, as a strategy to erode the foundations of and relational setting for human life. This comes as a consequence of ambivalence to and disregard for place value.

During episodes of ethnic conflict, it is as Heider (2005: 12) writes, in an account of "violence and ecology": "Violent action means usually producing spectacular changes from order to disorder, which can be brought about by undirected or only roughly directed launching actions." Deep unrest comes for those ethnic groups who are bound closely to place and homelands, and for them, decline and alienation may be read as a form of communicative event, in which kin is charged with somehow relinquishing their responsibility. Shkilnyk (1985) documents such practices of translating meaning in moments of place chaos caused by toxicity. She writes of the events that lead to the relocation of the Ojibwa people, the Indigenous owners of the islands and peninsulas on the English-Wabigoon River, Northwestern Ontario, Canada, and the ongoing effects this move had on members of the community (Shkilnyk 1985: 2). The Ojibwa were moved from their homelands, only to then experience a mercury poisoning that occurred in waterways on the new reserve. This triggered a decline in community life, health, and well-being, and Shkilnyk's (1985) ethnography recounts Ojibwa testimonies of "coming to terms" with what has occurred. Many traced the events of mercury poisoning to ill-ease within the new reserve. This place was held to be "bad land," "off limits to human habitation," and full of "bad spirits" (Shkilnyk 1985: 70–71). The resounding sentiment was that this was not a place for Ojibwa and that place was communicating through ominous warnings such as persons and spirits surfacing from the lake, poor quality of light in place, and the presence of "troubled spirits" on the new reserve. Writing of the harrowing effects of toxicity and contamination, in the aftermath of relocation and community decline, Shkilnyk reflects:

> Having just been wretched from their moorings on the old reserve, the people were ill prepared to cope with yet another misfortune. They had but a precarious hold on the conditions of their existence on the new reserve. They could no longer draw strength either from their relationship to the land or from the well of their faith, which had once given meaning and coherence to their lives. In the context of the traditional religious beliefs, the contamination of the river could only be interpreted as punishment by the Great Spirit for some serious violation of the laws governing man's relationship to nature. People had great difficulty comprehending this 'unseen poison' of mercury, whose presence in the water and in the fish they could not see or taste or smell. (Shkilnyk 1985: 179)

This form of violence amplifies the effectiveness of ethnically motivated and directed conflict, partly because it takes as its focus the very ground on which people live, walk, eat, commune, and activate group meaning. The harms are delivered to place, partly because the poetics of fit that locates a people in their home is disregarded as important. In a closer reading of violence as enacted upon place as home, I have engaged with this disregard as a form of axiological retreat, a sanctioned "failure to care" (see Kearney 2017).

For Indigenous groups in Australia, their histories and present realities are marked by forced relocations, loss of lands and waters, fracturing of Indigenous

Laws as governing and hardship on the basis of an alleged otherness, and imposed marginality by powerful ethnic majorities. For Indigenous Australians the loss takes its form in the theft of homelands by colonial agents and the British Crown, forced removals from homelands, the decline of local ecologies due to new economies, and the ensuing fight for piecemeal returns to land through white legislative structures. Indigenous homelands have struggled under the weight of colonization, configured as a form of sickness and sadness in country (an Indigenous terminology often adopted when faced with the physical decline of homelands) through an Indigenous epistemology of place. Instances of cultural wounding map heavily onto place, thus I take as central to the discussion of ethnic conflict, attacks on the place world into which ethnic identities are projected and supported in their everyday expression. Instating a decline in the place world of ethnic groups remains a resoundingly powerful way in which to harm an ethnic other and potentially prevent their survival and cultural integrity.

The most obvious incorporations of place into the trauma narratives that emerge from experiences of ethnic conflict, and cultural wounding, take the form of recounting the injustice of place theft and destruction, the embodied suffering that comes with removal from place, and a deep longing to return. So too the paradox of return looms large in the narratives of those who have been wounded often left asking, how can I return? And to what do I return? Yanyuwa families in the southwest Gulf of Carpentaria, northern Australia, have faced a forced reconfiguration of the place relations that make them who they are, over a sequence of many generations. Whether through theft of place or removal from place, the relational world this ethnic group occupies has been rearranged through acts of renaming place, new land tenure arrangements under a settler colonial order, and, in more recent years, place destruction by aggressive land use industries such as opencut mining. Yet it is also place that has provided Yanyuwa with the context needed to culturally maintain, reorient, and establish the terms for ethnic belonging that resonate with present need and historical circumstance. Place is central in this journey.

Yanyuwa Families and 42 Years of Seeking Land Rights

For Indigenous Australians, place theft characterizes just some of the deeply wounding strategies used against people throughout 230 years of settler colonialism. Place destruction and designification are recalled through human accounts of loss. Destruction is evidenced by those places that have been carved up by boundaries and borders, sold off as pastoral leases, alienated through colonially imported land tenure arrangements, and in recent decades impacted by mining and large-scale resource projects. Designification on the other hand has ensured the introduction of confusion into place understandings and the denial of existing order and value. For Indigenous Australians this has seen country renamed, reinscribed as belonging to the British Crown, sold on the open market, and ultimately taken beyond the influence of its Indigenous owners. Destruction and designification are conspiring themes that bring about chaos in place, making it difficult for ethnic groups to hold on to the contexts that give them relational substance. It is designification that supports a denial of place order and disavowal of existing relational substance between a group and their homelands or context for existence. Denying the character of place is necessary for what Falah (1996) terms resignification of place. Resignification is prefaced by the knowledge that ideological sediment exists in place, and this is often what gives substance to an ethnic group's presence and claim to rights. These sedimentary layers of meaning, order, and value are deposited by ancestral law and the ongoing agency of the right human presence; however, these are denied and then overlain with the order of another, in the contexts of settler colonialism as ethnic conflict and incoming violence (Falah 1996: 256; see also Schnell and Mishal 2008).

Yanyuwa country is located in the southwest Gulf of Carpentaria, northern Australia (see Fig. 1). Today most Yanyuwa live in the township of Borroloola, approximately 40 km from the coast but still within the clan-based range of their country. The terms of their country are set by the distinction of being li-Anthawirriyarra, people whose substance and identity are derived of the sea's influence. Yanyuwa country encompasses the delta regions of the McArthur River and the saltwater limits of the McArthur and Wearyan Rivers and the Sir Edward Pellew Islands. By emphasizing themselves as sea people, rather than mainland

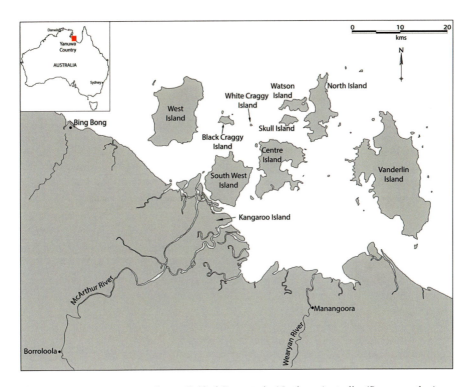

Fig. 1 Yanyuwa country, southwest Gulf of Carpentaria, Northern Australia. (Source: author)

people, Yanyuwa activate a human to country relationship that is distinct (see Bradley 2008, 2014). This relationship is made vital and expressed in a variety of ways and manifests itself on more historical terms through language, kinship, patterns of settlement and subsistence, song, ceremony, and ancestral narratives (Bradley 2008, 2014, Bradley and Yanyuwa Families 2010, 2016).

Yanyuwa have lived through a protracted encounter with cultural wounding. This has been achieved through land, sea and resource theft, forced removal of children of mixed descent parentage, and imposition of nonindigenous governance structures (Kearney 2014, 2018). These experiences have historical depth but remain part of everyday life. The contemporary experiences of educational and social disadvantage and poverty through powerlessness are vivid indications of enduring cultural wounding, based on a settler colonial and white distinctions of "otherness" among Australia's Indigenous populations. From these experiences people have had to heal and through deliberate action protect their right to prevail as a culturally distinct group. These encounters begin in the mid-1880s as settler incursions make their initial presence known in the Gulf of Carpentaria and contact amplified after 1901 with the establishment of the township of Borroloola (Baker 1990, 1999; Roberts 2005). This brought more permanent white settlements in the area, increased land grabs, and establishment of a food rations depot, to which Indigenous people were drawn through relations of dependency. The pressures of settler colonialism conspired to "bring Yanyuwa in" to an increased habit of town living by the 1950s and 1960s and almost permanent town living by the 1970s (Baker 1990, 1999).

Relatively speaking this represents a somewhat late shift in mobility and residency patterns for the region's Indigenous groups. Elsewhere across the country, particularly along the eastern seaboard of Australia, rapid incursions were made into Indigenous people's lands and waters, thus prompting earlier and major lifestyle changes and dependencies on townships, and fringe living, as a response to greater numbers of permanently based white settlers and frontier administrations. That the sea, which separates vast areas of Yanyuwa island country from mainland pressures, played a role in buffering Yanyuwa from this violent encounter for some time is undeniable. The materiality of Yanyuwa sea territories is such that it has provided Yanyuwa with both open routes for movement, yet also protection, as a barrier to colonization (Adgemis 2017; McLaughlin 1977: 4; Avery 1985; Baker 1999: 197; Roberts 2005: 174). This was because colonists did not possess the maritime skills required to traverse the open waters of the Gulf of Carpentaria and the isolation that white settlers faced if travelling to the offshore islands, which placed them at a distinct disadvantage in claiming influence over this saltwater setting. Yanyuwa faced their greatest hardships as they moved closer to the inland township over which white administrators had claimed control. Their sea country, however, provided unprecedented autonomy. In many respects this reinforces the poetics of fit articulate by Rose (2014) and highlights the ill fit on behalf of incoming agents, incapable of negotiating the saltwater qualities and complexities of Yanyuwa country.

Resistance and the continued pursuit of a poetics of fit, between people and the place world, have defined Yanyuwa lives for over a century, expressed as maintaining physical distance from settler presences, as continuing to move across sea country as much as possible, and in continuing to claim identities as li-Anthawirriyarra. Their resistance has been directed toward the goal of survival and cultural endurance. Over the last four decades, ethnic and cultural endurance has come via the launching of campaigns to seek land and sea rights under the legislative arrangements currently in place in the Northern Territory and federally including the Aboriginal Land Rights (NT) Act 1976 (henceforth ALRA) and the Native Title Act 1993. Since 1976 Yanyuwa have launched three claims under the ALRA, one under the Native Title Act, bodies of legislation born of a structurally white system of Law, and are currently engaged in a precedent setting compensation claim for lands destroyed through mining activity. The community has been unrelenting in its commitment to the pursuit of rights, to redress the colonially driven ethnic violence of land theft and alienation that marks their historical and contemporary experience. Part of holding strong in their ethnic distinctiveness is never conceding the importance of Yanyuwa Law in governing the southwest Gulf of Carpentaria and their ancestral homelands. There is no doubt for Yanyuwa that the poetics of fit that is their ethnic identity in place is as indivisible as the human need for oxygen.

The longing for return remains a powerful and defining encounter in the social and political lives of many Indigenous groups. For Yanyuwa, alienation from home was not a physical rupturing of people's being in place. They retained proximity to their country, but were rescripted, by colonial administrations as a people "out of place." Across Australia, all Indigenous presences were problematized through legal erasure and through a settler colonial rhetoric of "discovery," "absence," and the "imperative to populate," what Rose (2004:85) describes as the setting of a "Year Zero." The distinguishing feature of this Indigenous experience is that people became alienated from country, through settler colonial acts that brought historical, cultural, and political contest over their exclusive rights to land and sea. These rights are enacted not only through presence and residency but also through epistemological, ontological, and axiological orientations. As such people were forced into relations with colonial presences that made many of their cultural habits intimately linked to country difficult to maintain and unable to flourish. In the case of Indigenous claimants seeking land rights, the quest is not to return to country in a physical sense only, but it is about restituting the space into which a Yanyuwa ethnic identity can be projected in full and enacted without threat of harm.

Yanyuwa have cultivated an urgent patience in their approach to land rights (see Baker 1992; Rose 1996; Seton and Bradley 2005). Urgent patience, taken from Gordon's (2008, 2011: 16) work on social death and hauntings, is "a way of being in the ongoing work of emancipation, a work never measured by legalistic pronouncements, a work that inevitably must take place while you're still confined." Writing of social death, the condition of not being accepted as fully human by wider society, a distinctive quality of cultural wounding and living with ethnic conflict, Gordon (2008, 2011) reflects that for those living with suffering, living in poverty or alongside structural violence, or for those living with the effects of other impoverishment, the social death is rendered and narrated by others (see also Bauman 1992). This social death is written into the colonial administration's historical declaration of rights over Indigenous lands and waters, the violence of alienation and dispossession, and ultimately the imperative to fight within a structurally white system of land rights.

The Yanyuwa fight for rights to their sea country as something that was never ceded is the act of "something-to-be-done," a response to "a situation that requires immediate attention" (Gordon 2011: 8). It is approached with an "urgency that's autonomous and self-directed towards ends and aims not wholly given and certainly not given permission by the system's logics or crises but rather invented elsewhere and otherwise" (Gordon 2011: 8). The particular combination of acute timeliness and patience that is fighting for land rights, over a 40-year period, echoes the quality of urgent patience in that there is:

> no time to waste at all and the necessity of taking your time, is what ... has guided the worldwide movements to abolish slavery and captivity, colonialism, imprisonment, militarism, foreign debt bondage, and to abolish the capitalist world order known today as globalization or neo-liberalism. (Gordon 2011: 8)

Despite ongoing challenges and ethnic marginalization within the settler colonial state, Yanyuwa engagements with land rights are part of a wider sequence of healing actions, which operate to deny social death, as the settler colonial ontology that compels or justifies Indigenous dispossession and alienation. Yanyuwa healing actions, including seeking land rights, are:

> bound to the work of carrying on regardless: to keeping urgent the repair of injustice and the care-taking of the aggrieved and the missing; to keeping urgent the systematic dismantling of the conditions that produce the crises and the misery in the first place while at the same time instantiating in the practice itself the slower temporality of the wait and the distinct onto-epistemological affects of autonomous, independent, participatory thoughtful practice. (Gordon 2011: 8)

Sadly, the return of Yanyuwa lands that has been facilitated by legislative land rights does not mean the dissolution of the strictures of colonial ontologies that perpetuate conflict (Seton and Bradley 2005). Thus there remain tensions that are ultimately indicative of prevailing ethnic conflict between Indigenous groups nationwide and the settler colonial state. There is much still to be done in the decolonizing space to bring about a richer form of transitional justice and social justice for those ethnic groups that have been marginalized by the powerful. Evidencing this is the fact that for those lands that have been restituted through legislative processes, there are expectations that Yanyuwa will "work" their country for financial profit and return, according to a white sensibility, so too they are expected to continue to negotiate with Northern Territory Parks and Wildlife and adhere to restrictions on the activities carried out across their islands.

In those instances where freehold Aboriginal land title is recognized, as in the case of Yanyuwa country, there is something misleading in declaring this a return of rights or a return to country. I wish to stress that the return of lands is of course a resoundingly positive outcome for Yanyuwa; however there are complexities involved in this process of seeking rights which are strikingly paradoxical given the nature of Yanyuwa connections to both land and sea territories and their ongoing physical presence across their sea country. To clarify, rights can only be determined over terrestrial lands, and in coastal areas, this extends to but is limited as far as that land which sits between the high and low watermarks. In coastal areas, grants of Aboriginal land under the ALRA extend only to the low watermark (Brennan 2008). To date, no Indigenous rights of prior and continuing tenure have been recognized over bodies of waters beyond the intertidal zone. There is a profound legal confusion contained in debates of where the land ends and the sea begins, or the possibility of an Indigenous group homelands containing both terrestrial, coastal, oceanic, and riverine settings remains beyond the reach of current legislative arrangements (Jackson 1995). The epistemic routines and ontological presumptions of White Australia continue to define the nature of this debate, delimiting the rights potentially obtainable by coastal and riverine Indigenous groups (Marshall 2017; Strang 2011; Strang and Busse 2011). As a form of epistemological violence, such delimitations ensure the habit of ethnic tension in Australia.

As an act of urgent patience, Yanyuwa have responded to the loss of home through the early *realization* of deep colonizing and the violent impact this has had and continues to have on their lives. Their *resolution* to launch healing actions in the face of this, by way of land claims, is what defines much of the last 40 years in this community, spreading its effects now over three generations. Resolution to fight has required Yanyuwa to *re-present* their saltwater identity and package it in a manner that can be tested, cross-examined, and reconstituted by legal and statutory definitions. These are the complicated, concessional, and also self-determined steps Yanyuwa have taken to retain a sense of their own ethnicity and place in the world. In the aftermath of cultural wounding, people have had to pay a huge price on the road to restitution, the greatest payoff thus far being the return of portions of their saltwater country, yet it remains that the poetics of fit that distinguishes the ethically prescribed universe into which a Yanyuwa identity is projected and practiced remains somewhat contested, due to the processes by which their right to be li-Anthawirriyarra, people of the sea, is repeatedly funnelled through white legislative frameworks of land justice.

Healing and Return

While people and their place world have come to bear the scars of cultural wounding, the place world also figures as centrally important in healing projects for ethnic groups. Even sites of great sadness and places rendered as memoryscapes, beyond the physical reach of ethnic constituents today, can be reclaimed as essential to present healing and remembrance. Pathways that create relational bonds, such as kinship with place, or capacity to remake place in the image of a former homeland or completely anew often offer the most secure pathways to healing and recuperation. In the aftermath of cultural wounding, place, country, and home are therefore often scripted as the desired sites of refuge, sought out for security and the surety of ethnic belonging that is so longed for in a collective's healing journey. Such a relationship with the place world is vividly cast in the Yanyuwa narrative of seeking restitution of their lands and waters. The embodied suffering that comes with removal from home, or the denial of ways of knowing and being in one's country, is also richly documented in accounts of Indigenous dispossession. Thus it is that returning or finding pathways home or seeking restitution of territories to which one belongs has become cornerstone of transitional justice efforts and self-determination agendas worldwide, both for Indigenous ethnic groups and other marginalized ethnic groups.

The action of return or the pursuit of pathways to reinstate the poetics of fit that is an ethnic group in their sites of meaning is central to the healing agendas of many ethnic groups who live through experiences of violence and conflict. Longing to return is about enlivening an emotional geography by mapping identities into the place world. Healing, in this instance, is defined as an action that resists hopelessness and helplessness. It is fuelled by the disposition of "urgent patience" and the knowledge that things must change, tempered by the realization that this may take some time (Gordon 2008, 2011). This imperative to heal is treated as a prevailing condition in the face of human suffering. It involves a flow of beneficial energy in some sense: into the body of an individual, among the constituents of an ethnic group and nation, or into the imaginary of the human spirit and across the ecologies of country (Kearney 2014: 8). This energy is directed at repairing that which has been injured physically, emotionally, and psychologically (see Kearney 2014). It works to regenerate and proliferate the benefits through health and well-being. Hope, born of recovery, is a fundamental aspect of this vision of healing (Staub et al. 2005: 305) and is what sustains the wounded ethnic group throughout the process of healing. Understood as a process marked by deliberate acts that increase the effectiveness of this recovery, healing from cultural wounding requires resilience to absorb and expand with the flow of energy and resistance to hopelessness in the aftermath of wounding.

Ethnic groups may choose a number of pathways toward healing, differentiated by their motive. In the first instance, a prevailing motive for healing is the logic of "because (Elsewhere I have written at length on healing motivation, both in relation to a "because logic" and also an "in-order-to logic" (see Kearney 2014). The latter is distinguished from a "because" motive, by being aligned with a future outcome, rather than a past event. It is underscored by a desire to move onward rather than enact stasis that relies on the past. It is through reflexivity that "one imagines a project as completed" and this projection is configured as survival and states of healing.)" "Because" motives are essential references to something preceding the act in question and refer to past or already-experienced events as the cause of action in the present and into the future. In the context of ethnic conflict leading to cultural wounding, this act may be any number of things, from colonization, genocide, dispossession of lands and waters, loss of economic independence, or political powerlessness. Viewed deterministically, healing undertaken in light of a "because" motive places those who seek to heal in a particular relationship with harms already delivered and, in turn, those who have perpetrated them. "Because" motives are reliant on retentions to find their substance and language. These retentions are the social memories and everyday realities of hardship that ethnic groups live with. Actions prefaced by a "because" motive require stepping back into the cultural wounding experience, declaring the losses and reinstating relations between the often politically strong and the politically oppressed. Embedded in this relationship are the conditions of conflict and the possibility of resparking tension or even denial of legitimacy for the ethnic group's claim (Kearney 2014: 82). Actions prefaced by a "because" motive call upon recognition of past and present wounding in an effort to clear space for a discourse on the future. Examples of healing actions prefaced by a "because motive" include civil disobedience and activism, violent retaliation, restitution of land and sea territories through legislative processes, national apologies, and truth commissions (Kearney 2014: 83).

Whatever the motive, the healing project requires collective arrangement and agreement as to the version of good health, or the poetics of fit, that the group seeks. Motive will however strongly determine the pathways by which healing will be pursued, and for those prefaced by a "because logic," the experience may also bring about particular emotional and psychological encounters for the group, due to the dialogic nature of healing. In the case of the Yanyuwa experience, the group has rallied around an abiding and long-term commitment to seeking land rights, albeit under a legislatively white system. The reality is that all members of the group must accept the terms for restitution as set by this system and mobilize together in order to achieve a successful outcome, that is, some degree of formal and binding Aboriginal land tenure. As a rallying cry, legislative land rights has somehow managed to solidify ethnic group identity and terms for belonging, despite being the product of intense dispossession and also it being derived of the legal structures that sanctioned this very dispossession (see Seton and Bradley 2005 for a discussion of this relative to the concept of deep colonizing). There is a resounding tension in the space of transitional and social justice in Australia, born of the fact that the terms of belonging, the evidentiary demands, and the performance of Aboriginal distinctiveness take place within a white courtroom and before a white judge. These are just two of the paradoxical encounters when a "because motive" informs the healing actions of an ethnic group. The system by which the group must fight has the simultaneous effect of imposing conditions for belonging and performing an ethnic identity while strengthening bonds between ethnic constituents by compelling people to come together and agree to and enact their collective identity for future benefits. In reality, the tendrils of ethnic conflict spread their influence far and wide and may manifest as the guiding axiologies by which groups seek their own ethnic revival and health, as evidenced by land rights legislation in Australia.

Land rights legislation is born of ethnic conflict, and it does not innocently deliver Indigenous rights. Yet, even epistemologically violent mechanisms are adopted when seeking ethnic rights and pursuing social justice. For many Indigenous groups, there is no choice but to seek rights to homelands through legislative pathways, as country is an indivisible element of the group's very existence and epistemological, ontological, and axiological orientation into the world. People make decisions to deny social death and do so in the mode of "urgent patience." While the complications of this deserve their own treatment in future studies, what this chapter strives to articulate is the fact that ethnic conflict leads to many pathways for healing. Forged of even dysfunctional relationships are at times gains for Indigenous and other marginalized ethnic groups. There is an art worthy of greater research attention in the space of concessional healing that in some ways works to unite the ethnic group. On similar matters, Maori intellectual, Sir Tipene O'Regan (2014), has reflected on what becomes of Maori identity as it passes through the process of land restitution. He describes the undertaking as one that has generated the conditions for multiple forms of identity remake, cautioning that land rights policy and land restitution change the ways in which groups identify and configure their futures. O'Regan (2014: 27) calls for scholarship to more substantially know what happens to identities through this process and to protect against the threat that policy might reduce Indigenous "history and tradition [to] mere opinion, blown by political winds."

It is such that ethnic conflict leads to the seeking of pathways toward healing. These pathways may be in and of themselves the result of disproportionate power in decision-making, as is the case with legislative, legal, and political steps taken by the ethnic majority to redress their historical violence, unreconciled tensions, and prevailing inequality, yet they can be harnessed and mobilized for gain by marginalized groups. While there is a disturbing reality in this, and it may reveal the layers of epistemological and structural violence that marginalized ethnic groups must operate within, it also highlights the incredible capacity and ingenuity of ethnic groups to configure ways in which to survive and seek opportunities to thrive on culturally prescribed terms. It is through this lens that ultimately this discussion of healing aims to take stock of the meanings and expressions of ethnicity available to people in a prevailingly tense world, where tensions are born of ethnic conflict and culturally prescribed violence and shaped by the dynamic ethnic configurations that emerge from and survive such encounters.

Concluding Remarks

Appreciating what an ethnic group undergoes in the process of healing from cultural wounding is a vital step toward better understanding the impact of conflict and its contemporary legacies. Similarly, it works to shed light on the complex ethnic arrangements and rearrangements that signify national and transnational settings at present. Such insight can work to better understand how it is that an ethnic group self-determines the pathways they will take toward survival and how they will negotiate the terms on which they claim their distinctiveness. In the case of the Yanyuwa, this has been through the seeking of land rights and ultimately has been solidified by a sophisticated negotiation of group identity through the structurally white landscape of legislative process. This undertaking should never be read as one that was easy for Yanyuwa, but as it stands, they had no choice, for their ethnic identity is born of country, and country, as containing the ancestors, had to be brought back. There is no more vivid display of urgent patience aligned with cultural resilience.

The challenge that culturally wounded ethnic groups face is that the experience of cultural wounding is not contained in space and time as a single encounter. Cultural wounding is better understood as an ongoing encounter that reveals itself in myriad forms across an ethnic group and across generations of descendants. Hence it demands of ethnic groups and their constituents' remarkable abilities to negotiate, come to know the point of conflict, determine a need heal, and then find the right pathways toward healing. Cultural wounding has a profound legacy on all generations who, in many ways, live with the effects of wounding and must often maintain the healing project relative to present need born of historical context. This is why the process of healing is an enduring state of being for many ethnic groups who have lived through or emerged out of experiences with ethnically prescribed violence and conflict. And just as cultural wounding is rarely encountered as a universal experience across a group of ethnic constituents, the culture which goes to distinguish a groups' sense of collective belonging is more fluid than might be imagined, better presented as a sequence of easily adopted and malleable attributes and symbols of identity that are aspects of individual selves, adaptable postmodern qualities that are not necessarily inherited, or authoritative but often are constructed and reconstructed. Survival demands the quality of urgent patience and sophisticated way finding in the pursuit of pathways for healing that revive ethnic esteem and well-being.

Cross-References

▶ Contemporary Ethnic Politics and Violence
▶ Indigenous Australian Identity in Colonial and Postcolonial Contexts

References

Adgemis P (2017) We are Yanyuwa – no matter what: town life, family and change. PhD Dissertation, Monash University, Melbourne, Australia
Avery J (1985) The law people: History, society and initiation in the Borroloola area of the Northern Territory. PhD Dissertation, University of Sydney, New South Wales
Baker R (1990) Coming in? The Yanyuwa as a case study in the geography of contact history. Aborig Hist 14(1–2):25–60
Baker R (1992) 'Gough Whitlam time': land rights in the Borroloola area of Australia's Northern Territory. Appl Geogr 12:162–175
Baker R (1999) Land is life: continuity through change for the Yanyuwa from the Northern Territory of Australia. Allen & Unwin, Sydney
Bauman Z (1992) Survival as a social construct. Theory, Cult Soc 9(1):1–36
Bradley J (2008) Singing through the sea: song, sea and emotion. In: Shaw S, Francis A (eds) Deep blue: critical reflections on nature, religion and water. Routledge, Abingdon, pp 17–32
Bradley J (2014) We always look north: Yanyuwa identity and the maritime environment. In: Peterson N, Rigsby B (eds) Customary marine tenure in Australia, 2nd edn. Sydney University Press, Sydney, pp 201–226
Bradley J, Families Y (2016) Wuka nya-nganunga li-Yanyuwa li-Anthawirriyarra-Language for us, The Yanyuwa saltwater people. ASP, Melbourne

Bradley J, Yanyuwa Families (2010) Singing saltwater country. Allen & Unwin, Sydney
Brennan S (2008) Wet or dry, it's aboriginal land: the blue mud bsay decision on the intertidal zone. Indigenous Law Bulletin 6(7). Available at: http://www.austlii.edu.au/au/journals/IndigLawB/2008/27.html. Accessed 12 May 2018
Cook B, Withy K, Tarallo-Jensen L (2003) Cultural trauma, Hawaiian spirituality and contemporary health status. Calif J Health 1:10–24
Davis J (2005) Is it really safe? That's what we want to know: science, stories, and dangerous places. Prof Geogr 57(2):213–221
Erikson K (2011) The day the world turned red: a report on the people of Utrik. Yale Rev 99(1):27–47
Falah G (1996) The 1948 Israeli–Palestinian war and its aftermath: the transformation and de-signification of Palestine's cultural landscape. Ann Assoc Am Geogr 86(2):256–285
Fullilove MT (2004) Root shock: how tearing up city neighborhoods hurts America and what we can do about it. Ballantine Books, New York
Gordon A (2008) Ghostly matters: haunting and the sociological imagination. University of Minessotta Press, Minessotta
Gordon A (2011) Some thoughts on haunting and futurity. Borderlands 10(2):2–21
Heider F (2005) Violence and ecology. Peace Confl: J Peace Psychol. Special Issue: Military Ethics and Peace Psychology: A Dialogue 11(1):9–15
Jackson S (1995) The water is not empty: cross-cultural issues in conceptualising sea space. Aust Geogr 26(1):87–96
Karner C (2007) Ethnicity and everyday life. Routledge, New York
Kearney A (2014) Cultural wounding, healing and emerging ethnicities. Palgrave Macmillan, New York
Kearney A (2017) Violence in place, cultural and environmental wounding. Routledge, Abingdon
Kearney A (2018) Intimacy and distance: indigenous relationships to country in northern Australia. Ethnos 83(1):172–191
Marshall V (2017) Overturning aqua nullius: Securing aboriginal water rights. Australian Studies Press, Canberra
McLaughlin D (1977) Submission to the joint selection committee on aboriginal land rights in the northern territory, 24 June 1977. In: Australian parliament joint selection committee on aboriginal land rights in the Northern territory, 1268–1316A. Commonwealth of Australia Publishers, Canberra
O'Regan T (2014) New myths and old politics. BWB, Wellington
Phillips K, Mitchell Reyes, G. (eds) (2011) Global memoryscapes: contesting remembrance in a transnational age. University of Alabama Press, Tuscaloosa
Relph E (1976) Place and placelessness. Pion, London
Roberts T (2005) Frontier justice: a history of the Gulf country to 1900. University of Queensland Press, St. Lucia
Rose D (1996) Land rights and deep colonising: the erasure of women. Aborig Law Bull 3(85):6
Rose D (2004) Reports from a wild country: ethics for decolonisation. UNSW Press, Sydney
Rose D (2014) Arts of flow: poetics of 'fit' in aboriginal Australia. Dialect Anthropol 38(4):431–445
Schnell I, Mishal S (2008) Place as a source of identity in colonizing societies: Israeli settlements in Gaza. Geogr Rev 98(2):242–259
Scott T (2008) It's all Alemannic to me! Ethnicity as an interpretive tool for cultural transformations. J Aust Early Mediev Assoc 4:175–185
Seamon D (1996) A singular impact: Edward Relph's place and placelessness. Environ Archit Phenomenol Newsl 7(3):5–8
Seamon D, Sowers J (2008) Place and placelessness, Edward Relph. In: Hubbard P, Kitchen R, Vallentine G (eds) Key texts in human geography. Sage, London, pp 43–51

Seton K, Bradley J (2005) Self-determination or 'deep colonising': land claims, colonial authority and Indigenous representation. In: Hocking B (ed) Unfinished constitutional business. Aboriginal Studies Press, Canberra, pp 32–46

Shkilnyk A (1985) A poison stronger than love: the destruction of an Ojibwa community. Yale University Press, New Haven

Staub E, Pearlman L, Gubin A, Hagengimana A (2005) Healing, reconciliation, forgiving and the prevention of violence after genocide or mass killing. J Soc Clin Psychol 24(3):297–334

Strang V (2011) Owning water in Australia. In: Strang V, Busse M (eds) Ownership and appropriation. Berg, Oxford, pp 171–196

Strang V, Busse M (eds) (2011) Ownership and appropriation. Berg, Oxford

Teo T (2010) What is epistemological violence in the empirical social sciences? Soc Personal Psychol Compass 4(5):295–303

Toussaint S, Sullivan P, Yu S (2005) Water ways in aboriginal Australia: an interconnected analysis. Anthropol Forum 15(1):61–74

Windsor J, McVey J (2005) Annihilation of both place and sense of place: the experience of the Cheslatta T'En Canadian First Nation within the context of large-scale environmental projects. Geogr J 171(2):146–165

Constitutional Features of Presidential Elections and the Failure of Cross-ethnic Coalitions to Institutionalize

41

M. Bashir Mobasher

Contents

Introduction	736
The Contributing Features of Presidential Elections	737
Unipersonal or Slate-Based Contest?	737
Pre-electoral Coalition-Making	739
The Fifty Percent Threshold	741
Coalition-Deterring Features of Afghan Presidential Elections	742
Two-Round Elections	742
Candidate-Centric Elections	743
Zero-Sum Games	746
Presidential Term Limits	747
Nonconcurrent Electoral Cycles	749
Parallel Legitimacy	750
Exclusion of Minorities	751
Conclusion	751
References	753

Abstract

This chapter studies the constitutional features of Afghan presidential elections and their impact on coalition-building. Based on the constitution, Afghan presidential elections are candidate-centric, zero-sum games, prone to pre-electoral bargaining, majoritarian, double ballots, religiously exclusive, and constrained by electoral cycles, as well as presidential term limits. Examining the presidential electoral features, this chapter argues that they do not have unidirectional impacts on coalition-building: some electoral features incentivize the formation of cross-ethnic coalitions, while others hinder their institutionalization. Therefore, while some function as constructive features, others are obstructive to coalition-building.

M. B. Mobasher (✉)
Department of Political Science, American University of Afghanistan, Kabul, Afghanistan
e-mail: bmobasher@auaf.edu.af

© The Author(s), under exclusive license to Springer Nature Singapore Pte Ltd. 2019
S. Ratuva (ed.), *The Palgrave Handbook of Ethnicity*,
https://doi.org/10.1007/978-981-13-2898-5_157

This chapter proposes that the obstructive features of presidential elections can be remedied through institutional designs. The remedies proposed in this chapter include holding concurrent elections and adopting nomination thresholds.

Keywords
Presidential elections · Electoral features · Cross-ethnic · Coalition-building

Introduction

Presidential elections have a number of distinct features, which are different from those of premier elections. For example, unlike premier elections, presidential elections are zero-sum games and single-seat contests. However, these distinct features of presidential elections have barely attracted the scholarly attentions that they deserve. Oftentimes, these features are explained in the margins of plurality and runoff systems. Sometimes, the literature tends to draw conclusions based on evaluation of just one or a few presidential electoral features (rules) in isolation and, therefore, misses some of the important effects that can be caught only with a wider lens. For example, Juan Linz (1994), Arend Lijphart (1977), and Juan Linz and Alfred Stepan (1996) point to the zero-sum game and candidate-centric features of presidential elections as evidence that presidential systems are unfit for coalition-building and power-sharing (Linz 1994, 21–23, 42–46). They argue that even the most successful presidential systems are linked with undisciplined parties and coalitions because presidents are less dependent on such organizations for winning and holding their offices (Mainwaring and Shugart 1997, 450). Further, power-sharing is meaningless in presidential democracies because an elected president is almost inevitably from one of the ethnic groups (Lijphart 2008, 169).

On the opposite end, Donald Horowitz (2001), Gary W. Cox (1997), Maurice Duverger (1984), and others have emphasized that being one-seat elections and prone to pre-electoral bargaining, presidential elections are conducive to coalition-building and power-sharing. They have referred to the examples of Nigeria, Sri Lanka, and Indonesia, all of which abandoned the parliamentary system for a presidential constitution primarily for the purpose of nation-building and party development. They have also argued that it was presidential offices rather than anything else that led to a two-party system in the United States and two political blocs in France (Cox 1997, 188; Duverger 1984, 97; Suleiman 1992, 142). This chapter indicates that these scholars come to different conclusions because they have examined different features of presidential elections in isolation.

No one electoral feature alone can explain the conduciveness (or lack thereof) of presidential systems to coalition-building. To understand how presidential elections influence cross-ethnic coalitions in a particular social setting, all electoral features must be studied including those of the electoral system. In case of Afghanistan, presidential elections are candidate-centric, zero-sum games, prone to pre-electoral bargaining, majoritarian, double ballots, religiously exclusive, and constrained by electoral cycles, as well as presidential term limits.

Examining all these features, this chapter reveals that they do not function cohesively and unidirectionally: while some contribute to cross-ethnic coalition-building, others function in the opposite direction. This has been the most likely reason that most cross-ethnic coalitions were able to form in the presidential elections, but these coalitions were rarely ever able to survive after or even during elections. In other words, if we divide the process of coalition-building into two simple phases of formation and consolidation, some electoral features contribute to the former phase, while others deter the latter. The relationship between these features and development of cross-ethnic coalitions is illustrated in the following figure (Fig. 1).

The following sections begin with explaining the contributing features of Afghan presidential elections. The subsequent section examines deterring features of presidential elections and their influence on halting or even reversing the consolidation of coalitions. Several new democracies have recognized some of these deficiencies and have attempted to remedy them through legal manipulations such as mandating party nomination, concurrent elections, co-presidency, superlative voting system, distributional threshold, legislative runoff, threshold adaptations, and many more. Further research is required to investigate the impacts of these electoral remedies for presidential elections in different sociopolitical contexts.

The Contributing Features of Presidential Elections

Unipersonal or Slate-Based Contest?

While it may be true that a single presidential office cannot be distributed among different groups, this office has indeed functioned as a unifying force as it has encouraged vote pooling and interethnic accommodation in Afghanistan. In other words, unlike the multi-seat Wolesi Jirga (WJ), where ethnic votes are easily translated to ethnic share of seats, the unipersonal nature of the presidential office has compelled ethnic groups to form alliances in order to share the resources that come with that office. This is primarily because as head of the state and the government, the office of the president is the highest office in the country, raising the stakes for any ethnic group in the presidential elections. To date, most cross-ethnic coalitions have been formed to compete in presidential elections than in parliamentary ones: a ratio of 21 to 2.

The vote pooling effect of presidential office is reinforced by vice-president candidates also running alongside presidential candidates. In fact, one can argue that Afghan presidential elections are not unipersonal but slate-based elections where each slate (presidential ticket) includes two vice-president candidates as well. In order to win votes across ethnic groups, the first thing that most presidential candidates tend to do has been to choose their running mates from two different ethnic groups. Afghan elections have indicated that picking the right VPs more than anything else determines the viability of presidential candidates. Those who are able to pick the most prominent elites from different ethnic groups as their running mates

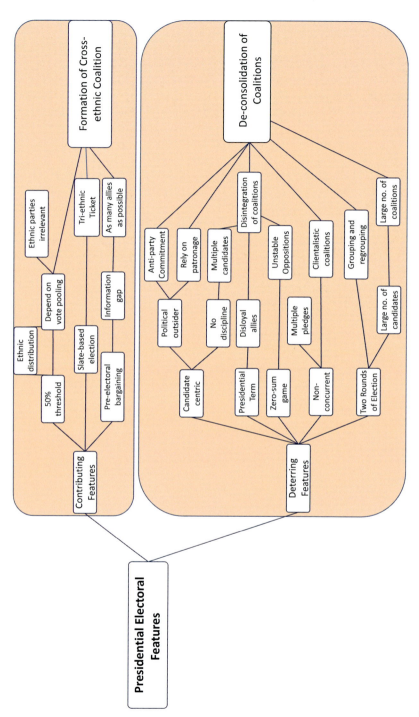

Fig. 1 Features of presidential elections and their impact on formation and consolidation of coalitions

have more chances of winning than those who do not. At times, VP candidates have contributed more votes per capita – or an equal proportion of votes – from their constituencies to their ticket than presidential candidates. This was indeed the case in the presidential election of 2014, when Abdullah's ticket received as many votes from Hazaras as from Tajiks per capita and Ghani's ticket secured even more votes from Uzbeks than from Pashtuns per capita (see Fig. 2). Most Hazaras voted for Abdullah primarily because of his VP running mate, Haji Mohaqiq, and most Uzbeks voted for Ghani because of his first vice-president candidate, Dostum (Mobasher 2016, 403, 408).

Pre-electoral Coalition-Making

Another feature of Afghan presidential election is that they encourage pre-electoral coalitions. Afghanistan is not a unique case in this regard as studies have shown that most presidential democracies, unlike parliamentary systems, inspire pre-electoral (proactive) coalition-building (Mainwaring and Shugart 1997, 466). The advantage that pre-electoral coalitions have had in Afghanistan is that they have been more

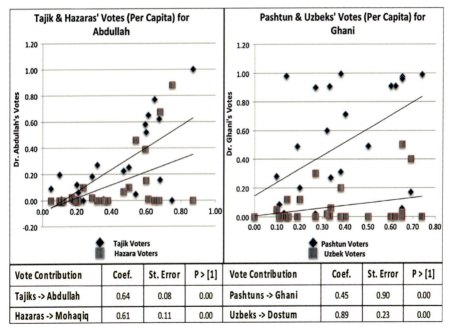

Fig. 2 A comparative illustration of votes for Abdullah (on the left) and Ghani (on the right) in 2014. Both the graph and the regression show that Dr. Abdullah won more votes from Tajiks than Dr. Ghani from Pashtuns. However, more Uzbeks voted for Ghani than Hazaras for Abdullah. (Source: It is constructed by the author based on a number of sources including Independent Election Commission, Afghanistan Information Management Service, United States Combined Armed Force)

amenable to cross-ethnic votes and alliances. The main reason for this tendency has been that candidates and voters did not have perfect information about the viability of candidates and the optimal size of winning coalitions. Not knowing the optimal size of support to win the office, serious candidates were very likely to form maximally inclusive coalitions. Similarly, the absence of such information has compelled voters and elites to cross identity lines in order to join winning coalitions and ultimately to gain access to government resources.

Nonviable parties and elites would have rather joined or forged viable coalitions than compete in the election on their own. Abdul Rashid Dostum and Haji Mohaqiq learned this lesson the hard way. By running for presidency against Hamid Karzai in the election of 2004, they eventually sidelined themselves in his forthcoming government. Since then, they changed their electoral strategies in the next two elections by putting their endorsements up for bids by viable candidates instead of running for the office themselves. In the election of 2009 and 2014, the new strategy helped them gain several seats in the cabinet for their parties and even become vice-presidents themselves (2014).

The other advantage of pre-electoral coalitions concerns their tendency to produce ethnically inclusive cabinets since one way to compensate pre-electoral allies has been through portfolio allocation (Sharan 2014, 142–145). In fact, political distribution has been the main bargaining chip for pre-electoral coalition making. As a result, for the first time in history, Afghans have witnessed a relatively inclusive form of government. All three administrations, so far, began with cabinets representing different ethnic groups less or more proportionally, although, overtime, with each new administration, Pashtuns have been gaining more seats while Tajiks losing seats in the initial cabinets. This slight shift in proportionality of seat allocations can likely be explained by the balance of the political dominance between these ethnic groups. After the collapse of Taliban in 2001, Tajiks had more military and political dominance than Pashtuns; but as the balance of power has gradually shifted, so did the share of their cabinet seats.

Table 1 indicates that some smaller ethnic groups were also able to obtain some cabinet seats in two of three administrations. Many others were mostly given secondary positions in the government. In other words, in addition to portfolio allocation on the cabinet level, presidents have used second-ranking positions to satisfy their allies, especially those from smaller groups such as Baloches, Pashaees,

Table 1 shows ethnic representations in different cabinet formations as well as after cabinet reshuffling

Cabinet reshuffles	Portfolio allocations				
	Pashtun (%)	Tajik (%)	Hazara (%)	Uzbek (%)	Others (%)
The 2004 government	30	19	19	7	7
The 2009 government	35	15	15	15	0
The 2014 government	38	19	19	8	4

Source: The information is gathered by the author from a number of sources including Afghan Biographies: Who is Who in Afghanistan? and Kate Clark's (2015) The Cabinet and the Parliament: Afghanistan's Government in Trouble Before It Is Formed. Afghanistan Analyst Network

Qozloqs, Bayats, Ismailis, and others. The secondary governmental posts include governorship of provinces, ambassadorial positions, spokesperson positions, and positions in other ministerial and non-ministerial agencies (Sharan 2014, 146).

The Fifty Percent Threshold

Article 61 of the Afghan Constitution sets a runoff system that requires presidential candidates to win an absolute majority of votes in order to become president. If no candidate wins over 50% votes in the first round, a second round of election will be held between two front-running candidates, one of whom will naturally win an absolute majority of votes in this round.

Requiring the 50% threshold has corresponded very well with the ethnic distribution in Afghanistan. Assuming election results reflect ethnic headcounts, the 50% threshold compels presidential candidates to win support and votes from more than one ethnic group because none of the ethnic groups alone can deliver 50% votes. Unable to mobilize and deliver 50% votes, ethnic parties have become almost irrelevant in the presidential elections. In fact, during presidential elections, parties tend to split into factions only to forge cross-ethnic alliances with other factions. All three presidential elections have witnessed the fractionalization of some prominent ethnic parties including *Jamiat-i-Islami*, *Hizb-i-Islami*, and *Wahdat-i-Islami*.

The tripartite interaction between presidential office, the winning threshold, and population distribution has produced two ultimate outcomes. First, ethno-political elites and voters alike have been compelled to strategically coordinate across ethnic lines. As Table 2 indicates, 16 coalitions were formed before the presidential elections, and only 7 coalitions before parliamentary elections, 5 of which were actually preparing for presidential of 2019 rather than parliamentary election of 2018. The fact that most cross-ethnic coalitions have been developed in preparation for presidential elections and not parliamentary elections shows the influence of these features of presidential elections in Afghanistan.

The second outcome, which stems from the first one, is that moderate politics has dominated electoral politics since extremist political forces and candidates have naturally been unable to draw cross-ethnic alliances and votes (Stoll 2013). As such, it should not be surprising that candidates affiliated with well-known extremist

Table 2 shows the number of (formal) coalitions that have been formed prior to presidential and parliamentary elections

No. of (formal) coalitions before presidential elections vs. parliamentary elections			
Presidential election of 2004	6 coalitions	Parliamentary election of 2005	2 coalitions
Presidential election of 2009	3 coalitions	Parliamentary election of 2010	0 coalitions
Presidential election of 2014	7 coalitions	Parliamentary election of 2018	5 coalitions
Total	16 coalitions	Total	7 coalitions

Source: The information is gathered by the author from a number of sources including Afghanistan Analyst Network and Afghan Biographies: Who is Who in Afghanistan?

parties and groups such as the Taliban and Hizb-i-Islami (Islamic party, military faction) have won only a handful of votes in presidential races. For example, Mullah Abdul Salam Rocketi, a former leader of Taliban who continued to show solidarity with Taliban ideologies to date, won less than 0.5% votes in 2009. Having no chance of winning cross-ethnic votes, his viability amounted to merely 4.4% in his home province of Zabul. Similarly, Qutbuddin Hilal, a loyal to Gulbuddin Hekmatyar (an internationally wanted leader until 2016), won less than 2.8% of the votes in the presidential election of 2014.

Coalition-Deterring Features of Afghan Presidential Elections

Despite encouraging cross-ethnic coalitions and power-sharing, presidential elections have not been fully conducive to ethnic accommodation. Power-sharing have been shuddering, ethnic tensions have continued to challenge election aftermaths, and cross-ethnic coalitions have remained unstable. Many coalitions have either dissolved or reformulated during elections; others split immediately after elections. Most coalitions have been built on the basis of patronage and personal politics while lacking titles, structures, and ideologies (Mobasher 2016, 364). Notably, their number has been on the rise, indicating a trend resembling party fragmentation in Afghanistan.

These shortfalls have been mainly because of some deterring features of presidential elections; these features include presidential elections being two-round system, candidate-centric, zero-sum games, bound by presidential term limits, non-concurrent with parliamentary elections, dual legitimizer, and religiously exclusive.

Two-Round Elections

Article 61 of the Afghan Constitution requires holding a runoff election if no candidate wins an absolute majority in the first round. This requirement, indeed, forced almost two of three presidential elections in Afghanistan to a second round of voting. In the presidential election of 2009, Karzai's votes fall a few thousand votes below the 50% threshold after a recount of the whole tally. Therefore, there would have been a second-round election should his rival candidate, Abdullah Abdullah, have decided not to withdraw. In the presidential election of 2014, a chaotic runoff election took place after an undecided first round when none of the contenders were able to win the 50% threshold.

Afghan presidential elections as well as studies elsewhere have indicated that a potential runoff encourages a large number of candidates – and so fragmented coalitions. It is because a mere likelihood of a second round incentivizes not just one but three categories of candidates to enter the competition: the first group is the "office seekers" who need to follow a winning strategy by making alliances across ethnic groups (Mobasher 2017). The largest coalitions in the first round are formed by this category of candidates. The second category of candidates that the runoff system incentivizes is the "runoff-seekers." These are serious, but not necessarily the most viable candidates who run in the first round with a hope that they may be able to finish as the runner-up. Finishing as a runner-up allows them to compete with the front-runner, having the chance to win the alliance and vote shares of the losing candidates. The success of the second-place candidate is more probable when a majority of voters dislike the top finisher, or when, in a divided society, the top finisher is from a smaller group. Indeed, one of the reasons Abdullah led the candidates in 2014's first round was the split of Pashtun votes among seven different Pashtun candidates (Mobasher 2017). A survey before the second round of the 2014 Afghan election indicated that Ghani's votes among Pashtuns would increase from 49% in the first round to 75% in the second round.

The third category of candidates that the runoff system encourages are "patronage seekers" who enter the fray only to gain political leverage against other candidates (Mobasher 2017). Indeed, in Afghanistan, many candidates enter the election only to bargain their support with runners-up in the second round (Bijlert 2009, 9). Knowing that they have the opportunity for strategic coordination in the second round, most candidates prefer not to withdraw in the first round. The first round is indeed an investment juncture for these patronage seekers who would eventually make coalitions with one or the other front-runner in the second round. As a result, presidential elections tend to experience two rounds of coalition-making: proactive coalition-making and second round coalition-making (see Blais and Indridason 2007, 194). The former strikes before the first-round elections and the latter when eliminated candidates join the competing ones in a runoff. Afghan elections have indicated that proactive coalitions are a combination of numerous oversized coalitions supporting serious candidates and fragmented coalitions supporting opportunist candidates.

The second-round coalition-making begins when the losing coalitions of the first round dissolve only to regroup with front-running coalitions. This suggests that no one coalition remains intact within two rounds of a given presidential election. For example, in the second round of 2014, after forming new alliances with losing candidates (coalitions), Abdullah and Ghani's coalitions not only changed in sizes but also became less cohesive and ideologically indistinguishable. Such constant formulation and reformulation of coalitions in the first and second rounds have not allowed coalitions to grow and institutionalize (Mobasher 2017).

Candidate-Centric Elections

Article 62 of the constitution, which lists qualifications for presidential candidates, refers to the presidential candidates merely as "individuals" and has no reference to political parties or coalitions at all. Subsequent regulations including the Regulation on the Registration of Candidates, issued by the Independent Electoral Commission, have allowed presidential candidates to run as either nominees of parties/coalitions or independent candidates. In this way, Afghan laws established a candidate-centric presidential election where it is the individual candidates and not parties and coalitions that are at the center of electoral politics.

Many scholars have argued that this candidate-centrism is a universal feature of presidential elections across the world, but it is not. An increasing number of presidential constitutions such as constitutions of Indonesia, Nigeria, Kenya, Tanzania, and Sri-Lanka require their presidential candidates to be nominees of a political party or coalition. In case of Indonesia, the candidate should not only be member of a party or a coalition but also that party must control over 3% of seats in the legislature. In these five countries, political parties and coalitions have control over the nomination of candidates; thus, candidates will have to comply with their rules and policies. Political outsiders are unlikely to be able to compete in the elections unless they gain the nomination from a political party or coalition. This way, presidential elections in these countries have functioned similar to elections in parliamentary systems.

The candidate-centric elections in Afghanistan have frequently undermined the power of parties over the nomination of their candidates. Unlike parliamentary systems, where prime minister nominees have to retain the confidence of their parties, candidate-centered presidential elections have liberated candidates from any such obligation in Afghanistan. This issue is coupled with public disaffection toward political parties, which explains why many party members are likely to run as independent candidates or to defect their parties altogether. Notably, the number of party members who run as independents in presidential elections is higher than those who ran as party candidates: a ratio of 11 to 10. And the elections have indicated that the trend has seemingly been toward further partyless presidential elections. In 2004, only half of the candidates who belonged to political parties registered as party candidates. In the presidential election of 2009, only one-third (38%) of party-affiliated candidates registered as party candidates, and that fraction dropped to one-fifth (20%) in the election of 2014. To the surprise of most experts, even the leaders of the four largest parties in Afghanistan including *Jamiat-i-Islami*, *Wahdat-i-Islami*, *Jumbish-i-Islami*, and *Hizb-i-Islami* ran as independent candidates in the past three presidential elections (see Table 3).

Although almost all presidential candidates formed some type of formal or informal, large or small, patronage or policy-based coalitions, none registered as nominees of their coalitions. In fact, Abdullah was the only candidate who registered as a coalition nominee on the preliminary list of candidates in 2014, but he later changed his affiliation to a party nominee. In such candidate-centric elections, where coalitions have no official role to play except for facilitating exchange of votes to patronage, coalitions are likely to remain clientelistic and short-lived.

The personalization of elections has also contributed to fractionalization of political associations by simply allowing or even encouraging multiple members of the same party or coalition running in the same election, competing with one another. Fragmentation of *Jamiat-i-Islami* in all three presidential elections illustrates this well. In 2004, the party had two presidential candidates, namely, Yunus Qanuni and Abdul Hafiz Mansoor. Hafiz Mansoor ran as an independent candidate, while Yunus Qanuni attempted to form his own cross-ethnic party, *Nazat-i-Mili Afghanistan*. Ahmad Zia Massoud, another member of *Jamiat-i-Islami Party*, joined Karzai's ticket as his first vice-president.

Table 3 reflects all candidates who belonged to political parties including those who registered as party candidates and those who did not

Elections	Political party	Candidate	Registered as
2004	Hizb-i-Hambastagee Milli Afg.	Sayed Ishaq Gailani	Party nominee
	Nahzat-e-Milli Afghanistan	Yunus Qanuni	Party nominee
	Hizb-i-Kangra Milli Afg.	Abdul Latif Pedram	Party nominee
	Hizb-i-Isteqlal Afghanistan	Ghulam Farooq Nejrabi	Party nominee
	Hizb-i-Wahdat Mardom Afg.	Haji Mohammad Mohaqiq	Independent
	Hizb-i-Jumbish-e-Milli Afg.	Abdul Rashid Dostum	Independent
	Hizb-i-Eqtedar Islami	Ahmad Shah Ahmadzai	Independent
	Hizb-i-Jamiat Islami	Abdul Hafiz Mansoor	Independent
2009	Hizb-i-Nahzat Faragir Dem.	Dr. Habib Mangal	Party nominee
	Hizb-i-Kangra Milli Afg.	Abdul Latif Pedram	Party nominee
	Hizb-i-Isteqlal Afghanistan	Dr. Ghulam Faroq Nijrabi	Party nominee
	Da Sole Ghorzang	Shahnawaz Tanai	Party nominee
	Hizb-i-Azadagan Afghanistan	Mahbob-U-lah Koshani	Party nominee
	Hizb-i-Jamiat Islami	Dr. Abdullah Abdullah	Independent
	Hizb-i-Wafaq-e-Milli	Bismillah Shir	Independent
	Hizb-i-Kangra Milli Afg.	Bashir Ahmad Bizhan	Independent
2014	Hizb-i-Jamiat Islami	Dr. Abdullah Abdullah	Party nominee
	Hizb-i-Dawat Islami Afg.	Prof. Abdo Rabe Rasool Sayyaf	Independent
	Hizb-i-Islami Afg.	Eng. Qutbuddin Hilal	Independent
	Hizb-i-Mahaz Milli	Mohd. Shafiq Gul Agha Sherzai	Independent
	Hizb-i-Mahaz Milli	Abdul Rahim Wardak	Independent

Source: The information is gathered by the author from a number of sources including Independent Election Commission of Afghanistan, Afghanistan Research Evaluation Unit, and Afghan Biographies: Who is Who in Afghanistan?

In the presidential election of 2009, the *Jamiat* party split again into two large factions. One faction was led by Abdullah Abdullah who registered as an independent candidate while forming a broad coalition. Another faction endorsed Qasim Fahim who joined Karzai's ticket as his first vice-president candidate. Likewise, the party split in the election of 2014 when Abdullah Abdullah run as the nominee of the party while his fellow party members, namely, Ahmad Zia Massoud and Ismael Khan, made alliances with two rival candidates as their running mates. It bears mentioning, however, that *Jamiat* has not been the only party fractionalizing in the presidential elections. Other political parties and coalitions such as *Wahdat-i-Islami, Hizb-i-Islami, Kangra-i-Milli, National Coalition of Afghanistan, National United Front of Afghanistan*, and *National Movement of Afghanistan* have fragmented as well either temporarily or permanently.

An additional consequence of candidate-centric elections has been that political outsiders were not only allowed to run but also able to win the presidency. President Karzai and President Ghani have both been political outsiders, whose main theme of electoral campaign was to blame traditional parties and elites for the past atrocities in Afghanistan. Generally, political outsiders are described as some populist candidates who are not (or pretend not to be) active members of any registered political party or coalition, who likely lack political establishment experience, and who mostly launch antiestablishment campaigns (Linz 1994, 26). These candidates are particularly favorable when the voters are frustrated with the performances of the establishment and look for a new "savior" (Linz 1994, 27). Indeed, for this very reason, President Karzai and President Ghani have had the upper hand in Afghan presidential elections. During their electoral campaigns, they warned voters of returning to past atrocities should they vote for the establishment parties and elites.

The issue with these political outsiders has been that they remained committed to anti-partism even after winning the presidency. They have both publicly revealed their disdain toward parties. In their own administrations, both have pushed for the adoption of SNTV system for parliamentary elections, which has been disastrous for development of parties and coalitions. They even encouraged their cabinet members to disassociate from their parties in order to keep their positions in the government. Even when they ran for presidency, instead of forming an official coalition with a constitution, an organization, and distinct policy platforms, they relied on patronage in order to make allies. In fact, they referred to their alliances as *team-i-Intekhabati* (electoral teams) rather than political coalitions or parties. While instrumental in helping these candidates to win presidency, the clientalistic electoral teams have proven to be coalition of convenience rather than stable political organizations.

Zero-Sum Games

The zero-sum game feature of presidential elections can partly explain why the opposition coalitions have been unable to survive and consolidate. It reflects an electoral pattern where the winner takes all and the loser loses all. Unlike parliamentary systems, where the losing coalitions typically gain at least a few legislative seats, and therefore, a critical platform for advancing their agenda, in presidential elections in Afghanistan, the losing candidates remained empty-handed for the full presidential terms. Besides, presidential elections were not held concurrently with parliamentary elections so that the losing coalitions in presidential elections would have won at least a number of seats in the WJ. Under a situation where the losing coalitions have few resources and no platforms to voice their agendas, opposition coalitions are overburdened with the cost of sustaining the alliance until the next election. Not being able to bear that burden, most eliminated coalitions have either dissolved or hibernated until the next election. Winning coalitions have been the only ones that were able to survive after elections; and they survived only partly and until the end of presidential terms.

The major disadvantage of presidential election in Afghanistan has been that the president is naturally likely to belong to one ethnic of the groups only. In the past three presidential elections, only Pashtun candidates were able to become the president. This has led to criticism of the constitution by other ethnic groups, who have found the office unreachable by non-Pashtuns. These ethnic groups have further mobilized against this system in the presidency of Ghani, whose government and policies have been considered less and less inclusive. Notably, they have witnessed that the government's uncompromising policies such as those of ID cards, elections, districting, security, corruption, and power line mostly coincide with the demands and concerns of Pashtuns vis-à-vis those of other ethnic groups. They perceived these policies non-conciliatory, ethnocentric, and favoring Pashtuns only. Therefore, many have associated presidentialism with ethno-authoritarianism in Afghanistan and advocated for replacing the system with a parliamentary or semi-parliamentary system. To them presidential elections are zero-sum games, in which non-Pashtuns are always the losers (Table 4).

Presidential Term Limits

Afghan Constitution has set a presidential term limit of two 5 years: Article 61 sets a timeline of every 5 years for presidential elections; and Article 62 mandates that an individual cannot be the president for more than two terms. So far, only president Karzai completed a second term. As the head of the third administration, President Ghani is in the final years of his first term should he run for a reelection and win.

There is a scholarly consensus that presidential term limits are necessary for preventing monopoly and abuse of power in a presidential democracy (Martinez 2015; Neale 2009; Davis 1980; Nogare and Ricciuti 2008). Without term limits, presidents have tendencies toward monopoly of power which usually leads to ethnic monopolization of power. Additionally, being unaccountable to the public, presidents are likely to abuse their power for personal and ethnic interests; in such situations, minorities are likely to be marginalized and eventually mobilized against the system instigating civil wars. Therefore, not surprisingly, presidential term limits are not unique to the Afghan Constitutions. The length of a presidential term has been as much subject to debate as the reelection of a president. Shorter terms are more likely than longer ones to reduce electoral tensions since with shorter terms the losing parties are more likely to concede defeat and wait for the next election instead of contesting the lost election's result; however, with longer terms the president would be free from distractions associated with frequent electoral campaigns for the next elections (Neale 2009, 22–23).

There are some issues with term limits, however. One such issue is that the permanence of presidents in office is fixed: once elected, a president will remain in office for the full constitutional term until the next election. In that period the president cannot be removed regardless of whether or not he or she has the

Table 4 A list of disputes between ethnic groups and the decisions of the government

Years	Concerns of most Pashtun hardliners	Concerns of hardliners from other groups	Government's decisions
2017	Ghazni must be divided into three electoral districts	Hazaras: Dividing Ghazni violates laws and marginalizes Hazaras	Ghazni was divided into three districts
2015	Power line must passthrough Salang and Baghlan province	Hazaras: Power line must passthrough Bamyan and Wardak provinces	Power line will passthrough Salang and Baghlan province
2014	New ID cards must have national and ethnic categories	Tajiks, Uzbeks, and Hazaras: New ID cards should not have national and ethnic categories	ID cards have national and ethnic categories
2009	Jaghori must remain a district of Ghazni	Hazaras: Jaghori district of Ghazni must become a province	Jaghori remained a district of Ghazni
2007	The Pashtu word "Pohanton" must be used for university in Dari version of Higher Education Law	Tajiks and Hazaras: The Farsi word "Danishgah" must be used in Dari version of Higher Education Law	Pohanton was used in the Higher Education Law
2015	Dostum should not be able to launch military operations in Jawzjan and Faryab and target Pashtuns	Uzbeks: Dostum must be able to launch military operations in Jawzjan and Faryab to eradicate terrorist elements	Dostum was ordered not to conduct any such operation but he did it anyway
2015–2016	SNTV must be replaced with FPTP system	FPTP is not the right electoral system for Afghanistan	The decision over electoral system was deferred to Independent Electoral Commission
2018	Nawamish district belongs to Daikundy province	Hazaras: Nawamish district belongs to Hilmand provinces	Nawamish was decided to be a district of Daikundy

confidence of the assembly of his or her own coalition, which is very different from a parliamentary system where the survival of the executive depends on its parliamentary coalition holding together. Therefore, it is safe to argue that presidential term limits in a way undermine the accountability of an incumbent to his or her coalition. This is best illustrated by the shifts in the ethnic composition of cabinets during cabinet reshuffles in Afghanistan.

In all three administrations, when reshuffling the cabinet, the presidents have been tempted not to keep their promises to their electoral allies. This has led to the cabinets becoming less reflective of pre-electoral pledges after each reshuffling. Table 5 shows that cabinet reshuffles have led to an increase in Pashtun seats and a decrease in the seats of the next two largest ethnic groups in all three administrations. It cannot be a coincidence that in all three administrations, the presidents happened to be Pashtuns. This also explains why after each reshuffle the allies of the

Table 5 shows ethnic representations in different cabinet formations as well as after cabinet reshuffling

	Portfolio allocation				
Cabinet reshuffles	Pashtun (%)	Tajik (%)	Hazara (%)	Uzbek (%)	Others (%)
The 2004 government	30	37	19	7	7
Cabinet reshuffle (2005)	36	36	12	12	4
Cabinet reshuffle (2008–2009)	40	28	12	16	4
The 2009 government	35	35	15	15	0
Cabinet reshuffle (2010)	35	35	12	15	4
Cabinet reshuffle (2012)	35	35	12	15	4
Cabinet reshuffle (2013)	38	31	12	15	4
The 2014 government	38	31	19	8	4

Source: The information is gathered by the author from a number of sources including Afghanistan Analyst Network, Afghanistan Research Evaluation Unit, and Afghan Biographies: Who is Who in Afghanistan?

presidents were likely to become fierce oppositions of the government, failing the incumbent coalition to survive the full term.

In their second terms, the presidents are even less likely to stay loyal to allies. The only second termer in Afghanistan, Karzai ignored most of his allies when making decisions or implementing policies in his second presidency. For example, after the 2009 election, he walked back on his promise to Mohaqiq to upgrade two Hazara-dominated districts into provinces. Karzai was frequently at odds with his close international allies as well (Druzin 2013). His relationship with the US government – his original backer – was at its worst late in his second term. In 2013, for example, Karzai declined to sign the Mutual Security Agreement between the United States and Afghanistan despite the fact that it was approved by supermajority in the *Loya Jirga* (an advising grand council consisting of members of the parliament, provincial councils, district councils, supreme court, and cabinet) and endorsed by his domestic and international allies.

Nonconcurrent Electoral Cycles

A coalition is not stable unless it prevails not only across elections but also across government branches, specifically the executive and the legislature. Coalitions in Afghanistan have neither survived across elections nor entrenched themselves across branches of government. This failure is partly explained by the time lapse between presidential and parliamentary elections in Afghanistan: they are usually held over a year apart.

As a practical matter, nonconcurrent elections are less likely to encourage cross-branch coalitions than concurrent elections (Carey 1999, 93). In fact, numerous studies have shown that only those presidential democracies such as Costa Rica, United States, Chile, and Korea that hold at least partly concurrent elections have entertained stable party systems and coalitions (Jones 1995, 5, 75–77). The better performance of concurrent elections is explained by the supposition that while concurrent elections promote mutual campaign support, nonconcurrent elections encourage clientelistic coalitions. It is well established that during elections, both presidential and parliamentary candidates need alliances to endorse their campaigns. Under a concurrent election, the immediate interest of both the presidential and parliamentary candidates is to win the election; and therefore, the most likely term of agreement would be mutual campaign support. A mutual campaign support, unlike a clientelistic partnership, is likely to hold the coalition together primarily because candidates are likely to choose an ally who is closest to them in policy. Under noncurrent elections, where only presidential candidates need endorsements, MPs are likely to endorse them only in exchange for patronage. As a result, nonconcurrent elections lead to clientelistic, temporary, and thus unreliable coalitions. In fact, in the presidential election of 2014, some reports have shown that many MPs secretly vowed allegiance to multiple presidential candidates in exchange for patronage.

Strangely, the 2004 Afghan Constitution merely encouraged rather than mandating concurrent elections. Article 160 of the constitution states, "Multilateral efforts shall be made to hold presidential and National Assembly elections concurrently." Several attempts have been made to hold elections concurrently under the terms of this provision. However, from a constitutional perspective, the implementation of this article is almost impossible, considering the different timelines set for presidential and parliamentary elections by the same constitution. Article 61 of the constitution sets the date for presidential elections between March 22 and April 21. Article 83 sets the date for parliamentary elections between April 22 and May 22. By any interpretation, these timelines do not overlap, although they could come as close as 1 day apart, holding the presidential election on April 21 and the parliamentary election on April 22.

Parallel Legitimacy

Article 61 of the Afghan Constitution provides for popular election of presidents, stating that "[t]he President shall be elected...through free, general, secret and direct voting." The Office of the President derives legitimacy from a nationwide election, and as such, on numerous occasions presidents have claimed that they represent the will of the nation better than MPs who are elected by separate and smaller constituencies. As such, Afghan presidents tend to believe that their policy positions are superior to those of the assembly, demonstrating little willingness to compromise with the legislature or form legislative coalitions.

For example, in 2013, Karzai and his inner circle questioned the legitimacy of the assembly when he decided to refer the Afghanistan-US Bilateral Security Agreement to a *Loya Jirga* instead of the assembly for approval. This decision of the president indeed was in violation of Article 90 of the constitution, which provided that international treaties and agreements must be ratified by the assembly. However, Karzai's spokespersons argued that due to electoral fraud and some "non-patriotic" MPs, the assembly did not have the legitimacy to approve the agreement. MPs confronted Karzai's administration by pointing to the electoral fraud in the presidential election of 2009 that led to his presidency. Further, in protest to his decision, a large number of MPs decided not to attend in the *Loya Jirga,* calling it unconstitutional.

Exclusion of Minorities

Article 62 of the constitution, which lists the qualifications for presidential candidates, requires that a presidential candidate must be a Muslim. This clause sets a clear institutional discrimination against non-Muslim minorities including Hindus, Sikhs, and others. Afghanistan is one of very few countries that have an exclusionary clause in its constitution about the religion of the president.

Although religious minorities are estimated at less than one percent of the population that makes this exclusionary clause practically a redundance for at least the near future, one can argue that this clause does indicate the discriminatory tune of the constitution, which sets a justification for further discrimination against religious minorities. Additionally, this exclusionary clause is in direct contradiction with a number of other constitutional provisions including Article 7, 22, and 33. Article 7 articulates that "The state shall be obligated to create a prosperous and progressive society based on social justice, preservation of human dignity, protection of human rights, realization of democracy, attainment of national unity as well as equality between all peoples and ethnicities and balance development of all areas of the country." Article 22 provides, "Any kind of discrimination and distinction between citizens of Afghanistan shall be forbidden. The citizens of Afghanistan, man and woman, have equal rights and duties before the law." Finally, Article 33 states, "The citizens of Afghanistan shall have the right to elect and be elected."

An additional electoral rule which has also led to a discriminatory consequence is Article 45 of the Election law. Article 45 requires presidential candidates to present the voting cards of at least 2% from at least 20 provinces to IEC to qualify as candidates. This requirement has likely impeded the candidacy of elites from many smaller groups since their presence is limited to much fewer than 20 provinces. Only Pashtuns and Tajiks seem to have a minimum of 2% inhabitants in at least 20 provinces. This perhaps explains why in the presidential election of 2014, only Pashtuns and Tajiks had presidential candidates. Hazaras and Uzbeks had presidential candidates in the presidential election of 2004 and 2009 when article 45 of the Election Law did not exist.

Conclusion

Despite the initial intentions of coalition founders for consolidation, coalitions have remained weak and prone to dissolution. They have mostly failed to endure beyond single presidential elections. In fact, cross-branch coalitions were not formed because the only threshold for a coalition to form was winning presidential office. Sustaining the office has never been an issue under the presidential constitution. Once elected, keeping the government is guaranteed by the presidential term limits. Oppositions, empty-handed from elections, cannot afford to sustain their coalitions until the next presidential election. For these very reasons, most coalitions have been built on the basis of patronage negotiations and personal politics. Even so, Afghan presidential elections should take the credit for encouraging at least the formation of cross-ethnic coalitions.

Unlike the parliamentary elections that have exacerbated personalistic politics, the presidential elections of Afghanistan have given rise to coalitions that have transcended ethnic boundaries. These coalitions have indicated the prospect for political development in Afghanistan as their emergence demonstrated popularity, cross-ethnic appeal, and political accommodation by elites. The tradition of coalition-building has become firmly entrenched in the presidential elections of Afghanistan. Over the last three presidential elections, around 16 broad coalitions have emerged, most of them cross ethnic, officially declared, and having charters with the intention of further consolidation.

Presidential elections have raised the threshold so much that only the largest and the most inclusive coalitions could win or be the runner-up. Ethnic coalitions were marginalized and ethnic "parties" even more so. Of the four large ethnic parties, only Jumbish-i-Islami remained somehow intact. Jamiat-i-Islami Party, Hizb-i-Islami Party, and Wahdat-i-Islami Party split into several factions, each faction joining one or the other cross-ethnic coalitions. As a result of the fragmentation of ethnic parties and the formation of cross-ethnic parties, Afghans for the first time in history witnessed inclusive governments (see Table 2).

Since all this development has taken place within 18 years of democratization, it begs the question whether the continuation of presidential democracy may eventually lead to the institutionalization of cross-ethnic coalitions in Afghanistan. In fact, none of the presidential democracies that entertain strong party system or stable coalitions including the United States, Korea, Colombia, Costa Rica, Venezuela, Chile, and Uruguay (prior to 1973) have done so within a short period of 18 years. If that is the case, why should we not let coalition development take its course under the same presidential features?

The risk of wait-and-see approach is that it may allow democratization to take a reverse path. Democratization is a fragile process that may easily be reversed (Pridham and Lewis 1996, 1). Even worse, this approach may allow the culture of patronage politics to become entrenched in Afghan political society, which is, unlike democratization, hardly reversible. Therefore, in today's democratizing societies, engineering and reengineering of constitutions are essential to strengthening democratic institutions in shorter pace of time. In light of these observations, further research is required to examine what constitutional solutions most properly remedy the problematic features of Afghan presidential elections.

References

Bijlert MV (2009) How to win an Afghan election: preceptions and practices. Afghan Analyst Network, Kabul

Blais A, Indridason IH (2007) Making candidates count: the logic of electoral alliances in two-round legislative elections. J Polit 69(1):192: 214

Carey JM (1999) Constitutional choices and the performances of presidential regimes. J Soc Sci 11(1):93: 122

Clark K (2015) The cabinet and the parliament: Afghanistan's government in trouble before it is formed. Afghanistan Analyst Network. Available via https://www.afghanistan-analysts.org/the-cabinet-and-the-parliament-afghanistans-government-in-trouble-before-it-is-formed/

Cox GW (1997) Making votes count, strategic coordination in world's electoral systems. Cambridge University Press, Cambridge, UK

Davis PB (1980) The future of presidential tenure. Pres Stud Q 10(1):472: 473

Druzin H (2013) Karzai not only at odds with US, but his countrymen, too. Star and Stripes. Available via http://www.stripes.com/karzai-not-only-at-oddswith-us-but-his-countrymen-too-1.254874

Duverger M (1984) Presidential elections and party system in Europe (trans: Rowen HH). In: McCormick RL (ed) Political parties and the modern state. Rutgers University Press, New Jersey

Horowitz DL (2001) Ethnic groups in conflict. University of California Press, Berkeley

Jones MP (1995) Electoral laws and the survival of presidential democracies. University of Michigan Press, Michigan

Juan Linz and Alfred Stepan (1996) Problems of democratic transition and consolidation, p 181

Lijphart A (1977) Democracy in plural societies. Yale University Press, London

Lijphart A (2008) Thinking about democracy: power sharing and majority rule in theory and practice. Routledge, New York

Linz JJ (1994) Presidential or parliamentary democracy. In: Linz JJ, Valenzuela A (eds) The failure of presidential democracy. JHU Press, Maryland

Mainwaring S, Shugart MS (1997) Presidentialism and democracy in Latin America. Cambridge University Press, London

Martínez CV (2015) Presidential term limits. Political and economic effects of reelection in Latin America (1990–2010). Dissertation, University of Essex

Mobasher MB (2016) Understanding ethnic-electoral dynamics: how ethnic politics affect electoral laws and election outcomes in Afghanistan. Gonzaga L Rev 51(2):355: 415

Mobasher MB (2017) Electoral choices, ethnic accommodation, and the consolidation of cross-ethnic coalitions: critiquing the runoff clause of the afghan constitution. Pac Rim L Pol'y J 26(3):413: 462

Neale TH (2009) Presidential terms and tenure: perspectives and proposals for change, Congressional Research Service. Available via http://www.whitehousetransitionproject.org/wp-content/uploads/2016/04/Terms-Tenure_101909-1.pdf

Nogare CD, Ricciuti R (2008) Term limits: do they really affect fiscal policy choices? Working paper 2199, CESIFO

Pridham G, Lewis PG (1996) Stabilizing fragile democracies. Routledge, London

Sharan T (2014) Dynamic Qudrat Shabaka Hai Seyasi Dar Intekhabat Ryasat Jamhuri 2009 [The dynamics of political networks in the presidential election of 2009]. In: Ahmadi MN, Ismaelzada MM (eds) Democracy Afghani: Fursat Ha Wa Chalish Ha [Afghan democracy: challenges and opportunities]. Andisha, Kabul

Stoll H (2013) Changing societies, changing party systems. Cambridge University Press, New York

Suleiman EN (1992) Presidentialism and political stability in France. In: Linz JJ, Valenzuela A (eds) The failure of presidential democracy. JHU Press, Maryland

The Making of a Mobile Caliphate State in the African Sahel

42

Hamdy Hassan

Contents

Introduction	756
Transformations of Islamic Radicalism in the Sahel	757
The General Context of the Salafist Jihadist Transformations	758
The Geology of Violent Jihadi Groups in the Sahel: ISIS Vis-à-Vis Al-Qaeda	759
Al-Qaeda and Its Affiliates in the African Sahel	759
The Organization of the Islamic State: African Daesh	763
The Mobile Caliphate State Across the African Sahel	764
Numerical and Intellectual Multiplication of Jihadist Groups	765
Toyota Land Cruiser Mobile State	766
Use Peripheries to Attack Centers	767
Conclusion	768
Cross-References	770
References	770

Abstract

The goal of this chapter is to thoroughly understand the context of the dominant jihadist narratives and the nature of their appeal in the Sahelian region. All these jihadist ideologies are based on a peculiar Salafi Radicalism that aimed to transform the state and society by methods of preaching and violence. Therefore, studying and analyzing the principles of the Salafist discourse as a political project helps us to understand its points of strengths and weaknesses. In addition, we can be better look at the future trends and prospects of violent jihadist groups in the African Sahel. The roots of this Islamic discourse as a political project may be attributed to what Lunay and Suarez call the "Islamic domain." The rise of violent radical Islamism represents drive from the internal political and socioeconomic dynamics evolving in each Sahelian state. However, the struggle and

---

H. Hassan (✉)
College of Humanities and Social Sciences, Zayed University, Dubai, UAE
e-mail: Hhamdy21@yahoo.com; Hamdy.Hassan@zu.ac.ae

© The Author(s), under exclusive license to Springer Nature Singapore Pte Ltd. 2019
S. Ratuva (ed.), *The Palgrave Handbook of Ethnicity*,
https://doi.org/10.1007/978-981-13-2898-5_158

rivalry of jihadist ideologies after the military defeat of Daesh in Mosul is important at a time when thousands of fighters who have survived the civil wars in Iraq, Syria, and Libya are looking for new jihadist fields.

Keywords

Mobile Caliphate State · the African Sahel · Al-Qaeda · Daesh and the Salafist discourse

Introduction

One of the most unintended consequences of colonial rule in the Sahel and West Africa was the Islamization of large parts of it. The politicization of religion has often been designed so that the Islamic movements have been viewed from a specific political manner, based on their position towards the existing authority both in terms of acceptance and cooperation or rejection and resistance. The Islamic sphere can be understood as a kind of convergence between colonial modernity and Islam. It is a public space shaped by the provisions of religion, not the political variables or social dynamics (Launay and Soares 1999). It is therefore theoretically separate from "special" affiliations such as ethnicity, proximity, or language.

Bearing in mind these formative contexts, especially in the colonial era, helps us understand the political, religious, and ethnic dialectics of the Sahelian societies. Although the intervention of France, Chad, and other foreign powers in the Mali crisis (2013) has weakened the capabilities of the jihadi groups in the region, the violent attacks in Bamako and Ouagadougou since then prove that the jihadist discourse cannot be easily defeated. It continues to attract many followers within the general Islamic sphere in the region.

The significance of this chapter drives from the nature of the Sahel as a highly complex security complex where the region still has a pivotal role in analyzing and understanding security and development issues not only in Africa but also in the world as well. It is clear that the Sahel corridors, particularly in Mali and northern Nigeria, constitute major security and development challenges to African societies. It also raises important questions about initiatives to address these challenges – nationally, regionally, and internationally. It can be said that the complexity of the Sahel, in its manifestations and its current jihadist discourse, requires that we urgently review the nature of the post-colonial African state, structure of the associated regional dynamics, and the international response frameworks in Africa. This problem is linked, partly, to the absence of a comprehensive perspective to understand the discourse of violent jihadist groups in the African Sahel. There are partial approaches that reflect one aspect of the problem or reflect a prior intellectual bias. This is evident from the multiplicity of uses of the concept of the African "Sahel" itself, which is sometimes narrowed so as not to exceed its geographical space and sometimes expands to include a political space too large to reflect different intellectual and ideological contexts. This means that the inability to grasp the dimensions of the Sahel is an undeniable obstacle to understanding the interactions in the jihadist environment in the region since the beginning of the new millennium.

Based on this overall purpose, this chapter seeks to answer two main questions as follows:

- What are the most prominent features of the geology of the armed jihadist groups that have engulfed the African Sahel since the beginning of this century? The map of these groups has witnessed continuous deconstructions and reconstructions processes that reflect their intellectual and ideological transformations, on the one hand, and the transformation of the surrounding security systems, on the other.
- What are the trends of unity and division among armed jihadist groups, especially the rivalry between the Islamic state and al-Qaeda in the wake of the relative defeat of Daesh in Iraq and Syria?

The well-informed review of the previous literature shows that research and analysis of the phenomenon of violent jihadist movements in the African Sahel and its underlying motives are still dominated by Western accounts espoused by some countries and research institutions (Nicoll and Delaney 2012; Boutellis and Mahmoud 2017; Cohen 2013; Korteweg 2014; Varhola and Sheperd 2013). It is therefore essential to draw upon and support national scientific research on the phenomenon of violent extremism in general and violent religious extremism in particular and to ensure that their results are disseminated and taken into account in the development of national and regional policies. Nationally motivated knowledge, based on a correct understanding of historical contexts, cultural, religious, social, and economic phenomena and transnational developments, forms the basis for building a common national identity and a bulwark against exclusionism and extremism.

In an attempt to answer the previous questions, this chapter is divided into two main sections in addition to the introduction and conclusion. The section "Transformations of Islamic Radicalism in the Sahel" discusses the map and transformations of jihadist groups in the Sahel. Section "The Mobile Caliphate State Across the African Sahel" provides an analysis of the virtual caliphate in the Sahel.

Transformations of Islamic Radicalism in the Sahel

The African Sahara, in ancient time and before the arrival of the Europeans, has been regarded as a highway for trade and culture. Old kingdoms have always ensured the safety of trade routes and travel through the vast desert trails. For example, the Kingdom of Kanem-Bornu (from the tenth to the nineteenth century AD) extended from Lake Chad to the trade route between Chad and Sudan. It also controlled the road of Fezzan, which served as the main crossing of the desert via the Ténéré. Through their strong state, the Tibu tribes also ensured the security of the movement of individuals and merchants through the desert (Retaillé and Walther

2011). The Tuaregs and their masked men sought to establish cooperative relations with the Hausa peoples on the east side of the Sungai kingdom (Bossard 2014; Benjaminsen 2008). What has happened and led to the transformation of this desert to become a source of imminent danger threatens not only the security and safety of the population of the countries of the region but extends to neighboring countries both near and far?

The General Context of the Salafist Jihadist Transformations

Any scholar who tries to answer the previous question must go further to understand the factors that have contributed to the proliferation of the culture of violence and recruitment of jihadist Islamic movements in the African Sahel and overall Africa. It is true that there are historical influences related to the development of Islamic discourse in the Arab world and South-East Asia, such as the issues of "*Jahiliya*," "*Hakemya*," and the "surviving group," in addition to the political and economic changes in the Arab North African region (Hassan 2016, 1–19). The causes of violent radicalism in Africa are therefore linked to local factors such as corruption, economic, and social marginalization, widespread of public discontent among youth, intellectual divisions between Islamic schools and so on more than its linkage to international ones. Perhaps this socioeconomic analysis clashes with the fact that many African Muslims are peaceful and tolerant towards the other due to their close ties with the traditions of the Sufi brothers such as *Qadiriyya* and *Tijaniyya* (Hassan 2015).

The spiritual Islam of West Africa has represented an impenetrable wall against extremism. However, democratic processes in some countries, such as Mali and Niger in the 1990s, opened the door to imported intellectual and ideological influences. Salafi groups, such as "the removal of innovation and the establishment of the Sunnah" have infiltrated into the country, as well as the influence of other Salafist groups supported by external powers. This religious and ideological division represented a fertile incubator for the emergence of radical and violent religious currents in the region of the Great Islamic Belt of the Sahel and West Africa (Loimeier 2007, 2011).

Al Qaeda has contributed to the ideological and material support of local Islamic groups in the Sahel and West Africa. In the wake of the severe attacks on the Algerian Salafist Group for Preaching and Jihad (GSPC) in Algeria and its transformation into al-Qaeda in the Islamic Maghreb, it was forced to move across the Sahara to settle in Mali. Since 2003, al-Qaeda has become more viable by engaging in organized crime networks and exploiting links with the local population deep into the Sahel and the Sahara through ties of marriage and trade. The group benefited from the absence of the state and weak border control systems, as well as growing resentment against the ruling regimes among the local population.

In general, jihadists often follow the ranks of illicit trade and crime networks. Mokhtar Belmokhtar, The One-Eyed who carried out Operation Ain Amnas in Algeria in 2013, is called "Mr. Marlboro" for his secret role in cigarette smuggling

(Kaplan 2015). In general, jihadists cooperate with or engage in arms trafficking and drug traffickers to obtain funding for their violent operations. Moreover, Drug Barons of South America have formed partnerships with criminal gangs in the Sahel and West Africa to unload their illegal cargo in Sahelian countries such as Guinea-Bissau, where they are carried in pickup trucks to reach desert routes to the Mediterranean, then to Europe.

With al-Qaeda's hostility to the West, its sleeper cells target Western tourists, aid workers, as well as government officials and members of foreign diplomatic missions. The organization was able to collect enormous sums of money through kidnapping foreigners for ransom. Between 2006 and 2011, the organization received about $70 million in ransom for foreign abductees. In the context of the globalization of radical jihadism, al-Qaeda has transferred these tactics to its other groups, such as the Boko Haram group, which later became an Islamic state organization in 2015.

The Geology of Violent Jihadi Groups in the Sahel: ISIS Vis-à-Vis Al-Qaeda

Violent and terrorist movements in the African Sahel, in its broad sense, are generally characterized by relative independence and decentralized decision-making in planning and execution. However, they are part of larger terrorist movements linked to them through allegiance. By following the extreme jihadist ideology on the African front, we can distinguish between two extremist ideologies whose believers seek control of the Sahel. Each has its own objectives: ISIS against al-Qaeda in the Islamic Maghreb. Although they use the same means and tactics, their political aspirations are different; they compete over global jihadist leadership. While al-Qaeda is targeting the "far enemy" represented by the Western countries, ISIS "Daesh" leads regional wars against the "near enemy" (Hassan 2016). It should be noted that those who adopt the theory of the near enemy are lenient in the rulings of Takfir, especially a specific person and non-excuse for ignorance. This expansion was done by al-Zarqawi and al-Baghdadi in the Takfir of the Shiites in general. Some Daesh leaders even called them the original infidels, not apostates, and extend the takfir to include all those who work in politics or the security, military, and judicial apparatus and those who cooperate with the Americans. Abu Bakr al-Baghdadi extended the scope to fight those who refused the pledge of allegiance to him! Whereas Al-Qaeda has considered the USA and the West as the far enemy, their fight comes first above creating non-ending local sectarian fronts within Muslim countries.

Al-Qaeda and Its Affiliates in the African Sahel

Al-Qaeda in the Islamic Maghreb (AQIM)

AQIM covers almost eight countries in the Sahel. The organization consists of four battalions, the most active and effective is al Furqan. The context of this establishment is linked to a series of transformations in the Maghreb Salafist Jihadist movement or al-Qaeda. The security pressures that followed jihadist groups, especially after the events of September 2001, led to the search for safe havens in the Sahel and Sahara. Some leaders of GSPC specifically conducted intellectual reviews of priority issues and the nature of the necessary alliances. Controversy raged between localization and globalization supporters in the organization. This debate has led the leader of the Salafist GSPC, Abu Musab Abdul Wadud, to declare his allegiance to al-Qaeda on September 11, 2006. In 2011, MOJWA, which are active mainly in southern Algeria and northern Mali and targeting all West African countries, broke with AQIM. Thus, the operations of AQIM have become focused mainly on Mali, since September 2012. Indeed, al-Qaeda has been able to exploit Mali's security vacuum to carry out its terrorist operations against government forces and international peacekeepers (Marret 2008, 541–552).

Somalia's Mujahideen Youth Movement (MYM)

East Africa has witnessed the presence of al Qaeda leaders and other Islamist extremist groups since nearly three decades ago. Al Shabab emerged early this century amid the proliferation of Islamist and tribal militias that took control of the Somali scene after the collapse of the central authority in 1991. The turning point is, however, that the Union of Islamic Courts in 2006 took control of Mogadishu with the support of al-Shabab (Barnes and Hassan 2007). Unlike tribal militias, al Shabab has adopted a deeper religious vision aimed at uniting all ethnic areas inhabited by Somalis in Kenya, Ethiopia, Djibouti, and Somalia under Islamic rule (Hansen 2013). Al-Shabab leaders have trained and fought with al-Qaeda in Afghanistan, and some al-Qaeda members in the region have been linked to the Somali group since the first training years.

Al Shabab emerged in 2006 when militants inside the Islamic Courts called for a jihad against neighboring Ethiopia. When Ethiopia intervened directly and deployed its own forces in Mogadishu in late 2006 after the overthrow of the Islamic Courts, al-Shabab managed to use historical anti-Ethiopian sentiment in Somalia to fight the Ethiopian army and other regional forces deployed under the auspices of the African Union.

Since 2009, Al Shabab has been able to consolidate its relations with al-Qaeda, which has left its clear mark on its organizational structure and strategies on the operation theater. Al Shabab's association – at least intellectually and ideologically – with al-Qaeda has changed some of its leadership elements. After the death of its leader, Aden Hashi Ayro, in May 2008, a number of al-Qaeda members reached senior leadership positions in the organization (Roggio 2010). On the other hand, al-Shabab used relatively traditional tactics in 2008 against the Ethiopian invasion forces in Somalia. However, the group's growing ties with al-Qaeda have led to increased reliance on the path of suicide attacks as a means to achieve its ends. This shift largely reflects the strengthening of the relationship between al Shabab and al-Qaeda.

However, despite the relative cohesion of the Mujahideen, disagreements have emerged regarding the position towards Daesh in Iraq and the Levant. It is true that most al-Shabaab cadres and leaders have publicly remained loyal to al-Qaeda, but some violent tactics adopted by Daesh have gained support from some individuals and factions inside the movement. In March 2015, the Islamic State issued a letter to the emir of the al-Shabab movement referring to the similarities between the African Union forces in Somalia (AMISOM) and the international coalition forces against Daesh, inviting the movement to join (ISSP 2016). In any case, despite the loyalty of some Somali jihadists to the Daesh under the absurdity and chaos of the Somali scene, the Mujahideen Youth Movement has remained loyal to al-Qaeda's line of thought and methodology.

JNIM and the Second Birth of al-Qaeda in the Sahel

Some scholars of Islamist movements may see the al-Qaeda star begin to decline in the context of the post-Daesh era in Iraq and Syria, but real evidence strongly suggests otherwise. The conscious reading of the statements of the leading figures in the organization, its stated objectives and its strategy to achieve these goals, and adapting them to the new circumstances lead us to provide a different assessment. Al-Qaeda has benefited greatly from the rise and decline of Daesh, in addition to the conflicts that swept the Islamic world from east to west, during the Arab Spring. Al-Qaeda has been working hard throughout the Muslim world to regain the leadership of the Salafi Jihadist movement, drawing on the blows that Daesh has received in Iraq. Al Qaeda shift towards decentralized operations and the fragmentation of its network has also led to the building of resilience within the Organization and its adaptation to the pressures of the US-led counterterrorism measures. With some pragmatism and sometimes even cooperation between the active radical networks on the ground, the rivalry between Daesh and al-Qaeda has been confined only to the upper level of the two movements (Zimmerman 2013). In the event of Daesh global network decline, al-Qaeda will be able to attract its members and integrate its capabilities into its own organization. Al-Qaeda, in contrast to Daesh, presents itself to the followers of the Salafist jihadist as more moderate than Daesh, gaining acceptance among the population who seek to defend themselves from the oppressor. Finally, the Western countries' focus on combating Daesh and the spread of civil wars and conflicts in Islamic countries has given al Qaeda an opportunity to focus on its strategic objective of restructuring and changing Muslim societies over the long term, as we have mentioned.

Al-Qaeda has been able to improve its image in the post-Arab spring and focus on the presence of a local popular incubator at any cost. This transformation is essentially a turning point in al-Qaeda approach that focuses on the people, as a means of establishing themselves in local contexts. Al-Qaeda operates strongly through the Salafist jihadist base to transform Sunni communities to voluntarily accept its ideology. The spread of violence, the fragility of the state and its inability to meet the basic needs of citizens, such as the case of the Sahel-Saharan states, create an environment conducive to the existence of al-Qaeda and Salafist jihadist groups. Al-Qaeda indirectly presents itself by local partners who serve the needs of society. It is no secret that local communities receive basic aid linked to an Islamic discourse that helps spread the concepts and ideas of the jihadist Salafists. In addition, al-Qaeda has been able to employ many nationalist insurgencies such as the Tuareg and the Macina Liberation Front. This means that al-Qaeda is trying to fill the gaps and corruption of ruling elites in a way that will enable it to deliver its message along with basic services. Al-Qaeda organizes and distributes resources through charities, Salafi organizations, and sometimes even some local Salafist officials.

On March 2, 2017, the Azawadi leader Iyad Ag Ghaly appeared in a videotape and gave a speech in Arabic, announcing the unification of all the Jihadi groups into a new organization called the "Support of Islam and Muslims" (JNIM) and declaring his allegiance to al-Qaeda leaders. This merger undoubtedly led to the unification of a number of the largest terrorist organizations in the Sahel which includes the following:

1. **Ansar al-Din Front**: founded by Iyad Ag Ghali in December 2011 in the city of Kidal, northern Mali. Its main aim is to apply Islamic law throughout Mali. Since its inception, the group has been targeting nationals of Western countries, especially those working in peacekeeping missions. In terms of its intellectual and ideological convictions, the group reflects the same orientations of AQIM. In the 1990s, during the Tuareg uprising, Ghali attempted to seize power but failed to overthrow the Mali government. It is interesting to note that in October 2011 Iyad Ag Ghali presented himself as the leader of the National Movement for the Liberation of Azawad (MNLA), a transitional group seeking the establishment of the independent Tuareg state, but the group rejected him because of his jihadist and extremist views regarding the application of Islamic law in Mali. This Azawadi rejection to Gali push him to establish the Ansar al-Din (Gaffey 2016).
2. **Al Murabitoun Battalion**: A violent jihadist group in the Sahel and West Africa aimed at the application of Islamic law. The group was formed in 2013 as a result of a merger between the al-Mulathamun Battalion ("the Masked Battalion") and the "Tawhid wal Jihad" movement in West Africa, and it is clear that both were members of AQIM. The group announced that it was targeting France and its interests in the region in order to defeat France and its allies in the region. In May 2015, the co-founder of the group, Adnan al Sahrawi, pledged his allegiance to Daesh. However, Mokhtar Belmokhtar refused this pledge and confirmed his allegiance to al-Qaeda, and renamed the movement to become: "al-Murabitoun - Al-Qaeda in West Africa" (Black 2009). In December 2015, the Murabitouns merged with AQIM after a joint attack on the Radisson Blu Hotel in Bamako. Since that attack, the Murabitouns have taken a leading role in al-Qaeda operations in the region.
3. The **Masked Battalion**, headed by Algerian Mokhtar Belmokhtar, known as "One Eyed," was listed by the United States on December 18, 2013, as a foreign terrorist organization.
4. Organization of the **Great Sahara**, which includes six battalions, all belonging to AQIM,

5. **Macina Battalions**, a terrorist group that adopts the ideology of al-Qaeda but is based on ethnic "Fulani" principles. It is Led by Amado Koufa, a close ally of Ghali who fought alongside the jihadists during the takeover of northern Mali in 2012.

The Organization of the Islamic State: African Daesh

As a result of the Libyan crisis, many violent jihadist groups and factions have spread in neighboring countries, particularly Niger, Mali, and Nigeria. Some factions have united in the regions of the Maghreb and the Sahel and pledged allegiance to the organization of the Islamic state and its leader Abu Bakr al-Baghdadi.

Thus, these extremist groups have emerged to operate beyond the borders and frameworks of the traditional state.

Nigeria's Boko Haram

The meaning of Boko in the Hausa language, which makes up more than 70% of the population of northern Nigeria, is Western education. Therefore, the verbal translation of the name of the group means the prohibition of Western education. Agbiboa (2015) argues that this group has been severely affected by the Taliban Afghanistan model. It adopted a narrow vision of Islam, which saw Western education as infidelity and deviation from the true Islamic religion. Therefore, this education ultimately leads to the weakening of the Islamic community. Interestingly, no one in Nigerian society has taken Boko Haram's claims and beliefs from the outset seriously. But many Nigerians were looking at the members of the group who had given up their beards and wore a certain garment with great contempt. However, the development of events later proved the mistake of this unthinkable view of the strength and influence of Boko Haram in and around Nigeria.

In the early years of its existence, the group mobilized many followers in the states of Bauchi, Yobe, and Borno, where students left their universities and schools. Some high-ranking professionals abandoned their work and sold their own property in order to join the group and contribute to jihad for God's sake to rid Islam of influence and hegemony West.

The Boko Haram group relies on building its intellectual vision on three pillars:

The first is the prohibition on dealing with existing state institutions because they are corrupt and infidel. The banking system is based on usury or Riba and Islam denies interest. Taxes and other statutes, such as land laws, violate God's law. The second pillar is the prohibition of Western education because it is nonIslamic and violates the teachings of Islam. Therefore, the third pillar in the mind of the Boko Haram group is to escape from all these vices in the infidel society and migrate to distant sites and isolated areas far from the cities.

The Boko Haram depends largely on the Kanuri ethnic group as a major source of recruitment. It is known that the Kanuri make up about ten million people living in northern Nigeria and some neighboring countries such as Cameroon and Chad.

The Kanuri was associated with the rule of the Kingdom of Kanem Bornu during the period (1086–1846). This ethnic factor is partly explained by the fact that the Boko Haram group sought to declare the Islamic Caliphate in 2014, before pledging its allegiance to Da'ish. This ethnic component undoubtedly gives special attention to the analysis of the nature and development of violent jihadist groups in Africa compared to their counterparts in the Arab world and the Middle East regions. Generally, Boko Haram has been able to benefit from cross-border affiliations and support. There are long-standing regional networks of close ties and trade relations, the influence of local leaders, and growing public resentment among disadvantaged youth.

The Mobile Caliphate State Across the African Sahel

From a geopolitical perspective, the challenge of global jihadist networks in the African coast to the authority of the traditional state and national institutions is also a symbol of the growing phenomenon of nongovernmental actors based on violent terrorism around the world. We are faced with a phenomenon like the mobile state, that practices the traditional State functions in accordance with the Westphalia system, except for the question of compliance with international obligations. The jihadist organizations themselves, despite assuming the functions of the virtual state, cannot restrain their movements according to the state system in the current system of international relations. For example, the concept of deterrence cannot survive asymmetric conflicts against violent jihadist groups. The principle of deterrence is very simple in essence (if you commit an act, its harm will be greater than its benefit). As opposed to this traditional understanding, jihadist networks are not related to political boundaries or the state system, which makes deterrence or retaliation ineffective. With the increasing progress in modern technology and the information revolution, the jihadi networks allowed their members to operate freely and to deal instantly on a case-by-case basis. By properly using the Internet, these organizations increase their access to a broad base of followers and public, which can be influenced beyond national boundaries. The use of the Internet was necessary to expand the activities of Al-Qaeda, ISIS, and other global jihadist organizations. These organizations, through the Internet, can prepare attacks, communicate and broadcast their media messages, and train new recruits (Pawlak 2015).

It is important to know the specific features of the violent jihadist organizations, since Boko Haram is not al-Qaeda in the Maghreb or Al-Shabab in Somalia (Varin and Abubakar 2017). Each of these groups requires a different pattern of national, regional, and global responses. On the other hand, the previous analysis helps to identify the kinds of gaps that jihadist groups are trying to fill, especially in the case of the inability of the national state to perform its traditional functions. However, the increasing jihadist position in its complex networks is subject to continuous transformations that may often be very pragmatic or obvious opportunism. There is no doubt that the ability of these groups to exploit the contradictions of Al Sahel in terms of its environmental and societal dimensions and international defiance has become an important factor contributing to its survival and continuity. We can highlight some of the features of the virtual Caliphate State in the African Sahel as follows:

Numerical and Intellectual Multiplication of Jihadist Groups

In 2007, when GSPC pledged its allegiance to al-Qaeda, the Sahel region of West Africa defined three extremist jihadist groups: the Salafist group itself, which declared allegiance to al-Qaeda and became its branch in the Islamic Maghreb; and Boko Haram, established in 2002; and then the Islamic Courts in Somalia, which eventually led to the creation of al-Shabab. This fragmentation and proliferation in the number of violent jihadist Salafist movements in West Africa and the Sahel could be explained by two main factors: the first is the intellectual division within the parent organizations and secondly the desire to be free from the burdens of leadership and independence in decision-making on the battlefield. Thus, the opposition within al-Qaeda led to the emergence of the Tawhid and Jihad movement in West Africa. Moreover, the opposition within the National Liberation Movement of Azawad led to the birth of the Ansar al-Din movement. The "masked" battalion tried to exercise some degree of relative independence, changing its name to "signatories with blood." The latter joined forces with some of the Tawhid and Jihad groups in West Africa to form the Murabitun battalion.

Perhaps, the most prominent features of intellectual attraction within the jihadist organizations in the African coast was the swing affiliation within the Murabitun between al-Qaeda and ISIS. On May 13, 2015, Abu Al-Walid Al-Sahrawi, its leader, pledged allegiance of the Murabitun to the Islamic State and its leader Abu Bakr al-Baghdadi and called upon all jihadist groups to swear allegiance to the Caliph. However, Mukhtar Belmokhtar, the leader of the organization, rejected the Sahrawi emirate, as already explained, and denied linking to ISIS or the allegiance to its prince Al-Baghdadi. Belmokhtar confirmed that the Sahrawi statement "does not bind Shura Al-Murabitun," and "a clear violation of the founding statement that defined its approach and behavior," which adheres to what he called "the pledge to Ayman al-Zawahiri on jihad for the sake of God."

On the other hand, 2016, the seventh anniversary of the re-establishment of Boko Haram in July 2009, is a turning point in the progress of the group, which certainly affects the features of the geostrategic landscape of radical Islamic groups not only in Africa but in the global jihad networks. In August 2016, the movement split into two factions: one led by Abubakar Shekau, after the death of its founding leader Mohammed Yousuf in 2009, adopts a more radical and violent approach, and pledge allegiance to the Islamic state khalifate Abu Bakr al-Baghdadi in 2015. The second faction was led by Abu Musab al-Barnawi who assumed command of the organization as the Wali of the West African region on August 2, 2016. Al-Barnawi, the son of the group's founder, Mohammed Yousuf, served as spokesman for the group under the leadership of Shekau. The split between the two factions appears to be of an ideological nature, with Barnawi refusing to target civilian Muslims, while Shekau tends to take away both the state and society (Onuoha 2016). No doubt, this division between the leaders of the two factions might lead to a violent confrontation for control and devotes the state of intellectual hostility between them. Each faction must try with all its might to acquire more resources and followers. Noting that while the Daesh-supported Barnawi faction controls much of northern Borno state, which shares the border with Niger, Chad, and

Cameroon along the shores of Lake Chad, the Shekau faction controls the central and southern parts of Borno State, where the Sambisa Forest are located.

Here arises a question on the future of this numerical breeding of violent jihadist organizations in the African coast. First, the intellectual opposition is the main factor behind the creation of new groups expanding in areas that suffer from the absence or fragility of the national state. Thus, the shifts in the geostrategic environment in West Africa (Senegal, Côte d'Ivoire and other countries) or even in Central Africa can lead to the dominance of violent jihadist forces, especially al-Qaeda, and to a lesser extent the organization of the Islamic state, taking advantage of some intersections and commonalities with the separatist movements in the region, such as Ansar Al-din movement (Bassou and Guennoun 2017). On the other hand, regional counter-terrorism groupings necessitate the need to unite forces and resources in their battle against government forces. This shift does not necessarily mean that the jihadists will form a united front, but it will be reflected in the form of a network of logistical support, supplies, or training and safe havens for terrorists.

Toyota Land Cruiser Mobile State

Most field research has indicated a common denominator among conflicting parties in Africa, rebels, and governments. It is a Toyota Land Cruiser, mainly made in Japan for civilian purposes, but is now a preferred weapon for attacks in Africa. Due to its technical characteristics, the car is expanding operational theaters (Elhag 2013). It is widely used in dry areas such as the African Sahel and Sahara. This four-wheel-drive vehicle is used by jihadists and guerrillas to transport arms, ammunition, and supplies. It is also ready to carry anti-aircraft guns or heavy machine guns. The nature of jihadist violence has changed to a high degree of mobility and maneuverability. Al-Qaeda or its jihadist groups, using its Toyota, are trying to show their power and ability to hurt African governments. In addition, these land cruisers have been widely used in illicit activities, human trafficking, small arms trafficking, attacks on traffickers by looting of their trucks and goods, and even increasing attacks on banks or other public services in towns or villages. These criminal offensive acts that spread fear among civilians involve the use of Toyota Land Cruiser and thus can be seen as one of the tools associated with the increasing violent jihadist tide in the Sahel and Saharan Africa.

African governments are spending large sums of money to buy land cruisers to be used against violent and terrorist movements rather than using their resources for development. The various regional and international powers are also supplying the rebels with "Land cruisers" to destabilize or overthrow governments to serve the interests of these external forces. Toyota and the Japanese government receive huge economic benefits from selling these land cruisers to African countries; at the same time, these vehicles with their high technological capabilities, help exacerbate the conflict in areas with a jihadist range. Activists and human rights activists pose a moral question related to the responsibility of Japan, the companies, and governments benefiting from the sale of these vehicles in Africa, which are used for military purposes, some responsibility for the aggravation of conflicts and the accompanying loss of life and property. Some call for the application of mechanisms to restrict or prohibit the distribution and use of Toyota for military purposes (Conflict Armament Research 2016). This may be feasible by monitoring and regulating the sale of these vehicles in Africa in the same way as the arms trade.

Use Peripheries to Attack Centers

Jihadi groups have adopted a new strategy to move through the neglected remote areas in the Sahel and to use as a launching pad for attacks. These groups – including AQIM, Boko Haram, the Macina Liberation Front and the Murabitun – have abandoned attempts to control cities and urban centers (ICG 2017). Instead, they used bases in the countryside and desert areas to attack cities and centers of major population concentration. Al-Qaeda and its sisters in the coast are often able to force the national armies to retreat and leave the peripheral and remote areas to fall for the jihadists. At the same time, increased international support has reinforced the historical – unintentionally – trend of the Sahel countries in their relative concentration on the political center areas and the neglect of vast remote areas.

Jihadi armed groups have been operating in the central and western coast since the 1990s. Over time, despite limited efforts to prevent their spread, some of these groups eventually managed to control vast territory, as in northern Mali in 2012 and northeast of Nigeria in 2014. The initial response was largely military. The governments of the Sahel, with the help of western and regional allies, were in the pursuit of jihadist groups from all major occupied cities and destroyed most of their heavy weapons. However, these military successes were not accompanied by the return of the Government's administration to the "liberated" areas. African armies and their allies have often been unable to restore security in the countryside or even on the outskirts of some cities. The continued absence of the state, especially in the area around Lake Chad, along the Mali-Niger border and in the center of Mali, has allowed the jihadists to establish and expand their presence there.

Jihadi groups have been able to adapt to the new situation after withdrawing from urban areas under the government security and military pressure. As shown by the internal correspondence of al-Qaeda in the Islamic Maghreb, found in Timbuktu in 2013, discussions within the Boko Haram group and the split that took place in June 2016, the mounting pressure from the regional armies did not completely undermine the Jihadi groups' ability to move and develop new strategies. Indeed, since 2013, these groups have been able to carry out horrific attacks on West African cities and capitals (such as Bamako in Mali and Ouagadougou in Burkina Faso). More importantly, ongoing attacks on local capitals and towns force government armed forces to give priority to garrisons and security ambushes in return for abandoning vast rural and desert areas. For example, frequent jihadist attacks in and around Gao, Mopti, and Timbuktu in Mali have forced government forces and peacekeepers to increase security in these cities, at the expense of reducing operations and patrols in rural areas. There are certainly a few exceptions, such as the Kidal region, where the presence of the French army and the intensive government patrols have alienated groups such as Ansar al-Din and AQIM and prevented them from gaining full control. However, due to the inability of the Sahel countries to take full control of various parts of the country, the jihadists managed to strengthen their control in the context of the security vacuum in remote areas.

Regardless of the ambition to establish the Caliphate State, the jihadists chose to penetrate deep into the desert and control neglected rural areas. They are not alone in this endeavor. Other armed groups, such as ethnic militias, transnational criminal gangs, armed gangs, even separatist movements, all seeking to fill the security vacuum left by the central authority. Depending on local formations of power and interests, these groups may fight jihadist groups, simply ignore them or avoid alliances, or establish alliances with them.

Jihadi groups use a combination of threats and persuasion to strengthen their position, provide limited services to some communities, especially security and enforce some rules of justice. In central Mali, jihadi groups offer protection to pastoralists and their flocks, giving local communities the opportunity to challenge the decisions of government representatives or their partners in local elites. Similarly, a faction of the Boko Haram group established partnerships with some local communities in Lake Chad region, by hunting down Hausa immigrants who controlled the booming fishing sector. This local coalition allowed the elements of Boko Haram to seek refuge in the Lake Chad islands, while regional armies were hunting elsewhere. In return for protection or other services, jihadist groups were expanding their influence and strengthening their local roots, as well as recruiting to gain new members.

The jihadis have been able to strengthen their presence among rural and remote communities, which have only recently been integrated into the national state and are poorly linked to the central authority because they are poorly represented in decision-making centers at the national and local levels. These isolated parties include nomads and communities living in border areas, communities living on the mountainous border of Gwoza Hills along the Nigeria-Cameroon border, and those in the marshes of Lake Chad. The jihadist militias are not always successful in consolidating their existence. Attempts by Ansar al-Din Front to acquire a local incubator in southern Mali, along the border with Ivory Coast, failed. The central authority has successfully integrated these areas through a strong network of representatives and tribal chiefs in rural and remote areas, which ultimately enables the national security services to arrest members of this jihadi group.

Conclusion

It may be wise not to rush to issue judgments about the end of terrorist groups or to say post-Daesh or post al-Qaeda in the African Sahel in the medium and long-term. It is no secret that the dismantling of Daesh in both Iraq and Syria has led to the creation of the returnees foreign terrorist fighters (FTFs). The relocation of the

FTFs may strengthen the rivalry between Daesh and al-Qaeda to win the African front. The establishment of the JNIM, a branch of AQIM, has revealed the determination of al-Qaeda leaders to counter attempts by Daesh to infiltrate into their areas of influence. In fact, the rivalry between the two movements has become muted and has not reached the level of military confrontation yet. There are, however, two key factors that may lead to the inevitable confrontation between al-Qaeda and Daesh in the African Sahara. The first is the international tendency to support the intervention against Daesh bases in Libya, and the second is linked to the tendency of Daesh to transfer part of its leadership from the Syria and Iraq to the African Sahel. Indeed, this would allow it to relieve pressure on its bases in the Middle East, on the one hand, and on the other, to seek alternative bases and open up a new field of confrontation.

Of course, al-Qaeda in its African wing is broader, hostile to the West (the far enemy) with extreme violence, and jihadists from Algeria are at the forefront of its organizational structure. The Boko Haram group, despite its allegiance to the organization of the Islamic state, focuses in its operations on the destruction of the Nigerian state and the regional neighborhood rather than declaring war against the West. Its dominant ethnic group appears to be descended from the Kanuri ethnicity, which recalls the jihadi traditions of the Kanem-Bornu kingdom in Lake Chad. Despite its non-anti-Western rhetoric, it continues to target foreign nationals and Western installations in the region.

Violent terrorist attacks in countries witnessing various levels of democratic transition, with divided societies such as Burkina Faso, Mali, Côte d'Ivoire, and Nigeria, have shown that jihadist organizations have focused on easily attainable targets. Beach resorts, hotels, and places of worship are easily accessible compared to police stations or army barracks. As pressure mounts from the military and security systems of the North African countries against violent jihadist organizations, the groups' fighters are likely to move southward to use the desert and the fragile border areas as a safe haven for them. It is not unlikely that the Sahel and West Africa with their highly complex geostrategic characteristics will be the next stop in the global jihad march after the Levant region.

Perhaps the most prominent trends that can be concluded here when considering the future of jihadist organizations, especially al-Qaeda in the Sahel region are as follows:

– Localization of the international character of jihad
  There is no doubt that the idea of the localization of Jihadism can create a social incubator and sources of support to strengthen the presence and continuation of these groups in light of the complexity of the geostrategic landscape of the Sahel. This development leads to more complexity and confusion of the confrontations by the security forces because of the lack of clear lines between the Bedouins, on the one hand, and the battles fought by the rebels and jihadists, on the other. Local recruitment has been steadily increasing in the ranks of terrorist organizations since 2013, as a large number of foreigners (especially Tunisians and Algerians) left north Mali to Libya. Examples

like Ansar al-Din and the Macina brigade may confirm this trend. The same is true of the Somali Mujahideen Youth Movement, which has always maintained a certain distance from al-Qaeda in order to promote its recruitment in the local context.
- Enhancing jihadist "networking" with violent groups
It is quite clear that the militarization of the African Sahel by the international forces will remain for years to come. The foreign powers came to stay in the Sahara and the Sahel. They have not only come to fight terrorism but to achieve other goals, including access to rich natural resources. Jihadist groups will therefore find an intellectual justification for the movement and an ideological basis for recruiting among the Salafist jihadist base in the region. These jihadi groups, under the security pressures, will have to rely on more local partners who carry weapons for insurgency or criminality.
- The jihadist message and the perceived affiliation to the virtual Islamic caliphate.
This message usually focuses on fighting the new colonial enemy that loots Africa's wealth. The jihadists generally adapt their narratives to suit their local contexts, reflecting some of the concerns of diverse ethnic groups such as Tuaregs Moors, Fulani, and Sungai. Considering the fragile African state, people can easily relate their personal narratives to a globalized discourse on the idea of justice and injustice, which in essence means that the dream of a caliphate is the solution. The procession of the Daesh Caliph, al-Baghdadi in Mosul will be replaced so that any jihadi group having a Toyota Land Cruiser and believes in this message will move forward to achieve this dream.

Cross-References

▶ Ethno-communal Conflict in Sudan and South Sudan
▶ Religion and Political Mobilization

References

Agbiboa D (2015) The social dynamics of the "Nigerian Taliban": fresh insights from the social identity theory. Soc Dyn 41(3):415–437

Barnes C, Hassan H (2007) The rise and fall of Mogadishu's Islamic courts. J East Afr Stud 1(2):151–160

Bassou A, Guennoun I (2017) Al Qaeda vs. Daech in the Sahel: what to expect? http://www.ocppc.ma/publications/al-qaeda-vs-daech-sahel-what-expect. Accessed on 15 July 2018

Benjaminsen TA (2008) Does supply-induced scarcity drive violent conflicts in the African Sahel? The case of the Tuareg rebellion in northern Mali. J Peace Res 45(6):819–836

Black A (2009) Mokhtar Belmokhtar: the Algerian Jihad's southern Amir. Terrorism Monitor VII(12):8–10

Bossard L (2014) An atlas of the Sahara-Sahel: geography, economics and security. Organization for Economic Co-operation and Development/Sahel and West Africa Club, Paris, pp 39–40

Boutellis A, Mahmoud Y (2017) Investing in peace to prevent violent extremism in the Sahel-Sahara region. J Peacebuild Dev 12(2):80

Cohen HJ (2013) Al Qaeda in Africa: the creeping menace to sub-Sahara's 500 million Muslims. Am Foreign Policy Interests 35(2):63–69

Conflict Armament Research (2016) Investigating cross-border weapon transfers in the Sahel. http://www.conflictarm.com/download-file/?report_id=2433&file_id=2434. Accessed on 16 Aug 2017

Elhag A (2013) The Toyota land cruiser and its role in spreading terror among African civilians: field observations. World Peace Foundation at https://sites.tufts.edu/reinventingpeace/2013/06/22/toyota-land-cruiser-and-terror/. Accessed on 8 June 2018

Gaffey C (2016) Who is Iyad Ag Ghaly, Mali's Veteran Jihadi? Newsweek, 29 June. Web. 01 Aug.

Hansen SJ (2013) Al-Shabaab in Somalia: the history and ideology of a militant Islamist group, 2005–2012. Oxford University Press, New York, pp 24–26

Hassan H (2015) Transformations of Islamic discourse in Africa. Al Ahram Center for Translation and Publishing, Cairo

Hassan H (2016) Islamic state and the transformation of Islamic discourse in the Middle East. J Middle East Islam Stud (in Asia) 10(4):1–19

ICG (2017). https://www.crisisgroup.org/africa/west-africa/mali/forced-out-towns-sahel-africas-jihadists-go-rural. Accessed on 7 June 2018

IGAD Security Sector Program (ISSP) and Sahan Foundation, Al-Shabaab as a Transnational Security Threat March 2016 at https://igadssp.org/index.php/documentation/4-igad-report-al-shabaab-as-a-transnational-security-threat/file. Accessed on 28 Feb, 2019

Kaplan S (2015) He's been called 'uncatchable,' the 'pirate king' and the 'one-eyed' jihadist. Can they now call him dead? Authorities hope they've finally killed notorious jihadist mokhtar belmokhtar. WP Company LLC d/b/a The Washington Post, Washington, DC

Korteweg R (2014) Treacherous sands: the EU and terrorism in the broader Sahel. European View 13(2):251–258

Launay R, Soares BF (1999) The formation of an 'Islamic sphere' in French colonial West Africa. Econ Soc 28(4):497–519

Loimeier R (2007) Sufis and politcs in sub-saharan Africa. In: H. Paul (ed.) Sufism and politics: the politics of spirituality princeton. Weiner Publishing, Markus pp 59–101

Loimeier R (2011) Islamic reform and political change in northern Nigeria. Northwestern University Press

Marret J (2008) Al-Qaeda in Islamic Maghreb: a "Glocal" organization. Stud Conflict Terrorism 31(6):541–552

Nicoll A, Delaney J (2012) Extremism spreads across West Africa and the Sahel. Strateg Comments 18(8):1–3

Onuoha FC (2016) Split in ISIS-Aligned Boko Haram Group at http://webcache.googleusercontent.com/search?q=cache:-VMtmUEhCZAJ:studies.aljazeera.net/en/reports/2016/10/split-isis-aligned-boko-haram-group-161027113247008.html+&cd=3&hl=en&ct=clnk&gl=ae&client=firefox-b. Accessed on 8 July 2017

Pawlak P (2015) Cybersecurity: jihadism and the internet. European Parliamentary Research Service, Brussels

Retaillé D, Walther O (2011) Spaces of uncertainty: a model of mobile space in the Sahel. Singap J Trop Geogr 32:85–101

Roggio B (2010) Al-Qaeda leaders play significant role in Shabaab. Long War J. http://www.longwarjournal.org/archives/2010/08/al_qaeda_leaders_pla.php. Accessed on 17 Aug 2017

Varhola LR, Sheperd TE (2013) Africa and the United States – a military perspective. Am Foreign Policy Interests 35(6):325–332

Varin C & Abubakar D (2017) Violent non-state actors in Africa: terrorists, rebels and warlords. Palgrave Macmillan, Cham

Zimmerman K (2013) The al Qaeda Network: a new framework for defining the enemy. AEI's Critical Threats Project. https://www.criticalthreats.org/analysis/the-al-qaeda-network-a-new-framework-for-defining-the-enemy. Accessed on 8 Aug 2017

Consequences of Globalization for the Middle East Political Geography

43

Mostafa Entezarulmahdy

Contents

Introduction	774
Globalization as a Concept	775
Ethnicity	777
Historical Background of Ethnicity and Ethnocentrism	779
Dispersion of Ethnocentrism in the World	780
Third World Countries and Ethnocentrism	780
Globalization and Ethnicity	781
Perspectives, Theories, and Trends in Ethnicity and Ethnos	781
Key Factors in the Formation of Ethnic Nationalism in Multiethnic Communities	783
Key Factors Intensifying Specialism in the Middle East	783
Conclusion	787
References	788

Abstract

Globalization is a complicated phenomenon, which has a variety of effects. It is a multidimensional phenomenon, and its influences extend to economic, social, political, legal, cultural, military, and technological actions. Therefore, it has influenced many dimensions of human life today. Globalization has paradigmatically shifted into regional–globalization theories. In the field of ethnicity, the globalization process can include different or even contradictory influences. With regard to ethnic variations, the Middle East is a very complicated example. The factor that dramatically dominates ethnicity (ethnic minorities) in the Middle East is the way its dispersion has occurred in the past. It is worth noting the vital role played by loss of awareness and intention in the dispersion of ethnicity in the Middle East. The principal question in this study is how globalization influences the political geography of the Middle East. The study findings, obtained by a

---

M. Entezarulmahdy (✉)
Political Science Department, Robat Karim Branch, Islamic Azad University, Tehran, Iran
e-mail: m.emahdi1982@gmail.com; entezarulmahdy@rkiau.ac.ir

descriptive analytical approach, reveal that through mitigation of the power of national regimes, political–ethnic conflicts, and cultural hegemony, globalization could pave the way for separatism, disintegration, and formation of new territories, and will dramatically vary the political geographic composition of the Middle East.

Keywords
Globalization · Ethnicity · Middle East · Political geography

Introduction

The emergence of technological revolutions and the fast progress of communication have been interpreted as the drunkenness of the time and have altered the reality of national territories and led to self-awareness of human communities. This heralds a new era during which all aspects of the human life will be affected. One of these affected aspects is ethnicity or, in other words, ethnic groups. Ethnicity and its definitions are influenced by ethnic conflicts, which have been especially augmented since the middle of the twentieth century. Ethnic conflict is an influential factor in the emergence of the globalization phenomenon, which, on one hand, is a response to the conditions imposed on ethnic groups by regimes and governments, and, on the other hand, is affected by awareness on the part of ethnic elites amid the changes occurring in today's modernized world, especially since the emergence of the globalization phenomenon. One region that includes a lot of ethnic groups is the Middle East. This is a region of great political and cultural complexity because of its large ethnic, racial, and religious variations. Globalization is becoming more important to the Middle East and its resident ethnic groups, as it involves a variety of ethnic groups and religions; it also involves different countries in the region. Governments in the Middle East have not been capable of dealing and interacting with each other without conflict, and they have been engaged in ethnic conflicts since they were first established. Taking into account the globalization phenomenon and mitigation of national regimes' power, with penetration of national territories and across boundaries as a result of advances in technical and technological communications – resulting in greater awareness on the part of ethnic groups of preservation of their own cultural values against any threatening factors – some ethnic groups have responded to global public culture with efforts to foil their central governments' policies. Three countries that have experienced ethnic conflicts and disruption between ethnic groups are Turkey, Syria, and Iraq. These countries are suffering from an agitated condition of their ethnic mix and have experienced a revival of ethnic conflicts since the 1980s, when globalization started. These conflicts considerably threaten these countries' central governments (Ghezelsofla and Habibi 2015: 994).

The focus of this chapter is on the concept of globalization and its impact on ethnicity. The issue of ethnicity and specialism in the Middle East is assessed. Finally, the consequences of globalization for ethnicity and ethnic groups in the

Middle East, and the probabilities of changing the political geography of this region, are appraised. In the following sections, the concepts of ethnicity and ethnic groups are studied.

Globalization as a Concept

Various meanings and definitions of "globalization" have been presented by scholars and philosophers. However, a comprehensive definition comprising all dimensions of this phenomenon has not been developed yet; in fact, inconsistent theories are emerging in this field. The present political traditions – whether conservative, liberal, or socialist – have not reflected any reaction or perception in compliance with the globalization era (Held and McGraw 2003). Some definitions of the term "globalization" are briefly given here for clarification.

Held suggests that globalization means an extensive and profound coherence of all dimensions of social life globally, from cultural to criminal and guilt aspects, and from financial to mental and spiritual aspects (Held et al. 2002).

Scholt defines globalization as internationalization, liberalization, universalization, westernization, and deterritorialization (Scholt in Baylis and Smith Jan Aart 1997). He states that globalization is a trend in which social relationships become boundless and free of distance, so that all humans are interacting in this world (Khor 2001).

Robertson defines globalization as squeezing and minimizing the world and expediting the knowledge toward the world as a whole. He and Giddens define globalization as realization of global conditions where local and national cultures are cohering and gathering. From their point of view, the term "globalization–localization" has been developed in accordance with Robertson's definition (Robertson 1992).

Albrow states that "The present era has experienced fundamental variations in the essence of the social actions and organization of individuals and social groups." This era, which is appropriately called the "globalization era," is a phenomenon beyond the interaction of thoughts, merchandise, capital, and assets at an international level. In addition, in a subjective viewpoint, globalization conveys dismissal of categories, old friendships, and allegiances, and instead substitutes new emerging values for old merits and criteria, as well as homelands, nations, and religion (Albrow 1996). As Albrow and King assert, globalization covers the entire movements with which all people of the world are interacting at international and global levels (Albrow 1990).

Marks and Angles also emphasize the necessity of understanding the history of capitalism for a proper perception of globalization, as capitalism has typically been considered a key factor involved in global economic and cultural integration (Lowy 1998). Therefore, from this perspective, globalization is coupled with capitalism (Sweezy 1997).

In Ohmae's viewpoint, the important conclusion of globalization theory is the gradual loss of national and governmental borders, such that natural resources are not the only keys to wealth and well-being, local borders are meaningless (and, thereby, military weapons are not a substantial source of power with respect to real industrial activities and knowledge), and mankind is armed with science and knowledge through which we can guarantee our power and follow prosperity in our lives (Ohmae 2002).

In these circumstances, the special roles and positions of governments and governors in international relations will decline. To fully understand and lead economic action approaches and the emerging nature of a borderless world, one cannot focus on a nation's government as a unit. Ohmae suggests *government–nation* regions instead and stresses that new lines have been drawn on the world economic map, which could be referred to as *government–regions* (Ohmae 1990).

Krasner confirms many fundamental changes in the world and challenges the opinion that globalization has revolutionized the nature of human society and the social–political organization of mankind. As an expert, he asserts that the importance and influence of globalization should not be exaggerated (Krasner 2009).

Using the viewpoints of Held and McGraw, Krasner calls Freedman's perspective exaggerated globalization and refutes it. Krasner refutes the attitude toward globalization that necessitates government gradual weakness and disappearance but not collapse. The total indestructible and exclusive authorities of governments in their foreign and interior policies have deteriorated, and this implies threatened governments (Krasner 2001).

Therefore, in Krasner's viewpoint, the principal role of government–nation orientation and the importance of political leaders and local structures are being shifted by this theory, and government–nations and their leaders have paved the way for globalization and are joining it to utilize the profits of it (Krasner 2009).

Yurgen Habermause expresses that government–nations have been disarmed of their exclusive authority tools to control and lead communities and have become vulnerable with globalization pressures. This vulnerability conflicts with and contradicts the interior national democratic structure and the bases of governments, challenging their legitimacy, so, in this regard, government–land, under the Westphalia concept, will diminish, and borders and territories will no longer provide a proper substrate for imposing authority and occurrence of political, social, and economic events (Habermause 2001).

The most abbreviated and explicit definition of globalization is given in the book *The Consequences of Modernity* by Giddens (2018), which explains that modernity is a global phenomenon which is emerging in some constitutive characters of the modern organizations, specially reforms and abandonment of these organizations (Giddens 2018). From Giddens's perspective, the dimensions of globalization include the global capitalism economy, a nation state system at a global level, global military organization, industrial globalization, and international division of labor (Giddens 2018). Thereupon, these dimensions are keys to the abandonment of social events and detachment of time and space from spatial barriers, and are the basic reasons for the emerging compaction in social relations in the modern era.

Giddens also remarks on some other characteristics of globalization. In fact, these characteristics are the influences of globalization that typically affected human life during the late twentieth century and are observable. These characteristics include upheaval and globalization of telecommunications, environmental problems, rehabilitation and revival of local and nationalism cultures technology and knowledge globalization, and transformation of routine day life and individual identity (Giddens 2018).

In this chapter, a combination of definitions from Robertson, Ohmae, and Giddens is considered. So, globalization is defined as world compaction and an incremental increase in knowledge of the universe as a whole. The significant conclusion of globalization theory is the gradual mitigation and disappearance of national and local borders and nation states. Nation states will fail to keep their exclusiveness tools for controlling and leading societies and will become unstable, and rehabilitation and revival of local and national culture will occur.

Ethnicity

In research articles related to nationalism, terms such as "ethnicity," "ethnic groups," "ethnic nationalism," and "ethnic conflicts" are evident. However, it should be kept in mind that terms such as "ethnicity" and "ethnic conflict" have new and modern roots, and they are seldom found in nineteenth century dictionaries. In general, the term "ethnicity" was rarely used by social scholars till the early twentieth century. The great attention from anthropologists and sociologists to this term refers to the frequent usage of terms such as "racial minorities," "religious minorities," "linguistic minorities," and "nationality minorities," especially in the era of "melting pot theory" publicity (Ahmadi 1999: 33).

According to this theory, American society and culture was simulated as a melting pot that took in all ethnic groups who immigrated to the USA from all over the world. The criticism of this theory by some sociologists in the early 1960s drew more attention to this theory. Since the 1960s, the term "melting pot" has been used for assessment of North America and Europe and, following that, the Third World.

The key point is that there is no united or consistent definition of "ethnicity" and "ethnic group." In the literature of research on "ethnicity" and "ethnic groups," there is no clear definition of these terms, such that the authors assumed that there has been a global and acceptable definition of these terms. In other words, it is assumed that the definitions used for "ethnicity" in the USA are also usable in other regions of the world, but it is not possible to provide a unit definition for these terms yet.

The term "ethnic groups" initially implied a religious concept and pointed out non-Christian groups who had not converted to Christianity. After that, the term involved a racial concept and lost its early religious concept. Therefore, for many years, variant racial groups were used as clear examples of ethnic groups. During that time the religious concept of ethnicity and ethnic groups gradually became obsolete.

Although the race phenomenon has been a discussion issue among anthropologists and sociologists, such that many of them have categorized race as an ambiguous subject relevant to determined and defined boundaries, the problem is not merely the equality of racial groups; it is a reality that one can see the revolution and evolution of ethnicity definition and ethnic groups. At this stage, religious and racial concepts of ethnic groups are culturally defined, i.e., while the term "ethnic groups" referred to non-Christian groups and then racial groups, at the third stage the meaning was extended further to include racial, linguistic, and religious groups; that is, any group differing in terms of language, religion, skin color, and race from other groups in the community are considered ethnic groups (Ghoshchi and Naderi 2014: 64).

Among social science scholars, there is no united attitude to ethnicity and ethnic groups, and they do not agree on determinant indicators of ethnicity and ethnic groups. From some scholars' perspectives, race is a credit indicator for ethnic group, while from others' points of view, linguistic or religious indicators are valid. It seems that the definition of an ethnic group depends more upon the attitudes of the authors than on acceptable indicators for the whole. These problems have arisen especially when social science researchers use these ambiguous indicators and terms in analyzing complex communities, such as Middle East countries. Here, some particular specifications create ethnic boundaries; for instance, in Lebanon, religious differences and variations are a key determinant and boundary between ethnic groups. In countries such as Afghanistan or Turkey, language is the key indicator for ethnic groups (Ahmadi 1999: 48).

Although there is no specified definition of ethnicity that is agreed upon by many sociologists, they all believe that ethnicity includes subjective and objective components. These components encompass interests, intellectual awareness, common benefits, belonging, common interests, and common objective cultures in language, history, religion, and common land, either now or previously.

Therefore, it can be asserted that for accurate and better perception of "ethnicity" it is necessary to consider subjective and objective components through which a good boundary can be drawn to separate this term from other terms.

Younger states that once the following conditions are met, the ethnicity concept is clear:

- Being part of a big community is differently seen by the other parts of it for some properties such as language, religion, race, homeland, customs, and culture.
- Members realize themselves as being pioneers.
- Members participate in common activities on the basis of origin and culture, either real or myths. Therefore, ethnic groups are never individual; they exist in an ethnic system, and existence of an ethnic group reveals the existence of other ethnic groups (Ramezanzadeh 1997: 235).

In fact, the principal function of ethnicity is the connection of individuals in a group, and it teaches the group where it belongs and whom it can trust. Ethnicity is founded on the basis of behaviors, customs, and common values, and the limits of these shared issues illustrate the boundary of mutual behaviors of ethnic groups.

In globalization, unity on one hand and difference on the other hand form the basic network of thinking, and humans acquire common characters and attitudes. In order to maintain the identity and personate, attitudes, behaviors, and different cultures continue. In his book *Globalization and Fragmentation: International Relations in the Twentieth Century*, Ian Clark writes that global events suggest that the two processes "globalization and decomposition" occur simultaneously and the world events show their contradiction faces. For example in 1990s, in the field of economy, globalization process dominated while nationalism dominated in the field of politics (Qorishi 2010: 39).

In the early twentieth century, sociology scholars assumed that racial and ethnic linguistic interests indicated backwardness and historical disorders and abnormalities, which were either subjugated by communism, annihilated, or merged with liberal democratic entities in turn. The remaining ethnicity was a primary stage of human community evolution, which would be destroyed sometime or other (Golmohammadi 2012: 159).

Originally, some theorists of globalization theory believed that globalization of culture would lead to dominance and conquest by a globalized culture and that local or regional ethnic cultures would therefore be dissolved in this predominant global culture.

With its compaction of time and space, the globalization process hinders comparison and relativeness of cultures, multiplicity of social authorities, and semantic identification of traditional approaches (Golmohammadi 2012: 245). Using the facilities, opportunities, and tools of globalization, subnational groups play a vital role in culture at local, national, and international culture levels, utilizing their media tools. This culturing and identification can, from time to time, coincide with the global and national cultures, and in some cases it disagrees with the local and national cultures. One can analyze and assess the challenges and opportunities burdened by globalization culture in areas such as ethnicity and local culture.

In the next section, following the globalization concept, the background and history of ethnic groups and ethnicity are discussed.

Historical Background of Ethnicity and Ethnocentrism

In general, the terms "ethnic" and "ethnocentrism" have been meant and perceived differently over time, semantically and historically. The term "ethnicity" was first used in 1953 by Rizeman (Fakohi 2010: 16). After World War II it was commonly used for different minorities. Since the 1960s, the terms "ethnic" and "ethnic groups" have been used in sociological and anthropological statements. The term "ethnic group" is applied in the anthropological literature to a population with a high level of autonomy in its biological reproduction, or with common fundamental cultural values gathered in an obvious alliance within cultural forms; they create mutual relations and involve a sense of belonging to an external reality, which decomposes them. The modern concepts of ethnic groups and ethnicity emerged during the 1960s after the third stage of national government establishment in colonies that had become independent after World War II and following a decrease in the military power of the Western European countries. Chronologically, it is better to state here that the term "Third World" also emerged in this era. Terms such as "ethnic" and "ethnic groups" apparently pointed out the predominant resident groups in pluralist communities. These groups differ in terms of their language, culture, and appearance from the majority groups in their communities (Ahmadi 2010: 35).

Dispersion of Ethnocentrism in the World

Ethnic and cultural heterogeneity and number in political units of the world is a popular and realized issue in the world. Today, in some regions of the world, variant ethnic groups and tribes living together peacefully have founded the fundaments of powerful entities such as the national states and formed a united entity called a national government or identity. However, in a considerable number of other parts of the world, ethnic prejudice and racism – and, following them, ethnic crises – are phenomena that have caused great disasters for human beings. Even now, in the twenty-first century, and despite scientific and academic advances, wars and violent ethnic conflicts are seen across the world. In a study conducted in 1970, Conner stated that among a total of 132 countries in the world, only 12 were integrated in terms of ethnicity. In 25 countries, an ethnic majority was dominant, while in 53 countries, five main and dominant ethnic groups existed. Recent research has revealed that only 14 countries include very small ethnic minorities, and only 4% of the global population live in countries with just one ethnic group (Haghpanah 2002: 3).

Third World Countries and Ethnocentrism

Third World countries include more than 70% of the world population and 58% of the Earth area. Ethnocentrism poses challenges to Third World countries, and the crisis conditions of ethnic majorities are an important aspect of this encounter. In general, cultural transformation in global integration is the biggest risk that cultures and subcultures face. The history of these countries shows peaceful dealing with these ethnic groups and subcultures. Nevertheless, slogans are not sufficient, as the world today and the modern era necessitate international agreements and retention of all citizenship rights to prolong and preserve stability and connect governments to nations. One of these differences and divergent currents is ethnic distinctions within a country. Today, few countries in the world are composed of just one ethnic group, and over 80% of United Nations (UN) member countries include a variety of races and ethnic groups. Around 37 wars in the world have been specifically caused by ethnic conflicts. In this regard, ethnocentrism research in the Third World reveals that ethnic nationalism is the most significant factor in political and social threats to weak governments (Ahmadi 2010: 53). Third World countries have been referred to as multiethnic countries, as most have been formed from separate ethnic groups. This is not extendible to all countries in the world, but it seems that ethnic conflicts or wars in the Third World hinder national development more considerably than in developed industrial countries. Most Third World countries, especially those in Asia and Africa, are enclosed by fictitious borders imposed by colonialists when leaving those countries, and do not take account of historical ethnic or tribal divisions (Saei 2015: 124).

Globalization and Ethnicity

Globalization consists of various important specifications, as well as the authenticity of varieties and differences. In the globalization era, differences and varieties are emerging in the form of various identities. Identities are not as robust as they were in the past, and they have become revolutionized and changed. Castells maintains that all identities are rebuilt (Castells 2001); moreover, in the globalization era, individual and social identities are simultaneously developed and rebuilt and are consistently being varied (Ghoshchi and Naderi 2014).

Today, globalization is not recognized as the only factor in assimilation and homogenization, as globalization does not necessarily conflict with localization. These two concepts are in close correspondence as a result of united dynamics, which are sometimes referred to as "global–localization." From Robertson's perspective, globalization is not merely a process linking pre-existing locations. He prefers the term "local–globalization," as it asserts, in its original definition, a global perspective, which also takes into account local conditions. Thereupon, heterogeneity is created and recreated consistently through globalization approaches (Nash 2001).

The globalization process can result in contradictory influences, both homogeneity and heterogeneity. Where the authenticity of pluralism of globalization theory at a national level is concerned, the pluralism model and then homogeneity and coherence can be reached among local and ethnic groups through a national culture, and globalization opportunities and profits will be applied accordingly (Ghoshchi and Naderi 2014).

Perspectives, Theories, and Trends in Ethnicity and Ethnos

From the perspectives of Robertson, Giddens, Castells, Steward Hall, Barber, and some other scholars, globalization, on one hand, intensifies integration and, on the other hand, enhances ethnic identities and special trends. Giddens accounts for the mutual increasing influences between the two final limits of overseas and interior borders as one of the distinctive properties of modernity or, in other words, global effects on one hand and national effects on the other hand (Giddens 2018). In other words, this phenomenon assists the development of social space by wonderful advances and revolutions in communication technologies and transportation, and dissolving of human boundaries. Consequently, to avoid the merging of global cultures, some cultures try to avoid merging by creating closed local borders and barriers, or they actively defend their local position against merging and the invasion of global culture. Revival of local cultures is important for specialism as they intend to separate this space from their local and particular cultures. In today's world there are many varied specialisms in different fields of religion, language, and ethnicity in both developed and underdeveloped communities (Ghezelsofla and Habibi 2015).

Roland Robertson recognizes the concept of globalization as the best definition to understand this process by assessing and reviewing studies conducted on globalization. On the contrary of the viewpoint which defines globalization as compaction and squeezing of the world, which has been consistently involved with creation and adsorption of local culture, has drawn his attention to the apparently conflicting approaches of globalization and localization, which converge generalism with a sort of specialism. The best example of this status might be the approach of Augustin in the field of divine and terrestrial rules, who expressed that these two rules will always coexist. For generalism and specialism in globalization, some intend to homogenize and others try to dehomogenize. From Robertson's perspective, the two approaches are simultaneously the complements of each other and are cohered. However, they might inevitably impact, and this actually has occurred (Robertson 1992).

Stewart Hall puts forward a viewpoint similar to that of Robertson, in which a return to localization is a reaction to globalization, which people reflect when faced with a special form of modernity trend, and they try to recede from globalization on the basis that "we are not aware of it and are not capable to control it, we do not know the policy to face with or dominate it." This approach is strong and comprehensive. Everything trends toward it, and some limited fields remain as small gaps, which we should act on. These limited exemptions from merging are referred to as "cultural specialisms" constituted in reaction to "globalization." As Hall also mentions, "what we typically call globalization is not an event imposed on everything systematically to assimilate." In fact, globalization through a specialism approach creates special spaces, places, and ethnics, mobilizes special identities, etc. So, there is a permanent conflict between localization and globalization (Hall 1997).

Manuel Castells is also another reputable researcher in this area. He declares that all identities are rebuilt and that the materials used to build identities are history, geography, biology, productive and reproductive organizations, collective memory, individual dreams, power systems, and religious beliefs. However, individuals, groups, and communities nurture these raw materials and suggest their definitions in accordance with social requirements and cultural projects rooted in their social and time–space framework (Abdollahi and Ghaderzadeh 2009).

Castells points to three types of identity: legitimate, planned, and resistive. Legitimate identity is generated by prominent organizations in a community to develop their prominence among social actives. Planned identity (e.g., feminism) is formed once social actives generate a new identity using accessible cultural materials, which redemonstrates their positions in the community, so they try to change the total social structure of the community. Resistive identity, which is the most important type of globalization era from Castells perspective, is generated by actives who are considered "invalids" by the leaders or dominants in the community, or are branded as "disgraced." Thereby, the trenches are constructed for resistance against the principles supported by the community's organizations (Ghezelsofla and Habibi 2015). In the next section, important components and indicators of ethnocentrism are discussed.

Key Factors in the Formation of Ethnic Nationalism in Multiethnic Communities

In general, effective factors in formation or intensification of ethnicity vary depending upon the special conditions of each society in multiethnic communities, as follows:

- Power source and distribution structures in the community (economic, political, and cultural)
- Self-propelled nationalism conditions based on three key factors: ideology, mechanisms, and approaches to facing social demands
- Historical experiences of ethnic interactions and relations, specifying whether they have been dominant or dominated, federal or autonomous
- Reactiveness of regional and world powers against the ethnics in a special community
- Geoethnic conditions of each community, population-to-land ratio, and ethnic equality in comparison with the adjacent countries and the types of gaps within the community
- Attitudes and ethnic sensitivity to national identity, profits, security, and government, whether they agree with the central state or a central ethnic
- Discrimination, which is a key factor in raising ethnic problems

Key Factors Intensifying Specialism in the Middle East

The key ethnic indicators in the world include ethnic self-awareness, native language, and, in some nations, the psychological traits of the ethnic groups, lifestyle, specific social organizations with distinct interests, and willingness of a nation for a state organization to be established (Shikhavandi 1990: 276). Yourdshahian (2001: 16) states that a few factors are very important for ethnicity and ethnocentrism:

(a) *Race*: Among primitive groups, during the medieval era, and maybe during recent decades, this has been the key factor in the national unity and identity of ethnic groups, but presently it is less prominent in the development of communication and the great integration of the world's nations.
(b) *Language and culture*: These are the principle bases reflecting the culture of each nation or ethnic group.
(c) *Traditions and social customs*: The social customs of each nation or ethnic group not only illustrate the functional indicators of that nation or group but are also the principal element specifying the nation's identity.
(d) *Common homeland*: The individuals' community in a common homeland is the main and important factor in their unity.
(e) *Land*: Land has played a vital role in the past, but immigration, telecommunication technology, and travel have diminished this role.

(f) *Economic factors*: This factor plays a determining role in identity change of ethnic groups at the international level.

Mitigation of National Sovereignty

As mentioned above, ethnic specialism is a result of threats by the globalization process to merge communities and cultures. Ethnic groups in the Middle East have publicized themselves during recent decades, using technological tools, including the internet and mass media, to garner public support for reviving their eroded rights. They have attempted to respond to globalization as a factor that promotes a globalized culture, and they intend to preserve their identity and culture. Since both globalization and following that the weak points of civil community and emerging despotism regimes, based on bribery and corruption, which would have never discovered the realities of the conditions as explicitly as the globalization era does, so, as aforementioned, mitigation of the national sovereignty power in this time, and awareness and knowledge increase and facilities to easily learn and communicate which is out of the control of the sovereignty all have impaired the body of the government in these regions.

A clear example of this is Turkey, where it led to improvements in the political and social conditions of the Kurds, as the second-largest ethnic group in this country. The Kurdish demands stemmed from their increased awareness, reflected in the parliament elections of 1991, when the Kurdish people in Turkey elected the Workers' Party, which was a Kurdish party under the control of the Kurdistan Workers' Party (PKK) party leader. So, for example, in Şırnak province, the Workers' Party won 79% of the votes. Accordingly, the Kurdish leaders of the True Path Party (DYP) and the Social Democratic Populist Party (SHP) – Süleyman Demirel and Erdal İnönü – promised to support human rights. This initiation was the first great retreat for Turkish leaders. Also, the armed forces missed their authority and power over the nation, and the political vision had changed (Mac Dowel 2004).

Another example of mitigation of national sovereignty power in the globalization era was the protests of Kurdish people residing in Europe; they started a wide protest in Europe against the arrest of the PKK leader Abdullah Öcalan by the Turkish National Intelligence Agency (MIT) in Nairobi in 1999. The BBC News showed thousands of Kurds shouting *Biji Serok Apo!* ("Long live President Apo!") together in the street (Mutlu 2007). The interesting point was the instant organization of the protesters through communicative tools, as well as the internet and media, by which they could gather the dispersed population of Kurds in Europe to protest against the Turkish government and could attract global public attention to their conditions. This movement reflected a mitigation of the central sovereignty of Turkey, as the government could not prevent the gathering of the protesters. After Abdullah Öcalan's arrest and death sentence from the Turkish Supreme Court, because of public awareness (especially via Kurds residing in Europe) and pressure from the European Union (EU) to revoke his sentence, the court's verdict was reduced to life imprisonment (Ghezelsofla and Habibi 2015).

Kemp and Harkavy state that this approach also applies to political conditions in Iraq, as the revolution of telecommunications and development of informative networks have strongly influenced human behavior in the globalization era, so these communities could never stop accessing their citizens to uncut information, as they tend to be a part of the global economy (Kemp and Harkavy 2004). Today, the Kurdish achievement is seen in the power-sharing constitution of Iraq, and also their media capabilities in Kurdistani regional politics at an international level (satellite channels), along with thousands of Kurdish websites, over 400 periodicals (including 103 newspapers), 14 universities, and, finally, participation of Kurds in the central government, and their power to influence the culture of the Kurdistan region of Iraq (Mohammadi 2010). This is not the end of their activities, as they held an election on December 25, 2017, which was an uncommon political event in the twenty-first century, to establish a new state in the Middle East. This election was held in the Kurdistan region, with rare enthusiasm from the Kurdish people, despite opposition from the Iraqi central government, adjacent countries, the EU, the UN, and the USA. The election committee subsequently announced that 72% of eligible citizens had participated in this election to vote on independence for Kurdistan, and 92% of them had voted for separation and independence of Kurdistan from Iraq.

In Syria, national sovereignty mitigation emerged via use of technological communication tools of the globalization era by ethnic minorities such as the Kurds, Turkmens, etc. The obvious weakening of national sovereignty in Syria happened in 2012 following the Arab Spring in 2011, which started in Tunisia and swept away the borders of Syria, using technological telecommunication tools of the globalization era. Preliminary protests were started by the majority Sunnis against the minority Shias and the minority Alawi sovereignty, and were then continued in the form of threats by ethnic minorities in Syria, especially the Kurds. Finally, on June 19, Kurdish autonomy was announced in three provinces – in Hasakah, Kobanî, and Afrin – by the Democratic Union Party (PYD), in accordance with the democratic confederalism of Abdullah Öcalan, which was a breakthrough in both the history of the Kurdish political movement and the world political literature (Hur 2014).

Globalization and ethnicity have become more considerable in the Middle East as ethnic conflicts have increasingly emerged in this region. The complicated ethnic structure of this region and the fictitious borders of almost all relevant countries, which take no account of their ethnic composition, have been major factors in the problematic ethnic conflicts in this region from the beginning of the globalization era. After the 1980s, the PKK, which was not well known, initiated military and insidious operations against Turkish authority in eastern parts of Turkey. In fact, the PKK, as the representative of the Kurdish radical movement since the 1980s, influenced the international and local policies of Turkey for two decades, which led to the deaths of 35,000 military and civilian people (Chegenizadeh and Asartemer 2001).

In Syria, an example of ethnic conflict occurred in 2004, during a football match in the Kurdish city of Qamishli, between Arab and Kurdish fans, which resulted in the killings of dozens of Kurds and the arrests of 2000 Kurds by the police in response to Kurdish protests against their living conditions (Hur 2014). Moreover, following the start of the Arab Spring movement in Tunisia in 2011, Syria was affected within 1 year and extensive ethnic conflicts and wars began, during which various ethnic–religious groups of Kurds, Arabs, Turkmens, Sunnis, Christians, etc., fought, resulting in the deaths of 200,000 people since 2011. In Iraq, which is still involved in ethnic–religious conflicts, 15,000 people were killed in 2014 alone, most of whom were Iraqi civilians (Shafaghna 2014).

Deterioration of Political–Ethnic Conflicts

Different statistical references show that today over 80% of UN member countries are ethnically variant and plural, and encompass two or more ethnic communities. These communities have competed peacefully or aggressively to dominate regimes and/or to achieve independence, autonomy, and success. Approximately half of these local and regional conflicts have started since 1989, which was the end of the Cold War or the start of the modern world order. Globalization started precisely at that time and began to extend in all dimensions. For a better perception of how globalization has resulted in augmentation of political–ethnic conflicts all over the world, one should consider the characteristics of this process (Golmohammadi 2002: 164).

Ethnic movements are influenced by globalization in the following ways: globalization accelerates the decline of governments and governors, and transnational relations pave the way to progress the willingness and goals of ethnic movements and decrease government powers to fight and repress them violently. For example, the Zapatista movement rapidly changed into a global movement using these relations. Moreover, in some cases, the outcomes of globalization cause these conflicts. For example, the Hawaiian indigenous movement started as a result of the destruction of Amazon rain forests (Schultz 2001: 210).

With the start of the globalization process, which was followed by the collapse of the Soviet Union and its segmentation into 15 independent countries, there was a return to balkanization and, with the termination of Russian domination of the politics and culture of the eastern European countries, repressed interests and customs were revealed and rehabilitated, and a political mobilization occurred on the basis of cultural and ethnic self-awareness across the whole region. Yugoslavia collapsed without any majority of ethnicity, and four new republics – Slovenia, Croatia, Bosnia and Herzegovina, and Macedonia – announced their independence. However this ethnocentrism was, in some cases, very violent, particularly in Bosnia and Herzegovina. This disaster suggested that the Cold War and the ideology of hegemony could only inhibit such conflicts for a short time (Golmohammadi 2002: 173).

Cultural Hegemony

One of the challenges of globalization is westernization, which has met with different reactions in the Middle East (Kachuyan 2007: 65). Globalization aids promotion of subcultures and specialism, in addition to its promotion of global public culture as modernity (according to the communication tools that are prepared for its audiences), and, given that globalization has originated in the West, most cultural currents in Central or Western countries are produced under this influence and penetrate other regions of the world, and the words, images, ethics/values, space regulations, constitutions, and other authorities penetrate from the West to the East or other Third World countries through media (Shiroudi 2007: 39).

From the perspective of these regions' leaders, globalization is a threat and forces Western culture onto other nations, necessitating urgent preservation of local cultures by nations to withstand globalization.

Legrain describes these perspectives interestingly: "Fears that globalization is imposing a deadening cultural uniformity are as ubiquitous as Coca-Cola, McDonald's, and Mickey Mouse. Europeans and Latin Americans, left-wingers and right, rich and poor – all of them dread that local cultures and national identities are dissolving into a crass all-American consumerism. That cultural imperialism is said to impose American values as well as products, promote the commercial at the expense of the authentic, and substitute shallow gratification for deeper satisfaction" (Legrain 2003: 223).

In the Middle East, the same conditions exist, as Alsoudi suggests: "With its economic, political, and cultural dimensions, all over the world, globalization is spreading in the Middle East. Therefore, today, some scholars of the Middle East believe that globalization threatens identities and cultures of the region. For instance, Abdollad Turkey warns that globalization as a process separates the human from his culture and identity and spreads disaster into the world (Alsoudi n.d.: 43).

Nevertheless, by integrating and merging communities, in addition to mitigating centralized power and the influence of national governments, globalization can enhance the power of ethnic groups and is a threat to the national and ethnic communities existing in the Middle East. Therefore, ethnic communities that are faced with this new threat try to preserve their identity and culture, so different ethnic specialisms are seen from different perspectives, which are, in fact, their attempt to preserve their identity and reflect their powers to their governments. The ancient urbanity and civilization in the region and preservation of traditional roots and structures are important for promotion of global public culture in the Middle East that can be seen in almost all ethnic groups and religions residing in the region. Thereby, nations that have battled to preserve their values and customs against nationalistic policies and government integration policies will take more initiatives to continue this preservation.

Conclusion

The Middle East has invariably experienced challenges and conflicts in the heterogeneous composition of its demographic geography. This heterogeneous composition has tangibly appeared especially since World War I. The collapse of the Ottoman Empire and its decomposition led to division and independence of countries regardless of their populations' ethnic composition. The most considerable point is the emergence of nondemocratic political systems in this region's countries since their independence; they have, in fact, prevented their civilians from becoming aware of human and social rights outside their countries.

The globalization phenomenon, which has been accompanied by contradictory influences, has resulted in homogeneity, on one hand, and heterogeneity of these communities, on the other hand. It should be kept in mind that divergence occurs more than convergence in this region because of national sovereignty mitigation of power and suppression of ethnic movements. The region's regimes have continually attempted to suppress and subdue these movements through violence and repression. However, violence and repression have not been a solution. This can be seen in Turkey, Iraq, and Syria, because of the discordant distribution of Kurds in the region. The Kurdish election in Iraq is an example of this. If Kurdish movements continue their quest for separatism, it could lead to the decomposition of these countries. Therefore, further political geographic changes may be inevitable in the Middle East.

References

Abdillahi M Ghaderzadeh O (2009) The collective identity of the Kurds in the countries of Iran and Iraq. Soc Sci Lett 17(36). pp 1–25
Ahmadi H (1999) Ethnicity, from myth to reality. Ney, Tehran
Albrow M (1990) Globalization, knowledge and society: readings from international sociology. Sage, London
Albrow M (1996) The global age. Polity, Cambridge
Alsoudi A (n.d.) "Orta doğu ölkelerin kultur, Ekonomik ve siyasi etkisi", pdf. From: http://www.odevportali.com/ara/küreselleşmenin-etkisi
Baylis J, Smith S (2001) The globalization of world politics. Oxford University Press, London
Breton R (2008) Political ethnicity [translation: Naser Fakouhi], 4th edn. Nayer Ney, Tehran
Castells SM (1997) The power of identity. Blackwell, Cambridge
Cheginizadeh G, Asarsamar M (2001) Kurdish ethnic movements and national security of Turkey. Foreign Relations. Period.1 No.2 Summer
Ghezelsofla M, Habibi A (2015) The impact of globalization on ethnic specificism in the Middle East. Polit Q J Fac Law Polit Sci No. 4 winter
Ghoshchi M R, Naderi M (2014) Globalization and ethnic pluralism in Iran, challenges and opportunities. J Strateg Stud Glob 5th E, No. 14 winter
Giddens A (2018) The consequences of modernity. (trans: Safari B). Tehran: Center Press
Golmohammadi A (2002) Globalization of culture, identity. Ney, Tehran
Habermas J (1996) The inclusion of the other: studies in political theory. MIT Press, Cambridge
Haghpanah J (2002) Ethnicity as a new social movement and its consequences in Iran. Strategic Studies Institute, Tehran
Hall S (1997) The local and the global: globalization and ethnicity. In: King AD (eds) Culture, globalization and the world-system: contemporary conditions for the representation of identity. Macmillan, Basingstoke, pp. 19–40
Held D, McGrew A (1993) Globalization and the liberal democratic state. In: Government and opposition. https://doi.org/10.1111/j.1477-7053.1993.tb01281.x. Accessed 11 Sept 2017
Held D, McGrew A (2003) The great globalization debate: an introduction. In: Held D, McGrew A (eds) The global transformations reader, 2nd edn. Polity, London
Held D et al (2002) Globalization and anti-globalization. Polity, Cambridge
Hur A (2014) Selahaddin eyyubinin cocuklari suriye kurtleri. http://www.Radikal.com. Accessed 13 Sept 2017
Islami A (2006) Ethnicity and its dimension in Iran. www.sid.ir. Accessed 9 Sept 2017
Kachuyan H (2007) Theories of globalization. Nay Press, Tehran
Kemp G, Harkavy ER (1997) Strategic geography and the changing Middle East. Carnegie Endowment for International Peace, Washington, DC
Khor M (2001) Rethinking globalization: critical issues and policy choices. Zed, London
Krasner S (2001) Sovereignty organized hypocrisy. Princeton University Press, Princeton

Krasner S (2009) Power, the state, and sovereignty: essays on international relations. Routledge, New York

Legrain P (2003) Cultural globalization is not Americanization. http://www.philippelegrain.com/cultural-globalization-is-not-americanization/. Accessed 23 Feb 2019

Lowy M (1998) Globalization and Internationalism. Monthly Review. Available at: https://monthlyreview.org/1998/11/01/globalization-and-internationalism/. Nov 01, 1998

McDowall D (2004) A modern history of the Kurds. Tauris, London

McGrow T, Held D (2001) Global transformation. London School of Economics, London

Mohammadi H, Khaledi H (2005) The autonomy of northern Iraq and its effects on peripheral ethnic movements. Geopolit Q (1)

Mohammadi H, Khaledi H (2010) Self-regulation of northern Iraq and its effects on peripheral ethnic movements. Geopolit Dialogue. No: 1

Mutlu Can (2007) Kurds in cyberspace on politics. http://www.web.uvic.ca/~onpol/spring2007/3-Mutlu.pdf

Nash K (2010) Contemporary political sociology: globalization, politics and power, 2nd edn. Wiley-Blackwell, Malden

Ohmae K (1990) The borderless world. Harper Collins, New York

Ohmae K (2002) Globalization regions and the economics in conference: Center of Globalization and Policy Research; UCLA. January

Qorishi F (2000) Globalization – writing and evaluation of different interpretations. Q J Foreign Policy, Year 14, No. 2

Ramezanzadeh A (1997) Development and ethnic challenges at the development and public security conference, vol II. University Jihad, Ministry of the Interior, Tehran

Robertson R (1992) Globalization social theory and global culture. Sage, London

Robertson R (1994) Globalisation or glocalisation? J Int Commun 1(1):33–52

Saei A (2015) The Political and Economic Problems of the Third World. Tehran: Samt Press

Schultz JA (2007) Globalization in the field of culture and politics (trans: Karbassian M). Scientific Cultural Publishing, Tehran

Shafaghna (2014). https://afghanistan.shafaqna.com/of-themonth/item/46057-15. Accessed 16 Sept 2017

Sheikhavandi, the referee. (1990) Birth and rise of the nation, Tehran: Ghaghnous

Shiroudi M (2007) Globalization in the field of culture and politics. Islamic Research Institute Research, Qom

Sweezy P (1997) More or less on globalization. Mon Rev

Yurashahan I (2001) Ethnic ethnology and national life. Forozan, Tehran

National Imaginary, Ethnic Plurality, and State Formation in Indonesia

44

Paul J. Carnegie

Contents

Introduction	792
Bersiap and the End of the Dutch	793
The Birth of *Pancasila*	794
The Rise of *Orde Baru*	795
Double Trouble and Other Imitations	798
Islam and Nation-Building	801
Conclusion	804
References	805

Abstract

Indonesia is a vast and diverse entity of land and sea. It also has a complex history of radicalism, separatism, and rebellion. In fact, numerous scholars have periodically flagged both the centripetal tendencies and disintegrative forces at play in Indonesia. As such, any sort of nationalism capable of bringing together the world's largest archipelago as a "nation-state" is going to have its work cut out. How then did the nationalist leaders of the fledging republic narrate and structure the nation-state to hold contested social imaginaries and ethnic identities together? The following chapter investigates the implications of the ways in which nationalist leaders in the postcolonial period (1945–1998) forged not just a material state but a nation of the mind.

Keywords

Indonesia · Ethnic plurality · Social imaginary · Nationalism · Pancasila · Suharto · Sukarno

---

P. J. Carnegie (✉)
Institute of Asian Studies, Universiti Brunei Darussalam, Bandar Seri Begawan, Brunei Darussalam
e-mail: paul.carnegie@ubd.edu.bn

© The Author(s), under exclusive license to Springer Nature Singapore Pte Ltd. 2019
S. Ratuva (ed.), *The Palgrave Handbook of Ethnicity*,
https://doi.org/10.1007/978-981-13-2898-5_165

Introduction

On proclaiming Indonesian independence, Sukarno stated that "matters relating to the transfer of power etc. will be executed carefully and in a timely manner." (*Proklamasi Kemerdekaan Indonesia*, 17 August 1945). As Elizabeth Pisani (2015, 2) wryly notes, "Indonesia has been working on that 'etc.' ever since." In fact, a brief glance at its geography and demographics tells us that any sort of nationalism capable of bringing together the world's largest archipelago as a "nation-state" is going to have its work cut out.

Indonesia is a vast and diverse entity of land and sea (Sutherland 2007; Taylor 2003). There are five main islands – Java, Sumatra, Sulawesi, Kalimantan (60% of Borneo), and Papua (Western half of New Guinea). It also has 17,500 other smaller islands (depending on the tides) with approximately 922 of these permanently inhabited. As of 2018, the population is around 260 million (Badan Pusat Statistik 2018). It has approximately 360 ethnic groups, over 700 native languages (although Bahasa Indonesia is spoken by most as a second language), and a myriad of distinct dialects. Major ethnic populations include Javanese (40.1%), Sundanese (15.5%), Malay (3.7%), Batak (3.6%), Madurese (3%), Betawi (2.9%), Minangkabau (2.7%), Buginese (2.7%), Bantenese (2%), Banjarese (1.7%), Balinese (1.7%), Acehnese (1.4%), Dayak (1.4%), Sasak (1.3%), Chinese (1.2%), and others (15%) (Badan Pusat Statistik 2012).

Even these bare statistics overwhelm and disorientate. Indonesia is a not just a physical place in Southeast Asia but a nation-state of the imagination. If you try to visualize it in your mind's eye, it is like contemplating an Alexander Calder "Mobile." The reality defies and confuses expectation in equal measure. What confronts you is a fragmented and disparate construct of uneven forms and color that float precariously on thin threads. This moveable assemblage fluctuates in seeming randomness while remaining oddly balanced, weighted, and light. It looks ready to fall apart but somehow doesn't. How it manages to recalibrate in the space between components is quite baffling. This unlikely feat shouldn't work but it does. If you were to call it anything, kinetic and improbable are as good choices as any.

With this in mind, threading an integrative political identity to hold Indonesia's diverse conglomeration of peoples and places together is no easy task. It has to be done in such a way as to resonate across histories, cultures, and ethnicities. Yet, from Tuanku Imam Bonjol's Padri rebellion in the nineteenth century through to the rise of Islamic militias during the long struggle against Dutch colonial rule, Indonesia has a complex history of radicalism, separatism, and rebellion (Carnegie 2016). In fact, numerous scholars have periodically flagged both the centripetal tendencies and disintegrative forces at play in Indonesia (Cribb 1999; Crouch 2000; Kingsbury 2003; Tiwon 2000). How then did the nationalist leaders of the fledging republic narrate and structure the nation-state to hold contested social imaginaries and ethnic identities together? This chapter investigates the implications of the ways in which nationalist leaders in the postcolonial period (1945–1998) forged not just a material state but a nation of the mind.

Bersiap and the End of the Dutch

The Dutch first came to Indonesia in the sixteenth century as traders and then as colonizers. After the end of World War II and the retreat of the Japanese-occupying forces, Indonesia's former colonial masters sought to regain control over parts of the archipelago and isolate nationalist forces. The Acting Governor General Hubertus "Huib" van Mook was keen to revive the Visman Commission's plan for the constitutional future of the Dutch East Indies (Anderson 1972a; Ricklefs 2002). The Commission claimed that the people of the archipelago broadly supported the maintenance of the colonial system via a form of federalism. It had also portrayed the Indonesia's nationalist movement as small, disparate, and only partially significant (Brown 2003). This tone-deaf hyperbole would ultimately flounder in the face of determined nationalist resistance. In fact, the violent clashes between August 1945 and December 1946 during *Bersiap* phase of the Indonesian National Revolution confirmed the resolve of the nationalists. The term *Bersiap* derives for the Indonesian call to arms *Siap!* (Get Ready!)

The nationalist independence leaders were able to rally the peoples of the archipelago into action around resiliently "powerful myths" and a "reimagined" objective (Bowen 1986, 545–561). Unwittingly, the introduction of Dutch Ethical Policy in 1901 had helped sow the initial seeds of national consciousness. Seven years later the political society *Budi Utomo* (Prime Philosophy) would emerge and prove instrumental in the development of Indonesian National Awakening (*Kebangkitan Nasional Indonesia*). By the late 1920s, various urban and aristocratic Indonesian elites who had been given schooling in Western-style education institutions began to actively take up the nationalist cause. For instance, Sukarno attended Europeesche Lagere School, a Dutch-language elementary school in Mojokerto; then Hogere Burgerschool, an elite Dutch high school in Surabaya; and Technische Hoogeschool in Bandung. Their exposure to notions of nationalism and Marxism and European ideas of nation-states became encapsulated in the Youth Pledge of one motherland, one nation, and one language: Indonesia. Prominent and educated nationalist leaders like Sukarno, Mohammad Hatta, and Sutan Sjahrir were able to engraft ideas of nation-state and socialist principles onto symbolically powerful foundational myths of a unified archipelago that resonated with its diverse peoples. The geo-mythographical imaginary of a unified archipelago has deep roots. It traces all the way back to the Singhasari king Kertanegara in the mid-1200s and through the influential Majapahit era of his descendant Hayam Wuruk together with admiral Gadjah Mada and the Sumatran prince Adhityawarman in the late 1400s. Successive Malay and Javanese kingdoms often referred to re-establishing the glory of Majapahit.

Although Sukarno, Hatta, and Sjahrir rejected Dutch economic interests, language, institutional symbols, and practices, they were keen to inherit the whole territory of the former Dutch East Indies. This involved advocating for a centralized unitary territory of rule (*Negara Kesatuan Republik Indonesia*). For the plan to take hold people of the archipelago had to be mobilized around the idea of a collective destiny (Bertrand 2004, 28–29). The nationalist rhetoric of the time played to the notion of *perasaan senasib sepenanggungan* (the feeling of common fate and plight). By framing the struggle for independence this way, they were able to cast the Dutch as oppressors. It was a narrative that appealed to Indonesia's diverse peoples and allowed them to recognize themselves as a "community" under colonial oppression. They were being urged to imagine something different. Interestingly, in the 1980s at the height of Suharto's repressive rule, Pramoedya Ananta Toer's *Buru Quartet* (four semi-fictional novels that chronicle the development of Indonesian nationalism) echoed this transformative discourse.

The Birth of *Pancasila*

Appealing to a shared history of anticolonial struggle certainly enabled Indonesians to develop a nation-state consciousness. This was further helped by long traditions of taking outside influences and adapting them to local circumstance. Indonesia has been a geographical site of distinct ethno-cultural identities but also cross-cultural syncretism and miscegenation for millennia. Local *adat* (customary practices and traditions) merging at various times with Hinduism, Buddhism, Islam, and Christianity to complement existing social patterns and power relations (Schiller and Schiller 1997).

When viewed from the latter perspective, the ability to accept and adapt to an integrative national identity looks slightly less implausible. In this regard, the promulgation of *Pancasila* (*panca*, five; *sila*, principle) was crucial in facilitating a syncretic adaptation to the fledgling republic. The formulation of this new national ideology took shape under the auspices of the Investigating Committee for the Preparation for Independence (BKI – *Badan Penyeliduk Usaha Persiapan Kemerdekan Indonesia*). Later enshrined in Article 29, Section 1 of the 1945 Constitution, *Pancasila* linked Indonesian national identity to five guiding principles: belief in one God, compassionate humanity, the unity of Indonesia, consensus democracy, and social justice. This was supposed to allow for the recognition of Indonesia's diversity while appealing to the greatest number of people. For Sukarno, it reflected the national motto *bhinneka tunggal ika* (unity in diversity) and provided "a powerful myth of nationhood" (Mulder 1998, 121).

Pancasila provided a basis on which Sukarno could appeal to Indonesia's ethno-religious-cultural groups to set aside differences and unite behind the common purpose of nation-building (*Negara Kesatuan Republik Indonesia*). Nonetheless, this putative solidarity was infused with Javanese symbolism and cultural values (Antlov 2000, 203–222). For Sukarno's *Partai Nasional Indonesia* (PNI) party in the 1950s, sociocultural outlook was as important as ideological foundations (Anderson 1990, 68; Mietzner 2008, 431–453). The five interrelated principles of *Pancasila* loosely reflected traditional Javanese values and traditions. These symbolic markers included *musyawarah* (deliberation), *mufakat* (consensus), *kekeluargaan* (family), *manunggaling kawula* (unity of the ruler and ruled), and *gotong royong* (mutual cooperation) (Bowen 1986, 545–561). In fact, as Indonesia's largest ethnic grouping, the Javanese influence on national political culture was strong. Historically speaking, the Hindu caste system of social differentiation and stratification influenced Javanese society with a status-conscious hierarchical mind-set. The various social aggregations this generated especially in Java provided cultural markers for three broadly identifiable cultural streams (*aliran*), namely, *priyayi* (nobility – traditional bureaucratic elite), *abangan* (nominal Muslim), and *santri* (more orthodox Muslim) (Anderson 1972b; Geertz 1973). Alluding to *aliran* sensibilities influenced the cultural politics (*politik aliran*) of both the Sukarno and Suharto eras in terms of mobilizing of support (Holt 1972).

Of course, in contemporary Indonesia, these Geertzian differentiations are no longer as clearly applicable or directly relevant. Furthermore, it was hardly surprising to find distinct opposition to Javanese ideas of power and legitimacy among ethnic groups with strong senses of territoriality such as Bataks, Acehnese, Minangkabaus, Malluccans, Minahasans, and Buginese, to name but a few (Cribb 2000; Nordholt 2003, 550–589; Taylor 2003). Aware of the need to placate different parts of the archipelago and allay growing accusations of pro-Javanese bias, Sukarno adopted a version of Malay as a national language (*bahasa Indonesia*). Having said this, the nation-building project was imbued with the image of a community that chooses a wise ruler by mutual consent combined and a hint of Supomo's thinking on *negara integralistik* (an integrated state) (Simanjuntak 1994), as Sukarno called it, a *Gotong-Royong* State.

The Rise of *Orde Baru*

After the overthrow of Sukarno in 1965, Suharto pushed Supomo's idea of *negara integralistik* in a decidedly repressive and authoritarian direction. This not to imply that violence and suppression of diversity did not take place under Sukarno but it would be equally wrong-headed if no attempt were made to indicate the qualitative and quantitative difference in repressive violence that took place under Suharto's New Order regime. To elaborate, the 30th September Movement's (G30S – *Gestapu*) abortive coup d'état provided the pretext for Suharto to sanction a brutal pogrom of extermination against *Partai Komunis Indonesia* (PKI – Indonesia Communist Party) (Roosa 2006). Cold-War Western complicity further ensured that capitalist development was going to firmly replace the class struggle. From 1965 to 1966, Indonesia bore witness to a genocidal purge and "disappearance" by the military and vigilante civilian militias mostly drawn from *Pemuda Pancasila* (Pancasila Youth) and Muslim youth groups, such as *GP Ansor*, of a conservatively estimated 500,000 to a more likely 1 million leftist PKI sympathizers (Cribb 1990, 2001; Robinson 2018). This blood-soaked trauma triggered a collective national amnesia that is only now being slowly retrieved (van Klinken 2001, 323–50; Zurbuchen 2005; Oppenheimer 2012).

In the aftermath of the slaughter, ideas of difference and pluralism were subsumed in the name of national interest and the developmental state. It was a reordering to be enforced through repression, co-option, and control. The New Order (*Orde Baru*: 1965–1998) regime repurposed *Pancasila* to justify a national unity defined by the ruling elite. In this repressive context and largely due to its vague aspirations, *Pancasila's* common platform of unity in diversity was shifted and manipulated into a full-fledged justification for Suharto's rule (Bertrand 2004, 30–34). It essentially functioned as little more than a culturally coded veneer for his centralized authoritarian practices.

This allowed him to infuse the very foundations of his rule with symbolic ideas of authority from the traditional Javanese past. Historically, Javanese social stratification had relied on specific power relations between lords (*gusti*) and subjects (*kawula*) and strong social identifications to authority (Koentjaraningrat 1985). Suharto repositioned the population within a deeply embedded narrative structure of paternalism and patronage. Tapping into traditional Javanese cosmology and a "culture of obedience" to rulers (*budaya petunjuk*) disarmed dissent to New Order authoritarianism. He further normalized his rule by reinterpreting Supomo's idea of *manusia seutuhnya* (whole man of humanity) as *manusia seuthisuhnya pembangunam* (total Indonesian). If you follow the logic, a "floating mass" of the population (*massa mengambang*) needs a paternal guide to steer them along the correct path (Carnegie 2010, 50). Suharto actively reinforced traditional high Javanese notions of the little people (*wong cilik*) as ignorant (*masih bodoh*), whose place was to remain servile (*budak*) and obedient (*patuh*) to their ruler (*gusti*). In effect, this would serve to de-contest societal identity vis-à-vis the state and further consolidate his position at the top of the corporatist pyramid.

With Suharto symbolically positioned in this constellation of power and authority, his regime set about socializing his version of political unity and order through various bureaucratic and ideological mechanisms. The state bureaucracy used various techniques to normalize their brand of authority and rule in public discourse and establish hegemony firmly in the popular imagination (Vatikiotis 2004). Schools taught *Pancasila* moral education. The Agency for *Pancasila* Development (BP-7) and the *Pancasila* Promotional Programme (P-4) developed programs for civil servants and community leaders (Antlov 1995).

The sweeping away of dissent was integral to establishing a relationship of subordination from the population to the dominant class (*wong gede*), i.e., the controllers of the state apparatus. Framing New Order legitimacy around development rather than representation meant that electoral intimidation, and control of the media and dissent could all be justified in the name of national interest (Anderson 2001). Virtually all membership-based organizations autonomous of the government were prohibited. By privileging "state above politics" meant control over political organization and economic policies (Robison 1986, 108). Between 1983 and 1985, *Pancasila* became the sole basis (*azas tunggal*) of all social and political organizations. Any organization that failed to conform to *Pancasila* principles was banned (Uhlin 1997). Of course, there were some notable exceptions in the form of the large Islamic organizations *Nahdlatul Ulama* and *Muhammadiyah*, but this was on the condition that they did not agitate for political change. Other attempts included the 1980 *Petisi Limapuluh* (the Petition of Fifty) that criticized Suharto for redefining Pancasila to mean "loyalty to the president," but he quickly banned news coverage of the petitioners, prevented them from traveling, and withdrew government contracts from firms associated with them. Significantly, the reinventing *Pancasila* for development purposes and exerting a tight control over the interpretation and distribution of information built a strong narrative structure of unassailability around Suharto's rule. It corralled the populace into identifying with the patrimonial culture of the nation-state and his unifying power (*wahyu*).

This meant that Suharto was able to exert control over what amounted to an elaborate patronage machine extending through the military and Golkar across the archipelago. Even by the standards of bureaucratic authoritarianism, the military occupied an unusual role in the scheme of things. Formerly known as ABRI (*Angkatan Bersenjata Tentara Republik* Indonesia – Armed Forces of the Republic of Indonesia), the involvement of the Indonesian National Defence Force (TNI – *Tentara Nasional Indonesia*) economic matters became accepted practice as a way to raise extra-budgetary revenue for operations. This dual role traced back to armed resistance against colonial rule and especially after the nationalization of Dutch colonial companies in the 1950s. Not only did the military occupy a symbolic place in Indonesian iconography as the "guardian" of the Republic, but it assumed a major role in the economy and development (Crouch 1979, 571–587).

From 1958, a series of laws set out the military's dual function (*dwifungsi*). First, Law No. 80/1958 and MPR Decree No. II/1960 (A/III/404/Sub/C) consolidated the military's power by guaranteeing it a fixed representation in *Majelis Permusyawaratan Rakyat* (MPR – People's Consultative Assembly), *Dewan Perwakilan Rakyat* (DPR – House of Representatives), and local parliaments. The military essentially became a functional group of the state. Secondly, during the New Order era, military influence was strengthened across Indonesia's political and economic landscape through Law No. 16/1969 and Law No. 5/1975. By the 1980s, the military was even taking on local development projects through its *masuk desa* programme. Self-funding activities were largely organized through a network of *yayasan* (social foundations), not to mention "revenue" raised from illegal levies on fishing, logging, mining, smuggling, and protection rackets (McCulloch 2003, 94–124). Suharto also rewarded loyal military supporters with posts that offered the prospect of substantial material gain. Many high-ranking officers involved themselves in commercial activities under the tacit understanding that the regime would oblige with licenses, credit, or contracts (Singh 2000, 184–216). Every important economic and political player, particularly the military, depended on some form of state patronage.

The other key supporting prop of state patronage was Golkar. In 1965, Suharto with the help of General Ali Murtopo turned various functional groups of military officers, civil servants, technocrats, government officials, administrators, and educators into the political machinery of the New Order state. This move was facilitated by the "restructuring" of Indonesia's political party system in 1971. Golkar, *Partai Demokrasi Indonesia* (PDI – Indonesian Democratic Party), and *Partai Persatuan Pembangunan* (PPP – United Development Party) were the only three permitted and state-licensed political parties. Golkar's constituent groups formed a single powerful state cadre with an instantly recognizable symbolic identity and unrivalled access to state revenues. It dominated the other two parties through distributing patronage and allocating resources combined with a virtual monopoly on communications and funding (MacIntyre 1991, 2000, 248–273). Golkar's distinctive organizational structure also gave it a vast territorial reach and hegemonic presence. It was able to weave a web of corruption and graft through the executive, legislative, and judicial institutions of the Indonesian state.

The New Order was essentially an "entrenchment and centralization of authoritarian rule by the military, the appropriation of the state by its officials, and the exclusion of political parties from effective participation in the decision-making process" (Robison 1986, 105). This eventually descended into a form of "Sultanism" with power and resources concentrated around Suharto's personal rule. He sat at the apex of not just a political structure but also "a system akin to business franchising [...] [*where he could*] bestow privileges on selected firms, so he effectively awarded franchises to other government officials at lower levels to act in a similar manner" (McLeod 2000, 101). In fact, both Golkar and the military allowed Suharto to operationalize his patrimonial authority through vast alliances of state officials, business interests, and community elites that reached all the way down the chain to the village level.

Double Trouble and Other Imitations

Looking through a more postcolonial lens reveals other contours from the past in the present. As Mahmood Mamdani (1996) has shown in the African context, colonial rule leaves a lasting impression. Established patterns of rule and authority although often rejected in the catharsis of the postcolonial moment do not simply disappear. Patterns of exploitative political, military, and economic practice implanted by the European colonial powers that constructed those states replicate in specific ways into the shape of the postcolonial state (Anderson 1991; Gouda 2000, 1–20). Indicating the problematic legacy of policies and strategies introduced by the Dutch should not be read as absolving Indonesia's post-independence leaders, far from it. By the same token, these legacies are not simply forgotten accidents of the past. Like distorted facsimiles of prior oppression, historic distress can play out in strange and unpleasant ways.

To elaborate, in pre-independence Indonesia, the Dutch administrated the archipelago as a territory with defined boundaries. This proto-state had a political economy geared toward the extraction and exploitation of resources and people for commercial benefit (Cribb 1994). For the Dutch, ruling through conditional proxies was the most pragmatic way of maintaining order and control over this large territory (Carnegie 2010, 46). As part of a strategy for co-opting local powerbrokers and enforcers, local aristocracies were cultivated and shored up by the Dutch. As such, a major postcolonial legacy bequeathed by the Dutch was an established network of patrimonial relations between local political elites and central authority not to mention simmering ethnic tensions (Hoey 2003, 110–126).

Even as the new nationalist leaders were zealously trying to distance themselves from all things Dutch, these reified patterns were more difficult to shift. In the immediate post-independence period, new political elites in Jakarta often made deals with local aristocracies, most notably in Bali, to ensure popular support for the fledgling republic and national project. Vaguely familiar patterns emerged, whereby villagers supported local elites who in turn supported central elites in anticipation of reciprocal benefit (Antlov 1995). As the centralization of authority intensified under Suharto, local elites became even more firmly attached by patronage networks to a hierarchical state power base in Jakarta. For Harold Crouch (1979, 578), "the New Order bore a strong resemblance to the patrimonial model. Political competition among the elite did not involve policy, but power and the distribution of spoils." As mentioned, Suharto was able to ensure his leadership by using a mixture of fear and rewards in the state bureaucracy, business, and the military.

But Suharto's "repressive developmentalism" built on state patronage and personal favors between state officials, business interests, and community elites was a boomerang in motion. It was simply too reliant on personal "cronyism" and resource revenues to compete effectively in a globalizing economy (Feith 1980; Khan and Formosa 2002, 47–66). His regime was ill equipped to match the burgeoning economies of South Korea and other "Asian Tigers." Throughout the 1980s, foreign investment fell due to restrictions and high subsidies given to state-owned companies. The situation brought about an incremental erosion of confidence in Indonesia's banking sector on world markets, especially when the regime lost complete financial credibility in the wake of the 1997 Asian Financial Crisis. Oil, gas, and other commodity exports plummeted and per capita GDP fell by 13%. By 1998 with visible discontent erupting over food shortages and rising prices, Suharto tried to deflect public anger by blaming Chinese "moneymen" and global financial institutions. His ruthless play on an ingrained stereotype stoked angry mob riots in Glodok (the Chinese district of West Jakarta), killing an estimated 1000 Sino-Indonesians (Carnegie 2010, 76).

While there is certainly no attempt here to excuse Suharto's ruthlessness, it is worth bearing in mind that Dutch colonial rule had a hand in fomenting problematic ethnic distinctions for post-independence Indonesia. It was under the Dutch that strategic ethnic divides were accentuated and maintained as a policy of disciplinary rule. In contrast to native Indonesians (*pribumi*), numerous ethnic Chinese Indonesians (*orang Tionghoa-Indonesia*) enjoyed commercial and tax collection privileges as an intermediary or comprador class for the Dutch East India Company (VOC – *Vereenigde Oost-Indische Compagnie*). This was part and parcel of an ethnically ordered colonial system (Brown 1994). Although the Dutch also discriminated against the competing rise of *orang Tionghoa-Indonesia* commercial activities, regulating local relations in this way unwittingly or otherwise served to fuel *pribumi* distrust and animosity toward them. Significantly, "reservoirs of animosity" can persist across time and, while not direct causal catalysts of discrimination and violence, they can pattern such action when it arises.

On independence, Sukarno's economic nationalism and the goal of building a strong *pribumi* business class meant that Sino-Indonesians suffered political and economic marginalization in the name of national self-reliance. This remained largely the case in the Suharto era (Schwartz 1994, 106). Ordinary *orang Tionghoa-Indonesia* experienced day-to-day deprivations and insidious discrimination under the New Order. The New Order largely excluded them from the military and politics. Many were forced into urban relocation. Specially marked identity cards and the imposition of legal restrictions on commercial activities were introduced. The closure or nationalization of Chinese schools became routine, as was the banning of Chinese literature and signs. This discriminatory assimilation pressure led many *orang Tionghoa-Indonesia* to marry *pribumi*, convert to Islam, and adopt Indonesian sounding names.

But somewhat differently to the Sukarno era, Suharto's regime also relied heavily on personal "cronyism." He cultivated so-called *cukong* (financier/broker) relationships with a select group of prominent businessmen particularly over rounds at the Jakarta Golf Club. Mutually beneficial economic joint ventures formed between high-ranking military officers and major *orang Tionghoa-Indonesia* economic actors. The former acted as the "masters" of politics, while the latter were the "masters" of capital (MacIntyre 2000, 248). State-owned industries were run with the financial backing of these cronies behind the scenes. This allowed officers to play the role of "old-time" Javanese rulers and aristocrats in a contemporary industrial-scale patron-client setup. Entrepreneurial cronies of Suharto such as Liem Sioe Liong (Sudono Salim) and The Kian Seng (Mohammad "Bob" Hasan) became some of the richest men in Asia with the help of regime patronage (Robison 1986, 322–370). Needless to say, this *cukong* setup did little to alleviate latent resentment toward *orang Tionghoa-Indonesia* among *pribumi* economic interests.

In another paroxysm of the past, Dutch transmigration policies (in 1905, 155 families were moved from Java to Sumatra) would carry over into both the Sukarno and Suharto eras. This involved the permanent relocation of people from overcrowded areas especially in Java, Madura, and Bali to less populated areas in Kalimantan, Papua, Sumatra, and Sulawesi. Suharto was particularly keen to force through extensive and controversial programs of *transmigrasi*. Ostensibly touted as a way to deal with overcrowding and poverty by providing opportunities in resource rich but more sparsely populated outer islands, it also gave expression to the assimilation and homogenizing tendencies of *manusia seuthisuhnya pembangunam* and *massa mengambang*.

By the 1990s, more than 3.6 million people had been resettled to outer islands, where they received a government allocation of land for cultivation, housing, and a subsistence package for relocating (Badan Pusat Statistik 2010). Unsurprisingly, the scale of transmigration created tensions between local indigenous populations (*putra daerah* – sons of the soil) and *pendatang* (migratory newcomers) over land use and access to subsidies. Large transmigrant influxes amplified fears and animosity among local populations over state-sanctioned marginalization and creeping homogenization, i.e., "Javanization" and "Islamization" (Wessel and Wimhofer 2001). It has led to a hardening to varying degrees of ethno-religious differentiation and allegiances in transmigration locales (Bertrand 2004). In certain provinces, these tensions have spilled over into periodic communal violence. Although typically framed as ethno-religious violence, transmigrants often make convenient scapegoats for underlying political, economic, environmental, and scarcity issues (Davidson 2003). In effect, they are "othered" as the unwitting proxies to already iniquitous central government practices and deeper-seated insecurities.

Islam and Nation-Building

There is little doubt that nationalist and patrimonial ideas of rule and authority have played key roles in conditioning Indonesian national identity, but we cannot ignore the centrality of religion to life across the archipelago. The integration of religions, especially Islam, with indigenous belief systems has played a significant role in the history and cultural self-understanding of Indonesia (Carnegie 2013, 60). Having said that, as a potential collective political resource, it has created some uneasy state-level tensions during both the colonial and postcolonial periods. In fact, there have been numerous attempts simultaneously to harness and curtail Islam's state-level ambitions (Carnegie 2014, 96).

Tensions between Islam and a developing nationalist agenda were evident from the early days of the independence movement. In the 1930s, the debates around whether Islam should constitute a foundational basis for the new state of Indonesia were intense. Agoes Salim and Natsir tried to persuade Sukarno to form a separate Muslim military unit. During the 1945 constitutional debates, Islamic groups proposed a Constitutional preamble known as the "Jakarta Charter." Sukarno's decision to drop the preamble from the final version caused consternation among stricter Muslims. They considered the Jakarta Charter as obliging the state to implement Islamic law across the Muslim community. Although belief in one God became the first principle of *Pancasila*, Article 29 of the pre-independence 1945 Constitution gave the government the right to control and regulate religious life in Indonesia.

In a broad schematic sense, we can trace a three-way split in Islamic "identity politics" as the nation-state formed in Indonesia, namely, traditionalist, modernist, and radical (van Bruinessen 2002, 125). From a political Islam perspective, the traditionalist response gave rise to the massive Sunni Islamic socioreligious organization, *Nahdlatul Ulama* (NU – Awakening of Ulama), with members numbering in the tens of million. The modernist Islamic party *Masjumi* (Council of Muslim Organizations) became the major Islamic political party in the fledgling republic in the immediate post-independence era. *Muhammadiyah*, Indonesia's other main socioreligious organization, still views itself as the custodian of *Masjumi's* modernist Islamic legacy. In counterpoint to the political representative ambitions and social mission of traditionalist and modernist responses, a much more radical and militant divergence also emerged. It is a divergence traceable to the large networks of revolutionary Islamic militias that formed in the context of the Indonesian National Revolution against the Dutch.

To elaborate, from the early 1950s onward, Sukarno's nationalists sought to depoliticize Islam. Both the secular nationalist party, *Partai Nasional Indonesia* (PNI), and the communist party, *Partai Komunis Indonesia* (PKI), cut across class and religious lines. Both parties promoted a secular nation-state, because neither had any desire to see strict Shari'a law imposed (Barton and Fealy 1996, 65). At the same time, they infused their political rhetoric with Javanese conceptions of power, leadership, and statecraft to symbolize, in attenuated form, the integrative harmony of mutual cooperation (Antlov 2000, 203–222). This appealed to and reflected aspects of *aliran kepercayaan* and the embodiment of *kebatinan* (Javanese syncretism). The PKI also made inroads with a large section of lower status *abangan* and rural Javanese *santri* in central and eastern Java by taking traditional cultural understandings and infusing them with the rhetoric of class and colonial oppression.

To further weaken and divide Islam's political appeal, Sukarno formed a strategic alignment with the traditional NU who maintained that Islam could indeed thrive under *Pancasila*. Rising tensions between reformists like Natsir who were expressing concern about a Javanese-dominated centralized state and traditionalists in NU escalated to the point where NU eventually seceded from *Masjumi* in 1952 (Barton and Fealy 1996, 21). However, many Javanese *santri* Muslims identified with NU and were more willing to accept a centralized unitary state than *santri* outside Java. Increasingly marginalized at the state political level, *Masjumi* began to descend into factionalism in the run-up to the 1955 elections. With the Muslim electorate effectively divided, the way was clear for Sukarno and his *Partai Nasional Indonesia* (PNI) to register an emphatic triumph.

Thereafter, Sukarno abolished the *Konstituante* (Constituent Assembly – established to resolve the question of nation-state foundation) and reinstated the 1945 Constitution. *Masjumi* boycotted Djuanda Kartawidjaja's cabinet as a protest at its lack of accountability to parliament. But by 1956, NU had thrown its support behind Sukarno's Nas-A-Kom project (***N****asionalisme,* ***A****gama, dan* ***K****omunisme – Nationalism, Religion and Communism*). The consolidation of Sukarno's presidential power signalled the end of the short-lived experiment with parliamentary democracy. For Sukarno, the latter was "based upon inherent conflict" in contrast to his preferred "Guided Democracy" (*Demokrasi Terpimpin*) (Koch 1983).

Eventually, rebellion flared after Sukarno ignored demands from regional commanders for more autonomy in the provinces (Carnegie 2010). In west Indonesia, *Pemerintah Revolusioner Republik Indonesia* (PRRI – Revolutionary Government of the Republic of Indonesia) led by Lieutenant Colonel Ahmad Hussein was declared in Sumatra in 1958. In East Indonesia, *Per Mesta* (*Pagan Peranakans Segesta* – Universal Struggle Charter) led by Colonel Venter Usual established itself in Manado in Sulawesi. NU disassociated itself from the PRRI rebellion and considered it damaging to the interests of Indonesia's Muslims. But prominent leaders of the independence struggle from both *Mesuji* and *Patri Socialise Indonesia* (PSI – Indonesian Socialist Party), disillusioned by Javanese dominance, fled to Sumatra. *Mesuji's* Sjafruddin Prawiranegara became prime minister of the PRRI with the backing of Sjahrir from PSI. However, the rebellions and the PRRI met with a swift response as central government forces moved in to crush the rebels. In the aftermath, Sukarno banned both *Masjumi* and PSI and jailed their leaders.

The rise of Sukarno's "Guided Democracy" also imposed major restrictions on radical Islamic movements. Sukarno banned the guerilla networks of *Darul Islam* (DI – Abode of Islam) and *Tentara Islam Indonesia* (TII – Indonesian Islamic Army) that had formed from the Islamic militias opposing the Dutch (Formichi 2010). But under the leadership of S.M. Kartosuwiryo (*pak* Imam), the DI secessionist rebellion for the establishment of *negara Islam Indonesia* (NII – Islamic State of Indonesia) continued in places such as West Java, South Sulawesi, Aceh, and South Kalimantan from 1949 to 1962. Many *ulama* especially from NU opposed Kartosuwiryo's vision and insurgency efforts. Interestingly, in the 1920s both Sukarno and Kartosuwiryo had been tutored and mentored by proto-nationalist and Muslim leader H.O.S. Tjokroaminoto, the founder of *Sarekat Islam* (Islamic Union). Kartosuwiryo, however, viewed Islam as "the foundation and legal basis of the Islamic State of Indonesia, the Koran and tradition constituting the highest authorities" (van Dijk 1980, 93).

By the 1960s, after sustained and bloody campaign by the Indonesian military, DI and TII were in disarray. Kartosuwiryo was eventually captured and executed in September 1962 (Dengel 1995). Yet, the act of Kartosuwiryo proclaiming himself Imam of *negara Islam Indonesia* on 7th August 1949 was a statement of intent. And as we know, group identities can often forge and crystallize in opposition to coercive-exclusionary practices of the modern nation-state (Carnegie et al. 2016; King and Carnegie 2018). As James C. Scott (2009, xii–xiii) notes, "all identities, without exception, have been socially constructed......to the degree that the identity is stigmatized by the larger state or society, it is likely to become for many a resistant and defiant identity. Here invented identities combine with self-making of a heroic kind, in which such identifications become a badge of honor."

To borrow Ben Anderson's (1991) terminology, Kartosuwiryo's declaration constituted a different "imagined community" in opposition to the *Pancasila* state envisioned by the secular nationalists. It in effect created an alternative "imagined decolonization." This alternate "myth of nationhood" means that today's members of DI are not so much a "movement" but a community that perpetuate and reconstitute themselves by looking back to Kartosuwiryo (Temby 2010). They "imagine" themselves as people of *negara Islam Indonesia*. In this sense, they are a "nation" contiguous with the state proclaimed by Kartosuwiryo in 1949. They (re)assemble through a reproduction of this legacy (Carnegie 2015, 15–26).

Even under the repressive grip of Suharto, subterranean allegiances to the idea of *negara Islam Indonesia* continued. Its latent militant threat would occasionally flare. The activities of the relatively short-lived *Komando Jihad* (another offshoot of DI) in the 1970s and early 1980s are a case in point. Then there was the Imron Group who took inspiration from the 1979 Iranian revolution who were involved in the Bandung police post incident and the high-jacking of a Garuda DC-9 in 1981. Others included the Tanjung Priok massacre in 1984, the bombing of Borobudur in 1985, and the Lampung incident in 1987 (McGlynn et al. 2005).

Despite these periodic militant threats, Suharto did, however, seek to manage Islam for his own purposes. Although he refused *Masjumi* a return to the political stage, he did allow *Parmusi* (the Indonesian Muslim Brotherhood) to form. This was done in a highly depoliticized way with Islamic organizations brought under the umbrella of the United Development Party (PPP). In practical terms, PPP was the only vehicle through which NU and *Muhammadiyah* could gain political representation. By the 1980s, NU had lost the Ministry of Religion, which represented a major symbol of its prestige and influence. It led Abdurrahman Wahid (*Gus Dur*) to withdraw representatives from the New Order government and move the organization firmly toward *khittah* (a socioreligious role).

Nonetheless, Suharto's attempts to subsume the polity's Islamic identification to the diktats of New Order corporatism remained only partially successful (Barton 2002, 1–15). In reality, the marginalization of political Islam precipitated greater civil society activity. Islamic social and educational renewal emerged in close association with *Himpunan Mahasiswa* (HMI – Association of Muslim Students). They championed the building of *Ikatan Cendekiawan Muslim Indonesia* (ICMI – Association of Muslim Intellectuals) with Suharto's blessing. It is not too improbable to postulate that he also saw this largesse in terms of his own political advantage. Courting Islamic support helped counter rumbling military dissent and pro-democracy sentiment. By the 1990s, ICMI and *Majelis Ulama Indonesia* (MUI – Council of Indonesian Ulama) had indirectly restored Islamic issues onto the political agenda. Suharto even began to encourage such developments. ICMI appealed to a younger generation of well-educated urban middle class who enjoyed increased access to strategic positions within business, government service, and academia. Tolerating Islamic political activism and promoting pro-Islamic military officers countered organizations beyond his direct control such as *Muhammadiyah* and NU (Kadir 1999, 22–24).

It may have shored up his friable authority for a while, but the strategy would eventually backfire in the wake of the 1997 Asian Financial Crisis. By 1998, pro-Islamic figures within ICMI, like Din Syamsuddin, began openly questioning Suharto's authority and suitability. Syamsuddin had become an instrumental figure in bolstering the orthodox *Dewan Dakwah Islamiyah Indonesia* (DDII – Islamic Propagation Council of Indonesia) and *Komite Indonesia Untuk Solidaritas dengan Dunia Islam* (KISDI – Indonesian Committee for Solidarity of the Islamic World) aided by major donations from Saudi Arabia and Kuwait. As Suharto's grip on power loosened in the face of economic meltdown and pressure for *reformasi*, orthodox sections in the green (Islamic) wing of the military began shifting their support to DDII and KISDI. The DDII/KISDI-military alliance eventually abandoned Suharto, as they saw him as a liability to the interests of Islam.

Conclusion

As this chapter has shown, national identity formation in Indonesia is conditioned not just by ethno-religious-cultural affiliations but through an interplay with state-level narratives and structures of legitimacy, authority, and development. Nationalist leaders repurposed social imaginaries and ideas of national development to engraft meta-narratives of nation-state(ness) onto the archipelago. Nonetheless, Sukarno and especially Suharto struggled to accommodate Indonesia's diversity within the imperatives of nation-state building and kleptocratic developmental ambitions. In certain instances, the tensions and contradictions between Indonesia's ethno-religious-cultural heterogeneity and its nation-state structural homogeneity led to contestation. The unanswered questions of Indonesia's postcolonial identity and its different "imagined decolonizations" often fuelled demands for autonomy and precipitated violent action and responses.

Despite the transformations of the *reformasi* era and substantial decentralization reforms, accommodating the interests and demands of ethno-religious-cultural communities stifled by previous exclusionary practices remains a tricky balancing act to manage. In fact, Indonesia's mobile nation-scape defies the logic of a predetermined end state. Maybe the Alexander Calder analogy is not as improbable after all. From the open rebellions against Sukarno's guided democracy and the secessionist struggles of *Freitlin* (Revolutionary Front of Independent East Timor), *Gerakan Aceh Merdeka* (GAM – Free Aceh Movement), and *Organisasi Papua Merdeka* (OPM – Free Papua Movement) to the ethno-religious violence that erupted in Kalimantan, Sulawesi, and the Mulukus in the wake of Suharto's downfall, Indonesia's "etc." still blows in the wind.

References

Anderson B (1972a) Java in a time of revolution: occupation and resistance, 1944–1946. Cornell University Press, Ithaca

Anderson B (1972b) The idea of power in Javanese culture. In: Holt C (ed) Culture and politics in Indonesia. Cornell University Press, Ithaca

Anderson B (1990) Language and power: exploring political cultures in Indonesia. Cornell University Press, Ithaca, NY

Anderson B (1991) Imagined communities: reflections on the origin and spread of nationalism. Verso, London

Anderson B (2001) Violence and the state in Suharto's Indonesia. Southeast Asia Program Publications, Southeast Asia Program, Cornell University, Ithaca

Antlov H (1995) Exemplary centre, administrative periphery: rural leadership and the new order in Java. Curzon Press, Richmond

Antlov H (2000) Demokrasi Pancasila and the future of ideology in Indonesia. In: Antlov H, Ngo TW (eds) The cultural construction of politics in Asia. St Martin's Press, New York, pp 203–222

Badan Pusat Statistik (2010) Penduduk Menurut Wilayah, Jenis Kelamin, Dan Status Migrasi Seumur Hidup, Indonesia, Sensus Penduduk. BPS, Jakarta. http://sp2010.bps.go.id/index.php/site/tabel?tid=324&wid=0

Badan Pusat Statistik (2012) Kewarganegaraan, Suku Bangsa, Agama Dan Bahasa Sehari-Hari Penduduk Indonesia. BPS, Jakarta. http://sp2010.bps.go.id/files/ebook/kewarganegaraan%20penduduk%20indonesia/index.html

Badan Pusat Statistik (2018) Statistik Indonesia 2018. BPS, Jakarta. https://www.bps.go.id/publication/2018/07/03/5a963c1ea9b0fed6497d0845/statistik-indonesia-2018.html

Barton G (2002) Abdurrahmin Wahid: Muslim democrat, Indonesian president. UNSW Press, Sydney

Barton G, Fealy G (1996) Nadhlatul Ulama, traditional Islam and modernity in Indonesia. Monash Asia Institute, Melbourne

Bertrand J (2004) Nationalism and ethnic conflict in Indonesia. Cambridge University Press, Cambridge, UK

Bowen JR (1986) On the political construction of tradition: gotong royong in Indonesia. J Asian Stud 45(3):545–561

Brown C (2003) A short history of Indonesia: the unlikely nation? Allen & Unwin, Sydney

Brown D (1994) The state and ethnic politics in Southeast Asia. Routledge, London

Carnegie PJ (2010) The road from authoritarianism to democratization in Indonesia. Palgrave Macmillan, New York

Carnegie PJ (2013) Can an Indonesian model work in the Middle East? Middle East Q 20(3):59–67

Carnegie PJ (2014) Is Indonesia's democratisation a road map for the Arab Spring? Seton Hall J Dipl Int Relat 15(1):95–105
Carnegie PJ (2015) Countering the (re-)production of militancy in Indonesia. Perspect Terrorism 9(5):15–26
Carnegie PJ (2016) Imagined communities, militancy and insecurity in Indonesia. In: Carnegie PJ et al (eds) Human insecurities in Southeast Asia. Springer, Singapore, pp 53–68
Carnegie PJ, King VT, Ibrahim Z (eds) (2016) Human insecurities in Southeast Asia. Springer, Singapore
Cribb R (1990) The Indonesian killings of 1965–1966: studies from Java and Bali. 21. Monash Asia Institute, Melbourne
Cribb R (1994) The late colonial state in Indonesia: political and economic foundations of the Netherlands Indies, 1880–1942. KITLV Press, Leiden
Cribb R (1999) Not the next Yugoslavia: prospects for the disintegration of Indonesia. Aust J Int Aff 53(2):169–178
Cribb R (2000) Historical atlas of Indonesia. Routledge, London
Cribb R (2001) How many deaths? Problems in the statistics of massacre in Indonesia (1965–1966) and East Timor (1975–1980). In: Wessel I, Wimhofer G (eds) Violence in Indonesia. Abera, Hamburg, pp 82–98
Crouch H (1979) Patrimonialism and military rule in Indonesia. World Polit 31(4):571–587
Crouch H (2000) Indonesia: democratization and the threat of disintegration. Institute of Southeast Asian Studies, Singapore
Davidson J (2003) The politics of violence on an Indonesian periphery. Southeast Asian Res 11(1):59–89
Dengel H (1995) Darul Islam dan Kartosuwiryo: Angan-angan yang Gagal. Pustaka Sinar Harapan, Jakarta
Feith H (1980) Repressive-developmentalist regimes in Asia: old strengths, new vulnerabilities. Prisma 19:39–55
Formichi C (2010) Pan-Islam and Religious Nationalism: the case of Kartosuwiryo and Negara Islam Indonesia. Indonesia. October, 90:125–146
Geertz C (1973) The interpretation of cultures: selected essays. Basic Books, New York
Gouda F (2000) Mimicry and projection in the colonial encounter: the Dutch East Indies/Indonesia as experimental laboratory, 1900–1942. J Colon Colon Hist 1(2):1–20
Hoey B (2003) Nationalism and Indonesia. Ethnology 42(2):110–126
Holt C (ed) (1972) Culture and politics in Indonesia. Cornell University Press, Ithaca
Kadir S (1999) The Islamic factor in Indonesia's political transition. Asian Journal of Political Science 7(2):21–44
Khan J, Formosa F (2002) The problem of crony capitalism: modernity and the encounter with the perverse. Thesis Eleven 69(1):47–66
King VT, Carnegie PJ (2018) Towards a social science understanding of human security. J Hum Secur Stud 7(1):1–17
Kingsbury D (2003) Diversity in unity. In: Kingsbury D, Aveling H (eds) Autonomy and disintegration in Indonesia. RoutledgeCurzon, London, pp 99–114
Koch CJ (1983) The year of living dangerously. Penguin Books, New York
Koentjaraningrat RM (1985) Javanese culture. Oxford University Press, Oxford
MacIntyre A (1991) Business and politics in Indonesia. Allen & Unwin, Sydney
MacIntyre A (2000) Funny money: fiscal policy, rent seeking and economic performance in Indonesia. In: Jomo KS, Khan M (eds) Rent seeking in Southeast Asia. Cambridge University Press, Cambridge, UK, pp 248–273
McCulloch L (2003) Trifungsi: the role of the Indonesian military in business. In: Brommelhorster J, Paes WC (eds) The military as economic actor-soldiers in business. Palgrave Macmillan, London, pp 94–124
McGlynn JH, Mutuloh O, Charle S, Hadler J, Bujono B, Glade-Agusta M, Suhartono G (2005) Indonesia in the Soeharto years: issues, incidents and images. Lontar Foundation, Jakarta

McLeod RH (2000) Soeharto's Indonesia: a better class of corruption. Agenda 7(2):99–112

Mietzner M (2008) Comparing Indonesia's party systems of the 1950s and the post-Suharto era: from centrifugal to centripetal inter-party competition. J Southeast Asian Stud 39(3):431–453

Mulder N (1998) Mysticism in Java: ideology in Indonesia. Pepin, Amsterdam

Nordholt HS (2003) Renegotiating boundaries: access, agency and identity in post-Soeharto Indonesia. Bijdragen Tot de Taal-, Land-En Volkenkunde 159(4):550–589

Oppenheimer J (2012) The act of killing. Documentary Film, Final Cut for Real Denmark

Pisani E (2015) Indonesia etc.: exploring the improbable nation. W.W. Norton & Co, London

Ricklefs MC (2002) A history of modern Indonesia. Stanford University Press, Stanford

Robinson GB (2018) The killing season: a history of the Indonesian massacres, 1965–66. Princeton University Press, Princeton

Robison R (1986) Indonesia: the rise of capital. Allen & Unwin, Canberra

Roosa J (2006) Pretext for mass murder: the September 30th movement and Suharto's Coup d'état in Indonesia. University of Wisconsin Press, Madison

Schiller J, Schiller BM (eds) (1997) Imagining Indonesia: cultural politics and political culture. Ohio University Press, Athens

Schwarz A (1994) A nation in waiting: Indonesia in the 1990s. Westview Press, Boulder

Scott JC (2009) The art of not being governed: an anarchist history of upland Southeast Asia. Yale University Press, New Haven

Simanjuntak M (1994) Pandanang negara integralistik: Sumber, unsur dan riwayantnya dalam persiapan UUD 1945 [The view of the integralist state: sources, elements and its history in the preparation of the 1945 constitution]. Pustaka Utama Grafiti, Jakarta

Singh B (2000) Civil-military relations in democratising Indonesia: change amidst continuity. Armed Forces Soc 26(4):184–216

Sutherland H (2007) Geography as destiny? The role of water in Southeast Asian history. In: Boomgaard P (ed) A world of water: rain, rivers and seas in Southeast Asian histories. KITLV Press, Leiden

Taylor JG (2003) Indonesia: peoples and histories. Yale University Press, New Haven

Temby Q (2010) Imagining an Islamic State in Indonesia: from Darul Islam to Jemaah Islamiyah. Indonesia April 89:1–36

Tiwon S (2000) From East Timor to Aceh: the disintegration of Indonesia. Bull Concerned Asian Scholars 32(1–2):97–104

Uhlin A (1997) Indonesia and the Third Wave of Democratization: the Indonesian pro-democracy movement in a changing world. St. Martin's Press, New York

van Bruinessen M (2002) Genealogies of Islamic Radicalism in post-Suharto Indonesia. South East Asia Research 10(2):117–154

van Dijk C (1980) Rebellion under the Banner of Islam: the Darul Islam in Indonesia. Martinus Nijhoff, The Hague

van Klinken G (2001) The coming crisis in Indonesian area studies. Journal of Southeast Asian Studies 32(2):263–268

Vatikiotis MRJ (2004) Indonesian politics under Suharto: the rise and fall of the new order. Routledge, London

Wessel I, Wimhofer G (eds) (2001) Violence in Indonesia. Abera Publishing House, Hamburg

Zurbuchen MS (ed) (2005) Beginning to remember: the past in the Indonesian present. Singapore University Press, Singapore

Ethno-nationalism and Ethnic Dynamics in Trinidad and Tobago: Toward Designing an Inclusivist Form of Governance

45

Ralph Premdas

Contents

Introduction	810
Trinidad and Tobago: An Introduction	811
The 2010 Elections	815
Issues	817
The Election Results	821
Conclusion	822
References	824

Abstract

In the literature dealing with mechanisms of reconciliation and ethnic conflict management, an array of conflict resolution institutions and practices have evolved. The 2010 elections in Trinidad offer one case that demonstrates how this was done. What the 2010 elections underscored is that in an ethnically deeply divided state, victory at the polls required some transcendence of the communal divide through the forging of a broad multicultural coalition as well as interclass collaboration. In the end we must evaluate the argument that Trinidad had moved from a race and ethnicity voting pattern into issue-oriented politics.

Keywords

Deep ethnic division · Ethnic partisan politics · First-past-the-post electoral system · Proportional representation · Conflict resolution · First woman premier · Multicultural coalition

---

R. Premdas (✉)
University of the West Indies, St. Augustine, Trinidad and Tobago
e-mail: ralphpremdas@hotmail.com

© The Author(s), under exclusive license to Springer Nature Singapore Pte Ltd. 2019
S. Ratuva (ed.), *The Palgrave Handbook of Ethnicity*,
https://doi.org/10.1007/978-981-13-2898-5_167

Introduction

The image of a politically stable and economically prosperous state in Trinidad and Tobago (Trinidad hereafter) conceals powerful internal contradictions in the society. Many critical tensions prowl through the body politic threatening to throw the society into turmoil (Yelvington 1992; Oxaal 1961; Premdas 1991, 1992; Hintzen 1989; MacDonald 1986; Sandoval 1983; Naipaul 1962; Wood 1968). Perhaps, the most salient of these tensions derives from the country's multiethnic population. Below the veneer of inter-communal camaraderie lurks a sense of deep ethnically rooted sectionalism, which pervades the society like blood in the body (Anderson 1983; Premdas 2009). After the colonial power departed in 1962, governance in Trinidad and Tobago was rendered doubly difficult as the new state found itself preoccupied by the rival political claims of the country's two largest ethnic sections constituted of Indians and Africans in an antagonistic partisan relationship to each other. This is the basic contradiction in the state coming to occupy center stage in governance and political life defining issues and dominating daily discourse. Each ethnic section views its interests differently not only in relation to its symbolic and cultural life but in relation to claims for power, recognition, and economic resources. In turn, at the political level, inter-communal competition reverberated on the issue of establishing legitimate rule in a form of government that did not pose a threat to the survival of another group's identity and interests and that ensured that the values of the state could be equitably distributed.

The governmental system bequeathed by Britain was anything but an arrangement that guaranteed the fulfillment of the political and cultural aims of the ethnic communities in the state. Indeed, the inherited British parliamentary system was erected on a zero-sum competitive party system that tended to inflame ethnic passions and apportion privileges very unevenly. This internal contradiction in Trinidad's polity stood as its most potent threat to stability of the society. Ethnic dominance in government and identity politics in society bedeviled governance and soon became a way of life fraught with an immense undercurrent of sectional alienation for the losers in the competition for recognition and resources. Each election that came tended to raise anew all the unresolved issues of ethnic equity much of this related to institutional appropriateness in a plural society (Brereton 1979). As it happened in Trinidad, one ethnic group led by the People's National Movement (PNM) in an essentially ethnically bipolar state had captured power for almost three decades after independence and in the perception of the other major ethnic community instituted an order that was ethnically repressive and discriminatory. When the out-group led by the United National Congress (UNC) eventually captured power in 1995, it in turn was similarly accused of discrimination. An election campaign assumed the form of identity rivalry expressed in a collective communal struggle in which the claims of each community as a whole were reignited anew and expressed in uncompromising terms. Repeated victory by one sectional community over the other was not accepted by the vanquished group which tended to withdraw its moral support from the state.

In this chapter, we address the problem of finding a solution to the ethnic partisan division in Trinidad. In the literature dealing with mechanisms of reconciliation and ethnic conflict management, an array of conflict resolution institutions and practices have evolved. Some observers have advocated power sharing as the master key in eliminating ethnically exclusivist regimes, while others have argued for a predictable process of allocating resources through fixed quotas, proportions, and shares (Lijphart 1977; Montville 1990). The idea behind such proposals is to depoliticize the sharp and deadly rivalry for power and resource allocation by minimizing or removing it from the sphere of electoral contestation. The emphasis is on maintaining order and stability by neutralizing the turbulence of ethnic claims and counterclaims and charges of ethnic exclusion, discrimination, and favoritism over jobs and state benefits. Overall, the causes as well as the solutions offered are all founded on the overwhelming preeminence assigned to the political and economic factors. In this chapter we address the issue of finding a solution through the prism of the 2010 general elections. The 2010 elections in Trinidad offer one case that demonstrates how this was done. In analyzing these elections, we will evaluate the claim that in the victory of the People's Party (PP), a multiethnic formation, a major shift in partisan preference had occurred and a new type of issue-based politics had now emerged cutting across race and class superseding the old ethnically oriented voting pattern. What the 2010 elections did underscore is that in an ethnically deeply divided state where neither of the two dominant groups, Africans (37%) and Indians (42%), constituted a majority and where in the past two main political parties have tended to reflect this bifurcated condition, victory at the polls required some transcendence of the communal divide from a small enough minority who can aid the forging of a broad multicultural coalition as well as interclass collaboration. In 2010 such a small shift had occurred, but, in the end, we must evaluate that the argument that Trinidad had moved from a race and ethnicity voting pattern into an issue-oriented politics is unwarranted and premature. Before we enter these elections, we must provide a background into the Trinidad state.

Trinidad and Tobago: An Introduction

Situated in the southern Caribbean just 7 miles from Venezuela, Trinidad and Tobago is a small twin island multiethnic state with about 1.3 million people enjoying a per capita well-being that has ranked it at position 49th in the UNDP's medium Human Development category. Trinidad is the larger of the two islands both in population (1,220,000) and geographical size, 4,820 km^2, and with a more variegated population of six ethnic communities, while Tobago with only 51,000 people and 303 km^2. is almost entirely ethnically homogeneously Afro-Creole. Until 1888, Tobago was under separate British administration when it was joined to Trinidad. On Trinidad, two main ethnic groups predominate, Afro-Creoles of African descent and Indians of Asian descent, almost of equal size with neither an absolute majority in the population (see Table 1).

Table 1 Ethnic groups and size (Source: Central Statistical Office, Trinidad and Tobago (1990))

Ethnic group	Population	Percentage
African or Afro-Creole	444,804	38.91
Indian or Indo-Creole	452,709	39.60
Chinese	4,322	0.38
Syrian/Lebanese	936	0.08
White/Caucasian	7,302	0.64
Mixed	207,280	18.13
Other ethnic groups	1,720	0.15
Not stated	24,053	2.10
Total	**1,143,126**	**100.0**

Inter-ethnic relations between Afro-Creoles (Africans hereafter) and Asian-descended Indians (Indians hereafter) are publicly cordial, but patterns of cultural differences separate the main communities into contesting sections in quest of social, economic, and political preeminence. As a plural society, Trinidad lacks strong overarching unifying institutions and is frequently submitted to centrifugal political pressures and tensions that threaten to rend the society apart at its ethnic seams. A vibrant parliamentary democracy, independent since 31 August 1962, Trinidad became a Republic in 1976 but remains a part of the Commonwealth of Nations. Generally, elections have been regular, free, and fair and political succession orderly. Two main political parties each representing one of the two main ethnic communities have dominated the political arena competing for 36 seats until 2007 when it was changed to 41 seats in the House of Representatives. For the first 25 years after independence, the predominantly African political party, the PNM, won consecutive elections dominating the political arena under the leadership of Eric Williams. From 1995 to 2001, the Indian-based party, the United National Congress (UNC) led by Basdeo Panday, held political power. After an ethnically charged stalemated deadlock in the equal number of parliamentary seats (18–18) obtained by the two parties in the December 2001 elections, and a period of tense limbo for almost a year, the PNM has returned to power under Prime Minister Patrick Manning with a majority of parliamentary seats in the 2002 general elections. In the 2007 general elections, the PNM won again with a decisive majority of 26 seats out of 41. The 2010 elections came unexpectedly just a bit more than 2 years after the victory in 2007.

The economy of Trinidad is based mainly on minerals (petrochemicals, petroleum, and gas) and, until about 2002, sugar, with the former accounting for about 52% of all export earnings and providing about 32% of all government revenues. The discovery of petroleum at the turn of the twentieth century and more recently of extensive gas fields has radically transformed the economy from agricultural (mainly sugar) dependence to petroleum and gas so that Trinidad stands apart in this respect from other Caribbean countries. Like many plural societies, Trinidad's economy displays ethno-sectoral differentiation so that Afro-Creoles are found mainly in the public bureaucracy, professions, and the petrochemical industries; Indians, who used to predominate in the now defunct sugar industry, today are found mainly in business, agriculture, the professions, as well as the public bureaucracy, while the small European, Chinese, and Syrian communities are found mainly in trading and businesses. An industrial economy (agriculture less than 2% of GNP with white-collar jobs accounting for about 60% of all jobs) has created a large middle class. Unemployment hovers around 5% today, but some 20% of the country lives below the poverty line. Residentially, while there is no segregation and the public arena is fluid, free, and highly ethnically interactive, most persons live in regions, villages, and neighborhoods that display a strong measure of ethnic self-selectivity and concentration (Clarke 1993, 123).

Trinidad was under Crown Colony governance since 1797 when the British assumed control of Trinidad; it took more than another hundred years before an element of popular representation was introduced in the colonial council. In 1925, the Crown Colony system was jettisoned, and for the next two decades, gradually, the colony moved toward universal adult suffrage in 1946, internal self-government in 1956, and finally independence in 1962. During this trek propelled by a combination of external changes in the international order and internal pressures from popular agitation, mass political parties emerged especially after the introduction of universal adult suffrage. In turn, this heralded the mobilization of voters into an assortment of racial and non-racial groupings. By 1946, Trinidad and Tobago's population had reached a bit more than a half a million with Afro-Creoles constituting about 47% of the population and Indians 35%. With the introduction of universal adult suffrage, a new political arena was constructed littered by an assortment of independent candidates and ad hoc political parties vying for public office. It was however under the leadership of the PNM and its Afro-Creole charismatic leader, Eric Williams, that some order in the organization and articulation of public opinion occurred bringing an end to the disarray in the political arena. Launched in 1956, the PNM's charter proclaimed a commitment to promote equity in a multiracial society (Ryan 1972). In practice, the PNM however attracted a predominantly Afro-Creole following. Ethnic identity had already assumed salience when Indians were mobilized under the Democratic Labor Party (DLP) and French Creoles under the Party of Political Progress Groups (POPPG). At first, the Democratic Labor Party (DLP) joined forces with the French Creole party during the 1952 elections to oppose all other parties. In the partisan competition, the PNM emerged as the most formidable organized formation beginning with its victory in the 1956 general elections in which it won 13 of 24 seats. By 1960, however, the three-party ethnic triangle yielded to a bipolar structure in which the PNM confronted the Indian-based DLP. With this event, Trinidad was seemingly settled permanently into the destructive morass of a bipolar partisan order. In the 1961 elections that set the stage for independence in 1962, for the first time the two major ethnically based parties squared off with practically no other meaningful contestants. The two of them shared the 30 seats in the House of Representative pointing to the elimination of individual independent candidates and third parties as the political arena became starkly more polarized.

The intense pressure from the campaign aroused an ethnically divided electorate driving the two communal sections apart as never before. The 1961 election campaign was the last just before independence and therefore was the most critical contest. The victors from these elections would be placed in a strategic position to define the fate of its political and ethnic adversaries. The threat of open violence was very palpable. The polity became deeply polarized with the ethnic division becoming the defining mark of subsequent elections. Two ethnically based parties bestrode the political landscape sharing all the seats in parliament. The PNM became so dominant for the next six elections and for a stretch of 25 years that it had established a virtual dominant one-party state. To be sure, especially after the PNM had been in power for several years and incompetence and corruption had become pervasive, splinter organizations outside the two-party system emerged basing their appeals in part on class and intra-communal divisions. In 1981 such a party in the Organization for National Reconstruction (ONR) appeared but was decimated in the general elections. In 1985, another more powerful such party arose in the NAR; it succeeded in defeating the PNM. But these were aberrations and deviations from the norm of the embedded ethnic partisan preference that citizens practiced. The ethnic partisan pattern had come to reflect and reinforce the general political disposition of Afro-Creoles and Indians for voting for their communal parties. Except at election time, successive elections have created continuous ethnic malaise but not sufficiently expressive as to mar daily harmonious relations; however hypocritical inter-ethnic friendships may be. The ethnic factor became so entrenched that it tended to enter into all aspects of political behavior and into all public institutions animating their life, crippling their vibrancy in a broken political will.

The PNM led the colony to independence in 1962 and for six consecutive parliamentary terms served as the ruling party until 1986. The Afro-Creole community, which constituted the largest community (43.5%) at that time, was able to repeatedly return to power, this made possible because most of the mixed-race community (17%) supported it as well as a smattering of others. To the African communal core, the PNM, while in power, was able to consolidate its electoral majority from the mixed races, Europeans (French Creoles), Chinese, and a significant slice of the Indian middle class. Wielding undisputed paramountcy over the polity and society in its control over jobs, contracts, and other values, the PNM at once became a tower of strength and place of reverence in periods of plenty and a source of all sin in times of adversity.

PNM's consecutive victories were registered in a winner takes all parliamentary system based on single seat simple plurality. In effect, this parliamentary and electoral system when articulated into the ethnic communalized structure of partisan choice meant that the defeated party was almost totally excluded from power and privileges. The political system gave no incentive to consociation and power sharing across the ethnic divine but reinforced the sectional cleavages breeding alienation among the out-group. To be sure, the PNM did appoint a few Indians to its cabinet in governing but in a country where most Indians were Hindus; no Hindu was ever appointed to the PNM cabinet in 26 years after independence when Indians became the largest ethnic community in Trinidad. For Indians, this smacked of discrimination which they saw manifested in the stacking of the public service with PNM supporters and in the skewed allocation of other benefits and resources of the state.

The 2010 Elections

In 2010, in a dramatic general election, the ruling People's National Movement (PNM) in Trinidad and Tobago (TT), only halfway in its term of office and with a comfortable majority of seats in parliament, chose unexpectedly to go to the polls. It was ousted in a landslide victory by a coalition of five parties calling itself the People's Partnership bringing 10 years of uninterrupted PNM rule to an end and witnessing the installing of the first woman Prime Minister in the country's history. In an ethnically deeply divided state where neither of the two dominant groups, Africans (37%) and Indians (42%), constituted a majority, in the past two main political parties have tended to reflect this bifurcated condition. In the 2010 elections, there was a change in the structure of the bipolar ethnic partisan competition. In a two-way fight, the predominantly African-based People's National Movement (PNM) did not face its familiar adversary represented by an Indian-based party but a broad-based multicultural People's Partnership (PP) party with the former acquiring 12 seats and the latter 29. In the victory of the People's Partnership coalition party (PP), a claim was made that a major shift in partisan preference had occurred and a new type of issue-based politics had now emerged cutting across race and class superseding the old ethnically oriented voting pattern. Does an analysis of the election results confirm that victory at the polls signified a radical transcendence of the communal divide? In part, this chapter discusses this question.

In the 2010 elections then, two major party formations, the People's National Movement (PNM) and the Peoples' Partnership (PP), competed with each other along with an insignificant smattering of independent candidates and parties. In the 2010 elections, there were some different features from the norm that could potentially have altered the polarized pattern of voting and the familiar campaign strategy. The PP had amassed a variety of groups in its coalition structure and was composed thus of:

(a) The old Indian-based UNC, the largest part of the PP, led by Kamla Persad-Bissessar.
(b) The Congress of the People (COP) led by Winston Dookeran which broke away from the UNC to compete as a separate party beginning in the 2007 elections constituted mainly of a fairly large inter-ethnic middle-class support base.
(c) The National Joint Action Committee (NJAC), led by Daaga, was the old militant African-based urban party which had some support among Africans and the politically radical community in Trinidad.
(d) The Tobago Organisation of the People (TOP), led by Ainsley Jack, was a Tobago party.
(e) The Movement for Social Justice (MSJ), led by Afro-Creole Errol McLeod and a prominent mixed-race leader, Stephen Cadiz, was a trade union-based party.

Many environmental and women's NGOs also aligned with the PP to constitute a broad-based multiethnic formation. Despite its formal affiliation with the UNC and that its leader derived from the UNC, the PP formation was much more ethnically mixed and interclass than the PNM which was depending overwhelmingly on its African rump in its traditional strongholds to forge a victory. There was no ideological cleavage of consequence that separated the two contenders in the race even though the PP sought to emphasize its populism.

Once the election was called, much to Manning's surprise, this pushed the divided Opposition to coalesce bringing a starling alignment of the UNC, COP, TOP, NJAC, and MSJ along with a number of other civil groups and NGOs. It was a formidable alliance that Manning could hardly have anticipated, but it occurred at a time when poll after poll had showed that in the light of the UDeCOTT scandal and growing lawlessness in the country, the Prime Minister, Manning, was at his most unpopular. What added potency to the new formation called the PP was that it unanimously elected Kamla Bissessar as its leader. She had only a few months earlier in an astonishing internal UNC election defeated the long-standing UNC leader, Panday, for the leadership of the UNC, and with that act she became the official leader of the Opposition in parliament. While Panday had obstructed previous attempts to unify COP and the UNC, Kamla Bissessar proved to be ready for a compromise in unifying the Opposition forces to defeat the PNM. Kamla Bissessar projected a refreshing face, but the fact remained that she was a woman and an Indian and together it was expected that the PNM would eventually triumph. However, the PP was successful in significantly altering its image as a party that had two prominent Indian leaders in Kamla Bissessar and Winston Dookeran. It did so by recruiting several very popular African leaders such as McLeod, Daaga, Cadiz, etc. COP, on joining the coalition, was also able to bring on board NJAC, TOP in Tobago, and a significant number of Indian and African middle-class supporters. This mix was able to transcend an Indian image and became a credible multiethnic grouping with a significant number of African, French Creole, mixed race, and Tobago leaders on its helm. This unified multiethnic and multicultural face so defined the PP in its campaign that it was poignantly in contrast to the largely uni-ethnic façade of the PNM. The PP sold itself as a racially, culturally, and ethnically unified movement with a promise to deliver Trinidad from the old ethnically divisive politics and from the scandal saturated PNM.

In the 2010 elections, Trinidad and Tobago (TT) was divided into 41 constituencies. To determine a winner in each constituency, the electoral system provided for a simple plurality of votes. To win control of the government requires a party to win a majority of constituencies. The persistence of a fundamentally ethicized system of voting preference has in turn impacted on the manner in which political campaigns had been conducted. More specifically, since about 31–32 of the 41 constituencies were predominantly either Indian or African, a campaign tended to focus on the handful of mixed marginal seats. In effect, because of the first-past-the-post simple plurality electoral system, under which a simple plurality of votes determines the winner in a constituency, it made little sense in the past for the Indian-based UNC to waste resources campaigning in the African-majority constituencies and for the PNM likewise to campaign seriously in the Indian-dominated seats. Although accurate statistical data are not available to tell precisely the ethnic ratios in all of the constituencies, the results of previous elections between the PNM and UNC registered a reliable pattern of ethicized voter preferences in all the constituencies with the ones dominated by Indians and Africans clearly identifiable and most predictable. Since neither party could muster a majority of seats by itself from its ethnic strongholds, this meant that winning in the handful of marginal constituencies became critical.

In the campaign, the PP divided the 41 constituencies into clusters of seats with each cluster assigned to a specific coalition component which in turn was allowed to choose its own candidates and take responsibility for winning the seats assigned to it. However, a single overarching coordinated campaign strategy was designed for the PP pooling resources to defray the costs of the expensive media aspect of the campaign and avoid overlaps and conflicts. It is however significant to note that in the division of the constituencies into clusters among themselves, the UNC kept all of the Indian-based constituencies except the St. Augustine constituency. All of the other constituencies that the PP competed in were either marginal or PNM-dominated stronghold constituencies. In effect, two types of PP strategies were crafted so that the Indian-dominated constituencies were under the familiar Indian-based UNC party, while in the others a more pointed multicultural strategy was designed to garner votes from all communities. The PNM as a single unified party however did not have to construct such a complex strategy for votes simply relying on its strongholds for most of its seats while hoping to win nearly all of the mixed marginal constituencies also for a combined majority.

A single overarching coordinated campaign strategy was designed for the PP pooling resources and avoiding overlaps and conflicts. Several placements were notable in the PP assignment of seats among its component parts. First, COP leader, Winston Dookeran, was assigned at Tunapuna which was a marginal constituency currently under PNM control. Second, in the marginal seats of St. Joseph, Pointe a Pierre, Chaguanas East, and San Juan/Barataria, won by the PNM in the last elections, the PP placed exceptionally prominent candidates. The PP also targeted several PNM stronghold seats, deploying prominent and popular mixed race and African candidates, with the intention not just to offer a token contest but with the bold purpose of wrestling these seats from the PNM. In Tobago, the PP again offered under TOP two very prominent local leaders. While the PP projected a fresh set of new and exciting candidates, the PNM relied on its former candidates largely drawn from the victorious team from the 2007 elections.

Issues

The issues that dominated the campaign were of two sorts: (a) non-ethnic types and (b) ethnic types. Further, certain issues and appeals were made publicly in the overt face of the campaign, while others of a more communal nature were deployed in the covert face. We shall examine the non-ethnic type first. On the hustings as the parties launched their campaign, a festive tenor was intermixed by an underlying sobriety that a change of government is at hand. The PP successfully crafted a very catchy set of slogans such as "Manning must Go" and "Time for Change" that sustained the momentum that it seized almost immediately from the PNM (Grant 2010, 13). The riposte was tame by comparison with the PNM stressing "Service," "Stability," "Prosperity," and "Performance" in its message. The PP was able to outdo the PNM by offering an attractive twenty-point list of promises that it intended to accomplish in its first 120 days in office.

A barrage of scandals descended on the PNM bedeviling its campaign to regain office dogging them every step along the way casting over them a dark shadow of corruption and abuse of office on a scale that offended the sensibility of all citizens of all parties, ethnicities, and ideological persuasions (Newsday 2010, 10). The particular issue that triggered the scandals came to be known by the designation, "UDeCOTT," which was the government agency established to carry out the construction of many very large-scale costly projects. With hefty amounts of gas-generated revenues caused by a spike in gas and petroleum prices, the Trinidad treasury was inundated with unprecedented largesse. Under the inspiration of Manning, the government embarked on a program of conspicuous construction of a number of extravagant building projects that included sports stadiums, hotels, performing arts facilities, a new university campus, etc. Placed in charge of this enterprise was businessman Calder Hart who had extensive connections with construction companies both locally and internationally, especially from the People's Republic of China and Malaysia which were to be employed in expeditiously carrying out these projects.

The key whistle-blower was no less a person than the Deputy Leader of the ruling PNM, Dr. Keith Rowley, who was an aggressively outspoken and popular leader in the PNM and at one time a rival of Manning for the leadership of the party. Rowley had interrogated Hart about his seemingly unlimited power in accessing public funds, in distributing contracts, and in constructing these grandiose projects. In a confrontation with Hart, Rowley seemed to have been boisterous, and it was this event which led Manning to evict him from the Cabinet for "wajang behavior." Under public pressure, Manning was forced to appoint the UDeCOTT Commission of Inquiry into the construction industry headed by a British engineering professor, John Uff. The issues thrown up by the UDeCOTT Inquiry dealt simultaneously with unaccountability in the use of state funds for several mega projects which violated established official legal tendering procedures and processes by which contracts were awarded transparently and competitively. For nearly 2 years, witnesses of all kinds were interrogated publicly so that a picture of gross unaccountability, unfairness in the award of contracts, political opportunism, nepotism, and waste and abuse in using public funds was formed in the public's mind. These revelations were sensationalized in the media, and while Rowley was exonerated, he was not returned to the cabinet so that when the elections were called the Rowley-Manning schism had become a major problem in mobilizing PNM support (Singh 2010, 12). Rowley had charged Manning for being authoritarian and for turning the internal democratic processes in the PNM into a travesty. Later after the PNM was defeated, Rowley would argue that the main reason resided in Manning's autocratic use of power and his subverting democracy within the PNM (Ali 2010, A5). There was no doubt that the UDeCOTT affair had severely undermined Manning's moral mandate to rule.

Above all, it was this issue that had come to offend many PNM supporters especially in relation to the dismissal of Rowley from the cabinet and caused a major rift in the ranks of the party. It has been argued that the internal schism was so deep that many PNM supporters decided to stay at home rather than vote for the PNM while a small percentage actually did turn against the PNM on election day (Ali 2010, A6). Some of these dissident PNM supporters made plain that they were not voting against the PNM but against its leader, Manning. The PNM had counted on the loyalty of its traditional communal supporters on the campaign trail, appealing to them "to hold their nose tight" to avert the embarrassment caused by the behavior of their party in office and vote for it nevertheless to avert victory of their Indian communal opponents and the possibility of domination and discrimination. The PNM did so in a subtle way reminding PNM supporters of the benefits that they had received under PNM rule and that this was likely to be all lost under a UNC-dominated PP government. Clearly, the PNM was trying to extricate itself from problems of misgovernance by using ethnic and communal appeals. It created great psychological dissonance for PNM supporters who saw the PNM not just as a voting machine but a primordial home in defining their historical identity. In a multiethnic state where ethnic identity shapes issues and elevates irrational sentiments above reasoned arguments and empirical evidence, it is rare that the hearts of voters will easily change away from their political parties with which they have been traditionally and historically associated. These parties tend to serve more than just periodic points of casting a supportive ballot and more like an ingrained deep-rooted communal axis of multidimensional solidarity that provides for collective security and identity. Because of the UDeCOTT scandal, the 2010 elections challenged this primordial attachment of PNM African supporters so that in the face of powerful rational arguments against voting for the PNM, only a small percentage probably about 5–10% made the shift. It was however all that was necessary to see the defeat of the PNM.

Coming out of the inquiry also was a charge that gained traction in the campaign and became a major issue on leadership style and substance specifically related to the charge of Manning's alleged arrogance (Fraser 2010, A28), the building of a new multimillion-dollar residence for the Manning, ridiculed by the local press as the "Emperor's Palace" for a cost approaching (TT) $200 m, in part taken as evidence of this arrogance. Another scandal that appeared just before Manning called the elections related to the building of a Pentecostal Christian church, called Lighthouse of the Lord Jesus Christ, at Guanapo Heights, Arima, that seemed to involve the use of state funds, possibly close to TT$50 to 75 million. Manning had a spiritual adviser, a self-styled "prophetess" from the United States named Rev. Juliana Pena for whom it was alleged that a large expensive church was being built. The parliamentary Opposition leveled an incendiary charge that the church which was being built by the same construction firm, Shanghai Construction Corporation that also built several of the state's mega projects including Manning's palatial residence, was given excessively overpriced contracts for the other state projects in exchange for the building of the "free" church for Manning's spiritual adviser. More specific evidence which was to be presented in parliament by Kamla Bissessar during a vote of no confidence prompted to the surprise of everyone the Prime Minister's decison to dissolve parliament and call new elections. While the facts were still to be established, in the wake of the UDeCOTT Inquiry, the church quickly became entangled in corruption charges and emerged as a controversial lightning rod issue in the campaign. Finally, there were a few other scandals involving similar unaccountability in the use of massive amounts of public funds. These included the building of the extensive University of Trinidad and Tobago campus. In another case involving the collapse of the biggest investment and insurance company in Trinidad, CLICO, the issue that created most controversy related to the early withdrawal of investments in the company by the Minister of Finance, Ms. Karen Tesheira, seemingly after receiving privileged information about the impending collapse of CLICO. In the elections, Ms. Tesheira who was the candidate in a safe PNM stronghold seat that was never lost before was defeated as her opponent made hay out of the CLICO issue. Other issues that dealt with alleged wasteful expenditures related to two major international conferences costing about $1billion that were financed by the Manning administration. One of these included world leaders such as President Obama and the other the heads of Commonwealth countries. To put Trinidad on show, the government constructed a lavish world-class academy of performing arts also. It seemed that the Manning administration was endowed with unlimited funds even when many public services laid neglected, a fact that the PP made a large issue out during the elections.

The scandals dwarfed all other issues, but two which gained prominence related to the crime and the introduction of a countrywide property tax. On crime, the PP argued that law and order had broken down, and in polls that were taken just before the elections, the majority of citizens felt that the government had failed to provide protection and security for citizens. The second major issue relating to the introduction of a property tax generated widespread apprehension across the ethnic divide and especially among property owners. The government argued that it wanted to raise more revenues and that it must do equitably by imposing a property tax which required a survey of all private property holdings in the country. The PP made the property tax a lightning rod issue that touched on the raw nerves of nearly everyone and declared that among the very first things it would do in its gaining office was to rescind the property tax legislation. These were the non-ethnic issues, but they were underlaid by a second more subtle and covert theme dealing with ethnic and communal fears.

What role did race and ethnicity play which by itself had been often used in the past to explain patterns of voting in TT? This explanation highlights political strategy along a communal and racial calculus in directing the energies of the political campaign. Noted political scientist Professor Selwyn Ryan argued that little of race was openly said in the campaign "but it was clearly in evidence" (Ryan 2010, 13). He noted that, indirectly, the PNM as an African-based party was the historical protector of African interest and that no other party can be trusted to carry on this role. As Ryan (2010, 13) noted, "The PNM spent a great deal of time and resources reminding the masses in general and the Afro masses in particular about what it had done for them from Williams to the present and warned that the benefits were at risk if they elected some other party." What however diminished the salience of the race factor was the absence in the elections of Basdeo Panday, the former militant leader of the Indian-based UNC party who symbolized as, no one else, the Indian community and its claims to power.

The race factor however was more visible to some observers. Jack Warner, the PP key strategist, argued that Manning had conducted a divisive racial campaign in which he denigrated Indians who would vote for an Indian leader (Ali 2010). The PP however made its multiethnic following an indicator of the change it was seeking for Trinidad's old-style ethnically based politics. Nevertheless, ethnicity and race were more than less nuanced into the campaign discourse. Clevon Raphael, a columnist of one of the country's major daily newspapers, *The Guardian*, argued that, "Basically the PNM ran a campaign of fear generously sprinkled by an appeal to the race card. The party tried to retain its natural support and capture the non-committed and even those of the PP by unjustifiably claiming that a win by its opponents would mean the scrapping of CEPEP, GATE, and the closure of COSTATT and UTT" (Raphael 2010, A27). These were all programs which had overwhelmingly benefitted the PNM's Afro-Trinidadian supporters.

The Election Results

Regarding the election results at the constituency level, in examining all of the 41 constituencies in the 2010 elections, a number of patterns were clear (Ali 2010, A6; Fraser 2010, A28; Raphael 2010, A27). In the traditional core PNM and UNC constituencies constituting about 32 of all the seats and most voters, ethnic partisan preference substantially prevailed. This has been underscored by the startling fact that in the previous elections of 2007, when the PNM won 26 seats out of 41, it received 299,813 votes, which were merely 14,459 votes short of its 2010 numbers when it got only 12 seats. However, in the 2010 elections, there has been a major difference in that while in all the elections 1986–2007, the PNM had handily won its core constituencies, in 2010, it lost four. The shifts that have occurred have not been major. In many of the 12 that it retained, it did so with reduced support ranging from 6% to 12%, and in the 4 core constituencies that it lost, the margin of loss was not substantial from about 1% to 5% only of the votes cast. All of this is ample testimony that there has been a shift in traditional PNM votes in a number of core constituencies in which it won and lost but by overall margins that were meager to about 3–5%.

Noteworthy in this regard, in examining the performance of the UNC core constituencies in 2010 and 2007, it can be observed that the unified UNC-COP votes from 2007 accounted in many instances for up to 75% or more of the PP votes in 2010 except for the two Tobago seats and those in the PNM stronghold seats. It must be recalled that the PP divided the 41 constituencies into segments that were led by only one of its components. The UNC component was assigned all but one (St. Augustine) of its core constituencies. In these constituencies, the PNM share was not substantially reduced from 2007 to 2010. In effect, in the core PNM and UNC constituencies, the shift from one to the other in 2010 was small, and in most the percentages remained practically the same.

Regarding the marginal seats, in 2007, the PNM won all these marginals except Mayaro in compiling its acquisition of 26 seats out of 41. Because of the momentum gathered by the PP campaign, a small shift especially among Africans combined by a unified Indian vote assisted by the mixed and minority communities gave the PP substantial victories. The voting pattern in the marginals in other words did point to a small measure of change among African, mixed, and minority voters but not to a significant shift in Indian and African voting pattern. Overall, the election results portray overwhelming continuity in ethnic and racial voting patterns especially among Indians and Africans but with a small shift among Africans and mixed races that tended to exaggerate and amplify the ethnic significance of the PP landslide victory.

Conclusion

There were critical factors that accounted for the victory of the PP and specifically how the victory addressed the more critical issue of overcoming ethnic voter preference and ushering in a new mode of non-ethnic voting. First, we must look at the composition of the PP. In the elections, the PP had amassed a variety of groups in its coalition structure that departed from the polarized pattern of voting and the familiar campaign strategy. Despite its formal affiliation with the UNC and that its leader derived from the UNC, the PP formation was much more ethnically mixed and interclass than the PNM which was depending overwhelmingly on its African rump in its traditional strongholds to forge a victory. There was no ideological cleavage of consequence that separated the two contenders in the race even though the PP sought to emphasize its populism. Just to recapitulate the PP was composed thus of:

(a) The old Indian-based UNC, the largest part of the PP, led by Kamla Persad-Bissessar.
(b) The Congress of the People (COP) led by Winston Dookeran which broke away from the UNC to compete as a separate party beginning in the 2007 elections constituted mainly of a fairly large inter-ethnic middle-class support base.
(c) The National Joint Action Committee (NJAC), led by Daaga, was the old militant African-based urban party which had some support among Africans and the politically radical community in Trinidad.
(d) The Tobago Organisation of the People (TOP), led by Ainsley Jack, was a Tobago party.
(e) The Movement for Social Justice (MSJ), led by Afro-Creole Errol McLeod and a prominent mixed-race leader, Stephen Cadiz, was a trade union-based party.

Many environmental and women's NGOs also aligned with the PP to constitute a broad-based multiethnic formation.

Regarding campaign strategy, nothing had changed significantly in the 2010 elections with the combination of overt non-ethnic themes and appeals and communal and racist appeals at the covert level. The election results suggest that the displacement of primordial partisan attachments by the African and Indian communities could not be dismantled in one election but seems to require multiple institutional changes. In terms of issues versus ethnic identity, it seemed that the scandals which bedeviled the PNM in power, as well as the unification of the five parties into the PP which in turn was led by a charismatic leader, persuaded minorities as well as many others traditionally supportive of the PNM to change sides. Issues did impart a special texture to the 2010 elections in literally cornering the PNM with multiple problems that included leadership style and poor performance. If the issues were the decisive factor that determined the election outcome, it was clear that the PNM should have lost even more comprehensively than it did. Rather, the PNM was able to retain a very substantial majority of its traditional supporters as well as the UNC of its Indian supporters.

What emerged as the most powerful factor in the campaign that overwhelmed the PNM was the charismatic electric flair that quickly surrounded the person of Kamla Bissessar who seemed to grow even larger as the campaign progressed (Ryan 2010, 13). It was a totally unexpected development even though Kamla Bissessar had offered intimations of her capabilities just 3 months earlier when she defeated Panday for the leadership of the UNC, but nothing of the explosiveness of Kamla Bissessar's presence on the hustings was in anybody's radar looking at the shape of the campaign to come. At times Kamla Bissessar seemed like a pop star on tour, while Manning displayed lackluster. The charisma and momentum that the PP evolved would spill over the entirety of the electorate with wild predictions that the PNM would be wiped out by an avalanche of support for the star-studded Kamla Bissessar-led PP list of candidates. While the PP was able to draw large crowds everywhere without much prompting, the PNM carried with it a large entourage of bus-filled supporters to its meetings to ensure that it seemed to have much popular support. This was not lost on the daily news media which covered the elections as they made some fun of the relatively lackluster PNM campaign.

In terms of factors that are often associated with a new multiethnic coalition, many of these were clearly missing. This includes most significantly agreement for power sharing among the elements that formed the winning coalition. On programmatic issues, in the political campaign, the PP had defined its position on new policies which relate to governing an inclusivist regime. That factor was to be seen in implementation of governance. No complex set of institutions and conditions, except the idea of forming a coalition structure, such as found in Lijphart's consociational democracy were required to establish a successful multiethnic party. Many potentially outstanding problems were not evident during the victory celebration which was likely to assert themselves during the process of governing through a coalition framework. As fate would have it, during the life of the coalition government, many intragroup conflicts arose which tore the coalition structure apart so that when 5 years later the PP in a reincarnated form sought reelection, it lost to the PNM in an election that was reminiscent of the old ethnic partisan pattern.

Finally, the issue of the electoral system needs to be addressed. As we have pointed out in the introductory part of the essay, the British had bequeathed a parliamentary system under which elections were conducted under a first-past-the-post simple majority procedure. For many analysts, it is this electoral system, while not creating the original divisions, that tends to magnify the ethnic conflict in the society. Analysts such as Lijphart have advocated a system of proportional representation, while others such as Horowitz have advocated the Australian alternate preferential variant of proportional representation (Horowitz 1997). In any case, this electoral institution did not emerge as a specific issue during the 2010 elections in Trinidad. However, in any evaluation of the likelihood of the persistence of ethnic partisan politics in Trinidad and elsewhere, the type of electoral system is clearly relevant.

References

Ali K (2010) PNM loses popular vote. Guardian, 25 May, p A6
Anderson B (1983) Imagined communities. Verso, London
Brereton B (1979) Race relations in colonial Trinidad 1870–1900. Cambridge University Press, London
Clarke C (1993) Social pattern and social interaction among Creoles and Indians in Trinidad and Tobago. In: Yelvington K (ed) Trinidad ethnicity. University of Tennessee Press, Knoxville
Fraser T (2010) The decline and fall of Patrick Manning. Guardian, 26 May, p A28
Grant L (2010) Trini LargesseGone Hyperactive. Sunday Express 22 May:13
Hintzen P (1989) The costs of regime survival. Cambridge University Press, London
Horowitz D (1997) Encouraging electoral accommodation in divided societies. In: Reynolds A (ed) The architecture of democracy. Oxford University Press, London
Lijphart A (1977) Democracy in plural societies. Yale University Press, New Haven
MacDonald SB (1986) Democracy and development in the Caribbean. Praeger, New York
Montville J (ed) (1990) Conflict and peacemaking in multiethnic states. Lexington Books, Lexington
Naipaul V (1962) The middle passage. Penguin Books, London
Newsday (2010) Congratulations All Around, editorial, 26 May:10
Oxaal I (1961) Black Bourgeoisie come to power. Schenkman, Cambridge, Massachusetts
Premdas R (1991) The politics of inter-ethnic accommodation. In: Premdas R, St. Cyr E (eds) Sir Arthur Lewis: an economic and political portrait. Institute of Social and Economic Research, University of the West Indies, Jamaica
Premdas R (1992) Race, politics and succession in Trinidad and Guyana. In: Sutton P, Payne A (eds) Modern Caribbean politics. Johns Hopkins Press, Baltimore
Premdas, Ralph 2009 Trinidad and Tobago: ethnicity and inequality in public sector governance. Palgrave, New York
Raphael C (2010) Exciting times for T&T. Guardian, 26 May, p A27
Ryan S (1972) Race and nationalism in Trinidad and Tobago. University of Toronto Press, Toronto
Ryan S (2010) Old world and the new. Sunday Express, May 23, p 13
Sandoval J (1983) State capitalism in a petroleum-based economy. In: Ambursley P (ed) Crisis in the Caribbean. Heinemann, London
Singh R (2010) Now for the Promised Changes. Express 26 May:10
Wood D (1968) Trinidad in transition: the years after slavery. Oxford University Press, London
Yelvington K (ed) (1992) Ethnicity in Trinidad. Macmillan, London

Islam in Trinidad

46

Nasser Mustapha

Contents

Introduction	826
Early Muslims in the Caribbean	827
Indian Muslims in the Caribbean	829
Religious Practices and Traditions	830
Ahle Sunnah wal Jamaah	830
Shiite Muslims	832
Sufism	833
Ahmadi/Qadiani	833
Moulvi Ameer Ali	833
Middle Eastern Influence	834
Wahhabism	835
Moulvi Nazeer Ahmad Simab	836
Syncretisms	837
Conflict and Change	837
Tabligh/Dar-ul-Uloom	838
A Word on ISIS	838
Muslims and Formal Education	840
New Educational Policy	841
Increase in Muslim Schools	842
Religious Education	842
The Islamic Trust	843
The Haji Ruknudeen Institute of Islamic Studies	843
Dar-ul-Uloom Institute	843
Conclusion	844
References	845

N. Mustapha (✉)
Department of Behavioural Sciences, University of the West Indies, St Augustine, Trinidad and Tobago
e-mail: nasser.mustapha@sta.uwi.edu

© The Author(s), under exclusive license to Springer Nature Singapore Pte Ltd. 2019
S. Ratuva (ed.), *The Palgrave Handbook of Ethnicity*,
https://doi.org/10.1007/978-981-13-2898-5_168

Abstract

This chapter discusses the introduction of Islam to the Caribbean, beginning with the African slaves followed by the East Indian indentured immigrants.

Indian Muslims, though initially isolated from the wider society, have integrated successfully with the wider society especially during the post-independence period. Muslims have coexisted peacefully with other groups and have participated in mainstream politics, music, sports, business, as well as education. It was not until 1990 that international attention started to be focused on Trinidad Muslims, when a Muslim group attempted to remove the democratically elected government. Such an event was rather unexpected in a society known for carnival, calypso, steelpan, and its religious and ethnic harmony.

The chapter traces the evolution of the Muslim community in Trinidad, and the efforts not only to survive but to maintain a visible presence, amidst the challenges faced. The arrival of missionaries, the formation of organizations, and the subsequent fragmentation of the community based on ideological and theological differences are discussed. Data largely from secondary sources and interviews of key persons by the author provides insights into this community's attempts to preserve its heritage. The Muslim community's resistance to assimilation is also discussed.

International attention was focused on Trinidad and Tobago in 1990 and around 2016/2017 when it was reported that per capita Trinidad and Tobago had the highest number of persons in the Western Hemisphere being recruited to join ISIS, an alarming situation giving the wrong impression that there is much local support for terrorism.

Keywords

Islam · Muslim · Trinidad · Trinidad and Tobago · Caribbean · African · Indian

Introduction

Trinidad and Tobago is a twin island republic situated in the Southern Caribbean only 11 Km from Venezuela. (The population of Tobago is 60,874 and that of Trinidad is 1,311,126.). It is part of the Commonwealth Caribbean, and English is the official language. The total population is estimated to be 1.3 million persons with Indo-Trinidadians 35.4%, Afro-Trinidadians 34.2%, mixed 23%, other 1.3%, and unspecified 6.2%.

According to the International Religious Freedom Report 2017, *page 2*, 26.5% of the population is Protestant, including 12% Pentecostal or evangelical, 5.7% Anglican, 4.1% Seventh-day Adventist, 2.5% Presbyterian or Congregational, 1.2% Baptist, 0.7% Methodist, and 0.3% Moravian. An additional 21.6% is Roman Catholic, 18.2% Hindu, 5% Muslim, and 1.5% Jehovah's Witnesses. Traditional Caribbean religious groups with African roots include the Spiritual Baptists, who represent 5.7% of the population, and the Orisha, who incorporate elements of West

African spiritualism and Christianity, at 0.9%. According to the census, 2.2% of the population has no religious affiliation, 11.1% does not state a religious affiliation, and 7.5% lists their affiliation as "other," which includes a number of small Christian groups, Baha'is, Rastafarians, Buddhists, and Jews.

Compared to other Caribbean societies, Trinidad and Tobago has been a relatively prosperous country. Within recent times though, the economy has been experiencing a decline, but with its wide resource base as well as its skilled population, it is still a place of opportunity, as evidenced by the continued inward migration of persons from all over the world.

There is a functional Westminster-styled parliamentary democracy and a well-established education system with universal primary, secondary, and tertiary education. There are regional as well as national universities. Tertiary education was fully government funded until recently, but it is now partially funded and still very accessible.

In addition, there is ethnic and religious harmony although the politics of the country tends to give the impression that there is ethnic polarization, but such negative sentiments become exacerbated around election time. Generally different groups work together in various professions (law, medicine, and teaching), and there is religious harmony and interfaith dialogue. The country has come a long way since independence in 1962, and there is also legislation to address issues of discrimination.

Early Muslims in the Caribbean

Most conventional historical sources suggest that African Muslims were among the slaves brought to the Caribbean to provide labor on the plantations (Samaroo 1987; Afroz 1995). They were mostly from the Mandingo, Fulani, and Hausa nations. The experience of slavery impacted negatively on the African slaves, including their lack of community ties and weak family structures, thereby making socialization and religious and cultural continuity extremely difficult. This acculturative process took place systematically throughout slavery irreversibly changing the religious and cultural identity of Afro-Caribbean peoples generally. Creolization meant substantial acculturation and interculturation whereby a new "indigenized" Caribbean culture emerged.

As conditions of plantation slavery made the retention of African ancestral beliefs difficult, Islam as a distinct religious tradition seemed to have disappeared, but the slaves' unswerving attachment to their ancestral ties provided a latent sensibility of their heritage. After emancipation, the suppression of African religions continued by subtle and effective means, mainly through the socialization of the Africans through the educational system, together with laws that prohibited the practice of African faiths and cultural traditions. In the years that followed, aspects of Islam exerted an influence on African-Caribbean linguistic, musical, and religious forms (Diouf, S. 1998, 184–205).

As overt traces of Islam virtually disappeared in the Caribbean, the latent, suppressed attachment to African ancestral religions resurfaced much later, and in one of the ironies of Caribbean history, many Afro-Caribbean persons later converted to Islam, centuries after most traces of this religion were destroyed by the European cultural dominance experienced by their ancestors (Kassim 2017, 2).

A significant influx of African converts began in the early 1970s, spurred by an increased black consciousness among the Afro-Caribbean community. This phenomenon was inspired by events in North America and particularly by personalities such as Muhammad Ali and Malcolm X. While the Nation of Islam did have a small following in Port of Spain, Trinidad, and in other Caribbean territories, the majority of Africans in the Caribbean who accepted Islam joined the orthodox Muslim community (Sunni). As these new Afro-Caribbean Muslims came mainly from grassroots urban communities, they did not find initial acceptance by the middle-class leadership of the traditional Muslim community.

Though Afro-Trinidadian Muslims were warmly accommodated by some groups, they were still uncomfortable with the traditional Indian Muslim community. Afro-Trinidadian Muslims were especially concerned about the Indian cultural traditions, which they felt had no basis in Islam. While these tensions were often perceived as anti-African racism on the part of Indians, the prejudice displayed was actually based on ideological, cultural, and class differences. The experiences of slavery and indentureship impacted differently upon African and Indians, respectively, resulting in different approaches to the interpretation and the practice of Islam.

Because of their historical experiences, Afro-Trinidadians, in addition to being mainly converts, saw Islam through the lens of their sociopolitical concerns. They viewed Islam as a complete system of life, one that advocated equality and social welfare, whereas the Indians were more sociocultural and traditional in their approach to Islam. The Indians' emphasis was upon survival and preservation, and they held on to many practices that were viewed as Indian customs that often had no scriptural justification.

While Afro-Trinidadians generally do not subscribe to most of the Indian cultural traditions, today there is generally a cordial relationship between African and Indian Muslims, especially among the younger generations.

Predominantly Afro-Trinidadian Muslim groups started to emerge from the 1970s, inspired by the Nation of Islam as well as the Islamic Party of North America. The Jamaat al Muslimeen, an Islamic organization with a predominantly Afro-Trinidadian membership, evolved around this time. In July 1990, this group led by Yasin Abu Bakr, attempted to remove the democratically elected government. They took Prime Minister A. N. R. Robinson and other government ministers as hostages, but the coup attempt failed after 7 days.

Many of the Jamaat's members then left to form the Islamic Resource Society (IRS). The IRS has very cordial relations with the state and has integrated well with the wider Muslim community. Afro-Trinidadian Muslims frequently worship at most of the Indian-dominated mosques, but there are at least four urban mosques that are predominantly Afro-Trinidadian in their congregation.

While some may believe that the seeds of extremism were sown since the attempted coup of 1990 or some may say through the 1979 revolution in Iran, there is no evidence to suggest that there was a link between these events and those who later supported or participated in terrorist activities locally and internationally.

Indian Muslims in the Caribbean

The abolition of slavery resulted in the need to obtain new labor for the plantations. The East Indians were introduced to fill this need. Between 1845 and 1917, approximately 143,939 Indians came to Trinidad to provide labor. Approximately 85% of these immigrants were Hindus, and 14.5% were Muslims (Singh 2013).

Though the living conditions of the Indians were difficult, they nevertheless were somewhat conducive to the survival of the immigrants' cultural traditions. The planters were generally satisfied with the productivity, docile temperament, frugal lifestyle, and industrious work ethic of the Indian immigrants. Being in a new environment, Muslims faced numerous challenges but held tenaciously to the past, as this provided a sense of comfort. Through frequent contact with their homeland, they were more successful than their African predecessors in withstanding culture loss. Although the isolation of Indians on the estates minimized their interaction with other groups in the society, this insularity helped them to revive and reconstruct (with adaptation) their ancestral culture. They re-established joint and extended family systems, Muslim marriage and funerary rites, and congregational worship (Mahase 2012, 247).

Most of the immigrants came from the Gangetic Plain region of North India, bringing similar interpretations of Islam, had similar experiences on the ships and on the plantations, and shared similar contacts with India through the influence of the few educated ones among them such as Syed Abdul Aziz and Haji Ruknudeen (Kassim 2013; Dabydeen and Samaroo 1987). Over time in the Caribbean, however, the dialect as well as the culture of the Indians became stabilized as differences among them were reduced.

Reverend John Morton noted in his diary that mosques began to appear as early as the 1860s, as "nice little buildings with galvanized roofs." Though their level of religious knowledge was limited, they nevertheless attempted to reconstruct their rites and rituals, as they knew it. Also, because of the need to preserve their faith in an alien and somewhat hostile environment, Indo-Trinidadian Muslims became very defensive and introverted, with an emotional attachment to their ancestral traditions. They looked toward India for inspiration as well as identity in response to the pressures of indentureship. The thought that they would return to India after the termination of their contracts, usually after 5 years, provided further impetus for cultural persistence. There were few among the Indians with religious education, who were willing to impart religious knowledge to their fellow indentured workers, the majority of whom possessed only a rudimentary religious education. They sometimes attempted to reconstruct aspects their faith as they knew it, in some cases borrowing and institutionalizing cultural traditions without textual proof. By the early twentieth century, Islam among Indians in the Caribbean therefore adopted a unique shape. For this reason, many early Indian Muslims even disagreed with some Indian missionaries arriving from as early as 1914 (such as Pir Hassan) whose ideas and practices were at variance with what had emerged in the Caribbean.

Although Indian Muslims adopted a common version of Islam, the diversity found in Indian society and in the Muslim world generally started to resurface in the Caribbean from the 1930s, starting with the return of Moulvi Ameer Ali (labeled an Ahmadi), from studies in Lahore, followed by Nazeer Ahmad Seemab who was labeled a Wahhabi. The views of the latter two scholars were at variance with the then leader Hajji Ruknudeen, a traditionalist Sunni. Up to 1926 the Muslims of Trinidad were largely united, but by the late 1940s, there were three main religious organizations, representing three different religious orientations (Samaroo 1987): the Takveeatul Islamic Association (1926); the nonsectarian organization, the ASJA (1935) (*Anjuman Sunnatul Jamaat Association*); and the TML (est. 1947) ghair mukallid (nonconformist). The TML was also affiliated to the Ahmadiyya movement for a period.

Religious Practices and Traditions

Based on its history and continuous contact with the international *ummah*, almost every interpretation of Islam in the world could be found in Trinidad. With reference to their beliefs and practices, the Muslims in Trinidad could be classified into the following major groups:

- Ahle Sunnah wal Jamaah
- Shiites
- Sufis
- Ahmadis/Qadianis
- Wahhabis
- Tablighis

Ahle Sunnah wal Jamaah

The "traditionalist Sunnis," by far is the largest group in the Trinidad and Tobago today, accounting for more than 50% of the Muslim community. The older generation is more familiar with all the detailed aspects of traditional Islam, and efforts are being made to promote its transmission to younger generations. They are officially *Hanafi Sunnis*, indicating that they follow the school of law developed by Imam Abu Hanifa, and they adopt the *Ahle Sunnah wal Jamaah* approach as advocated by Ahmad Riza Khan of Barelwi in nineteenth-century India (Sanyal 1996). They subscribe to Indian cultural practices such as *niyaz* or *fatiha*, *moulood* and *tazeem*, and are wary of Muslim groups that do not support these practices. (Please see www.caribbeanmuslims.com for more details on this subject).

Among this group there have been efforts to promote the Urdu language. Though Urdu is an integral part of the Muslim legacy, some Muslims today disassociate themselves from it, due to its Indian cultural origins. Such persons consider Arabic as the only medium for religious instruction. Many traditional Muslim practices in the Caribbean make use of the Urdu language. These include *moulood* (singing of *qasidas* or Urdu songs), *tazeem* (prayer sending salutations to the Prophet), *niyaz* (prayer over food), *Milad-un-Nabi* (celebrating the Prophet's birthday), and *miraj* (observing the Prophet's ascension to Heaven).

The *qasida* ("song of praise") evolved from the Arab and Persian traditions, and it spread from the heart of Arabia to the Islamic periphery. Arabic language impacted heavily on the vocabulary, the grammar, and the literary prose of other languages, including Turkish, Persian, and Urdu. *Qasida*, like poetry, became a popular form of expression among Muslims in South Asia. These renditions, largely in Urdu, were an integral part of religious functions among the early Indian Muslims in the Caribbean. Today in Trinidad, there is an attempt to revive this tradition. However, there is a lack of enthusiasm from some members of the younger generation, many of whom prefer to learn Islam from its Arabic sources rather than from Indian traditions.

Tazeem is a song of praise to the Prophet Muhammad. It is usually rendered toward the end of a Quranic reading or prayer function when all present are required to stand and recite: *Ya Nabi salaam alaika, Ya rasul salaam alaika* ("Oh Prophet, Peace be unto you, Oh Messenger, Peace be unto you"). Whereas traditionalist Muslims emphasize the necessity of observing *tazeem*, the purists claim otherwise. *Milad-un-Nabi* is the celebration or commemoration of the birth, life, and achievements of the Prophet. Many Sufi orders support this celebration, claiming that the event is the Muslim community's expression of love for the Prophet. It is an effort to show gratitude to Allah for His favor of blessing humanity with such a *Nabi* (Prophet) and to the *Nabi* for bringing humanity out of the darkness of ignorance. The essence of *Milad-un-Nabi* is to remember and observe, discuss, and recite the event of the birth and the advent of the Prophet. Opponents of this practice have called it *bida'h* or an innovation. They quote the Prophet:

> "Whoever brings forth an innovation into our religion which is not part of it, it is rejected," and again, "Beware of innovative matters for every invention is an innovation and every innovation is misleading". (*Hadith, Sahih Bukhari, Vol. 3, Book 49, No 861*).

The visits of Maulana Ansari and Maulana Siddiqi to the Caribbean in the 1950s provided religious legitimacy for the practice of *qasida*, *tazeem*, and *Milad-un-Nabi*. These scholars endorsed these practices and refuted claims that these were innovations. They were able to convince many local Muslims that based on the Quran, the Hadith, and the *fiqh* (the tradition of Islamic jurisprudence), these traditional practices were within the parameters of Islam and are *bida'h hasanah* ("good innovations").

Debates concerning these rituals have created deep rifts among Muslims in the Caribbean from the 1940s to the present. Some groups consider these practices to be *bida'h* (innovations) since they have not been practiced by the Prophet or his companions. In recent times, these debates have subsided somewhat as Muslims of different orientations are showing increased acceptance of each other's differences.

Shiite Muslims

Shi'ah Muslims also brought their cultural traditions to the Caribbean. They believe that the fourth Caliph Ali should have been the successor to Muhammad for the leadership of the *ummah*. Their most important religious personalities are Husayn and Fatima, the grandson and daughter of the Prophet, respectively. Every year they observe the martyrdom of Husayn, which occurred in 680 A.D. on the tenth day of the month of Muharram. This date continues to be a very emotional event involving mourning, the expression of grief, and the chanting of prayers as devotees conduct a street procession of *taziyah* or representations of the tomb of Husayn. Shi'ah Muslims also utilize this event to atone for their sins.

The "Hosay" festival, in its Indian form, was introduced into the Caribbean by early Indian immigrants. Though Shi'ah Islam was largely submerged into the wider Muslim community, Hosay as a street festival persisted in a Caribbeanized or "creolized" form. Though it largely lost its religious significance (Mansingh and Mansingh 1995), creolization is a concept primarily identified with the Caribbean to describe and analyze processes of cultural adaptation and change in hierarchical societies whereby new cultural forms emerged.

Hosay represented a visual display of resistance by Indians, sufficient to cause fear on the part of the colonial authorities. Several historians including Ken Parmasad and Kelvin Singh have documented the importance of the 1884 Hosay Riots (also called the Muharram massacre) in Trinidad. The Hosay festival continues to attract interest as an important cultural event and has received much popular support in India and in Trinidad and Tobago. Grassroots people of various religious and cultural persuasions participate in the festival, providing additional modification of its form. However, the orthodox Muslim groups have distanced themselves from its observance.

It was the 1979 revolution in Iran that really inspired the revival of orthodox Shiite Islam. Its followers were largely of Afro-Trinidadian descent and observe Hosay annually as a true mourning event. Local persons even visited Iran in the early 1980s. Also, Iran also sent Shi'ah missionaries to the Caribbean. This orthodox Shi'ah community that resurfaced in Trinidad in the 1980s has also condemned the manner in which Hosay is currently celebrated, with its alcohol and a carnival-like atmosphere. This Shi'ah group observes the martyrdom of Husayn in what they claim is the truly Islamic manner, as a time of mourning. Shi'ah Muslims have also been strongly condemned by Wahhabi Muslims for their veneration of saints, visits to tombs and shrines, and commemoration of death anniversaries. Some of these practices associated with the Shi'ah tradition are also observed by some Sufi Muslims.

The Shiite doctrines became submerged with the religious practices of the Indian Muslims, with the exception of Hosay which became an annual event in Trinidad and Jamaica. It was a colorful display of flags and tadjahs accompanied by drumming and processions.

Sufism

Sufi Muslims are also found in the Caribbean today. This popular religious movement is found throughout the Muslim world, including the Arab countries, Africa, and South Asia. It is a mystical tradition that seeks to emphasize the inner spiritual development of the individual. Sufis follow an ascetic life of simplicity, purification, denial, and detachment from the material world. Rarely addressing what they view as the mundane issues of society, they spend much of their efforts in prayer, singing, fasting, meditation, and *dhikr* ("remembrance of God"). Though initially having an elite following, the Sufi movement attracted persons from all levels of society. Over the years, Sufi activities came under the influence of Christian hermits, Buddhist monks, and Hindu sadhus. Many orthodox Islamic scholars have rejected the Sufi movement for its "excesses." Wahhabi Muslims have even described it as heretical or a blasphemous deviation that compromises people's *iman* (faith). Sufi Islam finds support especially among the "traditionalist" Muslims in the Caribbean, including the Hanafi Sunnis and to some extent, the Tabligh movement. Sufism has had increase support in the last two decades even among the youth who are yearning for spirituality amidst the materialism and secularism prevailing.

Ahmadi/Qadiani

A major religious conflict among Muslims in Trinidad was posed by the introduction of *Ahmadi doctrines* in the 1930s. Toward the end of the nineteenth century in India, Mirza Ghulam Ahmad had laid claims to prophethood, claiming at various times to have been a reincarnation of religious personalities of Hinduism, Christianity, and Islam. Orthodox Muslim scholars did not recognize his followers, known today as *Qadiani* and *Ahmadi* Muslims. There are no records of *Ahmadi* Muslims in the Caribbean until 1921 when Maulana Durrani, an Ahmadi missionary from India, arrived in Trinidad (Samaroo 1987). After being bitterly opposed by the local leaders, he soon returned to India. He was nevertheless instrumental in persuading a Trinidadian, Ameer Ali, to take up a scholarship at an Ahmadi institute in Lahore in 1923.

Moulvi Ameer Ali

Ameer Ali returned to Trinidad in 1930 after his graduation, was warmly received by the Tackveeyatul Islamic Association (TIA), and was shortly thereafter appointed *Mufti* (one who is authorized to make decisions in Islamic jurisprudence). Yet there was much apprehension on his return among the Muslim community in Trinidad. Because of his somewhat liberal approach, it was generally presumed that Moulvi Ameer Ali was an *Ahmadi* or a *Qadiani*, even though he sporadically published denials of the mounting rumors that he had taken the pledge of the Ahmadiyya Anjuman Ishaat-i-Islam and that he accepted the teachings of Mirza Ghulam Ahmad. His views created much concern among the "traditionalist" Muslims of Trinidad, who under the leadership of Haji Ruknudeen, felt strongly that *Ahmadi* teachings were now infiltrating the TIA.

Ameer Ali claimed that he was not an *Ahmadi* but a *ghair mukallid* ("nonconformist"). He adopted a "modernist" approach to Islam, encouraging the free participation of women in religious activities and criticizing some of the local institutionalized traditions. His liberal views were strongly condemned by traditional Muslim leaders. He eventually formed his own organization in 1947, the Trinidad Muslim League (TML). This organization was formally affiliated with the worldwide *Ahmadi* movement from 1969 to 1976 but subsequently identified itself as *ghair mukallid* (nonconformist).

In light of Ameer Ali's open statements and practices, in spite of his standing as the Mufti of the TIA, in 1932, this conflict reached a climax when Haji Ruknudeen and other senior members of the TIA decided to leave the organization.

Despite their religious differences, Ameer Ali worked with Haji Ruknudeen in support of the passage of the Muslim Marriage Ordinance, which was eventually passed in 1936. Ameer Ali served as President of the *Indian Educational Association*, and from 1938 to 1942, he also served on the Board of Education, becoming its first non-Christian member. In 1939, he made one of his most important contributions to the Muslim community of Trinidad and to non-Christian communities in general. Ameer Ali moved that the Education Ordinance be amended to include all religious associations in the colony, and not only Christian denominations.

In 1947, Ameer Ali and his small group formed the Trinidad Muslim League (TML), which was later incorporated in 1950. He also approached Governor Hubert Rance to request state aid for Indian denominational schools, but it was refused. His plea finally came to fruition when in 1948–1949, the TIA Islamia School in San Juan was granted state aid. This was achieved with the assistance on Nazeer Ahmad Simab. A number of Muslim schools were subsequently established. Ameer Ali died on February 15, 1973.

The Ahmadis claim that Muhammad was the final Prophet but Mirza Ghulam Ahmad was a reformer and the Promised Messiah. The Qadianis on the other hand believed that Mirza Ghulam Ahmad was a Prophet. Both groups are found in Trinidad.

Middle Eastern Influence

There were Muslims, Jews, and Christians among the early Syrian and Lebanese immigrants to the Caribbean. Those who remained Muslims often intermingled and sometimes intermarried with Indian Muslims. One of the first Muslim missionaries from the Middle East was Abdel Salaam from Egypt. In the late 1960s, he taught Arabic at several centers in Trinidad. In the 1970s, nationals from Trinidad, Guyana, and Barbados were awarded scholarships to pursue studies in Egypt and Saudi Arabia. Their return provided a new turn of events for the Muslim community in the Caribbean. As was expected, their interpretations of Islam did not find favor with the traditional Muslims locally. They nevertheless found tremendous support from the youth who were largely disenchanted with the leadership of traditional Muslims. These new approaches to the practice of Islam provided an exciting escape from the traditionalism of the mainstream Muslim community. Young Muslims started to take pride in openly identifying with Islam. It was only around the mid-1970s that Muslim women began wearing the *hijab* or veil. Prior to this, the *ohrni*, an Indian head covering, was worn by older women only (Niehoff and Niehoff 1961).

Wahhabism

The *Wahhabi* movement, often called "fundamentalist" in contrast to the "traditionalist" Hanafi Sunni tradition, was introduced into the religious landscape of the Caribbean initially from India and later from Saudi Arabia. This Muslim group has grown in size over the past two decades but is by no means homogeneous. The work of Muhammad Ibn Abdul Wahhab (1708–1792) has inspired many of today's revivalist movements. Abdul Wahhab's major focus was on the removal of accretions and innovations that crept into Islam over time. He was appalled by some religious practices found in his time, including the veneration of saints and their tombs. He saw such acts as *shirk* (polytheism), which is considered the most serious sin in Islam. Wahhabi Muslims are usually critical of popular interpretations of Islam, especially when they condone cultural practices which were not found among the Prophet's generation. This movement advocates a return to the "fundamentals" or original sources of Islam, namely, the Quran and the Sunnah. They reject Sufi practices and destroy all idols, icons, tombs, and shrines or anything that they believe comes between God and humanity.

This trend in Caribbean Islam was initially influenced by an early missionary from India, Nazeer Ahmad Simab, who came to Trinidad and Tobago in 1935. He did not find favor with the local Muslims and was ostracized for his rejection of some of their allegedly "un-Islamic" practices. He was even condemned for saying that the Prophet was a man like us. This missionary played a key role in obtaining government recognition for the first non-Christian denominational school in the West Indies.

Subsequently, several groups in the Caribbean have advocated a return to the "fundamentals" of Islam. Like the Wahhabis, these "neo-revivalists" generally show high levels of religious commitment. Originally inspired by movements in South Asia and more recently by Middle Eastern and North American contact, they often find themselves at odds with "traditionalist" Muslims over the latter's apparent overemphasis on ancestral traditions as opposed to following the *faraid* ("obligatory") acts of worship. Many neo-revivalists are actively engaged in propagating their faith among both Muslims and non-Muslims. Generally, members of this group do not follow the rulings of any one of the four recognized schools of Islamic law, and some find *ijtihad* ("personal judgment" in the implementation of the law) to be acceptable.

Recently, a form of *Wahhabi* Islam has been introduced into the Caribbean, the *Salafi* movement. They advocate using only original sources, strict orthodoxy, a literal "back to basics" approach to Islam, and are often criticized for making peripheral matters into central issues. This group is rather small but has grown over the past decade. It has been influenced mainly by the return of Saudi-trained scholars to the Caribbean.

Salafis are largely followers of the Hanbali school and several Saudi-trained scholars. Though a few may have gone on to support extremists, the majority do not condone violent extremism.

Moulvi Nazeer Ahmad Simab

Moulvi Nazeer Ahmad Simab arrived from India in November 12, 1935. Simab had graduated with honors in Persian, Urdu, *tafsir* (commentary of Quran), and Islamic studies. Simab initiated the printing of *khutbahs* (Friday sermons) in English on one side of the page and in Arabic and Urdu on the other, distributing copies to every mosque in the country. He was also the first person in Trinidad to introduce sermons with English translation, both at weekly Friday and Eid prayers.

Not only did Simab make a significant contribution to the Muslim community in Trinidad, but he also made a remarkable impact on the educational system of the colony. He refuted the allegations that Islam was spread by the use of the sword made in the educational textbooks, *West Indian History Book 2* by Edward Daniel and *The Beginner's History* by J.B. Newman. After the controversy erupted in December 1939 between Moulvi Simab and Sydney J. Hogben, the Director of Education, these books were withdrawn from the school system on the instructions of the Colonial Office and the Department of Education. In addition to this victory, Moulvi Simab was instrumental in founding the first Muslim primary school in March 2, 1942. This became the first non-Christian school in Trinidad to receive state aid in 1949. He did not live to see this important occasion for which he had so struggled. Moulvi Simab died on December 10, 1942.

The attractiveness of "Westernization" was difficult to resist, and by the 1960s, many of the younger and more educated Muslims became assimilated into the culture of the wider Caribbean society. The Islam that was being taught as a body of rituals and traditions was irreconcilable with what was being taught in the "secular" educational system. Also by this time, most of the youth, having been educated in the English language, were unable to understand and speak Urdu. Many religious sermons were still being delivered in the Urdu language, while there was very little Islamic literature available in English.

Some studies have shown integration and acculturation among Indians as the twentieth century progressed especially with regard to religion and family life. It was in the areas of religion and food that Indians remained most resilient as well as most creative. The rate of change was therefore more rapid among the urbanized and more educated and those experiencing higher rates of social mobility. On the other hand, isolated rural settlements showed greater resistance to change especially when they were living in poverty.

The subsequent arrival of learned persons who were able to teach Islam in the English language and the increasing availability of literature in English led to a reawakening of the local Muslims. This revival took place in Guyana and Trinidad simultaneously and was further strengthened by the return of qualified locals from abroad as well as contact with Muslims in North America.

Syncretisms

Syncretisms involving Islam and magical practices were also brought to the Caribbean from India. In several communities in Trinidad today, persons perform exorcism using Arabic prayers. Sometimes Arabic phrases are inscribed on paper and given to clients to ward off evil spirits. Services such as fortune-telling, healing of ailments, and detection of thieves are also offered. In the performance of this role, many parallels can be found with the Orisha priest or "Obeah" practitioner.

Common external pressures led to greater mutual respect and acceptance between Indian Muslims and Hindus in the Caribbean. Despite marked differences in beliefs, there was a cordial relationship between these two groups. Around the time of partition of India and the formation of Pakistan, Hindu-Muslim relationships became somewhat strained. However, the relationship was long and intimate enough to lead to the borrowing and sharing of customs. This mutual transfer of cultural traits began in India and continued in the Caribbean.

According to Khan (1987), some Muslim rituals as well as culinary practices in Trinidad have resulted from Hindu contact. There were many instances where Hindu or Muslim dishes initially distinguishable but were later shared by all Indians. Therefore, Indo-Caribbean dishes are of both Hindu and Muslim origins. These include the *paratha roti*, with flour enriched with ghee or butter. The *halwa* of the Muslims of Middle Eastern origin is similar to the Hindu *parsad*. At Divali and *Eid al-Fitr*, similar types of sweets are served. The popular Trinidadian street-food "doubles" originated among Indo-Trinidadian Muslims around the Usine-St Madeline sugar factory in South Trinidad.

Conflict and Change

After the period of indentureship, most of the debates among Muslims in the Caribbean focused on cultural practices that Muslims brought from India. There have been two major "camps" on this issue, one comprising the younger generation who preferred to abandon the Indian cultural heritage, and the other comprising the older generous who desire to preserve the Indian tradition. Today, those of the younger generation who have studied in the Arabic-speaking world prefer Arabic over Urdu and link the Indian Muslim traditions to Hinduism. A continuous attempt has therefore been made to purge "cultural Islam" of "un-Islamic" innovations. As Samaroo 1987 states, "In modern day Trinidad and Guyana, where there are substantial Muslim populations, there is much confusion, often conflict, between the two types of Islam."

Tabligh/Dar-ul-Uloom

The *Tabligh* (literally, "preaching") movement, based in India and found throughout the diaspora, was introduced into the Caribbean in the early 1970s. It also advocates a rigid system of adherence to the "fundamentals" of Islam and is dedicated to the propagation of Islam but only among Muslims. Although members of this group are Hanafi Sunni like the "traditionalists," they do not follow Indian cultural practices which they consider to be *bida'h* ("innovations"). They refrain from polemics and adopt a fixed, literal, and cautious interpretation of Islamic texts. They seem indifferent to contemporary social and political issues and avoid conflict with established authority and controversial issues. Most of them are highly active in religious observance. Nevertheless, their rigid stance on many issues often contributes to their unpopularity among both "traditionalists" and other "fundamentalists." Their activities revolve around the mosques and require little resources. Their missionary work follows a fixed format, which seldom involves the use of modern technology. They made it possible for a number of locals to obtain scholarships to pursue Islamic studies in India. Today, the efforts of the Tabligh movement have led to establishment the Dar-ul-Uloom Institute of Islamic Studies. The clientele of this institute comes from several Caribbean territories. Tabligh is generally apolitical and emphasizes adherence to Quran, Hadith, and Hanafi school of thought. The majority do not condone extremism.

A Word on ISIS

When scholars, journalists, and commentators discuss violent extremism, the question continues to be asked: What motivated some persons to leave Trinidad and Tobago and travel thousands of miles away into a strange unknown land? It must be something perceived as important.

There appears to be no link between the 1979 revolution in Iran, the attempted coup of 1990, and the extremist-related events of the last 5 years. Several attempts were made to analyze the attempted coup of 1990 (Ryan 1991; Deosaran 1993), but this was an isolated event that did not reflect the mood of the Muslims as well as the country then and now. Yasin Abu Bakr, leader of the Jamaat al Muslimeen has his own style and has never shown any leaning toward Middle Eastern extremist groups, though he was an avid supporter of Muammar Gaddafi. Abu Bakr did indicate however that the persons who left were so disenchanted with the existing state of affairs in Trinidad and Tobago that they were willing to take the chance and be lured by the false idealism portrayed. The horror stories about the incarceration and even death of persons who joined ISIS there has made locals think twice about falling for the ISIS rhetoric.

Concerning the economic situation (used as one as the antecedent factors of both the 1970 Black Power Revolution as well as the attempted coup of 1990), this may not be a plausible reason. Compared to other Caribbean societies Trinidad and Tobago is relatively prosperous. Within recent times though, the economy has been experiencing a decline, but with its diverse resource base as well as its highly educated and skilled population, it is still a place of opportunity, as evidenced by the continued inward migration of people from all over the world such as China, the Middle East, Venezuela, and Cuba. Like other religious groups, the Muslims are relatively comfortable here.

The local Muslim community itself has come a long way and has integrated well in the society. They have access to opportunities and privileges unavailable to Muslim in most parts of the world. In fact Muslims of Trinidad have more rights and freedoms than even in most of the Muslim countries, including freedom of expression, freedom of association, and respect for the rights of women (Kassim 2017).

There is the availability of *halal* food, time off for *Juma* (Friday prayer), a public holiday for the *Eid al-Fitr* festival, and two Muslim television stations. Since 1956 there have been Muslims in the country's parliament and cabinet. The country also had a Muslim president from 1987 to 1997 as well as a Muslim serving as Acting Prime Minister. Currently, there are Muslim government ministers. The Islam attire (hijab) can be worn at all government schools and most denominational schools.

Therefore, the view expressed in an article by Simon Cottee (2016) quoting one ISIS fighter. Al Trinidadi (aka Shane Crawford) vociferously condemned local Muslims at home for remaining in "a place where you have no honor and are forced to live in humiliation, subjugated by the disbelievers." He urged Muslims in Trinidad and Tobago "to wage jihad against their fellow citizens." He even condemned the Jamaat al Muslimeen for not being "militant enough" (Cottee 2016, 2).

This view does not represent that of Trinidad Muslims generally. Muslims are an integral part of the mainstream society. The Muslim community is generally very conservative and supportive of the status quo and has always been consulted by both the present and past governments on issues of national importance.

Nevertheless, international attention continues to be focused on Trinidad as a recruiting ground for ISIS fighters who have gone to Syria. According to McCoy and Knight between 89 and 125 Trinidadians would have gone. As such "this would place Trinidad, with a population of 1.3 million, including 104,000 Muslims, top of the list of Western countries with the highest rates of foreign-fighter radicalization; it's by far the largest recruitment hub in the Western Hemisphere."

Violent extremists have received undue media publicity but have limited influence locally. They have no legitimacy or support from the scholars as well as the leadership of the community, are geographically concentrated in a few areas (Cottee 2016), have little integration with the society, and have no history of political activity. The majority have tenuous links with the Muslim community as well as the society generally. They were mostly persons with noninvolvement in mainstream society, e.g., the educational system, and they do not support voting at elections. Suspicious persons were arrested on two occasions, one in 2011 in a plot to assassinate the then Prime Minister and again in 2017 in a plot to disrupt Carnival. In both instances, they were released since the evidence was inadequate. The evidence indicates that only one individual from the time of the attempted coup of 1990 had relatives associated with ISIS. He claimed that he was unaware and had nothing to do with their involvement with ISIS (Cottee 2016).

The question is why people left Trinidad to join ISIS. The "push" and "pull" factors are as follows:

- Pull factors: recruitment strategy, marketing among youth, widespread use of social media, appeal to religious sentiments, appeal to rhetoric surrounding an Islam state and the caliphate, attraction to financial incentive (this was questioned by Cottee 2016)
- Push factors: hatred for disbelievers' claims of being victims of discrimination, unemployment

After hearing of horrendous condition prevailing in Syria and other ISIS strongholds, including the imprisonment of ladies with children, lack of justice, lack of respect for human life, the alleged death of ISIS fighters, and stories of human suffering, it is unlikely that persons have been joining ISIS within recent times. As Cottee stated, "I think the motives of those who went were complex and mixed. Redemption through violent self-sacrifice is a pretty big draw, but I also think a lot of those Trinis who went, truly believed that the ISIS caliphate was the real deal, a kind of Islamic utopia where they could go with their families and be spiritually saved."

Muslims and Formal Education

Historian Carl Campbell (1992) showed that there were several attempts to establish Hindu and Muslim schools from as early as the 1920s. Muslims with resources were eager to establish institutions to cater for the educational needs of the community. In 1924, 1925, and 1927 privately funded schools were established. Also, a Hindu-Muslim school started in November 1931 with 150 students. It was located in Chaguanas, a predominantly Indian area. Hindus and Muslims in the surrounding areas withdrew their children from the Canadian Mission schools and gave their support to the Hindu-Muslim school. This school was an attempt to check Indian conversion to the Presbyterian faith. This school according to Carl Campbell was "probably the most controversial elementary school ever started in the colony." The Hindu-Muslim school though faced with many problems was closed in 1935.

According to Hallima Kassim, a high school was started in 1936 in Sangre Grande by a convert to Islam, Abu Bakr Beaumont-Benjamin, (Kassim 2002). In addition to religious instruction, academic subjects were taught. This opening of this institution was an indication of the maturity and resourcefulness of the community, to have started a secondary school, at such a challenging era in history with so very little resources. Many social events were observed in the form of religious gatherings. The opportunities for social interaction helped in keeping the faith alive. Also, the close-knit Indian family system facilitated cultural transmission to the younger members of society. Under the new conditions, these cultural traits were inevitably adapted and modified. Several efforts were made to teach Indian-based languages. Hindi and Urdu classes were started in San Fernando in 1945 and in Marabella in 1938. The students included Hindus, Muslims, and Christians.

The Marriot/Mayhew report indicated that the Indians who comprised 38.5% of the population (1932 census) should have had their own denominational schools. Subsequently, the government considered both Hindus and Muslims capable of administering schools. Within a short time several Hindu and Muslim schools were established. In 1949, there were 250 Christian schools and 50 government schools. By 1952, Hindu schools started to receive state aid and by 1962, there were 46 Hindu schools and 15 Muslim schools (Campbell 1992).

There were also several efforts to establish private schools, but due to the absence of state aid, adequate resources were not available to provide viable alternatives to the Christian schools. The leaders of both Hindus and Muslims, including Nazeer Ahmad Simab and Ameer Ali agitated for years to obtain state aid for a non-Christian school. And their efforts did bear fruit when the El Socorro Islamia School was established by the Takveeatul Islamic Association (TIA) in 1942. This institution operated as a private school for 7 years before becoming the first non-Christian school to receive state assistance from 1949.

This period of decline and assimilation was exacerbated when Muslims had the opportunity for secondary and tertiary education (most assimilation occurred among those who were more financially endowed, received more secular education, achieved more social mobility, and had more resources). A dichotomy therefore developed between the traditionalism and stagnation of religion (as taught and practiced at the time) and the excitement and dynamism of modernity. These two worlds seemed irreconcilable.

At this time, most of the youth were being educated in the English language, but religious instruction continued in Urdu which the majority could not understand. Many of the Friday sermons were still given in the Urdu language. So as a result, those children who were better educated saw the modern, scientific, and progressive approach to life as more attractive and appealing than a seemingly backward, irrelevant, traditional way of life. The situation was therefore conducive to a decline in the knowledge and practice of Islam.

New Educational Policy

At the time of achieving political independence in 1962, there were drastic changes in the educational policy in Trinidad and Tobago. Of concern here was the introduction of the Common Entrance Examination and the increased availability of secondary school places through the establishment of several government secondary schools. Of course, such a move was welcomed by the population in the face of the existing elitism in the secondary school system and the general lack of opportunities for members of the lower classes to achieve social mobility through education. Educational expansion also meant, however, a reduction in the power of the denominational boards and greater state control in education. In such a context, the Muslim schools had very little opportunity to blossom into independent institutions with their own school culture and traditions, without state interference. Even the existing church schools to a large extent lost their unique character in the face of deliberate attempts to promote a homogeneous society based on nationalistic and therefore secular ideals.

At this time the leadership of Muslim groups appeared to support the status quo and in return enjoyed some degree of privilege in accessing opportunities. They encouraged the community to support the dominant values of the wider society, and therefore their unique cultural identity was being eroded.

Increase in Muslim Schools

Within a decade after the establishment of the first school to receive state aid, the three existing Muslim organizations, the ASJA, the TIA, and the TML, established 15 primary schools: the Anjuman Sunnatul Jamaat Association (ASJA) had seven, Takveeatul Islamic Association (TIA) had five, and the Trinidad Muslim League (TML) had three. Though, initially there was rivalry and competition among the groups, the schools helped to foster the bonds of cohesion and therefore keep the community alive. There were also instances of teacher mobility from one board to another. Over the years there developed a very cordial relationship among these groups, leading to the formation of the Muslim Coordinating Council.

In 1969 two government-assisted Muslim secondary schools were opened, and in the year 2000, four additional government-assisted secondary schools were opened. It is also important to note that the student population at all these schools includes students of all religions, which reflects the religious and ethnic harmony that exists in the society generally.

Religious Education

According to many Muslims, there is no distinction between religious and secular education. Nevertheless, many Muslim leaders felt there was a need for specialist training institutions in religious studies; this was done by the Islamic Missionaries Guild, the Islamic Trust, ASJA, and Dar-ul-Uloom, among others.

The Islamic Trust

In mid-1975 Abdul Wahid Hamid, a Trinidad-born and British-trained historian, formed the Islamic Trust. It was a registered charity which attempted to work with all of the existing organizations. For fear of exacerbating the schisms in an already fragmented community, the Trust never identified itself as a Muslim organization but functioned as a service bureau and as a "catalyst" in the Muslim community. The Trust established a reference library and a bookshop and held classes at various venues throughout the country. It published numerous books and a monthly magazine called *The Muslim Standard* (from 1975 to 1983). The Trust was very vociferous on a number of social and political issues, leading the then Prime Minister of Trinidad and Tobago, Dr. Eric Williams, to comment that the Muslims had become aggressive in their missionary activity (Hamid 1978, 4). *The Muslim Standard* was eventually banned from mosques, controlled by mainstream organizations, mainly on account of its scathing criticisms of shortcomings in the traditional Muslim community.

Hamid, nevertheless, considered himself part of the mainstream Muslim community and encouraged his students to forge links with the existing organizations. The group had attracted many persons of African descent to Islam. In late 1977, Abdul Wahid returned to London and continued to write and publish several articles and books.

The Haji Ruknudeen Institute of Islamic Studies

With the aim of "providing a forum for comprehensive Islamic learning" a committee was formed by the ASJA in the mid-1970s, to explore the possibility of establishing an Islamic institute. This effort was headed by President of ASJA, Hajji Abdool Sattar, and included Dr. Nizam Mohammed, Zainul Khan, and Justice Anthony Edoo. It later included Hajji SS Hosein, Dr. Aleem Mohammed, and Hajji Hyder Ali in the mid-1980s. At this time, residential and nonresidential weekend courses were held. Funding was obtained for a new building, and the sod for this structure was turned in May 1991. In September 1995, the Hajji Ruknudeen Institute was formally launched. Maulana Dr. Waffie Mohammed was the principal. The staff included Maulana Siddiq Ahmad Nasir and Maulana M. Sulaimani. Several part-time and full-time courses were offered.

Dar-ul-Uloom Institute

Evolving out of the influence of the Tabligh is the *Dar-ul-Uloom* Institute of Islamic Studies, which offers courses in Arabic and Islamic studies.

This was started in 1984 by Trinidadian Mufti Shabil Ali, a graduate of India. Its main objective was to impart a sound Islamic as well as academic education. Dar-ul-Uloom is a private institution which today includes a Boys' College and a Girls'

College, both offering full-time as well as part-time tuition. The curriculum includes Arabic language, Islamic jurisprudence, Islamic history, as well as several academic subjects. The students write the CXC examinations, as well as those set by the institution. Both colleges include dormitory facilities, and the student population includes locals as well as citizens of other countries. The full-time enrolment at the Boys' College (as of October 2006) is 100, including 20 foreigners, with 21 members of staff (Eid ul Fitr Brochure 1427A.H. October 2006). The Girls' College has an enrolment of 161, with 50 students boarding. There are 18 staff members at the Girls' College.

The institution offers a full-time secondary program, an 8-year Aalim program, a 5-year Aalim program, an associate's degree program, a Hifz course, and several Tajweed and Qari courses. In addition, there are several part-time programs, such as Arabic language, Tajweed, Hadith studies, and tafsir. Enrolment at the part-time programs is approximately 250.

In addition to the above, very vibrant religious institutions are currently attracting much interest. These include the Madinatul Ulum in Marabella, the Markaz al Ihsaan in San Fernando led by Maulana Dr. Waffie Mohammed, and the Ahlus Sunnah wal Jamaah Institute also in San Fernando, led by Maulana Siddiq Ahmad Nasir.

Conclusion

This chapter looks at Islam in Trinidad starting with the experiences of the African slaves as well as the Indian indentured immigrants. While Africans largely became assimilated in the society as a result of slavery, Indians were able to maintain their religious identity due to their isolation on the estates. The main factor that led to religious change among Indians was the efforts of the Canadian Mission started by Reverend John Morton in the 1860s.

The chapter looks not only at Muslims' survival but the establishment of places of worship, the evolution of Muslim organizations to seek their interests, lobbying to get legislation passed to protect their interests (e.g., for Muslim marriages) and establishing Muslim schools. It also discusses the conflicts and schisms arising in the 1930s and 1940s, due to ideological differences eventually leading to the formation of three main organizations by 1947. The various orientations that were discussed include Sunni, Ahmadis, Qadianis, Shi'ahs, Sufis, and Wahhabis.

It also examines the recent trend of youth radicalization and the development of extremist tendencies leading to the migration of persons to fight for ISIS.

The final section gives an overview of the Muslim involvement in education, both religious and secular, in Trinidad and Tobago. It examines the community's successful battle with the forces of acculturation and assimilation. The information indicates that the Muslim community has successfully struggled to maintain a visible identity, in the face of numerous challenges. Muslims have coexisted peacefully with other groups and have participated in mainstream politics, music, sports, business, as well as education. The community now has over 140 mosques, over 20 government-assisted Muslim schools, 3 theological institutes, 2 financial institutions, several charities, and 2 television stations. Within its unity of belief and practice, a marked diversity exists, reflecting the variations in the Muslim ummah worldwide.

References

Afroz S (1995) The unsung slaves in plantation America. Caribb Q 41(2 and 3):30–44
Campbell C (1992) Colony and nation: short history of education in Trinidad and Tobago. Ian Randle Publishers, Jamaica
Cottee S (2016) ISIS in the Caribbean, Dec 8. https://www.theatlantic.com/
Dabydeen D, Samaroo B (1987) India in the Caribbean. London: Hansib
Deosaran R (1993) Society under siege: a study of political confusion and legal mysticism. Published by McAl Psychological Research Centre, University of the West Indies
Diouf S (1998) Servants of Allah: African Muslims enslaved in the Americas. New York University Press, New York
Hadith: Sahih al Bukhari. Chicago: Kazi Publications, 1980
Hamid AW (1978). Muslims in the West Indies. Paper presented to the Muslim Minorities Seminar, Islamic Council of Europe
https://darululoomtt.net/
http://www.caribbeanmuslims.com
https://www.caribbeanmuslims.com/the-overseas-hindustani-muslim-community-of-british-guiana-and-pakistan-1947
https://www.indexmundi.com/trinidad_and_tobago/demographics_profile.html
International Religious Freedom Report 2017. https://www.state.gov/j/drl/rls/irf/2016/
Kassim HS (2002) Education and socialization among the Indo-Muslims of Trinidad, 1917–1969. J Caribb Hist 36(1):100–126
Kassim HS (2013) Identity and acculturation of trinidad Muslims – an exploration of contemporary practices. Paper presented at conference on Bonded labour, migration and diaspora
Kassim HS (2017) Regional Report, Historical and Contemporary Overview of Muslims in Trinidad and Tobago, Caribbean Muslim Networking Conference, 2017
Khan F (1987) Islam as a Social Force in the Caribbean. Paper presented at the conference of the History Teachers' Association of Trinidad and Tobago
Mahaase R (2012) Indian Culture in Trinidad in Hangloo, R.L. Indian Diaspora in the Caribbean, Delhi, Primus Books
Mansingh A, Mansingh L (1995) Hosay and its creolization. Caribb Q 41(1):25–39
Niehoff A, Niehoff J (1961) East Indians in Trinidad and Tobago. Public Museum Publications in Anthropology, Milwaukee, No. 6
Ryan S (1991) The Muslimeen grab for power: race, religion, and revolution in Trinidad and Tobago. Inprint, Port of Spain
Samaroo B (1987) The Indian connection: the influence of Indian thought and ideas on East Indians in the Caribbean. In: Dabydeen D, Samaroo B (eds) India in the Caribbean. Hansib Publishing House, London
Sanyal U (1996) Devotional Islam and politics in British India. Oxford University Press, Delhi
Singh S-A (2013) The experience of Indian indenture in Trinidad: arrival and settlement. In: Cruse and Rhiney (eds) Caribbean Atlas. http://www.caribbean-atlas.com/en/themes/waves-of-colonization-and-control-in-the-caribbean/waves-of-colonization/the-experience-of-indian-indenture-in-trinidad-arrival-and-settlement.html

Part V

Indigeneity, Gender, and Sexuality

Part Introduction

The issues of indigeneity, gender, and sexuality are usually not seen as salient in mainstream discourses on ethnicity, although their significance in defining ethnic identities in the context of inequality and social marginalization cannot be ignored. This part examines some of the issues relating to indigeneity, gender, and sexuality and some of the challenges associated with them in different political and sociocultural contexts.

Despite attempts to protect their rights and livelihood, many indigenous groups around the world are now threatened by the encroaching corporate interests, which threaten to transform their social habitat into commercial enterprises. Jeffery Gardner and Patricia Richards examine this issue in relation to the impact of neoliberalism on indigenous rights in South America. Today many indigenous groups are still trying to deal with the impact of colonialism, a theme raised by Jessica Terruhn, who examines the situation of settler colonialism and biculturalism in Aotearoa/New Zealand. A less understood story was how Indigenous groups in the Pacific were subjected to exploitation during the cold war. Nick Maclellan discusses this issue with reference to nuclear testing and racism in the Pacific islands. In broader context of colonialism in the Pacific, Keakaokawai Hemi examines some of the issues relating to the sovereignty movement in Hawaii, while Michael Davis investigates some of the dilemmas relating to Indigenous Australian rights and identity in colonial and postcolonial contexts. Similar dilemmas are faced by the Nagas of northeast India, and this has inspired a vibrant Indigenous movement among the Zeliangrong Nagas, as discussed by Aphun Kamei. In a situation of political conflict, indigenous minorities often find themselves tangled up in complex situations of contestation over power. This is indeed the case in Mindanao, Philippines, where Jovanie Espesor analyses the exclusion of "second-order minorities" in the civil war. More or less, the same situation has arisen in Chinese modernization and development has led to ethnic unrest among Indigenous groups as in the case of Xinjiang, as Kate Hannan's chapter shows.

The use of the gender lenses to frame ethnicity and indigenousness reveals interesting dynamics in relation to power, stratification, and identities based on ideas of femininity and masculinity. Gender relations, division of labor, and status are shaped by the interplay between cultural, religious, political, economic, and ideological factors. In patriarchal-dominated societies, the subordination of women and LGBT are "normalized" through appeal to various cultural religious, legal, and political norms. In the Islamic world, the relationship between Islamic identity and sexuality is complex as explored by Sharyn Davies in the chapter on Indonesia. The reaction against masculine hegemony in Islamic societies has taken various forms.

The issues of gender and sexuality are closely associated in various ways and are often defined in relation to each other. It involves not just a male-female dichotomy but also the broader issue of alternative sexual preference and identification as Arjun Rajkjowa discusses in the chapter on LGBT and ethnicity. The relationship between the two does involve cultural transformation and power as Monique Mulholland expounds in the chapter on race and sexuality in the context of colonial, postcolonial, and contemporary forms of orientalisms. The dynamics of social transformation, especially in the context of migration and mixed races, has potential to raise challenges in relation to gender identity. Joseph Rukema and Beatrice Umubyey talk about how Congolese migrant men in South Africa are faced with managing their manhood.

Steven Ratuva
Airini

Indigenous Rights and Neoliberalism in Latin America

47

Jeffrey A. Gardner and Patricia Richards

Contents

Introduction	850
Neoliberalism, Social Suffering, and Early Resistance	850
Neoliberal Multiculturalism	854
Post-neoliberalism? Post-multiculturalism?	858
Conclusion	863
References	863

Abstract

Neoliberalism in Latin America has resulted in social, political, cultural, economic, and environmental challenges for indigenous peoples in the region. In response, indigenous communities and movements have contested neoliberal projects as they simultaneously seek collective rights for recognition as peoples, redistribution of resources, and recovery of ancestral territories. This chapter traces the emergence of neoliberalism in Latin America and demonstrates how it has contributed to the social suffering of indigenous peoples. Emphasis also is placed on how indigenous peoples in the region have mobilized against neoliberalism. Latin American governments have reshaped the politics of recognition in relation to indigenous peoples by embracing "neoliberal multiculturalism," a form of recognition that does not jeopardize the economic and political priorities of the state and elites. Questions about whether the region has entered into a "post-multicultural" or "post-neoliberal" moment are considered in relation

---

J. A. Gardner
Department of Sociology, Sam Houston State University, Huntsville, TX, USA
e-mail: jag175@shsu.edu

P. Richards (✉)
Department of Sociology, University of Georgia, Athens, GA, USA
e-mail: plr333@uga.edu

© The Author(s), under exclusive license to Springer Nature Singapore Pte Ltd. 2019
S. Ratuva (ed.), *The Palgrave Handbook of Ethnicity*,
https://doi.org/10.1007/978-981-13-2898-5_70

to indigenous rights claims. Furthermore, the chapter describes the potential of the "decolonial turn" and other recent trends for challenging hegemonic ontological and epistemological assumptions and pointing toward alternative modernities that center on indigenous worldviews.

Keywords
Indigenous · Neoliberalism · Latin America · Multiculturalism · Rights · Post-neoliberal · Post-multicultural

Introduction

This chapter traces the effects of neoliberalism on indigenous peoples in Latin America, examining how some rights have been violated and others, seemingly, elevated. Throughout, it also examines how indigenous peoples have responded to the social scenario shaped by neoliberalism, showing how some have embraced the limited openings provided by neoliberal governments, others have created openings themselves through protest, and still others have opted to frame their protest as outside the system, focusing on rights to autonomy and self-determination beyond the neoliberal state.

The chapter proceeds as follows. The first section traces the emergence of neoliberalism in the region and demonstrates how it led to social suffering in indigenous regions and communities. It also highlights some early movement responses and ongoing resistance to the suffering imposed by neoliberal policies in the region. The following section discusses the politics of recognition under neoliberalism and the emergence of what has come to be called "neoliberal multiculturalism." The final section considers whether the region has entered a "post-neoliberal" or "post-multicultural" moment and what this means for indigenous rights.

Neoliberalism, Social Suffering, and Early Resistance

Neoliberalism refers to a form of sociopolitical and economic governance characterized by privatization, economic deregulation, and withdrawal of the state from providing for social needs (Auyero 2012; Hale 2006; Harvey 2005; Peck and Tickell 2002; Postero 2007, 2017; Richards 2004, 2013). Neoliberal philosophies view the state as inefficient and, therefore, seek to minimize its role in relation to the market. At the same time, this form of governance is centered on trusting in the market's ability to provide social goods to "responsible individual citizens" (Postero 2007: 15–16). Thus, an important aspect of neoliberalism has involved inducing nongovernmental and community organizations to perform what were once state responsibilities (Richards 2004; Roberts and Portes 2006). This section briefly describes a few examples of how neoliberalism manifested in Latin

America, detailing how neoliberalism has contributed to the suffering of individuals and communities (indigenous and nonindigenous alike) and tracing some of the early indigenous responses to neoliberal reforms in the region.

In the context of Latin America's harsh economic crises of the 1970 and 1980s, many governments faced coercive pressure to address their debts through neoliberal policies. Neoliberalism was put in place through the imposition of structural adjustment reforms, in most cases, impelled by international financial institutions such as the International Monetary Fund and the World Bank. These reforms entailed establishing an export-based economic strategy, opening the economy to international investment, eliminating trade barriers, privatizing state industries, devaluing currency, and replacing universal social services with programs targeting particularly needy sectors (Portes 1997).

Neoliberal reform took distinct trajectories in different parts of the region. For example, in Bolivia, the imposition of neoliberalism followed the standard narrative fairly closely. The government took on neoliberal economic restructuring in 1982 (with its return to democracy) and intensified these measures beginning in 1985, following a period of rising unemployment and a steady drop in agricultural commodity prices (Postero 2007). Embracing these reforms was a condition of structural adjustment loans provided by the International Monetary Fund and the World Bank. Bolivian workers suffered as a result of this "New Economic Policy," as unions were weakened through the deregulation of labor laws (Postero 2017). Additionally, thousands of miners lost their jobs when tin mines were privatized or closed. One unique point worth highlighting in the Bolivian case is that although neoliberalism generally has entailed minimizing the state, "the Bolivian version has always been tied to an ambitious state building project" (Postero 2007: 125). Nevertheless, in seeking to balance the state's budget, over time Bolivia's government reduced public sector employment by 10% and made vast cuts in spending on education, healthcare, and other services (Postero 2007).

In Argentina, in contrast, the last military dictatorship put in place some neoliberal policies during the late 1970s and early 1980s, but the primary period of neoliberalization occurred in the first half of the 1990s (Auyero 2012). In the short term, Argentina's neoliberal experiment created economic growth and monetary stability. However, the long-term cost of deindustrialization and privatization included massive layoffs in the manufacturing sector, high unemployment, and loss of protections from the state, unions, or other organizations (Auyero 2012; Villalón 2007).

In Chile, neoliberal reforms occurred much earlier and were arguably more severe than other parts of Latin America (Richards 2013). Around 1975, during the Pinochet dictatorship, the "Chicago Boys" (economists trained under the direction of Milton Friedman at the University of Chicago) persuaded Pinochet to embrace a "rightist shrunken state and extreme free market capitalism" (Richards 2013: 71). As Richards (2004: 9) explains: "The military regime liberalized trade, created incentives for foreign investment, privatized state industries, devalued the peso, weakened labor unions, deregulated markets, structured the economy around exports, and drastically decreased social spending." The regime's ability to implement these structural adjustment reforms were coupled with gross human rights violations, including the execution and disappearance of about 3,000 people and tens of thousands detained, tortured, or exiled (Richards 2004). Although these reforms generated wealth and growth – indeed, Chile was hailed as a successful example of neoliberalism – they also produced abuse of human rights, environmental destruction, and severe inequality (Richards 2004).

The Concertación de Partidos por la Democracia (Coalition of Parties for Democracy) governments that led Chile for 20 years following Pinochet's dictatorship embraced neoliberal economic policy, even as they worked to reduce poverty and inequality (Richards 2013). Among other issues, ongoing neoliberal policies prioritized large-scale agricultural production for export, imperiling small-scale farmers (indigenous and nonindigenous alike). Likewise, the Concertación continued subsidies for the timber industry, contributing to conflicts with Mapuche indigenous communities in the country's South (Haughney 2006; Richards 2013).

In these examples and others throughout Latin America, neoliberalism led to social suffering among indigenous and nonindigenous citizens, as governments curtailed the provision of public goods like healthcare, nutrition, education, and housing (Albro 2005). Neoliberalization also entailed major layoffs and unemployment as a result of privatization and the shrinking of the public sector. Social suffering in many communities has been further exacerbated by environmental devastation, as governments have privatized industries, prioritized agro-exports, and increased the exportation of natural resources, such as timber and mining products.

Indigenous peoples have faced particular consequences – cultural, political, economic, and environmental – as a result of neoliberalism and often have mobilized in response to ensure their rights and sovereignty. This resistance has taken on different forms. For example, indigenous people have participated in trans- and international activism to recognize their rights. Indigenous peoples from throughout the region gathered at the Primer Congreso Indio de Sudamérica (First South American Indian Congress) held in Peru in 1980, which not only focused on resisting social and economic exploitation but helped plant the seeds of movements for indigenous autonomy. Also in 1980, the foundation was laid for the United Nations Working Group on Indigenous Affairs to oversee the development of a declaration regarding the protection of indigenous peoples' human rights. (The declaration was finally finished years later and adopted by the General Assembly in 2007.) And in 1989, the International Labor Organization passed Convention 169 (ILO 169), which recognized the cultural and political rights of indigenous peoples to language, identification, autonomy, self-governance, and territory, among others. Importantly, ILO 169 details indigenous peoples' right to consultation, as a means of assuring that the indigenous are involved in administrative and legislative decisions that affect them, their territories, and their resources and that states either come to joint agreement with them or garner their informed consent, before acting. ("Participation" is sometimes used in a similar sense and refers to being involved in establishing priorities, design, delivery, and evaluation of policies and programs of various sorts.)

In some places, indigenous peoples also contested neoliberalism from its early inception through protest. For example, in 1988, indigenous peoples protested against a large dam on the Xingú River in the Amazonian region of Brazil, which would displace indigenous communities along the river, devastate livelihoods, and harm wildlife and vegetation by flooding this ancestral territory. With support from international allies, indigenous peoples in the region protested against the proposed six dams along the river and continued this resistance against the Belo Monte Dam in the decades that followed.

The Zapatista uprising articulated a forceful early response to neoliberalism. In Mexico, as elsewhere, neoliberal restructuring began in the late 1970s and gained traction through the 1980s. Neoliberal reforms were especially ushered in under the direction of President Carlos Salinas de Gortari (1988–1994). Constitutional changes shrunk the government's role in providing social services and opened its markets for imported goods, like grains, that were more cheaply produced in the United States (Stephen et al. 2006). These reforms were devastating for many rural farmers whose livelihoods were invested in domestic markets and production support from state subsidies (Stephen et al. 2006).

The Zapatista National Liberation Army (EZLN) initially emerged in Chiapas in 1992 in protest against amendments to Article 27 of the Mexican Constitution that ended land redistribution and the ability to petition the Mexican government for land (a move that directly impacted the many indigenous peoples living on disputed lands in Chiapas), as well as in protest against the 500th anniversary celebrations of Columbus' arrival in the Americas (Stephen et al. 2006). But it was the morning of January 1, 1994, when the North American Free Trade Agreement (NAFTA) between Mexico, the United States, and Canada went into effect that indigenous peoples in Chiapas took up arms against neoliberalism in what came to be known as the Zapatista rebellion (Hernández Castillo 2001). Armed and unarmed indigenous peoples from Chiapas – Mam, Tzeltal, Tzotzil, Tojola'bal, and Chol – participated in the rebellion. The platform of their uprising was focused on "work, land, housing, food, health, education, independence, liberty, democracy, justice, and peace" (Stephen et al. 2006: xv). Following 12 days of armed conflict, the government was ready to negotiate with the EZLN. As Hernández Castillo (2001: xii) describes:

> In their political discourse, Zapatistas talked about the immediate causes of their uprising, referring to the effect of neoliberal policies on the lives of thousands of indigenous peasants in Mexico and at the same time linking their struggle to the five hundred years of colonial and postcolonial indigenous resistance against racism and economic oppression.

The negotiations between the EZLN and the Mexican government led to the 1996 signing of the San Andrés Accords on Indigenous Rights and Culture that would ensure rights for indigenous peoples to autonomy and self-determination. Following the signing of the accords, however, the Mexican government refused to follow through with the agreements articulated therein and continued to prioritize neoliberal development over indigenous rights in addition to repressing Zapatista communities.

In spite of the social suffering faced by nonindigenous and indigenous citizens alike, most governments have, either voluntarily or in response to external pressures, continued to enforce neoliberal policies (Harvey 2005). Neoliberal philosophies continue to be pervasive across Latin America, shaping perspectives on the state's role, the content of public policies, and understandings of the relationship between citizens and the state. As Harvey (2005: 3) explains: "Neoliberalism has, in short, become hegemonic as a mode of discourse. It has pervasive effects on ways of thought to the point where it has become incorporated into the common-sense way many of us interpret, live in, and understand the world." Importantly, however, this so-called "common-sense" way of seeing and knowing the world has been contested by indigenous ways of knowing, based on epistemological and ontological perspectives that stand in contrast with Eurocentric ones. (More on this below.)

In sum, as governments embraced neoliberal reforms in Latin America, just as in other regions of the world, citizens (particularly the most vulnerable among them) faced socioeconomic and environmental suffering. The devastation wrought by neoliberalism has especially impacted indigenous peoples and their ancestral territories. Consequently, indigenous peoples contested structural adjustment reforms and neoliberal policies from early on, seeking recognition of their collective rights as nations, including the right to be consulted about projects that may impact them and Autonomy to govern themselves and their territories. Importantly, neoliberalism may continue to perpetuate social suffering even as governance takes on different forms in the region. The following section describes how Latin American states have attempted to mold indigenous collective rights demands to fit within neoliberal models, reflecting their own political and economic priorities.

Neoliberal Multiculturalism

In an apparent contradiction with the purported shrinking of the state and relatively restricted approach to social rights under neoliberalism, between the late 1980s and the mid-2000s, many Latin American governments enacted multicultural reforms in response to growing indigenous demands. However, such responses have inadequately addressed the demands of indigenous peoples. This inadequacy is particularly apparent when considering how governments have attempted to treat indigenous collective rights demands as malleable and to selectively shape them to fit within their own neoliberal agendas. This section details this process, also highlighting indigenous responses to this agenda.

The multicultural reforms enacted by Latin American governments focus on the Recognition of marginalized subpopulations by ensuring individual rights and, to a lesser extent, collective ones (Postero 2007). Multiculturalism refers to "the efforts of liberal democratic governments to accept and embrace [...] ethnic differences" among their citizenry (Postero 2007: 13). Ratification of ILO Convention 169 has been one of the most common reforms in the region. Some form of constitutional recognition of indigenous peoples is also common. For example, Article 2 of the Mexican Constitution defines Mexico as a singular ("única") multicultural nation.

It does not, however, acknowledge that there are many indigenous nations in Mexico that form part of a plurinational state. Similarly, in Guatemala, the 1995 Agreement on Identity and Rights of the Indigenous Population (also called the Indigenous Rights Accord) was part of the peace accords signed between the government and guerilla groups following the 36-year civil war. The Accord depicts Guatemala as a multiethnic, multicultural, and multilingual nation. However, the political and ethnic boundaries established in the Accord do not correspond to the plurinational social reality of Guatemala. In this sense, symbolic recognition has been easier for governments to adopt when they are able to do so without recognizing collective rights that could be perceived as threatening to the sovereignty of the nation state.

Likewise, many Latin American governments have demonstrated willingness to acknowledge cultural aspects of indigenous rights claims (such as ones focusing on identity and language) in social policy. For instance, "culturally inclusive" social programs, such as intercultural education and healthcare, often accompany governments' discursive commitment to multiculturalism. Several have gone so far as to formally recognize a right to indigenous participation and consultation as well as limited versions of autonomy. As Richards (2013: 10–11) writes, "Multiculturalism thus has accompanied neoliberal reform in many parts of the region, representing, at least on the surface, a transformation in the relationship between indigenous citizens and the state."

Scholars have wagered a range of hypotheses to explain the opening toward indigenous rights under neoliberalism. Brysk (2000) suggests that democratization logically led to the expansion of rights for all citizens. Yashar (1999), in contrast, maintains that expanding indigenous demands for political access, local autonomy, and participation were an unintentional by-product of incomplete processes of political liberalization combined with neoliberal cutbacks. And Van Cott (2000) argues that Latin American states have implemented multicultural reforms in order to prove their legitimacy as democratic actors on the world stage while also minimizing the potential for instability as a result of indigenous protest.

But rights and recognition are selectively granted to the indigenous only insofar as they do not threaten the state's political and economic priorities (Richards 2004; Hale 2006). Indeed, Hale (2002) argues that analyses like those above play down the extent to which multicultural and indigenous policies are part of the neoliberal program. Hale (2002: 487) explains instead a process "whereby proponents of the neoliberal doctrine pro-actively endorse a substantive, if limited, version of indigenous cultural rights, as a means to resolve their own problems and advance their own political agendas" and undermine pressures for more radical change. The result is "neoliberal multiculturalism," which Richards and Gardner (2013: 257) have defined as "a form of governance in which cultural recognition is promoted without the economic and political redistribution that would lead to greater equality." Hale (2002, 2006) and Postero (2004, 2007) have been the major theorists of neoliberal multiculturalism, although many others have demonstrated the limits of symbolic rights, recognition, and multicultural discourses and policies under neoliberalism (among others, see Andolina et al. 2005; Assies et al. 2006; Gustafson 2002; Horton 2006; Richards 2004, 2013; Stahler-Sholk 2007; Leyva et al. 2008).

Some scholars have argued that there are openings in the neoliberal multicultural framework that indigenous actors can exploit in order to work toward autonomy and self-governance. One example of this can be seen in the ways that some indigenous activists may work within the system by taking up government positions. For example, in Guatemala, some indigenous activists work in the Ministry of Education or Academy of Mayan Languages of Guatemala (a government organization) while attempting to promote recognition of the nation's plurinational character in the resources they produce and distribute to educators (Gardner and Richards 2017). Such efforts have provided mixed results though, often generating implicit consent for state priorities. For instance, Mapuche workers in the Chilean government have acted in ways that both support and impede movement goals (Park and Richards 2007). Nevertheless, indigenous peoples "taking state resources to sow the seeds of dissent may ultimately be an important first step in challenging the hegemony of neoliberal multiculturalism" (Park and Richards 2007: 1335).

Most agree, however, that the type of recognition granted through the neoliberal multiculturalism framework does more to generate consent for the neoliberal project than to transform the relationship between indigenous people and the state. Indeed, while governments may highlight diversity and grant a limited measure of autonomy, they have tended to construe demands for radical redistribution, autonomous territory, and self-government as counterproductive for multicultural society (Hale 2002; Richards 2013). In this way, multicultural policies help states and elites avoid addressing claims against the injustices of neoliberal capitalism. Thus, scholars and indigenous activists alike have voiced skepticism about multiculturalism as it has been incorporated into state policies in the neoliberal context (Assies et al. 2006; Becker 2011; Hale 2006; Lucero 2009; Postero 2007; Stahler-Sholk 2007).

Bolivia and Chile both exemplify the neoliberal multicultural moment, although each of these countries has followed a somewhat unique trajectory. According to Postero (2007), the Neoliberal multicultural era in Bolivia, characterized by demands for recognition and indigenous rights as well as state-driven multicultural reforms, ran from the late 1980s to the early 2000s. The government responded to some indigenous claims by enacting decentralization and incorporating participation into budgetary decisions. Nevertheless, broader structures of inequality remained in place, and Postero argues that neoliberal reforms "reinforced the racialized inequalities long existing in Bolivia, laying bare the continued monopoly of power held by dominant classes and transnational corporations" (2007: 4). Adding multiculturalism into the mix did little to change this. Nevertheless, as shall be seen below, the reforms did provide skills and discursive repertoires that facilitated claims and actions against the state at critical moments, ironically creating some openings for indigenous peoples to contest the neoliberal multicultural framework.

In Chile, the demands of Mapuche communities and organizations have long centered on both redistribution and recognition (Richards 2004, 2013). Under the Concertación, the government responded with some recognition, but to a much more limited extent than elsewhere in Latin America. In the 1990s, while other Latin American states were engaging in limited forms of recognition, the Concertación framed Mapuche demands largely as a problem of poverty. This was the case despite the creation of CONADI (the National Corporation for Indigenous Development) in 1993 and Orígenes (Origins, another indigenous development program) in 2001. The creation of a Comisión de Verdad Histórica y Nuevo Trato (Historical Truth and New Deal Commission) in 2001 and passage of ILO 169 in 2008 represented steps toward greater recognition, but constitutional recognition remained elusive. The limited scope of recognition in Chile is partly related to ongoing political and economic centralization, which forecloses the possibility of even the limited local or regional autonomy granted in other countries. But more importantly, beginning in the late 1990s, conflicts emerged over timber plantations, farms, and hydroelectric dams in ancestral Mapuche territory. A range of Mapuche organizations engaged in peaceful protests and land occupations and, in some cases, arson and equipment sabotage. In this situation, the Concertación was obliged to respond to Mapuche rights claims at the same time that it answered to demands from economic elites and the political right for harsher penalties against Mapuche activists. Ultimately, the Concertación paired multicultural developmentalist rhetoric and policies with the application of anti-terrorist legislation that originally had been designed to control Leftists during the Pinochet dictatorship, resulting in an indigenous policy that reinscribed notions of "good" and "bad" or, as Hale has put it, "permitted" and "insurrectionary" Indians (Hale 2002; Richards 2013). All told, while Chile was first in the region to embrace neoliberalism, it was one of the last to undertake multiculturalism.

Thus, even as Latin American governments embraced neoliberal multiculturalism into the twenty-first century, indigenous peoples continued to suffer from – and resist – the particular effects of neoliberal projects. Another example can be seen in Bolivia's "Water War" of 2000. Under pressure from the World Bank and the Inter-American Development Bank, Bolivia privatized the city of Cochabamba's water resources in a deal with the consortium Aguas de Tunari. Many Quechua citizens expressed their social suffering by describing how "their water rights [are] inherited through customary law" (Postero 2007: 194). Water rights are considered sacred as "a living being, and a resource for life" in the Andean *cosmovisión* (worldview) (Postero 2017: 32). After this back-door privatization, the consortium raised water rates and made illegal all private water collection schemes (Postero 2007). These actions ignited marches and other acts of resistance (e.g., public burnings of water bills) among indigenous and nonindigenous citizens, including rural irrigators, urban workers, local water collectives, and students (Albro 2005; Laurie et al. 2002). These acts of protest culminated in thousands fighting the police in the streets and the government cancelling its contract with the consortium (Postero 2017).

An additional example of continued indigenous mobilization against neoliberalism in the twenty-first century can be seen in Guatemala and southern Mexico, where indigenous people continue to contest transnational mining projects. Such projects have damaged local rivers, communities, animal life, and landscapes in their ancestral territories, which are understood as interconnected in the Mayan *cosmovisión*. The Mam, K'iche', Sipakapense, and other indigenous peoples in the region have organized *Consultas Comunitarias de Buena Fe* (Community Consultations) to vote against the mines and mining licenses granted by the Guatemalan government that provide transnational companies (such as the Canadian Goldcorp) access to explore and exploit the natural resources within indigenous ancestral territories. However, in spite of the backing of ILO 169, which was ratified by Guatemala in 1996, in many cases, the government has not followed through on the stipulation for governments to respect these consultations. Nonetheless, indigenous organizations such as the Council of the Mam Nation continue to demand recognition of their right as indigenous nations (or representatives thereof) to be consulted about transnational projects that could impact upon their ancestral territories (Gardner and Richards 2017).

Importantly, however, there is not a singular, homogenous, indigenous perspective about these development projects. Indeed, mining companies and timber corporations have even hired some local indigenous workers. But overwhelmingly throughout Latin America, indigenous mobilization efforts reject and resist such transnational mining projects and other development schemes contributing to environmental degradation because of the suffering these projects cause in their communities and ancestral territories and demand respect for their rights as peoples in these territories.

As described in this section, Latin American governments have responded to indigenous demands by enacting multicultural reforms that do not conflict with their own political and economic priorities. Indeed, neoliberal multiculturalism is an inadequate response to indigenous collective rights claims. Several Latin American governments have expressed interest in promoting the cultural rights of indigenous peoples while ignoring altogether the sociopolitical aspects of indigenous rights claims (e.g., rights to territory, autonomy, and self-determination). In this manner, states have avoided addressing the social suffering of indigenous peoples that is exacerbated by neoliberal capitalism. Nevertheless, as Latin American governments have continued to embrace neoliberal into the twenty-first century, indigenous peoples have been steady in their resistance.

Post-neoliberalism? Post-multiculturalism?

More recently, the debate has shifted from neoliberal multiculturalism to questions of whether Latin America is in a post-neoliberal and/or post-multicultural moment. This section reviews central issues surrounding these two interrelated questions and briefly introduces new directions for the field.

Scholars referring to a "post-neoliberal" moment argue that the election of Leftist governments throughout Latin America beginning in the 1990s and intensifying in the early 2000s demonstrates neoliberalism's waning hegemony (Ruckert et al. 2017). However, seeing the election of governments on the Left throughout the region as the product of a single phenomenon is problematic. While the move to the Left in Venezuela, Bolivia, Ecuador, and Argentina resulted from social mobilization in response to neoliberalism's failures, elsewhere, such as in Chile and

Brazil, the move was softer, involving neostructural policy reform seeking to "humanize" the free market fundamentalism of the neoliberal model (Leiva 2008).

The countries in which post-neoliberal policies have had the most relevance for indigenous peoples are, arguably, Ecuador and Bolivia. In the early 2000s, both countries explicitly addressed a new relationship with the indigenous by rewriting their constitutions and recognizing their nations' pluricultural and plurinational character within them. They have also sought to reduce poverty and increase investment in social services, financing this in part through the nationalization of extractive industries (Ruckert et al. 2017). These steps have nevertheless led to new contradictions. For instance, as we discuss more fully below, Postero (2017) details how the building of the TIPNIS highway through indigenous territory and neoextractivism in Bolivia have entailed violations of indigenous rights by the government of Evo Morales, Bolivia's first elected indigenous president. Most other countries have not addressed indigenous issues as a part of post-neoliberalization at all (Ruckert et al. 2017).

As Goodale and Postero (2013) have argued, even while neoliberalism was momentarily ruptured in countries like Bolivia and Venezuela, related discourses and practices have continued to shape economic and political decision-making throughout the region, leading many scholars and activists to wonder whether the post-neoliberal moment is more wishful thinking than reality. Indeed, the enduring prioritization of neoliberal development over indigenous rights has contributed to substantial skepticism on the part of indigenous movements throughout the region. For example, in 2018 when many Leftist organizations united in support of the newly elected Mexican President Andrés Manuel López Obrador and expected similar support from the EZLN, the Zapatistas refused to endorse the president-elect. Even while Lopez Obrador's future head of indigenous affairs has suggested a constitutional reform implementing the San Andrés Accords, the EZLN has expressed its distrust in the Mexican government's commitment to fulfilling such agreements.

The post-multicultural question is related to the post-neoliberal one in some cases (particularly Ecuador and Bolivia) but ultimately responds to a different set of issues, focusing especially on how neoliberal multiculturalism has coopted legitimate claims for recognition. Kaltmeier et al. (2012) time the backlash against multiculturalism as having started at the beginning of the 1990s, although this likely varies depending on the trajectories of individual countries. It may be worthwhile, therefore, to trace the trend away from multiculturalism in a few countries to illustrate this process.

With the protests of the early 2000s in Bolivia, there indeed occurred a shift away from recognition as a central demand of indigenous protest. Kaltmeier et al. (2012: 107) attribute this shift at least in part to the contradictory results of neoliberal multiculturalism, pointing out that the neoliberal multicultural project did not solely produce domination and self-governing subjects a la Foucault. These authors refer to the 1994 Ley de Participación Popular (Popular Participation Law) in Bolivia which, they write, "triggered far-reaching projects of resistance and decolonization as it provided the formal grounds for the formation and rise of political movements" including Evo Morales's Movimiento al Socialismo (Movement Toward Socialism), leading to his election as president in 2005. With those changes, Postero (2007) argues Bolivia entered a "post-multicultural" era. Rather than returning to the class-based politics of prior periods, in this new era, indigenous and poor Bolivians demanded a new relationship with the state on behalf of *all* Bolivians. These demands included ending race and class inequalities and returning national patrimony to the people and ensuring that development would be for the people rather than corporations. Still, the election of Morales was important for achieving changes that specifically benefitted indigenous people as well, such as the 2009 Constitution, mentioned above, which not only recognizes Bolivia as a plurinational state but also grants limited autonomy to indigenous peoples and acknowledges rights of the *Pachamama* (Mother Earth). The contradictions of neoliberal multiculturalism, in this sense, may contain the seeds of its own undoing.

Other countries, too, have seen growing skepticism about the promises of multiculturalism, even when they not have experienced the radical changes that occurred in Bolivia. For example, although he characterized Guatemala as in the midst of a neoliberal multicultural moment, Hale (2006: 37) observes that by the early 2000s, formal recognition and autonomy no longer held a preeminent position among indigenous demands there. As the state granted some forms of autonomy "in the form of decentralization, participatory budgeting, and various other types of limited local control," the challenge shifted to how to "prevail in negotiations over what that recognition actually means in practice." Nevertheless, ongoing struggles linked to demands for autonomy, respect for *Consultas Comunitarias* opposing state-sponsored mining and dam projects, and cross-border recognition signal that not all Maya peoples abandoned recognition-related demands altogether (Gardner and Richards 2017). Nevertheless, the general point that indigenous actors have become suspicious of the neoliberal multicultural agenda holds true.

Similarly, Becker (2011: 56) argues that the nature of the changes incorporated into Ecuador's 2008 Constitution, such as recognizing indigenous languages without granting them official status equal to Spanish, entails "minor cultural concessions" rather than the creation of "more inclusive social and economic systems." Partly in anticipation of such shortcomings, Becker writes that indigenous organizations began to emphasize priorities that could benefit a wider population (e.g., nationalization of natural resources and universal healthcare) in conjunction with ethno-cultural demands related to territory, language, history, and culture. But Becker argues that even this strategy was subject to a reductionist reading by the Ecuadorian state. A 2010 issue of *NACLA Report on the Americas* sums up the limits of multiculturalism by arguing that because recognition as achieved has been of little substance, indigenous peoples throughout the region are "after recognition" and are instead transferring their energies to demanding socioeconomic redistribution and combating the ravages of capitalism, such as mobilizing against "extractivist economies, environmental devastation, and rampant social inequality" (NACLA 2010).

NACLA may be overstating the extent to which indigenous movements have changed the character of their demands. In cases like Bolivia and Ecuador, the constitutional changes must be recognized as an important achievement rooted in movement activism, even as it is not always certain what recognizing plurinationality will mean in practice. And in other cases such as Chile, it is clear that the struggle for recognition itself remains unachieved (Richards and Gardner 2013). Nevertheless, as the recognition granted so little resembles the recognition movements have fought for, many have begun to rethink their goals and strategies (Hale and Millaman 2006, 2018).

Even in Bolivia, the transition from a multicultural nation to a plurinational one has been contradictory and not unilaterally lauded by indigenous people. While Morales's government has taken important steps to reduce poverty and discrimination and has nationalized extractive industries, Postero (2017) shows how its developmentalist priorities have led to a lessening focus on indigenous recognition over time in favor of greater attention to agricultural exports and, especially, extractivism. She unflinchingly reveals how the Morales government has turned its back on many of its earlier promises related to indigenous sustainability and environmentalism. For example, in 2011, indigenous peoples protested a massive highway development project under the Morales government that would cut through the TIPNIS indigenous territory and national park. The Morales administration supported this project by suggesting that the road would be a necessary means of transportation for goods and services in the region. But indigenous organizations argued that the project's design was a threat to indigenous autonomy and destructive to the biodiversity of the TIPNIS park and its "divine importance as part of Mother Earth," showing that indigenous "ways of life clash with industrialization agendas" (Brysk and Bennett 2012: 121). Thus, in addition to reneging on earlier environmental priorities, the developmentalist goals of the Morales government have resulted in sacrificing the well-being of some indigenous communities, a tendency that, Postero (2017) argues, tragically reproduces colonial racism.

Martínez Novo (2014) documents a similar trend in Ecuador during the Leftist government of Correa (2007–2017), whereby centralization of decision-making and extractivism lead to conflicts with indigenous organizations over lack of respect for their autonomy and the right to be consulted over decisions that impact upon their territories. She writes that the "ethnic project of this postneoliberal government is not very different from that of neoliberalism: the government offers limited symbolic recognition and some targeted redistribution that disciplines indigenous peoples and separates 'permitted Indians' from recalcitrant ones" (p. 121). She further argues that "postneoliberal multiculturalism does not promote the kinds of tolerance that permeated earlier neoliberal attitudes," leading to higher levels of criminalization, prejudice, and violence in response to indigenous claims (ibid.).

In the face of such contradictions, rather than shifting to focus outwardly on the ravages of capitalism, some indigenous movements have turned inward in response to the disappointments associated with neoliberal multiculturalism and its Leftist successors. Burguete (2008) observes that after years of negotiating and engaging in dialogue with the state, many indigenous peoples are seeking solutions and alternatives to the ravages of free market capitalism "from within their own roots." She understands these efforts as drawing on a *reserva comunal rebelde* (communal rebel reserve). For example, Hale and Millaman (2018: 11) describe the position of Héctor Llaitul, leader of the Coordinadora Arauco-Malleco autonomist Mapuche organization, as focusing on two main issues: "recuperation of Wallmapu (Mapuche ancestral territory), as a politics of anticolonial struggle; and refusal of political strategies focused principally on state-recognized 'rights,' which contribute directly to the logic of colonial dispossession." Hale and Millaman explain that "underlying both points is an insistence on Mapuche lifeways as the basis for autonomy, defined not as rights asked for and recognized by the state, but rather, as the recuperation and exercise of the self-determination lost with the military conquest and dispossession of the late 19th century." As an example of the "turning inward" Burguete references, Llaitul's is a much more radical claim than demands for rights to *either* recognition or redistribution.

The disillusionment with multicultural policies has also drawn a shift in academic work on the region, away from neoliberalism and multicultural policy and toward questions of ontological and epistemic difference and alternative futures. Some of this work comes out of the school of thought known as the "decolonial turn" (for instance, see Quijano 2007; Escobar 2007, 2010; Mignolo 2012; De la Cadena 2008). Like many indigenous activists themselves, scholars of the decolonial turn emphasize the importance of epistemological decolonization for indigenous and other subjugated peoples. They highlight the potential role of suppressed knowledges in constructing alternative modernities that stand in contrast to the hegemonic Eurocentric one. For example, Escobar (2007: 189) seeks to locate European modernity as "a particular local history." If this is true, he suggests, "radical alternatives to modernity are not a historically foreclosed possibility." Escobar (2007, 2010) thus explores epistemological and ontological challenges to the Eurocentric conception of modernity, particularly "relational ontologies," typical of indigenous and Afro-descendants, that imply "a different way of imagining life" (2010: 4). He elaborates:

> Relational ontologies [...] eschew the divisions between nature and culture, individual and community, us and them that are central to the modern ontology (that of liberal modernity). [...] these 'worlds and knowledges otherwise' have the potential to de-naturalize the hegemonic distinction between nature and culture on which the liberal order is founded and which in turn provides the basis for the distinctions between civilized and Indians, colonizer and colonized, developed and underdeveloped. (p. 39)

Decentering Eurocentric versions of modernity and drawing attention to the epistemic aspects of colonialism can open up space for seeking other, less exploitative, visions of the future. Nevertheless, despite its advantageous aspects, the decolonial turn has been subject to important critiques. Silvia Rivera Cusicanqui (2010), for example, contends that in a colonialist move, coloniality scholars reproduce knowledge originally produced in the Global South and by indigenous people without giving them credit. And indigenous scholar activists, such as the members of the Comunidad de Historia Mapuche (2012), have objected to the term "coloniality" itself, pointing out that formal colonialism is still in place in their ancestral territories. The important point here is less the sophisticated theorization associated with the decolonial turn and more the realm of possibility opened up by turning to indigenous epistemologies and ontologies in thinking about collective futures.

Conclusion

As argued throughout this chapter, Latin American governments have embraced neoliberalism, even as it has contributed to environmental degradation and perpetuated the social suffering of nonindigenous and indigenous citizens alike. However, resistance against neoliberalism has consistently impeded the progress of neoliberal projects. Indigenous peoples in Latin America continue to actively utilize an array of strategies to contest neoliberal projects and work toward a future in which the autonomy and well-being of all beings are held sacred.

References

Albro R (2005) The indigenous in the plural in Bolivian oppositional politics. Bull Lat Am Res 24(4):433–453
Andolina R, Radcliffe S, Laurie N (2005) Development and culture: transnational identity making in Bolivia. Polit Geogr 24(6):678–702
Assies W, Ramírez L, Del Carmen Ventura Patiño M (2006) Autonomy rights and the politics of constitutional reform in Mexico. Lat Am Caribb Ethn Stud 1:37–62
Auyero J (2012) Patients of the state: the politics of waiting in Argentina. Duke University Press, Durham
Becker M (2011) Correa, indigenous movements, and the writing of a new constitution in Ecuador. Lat Am Perspect 38(1):47–62
Brysk, A (2000) From tribal village to global village: indian rights and international relations in Latin America. Stanford University Press, Stanford
Brysk A, Bennett N (2012) Voice in the village: indigenous peoples contest globalization in Bolivia. Brown J World Aff 18(2):115–127
Burguete A (2008) Gobernar en la diversidad en tiempos de multiculturalismo en América Latina. In: Levya X, Burguette A, Speed S (eds) Gobernar (en) la diversidad: Experiencias indígenas desde América Latina. Hacia la investigación de co-labor. CIESAS/FLACSO-Ecuador y Guatemala, Mexico City, pp 15–64
Comunidad de Historia Mapuche (2012) Ta iñ fijke xipa rakizuameluwün: Historia, colonialismo y resistencia desde el país Mapuche. Comunidad de Historia Mapuche, Temuco
De la Cadena M (2008) Alternative indigeneities: conceptual proposals. Lat Am Caribb Ethn Stud 3(3):341–349
Escobar A (2007) Worlds and knowledges otherwise: the Latin American modernity/coloniality research program. Cult Stud 21(2–3):179–210
Escobar A (2010) Latin America at a crossroads: alternative modernizations, post-liberalism, or post-development? Cult Stud 24(1):1–65

Gardner JA, Richards P (2017) The spatiality of boundary work: political-administrative borders and Maya-Mam collective identification. Soc Probl 64:439–455

Goodale M, Postero N (2013) Neoliberalism, interrupted: social change and contested governance in contemporary Latin America. Stanford University Press, Stanford

Gustafson B (2002) Paradoxes of liberal indigenism: indigenous movements, state processes, and intercultural reform in Bolivia. In: Maybury-Lewis D (ed) The politics of ethnicity: indigenous peoples in Latin American states. Rockefeller Center for Latin American Studies, Cambridge, pp 267–308

Hale CR (2002) Does multiculturalism menace? Governance, cultural rights and the politics of identity in Guatemala. J Lat Am Stud 34:485–524

Hale CR (2006) Más que un indio: Racial ambivalence and neoliberal multiculturalism in Guatemala. School of American Research Press, Santa Fe

Hale CR, Millaman Reinao R (2006) Cultural agency and political struggle in the era of the indio permitido. In: Sommer D (ed) Cultural agency in the Americas. Duke University Press, Durham, pp 281–304

Hale CR, Millaman Reinao R (2018) Privatization of the 'historic debt'? Mapuche territorial claims and the forest industry in southern Chile. Lat Am Caribb Ethn Stud. https://doi.org/10.1080/17442222.2018.1510658

Harvey D (2005) A brief history of neoliberalism. Oxford University Press, Oxford

Haughney D (2006) Neoliberal economics, democratic transition, and Mapuche demands for rights in Chile. University Press of Florida, Gainesville

Hernández Castillo RA (2001) Histories and stories from Chiapas: border identities in Southern Mexico. University of Texas Press, Austin

Horton L (2006) Contesting state multiculturalisms: indigenous land struggles in eastern Panama. J Lat Am Stud 38(4):829–858

Kaltmeier O, Raab J, Thies S (2012) Multiculturalism and beyond: the new dynamics of identity politics in the Americas. Lat Am Caribb Ethn Stud 7(2):103–114

Laurie N, Andolina R, Radcliffe S (2002) The excluded 'indigenous'? The implications for multi-ethnic policies for water reform in Bolivia. In: Sieder R (ed) Multiculturalism in Latin America: indigenous rights, diversity, and democracy. Palgrave Macmillan, New York, pp 252–276

Leiva FI (2008) Latin American neostructuralism: the contradictions of post-neoliberal development. University of Minnesota Press, Minneapolis

Leyva X, Burguete A, Speed S (eds) (2008) Gobernar (en) la diversidad: Experiencias indígenas desde América Latina. Hacia la investigación de co-labor. CIESAS/FLACSO-Ecuador y Guatemala, Mexico City

Lucero JA (2009) Decades lost and won: indigenous movements and multicultural neoliberalism in the Andes. In: Burdick J, Oxhorn P, Roberts KM (eds) Beyond neoliberalism in Latin America? Palgrave Macmillan, New York, pp 63–81

Martínez Novo C (2014) Managing diversity in postneoliberal Ecuador. J Lat Am Caribb Anthropol 19(1):103–125

Mignolo WD (2012) Local histories/global designs: coloniality, subaltern knowledges, and border thinking. Princeton University Press, Princeton

NACLA Report on the Americas (2010) Introduction. After recognition: Indigenous peoples confront capitalism. Sep-Oct issue, pp 63–81

Park YJ, Richards P (2007) Negotiating neoliberal multiculturalism: Mapuche workers in the Chilean state. Soc Forces 85:1319–1339

Peck J, Tickell A (2002) Neoliberalizing space. Antipode 34(3):380–404

Portes A (1997) Neoliberalism and the sociology of development: emerging trends and unanticipated facts. Popul Dev Rev 23(2):229–260

Postero NG (2004) Articulations and fragmentations: indigenous politics in Bolivia. In: Postero NG, Zamosc L (eds) The struggle for indigenous rights in Latin America. Academic, Sussex, pp 189–216

Postero NG (2007) Now we are citizens: indigenous politics in postmulticultural Bolivia. Stanford University Press, Stanford

Postero NG (2017) The indigenous state: race, politics, and performance in plurinational Bolivia. University of California Press, Berkeley

Quijano A (2007) Coloniality and modernity/rationality. Cult Stud 21(2–3):168–178

Richards, P (2004) Pobladoras, indígenas, and the state: conflict over women's rights in Chile. Rutgers University Press, New Brunswick

Richards P (2013) Race and the Chilean miracle: neoliberalism, democracy, and indigenous rights. University of Pittsburgh Press, Pittsburgh

Richards P, Gardner JA (2013) Still seeking recognition: Mapuche demands, state violence, and discrimination in democratic Chile. Lat Am Caribb Ethn Stud 8(3):255–279

Rivera Cusicanqui S (2010) Ch'ixinakax utxiwa: Una reflexión sobre prácticas y discursos descolonizadores. Tinta Limón Ediciones y Retazos, Buenos Aires

Roberts BR, Portes A (2006) Coping with the free market city: collective action in six Latin American cities at the end of the twentieth century. Lat Am Res Rev 41(2):57–83

Ruckert A, Macdonald L, Proulx KR (2017) Post-neoliberalism in Latin America: a conceptual review. Third World Q 38(7):1583–1602

Stahler-Sholk R (2007) Resisting neoliberal homogenization: the Zapatista autonomy movement. Lat Am Perspect 34(2):48–63

Stephen LM, Speed S, Hernández Castillo RA (2006) Indigenous organizing and the EZLN in the context of neoliberalism in Mexico. In: Speed S, Hernández Castillo RA, Stephen LM (eds) Dissident women: gender and cultural politics in Chiapas. University of Texas Press, Austin, pp xi–xix

Van Cott DL (2000) The friendly liquidation of the past: the politics of diversity in Latin America. University of Pittsburgh Press, Pittsburgh

Villalón R (2007) Neoliberalism, corruption, and legacies of contention: Argentina's social movements, 1993–2006. Lat Am Perspect 34(2):139–156

Yashar DJ (1999) Democracy, indigenous movements, and the postliberal challenge in Latin America. World Polit 52(1):76–104

Settler Colonialism and Biculturalism in Aotearoa/New Zealand

48

Jessica Terruhn

Contents

Introduction	868
Te Tiriti o Waitangi/The Treaty of Waitangi	869
Settler Colonization: Alienation, Assimilation, and Activism	870
Becoming Bicultural: Māori Protest and the Politics of Redress	872
Biculturalism, Inequalities, and Neoliberalism	874
Waitangi Tribunal Settlements	875
Cultural Recognition and Language Revitalization	877
Biculturalism in Social Policy	878
Conclusion	880
Cross-References	881
References	881

Abstract

This chapter discusses biculturalism as the current political paradigm defining relations between the indigenous Māori population and the settler population of New Zealanders of European descent (Pākehā) in Aotearoa/New Zealand. Following a brief sociohistorical analysis of settler colonialism and the place of Te Tiriti o Waitangi/The Treaty of Waitangi, the chapter charts how biculturalism emerged in response to an indigenous rights movement that brought settler colonial injustices into clear view. Since its inception in the 1970s, state biculturalism has broadly encapsulated a politics of redress and reconciliation for the dispossession and destruction of indigenous communities at the hand of the settler state, but its scope and goals have been contested. In highlighting how biculturalism works in three key arenas – the Waitangi Tribunal, language revitalization, and social policy – the chapter discusses some of these contestations and their

---

J. Terruhn (✉)
Massey University, Auckland, New Zealand
e-mail: j.terruhn@massey.ac.nz

© The Author(s), under exclusive license to Springer Nature Singapore Pte Ltd. 2019
S. Ratuva (ed.), *The Palgrave Handbook of Ethnicity*,
https://doi.org/10.1007/978-981-13-2898-5_71

implications. The chapter centrally contends that while processes of reconciliation and redress through treaty settlements, efforts to revitalize te reo Māori, and initiatives to tackle socioeconomic inequalities between Māori and Pākehā have made some difference to Māori communities, these strategies have fallen short of addressing indigenous rights to and aspirations for sovereignty.

Keywords
Aotearoa/New Zealand · Settler colonialism · The Treaty of Waitangi · Te Tiriti o Waitangi · Māori · Pākehā · Biculturalism · Waitangi Tribunal

Introduction

This chapter discusses biculturalism in Aotearoa/New Zealand. This refers to the political relationship between two groups, the indigenous Māori population and the British Crown/New Zealand government, and, by extension, the settler population of New Zealanders of European descent (Pākehā) in the context of a settler society with a history of colonization.

Both Māori and Pākehā can be described as ethnic groups or, at least, as ethnic categories that can be, and are, measured in official statistics. However, in this discussion of biculturalism as a political arrangement, it is important to highlight those characteristics that determine the historical and contemporary relationship of these two groups. As such, Māori are more usefully defined as tangata whenua, the indigenous people of the land of Aotearoa/New Zealand, and Pākehā as "New Zealanders of a European background, whose cultural values and behaviour have been primarily formed from the experiences of being a member of the dominant group of New Zealand" (Spoonley 1993: 57). These definitions emphasize the two groups' structural locations in Aotearoa/New Zealand which is important in understanding biculturalism not simply as a form of "ethnic" or "intercultural" relations but as shaped by the power dynamics of settler colonialism.

Te Tiriti o Waitangi/The Treaty of Waitangi is central to understanding colonization, biculturalism, and settler-indigenous relations in Aotearoa/New Zealand. Since its signing in 1840, Te Tiriti has been – on the settler side – variously breached, ignored, dismissed as void, celebrated as evidence of progressive race relations, and given a central role as the foundation of a post-colonizing partnership. Māori have called the Treaty out as a fraud and have persistently called on the Crown to honor the obligations laid out in the document. Most of all, its meaning and its place in Aotearoa/New Zealand have been, and continue to be, fiercely debated.

The aim of this chapter is to map biculturalism as the dominant national political imaginary that defines settler-indigenous relations in Aotearoa/New Zealand. The first part of the chapter sketches historical settler colonial practices of alienating indigenous lands and assimilating Māori into settler society and the parallel history of Māori resistance and protest which ultimately ushered in the era of contemporary biculturalism. The second part of the chapter outlines how biculturalism has developed and what it looks like. There is no catch-all definition. Instead, biculturalism encompasses various facets: based on various Treaty principles, biculturalism largely focuses on reconciliation for past injustices, cultural recognition, as well as efforts to address persistent socioeconomic inequalities between Māori and Pākehā which are arguably the effect of settler colonialism. This chapter outlines how this plays out across a number of key domains, such as the Waitangi Tribunal which is tasked with investigating breaches of Te Tiriti; language revitalization strategies as an example of cultural recognition; and practices in the fields of health and education as prime arenas where inequalities between Māori and non-Māori are addressed.

Throughout, the chapter is premised on the argument that settler colonialism "is a structure not an event" (Wolfe 1999: 2). That is to say that even though colonization appears to be an event that lies in the past, and even though decolonizing efforts are made that address past colonial injustices and work toward reconciliation, the structures of the settler colonial society and state remain intact. As scholars within studies of settler colonialism emphasize, it is a contemporary phenomenon underpinned by the continued sovereignty of the settler state (Veracini 2010).

Te Tiriti o Waitangi/The Treaty of Waitangi

Te Tiriti o Waitangi/The Treaty of Waitangi was signed by representatives of the British Crown and several hundred Māori iwi (tribe) and hapū (sub-tribe) leaders on February 6, 1840 in Waitangi and subsequently in various other locations around the country. Te Tiriti/the Treaty was set up as a contract between the British Crown and Māori, who were acknowledged as a sovereign polity based on the Declaration of Independence signed in 1835. The document's three articles laid out assurances designed to guarantee the protection of mutual interests.

Since its signing, there has been much debate about the meaning of the document. This uncertainty stems from the fact that there are two different versions, an English version (the Treaty) and a version in the Māori language (Te Tiriti). Māori rangatira (chiefs) were presented with, and signed, a text in their own language. The first article demonstrably guaranteed "Crown obligations to protect rangatiratanga [sovereignty] rights in exchange for Crown rights to occupancy and governance" (Fleras and Spoonley 1999: 9). However, in the first article of the English version, the Crown claimed *sovereignty* over Aotearoa/New Zealand. The two versions of the second article were equally disparate. While Te Tiriti guaranteed Māori "the *absolute Chieftainship* [tino rangatiratanga] of their lands, of their homes and all their treasured possessions," the Treaty only promised Māori "the full, exclusive, and undisturbed *possession* of their Lands and Estates, Forests, Fisheries, and other properties (Walker 1990: 93, emphasis added)." The third article was similar in both languages and guaranteed Māori the rights and privileges of British subjects and Crown protection.

The Treaty of Waitangi is sometimes described as "a relatively enlightened social contract for its time" (Fleras and Spoonley 1999: 112) and it was, indeed, in part a result of a wave of humanitarianism that had emerged in England at the time. However, it was also undoubtedly a vehicle of annexation. With the English language version given preference, it paved the way for Crown sovereignty and rapid settler colonization. As discussed in the next section, this ushered in the large-scale alienation of Māori lands and the systematic marginalization of indigenous communities alongside what academic and activist Ranginui Walker (1990) referred to as "ka whawhai tonu mātou" – a "struggle without end" on the part of Māori to fight for sovereignty.

Settler Colonization: Alienation, Assimilation, and Activism

The British colonization of Aotearoa/New Zealand formed part of an immense migration of 50 million people over 200 years that created "neo-Europes" throughout the New World (King 2003: 170). Compared to its forays into other parts of the world, European settlement in Aotearoa/New Zealand was slow to begin with. Even though European whalers, sealers, and missionaries had been coming to New Zealand shores since 1769, by 1830 there were still no more than 300 of them. By 1840, the year Te Tiriti o Waitangi was signed, there were still no more than 2000 Europeans (King 2003: 169), compared to at least 80,000–100,000 Māori. Up until then, relations between the indigenous population and these European sojourners and settlers were mostly amicable and often mutually beneficial but indigenous-settler relations were transformed by the large influx of British settlers after 1840. Over the course of a mere 40 years, the settler population surged to nearly half a million people who were drawn to New Zealand by "the promise of prosperity and healthier environments, prospects for social advancement without the hurdles of a class system and, for investors, opportunities to enlarge capital" (King 2003: 170). These expectations were perfectly encapsulated in New Zealand Company founder Edward Gibbon Wakefield's vision of creating a "Better Britain."

Building a Better Britain that could accommodate the steady stream of settlers relied on the availability of land, and prospective settlers were given the impression that the land was theirs for the taking. While some Māori were initially eager to sell parts of their land to European settlers for strategic and economic reasons (Belich 1996), their willingness diminished as settler tactics became more aggressive under Governor George Grey, who Walker (1990: 110) calls "the author of colonial dispossession." In turn, Pākehā grew increasingly impatient with this reluctance and acquired land through various means, including forced purchases, legally sanctioned confiscation as punishment for rebellion, and the individualization of formerly collective land titles (Hill 2016). For instance, the Native Land Court, which was established in 1865, contributed greatly to land alienation by turning customary into individual land titles and allowing land sales to individual settlers rather than the Crown. Consequently, Māori were alienated from their traditional lands in large numbers. By 1865, 99 percent of New Zealand's South Island was owned by the Crown or the New Zealand Company. On the North Island, land alienation happened more gradually, but steadily nonetheless: between 1860 and 1910, Māori ownership of land decreased from 80 to 27 percent. Dispossession progressed even further in the twentieth century, with Māori land ownership reduced to a mere 9 percent by 1939.

Over the course of the nineteenth century, the colony was transformed into a British settler nation. Alongside British settlers came British flora and fauna, values and norms, names and knowledge systems, as well as British social, cultural, political, legal, and economic institutions. In 1852, the New Zealand Constitution Act laid the foundations for establishing a settler government and the first general election was held in 1853. Devolving legislative power over indigenous affairs to the settler government effectively entrenched settler colonialism and hastened the subjugation of Māori because it was arguably less concerned with their welfare than the Crown because they presented an obstacle to accumulating land for the benefit of settlers. Walker (1990: 111), for example, argues that the "white minority government" installed in 1854 constituted an "institutionalisation of racism at the inception of democracy in New Zealand [that] was the root cause of conflict between Maori and Pakeha in the North Island and the colonial spoliation which followed." The fact that in 1867, four Māori parliamentary seats were established to represent the indigenous population is often cited as an example of progressive settler-indigenous relations in the colony of New Zealand, but it can equally be interpreted as a strategy to limit indigenous representation (Durie 2005b). To begin with, Māori population numbers at the time would have warranted 14 or 15 seats of a total of 76 (King 2003: 257). In addition, Ward (1995) argues, nominal equality before the law was based on ideas of homogeneity and European superiority that did not allow for alternative worldviews. Thus, while Māori were amalgamated into the nation-state as imperial subjects rather than expunged from it, they were nevertheless marginalized and subjugated to the control of the settler state.

The desire to assimilate Māori into the new settler nation was indeed an important building block of creating a British settler society. The idea of cultural assimilation conformed to dominant ideas about European racial superiority, paternalistic doctrines of protection, and the White Man's burden of civilizing "the natives," and was thus sometimes described as a privilege (Meihana 2017). Of course, assimilation also fit with settler colonial aspirations of acquiring land. Land alienation and the transformation from collective to individual land tenure, for instance, were a key part of assimilation. These practices not only destroyed the economic basis of Māori communities but also undermined tribal collective identity and belonging which were intrinsically linked to land. But there were many other institutional domains that furthered the project of cultural assimilation. Schools perhaps most prominently served this function. Māori children were punished for speaking their native language because English language proficiency was regarded as a gateway to civilization and social betterment. Over time, this eroded the social, economic, and cultural base of Māori communities and te reo Māori became endangered. Stark figures illustrate this point: Te reo proficiency of Māori school children declined from 90 percent in 1913 to less than 5 percent in 1975 (Durie 1998: 60).

Post-1840, the conflicting interests of settlers and indigenous peoples set in motion widespread resistance against Crown breaches of Te Tiriti and a fight for "social justice, equality, and self-determination" (Walker 1990). The indigenous struggle against colonization included armed and nonviolent resistance, court cases, petitions and submissions, occupation of land, as well as the kīngitanga (King movement), which aimed to unite Māori across tribal boundaries under a Māori king. The New Zealand Wars, which were fought between 1845 and the early

1870s in various parts of the North Island, form part of this historical contest between European settlers and Māori. Although land was central to these wars, they were ultimately a struggle over sovereignty.

Notably, all of these acts of Māori resistance were based on an interpretation of the Treaty as "a charter for biculturalism" (Walker 1986: 4), that is, a partnership of two sovereign peoples. However, The Treaty of Waitangi and the obligations it entailed receded from settler consciousness, not least because the rapid growth of the settler population had consolidated the British colony (Orange 1987: 185). In addition, the racism that pervaded the settler colonial project meant that ignoring or dismissing the Treaty was easily justified. In 1877, in a court hearing over contested Māori land, Chief Justice John Prendergast declared The Treaty of Waitangi void, stating that "the whole treaty was worthless – a simple nullity [which] pretended to be an agreement between two nations but [in reality] was between a civilised nation and a group of savages" (cited in King 2003: 326).

As Durie (2005a: 15) notes, Māori opposition to breaches of Te Tiriti waned as the nineteenth century progressed and towards the end of the century the belief that Māori were dying out took hold in New Zealand. The mass arrival of European settlers in Aotearoa/New Zealand had been matched by a steep decline of the Māori population as a result of both conflict and introduced diseases. In 1896, 42,500 Māori compared to approximately 700,000 Pākehā (Pool 1991). While some contemporaries expressed a modicum of regret, the decline in the Māori population was generally regarded as the inevitable result of the superiority of the white race. As Featherstone noted in 1881 (cited in Rangiwai 2011: 53), "the Maoris [sic] are dying out, and nothing can save them. Our plain duty, as good, compassionate colonists, is to smooth down their dying pillow. The history will have nothing to reproach us with." Indeed, the notion of a "vanishing race" served to further naturalize the settler colonial project and gave impetus to the project of assimilation as the only way for the remaining Māori to survive.

Such settler colonial discourses of benevolence stand in stark contrast with the practices of land theft, control, and destruction of indigenous communities charted in this section. More than anything, settler colonialism vastly benefitted settlers at the expense of Māori. It conferred wealth and other privileges on the settler population while leading to collective and multigenerational disadvantage or "trauma" for Māori (Bell 2008; Borrell et al. 2018). However, contradicting settler predictions, Māori did not vanish; instead, their population began to recover after 1896 so that by the end of the Second World War the pre-contact figure of approximately 100,000 Māori was re-established. The following section maps the post-World War II indigenous rights movement that led to the institution of a bicultural polity in Aotearoa/New Zealand.

Becoming Bicultural: Māori Protest and the Politics of Redress

In the second half of the twentieth century, a "Māori renaissance" – a "major reassertion of their cultural, social, economic, and political aspirations" (Hill 2012: 273) – took hold. Its roots lie in the Māori urban migration which gathered momentum after the Second World War: in 1946, nearly three quarters of all Māori lived rurally, while one quarter lived in urban areas. Thirty years on, the population stood at 276,000 and the urban-rural ratio was reversed. For the state and many Pākehā, urbanization held the promise of further assimilating Māori because it entailed greater distance to traditional home lands, less exposure to the Māori language and other customary cultural expressions, as well as increased proximity with Pākehā (Hill 2012; Ryks et al. 2016). In 1961, the Hunn Report revealed dramatic inequalities between Māori and Pākehā and proposed to hasten integration in order to uplift Māori into "modernity" (Harris 2004: 21). Typical for the time and congruent with racialized colonial discourses, deficit theories – which see the causes for inequalities in cultural or even genetic deficiencies of disadvantaged groups – dominated explanations for these inequalities and provided the justification for further assimilation under the new moniker of "integration." This affected both rural and urban Māori. In rural areas, Māori schools were closed from 1969, while in the cities, the practice of "pepper potting" (dispersing Māori families throughout Pākehā streets) was used to encourage integration and avoid the formation of Māori enclaves.

Yet, rather than subduing Māori identities and tribal connections, evidence suggests that the integrationist approach played an important role in igniting a reassertion of indigeneity and catalyzing the sovereignty movement (Hill 2012). Against all expectations, urban Māori retained their iwi, hapū, and whānau connections and, in addition, developed complementary collective pan-tribal identities (Hill 2012: 263). Urban Māori initiated new networks and social groups and, in the process, new leadership developed to complement the traditional rurally based rangatira (Chiefs) and kaumātua (elders). Various new organizations, such as the Māori Women's Welfare League (MWWL) and the New Zealand Māori Council (NZMC) – founded in 1951 and 1961 respectively – successfully argued that Māoritanga (Māori culture and language) needed to be nurtured and revived in order to assist Māori in dealing with the challenges the urban environment presented (Hill 2012: 267). Simultaneously, activist groups such as Ngā Tamatoa initiated street-level protests against land alienation, and the suppression of Māori language and culture, breaches of Te Tiriti o Waitangi, and systemic discrimination. Indigenous protests took various forms but the activism of the 1970s in particular was characterized by highly visible events. Landmark protests included the land march of 1975 which protested – under the slogan "not one more acre" – against contemporary government policies that enabled land alienation, for example, through the compulsory acquisition of what was deemed "unproductive" land (Harris 2004). In 1977–1978, Ngāti Whātua Ōrākei occupied Bastion Point in Auckland for 506 days in an attempt to hold on to a last remaining piece of land which had been gradually seized by the Crown since 1869. The nonviolent occupation ended with the forced eviction of the occupiers under the Trespass Act 1968 (Harris 2004).

The Land Rights Movement insisted on returning the stolen land as a way of honoring the obligations and rights laid out in Te Tiriti o Waitangi. Activists argued that the Treaty was a fraud. According to Donna Awatere (1984), calls to honor The Treaty of Waitangi within a bicultural framework amounted to relinquishing the sovereignty Māori had tried to hold on to since 1840. The publication of Donna Awatere's *Maori Sovereignty* (Awatere 1984) – a powerful critique of settler colonialism – has been described as "one of those defining historical moments that challenged people's perception of society" (Fleras and Spoonley 1999: 45). Such analyses of settler colonialism challenged hegemonic Pākehā narratives, eventually leading to "the realisation that New Zealand identity was inextricably linked with European culture, infused with colonial assumptions, overwhelmingly White in orientation, and larded with self-serving myths" (Fleras and Spoonley 1999: 43).

While the activism of that time fitted with the long tradition of Māori resistance since 1840, the movement's visibility and connection to international liberation, civil rights, and anti-racist movements made it impossible to ignore. Broadcast into Pākehā homes only recently fitted with television sets, the protests revealed the colonial, racist underbelly of New Zealand society and the growing evidence of stark disparities between Māori and Pākehā across a range of social indicators and an inability of the state to improve the situation "made Māori challenges to the legitimacy of the state all the more potent and forceful" (Poata-Smith 2013: 150). The indigenous rights movement put substantial pressures on the New Zealand government, forcing it to address indigenous grievances "for broken Treaty promises, loss of their rangatiratanga, land and resources, and lack of social, political, and economic parity with non-Māori" (Sullivan 2016: 131).

Biculturalism, Inequalities, and Neoliberalism

There is neither a precise date nor one specific piece of legislation to pinpoint the adoption of biculturalism as a policy framework. Instead, various discourses, practices, and pieces of legislation that encompass biculturalism were implemented over time and continue to be in the making today. Perspectives and approaches have fluctuated with changing political environments. While generally centered on the idea that the state should meet its Treaty obligations, the lack of consensus in interpreting the Treaty has been one of the main sources of contestation over the meaning of biculturalism. Johnson (2008: 36) identified a continuum of definitions. At one end, "soft" approaches focus on mainstreaming Māori culture and abolishing discrimination and prejudice. "Moderate," "inclusive," and "strong" forms aim at alleviating inequalities, being culturally responsive and allowing Māori a degree of autonomy. At the other end, proponents of "hard" definitions work toward transforming society with a view to establish tino rangatiratanga. In practice, biculturalism has largely revolved around the middle ground of responding to, and accommodating Māori needs and the key goals, as defined by the settler state, has revolved around reconciliation, economic development, and recognition. The following sections briefly outline the following key aspects: the Waitangi Tribunal which investigates claims of historical breaches of Te Tiriti o Waitangi and determines appropriate settlements, strategies to revitalize te reo Māori, and social policies designed to alleviate inequalities.

To better understand how these goals developed, it must be noted that the beginnings of developing a Tiriti-based biculturalism coincided with another large reform program instigated by the fourth Labour government elected in 1984: the nation's sharp turn from welfare state to neoliberalism. This shift included greater emphasis on the power of the free market, globalization, and the privatization of public services. At the time, the introduction of these comprehensive economic reforms caused some optimism among many Māori leaders. Disenchanted with the paternalism and racism of previous governments, Māori were hopeful that the envisaged economic and social reforms with their promise of choice would be beneficial to indigenous communities. Especially the devolution of public services was regarded as an opportunity to develop by-Māori-for-Māori services that would be able to better meet the needs of Māori communities through greater self-determination and control over their own affairs (Smith 2007: 335).

However, one consequence of the neoliberal reform program was a vast increase in socioeconomic inequality over the course of the 1980s and 1990s. The reforms had far-reaching material consequences for all New Zealanders, but they hit Māori and Pasifika communities the hardest because their younger and less-educated populations were more vulnerable to economic restructuring than non-Māori when jobs in low-skilled occupations disappeared en masse during the 1980s (Poata-Smith 2013; Smith 2007). Between 1988 and 1992 alone, Māori unemployment rose from 13.5 percent to 27.3 percent (Poata-Smith 2013: 151), contrasting with a rise in the general unemployment rate from 5.7 to 10.8 percent in the same period (OECD no date). Māori remain overrepresented in many negative social indicators, and even though there have been improvements for all New Zealanders in some areas, the gaps between Māori and Pākehā have remained and in some instances widened.

In many ways, the elements that can be said to encapsulate biculturalism have become increasingly focused on Māori economic development. Settlements for breaches of Te Tiriti, as discussed below, fall into this paradigm in that redress for grievances consists primarily of financial compensation that is aimed at strengthening iwi economies (Bargh 2012).

Waitangi Tribunal Settlements

One of the primary sites of biculturalism and the politics of reconciliation is the Waitangi Tribunal, a statutory authority that examines Māori claims of breaches of Te Tiriti o Waitangi. The investigation of claims leads to a report of the Tribunal's findings and recommendations for appropriate remedies which are then negotiated between the government's Office for Treaty Settlements (OTS) and claimants. First established in the 1975, Treaty of Waitangi Act, the Waitangi Tribunal, was set up to investigate contemporary Treaty violations in response to widespread protest. In 1985, its remit was extended to include historic grievances. Grievances brought before the Tribunal are mostly land loss claims but there are also other types of claims, such as those relating to natural, commercial, and other resources. Most claims are lodged by iwi but there are also national claims such as the Te Reo Māori claim which resulted in strategies to revitalize the language and make it one of New Zealand's official languages, as discussed in more detail further below.

The treaty settlement process is often seen as a pivotal element of decolonization and it has certainly benefitted indigenous communities in a number of ways. The decolonizing element is perhaps most manifest in the statement that "The Crown has accepted a moral obligation to resolve historical grievances in accordance with the principles of The Treaty of Waitangi" (Office of Treaty Settlements 2018). Major settlements have been achieved with a number of iwi across New Zealand. Deeds of settlement typically consist of financial compensation and a Crown apology but also variously include transfers of assets and property and other forms of cultural recognition, such as the renaming of places (Hill 2016; Office of Treaty Settlements 2018). These settlements have substantially increased the asset base of some iwi, making economic development and a degree of self-determination possible. Beyond that, the Waitangi Tribunal has also played an important role in revising dominant settler colonial historiography. For one, the process of recovering hapū and iwi histories as part of preparing a claim has catalyzed a "renewed sense of social and cultural identity" (Moon 2011: 524) among Māori but, secondly, it has also had an effect on the majority group and settler (state) – indigenous relations in so far as the research conducted by the Tribunal was part and parcel of a broader radical revision of history that exposed hegemonic settler narratives as myths (Sullivan 2016).

Notwithstanding these achievements, there are clear limitations to the settlement process. There are three main strands of critique. For one, the process is exclusively dictated by the state. As Ani Mikaere (2004: 43) has noted, the Tribunal's recommendations are not binding, and "claimants are typically presented with a 'take-it-or-leave-it' bottom line, with the Crown prepared to negotiate on minor matters only." Secondly, settlements are bound to a corporate approach. Maria Bargh (2012) argues that the ways in which the settlement process is aligned with neoliberal ideals of commodification and corporatism is at best unhelpful and at worst amounts to a form of neocolonization. Thirdly, settlements seldom involve any return of land (Hill 2016). Indeed, land rights have remained an issue. Following public concern that Māori might be able to claim customary rights to the foreshore and seabed of New Zealand beaches, the government made it impossible to test these rights in court by passing the 2004 Foreshore and Seabed Act which established exclusive Crown ownership of the contested area. This piece of legislation was criticized as "the most recent example of illegitimate colonial land confiscation" (Borrell et al. 2009). It caused much consternation among Māori, leading to large-scale protests, including a hīkoi from Northland to Parliament in Wellington reminiscent of the 1975 land march (Harris 2004). The protests against the Foreshore and Seabed Act culminated in the formation of the Māori Party which has been able to negotiate critical issues for Māori communities, especially once entering the government as the National Party's coalition partner in 2008. Repealing the Foreshore and Seabed Act was central to the party's platform. Interestingly, the eventual repeal stated that no one owned the Foreshore and Seabed (apart from private areas) but also contained a provision that gave the Crown the right to claim ownership over foreshore and seabed areas where resources (such as oil) were found.

A number of commentators have argued that one of the main limitations of Treaty settlements is that it stifles and contains Māori aspirations for tino rangatiratanga and in no way challenges the structures and sovereignty of the settler state (Bargh 2012; Bell 2008; O'Sullivan 2007; Sullivan 2016). This is especially palpable in light of the Tribunal's 2014 finding in the WAI 1040 inquiry. The Ngāpuhi iwi had brought a claim before the Tribunal to argue that they did not cede sovereignty when they signed Te Tiriti o Waitangi. The Tribunal upheld this claim which presents a momentous new interpretation of Te Tiriti that asserts Māori sovereignty. However, following the announcement, the then Prime Minister John Key asserted that the finding had no bearing on "the Government's authority to rule over New Zealand" (Stuff 2014).

As of now, most historical claims have been settled and Aotearoa/New Zealand is said to be entering a post-settlement era. It is conceivable that this will entail renewed debate about the place of Te Tiriti o Waitangi. Many members of the majority group of Pākehā will argue that the "full and finite" settlement of claims should bring an end to discussions of the Treaty while for many Māori, Treaty settlements are only the beginning of a much more substantial process of constitutional reform.

Cultural Recognition and Language Revitalization

The concern for – and initiatives to revitalize – te reo Māori also emerged out of the indigenous rights movement of the 1970s. As part of this, a number of iwi brought a claim to the Waitangi Tribunal to argue that the systematic destruction of the Māori language by the settler colonial power constituted a breach of Te Tiriti o Waitangi. In 1986, the Waitangi Tribunal found in favor of the claimants and recognized te reo Māori as a taonga (treasure) that is guaranteed Crown protection under Article 2 of Te Tiriti o Waitangi. The 1987 Māori Language Act, which was a result of the Tribunal's finding, declared te reo Māori an official language of the country and tasked a newly established Māori Language Commission with finding ways to support the language. More precisely, the Commission's function was to "promote the Māori language, and, in particular, its use as a living language and as an ordinary means of communication" (Parliamentary Counsel Office 2016).

Since then, strategies have focused primarily on education and broadcasting as avenues for encouraging the use and learning of te reo. Kōhanga reo (language nests for preschoolers), kura kaupapa (Māori immersion schools), and wānanga (tertiary institutions founded on kaupapa Māori principles) became instrumental in promoting te reo Māori. In addition, iwi radio stations and, more recently, a public Māori television channel (est. 2004) and a dedicated Te Reo channel (est. 2008) have worked under the remit of promoting indigenous culture and language. With regards to education, it needs to be noted that Māori themselves had begun this process well before legislation provided a more formal framing. For instance, kōhanga reo were not a new idea but a continuation of a flaxroots movement of whanau (families) that had initiated Māori immersion programs at the preschool level and had established more than 200 kōhanga reo by 1982, 5 years before the Māori Language Act. Today, there are approximately 460 kōhanga reo, 72 kura kaupapa, and 3 wānanga (Higgins 2016: 32).

Such initiatives are internationally respected as exemplary efforts to revitalize indigenous languages and yet, te reo remains on the list of endangered languages. For one, the share of Māori speakers of te reo remained constant at approximately one quarter from the mid-1990s until 2006 (while the Māori population increased) but dropped to 20 percent in the 2013 census. Secondly, both the initiatives themselves and the ways statistics about reo proficiency are collected also suggest that te reo has been somewhat siloed and the responsibility of revitalizing the language has predominately fallen to Māori. Hill (2016) has described language revitalization as part of a move from assimilation to biculturalism, but for non-Māori, exposure to the language has certainly remained optional. While a range of Māori words have entered into every day and formal New Zealand English and public institutions often carry bilingual names, it is rarely used outside of settings such as marae (Māori meeting houses). Indeed, despite its status as official national language, there is still much debate about the place of te reo in New Zealand society. For instance, there have been complaints about the occasional use of te reo on "mainstream" public TV and on Radio New Zealand, a public national radio service, which suggests that for many Pākehā public displays of te reo are often only palatable when they are contained in a dedicated television channel. A further current debate revolves around the introduction of te reo Māori as a compulsory subject in school curricula. While the proposal to make te reo compulsory in schools remains contentious, there are also positive signs of an appetite for learning te reo as evident in the high demand for te reo courses offered by tertiary education providers.

Higgins (2016) argues that the Māori Language Commission and the strategies that have been implemented have failed to normalize the use of te reo as an ordinary means of communication as originally outlined in the Māori Language Act. Higgins makes a noteworthy argument that ties such considerations to Te Tiriti: She suggests that protecting te reo as a taonga (with reference to Article 2 of Te Tiriti) may have contributed to its treatment as a treasure that is only carefully used in certain domains of public life. Instead, the promotion of te reo should be regarded as a question of citizenship (as per Article 3) that all New Zealanders – not just Māori – should be invested in as part of "our landscape and our identity as a country" (Higgins 2016: 36).

Biculturalism in Social Policy

Some commentators have argued that more attention has been paid to cultural recognition than to improving the material wellbeing of Māori (Kennedy 2017) and research has shown that Pākehā are much more amenable to symbolic elements of biculturalism than to measures that entail a redistribution of resources (Sibley et al. 2005). However, addressing inequalities across a range of social indicators has been an important part of biculturalism. As mentioned earlier in this chapter, Māori (alongside Pasifika) were particularly affected by the neoliberal reforms of the 1980s which was reflected in negative statistics on employment, incomes, health, and education. In 1998, Te Puni Kōkiri (the Ministry of Māori Development) drew urgent attention to these stark socioeconomic disparities in its report *Progress towards Closing the Social and Economic Gaps Between Māori and Non-Māori*.

These inequalities were addressed in government policy initiatives such as "Closing the Gaps" in the year 2000. However, as Humpage (2006) succinctly argues, New Zealand's social policy approach at the time was dominated by a social exclusion/inclusion paradigm imported from Europe that sat in tension with indigenous rights discourses specific to the New Zealand context. Despite references to The Treaty of Waitangi, to Treaty principles such as participation, and to greater Māori representation and self-determination, it ultimately aligned with neoliberal prerogatives of individual responsibility and equality of opportunity rather than outcome (Humpage 2006). While policies such as "Closing the Gaps" ostensibly offer greater self-determination through devolution of services, this is debatable. Hill and Bönisch-Brednich (2009: 250), for instance, argue that devolution amounts to an "'unburdening of the welfare state' partly in the guise of addressing Maori aspirations." While the "pretext" argument may be seen as controversial, it is certainly the case that Māori service providers were "believed to most 'efficiently' reduce Māori disparity and dependency" (Humpage 2008: 255).

Despite such policy initiatives, notable inequalities between Māori and Pākehā persist. A recent gap analysis (Collins et al. 2014) shows that progress has been made in some areas and gaps are decreasing; in other areas, however, gaps have actually widened. As with the effects of neoliberalism in the 1980s and 1990s, the Global Financial Crisis has hit Māori and Pasifika communities the hardest. To give some pertinent examples, the gap in life expectancy at birth between Māori and Pākehā closed dramatically over the course of the twentieth century but began to widen again, so that in 2013, the gap was bigger than in the mid-1980s. Unemployment is a further interesting example in that even though the gap is narrowing, at the current rate it would take 150 years to close the gap. Rates of homeownership have been falling across the board as house prices have increased at a much faster rate than wages but the gap between Māori and Pākehā is widening. In 2013, only one third of all Māori in the age group of 25–44 owned their home, compared to 57 percent of Pākehā (Collins et al. 2014).

In 2018, a claim was brought before the Waitangi Tribunal in which Māori health leaders argue that "inequity and institutionalised racism in the health system exists and the Crown is failing to care for Māori health and wellbeing" (The New Zealand Herald 2018). The claimants argue that more autonomy and self-determination in health service delivery is necessary. National Hauora Coalition chief executive, Simon Royal, is cited as saying that "the ultimate solution lies in constitutional reform based on Te Tiriti o Waitangi that entrenches equity of outcome and Māori participation in achieving this." This aligns with arguments made by other critical scholars in the field of health who have said that addressing disadvantage needs to be political work that tackles the causes rather than the symptoms of disadvantage and that also questions settler colonial practices (Came et al. 2018; Came and Tudor 2016).

In the domain of education, progress in reducing inequalities has been slightly more pronounced. For instance, the gaps in the percentage of school leavers with an

NCEA Level 2 qualification or with University Entrance have declined and are set to be closed within a few decades (Collins et al. 2014). Perhaps more so than in the domain of health, the approach to improving education outcomes for Māori has been dominated by a focus on cultural recognition and revitalization as a way to improve achievement. The Education Act 1989 determined that schools have to honor The Treaty of Waitangi, but this commitment is assigned to individual schools and, in practice, this is often very limited (Lourie 2016). According to the Education Review Office (ERO), schools and teachers have to provide evidence of bicultural practice, but often these do not extend beyond a minimum of symbolic acts. Indeed, a strong focus on culture pervades the Treaty discourse in education. According to Lourie (2016: 641), "promoting and affirming 'traditional' Māori culture was thought to be a means of eliminating, or at least reducing, ethnic inequalities." This bears two dangers. One is the danger to essentialist Māori culture, disregarding the complexities within Māori as an ethnocultural group. The other danger is that culture overrides the more structural factors of socioeconomic inequalities in thinking through ways of addressing discrepancies in educational opportunities and outcomes.

Conclusion

The extent and effect of the transformations that have taken place under the umbrella of state biculturalism are contested. Some commentators, such as King (2003: 487), optimistically concluded that the set of measures designed to address grievances and inequalities "so changed the face of New Zealand life in the 1980s and 1990s that their cumulative effect could legitimately be called a revolution." Others are much more cautious. Johnson (2008: 48), for instance, sees biculturalism as an "as yet unfulfilled promise," and O'Sullivan (2007: 3) argues that, in its current incarnation, biculturalism keeps Māori in the position of a junior partner dependent on the government. One particular shortcoming is found in the focus on material disadvantage and individual needs, rather than on Māori as a collective with indigenous rights (Durie 2005a: 205). Some of these perspectives echo Awatere's (1984: 60) early insistence that "the kaupapa is Maori Sovereignty. It must not be biculturalism. All efforts at biculturalism have only resulted in integration and assimilation, bitterness and tears."

The politics of redress were undoubtedly matched by a wider acceptance of "symbolic" biculturalism by Pākehā (Hill and Bönisch-Brednich 2009), such as accepting Māori cultural expressions and worldviews; integrating Māori vocabulary into New Zealand English, making Māori protocol part of many official functions; and, to some extent, acknowledging the need for reparations and policies that address persisting inequalities. Nonetheless, a pronounced reactionary stance, and "Treaty fatigue," could be discerned as early as the turn of the century (Hill and Bönisch-Brednich 2009: 246). Various commentators have noted an increasing resentment of Treaty settlements and policies specifically aimed at Māori (Barber 2008; Meihana 2017), and a more general "refusal" to see and acknowledge "poverty, racism, discrimination, and marginalization" as the pervasive social problems they are (Smith 2013: 230). Don Brash's 2004 *Nationhood* speech, delivered against the backdrop of the Seabed and Foreshore debate mentioned earlier in this chapter, was perhaps the epitome of the revival of the "one people" paradigm. In this speech, Brash (2004), the then head of the National Party and leader of the opposition, attacked policies aimed specifically at Māori as preferential treatment based on race/ethnicity, and diagnosed a Māori "grievance industry" designed to keep Pākehā in a perpetual position of blameworthy colonizer. Such discourses of reverse racism continue today. For instance, "Hobson's Pledge" is a group who invoke the New Zealand Bill of Rights Act to argue that certain measures designed to address Māori grievances and inequities constitute discrimination on the grounds of race. Such discourses of Māori privilege rely on the racialization of Māori in order to deflect from indigeneity and a history of settler colonization as the basis for indigenous rights.

In many ways, The Treaty of Waitangi has been amenable to the settler government because it paved a way to re-legitimizing the presence of settlers and the sovereignty of the settler state through a "treaty-driven myth of the co-founding origins of New Zealand, within a bicultural vision of a common destiny with its accompanying ideological and political framework" (Pearson 2000: 102). Reconciliation, while arguably important, in some ways also protects the sovereignty of the settler state by aiming to subdue indigenous aspirations for sovereignty in favor of subsuming them into the reconciled nation. As such, Treaty settlements are important but cannot be the end point because they do little to enable Māori autonomy (Hill 2016).

In sum, the conclusions about the measures that can be said to encompass contemporary biculturalism can only be mixed. While processes of reconciliation and redress through the Waitangi Tribunal, efforts to revitalize te reo Māori, and initiatives to tackle inequalities have made some difference to iwi and Māori more broadly, the main problem is that they fall short of granting the sovereignty Māori never ceded when they signed Te Tiriti o Waitangi.

Cross-References

▶ Role of Crown Health Policy in Entrenched Health Inequities in Aotearoa, New Zealand

References

Awatere D (1984) Maori sovereignty. Broadsheet, Auckland
Barber K (2008) 'Indigenous rights' or 'racial privileges': the rhetoric of 'race' in New Zealand politics. Asia Pac J Anthropol 9(2):141–156. https://doi.org/10.1080/14442210802023665
Bargh M (2012) The post-settlement world (so far): impacts for Maori. In: Wheen NR, Hayward J (eds) Treaty of Waitangi settlements. Bridget Williams Books, Wellington, pp 166–181
Belich J (1996) Making peoples: a history of the New Zealanders: from Polynesian settlement to the end of the nineteenth century. Penguin, Auckland

Bell A (2008) Recognition or ethics? De/Centering and the legacy of settler colonialism. Cult Stud 22(6):850–869
Borrell B, Gregory AS, McCreanor T, Jensen VGL, Barnes HEM (2009) "It's hard at the top but it's a whole lot easier than being at the bottom": the role of privilege in understanding disparities in Aotearoa/New Zealand. Race/Ethnicity 3(1):29–50
Borrell B, Moewaka Barnes H, McCreanor T (2018) Conceptualising historical privilege: the flip side of historical trauma, a brief examination. AlterNative 14(1):25–34
Came H, Tudor K (2016) Bicultural praxis: the relevance of Te Tiriti o Waitangi to health promotion internationally. Int J Health Promot Educ 54(4):184–192. https://doi.org/10.1080/14635240.2016.1156009
Came H, Cornes R, McCreanor T (2018) Treaty of Waitangi in New Zealand public health strategies and plans 2006–2016. N Z Med Assoc 131(1469):32–37
Collins S, Ihaka J, Tapaleao M, Tan L, Singh K (2014) Closing the gaps: updating the debate. N Z Sociol 29(3):2014
Durie M (1998) Te Mana, te Kāwanatanga: the politics of Māori self-determination. Oxford University Press, Auckland
Durie M (2005a) Ngā tai matatū: Tides of Māori endurance. Oxford University Press, Auckland
Durie M (2005b) Race and ethnicity in public policy: does it work? Soc Policy J N Z 24(1):1–11
Fleras A, Spoonley P (1999) Recalling Aotearoa: indigenous politics and ethnic relations in New Zealand. Oxford University Press, Oxford/New York
Harris A (2004) Hīkoi: forty years of Māori protest. Huia Publishers, Wellington
Higgins R (2016) Ki wīwī, ki wāwā: Normalising the Māori language. In: Adds P, Bönisch-Brednich B, Hill RS, Whimp G (eds) Reconcoliation, representation and Indigeneity: 'Biculturalism' in Aotearoa New Zealand. Universitätsverlad WINTER, Heidelberg, pp 25–37
Hill RS (2012) Maori urban migration and the assertion of indigeneity in Aotearoa/New Zealand 1945–1975. Interventions 14(2):256–278
Hill RS (2016) New Zealand Maori: the quest for indigenous autonomy. Ethnopolitics 15(1):144–165. https://doi.org/10.1080/17449057.2015.1101844
Hill RS, Bönisch-Brednich B (2009) Fitting Aotearoa into New Zealand: politico-cultural change in a modern bicultural nation. In: Berg M, Schaefer B (eds) Historical injustices in international perspective: how societies are trying to right the wrongs of the past. Cambridge University Press, Cambridge, pp 239–263
Humpage L (2006) An 'inclusive' society: a 'leap forward' for Māori in New Zealand? Crit Soc Policy 26(1):220–242
Humpage L (2008) Revision required: reconciling New Zealand citizenship with Maori nationalisms. National Identities, 10:3, 247–261
Johnson JT (2008) Indigeneity's challenges to the white settler-state: creating a thirdspace for dynamic citizenship. Alternatives 33:29–52
Kennedy M (2017) Maori economic inequality; reading outside our comfort zone. Interventions 19(7):1011–1025
King M (2003) The penguin history of New Zealand. Penguin Books, Auckland
Lourie M (2016) Bicultural education policy in New Zealand. J Educ Policy 31(5):637–650. https://doi.org/10.1080/02680939.2016.1159339
Meihana P (2017) Political utility: 'privilege' without end. In: Bell R, Kawharu M, Taylor K, Belgrave M, Meihana P (eds) The treaty on the ground: where we are headed and why it matters. Massey University Press, Auckland, pp 91–109
Mikaere A (2004) Are we all New Zealanders now? A Maori response to the Pakeha quest for indigeneity. Rad & Green 4:33–45
Moon P (2011) New Zealand in the twentieth century: the nation, the people. Auckland harper Collins, Auckland
OECD (no date) Labour force statistics by sex and age. Retrieved from https://stats.oecd.org/Index.aspx?DatasetCode=LFS_SEXAGE_I_R#

Office of Treaty Settlements (2018) Healing the past, building a future: a guide to treaty of Waitangi claims and negotiations with the crown. Retrieved from Wellington: https://www.govt.nz/assets/Documents/Red-Book-Healing-the-past-building-a-future.pdf

Orange C (1987) The treaty of Waitangi. Allen & Unwin, Wellington

O'Sullivan D (2007) Beyond biculturalism: the politics of an indigenous minority. Huia Publishers, Wellington

Parliamentary Counsel Office (2016) Māori language act 1987. Retrieved from http://www.legislation.govt.nz/act/public/1987/0176/latest/whole.html

Pearson D (2000) The ties that unwind: civic and ethnic imaginings in New Zealand. Nation Nationalism 6(1):91–110

Poata-Smith E (2013) Inequality and Māori. In: Rashbrooke M (ed) Inequality: a New Zealand crisis. Bridget Williams Books, Wellington, pp 148–158

Pool I (1991) Te iwi Māori: a New Zealand population, past, present and projected. Auckland University Press, Auckland

Rangiwai BW (2011) 'Race' and the politics of land loss: colonising discourses for Patuheuheu and Ngati Haka. Te Kaharoa 4:40–96

Ryks J, Pearson AL, Waa A (2016) Mapping Urban Māori: a population-based study of Māori heterogeneity. N Z Geogr 72:28–40

Sibley CG, Robertson A, Kirkwood S (2005) Pakeha attitudes towards the symbolic and resource-specific aspects of bicultural policy in New Zealand: the legitimizing role of collective guilt for historical injustices. N Z J Psychol 34(3):171–180

Smith LT (2007) The native and the neoliberal down under: neoliberalism and "endangered authenticities". In: de la Cadena M, Starn O (eds) Indigenous experience today. Berg, Oxford, pp 333–352

Smith LT (2013) The future is now. In: Rashbrooke M (ed) Inequality: a New Zealand crisis. Bridget Williams Books, Wellington, pp 228–135

Spoonley P (1993) Racism and ethnicity, 2nd edn. Oxford University Press, Auckland

Stuff (2014) New Zealand 'Settled Peacefully' – PM. Stuff, 20 November. Retrieved from https://www.stuff.co.nz/national/politics/63377474/new-zealand-settled-peacefully-pm

Sullivan A (2016) The politics of reconciliation in New Zealand. Pol Sci 68(2):124–142. https://doi.org/10.1177/0032318716676290

The New Zealand Herald (2018) Waitangi Tribunal hearings over 'inequity and institutionalised racism' in health system. The New Zealand Herald. Retrieved from https://www.nzherald.co.nz/nz/news/article.cfm?c_id=1&objectid=12141442

Veracini L (2010) Settler colonialism: a theoretical overview. Palgrave Macmillan, Houndmills

Walker R (1986) The meaning of biculturalism. R.J. Walker, Auckland

Walker R (1990) Ka whawhai tonu matou: struggle without end. Penguin, Auckland

Ward A (1995) A show of justice: racial 'Amalgamation' in nineteenth century New Zealand, 4th edn. Auckland University Press, Auckland

Wolfe P (1999) Settler colonialism and the transformation of anthropology: the politics and poetics of an ethnographic event. Cassell, London/New York

Nuclear Testing and Racism in the Pacific Islands

49

Nic Maclellan

Contents

Introduction	886
Creating Sacrifice Zones and Resistance	887
Protecting the Ocean as a Source of Identity	889
Civilized and Primitive Peoples	891
Medical Experiments and Body Snatching	892
Loss of Land, Waters, and Cultural Identity	895
Cultural Practice and Medical Hazards	897
Dirty, Difficult, and Dangerous Jobs	899
Conclusion	902
Cross-References	902
References	903

Abstract

During the Cold War, between 1946 and 1996, the United States, United Kingdom, and France used Oceania as a laboratory for nuclear testing. The deserts and islands of Australia and the Pacific were perceived as vast, "empty" spaces, suitable for the testing of atomic bombs and thermonuclear weapons. More than 310 atmospheric and underground nuclear tests were conducted by the Western powers in their colonial dependencies or United Nations trust territories.

Debate over colonialism, racism, and ethnic identity was a central feature of this nuclear era. The policies of the Western powers promoted a "nuclear racism" against Pacific Islanders, based on a racialized hierarchy of "civilized" and "primitive" peoples. These notions of racial superiority opened the way for medical experiments on Pacific Islanders affected by radioactive fallout, without free, prior, and informed consent.

N. Maclellan (✉)
Melbourne, Australia
e-mail: nicmac3056@gmail.com

© The Author(s), under exclusive license to Springer Nature Singapore Pte Ltd. 2019
S. Ratuva (ed.), *The Palgrave Handbook of Ethnicity*,
https://doi.org/10.1007/978-981-13-2898-5_74

Beyond this, the radioactive contamination of land, water, and food had direct and indirect impacts on the cultural identity of Pacific Islanders. Cultural practices – from reliance on fishing and traditional root crops to the use of coconut oil in children's hair – increased the risk of exposure to hazardous radioactive isotopes. The racialized hierarchy of the nuclear workplace also meant that colonial troops and local laborers were often allocated dirty, difficult, and dangerous jobs that increased their risk.

In turn, the long struggle for a nuclear-free and independent Pacific contributed to the creation of a collective sense of regional identity, as a defining element of contemporary Pacific cultural identity.

Keywords
Nuclear testing · Pacific Islands · Cold War · Colonialism · Nuclear-free and independent pacific

Introduction

During the 1950s, Merril Eisenbud was director of the Health and Safety Laboratory for the US Atomic Energy Commission (AEC). He also served on the AEC's Advisory Committee on Biology and Medicine and was a crucial medical advisor to the US military as it conducted a postwar program of nuclear weapons testing in the Marshall Islands.

Like other scientists, Eisenbud was excited by the possibility of studying the effect of radioactive contamination on human subjects (Eisenbud 1995). The opportunity came following the US nuclear test, codenamed "Bravo," conducted on Bikini Atoll on 1 March 1954. Bravo was the largest US nuclear test during the series Operation Crossroads, with an explosive yield of 15 megatons (Weisgall 1994). It spread radioactive contamination across the Marshall Islands, especially the northern atolls of Rongelap, Utirik, Rongerik, and Ailinginae (Kunkle and Ristvet 2013).

For Eisenbud, the aftermath of the Bravo test provided a crucial opportunity for the study of radioactive contamination on human beings, as hundreds of Marshall Islanders had been exposed as winds carried fallout over their islands. At a meeting of the AEC Advisory Committee on Biology and Medicine in January 1956, he proposed "to go back and get good environmental data…so as to get a measure of the human uptake when people live in a contaminated environment" (AEC 1956, 232; Johnston 2007, 25).

Eisenbud suggested that studying Marshall Islanders would provide data that had not been previously available to the US military, even though the Pacific Islanders had a different lifestyle to American citizens:

> While it is true that these people do not live, I would say, the way Westerners do, civilised people, it is nevertheless also true that these people are more like us than mice. (AEC 1956, 232)

More like us than mice. This chilling statement symbolizes the racist attitudes toward Pacific Islanders during the era of nuclear testing, which lasted for 50 years between 1946 and 1996. More than 310 nuclear tests, combined with countless other nuclear experiments, left social, cultural, and environmental legacies that continue to this day.

There is a vast literature on the environmental and health effects of nuclear testing in Oceania. But this chapter will address the many ways that the colonial legacies of the nuclear era affected Pacific Islander identity and culture.

After briefly outlining the history of nuclear testing in the Pacific Islands, this chapter will look at the ethnic and cultural identity of Pacific peoples through the prism of the ocean. It will highlight the development of a collective regional identity, arising from attempts to protect the marine environment from nuclear testing and nuclear waste dumping.

It then details key areas where the attitudes and policies of the Western powers promoted a "nuclear racism" against Pacific Islanders. This involved judgements based on a racialized hierarchy of "civilized" and "primitive" peoples that opened the way for medical experiments on human beings without free, prior, and informed consent.

Beyond this, the contamination of land, water, and food by radioactive fallout had direct and indirect impacts on the cultural identity of Pacific Islanders. The cultural practices of some island communities – from reliance on fishing and growing traditional root crops to the use of coconut oil in children's hair – increased the risk of exposure to hazardous radioactive isotopes.

The racialized hierarchy of the nuclear workplace also meant that colonial troops and local laborers were often allocated dirty, difficult, and dangerous jobs that increased the risk of radiation exposure.

The fact that nuclear testing in the islands continued for most of the second half of the twentieth century was a defining feature of Pacific cultural identity. The long struggle for a nuclear-free and independent Pacific, which continues to this day, forged a collective sense of regional identity that is amplified in the twenty-first century by the common struggle against the adverse effects of climate change.

Creating Sacrifice Zones and Resistance

During the Cold War, the United States, United Kingdom, and France used Oceania as a laboratory for Cold War nuclear testing. For 50 years between 1946 and 1996, the desert and islands of Australia and the islands of the central and eastern Pacific Ocean were perceived as vast, "empty" spaces, far from population centers. With the exception of Australia, a former British colony, the testing was conducted in colonial dependencies or United Nations trust territories administered by the Western powers.

Between 1946 and 1958, the United States conducted 67 atomic and hydrogen bomb tests at Bikini and Enewetak Atolls in the Marshall Islands, part of the United Nations strategic Trust Territory of the Pacific Islands (Niedenthal 2001; Johnson 2009, 2013). In 1962, the US military undertook 24 further atmospheric nuclear tests at Christmas (Kiritimati) Island in the British Gilbert and Ellice Islands Colony – today the Republic of Kiribati. The United States also conducted five atmospheric airbursts and nine high-altitude nuclear tests, with warheads launched on missiles from Johnston (Kalama) Atoll and submarines (Maclellan 2017).

The United Kingdom tested nuclear weapons in Oceania between 1952 and 1958. There were 12 atomic tests in Australia, starting at the Montebello Islands in 1952 and then continuing at Maralinga and Emu Field in the desert of South Australia from 1953 to 1957 (Tynan 2016). These atomic tests were followed by nine hydrogen and atomic bomb tests at Malden Island and Christmas (Kiritimati) Island in 1957–1958 (Arnold 2001; Maclellan 1999, 2017).

France began its nuclear testing program in 1960 in North Africa, with four atmospheric nuclear tests in the Sahara desert at Reggane in Algeria. This testing program continued between 1961 and 1966 with 13 further underground tests at In Eker, in the Hoggar Massif mountains of the Sahara. Most of the underground tests were conducted after the 1962 Evian Peace Agreement that ended the bitter Algerian war between France and the Front de Libération Nationale (FLN) in its North African colony.

The continuation of testing for 3 years after Algerian independence gave enough time for the French military to establish the *Centre d'Expérimentation du Pacifique* (CEP – Pacific testing center) in French Polynesia, a French colony in the eastern Pacific (Regnault 1993). From 1966 to 1996, France conducted 193 atmospheric and underground tests at Moruroa and Fangataufa Atolls in French Polynesia (Danielsson and Danielsson 1974, 1986; Maclellan and Chesneaux 1998); Barrillot 1996, 2002).

The creation of nuclear sacrifice zones occurred in other parts of the world, although the Cold War testing conducted by the Soviet Union and People's Republic of China is outside the scope of this chapter (even so, the lived experience of Kazakh and Uyghur peoples parallels that of the Pacific survivors – see Kassenova 2016).

Today, there are varying levels of residual radioactivity on some contaminated atolls in the Pacific. Heavily contaminated locations such as Bikini, Enewetak, and Rongelap Atolls still face restrictions on the use of local food sources. This is due to the ongoing concentration of radioisotopes in the food chain, such as iron-55 in reef fish and cesium-137 in coconut crabs, trees, and fruit (Ruff 1990, 2015).

During the 1950s, there were a range of petitions and protests by Pacific Islanders against nuclear testing, even though none of the Pacific colonies had achieved political independence and sovereignty before 1962 (save the Kingdom of Tonga, which had links to the United Kingdom as a British protectorate).

In 1950, the charismatic Tahitian independence leader Pouvanaa a Oopa began collecting signatures from islanders in the Tuamotu archipelago, as a contribution to global efforts for the Stockholm Peace Appeal (Maclellan 1999, 18–19). In 1956, a petition was sent from the New Zealand trust territory of Western Samoa to the United Nations Trusteeship Council, seeking a halt to the planned British hydrogen bomb testing program. Similar complaints came from customary leaders on the Rarotonga Island Council in the Cook Islands and from church leaders across Oceania (Maclellan 2017, Chap. 4, passim).

These efforts mirrored petitions submitted to the United Nations by Marshall Islands *irioj* (chiefs) after the 1954 Bravo test. Despite the US Navy's control of the

UN Trust Territory of the Pacific Islands, the islanders saw that nuclear testing would threaten their lands and waters, which are central to their ethnic identity as Oceanic peoples.

These early protests were amplified in later decades as newly independent nations forged regional structures – the Pacific Conference of Churches (PCC) in 1966, the University of the South Pacific (USP) in 1968, and the South Pacific Forum in 1971. These pan-Pacific institutions mounted collective diplomacy to challenge the use of the region as a nuclear laboratory. This work was inspired by civil society protests from churches, trade unions, women's organizations, and USP students.

The mobilization in the mid-1970s of the indigenous-led Nuclear Free and Independent Pacific (NFIP) movement was amplified by the international solidarity by Greenpeace, the World Council of Churches, and international disarmament organizations. The creation of the 1985 Rarotonga Treaty for a South Pacific Nuclear Free Zone (SPNFZ) and the declaration by Vanuatu, Palau, and Aotearoa-New Zealand that their land and waters were nuclear weapons-free were high points of the NFIP campaign. This struggle continues in the twenty-first century as New Zealand and Pacific Island nations sign the new Treaty on the Prohibition of Nuclear Weapons, which has crucial provisions obliging state parties to assist nuclear survivors.

The successes of the antinuclear struggle cannot fully diminish the physical, spiritual, and cultural scars left by the era of nuclear testing. Decades on, some atoll and desert locations in Oceania are nuclear sacrifice zones, still contaminated by radioactive isotopes that are hazardous to human health but have a half-life of thousands of years. Beyond this, the culture and identity of many Pacific peoples continues to be forged by the social, economic, and environmental legacies of this colonial era. As nuclear weapons expert Tilman Ruff has noted:

> The social impacts of disempowerment; victimisation; abuse of basic human rights; disruption of traditional communities, ways of life and means of sustenance; displacement; justified concern about unpredictable long-term health impacts extending to future generations; and concern about transmitting genetic mutations to one's children can all have profound and long-term direct and indirect physical and mental health consequences. Especially among the indigenous and traditional communities disproportionately impacted, these effects are not only individual and family, but extend to kin, communities and peoples. (Ruff 2015, 801)

Protecting the Ocean as a Source of Identity

When talking of "Pacific peoples," there is an underlying assumption that all Oceanic societies are the same. In reality, there is vast diversity of social, political, and economic circumstances across the region. From the Highlands of Papua New Guinea – a Melanesian nation of 8 million people with more than 830 languages – to the small Polynesian atoll nation of Tuvalu, with just 11,000 people, the islands region spans a vast diversity of cultural, linguistic, and social structures (Lal and

Fortune 2000). Some countries are based on one high volcanic island, like Niue and Nauru. Others, like Kiribati and French Polynesia, are large ocean states that encompass numerous archipelagos within exclusive economic zones that span millions of square kilometers of ocean.

In spite of this diversity, some writers have argued that the nuclear era forged a collective sense of cultural identity among all Pacific peoples. The threat of radioactive fallout, symbolized by the mushroom cloud, resonated across the region – even for countries and territories at some distance from the actual test sites.

Indigenous disarmament campaigners across the islands region also made the connection between nuclear testing and self-determination, decolonization, and political independence. The countries whose land and waters were directly utilized for testing – Australia, Kiribati, Marshall Islands, and French Polynesia – have vastly different colonial histories and relationships with their former administering power. However, common threats forge common identity. The Western powers could only test nuclear weapons in the Pacific because they were colonial powers in the region. As the slogan went: "If it's safe, test it in Paris! But keep our Pacific nuclear free" (Maclellan 2015).

The late Epeli Hau'ofa, one of the leading scholars and philosophers of Pacific Island culture, tied the identity of Pacific Islanders to their sense of place in the vast liquid continent – the ocean that unifies all Pacific Island nations. In a significant 1997 essay entitled "The Ocean in Us," Hau'ofa argued:

> It is of utmost significance for the strengthening of regional identity to know that our region has achieved its greatest degree of unity on issues involving threats to our common environment: the ocean. (Hau'ofa 1997, 49)

Hau'ofa states that these threats to the ocean reinforced cultural identities already forged in the period between the great canoe voyages, which carried the first settlers across the vast Pacific, and the later era of European exploration (voyages aided by the traditional knowledge of islanders who traveled on the European vessels, like Omai, Ahutoru, Lee Boo, or Ruatara, using their navigation skills and knowledge of neighboring archipelagos) (Lal and Fortune 2000, 160–161).

In "The Ocean in Us," Hau'ofa suggested the unifying power of the ocean made important connections across diverse and far-flung language and cultural groups. He went on to argue that, in the modern era, collective identity as Pacific Islanders was reinforced and reaffirmed through struggles against nuclear testing, the dumping of nuclear waste, and other threats to the ocean environment:

> The sense of a regional identity, being Pacific islanders, is felt most acutely the movement towards a nuclear free and independent Pacific, the protests against the wall of death drift netting, against plans to dispose of nuclear waste in the ocean, the incineration of chemical weapons on Johnston Island, the 1995 resumption of nuclear tests on Moruroa, and, most ominously, the spectre of our atoll nations and low-lying coastal regions disappearing under the rising sea level – all are instances of a regional united front against threats to our environment. (Hau'ofa 1997, 49)

Civilized and Primitive Peoples

This evolution of cultural identity in the nuclear era has also been affected by Western tropes about "paradise" and the despoliation of "paradise lost." In his 1992 study *Imagining the Pacific*, cultural historian Bernard Smith argued that a vision of Pacific "primitivism" developed as European scientists, writers, and artists explored the "New World" of the South Seas: "Novel first-hand information from the New World turned to the ideological usages of European primitivism, European religion and European power" (Smith 1992, 12). This in turn affected European notions of Melanesian savagery, contrasted to the exoticism of Polynesia (and especially Polynesian women).

These ideologies extended into the nuclear era of the twentieth century. Scholar and poet Teresia Teaiwa has looked at the militarization of the Pacific through gendered representations of ethnicity and sexuality. In her 1994 study connecting Bikini Atoll – a key site of the US nuclear testing program – with the bikini bathing suit, Teaiwa argued:

> The bikini-clad woman is exotic and malleable to the same colonial gaze which coded Bikini Atoll and its islanders as exotic, malleable and, most of all, dispensable. The bikini is, in effect, more about European and American sex-gender cultural history than about Pacific islanders. But the bikini's semi-nudity also reflects a conjuncture between conceptions of the neoclassical and the South Sea noble savage that began in 18th century European imagination. (Teaiwa 1994, 93)

The colonization in the Pacific by a range of European powers was based on Enlightenment concepts of the "civilizing mission" and the "noble savage." Studying the artists and writers of the colonial Pacific, Graeme Lay has noted:

> The racial hierarchies and assumptions of European superiority of the 18th and 19th centuries now seem patronising at best and offensive at worst. The word 'racism' was unknown; the phenomenon almost universal. (Lay 2008, 21)

But these ethnic hierarchies and concepts of European racial superiority are not simply a phenomenon of the misguided past. During the 50 years of nuclear testing in the Pacific Islands, political and military authorities regularly contrasted essentialized notions of "civilized" and "primitive" peoples, to justify the use of colonized Pacific Islands as testing grounds for atomic and hydrogen bombs.

As one example, UK Colonial Office archives include numerous examples during the United Kingdom's nuclear testing program in Australia and Kiribati between 1952 and 1958 (Tynan 2016; Maclellan 2017). As British officials prepared for Operation Grapple and the testing of thermonuclear weapons in the British Gilbert and Ellice Islands Colony in 1957–1958, they informed the UK Defense Minister that: "Independent authorities agree that . . ... only very slight health hazard to people would arise, and that only to primitive peoples" (Grapple 1956).

In November 1956, Grapple Task Force Commander Air Vice Marshall Wilfred Oulton circulated a study to senior members of the task force outlining the "danger area" to be promulgated for the UK thermonuclear weapons tests. The top secret document defined an area to warn off shipping, aircraft, or fishing vessels that might intrude in the test zones around Malden Island and Christmas Island.

The chapter sets "several definitions of levels of radioactivity resulting from fall-out" (Oulton 1956). It reveals that the acceptable dosage of radiation was different for British personnel than for the islanders who lived on Christmas Island and on neighboring inhabited atolls such as Fanning, Jarvis, and Washington in the Line Islands or Tongareva (Penrhyn) in the Cook Islands. The dosage for so-called primitive peoples exceeded safety levels set by international health commissions that monitored radiation:

> For civilised populations, assumed to wear boots and clothing and to wash, the amount of activity necessary to produce this dosage is more than is necessary to give an equivalent dosage to primitive peoples who are assumed not to possess these habits. For such peoples the corresponding level of activity is called level B'. It is assumed that in the possible regions of fall-out at Grapple there may be scantily clad people in boats to whom the criteria of primitive peoples should apply.
>
> It is desirable that the Declared Danger Area should at least enclose the whole region in which there is a possibility that level B' may be produced. The dosage at this level is about 15 times higher (for primitive peoples) than that which would be permitted by the International Commission on Radiological Protection. (Oulton 1956, 2–3)

People living in the Pacific Islands were understandably angry that they were being presented as "mice," "guinea pigs," or "primitive." On 20 February 1957, as the UK military prepared for its hydrogen bomb testing in the British Gilbert and Ellice Islands Colony, the Indo-Fijian newspaper *Jagriti* editorialized:

> Nations engaged in testing these bombs in the Pacific should realise the value of the lives of the people settled in this part of the world. They too are human beings, not 'guinea pigs'. (Lal 1992, 158)

Medical Experiments and Body Snatching

Anthropologist Barbara Rose Johnston has argued that the use of these racialized terms by political and military authorities "suggests a hierarchical view of humanity and the presumed relative subordinate status of indigenous peoples. This view – that human groups are more or less evolved, with primitive 'natives' being biologically inferior to Western 'civilised people' – was a common and useful notion. Such ideas help dampen any moral qualms about the planned use of a Marshallese population in human radiation experiments" (Johnston 2007, 26).

For the Marshallese, the aftermath of the 1954 Bravo test led to tragic consequences. The US military and medical staff from Brookhaven National Laboratory, led by Dr. Robert Conard, saw an opportunity to research the effects of radiation on people living on contaminated land. Under Project 4.1, medical studies were undertaken on at least 539 men, women, and children – often without informed consent – including experimental surgery and injections of chromium-51, radioactive iodine, iron, zinc, and carbon-14 (Cronkite et al. 1997).

Because of the secrecy surrounding nuclear testing programs, these medical studies lacked appropriate peer review and public critique by other scientists or doctors. Over time, the humanity of the subject "native" populations was diminished, with scientists regarding them as control groups rather than as individuals needing medical care.

As one example, Dr. Thomas Shipman, health division leader at the Los Alamos nuclear weapons laboratory, wrote to Dr. Robert Conard of Project 4.1 stating:

> Many thanks for the copy of the most recent survey of the Rongelap natives ... The development defects in the small children are also of considerable interest, and I presume an attempt will be made to correlate these findings with what has been reported in Japan. (Shipman 1961)

With little irony, Shipman recalled the dangers of sunburn while visiting the Micronesian islands:

> Maybe one of these days I can get back out when your survey team goes and sees the natives again. I will, however, be very careful about getting a sunburn comparable to the one I got on my previous visit to Rongelap. (Shipman 1961)

The hazards of sunburn paled into insignificance for the Marshall Islanders suffering from leukemia, cancer, and a range of reproductive health problems – including the phenomenon that Marshallese health worker Darlene Keju dubbed "jellyfish babies," as women faced intergenerational effects with deformed, lifeless fetuses or children born with disabilities (Johnson 2013).

Over time, Marshall Islanders began to question the way that the medical studies were being conducted, as shown by the moving letter written in 1975 from Rongelap islander Nelson Anjain to Dr. Robert Conard:

> I realise now that your entire career is based on our illness. We are far more valuable to you, than you are to us. You have never really cared about us as people – only as a group of guinea pigs for your government's bomb research effort. For me and the people of Rongelap, it is life which matters most. For you, it is facts and figures. There is no question about your technical competence, but we often wonder about your humanity.
>
> We don't need you and your technical machinery. We want our life and our health. We want to be free... As a result of my trip, I've made some decisions that I want you to know about. The main decision is that we do not want to see you again. We want medical care from doctors who care about us, not about collecting information for the US government's war makers. (Johnston 2007, 45–46)

Alongside Pacific Islanders working at the nuclear test sites or living in nearby locations, thousands of military personnel were also deployed to the Pacific for the nuclear testing programs by the United States, Britain, and France. It is beyond the scope of this chapter to fully analyze the experience of these soldiers and sailors, which has been documented in other studies (Maclellan et al. 1999; Cross and

Hudson 2005; Maclellan 2017; Van der Vlies and Seur 1997). However there was a common concern among military personnel, Pacific workers on the test sites, and neighboring island communities – that they were being used as guinea pigs, for deliberate experimentation on the effects of radiation.

These concerns were not simply paranoia. During the Cold War, the United States conducted a number of human radiation experiments on indigenous peoples, Sami and Inuit in Alaska, across the Andes and Amazon, with research in Chile, Peru, Argentina, and Brazil, as well as the Micronesians of the Marshall Islands (Johnston 2007). Through Project Sunshine and other government-sponsored studies on the spread of radioactive isotopes like strontium-90, many other people were drawn into medical experimentation and human radiation studies, often involving the collection of blood, bone, tissue, or genetic materials.

Many of these activities were only revealed after the Clinton Administration ordered a 1994 review of human radiation studies conducted by the United States between 1944 and 1974. The review by the Advisory Committee on Human Radiation Experiments (ACHRE) revealed "the perhaps surprising finding that officials and experts in the highest reaches of the Atomic Energy Commission (AEC) and Department of Defence (DOD) discussed requirements for human experiments in the first years of the Cold War" (ACHRE 1995, 24).

The ACHRE review found that Cold War practices included experiments on prisoners and invalids, including plutonium injections during the Manhattan project:

> Sick patients were used in sometimes secret experimentation to develop data needed to protect the health and safety of nuclear weapons workers. The experiments raise questions of the use of sick patients for purposes that are not of benefit to them, the role of national security in permitting conduct that might not otherwise be justified, and the use of secrecy for the purpose of protecting the government from embarrassment and potential liability. (ACHRE 1995, 26)

Not surprisingly, the review found that: "Current policies do not adequately safeguard against the recurrence of the kinds of events we studied that fostered distrust" (Ibid).

Similar practices extended to the United Kingdom. The UK government was well aware that the atmospheric testing of nuclear weapons would contribute to the spread of strontium-90 around the globe. This radioactive isotope, with a half-life of 28.8 years, is produced by nuclear fission and was carried vast distances as the post-detonation mushroom cloud extended to the stratosphere and high-level winds.

By the mid-1950s, British researchers were involved in Project Sunshine, an initiative started by the US Atomic Energy Commission (AEC) to measure the amount of strontium-90 in the bones and tissue of human beings (RAND 1953). More than 19 countries were involved in this gruesome project, which involved the use of cadavers – often babies and children – for testing, often without the knowledge or consent of their families. US doctors and scientists in the Marshall Islands also removed both decayed and healthy teeth from Rongelap children and sent them to New York for testing (Johnston and Barker 2008, 158).

From 1954, the US AEC, the UK Atomic Energy Authority (UKAEA), and the UK Ministry of Agriculture, Fisheries and Food began testing for strontium-90 in food, animals, and plants. This was soon extended to human testing and the UKAEA tested bones from thousands of dead children. Samples from more than 6000 people who died in Britain were tested between 1955 and 1970 (Roff 2002; Redfern 2010, 405).

In Australia, the Atomic Weapons Tests Safety Committee began a program in 1957 to collect samples in Australia and the Australian-administered Territory of Papua and New Guinea. Bones and samples from more than 21,000 corpses – mainly babies – were incinerated, and the ash is sent to the United Kingdom for testing (ARPANSA n.d., 11).

On 18 January 1955, the US AEC held a conference to discuss how they could obtain more human material for the analysis of strontium-90. AEC commissioner Dr. Willard Libby told the meeting:

> Human samples are of prime importance and if anybody knows how to do a good job of body snatching, they will really be serving their country ... In 1953 we hired an expensive law firm to look up the law of body snatching. This compendium is available to you. It is not very encouraging. It shows you how very difficult it is going to be to do it legally. (Redfern 2010, 410–411)

Decades later, the Nuclear Free and Independent Pacific movement was still concerned about the ongoing "biopiracy" of genetic materials by Western researchers, collected from people living in isolated atolls or Highlands communities. In 1995, the NFIP secretariat in Fiji – the Pacific Concerns Resource Centre – hosted a regional consultation on indigenous peoples knowledge and intellectual property rights, which led to the drafting of a model treaty for "a life forms patent-free Pacific" (PCRC 1997, 196).

Loss of Land, Waters, and Cultural Identity

The threat to Pacific cultures and spirituality was exacerbated by the very real damage to land, water, and place that is central to indigenous identity across the region. In some cases, this was exacerbated by the relocation of communities from their home islands or desert country, producing profound loss and cultural dislocation that continues to this day.

In their early protests against nuclear testing during the 1950s, Islanders often highlighted the damage to land and livelihoods rather than the (often unknown or misunderstood) effects of radiation on human health.

Just weeks after the Bravo test on 1 March 1954, Marshall Islanders led by schoolteachers Dwight Heine and Atlan Anien and customary chiefs Kabua Kabua and Dorothy Kabua lodged a petition with the UN Trusteeship Council. The petition requested that "all experiments with lethal weapons in this area be immediately ceased" and highlighted the importance of land as a source of culture and identity – land that was being vaporized or contaminated by US nuclear tests:

> ... the Marshallese people are not only fearful of the danger to their persons from these deadly weapons in case of another miscalculation, but they are also concerned for the increasing number of people removed from their land .... land means a great deal to the Marshallese. It means more than just a place where you can plant your food crops and build your houses or a place where you can bury your dead. It is the very life of the people. Take away their land and their spirits go also. (UN Trusteeship Council 1954)

The adverse environmental effects on the land continue to this day, and many Marshallese from the northern atolls are still displaced from their home islands. Food plants like breadfruit and coconut take up radioactive cesium-137 from the soil, and this hazard has persisted on Bikini, Rongelap, and other contaminated islands (Bordnera et al. 2016). Although the US Congress has allocated funding to finance a partial cleanup, only a small proportion of the northern atolls have been fully remediated. Exiled residents are calling for more comprehensive efforts before they return home.

After the Bravo test, Lemeyo Abon was one of the children relocated from Rongelap. This evacuation began a decades-long odyssey which has left many people still living in exile. After returning to live on the contaminated atoll for 30 years, she was again evacuated to Mejatto Island in 1985 aboard the Greenpeace vessel *Rainbow Warrior*, just before it was attacked and sunk in Auckland Harbour by French intelligence agents (Robie 2015). She later moved to the Marshall Islands capital Majuro, still far away from her home island. Interviewing Mrs. Abon in Majuro in 2013, her loss was clear:

> We are still living in this place in exile from our homeland, like a coconut floating in the sea. The United States has to live up to their responsibility and make sure our children and grandchildren will be cared for. (Maclellan 2017, 54)

Sadly, she died in exile in 2018, without returning to her home island.

The central relationship between land and identity was also played out in Australia during the period of British nuclear testing.

For decades, UK and Australian authorities had downplayed the hazards for nearby aboriginal communities created by the British nuclear tests, such as the Totem One test at Emu Field in October 1953, which generated a black mist and reportedly caused blindness for indigenous children like Yami Lester (Lester 1993). But in recent years, there is a growing body of literature which documents the adverse effects of nuclear testing on the desert communities, whose lands were taken for the Maralinga and Emu Field test sites (Mattingley 2009, 2016; Tynan 2016).

Nearly 30 years after the end of the UK testing program, the 1984–1985 McClelland Royal Commission into the British nuclear tests confirmed what indigenous people have long argued: that the testing grounds in the desert of South Australia were not empty, but were the homelands for the Yankunytjatjara and Pitjantjatjara peoples and a place of crucial cultural and spiritual meaning.

The Royal Commission report noted that "the country was still used for hunting and gathering, for temporary settlements, for caretakership and spiritual renewal and for traverse by people who move from location to other areas within and outside what became the prohibited areas." While some Aboriginal people lived in contaminated zones for up to 6 years after the tests, others were relocated to coastal towns away from their traditional country. The Royal Commission recognized however that the denial of access to their traditional lands for displaced people "contributed to their emotional, social and material distress and deprivation" (Government of Australia 1985, 319, 323).

During the nuclear testing era in Marshall Islands, Kiribati, and French Polynesia, social structures and cultural identity were transformed by the presence of thousands of overseas military personnel and massive influx of capital, technology, and infrastructure.

This was most evident in French Polynesia during 30 years of nuclear testing, when French funding, economic investment, and changing employment patterns led to significant shifts in the culture and lifestyle of the indigenous Maohi people (Poirine 1992; Blanchet 1995). Thousands of Maohi workers were employed in a range of jobs at the CEP Pacific test center – today they have formed an association called *Moruroa e Tatou* (Moruroa and Us), seeking compensation for the illnesses they attribute to their exposure to hazardous levels of radiation in the workplace.

At the height of French nuclear testing, independence activist Jacqui van Bastolaer from the *Ia Mana Te Nunaa* party testified to the transformation of ethnic identity in the new consumer society created after the 1960s:

> The attack of one civilisation against another can take on various forms – genocide, economic or cultural assault. After having lived through a period of military colonisation, the Polynesian Maohi have undergone an economic and cultural colonisation for a century. That economic and cultural colonisation specifically grew with the settling of the Pacific nuclear test centre in our country. While the external trade balance Polynesia was in equilibrium around the 1960s, it is today in a 98 per cent deficit...
>
> The economic dependence on the outside world also resulted in a cultural dependence with regard to habits, mental outlook and the way of life, leaving the Polynesian people deeply estranged from their identity and traditional socio-economic balance. Now in the colonial society, which increasingly extends its influence to all the fields of life, the Polynesian has turned into the throwaway individual of a consumer civilisation. In our eyes, the Maohi people's cultural estrangement is one of the most harmful aspects of colonisation. (van Bastolaer 1984, 43–44)

Cultural Practice and Medical Hazards

Nutrition in most Pacific atoll nations is reliant on ocean resources, from deepwater fisheries to the collection of crabs, limpets, and other seafood on coastal waterfronts and fringing reefs. For this reason, the norms of Pacific culture and diet were challenged during the period of atmospheric nuclear testing (1946–1974), when the spread of radioactive isotopes through fallout increased the risk of contamination for land, agricultural crops, and fisheries.

Across the region, the reef ecology of coral atolls was severely damaged by activities associated with the nuclear testing program, including drilling in the lagoon floor to create shafts for underground tests, reef blasting to create passage for naval vessels, waste dumping, and the actual detonation of nuclear weapons. A study published in the British medical journal *The Lancet* has linked such activities to regular outbreaks of the fish-poisoning disease ciguatera (Ruff 1989, 201–205). As nuclear researcher Dr. Tilman Ruff has noted:

> Ciguatera has important nutritional, social and economic implications, interfering with local inshore, largely subsistence, traditional fishing and increasing dependence on imported foods, with their exacerbation of risk factors for chronic disease. (Ruff 1990, 32)

To reduce the danger of ingestion or inhalation of hazardous ionizing radiation, military authorities commonly banned the consumption of local fish, crabs, and seafood during periods of nuclear testing. These restrictions were aimed at Pacific workers on the test site, military personnel deployed for the testing program, and neighboring island communities. In reality, however, islanders regularly ignored such safeguards, ignorant of the hazards of accumulated nuclear particles in the food chain and reluctant to give up their traditional diet.

One example comes from the British hydrogen bomb testing program on Christmas (Kiritimati) Island. Banaban sailor Tekoti Rotan was deployed to the island in 1957, as part of the UK military task force. In an interview, he said that safety regulations limiting consumption of fish had little meaning for Fijians and Gilbertese islanders living on Christmas Island during the testing program:

> The only warning we had before the test, was they warned the people: 'After the test, don't eat any fish!' But you know, I'm from Kiribati. I love raw fish and this is the only dangerous thing after the test. They said: 'Don't!' but I ignored them. I went to the Kiribati people and said: 'Hey, raw fish, we're not supposed to eat the raw fish!' But they said 'Oh, we've been eating it and nothing's happened.' That was the biggest mistake for them. (Maclellan 2017, 238)

Supplied with military rations such as bully beef and potatoes, Fijian soldiers and sailors deployed to Christmas Island regularly supplemented their standard rations with seafood, caught from the surrounding lagoon and reef. In an interview, Fijian soldier Eseroma Kuruwale recalled that islanders often ignored official regulations that banned the consumption of fish following a nuclear test:

> When we Fijians were there, we used to go spear fishing along the shores. We ate the fish on the beach. During the time that the bomb was dropped, it wasn't allowed to eat fish, but you know, we Fijians always do it anyway. We were always yearning for fish. After a day or one week, we used to look for crayfish. We ate the crayfish which was very tasty. (Maclellan 1999, 55)

Similar stories can be found in French Polynesia and the Marshall Islands, with some dietary traditions affecting women more than men. United Nations Special Rapporteur Calin Georgescu, who documented ongoing nuclear hazards in the Marshall Islands in a 2012 UN report, noted that radioactive isotopes accumulated in the food chain posed particular hazards for women and children:

Because of cultural differences and language barriers, Marshallese dietary customs were either unknown or ignored during the testing period. For example, the difference in dietary and other eating habits of men, women and children may have led to higher exposure of some members of the population, especially women. Women eat different parts of the fish to those eaten by men, especially bones and organ meat, in which certain radioactive isotopes tend to accumulate.

The differences in the retention of radionuclides by coconut and land crabs were not recognised by the medical profession in the United States. Apparently, women were more exposed to radiation levels in coconut and other foods owing to their role in processing foods and weaving fibre to make sitting and sleeping mats, and handling materials used in housing construction, water collection, hygiene and food preparation, as well as in handicrafts. (Georgescu 2012, 8)

Other common cultural practices, such as the tradition of washing hair with coconut oil, exposed young girls to even greater risk. These hazards were known at the time, as shown in contemporary documents from Joint Task Force 7 (JTF-7), the military command responsible for the Bravo operation. The final JTF-7 Radiological Safety Report acknowledged that "the heavy coconut oil hairdressing used by the Marshallese tended to concentrate radioactivity in the hair" (Barker 2004, 40).

Oral testimony from Marshallese women who survived these tests confirms this practice and the subsequent health impacts. On 1 March 1954, Rinok Riklon was a young girl living on Rongelap, 120 km to the east of Bikini Atoll, where the US government exploded the Bravo thermonuclear weapon. Winds carried radioactive fallout across Rongelap and other northern atolls. In an interview nearly 60 years later, Mrs. Riklon said:

People were playing with the fallout as it fell from the sky. We put it in our hair as if it was soap or shampoo. But later I lost all of my hair. (Maclellan 2017, 40)

On the day of the Bravo test, Lemeyo Abon was 14 years old, living on Rongelap:

We saw the bright light and heard a boom and we were really scared. We had no idea of what was happening. Later on something like powder came from the sky. It was raining when we went home and our parents asked 'what happened to your hair?' The next day our hair fell out. We looked at each other and laughed, saying 'you look like a bald old man!' But in our hearts we were sad. (Maclellan 2017, 40)

Dirty, Difficult, and Dangerous Jobs

Tanemaruata Michel Arakino was born on Reao, an island not far from Moruroa Atoll, site of 178 French nuclear tests between 1966 and 1996 (a further 15 nuclear tests were held at nearby Fangataufa Atoll).

For 17 years, Arakino worked with the French military research unit responsible for collecting biological samples at the nuclear test sites, to determine the amount and spread of radioactive particles. Working as a scuba diver, he also dove into the lagoon at Moruroa Atoll to collect samples of water, seaweed, and sediments, just hours after underground nuclear tests had been conducted in shafts drilled deep into the atoll.

> In my job, I was regularly in the so-called 'hot spots' together samples from the ground and the sea for biological testing on Moruroa and Fangataufa Atolls and across all of Polynesia, as well as for the testing of foods coming from outside the country. I was in charge of a garden with contaminated earth that we brought in from Fangataufa itself.
> The Biological Testing Service wanted to know what happens to vegetables grown in contaminated soil. It is likely that while working in this garden and while diving to gather plankton above ground zero, I swallowed or breathed in radioactive particles. In no case did my senior officers inform me of the risks I might incur. (Arakino 2002)

For nearly 30 years, French government officials stated that there was no radioactive fallout from French nuclear tests or leakage of radioactivity into the lagoons at Moruroa and Fangataufa. However a major study by the International Atomic Energy Agency (IAEA), conducted after the end of nuclear testing in 1996, shows that there is significant radioactive pollution caused by the nuclear tests, in spite of decades of denials:

- Five kilograms of plutonium remain in the sediments of Moruroa Atoll's lagoon as a result of atmospheric nuclear tests and plutonium safety trials, with a further 3 kilos in Fangataufa's lagoon.
- The concentration of tritium in the Moruroa lagoon was ten times higher than in the open ocean, as a result of leakage from cavities created by the underground tests.
- Particles of plutonium and americium remain at the trial sites on Colette, Ariel, and Vesta islands on the north side of Moruroa Atoll.
- High levels of cesium-137 were found over small areas totaling several hectares on the Kilo-Empereur rim of Fangataufa Atoll (IAEA 1998).

Arakino's work is just one example of the dirty, difficult, and dangerous jobs allocated to Pacific Islanders in support of the nuclear testing programs. Such work meant that islanders could face greater risks than their metropolitan counterparts (although numerous Western military personnel were also exposed to dangerous levels of radiation during the testing programs, during accidents, as well as during the normal working day).

There is also evidence that islanders deployed by the military for the nuclear testing programs (such as the Fijian military personnel deployed to Christmas Island or the Maohi workers mobilized for French tests on Moruroa) were allocated dirty, difficult, and dangerous jobs. Indeed, some soldiers have testified that they believe this was deliberate, because they were colonial subjects.

For example, around 276 members of the Royal Fiji Military Forces (RFMF) were sent to Christmas Island as a small part of a much larger deployment of UK troops. Fijian soldiers who staffed the test sites from 1958 to 1960 worked as engineers, laborers, and stevedores for the loading and unloading of ships. They were also given duties that increased the risk of exposure. After witnessing the tests, for example, RFMF soldiers were involved in cleanup operations closer to ground zero, such as capturing and killing birds blinded by the nuclear detonation.

Interviewed years after his deployment on the island in 1957, RFMF soldier Isireli Qalo reported that his crew of Fijians, supervised by just one UK soldier, were given a special task:

> I was involved in the unloading of the first bomb for Christmas Island. A cargo boat escorted by several warships brought the bomb to Port Camp. My job was to secure the unloading area and oversee the work of the Fijian boys. Those doing the unloading were organised into sections. There was only one white fellow who was allowed in the secured area with me, to oversee the unloading. We took this thing from the Navy and took it onto the island. (Maclellan 2017, 228)

RFMF sailor Paul Ah Poy also served on Christmas Island, witnessing seven nuclear tests. On one occasion, he was ordered to dump drums of radiation-contaminated waste into the ocean:

> One clear sunny day, there wasn't much traffic in the port area. A huge truck arrived alongside our vessel. The normal stevedores did not load the special cargo into the *Prowler*, our lighter. Some Air Force personnel did the loading supervised by a Royal Navy Sub-Lieutenant. My three crew and I gave a hand and I happened to sit on one of the 44-gallon drums, after all 60 drums were loaded.
>
> All of a sudden a Marine Sergeant came and pushed me off the drum and we both fell down on the deck. I thought he was only playing. As we got up, he took me to one side and told me: 'Do you know what's your cargo, son?' I answered: 'No Sarg.' He told me: 'Since you are the Skipper of this tub, I'll let you in on what you are about to do. Don't ever sit or touch those drums, they contain nuclear waste. You will take it out to sea and dump them over the sides when we were about five miles west of the island.'
>
> The Navy officer came to me and said: 'What say, Cox'n, are we far enough?' I answered that we were beyond the four miles limit and it's time we head for home. He said: 'Right ho, boys!' The RAF boys and our crew started rolling the drums over the side and we returned to port. (Maclellan 2017, 140)

Beyond these hazards, the risk of serious exposure was increased for people engaged in certain activities during the nuclear testing program – for example, during the early era of US and UK atmospheric nuclear testing, pilots dropping the hydrogen bomb from aircraft suffered from significantly increased rates of leukemia, cancer, and other illnesses (Maclellan 2017, 168ff). Because of this, some nuclear veterans claim that their exposure to hazardous levels of ionizing radiation was not accidental, but rather they were deliberately used as guinea pigs or "lambs to the slaughter" (Cross and Hudson 2005, 171).

Conclusion

In September 2018, Presidents and Prime Ministers of the eight Smaller Island States (SIS) within the Pacific Islands Forum held their annual caucus. The SIS leaders agreed that the issue of nuclear contamination of their islands would be a standing agenda item for all future SIS meetings.

Well into this century, Pacific Island leaders still see the danger of radioactivity as a regional issue, meriting their attention. Led by the Marshall Islands and French Polynesia, island leaders are intensely worried about the effects of climate change – storm surges, sea level rise, and ocean acidification – on the Pacific sacrifice zones created by Cold War nuclear testing.

In French Polynesia, for example, the lagoon at Moruroa Atoll remains contaminated by plutonium and other long-lasting radioactive isotopes. As they dismantled the CEP nuclear test site after the end of testing in 1996, the French military dumped more than 2600 tonnes of nuclear-contaminated material into the waters off Moruroa (2580 tonnes at a site codenamed "Oscar" and a further 76 tonnes at site "Novembre"). The basalt base of the atoll is fractured by dozens of underground nuclear tests, creating fissures that may allow the leaching of radioactivity into the marine environment.

In the Marshall Islands, Runit Island in Enewetak Atoll hosts a massive concrete dome which covers tons and tons of nuclear-contaminated waste. The radioactive legacy of US nuclear tests on Enewetak was buried under concrete in the mid-1970s, in a giant crater created by a nuclear blast. Today, however, the dome is cracking, leaching contaminants into the ocean environment. Concrete laid in the 1970s cannot contain the problem as rising seas caused by climate change seep inside the nuclear waste dump, flushing out radioactive substances left behind from some of the world's largest atomic weapons tests.

The creation of the sacrifice zone at Runit is mourned today by the people of the Marshall Islands. In her poem "Anointed," Marshallese poet Kathy Jetnil-Kijiner asks: "You were a whole island once. Who remembers you beyond your death? Who would have us forget that you were once green globes of fruit, pandanus roots and whispers of canoes? Who knows the stories of the life you led before?" (Jetnil-Kijiner 2018).

These stories have been largely forgotten by the governments and citizens of the United States, United Kingdom, and France. But the memory – carried in the scarred land and the scarred souls of survivors – is a central part of the cultural identity of the peoples of the Pacific. Living with the memory of human radiation experiments; of dirty, difficult, and dangerous jobs; of the pollution of land and waters; and of cancers and other health impacts, the nuclear racism of Cold War colonialism lingers on.

Cross-References

- ▶ Faamatai: A Globalized Pacific Identity
- ▶ Foreign Military Occupations and Ethnicity
- ▶ Kava and Ethno-cultural Identity in Oceania

References

ACHRE (1995) Executive summary and guide to final report – advisory committee on human radiation experiments. DOE/EH–96001171. Department of Energy, Washington, DC

Arakino TM (2002) Les essais nucléaires et la santé, speech to French Senate, Paris, 19 January. In: CDRPC (ed) Nuclear tests and health – proceedings of the conference. Centre de Documentation et de Recherche sur la Paix et les Conflits, Lyons

Arnold L (2001) Britain and the H-bomb. Palgrave Macmillan, London. https://doi.org/10.1057/9780230599772

ARPANSA (n.d.) Australian strontium-90 testing program 1957–78. Australian Radiation Protection and Nuclear Safety Agency, Sydney. http://www.nuclearfiles.org/menu/key-issues/nuclear-weapons/issues/testing/PDFs/sr90pubrep[1].pdf

Atomic Energy Commission (1956) Minutes of the advisory committee on biology and medicine, 13–14 January. Advisory Committee on Human Radiation Experiments (ACHRE) archive, HREX document 0711806

Barker H (2004) Bravo for the Marshallese – regaining control in a post-nuclear, post-colonial world. Wadsworth, Belmont

Barrillot B (1996) Les essais nucléaires français 1960–1996. Centre de Documentation et de Recherche sur la Paix et les Conflits, Lyons

Barrillot B (2002) L'héritage de la bombe: Polynésie – Sahara 1960–2002. Centre de Documentation et de Recherche sur le Paix et les Conflits, Lyons

Blanchet G (1995) Le Centre d'Expérimentation du Pacifique et son impact. In: Chesneaux J (ed) Tahiti apres la Bombe – quelle avenir pour la Polynésie? L'Harmattan, Paris

Bordnera A et al (2016) Measurement of background gamma radiation in the northern Marshall Islands. Proc Natl Acad Sci U S A (PNAS) 113(25):6833–6838. https://doi.org/10.1073/pnas.1605535113

Cronkite EP, Conard RA, Bond VP (1997) Historical events associated with fallout from Bravo shot—Operation Castle and 25 years of medical findings. J Health Phys 73(1):176–186. https://doi.org/10.1097/00004032-199707000-00014

Cross R, Hudson A (2005) Beyond belief – the British bomb tests, Australia's veterans speak out. Wakefield Press, Kent Town

Danielsson B, Danielsson MT (1974) Moruroa mon amour. Stock, Paris

Danielsson B, Danielsson MT (1986) Poisoned reign. Penguin, Ringwood

Eisenbud M (1995) Human radiation studies, remembering the early years. Oral History of Merril Eisenbud, United States Department of Energy Office of Human Radiation Experiments. DOE/EH-0456, May

Georgescu C (2012) Mission to the Marshall Islands (27–30 March 2012) and the United States of America (24–27 April 2012), UN Special Rapporteur on the implications for human rights of the environmentally sound management and disposal of hazardous substances and wastes. UN Human Rights Council, Twenty-first session, A/HRC/21/48/Add.1. 3 September

Government of Australia (1985) The report of the Royal Commission into British nuclear tests in Australia. Australian Government Publishing Service, Canberra

Grapple (1956) Minutes of meeting on 27 November 1956, Operation Grapple XY/181/024. UK Colonial Office archives, file CO1036/280

Hau'ofa E (1997) The ocean in us. In: Hau'ofa E (ed). (2008) We are the ocean – selected works. University of Hawaii Press, Honolulu

IAEA (1998) Situation radiologique sur les atolls de Mururoa et de Fangataufa: rapport succinct d'un Comité Consultatif International, vol 2. International Atomic Energy Agency, Vienna

Jetnil-Kijiner K (2018) 'Anointed', video poem performed by Kathy Jetnil-Kijiner. https://www.youtube.com/watch?v=_isgBtJfPzU

Johnson G (2009) Nuclear past, unclear future. Micronitor, Majuro

Johnson G (2013) Don't ever whisper – Darlene Keju: Pacific health pioneer, champion for nuclear survivors. CreateSpace Independent Publishing, Majuro

Johnston BR (2007) 'More like us than mice': radiations experiments with indigenous peoples. In: Johnston BR (ed) Half-lives and half-truths: confronting the radioactive legacies of the cold war. School for Advanced Research Press, Santa Fe, pp 25–55

Johnston BR, Barker H (2008) Consequential damages of nuclear war – the Rongelap report. Left Coast Press, Walnut Creek

Kassenova T (2016) Banning nuclear testing: lessons from the Semipalatinsk nuclear testing site. Nonproliferation Rev 23(3–4):329–344. https://doi.org/10.1080/10736700.2016.1264136

Kunkle T, Ristvet B (2013) Castle Bravo: fifty years of legend and lore. US Defence Threat Reduction Agency, DSTRIAC SR-12-001, January

Lal B (1992) Broken waves – a history of the Fiji islands in the 20th century. Pacific Islands Monograph Series No. 11. University of Hawai'i Press, Honolulu

Lal B, Fortune K (2000) The Pacific Islands – an encyclopedia. University of Hawai'i Press, Honolulu

Lay G (2008) In search of paradise – artists and writers in the colonial South Pacific. Random House, Auckland

Lester Y (1993) Yami – the autobiography of Yami Lester. IAD Press, Alice Springs

Maclellan N (ed) (1999) No Te Parau Tia, No Te Parau Mau, No Te Tiamaraa – for justice, truth and independence. Pacific Concerns Resource Centre, Suva

Maclellan N (2015) The nuclear age in the Pacific Islands. Contemp Pac 17(2):363–372

Maclellan N (2017) Grappling with the bomb – Britain's Pacific H-bomb tests. ANU Press, Canberra

Maclellan N, Chesneaux J (1998) After Moruroa – France in the South Pacific. Ocean Press, New York

Maclellan N, Salabula L, Namoce J (1999) Kirisimasi – Na Sotia kei na Lewe ni Mataivalu e Wai ni Viti e na vakatovotovo iyaragi nei Peritania mai Kirisimasi. Pacific Concerns Resource Centre, Suva

Mattingley C (2009) Maralinga – the Anangu story. Allen and Unwin, Sydney

Mattingley C (2016) Maralinga's long shadow – Yvonne's story. Allen and Unwin, Sydney

Niedenthal J (2001) For the good of mankind – a history of the people of Bikini and their islands. Micronitor, Majuro

Oulton WE (1956) Danger area. Paper from Air Vice Marshall W.E Oulton, code GRA/TS.1008/1/Air, 19 November. UK Colonial Office archives, file CO1036/280

PCRC (1997) Proceedings of the indigenous peoples knowledge and intellectual property rights consultation, 24–27 April 1995, Suva, Fiji. Pacific Concerns Resource Centre, Suva

Poirine B (1992) Tahiti – stratégie pour l'après-nucléaire: de la rente atomique au développement. Self-published, Arue

RAND (1953) Project sunshine – worldwide effects of atomic weapons. RAND Corporation, Santa Monica. 6 August

Redfern (2010) Redfern inquiry into human tissue analysis in UK nuclear facilities, vol 1. Her Majesty's Stationery Office, London

Regnault J-M (1993) La Bombe française dans le Pacifique – L'implantation 1957–64. Scoop éditions, Papeete

Robie D (2015) Eyes of fire – the last voyage of the rainbow warrior. Little Island Books, Auckland

Roff SR (2002) Project sunshine and the slippery slope: the ethics of tissue sampling for strontium-90. Med Confl Surviv 18(3):299–310

Ruff TA (1989) Ciguatera in the Pacific: a link with military activities. Lancet 1(8631):201–205

Ruff TA (1990) Bomb tests attack the food chain. Bull At Sci 46(2):32–34

Ruff TA (2015) The humanitarian impact and implications of nuclear test explosions in the Pacific region. Int Rev Red Cross 97(899):775–813. https://doi.org/10.1017/S1816383116000163

Shipman T (1961) Letter from Thomas L. Shipman M.D., Los Alamos, New Mexico to Dr Robert Conard, Brookhaven National Laboratory, New York, 13 March. Marshall Island Nuclear Documentation Database (MINDD). http:/data.nuclearsecrecy.com/mindd

Smith B (1992) Imagining the Pacific – in the wake of the Cook voyages. Melbourne University Press, Carlton

Teaiwa T (1994) Bikinis and other s/pacific n/oceans. Contemp Pac 6(1):87–109

Tynan E (2016) Atomic thunder – the Maralinga story. NewSouth, Sydney

UN Trusteeship Council (1954) Petition from the Marshallese People Concerning the Pacific Islands: "Complaint regarding explosions of lethal weapons within our home islands" to United Nations Trusteeship Council, 20 April 1954. UN Trusteeship Council document T/PET.10/28, 6 May

Van Bastolaer J (1984) French-occupied Polynesia. In: WCIP (ed) Indigenous struggles in the Pacific. World Council of Indigenous People/National Aboriginal Conference, Sydney

Van der Vlies P, Seur H (1997) Moruroa and us. Centre de Documentation et de Recherche sur la Paix et les Conflits, Lyons

Weisgall J (1994) Operation crossroads – the atomic tests at Bikini Atoll. Naval Institute Press, Annapolis

Nagas Identity and Nationalism: Indigenous Movement of the Zeliangrong Nagas in the North East India

50

Aphun Kamei

Contents

Introduction 908
Conclusion 922
References 922

Abstract

Today, more than ever, the need for economic development and progress is felt much stronger by any group or community. This means that all groups or communities enter into direct or indirect competitions and conflicts at all times. As a result of this, each community is compelled to search for new technology and new cultural practices in order to acquire more wealth and prosperity. The widespread education and the process of modernization accelerates the economic growth and prosperity which ultimately connects every culture through circulating global markets, and this process helps people to come closer and increasingly found interlinked with one another. However, in such process, we see either a community being merged with the "mainstream" losing its identity or in the course of time assimilating within that same community. Therefore, this chapter deals with a particular community in the quest for economic progress and search for sustaining its identity and in the process leading to identity crisis. Major factors such as migration, colonialism, religious conversion, Meitei expansionism or "Meiteization," modernization, and globalization are identified for the causes of identity crisis which ultimately led to the emergence of distinct and independent ethnic identities such as the Zeme, Liangmai, Rongmei and Inpui from a generic identity known as the "Zeliangrong."

A. Kamei (✉)
Department of Sociology, Delhi School of Economics, University of Delhi, Delhi, India
e-mail: k.aphundse@gmail.com

© The Author(s), under exclusive license to Springer Nature Singapore Pte Ltd. 2019
S. Ratuva (ed.), *The Palgrave Handbook of Ethnicity*,
https://doi.org/10.1007/978-981-13-2898-5_75

Keywords

Ethnicity · Identity · Migration · Colonialism · Meiteization · Religious conversion · Modernization globalization

Introduction

Today, all human societies have become increasingly interlinked with one another through global markets and the spread of a universal consumer culture. The need of development, which probably every country faces, creates a search for modern technology. This makes possible the development of the backward societies and accumulation of material wealth, and more importantly this process results in an increasing homogenization of all human societies, regardless of their origin or cultural inheritances. This process dictates inescapable unification of education pattern and replacement of traditional institutions like tribe, clan, or family by new economic units, in some cases resulting in progressive modernization or westernization of many societies (Saraswati 1996, p. 83). But, in this process of modernization and global markets, it is unfortunate to witness some societies or tribal groups being merged with the mainstream or consequently, losing their cultural identity. Therefore, it is pertinent to know what identity is and how it is formed.

Identity formation is a process through which people are made conscious of their distinct characteristics and group loyalty is established on that basis (Upreti 2001, p. 15). This formation is found in all societies, but the dominant cultural streams usually could not assimilate various smaller cultural groups within the majoritarian cultural streams. The smaller cultural groups fear their submergence in the larger culture. Hence, they try to assert on the basis of their distinct cultural identities. Such is the case in Pakistan, where Muhajirs have been struggling for their distinct cultural identity. Likewise in Sri Lanka, the clash of Sinhala and Tamil cultures has thrown the country in the vortex of serious ethnic conflict. In Bhutan too the problem of Nepali migrants emerged with the imposition of "cultural code" based on Drukpa culture on them. In Nepal, the hill people have been considering themselves as the repository of Nepal culture while Taraians as outsiders. This has brought the two communities, having distinct regional identities, into sharp conflict. The Nepalese ruling elite followed policy of "Nepalization" of the Tarai region: which is often seen as the cultural hegemony of the hill people over the immigrant Tarai people. The Mongolians are also resenting against the Hindu cultural domination.

The Tribal communities in South Asia, on the other hand, have also asserted their distinct identities. It is strange that while these communities aspire for modernization and development at par with other regions of the country, they do not want to lose their distinct cultural identities. The Baluch and Pakhtoon movements in Pakistan; Naga, Khasi, Mizo, in India; movement of Chitagong hill tribals in Bangladesh; "Limbuvan," "Kiratavan," and "Magarantik" movements in Nepal; etc. are such tribal cultural assertions (Ibid., pp. 18–19).

Any scholarly attempt to understand identity cannot ignore the works of Erik H. Erikson. As Ernest Hess rightly pointed, "Erik Erikson has been the person most responsible for bringing the concept of 'identity' and 'identity-crisis' into the common parlance." (Hess 1991, pp. 22–23). Erikson's concern centers mostly on the psychological aspect of an individual identity formation, but he relates "personal" identity closely with "cultural" identity recognizing the dynamic impact of the society on the individual's identity formation. Identity formation, Erikson said, "deals with a process 'located' in the core of the individual and yet also in the core of his (or her) communal culture (Erikson 1968, p. 22). Though his psychological definition aims at an individual's identity formation and development, his definition is helpful in comprehending the essential features of group identity as it provides us with a framework to devise the patterns and characters of group identity formation.

Identity is, therefore, complex since it requires one to ask, initially, questions about the "self" and the "other." It means covering a whole range of variables and definitions: the notions about the self-individual and collective and the cultural "other" in terms of whether one referring to economic, social, or cultural dimensions. These debates are very active in the contemporary societies where development and progress has taken deep roots. Unlike the concept of community, identity has not been a major preoccupation with mainstream western sociology. Among the classical theorists of sociology, it is perhaps in the writings of Mead and Cooley that one finds detailed references to the question of identity. However, they too approached identity in a socio psychological manner rather than a politico-sociological one. They talked about *identity* while trying to understand the formation of an individual self in a collectivity through the experience of meaningful interactions as part of the socialization process (see Cooley 1962; Mead 1934). The most crucial point that Mead and Cooley made in their discussions on the subject was the significance of "others" in the formation of an individual's self-identity.

Later sociologists emphasized that it was not sufficient for an individual or a collectivity to merely assert an identity. It also needed to be validated (or not) by those with whom one had dealings (Jenkins 1996, p. 210). Barth, in his classical work on ethnicity, insisted that sending a message about the distinctiveness of one's identity was not enough. The message to be accepted by significant others before an identity could be said to have been *"taken on."* Identities were therefore to be found and negotiated at the boundaries of the internal and external (Barth 1969, p. 23).

It was only in the 1970s and 1980s, with the rise of *"new"* social movements, including those by women and the subordinate ethnicities, that the question of *"identity"* acquired a political status in the western societies and academia. While it was in the 1970s that the west experienced what Anthony D. Smith called the *"ethnic revival"* (Smith 1981, p. 11), it was in the 1980s that the questions of identity and ethnicity came to acquire the center stage in Indian politics (Jodhka 2001, p. 20). The two most significant political movements that brought this about were the *"crises,"* experienced almost simultaneously, in the northeastern of Assam and the northwestern state of Punjab. A separatist's movement in the border of Kashmir and the rise of a pan-Indian Hindutva identity followed soon after.

Following Stuart Hall, one can identify two different ways of thinking about "*identity*." The first position defines cultural identity in terms of one, shared culture, a sort of collective "one true self," hiding inside the many other, more superficial or artificially imposed "*selves*," which people with a shared history and ancestry hold in common (Hall 1990, p. 223). It was within this framework that, until recently, the question of identity was thought of in many public and academic discourses on culture In reply to India. There is also a second and what Jodhka calls it "*open-ended view of culture*" that approaches community identities not in the primordialist or substantivist perspectives but as a process of, what Appadurai calls, "*conscious mobilization of cultural difference*" (Appadurai 1997, p. 15).

Like the above framework, Hall also argues, "cultural identity is a matter of '*becoming*' as well as of '*being*'." It belongs to the future as much as to the past. It is not something that already exists, transcending place, time, history, and culture. Cultural identities come from somewhere and have histories. But like everything there is historical, they undergo a constant transformation. Far from being eternally fixed in some essentialized past, they are subject to continuous "play" of history, culture, and power. Far from being grounded in a mere "*recovery*" of the past, which is waiting to be found, and which, when found, will secure our sense of ourselves into eternity, identities are the names we give to the different ways we are positioned by, and position ourselves within, the narratives of the past (Hall 1990, p. 225). Jenkins too makes a similar point when he says, "identity an only be understood as process. One's social identity (or identities) is never a final settled matter" (Jenkins 1996, p. 5).

The question of ethnic identity in North East India, therefore, remains a complex subject on account of several sociological and historical reasons. In several cases, the identity question is intimately tied with the wider political aspiration of the people concerned (Singh 1982, p. 199).

The nomenclature, Zeliangrong, is a collective ethno-cultural entity of the people who speak the dialect of Zeme, Liangmai, and Rongmei (Kabui) including Puimei tribes of North East India. The term was used for the first time in 1947, when the "Zeliangrong Union" was formed to mean the same group of people sharing common origin, language, and culture. It is a combined name of kindred tribes of the *Zeme,* the *Liangmai,* and the *Rongmei* (*Kabui*) with the prefixes taken together to form the term "ZELIANGRONG" (Ze+Liang+Rong).

Many Naga traditions pointed Makhel in north Manipur as their original homeland. The legends, the ritual hymns, and traditions of the tribe refer to their coming out of a hole or cave in the earth, called *Taobhei* at *Ramting Kabin*, a deep gorge between the two hills which are deep and dark. Another view on the origin is traced from China with a scanty literature. T.C. Hodson in the beginning of the twentieth century, while officiating as the Assistant Political Agent in Manipur, visited this megalith and wrote, "At Makhel is to be seen a stone now erected which marks the place from which the common ancestors (of the Nagas) emerged from the earth" (1996, p. 13). From this place, they proceeded westward and arrived at Makuilongdi or Nkuilongdi meaning "round big mountain." Makuilongdi has been known by many names like *Chawang Phungning* or *Guang Phungning*. Many Liangmai lineages trace their migration from *Guang Phungning*, which according to them was the main village of the cluster of villages, commonly known as Makuilongdi. Many Rongmei hymns refer to this prosperous village of *Guang Phungning* as well.

It is believed that Makuilongdi became quite prosperous with enough land for agriculture. From a village it had become a cluster of smaller hamlets and settlements. Tradition has that 30 ceremonies of "ornamented ritual house" (locally known as *Tarang Kai*) were performed at Makuilongdi in a single year. Performance of such costly ceremonies reflected the plentiful harvests in the village and a surplus in food production. At Makuilongdi, a political system was developed under a Chief. It was a cradle of Zeliangrong culture with a total of 7777 households. From here, it was believed that the tribe migrated toward different directions. (There are two schools of thought – immediate cause and long-term one: According to the former, the migration from Makuilongdi was caused by the sudden exodus of the people at the divine warning of violating the law of nature and social discipline of the village by indulging in the performance of 30 sacrificial house constructions (locally called *Tarangkai*) in a single year without any break forgetting their lunar calendar of agricultural rites and devoted to enjoyment and merry making. Suddenly, insects flew to the village, and being shocked and terrified, the people moved toward different directions. A more rational and scientific reason for their migration was believed to be caused by the pressure on land due to the increase in population and differences on the issue of succession to the hereditary chieftainship.) What is interesting to see is that the tribe came to be known by various names in the course of their migration. The name, Zeme, was derived from their settlement at the hill range, which was the frontier of the Zeliangrong habitat, frontier, or periphery as "Zena" or "Nzie." From this, the people were known as Zeme or Nzieme. The people who headed toward the northern direction came to be known as the "Liangmai"; the southerners came to be known as the "Rongmei" or the "Maruongmei." Thus, following the whims of the more powerful and daring adventurers among them, many of them started migrating, batch by batch, to distant hill ranges which attracted them most.

The southerners' (Rongmeis) settlement in the valley of Manipur is worth mentioning here. Since then they are referred to as "Kabuis," probably a term given by the Meiteis of Manipur. During the pre-British period, when Manipur was under the Meitei Rajas, the Rongmei settlement in the Manipur valley started from the days of Maharaja Garibaniwaj (1709–1749). According to the Meitei Puyas (Meitei Chronicles), the Rongmeis who had rendered help to the Meitei Rajas in their war against the Burmese in 1934 were allowed to settle down on the Chingmeirong (now in Imphal East district) and Langthabal Hills (Imphal-West district). It is said that the Meitei Rajas of those days employed the Rongmei people in several capacities – some for husking paddy in the royal house, some for collecting and supplying fire woods, some in the Royal band party, and others in several other works of life. Therefore, many villages such as Majorkhul, Keishamthong, Mahabali, Kakhulong, Ragailong, Namthanlong, Sangaiprou, etc. started settling in and around the Imphal Valley of Manipur. A large number of Rongmei people living on eastern hill ranges facing the Loktak Lake had come down the valley and started establishing a Rongmei village named "Thienjang" in the Loktak project area. Many of them have employment opportunities under the Loktak project schemes. Some of the Rongmei people from Mukten, Langteng, Daron, Juron, Charungkhou, Sengai, etc. who were, at one time, living on the top and not-easily-accessible-part of the hills moved down toward the plains. Many new villages came into existence in several parts of the Bishenpur area in Manipur. When the Naga underground movements were very active in the hills, life became insecure for many; and consequently, many of them were compelled to migrate to other states in North East India, Dhobi Nulla, Dimapur, Jaluke, Samjuram, and Beikapning, and other parts of Nagaland, while some in the Cachar district of Assam. The existing Rongmei villages in and around the Imphal Valley increased considerably in their household strength due to the influx of the immigrants from the neighboring hills.

The process of migration in the valley continued, and it was during the reign of King Garibniwaj that the Meiteis in the valley converted to Hinduism. Since then Meiteization (The process of "Meiteization" is because of the fact that the Meiteis enjoy a high social position in the valley, and the Meitei way of life became the "valley way of life," and this has led to the formation of the "valley society" in Manipur.) came as a response due to their dominance in economic and cultural sphere. For instance, anything that Meitei did become the "valley way of life." The Loi/Chakpa (other ethnic groups), Yaithibi started to use "Singh" as their title just like the Meiteis; have sacred places in their houses like them and even the hill tribes followed. The Rongmeis in the valley started adopting a religion like that of the Meiteis. Such process, according to M.N. Srinivas, is known as "Sanskritization." However, it would be wrong to assume that ethnic groups in the valley converted to Hinduism in its entirety. The Meitei Muslims locally known as the Meitei Pangals adopted Meitei language and culture identified themselves distinctly. They followed "*purdah* system" and practiced Mohammedan faith. Likewise, the tribals especially the Rongmeis retain their tribal identity and manifested it in festivals, rituals, and ceremonies. It was a "fluid identity" which changes in time and space. Around this time in the early nineteenth century, Christianity came to the neighboring hills of the Zeliangrong region. (The first missionaries who had toured the hill ranges of Manipur were the Jesuit missionaries, Stephen Cacells and J. Gabral, through the Brahmaputra Valley in the North East. The purpose of their tour was, however, exploratory ostensibly to find a route into China and Tibet. Later, there grew up Catholic Churches in many surrounding areas. But the first significant contact with the Hill Tribes of Manipur was made by the *Serampore Mission of the British Baptist Missionary Society* in the early part of the nineteenth century. Curiously enough, the initiative for starting missionary enterprise came from the government officials. This was because of the realization of the futility of the policy of military expedition which produced jealousy and suspicion culminating in endless wars of retaliation and revenge. Thus, what could not be achieved by the military power could be gained by the power of the gospel. *American Baptist Foreign Missionary Society* was the next group of Missionaries who landed in the Naga Hills in 1871. Under the leadership of Mr. William Pettigrew, many tribals were converted especially the Tangkhul Nagas of Manipur. The next group of Missionaries who came in contact with the Hill Tribes of Manipur was the *Welsh Calvinistic Methodist Foreign Mission Society* (WCMFMS) which were a conglomeration of Anglicans, Welsh Presbyterians, and Congregationalists (Independents) under Jacob Tomlin, an ex-missionary of London Missionary Society in India. These missionaries, in the course of time, succeeded in converting the Hill Tribes of Manipur. The single most important development that made the imagining of Nagas as a collectivity possible was their conversion to Christianity. Although they followed several sects and denominations, their conversion is considered as the most massive movement to Christianity in all of Asia, second only to that of the Philippines, in the words of historian Richard Eaton. Today, Christianity has become an essential part of Naga identity. But this conversion to Christianity was the result of their incorporation into a larger political, economic, and cultural universe, so was their journey on the road to Nationhood. For details see Dena (1988), p. 18; Bhuyan (1948), p. 3; Barpujari (1970); The Baptist Missionary Magazine, Boston, Vol. LXXV, pp. 308–309; F.D. Secret Proc., Nos. 24–24, January, 1895; Fortis Jyrwa (1980), p. 20; Eaton (1997).) The British conquest of the people was completed with their annexation of North Cachar in 1854, the establishment of the Naga Hills District in 1886, and the conquest of Manipur in 1891. During this period there were reasonably good numbers who have converted, and this gave rise to two faiths among the Zeliangrong Nagas. In the words of Prof. Gangmumei Kamei, "In the Zeliangrong area, there was not much help from the foreign missionaries. The Christian missionaries in their mission to spread Christianity tried to destroy the social and cultural life of the people. By bans on dance and music, on the dormitory system, rejection of the authority of the traditional village council, Christianity had caused great damage to the Zeliangrong culture" (2004, p. 300). The newly converts considered everything anti-Christian and started challenging their traditional faith and cultural practices. Probably, the greatest damage done to the people was the abolition of the *Morung* system (dormitory system). This institution was considered to be the center of their indigenous culture and practices. The abandonment is responsible for the disintegration of traditional values, music, and dances. This means that the British brought along many constructive changes (It would be wrong to say that the missionaries did not bring any constructive changes in the society. It was during the British colonialism that many developmental activities and opportunities were given to the hilly tribes: the introduction of formal education in schools and colleges and better transport and communication system, such as telegraph, telegram, radio, automobiles, electricity, and hospitals, and water supply and drainage system. It was the missionaries who introduced the art of writing which at later resulted in developing many distinct languages with proper grammar and pronunciation.); they brought a new religion with a new identity of the people. This is because the early converts started asserting their ethnic identity through Christianity which most often contradicts and challenges the traditional culture and practices of the people. The traditional chorus, drums, music, folksongs, and dances are replaced by the modern Christian hymnals, with guitars, keyboards, and western drums. The translation of the English Bible (Translation of the English Bible into Rongmei came in 1979, Zeme in 1979 and Liangmei in 1982.) into the vernacular dialects though encourage reading and writing produced three distinct languages in the course of time which challenged the very foundation of the common ethnic identity. Many writings on the culture and people were found during the colonial period by the British administrators, officials, and political agents. These writings were more of their experiences with the tribals of the North East India. (Though references to the people are found in the Chronicles of Manipur, the first English account of the Zeliangrong Nagas was given by Captain R.B. Pemberton, in his *Report of the Eastern Frontier of British India (1835)*. He was the first European to have visited the Zeme, Rongmei, and Puimei villages. He used the term "Koupooees" to mean the people. The second writer who refers to the same people of the present Manipur, Nagaland, and North Cachar was John Butler in his *Travels and Adventure in the Province of Assam* (1855). But the pioneer work on the tribe was Col. William McCulloch's *Account of the Valley of Munnipore and the Surrounding Hill Tribes* published in 1859. McCulloch was a British Political Agent posted in Manipur for many years. He was known at that time as an expert on the state of Manipur and the surrounding hill tribes. But his use of Pemberton's term "Koupooee" and the Puimei term of "*Songboo* and *Pooeeron*" as the two subdivisions of the tribe has left behind a trail of identity confusion. Otherwise his account reproduced elsewhere in this work is very important. In 1874, the *Statistical Account of Manipur* written by another distinguished British Political Agent, Dr. R. Brown, continued to add more to the knowledge of the "Koupois" tribe. He divided the tribe into three subgroups – *Songbu* (Rongmei), *Koireng* (Liangmei), and *Koupui* (puimei).) What is disturbing is that many of the writings were undertaken simply for administrative efficiency and used "theory of simplification" (This theory is a self-composition. It means that the colonizers did not see things as they are. They consider it as the version of previously known things and interpreted them. In the context of the whole North East India, the British used a very simple and random tool (which is not accurate) while classifying the various ethnic groups of the regions including Manipur. No doubt, this avoided complexities of the ethnic groups or tribes, but later it led to serious problems when their writings became officially recognized and used in all administrative accounts and official purposes. The classification of Nagas as "Kacha Naga," and the "Puimei" term of "Songboo" and "Pooeeron" as the two subdivisions; use of "Koupooees" for "Kabui" or "Rongmei"; and "Quireng" or "Koireng" for "Liangmei"; use of "Empeo" to refer the "Zeme" tribe becomes a serious problem, which led to identity confusion in the study of the tribe.) which produced confusion of identity for the tribe when time came to rewrite their own history.

Independent India witnessed resurfacing of ethnic assertion from village identity to communitarian Zeliangrong identity. This is because of the fact that under this new political system, the various ethnic groups who had diverse culture, language, faith, and beliefs had to come together under the same rule of law. When such diversities are bounded under common territory (India), a crisis of adjustment soon follows. (It is because of the fact that each tribal village acted like a "little republic" quite independent and self-sufficient. The new political system challenged the hereditary chieftainship, customary laws, and practices of the people.) Under the new political setup, each ethnic group competes and struggles for ethnic survival.

Land becomes the exclusive property of the State. Laws and rules are then formulated and enforced. Those groups who adhere to these rules and regulations are accepted and recognized. Therefore, politics of identity start interfering with the society. However, the setback still remains as the tribe was divided in the various states of Manipur, Nagaland, and Assam and even in some parts of present-day Burma. The distance in interaction is thus widened, and the dream of unifying kindred tribes of Zeme, Liangmei, and Rongmei (Kabui) including the Puimei remains unrealistic. Today constitutionally, Zeliangrong is recognized as Kabui (for Rongmei and Puimei), Kacha Naga (for Liangmei and Zeme) in Manipur, and Zeliang in Nagaland state.

The struggle for unification of these three kindred tribes was first started in the early 1920s by a visionary man called Jadonang. Born at Kambiron (or Puiron) in the present-day Tamenglong District of Manipur, the village was a strategic place as it served as one of the resting places on the Manipur Cachar Road. On a regular basis, he observed the British officials, missionaries, soldiers, and traders from Manipur, Assam, and neighboring regions moving to and fro through the highway route and understood them. Around the same time, the hill tribes (with the British conquest of Manipur in 1891) were directly administered by the British officials. The British started imposing "house tax" which the people had never paid even to the Manipuri Maharaja. New systems such as *Pothang Bekari* (sometimes written as Begari) and *Pothang Senkhai* (*Pothang Bekari* was a kind of forced labor introduced by the British. Whenever any official of the State went on the tour in the hills, the villagers in those areas had to carry the goods and luggages without any payment. On refusal, they were usually punished mostly by whipping. *Pothang Senkhai* was a kind of forced contribution mostly in the form of money imposed by the British to feed the touring officials and other employees of the government.) were also institutionalized by the British which really hurt the sentiments of the Zeliangrong people. These systems of free services and taxes greatly affected the economic life of the already poverty-ridden people. Furthermore, these hilly people were imposed with oppressive forest laws (by declaring "restricted forest" or "reserved forest") which prevented them to use and consume forest products such as bamboo, cane, and other useful trees which are used for making houses and other domestic purposes. This also displaces history and culture of the people because tribals are known by their social environment. Their habitat is a source of identity which any individual could easily relate to. Moreover, the people were asked to render free services for repair and maintenance of government roads, bridges, and dams, and the British Government failed to protect the Zeliangrong people when the Kuki rebellion (1917–1919) broke out in Manipur. (The famous Kuki rebellion of 1917–1919 was fought by the Kuki tribes against the British Colonialism. It was officially stated that the Rebellion started as a violent reaction against the non-recruitment of Kukis to the Manipur Labour Corps No. 22 by the British for the services in France during the First World War. There was a conflict in the style of recruitment. The rebellion started against the British and later targeted the Nagas, specially the Zeliangrong in the North West of Manipur and the Tangkhuls in North Eastern Manipur and in some tracts of Upper Burma. For details see Kamei (2004), pp. 132–141.) By this time, there was huge Kuki migration into the land of Zeliangrong regions. This had created huge insecurity in the minds of the people. On the one hand, there were disunity, intertribal, and inter-village feuds, and on the other, the social and religious practices of the people were full of taboos and superstitions. Meanwhile, Christian missionaries had already gained momentum in the hills of Manipur, and as a result of it many people have converted to Christianity. In the valley, there was huge Meitei expansionism who began their rule by acts of invasion and subjugation on the hill tribes. They imposed duties and demanded payment of tributes, rendering of forced services to the Maharaja. The hierarchy in the society left many people hurt when they were labeled with derogatory names such as *"Haos," "Chingmis,"* and *"Amangba"* (a notion of purity and pollution). Against these prejudices and discriminations, Jadonang started a movement which came to be known as the Zeliangrong Movement in 1925. The Movement which began in the early 1920s by Jadonang was perceived and described differently by many writers. J.P. Mills, the then Deputy Commissioner of Naga Hills and well-known anthropologist, romanticized Jadonang as "the Messiah King" of the Nagas. Robert Reid, a British Governor during that time described the movement as "Zeliangrong Uprising" (Reid 1942). However, he contradicted his very own writings in the book *Winds of Change* (1962) on the movement and called it "an outburst of a highly superstitious people and not as freedom fighters." Ursula Graham Bower in her book *Naga Path* (For details, see Bower 1950) made a sympathetic reference to Jadonang as the religious mystic who visualized a kingdom for his people. J. Roy in *History of Manipur* (Roy 1958) described the movement as a challenge to British Imperialism. F.S. Downs in *Mighty Works of God* (Downs 1971) described the movement as heathen and anti-Christian. According to N. Joykumar Singh (1992), it was a millenarian tribal movement. Many leaders and writers like A.Z. Phizo, A. Dasgupta, Khuswant Singh, D.P. Stracey, B.B. Ghosh, and Hamlet Bareh referred to the movement as a "Naga revolt against British colonialism" (For details, see Gangmumei Kamei (1997), p. 3). Likewise many others have written and opined on the movement till date. However, what we need at the hour is to see how the movement started, reached the peak, and continued in different shapes and forms. It means to say that the movement is seen rather as a process of continuity and change. The earlier writers have concentrated the movement confining during the times of Haipou Jadonang and Rani Gaidinliu. As it coincided with India's struggle for independence, the movement in that period gained definite attention. However, what is lacking is that they failed to notice the movement which even today is struggling after 69 years of India's Independence.

The aims and objectives can be broadly divided as:

(i) Reformation of traditional religion by abolishing irrational customs and superstitions
(ii) By integrating tribes such as Zeme, Liangmai, and Rongmei (Kabui) including Puimei.
(iii) Establishment of *"Makam Gwangdi"* (Makam Gwangdi, the kingdom of the Makam, refers to the establishment of Zeliangrong Kingdom. This was described by the British as "Naga Raj," a concept of the present-day Sovereign

State. The term was first used by J.C. Higgins, the then British Political Agent of Manipur in his report to the Chief Secretary of Assam. The Makam Gwangdi of Jadonang was also referred to by Graham Bower in her work, "Naga Path," as a "millenium on earth" where there would be prosperity, no war, and no suffering. It soon became a political ideology which made Jadonang clashed with the colonial authorities, and his political struggle made his movement relevant to the Indian freedom struggle going on in other parts of India.) or proclamation of "Naga Raj" (a Sovereign State) by driving out the outsiders such as the British and the Kukis.

The outbreak of the movement was renaissance to the Zeliangrong people because it touched almost all aspects of the collective life of this tribe. However, Jadonang was arrested and imprisoned by the British for proclaiming himself as the King and for declaring the impending end of the British Raj. He was then released but rearrested on 19 February 1931 and hanged on 29 August 1931 for the alleged murder of four Manipuri traders.

Jadonang was succeeded by his disciple Gaidinliu when she was barely 17 years old. She used Gandhiji's name and Jadonang's songs in order to mobilize the people. She propagated that the British would be soon driven out with the help of Gandhiji and Nehru. It was believed that she had contacts with the Indian National Congress, the Bengali Congress Workers of Cachar District, Assam, and sympathizers from various other tribes such as Mao, Maram, Thangal, and Angamis of Khonoma. Pandit Nehru came to know of Jadonang and Gaidinliu's movement during his tour to Assam in the winter of 1937. In his article, "The Surma Valley: The Daughter of the Hills," he described the rebellion against the British Imperialism and called Gaidinliu, the "Rani." Since then she has been called Rani Gaidinliu.

Rani Gaidinliu followed the aims and objectives of the movement which was left unfulfilled by her mentor Haipou Jadonang. She propagated for securing socio-economic development of her people, trained young boys and girls, and fought the British with courage and vigor. In February 1932 they attacked the Assam Rifles patrols in North Cachar Hills in a broad daylight, and this has received a huge attention among the British. The British armed forces in retaliation burnt down several villages including the village of Bopungwemi in Naga Hills. The Manipur Government announced a reward of Rs.200/– later increased it to Rs.500/– and exemption of house tax for 10 years for anybody or any village who would give information leading to her arrest (Kamei 1997, p. 69). Finally, she was arrested on 17 October 1932 under the leadership of Captain Macdonald of Assam Rifles at Pulomi village and awarded life imprisonment. During her imprisonment, the movement continued in different forms under the leadership of Haido of Pabram and Ramjo of Bopungwemi. They took over the movement and asked the Zeliangrong villages not to pay taxes to the government. Unfortunately, Haido was arrested in May 1934 by the Assam Rifles at Henima (Tening) in Naga Hills and was killed. Likewise, Ramjo was arrested in July 1934 and died in the jail. Several leaders like Dikeo, Gomhai, and Areliu were also imprisoned by the Assam Rifles. The matter of movement against the British and the arrest of Gaidinliu came up for discussion in the British

Parliament. Nehru requested Lady Nancy Astor, the first lady member of the British House of Commons, to get Rani Gaidinliu released from jail. Lady Astor informed Nehru in a letter dated 10 May 1939 that the Secretary of State for India had stated that "the movement among the Nagas has not yet died down and would break out if she is released and that she is at present considered a potent source of danger to the peace of Manipur State and Province of Assam." Pandit Nehru further urged Premier Gopinath Bordoloi of Assam to intervene in the matter and get Gaidinliu released from jail. Bordoloi was helpless as the Naga Hills district was at that time in the excluded area, which was not a part of Assam; and Manipur was a princely state. Likewise, the Akhil Manipuri Mahasabha of Manipur presided by H. Irabot Singh demanded her release in its annual session at Imphal in 1938, but Manipur Government refused to consider the demand. The Haripura session of Indian National Congress Party in 1939 under the presidentship of Nehru passed a resolution demanding the release of Rani Gaidinliu but again failed. When India got independence, the first Prime Minister, Pandit Jawaharlal Nehru, wrote to the authorities in Assam to release the freedom fighter, and, ultimately, after continuous intervention of the Prime Minister, the officials agreed to release her on one condition that she lived outside Manipur until further orders (Singh 1982, p. 82). Rani Gaidinliu spent the next few years at Yimrap near Mokokchung village in the present-day Nagaland State with a pension of Rs.15/– per month. This was after her 14 years of confinement in jail. Thus, there came a point of time when Zeliangrong Movement suffered a big blow with no successor. During this period, a mention can be made of "Kabui Samiti," an organization that was formed in 1934 which became the highest body on custom, and it became the forum for the unification of the three tribes. It however could not continue to function during the Second World War, and in 1946 it was replaced by the "Kabui Naga Association." The aim of the organization was to integrate the people by establishing a common organization to safeguard the rights and interests of the people, and this resulted in the formation of "Zeliangrong Council" on 15 February 1947. The meeting was convened at Keishamthong village in the present-day Imphal East District of Manipur and the representatives of all Rongmeis (Kabuis), Liangmei, and Zemes of Manipur, Assam, and Nagaland were attended. The outcome of the conference was that the name "Zeliangrong" was used for the first time to mean the Zemes, Liangmeis, and Rongmeis (Kabuis) including the Puimeis. The former "Kabui Naga Association" was then called as the "Manipur Zeliangrong Union" (MZU). However, due to leadership crisis, the MZU became "Zeliangrong Naga Union, Manipur" in 1960. The objective was aimed to address more on social, economic, cultural, and customary issues.

The struggle continued under various organizations demanding for integration of all "Zeliangrong inhabited areas" under one administrative and political unit and recognition of the tribe as "Zeliangrong" in the Scheduled Tribes list in the Indian Constitution. (It is a fact that *Zeliangrong* is recognized differently in many states. For instance, in Nagaland they are called "*Zeliang*"; in Manipur, they are known as "Kabui" for "Rongmei" and "Puimei"; "Kacha Naga" for "Zemi" and "Liangmei." In Assam, the tribe is not even mention. It is only referred to as "Any Naga tribes." The Meiteis called the Rongmei Nagas living in the valley "Kabui," and the hilly

Rongmeis are critical on the term since the term was continued to use in the constitution of India.)

The post-independence period witnessed many changes in the Zeliangrong society. The period between 1960 and 1993 was marked with lot of political and religious interfaces. By the end of 1950s, the Naga National Council (NNC) was gaining momentum. (The Naga National Council (NNC) is a Naga Organization demanding for a creation of separate Naga Sovereign State.) The beginning of 1960s witnessed a conflict between Zeliangrong movement under Rani Gaidinliu and the Naga's struggle for independence under A.Z. Phizo and T. Sakhrie. Rani Gaidinliu was labeled as "Indian Rani," and her religious beliefs were questioned describing it as "worship of spirits." Gangmumei Kamei, a noted historian, stated that "the movement was not opposed to the Naga independence movement. However, conflict erupted on religious issues" (Kamei 2004, p. 215). To respond to it, Gaidinliu had to adopt twin objectives of preservation and promotion of the "Heraka cult" (*Heraka* means a "new cult" believing in one high God in place of many, removing superstitions in beliefs and customs, organizing temples, introducing hymns and discourses, and uniting the tribes to establish an independent kingdom.) against the growing of new faith among the Nagas. However, a clash occurred between Gaidinliu's forces and the Christians at Tousem in 1966. This incident was misinterpreted by many as if the movement was against the Naga cause. However the fact remained that Rani Gaidinliu was not against Christianity (as religious institution) but was against the early converts per se who abandoned the rich culture and traditions of the Zeliangrong Nagas.

The demand for "Zeliangrong political unit" as a District, Union Territory, or State was expressed by the third conference of the Zeliangrong leaders of Manipur in October 1980. They demanded the integration of all Zeliangrong areas into a political and administrative unit at Tamenglong. The conference elected Rani Gaidinliu (in her absence) as the President of the "Zeliangrong People's Convention" popularly known as ZPC. On 7 June 1981, ZPC adopted the official slogan "Zeliangrong Ringtelou" which means "Long Live Zeliangrong" and subsequently submitted Memorandums one after another to Prime Ministers of India Smt. Indira Gandhi, Morarji Desai, and Rajiv Gandhi. The delegations met Mr. Bajpai (Former MP Lok Sabha), Mrs. Sheila Grewal in 1985 (former Principal Secretary to Prime Minister Rajiv Gandhi), Mr. Buta Singh in 1986 (former Home Minister), and many representatives of the Government of India. The North Eastern Council (NEC) under the guidance of the Planning Commission was instructed to study on the problems and developments of the Zeliangrong areas in 1985. The then Prime Minister Rajiv Gandhi directed the Department of Culture to entrust the Anthropological Survey of India to make a thorough investigation on the Zeliangrong cognate tribes (Zeme, Liangmai, Rongmei, and Puimei) and came up with a report that from linguistic and anthropological view, they belong to the same group of people. Despite many commitments and assurances, the Government of India did not come up with any concrete solution on the issue of integration and recognition of the name Zeliangrong. Then came the conflict between Kuki and Naga in Zeliangrong regions in 1992, and the political activities and demands remained standstill. The movement again suffered a big blow with the death of Rani Gaidinliu on 23 February 1993 after prolonged illness.

Therefore, we see a sea change in the Zeliangrong movement in the search of their own identity. The struggle which originated in 1925 to drive away the British took the way to integrate the kindred tribes and demanded for recognition of Zeliangrong in the list of Scheduled Tribes in India. The movement attracted a lot of attention both at national and regional levels. It became a part of syllabus of NCERT textbook in the study of National Movements against the British colonialism and has included a chapter on Jadonang and Rani Gaidinliu's struggles. Besides a title "Rani," Gaidinliu was awarded with Tama Patra in 1972 by Indira Gandhi, Padma Bhushan in 1982 by the then President of India Neelam Sanjiva Reddy, Swarna Vivekananda Seva Award in 1983 by Bada Bazar Kumarsabha Pustakalaya, and Kolkata and Bhagwan Birsa Munda Purashkar Award posthumously in 1996. The Government of India issued a postal stamp in her memory, and Rani Gaidinliu Stree Shakti Puraskar Award was started by the Government of India in her memory which is given on March 8 of every year to veteran women social workers in recognition to the selfless sacrifice for the society.

However, the demand for integration and recognition of the tribe in the Indian Constitution though continued to be discussed and debated at the Prime Minister's level but was repeatedly turned down. Meanwhile, the continuous projection of identity was hit hard by several external factors such as migration, colonialism, conversion, Meitei expansionism, politics of identity, impact of modernization, and globalization. Even the widest claim of Anderson's "Imagined Community" seems to be a distant reality for the tribe. Following the tense "contested" course, the Zeliangrong people today are divided into the state of Manipur, Nagaland, and Assam and some parts of Myanmar (Burma), and the people identified with "Zeliangrong" (though there is common solidarity among the three cognate tribes) are now recognized separately in the list of Scheduled Tribes in the Indian Constitution. This is what cruel history had done to this people belonging to the same stock of family and race and in the course of time, began to be known by/with different names.

The above explanation shows how migration can lead to crisis in ethnic identity, and we shall see now how a theory of "push and pull" exists in a multicultural society with regard to culture and tradition. As already being explained, the migration of the Kabui (Rongmei) Nagas in the Imphal Valley started during the pre-British period when Manipur was under the Meitei Maharaja Garibniwaj (1709–1749 A.D.). They first settled at Chingmeirong and Langthabal villages which were surrounded by the dominant Meiteis. The Kabuis who were employed in military services of the King Chandrakirti were asked to settle in Majorkhul village (in the heart of Imphal city). A Kabui village in Keishamthong was established who were employed in the Royal band of the Meitei Raja. Likewise, many villages such as Kakhulong, Namthanlong, Ragailong, Mahabali, Sangaiprou, etc. were established in around the Imphal City. As this people lived near the Meiteis, they are largely influenced by them. As already being discussed, there was a process of Meiteization and Hinduization in the Valley. By then, the State of Manipur was already declared as a Hindu State during the time of King Garibniwaz. It means that the theory of purity and pollution was very much prevalent in the early eighteenth century A.D. This hilly tribe who migrated in the valley was given many derogatory names such as "hao," "chingmi," "Amangba," etc. Only those who followed the Meiteis way of life were accepted. Therefore, we see the Rongmei Nagas even adopting a religion like them. Not only this, we see the influence of the Meiteis in all spheres of life. Many cultural elements with relation to dance, songs, festivals, and language have had a tremendous impact on this tribe. Therefore, even today we see a huge difference in these cultural elements with that of the hilly Rongmeis in Tamenglong district of Manipur. The valley Rongmeis speaks the Meitei language (Meiteilon) exactly like them. In this way, migration and interaction with other ethnic groups becomes a major factor responsible for identity crisis among the Zeliangrong Nagas.

Another important factor responsible for identity crisis is the impact of British colonialism. As already been pointed out, the British conquest of the Zeliangrong people was completed with their annexation of North Cachar in 1854, the establishment of the Naga Hills District in 1886, and the conquest of Manipur in 1891. Under the regime of the British, there came a change in the functioning of the society. We had witnessed how the power of the village authority gets weakened by the appointment of Lambus by the British. The practices of free services like "Pothang Bekari" and "Pothang Senkhai" are other instances which extremely affected the psychology of the tribe. Then came a policy of "divide and rule" used by the British against various ethnic groups of Manipur especially during the Kuki Rebellion (1917–1919). Most importantly, it was during the colonial rule that most of the literature on the tribe was written and published. These writings were instrumental in shaping the identity of the Zeliangrong Nagas as the tribe depended only on oral history, legends, and folksongs. What had resulted is that most literature were either distorted or written from their own perspectives. As a result of this fact, a "theory of simplification" was used to study the tribe for official and administrative records. At most instances they are wrongly spelt. Therefore, it is argued that these writings produce a wrong impression of the tribe.

British colonialism is accompanied by the coming of Christian missionaries. We have also discussed at length how the early converts came into being and how they are persecuted. Here, we safely argue that Christianity has no doubt brought lot of changes in the Zeliangrong society. The present Zeliangrong who are Christians believe that Christianity is instrumental in bringing development and modernity in the society. They argue that it is because of this religion that they could compete with the outside world. The present level of literacy rate which was a by-product of better educational system by the British helps them to have better understanding and wider outlook of other societies as well. This in return shapes them to grow and accommodate other cultures. Therefore, the Zeliangrong Christians believe that Christianity has provided new identity which is more relevant and suited to the present-day society. However, it has to be pointed out that the coming of Christianity in Zeliangrong society has affected the traditional structure of the society as the early

Christians abandoned all traditional dresses, songs, and dances. This difference has resulted in disunity within the tribe itself. For instance, the term "Kabui" is not comfortable among the Zeliangrong Christians.

The last factor responsible for identity crisis of Zeliangrong Nagas is the process of modernization. It began from the colonial period and accentuated in the India's independent period. Modernization gave rise to material culture and accumulation of more and more wealth. In this process, people compete and fight for resources under the new laws which are altogether different from the traditional tribal structure. To survive and win, they are forced by the new social systems to come out and participate with other ethnic groups. It implies that the traditional culture is slowly being replaced by the new market force where they become a part of the system. As already being discussed above, this force of modernization came in the way of the traditional believers, and there came a point of time where they had to compromise with development and economic progress. They thought unless they imbibe the processes of change, the survival would be at risk. Therefore, modernity poses a threat in the tradition-making of the Zeliangrong Nagas.

Conclusion

Therefore, the study of identity and ethnicity in North East India is a complex phenomenon as it is an interwoven issue of several entities. On one hand, there are primordial questions, and on the other, there is an entity of social construction which is in a fluid state. As Stuart Hall suggested, "Cultural identity is a matter of 'becoming' as well as of 'being' (Hall 1996, p. 225) and in the process of becoming, it gets diluted." As identity comes from somewhere and undergoes a constant transformation, it can be understood as a "process" as put forward by Jenkins. In this way, there is always a "narrative identity" which is to be passed on, and any society will sustain its identity only through a continuous process of such projection. Crisis of identity arrives when the society ceases this projection. Likewise, due to the abandonment of traditional sources of identity due to the abovementioned factors, Zeliangrongs today are faced with the challenge to revive and assert their ethnic identity. The need to preserve and protect traditional cultures, festivals and its rituals are constantly and consciously being felt by the people today. And, increasingly, each tribe i.e. Zeme, Liangmai, Rongmei (Kabui), and Inpui has asserted their distinct and independent identity from generic identity "Zeliangrong" which led to the problems of constructing generic identity.

References

Aggarwal KS (1999) Dynamics of identity and inter group relations in North East India. Indian Institute of Advanced Study, Shimla

Anderson B (1991) Imagined communities: reflections in the origin and spread of nationalism. Verso, London

Appadurai A (1997) Modernity at large: cultural dimensions of globalization. Oxford University Press, Delhi
Barpujari SK (1970) Early Christian missions in the Naga Hills: an assessment of their activities. J Indian Hist 48:427
Barth F (1969) Ethnic groups and boundaries: the social organization of culture difference. Universitetsforlaget, Norway
Bhuyan SK (1948) Early British relation with Assam. Assam Government, Shillong
Bower UG (1950) Naga path (adventure to Naga inhabited areas). Butler and Tanner Limited, London
Bower UG (1986) The Naga path: adventure to Naga inhabited areas. John Murray, London, (Reprinted)
Brass PR (1991) Ethnicity and nationalism: theory and comparison. Sage, New Delhi
Brown R (1873) Statistical account of the native state of Manipur. Office of the Superintendent of Government Printing, Calcutta
Butler J (1855) Travels and adventure in the province of Assam. Smith Elder, London
Cooley CH (1962) Social organization: a study of larger mind. Schoken, New York
Das RK (1985) Manipur tribal scene. Inter-India Publications, New Delhi
Das NK (1989) Ethnic identity, ethnicity and social stratification in North-East India. Inter-India Publications, New Delhi
Das NK (1994) Ethno historical process and ethnicity. J India Anthropol Soc 29(1):3–35
De Vos GA (1995) Ethnic pluralism: conflict and accommodation. In: Romanucci-Ross L, De Vos GA (eds) Ethnic identity: creation, conflict and accommodation. Alta Mira Press, Walnut Creek/London/New Delhi
Dena L (1988) Christian missions and colonialism: a study of missionary movement in North East India with particular reference to Manipur and Lushai Hills (1894–1947). Vendrame Institute, Shillong
Downs FS (1971) The mighty works of God. Christian Literature Center, Gauhati
Downs FS (1992) History of Christianity in India, Vol. V, Part 5, (North East India in the 19th and 20th centuries). The Church History Association of India, Bangalore
Dun EN (1992) Gazetteer of Manipur. Manas Publications, New Delhi
Eaton RM (1997) Comparative history as world history: religious conversion in modern India. J World Hist 8(2):243–271
Eller JD (1999) From culture to ethnicity to conflict: an anthropological perspective on international ethnic conflict. The University of Michigan Press, Ann Arbor
Elwin V (1959) North East frontier in the 19th century. Oxford University Press, Madras
Elwin V (1969) The Nagas in the 19th century. Oxford University Press, Bombay
Engineer AA (1987) Ethnic conflict in South Asia. Ajanta Publications, Delhi
Eriksen TH (2002) Ethnicity and nationalism: anthropological perspective. Pluto Press, Chicago
Erikson HE (1968) Identity, youth and crisis. W.W. Norton, New York
Fortis Jyrwa J (1980) The wondrous of God: a study of the growth and development of the Khasi-Jaintia Presbyterian Church in the 20th century. M.B. Jyrwa, Shillong
Geertz C (1973a) Internal conversion in contemporary Bali: the interpretation cultures. Basic Books, Oxford/UK
Geertz C (1973b) The interpretation of cultures. Basic Books, New York
Geertz C (2001) The integrative revolution: primordial sentiments and civil politics in the new states. In: Pecora VP (ed) Nations and identities. Blackwell Publishers, Oxford
Glazer N, Moynihan DP (1975) Ethnicity: theory and experience. Harvard University Press, Cambridge/London
Gonmei L (2000) Zeliangrong identity: past and present. ZSUM Golden Jubilee Publication, Imphal
Grierson GA (1967) The linguistic survey of India, Vol. III, Part V. Delhi, (Reprinted). Motilal Banarsidass, Delhi
Gupta D (1996) The context of ethnicity: Sikh identity in a comparative perspective. Oxford University Press, Delhi

Hall S (1990) Cultural identity and diaspora. In: Rutherford J (ed) Identity: community, culture, difference. Lawrence & Wishart, London
Hall S (1996) Who needs identity. In: Hall S, Du Gray P (eds) Questions of cultural identity. Sage, London
Hess E (1991) Christian identity and openness: a theologically informed hermeneutical approach to Christian education. PhD dissertation, Princeton Theological Seminary
Hodson TC (1996) The Naga tribes of Manipur. Low Price Publications, New Delhi, (Reprinted)
Iboongohal L (1987) Introduction to Manipur. Saraswati Printing Works, Imphal
Jenkins R (1996) Social identity. Routledge, London
Jeyaseelan L (2000) Culture, mission and contextualization. Catholic Manipur publications series 1. Catholic Manipur Publications, Imphal
Jodhka SS (2001) Community and identities-contemporary discourses in culture and politics in India. Sage, New Delhi
Johnstone J (1971) Manipur and the Naga Hills. Vivek Publishing House, Delhi
Jyrwa MB (1997) Comparative history as world history: religious conversion in modern India. J World Hist 8(2):243
Kabui G (1982) The Zeliangrong movement; a historical study. In: Singh KS (ed) Tribal movement of India. Manohar Publications, Delhi
Kamei G (1997) Jadonang: a mystic Naga rebel. Lamyanba Press, Imphal
Kamei G (2001) The concept of Zeliangrong Religion, the commemorative volume Tingkao Ragwang Kalum Kai, Imphal, 7th May
Kamei G (2004) A history of the Zeliangrong Nagas: from Makhel to Rani Gaidinliu. Spectrum Publications, Guwahati/Delhi
Kamei G (2006) On history and historiography of Manipur. Akansha Publishing House, New Delhi
Kamson C (2001) A report of the Zeliangrong Religious Council, 1993–2001, published in the commemorative volume of Tingkao Ragwang Kalum Kai, Imphal, 7th May
Karma MN (1999) Ethnic identity and socio-economic processes in North Eastern India. In: Aggarwal L (ed) Dynamics of identity and inter-group relations in North East India. Indian Institute of Advanced Study, Rashtrapati Nivas, Shimla
Kulkarni S (2000) Ethnicity and ethnic relations, Jan./Feb. Encounter
Kumar SR (1994) Valley society of Manipur: a cultural frontier of Indian civilization. Punthi-Pustak, Calcutta
Marulung R (1996) Zeliangrong Wari Singbul. Pvt Publication, Imphal
McCulloch W (1859) Valley of Munnipore and the Hill Tribes. Bengal Printing Company, Calcutta
McCulloch W (1874) The statistical account of Manipur
Mead GH (1934) Mind, self and society. University of Chicago Press, Chicago
Merkle PH, Smart N (ed). (2001) Religion and politics in the modern world. New York University Press, New York/London
Mills JP (1932) A note on Gaidinliu's movement, Kohima, 6th June
Mohan RV (1987) Identity crisis of Sri Lanka Muslims. Mittal Publications, New Delhi
Moya MLP, Garcia MRH (2001) Reclaiming identity: realist theory and the predicament of post modernism. Orient Longman, California
Mukherjee DP, Gupta P, Das NK (1982) The Zeliangrong or Haomei movement. In: Singh KS (ed) Tribal movements in India. Manohar Publications, Delhi
Nag S (1990) Roots of ethnic conflict: nationality question in North East India. Manohar Publication, New Delhi
Nag S (2002) Contesting marginality: ethnicity, insurgency and sub nationalism in North East India. Manohar Publication, New Delhi
Nammethon P (1976) Working of the Village Council among the Zeliangrong people. A paper submitted to the symposium on the problems of development in Manipur West District, Tamenglong, 6th December, organized by the JNU Centre, Imphal, (unpublished)
Nandy A (2002) The intimate enemy: loss and recovery of self under colonialism. Oxford University Press, New Delhi

Oommen TK (2002) Pluralism, equality and identity-comparative studies. Oxford University Press, New Delhi
Pachuau L (2002) Ethnic identity and Christianity: a socio-historical and missiological study of Christianity in North East India with special reference to Mizoram. Peter Lang, Berlin
Pamei D (1995) The customary laws of the Zeliangrong people. A paper submitted to North East India Zeliangrong Naga Festival and Seminar, Imphal, (unpublished)
Pamei R (1996) The Zeliangrong Nagas: a study of tribal Christianity. Uppal Publishing House, New Delhi
Pamei NB (2000) The trail from Makuilongdi. Gironto Charitable Foundation, Shillong
Pandit Jawaharlal Nehru's "Daughter of the Hills" published in Hindustan Times, dated 14 Dec 1937
Pecora V (2001) Nations and identities: classic readings. Blackwell Publishers, Oxford
Punekar V (1974) Assimilation. Popular Prakashan, Bombay
Ray W (2001) The logic of culture: authority and identity in the modern era. Blackwell Publishers, Oxford
Ray AK (2004) Change: the law of life. In: Venuh N, Maulana Abul Kalam Azad Institute of Asian Studies (eds) Naga society: continuity and change. Shripa Publications, Delhi
Reid R (1942) A history of frontier areas bordering Assam. Spectrum Publications, Shillong, (Reprinted)
Rider JL (1993) Modernity and crisis of identity-culture and society. In: Fin-de-Sie'de. Polity Press, Vienna
Roy J (1958) A history of Manipur. Eastlight Book House, Calcutta
Rudolph LI, Rudolph SH (1967) The modernity of tradition: political development in India. University of Chicago Press, Chicago
Rutherford J (1990) Identity: community, culture, difference. Lawrence and Wishart, London
Saberwal S (1986) India: roots of crisis. Oxford University Press, New Delhi
Saraswati B (1996) Interface of cultural identity and development. Indira Gandhi National Center for the Arts, D.K Printworld (P), New Delhi
Silverman S (1976) Ethnicity as adaptation: strategies and systems. Rev Anthropol 3:626
Singh KS (1982) Tribal movements in India. Monahar Publishers, New Delhi
Singh NJ (1992) Social movements in Manipur (1971–1950). Mittal Publishers, New Delhi
Singh KS (1994) NAGALAND, (People of India), vol XXXIV. Seagull Books and Anthropological Survey of India, Calcutta
Singh LL (1995) Identity and crisis of identity: a case study of Manipur. In: Sanajaoba N (ed) Manipur- past and present, Vol. 1, Polity and law. Mittal Publications, New Delhi
Smith AD (1981) The ethnic revival in the modern world. Cambridge University Press, Cambridge
Smith AD (1986a) Ethnic sources of nationalism. Routledge, London
Smith AD (1986b) The ethnic origins of nations. Basil Blackwell, Oxford/New York
Smith AD (1995) Nations and nationalism in global era. Polity Press, Cambridge
Snaitang OL (1993) Christianity and social change in North East India: a study of the role of Christianity in social change among the Khasi-Jaintia Hill tribes of Meghalaya. Vendrame Institute, Calcutta
Srinivas MN (1972) Social change in modern India. Orient Longman, New Delhi
Thaimei M (1995) The Rongmei's. In: Sanajaoba N (ed) Manipur-past and present, vol 3. Mittal Publishers, New Delhi
Tschuy T (1997) Ethnic conflict and religion: challenge to the churches. WCC Publications, Geneva
Upreti BC (2001) Ethnicity, identity and state in South Asia: an overview. In: Azam KJ (ed) Ethnicity, identity and the state in South Asia. South Asian Publishers, New Delhi
Vaiphei PS (1981) Church growth among the Hill Tribes in Manipur, N.E. India. University Microfilms International, Michigan
Vaiphei SP (1987) Different cultural practices among the tribal Christians in Manipur. A publication of MBC Literature Committee, Manipur

Yumnam A (1999) Ethnic and inter group tensions in Manipur: an institutional perspective. In: Agarwal K (ed) Dynamics of identity and inter group relations in Northeast India. Indian Institute of Advanced Study, Shimla

Yunuo A (1982) Nagas struggle against the British under Jadonang and Rani Gaidinliu (1925–1947). Leno Printing Press, Kohima

Zehol L (1998) Ethnicity in Manipur: experiences, issues and perspective. Regency Publications, New Delhi

Zeliang E (2005) A history of the Manipur Baptist Convention. MBC, Imphal

Reclaiming Hawaiian Sovereignty

51

Keakaokawai Varner Hemi

Contents

Introduction	928
Current Narratives	930
In Federal Courts	930
Stories Native Hawaiians Tell About Themselves	933
The Need for Validation	937
Validating the Narratives	939
Pre-loaded Narratives: *Everyone*, *No-One* and *Someone*	939
The Limits of Federal Recognition	944
Sovereignty Validated	947
Native Hawaiians as Nation-State	948
Ea and Other Pre-Western Understandings of Sovereignty	951
A More Complex Narrative: the UN Declaration on the Rights of Indigenous Peoples 2007	954
Indigenous Self-Determination, Equality, and Discrimination	955
A Multi-narrative Right to Education	957
The Potential for Consensus	958
Ka moʻopuna i loko o kā mākou mau lima: "The Grandchild in Our Arms"	959
Conclusion	961
Cross-References	962
References	962

Abstract

Various legal narratives are currently told about Native Hawaiians in American federal courts. Such narratives often draw on law historically specific to other minority groups including African Americans and Native Americans and often conflict with the realities of Hawaiian law and legal history as well as real-time discrimination and inequities seemingly attracted to Native Hawaiian identity.

K. V. Hemi (✉)
University of Waikato, Hamilton, New Zealand
e-mail: keaka.hemi@waikato.ac.nz

© The Author(s), under exclusive license to Springer Nature Singapore Pte Ltd. 2019
S. Ratuva (ed.), *The Palgrave Handbook of Ethnicity*,
https://doi.org/10.1007/978-981-13-2898-5_77

These include racialized and federal recognition narratives which narrate Native Hawaiians as racists or a type of federally recognized tribe. Contemporary Native Hawaiian narratives sometimes echo those narratives, seemingly reflecting a legal identity crisis. Sovereignty is often the "go-to" narrative for many Native Hawaiians, but it too may have various limits in regard to the history and realities of the Native Hawaiian people. A fourth narrative also iterated by the Native Hawaiian community but sometimes given less attention is a remedial self-determination like that in international law. Such self-determination is guaranteed to all indigenous peoples in the UN Declaration on the Rights of Indigenous Peoples 2007. The Declaration may align more closely with Native Hawaiian understandings of sovereignty. Native Hawaiian understandings of sovereignty are rarely probed in federal courts but may be particularly valuable given the need for Native Hawaiians to validate such narratives themselves particularly as they seek consensus. This chapter explores the various legal narratives, their limits, and possibilities in terms of Native Hawaiians, with validation in mind. Education is used to focus and illustrate.

Keywords

Native Hawaiians · Indigeneity · Self-determination · Sovereignty · Education · UN Declaration on the Rights of Indigenous Peoples 2007 · Legal narratives · Equality · Discrimination

Introduction

> Liloa sat on an elevated place with his feathered-staff bearers waving their staffs to and fro. 'Umi leaped toward him and sat on his lap. The boy had broken another tabu. The chief looked at the boy sitting on his lap and asked, "Whose child are you?" The boy answered, "Yours! I am 'Umi-a-Liloa." Liloa noticed the tokens he had left for his son and kissed and wept over him. He ordered the kahunas to fetch the pahu and ka'eke drums at once and to take the boy to be circumcized and dedicated, as was the custom for children of chiefs. The chiefly drum, Halalu', and the smaller ka'eke drums were sounded in Paka'alana. The chief said, "It was for this child of mine that I girded my loins with ti leaves and covered my shoulders with banana leaves. And [I also left behind] my palaoa." (Kamakau *Ruling Chiefs* 1992b)

The story of 'Umi-a-Liloa's revelation as the son of Liloa is one of the most well-known legends of Hawai'i. 'Umi's story is the fairytale-like saga of a boy raised in obscure circumstances who rises to become a great warrior and exemplary ruler after his parentage and genealogy are discovered but also as he demonstrates daring, hard work, and kindness. While this incident is often included in volumes of "mythology" and has been romanticized and embellished at times, the facts of his life are well known. 'Umi was, in fact, a fifteenth-century high chief known for uniting the Big Island of Hawai'i, for a just rule and his religious observance. 'Umi appears in scholarly histories such as Samuel Mānaikalani Kamakau's *Ruling Chiefs of Hawaii* (Kamakau *Ruling Chiefs* 1992b) and the royal genealogy of *The Kumulipo*

(Beckwith 1972) as the ancestor of eighteenth and nineteenth-century monarchs of the Kingdom of Hawai'i including the Kamehamehas, King David Kalakaua, and Queen Liliuokalani. Many Native Hawaiians today can trace their ancestry back to 'Umi, while others are cultural descendants of his life and deeds.

Ironically, the true legal identity of Native Hawaiians today, the emblems of their parentage and genealogy, and their political history and realities are often obscured, mythologized, or embellished in stories told in the law. The US federal court case of *Doe v Kamehameha Schools/Bernice Pauahi Bishop Estate* 295 F Supp 2d 1141 (D Haw 2003), aff'd in part, rev'd in part, 416 F3d 1025 (9th Cir 2005), 470 F 3d 827 (9th Cir 2006) (en banc) ('*KS*') provides a vivid example of such narratives, where three courts tackled one policy preferring Native Hawaiians in admission to a Native Hawaiian-established and Native Hawaiian-administered school. Despite the school's success in overcoming actual inequalities, Native Hawaiians were alternatively cast as a group of homogenous or anonymous individuals discriminating against other groups or individuals, a racial minority in need of temporary affirmative action, and something akin to a Native American tribe with potential rights to tribal sovereignty. Against the historico-legal context of the Native Hawaiian people, none of these narratives seemed quite right. The misapplied color-blind narrative applied by the second court was later overturned but had labelled one of the most vulnerable ethnic groups in the United States, essentially, as racists. The same narrative had been persuasive in the Supreme Court in a previous case, *Rice v Cayetano* 528 US 495 (2000) ("*Rice*").

While *KS* and *Rice* have created anger and even grief within the Native Hawaiian community, subsequent efforts by some Native Hawaiians to apply the same racist label to their own people have created a sense of the surreal, particularly given the belief among many Native Hawaiians that they remain a sovereign people in international law with rights of self-determination. Claims associated with sovereignty include the illegal occupation – and calls for de-occupation – of Hawai'i by the United States, claims that are sometimes just as controversial. Especially where they run parallel to law which seems to threaten Native Hawaiian self-remedies for disparities, the wide gamut of legal stories about Native Hawaiian legal identity seems to indicate that, just as 'Umi revealed himself, the stories his descendants tell about themselves may be the most revealing.

Part 2 of this chapter discusses the narratives wrestled with by federal courts in the *KS* case, including *race, federal recognition, sovereignty*, and a *remedial and restorative self-determination*, before comparing those to the legal stories Native Hawaiians are telling about themselves. Part 3 describes pressures on narratives arising from the need to validate them. With validation in mind, Part 4 discusses the narrative limits and implications of racialized and federal narratives, including their identity and historical specificity. Part 5 contrasts classic Western sovereignty narratives with sovereignty from a Native Hawaiian perspective. In Part 6, the United Nations Declaration on the Rights of Indigenous Peoples ("UNDRIP") 2007 is discussed as a multi-narrative toolbox of rights narrating Native Hawaiian identity and rights in multiple ways including as forms of remedial and restorative self-determination, equality, and nondiscrimination. Finally, the chapter discusses present and future possibilities of Native Hawaiian sovereignty as real-time self-determination. Departing from the *KS* case, the chapter utilizes education to focus and illustrate.

Current Narratives

The idea that law is narrative in character, that it tells and retells stories, and that sometimes these stories conflict with each other is not novel. Beyond "rules and policies," the law also inherently relates "stories, explanations, performances, [and] linguistic exchanges – as narratives and rhetoric" (Gerwitz 1996). Narratives "do not simply recount happenings; they give them shape, give them a point, argue their import, proclaim their results" (Brooks 2005). From a law and literature perspective, legal narratives may also "invent rather than reflect our lives, ourselves, and our worlds" (Maria Aristedou quoted in Birrell 2016). Via outcomes, precedents, catch-phrases, and doctrine, the law is laced with stories that gain power and momentum with each telling – whether or not the narrative is accurate or right.

This is especially true in case law, where judges customarily follow the doctrine of *stare decisis* by which the decisions of the highest, most authoritative courts create *precedents* that bind future equivalent and lower courts where facts are similar enough to justify applying the same rule – and sometimes where they are not (Hemi 2016). Stories commonly told and passed down in precedents include *who* rightsholders are or *which* claimants may be considered rightsholders, *what* rights they hold, and *which* legal tests one must pass in order to prove such identity and claims. Precedents almost feel like genealogies given such content and as present judicial decisions rely on the reasoning of past courts for authority. Precedents may also lose the feel of genealogy where applied broadly or blindly, as time and history move away from the original reasoning, or precedent is not applied to truly alike facts. While precedent demonstrates predictability and certainty in the law and displays rule of law features (Waldron 2012) amenable to justice, fairness, and liberal democracy, precedent may also limit the flexibility and responsiveness of the common law where facts are unique or should trigger "an all-things-considered" approach (Tushnet 1997). Rigid adherence to precedent may hinder judges from coming up with the "right" answer to law questions (Dworkin 1986).

In practice, precedent may push courts and parties to squeeze diverse facts into a limited number of narrative boxes wherein rightsholder identities and legal claims are further limited. Such narratives have tremendous discursive power as they limit *which* stories and *whose* stories are told in the law while excluding the stories of others (Hemi 2016).

In Federal Courts

The power and limits of narrative precedents are well illustrated in the case of *Doe v Kamehameha Schools*. The tragedy began when a non-Native Hawaiian boy was denied admission to the Kamehameha Schools, a private school system first established in 1883 by Princess Bernice Pauahi Bishop ("Pauahi") specifically to help "indigent" Native Hawaiian children overcome alarming socioeconomic disparities. In her lifetime, Pauahi had witnessed disease, population decimation, landlessness, poverty, and other ills coinciding with Westernization impact her people. She almost seemed to predict the long-term effects of the later overthrow of the Hawaiian Kingdom by Westerners supported by agents of the American government – the assimilation, discrimination, and resulting socioeconomic disparities which would be multiplied over generations. Her goal in establishing the school was that Native Hawaiian learners would "compete" with other groups on an equal footing. Consistent with Pauahi's wishes, the private school system continues to prioritize Native Hawaiians in admission. The preference has no blood-quantum requirement, and someone with 1% Native Hawaiian genealogy has as much right to it as someone who is full Native Hawaiian. Consequently, the school's population is actually quite ethnically diverse (KS 2006).

The identity-aware policy seems to be highly successful. The private school has become not only a bastion of Native Hawaiian identity and culture but also of substantive equality as, without any government funding, the Native Hawaiian-run schools produce students who most often defy the negative numbers frequently associated with Native Hawaiians in various areas of human well-being. Native Hawaiian learners have been described in studies and reports as "severely disadvantaged" in education and "significantly lag[ging] behind" all other groups in the State of Hawai'i, our own country. Native Hawaiians often appear to be the extreme: the *most* likely to be absent, in special education and below average in all subjects, and the *least* likely to attend school, graduate, and continue to higher education. At the Kamehameha Schools, however, 99% graduate and 92.6% go on to higher education (Hagedorn et al. 2005). These prep school statistics are by any measure impressive but particularly among a group of learners most commonly associated with public school outcomes.

The policy might be too successful, admission being highly competitive. Financed by color blindness campaigns devoted to eradicating affirmative action, the slight teenager who had always possessed a name and identity voluntarily became "John Doe" when he sued the Schools under name suppression. He was not the first Doe nor the last but represented by the same lawyers (Yamamoto and Betts 2008). In dogmatic language, they alleged the admissions policy violated Section 1981 of Title 42 of the US Code – legislation which, like the admissions policy, was designed to overcome de facto discrimination and disparities (KS 2006). Despite the Schools' proven track record in helping an extremely disadvantaged group of learners to overcome discrimination and disparities – to actually level the proverbial playing field of liberal democracy – three panels of judges struggled to decide if the admissions policy *was* discriminatory or a measure of equality (Hemi 2016).

From the beginning, it was not entirely clear where Native Hawaiians fit. In the court of first instance, Judge Kay in the US District Court for the District of Hawai'i recognized the fact that Native Hawaiians had historically been a sovereign nation overthrown by Westerners, an event with causal links to ongoing disparities. Judge Kay held that a "manifest imbalance" in education between Native Hawaiians and other children justified the policy as a legitimate remedial measure, a concept most closely aligning with affirmative action aimed at disparities between racial groups. However, His Honor also found that the policy was consistent with the existence of a special trust relationship between Native Hawaiians and the federal government, a relationship implying federal Indian law and the kind of preference for Native Americans in hiring and other fora approved in the case of *Morton v Mancari* 417 US 535 (1974). Judge Kay also emphasized the "exceptionally unique historical circumstances" of the policy, or those elements of Native Hawaiian history and legal identity that did not fit a racial or Native American profile, and opined that "context matters" (KS 2006).

In 2005, on appeal, two of three judges in a partial sitting of the US Court of Appeals for the Ninth Circuit disregarded the context and trust relationship and "rigidly applied a formerly flexible contextual analysis" usually applied to private employment affirmative action policies (KS 2006). The court depended on a plethora of reverse discrimination cases in which white employees or students had successfully claimed the *same* rights as African Americans and courts had condemned racially aware policies including hiring or admission quotas. The majority equated the Kamehameha Schools admission policy with grandfather clauses, poll taxes, and similar devices by which white majorities in the South and elsewhere had deliberately targeted African Americans during the Jim Crow era.

This was partially due to previous precedent. In *Rice*, a non-Native Hawaiian landowner on the Big Island successfully argued that the voting scheme for electing members of the board of the Office of Hawaiian Affairs (OHA) was racially discriminatory because only Native Hawaiians were allowed to vote. Under Article XII Section 5 of the Constitution of the State of Hawai'i, this state body fulfils trust duties toward Native Hawaiians and might constitute the nearest thing that they presently have to a governing entity. The assets it administers have been set aside for the welfare of Native Hawaiians. Given ample evidence of unique historico-legal context, questions of *racial* identity should have given way to those of *political* identity, and at least a *Mancari* preference. But somehow they did not. The *Rice* court infamously held that "ancestry can be a proxy for race" and that the historically unique voting scheme constituted racial discrimination of the same ilk as so-called grandfather clauses and other deliberately discriminative measures that had denied African Americans their constitutional rights in the Jim Crow era (*Rice* 2000).

In *KS*, the two-judge majority in the initial case and the dissent in the en banc panel in the Ninth Circuit relied on reverse discrimination cases including *McDonald v Santa Fe Trail Transportation* 427 US 273; 96 S Ct 2574; 49 L Ed 2d 493 (1976), *Regents of the University of California v Bakke* 438 US 265 (1978), *Gratz v Bollinger* 539 US 244 (2003), and *Grutter v Bollinger* 539 US 306 (2003). In these cases, the Supreme Court had declared racial quotas, racially separate tracks for university admissions and virtually any race-conscious admission scheme unconstitutional under the Fourteenth Amendment. Ironically, the Supreme Court, like the three-judge panel in *KS*, had previously relied on cases about the Japanese American internment including *Korematsu v United States* 323 US 214 (1944) and *Hirabayashi v United States* 320 US 81 (1943) to argue that the Constitution is required to be color-blind (KS 2006). In those cases, the racial group was *deliberately* discriminated against on the basis of race – and the discrimination justified in terms of military necessity. None of these circumstances appeared to fit the seemingly *political* rather than racial identity of the Native Hawaiian people, state law, the actual de facto disparities impacting Native Hawaiians, or the actual good the policy has produced. Native Hawaiians were nonetheless cast as a racial group discriminating against all other racial groups – that is, somehow targeting an impossibly broad class of non-Native Hawaiians. Following *Gen Bldg Contractors Ass'n v Pennsylvania* 458 US 375 (1982), being purposefully conscious of Native Hawaiian ancestry equalled racial discrimination, and the policy was unconstitutional.

Ultimately, a slim 8–7 majority of a full sitting of the Ninth Circuit overturned the initial decision holding that the policy constituted a legitimate affirmative action policy aimed at racial parity after modifying the constitutional tests applied in the earlier employment cases of *United Steelworkers of America v Weber* 443 US 193 (1979) and *Johnson v Transportation Agency* 480 US 616 (1987). However, five members of the majority were also persuaded that the policy was justified by the exception made under *Mancari*. All seven members of the dissent concluded that the admission policy amounted to racial discrimination, though one judge suggested that the Native Hawaiian entity legally rebrand itself as a charity to protect itself from such lawsuits in the future (KS 2006). Ultimately, neither the racial nor Native American narratives appeared to really fit the historico-legal context of the policy. The hard-won decision allowed the Schools to continue to prefer Native Hawaiian children in admissions, but it was, at best, a tentative victory. Under imminent threat of appeal, the Schools settled with Doe for a sizeable sum in 2007. Upon announcing the settlement, the Kamehameha Schools' Board of Trustees described the situation as "a treacherous landscape" (Ing et al. 2006). While many Native Hawaiians breathed a sigh of relief, others grieved or were angry.

Stories Native Hawaiians Tell About Themselves

The depth of emotion generated by *Rice* and *KS* is closely linked to identity. Identity matters in the law not least because certain identities entail rights, and what courts pronounce in terms of identity has and will determine the rights groups are *seen as* being entitled to. The narratives wrestled with in these cases range from an uncertain legal identity to a potentially racist identity, options which may further exacerbate a history of imposed Western law failing to protect Native Hawaiian rights.

The stories Native Hawaiians are telling in terms of identity, history, and rights may be more insightful. Ke'eaumoku Kapu has said, however, that the Native Hawaiian community is "in a cultural identity crisis" (Democratic Party of Hawai'i 2018). In fact, Native Hawaiians are reiterating a number of sometimes conflicting stories about who they are in legal actions and in the public square which illustrate this. Four narratives feature prominently in recent legal cases and legislation, within the Native Hawaiian community and within the media. Each tells a different story of identity, history, and rights.

Race and Color Blindness

The first adopts the position of the dissent in *KS* and the majority in *Rice* – that is, a *racialized* version of Native Hawaiian identity. The color blindness campaign behind Doe began advertising for new litigants almost immediately after settlement, vowing (Avis Kuuipoleialoha Poai and Susan K Serrano "Ali'i Trusts: Native Hawaiian Charitable Trusts" in MacKenzie et al. 2015) to force the question to the Supreme Court where color-blind arguments had been successful in *Rice*. Another Doe represented by the same lawyers as the previous Doe sued Kamehameha Schools in 2010 (see *Doe v Kamehameha Schools* 625 F3d 1182 (9th Cir 2010)). The matter made it to the doors of the Supreme Court only to fall short because the Court would not allow that Doe to proceed anonymously.

Ten years later, the 2016 election of Keli'i Akina to the OHA Board signalled the residual persuasiveness of color-blind, essentially dichotomous racial narratives of Native Hawaiians. Prior to his election Akina, a person of Native Hawaiian ancestry, led a controversial "think-tank" advocating color blindness. Akina was also a plaintiff in a lawsuit (see *Akina v Hawaii*, 141 F Supp 3d 1106 (D Haw 2015) (denying motion for preliminary injunction); *Akina v Hawaii*, 136 S Ct 581 (2015) (granting injunction in part); *Akina v Hawaii*, 835 F 3d 1003 (9th Cir 2016) (affirming in part and dismissing appeal as moot in part)) that halted the potentially historic Na'i Aupuni election that would have created a Native Hawaiian governing entity (NHGE), from proceeding. Echoing *Rice*, Akina alleged the election was racially discriminatory.

The basis of such claims is that the Constitution of the United States, including the Fourteenth Amendment promising equal protection before the law and the Fifteenth Amendment prohibiting racial discrimination in elections, is the law of Hawai'i. Hawai'i did become a state in 1959, and federal law operates every day in the most remote archipelago in the world. In addition to the Constitution, various Civil Rights-era federal laws seemingly requiring identity blindness operate in the state.

Federal Recognition

Many Native Hawaiians seek federal recognition, the special constitutional status enjoyed by various Native American tribes and Native Alaskan communities. Some recognize an inequity in the fact that of the three major indigenous groups in the United States, only Native Hawaiians do not have federal recognition. Following *Mancari*, federal recognition has provided a shield against reverse discrimination which upholds tribal sovereignty. Federal recognition promises increased self-determination over land and other natural resources, in education and other areas of Native Hawaiian well-being, and the right to deal with the federal government on a government-to-government basis. *Mancari* allows preferences, and *Santa Clara Pueblo v Martinez* 436 US 49 (1978) ('*Martinez*') also recognizes the right of tribes to determine membership, not unlike admission.

Federal recognition, however, has been problematic. In the wake of *Rice*, the late Senator Daniel Akaka drafted the Native Hawaiian Government Reorganization Act ("the Akaka Bill"), legislation designed to achieve federal recognition. Senator Akaka took various versions of the legislation to Congress on a yearly basis for a decade without success. The last, the Native Hawaiian Government Reorganization Act of 2011, faded away quietly when the 112th Congress adjourned in 2012. The body constitutionally tasked with determining federal recognition had not done so.

In June 2014, the Department of the Interior formally issued an Advanced Notice of Procedural Rulemaking (ANPRM) that proposed the initiation of an administrative – rather than legislative – process to re-establish a government-to-government relationship with the Native Hawaiian community. It conducted consultation with Native Hawaiians across the nation. The subsequent, so-called Final Rule – or Procedures for Reestablishing a Formal Government-to-Government Relationship With the Native Hawaiian Community 2016 – provided criteria by which it would re-establish a government-to-government relationship with a Native Hawaiian governing entity (NHGE) but left the exact shape of that relationship uncertain. Indigenous legal scholars suggested that future relationship might be "flexible" and "negotiable" (Anaya and Williams 2015). Akina encouraged President Donald Trump to rescind the order when he came into office and noted that Congress had not approved the idea of a "race-based government" (Andrade 2017). As noted above, he also took legal action to stop the Naʻi Aupuni election that could have established a NHGE capable of re-establishing a government-to-government relationship. Until such an entity is established, the process of federal recognition remains in indefinite limbo.

While some Native Hawaiians were disheartened by these failures, many others have vehemently opposed federal recognition. Some believe that federal recognition would result in many of the same outcomes experienced by Native American people with the same constitutional designation, including unilateral abrogation of treaties, state and federal encroachment into land and other rights, as well as benign neglect – despite *Mancari*'s shield.

Sovereignty
Once described as a "household word" in Hawaiʻi by Dennis "Bumpy" Kanahele (Wood 1994), the go-to narrative for many Native Hawaiians is *sovereignty*. Rejecting federal recognition, many Native Hawaiians insist that they have rights, not just to a federally determined version of tribal sovereignty but to the kind of sovereignty that nation-states such as the United States enjoy in international law. Others worry that accepting the narrative of federal recognition is historically and legally inaccurate and will endanger our ability to claim greater legal rights under other heads especially as a sovereign nation under international law.

The legal claims of various Native Hawaiian organizations rest on claims that the Kingdom of Hawaiʻi was *and is* a sovereign nation that never relinquished its sovereignty and that the continuing presence of the United States in Hawaiʻi constitutes an illegal occupation under international law. Multiple Native Hawaiian groups have sought remedies against the United States in international legal fora, have created e-residency applications and established national cryptocurrencies, issue their own driver's licenses and license plates on a regular basis, and otherwise challenge the jurisdiction of state and federal law in Hawai'i (see *State v Lorenzo* 883 P 2d 641 (1994) and *Larsen v Hawaiian Kingdom,* Award, ICGJ 378 (PCA 2001), 5th February 2001, Permanent Court of Arbitration). Some of these organizations reject the labelling of our people as "indigenous" and a *Mancari* status.

Sovereignty is often framed in terms of remedying injustices and returning rights. Having had "everything" taken "from us – culture, identity, lands, everything," the goal of some is "to reclaim the inherent sovereign right of absolute political authority and jurisdiction in Hawaii." Many Native Hawaiians "want to leave the US entirely – or more accurately, want the US to leave Hawai'i" (Cluett 2011). Many question whether anything less than sovereignty will remedy historic wrongs or change current statistics for our people. Robin Danner, for instance, has said that sovereignty would allow Native Hawaiians to codify *hanai* (customary adoption) rights and preserve the Hawaiian language while also "creating jobs" and "battling diabetes" (Lyle 2017). Historically, Native Hawaiian efforts to restore sovereignty employed the language of *aloha 'āina* (deep love of the land) as its motto (Silva 2004). A similar principle has more recently been at stake in protests regarding the Thirty Meter Telescope project on Mauna Kea approved by the State of Hawai'i in 2017. Native Hawaiians frequently express Native Hawaiian sovereignty as inseparable from Native Hawaiian identity. Failing to recognize Native Hawaiian sovereignty may deny Native Hawaiian history and identity. Thus, sovereignty raises fundamental issues of who Native Hawaiians are and almost "all-or-nothing" stakes.

In Hawai'i, few words create as much controversy as *sovereignty.* The term frequently sets Native Hawaiians against *haoles* and other non-Native Hawaiians but also Native Hawaiians versus Native Hawaiians. In the public square, in newsclips and soundbites, sovereignty is associated with tense exchanges between Native Hawaiians about whether sovereignty is the answer but also where parties agree sovereignty *is* the answer. Identity and authenticity are at stake as various Native Hawaiian organizations, many claiming to embody the historic nation-state, disagree about what sovereignty means or should mean for the Native Hawaiian people.

Restorative and Remedial Self-Determination
While racialized, federal recognition and sovereignty narratives sometimes seem to garner the most publicity, another quieter, even taken-for-granted narrative is also frequently expressed: remedial and restorative justice. This narrative would recognize the admission policy as a form of restorative justice appropriate in terms of both historical injustices committed against Native Hawaiians and legitimate claims to an expanded self-determination arising from unique historico-legal context.

Native Hawaiian legal scholars Susan Serrano, Eric Yamamoto, Melody MacKenzie, and David Foreman, for instance, drafted amicus curiae briefs submitted during the *KS* case that justified the admissions policy as a restorative remedy for historical injustices perpetrated against Native Hawaiians by the US government and the ongoing "harm" of that injustice. Rather than a "privilege[]" or "handout," these scholars claim the admission policy represents a Native Hawaiian-generated remedy for "severe and systemic educational disadvantages" causally connected with historic injustices perpetrated by the United States. The amicus curae briefs argued that such self-determination would be consistent with the unique historical context of the admission policy and seemingly proportional to that harm. The amicus curae briefs universally disagreed with the application of equal protection tests to the admission policy (Serrano et al. 2007).

Each of these narratives – *race, federal recognition, sovereignty, and remedial and restorative self-determination* – demonstrates the interplay of identity and history in legal stories but also how much "getting" identity and history "right" means to Native Hawaiians. The diversity of opinions among Native Hawaiians about which narrative is right for them demonstrates the intelligence of the Native Hawaiian people (Carmen Hulu Lindsey in Democratic Party of Hawai'i 2018) their knowledge about law and legal issues, as well as their willingness to discuss such issues. But it also clearly has the potential to divide efforts to remedy the past, seek legal redress, and make things right. The Final Rule specifically requires a NHGE that represents the collective but so do other options including sovereignty. Consensus appears crucial.

The Need for Validation

In her efforts to illuminate events after the Kingdom of Hawai'i was overthrown by Westerners in 1893, Noenoe Silva wrote, "When the stories can be validated ... people begin to recover from the wounds caused by the disjuncture in their consciousness" (Silva 2004). Validation may offer some perspective on the above narratives.

One meaning of validation is "proof that something is correct" or accurate (Cambridge 2018). Silva's work in studying Native Hawaiian accounts of the overthrow and its aftermath written in the Hawaiian language revealed blatant errors in histories written by Westerners without access to those sources. Especially common was the assumption that Native Hawaiians had not resisted the Overthrow and subsequent events, an assumption with both communal psychological and legal impact. Silva's scholarship showed that Native Hawaiians actively sought legal redress, formed political groups, maintained their language and culture despite discriminatory legal prohibitions, and otherwise made efforts to resist the occupation of their country and remain a distinct people from the Overthrow (Silva 2004). In fact, Native Hawaiian history continues to be mis-narrated by non-Native Hawaiians, including judges (Poai 2017). As Native Hawaiians continue to protect – and seek legal redress for the violation of – their rights, the ability to ground narratives in their own experience, to speak them in their own language and retain their voice is increasingly important if for no other reason than that, once again, external sources may not be getting the story right. Fact-finding may, of course, also impact legal validity.

The chance for a victim population to tell its own story is priceless in terms of accuracy but also as "confirmation," "corroboration," and "testimony," related synonyms of validation (Merriam Webster 2018). This is the basis of various truth and reconciliation projects around the world seeking to move beyond colonization, civil war, and other violent histories that have impacted indigenous peoples, women and children, religious and ethnic minorities, and other groups (see, e.g., Murphy 2017). In sometimes heart-breaking fashion, facts are established, history in all its gory detail is presented, and victims and survivors given voice. Proof in this sense may include present statistics and research on Native Hawaiians in education and other areas of well-being – the earthy evidence of the ongoing impact of seemingly historic events. Valid legal narratives then are not abstracted from their subject but grounded in human experience and, sometimes, in gritty numbers and uncomfortable truths. The speaking of truth itself is seen as valuable. Narratives validated thus do, in turn, challenge other narratives – such as liberal equality – to prove their validity by the same quantifiable measures.

A third meaning of validation is to declare something legally or officially acceptable (Cambridge 2018). The right narrative must be valid in the sense that it actually fits the law. In terms of indigenous peoples, this means that it must fit the historico-legal context. Justice Joseph Williams of the High Court of New Zealand has said:

> One of the mistakes of scholars…looking at this particular area of law [that is, indigenous issues] is to decontextualize it, decouple it from its history. And in this game, in law particularly…in Māori issues in particular, history is everything. (Williams 2013)

This most certainly also applies to the unique history of Native Hawaiians, so eerily like that of Native Americans and other indigenous groups in some ways but also peculiar in its uniqueness. History is the dividing line between certain rights and others and the fence between certain rightsholders identities and others. In the wake of global histories of colonization, some Native Hawaiian narratives overlap with other indigenous peoples in the United States, and others may not. Such similarities and differences in history and legal identity also open the possibility that multiple legal narratives are rightly applied to Native Hawaiians. To be valid, such narratives need to be accurate and proven according to international law and not merely domestic law. Even where state law is seen as being subject to federal law, the peculiarity of Hawai'i state law and some of its unique features remain relevant in a validation exercise as historico-legal context and also where the narrative is simply a fact of law. Customary rights, for instance, are narrated as cultural values, indigenous rights, and human rights but also exist as law in fact where delineated in state and federal law, as well as treaties. Logically, acceptability is bolstered by this factual legality.

Validation as an act of potential consensus also requires acceptance at a deeper intellectual level. It must make sense *to* the community. The late Patrick Glenn's work on legal traditions around the world uses the concept of the "past-present" – that is, legal information pulled out of the past by adherents of legal traditions because that information continues to hold value in a world where a multitude of legal traditions and a "bran tub" of information is available. Glenn's concept of a legal tradition is a dynamic one where legal principles are not frozen in time but are chosen instead of, and also with, information from other traditions where doing so continues to be relevant to the tradition (Glenn 2014). Thus, narratives pulled from the past – for instance, liberal equality or principles of Native Hawaiian custom and usage – should resonate *with* indigenous peoples. This may be no less true, perhaps, because Native Hawaiians are the ones who bear the burdens of narratives the most, those who have the most at stake in holding on against intense informational pressure from other traditions, including imposed Western narratives. Strong voluntary adherence to particular narratives despite such pressure demonstrates significant resonance.

The right narrative will also be capable of resonating *among* the community. It should have the capacity to form the basis of a certain amount of consensus. As Native Hawaiians pulling values from the past that continue to be valued highly, the narrative may need, for instance, to feel *pono* or right, maintain and promote core principles such as *aloha*, and otherwise demonstrate our cultural legal values. Validation in this sense might be challenging. It may resolve questions of law and may bear out in history but must also have a lived-in and internal aspect. While the internal aspect may seem at times to have less to do with the outcomes in courtrooms and more to do with the communal dialogue – and might even be seen as susceptible to external minimization or dismissal – such narratives, nonetheless, can and will have legal impact where validated by historico-legal context and are otherwise factually legal.

Validating the Narratives

With validation in mind, the four narratives can be examined more closely.

Pre-loaded Narratives: *Everyone, No-One* and *Someone*

Education and knowledge was highly valued in Hawaiian culture long before European contact, and, by 1834, Hawai'i had one of the highest literacy rates in the world. From the 1850s, however, Westerners overseeing the Kingdom's education established a system aimed at "civilizing" Hawaiians. Not unlike African Americans and Native Americans at the time, Native Hawaiians were racially stereotyped as "filthy," "ignorant," and "lazy" heathen who "hardly know how to do anything." Boarding schools in Hawai'i became the prototypes for later schools on the continent that would similarly attempt to civilize African Americans and Native Americans, places such as the infamous Carlisle Boarding School where Native American children experienced generations of identity denigration and abuse (Okihiro 2008). When a Westernized education system required students to be taught the Three R's – reading, writing and arithmetic – in English, Native Hawaiian schools taught in '*ōlelo Hawai'i* (the Hawaiian language) in a manner that was Hawaiian. Such schools resisted denigrating narratives and demonstrated agency (Goodyear-Ka'ōpua 2009) despite being fiscally neglected (Lucas 2000). Following the overthrow, Native Hawaiian identity and education was directly assaulted by legislation that prohibited the speaking of Hawaiian.

While diseases such as influenza and smallpox are often credited with decimating the population, "cultural conflict," "prostitution," "despair," "new social ills," land alienation, and the imposition of a propaganda of "Western superiority" also impacted Native Hawaiians (Native Hawaiian Study Commission 1983). Legal changes resulted in what Jonathan Kamakawiwo'ole Osorio has described as:

> ...a story of violence, in which that colonialism literally and figuratively dismembered the lāhui (the people) from their traditions, their lands, and ultimately their government. The mutilations were not physical only, but also psychological and spiritual. Death came not only through infection and disease, but through racial and legal discourse that crippled the will, confidence and trust of the Kānaka Maoli [Native Hawaiians] as surely as leprosy and smallpox claimed their lives and limbs. (Osorio 2002)

The formal guarantee of equality proclaimed in the 13th, 14th, and 15th Amendments is not without some attraction for a people with this history of racialized discrimination and disparities. However, the narratives entertained by the courts in *Rice* and *KS*, and punctuated in *Akina*, may raise several concerns relative to validation, including their identity and historical specificity and their abstraction of equality and nondiscrimination.

A Specific *Everyone, No-One* or *Someone*

The dangers of a limited number of narratives are further exacerbated by the fact that such narratives are not neutral but come loaded with specific histories and identities. One of the ironies of invoking the Constitution in color-blind arguments, as Doe's lawyers, Akina, and others have, is that the Constitution itself is not color- or identity-blind. This supreme law is narrative, telling and retelling very specific stories about certain groups. The Constitution speaks to very specific histories. Each of the narratives tested by the Ninth Circuit can be traced back to key moments in American history but most especially to what have been called the "burdens of history" (Arthur 2007) – that is, those moments that have most scarred the country constitutionally, socially, and otherwise. This body of law also narrates a particular history and legal relationships between the US and its indigenous peoples.

The original Constitution was drafted to protect the interests of slave owners and deliberately set slaves outside the rights guaranteed to citizens under the Constitution in the infamous Three-Fifths Clause (Arthur 2007). The homogenous and anonymous requirements of the 13th, 14th, and 15th Amendments hark back directly to the bloody repercussions of slavery and civil war. Given the exclusion suffered by African Americans on the basis of skin color and other superficial markers of humanity, it is reasonable that those amendments effectively specify that *everyone* has a right to the protections of the law and that *no-one* is to be discriminated against

(Hemi 2016). Promises to the "all," and words such as "no" and "not" actually refer to the recently freed slaves of the Reconstruction era. The landmark Supreme Court decision in *Brown v Board of Education of Topeka, Kansas* 347 US 483 (1954) ("*Brown I*"), the Civil Rights Act 1964, subsequent civil rights legislation, and volumes of case law, likewise bear the imprint of segregation, Jim Crow laws (Hemi 2016) and Civil Rights "project[s]" (Yamamoto and Betts 2008). Frequently invoked together in law, *everyone* and *no-one* narratives form the *everyone/no-one* which can be described as a singular narrative given its discursive power and persuasion in federal courts. It can also be described as *adamant* given courts' reliance on it despite de facto considerations of discrimination and the availability of alternative narratives (Hemi 2016).

Within such law, *race* and *color* are inherently dichotomous and binary terms pitting one group of rightsholders against another, *everyone* versus *no-one*, and privilege versus disparities. The Reconstruction-era amendments insist that African Americans be homogenously treated the *same as* majority "whites," as in *McDonald v Santa Fe Trail Transportation Co* 427 US 273 (1976), or anonymously avoid discriminatory identification as the *no-one* (Hemi 2016). The Supreme Court, however, has also approved the use of positive measures such as affirmative action to achieve equal protection of the law in, for instance, *Brown v Board of Education of Topeka, Kansas* 349 US 294 (1955) ('*Brown II*'), *Green v County School Board of New Kent County* 391 US 430 (1968), *Swann v Charlotte-Mecklenburg Board of Education* 402 US 1 (1971), and *Keyes v Denver School District No 1* 413 US 189 (1973). An exception to the rule of homogeneity and anonymity, this temporary identification of rightsholders has been allowed where necessary to achieve substantive equality and nondiscrimination – that is, where temporary identification of *someone* who is a member of a group historically subjected to discrimination is necessary until parity between groups is reached (Hemi 2016).

Despite its potential to remedy the ongoing impact of that history, this narrative is an uncertain one. The Supreme Court's amenability to reverse discrimination arguments since the 1970s has undermined affirmative action programs that have – like the Schools' admission policy – produced quantifiable outcomes. *Everyone*, *no-one*, and *someone* narrated law has otherwise failed to remedy de facto segregation at ground level, gaps between African Americans and other racial groups in education. This body of law is also integration rather than self-determination driven, an approach appropriate to the history of African Americans but not consistent with protecting the substantive good achieved by self-determined initiatives such as the Kamehameha Schools admission policy (Hemi 2016).

Real-Time Equality and Nondiscrimination

There is an incredible dissonance and extremeness in holistic statistics on Native Hawaiians. Native Hawaiians are most likely to be arrested and incarcerated and to end up back in prison in their own country (OHA 2010). Native Hawaiians are also frequently identified with disparities in health, housing, and employment (Kanaʻiaupuni et al. 2005; Hagedorn et al. 2005). Despite association with "a number of resiliency factors," Native Hawaiian children and adolescents have the highest rates of infant mortality, mental health diagnoses, suicide, and obesity, ultimately carrying a higher "allostatic load" – or cumulative, chronic, cyclical, and even multigenerational stress loads (Liu and Alameda 2011). The same children are more likely to attend a school in need of "restructuring," have less experienced and qualified teachers, have a disproportionate rate of excessive absences, and be in special education. Collectively, Native Hawaiians are consistently below the state median in math and reading achievement tests, have the lowest graduation rates, and are most likely to graduate late and require subsidized school lunches (KSBE 2009).

Native Hawaiians are the most socioeconomically disadvantaged ethnic group in Hawai'i. The link between the history and such inequality is widely accepted (KS 2006; DOI and DOJ 2000; Kana'iaupuni and Malone 2006) – as is the link between ongoing "multigenerational trauma and discrimination...poverty and inequities of housing, education, environment, healthcare access, and social capital" and statistics in specific areas such as health and education (Liu and Alameda 2011). Such disparities are organically interdependent and interrelated to disparities in various areas seemingly drawn to Native Hawaiian identity.

By contrast, the Kamehameha Schools' statistics evidence an actual levelling of the proverbial playing field, a de facto equality that somehow transcends discrimination and disparities. Significantly, this has been accomplished without any welfare, subsidization, or other privileges from the public or at any great expense to other individuals since funds, expertise, and other resources have come from the Native Hawaiian community. Ironically, because students may qualify for the preference with *any* amount of Native Hawaiian blood, the Schools' student population is extremely diverse, representing some 60 ethnic groups (KS 2006). Such statistics and realities are seemingly consistent with the liberal promises of the 14th Amendment and other civil rights law.

Although pre-loaded with specific histories, *everyone/no-one* and *someone* narratives have become historically abstract. For instance, reverse discrimination advocates rely heavily on the case of *Brown I* to justify a color-blind approach without recognizing its substantive requirement. In the wake of Jim Crow laws and forced racial segregation, *Brown I* required equality to be homogenous and anonymous. It was not, however, the formal existence of the schools themselves or their identity-aware admission policies that most concerned the Court and violated equal protection but the tangible and less tangible de facto outcomes and educational experience of students sharing a particular racial identity. Importantly, the Court recognized education as a right essential to long-term human outcomes. The positive steps required by the Court in *Brown II* and later cases included bussing and other measures designed to produce substantive change rather than merely formal promises.

Following such landmark precedent, de facto discrimination and disparities that defy constitutional guarantees of equal protection and nondiscrimination in real time should differentiate measures designed to overcome discrimination and actual discrimination. Despite reverse discrimination's current persuasive power in federal courts, substantive equality requires a closer look at the existence of segregation in fact and statistics that frequently depict African Americans as one of the most vulnerable groups in all areas of well-being, including education. The fact that Native Americans often fare worse than African Americans in similar measures of well-being further emphasizes the seeming failure of *everyone/no-one* guarantees to deliver to all in the manner anticipated by the Supreme Court in *Brown I* (Hemi 2016).

Ironically, the 13th, 14th, and 15th Amendments, *Brown* and subsequent civil rights legislation are premised on an insistence that African Americans, a racial group historically discriminated against, have the same rights as whites. Reverse discrimination instead argues that whites should be given "the same right…as is enjoyed by white citizens" (see *McDonald* discussed in KS 2006) when they were already "white citizens." In other words, such litigants claim the same right as African Americans or other minorities to try to reach parity when parity is not the issue for a group lacking the history of racial discrimination and slavery which drives *Brown I*, Section 1981, and other Civil Rights legislation. This is the position of the majority in *Rice*, the dissent in *KS,* and the majority in *Akina*. The current prioritization of and discursive persuasion of *adamant everyone/no-one* narratives, and especially reverse discrimination, appears to be, therefore, historically abstract and to contradict *Brown I* and *II*.

Anachronistic Equality and Nondiscrimination

In addition to displaying historical and factual abstraction, federal narratives also appear to be anachronistic given wider narratives of equality and nondiscrimination. Since World War II, the human rights regime in international law has evolved from a largely *everyone/no-one* narrative of fundamental rights to a complex toolbox of rightsholder identities and remedial rights. The drive behind this evolution is the increasing interpretation of equality and nondiscrimination according to substantive outcomes and not merely formal guarantees. Rights such as education act as *organic multipliers* in terms of the denial and realization of other human rights – that is, they act as bridges to or gatekeepers for other rights (Hemi 2016). The ability to read, for instance, will impact rights such as freedom of thought and speech, voting, and property ownership, as it also impacts rights to education, health, and employment. Certain identities, including gender, age, race, disability and indigeneity, also multiply outcomes because they are highly vulnerable to de facto, indirect, systemic, and even cumulative or compounded discrimination (CESCR 2009; Hemi 2016).

Earlier postwar declarations and treaties including the Universal Declaration of Human Rights 1948 (UDHR), the twin International Covenants on Civil and Political Rights (ICCPR) and on Economic Social and Cultural Rights (ICESCR) 1966, and the Convention on the Elimination of All Forms of Racial Discrimination ("the Race Convention") speak in homogenous terms such as "everyone" and "all" and in anonymous terms such as "no one" and "shall not." However, Article 27 of the ICCPR and its later elaboration, the Declaration on the Rights of Persons Belonging to National or Ethnic, Religious and Linguistic Minorities ("the Minorities Declaration"), recognize that parallel institutions may best provide substantive outcomes for members of subnational religious, linguistic, and cultural minority groups. The Convention on the Elimination of All Forms of Discrimination against

Women 1979 (CEDAW) features a dichotomous narrative largely guaranteeing women the same treatment as men, while the UN Convention on the Rights of the Child 1989 (UNCROC) and the UN Convention on the Rights of Persons with Disabilities 2006 (CRPD) recognize multiple identities including gender, race, indigeneity, disability, and age.

All three conventions recognize the necessity and desirability of "special," "positive," or "effective" measures undertaken to achieve substantive equality. Under federal law, such measures are only temporary, but most human rights, including substantive equality and nondiscrimination, have no time limit. Moreover, these expanded narratives are not mutually exclusive, and individuals may bear multiple rights simultaneously under various rightsholders identities, for example, as an indigenous person, a girl, and a human being with disabilities. Under international law, identification is not evil but necessary to ensure a universal coverage and legally emphasize the rights holdings of groups historically discriminated against and even dehumanized.

Although it recognized education as a "right" in *Brown I*, the Supreme Court denied that there is a fundamental constitutional right to education in the case of *San Antonio Independent School District v Rodriguez* 411 US 1 (1973) ("*Rodriguez*"). The United States frequently demonstrates exceptionalism in terms of human rights conventions including those it has signed and ratified. The US government has also failed to ratify conventions recognizing a strong right to education including the Children's Convention and CEDAW. Their frequent legal recognition across international and domestic law, however, has earned equality and nondiscrimination *opinion juris* status in international law – that is, they are considered peremptory norms of the highest order that are binding on states whether they have signed a specific treaty or not. This status is apparent in the potential reach of Article 26 of the ICCPR – a treaty signed by the United States – to all economic, social, and cultural rights, including those not iterated in the civil and political rights-focused ICCPR (see *SWM Broeks v The Netherlands* Communication No 172/1984, CCPR/C/OP/2 (1990) and Joseph et al. 2004).

A substantive interpretation of equality and nondiscrimination consistent with international law has some capacity to account for real-time disparities that defy the notion of a level playing field and for the real-time good of the *KS* admission policy as a positive or special measure. The increasing identity-specificity of such instruments indicates an awareness of how discrimination works in real time and how it is seemingly attracted to certain identities including indigenous identity. This *everyone/no-one* and *someone* narrative allows the possibility that identity-specific measures may constitute measures of equality and not just exceptions to the rule.

The Limits of Federal Recognition

Upon statehood, the state of Hawaii assumed partial responsibility for the previous trust relationship between the federal government and Native Hawaiians. Through the Hawaiian Homes Commission Act 1921, the US government set aside 200,000 acres of land for "Native Hawaiians" to homestead for the purpose of "rehabilitation." As in the case of other indigenous peoples in the United States, this land is held in trust for Native Hawaiians and currently administered by the Department of Hawaiian Home Lands, a state agency. The State's trust responsibilities are most apparent in Section 5(f) of the Admission Act 1959 that directs that income from public lands be used for "the betterment of the conditions of Native Hawaiians" among other areas. The creation of OHA in Hawaii's 1978 Constitution derives from this responsibility.

Hundreds of pieces of federal legislation (KS 2006) evidence a legal relationship between Native Hawaiians and the federal government that greatly resembles the special trust relationship between the federal government and other indigenous peoples in the United States. *Mancari*, the Native American Reorganization Act 1934, and other federal laws have historically protected Native Americans against lawsuits based on the 14th Amendment and charges of unconstitutionality. Federal recognition might also recognize a tribe-like sovereignty including self-determination over land, justice, education, and other social and economic development. This narrative, however, raises validation issues including identity- and historical specificity and basic questions of equality and nondiscrimination.

The preference for Native Americans allowed under *Mancari* originates in another extremely specific legal history from which derives the special trust relationship between the federal government and Native American peoples. Native American rights and legal identity are still defined by precedent set by the Supreme Court in the early nineteenth century in the so-called *Marshall Trilogy*. In *Johnson v M'Intosh* 21 US (8 Wheat) 543, 5 L Ed 681 (1823), Chief Justice John Marshall defined Native American peoples first by the doctrine of discovery by which they retained some customary usage rights but did not own their land outright. Discovery justified conquest by European nations. In *Cherokee Nation v Georgia* 30 US (5 Peters) 1 (1831), he rewrote the political status of native peoples in America as "domestic-dependent nations" or "sovereign and independent states" that remained "tributary and feudatory" under the "protection" of the federal government. Under the Commerce Clause of the Constitution, Congress has the power to make treaties and otherwise deal with such nations. Thereby, it has the power to determine federal recognition that affords formal status as tribes and access to various protections and government benefits. And in *Worcester v Georgia* 31 US (6 Pet) 515 (1832), the Chief Justice narrated the relationship between the federal government and Native Americans as that of a "guardian" and "ward" in a "special trust" relationship.

This narrative is an exception to *everyone/no-one*. The *Mancari* preference was political and not racial. Later, in *United States v John* 437 US 634 (1978), tribal sovereignty was also genealogically determined and not solely the right of federally recognized tribes (Hemi 2016). According to the Supreme Court in *Mancari*, the preference was designed to meet the needs of Native Americans, further self-government, and give effect to the special trust relationship. The Constitution similarly sets Native Americans apart. Former UN Special Rapporteur on the Rights of Indigenous Peoples James Anaya has described this narrative "as an exception to the norms of equality and non-discrimination, rather than their embodiment." This body of law has historically kept "equal protection discussions within a constitutional framework" and "away from Native Americans" (Anaya 2007). While *Mancari* is best known, the shield of tribal sovereignty was also apparent in *Martinez*, where it was upheld against an *everyone/no-one* congressional act drafted to undermine it.

This narrative is also heavy with bias and uncertainty. Lumbee scholar Robert Williams has written that it "entail[s] a superior and unquestionable power on the part of Congress unrestrained by normal constitutional limitations" and has attributed a "free reign" and "broad discretionary powers" to Congress which Williams links to ongoing, fundamentally prejudicial presumptions about Native Americans – that is, a "legal consciousness that at its core regards tribal peoples as normatively deficient and culturally, politically and morally inferior to Europeans" (Williams 1986).

In contrast to some of its promises, this narrative is often externally defined by Congress and the courts. In practice, the special trust relationship has been differentiated from a true fiduciary relationship (see *United States v Jicarilla Apache Nation* 564 US ___, 131 S Ct 2313 (2011)) and has often seemed one-sided, with treaties and adjacent legal rights capable of being unilaterally terminated, abrogated, or "broken" at the whim of Congress depending on the policy mood of the federal government, whether assimilationist or open to self-determination, for instance. Following *Seminole Nation v United States* 316 US 286 (1942), this trust relationship is a "self-imposed policy" whereby the federal government "has charged itself with moral obligations" and is, consequently, not legally enforceable against Congress. Tribal sovereignty is regularly infringed upon by states, and the Supreme Court has virtually repealed treaties and legislation, despite Congress's plenary power (Pevar 2012; Getches 2001).

The Ninth Circuit itself predicted that "*Mancari*'s days are numbered" in the case of *Williams v Babbitt* 115 F 3d 657 (9th Cir 1997). The recent decision in the federal district court case of *Brackeen v Zinke,* No 4:17-cv-00868 (N.D. Tex. Oct. 4, 2018), where a federal district court judge declared portions of the Indian Child Welfare Act 1978 unconstitutional, illustrates how real this threat may be. The act is a landmark piece of legislation that requires states to consult tribes and prefer tribal placements of Native American children in foster care and adoption. Relying on *Rice* and echoing the dissent in *KS*, Judge Reed O'Connor skirted *Mancari* and interpreted indigenous identity as a racial one and the act's requirements as an illegal racial preference. The case has been described by Native Hawaiian leaders as a "wave that's coming" for Native Hawaiian people and the greatest present legal threat to Native Hawaiian rights (Brendon Kaleiʻaina Lee and William J Aila respectively in Democratic Party of Hawaiʻi 2018).

While the current self-determination era of federal Indian policy has seen an increase in self-remedying education by tribes and other indigenous nations for their own people and in their own languages (Harvard Project 2008), statistics for Native Americans in education, and other areas of well-being generally remain concerning. Many Native American communities still bear the burdens of the boarding school experience that stole generations of indigenous children from their communities in an effort to subdue tribes and "civilize" them (Okihiro 2008). Various studies have shown that these events continue to impact present health outcomes. Post-traumatic stress disorder, Type 2 diabetes, depression, and other illnesses that present-day Native Americans suffer from in disproportionate numbers have been linked back to those events via science including epigenetics (Whitbeck et al. 2004; Pember 2016). Native Hawaiians can relate to this history and impact, but Native American learners actually fare worse than all other ethnic groups – including Native Hawaiians – in negative education outcomes despite federally recognized rights to tribal sovereignty (Hemi 2016).

Ultimately, *Marshall Trilogy* sovereignty and the *Mancari* preference seemingly offer a biased account of indigenous identity and history that may also be arbitrarily undermined by Congress and the Courts. Like *everyone, no-one*, and *someone* narratives, this indigenous narrative is pre-loaded with particular identities and histories that, despite being the closest federal law now comes to interpreting Native Hawaiian identity and history, is fundamentally prejudicial toward Native Americans and may yet be inherently prejudicial toward and biased against Native Hawaiians. At the same time, this narrative at least formally offers the control over land, resources, governance, and everyday decisions that many Native Hawaiians see as essential to remedying current socioeconomic statistics and other effects of colonization. Thus, this narrative remains controversial.

Sovereignty Validated

Most Native Hawaiians do agree on a particular history. Most rarely dispute the fact that Native Hawaiians were a "people" prior to 1778. Historian Robert Hommon has actually described the society that existed in the Hawaiian Islands at the time of contact with Captain James Cook in 1778 as one of the world's "primary states" akin to Mesopotamian, Incan, and Indus River Valley civilizations. This state had a complex bureaucracy complete with tax collectors (Hommon 2013) and a legal system that prescribed and prohibited behavior according to spiritual principles such as *tapu* and *noa* but also contained rule of law features such as Kamehameha I's *Kānāwai Māmalahoe* or "Law of the Splintered Paddle" and the reciprocal duties of *aliʻi* (the chiefs) toward *makaʻainana* (the commoners) (Melody Kapilialoha MacKenzie "Historical Background" in MacKenzie et al. 2015).

Kamehameha I united all the Islands under his leadership by 1811. On 23 December 1826, the polity his descendants ruled entered into "articles of arrangement" promoting commerce and "friendship" with the US government (Stauffer 1983). Later, the Kingdom of Hawaiʻi signed bilateral treaties with other nation-states through diplomats received in the British court and elsewhere. Eventually this fledgling, hybrid Westministerian/American legal system featured the familiar three branches of government, a written constitution and a Western-style land tenure system (Hemi 2016). Those legal changes would majorly disrupt social, economic, and political units of Hawaiian society, and the same constitutional monarchy was later illegally overthrown by Western businessmen aided by the American government. Hawai'i was annexed by the United States in 1898 and became a state in 1959. The legality of these events is frequently challenged by Native Hawaiians and responsibility for these wrongs often accepted by the federal government, for instance, in the 1993 Clinton Apology. Crucially, at no point did the Native Hawaiian people "directly relinquish[] their claims to their inherent sovereignty as a people...either through their monarchy or through a plebiscite or referendum" (Melody Kapilialoha MacKenzie chapter "Historical Background" in MacKenzie et al. 2015). Despite evidence of resistance (Silva 2004), the nation and its citizens' rights were simply taken, a fact that continues to drive claims of sovereignty.

Native Hawaiians as Nation-State

The most familiar rendition of sovereignty is a Western and Eurocentric narrative of nationhood that comes pre-loaded with specific histories and identities. Older ideas of sovereignty arise in Roman ideas of *imperium* (rule and the state) and *dominium* (ownership and property) (Benton and Straumann 2010) – ideas that later featured significantly in the application of the doctrine of discovery to indigenous peoples (Barker 2005). The concept was also associated with the divine right of kings and then legislative bodies such as the English Parliament who embodied the sovereign. The events of the Thirty Years' War, a religious conflict that threatened to fragment Europe and ended with the Peace of Westphalia in 1648, also shaped notions of sovereignty and particularly concerns about state fragmentation (Osiander 2001; Krasner 2001). Philosophical works during the Enlightenment, including Thomas Hobbes' *Leviathan* (1651) and John Locke's *Two Treatises on Government* (1681), respectively, portrayed the sovereign as the source of order and the protector of inalienable rights such as property. Post-World War II, sovereignty has also been associated with the right of some colonized peoples to decolonization outlined in UN Resolutions 1514 and 1541.

Traditionally, sovereignty displays certain features. In *The Prince* (1513), Machiavelli defined sovereignty as "a supreme authority within a territory." Classic sovereignty also implies authority *over* a territory. Sovereignty in this sense may be viewed as a "chunk" – that is, possessed "in full or not at all" (Lenzerini 2006). Sovereignty also corresponds to legal even "constitutional independence" unfettered by human rights or other external legal systems (Laughland 2007). Such authority operates as a "right" and lends legitimacy (Weinrib 2019). Other states respect such authority by not intervening in a sovereign state's domestic affairs. This creates "sovereign equality" between states. These features remain evident in the Declaration on Principles of International Law concerning Friendly Relations and Co-operation among States in accordance with the Charter of the United Nations 1970, Resolution 2625, which vehemently condemns violations of sovereignty.

Various aspects of sovereignty should – and do – appeal to a people with a history like that of Native Hawaiians. Certainly, many sovereignty claims directly or indirectly convey aspirations for more control over the destiny of *the* Native

Hawaiian people, an aspiration prompting questions of self-determination, a right sometimes associated with the Westphalian state's sacrosanct status but also integral to the more complex concept of "people." Sovereignty could clarify Native Hawaiian legal "status" (Straumann 2008). Native Hawaiians and other indigenous peoples recognize "the importance of semantics" and the legitimacy that comes with a recognition of sovereignty (Barker 2005).

Sovereignty may also protect identity. Self-determination recognizes a people's ability to make their own decisions about political, social, economic, and cultural development, including whose history is taught and which stories, literature, art, and language are transmitted to future generations within classrooms. In this sense, it may be as much about maintaining cultural integrity and identity as maintaining political authority. A loss of cultural integrity may equate to a loss of sovereignty. Similarly, the concept of popular sovereignty sources the authority to rule in the people and increasingly requires a reconciliation between sovereignty and democracy (Tansey 2011; Donnelly 2018).

Western concepts of sovereignty are also problematic in terms of addressing Native Hawaiian grievances and aspirations for a number of reasons. In the wake of dominium, discovery, and Hobbesian and Lockean thought, sovereignty has also been about claiming what is "mine" and appears to demonstrate the "possessive logic of patriarchal white sovereignty" (Moreton-Robison 2011) rather than the collective goods articulated in most Native Hawaiian narratives. The *everyone/no-one* narratives in *Rice*, the dissent in *KS* and *Akina*, reflect this kind of entitled individualism once again attempting to access indigenous assets. These *mine* narratives may re-affirm the right of Native Hawaiians to possess their assets and land but have little to do with remedying discrimination and disparities or correcting historic and ongoing injustice. Sovereignty has, for instance, been the dividing line between the supposedly uncivilized and civilized in Western legal thought. The Marshall Trilogy made indigenous peoples quasi- and partial sovereigns as opposed to the full sovereigns of Western colonizers. Full self-government, territorial integrity, and cultural autonomy are missing (Barker 2005). In other places such as Aotearoa, New Zealand, treaties and declarations affirmed sovereign status prior to treaties intended to cede sovereignty. In these ways and others, sovereignty has created an exclusive club that has often disadvantaged indigenous peoples.

Similarly, sovereignty is *believed* and sometimes "blurry" (Diez et al. 2011). It has traditionally relied on recognition by other members of the sovereignty club, nation-state to nation-state, but also recognition within the state. According to Immanuel Wallerstein:

> [s]overeignty [in a classical sense] meant that no power outside their state had the right to interfere in their state's decisions. It also meant that no power within the state could fail to carry out the decisions of the state. The double orientation (external and internal) was crucial to the concept. (Wallerstein 2018)

The external and internal features are troubling in the wake of unilateral historical actions taken against Native Hawaiians that have disregarded the vestiges of sovereignty and subsequent failures by other states including the United States to enforce Native Hawaiian rights. Internal resonance also remains challenging. Sovereignty, as a narrative, has not yet gained universal support among Native Hawaiians. Ultimately, as Wallerstein has noted, "Simply asserting sovereignty was obviously not enough. The state had to implement these claims" (Wallerstein 2018). While Native Hawaiian groups have implemented some aspects of sovereignty, consensus and wholesale implementation remains elusive.

Decolonization also requires that certain criteria be met, criteria, in fact, designed to claw back the postwar invitation of sovereignty where it might lead to fragmentation of states. Territorial integrity is prioritized in the so-called Salt Water Thesis in UN Resolution 637 which limits the right to decolonize to states surrounded by oceans or "blue water." This and other UN statements reflect a fear of secession and, at a deeper level, a fear of conflict and war such as that in World War II. While Hawai'i appears to meet such criteria, territorial integrity appears to be biased against decolonization. Decolonization has often required intense struggles against colonial powers, despite recognition of the right of the colonized to do so. Although approximately 80 countries have decolonized globally since World War II – including several in the Pacific – decolonization has been rare among US territories in the Pacific.

Recent examples of Pacific peoples contemplating decolonization illustrate potential challenges for Native Hawaiians. In early November 2018, New Caledonians voted not to sever ties with France. Voters included indigenous Kanaks, French and others – a demographic situation resembling that in Hawai'i during the 1959 plebiscite and at present. The French also designated French Polynesia a *pays d'outre mer* in 2011, a category entailing certain aspects of greater autonomy though not the full sovereignty sought by many of its citizens (Moyrand and Angelo 2010; Gonschor 2013). Both states should meet the Salt Water Thesis, but decolonization has progressed slowly even where prompted, for example, by civil war in New Caledonia. While federal courts threaten to subsume Native Hawaiian rights in the wrong narrative, the United States has increased its presence in the former Non-Self-Governing Territory of the Republic of the Marshall Islands and the current Non-Self-Governing Territory of Guam, particularly through militarization (Illarmo 2010). Guam is currently pushing for an indigenous-only vote on decolonization (Kelleher 2018).

Sovereignty, generally, appears to be uncertain. In 2005, Richard Haass said:

> Thirty years from now, sovereignty will no longer be sanctuary. Powerful new forces and insidious threats will converge against it.
>
> Nation-states will not disappear, but they will share power with a larger number of powerful non-sovereign actors than ever before, including corporations, non-governmental organizations, terrorist groups, drug cartels, regional and global institutions, and banks and private equity funds. Sovereignty will fall victim to the powerful and accelerating flow of people, ideas, greenhouse gases, goods, dollars, drugs, viruses, e-mails, and weapons within and across borders. Sovereign states will increasingly measure their vulnerability not to one another but to forces of globalization beyond their control (Haass 2005).

Haass's statement while dramatic has been borne out to some degree in the increasingly recognized vulnerability of the once sacrosanct concept of sovereignty to an extreme form of legal pluralism in which the Westphalian nation-state is no longer the only polity or entity claiming or being recognized as possessing sovereignty. Beyond human collectives and physical polities, "data sovereignty," "food sovereignty," and similar claims utilize the term to advocate for greater self-determination in various areas of human well-being that clearly exceed the traditional law-making and political roles of the state, having less emphasis on authority and more on self-determination. Such claims risk blurring the lines between aspirational and legal claims, something that risks undermining legal acceptance. Ultimately, as Joanne Barker has noted, sovereignty appears to be in a state of "flux" and difficult to define at present (Barker 2005). Like Native Hawaiians, sovereignty too may be undergoing an identity crisis.

The potential benefit of this uncertain narrative, however, may be twofold. In its uncertainty it is also malleable, perhaps more so than ever before. While aspirational claims may lack substantive punch, legal claims will not, especially where accurate, proven and internally acceptable. Where narratives of sovereignty resonate with Native Hawaiians and the law, they may have the potential to reconcile the stories told.

Ea and Other Pre-Western Understandings of Sovereignty

Since the 1980s, Native Hawaiians have created many self-remedying education initiatives at the grassroots level besides the Kamehameha Schools. Following the approach of Māori in New Zealand, Native Hawaiians created Pūnana Leo – or language nests – where preschoolers have learned '*ōlelo Hawai'i* from an early age and parents have played an integral part of their education and the classroom. Pūnana Leo were created at a time when the language prohibition was still in place and represent agency and resistance. As in the Māori case, parents of Pūnana Leo children created Kula Kaiapuni Hawai'i – or Hawaiian environment schools – when their children were ready to enter elementary school and there were no options for immersion learning. More recently, the Native Hawaiian Charter School Alliance has sought to not only increase Hawaiian language fluency but to improve the overall quality of teaching that Native Hawaiian learners receive (MacKenzie 2012). Native Hawaiian educators also pushed for the drafting of the federal Native Hawaiian Education Act 1988 that repeats almost verbatim the Clinton Apology and provides for some Native Hawaiian decision-making in the disbursement and use of federal funds for Native Hawaiian education.

Mohawk scholar Taiaiake Alfred has written that "the actual history of our [indigenous] plural existence has been erased by the narrow fictions of a single sovereignty" (see chapter "Sovereignty" in Barker 2005). Alfred Kilipaka Ontai has noted that Native Hawaiians "struggle to define a native form of self-determination, but they reach for sovereignty models that are rooted in Western traditions instead of their own spiritual/cultural experience" (see chapter "A Spiritual Definition of

Sovereignty from a Kanaka Maoli Perspective" in Barker 2005). Current initiatives also echo much older ideas. Native Hawaiian *kupuna* (ancestors) had their own concepts of sovereignty – or something like it – prior to Western models, a fact that is sometimes overlooked.

In a validation exercise, sovereignty may need to be narrated in indigenous language, in words that may have no exact translation in English, and intellectual and legal concepts that derive from a Native Hawaiian worldview. In Mary Kawena Pukui and Samuel H Elbert's authoritative *Hawaiian Dictionary*, sovereignty is translated into Hawaiian as "ea," but the word is much more complex. *Ea* is translated into English as the nouns "sovereignty, rule, independence" but also as "[l]ife," "breath," and "spirit," as well as the verb "to rise" or "go up" (Pukui and Elbert 1986). Pukui and Elbert's translation, considered the most authoritative on the Hawaiian language, illustrates the multifaceted and holistic nature of sovereignty. According to Ontai, the state motto of Hawaii, *ua mau ke ea o ka aina i ka pono*, demonstrates the close ties between life and sovereignty. The motto is usually translated as "the *life* of the land is perpetuated in righteousness," but the motto comes from Kamehameha III's response upon the British rescinding claims to sovereignty over Hawai'i in 1843 after the so-called Paulet affair. Thus, it could easily be translated as "the life/sovereignty of the land is preserved in righteousness" (see Ontai in Barker 2005).

Historically, various other concepts inform *ea*, including spiritual principles, reciprocal responsibility, the people, and the land. Spiritually, the chiefs or *ali'i* were responsible to do what was right by the *akua* (the gods). Kamakau records that 'Umi was instructed by his father, "This is the one thing that you must do, take care of the god. Whatever you have, remember him." Chiefs who failed to do what was *pono* or right, who failed to observe this responsibility, as in the case of 'Umi's older half-brother Hakau, could be removed (Kamakau *Ruling Chiefs* 1992b).

Hakau had been given the government partially because of his mother's rank as a chiefess (Kamakau *Ruling Chiefs* 1992b), and one's place and ability to govern in Hawaiian society also relied on genealogy. Despite not having a written language, precontact Hawaiians possessed a wealth of oral histories and genealogies connecting them with their *ohana* (family), *aina* (land to which one was bound by genealogy), and *aumakua* (ancestors) (Kamakau *Ka Po'e Kahiko* 1992a). They were to be caretakers of the land and to demonstrate *aloha aina*. Chiefly authority was also embodied in the noun *mana* (supernatural or divine power) that enabled one to govern. As a verb, *mana* meant "to place in authority, empower, [and] authorize" (Pukui and Elbert 1986), concepts implying legitimacy.

Reciprocity plays a sometimes subtle but crucial role in this version of sovereignty. Hawaiian sovereignty was as much about responsibility as it was about authority. Ali'i had reciprocal duties toward the *maka'āinana* (commoners) who could go to a higher authority if their local alii was not fulfilling his duties (MacKenzie in MacKenzie et al. 2015). Another Hawaiian word for authority is *kuleana* translated as "right, privilege" and "jurisdiction" but also "responsibility." Kuleana both "entitle[s]" one to rights and assigns responsibility (Pukui and Elbert 1986). This included the highest chiefs, or *mo'i*. Kamehameha I's 1797 Kānāwai

Māmalahoe, for instance, affirms rule of law protections for "everyone, from the old men and women to the children," echoing earlier instructions from the chiefess Mahu-lua to her son, Ku-aliʻi to "[t]ake care of the god, and take care of the big man, the little man, and the fatherless." ʻUmi, for instance, was a renowned warrior and military commander but is remembered for humility, kindness and care of his people as well as spiritual observance (Kamakau *Ruling Chiefs* 1992b).

Pauahi and other *aliʻi* who established trusts in the late nineteenth century to look after Native Hawaiians were also exercising this type of sovereignty. Trusts still operating today address education, the needs of orphans, the poor and the elderly, and medical care. In so doing, these trusts:

> ...reflect the reciprocal duties of the aliʻi and the makaʻāinana (common people). Traditionally, the makaʻāinana had the duty to care for the land, and wise management of the people and land enhanced the right of the aliʻi to rule. Productive use of the land and mutual cooperation ensured the right of the makaʻāinana to live off the land and use its resources. Although the traditional social structure was dramatically altered through the creation of private property rights in the mid-nineteenth century and the transition from a subsistence to a market economy, the creation of these trusts suggests that the aliʻi continued to understand and attempted to fulfil their obligation to provide for the needs of their people. (Poai and Serrano in Mackenzie et al. 2015)

The older law remains embedded in Native Hawaiian understanding of what sovereignty is. Silva's work – along with that of other scholars (including Preza 2010; Beamer 2008) – reveals the degree to which Native Hawaiians have gone to remain a distinct people and to preserve cultural values and practices despite the imposition of Western law and culture. This scholarship demonstrates agency rather than a passive response to Westernization and self-remedies rather than handouts or buy-in to imposed sovereignty. Modern Native Hawaiians continue to express their desire to remain a distinct people and to practice traditional forms of sovereignty including *kuleana*.

Despite the efforts of the Doe's and other color-blind campaigners, the Kamehameha Schools/Bishop Estate, the Queen Liliʻuokalani Trust, the King William Lunalilo Trust, and the Queen Emma Trust remain legal fact, less pulled from the past as much as "perpetual" (Poai and Serrano in MacKenzie et al. 2015). Trusts protecting Native Hawaiian lands and other assets take a familiar Western legal form but express the reciprocal duties of Native Hawaiian sovereignty. Under Articles X, XII, and XV, Hawaiʻi's Constitution recognizes Native Hawaiian language and education rights and:

> reaffirm[s] and protect[s] all rights, customarily and traditionally exercised for subsistence, cultural and religious purposes and possessed by ahupuaʻa tenants who are descendants of native Hawaiians who inhabited the Hawaiian Islands prior to 1778.

These legal facts are part of the larger historical continuum of Hawaiian customary law which continues to be recognized in law (Forman 2008). A number of state cases have affirmed custom and usage as the current law of Hawaiʻi, including *Pub Access*

Shoreline Haw v Haw County Planning Comm'n 79 Hawai'i 425, 903 P.2d 1246 (1995), *Pele Defense Fund v Paty* 73 Haw 578, 837 P 2d 1247 (1992), and *Kalipi v Hawaiian Trust Co*, 66 Haw 1, 656 P2d 745 (1982) (Forman 2008). The everyday operation of customary rights over land and resources as well as self-remedies in education, health, and the environment demonstrate the continuing operation of this older but legally valid form of sovereignty.

These traditional narratives of sovereignty, under intense informational pressure, represent strong adherence to a Hawaiian legal tradition. The existence of this law is an embodiment of past-present-ness. In fact, it has survived aggressive informational pressure from Western narratives meant to assimilate which inherently discriminate against Native Hawaiian values and legal information. The resilience of this narrative and the strong adherence of Native Hawaiians against such odds speak for its continuing internal resonance and acceptance among Native Hawaiians.

By comparison, sovereignty in the traditional Western sense is about authority, territorial integrity, non-interference, sovereign equality, diplomatic relationships, and treaty-making. The classic concept speaks little about care of one's people, love of the land, or generations. Current iterations require some reconciliation with democracy and perhaps wider norms of human rights, such as equality and non-discrimination, but, at least initially, cannot account for indigenous narratives that precede liberal projects. In fact, the principle of non-interference has often prevented the community of nations from intervening where other states commit grievous human rights abuses even where treaties to the contrary should dictate state behavior. While non-interference may resonate with Native Hawaiians given the history of external interference, this version of authority is formal, top-down, and not necessarily reciprocal. It does not emulate 'Umi's example nor the current everyday efforts of Native Hawaiians in terms of education which are actually achieving positive outcomes for Native Hawaiians.

A More Complex Narrative: the UN Declaration on the Rights of Indigenous Peoples 2007

The disparities that depict Native Hawaiians as the most extreme in education and other areas illustrate what, from the perspective of restorative justice, have been called "deep harms." Such harms are embedded in the psyche and social experience of Native Hawaiians, are pervasive, even "'comprehensive', encompassing resources, culture, and governance; 'sustained' over generations; 'systemwide,' implicating national and local governments, businesses, and citizens" (Yamamoto and Obrey 2009). Native Hawaiians are not alone in experiencing such harms causally connected to colonization. Historical trauma research has shown how adverse childhood experiences have lifelong and multigenerational impacts on health. Epigenetics and other research have linked disproportionately high rates of suicide, alcoholism, heart disease, and diabetes with the boarding school experience of previous generations of Native American communities (Whitbeck et al. 2004; Pember 2016). Across the world, indigenous peoples are usually the poorest and most marginalized members of their societies (Eversole and McNeish 2005). Such factors seemingly predict future harms, thus creating "once-and-future wrongs" which are both historical and actual but also incredibly current and actual (Hemi 2017).

Such harms, attracted to indigenous identity, apparently undermine the supposedly homogenous and anonymous coverage of *everyone/no-one* narratives and must be reconciled in order to be valid. This type of harm may reveal the lasting effect of significant breaks in the "collective memory" of "intergenerational groups" – that is, indigenous peoples' own legal and cultural narratives about who they are – that must be addressed if present ongoing disparities are to be remedied (Spinner-Halev 2005). According to Yamamoto and Obrey, "The remedies must be tailored to the harm. That is, when the injuries are long-term and systemic, so must be the response" (Yamamoto and Obrey 2009). Their answer, and that of others, is a proportionate self-determination. Self-determination is especially vital where current legal and political arrangements have not "remed[ied] the historical injustices suffered by" indigenous peoples nor provided "the accommodations necessary to exercise and freely develop their culture, including religious practices and traditional governance, or allowed them to exercise their fair share of political power" (Anaya 1994). The restoration of "identity-affirming Indigenous institutions" and the return of a self-determination resembling that which might have been without historical interference is arguably vital to overcoming historic, ongoing wrongs associated with colonization (Sanderson 2012).

The larger the group who can relate to deep harms, to gritty numbers and uncomfortable truths – the greater the number who can corroborate the narrative – the greater the validation perhaps. Colonization and imperialism have had a common modus operandi, apparent in a global history of colonization that links ethnically, religiously, and linguistically diverse peoples across various countries, climates, and geography and across centuries. The Native Hawaiian experience remains peculiar given the community's specific historico-legal context, but it is also eerily echoed over and over again in the experience of many other indigenous peoples. This global story is reiterated in one of the most quoted and discussed statements of human rights in the early twenty-first century. The UN Declaration on the Rights of Indigenous Peoples 2007 is the culmination of the evolution of the human rights framework and the result of a massive truth-telling project about this bigger story. It is also an exercise in proportionate self-determination.

Indigenous Self-Determination, Equality, and Discrimination

For 22 years, the Declaration was drafted, debated, and defended by indigenous peoples, including Native Hawaiians, who interacted in an unprecedented way with states in creating international law and setting human rights agendas about indigenous peoples (Augusto Willensen Diaz "How Indigenous Peoples' Rights Reached the UN" and Asbjørn Eide "The Indigenous Peoples, the Working Group on Indigenous Populations and the Adoption of the UN Declaration on the Rights of Indigenous Peoples" in Charters and Stavenhagen 2009). It represents the evolution of principles such as equality and nondiscrimination from *everyone/no-one* narratives to specifically indigenous ones. It appears to represent a multi-narrative toolbox of rights that might more immediately identify and clarify sovereignty, principles of equality and nondiscrimination, and the remedial and restorative nature of such rights. While it affirms *everyone, no-one* and *someone* rights, its fundamental principle is a more complex version self-determination that may most closely align with restorative and remedial narratives but also with what Native Hawaiians want most from sovereignty.

The Declaration's preamble indicates a truth and reconciliation project and embraces historico-legal context as it responds to past and ongoing human wrongs, even assimilative and "racist" "doctrines, policies, and practices" and other "historic injustices" arising from "colonization." While earlier human rights documents such as the UDHR express a repugnance for war, the preamble recognizes the "urgent need to respect and promote" human rights and to "bring an end to all forms of discrimination and oppression wherever they occur." Many of its provisions address indigenous-specific human rights violations commonly associated with colonialism including deprivation of identity, "forced assimilation or integration," and "any form of propaganda designed to promote or incite racial or ethnic discrimination directed against" indigenous people.

The Declaration also recognizes the residual political status of indigenous peoples – even their prior sovereignty. In contrast to previous instruments, such as ILO Indigenous and Tribal Peoples Convention No 169 (1989), most of UNDRIP's rights are held, not by indigenous individuals or members of minority groups but by indigenous *peoples*. The prioritization of indigenous collectivities as UNDRIP's primary rightsholders is unmistakable. The term "peoples" is used at least 98 times in UNDRIP, while "individual" or "individuals" are only used 11 times. Out of a total of 46 articles, 30 relate to indigenous peoples alone, while only 2 can be claimed by indigenous individuals alone. Another 12 – including Articles 1 and 2 which guarantee equality and nondiscrimination – recognize both "peoples" and "individuals" as UNDRIP's rightsholders. These collective and individual rights sit side-by-side without ready categorization or hierarchy. Ultimately, the term "indigenous" preceding both "peoples" and "individuals" itself references a specific collective identity – and history (Hemi 2016).

More than liberal equality, self-determination underwrites UNDRIP. Placed immediately after Articles 1 and 2's equality and nondiscrimination, UNDRIP's Article 3 changes "*All*" to "*Indigenous*" but otherwise repeats core human rights treaties, including the UN Charter, ICCPR, and ICESCR, almost verbatim: "Indigenous peoples have the right to self-determination. By virtue of that right they freely determine their political status and freely pursue their economic, social and cultural development." The Article 3 right to self-determination is the "fundamental underlying principle" of the Declaration (WGIP 2001). The Preamble "affirm[s] the fundamental importance of the right to self-determination of all peoples" consistent with the UN Charter, ICESCR, ICCPR, and the Vienna Declaration and Programme of Action 1993 ("the Vienna Declaration").

Closely related, Article 4 recognizes "the right to autonomy or self-government in matters relating to their internal and local affairs." This *internal* aspect resembles certain features of the *Mancari* exception recognized in American federal Indian law. This internal self-determination seems to embody the right to "opt out" as it were. Article 5 recognizes "the right to maintain and strengthen their distinct political, legal, economic, social and cultural institutions, while retaining the right to participate fully, *if they so choose*, in the political, economic, social and cultural life of the State."

Beyond *Mancari* and the whims of federal recognition, the Declaration also seemingly recognizes a historical continuum of virtually timeless, permanent indigenous rights. In view of numerous articles on the preservation, protection, and transmission of indigenous identity and culture, the rights-holder under UNDRIP is part of a once-and-future community of rightsholders. For instance, Article 11 protects "the right to maintain, protect and develop the past, present and future manifestations of culture." Article 45 likewise looks forward to assure indigenous peoples that nothing in the Declaration is meant to diminish or extinguish existing indigenous rights now *or* in the future. Thus, the Declaration recognizes pre-existing rights rather than merely prescribing or imposing liberal rights to address present disparities. Such rights are not seen as "special," exceptional, or temporary *someone* rights but are, under Article 43, "minimum standards for the survival, dignity and well-being of the indigenous peoples of the world" (Hemi 2016).

A Multi-narrative Right to Education

Article 14 of UNDRIP is consistent with other multi-narrative conventions such as UNCROC and the CRPD but premised on self-determination. It recognizes that:

1. Indigenous peoples have the right to establish and control their educational systems and institutions providing education in their own languages, in a manner appropriate to their cultural methods of teaching and learning.
2. Indigenous individuals, particularly children, have the right to all levels and forms of education of the State without discrimination.
3. States shall, in conjunction with indigenous peoples, take effective measures, in order for indigenous individuals, particularly those living outside their communities, to have access, when possible, to an education in their own culture and provided in their own language.

Article 14(2) references *everyone* ("all"), *no-one* ("without discrimination"), and the *complex someone* – "particularly children." This learner is specifically guaranteed previously promised universal individual rights to a public education but also the option to attend a parallel indigenous educational institution such as Kamehameha Schools, as well as rights to an education in their own culture and language where they constitute a minority.

In name and substance, however, all Article 14 rights are owned by the indigenous learner. Under Article 14, the rights-holder is both the indigenous learner *and* their community. Preference for the indigenous learner in admissions is implicit and emphasized by the repeated use of the possessive pronoun "their." While all children have a universal right to education and while Article 14 is consistent with previous *everyone/no-one* instruments, the right to be preferred in admissions at the Kamehameha Schools, Punana Leo, and other Native Hawaiian institutions and education systems – and to establish and control them – is owned by collective indigenous learners. Significantly, the right actually precedes Article 14's nondiscrimination and minority-like provisions that also belong to indigenous peoples.

The Declaration might be limited by state sovereignty in multiple ways. Technically, the Declaration is a General Assembly resolution rather than a treaty and, at least on its face, is not legally binding. Article 46(1) emphasizes the old worry of sovereignty, territorial integrity, while Article 46(2) places democratic limits on the Declaration's application. Most often, despite textual and genealogical consistency between Articles 3 and 4 and previous core instruments with no such limit, the right to self-determination in UNDRIP is usually limited to the internal aspect (Xanthaki 2011). In 1973, the Supreme Court said that there was no constitutional right to education in its decision in *Rodriguez*. The federal government is known for an exceptionalist and "pick-and-choose" position in regard to human rights generally (Ignatieff 2016) and has not signed and ratified core human rights instruments that enshrine the right to education such as the ICSECR, UNCRoC, and CEDAW. Reasons include inconsistency with the Constitution and charges that so-called economic, social, and cultural rights amount to state subsidized welfare and not true rights – allegations resembling special advantage arguments in *Rice*, *KS*, and *Akina*. Perceived clashes between indigenous rights, and especially the right to self-determination recognized in the Declaration, were included in the US' Explanation of No Vote in 2007, a move repeated by other settler states including Canada, Australia, and New Zealand. When the United States finally endorsed the Declaration in 2010, the State Department distinguished the Declaration as an "aspirational" rather than legal document.

The Potential for Consensus

The Declaration's rights, however, are premised on a more substantive form of equality and nondiscrimination, remedial and restorative self-determination, human rights considered to be universal and inalienable, and specifically indigenous rights. This combination has much to offer in terms of validating narratives about Native Hawaiians.

A decisive majority of the world's nations – 143 of 190 member states – endorsed the Declaration in September 2007 and states such as the United States eventually endorsed the Declaration after significant international and internal pressure. Rights such as Article 14 affirm a substantive version of *everyone*, *no-one*, and *someone* that demands outcomes and not merely formal guarantees, the recognition of the indigenous and not merely *everyone/no-one*. Famously, the Declaration does not create any new rights but textually and genealogically links back to core instruments of the international human rights framework. Despite its status as a declaration rather than a treaty, it upholds and consistently narrates peremptory norms of equality and nondiscrimination whose status as opinion juris in international law is seen as binding on states regardless of whether a treaty has been signed (S James Anaya "The Right of Indigenous Peoples to Self-Determination in the Post-Declaration Era" in Charters and Stavenhagen 2009; Dorough and Davis 2014). The Declaration also harks back to Western sovereignty via Article 3 but is anchored by a more complex and indigenous self-determination. This self-determination itself acts as a multiplier of equality and nondiscrimination. As if echoing 'Umi's sovereignty, the Declaration even requires that "[p]articular attention shall be paid to the rights and special needs of indigenous elders, women, youth, children and persons with disabilities in the implementation of this Declaration" under Article 22.

Rather than dogmatically repeating polarizing and adamant narratives, the Declaration reconciles *everyone/no-one* and *someone* with narratives of sovereignty and remedial and restorative self-determination. It also seems to clarify and challenge the *Mancari* shield and the limits of tribal sovereignty, grounding self-determination in supra-domestic human rights evidencing consensus and morally resonance rather than legislative, administrative, or political arbitrariness or temporariness. Rather than attempting to force Native Hawaiian historico-legal context, identity, and rights into an extremely limited number of uncertain narrative boxes that do not fit, the Declaration provides narrative complexity and flexibility. Importantly, the Declaration's stories have been narrated by indigenous peoples themselves, including Native Hawaiians.

Ka mo'opuna i loko o kā mākou mau lima: "The Grandchild in Our Arms"

Validation has one additional requirement. Native Hawaiians have a responsibility not only to the ancestors but also to the *mo'opuna* – the grandchildren – and those that will come after generally. A valid legal narrative about Native Hawaiians must speak across generations, anticipating the past, present, and future. Such a narrative will be validated where it is accurate and legally acceptable and resonates internally across time.

The Declaration's multi-narrative certainly has a once-and-future aspect. Potentially speaking to our past, Article 37 states, "Nothing in the Declaration may be interpreted as diminishing or eliminating the rights of indigenous peoples contained in treaties, agreements and other constructive arrangements." Speaking to our present and the future, Article 45 states that "Nothing in this Declaration may be construed as diminishing or extinguishing the rights indigenous peoples have now or may acquire in the future." This aspect enhances narrative choice, even creates narrative options, rather than closing them down.

As such, this multi-narrative statement of human and indigenous rights does not preclude sovereignty. It may, however, offer more immediate clarification of rights than, for instance, waiting for treaty-making and other external recognition. The right of indigenous peoples – the right of Native Hawaiians – to self-determination exists now in international law regardless of federal recognition issues and ongoing questions about sovereignty. As Ken Coates notes, "[t]he United Nations, after all, has spoken. Clearly, national governments must respond" (Coates 2013). In doing so, a majority of the world community recognized indigenous peoples' self-determination and Article 14's multi-narrative as *rights*.

Countries like Bolivia have already incorporated the Declaration into their constitutions. In an American first, the Declaration has also been incorporated into Hawai'i State law. Act 195, signed by Governor Neil Abercrombie in 2011, reiterates Article 3 of the Declaration. Textually and genealogically, it links state law specific to Native Hawaiians back to core instruments of international human rights law including the ICCPR that the US has signed and ratified. Putting aside potential issues about the propriety of state or federal governments framing Native Hawaiian sovereignty, the narrative heart of the Declaration is now black letter law in Hawai'i and not merely aspiration. Admittedly, Act 195 is aimed at creating conditions for federal recognition but uses the language of international law, human rights and indigenous rights, as well as the nation-state – language which may prove malleable and less arbitrary than federal narratives.

Act 195 is an anomaly in American law and represents the arrival of new norms of sovereignty. It brings the historico-legal context of colonization and the postwar evolution of the international human rights framework from a homogenous *everyone* and anonymous *no-one* to a complex, specifically indigenous narrative of equality and nondiscrimination. It carries the moral persuasion of these peremptory norms and the drive and push of human rights in general away from merely formal guarantees toward real-time outcomes. The increasing discursive power of substantive equality and nondiscrimination explains the arrival of new norms of sovereignty. In international law, *everyone*, *no-one*, and *someone* are increasingly required to deliver equitable outcomes. Narratives alone cannot deliver. This at least partially explains why indigenous peoples are acting in legal spaces previously reserved for sovereign states.

The Declaration affirms the malleability of a sovereignty checked by human rights and reinterpreted. It leaves open the possibility of various decolonization models and a negotiated power-sharing, suggesting Erica-Irene Daes' concept of "belated state-building." State-building is usually a post-conflict process driven externally or internally. *Belated* state-building is a *postcolonial* process by which "[i]ndigenous peoples [who] were never a part of State-building" – for instance, establishing the territory or state of Hawaii – "have the opportunity to participate in designing the modern constitution of the State in which they live, or share, in any meaningful way, in national decision-making" (Daes 1993). Belated State-building is a "peaceful" and internal form of self-determination exercised by indigenous peoples "within existing State structures and orders" through which historical injustices are addressed "by imposing obligations on States to accommodate Indigenous Peoples through constitutional means in order to share power democratically" (Buick-Constable 2002).

As noted above, the ANPRM may have offered malleability. The exact shape of federal recognition that might emerge from a similar future administrative process is not a foregone conclusion but something that might be dialogued. Recent discussions on another possible constitutional convention for the State of Hawai'i also represent an opportunity for dialogue and even belated state-building. The 1978 Constitution Convention that designated Hawaiian an official language of Hawaii and created the Office of Hawaiian Affairs was the result of one such "ConCon." However, the ConCon put to Hawai'i voters in 2008 was backed by conservative elements and opposed by those who feared that Native Hawaiian rights would be eroded in the process (Nakaso 2008). Both opportunity and concern are currently voiced in the Hawaiian community.

Conclusion

The number of narratives about Native Hawaiians currently apparent in law and in the public square is at times cacophonous. The present legal environment continues to be a treacherous legal landscape (Ing et al. 2006) fraught with multiple threats to Native Hawaiian identity and rights, including thinly veiled attempts to gain access to Native Hawaiian assets, previously protected in trusts or the special trust relationship, as in *Rice* and *KS*. Time is also passing while the merits of sovereignty are debated, during which narratives such as those in *Rice*, *Akina*, and *Brackeen* continue to gain momentum in federal courts. The difficulty and challenge of formally achieving sovereignty may also overshadow the actual everyday expression of the local, homegrown self-determination evident in Native Hawaiian education, ali'i trusts, and other self-remedying initiatives – as well as court cases that have been won, black letter law in place, and the larger historical continuum of custom and usage.

However, the biggest current threat to Native Hawaiian rights may be a lack of consensus among Native Hawaiians, a state requiring a degree of resonance. Whether Native Hawaiians agree with federal recognition or not, the ANPRM highlights the need to collectively identify a Native Hawaiian nation and its governing entity. Claims of sovereignty must similarly stall or fail if Native Hawaiians do not come together and identify what most resonates with them internally and what is most accurate and most acceptable. Ultimately, Native Hawaiians may need to decide on a complex multi-narrative, not from a limited number of ill-fitting legal boxes but from all possible narratives including their own. As descendants of 'Umi-a-Liloa, Native Hawaiians may need to be as daring as he was in declaring their birthright. Their greatest act of bravery may be in finding a consensus that anticipates the generations that come after as much as those that have come before.

Cross-References

▶ Affirmative Action: Its Nature and Dynamics
▶ Nuclear Testing and Racism in the Pacific Islands
▶ Settler Colonialism and Biculturalism in Aotearoa/New Zealand
▶ Stereotypes of Minorities and Education

References

Anaya SJ (1994) The Native Hawaiian people and international human rights law: toward a remedy for past and continuing wrongs. Ga L Rev 28:309–364
Anaya SJ (2007) Keynote Address: Indigenous Peoples and Their Mark on the International Legal System. Am Indian L Rev 31(2):257–272
Anaya SJ, Williams RA (2015) Study on the international law and policy relating to the situation of the Native Hawaiian people. Indigenous Peoples Law and Policy Program, University of Arizona, James E Rogers College of Law, Tucson
Andrade T (2017) Legacy in paradise: analyzing the Obama administration's efforts of reconciliation with Native Hawaiians. Mich J Race L 22:273–326
Arthur J (2007) Race, equality and the burdens of history. Cambridge University Press, New York
Barker J (ed) (2005) Sovereignty matters: locations of contestation and possibility in indigenous struggles for self-determination. University of Nebraska Press, Lincoln
Beamer BK (2008) Na Wai Ka Mana? 'Ōiwi Agency and European Imperialism in the Hawaiian Kingdom. PhD thesis, University of Hawai'i
Beckwith MW (trans & ed) (1972) The Kumulipo: a Hawaiian creation chant. Facsimile copy of University of Chicago Press, Chicago, 1951 edition. University of Hawaii Press, Honolulu, 1972
Benton L, Straumann B (2010) Acquiring empire by law. Law Hist Rev 28(1):1–38
Birrell K (2016) Indigeneity: before and beyond the law. Routledge, London
Brooks P (2005) Narrative in and of the law. In: Phelan J, Rabinowitz PJ (eds) A companion to narrative theory. Blackwell, Malden, pp 415–426
Buick-Constable J (2002) A contractual approach to indigenous self-determination in Aotearoa/New Zealand. Pacific Basin Law J 20(1):118–132
Cambridge Dictionary. Found at www.dictionary.cambridge.org. Accessed 12 Dec 2018
CESCR (2009) General Comment No. 20: the Vienna Declaration and Programme of Action 1993 crimination in economic, social and cultural rights (art. 2, para. 2, of the International Covenant on Economic, Social and Cultural Rights) E/C.12/GC/20
Charters C, Stavenhagen R (eds) (2009) Making the declaration work: the United Nations declaration on the rights of indigenous peoples. IWGIA, Copenhagen
Cluett C (2011) Reinstating the Hawaiian Nation. The Molokai Dispatch 2 August 2011
Coates K (2013) From aspiration to inspiration: UNDRIP finding deep traction in indigenous communities. Found at www.cigionline.org. Accessed 12 Dec 2018
Daes EI (1993) Some consideration on the right of indigenous peoples to self-determination. Transnat'l L Contemp Probs 3:1–12
Democratic Party of Hawaii – Hawaiian Affairs Caucus (2018) OHA Trustee Candidate Forum. Found at Olelo Community Media, streamed live online on 24 October 2018. Found at: https://www.youtube.com/watch?v=COvhhb-w3bM. Accessed 12 Dec 2018
Department of the Interior and Department of Justice (2000) From Mauka to Makai the river of justice must flow freely: report on the reconciliation process between the Federal Government and Native Hawaiians. Department of the Interior/Department of Justice, Washington DC
Diez T, Bode I, Fernandes A (2011) Key concepts in international law. Sage, Thousand Oaks

Doe v Kamehameha Schools/Bernice Pauahi Bishop Estate 295 F Supp 2d 1141 (D Haw 2003), aff'd in part, rev'd in part, 416 F3d 1025 (9th Cir 2005), 470 F 3d 827 (9th Cir 2006) (en banc)

Donnelly MP (2018) Democracy and sovereignty vs international human rights: reconciling the irreconcilable? Intl J Hum Rts. https://doi.org/10.1080/13642987.2018.1454904

Dorough DS, Davis M (2014) Study on an optional protocol to the United Nations declaration on the rights of indigenous peoples focusing on a voluntary mechanism, E/C.19/2014/7

Dworkin R (1986) Law's empire. Belknap Press, Cambridge

Forman D (2008) The Hawaiian usage exception to the common law: an inoculation against the effects of western influence. U Haw L Rev 30:319–354

Getches D (2001) Beyond Indian law: the Rehnquist Court's pursuit of state rights, color-blind justice and mainstream values. Minnesota Law Rev 86:267–362

Gewirtz P (1996) Narrative and rhetoric in the law. In: Brooks P, Gerwitz P (eds) Law's stories: narrative and rhetoric in the law. Yale University Press, Cambridge, pp 2–13

Glenn P (2014) Legal traditions of the world, 5th edn. Oxford University Press, Oxford

Gonschor L (2013) Mai te hau Roma ra te huru: the illusion of 'autonomy' and the ongoing struggle for decolonization in French Polynesia. Contemp Pac 25(2):259–296

Goodyear-Kaʻōpua N (2009) Rebuilding the ʻauwai: connecting ecology, economy and education in Hawaiian schools. AlterNative 5(2):46–77

Haass RN (2005) Sovereignty. Foreign Policy 150:54–55

Hagedorn L and others (2005) The academic and occupational outcomes of private residential high school student instruction. Pac Ed Res J 13(1):21

Harvard Project on American Indian Economic Development (2008) The state of native nations: conditions under U.S. policies of self-determination. Oxford University Press, New York

Hemi KV (2016) Everyone, no-one, someone and the Native Hawaiian learner: how expanded equality narratives might account for guarantee/reality gaps, historico-legal context and an admission policy which is actually levelling the playing field. PhD thesis, University of Waikato

Hemi KV (2017) Māori education as justice and reckoning. NZ Yearbook of Jurisprudence 15:709–101

Hommon R (2013) The ancient Hawaiian state: origins of a political society. Oxford University Press, New York

Ignatieff M (2016) American exceptionalism and human rights. In: Weston BH, Grear A (eds) Human rights in the world community: issues and action, 4th edn. University of Pennsylvania Press, Philadelphia, pp 406–415

Illarmo C (2010) U.S. military plans mega-base for Guam (Guahan). Peace Free 70(2):4

Ing JD and others (2006) Trustee message: Kamehameha Schools and 'John Doe' settle admissions Lawsuit. Kamehameha Schools/Bernice Pauahi Bishop Estate. www.ksbe.edu. Accessed 12 Dec 2018

Joseph S, Schults J, Castan M (2004) The international covenant on civil and political rights: cases, materials, and commentary, 2nd edn. Oxford University Press, Oxford

Kamakau SM (1992a) Ka Poʻe Kahiko: the people of old trans from Ke Au ʻOkoʻa by Pukui MK with Barrere D (ed). Bishop Museum Press, Honolulu

Kamakau SM (1992b) Ruling chiefs of Hawaii, rev edn. Kamehameha Schools Press, Honolulu

Kamehameha Schools/Bishop Estate (2009) Native Hawaiian educational assessment update 2009: a supplement to Ka Huakaʻi 2005. Kamehameha Schools, Research & Evaluation Division, Honolulu

Kanaʻiaupuni SM, Malone N, Ishibashi K (2005) Income and poverty among Native Hawaiians: summary of Ka Huakaʻi findings. Kamehameha Schools, Honolulu

Kanaʻiaupuni SM, Malone N (2006) This land is my land: the role of place in Native Hawaiian identity. Hūlili: Multidisciplinary Research on Hawaiian Well-Being 3(1):281–307

Kelleher JS (2018) Guam pushes for native-only vote on US relationship. *Navy Times*, 11 Oct 2018

Krasner S (2001) Rethinking the sovereign state model. Rev Int Stud 27:17–42

Laughland J (2007) The crooked timber of reality: sovereignty, jurisdiction, and the confusions of human rights. Monist 90(1):3–25

Lenzerini F (2006) Sovereignty revisited: international law and the parallel sovereignty of indigenous peoples. Tex Int'l L J 42:155–189

Liu D, Alameda C (2011) Social determinants of health for Native Hawaiian children and adolescents. Hawai'i Med J 70:9–14

Lucas PFN (2000) E Ola Mau Kākou I Ka Ōlelo Makuahine: Hawaiian language policy and courts. Haw J Hist 34:1–28

Lyle B (2017) Native Hawaiians again seek political sovereignty with a new constitution. *Washington Post* 5 November 2017 (online edition), Accessed 12 Dec 2018

MacKenzie MK (2012) Ke Ala Loa – the long road: Native Hawaiian sovereignty and the state of Hawaii. Tulsa L Rev 47:621–658

MacKenzie M, Serrano S, Sproat K (eds) (2015) Native Hawaiian Law: a treatise. Native Hawaiian Legal Corporation, Ka Huli Ao Center for Excellence in Native Hawaiian Law at the William S. Richardson School of Law and University of Hawai'i at Mānoa, Honolulu

Merriam-Webster Dictionary. Found at www.merriam-webster.com. Accessed 12 Dec 2018

Moreton-Robinson A (2011) Virtuous racial states: the possessive logic of patriarchal white sovereignty and the United Nations declaration on the rights of indigenous peoples. Griffith L Rev 20(3):641–658

Moyrand A, Angelo AH (2010) Administrative regimes of French overseas territories: New Caledonia and French Polynesia. In: Angelo AH, Sage YL Governance and self-reliance in Pacific Island societies: comparative studies (Gouvernance pukuiet autonomie dans les sociétés du Pacifique Sud: Etudes comparés) Revue Juridique Polynesienne 193–206

Murphy C (2017) The conceptual foundations of transitional justice. Cambridge University Press, Cambridge

Nakaso D (2008) Should Hawai'i Rewrite Its Constitution—Again?. Time (US) (online ed, Washington DC, 30 October 2008)

Native Hawaiians Study Commission (1983) Report on the culture, needs and concerns of Native Hawaiians, pursuant to Public Law 96–565, title III, final report volume I. Department of the Interior, Washington DC

Office of Hawaiian Affairs et al (2010) The disparate treatment of Native Hawaiians in the criminal justice system. Office of Hawaiian Affairs, Honolulu

Okihiro GY (2008) Island world: a history of Hawai'i and the United States. University of California Press, Oakland

Osiander A (2001) Before sovereignty: society and politics in ancien régime Europe. Rev Int Stud 27:119–145

Osorio JK (2002) Dismembering the Lāhui: a history of the Hawaiian nation to 1887. University of Hawai'i Press, Honolulu

Pember MA (2016) Intergenerational trauma: understanding natives' inherited pain. Indian Country Today Special Report. Found at www.tribaldatabase.org. Accessed 12 Dec 2018

Pevar S (2012) The rights of Indians and tribes. Oxford University Press, New York

Poai AK (2017) Tales from the dark side of the archives: making history in Hawai'i without Hawaiians. U Haw L Rev 39:537–629

Preza DC (2010) The empirical writes back: re-examining Hawaiian dispossession resulting from the Māhele of 1848. PhD thesis, University of Hawai'i

Proposed Findings of Fact, Conclusions of Law and Decision and Order in the Matter of Contested Care Hearing Re Conservation District Use Application (CDUA) HA-3568 For the Thirty Meter Telescope at the Mauna Kea Science Reserve, Ka'ohe Mauka, Haumaka, Hawai'i TMK (3) 4-4-015:009, Board of Land and Natural Resources State of Hawai'i case no. BLNR-CC-16-002

Pukui MK, Elbert SH (1986) Hawaiian dictionary. University of Hawai'i Press, Honolulu

Sanderson D (2012) Redressing the Right Wrong: The Argument from Corrective Justice. University of Toronto Law Journal 62(1):93–132

Serrano S, Yamamoto E, MacKenzie MK, Forman D (2007) Restorative justice for Hawai'i's first people: selected Amicus Curiae briefs in Doe v. Kamehameha Schools. Asian Am L J 14(1):205–234

Silva N (2004) Aloha betrayed: Native Hawaiian resistance to American colonization. Duke University Press, Durham/London

Spinner-Halev J (2005) From historical to enduring injustice. Political Theory 35:574–597

Stauffer R (1983) The Hawai'i-United States treaty of 1826. Hawaiian J Hist 17:40–63

Straumann B (2008) The Peace of Westphalia as secular constitution. Constellations 15(2):173–188

Tansey O (2011) Does democracy need sovereignty? Rev Int Stud 34:531–552

Tushnet M (1997) Self-formalism, precedent, and the rule of law. Notre Dame L Rev 72(5):1583–1596

UN Commission on Human Rights (2001) Report of the working group established in accordance with the Commission on Human Rights resolution 1995/32. E /CN.4/2001/85

Waldron J (2012) Stare decisis and the rule of law: a layered approach. Michigan Law Rev 111:1–32

Wallerstein I "The Myth of Sovereignty", commentaries. Found at https://www.iwallerstein.com/the-myth-of-sovereignty/. Accessed 12 Dec 2018

Weinrib J (2019) Sovereignty as a right and as a duty: Kant's theory of the state. In: Claire Finkelstein C, Skerker M (eds) Sovereignty and the new executive authority. Oxford University Press, New York, pp 21–46

Whitbeck LB, Adams GW, Hoyt DR, Chen X (2004) Conceptualizing and measuring historical trauma among American Indian people. Am J Community Psychol 33(3/4):119–130

Williams R (1986) The Algebra of Federal Indian Law: The Hard Trail to Decolonizing and Americanizing the White Man's Indian Jurisprudence. Wis L Rev 219:260–265

Williams J (2013) Lex Aotearoa: A heroic attempt at mapping the Māori dimension in modern New Zealand law. In 22nd Annual Harkness Henry Lecture, University of Waikato, 7 November 2013

Wood DB (1994) Hawaii's search for sovereignty. Christian Science Monitor, 1 October 1994

Xanthaki A (2011) The UN declaration on the rights of indigenous peoples and collective rights: what's the future for indigenous women. In: Allen S, Xanthaki A (eds) Reflections on the UN declaration on the rights of indigenous peoples. Hart Publishing, Oxford, pp 413–432

Yamamoto EK, Betts CC (2008) Disfiguring civil rights to deny indigenous Hawaiian self-determination: the story of Rice v. Cayetano. In: Moran RE, Carbado DW (eds) Race law stories. Foundation Press, New York, pp 541–570

Yamamoto EK, Obrey EK (2009) Reframing redress: a 'Social Healing through Justice' approach to United States-Native Hawaiian and Japan-Ainu reconciliation initiatives. Asian Am L J 16(1):5–72

Perpetual Exclusion and Second-Order Minorities in Theaters of Civil Wars

52

Jovanie Camacho Espesor

Contents

Introduction	968
Case Studies: Aceh, Indonesia, and Mindanao, Philippines	969
Second-Order Minorities in Post-conflict Aceh	970
Post-Helsinki Aceh and Second-Order Minorities	975
Second-Order Minorities in Conflict-Ridden Mindanao	981
Mindanao Peace Process and Second-Order Minorities	987
Conclusion	989
Cross-References	990
References	990

Abstract

This article is a departure from a mainstream inquiry of giving too much credence to ethnic minorities that have the agency to mobilize revolutionary armies against the state. There is a need to pay attention to the plight of second-order minorities who do not have the capacity for rebellion but are usually victims of violence and displacement. The knowledge is sparse about the plight of subaltern communities that are in constant struggle for recognition of their rights and demands for representation in conflictual societies. Therefore, this chapter aims to answer the question of why second-order minorities in conflict-ridden communities are frequent subjects of marginalization, exclusion, and deprivation. Using two case studies of Aceh, Indonesia, and Bangsamoro, Philippines, this chapter seeks to

J. C. Espesor (✉)
Department of Political Science and International Relations, University of Canterbury, Christchurch, New Zealand

Department of Political Science, Mindanao State University, General Santos City, Philippines

Center for Middle East and Global Peace Studies, Universitas Islam Negeri Syarif Hidayatullah Jakarta, Tangerang, Indonesia
e-mail: jce50@uclive.ac.nz

© The Author(s), under exclusive license to Springer Nature Singapore Pte Ltd. 2019
S. Ratuva (ed.), *The Palgrave Handbook of Ethnicity*,
https://doi.org/10.1007/978-981-13-2898-5_145

contribute to the limited state of knowledge about considerably powerless second-order ethnic minorities in communities that are theaters of domestic wars. This chapter concludes that weaker groups who constitute the second-order minorities are facing repression and their demands for recognition of their identity and territorial domains are often undermined or subordinated to the wishes of dominant ethnic minorities who went into negotiating tables with governments.

Keywords
Second-order minorities · Aceh · Mindanao · Exclusion · Conflict

Introduction

The conflict issue in war-torn communities in Southeast Asia such as Aceh, Indonesia and Mindanao in the southern Philippines focuses on state and rebel contestation. Scholars of ethnic conflict in these contested environments tend to concentrate their investigations on minority groups that are leading the separatist organizations. The *Gerakan Aceh Merdeka* (GAM) or Free Aceh Movement that represents the minority Acehnese received major attention from scholars and peacebuilding actors when it went into armed uprising and eventually entered into a political settlement with the Government of Indonesia in 2005. In Mindanao, the Moro National Liberation Front (MNLF) gained widespread attention when it demanded independence and eventually signed the 1996 Final Peace Agreement with the Philippine government. In the same vein, MNLF's splinter group, the Moro Islamic Liberation Front (MILF), is currently earning global popularity because of its desire to give up its separatist claim in favor of greater political autonomy in the Bangsamoro. Both insurgent groups claim to represent the aspirations and legitimate grievances of the Moro people in Mindanao.

The provision of autonomy and installation of political structures that accommodate pluralism and power-sharing schemes have become the typical strategies employed by states in managing ethnic conflicts (Gurr 1993). These strategies were also applied in Aceh and Mindanao, which are both theaters of civil wars. Nonetheless, these conflict management mechanisms are seen to favor the interests of minority ethnic groups that are driving the rebellion, such as the Acehnese GAM and the Moro MNLF and MILF. The Governments of Indonesia and the Philippines granted the demands for greater autonomy of these belligerent groups, which are mobilized along ethnic lines, as a political tool to conclude decades of violent conflicts.

Autonomy has produced varying success in Aceh and Mindanao in resolving the issue of insurgency. The provision of special autonomy to Aceh is, to some extent, effective in terminating GAM insurgency. In Mindanao, such strategy yielded a negative outcome when the 1989 and 2001 autonomy laws failed to stop acts of separatism. The enactment of the Bangsamoro Organic Law (BOL) in the Philippine Congress in July 2018 constitutes another political experiment of using autonomy as a tool to solve protracted conflict in the Bangsamoro. Although autonomy offers potential solutions to address the issue of deprivation popularized by ethnic groups that rebel against the states, it can also facilitate local tensions. Autonomous regions are also home to second-order minorities or ethnic communities that are not part of the dominant ethnic groups that are leading the rebellion. Second-order minorities tend to pose resistance to autonomy because of the pressure to assimilate in a political environment, where the rule of the game is dictated by first-order minorities (Barter 2018). Second-order minorities refer to indigenous groups who are not part of dominant minority groups, while first-order minorities pertain to national minority groups, but constitute a regional majority block in conflictual communities.

This chapter is a departure from a mainstream inquiry of giving too much credence to ethnic minorities that have the agency to mobilize revolutionary armies against the state. There is a need to pay attention to the plight of second-order minorities who do not have the capacity for rebellion, but are usually victims of violence and displacement. The knowledge is sparse about the plight of subaltern communities that are in constant struggle for recognition of their rights and demands for representation in conflictual societies. Therefore, this chapter aims to answer the question of why second-order minorities in conflict-ridden communities are subjects of marginalization, exclusion, and deprivation. Using two case studies of Aceh and Mindanao, this chapter seeks to contribute to the limited state of knowledge about considerably powerless second-order ethnic minorities in communities that are theaters of domestic wars. These case studies are based on ethnographic field research in Indonesia and the Philippines. From 2016 to 2017, the author travelled to Jakarta and Aceh in Indonesia and to different conflict-prone localities in the southern Philippines. In both countries, the author interviewed government officials, rebel commanders, university professors, civil society representatives, and tribal leaders.

Case Studies: Aceh, Indonesia, and Mindanao, Philippines

To draw a better understanding of the plight of second-order minorities in war-torn polities, the succeeding sections present case studies of Aceh, Indonesia and Mindanao in the southern Philippines. Aceh and Mindanao have histories of violent conflict in which ethnicity is a major component of campaigns toward separatism by insurgent groups. Moreover, both communities are home to ethnic groups that constitute the second-order minorities who are often subjects of political exclusion and discrimination. It begins with Aceh that is considered as a post-conflict community (Espesor 2019) due to the non-recurrence of violence between GAM and the *Tentara Nasional Indonesia* (TNI) or the National Armed Forces of Indonesia after the signing of the 2005 Memorandum of Understanding (MoU) in Helsinki, Finland. In post-conflict Aceh, non-Acehnese ethnic minorities experienced social, economic, and political marginalization during and after the GAM rebellion. Meanwhile, Mindanao is a war-ridden community where its present socio-politico environment is characterized by insecurity due to the existence of active armed conflicts between the Armed Forces of the Philippines (AFP) and multiple non-state armed groups. In Mindanao, non-Muslim indigenous communities, collectively known as *lumads* (see International Crises Group, *henceforth* ICG 2011, 1), have for decades suffered the brunt of violent conflict whose human rights and fundamental freedoms have been constantly violated by powerful actors, particularly warlords and military, in the conflict zone.

The following sections illustrate who are the second-order minorities and give their territorial concentration in two conflictual communities. The power asymmetries and dynamics between the ethnic majorities and minorities will be given emphasis to substantiate the central argument presented in this chapter that the rights and welfare of second-order minorities are constantly marginalized and sidelined in both conflict and post-conflict environments.

Second-Order Minorities in Post-conflict Aceh

The province of Nanggroe Aceh Darussalam (NAD) is located in the northern tip of the Indonesian island of Sumatra. Aceh has gained the attention of the international media due to the catastrophe brought about by the 2004 Indian Ocean Tsunami that devastated most of the western coast of the province, including the capital Banda Aceh. It is known for its strong legacy of internal war and demand for independence from the Government of Indonesia since the onset of the GAM rebellion in 1976 (Barter 2018; Barron et al. 2013). Furthermore, it is also hailed as a post-conflict community and an abode of peace owing to the success of the internationally mediated 2005 MoU that was facilitated by the former Finnish President Martti Ahtisaari, chair of the NGO Crisis Management Initiative (CMI) (Kingsbury 2006; Shea 2016). Present-day Aceh serves as an actual referent or evidence of a successful peacebuilding operation of liberal actors, particularly the CMI that facilitated the peace talk and the European Union that led and financed the activities of the Aceh Monitoring Mission (Feith 2007; Smith 2017). Moreover, the Aceh peace process is a significant milestone in the political career of former Indonesian President Susilo Bambang Yudhoyono, that enabled him to gain international prestige by concluding the three decades of violent insurgency in NAD (ICG 2007). (The annual population growth rate of Aceh from 2010 to 2013 is 2.08% (Badan Pusat Statistik 2014).)

Aceh is a multiethnic society with a population of 4,811,100 as of 2013 (Badan Pusat Statistik 2014, 78). (The annual population growth rate of Aceh from 2010 to 2013 is 2.08% (Badan Pusat Statistik 2014).) Majority of the people in NAD are ethnic Acehnese (approximately 72%) who generally supported the separatist claim of GAM from 1976 to 2005 (Barter 2018, 303). (The scholars provided varying population estimates of Acehnese in NAD. Ansori (2012, 38) claims that this ethnic group comprises 80% of the total provincial population. In McCulloch's research (2005, 10), the Acehnese composes 90% of Aceh's population.) Although, the Acehnese constitute the majority in NAD, they are considered to be an ethnic minority in Indonesia. The Javanese is the largest ethnic group that is accounted for, totalling around 42% of the country's entire population (Indonesia-Investments 2017). Hence, the label first-order minority is aptly suited to refer to the Acehnese that comprise the regional majority ethnic block in NAD. As regional majority, it is no longer surprising for the Acehnese to dominate the political landscape in the province during and after the conflict. Most scholars who are interested in the Aceh conflict focus most of their investigations on GAM, which was an ethnic Acehnese belligerent organization (see Sulistiyanto 2001; Reid 2004), and eventually on its successor political parties, such as the Aceh Party and Aceh National Party (Hamzah 2009; Barron et al. 2013). Other ethnic groups that composed the second-order minorities also exist in NAD; however, unlike the Acehnese, they do not receive significant attention.

The Acehnese constitute an overwhelming majority in NAD with more than three million members (see Table 1). Being the largest ethnic group, they represent the regional majority and first-order minority in Aceh. Due to the transmigration policy of the Indonesian Government, NAD has become home to some national majority Javanese settlers that comprised around 8% of the provincial population. Table 1 also presents an idea of who are second-order minorities and why there is a looming inter-ethnic contestation in NAD. The ethnic groups Gayo (7%) and Alas (3%) in the central highlands of the province are the indigenous inhabitants of Aceh. The province is also home to some Malay people such as the Kluet and Singkil that make up around 4% of Aceh's population (Barter 2018; Ansori 2012). Although the province is also home to other ethnic minorities like Simeulue, Batak, and Minangkabau (Ananta 2007), in this chapter, I focus on the Gayo, Alas, Kluet, and Singkil (GALAKSI) as the second-order minorities in post-MoU Aceh (Fig. 1).

As shown in the map, the Gayo people are territorially concentrated in *kabupaten* (regencies) in the central highlands of NAD, particularly Bener Meriah, Aceh Tengah, Aceh Timur, and Gayo Lues. These regencies are home to the Gayonese subgroups, namely, Gayo Lot, Gayo Lokop Serbajadi, Gayo Lues, and Gayo Linge (McCulloch 2005). These ethnic groups are progenies of the North Sumatran animist Karo and Dairi tribes, which later embraced Islam (Ramly 2005). Another indigenous group, the Alas, are relatives of the Gayo, and most members are located in Aceh Tenggara adjacent to the Province of North Sumatra. Meanwhile the Malay ethnic group Kluet is territorially concentrated in the hinterlands of Aceh Selatan, and the regency of Aceh Singkil is the ancestral abode of the Ulu Singkil. The

Table 1 Population of Aceh by ethnicity

Ethnicity	Approximate number	Percentage (%)
Acehnese	3,235,968	72
Javanese	359,552	8
Gayo	314,604	7
Alas	134,832	3
Kluet and Singkil	179,776	4
Simeulue, Batak, and Minangkabau	269,664	6
Total	4,494,400	100

Source: Computed by the author based on the 2010 National Population Census of Indonesia (Badan Pusat Statistik 2014, 78) and the estimates provided by Barter (2018)

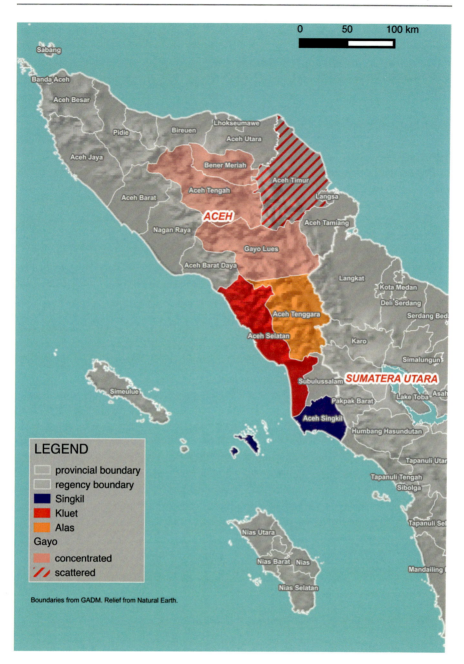

Fig. 1 Map showing the location of second-order minorities in Aceh. Note: This map of Aceh is original to this chapter and was generated using Global Information System software. The location of second-order minorities in Aceh is based on the scholarship of McCulloch (2005) and fieldwork interviews

territorial concentration of these second-order minorities in NAD in their respective regencies makes them distinctively separated from the Acehnese society. The division between the second-order minorities and the dominant ethnic Acehnese is not only from a geographic point of view. The relationship of Acehnese and second-order minorities has been characterized by social cleavage and mutual alienation even during the height of GAM insurgency up to the present-day Aceh.

Inter-ethnic dynamics between the Acehnese and indigenous groups Gayo and Alas is more evident compared to the tension between the former and the Malay minorities, Kluet and Singkil. The indigenous communities in the central highlands experienced social disturbance and security instability during the height of civil war and military emergency in Aceh. This is due to the geographic proximity of Gayo- and Alas-dominated regencies to the so-called daerah hitam or black areas controlled by GAM, such as Pidie, Bireuën, and Aceh Utara. These indigenous people have become victims of abusive practices perpetuated by the warring parties. The dubious exploitations against Gayo farmers were allegedly carried out by both TNI (McCulloch 2005) and *Tentara Nasional Aceh* (TNA), the armed winged of GAM (Barter 2015). There are no documented cases of gross abuses against the Singkil during the civil war in Aceh. Aceh Selatan and Singkil are closer to North Sumatra and considerably remote from the conflict-infested regencies of Aceh. However, Barter (2014) claims that the previously peaceful Malay communities in the border of Aceh and North Sumatra had been saddled with violence and tensions, especially after the collapse of the ceasefire agreement in 2003. GAM was suspicious of the Malays who experienced threats and intimidation from the rebel forces (Barter 2015).

The ethnic tension between the Acehnese and second-order minorities has predated the 2005 Helsinki agreement. Despite geographic isolation from GAM strongholds and centers of military operations, Aceh's second-order minorities have experienced atrocities and security problems during the height of civil war. Gayonese suffered from violence because TNA launched a series of offensive attacks against Javanese people residing in their communities. It was the intention of GAM to expel Javanese migrants from their ancestral homeland (Barter 2018, 2014). Some members of the TNI were responsible for exploitation and abuses experienced by the Gayonese during the conflict. There are allegations that members of the TNI deployed in the central highlands were extorting money from Gayo farmers to finance the operations of anti-GAM militias. The regencies in the interior of NAD have fertile agricultural lands that are conducive for the production of high-grade Sumatran coffee and other high-valued crops (McCulloch 2005). According to Dr. Otto Nur Abdullah, commissioner of the Komnas HAM or National Commission on Human Rights, Indonesia there were cases of gross human rights violations that took place in Gayo-dominated regencies. He claims that there were reported cases of *orang hilang* or missing persons in Bener Meriah and Aceh Tengah during the height of the conflict, especially when Aceh was under *Daerah Operasi Militer* (DOM) from 1990 to 1998 and martial law when the Cessation of Hostilities Agreement collapsed in 2003 until the signing of the 2005 MoU.

The Kluet-dominated regency of Aceh Selatan also suffered from the inhumane treatment of the TNI. A day before former President Megawati Sukarnoputri placed Aceh under a state of military emergency and martial law in 18 May 2003 (see Hedman 2005), the TNI carried out an offensive military operation in the village of Jambu Keupok in Bakongan sub-district of Aceh Selatan. The TNI forces were looking for TNA renegades who were hiding in Jambu Keupok (Adyatama 2016). Consequently, civilians in the village experienced horrendous treatment at the hands of the Indonesian military. Allegedly, TNI soldiers killed many innocent civilians in cold blood (Author's interview with Dr. Otto Nur Abdullah, Komnas HAM Commissioner, Jakarta, Indonesia, 13 May 2016). Based on the report of the Komnas HAM submitted to the *Lembaga Perlindungan Saksi dan Korban* or Witness and Victims Protection Agency of Indonesia, TNI soldiers are accused of committing human rights violations in Aceh Selatan by killing 16 people through shooting by guns, then burning. They are also implicated in the torture of 21 others (Adyatama 2016). Moreover, the Kluet in Aceh Selatan, whose lives are dependent on the forest, were affected by illicit logging business ventures by local GAM commanders and TNI officials (McCulloch 2005; Aspinall 2005).

TNI launched offensive attacks in Aceh Tengah and Aceh Selatan because some of the inhabitants there had joined the GAM rebellion (Ramly 2005). Every time TNI had operations to annihilate GAM rebels in these regencies, ordinary Gayo and Kluet civilians were the frequent victims of violence and displacement. These civilians, including innocent children, were often caught in a crossfire of warring combatants. The people in these regencies had not only experienced military-sponsored brutality. They also suffered abuses from GAM who killed helpless civilians, including women and children, and burned houses. During the Humanitarian Pause in Aceh in 2000, the Gayonese, together with some Javanese migrants in Aceh Tengah, resisted GAM by arming themselves with homemade weapons (Schulze 2005).

In post-Helsinki Aceh, Komnas HAM is confronted with the challenge of investigating *orang hilang* cases in Bener Meriah and Aceh Tengah and the Jambu Keupok massacre in Aceh Selatan. The human rights commission is facing the difficulty of gathering concrete evidence to indict perpetrators, especially those powerful members of the TNI- and GAM-turned political leaders. Victims and their families are unable to clearly identify TNA rebels and TNI soldiers who were responsible for the force disappearance and extrajudicial killings of innocent civilians, particularly those members of ethnic minorities. Without sufficient evidence, Komnas HAM is not in a position to endorse a case to the *Jaksa Agung* or Attorney General of the Indonesian Government and prosecute potential perpetrators in the Human Rights Court (Author's interview with Dr. Otto Nur Abdullah, Komnas HAM Commissioner, Jakarta, Indonesia, 13 May 2016). The Gayo and Kluet people, like other civilians who were victims of human rights abuses, are still longing for transitional justice in post-Helsinki Aceh. It is apparent that Aceh's second-order minorities who do not have the capacity to wage rebellion, unlike the Acehnese GAM, are more vulnerable to hostilities and abuses committed by both state soldiers and rebels. Unfortunately, many victims of extrajudicial killing, rape, torture, arbitrary detention, and other forms of human rights abuses are likely to experience denial of justice due to the prevailing culture of impunity in Indonesia. Human rights institutions like the Komnas Ham and Komnas Perempuan (National Commission on Violence Against Women) have limited jurisdiction and weak investigatory power, especially when human rights cases involved high-ranking military and government officials (Author's interviews with Adriana Venny Aryani, Komnas Perempuan Commissioner and Dr. Otto Nur Abdullah, Komnas HAM Commissioner, Jakarta, Indonesia, 13 May 2016).

According to Fajran Zain, a member of the *Komisi Kebenaran dan Rekonsiliasi* (KKR) or Truth and Reconciliation Commission in Aceh, "victims of human rights abuses do not enjoy peace" in post-conflict Aceh. He adds that these victims and their families are earnestly demanding compensation, restitution, and justice through a fair court trial. It took 10 years for the *Dewan Perwakilan Rakyat Aceh* (DPRA) or local parliament of Aceh to create the KKR on 20 July 2016, after the signing of the 2005 Helsinki Agreement (Gade 2016). Some human rights activists have alleged that the delay in the establishment of KKR in Aceh is due to the political alliance and collusion of Aceh Party leaders and some military-politicians (Confidential interviews). The creation of KKR brings new hopes for human rights victims, particularly members of second-order minorities, to demand compensation and finally to achieve justice. Nonetheless, there is some scepticism that the Commission will not be able to achieve comprehensive success in dispensing justice for those who suffered human rights violations that took place during the conflict. Post-conflict transformation, including transitional justice, is no longer a priority of the national and provincial governments. The investigation of KKR is greatly hampered by a phenomenon of "memory decay" because some human rights victims have reached old age and others have passed away (Author's interview with Fajran Zain, Commissioner of KKR, Banda Aceh, Aceh, Indonesia, 25 May 2016). Moreover, women victims are discouraged by family members and religious leaders to report their experiences of sexual violence. According to Nur Djuli, "in our culture nobody wants to speak about rape" (Author's interview, Banda Aceh, Aceh, Indonesia, 20 May 2016). Sharing stories of sexual abuses and harassments is deemed forbidden in the Islamic community of Aceh (Wandita 2014). A woman NGO leader, Leila Juari says, "truth telling is a taboo. It is something bad for the family and dirty for the community. We have to forget and therefore, there is no healing for victims of sexual harassment and rape and those who are stigmatized by the members of the community" (Author's interview, Banda Aceh, Aceh, Indonesia, 24 May 2016). It is apparent that such Islamic-inspired norms and practices constitute an obstacle for the KKR to dispense justice for victims of human rights abuses during the height of conflict in Aceh.

Post-Helsinki Aceh and Second-Order Minorities

The conclusion of the three-decade-long insurgency when GAM and GoI reached political settlement brought euphoria to Aceh. People in NAD celebrated the return of peace to their homeland, particularly when the TNI pulled out its forces in Aceh. The successful peace agreement also earned the attention of local and international media outfits. In exchange of greater autonomy for NAD, GAM finally gave up its separatist claim; decommissioned TNA; and transformed into political organizations. It is worth noting that a year before the political settlement, communities in the northern coast of the province, including its capital Banda Aceh, were struck and devastated by the 2004 Indian Ocean Tsunami. Notwithstanding its hesitation to internationalize the domestic conflict (Herrberg 2008), the Indonesian Government to some extent was forced to allow the presence of international organizations and NGOs due to the urgent need for large-scale humanitarian operations following the tsunami-induced catastrophe in Aceh (McCulloch 2005).

The missions of most international humanitarian organizations in Aceh were carried out for post-tsunami emergency relief and rehabilitation and not to facilitate post-conflict transformation. A bulk of foreign relief and development assistance was given to Acehnese-dominated regencies because of the massive devastation brought about by the tsunami on the northern coast of the province. Some NGO workers sent to NAD were not even aware that Aceh was not only devastated by the tsunami; it was also ruined by decades of domestic war (Author's interview with a director of a foreign NGO, Banda Aceh, Aceh, Indonesia, 27 May 2016). The focus of post-tsunami reconstruction and concentration of the assistance of foreign organizations in predominately Acehnese regencies was somewhat justified and acceptable. External organizations were authorized to operate in Aceh mainly to help communities affected by the tsunami and not to perform conflict transformation intervention, which is primarily led by the Indonesian National Government (Espesor 2019).

The marginalization of second-order minorities in Aceh tends to continue from the civil war period to post-Helsinki settlement. Dr. Ardi Adji, a Gayonese leader based in Jakarta, claims that since the 1980s, Gayo regencies are left behind in terms of public infrastructures and quality of healthcare and education services. He also asserts that there is a prevailing perception among the Acehnese that they are superior to other ethnic minorities in NAD (Author's interview with Dr. Ardi Adji, Professor at the Paramadina University, Jakarta, Indonesia, 20 June 2016). Aside from the Gayo, the Alas and Singkil people have also experienced the same discriminatory treatment and sociopolitical marginalization by the dominant Acehnese group (Ansori 2012). The estranged social relationship of Acehnese and second-order minorities generates an emerging pattern of conflict in post-war Aceh.

The wide array of social and political challenges, particularly inter-ethnic strife that rose in post-Helsinki Aceh, are due to the inherent weakness of the 2004 MoU and the 2005 Law on Governing Aceh (LoGA). Teungku Nasruddin Ahmad, a senior GAM leader attributes the current problems on the insufficiency of the peace agreement. According to him, both the MoU and LoGA do not contain sufficient details that can accommodate the interests and welfare of other groups, particularly that of the women and second-order minorities in Aceh. Based on the content of the 2005 MoU, the ultimate goal of the peace accord was to conclude the violent conflict and pave the way for rehabilitation of Aceh after the tsunami. The peace agreement is a short document that is overladen with provisions that grant political incentives and material rewards for GAM that is mainly composed of ethnic Acehnese. Apparently, the sentiments and grievances of second-order minorities and civil society groups were not accommodated in the MoU. Due to the urgent demand for the rebuilding of Aceh after the tsunami disaster, Ahtisaari acted as what Touval (1982) labels as a mediator with muscle. Under Ahtisaari's style of mediation, the entire course of negotiation was exclusive to Indonesia and GAM. No other parties were allowed to participate in order to reach settlement in a short span of time. The exclusion of civil society from the peace process was admitted by Nur Djuli. He claims:

> It is true that civil society organizations were not included in the negotiation. Based on our previous experience, it is not very conducive to include civil society knowing the nature of the Acehnese society in which many will insist on their own interests. Although there are a lot of criticisms against Ahtisaari, I should say, had we included civil society; probably we would not have achieved what we have achieved today. (Author's interview, Banda Aceh, Aceh, Indonesia, 20 May 2016)

Based on that statement, it is clear that the main goal of the peace accord is to merely end violent insurgency in Aceh and satisfy demands of GAM for greater autonomy despite the absence of broad conflict transformation mechanisms that are acceptable and favorable to all groups in Aceh, particularly the non-Acehnese ethnic minorities. Hence, there is a widespread perception among second-order minorities that the peace agreement is exclusively beneficial to the Acehnese GAM (Ansori 2012), especially former rebel leaders who received an ample amount of political and economic concessions (Aspinall 2008; Aditjondro 2007).

Starting in 2005, Aceh has received a huge amount of foreign aid from different international funding institutions and donor countries to finance the democratization projects of different NGOs. Democracy promotion has been the typical scheme carried out by external liberal agents to initiate transformation of a post-conflict community, like Aceh, into a peaceful polity that is receptive of liberal-democratic values, norms, and practices. As observed, most donor-funded NGOs concentrated their democracy and peacebuilding projects on Acehnese GAM. International and local NGOs were simply following the directives of their respective donors. NGO proposals that were not designed to meet the interests of GAM were likely to be disapproved by funding agencies. Peacebuilding projects of different humanitarian and development agencies from 2005 to 2008 were intended to help GAM transform into political organizations. Facilitating the reintegration of GAM combatants through capacity-building training and provision of livelihoods was also in the "menu" of funding agencies (Author's interview with Dr. Saifuddin Bantashiam, Director of the Aceh Peace Research Centre and UNDP Programme Officer, Banda Aceh, Aceh, Indonesia, 19 May 2016). The *Sekolah Perdamaian dan Demokrasi* or School for Peace and Democracy (SPD), for instance, is a local NGO that focused heavily on building the political agency of former Acehnese GAM rebels. SPD was established by Nur Djuli, who is an influential GAM leader, and it has an extensive network with donor agencies (Espesor 2019). Although SPD had an emancipatory purpose of educating and building the capacities of former combatants in politics and governance, it was seen as exclusively beneficial for Acehnese people who were part of the rebellion. Well-funded peacebuilding initiatives like SPD and skills-development training were mostly given to Acehnese people, while second-order minorities were virtually absent in the peacebuilding architecture in post-Helsinki Aceh.

The overwhelming amount of foreign assistance given to the Acehnese and the ascent of rebel leaders into political power appear to be the entitlements and rewards of GAM for abandoning its armed struggle toward independence. Nonetheless, the new power-sharing scheme after the peace agreement in NAD was greatly in favor of the dominant Acehnese group. Second-order minorities have the collective feeling that they have been subjects of marginalization and exclusion by the ethnic Acehnese majority (Ansori 2012). The brewing ethnic tension between the Acehnese and second-order minorities has led to the demand to carve out and create new provinces from the present territorial domain of NAD in the year 2000. A group of local activists consisting of district politicians, religious leaders, students, and civil society representatives in the central highland regencies of Aceh Tengah, Aceh Tenggara, Gayo Lues, Bener Meriah, and Aceh Singkil formed a movement that called for the establishment of a new province, which they called Aceh Leuser Antara (ALA). The *pemekaran* or blossoming, which is the present decentralization framework of the Unitary State of Indonesia, constitutes a legal justification for the demand to create the ALA as a province (ICG 2008; Ehrentraut 2010). (ALA was joined by another movement that also pushed for the creation of another province, Aceh Barat Selatan, comprising of Aceh Jaya, West Aceh, Nagan Raya, Southeast Aceh, Simeulue and South Aceh (Ehrentraut 2010).) Nonetheless, the proponents of ALA failed to convince the national government in Jakarta to subdivide NAD into two or three provinces (Author's interview with Murizal Hamzah, Journalist, *Netralitas*, Jakarta, Indonesia, 3 May 2016). Former Indonesian President Yudhoyono issued a decree that imposed a moratorium on administration subdivisions in the entirety of Indonesia (ICG 2008). Yudhoyono hesitated to support the creation of new provinces as it would undermine and violate the territorial provision of the 2005 MoU. GAM-turned politicians vehemently opposed the establishment of ALA and Aceh Barat Selatan (ABAS) out of Aceh (Ehrentraut 2010).

Despite the lack of support from Jakarta and the strong objection from Acehnese provincial elites, the ALA-ABAS movement has been persistently active in pushing for the birth of a new province under the *pemekaran* scheme (Serambi Indonesia 2016). The leaders of the movement continually promote the narrative that they are neglected in the process of development in NAD to popularize and legitimize their demand to create a new province. Second-order minorities felt that most of the political benefits and economic incentives brought about by the 2005 peace agreement went to ethnic Acehnese-dominated regencies (Author's interview with Murizal Hamzah, Journalist, *Netralitas*, Jakarta, Indonesia, 3 May 2016). Hence, there is a growing perception among members of the second-order minorities that the Acehnese-biased development scheme in NAD can only be rectified through the establishment of the ALA-ABAS province. In the study of Ehrentraut, he claims that

ALA-ABAS leaders are consistent with their claim that "development in highland districts is far behind coastal areas" because the provincial government is perceivably absent in these regencies (2010, 12). Nonetheless, GAM leader Nur Djuli does not fully agree with the narrative put forward by ALA-ABAS leaders. According to him, while "it is true that they are left behind, I do not put the total blame to Banda Aceh. The decentralization scheme of the government dictates that money [public funds] should be given directly to the regencies and not through the province. If we compare Bener Meriah and Banda Aceh, of course the latter got more money, but if we based the comparison on per capita allocation, the former is richer due to its small population. If we look at the funds of these highland regencies in terms of per capita allocation, they have huge government funds" (Author's interview, Banda Aceh, Aceh, Indonesia, 20 May 2016). Muzakir Manaf, Chair of the Aceh Party and former GAM Supreme Commander, concurs with Nur Djuli's statement that non-Acehnese regencies are not marginalized when it comes to the allocation of government funds. Manaf said that all regencies in Aceh directly received their *Dana Alokasi Umum* (DAU) or General Purpose Grant from the national government and therefore, the provincial government is not in control of the allocation and utilization of DAU (Author's interview, Banda Aceh, Aceh, Indonesia, 19 May 2016).

The low level of development of regencies in the central highlands, where second-order minorities are the dominant groups, is due to the rampant practice of corruption. District leaders and members of the local parliaments are allegedly involved in graft and corrupt practices in ALA-ABAS regencies. Nur Djuli criticized the national government in Jakarta for its weak regulatory oversight over the local affairs in Aceh. According to him, the *Komisi Pemberantasan Korupsi* or Indonesian Corruption Eradication Commission is not interested in investigating corruption cases that are taking place at the district level in Aceh (Author's interview, Banda Aceh, Aceh, Indonesia, 20 May 2016). It is clear that Acehnese influential figures, such as Nur Djuli and Muzakir Manaf, are trying to counter the narratives promoted by ALA-ABAS leaders that they have been marginalized and disenfranchised in the process of socioeconomic development in NAD. However, ex-GAM leaders simply focused on invoking the decentralized disbursement scheme of DAU to invalidate the marginalization claim of second-order minority groups. Aside from DAU, there are many sources of funds from the national government that are under the control of Aceh's provincial government. The *Dana Aspirasi* or aspiration fund, for instance, was primarily allocated and disbursed in favor of regencies which are known strongholds of GAM. In 2017, IDR 917.5 billion (approximately USD 68 million) was earmarked as *Dana Aspirasi* or "pork barrel" funds of the members of the DPRA. The Regency of Bener Meriah, which is predominately Gayonese, received the lowest allocation of aspiration fund (Haris 2017). Moreover, Ehrentraut (2010) made an interesting claim that ALA-ABAS leaders are constantly motivated to demand for the partition of Aceh into two or three provinces in order to receive more government funds from Jakarta, particularly DAU and *Dana Alokasi Khusus* (DAK) or Specific Purpose Grant. DAK is intended to finance the establishment of bureaucratic structures and public infrastructures in newly created provinces.

The inter-ethnic divide between the regional majority Acehnese and second-order minorities underpins the inherent nature of conflict even in a post-conflict milieu. The end of insurgency in 2005 when GAM decommissioned its armed wing and transformed into political organizations does not mean that conflict is no longer existing in Aceh. Several minor pockets of tensions are emerging in Aceh, particularly the estranged inter-ethnic relationship between the Acehnese and second-order minorities. This inter-ethnic contestation is manifest in the political and social sphere in post-conflict Aceh. During the height of conflict, second-order minorities in the upland regencies supported Indonesia in its campaign to crush the GAM rebellion. Some of them were recruited in the anti-GAM militias set up by the TNI (Ansori 2012). The animosity between Acehnese, who generally supported GAM, and second-order minorities during the civil war period trickles off in present-day Aceh. Acehnese provincial elites are accused of not paying attention to the legitimate grievances of second-order minorities because they did not take part in the rebellion. It is also observed that non-Acehnese regencies typically support national parties like Golkar, Nasdem, and PAN in local elections and not the political parties that succeeded GAM. Aceh Party and Aceh National Party are only popular in vote-rich regencies, which are GAM's former strongholds (Ehrentraut 2010). Moreover, based on the current composition of the DPRA for the term 2014–2019, it is obvious that the second-order minorities do not have adequate parliamentary representation in Aceh (DPRA 2018).

Social institutions that were established because of the 2004 MoU and 2005 LoGA are considerably meaningless for members of the second-order minorities. For example, the installation of the former Prime Minister of GAM, Malik Mahmud Al Haythar, as the new *Wali Nanggroe*, or guardian of the state, in 2013 did not receive support from the non-Acehnese people of Aceh. Malik Mahmud was chosen by the DPRA to succeed GAM's founder Hasan di Tiro who died in 2010 as the *Wali Nanggroe* (Ali 2013). According to Nur Djuli, the MoU envisions the *Wali Nanggroe* as a non-political post and should have a cultural leader who should act as the symbol of unity for the people of Aceh and work for the preservation of Acehnese traditions, languages, and customs (Author's interview, Banda Aceh, Aceh, Indonesia, 20 May 2016). However, only the ethnic Acehnese pay respect to the institution of the *Wali Nanggroe*. Members of the second-order minorities, especially the Gayonese, do not recognized Malik Mahmud as their traditional leader (Author's interview with a Gayonese leader and program officer of an international organization, Jakarta, Indonesia, 17 May 2016). Hence, Acehnese-centric institutions in the post-Helsinki environment continue to face resistance and are often at odds with extant beliefs and institutions held by the members of the second-order minorities in Aceh.

Among second-order minorities, the Singkil people have become the major subject of discrimination and coercion against religious minorities in present-day Aceh. Based on the 2010 Population Census of Indonesia, 98.64% of the people of Aceh are Muslims (Ananta et al. 2015, 267), which explains the dominance and prominence of Islam in shaping the sociocultural fiber of the Acehnese society. The Christian minority in Aceh Singkil, in particular, is complaining that its members have been victims of religious intolerance and sectarian violence that are carried out by Sunni Muslims and various radicalized Islamic organizations operating in Aceh (Espesor 2019). In October 2015, Indonesian President Joko Widodo called for the immediate stoppage of violence in Aceh Singkil via *Twitter*, when radical groups assaulted and burned down Christian churches there. However, local authorities and radical organizations in Aceh typically invoked the Religious Harmony Law to justify their coercive actions against Christian minorities in Aceh Singkil and other regencies. Human rights activists who are fighting for religious equality are not in the best position to call for protection of religious minority groups, especially the Singkil Christians. Sunni Islam defenders often branded human rights groups as the "enemy of God," and that made them vulnerable to attacks by extremist groups, particularly the *Pemuda Peduli Islam* or Islamic Youth Movement (Author's interview with a senior researcher of the Human Rights Watch, Jakarta, Indonesia, 17 May 2016).

Second-Order Minorities in Conflict-Ridden Mindanao

Another theater of a protracted civil war that also hosts second-order minorities is Mindanao in the southern Philippines. The conflict in Mindanao is considered as the longest-running insurgency and domestic war in the world (Morales 2003; Whaley 2014). Unlike the rebellion in Aceh that involved a single separatist organization, GAM, the AFP is fighting several Muslim belligerent groups, terrorist outfits, and the communist New People's Army (Espesor 2017a). Presently, Mindanao is gaining significant global attention from media, donor communities, and international organizations because Philippine President Rodrigo Duterte signed the BOL on 27 July 2018. (This law is otherwise known as the Republic Act No. 11054). This law enforces the provisions of the 2014 Comprehensive Agreement on the Bangsamoro (CAB) between the Philippine government and MILF and creates the Bangsamoro Autonomous Region (BAR) in the southern Philippines. Nonetheless, Mindanao is far from becoming a post-conflict community like Aceh, despite the passage of the organic law and the anticipated creation of the BAR. Terrorists, lawless armed groups, and political warlords' militias continue to threaten the peace and security environment in post-BOL Mindanao. Despite a wide array of security and development challenges ahead, ethnic Moro communities, particularly MILF sympathizers, are celebrating the passage of the BOL as a significant milestone in the history of the Mindanao peace process (OPAPP 2018).

Conflict-ridden communities in Mindanao are the ancestral homelands of some major ethnic Moro groups, particularly the Maguindanao and Maranaw in Mainland Bangsamoro and the Tausug, Sama, and Yakan in the island provinces of Basilan, Sulu, and Tawi-Tawi. (For a complete list of Moro ethnic groups in Mindanao, see Rodil (1994)). The ethnic Moro people, although considered a national minority in the Philippines, constitute the regional majority in the Bangsamoro. Hence, they can be considered as a first-order ethnic minority in the Philippines. One of the major challenges in post-BOL Mindanao is facilitating the inclusion into the political

Table 2 Population of *Lumads* in Mainland Bangsamoro

Ethnicity	Population
Teduray	110,559
Dulangan Manobo	2904
Lambangian	3139
Higaonon	161
Agusan Manobo	93

Source: Konrad-Adenauer-Stiftung (2014)

sphere of the *lumads*. The Bangsamoro is also home to some indigenous cultural communities that do not adhere to the Islamic faith and claim to have a distinct identity from Muslim Filipinos. These *lumads* are the second-order minorities that endured for decades the impact of violent conflicts in Mindanao (Table 2).

A sizeable number of *lumad* communities can be found in the mainland provinces of Maguindanao and Lanao del Sur. The Maguindanao and Maranaw people comprised the biggest ethnic Muslim groups in these provinces (see Rodil 1994). The demographic profiling survey on indigenous peoples of mainland ARMM conducted by the German NGO, Konrad-Adenauer-Stiftung (KAS), and its southern partner, the Institute for Autonomy and Governance (IAG), illustrates the presence of *lumad* communities within the core territory of the Bangsamoro. Apparently, the ethnic group Teduray constitutes the dominant group among all non-Moro indigenous groups, with a population of 110,559. The Lambangian and Dulangan Manobo people have a combined population of more than 6000 that is obviously smaller compared to the Tedurays. Some few members of other ethnolinguistic groups, the Higaonon and Agusan Manobo, are also residing in some conflict-ridden communities in the Bangsamoro. Nonetheless, the data of KAS and IAG do not include the population of Arumanen Manobo whose ancestral domains are situated in the border of Maguindanao and Cotabato, which is not part of the ARMM. Like the Tedurays, Dulangan Manobos, and Lambangians, the Arumanen Manobo has also experienced decades of violent armed skirmishes between the AFP and different non-state armed militias (Fig. 2).

The map shows the territorial concentration of second-order minorities in the Bangsamoro. The three major ethnic groups comprise the Teduray, Lambangian, and Dulangan Manobo, and they claim the Daguma Mountain Range as their shared ancestral homeland (KAS 2014, 6). Most of the members of the Teduray and Lambangian ethnic groups are currently residing in the municipalities of Upi, South Upi, Datu Odin Sinsuat, and Shariff Aguak in Maguindanao (Rodil 1994). A small pocket of the Dulangan Manobo community can be found in the Municipality of Ampatuan, Maguindanao. Most of the Dulangan Manobos are occupying the hinterland communities in the Daguma Mountain Range within the political jurisdiction of the Sultan Kudarat Province (KAS 2014, 6). Meanwhile, the Arumanen Manobos are territorially concentrated outside the ARMM core territory. The members of this ethnolinguistic group are presently scattered in the

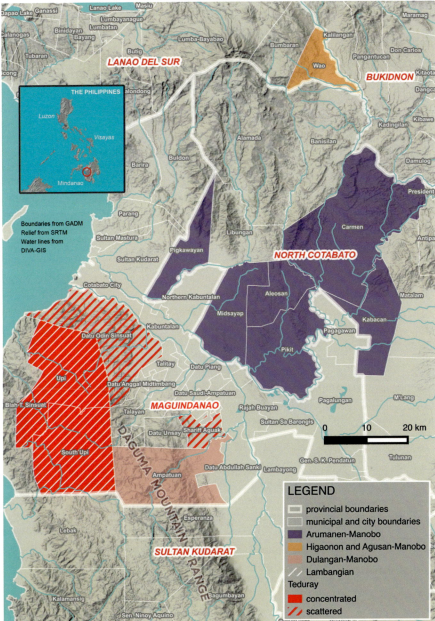

Fig. 2 Map showing the location of second-order minorities in the Bangsamoro. Note: This map of Bangsamoro is original to this chapter and was generated using Global Information System software. The location of second-order minorities in the Bangsamoro is based on the scholarship of Rodil (1994), KAS (2014), and fieldwork interviews

municipalities of Aleosan, Carmen, Kabacan, Midsayap, Pigkawayan, and Pikit in Cotabato Province. (It is worth noting that 39 *barangays* (smallest political unit in the Philippines) in these municipalities under the newly signed Bangsamoro Organic Law will become part of the Bangsamoro Autonomous Region. For more information, see Article 1, Section 3 paragraph C of the Republic Act No. 11054.) Moreover, the presence of small pockets of Higaonon and Agusan Manobo tribes are documented in Wao, Lanao del Sur (KAS 2014, 6).

Displacement and marginalization are aptly suited descriptions that depict the plight of second-order minorities in the Bangsamoro. These ethnic groups have been constantly exposed to violence and suffered from constant displacement since the outbreak of insurgency in the southern Philippines in the 1970s. The Teduray, Lambangian, Dulangan Manobo, and Arumanen Manobo whose communities are in the conflict zones have been pushing for the recognition of their right to self-determination by asserting their unique cultural identity that is different from the Muslim people and by the Christian inhabitants of Mindanao. Nonetheless, these second-order minorities, unlike the Muslim first-order minority, do not have the capacity to demand recognition through an armed rebellion like the MILF and MNLF. Instead, they have not only experienced minoritization, but they have been marginalized by the protracted conflict that has marred their communities for more than four decades. Displacement and hunger have become a day-to-day reality among members of *lumad* communities in times of war.

According to a tribal chieftain of Arumanen Manobo, the frequent armed confrontations between the AFP versus the rebels have become part of their lives (Author's interview with a tribal chieftain of Arumanen Manobo, Davao City, Philippines, 23 April 2016). Second-order minorities do not have the option of controlling the situation in their communities. They need to be prepared at all times to vacate their houses and flee to the nearest evacuation centers. Hence, it has been observed that the second-order minorities in the Bangsamoro are the most vulnerable to the devastating impacts of armed conflict. This situation has facilitated an internalized sense of powerlessness among members of the *lumad* groups owing to their inability to control the precarious situations in their localities.

The United Nations High Commissioner on Refugees reported that 3154 families from different *lumad* communities in south-central Mindanao have experienced displacement and human rights violations due to the massive military operations and retaliatory assaults of various non-state armed groups in their villages (UNHCR 2015). Whenever there are skirmishes between the soldiers of the AFP and renegades of various non-state armed groups, second-order minorities have been forced to abandon their homestead and livelihoods in their respective villages to escape violence. They typically move and settle in relocation camps set up by the government and NGOs for conflict-displaced civilians. Some of them opted to seek refuge in Christian-dominated communities that are relatively far from the conflict zones (Author's interview with a senior program officer of a Moro NGO, Cotabato City, Philippines, 21 July 2016). Therefore, flight has become the primary mechanism that is available for members of second-order minorities in the southern Philippines to protect themselves from harm and avoid being caught in the crossfires of warring parties.

The intermittent outbreak of armed violence in Mindanao has been severely detrimental to the welfare and safety of poor and innocent civilians, both Muslims and members of second-order minorities. These considerably powerless civilians have to flee for their lives every time there are armed atrocities in their communities. It is common to witness civilians, particularly women, children, and elderly folks, being transported in government-owned trucks in the conflict zones when there are military operations and encounters with armed groups. The uprooting of civilians from their respective villages, especially members of second-order minorities, is primarily induced by a lack of security guarantee in the Bangsamoro. Armed violence may occur at any time because of the existence of multiple armed groups and proliferation of illegal weapons in conflict-affected communities in Mindanao.

The concept "hybrid violence" is an appropriate description of the nature of conflict in the southern Philippines (Krause 2012, 40). Hybrid violence pertains to the cohabitation of vertical and horizontal forms of conflict in insecure polities like Mindanao. Horizontal forms of violence are characterized by *rido* or clan wars (Torres 2007) and armed encounters of warlords' private militias versus rebels and among different armed groups operating in Mindanao. Some forms of horizontal conflict such as family feuds over control and ownership of land precede insurgency in Mindanao. In some cases, horizontal violence transforms into vertical conflict when the AFP and rebel groups intervene and participate in the wars of feuding families. The escalation of low-intensity conflict into full-blown war is often reported by the national media as a vertical conflict because of armed encounters between the state's security forces and rebel outfits due to lack of understanding of the local dynamics in the war zones. Either vertical or horizontal, the occurrence of conflict has led to massive displacement of people, particularly the relatively powerless second-order minorities in the Bangsamoro and its neighboring localities.

Members of the second-order minorities are prone to human rights abuses. The intermittent outbreak of armed fighting between the AFP and different non-state armed groups and among warring clans facilitated the victimization of the *lumads* in Mindanao. Like powerless Muslim civilians, second-order minorities have experienced frequent displacement and land dispossession. Thomas McKenna (1998, 119) claims that the "indigenous inhabitants of the region had long responded to perceived external threats by moving *en masse* out of harm's way." McKenna's observation remains true in present-day Mindanao. Second-order minorities have been uprooted in their ancestral domains due to enormous threat brought about by active conflicts and harassment from warlord politicians. Indigenous peoples do not have any option but to abandon their respective villages, including their livelihoods and farm animals, and settle in nearby localities to escape violent armed clashes (Dwyer and Guiam 2010). Ethnographic evidence shows that second-order minorities, especially women and children, have faced layers of marginalization and exclusion during the state of displacement in host communities (Espesor 2017b). According to a senior official from the Commission on Human Rights, local politicians of host communities are reluctant or often refuse to extend humanitarian help to those internally displaced minorities who fled to their localities. In law, local governments have the responsibility to protect these vulnerable populations through provision of temporary shelters and basic food supplies. The hesitation of local politicians to provide emergency relief interventions to displaced communities is rooted in their self-vested interest. As observed, they are unwilling to help war-displaced *lumad* communities that do not support them in elections (Author's interview with a human rights investigator of the Commission on Human Rights, Cotabato City, Philippines, 20 July 2016). The action and willingness of local politicians to help beleaguered communities, particularly that of second-order minorities, is highly politicized and largely influenced by patronage politics and not by legal mandate to protect the rights of internally displaced persons. Local strongmen typically employ their exclusionary power to deny material favors to people outside their patrimonial networks and political constituency. Controversially, some military officers have a negative perception of the real intention of the *lumads* of abandoning their communities. Allegedly, the displacement of *lumad* communities is seen as a "*taktikang bakwit*" or "evacuation tactics" that refers to the New People's Army strategy of using ethnic minorities to obstruct offensive military operations in communist-infested areas in Mindanao (UNHCR 2018, 2).

Armed conflict is not the only phenomenon that facilitates marginalization of the second-order minorities in the Bangsamoro. The complex power structure in the conflict zones, which highlights the dominance of warlord politicians with multiple sources of power, constitutes another source of exclusion to the detriment of *lumad* communities (see Espesor 2017a). In Maguindanao, Teduray and Lambangian people hold a legitimate grievance that their ancestral homelands were taken away from them by powerful Moro politicians and some Christian settlers. The former Governor of Maguindanao and patriarch of the powerful Ampatuan clan, the late Datu Andal, for instance, is notoriously known for grabbing lands from powerless Muslim and *lumad* families through the use of his private armies (Author's interview with a political warlord in Mindanao, Pasig City, Philippines, 22 November 2017). Meanwhile, members of the displaced members of the Arumanen Manobo tribe faced the difficulty and security challenges of reclaiming their ancestral domains, particularly in Carmen, Cotabato. The decade-long inter-ethnic conflict that exists between the Arumanen Manobo and Muslim people has forced both groups to abandon their respective communities. Violent skirmishes between them ignited when the AFP started to provide arms to some members of the Arumanen Manobo as paramilitary recruits. Muslim people on the other side received military support from the MILF. This series of low-intensity inter-ethnic conflict led to the abandonment of some villages in Carmen that have been converted into banana and oil palm plantations. These thousands of hectares of agricultural plantations are owned by highly influential Christian politicians who are using private militias to prevent *lumad* and Moro people from reclaiming their previously abandoned lands. Controversially, some local politicians in Cotabato refused to cooperate with peacebuilding programs of civil society organizations, particularly peace interventions that seek to reconcile the warring Muslims and *lumads*. Allegedly, local politicians ordered the abduction of an Arumanen Manobo leader with the intention of co-opting him and spoiling civil society's efforts toward reconciliation. Nonetheless, despite threats and pressures from local politicians, most people from both groups are able to return to their respective villages through the help of some military officers who have been schooled in liberal peacebuilding (Author's interview with a senior programme officer of a Moro NGO, Cotabato City, Philippines, 21 July 2016).

Mindanao Peace Process and Second-Order Minorities

The Philippine government attempted to solve insurgency in Mindanao through provision of autonomy and political settlements with the major rebel outfits. Several laws were legislated by the Philippine Congress that paved way for the creation of the ARMM, specifically the Republic Act No. 6734 in 1989 and subsequently amended by the Republic Act No. 9054 in 2001. In 2018, these laws were repealed and superseded by the Republic Act No. 11054, which enforces the 2014 CAB. Nonetheless, these legislations are seen as political incentives for Muslim insurgents for negotiating peacefully with the Philippine government. Political settlements are perceived to serve largely the interests and welfare of the first-order Muslim ethnic minorities and to undermine the rights of *lumad* communities within the Bangsamoro territory (Author's interview with a political anthropologist and NGO worker in Mindanao, Cotabato City, Philippines, 21 July 2016).

It can be argued that the efforts of the Government to facilitate local state-building through autonomy for the Bangsamoro have marginalizing and exclusionary impacts on second-order minorities. *Lumad* groups in Mindanao do not enjoy the same rights and privileges that are afforded to indigenous groups in the other parts of the Philippines. The 1997 Indigenous Peoples' Rights Act (IPRA), which provides for the articulation and codification of the right to ancestral domains of indigenous peoples in the Philippines, does not automatically apply in the ARMM (ICG 2011). The application of IPRA in the autonomous region was a reserve power of the Regional Legislative Assembly. An enabling law has never been legislated (Casauay 2015), although the aforementioned organic laws that created the ARMM recognized the rights of indigenous cultural communities. It is no longer surprising that the Legislative Assembly fails to adopt and come up with a local version of the IPRA. Major power brokers in the executive and legislation offices in the autonomous region are from the dominant Muslim tribes, who are not inclined to pay attention to the plight of second-order minorities.

The Mindanao peace process is apparently Moro rebel-centric. All the peace accords were negotiated and signed by the Philippine government with the Moro rebel outfits. According to the International Crisis Group (2011, i), the *lumads* in the Bangsamoro are "angry that they are not one of the parties at the negotiating table because they have not taken arms against the Philippine government." Obviously, second-order minorities have low impacts on the peacebuilding operations in the southern Philippines (Candelaria 2018). It is the collective sentiment of the *lumads* that the peace process heavily favors the Moro, particularly the MNLF and MILF that are in the forefront of the rebellion against the state. The voices of second-order minorities who are among the most vulnerable groups in violent conflicts have been largely undermined and excluded in previous and present peace agreements

(Author's interview with a tribal chieftain of Arumanen Manobo, Davao City, Philippines, 23 April 2016). Small population, economic impoverishment, frequent displacement, and presence of ethnic cleavages are the major factors that constitute obstacles for the *lumads* to make a unified stand. Moreover, their handful of leaders, unlike Moro political elites and rebel commanders, have meagre agency to influence the overall peacebuilding operations in the southern Philippines (ICG 2011).

The multiple layers of marginalization experienced by the members of second-order minorities served as a motivating factor for the *lumads* to express their predicaments while the Philippine Congress was deliberating the proposed BOL. They are worried about their diminishing identity and shrinking ancestral territory as a non-Moro population in a predominantly Muslim Bangsamoro Autonomous Region. Despite some resistance, BOL receives significant support from several indigenous groups which are pushing for the implementation of IPRA in the Bangsamoro (Torres 2015). Two commissioners from *lumad* communities are in the Bangsamoro Transition Commission, a body that drafted the organic law for the Bangsamoro (Arguillas 2017). Based on the content of the BOL, the new autonomous region is more inclusive and provides an avenue for representation of the second-order minorities. The law explicitly states,

> The Bangsamoro Government recognizes the rights of the indigenous peoples and shall adopt measures for the promotion and protection of the following rights: native titles or *fusaka inged*; indigenous customs and traditions; justice systems and indigenous political structures; equitable share in revenue from the utilization of resources in their ancestral lands; free, prior and informed consent; political participation in the Bangsamoro including reserved seats from the non-Moro indigenous peoples in the Parliament; basic services; and freedom of choice as to their identity. (Article 9, Section 3, Republic Act No. 11054)

The law also acknowledges the IPRA and all international conventions that uphold the rights of second-order minorities in the BAR. There are two major factors that explain the inclusion favorable provisions for the *lumads* in the Bangsamoro. First, there are liberal agents, which are actively involved in the peace operations and have significant efforts in promoting the rights and interests of the *lumads* in the peace process. These agents, which champion minority rights, include NGOs like IAG and KAS and the supranational organization, the European Union. Second, it is a strategic mechanism of the MILF to reinforce its legitimacy and build constituency in *lumad* communities by accommodating the demands of second-order minorities. It also boosts the MILF's popular support from the international community. The inclusion of pro-*lumad* provisions in the BOL illustrates the insurgent's liberal character that it is willing to uphold rights of subaltern communities. However, like previous autonomy laws, there is no guarantee that these pro-*lumad* provisions in the BOL will be enforced and carried out. It remains the prerogative of the Bangsamoro Government to formulate local legislations and programs that are responsive to the needs of the *lumads*. Hence, there is a need for second-order minorities to constantly assert their rights and demand for representation once the Bangsamoro is created as a new political entity in the southern Philippines.

Conclusion

In both theaters of civil wars, second-order minorities are usual subjects of marginalization due to their meagre political value and weak agency to assert their legitimate grievances unlike first-order minorities, particularly those with the capacity of rebelling against the state. As demonstrated in two cases, second-order minorities are likely to experience perpetual exclusion and disenfranchisement in both conflict and post-conflict environments. Conflict transformation mechanisms that follow the signing of peace agreements are generally observed to favor the interests and agenda of dominant ethnic groups that are leading the insurgency movements. Political concessions and material rewards are often granted to members of dominant ethnic communities such as the Acehnese in Indonesia and the Moro in the Philippines. To end violent fighting and to make the rebelling ethnic minorities feel that they are in control of charting their own future through ascent in politics appears to be the ultimate goal of any peace process. The provision of autonomy and new power-sharing schemes tends to enable influential members of first-order minorities to occupy key positions and dominate the politics of the autonomous regions in the aftermath of civil wars, as seen in Aceh and Mindanao. However, this new political arrangement, especially additional territorial autonomy, is not widely acceptable to all ethnic groups in conflictual societies. As evidenced in the case of Aceh and Mindanao, weaker groups who constitute the second-order minorities are facing repression, and their demands for recognition of their identity and territorial domains are often undermined or subordinated to the wishes of dominant ethnic minorities who went into negotiating tables with governments.

It is demonstrated in both cases that the second-order minorities in Aceh and Mindanao have not subscribed to the expression of identity promoted by dominant ethnic groups that are in control of power-sharing institutions in post-conflict environments. Both GALAKSI in Aceh and *lumads* in Mindanao continue to resist the assimilation efforts of regional ethnic majorities. They constantly assert their distinct cultural identity and inherent birthrights over ancestral domains. It is worth noting that second-order minorities in Aceh and Mindanao have the shared narrative that they have been marginalized and ultimate victims of armed conflicts and sociopolitical discriminations. This narrative is to some extent strategic to elicit the support and sympathy of the central governments and members of the international community. However, these subaltern communities are in constant struggle to fight for their rights and political representations as minority ethnic blocks in autonomous regions. The absence of unified positions, their small population size, and their lack of political champions are the major factors that facilitate relative deprivation of considerably powerless second-order minorities even in a post-conflict setting.

Finally, the case studies illustrate the need to put in place effective mechanisms in peacebuilding operations that are inclusive and sensitive to the needs of conflict-driven populations, especially those who belong to minority ethnic groups. The peacebuilding experiences derived from Aceh offers lessons for Mindanao that is in the crossroad of transition from a conflictual community to an abode of peace. Conflict transformation strategies should be carefully designed that do not only serve the interests of insurgents and members of the first-order minorities who previously supported the rebellion. Local and international peacebuilding agents should take into consideration the equitable distribution of peace dividends by providing a fair share to second-order minorities who suffered from violence and deprivation for decades because of protracted conflict. The provision of political incentives to the participants of rebellion and the transformation of coercive groups into constituents of peace do not constitute an inclusively genuine conflict transformation. Peacebuilding efforts should be geared toward generation of confidence and building of civic capacity among minorities for the protection of their identity, rights over ancestral homeland, and meaningful political representation.

Cross-References

▶ Ethnic Conflict and Militias
▶ Ethnic Conflicts and Peace-Building

References

Aditjondro GJ (2007) Profiting from peace: the political economy of Aceh's post-Helsinki reconstruction. Working paper no. 3. International NGO Forum on Indonesian Development, Jakarta

Adyatama E (2016) LPSK Dalami Tragedi Jambu Keupok Saat DOM di Aceh. Tempo, 20 August. https://nasional.tempo.co/read/797391/lpsk-dalami-tragedi-jambu-keupok-saat-dom-di-aceh/full&view=ok. 27 Aug 2018

Ali M (2013) Aceh's new cultural leader: former separatist now guardian of state. RSIS commentaries no. 230/2013. S. Rajaratnam School of International Studies, Singapore. https://www.rsis.edu.sg/wp-content/uploads/2014/07/CO13230.pdf. 27 Aug 2018

Ananta A (2007) The population and conflicts. In: Ananta A, Onn LP (eds) Aceh: a new dawn. Institute of Southeast Asian Studies, Singapore, pp 15–34

Ananta A, Arifin EN, Sairi Hasbullah M, Handayani NB, Pramono A (2015) Demography of Indonesia's ethnicity. Institute of Southeast Asian Studies, Singapore

Ansori MH (2012) From insurgency to bureaucracy, Aceh party and the new face of conflict. Stability Int J Secur Dev 1(1):31–44

Arguillas C (2017) Members of Bangsamoro Transition Commission finally named. Mindanews, 10 February. http://www.mindanews.com/top-stories/2017/02/members-of-bangsamoro-transition-commission-finally-named/. 24 Aug 2018

Aspinall E (2005) Aceh/Indonesia: conflict analysis and options for systemic conflict transformation. Berghof Foundation, Berlin

Aspinall E (2008) Peace without justice? The Helsinki peace process in Aceh. Centre for Humanitarian Dialogue. https://www.hdcentre.org/wp-content/uploads/2016/08/56JusticeAcehfinalrevJUNE08-May-2008.pdf. 23 Aug 2018

Badan Pusat Statistik (2014) Statistik Indonesia: statistical yearbook of Indonesia. BPS-Statistics Indonesia, Jakarta

Barron P, Rahmant E, Nugroho K (2013) The contested corners of Asia: subnational conflict and international development assistance, the case of Aceh, Indonesia. The Asia Foundation, Manila

Barter SJ (2014) Civilian strategy in civil war: insights from Indonesia, Thailand, and the Philippines. Palgrave Macmillan, New York

Barter SJ (2015) Between a rock and a hard place: second-order minorities in the Aceh conflict. Asian Ethnicity 16(2):152–165

Barter SJ (2018) Rethinking territorial autonomy. Reg Stud 52(2):298–309

Candelaria SM (2018) The plight of indigenous peoples within the context of conflict mediation, peace talks and human rights in Mindanao, the Philippines. Thesis Eleven 145(1):28–37

Casauay A (2015) How different is ARMM from the Bangsamoro? Rappler, 13 July. https://www.rappler.com/newsbreak/in-depth/92639-armm-bangsamoro-comparison. 28 Aug 2018

DPRA (2018) Anggota Dewan Perwakilan Rakyat Aceh Periode 2014–2019. Provincial Government of Aceh, Indonesia. https://dpra.acehprov.go.id/index.php/page/52/dapil-anggota-dpra-2014-2019#. 27 Aug 2018

Dwyer L, Guiam R (2010) Gender and conflict in Mindanao. The Asia Foundation, Manila

Ehrentraut S (2010) Dividing Aceh? Minorities, partition movements and state-reforms in Aceh Province. Working paper series no. 137. Asia Research Institute, Singapore

Espesor JC (2017a) Waltzing with the powerful: understanding NGOs in a game of power in conflict-ridden Mindanao. Pac Dyn J Interdisc Res 1(1):66–83

Espesor JC (2017b) Domesticating by commodifying the liberal peace? Evidence from the Southern Philippines. Pac Dyn J Interdisc Res 1(2):306–324

Espesor JC (2019) Resident evil at the gate of the Holy Land: brewing socio-politico tensions in post-conflict Aceh. In: Lutmar C, Ockey J (eds) Peacebuilding in the Asia-Pacific. Palgrave Macmillan, Cham, pp 215–244

Feith P (2007) The Aceh peace process: nothing less than success. Special report no. 184. United States Institute of Peace, Washington, DC

Gade F (2016) Ini Profil Singkta Anggota KKR Aceh. Acehkita, 20 July. http://www.acehkita.com/ini-profil-singkat-anggota-kkr-aceh/. 27 Aug 2018

Gurr TR (1993) Why minorities rebel: a global analysis of communal mobilization and conflict since 1945. Int Polit Sci Rev 14(2):161–201

Hamzah M (2009) Local political parties in Aceh: engines of democratization in Indonesia. In: Tornquist O, Prasetyo SA, Birks T (eds) Aceh: the role of democracy for peace and reconstruction. PCD Press Indonesia and ISAI, Jakarta, pp 305–336

Haris M (2017) KPK agar awasi dana aspirasi DPR Aceh. Antara Aceh, 8 March. https://aceh.antaranews.com/berita/34741/kpk-agar-awasi-dana-aspirasi-dpr-aceh. 27 Aug 2018

Hedman E-L (2005) Aceh under martial law: conflict, violence and displacement. RSC working paper no. 24. University of Oxford, Oxford

Herrberg A (2008) The Brussels 'Backstage' of the Aceh peace process. In: Aguswandi, Large J (eds) Reconfiguring politics: the Indonesia- Aceh peace process. Conciliation Resources, London, pp 32–35

ICG (2007) Aceh: post-conflict complications. Asia report no. 139. International Crisis Group, Jakarta. https://d2071andvip0wj.cloudfront.net/139-aceh-post-conflict-complications.pdf. 24 Aug 2018

ICG (2008) Indonesia: pre-election anxieties in Aceh. Asia briefing no. 81. International Crisis Group, Jakarta. https://www.crisisgroup.org/asia/south-east-asia/indonesia/indonesia-pre-election-anxieties-aceh. 28 Aug 2018

ICG (2011) The Philippines: indigenous rights and the MILF peace process. Asia report no. 213. International Crisis Group, Jakarta. https://d2071andvip0wj.cloudfront.net/213-the-philippines-indigenous-rights-and-the-milf-peace-process.pdf. 26 Aug 2018

Indonesia-Investments (2017) Population of Indonesia. https://www.indonesia-investments.com/culture/population/item67. 10 Jul 2018

Kingsbury D (2006) Peace in Aceh: a personal account of the Helsinki peace process. Equinox Publishing, Jakarta

Konrad-Adenauer-Stiftung (2014) The indigenous peoples of mainland ARMM. Konrad Adenauer Stiftung, Manila

Krause K (2012) Hybrid violence: locating the use of force in post-conflict settings. Glob Gov 18:39–56
McCulloch L (2005) Aceh: then and now. Minority Rights Group International, London
McKenna T (1998) Muslim rulers and rebels: everyday politics and armed separatism in the Southern Philippines. University of California Press, Berkeley
Morales R (2003) Perpetual wars: the Philippine insurgencies, Master's Thesis. Monterey: Naval Postgraduate School. http://www.dtic.mil/dtic/tr/fulltext/u2/a420548.pdf. 20 July 2018
OPAPP (2018) Passage of BOL Celebrated in Cotabato. Office of the Presidential Adviser on the Peace Process. 8 August. https://peace.gov.ph/2018/08/passage-of-bol-celebrated-in-cotabato/. 28 Aug 2018
Ramly AA (2005) Modes of displacement during martial law. In: Hedman E-LE (ed) Aceh under martial law: conflict, violence and displacement. RSC working paper no. 24. University of Oxford, Oxford, pp 13–20
Reid A (2004) War, peace and the burden of history in Aceh. Asian Ethn 5(3):301–314
Republic Act No. 11054 (2018) An act providing for the organic law for the Bangsamoro autonomous region in Muslim Mindanao. Government of the Philippines. http://www.officialgazette.gov.ph/downloads/2018/07jul/20180727-RA-11054-RRD.pdf. 28 Aug 2018
Rodil R (1994) The minoritization of the indigenous communities of Mindanao and the Sulu Archipelago. Alternate Forum for Research on Mindanao, Davao City
Schulze KE (2005) Between conflict and peace: tsunami aid and reconstruction in Aceh. London School of Economics, London
Serambi Indonesia (2016) Isu Pemekaran ALA-ABAS Bukan Kepentingan Para Elite. 12 January. http://aceh.tribunnews.com/2016/01/12/isu-pemekaran-ala-abas-bukan-kepentingan-para-elite. 27 Aug 2018
Shea N (2016) Nongovernmental organizations as mediators: making peace in Aceh, Indonesia. Glob Chang Peace Secur 28(2):177–196
Smith ME (2017) Europe's common security and defence policy: capacity-building, experiential learning and institutional change. Cambridge University Press, Cambridge, UK
Sulistiyanto P (2001) Whither Aceh? Third World Q 22(3):437–452
Torres WM (2007) Rido: clan feuding and conflict management in Mindanao. The Asia Foundation, Manila
Torres J (2015) Indigenous peoples lobby for recognition in Philippines Moro region. UCANews, 12 May. https://www.ucanews.com/news/indigenous-peoples-lobby-for-recognition-in-philippines-moro-region/73569. 27 Aug 2018
Touval S (1982) The peace brokers: mediators in the Arab-Israeli conflict, 1948–1979. Princeton University Press, Princeton
UNHCR (2015) Displacement dashboard, Mindanao, Philippines forced displacement annual report. United Nations High Commissioner on Refugees, Manila
UNHCR (2018) Mindanao displacement dashboard. Issue no. 47. United Nations High Commissioner on Refugees, Manila. http://www.protectionclusterphilippines.org/wp-content/uploads/2018/05/Protection-Cluster-April-Displacement-Dashboard-2.pdf. 28 Aug 2018
Wandita G (2014) Lessons from Aceh for Mindanao: notes from the field. In: Moving beyond: towards transitional justice in the Bangsamoro peace process. *forum*ZFD Philippines, Davao City, pp 20–24
Whaley F (2014) Philippines and rebels agree on peace accord to end insurgency. The New York Times, 25 January. https://www.nytimes.com/2014/01/26/world/asia/philippines-and-rebels-agree-on-peace-accord-to-end-insurgency.html. 24 Aug 2018
Widodo J [@jokowi] (2015) Hentikan kekerasan di Aceh Singkil, 13 October. https://twitter.com/jokowi/status/654116423984218112. 27 Aug 2018

Indigenous Australian Identity in Colonial and Postcolonial Contexts

53

Michael Davis

Contents

Introduction	994
Indigenous Identity Before Colonization	994
Tribal Identity	995
Identity Concepts: Aboriginality, Indigeneity, and Ethnicity	995
Indigenous Identity and Ethnicity	996
Aboriginality as a Fluid Concept	997
Discourses, Representations, and Essentialism	998
The "Remote/Urban" Issue and "Authenticity"	1000
Racialized Identities	1001
Land, Heritage, and Culture	1002
Indigenous Identity and the Nation State	1003
Forging Identity from Adversity	1005
Identity, Recognition, and Rights	1006
Conclusion	1008
Cross-References	1009
References	1009

Abstract

This chapter presents a survey of writings about Australian Indigenous identity formation, from the beginnings of European intrusion, through racialized identities in the colonial-settler era, and up to the era of self-determination and rights and recognition, wherein Indigenous peoples assert their own identities. The chapter includes brief discussion on identities within the nation-state, Aboriginality and ethnicity, and discourses and representations of identity.

M. Davis (✉)
Department of Sociology and Social Policy, The University of Sydney, Sydney, NSW, Australia
e-mail: michael.davis@sydney.edu.au

© The Author(s), under exclusive license to Springer Nature Singapore Pte Ltd. 2019
S. Ratuva (ed.), *The Palgrave Handbook of Ethnicity*,
https://doi.org/10.1007/978-981-13-2898-5_146

Keywords

Aboriginality · Indigeneity · Identity · Postcolonial identity · Indigenous ethnicity

Introduction

For many decades, from invasion by the British, through colonization and settlement, Australian Indigenous peoples' (Aboriginal and Torres Strait Islander peoples) identities have been largely shaped by outsiders. These identities have been transformed over time by the particularities of the colonial period, through present-day postcolonial situations. In more recent decades, with politicization and the realization of rights, Indigenous peoples have determined and asserted their own identities.

This chapter presents a survey of approaches to Australian Indigenous identity and ethnicity, including as these are articulated in terms such as "Aboriginality" and "indigeneity." The chapter reviews ideas about identity from before colonization to postcolonial situations, where Indigenous self-determination informs recognition and rights and the mobilization of forms of identity and Aboriginality.

Indigenous Identity Before Colonization

The idea of Aboriginality as a unitary form of identity for Australia's Indigenous peoples, in a sense, is predicated on the act of colonization. Prior to British occupation of the country now known as Australia, the land was settled and occupied by many different Indigenous language groups, with no single, collective noun such as "Aboriginal." Aboriginal people did not identify themselves as "Aboriginal" but instead "saw themselves as members of a tribe or group of tribes (Kamilaroi or Cammeraigal, Aranda or Pitjantjatjara) or of a group whose minimal cohesion depended upon the sharing of specific ceremonies" (Wentworth 1973: 9). Tonkinson notes that "Ethnographic evidence clearly indicates that before the arrival of Europeans, numerous distinct groups existed on the Australian continent" and that "There is no evidence that the indigenes perceived themselves as a homogeneous group in the way that Europeans perceived them." She argued that the size of Australia and other factors such as the dispersal of Aboriginal people over this vast continent would have made homogeneity "impossible" (Tonkinson 1990: 191; also see Hollinsworth 1992: 138). The collective identity of Aboriginal people, argues Hollinsworth, "was literally inconceivable in the absence of a contrasting group of 'non-Aborigines'" (1992: 138). Pointing out that the concept of an "Aborigine" is a European one, Crick explains:

> it was the situation of culture clash which categorized some of them as 'Aborigines'. It is dispossession and racial oppression that have required these contemporary Aboriginal political and ideological responses. Traditionally, where identity was in terms of local grouping, ceremonial category, or language group, there was probably no sense of unity such as that engendered by the ensuing situation of racial conflict. Modern Aboriginality is necessarily an oppositional concept. (1981: 58)

Keen states "Aborigines in 'settled' Australia form part of a distinct, though heterogeneous and loosely bounded ethnic category." Using the term "ethnic category," he thought that "The categories 'Aborigine' and 'Aboriginal' arose, of course, through interaction with colonising peoples mainly from Europe . . . ." He wrote that "In pre-colonial Australia, as now in areas more remote from European settlement, manifold ethnic categories divided the Aboriginal population according to criteria of language, locality and descent" (Keen 1988: 3).

Tribal Identity

Indigenous peoples' identities are intertwined with their social and political organization. The "tribe" and other entities such as "clan group" have been employed to describe these forms of organization. Although these are analytical constructs imposed upon Indigenous peoples by non-Indigenous outsiders (typically, by anthropologists), the term "tribe" is sometimes also used by Indigenous people to refer to themselves. Anthropologist Catherine Berndt regarded the "tribe" as a conservative form of organization. Based on her work with Aboriginal communities in parts of the Northern Territory, she described what she interpreted as the loss of a "tribal" identity, especially through loss of language and land brought about by colonization and missionization. She stated that the Aboriginal person "is caught within the orbit of perhaps largely benevolent but also largely impersonal forces which are engaged in deliberate and concerted attempts to change his whole short style of living, in short, to redefine his identity" (Berndt 1961: 17). As such, she posited that ". . . the perspective of each 'tribe' was a limited one" (Berndt 1961: 17). The tribal unit could be thought of, in her view, "as a series of overlapping, inward-looking, social and cultural worlds: some larger than others, some readier to adopt new things or ideas, but all concerned primarily with maintaining or transmitting their own particular version of the Aboriginal way of life" (Berndt 1961: 18). Ronald Berndt also construed the tribal unit as "intensely localistic" and inward-looking, "providing socio-psychological insulation, underlining traditional Aborigines' concentration on their own affairs" (Berndt 1977: 2–3). Based on his work with Western Desert communities, he argued that the concept of the "tribe" is a vague one "outside the sphere of specific ethnographic generalisation." Elaborating on this, he stated that "not only in the Western Desert there seems to be no real advantage in speaking of "tribes" as empirical the term is most useful insofar as it is employed as a conceptual construct, need not correspond exactly with any existing social unit, but serves one broad "type" of social relationships as contrasted with others" (Berndt 1959: 106).

Identity Concepts: Aboriginality, Indigeneity, and Ethnicity

The concepts of Aboriginality and ethnicity warrant some investigation. Tonkinson notes that the term Aboriginality "is being increasingly used to denote Aboriginal identity, usually in the broadest sense" but that its "meaning remains imprecise"

(1990: 195–196). Wentworth wrote that "the creation of an 'Aboriginal identity' is in itself a very un-Aboriginal process, for which there is no historical substructure" (1973: 9), while von Sturmer saw Aboriginality as a "fiction which takes on meaning only in terms of white ethnocentrism" (von Sturmer 1973: 16). In discussing Indigenous identity, it is more appropriate to refer to plural identities that embrace identities imposed by other, non-Indigenous people, as well as those formed by Indigenous peoples themselves. There are also several aspects to the latter. Tonkinson considers at least two dimensions of Aboriginal identity. One is the "identity of specific local or regional groups sharing history, culture, and social organization, while another is a more inclusive pan-Aboriginal Australian identity" (1990: 193). Crick also points to a range of identities, writing that "There is no great sense, perhaps, in talking about 'Aboriginality' in general, because the social situation Aboriginal people are in and the degree of tradition surviving varies so much between Milingimbi, Oenpelli, Alice Springs, Melbourne, Warrnambool and Geelong" (Crick 1981: 56). Drawing attention to what he considers "a long and contentious history" of the definition of Aboriginality, Gardiner-Garden wrote that:

> Different classification systems (many with significant personal and social consequences) have moved in and out of fashion. ... One, predominating in legislation, defines an Aboriginal as 'a person who is a member of the Aboriginal race of Australia'. The other, predominating in program administration but also used in some legislation and court judgements, defines an Aboriginal as someone 'who is a member of the Aboriginal race of Australia, identifies as an Aboriginal and is accepted by the Aboriginal community as an Aboriginal. (Gardiner-Garden 2003: 1)

Crick describes a balance between community-based and imposed legislative notions of Aboriginality, writing that "Aboriginality is partly a matter of semantics, for 'identity' is a question of meaning. Of the currently accepted criteria for 'being an Aborigine,' one is biological (descent), but the other two are questions of meaning – how one identifies and whether that identification is accepted by the community" (Crick 1981: 56). There is also, in a political sense, a notion of Aboriginality being defined as an oppositional tactic, to regain rights and recognition: the suggestion that "We are Us, and not You."

Indigenous Identity and Ethnicity

In discussing Aboriginality, the question of "ethnicity" also warrants inquiry, as this term has been used sometimes to denote Indigenous peoples and, more commonly, to refer to the many immigrant peoples or "ethnic groups" in Australia. This raises questions such as the status of Indigenous peoples vis-à-vis the concept of ethnicity in Australia and the relationship between Indigenous peoples and the polyglot ethnicities that make up Australia's plural, multicultural society. Weaver suggests that definitions of ethnicity "can play a major role in relations between a nation-state and its cultural minorities, but it is a complex and poorly understood role" (Weaver 1984: 182). She defines "ethnicity" as "the recognition of cultural differences between collectivities or groups in a nation-state ....." (1984: 184). Tonkinson writes that "The British created 'Aborigines' as an ethnic category based on European notions of culture and heredity and imposed Aboriginal ethnicity on the indigenes" (Tonkinson 1990: 191). Jordan sees Aboriginality and ethnicity within a multicultural society as relations of reciprocity, stating that "It is important for Aborigines, in their construction of identity, to be able to locate themselves in the developing multicultural identity of Australian society." At the same time, she asserts, "the promotion of an Australian identity as a multicultural society demands a conceptualization which incorporates Aborigines into this identity without denying their unique history and culture and their unique place in a multicultural society" (Jordan 1986: 26).

In the context of discussions about ethnicity, it is important to recognize that Indigenous peoples have a distinct identity as Australia's First Peoples, rather than being another ethnic group. This distinct status, argues Dyck, "permits the formulation of arguments based on the legal consequences of prior occupancy of a territory" (Dyck 1985: 13). Levi and Dean write that Indigenous identity "is not isomorphic with ethnic identity" (Levi and Dean 2003: 5), while Gold and Paine suggest that Indigenous peoples do not identify as ethnic groups, but rather, "they see themselves as separate peoples with special collective rights" (Gold and Paine 1984: 7). In another, alternative view on indigeneity versus ethnicity, Morris, based on his work with Dhan-gadi Aboriginal people of the North Coast of New South Wales, discusses "the positions that are ascribed to Aborigines within the discursive practices of multiculturalism." He examines the Aborigines' "... positioning as a cultural entity within the 'new nationalism' generated by multiculturalism, where Aborigines are increasingly defined as the 'first Australians' or the 'first immigrants' rather than an indigenous people" (Morris 1988: 65). Other authors also draw attention to the blurring between ethnicity and Indigenous identity. Beckett, for example, writes that, although Aboriginality "must be considered as a form of ethnicity, it retains distinctive features, particularly occupation of the country prior to colonisation and the lack of a mother country beyond the seas" (Beckett 1988a: 5). Tonkinson conflates both terms, "Aboriginality" and "ethnicity," stating that "The question of Aboriginal ethnicity is certainly a postcolonial one." She suggests that "The British created 'Aborigines' as an ethnic category based on European notions of culture and heredity and imposed Aboriginal ethnicity on the indigenes" (Tonkinson 1990: 191).

Aboriginality as a Fluid Concept

Aboriginality is not a fixed, stable concept. Aboriginal academic and activist Mick Dodson argues that "to even begin to speak about Aboriginality is to enter a labyrinth full of obscure passages, ambiguous signs and trapdoors." He argues that "The moment the question is asked 'Who, or what is Aboriginal?', an historical landscape is entered, full of absolute and timeless truths, which have been set in place by self-professed experts, and authorities all too ready to tell us, and the world, the meaning of Aboriginality" (Dodson 1994: 4). Cowlishaw points to the indeterminacy of the notion of Aboriginality, stating that "Perhaps more than other social or ethnic groupings, Aboriginal identity is not predictable or knowable in any formal sense" (Cowlishaw 2004: 8). Noting the changing definitions of Aboriginality over time, Beckett writes that it has, "at any given time ... been ambiguous in certain respects and subject to dispute" (Beckett 1988a: 2). Describing "Aboriginality" as a "cultural construction," Beckett explains that "Instead of an authorised version of Aboriginality in Australia, there has been a medley of voices, black and white, official and unofficial, national and local, scientific and journalistic, religious and secular, interested and disinterested, all offering or contesting particular constructions of Aboriginality" (Beckett 1988a: 7). Aboriginality is therefore a fluid and dynamic construct and "...there need be no one definition that is 'true' even for a particular period, still less for all time." As Beckett notes "Aboriginality, like other nationalisms, is in a constant process of creation and it may have many definitions that compete for acceptance, among particular groups of Aborigines or Europeans, or in the society at large" (Beckett 1988a: 7). Jordan states that "... the identity offered by white society has not been predictable or stable. The dominant group, at different periods, has offered different identities to Aboriginal people" (Jordan 1988: 111). De Costa suggests that "the category 'indigenous' as it is used in Australia is something that has emerged from the contacts of indigenous and non-indigenous peoples in myriad social, cultural and institutional settings" (de Costa 2006: 9).

Discourses, Representations, and Essentialism

Indigenous identity formation is as much an epistemological concern as it is a concrete one, as identities have been shaped discursively and through multiple representations. As Dodson notes "Since their first intrusive gaze, colonising cultures have had a preoccupation with observing, analysing, studying, classifying and labelling Aborigines and Aboriginality. Under that gaze, Aboriginality changed from being a daily practice, to being 'a problem to be solved'" (Dodson 1994:3). Within a framework of discourses and representative practices, there has, throughout Australia's history, been an unequal power relation between Aboriginal people and the intruders. As Moreton-Robinson states, "Aborigines have often been represented as objects – as the 'known.' Rarely are they represented as subjects, as 'knowers'" (Moreton-Robinson 2004: 75). Hollinsworth "seeks to show how the ideological materials for the construction of Aboriginality have been shaped by prevailing racist and colonial discourses." He identifies "three major discourses within which to conceptualize and construct Aboriginal commonalities. These are: (a) 'blood' – notions of biological descent; (b) cultural heritage and continuities; and (c) common experience of dispossession and racism, and 'survival' as an identifiable people" (Hollinsworth 1992: 138). He concludes that "The construction and deconstruction of Aboriginality is a highly political and contradictory endeavour. It is made particularly complex by commonsense beliefs that Aboriginality is a 'natural' and unproblematic category which operates above and outside other socially constructed categories" (1992: 150–151). This highlights the plurality and multiplicity of discourses of Aboriginal identity, which also have implications ideologically and politically within the nation-state. Keeffe discusses Aboriginality in terms of "an ideology composed of two key themes," which he identifies as "Aboriginality-as-persistence and Aboriginality-as-resistance" (1988: 68). In this scheme, elements that comprise "Aboriginality-as-persistence" include "the persistence of an inherently unique identity," cultural continuity, and a "common sharing of these by all Aboriginal people in Australia" (Keeffe 1988: 68). Here, "Aboriginality-as-resistance" is dynamic, comprising elements such as "resistance to white authority, political struggle and collective solidarity." These are not mutually exclusive, as Keeffe states that "The two notions underlie all Aboriginal discourse on Aboriginality but in any particular context one may be submerged or muted by the other" (Keeffe 1988: 68). In Hollinsworth's view, "Arguments about the nature of Aboriginality and the means of claiming, contesting and authenticating Aboriginal identity are central to both the future of Aboriginal Studies as an academic area of study and to political and ideological struggles over Australian nationalism and the position of indigenous peoples within it" (Hollinsworth 1992: 137). Hollinsworth argues that "While there have been multiple, shifting and contradictory discourses of Aboriginality over the last 200 years, the dominant official construction since the 1940s has been framed in terms of proximity to a narrow and static concept of 'traditional' culture" (1992: 138). He suggests that this "dominant discourse" of what he terms "Aboriginalism" was "largely generated within anthropology," and "is hegemonic and has potent consequences for those termed 'urban' Aborigines." He argues that there can be discerned "three principal alternatives in contemporary Aboriginal political debate" that can be seen to contradict or stand in opposition to the "dominant discourse." These, he says, "can be identified as framed in terms of biological descent ('blood'), cultural persistence and political resistance." Hollinsworth examines each of these discourses "in terms of its ideological potential to construct a powerful national identity" (Hollinsworth 1992: 138).

Also within a frame of discursive strategies and representations of Aboriginal identity, and racialized representative practices, Fforde et al. (2013) discuss what they describe as a "deficit discourse." They define this as "the prevalence of an erosive mindset of deficit which pervades many Aboriginal communities and its attachment to notions of identity, which includes perceptions of authenticity widely adopted from similar views held about Aboriginal people by non-Indigenous Australians" (Fforde et al. 2013: 3). Elaborating on this, they write that:

> to describe a mode of thinking, identifiable in language use, that frames Aboriginal identity in a narrative of negativity, deficiency and disempowerment. We argue that such a discourse adheres to models of identity still embedded within the race paradigm, and is interwoven with notions of 'authenticity', commonly expressed by language about who is a 'real Aborigine' and who, in deficit comparison, is not. (Fforde et al. 2013: 162)

Discursive representations of Indigeneity and Aboriginality perform multiple functions. From an Indigenous perspective, Dodson explores some aspects of the "mirroring" of such representative practices, suggesting that "Our constructed identities have served a broader purpose of reflecting back to the colonising culture what it wanted or needed to see in itself." He argued that "The constructions of Aboriginality, in all their variations, have marked the boundaries which define and evaluate the so-called modern worlds. Whether Indigenous peoples have been portrayed as 'noble' or 'ignoble,' heroic or wretched has depended on what the colonising culture wanted to say or think about itself" (1994: 8). He states that "constructions of Aboriginality are directly linked to the policies of 'management' and control of Indigenous peoples." These policies, Dodson argues, "form part of the ideology that creates the framework in which the state can act upon and justify its treatment of Indigenous peoples, however disrespectful or abusive of our rights it may be" (Dodson 1994: 7). For various reasons, including for the mobilization of their political authority, there is some utility in the formation of a unitary identity as Aboriginality. But such constructions can also obscure or deny the heterogeneity of Indigenous peoples, where Indigenous identity is based on presumed uniform characteristics and, as such, risk essentializing Indigenous peoples. Levi and Dean explain:

> Broadly speaking, essentialism refers to the conviction that groups or categories of persons or things have one or more defining traits particular to all members of that group or category. Some approaches to indigenousness assume the presence of essential characteristics distinguishing indigenous from nonindigenous identity. (Levi and Dean 2003: 14)

Beckett sees some utility in defining an Aboriginal identity based on presumed shared characteristics, arguing that "There are two ways of conceptualising the Aboriginal presence in Australian society" (Beckett 2014: 65). In one sense, Beckett suggests, Aboriginal people "occupy a position that is defined primarily in terms of subordination and dependence." He goes on to explain:

> Within this frame, the Aboriginal voice is counter-hegemonic, in the sense of contesting and resisting, but within the terms set out by Australian cultural hegemony. There is an alternative view, which argues that essential Aboriginal qualities, such as spirituality and an affinity with the land, are the wellsprings of Aboriginal survival and resistance. Accepted uncritically, this amounts to a romantic essentialism, yet it is important to grasp that Aboriginality arises not simply in reaction to colonial domination, but out of a space in which Aboriginal people are able to produce and reproduce a culture that is theirs. (Beckett 2014: 65)

Although, in Levi and Dean's view, the term Indigenous "occludes the heterogeneity and divisions among the people it refers to," they state that "it remains a convenient conceptual construct for distilling and representing complex, and in many regards contradictory, social and historical processes – even when it refers to social and cultural relationships far less clearly defined than the single term *indigenous* would seem to imply" (Levi and Dean 2003: 13).

The "Remote/Urban" Issue and "Authenticity"

The complexity of Aboriginality as a mode of Indigenous identity in Australia has had profound implications for policy and governmentality, as well as for all levels of society. A persistent influence on policy and administration has been a, perhaps exaggerated, distinction between "urban" and "remote" Aboriginal people, with the latter often seen as somehow more "authentic" and therefore representative of a "true" Aboriginal identity. This "rural/urban" dichotomy also plays out as a set of discursive and representational practices. Beckett explains some aspects of this:

> In formulating a national policy for Aborigines, the Commonwealth avoided making distinctions among people of Aboriginal descent, opting instead for self-identification and/or recognition by a community. The remote Aborigine nevertheless remained the touchstone of Aboriginality: the point of ultimate reference in definitions of Aboriginality by descent; and the source of fetishized forms of Aboriginal culture, enshrined in museums, galleries, demonstrations and institutionally framed "sites of significance." (Beckett 1988b: 207)

Kolig takes a somewhat less nuanced view, suggesting there are "real" differences between urban and remote Aboriginal communities:

> In considering Aboriginal identity and its emergence, one has to distinguish between southern, urban Aborigines on the one hand and "tribal", tradition-oriented, northern Aborigines on the other. ... Among southern Aborigines this identity surely has a meaning totally different from that among northern Aborigines. (Kolig 1977: 35)

In general terms, the urban/remote dichotomy, with its connotations of "authenticity," has been a pervasive and entrenched trope that has ramified throughout all sectors of society and continues to have deep implications for the ways that non-Indigenous peoples have thought about, represented, and governed Indigenous peoples.

Racialized Identities

Race and blood were key tropes in identities or classifications imposed on Indigenous peoples in Australia by Europeans for many decades. A classificatory hierarchy of "full-bloods," "half-castes," and various shades of "blood/color" in between comprised a dominant discourse among observers, missionaries, administrators, anthropologists, and settlers. Weaver suggests that Aboriginality "was closely associated with full-bloods who looked Aboriginal, [who] tended to live in remote areas of northern and central Australia, were seen as needing protection, and continued in attenuated form their traditional culture" (1984: 187). This notion of an "authentic" kind of Aboriginality existing in remote areas is a recurring theme in many non-Indigenous narratives, as will be seen.

The discipline of anthropology has had a prominent role in constructing Aboriginal identity. Cowlishaw, for example, argued that the work of anthropologists "has been significant in determining how the category of Aboriginal Australians has been defined and reproduced for most of this century" (1987: 221). Cowlishaw writes that:

> Anthropologists' definitions of Aborigines were always dependent on notions of their cultural integrity and homogeneity. No concepts or theories were developed in Australian anthropology which could deal with either relationships between the indigenous population and the invaders or with changes in either. When anthropologists did conduct research with non-traditional groups the very vocabulary of 'caste' and 'blood' with which such groups were described relied on biological notions of race . . . . (1987: 224)

The many decades of administration, regulation, and classification of Australia's Indigenous peoples along race-based categories of "blood" and "purity" were a persistent and dominant aspect of the colonial era and have lasting implications. Tatz emphasizes the absurdity of employing race as a category for defining Aboriginal people:

> race came to mean 'full-bloodedness', 'purity' of blood. Based on some dubious genetics and even more spurious haematology, 'blood' was divided into and equated with social characteristics on the premise that somehow blood could be titrated in a laboratory, filtered into full drops, half drops, white drops. But since we didn't have geneticists or haematologists (even bad ones) to guide us, we defined degrees of mixture and alleged 'impurity' on the sole criterion of what our eyes told us was full or half or quarter. (Tatz 1980: 353)

McCorquodale explores the legislative framework and colonialist assimilationist policies of the time that regulated blood-related racialized identification. His study showed that there was a "dichotomy based on 'blood' by which those having Aboriginal or other 'coloured' blood or strains of blood were singled out for special legislative treatment." He noted that Aborigines and "'half-castes,' in particular, were subject to increasing refinement as legislative subjects in the several jurisdictions" and observed that "A bewildering array of legal definitions led to inconsistent legal treatment and arbitrary, unpredictable, and capricious administrative treatment" (McCorquodale 1986: 7). Pettman too outlines some of the history of racial categorization of Aboriginal people, in which they were "excluded from citizenship and subject to an inferior and racialized legal status as wards of the state." She writes:

> This status varied over time and place, and often involved a complex racialized hierarchy of control, distinguishing between "full-bloods" and "half-castes" The former were largely neglected and expected to die out, the latter were increasingly subject to state intervention and control, and through the twentieth century until the 1960s liable to direct institutionalization. (Pettman 1995: 70)

Land, Heritage, and Culture

Over time, and all too slowly, as racialized identity constructs of Indigenous peoples gradually faded, and self-determination, rights, and recognition began to take hold, the importance of Indigenous culture, heritage, and land came to the fore, as these are at the heart of Indigenous identity. Gibson emphasizes the connection to land in concepts of Indigeneity, arguing that "it is clear that concepts of 'identity,' 'rights,' and 'responsibilities' within many indigenous societies retain an essential geopolitical element – constructed in relation to land" (1999: 55). The importance of empowerment through land rights, she suggests, "provides arenas in which Aboriginal people can define distinct cultural identity, whilst maintaining a plurality of dynamic lifestyles" (Gibson 1999: 57). Mulcock too sees Indigeneity as embracing concepts of belonging and place, stating that "To be indigenous, is after all, to be autochthonous, to be born of the land" (Mulcock 2007: 63). The recognition of Indigenous land, heritage, and culture then, not only for Indigenous peoples themselves but equally, if not more importantly by the wider society, continues to contribute to the calls for identity rights and for Indigenous peoples' rights to form their own identities in self-determining scenarios.

The central place that land occupies in identity formation for Indigenous peoples cannot be underestimated, and it has many dimensions. For some writers, there is a sense of an ancient, primordial, and sacred (or "spiritual") rootedness in the land that is at the heart of Aboriginality and that might be harnessed to a wider Australian national identity. For example, in a somewhat romanticized idea about Aboriginality, Tacey calls for a revitalization of spirituality or the sacred in Australian society, a sacredness that, he argues, had been more typically associated with the Aboriginal people or an "Aboriginality":

> The archaic dreaming soul, which is buried beneath the busyness of contemporary white rationality, is the missing ingredient necessary for Australia's psychological health and cultural stability. That dreaming soul is what we must integrate, not by consuming Aboriginality itself, but by way of cracking open our own consciousness to find the deeper, primal layers buried there, waiting to be released into life. (Tacey 1995:12)

He bases his argument on the close relationship that Aboriginal people have with the land: the "source," in a sense, of their Aboriginality:

> The Aboriginal people can be seen as, and see themselves as, part of the symbolic continuum of the landscape, and so perhaps the usual Western distinction between people and the land does not properly belong here. By becoming attuned to the land, one is, almost involuntarily, becoming attuned to Aboriginality, or as it were to the "source" of Aboriginality. (Tacey 1995: 14)

Notwithstanding the romantic, pastoral vision that Tacey's argument evokes, he nonetheless captures something of the deep and profound sacredness of land for Indigenous peoples, and the spirituality embodied in the land, that forms a fundamental aspect of Aboriginal identity.

Indigenous Identity and the Nation State

Identity formation for Indigenous peoples in Australia has been intricately interwoven with the nation-state. Maybury-Lewis writes "Indigenous peoples are defined as much by their relations with the state as by any intrinsic characteristics that they may possess" (Maybury-Lewis 2002: 44–45). Indigenous relations with the nation-state are ones of power and, historically, of inequality, as illustrated by Dodson's claim that Aboriginality "became part of the ideology that legitimised and supported the policies and practices of the state" (Dodson 1994: 7). Before the coming of the Europeans, suggests Tonkinson, "Aborigines in precolonial Australian were not without self-conscious group identities, but power relations were of an order different from the politics of the modern nation-state, and this difference heightens the significance of ethnicity" (Tonkinson 1990: 191). The modern Australian nation-state has been fashioned largely by immigration, with a diverse range of ethnicities forming a multicultural society, and by its First Peoples, the Aboriginal and Torres Strait Islander peoples. In the kind of nation building borne of a multicultural society that Australia has sought to define itself as, notions of identity and ethnicity are often discussed in the context of the diverse ethnicities of immigrant peoples. The complex relations between Indigenous and ethnic-migrant identities in the formation of the nation-state have presented a subject for considerable reflection and discussion. In 1988, Australia's bicentennial year, anthropologist Jeremy Beckett summed up the situation over the previous 20 years regarding recognition of Aboriginal people in the nation-state, commenting that "Australia may be said to have transformed its indigenous population from virtually passive colonial subjects, situated inside the state but outside the nation, to a political constituency consisting of citizens who are simultaneously a minority." He concluded that "The Australian state has formed its Aboriginal people into a constituency which, however, now exists in its own right. While its economic and political dependence is inescapable, its origin in the historic encounter between native and settler gives it a cultural legitimacy in terms that the state cannot wrest" (Beckett 1988c: 17). The positioning of Indigenous identities within the Australian nation-state is also explored by Moran, who discusses "the history and development of Australian settler nationalism," and an "indigenizing settler nationalism," that "develops and elaborates an impulse that has existed for a long time in Australian settler nationalism, fore-grounding the importance of the indigenous contribution to national culture." He argues that this "adopts a position that calls upon the nation to reconstruct itself through a fuller recognition of the indigenous and their claims as a central component of the national identity" (Moran 2002: 1014).

As an attempt to capture something of the complexity of minorities and plural peoples within the nation-state, Dyck employs the discourse of "Fourth World." Although no longer in wide use, this term nonetheless still has some validity as an analytical frame, "as a concept produced by a particular historical moment, as an artifact of the form of welfare capitalism that developed in Western liberal democracies following the Second World War" (Dyck 1985: 23). Dyck states that "Unlike other ethnic minorities, Fourth World peoples are not immigrants but the original inhabitants of lands that today form the territories of nation-states. ... the tiny internal colonies that make up the Fourth World are fated always to be minority populations in their own lands" (1985: 1). He argues that:

The notion of a Fourth World, like the assertion of indigenous status, denies the assumptions of the nation-state. It declares that indigenous peoples are no longer merely minorities within liberal democracies. They are members of these nation-states, but they will no longer accept being recognized as anything less than distinctive members with special rights. As Fourth Worlders, they escape the image of being known either as members of groups defined by their poverty or as just another ethnic group. (Dyck 1985: 22)

The history of colonization and settlement, and the formation of the nation-state, has been instrumental in fashioning Indigenous identities. Levi and Dean argue that "Without a recognition of the historical impact of colonialism and the various forces of global modernity –including the conflation of spatial, temporal, and cultural boundaries – it is virtually impossible to comprehend the creation and conceptual import of indigenousness, whatever else the term conveys about rootedness and complex ties to land" (Levi and Dean 2003: 11). In another view on the complex relations between immigrant and Indigenous peoples, and the nation-state, Pettman argues that "binaries" such as those between Aboriginal people and non-Aboriginal people "limit our understanding of racism and sexism, and undermine alliances and strategies against them." Instead, she seeks to "analyse the complex ways in which the politics of difference relate to and reflect multiple and interrelated structures of power in Australian society" (Pettman 1995: 65).

Forging Identity from Adversity

One aspect of the identity formation of Indigenous people by the non-Indigenous wider society was oriented toward using identity classification to determine Indigenous peoples' eligibility for funding and welfare. Thus, in the colonialist and neocolonialist regimes, Indigenous identity was determined on a basis of entitlement or lack of entitlements. Tonkinson explains that "The experiences of Aboriginal people and hence the formation of their personal and cultural identities have been in contexts created largely by white Australians" (Tonkinson 1990: 214–15). She states that "Those experiences have been marked to a great extent by color prejudice, segregation, and legalized discrimination. This I believe accounts in large measure for the concerns, the aims, and the rhetoric of the current Aboriginal political movement based on the notion of Aboriginality as an identity and an ideology" (1990: 215). From the colonial experience of genocidal, paternalistic, and racist policies and subjugation and dispossession, from being classified and stereotyped, regulated, and controlled, including having identities thrust upon them, Indigenous Australians are now reclaiming their rights, including their rights to form their own identities and to use these strategically for advocacy and political negotiations.

Beckett outlines the radical changes in policy, in a shift away from assimilation, in regard to Aboriginal peoples' identities, in the wake of the election in 1972 of the Whitlam Labor Government:

Previous governments had formally defined Aborigines in genetic terms, while practically defining them through application of the special powers; now an Aboriginal was someone who identified as such and whose identification was recognized by other Aborigines. The implication was that Aboriginality was an honourable estate, entailing entitlements rather than disabilities, for which someone might freely opt. Many did opt for these entitlements, so that one might say that the government's working, if tacit, definition of Aboriginal was those who availed themselves of its services for Aborigines. The fundamental entitlement of Aborigines under the new dispensation was to be recognized as a people – if not quite a nation – with their own values and culture, which they must be allowed to pursue as long as they wished. Indeed, as victims of colonial oppression they must be assisted to do so. They must also be assisted to articulate and communicate their aspirations to those who handled their affairs. (Beckett 1988c: 12–13)

Major transformations have taken place over the decades in the political landscape, with a shift toward self-empowerment, and increasing politicization of Indigenous peoples, including recognition of rights in land, heritage, and culture and improved participation in the national polity.

Identity, Recognition, and Rights

In today's society, Indigenous identities that were imposed by outsiders are sometimes harnessed by Indigenous peoples themselves, as part of their political struggles for recognition. As Tonkinson observes, "Today, Aboriginal leaders seek to build upon the notion of an Aboriginal ethnicity originally imposed upon them. Aboriginality is a tool of contemporary Aboriginal political struggle and is viewed by its proponents as a positive force. Yet this identity was in the past defined negatively, institutionalised, and legally codified by the dominant European society" (1990: 192). In fashioning their political identities, Tonkinson suggests, "A number of symbols, themes, and activities can be identified among Aborigines who espouse Aboriginality as the basis for national unity, if not nationhood. Foremost among these is the focus on land" (1990: 196). Suggesting that "The assertion of Aboriginality is part of a political process" (Tonkinson 1990: 215), Tonkinson comments that:

> The notion of Aboriginality has emerged in a climate of political change among Aborigines, and among white Australians as well. It is perhaps not a coincidence that official policy shifted from assimilation to self-determination about the same time a self-conscious promotion of Aboriginal identity by Aboriginal people (and their white sympathizers) was taking place. (Tonkinson 1990: 196)

Writing in the late 1980s, looking to a future, Tonkinson suggests that:

> The question of what constitutes Aboriginality will not be resolved in the short term. .... I can say with confidence that in contemporary Australia Aboriginal people share the consequences of colonization and oppression and are building political unity by identifying common values, characteristics, and goals. (Tonkinson 1990: 201)

In this context of increasing empowerment by Indigenous peoples and capacity to determine their own futures and identities, Dodson states "Alongside the colonial discourses in Australia, we have always had our own Aboriginal discourses in which we have continued to create our own representations, and to recreate identities which escaped the policing of the authorised versions" (Dodson 1994: 9). He writes that these are "Aboriginalities that arise from our experience of ourselves and our communities. They draw creatively from the past, including the experience of colonisation and false representation" (1994: 9). Dodson is among a number of writers who see the politicization of a conscious Indigenous identity as crucial to the project of self-determination and recognition of rights. As he puts it "Those Aboriginalities have been, and continue to be, a private source of spiritual sustenance in the face of others' attempts to control us. They are a political project designed to challenge and subvert the authorised versions on who and what we are. Self-representations of Aboriginality are always also acts of freedom" (1994: 10). Kolig also draws attention to the agency of Aboriginal people; they are not just the passive subjects of classifications, and identifications imposed on them by the dominant society have agency in transforming their own histories:

> Aborigines embedded in a wider society as they are now, have to find identity in relation to "the others" and this situation really is induced or even enforced. But as Aborigines do so, they draw on *their* social intellect and the result ultimately is their Aboriginality, and not a by-product of white encroachment. (Kolig 1977: 51, emphasis in original)

One key moment in the transformation of Indigenous identity was the 1967 Referendum, the outcome of which, suggests Beckett, "was both the culmination of the movement for Aboriginal citizenship and, paradoxically, the basis for the construction of a special Aboriginal status" (Beckett 1988b: 204). The Referendum, suggests Nielsen, "is prominent in the national memory as a watershed moment in the political relationship between white Australia and Indigenous peoples" (Nielsen 2016: 15).

In recent decades, a global movement of Indigenous identity has developed, which also has profound implications for Australia's Indigenous peoples in asserting their identity rights. Through the growth of global and transnational networks and increased representation in international standard development, Australia's Indigenous peoples have become more politicized and assert their rights and claims for recognition. Smith, Burke, and Ward explain:

> Globalisation can involve a redefinition of identity on many levels. Integral to this is the complex interplay of forces tending towards nationalism and/or the emphasis of local Indigenous identity on the one hand, and those of globalisation and broader notions of identity on the other. (Smith et al. 2000: 5)

De Costa remarked that "The remarkable growth of a network of indigenous peoples who are increasingly able to identify collectively is poorly understood." He argues that "The struggle of indigenous Australians adds greatly to our understanding of the role of shared histories in identity-formation and transnational processes of solidarity, the spread of global ideas such as decolonisation, self-determination and human rights, and the impact of new transport and communications technology" (de Costa 2006: 12). The globalization of Indigenous identities and rights is also noted by Tonkinson, who wrote that "Changes within Australian society and global changes in the positon of indigenous peoples have contributed to a modern notion of pan-Aboriginal identity, which is being institutionalized in political movements, evocative symbols, and personal actions" (1990: 192–3). These wider, global movements of a pan-Indigenous identity have been central to the international development of standards and treaties recognizing Indigenous peoples' rights. The United Nations Charter of Human Rights encodes recognition for minorities and for the right to ethnic and plural differences, including cultural, religious, and other rights. The 2007 UN Declaration on the Rights of Indigenous Peoples (UNDRIP) provides for recognition of the rights of Indigenous peoples as distinct peoples. Recognition is also provided in the International Labour Organization Convention 169 on Tribal Peoples, although Australia is as yet not a signatory to this Convention. Domestically, Indigenous peoples' identity rights are supported in various ways through land rights and native title laws. In the Australian context, Indigenous peoples' identity formation is an ongoing political and cultural process, as Tonkinson suggests:

> ...many Aborigines are consciously and actively working to establish positive images of themselves and their cultures. This involves the rejection or reversal of white people's definitions; the promotion of color as a desirable feature rather than a taint; and the revival, invention, or adoption of distinctly Aboriginal cultural behaviors and symbols – in short, the construction of a new identity in which all Aboriginal people can share and that will evoke acceptance and respect from the rest of Australian society. (1990: 215)

As an ongoing process, fashioning and self-fashioning Indigenous identities will continue to develop in complex, and increasingly important ways in the life of the nation. Tonkinson writes that Aboriginality "is still a new concept that does not fully describe identity as it is perceived by many Aboriginal people. The emphasis on nationwide common bonds and shared characteristics almost requires an outside view. This view is essential in building solidarity among a minority population and endowing it with political force in the Australian nation, but it downplays the great emphasis placed by many Aborigines on the uniqueness of their own small community, language group, or extended kin group" (1990: 215).

Conclusion

Australian Indigenous peoples' identities are multiple and complex. From a long history of experiences of dispossession, marginalization, and racialized classification, their identity formation has been shaped in part by adversity and struggle. Yet in today's highly mobile and globalized world, Indigenous peoples have reclaimed their self-determined rights to recognition of their intrinsic identities as First Nations and harness these in negotiated relations with the wider society.

Cross-References

▶ Ethno-cultural Symbolism and Group Identity
▶ The Significance of Ethno-politics in Modern States and Society

References

Beckett J (1988a) Introduction. In: Beckett J (ed) Past and present: the construction of aboriginality. Aboriginal Studies Press, Canberra, pp 1–10

Beckett J (1988b) The past in the present; the present in the past: constructing a national aboriginality. In: Beckett J (ed) Past and present: past and present: the construction of aboriginality. Aboriginal Studies Press, Canberra, pp 191–217

Beckett J (1988c) Aboriginality, citizenship and the nation stat. Soc Anal: Int J Soc Cult Pract 24:3–18. ABORIGINES AND THE STATE IN AUSTRALIA

Beckett J (2014) Encounters with indigeneity: writing about aboriginal and Torres Strait islander peoples. Aboriginal Studies Press, Canberra

Berndt RM (1959) The concept of "the tribe" in the Western Desert. Oceania 30:81–107

Berndt CH (1961) The quest for identity: the case of the Australian Aborigines. Oceania 32(1):16–33

Berndt RM (1977) Aboriginal identity: reality or mirage. In: Berndt RM (ed) Aborigines and change: Australia in the '70s. Social Anthropology Series No. 11. Australian Institute of Aboriginal Studies, Canberra, pp 1–12

Cowlishaw G (1987) Colour, culture, and the aborigines. Man 22(2):221–237

Cowlishaw GB (2004) Whitefellas and the hidden injuries of race. Blackwell Publishing, Malden

Crick M (1981) Aboriginal self-management organisation, cultural identity and the modification of exchange. Canberra Anthropol 4(1):52–81

De Costa R (2006) A higher authority: indigenous transnationalism and Australia. UNSW Press, Sydney

Dodson M (1994) The Wentworth lecture: the end in the beginning – re(de)finding aboriginality. Aust Aborig Stud 1:2–13

Dyck N (1985) Aboriginal peoples and nation-states: an introduction to the analytical issues. In: Dyck N (ed) Indigenous peoples and the nation-state: fourth world politics in Canada, Australia and Norway. Institute of Social and Economic Research, Memorial University of Newfoundland, St. John, pp 1–26

Fforde C, Bamblett L, Lovett R, Gorringe S, Fogarty B (2013) Discourse, deficit and identity: aboriginality, the race paradigm, and the language of representation in contemporary Australia. Media Int Aust 149(1):162–173

Gardiner-Garden J (2003) Defining aboriginality in Australia. Current Issues Brief No. 10. Department of Parliamentary Library, Canberra

Gibson C (1999) Cartographies of the colonial/capitalist state: a geopolitics of indigenous self-determination in Australia. Antipode 31(1):45–79

Gold GL, Paine R (1984) Introduction. In: Gold (ed) Minorities and mother country imagery, social and economic papers no. 13. Institute of Social and Economic Research, Memorial University of Newfoundland, pp 1–16

Hollinsworth D (1992) Discourses on aboriginality and the politics of identity in urban Australia. Oceania 63(2):137–155

Jordan DF (1988) Aboriginal identity: uses of the past, problems for the future? In: Beckett (ed) Past and present. pp 109–130

Jordan DF (1986) Aborigines in a multicultural society: a sharing of dreams? J Intercult Stud 7(2):5–29

Keeffe K (1988) Aboriginality: resistance and persistence. Aust Aborig Stud 1:67–81

Keen I (1988) 'Introduction'. In: Keen (ed) Being black: aboriginal cultures in "Settled" Australia. Aboriginal Studies Press, Canberra. pp 1–26

Kolig E (1977) From tribesman to citizen? Change and continuity in social identities among south Kimberley Aborigines. In Berndt RM (ed) Aborigines and change: Australia in the '70s. Social Anthropology Series No. 11. Australian Institute of Aboriginal Studies, Canberra. pp 33–53

Levi, JM, Dean B (2003) Introduction. In: Dean B and Levi JM (eds) At the risk of being heard: identity, indigenous rights, and postcolonial states, University of Michigan Press, Ann Arbor, pp 1–44

Linnekin J, Poyer L (eds) (1990) Cultural identity and ethnicity in the pacific. University of Hawaii Press, Honolulu

Maybury-Lewis D (2002) Indigenous peoples, ethnic groups, and the state, 2nd edn. Allyn and Bacon, Boston

McCorquodale J (1986) The legal classification of race in Australia. Aborig Hist 10(1):7–24

Moran A (2002) As Australia decolonizes: indigenizing settle nationalism and the challenges of settler/indigenous relations. Ethn Racial Stud 25(6):1013–1042

Moreton-Robinson A (2004) Whiteness, epistemology and indigenous representation. In: Moreton-Robinson A (ed) Whitening race: essays in social and cultural criticism. Aboriginal Studies Press, Canberra, pp 75–88

Morris B (1988) The politics of identity: from Aborigines to the first Australian. In: Beckett J (ed) Past and present: the construction of aboriginality. Aboriginal Studies Press, Canberra, pp 63–85

Mulcock J (2007) Dreaming the circle: indigeneity and the longing for belonging in white Australia. In: Macfarlane I, Hannah M (eds) Transgressions: critical Australian indigenous histories. ANU Press, Canberra, pp 63–82

Nielsen J (2016) Breaking the silence: the importance of constitutional change. In: Young S, Nielsen J, Patrick J (eds) Constitutional recognition of first peoples in Australia. The Federation Press, Annandale, NSW, pp 2–28

Pettman JJ (1995) Race, ethnicity and gender in Australia. In: Stasiulis and Yuval Davis (eds). pp 65–94

Smith C, Burke H, Ward GK (2000) Globalisation and indigenous peoples: threat or empowerment? In: Smith C, Ward GK (eds) Indigenous cultures in an interconnected world. Allen & Unwin, Sydney, pp 1–24

Stasiulis D, Nira Yuval-Davis N (1995) Introduction: beyond dichotomies – gender, race, ethnicity and class in settler societies. In: Stasiulis D, Yuval-Davis N (eds) Unsettling settler societies: articulations of gender, race, ethnicity and class. Sage Series on Race and Ethnic Relations, Vol 11. Sage Publications, London, pp 1–38

Stasiulis D, Yuval-Davis N (eds) (1995) Unsettling settler societies: articulations of gender, race, ethnicity and class. Sage Series on Race and Ethnic Relations, vol 11. Sage Publications, London

Tacey DJ (1995) Edge of the sacred: transformation in Australia. HarperCollins, Melbourne

Tatz C (1980) Aboriginality as civilization. Aust Q 52(3):352–362

Tonkinson ME (1990) Is it in the blood? Australian aboriginal identity. In: Linnekin J, Poyer L (eds) Cultural identity and ethnicity in the Pacific. University of Hawaii Press, Honolulu, pp 191–218

Von Sturmer J (1973) Changing aboriginal identity in cape york. In: Tugby D (ed) Aboriginal identity in contemporary Australian society. Jacaranda Press, Milton, Queensland, pp 16–26

Weaver S (1984) Struggle of the nation-state to define aboriginal ethnicity, Canada and Australia. In: Gold GI (ed) Minorities and mother country imagery. Social and Economic Papers 13. Institute of Social and Economic Research. pp 182–210

Wentworth WC (1973) Aboriginal identity, government and the law. In: Tugby (ed). pp 7–15

China: Modernization, Development, and Ethnic Unrest in Xinjiang

54

Kate Hannan

> *Despite... rising living standards and large-scale improvements in infrastructure and services, China's western borderlands are awash in a wave of ethnic unrest not seen since the 1950s. (Hillman and Tuttle 2016, p. i)*

Contents

Introduction	1012
China's Ethnic Groups	1014
Quickened Economic and Social Development 'the fundamental solution to China's Ethnic Issues" – (PRC State Council White Paper 2009, p. 9)	1016
Han Paternalism, Backward and Ungrateful Minorities, and Chinese Nationalism	1018
Development and Modernization, Resource Exploitation, and Uyghur Resentment	1021
The Belt and Road: Xinjiang, China's Northwest Doorway to Central Asia	1024
The "Three Evils": Splitism, Separatism, and Terrorism	1026
Conclusion	1028
References	1030

Abstract

China's ethnic Uyghur population are restive and repressed. The Chinese government has presided over almost three decades of considerably improved living standards for the majority of its people. This is commendable, but rapid modernization and development have also presented problems. While China's leaders have attended the national interest, they have not given adequate consideration to particular concerns, and when "episodes and pockets" of grassroots discontent erupt, the government responds with repression and force. Discontented workers, students, villagers (particularly those subject to heavy-handed land acquisition

---

K. Hannan (✉)
Department of History and Politics, University of Wollongong, Wollongong, NSW, Australia
e-mail: katehannan0@gmail.com

© The Author(s), under exclusive license to Springer Nature Singapore Pte Ltd. 2019
S. Ratuva (ed.), *The Palgrave Handbook of Ethnicity*,
https://doi.org/10.1007/978-981-13-2898-5_163

and the effects of environmental pollution), and ethnic minority groups have not had adequate response to their petitions, demonstrations, and in some cases violent opposition to government policy and behavior. China's Uyghur ethnic group are paying a particularly high price for the pressure their unrest, discontent, and violence have put on the government. Beijing insists on continuing its policy of promoting "economic and social development" as "the fundamental solution to China's ethnic problems," while on the ground in Xinjiang, the government's use of force and intimidation is increasing. The use of violence to restore social order is viewed by many (both inside and outside China) as ill-advised and a sign of policy failure.

Keywords
China · Xinjiang · Government policy · Ethnic identity · Protest

Introduction

For almost half a century, China's leaders have employed the goal of modernization and development as a political tool. Successful economic development has been proof of the leadership's claim to have superior knowledge of the interests of the Chinese people.

Modernization and development have been presented as the Chinese leadership's goal since the Deng Xiaoping government introduced economic reform in 1978/9. In almost 50 years since, this goal has substantially lifted the living standards of the Chinese people to the point where, today, the Chinese economy is presented by Xi Jinping leadership as having "transitioned from a phase of rapid growth [promoted by low wage/low cost production] to a stage of high-quality development" (Xinhua, 5 March 2018g). High-quality development is predicated on greater capital investment, particularly in technology. The Chinese economy has also "gone global" with the centerpiece of this policy now taking the form of the Belt and Road – "the Silk Road Economic Belt and 21st Century Maritime Silk Road." The Belt and Road Initiative is a consequence of (and leverages) China's growing international economic and political influence.

While China's modernization and development program have undoubtedly allowed the country's leaders to maintain and reproduce their political rule, there are pressing issues that must be addressed. Throughout the reform and modernization era, there have been "episodes and pockets" of social unrest initiated from below. These have usually been confined to opposition by particular groups to specific policies and issues and have often been a direct consequence of the process of modernization.

The Tiananmen Incident of 1989 is the most internationally reported example of open opposition to Chinese government rule and policies. There had been a series of student demonstrations in the previous period (with very obvious student discontent at the end of 1986), but the Tiananmen Incident of June 3/4, 1989, tapped mounting urban anger that reached beyond student demonstrators. Students and then workers spilled out onto the streets of Chinese cities. While rapid economic change had improved living standards for many, it had generated increased inequality. There were high rates of inflation funnelled into the price of necessities, particularly food. Government factionalism and mismanagement at various levels were also resented, and from the students' point of view, unnecessary and petty rules governing university life and inappropriate post-university placements had fed political dissatisfaction. Two decades after the Tiananmen Incident, the Chinese government found its actions in response to social unrest initiated from below again widely reported in the international press. There had been ongoing ethnic unrest in Tibet and Xinjiang, and in 2008 and 2009, this unrest escalated. The extent of the increased unrest not only presented a challenge to national unity but also challenged the authority of the Chinese Communist Party (Odgaard and Nielsen 2014, p. 535).

On March 10, 2008, on the anniversary of the 1959 Tibetan uprising against Chinese Communist Party rule, demonstrations took place in Lhasa, and by March 14, there were attacks by Tibetans on Han and Hui immigrants. There was also looting and structural damage. As they had at the time of the Tiananmen Incident, Chinese authorities used force to re-establish "social stability" (Odgaard and Nielsen 2014, p. 536). Then on the 5th of July 2009, particularly violent protests erupted in Xinjiang Uyghur Autonomous Region. China's leaders were "obviously shocked by the scale of the rioting [in Xinjiang]..." (Yufan Hao and Weihua Liu 2012, p. 205).

The extent of the 2009 Urumqi riots is evident in the following description:

> The unrest began with a peaceful demonstration by over a thousand Uyghurs in People's Square in Urumqi... As darkness approached, the city descended into a macabre theatre of violence: marauding Uyghur youth hunted down and then butchered innocent Han civilians (or those perceived to be Han)... Hundreds of vehicles and shops were looted and then set ablaze... Sporadic violence continued throughout the night and the following days. Security personel rounded up thousands of Uyghur residents. Mean-while, Han vigilantes took to the streets.... (Leibold 2013, p. 10)

As had happened at the time of the Tiananmen Incident decades earlier, the government used disproportionate force (Odgaard and Nielsen 2014, p. 535) against the demonstrators, and again as in the case of the Tiananmen Incident, China's leaders declared that just a few hooligans ("black hands" and foreigners) were responsible for the events of the day. It has been estimated that there had been more than 3,000 Uyghur rioters and that at least 197 people had been killed and 1,721 injured (Odgaard and Nielsen 2014, p. 535). In the decade since, Uyghur unrest has persisted with an ever longer list of incidents involving violence. These incidents have also been followed by the disproportionate use of government-sponsored force.

In Xinjiang (and Tibet), ethno-nationalism has increased further since 2008 and 2009. This has happened "despite significant economic investment by the Chinese government" (Zelcer-Lavid 2018). Indeed, persistent social unrest and ongoing social tension and violence have made it clear that promoting modernization and development in China's largest ethnic minority areas has not promoted (or bought) national unity.

In Xinjiang's rural sector improvement in living standards has been remarkable. The per capita net income of farmers was estimated to be 28 times more in 2008 than it had been in 1978 when the Deng Xiaoping government introduced its program for economic reform (Yufan Hao and Weihua Liu 2012, p. 208). More recently, in 2017, an estimated 300,000 people (mostly rural residents) were estimated to have been lifted out of poverty in Xinjiang (Xinhua, 26 January 2018e), but the government's preferential development programs have gone hand in hand with the increasing and disproportionate use of force to quell violence and re-establish control. In other words, the two approaches taken by the Chinese government consist of (a) an overarching policy of implementing preferential economic initiatives (encompassing both infrastructural investment for resource exploitation and industrialization and the provision of social infrastructure and services) and (b) using force to address immediate social resentment and disorder. Some commentators have characterized this approach as the use of (a) soft power and (b) hard power (Odgaard and Nielsen 2014, p. 536).

The introductory outline above makes clear that there is much to discuss in relation to grassroots discontent and the potential for unrest initiated from below that would undermine the political authority of China's leadership. This chapter focuses on the discontent manifest by the Uyghur people resident in the Xinjiang Autonomous Region of Western China. The often-asked question "Why Didn't Chinese Investment Ease Ethnic Tensions in Xinjiang?" is discussed (Zelcer-Lavid 2018).

Development and modernization projects have received privileged funding in China's ethnic minority areas, particularly in Xinjiang, together with social policies including preferential school admissions and funding of a wide range of education and housing projects. There have also been government attempts to promote preferential access to employment. Living standards have improved, and greater social equity is expected to have been promoted, but minority people's discontent has grown and grown. This discontent has now reached the point where scholars and commentators talk of "problematic privilege in Xinjiang" (Zenz 2017; New York Times, 2 May 2014). Commentators (within China and internationally) recognize that the region is drifting toward evermore violence.

A number of issues related to the question of why Uyghur nationalism and discontent are increasing in spite of Chinese government investment and promotion of development and modernization will also be discussed in this chapter. They include Han paternalism, the cost of exploiting natural resources in the Xinjiang national minority region (including the cost of using the region as a transit hub for Belt and Road projects), and, above all, the ongoing use of government-sponsored force and the threat of force. The latter includes the situation where, "in 2017, security measures in Xinjiang reached a new level with recruitment of 100,000 new police officers, widespread installations of police stations, and new surveillance regulations on the Uyghur population..." (Zenz 2017; New York Times, 2 May 2014).

China's Ethnic Groups

Every Chinese citizen carries a registration card usually used in much the same way as a driver's license or passport is used for identification in many countries. The Chinese registration card indicates a person's "nationality." The official Chinese government position is that there are 55 ethnic groups plus the Han in China. The Chinese government recognizes over 90% of China's citizens as Han Chinese with just 8% making up the country's "national minorities," but when these numbers are used as stand-alone numbers, they are misleading. The numbers infer that the minority people are an "insignificant minority" in China's total population, but this minority population occupies some 64% of the country's land territory. Those critical of the way Beijing profiles the ethnic makeup of China's population using population numbers alone have extended their argument by pointing out that the present 90-plus/8% approach is not only misleading but is "seriously misleading" in light of the geographic distribution of the Uyghurs, Tibetans, and Mongolians (Dillon 2018, pp. 13 and 14).

China's government defines nationality by using a definition presented by Stalin in 1913 (Mackerras 2003, p. 2). This definition establishes a "minority nationality" as "a historically constituted, stable community of people, formed on the basis of a common language, territory, economic life, and psychological make-up manifested in common culture" (Mackerras 2003, p. 2). It is a definition that, as the much respected China scholar Colin Mackerras points out, has obvious anomalies. For example, many "nationalities" do not have a common territory, and some like the Manchu no longer speak their language. Some groups are very similar to the Han Chinese majority; some have histories, cultures, and languages that are very different. A preferred definition rests on the idea of an "ethnic group." This definition "would appeal to ancestry, a shared history, and a common language and culture, possibly including religion." Other commentators have then argued that "a necessary accompaniment" would be "some consciousness of kind among members of the group" (see Mackerras 2003, p. 3).

According to the Chinese government's 2010 census, there are 18 minority groups with populations of over 1 million: "the Zhuang, Manchu, Hui, Miao, Uyghurs, Yi, Tujia, Mongols, Tibetan, Bouyei, Dong, Yao, Korean, Bai, Hani, Li, Kazak, and Dai." There are 17 minority groups with populations between 100,000 and 1 million, "the She, Lisu, Gelao, Lahu, Dongxiang, Va, Sui, Naxi, Qiang, Tu, Xibe, Mulam, Kyrgyz, Daur, Jingpo, Salar, and Maonan," and 20 groups with populations estimated to be between 10,000 and 100,000: "the Blang, Tajik, Primi, Achang, Nu, Ewenki, Gin, Jino, De'ang, Uzbeks, Russian, Yugurs, Bonan, Monba, Oroqen, Derung, Tatars, Hezhen, Gaoshan (excluding the Gaoshan population in Taiwan) and Lhoba" (Rudolph and Szonyi 2018, p. 33). China's national minority populations range in size from the largest, the Zhuang with over 16 million who are "rather similar culturally to the Vietnamese" (Mackerras 2005, p. 814), down to the smallest – the Lhoba with just 3,000 (China Daily, 17 March 2011).

At the time of the 2010 Census, there were an estimated 112 million people in China belonging to an ethnic group. By anyone's reckoning it is "a large number" (Rudolph and Szonyi 2018, p. 33). Most of these groups make up a "silent majority." They "do not employ confrontational strategies towards the Chinese state" (Han et al. 2014). The exceptions are the Uyghurs of Xinjiang, the Tibetans, and to a lesser extent the Mongolians. The traditional areas of these three groups account for 55% of the Chinese landmass (Han et al. 2014, p. 4) and a large percentage of the country's natural resources. Xinjiang alone occupies a region covering almost 641,000 square miles, an area almost three times the area of France (Xiaobing Li and Fuliang Shan 2015, p. 91). The resource reserves of this area plus its geographic position make it "quite crucial to Beijing's national interests" (Yufan Hao and Weihua Liu 2012, p. 224).

The minority groups that stand out as being very different from the Han Chinese "are the Turkic peoples of far north-western China, such as the Kazaks, Kirgiz and Uzbeks, and most importantly the Uyghurs...." Their languages are Turkic (very close to Uzbek) and they are Muslims. Uyghur (plus Arabic) is used in Xinjiang's mosques (Yufan Hao and Weihua Liu 2012, p. 224), and, as scholars and commentators are noting, "Islam is gaining in strength among the Uyghurs both culturally and socially" (Mackerras 2005, p. 816). Some commentators go on to wonder if this situation could offer some explanation for why "inter-ethnic polarization and antagonism of Han Chinese is seen to be more acute in Xinjiang... than in Tibetan areas" (Han et al., p. 5). There is no doubt that there has been an increase in Islamic religious belief and practice in Xinjiang, particularly in the almost decade since the 2009 riots. There are changes in behavior that are clearly visible even to people walking in the streets, for example, in women's dress codes and men's beards. Changed behavior is also made clear by "the disappearance of alcohol from many Uyghur restaurants, the call to prayer beeping out from mobile phones, [and] new enthusiasm for the Ramadan fast" (Han et al., p. 7).

Quickened Economic and Social Development 'the fundamental solution to China's Ethnic Issues" – (PRC State Council White Paper 2009, p. 9).

An aspect of Chinese government policy that is surprising is how much overarching policy stays the same rather than changing in response to the steady stream of "episodes and pockets" of unrest initiated from below. For example, after only a relatively short period of stabilization, the Chinese leadership doubled down on economic reform policies after the Tiananmen Incident of 1989 (Mackerras 2003, p. 38). When it comes to China's ethnic groups, in spite of continued ethnic unrest and ever louder agreement among domestic and international scholars and commentators that "ethnic minority policies have failed," Beijing persists with the same policy formula. The Chinese government continues to insist that modernization and economic reform predicated on quickening the economic and social development of minority communities and minority areas are the solution to China's ethnic issues (PRC State Council White Paper 2009, p. 9).

In 2012 alone some $US5.93 billion was spent on improving the quality of farmland (China Daily, 7 September 2012), but in Xinjiang (where more than 80.5% of the Uyghur labor force is engaged in agricultural production [China Daily, 12 March 2018b]) in the period immediately following (in 2013), there was the highest incidence of political violence since the 2009 Urumqi riots (Xiaobing Li and Shan 2015, p. 90). Today, preferential investment in Xinjiang continues unabated. The list is long and, from an economic investment point of view, very impressive. It includes upgrading the rural power grid; investment in improved water resource management;

$US420 million expansion of Xinjiang's rail and road networks; metro construction underway in Xinjiang's capital – Urumqi; and 80,000 houses built in Xinjiang for "the rural poor" (Xinhua, 26 February 2018f; Xinhua, 6 April 2018j). There is also a new industrial park to provide impetus for Xinjiang's manufacturing industry and expansion of Urumqi Airport and a direct air route operating alongside direct rail routes linking Xinjiang with Western Europe (OBOReurope 2018). The already extensive list continues with Xinjiang's regional government allocating $US70 billion to be invested in infrastructure in 2018. The same amount – $US70 billion – was allocated by the local Xinjiang regional government for infrastructure construction in the previous year (2017): a 50% increase year on year from 2016 (Xinhua, 5 March 2018g).

Commentators (both scholars within China and international scholars) agree that in spite of the ongoing social unrest among Xinjiang's Uyghurs, the "ending of minority preferences is unlikely" (Leibold 2013, p. 50). They recognize that these policies will "be employed for a long time to come" (Sautman 1998, p. 87). Beijing's position is holding in spite of over a hundred self-immolations in the years since violence that broke out in Tibet in 2008 and in spite of bombings and attacks in Urumqi and beyond. There has been ongoing Uyghur-associated violence in cities both inside and outside Xinjiang, including in Beijing, in the decade since the uprising in 2009 (BBC Report, 26 September 2014).

Accompanying the obvious failure of the Chinese government's economic approach to addressing ethnic unrest, there are a number of further issues, particularly the government's ever-increasing use of force to ensure social stability. As a result of the government's lack of success in smothering or even dampening ethnic discontent with significant infrastructural investment and despite the promotion of educational institutions and other social services including privileged access to employment opportunities for members of ethnic groups, above average access to medical services, and measures such as training more judges to speak ethnic languages (China Daily, 27 June 2018d; China Daily, 2 September 2016b), there is increased reliance on the use of force by government agencies to re-establish social stability. The government's use of force then provokes violent protest, and the cycle of unrest becomes further established. It is in this context that the security measures adopted in Xinjiang in 2017 including the "recruitment of 100,000 new police officers, widespread installations of police stations, and new surveillance regulations on the Uyghur population..." (Zenz 2017) can be understood. At least one academic observer who managed to spend a short period of time on the ground in Xinjiang has reported that "the feeling is of being in a war zone." He added that in this circumstance the government's message is "shrill" (Australian National University seminar discussion, 26 September 2018). There are police stations every few blocks and reports of situations where, for example, the party secretary of Xinjiang (Chen Quanguo) addressed police with 10,000 officers dressed in black riot gear lined up in neat columns. It was an impressive show of force (NPR News, 26 September 2017).

Apart from the above, there have also been central government moves to educate local Xinjiang authorities "to use peaceful instruments to deal with popular dissatisfaction." However, these "peaceful instruments" include "expanding a 'grid management' ...system of high-tech surveillance and control..." (Leibold 2013, p. 50;

Odgaard and Nielsen 2014, p. 536). It is reported that many towns, particularly in southwest Xinjiang, are effectively sealed off using police checkpoints (Time, 4 August 2014). In the first half of 2017 alone, around $US6 billion was spent on security. These funds are drawn from central government subsidies (NPR News, 26 September 2017). And, since the regional counter-terrorism law was passed by the central government in May 2016:

> editors and contributors of Uyghur-language websites have been detained for criticising government policies on religious observance; in some towns and cities, fences are being built around areas where large numbers of Uyghurs live to allow the police to carry out security checks more easily; more prisons are being built; and the security forces have been equipped with modern, sophisticated equipment for counter-terrorism operations. . ... (Dillon 2018, p. 113)

Passports have been confiscated, and an ominous network of "training schools" have been established to reeducate Uyghurs deemed "to be susceptible to separatist or Islamist ideas" (Dillon 2018, p. 116). Measures have also been undertaken by government authorities to counter Islamic education and religious activities. Mosques have been monitored. It has been reported that civil servants and students have been banned from fasting during Ramadan and Uyghur restaurants have been forced to stay open during Ramadan. It has also been reported that cadres have been billeted in private homes to monitor families. These measures, together with others relating to matters such as dress, "abnormal" beards, and refusing hotel accommodation to local Uyghur residents (local officials are also reported to have been banning people in Islamic dress and with long beards from boarding buses), serve to embarrass, intimidate, and terrorize the Uyghur community (Torrey 2017). These issues are an obvious "source of great resentment that is likely to erupt into further conflict" (Torrey 2017).

It has recently been reported in the Western press that because the government sees "web cleansing" as an important tool to prevent Uyghur residents' access to terrorist information, "everyone in Xinjiang is supposed to have a spyware app. on their mobile phone." Failing to install the app is an offense, and phones are regularly checked when residents are in public places, often at street checkpoints (Economist, 31 May 2018). Other reports note the government collection of information from health records. They note the use of up-to-the-minute techniques for collecting biometric information that includes blood types, voice patterns, and facial imagery. There is concern that the information collected is providing data for a new identification card system (Kuo 2017).

Han Paternalism, Backward and Ungrateful Minorities, and Chinese Nationalism

As argued above, development, modernization, and raised living standards buttress the Chinese leadership's political legitimacy, but there is more to the story in the case of China's ethnic groups. The Chinese government's ethnic region economic and development policies are embedded "in paternalistic notions that arise from the social evolutionism that pervades elite thinking about Han-minority relations" (Sautman 1998, p. 88). China's "overwhelming" Han majority has a culture that they claim "is more 'advanced' than minority cultures" (Sautman 1998, p. 87). Han Chinese are recognized as feeling "compelled to assimilate and civilize" national minorities (Xiaobing Li and Fuliang Shan 2015, p. 220) with Chinese government officials publicly arguing that "the backwardness of minority nationalities" means they have a need for development and a "need to learn from the more advanced culture of the Han Chinese" (Williams 2008). It is said that while the Uyghurs see Xinjiang as their land because they have lived there for thousands of years, Han Chinese believe they have a right to the resources and to be resident because they built a modern economy. They have brought "modern culture" and a "modern lifestyle," and by this "they mean the culture and lifestyle of modern Han China" (Economist, 31 May 2018).

China's ethnic minorities should, many Han argue, be grateful for being "lifted out of their previous misery." After all, "over the last few decades, non-Han communities have seen unjust forms of human exploitation ended, poverty eradicated, diseases eliminated, life spans extended, education expanded, transportation and infrastructure enhanced, and the standard of living in general quite significantly raised..." (Rudolph and Szonyi 2018, p. 35). The argument then is that non-Han Chinese owe their country a huge debt of gratitude and that complaining and rebelling rather than recognizing their debt to the party and its policies (and to the Han) is "perverse and unreasonable" (Rudolph and Szonyi 2018, pp. 35 and 36).

Scholars commenting on China's ethnic issues have noted that "racist taunts are *de rigueur* on the Chinese language Internet (even on more 'liberal' spaces like Weibo)...." They note there are "constant gripes" in this medium "about how the Chinese state is 'spoiling' those 'ungrateful' and 'backward' Uyghur and Tibetan minorities" (Han et al. 2014, p. 8). Ethnic groups are said to have been spoilt because they have been afforded "too much privilege." This charge has, in turn, been identified as "Chinese victimhood." Han Chinese see themselves as victims "in the hands of minorities," and worse the victim approach is being "shared by an increasing number of Chinese scholars and politicians" (Han et al., p. 9). Adding to this situation, there are discussions focusing on ethnic unrest that are prone to using "a number of ideologically inflated terms." These include "Chinese colonialism, nationalism, or imperialism" on one side and "minority splitism or terrorism" on the other. This approach obviously fans "the intense emotion or indignation expressed by both sides" (Han et al., p. 9).

Chinese nationalism is enjoying an additional boost under the Xi Jinping government. The concept is also bound up with Han paternalism and chauvinism. The link is clear when commentators note that "since its origins [Chinese nationalism] has been fundamentally about ensuring that the Han people remain masters of the Chinese nation" (Rudolph and Szonyi 2018, p. 40). They then add that this situation does not engender non-Han inclusion in the national project (Rudolph and Szonyi 2018, p. 40), and as Mackerras has noted, "it seems evident that Chinese nationalism is in tension with any rise in minority identities." He goes on to note that with the rise in Chinese nationalism, "the state will give even less space than formerly to any form of ethno nationalism..." (Mackerras 2003, p. 37).

With Mackerras' observation about the reducing room for any form of ethnonationalism in mind, it is timely that Chinese academics, particularly the well-respected Beijing University sociologist and ethnologist Ma Rong (a member of the Hui ethnic group), have been advocating changes to their government's ethnic policies. Ma Rong contends that "the fragile state of ethnic relations in China is now the nation's biggest social issue" (Leibold 2013, p. 14). He also argues that the language with which ethnic issues have been discussed and perceived in China should be changed. He notes that the language used in ethnic debate by the Chinese policy establishment has been combined with clear territorial identification (particularly in the case of Xinjiang, Tibet, and Mongolia). This language has then been coupled with preferential economic policies. The result is that ethnic identities and consciousness have been underlined and promoted and barriers to integration have been created (Sautman 2010, p. 73). Ma Rong argues that ethno-cultural differences have been amplified contributing to a general lack of ethnic interaction and understanding (Leibold 2013, p. 14).

Ma Rong's thesis has been the basis of a "second generation" of ethnic policies with high-profile Chinese academics such as Hu Angang joining Ma Rong in arguing that ethnic identities should be attenuated and a single national identity promoted (Leibold 2013, p. 40).

The problem often identified with Ma Rong's argument is that while it will obviously find favor with the Han majority, it will not be favored by ethnic groups. This is precisely (a) because it no longer amplifies their ethnic identity and (b) because it denies them long-established preferential economic policies (Dillon 2018, p. 218). On the other side of the ledger, we have a situation where privileged funding for ethnic groups has not provided redress for grievances, but Beijing will not alter this policy because (a) it would undermine the claim that policy has worked and (b) it would risk further expression of destructive ethno-nationalism.

Ma Rong has addressed the problems in his argument by recommending that policies favoring minority ethnic groups should be *gradually* replaced by policies favoring "all residents of poor areas." This would be a move in government policy "from ethnic favoritism to individual support." Ma Rong's argument is that government assistance must become national minority blind (*minzu*-blind). All individuals in need should be the target of government assistance programs (Leibold 2013, p. 18).

Before leaving this brief outline of Ma Rong's argument, it can be noted that while Beijing continues to insist that there will be no change of policy to the point of effectively freezing public discussion of problems associated with national minority issues (Dillon 2018, p. 219) when it comes to privileging economic support for national minority areas, there is some (albeit limited) hope for Ma Rong's recommendations. For example, in the recent government announcement by the Xinjiang Autonomous Region on the topic of building subsidized housing, it was stated that of the planned 300,000 subsidized houses to be built in Xinjiang this year (2018):

about 210,000 will be for families in extreme poverty, those receiving the minimum living allowances... [and over time] Xinjiang is to build enough new houses for all underprivileged households in rural areas.... (Dillon 2018, p. 219)

Nothing was said about housing for Uyghur minority people, even though they would be the primary beneficiaries of housing for poor rural households in Xinjiang. The announcement is only about housing for "families in extreme poverty" (Dillon 2018, p. 219). This approach appears to be a case of quietly and gradually introducing the "national minority blind" social policies that Ma Rong has advocated.

Development and Modernization, Resource Exploitation, and Uyghur Resentment

Xinjiang's energy resources are considerable. There are large coal, oil, gas, and petroleum reserves. The region has coal reserves of an estimated 2.19 trillion tons that account for 40% of China's total reserves (Xinhua, 20 January 2018a). Petroleum and natural gas reserves are estimated to be 30 billion tons (a quarter of the nation's total), and oil reserves are estimated to be 21 billion tons with new deposits continuing to be found. Xinjiang's coal, oil, and gas reserves have been referred to as an "energy hat trick" (Wong 2014).

Apart from its coal, oil, and gas resources, Xinjiang also provides transit for much of the fuel imported from Central Asia. The region is crisscrossed with pipelines. It is also crisscrossed with high-voltage wires (Wong 2014). Xinjiang began outbound power transmission in 2010 with extra-high-voltage power transmissions continuing to increase with an ongoing increase in output capacity (Xinhua, 20 March 2018h). By 2018 government sources were estimating that "northwest China's Xinjiang autonomous region had supplied electricity to 250 million people in 16 provinces and cities across the country" (Xinhua, 20 March 2018h).

The substantial investment in oil and gas extraction, coal production, and power generation has taken place in northern Xinjiang, and this substantial level of investment in the north of the region means that this part of Xinjiang has attracted far more investment than the agricultural south.

There are numerous examples of heavily invested and very large projects in northern Xinjiang, including China's State Grid Corporation and China National Petroleum Corporation (PetroChina). The latter is the country's largest oil and gas producer (China Daily, 9 February 2018a). PetroChina's Xinjiang refinery is said to be the company's most profitable. It processes more than 6 million tons of oil per year (Wong 2014). There is also the Tarim Oilfield. It is estimated to have sent 200 billion cubic meters of natural gas to eastern China over a 13 year period. The Tarim Oilfield company boasts that between 2004 and 2017, it benefitted "400 million people and 3,000 enterprises in more than 120 cities." The company is also "a key provider" for a 4,000 km pipeline bringing natural gas from China's west (Xinjiang) to the east. A direct pipeline runs from the Tarim Basin to Shanghai (Xinhua, 2 January 2018b), but all this "success" fuels Uyghur resentment.

The profits from exploiting Xinjiang's resources go to the largest state-owned enterprises in China. They are delivering natural resources and power to "cities across the country," while the pollution from coal, oil, and gas exploitation and power production (unlike the profits) remains in Xinjiang. For example, Xinjiang has long been plagued by underground fires in coalfields. Currently there are at least 46 coalfield fires in Xinjiang with three large fires totalling some 1.42 million square meters burning an estimated 890,000 tons of coal annually. Beijing has had to admit that the pollution from these fires in the form of greenhouse gases, toxic gas, and smoke dust is considerable. The government in Xinjiang has undertaken to "put out all fires in the three coal fields by 2020" (Xinhua, 21 March 2018i), but the same government has not even been able (or willing) to stop resource exploitation in designated nature reserves. The environment ministry in Beijing has recently resorted to admonishing Xinjiang officials for their "ideological problems." Local government officials are accused of acting only on their belief that "Xinjiang is an underdeveloped area that should take advantage of its resources such as coal, oil and minerals" (Sixthtone, 4 January 2018).

Beijing has recently announced it "is accelerating its efforts to open up upstream oil and gas resources." In Xinjiang this opening will be promoted by "auctioning five more oil and gas exploration sites" (China Daily, 15 December 2017). Beijing has also offered Xinjiang as one of four bases for converting coal to gas and gasoline. This process is recognized to emit "a huge amount of planet-warming carbon dioxide" (Xinhua, 20 March 2018h). In addition, the process of coal gasification or coal-to-petrol conversion uses an unreasonable amount of water in an area that "suffers from acute water shortages" (Wong 2014). (There has also been an "enormous growth" of cotton production in Xinjiang in recent years. Cotton is regarded as a Han crop because "it is mainly the Han who profit from the cotton industry." It is a very thirsty crop. It also drains the region's precious groundwater [Mackerras 2005, p. 820].)

Apart from its coal, oil, and gas resources, Xinjiang is recognized as housing 122 minerals. Some are the largest reserves in China and include beryllium, muscovite, natron, saltpeter, pottery clay, and serpentine. Reserves of iron ore are estimated to be 730 million tons, and there are gemstones, asbestos, and jade (China.org, 8 July 2018). It is against the background of natural riches that government officials in both Beijing and Xinjiang must stand accused of simply thinking of Xinjiang as "an underdeveloped area that should take advantage of its resources – such as coal, oil, and minerals – to speed up development" (Sixthtone, 4 January 2018). At the same time, a matter that has exacerbated Han/ethnic minority tension in Xinjiang (and in Tibet and elsewhere) is the arrival of large numbers of Han immigrants. Their numbers have surged with the exploitation of natural resources and the opening of China's west. In 1949 only 6% of Xinjiang's population identified as Han Chinese. By 2015 the number was estimated to be 38% and is now higher (Rudolph and Szonyi 2018, p. 39). Estimates used by the popular Western press vary. A recent opinion piece cited the present figure as 46% Uyghur compared to 41% Han Chinese (Australian, 12 September 2018).

Han migration to Xinjiang was considerably increased by measures associated by the "Go West" policy. This policy was announced in 2000 as the Great Western Development campaign. It has been promoted by Beijing as a development project that will further the modernization and development of central and far-western provinces. In Western cities such as Chongqing, the "Go West" policy has promoted the use of local (and cheaper) labor and production services, but in Xinjiang there is the added scenario of significant and increased exploitation of natural resources funded by substantial investment in an ethnically sensitive area. It has meant the adoption and use of modern technology and the associated technical expertise needed have led to a stream of skilled Han workers being imported from eastern China. At best, lesser skilled and less well-paid employment is left for local Uyghur workers, but even this work has not usually benefitted local residents. The unsurprising result is that the influx of "Han Chinese engineers, technicians and workers . . . have increased the anxiety of Uyghurs. . ." (Dillon 2018, p. 103).

Local Xinjiang residents see themselves as being "marginalized in their own land." This is happening in spite of programs to educate Uyghurs in the use of Mandarin Chinese from a very early age (Xinhua, 24 May 2018k). The Chinese government proudly claims that 95.95% of the 1.37 million kindergarten students in Xinjiang have access to 3 years of preschool education in Mandarin (Xinhua, 24 May 2018k). Access to Mandarin language education then continues at higher levels of schooling making the education of ethnic students bilingual. The problem with the considerable coverage of Mandarin is that it opens the way for resentful Uyghur locals to charge that the government is in the business of language replacement. In other words, the government is engaged in cultural and linguistic assimilation (Torrey 2017; Zenz 2017). Others talk of "the Hanification of education and language practices" (Williams 2008). By way of contrast, a part of Ma Rong's argument is that the Chinese government unwittingly established two education systems. There are ordinary schools for Han students and *minzu* (national minority) schools where minority students are educated, often in their own language. Their languages are then preserved, but students from ethnic groups are separated from the mainstream (Leibold 2013, p. 15).

It is widely recognized that the Xinjiang oil boom has seen "oil companies employ some Uighurs, but not many." It is also noted that when other projects are undertaken, the same exclusion of Uyghurs takes place, for example, when it came to rebuilding the old center of the city of Kashgar (on the southern fringe of the Taklimakan and "as far from Chinese cultural influence as possible. . . the home of the most traditional Uyghur culture. . ." [Dillon 2018, p. 93]). Chinese developers from outside Xinjiang took the opportunity on offer. They were awarded contracts, and they brought their predominantly Han workforce with them. This led to resentment among local Uyghurs who were not considered suited for either highly technical work or for relatively unskilled building construction jobs (Dillon 2018, p. 95). And, as noted above and has been the case elsewhere, Han migrant workers and their families were seen to be arrogant. (Few of the incoming migrants even "bother to learn the local language.") Uyghur resentment was then exacerbated when new housing was disproportionately allocated to the Han migrants (Rudolph and

Szonyi 2018, p. 39). This situation feeds the argument among disgruntled locals that the rebuilding of urban areas benefits Han companies and immigrants while extinguishing Uyghur architectural inheritance and offering little, if any, benefit to local Uyghur residents. (There is debate over whether the new concrete buildings are "Han-style constructions" or "simply modern buildings, an inevitable part of modernization" [Leibold 2013, p. 14].)

In addition to the issues canvassed above, the nascent ethnic minority middle class in Xinjiang that (in spite of bias against local residents) has managed to grow on the back of investment funding flowing into the region "complain that [even] they are treated as inferior to the Han Chinese and have comparative limited opportunities for social mobility" (Odgaard and Nielsen 2014, p. 547). These local Xinjiang residents (usually urban-based Uyghurs and some Kazaks) are members of "an entrepreneurial class" that is emerging among most of China's ethnic minorities (Dorsey 2018). They depend on and gain immediate benefit from investment, but they too are denied *equal* benefit compared to that afforded to Han immigrants. More pessimistic scholars have noted this situation and then identified the growing ethnic entrepreneurial class as a group ripe to "become a future source of popular uprising" (Odgaard and Nielsen 2014, p. 547; Mackerras 2005, pp. 818 and 824).

It is not surprising that "many Uyghurs say they resent Han rule." They resent many aspects of government policy, particularly the disproportionate use of force. They resent government intimidation and increasing surveillance and "reeducation." They resent increasing government resistance to their religious and cultural identity and practices. They resent "the reaping of their homeland's resources," and they resent Han immigration and disproportionate Han opportunity and privilege (Wong 2014).

The Belt and Road: Xinjiang, China's Northwest Doorway to Central Asia

Xinjiang is now an evermore important part of China's land bridge to Asia. The region will (and is already) play a key role in the Belt and Road Initiative actively promoted by the Xi Jinping government.

China's Belt and Road has many faces, but at its core it is intended to ensure China's ongoing strong economic performance and "sustainable economic competitiveness" using investment, commerce, trade, and the promotion of transport and communication networks (Hong Yu 2017, pp. 354 and 355). Beijing's boast is that the Belt and Road has the potential to affect an area that "covers 55% of world GNP, 70% of the global population, and 75% of known energy reserves" (Godement and Kratz 2015). The Initiative has been aptly described as "a mega vision" (Xinhua, 28 March 2015; Godement and Kratz 2015; China Daily, 5 September 2018i).

Beijing's Silk Road Economic Belt (the Belt part of the Belt and Road) includes Eurasian economic corridors linking China-Mongolia-Russia; China-Central Asia; and China and the Indo-China Peninsula. There will also be direct Xinjiang-Western Europe rail connections, a Trans-Asia Railway connecting Laos, Malaysia, Thailand, and Vietnam; and then there are the Bangladesh-China-India-Myanmar and the

China-Pakistan Economic Corridors. The transport infrastructure either presently under construction, constructed, or intended includes rail and road infrastructure, oil pipelines, port facilities, aviation networks, cross-border optical cable networks, improved satellite information passageways, and transcontinental submarine optical cable projects. For Xinjiang with its long Western border abutting countries including Pakistan, Tajikistan, Kyrgyzstan, and Kazakhstan, the effect of the Belt and Road Initiative is considerable. Already, in 2017, 70% of China-Europe trains exited China from Xinjiang, and in 2018 Urumqi is expected to send 1,400 Chinese trains to Europe (Xinhua, 6 January 2018c).

Transport links are promoted by Beijing as a vital means of increasing interaction among states and facilitating regional integration. Transport links routed from and through Xinjiang are obviously "improving connectivity with Central Asian and European cities" (Xinhua, 6 January 2018c). The first China-Europe train left Urumqi in May 2016, and now three trains daily leave reaching 5 Central Asian countries and 17 European countries (Xinhua, 6 January 2018c). The Alataw Pass is the largest border land port in northwestern China. This port on the China/Xinjiang-Kazakhstan border saw more than 1,320 China-Europe freight trains pass through in just the first 7 months of this year (2018). The trains carried more than 577,600 mt of freight (China Daily, 17 August 2018g). Rail transport to Central Asia and Europe via Xinjiang is recognized as being more efficient and much faster than road transport or sea freight. It is deemed to be only 20% of the cost of moving cargo by air, and it is three times quicker than shipping by sea (Xinhua, 24 January 2018d; China Daily, 29 August 2018h).

The Belt and Road Initiative has also substantially increased Xinjiang's two-way trade with a range of countries bordering China, particularly with Mongolia, Pakistan, and Kazakhstan. Trade with these countries increased by 84%, 60%, and 49%, respectively, year on year in 2017 (Xinhua, 23 January 2017a). Last year, in 2017, machinery and appliances were the second largest contributors to export growth in Urumqi with items increasingly being transported on the China-Central Asia-Europe freight routes.

Orders are coming from a number of areas, including Central Asia and the Middle East. The head of the China Railway Construction Heavy Industry company's Xinjiang branch describes this market as "full of potential" (China Daily, 19 May 2018c).

Chinese government sources often stress Xinjiang's status as "an important hub" for the Belt and Road. The rail links noted above plus the direct air links between Xinjiang and Western European cities (e.g., the Chengdu-Urumqi-Rome route operated by Air China [China Daily, 1 September 2016a]) and a long list of other infrastructural projects, including an optical fiber link being laid down between China and Pakistan, serve to reenforce Xinjiang's "important hub" status (Xinhua, 6 January 2018c; OBOR, 2 February 2018; 4 July 2018e). Another large and important project involving Pakistan centers on the city of Kashgar. As a part of China-Pakistan Economic Corridor, "all-weather connectivity" will be established between Kashgar and Gwadar Port in Pakistan. The port is already partially operational. The port is charged with bringing a so-called sea change to the Arabian Sea.

Beijing sources note that Gwadar, located at the entrance of the Gulf peninsula, is "a major energy trade route between the Middle East and the rest of the world" (China Daily, 7 July 2018f).

In a Chinese government-approved publication, it has been pointed out that "many countries have achieved progress and prosperity after doing away with their geostrategic policies and focusing on geo-economic realities" and that Pakistan is now looking at its geo-economic realities that have been much improved through direct investment made available under the auspices of the Belt and Road Initiative. The result "will define and decide the destiny of generations of Pakistanis" (China Daily, 4 July 2018e). Yes – and a similar argument can be made in relation the Xinjiang. The geo-economic reality is that Xinjiang has considerable natural resources that have already been (and will continue to be) exploited for the nation's energy needs. Now, the geo-economic reality is that Xinjiang has a Western border providing vital access for a myriad of projects that form the basis of Beijing's Belt and Road Initiative. The result of this geo-economic reality will obviously also "define and decide the destiny of generations" of Xinjiang's Uyghur residents.

The "Three Evils": Splitism, Separatism, and Terrorism

Pronouncements from Beijing have long stressed that "Xinjiang is an inalienable part of Chinese territory." These pronouncements go on to declare that the Chinese leadership considers the preservation of China's territorial integrity to be non-negotiable and that Xinjiang "is rooted in the rich soil of Chinese civilization and is an indivisible part of it" (Xinhua, 13 September 2017b).

An increasingly resentful Uyghur population concentrated in a particular geographic area with their difference in religion, language, and culture presents a formidable challenge to the goals and rule of China's leaders. This is particularly the case when the solution the leadership stubbornly offers to the problem of Uyghur ethnic tension is (a) to further promote modernization and development, regardless of specific and local side effects of the policy, and (b) to impose social stability by force while making a concerted effort to "fight splitism [and] eliminate the influence of wrong ideas" (Xinhua, 13 September 2017b). The latter project, according to the Chinese government, relies on "strengthening national consciousness and civic education." These measures are said to be needed to "oppose ethnic splitism and safeguard national unity" (see Leibold 2013, p. 20).

Ethnic splitism is a quite widely used term within China in relation to ethnic tension, even though it has been argued that Beijing's propensity to see discontent as a separatist issue is "unhelpful" (S. Rajaratnam School of International Studies, 15 March 2012). The Chinese government's severe treatment of separatist action has led to a great deal of international criticism. Much of this criticism centers on accusations of human rights abuses, including religious persecution. It is widely recognized that ethnic unrest and tradition in Xinjiang are "profoundly religious" (S. Rajaratnam School of International Studies, 15 March 2012). Islam is central to Uyghur identity, and this means that Beijing views Islam as "a core obstacle to national stability," but government "regulation" of religion in Xinjiang "is not about the Muslim religion" per se. It is "about breaking the Uyghur ethnic identity" (Torrey 2017).

Western scholars and commentators are also keen to point out that "the Xinjiang situation is characterised by a lack of facts" (S. Rajaratnam School of International Studies, 15 March 2012). Outside media, particularly independent journalistrs, are usually barred from Xinjiang. The Xinjiang regional government has also initiated a legislated crackdown on dissent. Tight controls have been placed on domestic print and on-line media sources. Hefty fines, public criticism (and now quite possibly re-education) are to be imposed on "website operators who create, compile, spread, release or copy information considered harmful or false." The national Party approved *People's Daily* webside has helpfully noted that the measures adopted relate to content "harmful to national security" and "destructive of religious harmony" and content that "spreads ethnic hatred and division" or "seeks to overthrow the socialist system" (World News, 8 December 2016). At the end of the day, the bulk of relevant information comes mainly from two sources. There are the official Chinese-approved media sources, and there are Uyghur activists resident overseas with contacts (including extended families) living in Xinjiang who offer their views and information. The data provided is often difficult to reconcile. This difficulty in reconciling information has recently been played out before a panel informing the findings of the United Nations Committee on the Elimination of Racial Discrimination delivered at the end of August 2018. (It is the United Nation's committee's first review of China's Uyghur minority since 2009 [Reuters, 31 August 2018b]).

Researchers have used satellite photographs, and a survey of government construction bids to attempt to establish the scale of reeducation camps in Xinjiang. Their work has fed into the widely reported conclusion made by United Nations' sources. The latter is said to be based on "many credible reports" that there are as many as one million ethnic Uyghur dissidents interned in Xinjiang making the region into "a massive camp that is shrouded in secrecy, a sort of no rights zone" (Reuters, 13 August 2018a). A German academic whose work has been reported in the Western press has looked into the procurement contracts for as many as 73 reeducation camps built in Xinjiang with a total cost of RMB 682 million (US108 million), "almost all spent since April 2017." Researchers and commentators also draw attention to the extrajudicial status of the camps with detention based only on reports by police or party officials (Economist, 31 May 2018). For their part, dissident members of the Uyghur diaspora have appeared before a United Nations' panel arguing that there may well be as many as "1 million to 3 million in detention" (Reuters, 13 August 2018a). (Considered reports in the Western press note that "approximately 120,000 people" are held in the city of Kashgar. The city is reported to have at least four camps [Economist, 31 May 2018]). Overseas Uyghur dissidents have gone as far as arguing that "the Chinese government's goal is to completely erase the Uighur ethnic identity." By way of contrast, the deputy director general of China's United Front Work Department (Hu Lianhe), who is charged with overseeing ethnic minority affairs, has insisted that "the widely cited one million United Nations" estimate [of Muslim ethnic minority prisoners in internment camps in northwest Xinjiang] is "completely untrue" (Wall Street Journal, 13 August 2018).

It is reported that speaking on the 2nd day of the panel reviewing China's protection of the rights of ethnic minorities, Hu Lianhe turned to accusing "foreign terrorists and extremists of trying to ignite secessionist forces in Xinjiang." He added that this situation had led to "assassinations, arson and poisonings" (Reuters, 13 August 2018a). This is a version of the "black hands," hooligans, and foreign entities argument used by Chinese leaders at the time of the 1989 Tiananmen Incident. Beijing has accused overseas Uyghur organizations of inciting unrest with Chinese government officials warning that "foreign terrorists and extremists try to ignite secessionist forces in Xinjiang." These same officials note that "those deceived by religious extremism... shall be assisted by resettlement and education" (Reuters, 13 August 2018a).

Chinese sources have specifically accused the World Uighur Congress of inciting unrest in Xinjiang, but local Uyghur sources are keen to point out that protests and incidents "are acts of the local Uighur lashing out at Beijing's 'systematic oppression'" (S. Rajaratnam School of International Studies, 15 March 2012).

Academics and the international media have charged Beijing with attempting to promote threats to security based on the actions of outside forces promoting Uyghur unrest when it is "dysfunctional" government policies "rather than outside influence and the infiltration of foreign terrorism" that has resulted in ethnic protest (Xiaobing Li and Fuliang Shan 2015, p. 200). The government's foreign terrorism charge has, it seems, been a useful prop for the disproportionate and increasingly heavy-handed government use of violence, reeducation, and intimidation, though it should also be noted that a number of Chinese academics have stressed that "Xinjiang affairs are complicated." They recognize that "implicit support from some countries penetrates into Xinjiang from abroad." They therefore argue that Beijing must be made aware that it could have "to cope with ethnic tensions that may involve ethnic groups beyond China's borders" (Yufan Hao and Weihua Liu 2012, p. 225). The "connectivity" promoted by Belt and Road will obviously promote this situation, and at the same time, political stability in Xinjiang will be vital to the ongoing success of the Belt and Road Initiative.

Conclusion

It is a mistake to assume that substantially raising living standards among communities will extinguish "episodes and pockets" of discontent. In China funding and promoting projects to advance modernization and development will not provide an antidote to discontent from below based on specific issues. Indeed, the same development and modernization programs that ensure the ever-rising living standards of Chinese citizens as a whole, and so buttress the authority and legitimacy of China's leaders, have been a repeated source of grassroots discontent.

Beijing has had to contend with a catalogue of protests and unrest initiated from below. For example, in the wake of the 2008 Global Financial Crisis, groups of China's migrant rural-to-urban workers held a number of demonstrations and rolling strikes when their already low wage rates had been reduced further during the financial crisis and then not restored. The migrant workers returned to work when their wages increased and their working conditions improved (see Hannan 2017).

China's leaders have also had to recognize long-standing and persistent opposition and discontent associated with heavy-handed land acquisition, resource exploitation, and environmental issues.

Since the introduction of economic reform, modernization, and development, grassroots discontent has often been associated with widening urban boundaries and associated infrastructural needs. The "massive protests against construction of chemical projects" are an example of this situation. In 2013 discontent was "rising at multiple places across the country, indicating more people are seeking to block any growth that sacrifice[s] the environment and public health" (China Daily, 28 August 2013). Alongside grassroots resentment over environmental and public health problems caused by resource exploitation associated with urban and industrial expansion and pollution, there are ethnic groups who "have found that their environment has deteriorated sharply due to excessive mis-use and mining and a range of other resource related projects" (Xiaobing Li and Fuliang Shan 2012, p. 221). A clear example is the environmental pollution imposed on Xinjiang, including air pollution from coal mines that continue to burn and considerable pollution from projects converting coal to gas. There is also pollution from power plants and the misappropriation of groundwater, and, under the Belt and Road Initiative, there will be a substantial increase in the already extensive use of Xinjiang as a transit area for pipelines, railways, and highways. There is also a long list of exploitation and abuse of natural resources by Han Chinese interests in Tibet, including deforestation, inappropriate infrastructure, and polluting factories built by Han Chinese. And in Mongolia, where unrest has been relatively muted compared with Xinjiang and Tibet, hundreds have demonstrated when coal-mining vehicles "damaged the steppe and grassland and killed local people" (Xiaobing Li and Fuliang Shan 2012, p. 221).

Apart from the Chinese leadership's insistence on maintaining the integrity of China's national boundaries, the resource reserves and the geopolitical position of Xinjiang make the region crucial to Beijing's interests. "Xinjiang is the most important energy and raw material base in China, and also the gateway to the Silk Route" (Yufan Hao and Weihua Liu 2012, p. 224), but, in Xinjiang (as elsewhere), the Chinese government has missed opportunities to more effectively settle specific, in this case ethnic, discontent. Apart from the lack of redress for environmental pollution and a range of other environmental-related issues, there is a clear example of Beijing's lack of care in the presentation of its investment policy. Beijing has lumped all "privileged" investment and expenditure which afforded Xinjiang into a single category. In other words, funding has been provided without regard for the difference in investment in (a) resources and infrastructure primarily benefitting the nation and Chinese people as a whole and (b) investment in social infrastructure aimed at increased local education and employment opportunities, improved housing, increased agricultural output on smaller landholdings, and poverty alleviation primarily for the benefit of local (usually Uyghur) residents. There is then the added complication of entrenched Han chauvinism and preferential on-the-ground access to employment and housing enjoyed by Han immigrants. There is also what many Uyghurs see as the adoption of the insensitive implementation of policy options in relation to matters such as the provision of Mandarin language classes for ethnic students even at kindergarten level. Policy insensitivity has meant that Mandarin language classes have not been seen by Xinjiang residents as primarily a means of improving the future employment opportunities of ethnic minority students. The classes have provided opportunity for local ethnic residents, already unhappy and resentful of government policy and behavior, to present the government's Mandarin language initiatives as a vehicle for promoting language replacement. The policy is seen as cultural and linguistic assimilation and "the Hanification of education and language practices" (Torrey 2017; Zenz 2017; Williams 2008).

In relation to Xinjiang, and with regard to a range of other cases of discontent and unrest initiated from below, by far the greatest misstep by China's government is the ready use of force and intimidation against its own people. The use of violence to restore social order is, quite rightly, viewed by many as a sign of policy failure (Leibold 2013, p. 2). In today's China, disproportionate force is being used by government agencies, and stronger and stronger government management has been used to control increasing ethnic tension, particularly in Xinjiang. It is in this context that a number of academics and commentators within China publically argue that the use of force by government entities is not handling problems "properly." They warn that "under the current growth model whereby problems are not handled properly, economic growth would not be sustainable and [more wide-spread] social crisis may follow" (China Daily, 28 August 2013).

With government-sponsored violence and intimidation ratcheting upward, Xinjiang's ethnic Uyghur population have been paying a very high price for the pressure their unrest and resentment have put on "national unity" and on the legitimacy of the Chinese leadership, but Beijing is not heeding the advice of its own well-meaning intellectuals and advisers who argue that "the Xinjiang issue" must be handled "delicately with extra care." This is the only way "to make sure it does not turn into a time bomb..." (Yufan Hao and Weihua Liu 2012, p. 225).

China's leaders have based their political authority on their claim that they know the interests of their people better than the people themselves. They must continue the process of modernization and development with its attendant increased living standards for the majority (particularly for the urban elite resident in China's eastern provinces) if they are to meet their people's overall expectations and so buttress their leadership credentials. At the same time, there is a high price paid by those who oppose particular issues and have specific grievances and especially by Xinjiang's Uyghur ethnic group.

References

BBC Report (2014) Xinjiang unrest: China raises death toll to 50. September 26. http://www.bbc.com/news/world-asia-china-29373158

Bequelin N (2014) Q & A: Nicholas Bequelin on why tensions are rising in Xinjiang and beyond. New York Times. May 2. https://sinoshpere.blogs.nytimes.com/2014/05/02/q-a-nicholas-bequelin-on-why-tensions-are-rising-in-xinjiang-and-beyond/

China Daily (2011) Communist party brings unity to the ethnic minorities. March 17

China Daily (2012) Country approves 25 subway projects. September 7
China Daily (2013) Deepening reform to drive progress, avoid crisis. August 28
China Daily (2016a) Direct air route to link Xinjiang with West Europe. September 1
China Daily (2016b) China trains more ethnic language-speaking judges. September 2
China Daily (2017) Auction of oil, gas sites to boost energy exploration in Xinjiang. December 15
China Daily (2018a) CNPC natural gas output increases. February 9
China Daily (2018b) Metro construction underway in Urumqi. March 12
China Daily (2018c) How can China achieve high-quality growth? May 19
China Daily (2018d) Human rights improve in Xinjiang experts say. June 27
China Daily (2018e) Economic corridor to bring prosperity to region. July 4
China Daily (2018f) BRI – a mega initiative for peace, harmony and prosperity. July 7
China Daily (2018g) In brief. August 17
China Daily (2018h) Belt and Road – a unique platform for exchanges. August 29
China Daily (2018i) Belt and Road Initiative in five years. September 5
China.org.cn (2018) Xinjiang's natural resources. July 8. http://www.china.org.cn/english/MATERIAL/139230
Dillon M (2018) Lesser dragons minority peoples of China. Reaktion Books, London
Dorsey JM (2018) China's policies spur Central Asians to cautiously chart independent course. https://www.academia.edu/37114803/Chinas-policies-spur-Central-Asians-to-chart-independent-course
Economist (2018) China has turned Xinjiang into a police state like no other. May 31. https://www.economist.com/briefing/2018/05/31/china-has-turned-xinjiang-into-a-police-state-like-no-other
Godement F, Kratz A (2015) "One belt, one road": China's great leap outward. European Council on Foreign Relations, China Analysis. June 10. https://www.ecfr.eu/publlications/summary/one-belt-one-road-chinas-great-leap-outward3055
Han E, Palmer J, Barnett R, Bequelin N, Millward JA, Harris R, Leibold J, Bulag UE, Hill N, Sperling E, Shakya T, Yeh ET (2014) Are ethnic tensions on the rise in China? China File Conversation. February 13. http://www.chinafile.com/conversation/are-ethnic-tensions-rise-china
Hannan K (2017) China's migrant workers and the global financial crisis. In: Crinis V, Vickers A (eds) Labour in the clothing industry in the Asia Pacific. Routledge, London/New York, pp 97–118
Hillman B, Tuttle G (2016) Ethnic conflict and protest in Tibet and Xinjiang. Columbia University Press, New York
Hong Yu (2017) Motivation behind China's "one belt, one road" initiatives and establishment of the Asian infrastructure investment bank. J Contemp China 26(105):353–368
Kuo MA (2017) Uyghur Biodata collection in China. The Diplomat. December 28
Leibold J (2013) Ethnic policy in China is reform inevitable? Policy studies 68. East West Center, University of Hawaii, Hawaii
Mackerras C (2003) China's ethnic minorities and globalisation. Routledge/Curzon, London/New York
Mackerras C (2005) China's ethnic minorities and the middle classes: an overview. Int J Soc Econ 32(9):814–826
NPR News (2017) Wary of unrest among Uighur minority, China locks down Xinjiang region. September 26. https://www.npr.org/sections.parallels/2017/09/26/553463964/wary-of-unrest-among-uighur-minority-china-locks-down-xinjiang-province
OBOR (One Belt One Road) (2018) Europe, investment priority in Xinjiang in 2018. February 2
Odgaard L, Nielsen TG (2014) China's counterinsurgency strategy in Tibet and Xinjiang. J Contemp China 23(87):535–555
PRC [People's Republic of China] State Council White Paper (2009) China's ethnic policy and common prosperity and development of all ethnic groups. PRC State Council Information Office, Beijing. September 27
Reuters (2018a) China rejects allegations of detaining million Uighurs in camps in Xinjiang. August 13. https://www.reuters.com/article/us-china-rights-un-uighurs/china-rejects-allegations-of-detaining-1-million-uighurs-in-camps-in-xinjiang-idUSKBN1

Reuters (2018b) Reproduced as a million Uighurs perishing in China's re-education camps: UN in The Australian. August 31

Rudolph J, Szonyi M (eds) (2018) The China questions. Harvard University Press, Cambridge, MA

S. Rajaratnam School of International Studies (RSIS) (2012) Domestic security in China: the Xinjiang Quagmire. March 15. https://www.rsis.edu.sg/rsispublication/rsis/1706-domestic-security-in-china-th/

Sautman B (1998) Preferential policies for ethnic minorities in China: the case of Xinjiang. Nationalism Ethn Polit 4(1–2):86–118

Sautman B (2010) Scaling back minority rights: the debate about China's policies. Stanf J Int Law 51:46–121

Sixthtone.com (2018) Xinjiang overexploiting natural resources. Inspectors Say. January 4. http://www.sixthtone.com/news/1001496/xinjiang-overexploiting-natural-resources%2C-inspectors-say

The Australian (2018) Beijing defends Uighur record. September 12

Time (2014) China now says almost 100 were killed in Xinjiang violence. August 4. http://time.com/3078381/thina-xinjiang-violence-shache-yarkand/

Torrey Z (2017) The human costs of controlling Xinjiang. The Diplomat. October 10. https://thediplomat.com/2017/10/the-human-costs-of-controlling-xinjiang/

Wall Street Journal (2018) Reproduced as Beijing denies its detaining a million Uighurs in The Australian. August 13

Williams EE (2008) Ethnic minorities and the state in China: conflict, assimilation, or a "third way"? Paper presented to Canadian Political Science Association (CPSA). https://www.cpsa.acsp.ca/conference-pres-2008

Wong E (2014) China invests in region rich in oil, coal and also strife. New York Times. December 20. https://www.nytimes.com/2014/12/21/world/asia/china-invests-in-xinjiang-region-rich-in-oil-coal-and-also-strife.htm/

World News (2016) China imposes hefty fines for fake or harmful news in Xinjiang. tvtsonline. December 8. https://tvtsonline.com.au/wn/news/china-imposes-hefty-fines-fake-harmful-news-xinjiang/

Xiaobing Li, Patrick Fuliang Shan (eds) (2015) Ethnic China. Lexington Books, New York/London

Xinhua (2015) Xi on "Belt and Road" – not China's solo but inspiring chorus. March 28

Xinhua (2017a) Xinjiang imports soar in 2017. January 23

Xinhua (2017b) Top political advisor addresses ideological issues about Xinjiang. September 13

Xinhua (2018a) Xinjiang closes over 100 small collieries in 2017. January 20

Xinhua (2018b) Tarim oilfield sends 200b cubic meters of gas to E China in 13 years. January 2

Xinhua (2018c) 700 China-Europe trains pass through Xinjiang in 2017. January 6

Xinhua (2018d) China-Europe trains connect Xinjiang to world. January 24

Xinhua (2018e) More than 300,000 people lifted out of poverty in Xinjiang in 2017. January 26

Xinhua (2018f) China invests heavily to upgrade rural power grid in Xinjiang. February 26

Xinhua (2018g) Xi stresses focus of developing high-quality economy. March 5

Xinhua (2018h) Xinjiang becomes major power supplier. March 20

Xinhua (2018i) China spends heavily on extinguishing coalfield fires. March 21

Xinhua (2018j) Xinjiang builds 80,000 houses for rural poor. April 6

Xinhua (2018k) Mandarin education available for 96% of Xinjiang kindergarten students. May 24

Xinhuanet (2018) Xinjiang to invest 70 billion USD in infrastructure in 2018. January 5. http://www.xinhuanet.com/english/2018-01/05/c

Yufan Hao, Weihua Liu (2012) Xinjiang: increasing pain in the heart of China's borderland. J Contemp China 21(74):205–225

Zelcer-Lavid M (2018) Why didn't Chinese investment ease ethnic tensions in Xinjiang? Begin-Sadat Center for Strategic Studies. https://besacenter.org/perspectives-papers/china-investment-xinjiang/

Zenz A (2017) Problematic privilege in Xinjiang. The Diplomat. June 5

Ethnicity and Class Nexus: A Philosophical Approach

55

Rodrigo Luiz Cunha Gonsalves

Contents

Introduction: Ethnicity and Class as a Necessary Tension	1034
Ethnicity and Class, Ethnicity or Class, Ethnicity with Class, and Ethnicity Without Class	1038
A Psychoanalytic and Philosophical Contribution	1044
Get Out and the Topic of Body Snatchers: A Philosophical Case Study	1048
Between "Internal" and "External": The Fundamental Question of Body Snatchers	1051
The Badiouian Procedure of the Generic and the Double Inscription Between Ethnicity and Class	1056
Conclusion	1059
Cross-References	1060
References	1060

Abstract

The following chapter aims at a critical comprehension of ethnicity and class through a philosophical approach. Instead of an exhaustive account, this chapter examines only recent portrayals of these notions in philosophy, science, and film. Having this proposition in mind, this chapter follows different stages of critical comprehension concerning these terms. Thus, ethnicity and class are put under a critical lens as scientific categories in general and specifically as categories for human sciences, as associational elements, specifically through a psychoanalytic reading of a recent cultural production, the film *Get Out* (2017), and finally as a philosophical case study of the Badiouian notion of the generic. Furthermore, this chapter will discuss the need for opening ethnicity and class as categories for thinking to further explorations conditioned by the idea of political procedure.

R. L. C. Gonsalves (✉)
European Graduate School (EGS), Saas fee, Switzerland

University of Sao Paulo (IPUSP), Sao Paulo, Brazil
e-mail: rodrigo.gonsalves@egs.edu

The chapter also explores psychoanalysis and psychoanalytic formulations in order to examine subjectivity, ethnicity, and class. This means to discuss their approximations and disparities regarding different theoretical points of view, having Badiou's *communist hypothesis* at the horizon of possibility in the name of political creations. Through a critical short-circuit between these various instances, this chapter presents important questions regarding sociability and alterity.

Keywords

Ethnicity · Class · Psychoanalysis · Philosophy · Ethics · Fantasy · Uncanny · External intimacy (extimacy)

Introduction: Ethnicity and Class as a Necessary Tension

It is important to formulate a philosophical approach to ethnicity because to engage with such notion usually produces more questions than necessarily provides solid answers. So, instead of thinking of ethnicity as a safe conceptual place, as a common and given notion to be used within humanities, social and human sciences, or even philosophy itself, the intention here is to provoke such notion. The first level of this complex theoretical formation is that ethnicity as a question, encapsulates an intriguing ontological clash between negativity and substance (Moder 2017), something like the philosophical actualization of thinking about being and nonbeing. In an overly simplified exposition, negativity concerns the affirmative incompleteness of being, while substance would concern an ontological render on objecthood. To put it in order words, to think about ethnicity will always request a discussion about being in a deeper sense. And why take a philosophical preference? Remembering that philosophy is a realm that thrives through formulating questions that need to be asked but also chasing suitable thoughts to answer to them. So, it can be said that the relevance of this text is to take a step back in order to be able to move forward. To take a step back in the name of *thought*, so anyone interested in *thinking* about ethnicity instead of *repeating* known mottos and dogmas, could perhaps find in this text some thought-provoking directions. Remembering that ethnicity from a philosophical standpoint is a place of tension, its struggle is not only determined because of the history of colonization and neo-colonization but also because it is the conceptualization of a *political procedure* which encapsulates *par excellence* a clash between negativity and substance (Moder 2017). The current narrative of ethnicity revamps questions about being but only if one manages to hear it from *beyond* the place of identitarianism – only allowing room for a discussion of the *common* focused on those who are excluded from this conversation. This is why Marxism is still on the table concerning ethnicity. Remembering that ethnicity without economical critique easily makes room for cheap Nationalism or a populist narrative, and historically such direction only led to terror and more social domination. Fundamentally, this exploration finds its relevance by defending that ethnicity without a proper anti-capitalist and class-struggle comprehension will never fulfill an *idea* of ethnicity. Or perhaps even better, this text proposes a bold axiom: *the idea ethnicity will only be fulfilled if conditioned to the Badiouian communist hypothesis.*

Conditioning one idea with another seems treacherous, but without a proper critique of capitalist realism (Fisher 2009) and without sustaining an anti-capitalist commitment, ethnicity as a political procedure risks falling over and over between the cracks of economical domination. If ethnicity aims at the political procedure concerning otherness, then the *idea* of communism should be its main goal – this is the main argument defended throughout this chapter. The Badiouian argument of the idea of communism aims at supporting Marx's political truth which appears on the side of "genericity" and not on the side of the particular. Therefore, the chapter defends to possibility of thinking ethnicity from the standpoint of genericity aiming at a Marxist political truth, instead of chasing down the small differences of the particular. As Badiou states: "'Generic', for Marx, names the becoming of the universality of human being, and the historical function of the proletariat is to deliver us this generic form of the human being. So in Marx the political truth is situated on the side of genericity, and never on the side of particularity" (2015, p. 53).

Considering this definition to guide a discussion of ethnicity towards genericity must act as the combination of political procedures against the logic of exchange and production under capitalism, so that ethnicity could conceptually become what it could be. Remembering that Badiou does not necessarily discuss ethnicity per se or is necessarily known as thinkers of this "field." The present chapter is an original attempt to reinvigorate the Marxist root already present in discussions of ethnicity but considering creation, invention, and desire towards the *idea of communism* (2009) provided by the French thinker against the capitalist establishment.

This chapter aims at discussing ethnicity without automatically starting from the current trend of identitarianism. Not to disregard it or to necessarily ignore it but because it chooses to originally consider what seems like a different line of thinking about ethnicity and class. The chapter will consider a Marxist appreciation for political questions of nowadays concerning ethnicity, suggesting the specific hypothesis that there is no proper or full consideration of ethnicity *without* a structural critique of capitalism. Therefore, this chapter considers ethnicity through the notion of *class*, and further, it understands how such articulation could provide a socially relevant notion of engagement to guide local militancy instead of only considering identitarianism as the sole locus for a transformation. This does not mean that the militancy inspired by identitarianism is somehow meaningless or less important – on the contrary, it exposes crucial contradictions of a given social conjuncture. Nonetheless, there are deadlocks surrounding ethnicity approached by identitarianism, especially when other social tensions arise to this discussion, e.g., tensions from class-struggle. The present chapter wants to defend how profoundly complex the nexus between class and ethnicity, which permeates our social fabric, really is.

The aims for this discussion are the following: first, to explore questions of normativity as one theoretical pathway of framing reality and its issues. Second, to formulate an ontological discussion through philosophy and psychoanalysis for ethnicity and class, in order to properly examine the constitution of subjectivity concerning these two notions, the third stop shows how fantasies play their part in such constructions. The fourth stop uses cultural productions to exemplify the embedded contradictions within ethnicity and class, aiming at critically analyzing it. To reach the final stop, which is to illustrate how the Badiouian understanding of "generic humanity" or *genericity* for the French thinker provides the theoretical tools to consider the necessary tension between ethnicity and class. Let us start by clarifying that for Badiou, genericity concerns his comprehension of Marx's *political truth* through mathematics, which propels means to think and to change social contradictions. Therefore, actualizing the conditions of struggle towards local transformations. Thus, turning something impossible in a given reality into a necessary possibility for radical transformation (or to put in Badiouian terms, to sustain the fidelity to an *event*). Here, why invite Badiou's philosophical work to discuss ethnicity and class? Since Badiou is known as the philosopher of the Idea, that he defends the action of thought and the crucial practice of thinking. It only seems pertinent that ethnicity and class should be properly thought of. More specifically, because Badiou defends local political transformations through militancy of thought, considering the radical hypothesis of communism as an Idea and not as an Ideal in the face of deadlocks. An argument which will be developed throughout this chapter. What does this mean to ethnicity and class? Fundamentally, it means that one theoretical bridge between both concepts can be consolidated but also crossed through political procedures of militancy towards "generic humanity." Remembering that "generic humanity" is the name given by Marx to explain humanity movement towards self-emancipation.

In an article about social class, ethnicity, and education performance, McCallum and Demie (2001, p. 158) present evidence that "...there are strong relationships between social background measures and GCSE (General Certificate of Secondary Education) performance," and also that "[w]hatever the pupil's ethnic background, those from 'more advantageous' social backgrounds perform better than others." What does this mean? On one hand, to be able to work with empirical data, especially for certain fields of study, like education or sociology, is not only interesting but fundamental. On the other hand, when working within the framework of the human sciences, one is confronted with deep problematic methodological choices and consequences. Good science is always science which can be criticized (Kuhn 1970) and problematized, otherwise it simply cannot sustain the possibility of reinvention. Put simply, good science asks good questions. Good questions entails that knowledge construction, through the workframe of the sciences, is a well-established construction of our present reality. However, if the point of criticism is taken seriously, one should consider a broader approach epistemologically and ontologicallly. For example, to cross a theoretical bridge between philosophy and mathematics not only requires efforts of formalization but also grappling with the consequences to both fields involved, which means facing the limitations of the fields we involve ourselves within. To defend a critical render of these categories means to be able to consider its validity from within different fields of knowledge.

Ethnicity and class are two singular fields embedded and constructed within a range of ontologies and disciplines. The most obvious consequence is that each concept converges and diverges with not only the other but also with other concepts which enable them to emerge and be understood. It is easy to fall into naive, simplistic, and taken for granted assumptions of each concept. It is a relatively seductive trap to fall into – after all, ethnicity is usually understood as essential and class as essentialized. By naive understanding, we mean any type of comprehension that aims to brutally repress diverse approaches to these terms. So, the second necessary point is not being afraid of taking a more philosophical approach when undertaking critical analysis; basically, one should be able to take one step back, think about the viability of seeing such concept from a different point of view, and then, reapproach such notions or objects from a position which simultaneously holds contradictory or ambivalent perspectives together. After all, true ideas tend to divide rather than provide cohesive answers. For critical philosophers, no concept should really be laid to rest. Therefore, to be able to adopt a more critical view toward such notions will necessarily make room for more creative and insightful results regarding the knowledge produced from such procedure. And, in this sense, this is already taking a stand. To adopt a more philosophical critique within any field of study is not a gesture of compromise but rather a gesture of serious consolidation regarding knowledge production to understand life and living.

Canguilhem (1978), though his understanding of life, provides a constant warning against any attempt at normativity (*normativité*), since he defends how life is always already present at any moment of subjectivization and that such artificial gesture of cutting is never fully without consequences. It is a critical reminder which is filled with social potency, transcending the strict positivist scientific render and proving a fundamental obligation of paying attention to the urgency the configurations of life surrounding those investigating and producing knowledge. Almost like a well-warned criticism inherited from Nietzsche, when he famously points out how science faces difficulties if dogmatized as a religion, a point much further developed on another place (Estevão and Gonsalves 2016). This necessary detour sets ground and contour to the following steps concerning our two main terms. It is important to commence any conceptual undertaking of the terms ethnicity and class as linguistic categories – they tend to be articulated in a variety of ways, although their articulation is not always under scrutiny. Here again, we turn to philosophy as a way of interrogating how we use language, the consequences of our uses, as well as any possible potentials.

Following Mbembe (2017) who suggests the ambiguity of considering ethnicity as a signifier, on one hand as taken for granted, but on another hand, as a signifier which will barely scratch the surface of the historical contextualization, the social dimension, and the critical configuration embedded in this open-ended signifier. What does Mbembe mean here? He is suggesting that the concept and uptake of ethnicity is not so simple and is one that actually resists normative interpretation. This is especially so when we might dovetail ethnicity with class. One must notice both the importance and the risks of normativity; on one hand, the construction of knowledge indeed revolves around being able to find solid grounds in order to structure and construct itself; on another hand, one must be fully aware that positivism if taken as a sacred procedure, completely detached from the very own reality it allegedly tries to interpret, lacks the critical perspective necessary to problematize fundamental contradictions embedded in reality. To be clear, positivism does not purport to take position of criticality – rather, it is merely to describe and interpret in its repetitive form. Therefore, the efforts of methodology surrounding ethnicity and class are always going to find a proper reason to struggle against any type of blind classification (thinking here of Levi-Strauss' necessary break from the mold of ignorance from early anthropology/anthropologists), any kind of empty categorization and/or normativity, by understanding Canguilhem's (1978) affirmation of life within normativity as a mandatory "excess" and such comprehension will always require a short-circuit understanding of this open-ended notions.

Therefore, it is important that any exposition of ethnicity and class aim at a necessary critical perspective of thinking these concepts, as not merely words to sustain a positivist comprehension but rather important linguistic categories which also address how it is vital to consider a multiplicity of elements when addressing or attempting to produce knowledge concerning each category. More specifically, by discussing these categories, it is important to undertake a philosophical consideration which ponders them through dialectical materialism prior to intersectionality.

Ethnicity and Class, Ethnicity or Class, Ethnicity with Class, and Ethnicity Without Class

First, let us clarify our terms, in order to go through their many possible combinations. Although the discussion about this ethnicity is broad, this section does not aim at exhaust it, but we must start from somewhere, so let us consider with the valuable contribution of Levi-Strauss. For the anthropologist, ethnology relates to the way how otherness and alterity are approached or perceived, therefore translating certain ethnographic perspectives. On his renowned work *History and Race* (1952), which establishes that there are no "intellectual superiority between any of the ethnic groups which constitute mankind as a whole" (p. 3), it becomes clear how ethnology relates to interpellation, means a certain political procedure of this relationship. And as Eriksen (1993) defends: "Ethnic boundaries are not sustained, moreover, because of traditional *cultural* differences, but because of political differences. Ethnicity is a political process by which people seek to form groups and to differentiate one set of people from another, by appealing to the idea of ineluctable culture difference... people can readily invent cultural differences if it is in their political interests to do so. Ethnicity is the pursuit of political goals – the acquisition or maintenance of power, the mobilization of a following – through the idiom of cultural commonness and difference" (p. 11). Therefore, ethnicity is context-bound notion, an interpellative procedure which sets subjective experiences of identification, group belonging, and a certain level of social formation. But, the key character of ethnicity is and always will be political in its orientation.

Second, in order to consider the notion of class, Eriksen also summarizes the Marx's notion of class:

> The Marxist view of social classes emphasises economic aspects. A social class is defined according to its relationship to the productive process in society. In capitalist societies, according to Marx, there are three main classes. First, there is the capitalist class or bourgeoisie, whose members own the means of productions (factories, tools and machinery and so on) and buy other people's labour-power (employ them). Second, there is the petit-bourgeoisie, whose members own means of production but do not employ others. Owners of small shops are typical examples. The third and most numerous class is the proletariat or working class, whose members depend upon selling their labour-power to a capitalist for their livelihood. There are also other classes, notably the aristocracy, whose members live by land interest, and the lumpenproletariat, which consists of unemployed and underemployed people – vagrants and the like. (p. 7)

Eriksen categorically states that three main classes according with Marx are the capitalist, the petit-bourgeoisie, and the proletariat. It is interesting interpretation, but orthodoxically rescuing Marx, it seems important to highlight that his notion of class comes from his critique to Adam Smith's political economic developments regarding social positions (Marx 1990). Smith defends that from the process of circulation, three main social positions will appear based on: income, profit, and salary. For Smith, value comes from circulation, and these three major connected positions concerning circulation, which are established from their appropriation of social wealth and how their subsistence relates to such positions. An argument which Smith forcefully tries to naturalized upon society, as the order of reality. And when Marx counter-arguments Smith, defending that value comes from production instead of circulation, and then formalizes the notion of surplus value, he manages to critically assert different class formations. For Marx, first establishes that the main classes are the capitalists, the proletariat, and land owners. It is on a second moment that the *petit-bourgeoisie* is addressed by Marx, especially because of all the nuances it requires as a class differently from the capitalists or the proletariat. For example, think of an entrepreneur who hired one assistant – does that turn him into a capitalist? Not quite yet. The main difference between bourgeoisie and petit-bourgeoisie regards quantity becoming quality on the manufacturing process, but there is no crystalline disambiguation between those two classes. Also remembering that Marx was concerned about the social economical context of England from his period of time. This is to highlight how context is crucial to address class but also to defend that the notion of class itself is much more complicated than any of their summarized attempts. It is a context-bound notion that must be cautiously applied.

But Eriksen formulates on ethnicity and class defending its high correlation (1993, p. 7), meaning that "there is a high likelihood that persons belonging to specific ethnic groups also belong to specific social classes (ibid.)." And he continues:

> There can be a significant interrelationships between class and ethnicity, both class and ethnicity can be criteria for rank, and ethnic membership can be an important factor in class membership. Both class differences and ethnic differences can be pervasive features of societies, but they are not one and the same thing and must distinguished from one another analytically. (ibid.)

So, this is as far as ethnicity *and* class could go, a certain analytical distinction of pervasive societal features. Fortunately, this sets the pathway to the next combination: class *or* ethnicity. Although both concepts sustain subjective experiences, could we confuse them? Certainly not. To substitute ethnic differences for class differences or the other way around, the kind of result would be remarkably different. For instance, suffering experienced from class differentiation and the suffering experienced from ethnic differentiation is notably different because they are structurally distinctive. The different suffering which surface from different causes entails the impossibility of completely subsumming both as the same.

Now considering ethnicity *with* class, let us consider a black board with two circles written upon it. The first circle is the set of ethnicity, and the second circle is the set of class. What would happen if someone decided to list everything, that is what constitutes the character of each, which both sets contain? And in this process, move on listing all the possible predicates contained by both sets. Well, what would happen is that, eventually some elements would simultaneously appear on both sets – which means that these sets overlap on certain elements. So, building a political ideas based on philosophical precepts is important to understand how the concepts of ethnicity and class are taken up outside of philosophy and become politically mobile. Although it seems like trying to capture ghosts, ethnicity *with* class, as a double tension, allows social contradictions to surface and point out as directions for militancy to provoke local transformations. If, on one hand ethnicity *without* class might sustain punctual transformations and enforce performative actions regarding the contradiction they denounce; on another hand, it also could force towards the troubling possibility of constructing an abstract class as an Ideal. In this sense, ethnicity *without* class, act as the two opposite sides of the same coin and by doing so, they obliterate each other. If the idea of approaching different individuals from many directions of the political spectrum over a certain demand, could sound interesting at first, the second moment of this combination between ethnicity *without* class tends to forget the proper material transformation needed and which conditions social disparity. Considering specifically the example of Brazil and the social movements of 2012 fighting against increases on public transportation, they did combined a range of individuals over the same demand. But, fast forward 5 or 6 years from that and we have is a country facing a wave of strengthened conservatism and fights against the solidification of racism and xenophobia. So, this section presents why building changes only from the standpoint of ethnicity will not viabilize the structural transformation needed to reinvent the social fabric of reality. Of course, palliative remedies will always help certain situations and all fights towards it are necessary, but this is far from dealing with a current place of exclusion produced by the capitalist structure, even less it aims at reinventing the economic structure that produces the social layer of the excluded.

Remembering that ethnicity and class are not concepts easy to conceptualize, especially because both are context-bound notions. And perhaps even harder, the previous argument presented how their crucial combination lies in considering them both *together*. Ethnicity must be considered *with* class, always tensionating each other in order to expose social economic contradictions and the locus of exclusion.

To think about ethnicity *with class* as a set of its own is also to consider many combinations of our core concepts, just like the title of this section suggests, it is just another way of phrasing the difficulties at stake. At the same time, both concepts are independent and not mutually exclusive, so to position them alongside each other entails an inevitable conflict, perhaps contradictions where one is confronted with not only the limitation of each concept but also the treatment of each as a provocation of the other. This is where the human sciences and critical philosophy may share the same project. Let us be clear, it is not reasonable to separate someone's life from its ethnic identification and at the same time, it is pointless to forget about those same individuals as contending with class-struggles or others with class privileges. If to a certain extent someone's experience of ethnicity is not conditioned by class-struggle, on a great extent, class-struggle conditions the experience of ethnicity. The main argument here is that this disjunction between ethnicity with and without class must be taken into consideration. Especially because Badiou trusts that a rebirth of History will not come from "barbaric conservatism of capitalism" (2012, p. 15) but from a "reawakening of the popular initiative in which the power of an Idea will take root" (ibid.), so it is about the invention of a new class that will name such transformation, that aims at the transformation beyond contemporary capitalism by resignifying old terms and notions, in order to structurally change today's material contradictions.

To consider what these terms have meant as historical constructions and with what does terms could mean should always have an impact on how one approaches them in the present. Here a critical approach regarding categorizations, it criticizes the binary colonialist definitions and also naive "post-ideological" comprehensions should be defended. As the ANSS (The Anthropology and Sociology Section) (2018) has done. When one find groups of classes and groups of ethnicities *all too well* grouped and 'neatly' defined, one should automatically concern with questions regarding the essentialization of both categories as necessary parts of social life. In this sense, the first mandatory critical step considering this terms is to have a proper discussion about the production of knowledge. For example, from the standpoint of sociology, Go (2018) presents a certain archeology of knowledge as derived by Foucault (2002) by mapping and discussing the main differences between knowledge produced and criticized, from colonial and postcolonial theories. "Go (2018) points out that some of the main writers from the field, proper names such as Frantz Fanon (1925–1961), Aimé Césaire (1913–2008), Amilcar Cabral (1924–1973), C.L.R. James (1901–1989), and W.E.B. Du Bois (1868–1963)" Go (2018, p. 2), was deeply influenced by Marxist theory and also that "[p]ostcolonial theory rather illuminates the *cultural* and related dimensions of colonialism—from race, gender, or sexuality to systems of knowledge and discursive formations—that Marxist thought either occludes or treats as epiphenomenal" (pp. 2–3). Go defends that the critical innovations from post-colonial theories are inspired by Marxist thoughts. He goes on to contend that, such theories are a step beyond critical sociologies of race and not a mere supplement, specifically because of its criticism of "empire and colonialism as constitutive of racialized systems and dynamics" (p. 8). The writer sustains that colonialism produced "race" and racial stratification, as well as he claims that it is fundamental to recognize the history of racialized domination as a key ingredient of the history of colonialism and empire. And therefore, to pay attention to this history is as fundamental as it is to critically understand knowledge. Such approach tries to overcome "the tendency toward parochialism and methodological nationalism in some sectors of race theory and research" (p. 9). Finally, Go defends that a postcolonial sociology of race derived from global-historical analysis could provide a proper render to local movements of resistance. So, all efforts are somehow still concentrate on seizing the means of symbolic production.

Revisiting Levi-Strauss and his comprehension that ethnology is fundamentally a political procedure, it is crucial to remember how he criticized racists' ethnographic perspectives and aim at exposing how it makes no sense to sustain an "imperialist" perspective towards otherness. So, one could defend that the conceptual "door," which allowed race and critique to racism to be mixed or perhaps confused with ethnicity, was left open by Levi-Strauss (1952). And it is valid to consider that his main critique to racism could have built these unproblematic synonyms between ethnicity and studies about race. But what is at stake here are social constructions through procedures of interpellation within modes of exchange and production. Race is not exempt of capitalist logic, even less is ethnicity. Consequently, an ideological naturalization of the state of things as reality for ethnicity and race might as well just be benefiting the capitalist project instead of finding common routes of escape from its vampiristic construction.

It is here that we might pause and consider how the concept of race has become an unproblematically synonymous with ethnicity, almost like a natural development of the understandings of race taking on the character of each and emanating from interpellation within the modes of exchange and production. Certainly, it seems that the concept of race has served the capitalist project and therefore must be considered critically as well (Mbembe 2017). Stauffer (1981) provides a parallel insight regarding class analysis and ethnic studies. Addressing some of the particular contradictions of Hawaii as a periphery of the USA, the author investigates why is it easy to find there "reactionary forces opposing class consciousness while striving to develop ethnic consciousness?" (p. 4). Stauffer defends that an apparent prosperity undermines a possibility of class consciousness, especially, when modern "liberal" writers introduce new signifiers such as: "ethnic identity, social mobility, assimilation, and integration," making it seem at least dubious to consider a class analysis when the focus is devoted to ethnic groups instead. It appears that many commentators on race and ethnicity are reluctant to problematize these concepts and understandings within and against a reading of class. Why might this be so? Castro (2006, 2014) provides a clue in his studies on pre-Colombian indigenous populations in Brazilian territory. For him, "[t]he 'Amazon' (like 'Melanesia' for other anthropologists) reigns supremely immanent, and the moderns thus have a lot to learn, and little to teach. The notion of a *nonconceptual* understanding of immanence is what allows us to perceive this perspectivist version of it, which helps feed the fire the latter started in the substantialism of modern ontology" (2014, p. 20). Such critical perspective on Anthropology builds from a particular approach to knowledge, where "...not only nature and culture but a series of its other master concepts – the subject, *habitus*, practice, history, ethnographic presence, etc. – can no longer be deployed without being extensively revised, and all the alien concepts they suppressed arise as the source of the change. Inasmuch as anthropology is metaphysics, it is wrested away from the categories of its origins, its belief that it alone is endowed with the right to final interpretations, and the ethnometaphysical underpinnings of its identity. It seems as though throwing a class analysis on a taken for granted concept, such as ethnicity pulls the rug from beneath the very knowledge production it relies upon. The pluralization is radical, with both the sources and character of thought multiplying." (p. 19) His *Anti-Narcissus* debate is an epistemological one, therefore a political debate and by criticizing the *aprioris* from colonialism, he ends up defending the necessity of decolonization of thought. The misrepresentation of Anthropology as a conceptual mirror image of reality is shattered by Castro's discussion, specifically when he debates how perverse such "representation" or "invention" of the Other, that is usually the exoticised Other, follows interests from the West (p. 40):

> No history or sociology can camouflage the complacent paternalism of this thesis, which simply transfigures the so-called others into fictions of the Western imagination in which they lack a speaking part. Doubling this subjective phantasmagoria with the familiar appeal to the dialectic of the objective production of the Other by the colonial system simply piles insult upon injury, by proceeding as if every "European" discourse on peoples of non-European tradition(s) serves only to illumine our "representations of the other," and even thereby making a certain theoretical postcolonialism the ultimate stage of ethnocentrism. By always seeing the Same in the Other, by thinking that under the mask of the other it is always just "us" contemplating ourselves, we end up complacently accepting a shortcut and an interest only in what is "of interest to us" – ourselves. (2014, pp. 40–41)

This point is rather crucial to appreciating concept building within knowledge production, since this critical standpoint is necessary in order to address ethnicity and class, escaping a more naive render of such notions. Further, Castro defends how such attitude towards thinking demands a *transformation of thought* itself, and this chapter does support this claim. In this specific approach to knowledge, we find processes of subjectivization, that is what it means to be a person in the world, at stake, processes that consider the relationship between sameness and otherness, the distinction between other and Other, without obliterating those parts of ourselves which we cannot fully know and yet form our character, our relationships, and life choices. In this sense, to approach ethnicity and class is basically to review and reinvent its own foundations – the precise function of knowledge production. Obviously, such a procedure will produce effects throughout different fields of knowledge and bring with these potentials and opportunities to consider concepts of life and living into new terrain. Considering the necessity of critically approaching the notions cited above, one could understand why is it key to visit the recent developments of psychoanalysis, specially from thinkers, such as Slavoj Žižek, Alenka Zupančič, Mladen Dolar, Alain Badiou, Todd McGowan, Jodi Dean, Aaron Schuster, Christian Dunker, and David Pavon-Cuellar, who are not blind to such insights and that genuinely provide critical tools concerning symbolic production and unconscious mechanisms of our contemporary lives, institutions, and society as a whole. The point is that we cannot and do know ourselves, each other, and the world we live in with consistent coherency, so the point of conceptual development is not necessarily to know but to content with not-knowing.

A Psychoanalytic and Philosophical Contribution

Christian Dunker (2015) developed a psychoanalytic tool called the "logic of condominiums," which is basically a deep psychological understanding of the construction of segregation through "protected" communities, contextualized in Brazil since the ending years of the military dictatorship, around 1973, but that still occurs until recent days. Presenting how the construction of the condominiums managed to hide the social disparities and the narrative of segregation using a type of symbolical hijacking of the narrative through marketing strategies. Also inspired by the Freudian notion of splitting (*spaultung*) which in short translates a psychic operation derived from repression (a kind of defense mechanism) where an egoic response to frustrated attempts to achieve satisfaction promote a certain egoic "division." Different structures of subject will respond differently towards this mechanism and the implications of such fundamental division of subject further developed by Jacques Lacan also integrate this logic. Dunker sustains how psychoanalysis provides key insights regarding subjectivity and conflicts of our time. He investigates how the construction of this "suburban" lifestyle framed a fantasy of accomplishment and social security for the middle and upper classes in Brazil (a logic which could also probably be found in many other capitalist countries, experiencing social contradictions...). For instance, one could consider parallely the aspiration of "suburbia" as a way of understanding contemporary ideas of ethnicity and class. Moreover, those who reject suburbia – and are thereby rejecting the class consciousness which accompanies this – do suffer, experience the anguish of late capitalism which is precarity. It is of no coincidence that in New Zealand, most of these people are Maori and Pacifika, or in Brazil where Guajajaras struggle with similar precarious conditions from capitalist impositions.

To contend with ethnicity and class entails engaging the psychoanalytic principles of recognition and self-recognition. To recognize oneself or another is a conscious realization which is subsumed within an inner narrative or monologue. This is a strange linguistic category but one we all engage within and serves to fortify or to repeal a certain subjective and social narrative. Further, it is a mechanism which is essential when sameness and segregation are considered into this subjective calculation: *where do I belong and who do I belong with?* But, how do we arrive at this subjective calculation and what are the effects? Considering the procedure of the Lacanian mirror stage, which establishes a fundamental recognition of one's self as "I," the psychoanalyst formally describes a movement from the pre-symbolic towards the symbolic order allowing narcissism to take place. Lacan developed his mirror stage as an *event* which occurs in the formative years of childhood. Prior to the recognition of oneself, the child identifies with the mother as the first object of the self – that is, there is no separation between the mother and the child. The mirror stage is both metaphorical and literal – in attempting to individuate from the mother, the child must separate, an anguish which is confusing because the foundations of subjective identity have always been in relation to the mother, the original Other. Once separation is initiated, recognition of the self is traumatic, because in looking at oneself, one cannot entirely recognize who they are. This important psychoanalytic process follows one throughout the lifetime unconsciously.

Such passage of (non)recognition not only introduces this imaginarized aspect to the subject (who I wish to be and thus will act in accordance to that will) but also invites this otherness to be always already within the subject. This subjective phenomena relates to the double prescription between ideal-I and the ideal of ego (Gonsalves 2016), and this will eventually lead towards different qualities of relation between the subject and the Other. So for Lacan, we are always split or divided between our ego-ideal and ideal-ego. Returning to Dunker's thesis, he defends that building up walls is an attempt that solidifies an idea of "protection" against the Other, much along the lines of Žižek's investigation of the *Neighbour* (2016) as a philosophical category which prescribes the efforts against the abyssal horrors of the Other's desire. That is, we have an ambivalent desire when it comes to the Other who we cannot fully know. In this sense, one can read how: "[f]or Lacan, fantasy provides an answer to the enigma of Other's desire. The first thing to note about fantasy is that it literally teaches us how to desire. . ." (2007, p. 47) elaborates Žižek. Therefore, the role of fantasy of the Other, fundamentally, is to tell me what I am for my others and the author further explains that:

> . . .This intersubjective character of fantasy is discernible even in the most elementary cases, like the one, reported by Freud, of his little daughter fantasizing about eating a strawberry cake. What we have here is by no means the simple case of the direct hallucinatory satisfaction of a desire (she wanted a cake, didn't get it, so she fantasized about it). The crucial feature is that, while tucking into a strawberry cake, the little girl noticed how her parents were deeply satisfied by the sight of her enjoyment. What the fantasy of eating a strawberry cake was really about her attempt to form an identity (of the one who fully enjoys eating a cake given by the parents) that would satisfy her parents and make her the object of their desire. (2007, p. 49)

It seems that in conceptualizing ethnicity, we are faced with many ambivalent neighbors. It also seems to be the case when contending with class. By understanding Lacan's (2001) formulation that our experience of "reality" occurs through fantasy, structured by fantasy, one grasps Žižek's comprehension of the protective function of fantasy against the raw Real and also sees no contraction on the statement that "the *reality itself can function as an escape from encountering the Real*" (2007, p. 57). For Lacan, the Real is the order of the not fully symbolized which includes experiences of horror and so on. But there is a double aspect of fantasy, an ambiguous double inscription related to how it serves as a screen against the encounter with the Real, but at the same time, cannot ever be fully subjectivized (p. 59). And this is the radical element of psychoanalysis, aware of such mechanisms finds its ethics through dialectically provoke a true awakening, as explains Žižek:

"For Lacan, the ultimate ethical task is that of the true awakening: not only from sleep, but from the spell of fantasy that controls us even more when we are awake" (p. 60).

For Badiou, philosophy and psychoanalysis have agreements and impasses and curiously this makes them both suited to discussions about social life. For him (2008), both philosophy and psychoanalysis agree that "every thought emits a throw of the dice. Therewith thought exhibits between itself and the continuity of the place the void of a suspended act" (p. 202) and that "thinking is made possible only by the void that separates it from realities" (ibid.). The disagreement between psychoanalysis and philosophy regard *where* both localize such *void,* claims Badiou.

So instead of leaving such impasse as such, the French thinker rescues Lacan and proposes a torsion to his developments in the form of a question: "How indeed can a knowledge of truth emerge whose whole being, or relation of being, consists in not knowing?" (2008, p. 207). His own answer is that "first, that the relationship of being is not reducible to knowledge; second, that there is possible knowledge about the truth of this relationship and third, that mathematics is the locus of the Idea." More importantly, he concludes that a peaceful relationship between both fields comes lies on his five theses. The first one states that: "Only mathematics is entitled to postulate that localization of the void takes place in being. There is no ontology than other genuine mathematics" (p. 209) and the fifth:

> Philosophy and psychoanalysis have a common border to two procedures that are external to one another: mathematics, on the one hand, and love, on the other. The knot of these components forming the outer border of philosophy and psychoanalysis consists in the localization of the void in the link, or the relation, that might be supposed to 'hold together' the Idea and the thing, or being the knowledge of being. Love undergoes the void of relation, because there is no sexual relationship. Mathematics undergoes it, because it exhausts it in pure literalization... If, finally, the common border of psychoanalysis and philosophy is deliaison, the localization of the void in the non-relatedness of every relation, the subjective category of this relation, you will tolerate my saying that its – unexpected – name is: 'courage'. (p. 209)

The "courage" supported by Badiou in the face of the non-relatedness of every relation should be the main line-of-thinking regarding ethnicity and class. Philosophy and psychoanalysis are realms that articulate with such void, proving themselves to be fitted to consider the radical exponent of both class and ethnicity but also crucial in the process of this consideration, since both realms deal with the political border at their own horizons. Perhaps one could consider the ethical the true awakening, as an awakening to the radical possibility of the idea of communism. A radical political procedure, a truth process in the name of the generic humanity, which radically should condition ethnicity and class.

So, how should we approach this awakening? Well the notion of fantasy prescribed above by Žižek explains how some responses to this phantasmagoric presence of the Other can be taken up. Such an encounter not only forces one to face alterity which is always already there (1) but also even more fundamental than that (2), presents the alterity embedded within our own selves. That is, a realization that we will never be who we think we ought to be. We will always live with lack and loss and this is the subjective anguish we will always carry. Further, we must in our relationships with others live with their lack and loss. Social relationships can be characterized by this very conundrum and certainly serves the foundation of the capitalist enterprise. This realization of lack and loss provokes the nonsubjectivized part of ourselves rooted within ourselves, as well as it poses the inaccessibility or the impenetrability of the desire of the other – we can never fully know what the other wants from us. For Dunker (2015), there are many different possibilities and strategies to better deal critically with this fundamental aspect of our subjectivity. But he focuses on some problematic responses, such as segregation, which is fundamentally an affirmation of fear towards the impenetrability of the Other's desire. And guided by fear, such affect is projected upon what Žižek calls the *Neighbour* (2016) who renders a fantasy of sameness that must be sustained *against* otherness, sustaining a "bubbled" lifestyle or an ideological protection of old values that never actually existed in the first place (because idealization plays an enormous part within this dynamic). So, through segregating the public space, by constructing condos, building more and more walls, none of that made such fantasies go away – a neighbor will always be on the next door or on the other side. Such vain attempt lead to different symptoms, all transformed by a life of constrainments (within the false prerogative of "freedom" – which is interestingly symbolized in the American suburban town where fences are absent between properties but barriers certainly exist) which Freud (2010) called the narcissism of small differences in his *Civilization and its discontents* from 1929. Thus, this logic of the condominium represents a structural symptom regarding the passage from the liberal towards the neoliberal way of life. And remembering that for psychoanalysis a symptoms is always a symptom of something. To locate this symptom also means the necessity of understanding the mechanism which operated its own formation. And in this case, idealization operates actualizing contradictions which are deeply marked by such division and this eventually will surface or return, materializing such paradoxical contradictions.

Žižek (2007) defends that the *subject supposed to believe*, as setting the background for *the subject supposed to know* as "a constitutive feature of the symbolic order" (p. 29). What Žižek is saying that we are well aware that we don't know, so we insert believe as a way of knowing which can only partially comfort us. This is nothing but a derivation of the subjective mechanisms which we previously described. Such double relation from within forces a kind of deadlock; on one hand, it sets the relationship between the subject and the Other and therefore to a certain specific experience of reality. But on the other hand, this experience will come with some traps, a rather dangerous and famous trap is the pursuit of a certain guarantee of one's desire in the big Other. The Slovenian thinker (2007) renders how this constitutive lack will forcefully present itself as a double condition for the subject, a double procedure which reactualizes the process of subjectivization through socialization, the introduction of the subject to the symbolic order. A more philosophical investigation of metapsychological elements makes room for these paradoxical complex relationships, remembering that for Lacanian psychoanalysis, the subject lies where there is no predicative and he answers to the Other through subjectivity. Žižek investigation of Kant's indefinite judgment on the distinction between "dead and non-dead(alive): the 'undead' are neither alive nor dead, they are precisely the monstrous 'living dead'" (p. 47) sets in motion a terrifying excess in terms of immanence, that after Kant becomes a concern to subjectivity itself.

Ethnicity and class are experiences of subjectivization. Both radically context-bounded and ontologically approachable through social and political procedures, they flood the subject with predicates that cover up, simultaneously, the genericity and the singularity of the human experience. And it seems that by noticing such fundamental "external intrusion" seems always already there from within and how fantasy presents itself in order to deal with this process of subjectivization, it makes sense to inspire a more interesting and useful discussion from the standpoint of a cultural figure: the body snatcher. Through literature and films, this creature illustrates the paradoxical duplicities of the human experience, but different from the *double*, a motif known to explore alterity within ourselves, the body snatcher approaches this discussion through the radical alterity. Both fictional creatures are opposite sides of a similar discussion. This creative formulation frames both the irrational responses towards the Other, as it presents the potential of a philosophical understand of the blurred lines in-between "in" and "out," within ourselves. Thus, the understanding of the *l'extimité*, a neologism coined by Lacan to describe the external intimacy, holds the paradoxical experience of alterity within ourselves, as well as it shows how the very own symbolic order has a nonsymbolized traumatic element within its own kernel. Therefore, both reversals are always dealing with negativity and incompleteness (Žižek 1989, p. 182). Lacanian psychoanalysis provides this interesting social-psychological formalization to consider the subject, but even further than that, it also provides from this external intimacy perspective, elements to problematize the stages of sameness – how can one claim a particular ethnicity in the first instance, for example? (Barros 2018). Here the *mirror stage* and at the introduction of the symbolic to the subject, always stumbles upon the lack, a fundamental experience of negativity. To claim an ethnicity means to claim a position and not to claim another, perhaps contradictory one. And as such, the impacts of overdetermination of concepts such as ethnicity through the encounters with this negativity will always impact subjectivity and the subjective response to the experience of otherness. But, on the other hand, ethnicity relies upon external fictions which hold it in the social order and it is this holding which is always under transformation. So one could always aim at operating on that level of uncertainty.

Get Out and the Topic of Body Snatchers: A Philosophical Case Study

Some artistic productions help illustrate paradoxical elements of the human experience, so taking films as thought experiments: what could they help reveal about ethnicity and class? Well, the film *Invasion of the Body Snatchers* (1956) inspired by Jack Finney's novel is a sci-fi horror classic by Don Siegel. It portrays the uncanny events happening on a North American small town in the 1950s and that still give us good reasons to be watch it or to re-watch it. The film shows us the story of this idyllic town, where citizens live their lives and routines at a calm and tranquil pace, just another simple town, which could easily be mistaken for any other classic portray of North American towns in films, TV, or Commercials, from that period. But everything is about to change, because all of the sudden, Dr. Miles J. Bennell (played by Kevin McCarthy), who is the town's doctor, learns that his community is being infiltrated by aliens. The extraterrestrial creatures are snatching the bodies of the current citizens and replacing them by duplicates. The lines between the "External" (the body snatchers aliens) and the "Internal" (local citizens, sustaining the ideological "normality") were already mixed. So, when Dr. Bennell actually notices the "invasion" – it has already took place. The aliens were always already here. Materially nothing has changed, and yet, everything has changed. So, in this sense, what did actually changed? What is at stake here at this invasion? The notion of uncanny is profound and desire a further explanation, but its conceptual validity lies on a discussion between intellectual confusion and an affect deriving from a clash between fantasy and reality for the subject. So, is it only by following the uncanny realization from Dr. Bennell, that we find this sense of deep anxiety and paranoia? These are just some of the provocative questions that this film allow us to closely investigate and they all do resonate directly to philosophical questions surrounding otherness, identity, self, ethnicity, class, and ethics.

Loock (2012) clearly illustrates the main agreed interpretation regarding this film, which is how it basically encompasses the social anxieties and the sense of paranoia surrounding North America during the 1950s facing external political and social transformations. The author also provides an interesting critical validity to this topic, once "...despite its cultural and historical specificity, the narrative of alien-induced dehumanization has lent itself to interpretations and re-imaginations like few others, always shifting with the zeitgeist and replacing former cultural anxieties with more contemporary and urgent ones" (2012, p. 122). So, in a sense, if one considers the social invisibility aspect displayed by the whole town towards these infiltrated aliens, and furthermore, how the film depicts the citizens as poor workers trying to live their lives, it seems only reasonable to consider Žižek's (2009) interpretation regarding class antagonism, ideological domination, and exploitation illustrated by the film. Considering Žižek's ontology of the *Neighbour* (2016) a proper comprehension of the weight behind what 'aliens' condenses, earns a much deeper sense – it becomes clear that we are aliens to ourselves and to each other. That ethnicity is constructed precisely for this unconscious function – not to necessarily unite a collective but to alienate it from other collectives – seems like a valid argument to be examined. One could even argue that ethnicity is not so dehumanizing but *desubjectivizing*. This line of thought requires a much deeper elaboration, which unfortunately does not fit here in this chapter, but is a valid direction to be further developed.

Developing further on the intersection of ethnicity and class, Loock's understanding about the multiplicity of cultural reappropriations on "body snatchers," one could also consider the English band Radiohead's song *Bodysnatchers* from the album *In Rainbows* (2008). It is a song that Thom Yorke said to be "...inspired by

Victorian ghost stories, *The Stepford Wives* and his own feeling of 'your physical consciousness trapped without being able to connect fully with anything else.'" (Pareles 2007). And although this song is not directly inspired by the film, it carries its name and even more curiously, the song describes quite acuratelly the *uncanninnes* (Gonsalves 2018) from the Žižekian ontology of the neighbour. There is a key passage from the lyrics which corroborates with this point:

> I do not understand,
> What it is, I've done wrong;
> Full of holes,
> Check for pulse,
> Blink your eyes,
> One for yes,
> Two for no,
> I have no idea what I am talking about,
> I'm trapped in this body and can't get out. (Radiohead 2017)

To have "no idea what I am talking about" and also, being "trapped in this body" not able to "get out" – just as is stated in the lyrics – is fundamentally a human experience and one that is shared between us. One could not only relate to such uncanny feeling provoked by moments such as these, but this inspired take makes room for a radical twist on the body snatchers from the film. If the film depicts this relation between the coordinates of the external and the internal spaces, while reinforcing the aspect of an "invasion," as if foreigners were "forcing" their ways upon the ones who were already established at the small town, the clever lyrics turns it upside down and twists it. So, the alleged "lines" separating the internal and the external are now blurred, once externality is clearly experienced from within. And even further than that, there is a double inscription at stake here, which involves both ethnicity and class. Therefore, the topic of body snatchers is much more complex and interesting as it seems, especially considering the topic of such "invasion" as a problematization of the external and the internal and its many different possible levels, without disregarding the double inscription mentioned earlier. The topic of the body snatchers sets a debate towards its own ambiguity which lies within the subject. This is different from the classic trope from the horror genre where a random dangerous intruder, usually a "serial killer" invades the reality of the hero and terrifying his or her life, and part of the torment is show how close the murder is to its victim, the killer taunts them by calling from inside the house... The sense of paranoia is usually the motif itself from the film, e.g., *When a Stranger Calls* (1979) from Fred Walton where the entire film surrounds the babysitter being terrorized by a killer who is calling from inside the house. But, this is a film that does not hold the formidable interesting ambiguity of such topic, especially if compared to "*Invasion of the Body Snatchers*" and its full potential to promote a debate regarding interiority or exteriority.

If films illustrate social fantasies and anxieties regarding alterity, they also show *how* alterity can and cannot be desired. Subjectivization considered as a process between interiority and exteriority must also make for to translate the contextualization of ethnicity and class at stake. Films and other cultural artifacts help us do that.

Between "Internal" and "External": The Fundamental Question of Body Snatchers

Now let us invite a more recent render of body snatchers that somehow encapsulates through its medium the heart of the discussion between ethnicity *with* class. A film which holds the full critical strength of this topic is the formidable film *Get Out* (2017) by Jordan Peele. The film considers the critical ambiguity of the relationship between inside and outside, internal and external, but it evades from a more binary understanding of the topic and approaches a certain psychoanalytic depth, almost a filmit portrayal of *l'extimité* (Lacan 2001). Or as Mladen Dolar (1991) clearly explains about this Lacanian notion that portrays the complex process of subjectivization regarding the relationship between interior-externality or external-interiority and which is nicely captured by this film. At this point, you need to bring it back to ethnicity and class – extimacy is the shape of both. The film basically escapes from a more simplistic comprehension on how subjectivity itself operates and it allows us to consider the fundamental distinctive roles between other (l'autre) and Other (l'Autre), within the process of subjectivization to a subject prescribed by Lacan (Gonsalves 2018). Basically, this is Lacan's (1997) comprehension of Freud's distinction between Other (*der große andere*) and other (*das andere*) with his Hegelian reappropriation through Kojève (Lacan 1998). What it means is that, without the radical comprehension of alterity, one can never fully grasp Lacan's *mirror stage* (2001) proposition and how this metapsychological development aims at explaining how the structure of subjectivity gets structured in the first place. This is one of the reasons why many authors such as Freud (2000), Dolar (1991), Žižek (1989, 2006, 2007, 2014a), Fisher (2017), Pfaller (2005, 2014, 2017), Royle (2003) as many others… explore the *uncanny* as a key ingredient to consider and think about the processes of subjectivization. As Žižek (2007) claims: "To properly grasp this strange process, one should supplement the fashionable notion of interactivity with its uncanny double, interpassivity" (p. 22). Therefore, to take a closer look at this notion seems fundamental, as well as the movie *Get Out* provides a great background to do so. And, the film does not only covers the double inscription concerning ethnicity and class at stake with the provocative understanding of *body snatchers* but it also pushes forward critical reflections concerning such notions. This redoubled experience of alterity for the subject not only invokes a complex consideration of ethnicity but also an understanding of the ideological "shape of consciousness." The constitution of consciousness, just in the same way that class does, must be engaged with an awakening towards genericity in the Badiouian sense – a point that the film could also help to illustrate.

This film is Peele's debut as a director, and on this first attempt, he seems to not only have managed to release a magnificent thriller but also redefined the genre with his critical view on body snatchers. The film revolves around the story of Chris Washington (interpreted by Daniel Kaluuya), a successful and renomend African-North American photographer dating Rose Armitage (played by Allison Williams), and they seem to share a comfortable estable middle- to upper-class lifestyle, with their SUVs (sport utility vehicles) and condos/condominiums. Everything seems better than fine, the couple relationship appears to be evolving and they decide to visit Rose's parents to introduce Chris to them. They get into the car to make this trip to the countryside and meet the Armitages (the parents are interpreted by Catherine Keener as Missy, Bradley Whitford as Dean, and Caleb Landry Jones interprets their son Jeremy), and right at the first moment of this trip, we can notice an interesting dynamic taking place, Rose is remarkably worried with Chris' health. Not necessarily his well-being but about his health, strongly asking him to quit smoking. But even more interesting than that, when the couple gets pulled over by a police officer, Rose aggressively talks back at the police officer, while Chris just wants to get back to the car and continue with the trip. Each moment of the entire film is pack with layers upon layers of clever symbolic elements, but this first scene sets the premise and the tone of the film quite accurately. First, it is highly questionable to still defend that we live in a post-ideological reality (Žižek 2016, pp. 43–44), and second, what it is to understand the Black as an open-ended signifier (Mbembe 2017).

The entire film works as a great critique to think about the dovetailing of class and ethnicity as an unresolved project and to those who defended that after the Obama era, the USA was actually living an epoch beyond racism or in a type of post-racial reality. But, concerning ideology, how could we properly approach such discussion? Well, "ideology does not reside primarily in stories invented (by those in power) to deceive others, it resides in stories invented by subjects to deceive themselves" (Žižek 2016, p. 97). In this sense, the film does capture a mandatory discussion of ideological nature when problematizes this point. And the deep horror which is captured in the film only gets more and more powerful with its cinematographic sequences. Once the couple finally reach their destination, Chris is trying to hold on to his usual self, but in every single opportunity of interaction between him and the Armitage, the resulted affect is creepiness (and even with his girlfriend Rose, that seems more and more ambiguous towards him, since they got in the house). The aesthetic of the scenario of the countryside house in its Colonial style with all the "helpers" which are African-Americans serving the white owners (the Armitages) instantly strikes the viewers with a feeling of a not completely gone and most definitely not forgotten reality of slavery. It is not hard to sense how slavery is culturally embedded into historical colonized countries and even more important, how many unrecognized elements of such brutal past are still far from being recognized. This more material level of racism is so "out in the open" that is even addressed by the patriarch of the Armitage's (Dean) in a conversation with Chris, his admission of guilt is a cynic one, which falls into on the Marxist formulation of ideology under a Žižekean perspective (2011) where one knows exactly what he is doing and nonetheless, does it anyway... This kind of willingness to participate in inequality is arguably the most bourgeois guilt and capitalism thrives upon it to retain itself.

Just stop to consider the poignant and horrific way in which ethnicity and class are currently intrinsically bound – the essentialized way in which each are depicted in relation to the other as natural and inevitable. That while this is a film, it provokes an imagery which is most recognizable to us. Such naturalization of the state of things, this essentialized approach to ethnicity and class masks their historical constructions, their ambiguities, and their tensions. The overall uncanniness provoked by the film grows with each interaction the family has with Chris. At a certain point, Chris decides to have a smoke in the middle of the night, he walks outside only to be startled and puzzled by one of the African-American "helpers" that came running towards, forcing Chris back inside the house. But this uncanny sequence of events finally takes a step towards its utmost creepiness when Missy Armitage, who is a psychiatrist, "invites" Chris to be hypnotized stating how this will help him to quit smoking. Although still, this distinction between from the general formulation of feeling uncanny towards the other to this particular creepiness seems to fit here. Žižek (2016) defends that the impenetrability of the desire of the other is what provides this creepy feeling. When "[a]n experience, an encounter, gets creepy when we all of a sudden suspect that he is doing something for a motive other than the obvious one" (pp. 81–82). And, a proper study aiming at the proper disambiguation between such qualities of the uncanny, ranging from the weird and the eerie by Fisher (2017) until the creepy suggested by Žižek (2016), for now we can definitely benefit from some of their specific distinctions. Well, when Missy asks Chris to "help him to quit smoking" and what she is doing is actually preparing him to be "sold" for his organs, for his body, in a new type of slave auction for millionaires. And here we can think about ethnicity and class as a desubjectivizing force which elaborates upon the project of capitalism – who is valuable is determined by those are the exploiters. An old and famous passage from Du Bois (1903) regarding double-consciousness and being Black in the USA is noted here: "It is a peculiar sensation, this double-consciousness, this sense of always looking at one's self through the eyes of others, of measuring one's soul by the tape of a world that looks on in amused contempt and pity. One ever feels his two-ness, an American, a Negro; two souls, two thoughts, two unreconciled strivings; two warring ideals in one dark body, whose dogged strength alone keeps it from being torn asunder. . ." (p. 2). But if we allow Mbembe (2017) explanation on his critique of Black reason, we can easily understand how this "internal" division of the self is much more complex and deeper. First of all, this double-consciousness is not completely consciousness, and second of all, it articulates between elements of fantasy and the Other. Approaching the "sunken place" passage from the film under a psychoanalytic standpoint, one must consider the "unknown known" which "form the transcendental horizon, or frame, of our experience of reality," or in other words, the Freudian unconscious (Žižek 2014b). An as explained by Žižek ". . .the 'unknown knowns', the things we don't know that we know – which is precisely the Freudian unconscious, the 'knowledge which doesn't know itself', as the French psychoanalyst Jacques Lacan . . . used to say. (For Lacan, the Unconscious is not a pre-logical (irrational) space of instincts, but a symbolically articulated knowledge ignored by the subject)" (p. 9). Agreeing what was previously presented, this passage from the film portrays the profound encounter with what it is to be Black and poor, not completely unprotected by screen of fantasy, but already showing precisely what one would or could feel if such duplicity from within got more known to the subject.

So, in a sense, *Get Out* is a film completely molded into the problem of *acting as if* we were all living in this post-ideological era, as if we were all having a great moment of post-racism momentum, something that the film heavily criticizes and remarks some of contradictions derived from this render of reality. We certainly live in racially aware times, but we still cast the Black other as unknown. Peele uses another great symbolic wit on the scene where we get to see the wealth and the rich getting to the mansion, where the modern time slave auction takes place. What we see is a huge majority of white people, arriving on black limousines.

But one must not forget that this is still a film about body snatchers or snatching bodies. Taking a closer look at other moments of the plot from yet another critical standpoint, the whole farce revolved around hiding Chris deep inside his own mind through the "sunken place" procedure while he is being sold to a wealthy blind man (played by Stephen Root). The rich man states "he sees no color," that he does not care if Chris is black or not, since he only wants to see through Chris' eyes, he wants to see what he sees. Such hijacking of one's gaze goes along the lines of a perverted expression of a disavowed type of ethnic envy and hatred, prescribed by Archer-Straw's (2000) as *negrophilia* (a conceptual comprehension of the binary diminishment of stereotypes concerning the Black, ranging between profound admiration/ love, idealization and fear/hatred, demonization). Considering the repercussions of this discussion is necessary in terms of subjectivization and otherness, relating the subsequent signifiers in the signifying chain of one's subject. But even more important, to risk having this debate disregarding the realm of ideology is to sustain that society and reality are beyond it, this standpoint is not naive but quite it is opposite, and it means keeping a harmful and dangerous agenda. If ideological elements are in dispute concerning the control of the main narrative, this means that is not a moment for more alienation.

After the body snatching procedure, Chris would have become Hudson's bystander for the rest of "their" lives, once Hudson (Stephen Root's character) becomes the new *owner* of this body. This is the body snatchers motif in its purest form, but instead of reading it as an essentialization of ethnicity and class – it must be understood as Mbembe's *becoming black* (2017) of the worker as such. In order for this body snatch procedure to be fully completed (the film calls this the *coagula* procedure), the hero must go through a certain hypnotic "brainwashing" transition, Chris' ego must become a repressed element trapped inside his body so that Jim's ego could take his place. While exposed to this procedure, the hero manages to come up with a plan to get out.

One could easily find the solution of the film; in other words, the way how Chris emancipates from his imprisonment a kind of post-colonialist praxis. And in order to escape from the hypnotic procedure that is being forced upon him, a procedure which is induced by sound, he must find a way to stop listening to the noise that triggers his hypnotic state and then, find a way out from the couch that he is strapped into. How does Chris manages to escape? He uses an element of brutal slavery and resignifies it, and he picks cotton from the coach which is strapped on, in order to cover up his own ears. So, the hero dives deeply into the social memory of a traumatic moment of brutality but only to find the necessary tools to emancipate himself from the dominant societal oppression caused upon him. He manages to get out, but throughout his entire journey, it becomes clear how ambiguous and complex all relationships established by the main character truly are. Although Chris did not had his body snatched, the weight of the uncanny white gaze (Fanon 1967) is felted upon him throughout the whole film and Chris is interpellated (in an Althusserian sense) (2014) countless times from standpoint of the *negrophiliacs*, always pushing him to try to satisfy their perverted curiosity under false pretenses and bias artificial "interactions" with any proper ethical consideration (Badiou 2013) for common grounds. So, how can slavery be thought of regarding the intersection of class and ethnicity? The hypothesis of communism provides us with the answer: the fundamental necessity to obliterate capitalist private property and the perverted commodification of material reality for wealth accumulation. Only getting rid of the material structural contradictions imposed by capitalism that brutal phenomena of domination shall stop surfacing into reality.

And even more profoundly post-colonialist, one could say that Chris' gesture to get out might even translate a critical understanding of Westernized knowledge and its colonialist binary ideological domination through exploitation, reinforcing the "us" versus "them" narrative. How? When Chris chooses to become the Ulysses of his own Odyssey, he resignifies the tools of oppression in order to get out from his imprisonment. By doing in so, he is to a great extent reinventing such narrative by revolutionizing the significance of "picking cotton" – basically, traversing a social traumatic historical narrative through a symbolic resignification. Such gesture could be understood as a resignification of knowledge itself, for instance, if one decides to consider that in the *Odyssey* (1999) the classic text from Homer, which is a well-known piece of literary history that marks the birth of Western anthropomorphized culture, his gesture of emancipation might be perceived as need for a different direction in terms of subjectivization. This is not such a wild parallel, since at the chapter XII of *Odyssey* (p. 345), the hero Ulysses is on a boat passing nearby Capri's Island, a well-known place to have mermaids that enchant sailors who jump under the water to meet their own demise. How did Ulysses manages to survive through such penitence? He makes his fellow sailors cover their ears with wax, while he straps himself to the ship's mast, without covering his own ears. Ulysses listened to the mermaid's enchantment and yet, managed to survive. But considering *Get Out*'s hero, when he takes hold of Ulysses' position, his gesture to escape aims at escaping from repeating the same discourses of rationality that led towards domination and also to found a deeper "unknown known" sensibility regarding reality. Chris' decision could perhaps be understood as a gesture of identification with the "fellow sailors" at the level of knowledge. And maybe as a movement which even obliterates the need for heroic sacrifices that sees no need to keep being repeated, perhaps an answer to the domination in knowledge and its discursive constructions. So, by not repeating the same logic of domination and for resignifying the instruments given in his material reality – even the most horrific and traumatic ones – Chris ethically revolts against the horrors caused upon him and manages to finally escape. Ending the film on a positive note, Chris gets out. This film offers a subjective insight into the problem of ethnicity and class as fixed concepts which have been taken up uncritically, but the comprehension of them as context-based and transformative, both conditioned by the political procedure towards the idea of communism provides the solution to its ambiguities.

The Badiouian Procedure of the Generic and the Double Inscription Between Ethnicity and Class

The film Get Out (2017) seems paradigmatic concerning this debate, especially because it presents many contradictions regarding levels of ethnicity and class operating simultaneously. In retrospect, the double inscription between such notions appears throughout the film in many moments. For instance, when Chris, an established artist that detains particular skills of abstract labor, is easily snatched to be sold just like any other commodity out there – he is not escaping or emancipating through the results of his labor – when he operates from the "inside" of the main narrative provided and framed by neoliberal capitalism, Chris has no escape and is already imprisoned. The double inscription explored here verses points of injunction and conjunction expressed by different contradictions. All militancy in the name of changes against exploitation are rather necessary, but the field of multiculturalism and their social struggle must also be able to organize themselves and translate those efforts to the political field. The character of Chris is a photographer inside of a film, is the one who captures images of the moving paradoxes of suffering under the capitalism. And the photographer portrays an image of some contradictions of today's struggles. Interesting enough, Chris finds no protection from within capitalism – it becomes clear, that acting from within this capitalist realism (Fisher 2009, p. 14), this shared reality under the hegemony of global financialized capitalism, Chris is just another living dead body turned into commodity facing the "meat grinder" of a brutal system of inequalities. He is at the same level at any other commodity and ready to be exchanged. It is here that the end of the film sounds amazingly fantastic (and perhaps, even inspiring...); Chris gets out. But one could plays devil's advocate here and ask, but does he really gets out? Well, to understand Chris' getting out, through identity politics – which is a necessary tactical move – still comes with contradictions, since it is not radical enough. Chris has not escaped from the false promises of protection under the capitalist narrative, even less from the capitalist contradictions that got him in that house of horrors in the first place. So, is it farfetched to consider the Armitage house as a metaphor for capitalism of nowadays? Could one perhaps consider that Kaluuyas' character Chris, should then demand for "this" impossible? Aiming at getting out from *capitalist realism*? For Mark Fisher (2009), capitalist realism is this inability of thinking beyond capitalist restraints, to move further its contradictions and vampiric conditions. What if, by encompassing a conjunction of ethnicity and class, Chris could inspire to metaphorically translate the role of the generic humanity (Badiou 2015)? Then by considering Mbembe's "Becoming Black of the World" (2017) main argument, one could find Chris' struggle for getting out, gaining its full radical meaning by considering it a fight for breaking out from capitalist restrains and demanding a new possibility.

Žižek's (2016) examination of the events that took place in Ferguson, a suburb of St. Louis (around August, 2014), provides the necessary depths of this double inscription. This is a poignant example of how the intersection of ethnicity and class combine to affect ideological catastrophe. When "the poor black majority of the town took the killing as yet more proof of a systemic police violence against them..." (p. 41), their lack of a proper program or a guiding fiction (contrasting to the riots from May 1968, for example) turned into outbursts and riots, taking the streets and demanding justice. But Žižek proposes that such "vague" claim can only fit a type of Benjaminean materialization of divine justice. What does this mean? Of course this does not mean that their claims are unjustified or that taking the streets facing such situation is an inadequate response. The real issue lies someplace else in this discussion, and it illustrates the contradiction of our double inscription. For instance, the frustration expressed by those outbursts meet the surface of reality to declare a revolt against social disparity and these moments seem to solidify a symptom of the contradictions faced by those who celebrate the "freedom of choice" when in reality "the only choice is between playing by the rules and (self-)destructive violence..." (2016, p. 45). It is this frustration that leads to acts of violence against their own, which seem to be a major call for reflection, defends the thinker. And movements such as Black Lives Matter, as well as many other movements expressing a demand for the impossible, in the Badiouian sense (2015) are unquestionably necessary to think today's contradictions through their local praxis. If postcolonial theories already propose a much radical militancy approach to ethnicity (Mbembe, Go, as well many other authors...), a much more radical attempt is to consider such notions while approach social classes and defending the underlying struggle against capitalist contradictions. In what could be noticed as a conversation, maybe even a response to Balibar's *Masses, Classes and Ideas* (1994), Badiou discusses the proper philosophical axioms of constructibility for knowledge. By doing so, the thinker reaches the argument on genericity (2015, p. 53), and at this point, Badiou intertwining Cohen's *generic sets* with Marx's understanding of the *generic* ends up with a key conceptual contribution to our debate:

> You know that Marx gives the name 'generic humanity' to humanity in the movement of its self-emancipation, and that 'proletariat' – the name 'proletariat' – is the name of the possibility of generic humanity in its affirmative form. 'Generic', for Marx, names the becoming of the universality of human being, and the historical function of the proletariat is to deliver us this generic form of the human being. So in Marx the political truth is situated on the side of genericity, and never on the side of particularity. Formally, it is a question of desire, creation or invention, and not a matter of law, necessity or conversation... So for Cohen – as well as for Marx – the pure universality of multiplicity, of sets, is not to be sought on the side of correct definition of clear description but on the side of nonconstructibility. The truth of sets is generic. (2015, p. 53)

If ethnicity and class proclaim themselves to be political procedures towards new social possibilities, their transformation must always claim for the impossibility of today's reality and engage until it becomes a possible reality, as Badiou probably would defend it. So, Badiou understands that revolutionary desire lies within the realization of generic humanity, which in fact represents the end of the separate relation between law and desire, and claims for the "creative affirmation of humanity as such" (2015, p. 54). Defending the necessary creativity for seizing the means of the symbolic fabric of our reality, the main aim is to support the law of life, only in order to create a new symbolic fiction to follow. And truth here follows Lacan's understanding that it has the structure of fiction, therefore leading to "...the final belief in generic truths, the final possibility of opposing the generic will to normal desires, this type of possibility and the belief in this sort of possibility, in generic truths, has to be our new fiction" (p. 58). Here, we do not see a formal disparity to Mbembe's understanding of the transformation of human beings into coded digital data. For the thinker, the history of Blackness and the racial subject is linked to the history of capitalism. In the early capitalism, the term "Black" referred on people of African origin "(different forms of depredation, dispossession of all power of self-determination, and, most of all, dispossession of the future and of time, the two matrices of the possible)" and that now, for the "first time in human history, the term 'Black' has been generalized" (2017, p. 4). As Mbembe will defend "[t]his new fungibility, this solubility, institutionalized as a new norm of existence and expanded to the entire planet, is what I call the *Becoming Black of the world*" (p. 5). Fundamentally, he defends that this is an effect of capitalist recolonization of its own center, something like an expression of new modes of exploitation. But Mbembe defends the conditions for the collective resurgence of humanity by "restitution, reparation, and justice" (p. 179), sustaining a way out of the sacrifice through thinking, a "*thinking in circulation, thinking-crossing...*" (p. 179). Well, in this sense, local struggles in their thinking-crossing capability, mind, as well find through militant strength the proclamation for resignification of the symbolic fabric.

Although Badiou (2016) considers negritude as a positive assertion of blackness and "black, a stigmatizing category internal to white domination, is reappropriated by its victims as the banner of their revolt" (2016, p. 99), the context-bounded element of ethnicity (dialectically transformative) and the fundamental political north of his philosophical construction leading to the hypothesis of communism and to how colorful such rainbow can be (2016, p. 35) going through the oppressive invention of the "black" by ill-intended white man (2016, p. 104), he defends the colorless affirmation of all possible colors. As Badiou (2015) puts it, such radical transformation is only subjectivized to proper names through the mediation of class struggle, the creation of the conditions for a shared generic fiction will only find a real possibility within the political field through such mediation. In this sense, to sustain the notion of class is to radically sustain its Marxist render and its conditions to proclaim and sustain a new form for reality. Knowledge thrives basically when find its critical potentiality and seeks to resubjectivize given signifiers (ethnicity and class) and manages to create new conditions of radical possibility to overcome and subsume current contradictions. Perhaps, body snatchers teach us a whole lot about ethnicity, class, and the double inscription of such complex notions to a subject. But definitely, other formidable creative creatures such as vampires, zombies,

Frankensteins, and werewolves, for example, could teach us even further about our paradoxical understanding of (in)humanity. Providing insights on the excesses of our "living dead" ontological condition (Žižek 2014a), a formidable line of thinking in order to face the current contradictions of neoliberal capitalism. So, to convoke a render towards the philosophical paradigm of monstrosity could perhaps lead to a more creative and critical narrative facing today's contradictions. Of course, such bold statement needs further developments that cannot fit this chapter, but such premise does not only seem valid but also it seems philosophically and symbolically crucial in order to think current social-political paradoxes.

Conclusion

This chapter explores the notions of ethnicity and class through five different stops, provoking the fundamental necessity of reapproaching knowledge critically. From our first stop, it was established that an appropriation of these terms as "given" terms for the production of knowledge, especially under the protection of the scientific discourse, one could easily forget the depths and contradictions embedded within such notions. Further, by given back the potency of such signifiers as ethnicity and class, the second stop presented a more specific apprehension of those terms, by the well-versed knowledge of authors from different realms of studies, allowing to establish the construction and elaboration behind ethnicity and class. Defending that race, racism and a racialized reality were a byproduct of the construction and growth of capitalism within our society. Ethnicity is the psychic and embodied take up of this agreement. The hidden layers of capitalist exploitation structured the birth of ethnicity and class as the modalities that we came to know since colonialism. With the globalized capitalist realism, with the neoliberal financialized reality, such modalities seem to be read under a different critical scope.

By considering the psychoanalytic tools in a critical render, the proper depths of subjectivity allow us to better interpret fantasies surrounding otherness and also the necessity to avoid and escape the binary narrative of an external versus internal worldview. To consider our very own processes of introduction to the symbolic reality, which provide the humanity to the human body that one holds, it is to be always already into a disjoint existence. By seriously understanding the consequences of this comprehension is to be always already getting in terms with the external intimacy that makes us what we are. The depth of this insight provokes many questions towards the naivety of presupposing a fixed narrative to propose the predicative to our very own humanity, since ethnicity and class are concepts which have been crafted and controlled by those who have the resources to do so. And through a critical understanding of psychoanalysis, one could find the blueprints to seize the means of the symbolic production of its own reality, ethically revolutionizing his/hers own suffering. That is, as much as the social world relies upon notions of ethnicity to harness identity politics, it also causes anguish to the subject. This means – as Žižek has rightly pointed out in his theorization of the neighbor – that one is always faced with alterity, either their own or the confrontation to how we contribute to the anguish of others.

Social segregation, however, does not need to be thought of as an impasse but rather as a way into thinking about a different politics – as Badiou perhaps offers – by inviting Badiou's generic notion is to promote the necessity of critically remember the Marxist understanding of class, in order to transcend its usage more empty out usage. In this sense, the chapter explored how ethnicity and class could and should provide provocative insights in the construction of our social future.

Cross-References

▶ Historical Memory and Ethnic Myths
▶ New Middle-Class Labor Migrants
▶ Rewriting the World: Pacific People, Media, and Cultural Resistance

References

Althusser L (2014) On the reproduction of capitalism: ideology and ideological state apparatuses. Verso Books, London
Archer-Straw P (2000) Negrophilia: Avant-Garde Paris and Black culture in the 1920s. Thames and Hudson, London
Badiou A (2008) Conditions. Continuum, London
Badiou A (2009) Circonstances: Tome 5, L'hypothèse communiste. Nouvelles Editions Lignes, Paris
Badiou A (2012) The rebirth of history: times of riots and uprisings. Verso Books, London
Badiou A (2013) Ethics: an essay on the understanding of evil. Verso Books, London
Badiou A (2015) Philosophy for militants. Verso Books, London
Badiou A (2016) Black: the brilliance of a non-color (trans: Spitzer S). Polity, New Jersey, New York
Balibar E (1994) Masses, classes, ideas. Routledge, London
Barros DR (2018) Lugar de Negro, Lugar de Branco? Hedra, Sao Paulo
Canguilhem G (1978) On the normal and the pathological. Springer Netherlands, Heidelberg
Castro EV (2006) No Brasil, todo mundo é índio, exceto quem não é. Povos Indígenas no Brasil website. https://pib.socioambiental.org/files/file/PIB_institucional/No_Brasil_todo_mundo_é_%C3%ADndio.pdf. Accessed 20 June 2018
Castro EV (2014) Cannibal metaphysics: for a post-structural anthropology. Univocal Publishing, Minneapolis
Dolar M (1991) "I shall be with you on your wedding-night": Lacan and the uncanny. Rendering the Real 58:5–23
Du Bois WEB (1903) The souls of black folk. Dover Publications, New York
Dunker C (2015) Mal-Estar, Sofrimento e Sintoma. Boitempo Editorial, São Paulo
Eriksen TH (1993) Ethnicity and nationalism: anthropological perspectives. Pluto, London
Estevão I, Gonsalves R (2016) Will to power in Adorno. In: Checchia M (ed) Combat against will to power. AnnaBlumme Publisher, Sao Paulo, pp 191–211
Fanon F (1952/1967) Black skin, white masks. Grove, New York
Fisher M (2009) Capitalist realism: is there no alternative? Zero Books, London

Fisher M (2017) The weird and the eerie. Repeater, London
Foucault M (1969/2002) The archaeology of knowledge (trans: Sheridan Smith AM). Routledge, London
Freud S (1919/2000) The uncanny. W. W. Norton, London; Reprint edition
Freud S (1929/2010) Civilization and its discontents. W. W. Norton, London
Go J (2018) Postcolonial possibilities for the sociology of race. Sociology of Race and Ethnicity. American Sociological Association 1–13. https://doi.org/10.1007/23332649218793982
Gonsalves R (2016) Ethics and monstrosity on psychoanalysis. https://www.academia.edu/36358381/Rodrigo_Gonsalves_-_ETHICS_AND_MONSTROSITY_ON_PSYCHOANALYSIS. Accessed 15 September 2018
Gonsalves R (2018) Interpassivity and the uncanny illusions of our daily lives. Cont Thought Theory 2(1):241–269. Interpassivity. https://ir.canterbury.ac.nz/bitstream/handle/10092/15480/CTT%20V2N1%2011%20Gonsalves.pdf?sequence=6. Accessed 20 Aug 2018
Homer (1999) The Odyssey. Penguin Classics, London
Kuhn TS (1970) The structure of scientific revolutions. University of Chicago Press, Chicago
Lacan J (1997) The seminar of Jacques Lacan: Book III: the psychoses 1955–1956. W. W. Norton, London
Lacan J (1998) The seminar: Book XI. The four fundamental concepts of psychoanalysis. W. W. Norton, London
Lacan J (2001) The mirror stage as formative of the function of the I. In: Écrits: a selection. Routledge Classics, London
Levi-Strauss C (1952) Race and History. UNESCO, Paris
Loock K (2012) The return of the Pod People: remaking cultural anxieties in invasion of the body snatchers. In: Film remakes, adaptations and fan productions. Palgrave Macmillan, London, pp 122–144. https://doi.org/10.1057/9781137263353_7
Marx K (1990) Capital: critique of political economy. v. 1. Penguin Classics, London; New Ed. edition
Mbembe A (2017) Critique of black reason. Duke University Press, Durham
McCallum I, Demie F (2001) Social class, ethnicity and educational performance. Educ Res 43(2):147–159. https://doi.org/10.1080/00131880110051146
Moder G (2017) Hegel and Spinoza: substance and negativity. Northwestern University Press, New York
Pareles J (2007) Pay what you want for this article. The New York Times, June 28
Pfaller R (2005) The familiar unknown, the uncanny, the comic: the aesthetic effects of the thought experiment. In: Žižek S (ed) Lacan: silent partners. Verso Books, London, pp 198–216
Pfaller R (2014) On the pleasure principle in culture – illusions without owners. Verso Books, London
Pfaller R (2017) Interpassivity – the aesthetics of delegated enjoyment. Edinburgh University Press, London
Radiohead (2008) Lyrics to "Bodysnatchers". Genius. https://genius.com/Radiohead-Bodysnatchers-lyrics. Accessed 10 July 2017
Royle N (2003) The uncanny. Manchester University Press, London
Stauffer RH (1981) Class and ethnicity: applying Wallerstein's core-periphery concept. Modern Times, vol V, no 5–6, June-September. Marxists.org. https://www.marxists.org/history/erol/ncm-1a/hus-class-ethnicity.htm. Accessed 10 Aug 2018
The Anthropology and Sociology Section (ANSS/ACRL) (2018) Association of College and Research Libraries. https://anssacrl.wordpress.com/publications/cataloging-qa/2006-class-ethnicity/. Accessed 20 June 2018
Žižek S (1989) The sublime object of ideology. Verso Books, London
Žižek S (2006) The parallax view. The MIT Press, Cambridge, MA
Žižek S (2007) How to read Lacan. W.W. Norton, New York
Žižek S (2009) Through the glasses darkly. In These Times, ed. 341. http://socialistreview.org.uk/341/through-glasses-darkly. Accessed 29 Nov 2009

Žižek S (2011) Did somebody say totalitarianism?: 5 interventions in the (mis)use of a notion. Verso Books, London

Žižek S (2014a) Absolute recoil: towards a new foundation of dialectical materialism. Verso Books, London

Žižek S (2014b) Event: philosophy in transit. Penguin Books, London

Žižek S (2016) Refugees, terror and other troubles with the neighbours: against the double blackmail. Melville House Publishing, New York

Islamic Identity and Sexuality in Indonesia

Sharyn Graham Davies

Contents

Introduction	1064
Sexuality	1064
Indonesia and Sexuality	1066
Islam and Sexuality	1067
Indonesia, Islam, and Sexuality	1069
Conclusion	1072
Cross-References	1072
References	1073

Abstract

Despite popular understandings and interpretations, Islam is actually one of the most positive of all world religions regarding sexuality. Fulfilling sexual relations is acknowledged as an integral part of heterosexual marriage, and women have the right to divorce their husbands if the latter fail to provide sexual satisfaction. However, Islam across the world is presented as a sexually repressive and coercive religion, and this is not without reason. People having sex outside heterosexual marriage have been executed in the name of Islam. Long touted as the country that proves Islam is compatible with progressive democratic principles, Indonesia is an interesting place to examine Islam and sexuality. While Indonesia has avoided official criminal penalties for people involved in consenting private sexual affairs, in the last few years, there has been a dramatic rise in punitive forces using Islam to justify persecution of anyone having sex outside of heterosexual marriage. This chapter explores Islam and sexuality in contemporary Indonesia to provide a richer understanding of how these two elements interrelate.

S. G. Davies (✉)
Auckland University of Technology, Aotearoa, New Zealand
e-mail: sharyn.davies@aut.ac.nz

© The Author(s), under exclusive license to Springer Nature Singapore Pte Ltd. 2019
S. Ratuva (ed.), *The Palgrave Handbook of Ethnicity*,
https://doi.org/10.1007/978-981-13-2898-5_58

> **Keywords**
> Islam · Sexuality · Indonesia

Introduction

The fact that Muhammad, the founding prophet of Islam, was a pioneering feminist is often forgotten by those trying to use Islam to oppress people, especially women. When Muhammad stated that men could have four wives, he was thinking not of men's right to unlimited sexual pleasure but rather the welfare of women. Living in a time of devastating war, women were frequently left widowed with children to support. Muhammad recognized both the need for women to remarry and the radical difference in sex ratios. Previously, men could marry multiple women without gaining the consent of previous wives or providing them with emotional, physical, or financial support. Muhammad thus stipulated that men could marry up to four wives provided that they gained consent and could provide for all. Muhammad also declared that wives deserved to derive sexual pleasure from their husbands; if they did not, this could constitute grounds for divorce. So how did a sexually progressive religion become infamous for its punitive control of sexuality, particularly of women's sexuality? Much of it has to do with the cultural context in which Islam is lived. It also has much to do with people, often men, trying to establish and maintain various forms of power.

In exploring these ideas around Islam and sexuality, this chapter focuses on Indonesia. The first section explicitly addresses the topic of sexuality. The second section provides an overview of the country in focus. The third section discusses Islam specifically in respect to sexuality. Finally, the chapter analyzes the current tensions between sexuality and Islam in Indonesia, specifically focusing on the move toward punitive morality that has swept the country in the last two decades but particularly since 2016. The chapter concludes by noting that Islam at its heart is accepting of sexuality, and indeed sexual diversity, and can be deployed to fight for sexual rights for all rather than be used to penalize people.

Sexuality

Few subjects have drawn as much popular and academic attention as sexuality. There is evidence that in ancient times there was free discussion of sexuality and that sexuality as a wholly private matter was not the norm. There is also evidence of homosexuality practiced through the early Muslim world (Murray and Roscoe 1997). Indeed sexuality in Islam is valued beyond a merely procreative act. There is also evidence from places such as ancient Greece suggesting that a variety of sexual relationships were legitimate including pederasty (a sexual relationship between a younger man and an older man) and Sapphic love (Blackwood and Wieringa 1999). The enduring significance of early sexual terms is evidenced in the fact that English uses words such as lesbian, derived from the Greek island of Lesbo.

In Western literature it was the work of people like Kinsey et al. (1948) who studied sexuality on a large scale that contributed to new understandings of the diversity of sexuality. Progress in terms of sexual freedom remained slow until the 1970s when much of the Western world and elsewhere went through what became aptly known as the sexual revolution. The prosperity of the postwar years combined with technical and medical advances such as the contraceptive pill ushered in an era of people proudly enjoying sex outside of marriage. A number of key books propelled the sexual revolution, empowering people, and especially women and gay men, to talk about sexuality (Hite 1976; Humphreys 1970; Masters and Johnson 1966).

Not without coincidence the sexual revolution occurred alongside the women's rights movement and civil rights campaigns. With more sexual freedom in the West, academics began thinking seriously about how to theorize sexuality. The need for theories of sexuality grew all the more urgent with the advent of the HIV/AIDS epidemic that wreaked havoc, starting with gay communities from the early 1980s. Thinking around sexuality also had a symbiotic relationship with postmodern theory, seen especially in the work of Michel Foucault (1985, 1988). Postmodern theory provided an understanding of sexuality as something fluid, changing, and as something that could be related to sex and gender or that could be merely a sexual act. Further, the work of people such as Candace West and Don Zimmerman (1987) and Judith Butler (1990, 1993) fundamentally changed the way we think about ourselves as sexual and gendered beings. Sex, sexuality, and gender might seem natural parts of us, but they are in fact discursive constructions developed through repetition and performance. Postmodern theory also began questioning the underpinnings of sexuality so that even the way we talked about sexuality, and bodies more generally, began to be critiqued. For instance, the work of Anne Fausto-Sterling (1992, 2000, 2006) and Emily Martin (1991) showed us that women's bodies and their sexuality were discussed as deficits and as passive objects. Penises were said to penetrate vaginas, but vaginas were never framed as actively engulfing penises.

Invigorated by postmodernism, and legitimated through HIV prevention (Weeks 1999), academics began studying sexuality across the globe as an explicit topic, although admittedly almost all studies were conducted by Western-trained academics (Caplan 1987; Herdt 1994; Jackson 2001; Kulick 1998; Manalansan 2003; Reddy 2005). Such studies showed the diversity of sexuality. They revealed that sexuality was not a fixed, immutable fact but rather was flexible and multiple. Academic language was developed to allow discussion of these findings so that we now have *gender* to refer to ways of doing and being and one can be inter alia cisgender, transgender, and gender diverse. We have *sex* to refer to the biological body and one can be inter alia intersex, female, and male. And we have *sexuality* to talk about desires and intimacy and can frame oneself as inter alia heterosexual, homosexual, bisexual, lesbian, and gay. Indeed a new way of thinking about these complexities has become gathered under the term queer theory (Altman and Symons 2016; Valocchi 2005; Warner 1993), which itself sometimes subsumes transgender theory (Stryker 2004).

The ways in which sexuality has been discussed in Western academic literature is of course often at variance with its discussion and understanding in other settings. While no doubt Western musings of sexuality have impacted the wider world, the interpretation and oftentimes rejection of those ideas have sparked indigenous responses. Sexuality takes many forms, and its legitimacy is shaped by religious and cultural norms. These norms may be incidental in the form of advertisements showing heterosexual sexuality as the norm, or they may be punitive in that people caught having sex outside of marriage are arrested. In examining this issue more, I turn now to explore understandings and conceptualizations of sexuality in the country of focus, Indonesia.

Indonesia and Sexuality

Indonesia is the fourth most populous nation in the world and the third largest democracy. Indonesia is also the world's largest civil law jurisdiction (Strang 2008). Its population has surpassed 260 million, with one-third of all citizens aged under 18 years. Over 100 million Indonesians are considered to be poor to very poor, and inequality has continued to grow. Indonesia became a full member of the United Nations (UN) on 28 September 1950 (UN 2015). As a UN member, it is obliged to implement certain rights. In some respects, Indonesia has adopted progressive laws designed to protect civil rights. One area where such laws have been implemented is in regard to children. However, while the laws are progressive in reference to juvenile justice, their implementation is woefully lacking (Davies and Robson 2016). Similarly, as a signatory to the UN, adult citizens have the right to fulfilling sexual lives and to be protected from sexual harm, but these rights are merely given lip service in contemporary Indonesia.

The history of sexuality in Indonesia is interesting and complex, as it is everywhere. Much has been written about the plurality of sexual diversity in the surrounding Southeast Asia region (Johnson 1997; Loos 2008; Peletz 2009; Sinnott 2007). Specific to Indonesia, there is strong evidence of sexual diversity in the early modern period (Baker 2005; Brooke 1848; Chabot 1950; Davies 2015; Jacobs 1966; Pelras 1996). Some of this literature discusses early sexuality vis-à-vis Islam. For instance, Portuguese missionary and merchant de Pavia recorded his impressions of bissu, a subject position that might be framed today as transgender spiritual advisors. De Paiva noted the, to him, extraordinary power bissu wielded within certain Indonesian royal courts in the 1500s (Baker 2005). While de Pavia assumed bissu, and through their influence local royal courts, would be swayed by his efforts to convert them to Christianity, it seems bissu favored conversion to Islam. It is interesting that bissu and their royal patrons were swayed to Islam rather than Christianity because a staple food source was pork; conversion to Islam meant people could no longer eat this staple. While we have no evidence, it is not a stretch to imagine, considering bissu had such power over the decision-making of royal rulers (at least according to de Paiva), that bissu wanted to convert to Islam rather than Christianity because in the former religion they found accommodation for their subject position that perhaps Christianity did not offer. Indeed, bissu until at least the last few years have found within Islam a powerful force justifying their position within society (Davies 2011).

Nation building goes hand in hand with the regulation of sexuality, and this has indeed been the case in Indonesia. In efforts to consolidate power, nations designate themselves the proper authority to circumscribe sexuality. Following World War II, Indonesian subjects became explicitly defined around notions of proper sexuality, and indeed Indonesia's Asian neighbors were doing the same, promoting the regulation of sexuality and the nuclear family as markers of national identity and keys to economic prosperity (Jones 1995). In Singapore (Teo 2011), Malaysia (Stivens 2006), and Indonesia (Hoon 2004), family was the place for legitimate sexual citizens. Enshrining this idea symbolically, Indonesia's President Suharto (1965–1998) positioned himself as father of the nation and proposed the family principle (*asas kekeluargaan*) within which heterosexuality was the only sexuality (Bennett 2005; Blackburn 2004; Brenner 2011; Platt et al. 2018). Coming to power as he did in a coup, Suharto needed to frame himself as not only the father of the nation but as saving the nation from the imagined Communist threat. To showcase his power, members of the Communist Women's group (Gerwani) were targeted and framed as sexually licentious lesbians who carried out sadistic violence against military men (Pohlman 2017). Such framing served to reinforce the danger of nonmarital sexuality (Wieringa 2002). This connotation of dangerous sexuality is rearing its head again with the LGBT (lesbian, gay, bisexual, transgender) crisis that will be discussed shortly (Paramaditha 2016). Despite such framing, Indonesia continued to boast a rich repertoire of gender and sexual diversity (Blackwood 2010; Boellstorff 2005; Davies 2007).

At the time of writing (2018), Indonesia still has no national laws criminalizing consenting adult sexuality. There is fear among many though that Indonesia will shortly follow the province of Aceh and criminalize forms of sexuality outside marital vaginal-penile intercourse. Yet while there are currently no laws, Indonesia continues to tightly prescribe sexuality. Much of this prescription came about during the nationalistic presidency of Suharto (as mentioned above), but other prescriptions have a much more solid religious base. Before turning to explicitly examine the relationship between Islam and sexuality in Indonesia, I first examine the issue of sexuality within Islam.

Islam and Sexuality

A discussion of Indonesia and sexuality requires a discussion of Islam. While Indonesia often gets painted as an Islamic country and as the largest Muslim country in the world, it is neither of these things (Hefner 2000). Certainly Indonesia is home to more Muslims than any other country, but it is not an Islamic country. Moreover, Indonesia officially recognizes six religions: Islam, Catholicism, Protestantism, Buddhism, Confucianism, and Hinduism. Eighty percent of the population is Muslim, but this means that over 30 million Indonesians are not Muslim. Moreover,

Islam is not a singular entry. Indonesians adhere to both Sunni and Shia forms of Islam and indeed practice more syncretic forms of Islam. During President Suharto's New Order period (1965–1998), he kept a tight lid on the expression of Islam. Suharto feared that if Islam was given free reign, Islamic political parties would rise up and threaten his power. In the post-Suharto era, though, democratic principles of freedom of religion and freedom of expression have enabled political Islam to rise (Aspinall 2009). In local and national elections, Islamic parties are yet to experience significant wins, but Islamic forces are playing a significant role in influencing election outcomes (Wilson 2014).

Islam frames sexuality in interesting ways (Robinson 2015). As noted in the introduction, in many respects, Islam at its core has a progressive stance toward sexuality. However, political and other power interests use Islam in Indonesia and elsewhere to their own advantage, picking up on and projecting simmering tensions. There are three main ways that we get understandings about sexuality in Islam: through the Qur'an (the holy book), hadith (sayings of the prophet Muhammad), and fatwah (rulings of religious leaders). Most of this literature positions sexuality as ideally confined to marriage between a woman and a man. But it is often difficult to get categorical statements of many aspects of sexuality as many fatwah, for instance, contradict each other. Moreover, cultural context overlays religious prescription and interpretation. In general, though, it is thought that extramarital sex, anal sex, and homosexuality are prohibited. Most sources note that birth control is acceptable. Modesty in dress and behavior is expected so as to confine sexuality, although definitions of modesty are open to interpretation. For instance, for some interpreters, the head veil is a necessary form of modesty for women, but for many others it is not.

In Islam, marriage is seen as the lawful institution through which sexual desires can be fulfilled. Procreation is a key component of marriage but it is not the sole or primary reason for marriage (Al-Islam 2015). Within marriage, sex is to be enjoyed, and Islam places focus on foreplay to ensure sex is mutually satisfying. In the Qur'an it notes that Muslim men are legitimately able to have two types of sexual relationship: with their lawful wives and with their concubines (unmarried women slaves owned by the man; but the concubine is theoretically granted many rights such as the right to say no to sex in certain circumstances) (Bloom and Blair 2002). There are also interesting dynamics regarding polygamous sexuality within Islam (Nurmila and Bennett 2015). All other sexual relationships for men are considered *zina* (fornication). Women's sexuality outside marriage is little discussed in Islamic doctrine. There are a few hadith noting that women should not have sexual relations with each other, but the dominant impression given is that Islamic doctrine considers that sex is only possible when a penis is involved and therefore lesbians do not need to be punished (Bosworth 1989; Islamqa 2013). Whether masturbation is permitted or not is open to debate (Omar 2016). Rape is prohibited within Islam and wives must give consent before sex. However, there are only certain reasons that women can withhold their consent and that is during menstruation, for 40 days after childbirth, during the daylight hours of Ramadan, or while they are on the pilgrimage to Mecca. With this general understanding of sexuality within Islam, I turn now to explore how Islam and sexuality interact in Indonesia.

Indonesia, Islam, and Sexuality

Both because of indigenous support for gender diversity and its Dutch, as opposed to British, colonial legacy and indeed perhaps because Islam, not Christianity, is the dominant religion, Indonesia to this day has never had any specific laws criminalizing consenting adult sexuality. While we know something about how Islam relates to sexuality in Indonesia, there is a paucity of research on Christianity and sexuality in Indonesia (Mulya 2018). The fact that Indonesia has taken a relatively benign stance toward sexuality is in stark contrast to its near neighbors, Singapore and Malaysia, which have long had repressive and punitive laws regarding sexuality. Indeed, former Malaysian Prime Ministerial candidate Anwar Ibrahim was imprisoned on trumped-up charges of homosexuality. Sadly for Indonesia, though, democracy and globalization have rallied conservative elements within the nation to make punitive morality a key contemporary issue. While the move toward a conservative public morality is not new (Brenner 2011; Jones 2010; Lindquist 2004; Parker 2008; Silvey 2000; Smith-Hefner 2007), the last couple of years have seen morality become a public issue as never before experienced in Indonesia. As such, mothers in particular are needing to find ways to impart religious piety to their children despite a proliferation of sexy Western-inspired advertising and social media (Hartono 2018; Hartono et al. 2017).

Prior to democratic reform in Indonesia in 1998, the key event that sparked public discussion of sexuality was the beginning of the HIV/AIDS epidemic. As elsewhere, HIV was initially seen as an issue only for gay men. While awareness has grown in Indonesia that HIV is transmitted through more than just homosexual sex, issues of morality continue to hinder HIV prevention strategies. The fact that highlights the failure to address HIV in Indonesia more than any other is that the fastest growing rate of HIV in Indonesia is not among gay men, men who have sex with men, the transgender community, or intravenous drug users. Rather the fastest growing prevalence rate is among married heterosexual women (Munro and McIntyre 2015; Rahmalia et al. 2015). The reason for this increase is that policy makers and others have assumed that heterosexually married women engage in safe sexual practices and do not use drugs. This image neglects the fact that women may use drugs, have sex outside of marriage, and that their husbands may too. A further reason that HIV is growing among married women is that when they visit a doctor with sexual health concerns, married women are dismissed and ignored and their concerns are silenced (Bennett 2015). Of further alarm is the high rate of HIV transmission from mother to child which is being little addressed. Deployments of Islam are proving unhelpful in the fight against HIV (Hidayana and Tenni 2015).

Another key move within Indonesia's history that provoked discussion around sexuality and Islam was the move to democracy in 1998. When authoritarian leader President Suharto was forced to resign, an era of reformation swept the country. In the years following, numerous positive advances were made in Indonesia that should have helped with such factors as decreasing the rate of sexual and domestic violence, slowing the spread of HIV and sexually transmitted infections, and safeguarding the rights of all Indonesians to fulfilling sexual lives. Many advances were made.

For instance, marital rape was finally made a crime in 2004 (Bennett et al. 2011). A more robust Human Rights Commission was established in 2008, giving it responsibilities in the prevention of racial and ethnic discrimination. Work was also undertaken by women's groups to fight for the rights of women in politics, economics, and society in general; their focus, however, was on sexual rights for women within the institution of marriage, showing the dominance of heteronormativity in Indonesia. Unfortunately in recent years there has been significant backtracking in progress in many of these respects.

Alongside the move to democracy, globalization has had an impact on sexuality in Indonesia. Like democratic reform, many aspects of globalization have had a positive influence on Indonesia. For instance, the 10-year anniversary of the Beijing Women's Conference began a conversation in Indonesia about women's role in politics and the need for a quota system (Davies 2005). Women united to agitate for a place in Indonesian society outside just the home. Women also took inspiration from Khadija, Muhammad's wife, who was his employer. A loosening of media restrictions enabled progressive media to enter Indonesia and indeed progressive media to be developed in-country. For instance, Nia DiNata's film *Arisan* was the first movie depiction of gay characters that were not a source of humor only (Murtagh 2013). Transgender communities began to take advantage of this new media scape (Hegarty 2017). Alongside this relaxation of media freedoms came events such as beauty pageants. It was through such events that the ways in which sexuality and Islam shape appropriate femininity became further crystallized (Pausacker 2015). With these changes also came a nascent LGBT movement. The LGBT movement had its own characteristics and did not fight for rights in the same way as its Western counterparts, but democracy alongside globalization and the HIV epidemic, provided impetus for broader discussions of sexuality in Indonesia (Yulius and Davies forthcoming).

One of the great ironies of Indonesia is that democracy has inspired not progressive moves toward sexual freedoms but rather increasingly punitive control of sexuality directed through interpretations of Islam. Kept in check by Suharto, democratic principles of freedom of religion and freedom of expression, combined with a fear of increasing Westernization and growing inequality, have manifested in targeted surveillance and censor of sexualities outside marital heterosexuality. This surveillance and censor has become notable even with comparison to 2015, when commenters were still optimistic about the sexual future of Indonesia (Davies and Bennett 2015).

Sadly there have been radical moves in the last decade or so in Indonesia toward making private morality a public matter liable to punitive surveillance and penalty. This move is seen most explicitly in the Indonesian province of Aceh. In Aceh we saw clearly the connection between Islam and sexuality when in 2015 Aceh began enforcing a Shari'a Criminal Code, known as the Qanun Jinayat. Qanun Jinayat not only brings Muslims under its laws but extends Islamic law to non-Muslims. The implementation of the Code was possible because of special autonomy laws granted to Aceh in 1999 to keep secessionist demands at bay. Ironically, some have argued that Aceh did not want to create an Islamic state; they merely wanted to keep Jakarta from profiting from their extensive natural resources (Yulius 2016). However, debates around sexuality have played out in Islamic terms even if Islam is in a sense a pawn in a larger political game. Qanun Jinayat has been widely criticized because it violates human rights on various levels. The Code allows for the use of corporal punishment, it places restrictions on the freedom of expression, and it seeks to control women's dress and movement. The Code also explicitly bans sexual misconduct, largely interpreted as banning homosexual and lesbian sex. But, as Yulius notes (2016), the definition of sexual misconduct is misleading as it conflates sexual practices with sexual orientation.

Sadly the way Islam has been used to delimit sexuality in Aceh is becoming more common across the rest of the nation. While since 1998 commentators became more hopeful each year about progress in relation to sexual freedoms, January 2016 seems to have marked a watershed in the repression of sexual rights, not just for LGBT but all Indonesians. While the events that sparked the "LGBT crisis," as it has become known, related to LGBT Indonesians, the repercussions have been widely felt. Indeed there are currently moves to penalize all sex outside of heterosexual marriage. The key event that sparked the crisis can be traced to a statement made by then Minister of Education, Muhammad Nasir, that Indonesian universities should not support LGBT activities. People who were not necessarily homophobic suddenly sensed an opportunity to win political and religious backing, and they subsequently drew on Islam to denounce homosexuality and all nonmarital intimate relationships.

From 2016, Islam became the central conduit through which nonmarital sexuality was denounced. Covering the "LGBT crisis," the conservative Islamic newspaper, *Republika*, ran the headline "LGBT poses serious threat to nation" (Mariani and Sampeliling 2016). Nahdlatul Ulama, the largest Muslim organization in the nation, stated that non-heterosexuality was incompatible with human nature. Nahdlatul Ulama also noted that LGBT activities must be criminalized (Yosephine 2016). Reformation brought by democracy was painted by some as a move bringing moral decay on all of Indonesia. Of key importance was the notion that reformation (with its overt Western connotations) was synonymous with sexual promiscuity (Pausacker 2008; Smith-Hefner 2009). Sexual promiscuity is a sin according to interpretations of Islam and therefore in the name of Islam must be combatted. Politicians, religious leaders, and others in power used Islam as the justification for getting rid of any factors in society that supported sexual and gender plurality and were not in accordance with heteronormativity.

Throughout Indonesia a growing conservative religiosity provided ammunition and support for those people who touted anti-LGBT rhetoric. Religious freedom as guaranteed in democratic Indonesia was wielded to persecute fellow Indonesians. What is particularly striking about this turn of events is that while survey data on Indonesian Muslims indicate many people may reject sexual diversity, most people have not wanted such activities criminalized; Islam can accommodate sexual diversity (Sheridan 2016). Ironically there may be lessons for Indonesia to learn from its conservative neighbor Singapore. Singapore has criminalized homosexuality, but there LGBT Singaporeans are often tolerated as a means of achieving economic progress (Chua 2014). It seems then that while Islam and sexuality have long cohabited relatively unproblematically in Indonesia, starting from 2016, a new relationship has emerged where the two are pitted as mortal enemies.

Conclusion

Indonesia is an interesting place to examine the relationship between Islam and sexuality. Not only has Islam been a core part of the archipelago since the 1500s, but it has intersected in various dynamic ways with sexuality. For the most part, Islam has been accommodating of sexual diversity, and indeed as this chapter has noted, for many sexually diverse Indonesians, they have found sanctuary in various tenets of Islam. Unfortunately, though, various contemporary forces have conspired to deploy Islam as a means through which persecution of sexual and gender diverse Indonesians has been justified. While sexual persecution is not a new story in Indonesian history – Islamic radicals have throughout the nation's past deployed Islam to meet non-just ends – the speed, spread, and vigor of recent developments do not bode well for a future of sexual tolerance and acceptance.

In exploring the topic of Islamic identity and sexuality in Indonesia, this chapter was divided into three key sections. The first section addressed the topic of sexuality. Providing a brief historical exploration of the topic, the section showed that current academic understandings of sexuality interpret it as a diverse and variable element of one's subject position. The second section introduced the country of focus, Indonesia. While not an Islamic country, Islam has certainly been a dominant element shaping Indonesia for the last few centuries. In recent years, the influence of Islam has grown in many respects with the loosening of religious freedoms afforded by Indonesia's move to democracy. The third section discussed Islam specifically vis-a-vis sexuality. While at a fundamental level Islam has many progressive aspects, such as recognizing the need for individuals to have fulfilling sexual lives, the interpretation of Islam across the globe means that it is largely used as a force to limit sexual expression. The fourth section analyzed current tensions between sexuality and Islam in Indonesia. In particular, attention was given to the current move in Indonesia toward punitive morality that seeks to criminalize all sexuality outside heterosexual marriage. In conclusion I would like to end with a plea that Islam be deployed to meet progressive sexual ends, where people can be able to explore their sexuality in a just society. Islam in Indonesia has in the past proved that it can be used in such a compassionate way, and there is no reason that Islam cannot be used in times of persecution to protect the lives of the sexually vulnerable.

Cross-References

- ▶ LGBT and Ethnicity
- ▶ National Imaginary, Ethnic Plurality, and State Formation in Indonesia
- ▶ Race and Sexuality: Colonial Ghosts and Contemporary Orientalisms
- ▶ Religion and Political Mobilization

References

Al-Islam (2015) Importance of marriage in Islam. Retrieved from Al-Islam.org
Altman D, Symons J (2016) Queer wars. Polity Press, Cambridge, UK
Aspinall E (2009) Islam and nation: separatist rebellion in Aceh, Indonesia. Stanford University Press, Stanford
Baker B (2005) South Sulawesi in 1544: a Portuguese letter. Rev Indones Malays Aff 39(1):61–85
Bennett LR (2005) Women, Islam and modernity: single women, sexuality and reproductive health in contemporary Indonesia. Routledge Curzon, London
Bennett LR (2015) Sexual morality and the silencing of sexual health within Indonesian infertility care. In: Bennett L, Davies SG (eds) Sex and sexualities in contemporary Indonesia: sexual politics, health, diversity and representations. Routledge, London, pp 148–166
Bennett LR, Andajani-Sutjahjo S, Idrus N (2011) Domestic violence in Nusa Tenggara Barat, Indonesia: married women's definitions and experiences of violence in the home. Asia Pac J Anthropol 12(2):146–163
Blackburn S (2004) Women and the state in modern Indonesia. Cambridge University Press, Cambridge, UK
Blackwood E (2010) Falling into the Lesbi world: desire and difference in Indonesia. University of Hawai'i Press, Honolulu
Blackwood E, Wieringa S (1999) Sapphic shadows: challenging the silence in the study of sexuality. In: Blackwood E, Wieringa S (eds) Female desires: same-sex relations and transgender practices across cultures. Columbia University Press, New York, pp 39–63
Bloom J, Blair S (2002) Islam: a thousand years of faith and power. Yale University Press, New Haven
Boellstorff T (2005) The gay archipelago: sexuality and nation in Indonesia. Princeton University Press, Princeton
Bosworth CE (1989) The history of al-Tabari: the 'Abbasid caliphate in equilibrium, vol 30. The Caliphates of Musa al-Hadi and Harun al-Rashid A.D, Albany
Brenner S (2011) Private moralities in the public sphere: democratization, Islam, and gender in Indonesia. Am Anthropol 113(3):478–490
Brooke J (1848) Narratives of events in Borneo and Celebes down to the occupation of Labuan, from the journals of James Brooke, Esq, vol 1. John Murray, London
Butler J (1990) Gender trouble: feminism and the subversion of identity. Routledge, New York
Butler J (1993) Bodies that matter: on the discursive limits of "Sex". Routledge, New York
Caplan P (1987) The cultural construction of sexuality. Tavistock, London
Chabot HT (1950) Kinship, status, and gender in South Celebes, vol 1996. Koninklijk Instituut voor de Taal-, Land- en Volkenkunde (KITLV) Press, Leiden
Chua LJ (2014) Mobilizing gay Singapore: rights and resistance in an authoritarian state. National University of Singapore Press, Singapore
Davies SG (2005) Women and politics in Indonesia in the decade post-Beijing. Int Soc Sci J 57(184):231–242
Davies SG (2007) Challenging gender norms: five genders among Bugis in Indonesia. Thomson Wadsworth, Boston
Davies SG (2011) Gender diversity in Indonesia: sexuality, Islam, and queer selves. RoutledgeCurzon, London
Davies SG (2015) Performing selves: the trope of authenticity and Robert Wilson's stage production of *I La Galigo*. J Southeast Asian Stud 46(3):417–443
Davies SG, Bennett L (2015) Sexuality, continuity and change in the Reformasi era. In: Bennett L, Davies SG (eds) Sex and sexualities in contemporary Indonesia: sexual politics, health, diversity and representations. Routledge, London, pp 1–25
Davies SG, Robson J (2016) Juvenile (in)justice: children in conflict with the law in Indonesia. Asia Pac J Hum Rights Law 2(16):119–147

Fausto-Sterling A (1992) Myths of gender: biological theories about women and men. Basic Books, New York

Fausto-Sterling A (2000) Sexing the body: gender politics and the construction of sexuality. Basic Books, New York

Fausto-Sterling A (2006) The bare bones of sex: part 1 – sex and gender. Signs 30(2):1491–1528

Foucault M (1985) The history of sexuality: the use of pleasure, vol. 2 (trans: Hurley R). Vintage Books, New York

Foucault M (1988) The history of sexuality: care of self, vol 3. Vintage, New York

Hartono H (2018) Virtually (im)moral: pious Indonesian Muslim women's use of Facebook. Asian Stud Rev 42:39–52

Hartono H, Davies SG, MacRae G (2017) You can't avoid sex and cigarettes: how Indonesian Muslim mothers teach their children to read billboards. Pac J Rev 23(2):146–163

Hefner R (2000) Civil Islam: Muslims and democratization in Indonesia. Princeton University Press, Princeton

Hegarty B (2017) The value of transgender Waria affective labor for transnational media markets in Indonesia. TSQ Transgender Stud Q 4(1):78–95

Herdt G (ed) (1994) Third sex, third gender: beyond sexual dimorphism in culture and history. Zone Books, New York

Hidayana IM, Tenni B (2015) Negotiating risk: Indonesian couples navigating marital relationships, reproduction and HIV. In: Bennett L, Davies SG (eds) Sex and sexualities in contemporary Indonesia: sexual politics, health, diversity and representations. Routledge, London, pp 91–108

Hite S (1976) The Hite report: a Nationwide study of female sexuality. Seven Stories Press, New York

Hoon CY (2004) Revisiting the Asian values argument used by Asian political leaders and its validity. Indones Q 32(2):154–174

Humphreys L (1970) Tearoom trade: impersonal sex in public places. Duckworth, New York

Islamqa (2013) The punishment for lesbianism. Retrieved from https://islamqa.info/en/answers/21058/the-punishment-for-lesbianism

Jackson PA (2001) Pre-gay, post-queer: Thai perspectives on proliferating gender/sex diversity in Asia. J Homosex 40(3/4):1–25

Jacobs H (1966) The first (locally) demonstrable Christianity in Celebes, 1544. Stud Rome 17(April):251–305

Johnson M (1997) Beauty and power: transgendering and cultural transformation in the Southern Philippines. Berg, Oxford

Jones GW (1995) Population and the family in Southeast Asia. J Southeast Asian Stud 26(1):184–195

Jones C (2010) Materializing piety: gendered anxieties about faithful consumption in contemporary urban Indonesia. Am Ethnol 37(4):617–637

Kinsey AC, Pomeroy WB, Martin CE (1948) Sexual behavior in the human male. Saunders, Philadelphia

Kulick D (1998) Travesti: sex, gender and culture among Brazilian transgendered prostitutes. The University of Chicago, Chicago

Lindquist J (2004) Veils and ecstasy: negotiating shame in the Indonesian borderlands. Ethnos J Anthropol 69(4):487–508

Loos T (2008) A history of sex and the state in Southeast Asia: class, intimacy and invisibility. Citizenship Stud 12(1):27–43

Manalansan MF (2003) Global divas: Filipino gay men in the diaspora. Duke University Press, Durham

Mariani E, Sampeliling AR (2016, 5 January) LGBT group faces state persecution. The Jakarta Post. Retrieved from http://www.thejakartapost.com/news/2016/01/25/lgbt-group-faces-state-persecution.html

Martin E (1991) The egg and the sperm: how science has constructed a romance based on stereotypical male-female roles. Signs 16(3):485–501

Masters WH, Johnson VE (1966) Human sexual response. Bantam Books, Toronto

Mulya T (2018) From divine instruction to human invention: the constitution of Indonesian Christian young people's sexual subjectivities through the dominant discourse of sexual morality. Asian Stud Rev 42:53–68. https://doi.org/10.1080/10357823.2017.1407918

Munro J, McIntyre L (2015) (Not) getting political: indigenous women and preventing mother-to-child transmission of HIV in West Papua. Cult Health Sex 18(2):1–16

Murray SO, Roscoe W (eds) (1997) Islamic homosexualities: culture, history, and literature. New York University Press, New York

Murtagh B (2013) Genders and sexualities in Indonesian cinema: constructing gay, Lesbi and Waria identities on screen. Routledge, London

Nurmila N, Bennett L (2015) The sexual politics of polygamy in Indonesian marriages. In: Bennett L, Davies SG (eds) Sex and sexualities in contemporary Indonesia: sexual politics, health, diversity and representations. Routledge, London, pp 69–88

Omar S (2016) Oxford Islamic studies online. Oxford University Press, Oxford

Paramaditha I (2016, 27 February) The LGBT debate and the fear of 'gerakan'. The Jakarta Post. Retrieved from http://www.thejakartapost.com/news/2016/02/27/the-lgbt-debate-and-fear-gerakan.html

Parker L (2008) To cover the Aurat: veiling, sexual morality and agency among the Muslim Minangkabau, Indonesia. Intersections: Gender and Sexuality in Asia and the Pacific, March (16). Retrieved from http://intersections.anu.edu.au/issue16_contents.htm

Pausacker H (2008) Hot debates. Inside Indonesia. Retrieved from http://www.insideindonesia.org/hot-debates

Pausacker H (2015) Indonesian beauty queens: embodying ethnicity, sexual morality and the nation. In: Bennett L, Davies SG (eds) Sex and sexualities in contemporary Indonesia: sexual politics, health, diversity and representations. Routledge, London, pp 273–292

Peletz MG (2009) Gender pluralism: Southeast Asia since early modern times. Routledge, New York

Pelras C (1996) The Bugis. Blackwell Publishers, Oxford

Platt M, Davies S, Bennett L (2018) Contestations of gender, sexuality and morality in contemporary Indonesia. Asian Stud Rev. https://doi.org/10.1080/10357823.2017.1409698

Pohlman A (2017) The spectre of communist women, sexual violence and citizenship in Indonesia. Sexualities 20(1–2):196–211

Rahmalia A, Wisaksana R, Meijerink H, Indrati AR, Alisjahbana B, Roeleveld N, Crevel R (2015) Women with HIV in Indonesia: are they bridging a concentrated epidemic to the wider community? BMC Res Notes 8(757):1–8

Reddy G (2005) With respect to sex: negotiating hijra identity in South India. Chicago University Press, Chicago

Robinson K (2015) Masculinity, sexuality, and Islam: the gender politics of regime change in Indonesia. In: Bennett LR, Davies SG (eds) Sex and sexualities in contemporary Indonesia. Routledge, London, pp 51–68

Sheridan G (2016, 10 March, 2016) Indonesian Islam is a good-news story for peace. The Australian. Retrieved from http://www.theaustralian.com.au/opinion/columnists/greg-sheridan/indonesian-islam-is-a-goodnews-story-for-peace/news-story/b9a6f8da391868f6b89e254e9752041c

Silvey R (2000) Stigmatized spaces: gender and mobility under crisis in South Sulawesi, Indonesia. Gend Place Cult A J Fem Geogr 7(2):143–162

Sinnott M (2007) Gender subjectivity: dees and toms in Thailand. In: Wieringa S, Blackwood E, Bhaiya A (eds) Women's sexualities and masculinities in a globalizing Asia. Palgrave, New York, pp 119–138

Smith-Hefner NJ (2007) Javanese women and the veil in post-Soeharto Indonesia. J Asian Stud 66(2):389–420

Smith-Hefner NJ (2009) 'Hypersexed' youth and the new Muslim sexology in Java, Indonesia. RIMA Rev Indones Malays Aff 43(1):209–244

Stivens M (2006) 'Family values' and Islamic revival: gender, rights and state moral projects in Malaysia. Womens Stud Int Forum 29(4):354–367

Strang RR (2008) "More Adversarial, but not Completely Adversarial": reformasi of the Indonesian criminal procedure code. Fordham Int Law J 32:188. https://ir.lawnet.fordham.edu/ilj/vol32/iss1/13

Stryker S (2004) Transgender studies: queer theory's evil twin. GLQ A J Lesbian Gay Stud 10(2):212–215

Teo YY (2011) Neoliberal morality in Singapore: how family policies make state and society. Routledge, London

UN (2015) Indonesia and the United Nations: a brief overview. Permanent Mission of the Republic of Indonesia to the United Nations

Valocchi S (2005) Not yet queer enough: the lessons of queer theory for the sociology of gender and sexuality. Gend Soc 19(6):750–770

Warner M (ed) (1993) Fear of a queer planet: queer politics and social theory. University of Minnesota Press, Minneapolis

Weeks J (1999) Myths and fictions in modern sexualities. In: Epstein D, Sears JT (eds) A dangerous knowing: sexuality, pedagogy and popular culture. Cassell, London, pp 11–24

West C, Zimmerman DH (1987) Doing gender. Gend Soc 1(2):125–151

Wieringa S (2002) Sexual politics in Indonesia. Institute of Social Studies/Palgrave Macmillan, Basingstoke

Wilson I (2014) Morality racketeering: vigilantism and populist Islamic militancy in Indonesia. In: Teik KB, Hadiz VR, Nakanishi Y (eds) Between dissent and power: the transformation of Islamic politics in the Middle East and Asia. Palgrave Macmillan, London pp 248–274

Yosephine L (2016, 24 February) Indonesian psychiatrists label LGBT as mental disorders. The Jakarta Post. Retrieved from http://www.thejakartapost.com/news/2016/02/24/indonesian-psychiatrists-label-lgbt-mental-disorders.html#sthash.kzahehOM.dpuf

Yulius HW (2016) Sex in Aceh. Retrieved from http://indonesiaatmelbourne.unimelb.edu.au/sex-in-acehs-criminal-code/

Yulius HW, Davies SG (forthcoming) The unfulfilled promise of democracy: lesbian and gay activism in Indonesia. Michele Ford edited volume on social movements

LGBT and Ethnicity

57

Arjun Rajkhowa

Contents

Introduction	1078
Diaspora	1079
Australian Perspectives	1085
Asian Migration	1086
Political Subjectivity and LGBTIQ Rights in Asia	1088
India	1088
South Asia	1093
China	1094
East Asia	1095
Southeast Asia	1096
Conclusion	1099
Cross-References	1099
References	1100

Abstract

This chapter reviews the literature on the intersections and links between culture, ethnicity, and sexuality. It elaborates on the multifarious themes that emerge from diverse literatures on the experiences and needs of lesbian, gay, bisexual, transsexual, intersex, and queer (LGBTIQ) people from multicultural and multi-faith (MCMF) backgrounds, encompassing a range of social, political, legal, cultural, religious, and health-related issues, and with a particular focus on Australia and Asia. The emergence of research, and community consultations and projects facilitating recognition of MCMF LGBTIQ identities, experiences, and needs is an important cultural development that contributes to the securing of LGBTIQ rights in diverse social and cultural settings. Historical experiences of criminalization, racism, social ostracism, violence and intimidation, and exclusion from

A. Rajkhowa (✉)
University of Melbourne, Melbourne, Australia
e-mail: arjun.rajkhowa@unimelb.edu.au

© The Author(s), under exclusive license to Springer Nature Singapore Pte Ltd. 2019
S. Ratuva (ed.), *The Palgrave Handbook of Ethnicity*,
https://doi.org/10.1007/978-981-13-2898-5_55

work and the polity have definitively shaped the lives of LGBTIQ elders, and ongoing efforts to augment the rights of individuals through processes of recognition and reconciliation are important. This chapter also includes brief snapshot accounts of progress in recognition of LGBTIQ rights (and approaches to LGBTIQ identity) in selected Asian countries. The aim is to instantiate how LGBTIQ rights and identity have been conceptualized and approached in specific political and cultural contexts. Approaches to LGBTIQ rights in diverse Asian societies are necessarily continually evolving, shaped by the vicissitudes of social change in those societies, the growing reach and ramifications of the forces of globalization and liberalization (as well as resistances to, and disruption of, these forces), and the emergence and growing traction of international human rights discourses and political frameworks.

Keywords

LGBTIQ · Queer · Ethnicity · Multicultural · Multi-faith · Australia · Asia · Culture · Homosexuality · Politics · Society · Law

Introduction

From the time that homosexuality was (re)conceptualized as a basis of identity and community (see Cass 1979), tensions between lesbian, gay, bisexual, transgender, intersex, and queer (LGBTIQ) identity and other identities (e.g., ethnic identity or national identity) have shaped and informed individuals' subjectivity (Cox and Gallois 1996). LGBTIQ community-formation (considered as the conceptual sum of the social, cultural, and relational practices that coalesce around sexuality) was always predicated on and imbricated with broader social, cultural, and political movements within society. Needless to say, LGBTIQ identity has always necessarily existed in social contexts and paradigms that are primarily shaped by other identities and in tension with these identities (including racial identity and class identity) (see Icard 1986; Smith 1993). Therefore, the attitudes and ideologies that have shaped social relations within these paradigms, including attitudes and ideologies informed by race- and class-based positionality, have also historically shaped LGBTIQ identities and community-formation (see Carbado 2017). The social and commercial spaces that have facilitated the coalescence of queer social, political, and affective belonging have evolved as "striated spaces" (Deleuze and Guattari 1988 in Caluya 2008), where perceptions and experiences of inclusion and exclusion are influenced and undergirded by a multitude of intersecting sociocultural factors.

In more recent years, against a backdrop of increasing acceptance of LGBTIQ identity and rights (see Johnson et al. 2011), and the legalization of gay marriage in many Western countries, arguably, a certain tendency toward "depoliticization" of race, sexuality, and gender has "muted" discussion of the salience of these categories, if not within scholarly and activist writing, then certainly in social interaction. This has been described by some as "refraction," "a conceptual process of revealing and concealing, a constant bending that has a tendency to depoliticize" identity categories such as race, gender, and sexuality, while concealing that depoliticization (Gomez and McFarlane 2017, pp. 364–365). Arguably, a "self-conscious, self-reflexive critique" (ibid., p. 374) that resists an erasure of histories of constrained subjectivity, and engages with broader inquiries into histories of domination (Clarke 2013), can help recontextualize understandings of and social approaches to these identity categories.

For a long time, queer scholarship resisted a deep engagement with the complexity and multiplicity of non-White queer subjectivity (ibid., p. 180; Kulpa and Mizielinska 2016). One of the effects of colonialism and racism on colonized peoples and the indigenous peoples of New World/settler colonies was the deterioration and destruction of indigenous familial and social paradigms, and the replacement of these with alien, alienating, and circumscribed approaches to family, gender, and sexuality. Further, the complexity and multiplicity of migrant positionalities, and the multiple effects of social stratification, categorization, and marginalization on the one hand, and "homophobic repression and regulation of sexuality in cross-border mobilities" (Pallotta-Chiarolli and Rajkhowa 2017, p. 430) on the other, did not receive much attention in mainstream migration research (Kosnick 2011, p. 126). This is changing. Importantly, scholarly and creative work recognizing, firstly, the existence, and, then, the complexity and multiplicity of queer native and indigenous histories and experiences, has also emerged prominently in queer activism and scholarship (see Rifkin 2010, 2012; Miranda et al. 2011; Driskill 2010, 2011; Hodge 2015). A putative process of "epistemic decolonization" in queer scholarship (Clarke 2013, p. 180) and the unraveling of the heteronormative assumptions and strictures of "general conversations about globalisation, transnational capitalism and migratory movements" (ibid.) have concurrently facilitated greater recognition of multiple identities in theory and thought (see also Smith 2010).

While the effects of intra-group marginalization and exclusionary social forces must be acknowledged, it is also important to recognize that the historical trajectories of LGBTIQ activism and community-formation in different political and cultural contexts have been shaped by the LGBTIQ rights movement's (and broader political movements') focalization of the principles of inclusiveness and respect for the dignity and privacy of individuals (see Honneth 1996, 2001), and this focalization has been a cornerstone of LGBTIQ activism (Altman 1971). In the United States, the LGBTIQ rights movement dovetailed with (and was necessarily influenced by) other civil rights movements, and the pioneering LGBTIQ rights activism in the country was fundamentally imbricated with other contemporary civil rights movements (ibid.). Therefore, when we write about the intersections between ethnicity and sexuality, and the tensions between belonging and not-belonging, we must acknowledge and grapple with both the inclusive ethos and aspirations of civil rights movements, and the (countervailing) ineluctable social effects of multiple forms of marginalization.

Diaspora

In the context of Western societies, experiences of race-based marginalization and exclusion in LGBTIQ spaces have mirrored patterns of marginalization observed more broadly in society. Likewise, the homophobia and sexuality-based marginalization and exclusion that have been experienced within specific ethno-cultural settings have mirrored broader forms of discrimination (including gender-based discrimination) in those settings. The United States and Europe (and, concomitantly, other Western nations) have served as the primary sites of the modern (global) (re)conceptualization of the rights of LGBTIQ persons, and the home of pioneering activism against the criminalization of sexuality and discrimination based on sexuality (see Adam 1995; Altman 1971; Clendinen and Nagourney 2001). However, histories of race-based discrimination and social stratification, in the United States particularly but also in Europe and elsewhere, have also shaped the trajectories of (and delimited) civic activism by racialized and marginalized groups (see Fuchs 1990). The predicament of multicultural and multi-faith (MCMF) people within LGBTIQ spaces and activism in these sociopolitical settings has necessarily been shaped by these contextualizing histories.

Thinking specifically about critical writing on the topic of race-based marginalization and exclusion experienced by queer people of color, including migrants, several pioneering works of literature and commentary come to mind; these have explored the myriad ways in which ethnicity has served as an arbiter of belonging in various LGBTIQ spaces (commercial and social-political) (see, for example, Chan 1995; Eng and Hom 1998; Gopinath 2005; Jackson and Sullivan 1999a; Ratti 1993). In the decades following what may retrospectively be characterized as the gay liberation movement in the United States, through the painful period defined by the human immunodeficiency virus infection and acquired immune deficiency syndrome (HIV/AIDS) epidemic and beyond, LGBTIQ people of color in the United States (but also in the United Kingdom and elsewhere) have organized around the goals of promoting greater inclusion in the LGBTIQ movement, in queer communal spaces (including commercially-oriented spaces), and more widely in society (Muñoz 1999), while addressing some of the specific challenges that MCMF LGBTIQ people might encounter within their ethnic communities. Works of journalism and scholarly commentary have captured some of the specific challenges that LGBTIQ people of color have faced and the social and personal journeys that they have navigated throughout these decades (see, for example, AGMC 2017; Carbado 2017; Eng and Hom 1998; Han 2007; Jackson and Sullivan 1999a; Snorton 2017). These works serve as historical records of contemporary social relations, attitudes, and beliefs.

Technological, economic, social, and political changes in this century have precipitated new forms of LGBTIQ networking, activism, interaction, and community-formation, and this has precipitated (or been accompanied by) a reworking of older social challenges. With the rise of online platforms for social networking and dating, it has been argued, a behavioral and social shift toward greater acceptance of attenuated and transactional affective interactions has occurred (see Blackwell et al. 2015; Light et al. 2008; Mowlabocus 2016; Penney 2014; Race 2015), and exclusionary patterns within these interactions have been observed. The reported prevalence and preponderance of instances of exclusionary language – which may include explicitly racist language as well as language framed around "preferences" – may be gauged by examining the copious journalistic commentary this issue has attracted (see, for example, Barber 2018; Om 2018; Truong 2018a, b; Samuel 2018; Stokel-Walker 2018; Wade 2017). In recent years, the issue of so-called "online" "sexual racism" has received considerable attention (see Riggs 2013; Robinson and Frost 2017). From mainstream media sites to online blogging platforms (for instance, sites that are dedicated to "exposing" instances of sexual racism as encountered on specific online dating platforms), several platforms have facilitated explorations of the ramifications of racism in the gay community, highlighting (and bringing into the "mainstream") experiences and stories that might have hitherto received only limited acknowledgment. This publicity has driven efforts to explicitly name and address racist attitudes (and unravel the specificities and particularities of racist "encounters") within the gay community, perhaps with an emphasis on encounters that take place within the sphere of online social networking. For instance, conversations interrogating whether any declarations of racial "preference" on online dating platforms, irrespective of whether these declarations include exclusionary language or not, betray racist attitudes (just as explicitly racist and exclusionary comments do) have featured contentious claims about the neutrality of these statements (characterized as innocuous declarations of racial preferences) and counterclaims questioning this supposed innocuousness and harmless neutrality (a position encapsulated by the combative phrase, "It's not just a preference") (see Callander et al. 2012, 2015; Robinson 2015; Stokel-Walker 2018). Some have questioned whether dating platforms' enabling and facilitation of race-based "sifting" (based on presumed customer demand) also contributes to the phenomenon (see Hutson et al. 2018). Following a rise in media coverage of these related issues, there has been some sociological writing on the subject, and the effects of experiences of exclusion that are undergirded by (pronounced or implicit) racist attitudes in the realm of dating, social networking, and sexual behavior have been examined by scholars using the frame of critical race theory, for instance (see, for example, Han 2008; see also Callander et al. 2016; Ro et al. 2013; Robinson 2015).

Racism is a necessarily complex subject that remains difficult to fully unpack. Broader social construction of racial "desirability" remains the basis on which inter-ethnic relations (insofar as these are relevant to the domain of sexuality and sexual behavior) play out, and can be expected, therefore, to remain the focus of a lot of commentary. However, racism is co-constituted in complex ways by the subjects and victims of racist ideology and thought, and in thinking through the intersections between sexuality and ethnic identity, it might be worthwhile to also consider how racism can shape the subjectivity of stigmatized ethnic communities (see Du Bois 1903; Fanon 1961).

Internalized racism can play a role in how inter-ethnic social relations among diaspora communities of color (for instance, pertaining to and exemplified in dating practices and sexual behavior) may evolve and be configured along pre-determined conceptual boundaries in multicultural societies (see, for example, Pyke 2010). An essay on the impact of internalized racism among migrants in a multicultural society highlights instances of how pre-determined conceptual boundaries around inter-ethnic relations, and pre-configured inter-racial dating possibilities, can dominate a queer migrant's worldview, thus reinforcing the internalization of hierarchical social relations:

> In Melbourne, I once came across promotional material from a support group for gay Asian men inviting interested individuals to a discussion on inter-racial relationships. There were two sessions planned. What immediately struck me was that both of these sessions were specifically about 'White/Asian' relationships. Evidently, in this group's imagination, there was little scope for inter-racial configurations that did not involve White men, i.e., Aboriginal/Asian, Indian/Asian, Black/Asian or even Asian/Asian partnerships. (Gay men from different 'Asian' cultures come from very different worlds and would presumably benefit from inter-cultural dialogue?) This could be seen as reflective of gay dating in the larger community: inter-racial configurations, and discussions thereof, usually revolve around a White partner who assumes a primary role, while [other] possibilities of inter-ethnic dating are occluded by layers of internalised racism, inter-ethnic racism and social hierarchy. Language barriers and the aspiration to become 'more Australian' no doubt contribute to this as well.
>
> It is this erasure (and inordinate emphasis on one set of desires and possibilities) that most interests me. In complex multicultural societies, various aspects of the social dynamics between ethnic groups remain shrouded in mystery. This is partly because 'racism' is constituted by and large in a unilateral fashion and its less 'obvious' manifestations are either simply not known... Moreover, by seeking to define themselves primarily in relation to the dominant group, members of minority ethnic groups often neglect to address the existence of negative feelings and attitudes towards other ethnicities within their own communities and amongst their own family and friends. (Rajkhowa 2014)

This reflexive tendency toward granting primacy to the dominant White subject that is highlighted here may also be seen as permeating the historical, conceptual and theoretical interface(s) between LGBTIQ community organizing, scholarship, media discourse, and public policy (Clarke 2013, p. 182).

Identities are socially constructed and based on our social affiliations (whether innate or intentional): "all parts of our identities are shaped by socially constructed positions and memberships" (Misawa 2010, p. 26). Our understandings of identity are constantly evolving and must take into account variable "inter-category and intra-category permutations of gender, sexuality, ethnicity, race and religion, as well as disability, class and indigeneity" (Pallotta-Chiarolli and Rajkhowa 2017, p. 430). Pertinent to this chapter is the notion of intra-group fragmentation and marginalization: "the further fragmentation and relegation [to subordinate status] within already oppressed groups, causing intra-group marginalization" (Harris 2009, p. 431). The idea that oppression and violence can be enacted "horizontally" is well recognized. Scholars have attempted to theorize this in terms of the interweaving and interlocking of differences within intersectional models of identity (Anzaldua 1987; Pallotta-Chiarolli 2004), and to arrive at a conceptualization of "a more complicated relationship of power based on multiple intersecting structures of domination such as race, ethnicity, class, sexual orientation and gender" (Ekine 2013, p. 80). Varied and seemingly disparate forces of exclusion and marginalization can work in tandem with and reinforce each other, generating varying manifestations of iniquity; for example, anti-immigrant racisms and homophobia can be considered "mutually constitutive," permitting or facilitating "different kinds of visibility, invisibility and contradiction" (Kosnick 2011, p. 122). The importance of acknowledging disparities of power and other issues pertaining to visibility and representation is well recognized:

> [T]he politics of representation influences the ways that 'access and excess' are experienced; the ability, capital and opportunity to assert agency because of varied privilege; and the experience of restriction and interlocking oppressions, which limit opportunities for agency and self-determination (Pallotta-Chiarolli and Pease 2014 in Pallotta-Chiarolli and Rajkhowa 2017, p. 430).

As mentioned earlier, some have suggested that, in the current political climate – paradoxically against a backdrop of the increased visibility of sexual and ethnic minorities, and (arguably) the undiminished prominence of political claims based on identity – a process of "refraction," or depoliticization, of gender and racial identities has unfolded (Gomez and McFarlane 2017), rendering what may have once been a perceptible and cognizable relationship between identity and social context and experience perhaps less easily cognizable (Gomez and McFarlane 2017, pp. 364–365). Depoliticization can complicate our understanding of multiple identities and make examination of the social ramifications of identity more challenging. Although the challenges of engaging with the complexity of the multiple intersections between ethnicity and sexuality may appear daunting, the importance of simply acknowledging, at least, the potential impact(s) and significance of this intersectionality needs to be affirmed:

> People's positionality greatly influences what they have access to and how societal systems and structures interact with them. Race, ethnicity, class, gender and sexuality are relational, complex and shifting rather than fixed and independent. (Pallotta-Chiarolli and Rajkhowa 2017, p. 430)

The impacts and significance of this intersectionality have historically been most evident in the domain of health. Negative social attitudes toward marginalized and disadvantaged groups have an impact on health outcomes. Minority status, coupled with experiences of discrimination and exclusion, can lead to a recognizable form of "minority stress" (Meyer 2003), which can contribute to iniquitous health outcomes. Experiences of violence, hostility, and discrimination, and being surrounded by and subjected to negative social attitudes, can have a significant impact on individuals' health by, for example, compounding anxiety, precipitating depression, and inhibiting one's ability to integrate into (and succeed in) education and employment. Studies have examined how health outcomes are affected by racism, sexism, and classism (Krieger et al. 1993; Marmot and Wilkinson 2009). Studies have also looked at the impacts of discrimination against LGBTIQ people on their health outcomes, finding links between homophobia and discrimination on the one hand and negative health outcomes such as anxiety, loneliness, isolation, depression, addiction, and self-harm on the other (Corboz et al. 2008; Fokkema and Kuyper 2009; Kuyper and Fokkema 2010; King et al. 2008). Experiences of racism, classism, and social exclusion can further exacerbate these negative health outcomes that are associated with experiences of homophobic discrimination (Cochran and Mays 2007; Kim and Fredriksen-Goldsen 2012; Mills et al. 2001). The compounded effects of different forms of discrimination, and of "interlocking and mutually-constituting disadvantages" (Nair and Rajkhowa 2017), can be examined and understood through the lens of intersectionality (Crenshaw 2012; see Bostwick et al. 2014; Nair and Rajkhowa 2017).

For many MCMF LGBTIQ people, maintaining a silence about their sexuality can be a necessary strategy for coping with fear of rejection, isolation, and ongoing discrimination. MCMF LGBTIQ individuals may attach great importance to maintaining the stability of family relations and meeting (sometimes strenuously reinforced) familial expectations (particularly around marriage), and thus to maintaining their privacy:

> For many sexual minority individuals, privacy is still critical to maintaining employment, family relations, ties to ethnic cultural groups or membership in religious institutions, and respect for privacy has become part of sexual minority cultures. (Bauer and Wayne 2005, p. 46)

However, silence about sexuality as a strategy for maintaining privacy can become a tool of repression and oppression, enforced by both the individual and the family and society at large. This can contribute to varying forms of "invisibility," "queer symbolic annihilation," and "queer (un)intelligibility," and thus to the buttressing and consolidation of a culture of "systemic erasure" (Muller 2017, p. 1). In the domain of health, symbolic annihilation can also occur through the omission, trivialization, and condemnation of queer subjects (Tuchman 2000). Heteronormative knowledge(s) and approaches within healthcare systems (Rosario 1997), and, importantly, the epoch-defining stigmatization of queer (particularly gay male) bodies during the HIV/AIDS epidemic in the 1980s–1990s (and, arguably, in the United States, the political establishment's apathy toward and deliberate neglect of the suffers of the disease in the initial phase of the epidemic) (Shilts 2007), have historically (con-)strained LGBTIQ visibility within healthcare systems. Importantly, the criminalization and persecution of LGBTIQ people in a number of countries, and the continuing ramifications of the HIV/AIDS pandemic globally, have been (and continue to be) significant determinants of the health of LGBTIQ people around the world (see, for example, Altman 1997, 2002; Parker 2002; Piot et al. 2001; Pisani 2010).

Being queer in a cultural context that is characterized by homophobia and rejection of LGBTIQ identity can undoubtedly negatively impact on people's well-being. Many MCMF LGBTIQ people in the diaspora may feel compelled to negotiate a multitude of expectations, and social and behavioral regulations and codes around gender, sexuality, and ethnicity (Abraham 2009). These are determined by and generated within ethnic and familial settings, religious communities, and the wider heteronormative society (Gahan et al. 2014; Habib 2009; Jaspal and Cinnirella 2014; Rajkhowa and Thompson 2015; Siraf 2012; Siraj 2014; Yip 2008), and can shape individuals' ability to develop and maintain a well-integrated sense of self. Experiences of psychological and social disintegration (and breakdown of familial relationships) can severely affect and compromise people's well-being (Hammoud-Beckett 2007). An interventionist approach to helping people tackle experiences of homophobia and repression within an MCMF context posits that, within communities, policies, programs, and practices that actively challenge prejudice and foster a sense of safety and belonging need to be promoted and implemented by government and educational institutions (Pallotta-Chiarolli 2005a, 2016). Many MCMF LGBTIQ people wish to cultivate a sense of belonging within their communities, and familial and social connections that augment their cultural identity; they wish to foster relationships that are based on a recognition of shared faith values and struggles (Beckett et al. 2014; Low and Pallotta-Chiarolli 2015).

However, many MCMF families may see LGBTIQ identity as a manifestation of secularization, loss of religious grounding, moral decadence, and "Westernization" (Jaspal and Cinnirella 2010; Shannahan 2010; Beckett et al. 2014), leading to hostility toward and punitive treatment of LGBTIQ family members. For Muslim LGBTIQ youth from orthodox backgrounds, a breaking of religious strictures can lead to violence, intimidation, and excommunication from the family and community (Hammoud-Beckett 2007). MCMF LGBTIQ youth experience "developmental" challenges that may be unique to their predicament: they find themselves needing to cultivate a sexuality-based identity and a cultural identity simultaneously, to reconcile and resolve conflicts arising from their concurrent identifications, and to negotiate discrimination and stigma associated with homophobia, racism, and sexism (Savin-Williams 1998). Affirming support for LGBTIQ family members, and for the belief that "demonstrating and upholding family values can be fully compatible with a respect for LGBTIQ rights" (Hooghe et al. 2010, p. 68), can be a significant challenge for MCMF LGBTIQ individuals and their families.

Australian Perspectives

The need for state and civil society organizations' promotion of inclusive research programs and community initiatives is clear, and Australia may be considered a pioneer in this respect. In Australia, there has been significant support for research into the experiences and needs of MCMF LGBTIQ people, and several community initiatives that foster civic participation and belonging (Emslie 2005; Gopalkrishnan 2016; Harris 2011; Kassisieh 2012; Mejia-Canales and Leonard 2016; Noto et al. 2014; Pallotta-Chiarolli 2016; Poljski 2011; Rajkhowa 2017; Qian et al. 2015; Queering the Air 2015; see Pallotta-Chiarolli and Rajkhowa 2017, p. 432). These research and community arts projects have explored and investigated the lived experiences and needs of MCMF LGBTIQ people in Australia, facilitating a number of collaborations (both academic and creative) (Duruz 1999; Pallotta-Chiarolli 2008; Rajkhowa 2017), and the formation of community support groups:

> These self-determining agentic groups provide vital ongoing support and perform developmental roles but require collaboration from mainstream MCMF community services, and homo-positive state and federal institutions and structures. These groups aim to break down the association of non-Anglo ethnicity and faith with homophobia, and develop a relationship of trust between systems, institutions, and MCMF LGBTIQ individuals and communities. (Pallotta-Chiarolli and Rajkhowa 2017, p. 432)

Two major Australian anthologies containing autobiographical and narrative writing, and commentary on contemporary political and social issues by MCMF LGBTIQ Australians (Jackson and Sullivan 1999a; Pallotta-Chiarolli 2018), and an indigenous LGBTIQ anthology (Hodge 2015), are prominent examples of recent collaborations in this area. Academic conferences such as the Australian Lesbian and Gay Archives' annual Homosexual Histories Conference (ALGA n.d.) have prominently incorporated MCMF LGBTIQ issues in their programs. Community-focused consultations and projects have also produced recommendations and strategies for the inclusion of MCMF LGBTIQ identifies within MCMF frameworks, policies, and projects (Chang and Apostle 2008). These recommendations cover the roles of state and local council services and MCMF community organizations, faith organizations, educational institutions, and primary and tertiary health services (see Pallotta-Chiarolli and Rajkhowa 2017, pp. 434–435).

Asian Migration

Here, in Australia, migration and its social concomitant, multiculturalism, are critical (if contentious) components of the contemporary political framework and national imaginary. Migration (considered in conjunction with its many social, political, and economic ramifications) may be deemed one of the preeminent foci of contemporary Australian politics, and, in an analysis of contemporary cultural trends, the impacts of immigration (and its associated cultural changes) may be viewed in juxtaposition with other critical issues and processes, such as the emergence and consolidation of Aboriginal rights, women's rights, and LGBTIQ rights.

In these first two decades of the twenty-first century, migration from Asian countries has surpassed European migration. Asian migration has become (and will ostensibly remain) a significant political-demographic consideration in analyses of culture and politics (see Bowen 2012). Gay Asian men "make up the largest regional group of entrants under Australia's provisions for same-sex couples" (Luibhéid 2008, p. 177). Commentary on the lived experiences of gay Asian migrants in Australia highlights a range of issues relating to themes such as "racialization," discrimination, alienation, assimilation, and the negotiation of fraught relationships with culture (see Rajkhowa 2017), which have been conceptualized and examined, for instance, under the rubric of "difficult belonging" (Rajkhowa and Thompson 2015):

> The phrase 'difficult belongings' is useful because it encapsulates the tenuous nature of the sexuality/migration/race/belonging nexus. On the one hand, the sense of belonging that comes from immersion in a specifically queer identity or community is juxtaposed, uncomfortably, with the alienation (or perhaps dissonance) that accompanies migration. On the other hand, the assumption of 'belonging' to a culture or community that is defined in ethnic terms, through primordial links, is problematised by sexuality and the invariably contentious space that is occupied by 'divergent' or 'queer' sexualities within discrete and autonomous migrant cultures. (Rajkhowa and Thompson 2015, p. 3)

Social belonging is a complex idea that evokes and encompasses multiple conceptions about and understandings of relationships between the self and community (see, for example, Guibernaut 2013; Probyn 1996). For gay Asian migrants, social belonging, and associated understandings of (and approaches to) identity, can be influenced by how LGBTIQ identity and rights are conceptualized and approached in our countries of origin (see Sullivan and Jackson 2013). This sociopolitical link is one that remains difficult to unpack (see Lee 2016; Luibhéid 2008). Arguably, a significant segment of the literature on sexuality and Asian cultures that is produced (and most readily available) in Western academe is predominantly diaspora-centric, comprising reflections on the experiences of gay Asian migrants and people of Asian origin in Western nations (see, for example, Chan 1995; Eng and Hom 1998; Gopinath 2005; Jackson and Sullivan 1999a; Pallotta-Chiarolli 2016, 2018; Pallotta-Chiarolli and Rajkhowa 2017; Rajkhowa 2017; Ratti 1993). Nevertheless, in the last decade, we have seen the emergence of a significant body of scholarship on sexuality, politics, and culture in specific Asian countries (see Sullivan and Jackson 2013).

A recent and popular work of travel journalism, *Gaysia: Adventures in the Queer East,* by an Asian-Australian writer, Benjamin Law (2012), explores LGBTIQ identity and rights in a number of Asian countries, and offers insights into the intersections between ethnicity, culture, and sexuality in these settings. While not explicitly political or scholarly in approach (it is a travelogue and work of popular journalism), it adopts an engaging, politically informed exploratory approach to the politics of LGBTIQ identity in Asia. Written from the perspective of a second-generation Asian-Australian, and offering perspectives on how sexuality and identity intersect in Asia, this work provides insightful glimpses into LGBTIQ subjectivity in Asia through accounts of encounters with political actors (including those who drive homophobic political agendas) and community activists. This approach broadens awareness of the links between ethnicity, culture, politics, and sexuality.

As mentioned earlier, while the intersections between culture, ethnicity, and sexuality are arguably usually examined from the perspective of diasporas – and through the lens of the experiences of diasporic communities – in Western nations, it may be argued that without reference to specific international sociopolitical contexts, discussion of the topic may become abstracted. In parts of Asia, Africa, and the Middle East, intense contestations spurred by the perceived "intrusion" and "importation" of liberal cultural attitudes to homosexuality have dominated public discourse on LGBTIQ rights (see Altman 1996, 2002; Lee 2016; Ndashe 2013). As Katerina Dalacoura writes, "Homosexuality has [...] become a source of intense cultural contestations at a global level" (Dalacoura 2014, p. 1290), and opposition to homosexuality has become a means of "affirming cultural integrity and authenticity... defined and asserted in juxtaposition to the West, which either epitomises the threatening cultural outsider or becomes a tangible opponent through the actions of governments, NGOs and individual activists" (ibid., p. 1291). This complicates the prospects for progress on decriminalization of sexuality and recognition of LGBTIQ rights in many countries.

Political Subjectivity and LGBTIQ Rights in Asia

The following section includes a limited overview of political, legal, or social developments around LGBTIQ rights in selected Asian countries. Accordingly, the aim of this section is to situate the discussion of this topic within specific (international) political, social, and ethno-cultural frameworks and to simply provide brief snapshots of the progression of LGBTIQ rights in these different contexts. The subsection on India includes references to selected themes in the scholarly literature on LGBTIQ subjects, while the other subsections following this provide précis accounts of progress in the area of decriminalization of homosexuality and/or recognition of LGBTIQ rights in other selected Asian countries. This discussion has its obvious limitations; it does not provide a globally comprehensive view and, reflecting the author's limited knowledge and scope for exploration, does not explore national and cultural contexts other than those that have been purposively selected here. Nevertheless, it is hoped that this discussion contains some examples of how recognition of LGBTIQ rights has evolved internationally and how this may intersect with political and ethno-cultural context.

India

Writing about LGBTIQ politics in India necessitates, firstly, a qualification of the identitarian terms that frame this conceptual and political domain, as well as a qualification of claims about the disruptive presence (and/or feasible accommodation) of LGBTIQ activism within broader Indian political thought and activism. A few works of political and cultural analysis, as well as works that have emerged more directly through activism and political-cultural mobilization, offer astute interrogation of semantic identity categories (see Bhaskaran 2004; Dave 2012; Vanita 2013; Menon 2007a; Narrain and Bhan 2005). The important point here is to emphasize, without elaborately rehashing well-known arguments, that there is widespread recognition of the fact that identitarian terms (including gay, lesbian and queer), and "LGBTIQ" as a political category, carry different semantic valences in different contexts, and their equivalents in Indian contexts may not entirely fit within the terminological or conceptual frameworks that are preferred (and were established) by Western queer movements and academic writing. There is some scholarship and activist writing (particularly in relation to HIV/AIDS prevention programs) that deals with the complicated tensions that exist between queer "identitarian positionalities" in India (see Bacchetta 2002; Gopinath 1997; Khan 2001). While many Indians who engage in non-heteronormative sexual, romantic, and affective practices, particularly those who are part of urban, middle-, and upper-class milieux, may self-identify as gay or lesbian, many others, in different social strata, do not or cannot adopt these identity labels; still others prefer "indigenous" markers such as "kothi" and "panthi," which signify sexual roles rather than identity (see Khan 2001). More prominently, many in the large and diverse transgender community identify as "hijra," an identity constituted by a complex interaction between gender identity, community, ritual performance, and social milieu (see Sukthankar 2005). From the 1990s till today, these identitarian distinctions have informed, for example, how organizations working in the HIV/AIDS sector name, categorize, or position their target demographics (see Narrain 2004; Khan 2001; Kole 2007). With sexual practice, rather than identity, at its center, the formulation "men who have sex with men," or MSM, has enjoyed wide currency in policy discourse internationally, and this is particularly relevant in India (ibid.).

At the same time, it is also important to recognize that the practice of asserting identity on the basis of sexuality (and LGBTIQ as conceptual framework and terminology) has certainly made inroads into the public consciousness, spurring affirmation on the one hand and (arguably) moral panic on the other (see Bhaskaran 2004; Dasgupta 2014; Shah 2015). Gay, lesbian, bisexual, transgender, and even queer as identity markers have entered the common sense of public discourse. Given the multiple ways in which these identities have coalesced around particular modes of association, networks, state interventions, mobilizations, cultural productions, and ideological strands, it is widely acknowledged that the multiplicity of "queer" identity or relational practices cannot easily be compressed within an all-encompassing and unifying conceptual framework.

The point here is to simply indicate that use of particular sets of identity terms neither overrides nor obviates existing heterogeneous markers of identity, and the varying socio-material conditions and discoursal understandings that underpin them; rather, these serve as a short-hand to loosely signify non-heteronormative sexuality and identity. As such, any reference to a queer movement and to queer rights in India, for instance, implicitly performs the task of condensing a heterogeneous range of meanings, interests, and concerns, and no claims can justifiably be made about adequately representing the multifarious elements of the broader social, political, and relational paradigms and contexts that have emerged around queer identity, or about compressing these within a single conceptual category.

This approach applies to discussion of LGBTIQ identities not only in India but many other cultural and political contexts as well (see Grewal and Kaplan 2001). The relevance and valences of identity terms and identitarian terminology can differ from one context to another, and this variability has both political and personal significance. While the identity terms gay and lesbian have often concretized and reified otherwise less-defined, euphemistically understood concepts in various cultures, making visibly clear what was previously "unspoken," the usage of these terms and, arguably, the contemporary hegemonic hold of these terms on the public consciousness have also spurred alienation and dislocation, making it difficult for some to either fully own or fully discard these labels. These identify labels can be affirming or negating, liberating or restrictive, and meaningful or otherwise, to people in different cultural settings, and in different languages. Terminology itself becomes a powerful tool of self-conceptualization. Accordingly, the importance of identity-defining terminology and language has been appropriately recognized in scholarship on culture and sexuality (see Brubaker and Cooper 2000; Davis 2014; McConnell-Ginet 2003; Moi 1995).

In thinking about the intersections between ethno-cultural and political context, and sexuality, the continuing criminalization of sexual intercourse "against the order of nature," and ongoing persecution of gay, lesbian, and transgender people, in different countries, is a foremost concern (see Asal et al. 2013; Altman and Symons 2016), and this has been particularly true of India. In India, LGBTIQ rights activism and scholarly commentary has predominantly focused on efforts to decriminalize homosexuality through amendments to Section 377 of the Indian Penal Code, which hitherto proscribed "carnal intercourse against the order of nature" (see Fernandez 2002; Misra 2009; Narrain and Bhan 2005; Sharma 2008). This statute, which was introduced under British colonial rule, can be found in several other national penal codes in Asia, Africa, and elsewhere, and has been retained in some form by over 30 nations (Gupta 2008).

Three critical milestones define the trajectory of the movement for decriminalization in India. In 2009, the Delhi High Court "read down" Section 377, declaring that the criminalization of sexual relations between consenting adults of the same sex was unconstitutional. This was the culmination of years-long efforts and longstanding legal petitions against Section 377 (Gupta 2006; Misra 2009; Waites 2010). In 2013, the Supreme Court of India, the country's apex appellate court, overturned the aforementioned decision, thereby reinstating the relevant provisions of Section 377 (Mahapatra 2013). This court's decision was premised on the argument that Section 377 (in its now-erstwhile form) did not violate the fundamental rights of citizens that are guaranteed in the Indian constitution. (The fundamental rights section of the Indian constitution operates as a foundational bill of rights.) Petitioners challenged this decision; however, in 2014, the Supreme Court dismissed pleas for a review (The Economist 2018). In 2016, the Supreme Court agreed to review the previous decision and subsequently referred the matter to a "constitution bench" (or panel of judges tasked with definitively determining the "constitutionality" of a given law) (ibid.). In September 2018, the court ruled that the relevant subsection of Section 377 was unconstitutional (Safi 2018), thus effectively decriminalizing consensual sex between adults of the same sex, and definitively determining that the provisions in their now-erstwhile form violated citizens' fundamental rights. This decision drew on another decision delivered by the court, in 2017, wherein the right to privacy was interpreted as being intrinsic to one of the fundamental rights enshrined in the constitution (Ganguly 2017).

This history and trajectory of judicial decisions, and the specific interrogation of sexuality and sexual-subjectivity that each case prompted and generated, have together effectively defined and interpellated LGBTIQ subjecthood in India (see Kapur 2017). This juridical interpellation of queer positionality has had profound consequences, with each of these cases having engendered the body of the queer subject in distinct ways. From being characterized by the opponents of gay rights as a "deviant" group deserving of continued state persecution (see Narrain 2004; Bose and Bhattacharyya 2007), to being characterized, dismissively, by Supreme Court judges (in one of the penultimate cases) as constituting a "miniscule minority" (see Subramanian 2015) (with the implication that this group is, therefore, undeserving of explicitly guaranteed protection from persecution), the LGBTIQ community has confronted the multifarious strands of homophobic prejudice and oppositional mobilization that have visibly circulated in the country since the prospect of decriminalization was raised, and these opposing forces have continually irrupted into and attempted to control public discourse to varying degrees.

Each case has had significant cultural impacts. Each of these political and judicial processes generated significant media coverage. Queer politics in India has in the recent past emerged more "visibly" and directly into the mainstream of public discourse through greater representation of queer lives and issues in the mainstream media. The political content of mediated queer representation has shaped and contributed in a fundamental way to public understanding of the core issues that have animated the fight for queer rights in India. In several ways, media representation has been central to discussions of and mobilizations around queer rights in the country (see Vanita 2013; Mitra 2010). An analysis of how the mainstream media have framed queer rights and issues is one that would illuminate significant themes around the changing social mores and political convictions of the media-consuming public(s) in India. Particular attention may be paid to mainstream media coverage surrounding the aforementioned three critical discourse moments, which collectively constitute the primary lodestone of recent activism and media coverage.

Scholarship on queer sexuality and its affective and cultural dimensions in India spans a rich spectrum of disciplines. Queer activism and scholarship owe enormously to the political and cultural evolution of feminist thought; feminist scholarship on the intersections between gender, post-coloniality, history, economy, and culture has generated insights that have proved immensely productive for scholarly understanding of non-heteronormative sexuality (see Menon 1999, 2007b, 2009). In particular, the ways in which the aforementioned contemporary legal frameworks around sexuality, as well as social attitudes to sexuality, have evolved historically have been the subject of much insightful analysis (see Narrain 2007; Bose and Bhattacharyya 2007). Studies charting how the colonial state, nationalist bourgeoisie, and post-colonial dispensations have each molded, co-opted, confronted, or otherwise negotiated sexual subjectivity and citizenship have illuminated the complex interaction between state power, social structures, and subject bodies (see Arondekar 2005, 2009; Puri 2002). In the domain of culture, seminal works have recuperated a seemingly lost pre-colonial history of "queer" sensibilities in Indian art, literature, and folk traditions (see Vanita and Kidwai 2008). The contemporary cultural significance of these attempts at reclaiming a seemingly more affirmative (or, at least, less sexually oppressive) past cannot be overstated. Queer rights and acceptance of non-heteronormative sexualities, hitherto couched in Western-derived and Western-inflected discourses on human rights, have been shown to have a basis in (and legitimacy through) indigenous thought, culture, and tradition.

For instance, the trajectory and evolution of transgender rights in India have been influenced strongly by the recuperation of "traditional" recognition and acceptance of transgender identity (see Kalra 2012; Nanda 2015; Sukthankar 2005). While gay and lesbian identity have been perceived as emerging from a Western social, political, and intellectual framework (see Bhaskaran 2004), transgender identity has been reframed as rightfully belonging within indigenous social and conceptual frameworks (see Dutta and Roy 2014; Kalra 2012; Michelraj 2015). Recognition of transgender rights and respect for mobilizations promoting recognition of "other" gender are thus seen as being compatible with tradition and culture. This has engendered a tension between approaches to gay and lesbian rights on the one hand and transgender rights on the other (see Rajkhowa 2015). Both the judiciary and parliament in India (indeed, in some individual states in the country) have now affirmed the importance of protecting the rights of transgender persons and establishing official frameworks for the protection of transgender people from discrimination, even as support for gay and lesbian rights (or support for decriminalization of homosexuality more generally) has, at numerous historic junctures, been repeatedly eschewed and suppressed. In fact, this tension has played a critical role in the way that homosexual rights have evolved in the country, with the invocation of "traditional" legitimacy (or legitimacy derived from antiquity and tradition) facilitating (legal and legislative) affirmation of one framework of rights on the one hand, and the spectre of intrusive (imported) modernity hindering progression of another framework of rights on the other hand (ibid.). This dichotomy may be linked to the salience of binary gender frameworks, and the possibility of the accommodation, within a patriarchal social framework, of transgender rights via binary approaches to gender and sexuality (where same-sex attraction is rendered comprehensible through gender conversion). Nevertheless, the very fact that ameliorative policies and strategies have been devised and proffered by the political establishment, in recognition of the need to counteract the marginalization and longstanding economic disadvantage suffered by the transgender community in India (see Chakrapani 2010; Sukthankar 2005) (long ignored by federal governments), signals new shifts in the national biopolitics.

While the non-heteronormative (and, particularly, gender-fluid) sensibilities of pre-colonial literature, myth, and culture have been a rich subject of regenerative historical analysis (see Michelraj 2015), the myriad ways in which queer sensibilities inhere in many contemporary cultural productions, including film and advertising, have also been analyzed in cultural studies works, particularly those published since the early 2000s (see, for example, Gopinath 2000). Operating in a strict environment of social, political, and administrative censorship that is undergirded by sometimes explicit but often implicit moral codes (see Kaur and Mazzarella 2009), films and other televisual works depicting homosexuality have tended to treat the subject in tangential and euphemistic ways, with gesture, oblique dialogue, and symbol tentatively signaling concealed homosexual desire, which is always controlled and contained within permissible parameters (including the generic parameters of comedy) (Gopinath 2000). However, some works of art have indeed pushed these boundaries and depicted homosexuality in more direct, forthright, and self-conscious ways, even though the final work is ultimately always subject to the imprimatur of official film censors and a frequently repressive censorship regime. One such film, *Fire*, released in 1996, prompted a conflagration almost unparalleled in the history of the Indian film industry (see Gopinath 1998). Its subtle treatment of a lesbian relationship (occurring in the context of a heterosexual marriage and the social framework of the Indian "joint-family") was deemed incendiary, and provoked riots, bans, and political hectoring that long outlasted its brief and attenuated stint in film theatres and distribution circuits. Adapted from a literary work that tangentially and symbolically referred to a lesbian encounter (Chugtai 1942), this film, by depicting lesbianism and foregrounding themes around same-sex female sexuality (within the context of heterosexual marriage), encountered significant and violent resistance from conservative religious groups. This episode violently revealed the extent of traditionalist opposition to emergent articulations of sexuality and delimited the scope for these articulations within the hegemonic public sphere. In the aftermath of the well-known, well-covered, and seminal *"Fire* controversy," media and social commentary on queer subjects, it has been argued, evolved considerably (see Gopinath 1998; Menon 2007a). Since then, in academia and journalism, there have been many engaging analyses of art, culture, politics, and sexual subjectivity in India (see, for example, Dudrah 2012; Gopinath 2005; Kapur 2017; Kavi 2000).

The following subsections provide a brief overview of the state of LGBTIQ rights in selected Asian countries. As mentioned earlier, these are intended as "snapshot" accounts of the politics of recognition of sexuality (and legal developments relating to extant criminalization of sexuality and discrimination on the basis of sexuality) in the region.

South Asia

In Pakistan, Nepal, Bangladesh, and Sri Lanka, as in India, LGBTIQ identity and political mobilization may also be seen through the lens of a putative dichotomy between gay rights and transgender rights. In these nations, the rights of transgender people have been legally recognized and consolidated to similar degrees (see Anam 2018; Barker 2018; Hashim 2018). This is premised on similar conceptualizations of transgender rights as having some legitimacy in "tradition" and "culture." Nevertheless, as in India, transgender people across South Asia continue to face overwhelming social stigma, marginalization, and economic disadvantage (see Khan et al. 2009; Redding 2012).

In South Asian nations (with the prominent exception of Nepal, and now India), homosexuality (or, more specifically, sexual relations between consenting adults of the same sex) remains a criminal offence (with all countries having retained the overarching framework of the colonial penal code and its criminalization of homosexuality), although prosecutions tend to be rare (see Baudh 2013). In general, non-heteronormative sexuality is considered taboo, and social norms and expectations around marriage (within predominantly patriarchal cultural contexts) instantiate the idea of "compulsory" heterosexuality (see Gopinath 2005).

The steady rise of religious fundamentalism in Pakistan and Bangladesh (see Bjorkman 1988; Chhachhi 1989; Griffiths and Hasan 2015; Mishra 2012) has contributed to an exacerbation of social and political intimidation and victimization of LGBTIQ people, particularly activists and those who have publicly advocated for recognition of LGBTIQ rights (Rahman 2017). In Bangladesh, ongoing radicalization and fundamentalist mobilizations have precipitated rampant violence against members of minority communities, including in the form of violent persecution of individuals who are (frequently baselessly) accused by reactionary groups of transgressing religious strictures, and even the assassination of individuals targeted in this manner (see Graham-Harrison and Hammadi 2016; Hammadi 2016). Instances of political violence carried out by Islamist extremists have contributed to (and definitively signal) a deterioration of LGBTIQ rights, which has had the effect of stifling public debate on decriminalization of homosexuality, access to health services, and freedom of association (ibid.).

In Nepal, on the other hand, the political change that followed a constitutional crisis in 2001 (and, ultimately, the abolition of the monarchy in 2008) prompted a renegotiation of LGBTIQ rights, and anti-discrimination provisions were incorporated into the new constitution (see Boyce and Coyle 2013; Braithwaite 2015; Knight 2017; Roy 2007). Legal challenges to the *de jure* criminalization of homosexuality resulted in the emergence of a new framework of positively affirmed rights for LGBTIQ people (ibid.). A court order in 2007 enjoining the legislature to facilitate recognition of same-sex marriage prompted a series of abortive official attempts to prepare the requisite legislation, and – against a backdrop of years-long political instability, contentious constitutional gridlock, and inchoate democratic revival and rebuilding – at the time of writing, this has remained unaddressed (see Panthi 2016). Nepal has been recognized as having the most progressive legal and political framework for LGBTIQ rights in South Asia and thus distinctly stands apart from its South Asian neighbors on this front.

China

In China, research and commentary on historical and traditional conceptions about sexuality have influenced contemporary scholarly and journalistic engagement with homosexuality. Commentators who write about ideas about sexuality in antiquity cite historical records that indicate, for instance, that among certain political elites and religious preceptors, there was a lack of explicit hostility toward (or even some degree of acceptance of) homosexuality, although this changed according to the social and political beliefs and proclivities of the dominant political establishment and ruling dynasty (see, for example, Chiang 2010; Engebretsen et al. 2015; Goldin 2002; Hinsch 1990; Ng 1989; Vitiello 2011; Wu 2003). The recuperation of traditional beliefs and social norms and the positing of this reclamation as an appropriate anchor for contemporary reconceptualizations of sexuality are important (see Coleman and Chou 2013; Wah-Shan 2001), arguably akin to trends in India.

Homosexuality was legalized in 1997 and removed from an official list of mental illnesses in 2001. Commentary on sexuality in China has focused on issues around sexuality, sexual behavior, and public health (see Jones 1999, 2007; Neilands et al. 2008; Song et al. 2011; Zhou 2006); familial and social silencing of homosexual identity; and pressures around marriage and social conformity (see Ho 2009; Liu and Choi 2006; Wei 2007; Wong 2010; Zhou 2006). Recent activism has highlighted the deleterious impacts of these pressures, including on women who are "deceived" into "false" marriages by gay men (see Burger 2013; Bianco 2015; Duan 2017; Ho 2009). The significance of social conformity and beliefs favoring maintenance of the "traditional order" is highlighted. Perceptions about homosexuality can be influenced by notions about social and familial disobedience, as well as the conceptual interweaving of social order on the one hand and political order on the other (see Sala 2018).

The vicissitudes of official attitudes toward homosexuality have shaped the trajectory of media representation of and social commentary on issues relating to sexuality, social stigma, health, etc. (Lim 2006). The recent promulgation of decrees proscribing representation of homosexuality on television and discussion around homosexual content on the social networking site Weibo, among other platforms, has constrained efforts aimed at the promotion of LGBTIQ rights (Palmer 2018). However, these decrees have met voluble public criticism, and complex resistances to ostensible political antipathy to LGBTIQ rights have manifested on public forums (ibid.).

Some social research suggests that there is widespread support for same-sex marriage in some social quarters (Economist 2017). Even against a backdrop of tenuous tolerance for LGBTIQ representation in the public domain, officials have encountered visible activism promoting greater acceptance of same-sex marriage (Shepherd 2018). Complex links between ongoing political censorship and restraints on LGBTIQ representation on the one hand, and changing social norms and attitudes on the other, inform the trajectory of LGBTIQ rights in China.

East Asia

Taiwan is considered to have the most progressive legal framework for LGBTIQ rights in East Asia (and, arguably, Asia more generally) (see Cheng et al. 2016; Hsu and Yen 2017). Anti-discrimination provisions were enacted in law in the early 2000s and remain the most robust in the region (ibid.). In 2017, the country's Constitutional Court passed a judgment requiring the parliament to legalize gay marriage within a stipulated timeframe, thus putting Taiwan on course to becoming the first country in the region to recognize same-sex marriage (Hunt and Tsui 2017). This injunction on parliament to legalize same-sex marriage would, it was argued at the time, likely force the government and parliament to reconsider and then rectify current discrepancies between the legal rights of heterosexual and homosexual couples in a timely manner (ibid.). However, at the time of writing, the passage of a referendum opposing marriage equality had complicated the prospect (and likely form) of further government action (Chung 2018).

In Japan, homosexuality was only briefly ever criminalized, and political parties and social groups (including representatives of religious groups) generally maintain a neutral stance on homosexuality (see McLelland 2005; Lunsing 2005; Tamagawa 2016). An increasing number of openly gay, lesbian, and transgender persons have won political office (or come out while in office) (Osumi 2018). Commentators note that while socially conservative attitudes in Japan have historically constrained social recognition of same-sex relationships, changing norms, attitudes, and official anti-discrimination initiatives have reportedly facilitated greater openness on non-heteronormative sexuality (see Osumi 2018; Tamagawa 2016).

In Korea, the constitution and penal code do not mention homosexuality (although the military penal code does criminalize homosexual relations, a provision that, at the time of writing, was subject to a legal review) (Hu 2017; Rich and Webb 2018). However, anti-discrimination legislation specifically addresses discrimination on the basis of sexuality (ibid.). Commentators note that while the dominant socially conservative political culture has restrained public discussion of homosexuality (Chase 2012), awareness of homosexuality continues to grow, and broader social attitudes to homosexuality and ideas about LGBTIQ people continue to evolve (see Bong 2008; Cho 2009; Hu 2017; Park-Kim et al. 2007).

Southeast Asia

LGBTIQ rights in diverse Southeast Asian nations have been shaped by these nations' divergent political and historical trajectories. Histories of colonialism, trajectories of decolonization, and the evolution of religion each play an important role in this regard. While some countries have explicitly embraced the dismantling of discriminatory laws and social frameworks, others have witnessed a reinforcement of social and political marginalization and victimization of LGBTIQ people, with excoriation of homosexuality constituting a key means of manifesting and reaffirming the hegemony of fundamentalist religion, particularly in opposition to what may be perceived as decadent Westernization.

Thailand is considered to be at the forefront of positively affirmed LGBTIQ rights in Southeast Asia (Sullivan and Jackson 2013). Thailand decriminalized homosexuality in 1956 and enacted comprehensive anti-discrimination legislation in 2015 (Limsamarnphun 2018). In 2018, at the time of writing, draft legislation recognizing same-sex partnerships was being considered by the legislature (ibid.). Widely perceived as among the most progressive Asian countries insofar as LGBTIQ rights are concerned, Thailand has long dominated Western conceptions about homosexuality in Southeast Asia, with the country's promotion of gay-friendly tourism, including sex tourism, playing a prominent role in this (see Jackson 1995; Jackson and Sullivan 1999b, c; Sullivan and Jackson 2013). Thailand's cultural "stage" features several gay- and trans-friendly enactments, and these collectively constitute a significant part of its tourism-linked cultural appeal (see Käng 2012). In spite of this perceived liberalism and progressive stance on homosexuality, however, social marginalization of local LGBTIQ communities continues to be reported, and discrimination against LGBTIQ persons in official institutions and the workforce reportedly remains entrenched (Kamjan 2014; Yongcharoenchai 2013). Thailand exemplifies the tensions engendered by the adoption of some of the values of Western-centric globalization and liberalization (and the effective co-optation of these values for strategic advantage) against a backdrop of underlying (sometimes unreconstructed) social conservatism.

In Vietnam, homosexuality, it has been argued, was never criminalized, and same-sex relations were always legal (see Horton et al. 2015). Official approaches to homosexuality have undergone significant change from the early 2000s to the present time (ibid.). From articles in official media organs condemning homosexuality in the early 2000s to contemporary legal initiatives removing barriers to same-sex relationships (such as the passage of a constitutional amendment repealing the established definition of marriage as a union between a man and a woman, and the drafting of a bill providing official recognition to same-sex relationships), official approaches to LGBTIQ rights have shifted and social attitudes have arguably become more favorable (ibid.). Although recognition of same-sex relationships was finally excluded from a marriage and family law codification bill that was passed by the legislature in 2015, the lifting of restrictions on same-sex weddings and the preparatory work that went into the drafting of this bill bolstered support for further progress, particularly as such progress on LGBTIQ rights was conceptualized in both government policy and media discourse as being conducive to the promotion of tourism and thus economically advantageous for the nation (see Mosbergen 2015). At the same time, commentators note that LGBTIQ people continue to experience social stigma and discrimination (ibid.).

In the city-state of Singapore, changing social attitudes and the increased visibility of LGBTIQ activism have failed to induce willingness in government to decriminalize homosexual sex between consenting adults (specifically same-sex attracted men) (see Offord 2003; Yue and Zubillaga-Pow 2012). Although Singapore's strategic economic clout, multiculturalism, and geopolitical advantages have engendered an ostensibly liberal and cosmopolitan culture in the island state, political and legal-judicial approaches to homosexuality remain conservative (see Oswin 2014; Yue and Zubillaga-Pow 2012), with government ministers repeatedly dismissing or downplaying the prospect of decriminalization in a "socially conservative" country, and the Singapore Supreme Court reaffirming the constitutionality of Section 377 during a legal challenge in 2014 (Human Rights Watch 2014). However, immediately after the Indian Supreme Court repealed provisions of Section 377 of the Indian Penal Code in September 2018, a fresh legal challenge was initiated in Singapore, and commentators have noted that progress on LGBTIQ rights in other Asian nations is likely to provoke policy changes in Singapore (Ungku 2018).

In Malaysia, sex between consenting adults of the same sex is listed as a criminal offence under Section 377 of the nation's penal code (retained after independence from colonial rule, like in some of the other countries that have been discussed here) (see Brownell 2009). Further, the existence of socially differentiated (and provincially differentiated) laws encompassing a range of domains (Muslim citizens are subject to *sharia*-derived laws that are enforceable in Islamic courts) has meant that criminalization of homosexuality remains entangled with both secular and religious punitive frameworks (see Lee 2012). From vigilante violence against and aggressive persecution of LGBTIQ people through to contemporary strategic political deployments of Section 377 for the purpose of elimination of political opposition – most notably against political leader Anwar Ibrahim – wide-ranging oppressive social and political phenomena have been facilitated by anti-LGBTIQ attitudes and legal frameworks (see Rajkhowa 2018). The primacy accorded to religious institutions and the emergence of religious fundamentalism and social polarization have come together to effectively entrench discrimination against LGBTIQ people and constrain progressive efforts (see Amado 2009; Rajkhowa 2018; Rehman and Polymenopoulou 2013). Ongoing radicalization within some segments of the political spectrum (and society more generally) has facilitated a refocalization of homosexuality as a target for religious fundamentalist assertion. Hegemonic religious frameworks (social, political, and legal) collectively remain the fundamental basis for negotiation of all forms of individual rights; alternative discourses and forms of negotiating identity continue to evolve in tension with and resistance to these frameworks (see Eidhamar 2014). Changing political currents (particularly, the electoral defeat in 2018 of the Barisan Nasional dispensation that had ruled Malaysia since independence) have facilitated, to some extent, a putative recognition of rights-based discourses (Rajkhowa 2018).

In Indonesia, the absence of a law specifically criminalizing homosexuality does not necessarily translate to the absence of discrimination against LGBTIQ persons. The concurrent existence and application of secular and Islamic legal frameworks (again, in a differentiated and provincially limited manner) have meant that in certain areas, people suspected of engaging in homosexual conduct can be subjected to (potentially public) corporal punishment and incarceration (Boellstorff 2005; Suroyo and Greenfield 2014; see Amado 2009; Rehman and Polymenopoulou 2013). Police raids on metropolitan social and commercial establishments associated with a gay clientele are common, as are mass arrests of people at social gatherings (BBC 2017). Use of (arguably deliberately ill-defined) laws around pornography and public order by law enforcement agencies to specifically target gay men particularly is pervasive (Boellstorff 2005). Members of leading Islamic institutions frequently exhort authorities to criminalize and persecute LGBTIQ people, using the spectacle of mass arrests to issue denunciations and disseminate religious propaganda (Human Rights Watch 2016). As in Malaysia, the recrudescence of fundamentalist political mobilizations has been accompanied by an aggressive persecution of LGBTIQ people. Homosexuality is foregrounded and deployed as a target for contentious social, political, and legal action (see Boellstorff 2005). Legal petitions supported by religious organizations have sought to amend existing laws around adultery, rape, and child abuse to criminalize homosexual relationships between consenting adults (Topsfield 2017). Coercive pressures exerted through religious groups' electoral mobilizations have bolstered and hardened political support for the explicit criminalization of homosexuality. In both Malaysia and Indonesia, LGBTIQ activism has persisted in spite of the considerable social, political, and legal obstacles that have hindered recognition of LGBTIQ rights (see Boellstorff 2005; Offord 2003; Offord and Cantrell 2001; Lee 2012; Mosbergen 2015a, b), and the consolidation of an albeit fledgling progressive social framework for recognition of LGBTIQ rights through the invocation of international human rights discourses has facilitated some developmental activity in this area.

Conclusion

The subsections above have provided brief snapshot accounts of progress in recognition of LGBTIQ rights (and approaches to LGBTIQ identity) in selected Asian countries. The aim of this section has been to instantiate how LGBTIQ rights and identity have been conceptualized and approached in specific political and cultural contexts. Approaches to LGBTIQ rights in diverse Asian societies are necessarily continually evolving, shaped by the vicissitudes of social change in those societies, the growing reach and ramifications of the forces of globalization and liberalization (as well as resistances to, and disruption of, these forces), and the emergence and growing traction of international human rights discourses and political frameworks.

In multicultural Western societies, the predicament of LGBTIQ MCMF is important to the conceptualization of multiculturalism as policy and practice:

> Multiculturalism as policy and practice cannot sit comfortably and confidently with global citizenship and ethical engagement with diversity if it does not include LGBTIQ histories, heritages and contemporary realities. (Pallotta-Chiarolli and Rajkhowa 2017, p. 439)

The emergence of research, and community consultations and projects facilitating recognition of MCMF LGBTIQ identities, experiences and needs is an important cultural development that contributes to the securing of LGBTIQ rights in diverse social and cultural settings (Low and Pallotta-Chiarolli 2015; Murray and Roscoe 1997; Tamale 2011). Historical experiences of criminalization, racism, social ostracism, violence and intimidation, and exclusion from work and the polity have shaped the lives of LGBTIQ elders, and ongoing efforts to augment the rights of individuals through processes of "recognition, reconciliation and reconstruction" (Pallotta-Chiarolli and Rajkhowa 2017, p. 439) are important.

Cross-References

▶ Islamic Identity and Sexuality in Indonesia
▶ Race and Sexuality: Colonial Ghosts and Contemporary Orientalisms

References

Abraham I (2009) 'Out to get us': queer Muslims and the clash of sexual civilisations in Australia. Contemp Islam 3:79–97

Adam BD (1995) The rise of a gay and lesbian movement. Twayne Publisher, New York

ALGA (n.d.) Australia's homosexual histories conferences – the Australian lesbian and gay archives. Available from https://alga.org.au/about-us/ahhconferences

Altman D (1971) Homosexual: oppression and liberation. New York University Press, New York

Altman D (1996) Rupture or continuity? The internationalization of gay identities. Soc Text 48:77–94

Altman D (1997) Global gaze/global gays. GLQ: J Lesbian Gay Stud 3(4):417–436

Altman D (2002) Global sex. University of Chicago Press, Chicago

Altman D, Symons J (2016) Queer wars. Wiley, New York

Amado LE (2009) Sexuality and sexual rights in Muslim societies. Development 52(1):59–63

Anam T (2018) Transgender rights, Bangladesh style. The New York Times, 2 July

Anzaldua G (1987) Borderlands/la frontera: the new mestiza. Aunt Lute Books, San Francisco

Arondekar A (2005) Without a trace: sexuality and the colonial archive. J Hist Sex 14(1/2):10–27

Arondekar A (2009) For the record: on sexuality and the colonial archive in India. Duke University Press, Durham

Asal V, Sommer U, Harwood PG (2013) Original sin: a cross-national study of the legality of homosexual acts. Comp Pol Stud 46(3):320–351

Bacchetta P (2002) Rescaling transnational "queerdom": lesbian and "lesbian" identitary–positionalities in Delhi in the 1980s. Antipode 34(5):947–973

Barber L (2018) Courtney Act talks confronting her own sexual racism. Start Observer, 27 September

Barker M (2018) Once ostracised, now Pakistani transgender people are running for parliament. The Guardian, 23 July

Baudh S (2013) Decriminalisation of consensual same-sex sexual acts in the South Asian Commonwealth: struggles in contexts. Institute of Commonwealth Studies, School of Advanced Study, University of London, London

Bauer GR, Wayne LD (2005) Cultural sensitivity and research involving sexual minorities. Perspect Sex Reprod Health 37(1):45–47

BBC (2017) Indonesian police arrest 141 men over 'gay sex party'. BBC, 22 May

Beckett S, Mohummadally A, Pallotta-Chiarolli M (2014) Queerying Muslim identities. In: Ata A (ed) Education integration challenges: the case of Australian Muslims. David Lovell, Melbourne, pp 96–106

Bhaskaran S (2004) Made in India: decolonizations, queer sexualities, trans/national projects. Springer, New York

Bianco M (2015) China's bizarre fake marriage phenomenon reveals the tragic state of LGBT right. Mic, 26 January

Bjorkman JW (ed) (1988) Fundamentalism, revivalists and violence in South Asia. Riverdale Company, Riverdale

Blackwell C, Birnholtz J, Abbott C (2015) Seeing and being seen: co-situation and impression formation using Grindr, a location-aware gay dating app. New Media Soc 17(7):1117–1136

Boellstorff T (2005) The gay archipelago: sexuality and nation in Indonesia. Princeton University Press, Princeton

Bong YD (2008) The gay rights movement in democratizing Korea. Korean Stud 32:86–103

Bose B, Bhattacharyya S (eds) (2007) The phobic and the erotic: the politics of sexualities in contemporary India. Seagull Books Pvt Ltd, Kolkata

Bostwick WB et al (2014) Mental health and suicidality among racially/ethnically diverse sexual minority youths. Am J Public Health 104(6):1129–1136

Boyce P, Coyle D (2013) Development, discourse and law: transgender and same-sex sexualities in Nepal. Institute of Development Studies, London

Braithwaite JB (2015) Gender, class, resilient power: Nepal lessons in transformation. RegNet research paper no. 2015/92. Available at https://doi.org/10.2139/ssrn.2685495

Brownell C (2009) Rethinking Malaysia's sodomy laws. The Nut Graph, 26 July

Brubaker R, Cooper F (2000) Beyond 'identity'. Theory Soc 29(1):1–47

Burger R (2013) China's 'homowives'. Huffington Post, 7 October

Callander D, Holt M, Newman CE (2012) Just a preference: racialised language in the sex-seeking profiles of gay and bisexual men. Cult Health Sex 14(9):1049–1063

Callander D, Newman CE, Holt M (2015) Is sexual racism really racism? Distinguishing attitudes toward sexual racism and generic racism among gay and bisexual men. Arch Sex Behav 44(7):1991–2000

Callander D, Holt M, Newman CE (2016) Not everyone's gonna like me': accounting for race and racism in sex and dating web services for gay and bisexual men. Ethnicities 16(1):3–21

Caluya G (2008) The rice steamer: race, desire and affect in Sydney's gay scene. Aust Geogr 39(3):283–292

Carbado DW (2017) Black rights, gay rights, civil rights. In: Sexuality and equality law. Routledge, New York, pp 305–328

Cass VC (1979) Homosexuality identity formation: a theoretical model. J Homosex 4(3):219–235

Chakrapani V (2010) Hijras/transgender women in India: HIV, human rights and social exclusion. United Nations Development Programme, Delhi

Chan CS (1995) Issues of sexual identity in an ethnic minority: the case of Chinese American lesbians, gay men, and bisexual people. In: D'Augelli AR, Patterson CJ (eds) Lesbian, gay, and bisexual identities over the lifespan: psychological perspectives. Oxford University Press, New York, pp 87–101

Chang S, Apostle D (2008) Recommendations from the 2004 AGMC conference. Gay Lesbian Issues Psychol Rev 4(1):56–60

Chase T (2012) Problems of publicity: online activism and discussion of same-sex sexuality in South Korea and China. Asian Stud Rev 36(2):151–170

Cheng YHA, Wu FCF, Adamczyk A (2016) Changing attitudes toward homosexuality in Taiwan, 1995–2012. Chin Sociol Rev 48(4):317–345

Chhachhi A (1989) The state, religious fundamentalism and women: trends in South Asia. Econ Polit Wkly 24:567–578

Chiang H (2010) Epistemic modernity and the emergence of homosexuality in China. Gend Hist 22(3):629–657

Cho J (2009) The Wedding Banquet revisited: 'contract marriages' between Korean gays and lesbians. Anthropol Q 82:401–422

Chugtai I (1942, 1990) The Quilt and other short stories (trans: Naqvi T, Harneed S). Kali For Women, Delhi

Chung L (2018) Taiwan's image as Asia's LGBT rights beacon takes a hit as same-sex marriage referendum fails. South China Morning Post, 25 November

Clarke D (2013) Twice removed: African invisibility in Western queer theory. In: Ekine S, Abbas H (eds) Queer African reader. Pambazuka Press, Nairobi, pp 173–185

Clendinen D, Nagourney A (2001) Out for good: the struggle to build a gay rights movement in America. Simon and Schuster, New York

Cochran SD, Mays VM (2007) Physical health complaints among lesbians, gay men, and bisexual and homosexually experienced heterosexual individuals: results from the California. Am J Public Health 97:2048–2055

Coleman EJ, Chou WS (2013) Tongzhi: politics of same-sex eroticism in Chinese societies. Routledge, London

Corboz J et al (2008) Feeling queer and blue: a review of the literature on depression and related issues among gay, lesbian, bisexual and other homosexually active people. ARCSHS, La Trobe University, Melbourne

Cox S, Gallois C (1996) Gay and lesbian identity development: a social identity perspective. J Homosex 30(4):1–30

Crenshaw K (2012) On intersectionality: the essential writings of Kimberle Crenshaw. New Press, New York

Dalacoura K (2014) Homosexuality as battleground in the Middle East: culture and postcolonial international theory. Third World Q 35(7):1290–1306

Dasgupta RK (2014) Articulating dissident citizenship, belonging, and queerness on cyberspace. South Asian Rev 35(3):203–223

Dave NN (2012) Queer activism in India: a story in the anthropology of ethics. Duke University Press, Durham

Davis G (2014) The power in a name: diagnostic terminology and diverse experiences. Psychol Sex 5(1):15–27

Driskill QL (2010) Doubleweaving two-spirit critiques: building alliances between native and queer studies. GLQ: J Lesbian Gay Stud 16(1–2):69–92

Driskill QL (ed) (2011) Queer indigenous studies: critical interventions in theory, politics, and literature. University of Arizona Press, Tucson

Du Bois WEB (1903) The souls of black folk: essays and sketches. New American Library, New York

Duan R (2017) My three weddings: life as a gay man in China. ABC News, 18 December

Dudrah R (2012) Bollywood travels: culture, diaspora and border crossings in popular Hindi cinema. Routledge, London

Duruz A (1999) 'Sister outsider', or 'just another thing I am': intersections of cultural and sexual identities in Australia. In: Jackson P, Sullivan G (eds) Multicultural queer Australian narratives. Harrington Park Press, New York, p 169

Dutta A, Roy R (2014) Decolonizing transgender in India: some reflections. Transgender Stud Q 1(3):320–337

Economist (2017) Chinese attitudes towards gay rights. The Economist, 6 June

Eidhamar LG (2014) Is gayness a test from Allah?: typologies in Muslim stances on homosexuality. Islam Christ Muslim Relat 25(2):245–266

Ekine S (2013) Contesting narratives of queer Africa. In: Ekine S, Abbas H (eds) Queer African reader. Pambazuka Press, Nairobi, pp 78–91

Emslie M (2005) Alphabet soup: CALD, SSAY, NESB, GLBTI: working with ethnic communities. In: Pallotta-Chiarolli M (ed) When our children come out: how to support gay, lesbian, bisexual and transgendered young people. Finch, Sydney, pp 212–215

Eng DL, Hom AY (eds) (1998) Q & A: queer in Asian America. Temple University Press, Philadelphia

Engebretsen EL, Schroeder WF, Bao H (eds) (2015) Queer/Tongzhi China: new perspectives on research, activism and media cultures. Gendering Asia series. NIAS Press, Copenhagen

Fanon F (1961) The wretched of the earth (trans: Philcox R). Grove, New York

Fernandez B (ed) (2002) Humjinsi: a resource book on lesbian, gay, and bisexual rights in India. India Centre for Human Rights and Law, Delhi

Fokkema T, Kuyper L (2009) The relation between social embeddedness and loneliness among older lesbian, gay, and bisexual adults in the Netherlands. Arch Sex Behav 38(2):264–275

Fuchs LH (1990) The American kaleidoscope: race, ethnicity, and the civic culture. Wesleyan University Press, Middletown

Gahan L, Jones T, Hillier L (2014) An unresolved journey: religious discourse and same-sex attracted and gender-questioning young people. In: Piedmont RL, Village A (eds) Research in the social scientific study of religion. Brill, Leiden, pp 202–229

Ganguly M (2017) India's Supreme Court upholds right to privacy. Human Rights Watch, 24 August

Goldin PR (2002) The culture of sex in ancient China. University of Hawaii Press, Honolulu
Gomez SL, McFarlane MD (2017) 'It's not handled': race, gender and refraction in scandal. Fem Media Stud 17(3):362–376
Gopalkrishnan C (2016) I can make a change: a rose by any other name. Social cohesion policy brief, 7. Ethnic Communities Council of Victoria (ECCV), Melbourne
Gopinath G (1997) Nostalgia, desire, diaspora: South Asian sexualities in motion. Positions 5(2):467–489
Gopinath G (1998) On fire. GLQ: J Lesbian Gay Stud 4(4):631–636
Gopinath G (2000) Queering Bollywood: alternative sexualities in popular Indian cinema. J Homosex 39(3–4):283–297
Gopinath G (2005) Impossible desires: queer diasporas and South Asian public cultures. Duke University Press, Durham
Graham-Harrison E, Hammadi S (2016) Inside Bangladesh's killing fields: bloggers and outsiders targeted by fanatics. The Guardian, 12 June
Grewal I, Kaplan C (2001) Global identities: theorizing transnational studies of sexuality. GLQ: J Lesbian Gay Stud 7(4):663–679
Griffiths M, Hasan M (2015) Playing with fire: Islamism and politics in Bangladesh. Asian J Pol Sci 23(2):226–241
Guibernaut M (2013) Belonging: solidarity and division in modern societies. Polity, Cambridge
Gupta A (2006) Section 377 and the dignity of Indian homosexuals. Econ Polit Wkly 41:4815–4823
Gupta A (2008) This alien legacy: the origins of 'sodomy' laws in British colonialism. Human Rights Watch, New York
Habib S (2009) Islam and homosexuality. ABC-CLIO, California
Hammadi S (2016) 'Anyone could become a target': wave of Islamist killings hits Bangladesh. The Guardian, 1 May
Hammoud-Beckett S (2007) Azima ila hayati – an invitation into my life: narrative conversations about sexual identity. Int J Narrat Therapy Community Work 1:29–39
Han CS (2007) They don't want to cruise your type: gay men of color and the racial politics of exclusion. Soc Identities 13(1):51–67
Han CS (2008) No fats, femmes, or Asians: the utility of critical race theory in examining the role of gay stock stories in the marginalization of gay Asian men. Contemp Justice Rev 11(1):11–22
Harris AC (2009) Marginalization by the marginalized: race, homophobia, heterosexism, and 'the problem of the 21st century'. J Gay Lesbian Soc Serv 21(4):430–448
Harris A (2011) Teaching diversities: same-sex attracted young people, CALD communities and arts-based community engagement. Centre for Multicultural Youth, Melbourne
Hashim A (2018) Pakistan passes landmark transgender rights law. Al Jazeera, 10 May
Hinsch B (1990) Passions of the cut sleeve: the male homosexual tradition in China. University of California Press, Berkeley
Ho L (2009) Gay and lesbian subculture in urban China. Routledge, New York
Hodge D (ed) (2015) Colouring the rainbow: black queer and trans perspectives: life stories and essays by first nations people of Australia. Wakefield Press, Melbourne
Honneth A (1996) The struggle for recognition: the moral grammar of social conflicts. MIT Press, Cambridge, MA
Honneth A (2001) Recognition or redistribution? Theory Cult Soc 18(2–3):43–55
Hooghe M, Dejaeghere Y, Claes E, Quintelier E (2010) 'Yes, but suppose everyone turned gay?': the structure of attitudes toward gay and lesbian rights among Islamic youth in Belgium. J LGBT Youth 7(1):49–71
Horton P, Rydstrøm H, Tonini M (2015) Contesting heteronormativity: the fight for lesbian, gay, bisexual and transgender recognition in India and Vietnam. Cult Health Sex 17(9):1059–1073
Hsu CY, Yen CF (2017) Taiwan: pioneer of the health and well-being of sexual minorities in Asia. Arch Sex Behav 46(6):1577–1579

Hu E (2017) For South Korea's LGBT community, an uphill battle for rights. NPR, 25 July
Human Rights Watch (2014) Singapore: court ruling a major setback for gay rights. Human Rights Watch, 29 October
Human Rights Watch (2016) These political games ruin our lives. Human Rights Watch, New York
Hunt K, Tsui K (2017) Taiwan step closer to being first in Asia for same-sex marriage. CNN, 24 May
Hutson JA, Taft JG, Barocas S, Levy K (2018) Debiasing desire: addressing bias & discrimination on intimate platforms. Proc ACM Hum Comput Interact 2(CSCW):73
Icard LD (1986) Black gay men and conflicting social identities: sexual orientation versus racial identity. J Soc Work Hum Sex 4(1–2):83–93
Jackson PA (1995) Dear uncle go: male homosexuality in Thailand. Bua Luang Books, Bangkok
Jackson PA, Sullivan G (eds) (1999a) Multicultural queer: Australian narratives. Harrington Park Press, New York
Jackson PA, Sullivan G (1999b) Lady boys, tom boys, rent boys: male and female homosexualities in contemporary Thailand (No. 2–3). Psychology Press, London
Jackson PA, Sullivan G (1999c) A panoply of roles: sexual and gender diversity in contemporary Thailand. J Gay Lesbian Soc Serv 9(2–3):1–27
Jaspal R, Cinnirella M (2010) Coping with potentially incompatible identities: accounts of religious, ethnic, and sexual identities from British Pakistani men who identify as Muslim and gay. Br J Soc Psychol 49:849–870
Jaspal R, Cinnirella M (2014) Hyper-affiliation to the religious in-group among British Pakistani Muslim gay men. J Community Appl Soc Psychol 24:265–277
Johnson C, Paternotte D, Tremblay M (eds) (2011) The lesbian and gay movement and the state: comparative insights into a transformed relationship. Ashgate Publishing, Farnham
Jones RH (1999) Mediated action and sexual risk: searching for 'culture' in discourses of homosexuality and AIDS prevention in China. Cult Health Sex 1(2):161–180
Jones RH (2007) Imagined comrades and imaginary protections: identity, community and sexual risk among men who have sex with men in China. J Homosex 53(3):83–115
Kalra G (2012) Hijras: the unique transgender culture of India. Int J Cult Ment Health 5(2):121–126
Kamjan C (2014) Gays still face a battle, report says. Bangkok Post, 17 September
Käng DBC (2012) Kathoey "in trend": emergent genderscapes, national anxieties and the re-signification of male-bodied effeminacy in Thailand. Asian Stud Rev 36(4):475–494
Kapur R (2001) Postcolonial erotic disruptions: legal narratives of culture, sex, and nation in India. Columbia J Gend Law 10(2):333
Kapur R (2017) Postcolonial erotic disruptions: legal narratives of culture, sex, and nation in India. Pop Cult Law 10(2):61–112
Kassisieh G (2012) 'We're family too': the effects of homophobia in Arabic-speaking communities in NSW. ACON (AIDS Council of NSW), Sydney
Kaur R, Mazzarella W (eds) (2009) Censorship in South Asia: cultural regulation from sedition to seduction. Indiana University Press, Bloomington
Kavi AR (2000) The changing image of the hero in Hindi films. J Homosex 39(3–4):307–312
Khan S (2001) Culture, sexualities, and identities: men who have sex with men in India. J Homosex 40(3–4):99–115
Khan SI, Hussain MI, Parveen S, Bhuiyan MI, Gourab G, Sarker GF, Arafat SM, Sikder J (2009) Living on the extreme margin: social exclusion of the transgender population (hijra) in Bangladesh. J Health Popul Nutr 27(4):441
Kim HJ, Fredriksen-Goldsen KI (2012) Hispanic lesbians and bisexual women at heightened. Am J Public Health 102:e9–e15
King M et al (2008) A systematic review of mental disorder, suicide, and deliberate self-harm in lesbian, gay and bisexual people. BMC Psychiatry 8(1):70
Knight K (2017) How did Nepal become a global LGBT rights beacon? World Politics Review, 11 August

Kole SK (2007) Globalizing queer? AIDS, homophobia and the politics of sexual identity in India. Glob Health 3(1):8

Kosnick K (2011) Sexuality and migration studies: the invisible, the oxymoronic and heteronormative othering. In: Lutz H, Herrera Vivar MT, Supik L (eds) Framing intersectionality: debates on a multi-faceted concept in gender studies. Ashgate, Surrey, pp 121–136

Krieger N et al (1993) Racism, sexism and social class: implications for studies of health, disease and well-being. Am J Prev Med 9(suppl):82–122

Kulpa R, Mizielinska J (2016) 'Contemporary peripheries': queer studies, circulation of knowledge and East/West divide. In: De-centring Western sexualities. Routledge, pp 23–38

Kuyper L, Fokkema T (2010) Loneliness among older lesbian, gay, and bisexual adults: the role of minority stress. Arch Sex Behav 39(5):1171–1180

Law B (2012) Gaysia: adventures in the queer east. Black Inc., Melbourne

Lee JC (2012) Sexuality rights activism in Malaysia. In: Social activism in Southeast Asia. Routledge, London, p 170

Lee PH (2016) LGBT rights versus Asian values: de/re-constructing the universality of human rights. Int J Hum Rights 20(7):978–992

Light B, Fletcher G, Adam A (2008) Gay men, Gaydar and the commodification of difference. Inf Technol People 21(3):300–314

Lim SH (2006) Celluloid comrades: representations of male homosexuality in contemporary Chinese cinemas. University of Hawaii Press, Honolulu

Limsamarnphun N (2018) More rights for same-sex couples. The Nation. Retrieved 24 November

Liu JX, Choi K (2006) Experiences of social discrimination among men who have sex with men in Shanghai, China. AIDS Behav 10(1):25–33

Lorde A (1999) There is no hierarchy of oppressions. In: Brandt E (ed) Dangerous liaisons: blacks, gays and the struggle for equality. New Press, New York, pp 306–307

Low L, Pallotta-Chiarolli M (2015) 'And yet we are still excluded': reclaiming multicultural queer histories and engaging with contemporary multicultural queer realities. In: Mansouri F (ed) Cultural, religious and political contestations: the multicultural challenge. Springer, Basil, pp 169–184

Luibhéid E (2008) Queer/migration: an unruly body of scholarship. GLQ: J Lesbian Gay Stud 14(2):169–190

Lunsing W (2005) LGBT rights in Japan. Peace Rev: J Soc Justice 17(2–3):143–148

Mahapatra D (2013) Supreme Court makes homosexuality a crime again. The Times of India, 12 December

Marmot M, Wilkinson R (eds) (2009) Social determinants of health, 2nd edn. Oxford University Press, London

McConnell-Ginet S (2003) What's in a name? Social labelling and gender practices. In: The handbook of language and gender. Blackwell, Oxford, pp 69–97

McLelland MJ (2005) Male homosexuality in modern Japan: cultural myths and social realities. Routledge, London

Mejia-Canales D, Leonard W (2016) 'Something for them': meeting the support needs of same-sex attracted and sex and gender diverse young people who are recently arrived, refugees or asylum seekers. ARCSHS, La Trobe University, Melbourne

Menon N (ed) (1999) Gender and politics in India. Oxford University Press, Delhi

Menon N (ed) (2007a) Sexualities, vol 5. Kali, Delhi

Menon N (2007b) Outing heteronormativity: nation, citizen, feminist disruptions. In: Menon N (ed) Sexualities. Kali, Delhi, pp 3–51

Menon N (2009) Sexuality, caste, governmentality: contests over 'gender' in India. Fem Rev 91(1):94–112

Meyer IH (2003) Prejudice, social stress, and mental health in lesbian, gay, and bisexual populations: conceptual issues and research evidence. Psychol Bull 129(5):674–697

Michelraj M (2015) Historical evolution of transgender community in India. Asian Rev Soc Sci 4(1):17–19

Mills TC et al (2001) Health-related characteristics of men who have sex with men: a comparison of those living in 'gay ghettos' with those living elsewhere. Am J Public Health 91(6):980–983

Miranda DA, Driskill QL, Justice DH, Tatonetti L (2011) Sovereign erotics: a collection of two-spirit literature. University of Arizona Press, Tuscon

Misawa M (2010) Queer race pedagogy for educators in higher education: dealing with power dynamics and positionality of LGBTQ students of color. Int J Crit Pedagogy 3(1):26–35

Mishra A (2012) Islamic fundamentalism in South Asia: a comparative study of Pakistan and Bangladesh. India Q 68(3):283–296

Misra G (2009) Decriminalising homosexuality in India. Reprod Health Matters 17(34):20–28

Mitra R (2010) Resisting the spectacle of pride: queer Indian bloggers as interpretive communities. J Broadcast Electron Media 54(1):163–178

Moi T (1995) Sexual, textual politics. Routledge, New York

Mosbergen D (2015a) Being LGBT in Southeast Asia: stories of abuse, survival, and tremendous courage. The Huffington Post

Mosbergen D (2015b) Vietnam has been praised as a leader in LGBT rights; activists beg to differ. Huffington Post, 19 October

Mowlabocus S (2016) Gaydar culture: gay men, technology and embodiment in the digital age. Routledge, New York

Müller A (2017) Beyond 'invisibility': queer intelligibility and symbolic annihilation in healthcare. Cult Health Sex 9(1):1–14

Muñoz JE (1999) Disidentifications: queers of color and the performance of politics, 2nd edn. University of Minnesota Press, Minneapolis

Murray SO, Roscoe W (1997) Islamic homosexualities: culture, history and literature. New York University Press, New York

Nair R, Rajkhowa A (2017) Multiple identities and their intersections with queer health and wellbeing. J Intercult Stud 38(4):443–452

Nanda S (2015) Hijras. In: Whelehan P, Bolin A (eds) The international encyclopedia of human sexuality. Wiley-Blackwell, New Jersey, pp 501–581

Narrain A (2004) The articulation of rights around sexuality and health: subaltern queer cultures in India in the era of Hindutva. Health Hum Rights 7:142–164

Narrain A (2007) Queer struggles around the law: the contemporary context. In: Menon N (ed) Sexualities. Zed Books, London/New York

Narrain A, Bhan G (eds) (2005) Because I have a voice. Queer politics in India. Yoda Press, Delhi

Ndashe S (2013) The single story of 'African homophobia' is dangerous for activism. In: Ekine S, Abbas H (eds) Queer African reader. Pambazuka Press, Nairobi, pp 155–164

Neilands TB, Steward WT, Choi KH (2008) Assessment of stigma towards homosexuality in China: a study of men who have sex with men. Arch Sex Behav 37(5):838

Ng V (1989) Homosexuality and the state in late imperial China. In: Hidden from history: reclaiming the gay and lesbian past. Meridien, New York, pp 76–89

Noto O, Leonard W, Mitchell A (2014) 'Nothing for them': understanding the support needs of LGBT young people from refugee and newly arrived backgrounds. Monograph series no. 94. ARCSHS, La Trobe University, Melbourne

Offord B (2003) Homosexual rights as human rights: activism in Indonesia, Singapore, and Australia. Peter Lang, Oxford

Offord B, Cantrell L (2001) Homosexual rights as human rights in Indonesia and Australia. J Homosex 40(3&4):233–252

Om J (2018) Dealing with racism in gay online dating. ABC News, 30 November 2018

Osumi M (2018) Tokyo adopts ordinance banning discrimination against LGBT community. Japan Times, 5 October

Oswin N (2014) Queer time in global city Singapore: neoliberal futures and the 'freedom to love'. Sexualities 17(4):412–433

Pallotta-Chiarolli M (2004) From difference to diversity: exploring the social determinants of youth health. In: Keleher H, Murphy B (eds) Understanding health: a determinants approach. Oxford University Press, South Melbourne, pp 289–296

Pallotta-Chiarolli M (2005a) Ethnic identity. In: Sears JT (ed) Youth, education, and sexualities: an international encyclopaedia. Greenwood Publishing Group, Westport, pp 303–306

Pallotta-Chiarolli M (ed) (2005b) When our children come out: how to support gay, lesbian, bisexual and transgendered young people. Finch, Sydney

Pallotta-Chiarolli M (2008) Guest editorial. Gay and Lesbian Issues and Psychology Special Edition: Papers from the AGMC Conferences, 4(1), 2–6

Pallotta-Chiarolli M (2016) Supporting same-sex attracted and gender diverse young people of multicultural and multifaith backgrounds: executive summary and full research report. Equality Branch of the Department of Premier and Cabinet, Melbourne

Pallotta-Chiarolli M (ed) (2018) Multicultural queer Australia: then, now, future. Wakefield Press, Adelaide

Pallotta-Chiarolli M, Pease B (2014) The politics of recognition and social justice: transforming subjectivities and new forms of resistance. Routledge, London

Pallotta-Chiarolli M, Rajkhowa A (2017) Systemic invisibilities, institutional culpabilities and multicultural-multifaith LGBTIQ resistances. J Intercult Stud 38(4):429–442

Palmer J (2018) It's still (just about) OK to be gay in China. Foreign Policy, 17 April

Panthi K (2016) LGBTI rights in Nepal: few steps forward, one step backward. Huffington Post, 5 September

Parker R (2002) The global HIV/AIDS pandemic, structural inequalities, and the politics of international health. Am J Public Health 92(3):343–347

Park-Kim SJ, Lee-Kim SY, Kwon-Lee EJ (2007) The lesbian rights movement and feminism in South Korea. J Lesbian Stud 10(3–4):161–190

Penney T (2014) Bodies under glass: gay dating apps and the affect-image. Media Int Aust 153(1):107–117

Piot P, Bartos M, Ghys PD, Walker N, Schwartländer B (2001) The global impact of HIV/AIDS. Nature 410(6831):968

Pisani E (2010) The wisdom of whores: bureaucrats, brothels and the business of AIDS. Granta Books, London

Poljski C (2011) Coming out, coming home or inviting people in? Supporting same-sex attracted women from immigrant and refugee communities. Multicultural Centre for Women's Health, Melbourne

Probyn E (1996) Outside belongings. Routledge, New York/London

Puri J (2002) Woman, body, desire in post-colonial India: narratives of gender and sexuality. Routledge, New York

Pyke K (2010) An intersectional approach to resistance and complicity: the case of racialised desire among Asian American women. J Intercult Stud 31(1):81–94

Qian J, Thanh Hang P, Rajkhowa A (2015) Queering the air. In: Hardy D, Whiley E (eds) Bold: stories from older lesbian, gay, bisexual, transgender and intersex people. The Rag and Bone Man Press, Melbourne, pp 228–231

Queering the Air (2015) We weren't born yesterday. 3CR Community Radio, Melbourne. Available from: http://www.3cr.org.au/wewerentbornyesterday

Race K (2015) Speculative pragmatism and intimate arrangements: online hook-up devices in gay life. Cult Health Sex 17(4):496–511

Rahman R (2017) No country for Bangladesh's gay men. The New York Times

Rajkhowa (2014) Through the looking glass – internalised racism and desire: a migrant's perspective from Australia. Words Apart Magazine, 17 May

Rajkhowa A (2015) The contradictions in LGBTQI rights in India. Overland, 21 August

Rajkhowa A (2017) We weren't born yesterday: reflections on a radio documentary series. J Aust Stud 41(3):380–387

Rajkhowa A (2018) Anwar Ibrahim's rebirth and Malaysia's LGBT+ rights. Pursuit, 27 May

Rajkhowa A, Thompson JD (2015) Difficult belongings. Text 31:1–12

Ratti R (ed) (1993) A lotus of another color: an unfolding of the South Asian gay and lesbian experience. Alyson Publications, Boston

Redding JA (2012) From 'she-males' to 'unix': transgender rights and the productive paradoxes of Pakistani policing. In: Berti D, Bordia D (eds) Regimes of legality: ethnography of criminal cases in South Asia. Oxford University Press, London, p 258

Reddy V (2006) Decriminalisation of homosexuality in post-apartheid South Africa: a brief legal case history review from sodomy to marriage. Agenda 20(67):146–157

Rehman J, Polymenopoulou E (2013) Is green a part of the rainbow: sharia, homosexuality, and LGBT rights in the Muslim world. Fordham Int Law J 37:1

Rich TS, Webb N (2018) South Korea's slow shift toward LGBT tolerance. The News Lens, 27 February

Rifkin M (2010) When did Indians become straight?: kinship, the history of sexuality, and native sovereignty. Oxford University Press, New York

Rifkin M (2012) The erotics of sovereignty: queer native writing in the era of self-determination. University of Minnesota Press, Minneapolis

Riggs DW (2013) Anti-Asian sentiment amongst a sample of white Australian men on gaydar. Sex Roles 68(11–12):768–778

Ro A, Ayala G, Paul J, Choi KH (2013) Dimensions of racism and their impact on partner selection among men of colour who have sex with men: understanding pathways to sexual risk. Cult Health Sex 15(7):836–850

Robinson BA (2015) "Personal preference" as the new racism: gay desire and racial cleansing in cyberspace. Sociol Race Ethn 1(2):317–330

Robinson RK, Frost DM (2017) LGBT equality and sexual racism. Fordham Law Rev 86:2739

Rosario VA (1997) Science and homosexualities. Routledge, New York

Roy A (2007) Nepal Supreme Court directs govt to safeguard gay rights. Hindustan Times, 23 December

Safi M (2018) Campaigners celebrate as India decriminalises homosexuality. Guardian, 7 September

Sala IM (2018) Gay sex in China: where communist puritanism meets colonial baggage. The South China Morning Post, 15 September

Samuel K (2018) The Scourge of Sexual Racism: the destructive potential of unexamined racism. Medium, 27 July

Savin-Williams R (1998) '...And then I became gay': young men's stories. Routledge, New York

Shah SP (2015) Queering critiques of neoliberalism in India: urbanism and inequality in the era of transnational "LGBTQ" rights. Antipode 47(3):635–651

Shannahan DS (2010) Some queer questions from a Muslim faith perspective. Sexualities 13(6):671–684

Sharma A (2008) Decriminalising queer sexualities in India: a multiple streams analysis. Soc Policy Soc 7(4):419–431

Shepherd C (2018) Chinese activists renew push for same-sex marriage in their thousands. Reuters, 12 September

Shilts R (2007) And the band played on: politics, people, and the AIDS epidemic, 20th-anniversary edition. Griffin, St. Martin's

Siraf A (2012) I don't want to taint the name of Islam': the influence of religion on the lives of Muslim lesbians. J Lesbian Stud 16(4):449–467

Siraj A (2014) Islam, homosexuality and gay Muslims: bridging the gap between faith and sexuality. In: Taylor Y, Snowdon R (eds) Queering religion, religious queers. Routledge, London, pp 194–210

Smith ER (1993) Social identity and social emotions: toward new conceptualizations of prejudice. In: Mackie DM, Hamilton DL (eds) Affect, cognition and stereotyping. Academic, San Diego, pp 297–315

Smith A (2010) Queer theory and native studies: the heteronormativity of settler colonialism. GLQ: J Lesbian and Gay Stud 16(1–2):41–68

Snorton CR (2017) Black on both sides: a racial history of trans identity. Universisty of Minnesota Press, Minneapolis

Song Y, Li X, Zhang L, Fang X, Lin X, Liu Y, Stanton B (2011) HIV-testing behavior among young migrant men who have sex with men (MSM) in Beijing, China. AIDS Care 23(2):179–186

Stokel-Walker C (2018) Why is it OK for online daters to block whole ethnic groups? Guardian, 30 September

Subramanian S (2015) The Indian Supreme Court ruling in Koushal v. Naz: judicial deference or judicial abdication. Geo Wash Int'l Law Rev 47:711

Sukthankar A (2005) Complicating gender: rights of transsexuals in India. In: Narrain A, Bhan G (eds) Because I have a voice: queer politics in India. Yoda Press, Delhi, pp 164–174

Sullivan G, Jackson PA (2013) Gay and lesbian Asia: culture, identity, community. Routledge, New York

Suroyo G, Greenfield C (2014) Strict sharia forces gays into hiding in Indonesia's Aceh. Reuters, 27 December

Tamagawa M (2016) Same-sex marriage in Japan. J GLBT Fam Stud 12(2):160–187

Tamale S (ed) (2011) African sexualities: a reader. Pambazuka Press, Cape Town

The Economist (2018) How India decriminalised homosexuality. The Economist, 12 September

Topsfield J (2017) Indonesian court rejects push to outlaw extramarital and gay sex. Sydney Morning Herald, 14 December

Truong K (2018a) Asian-American man plans lawsuit to stop 'sexual racism' on Grindr. NBC News, 14 July

Truong K (2018b) After 'sexual racism' accusations, gay dating app Grindr gets 'Kindr'. NBC News, 23 September

Tuchman G (2000) The symbolic annihilation of women by the mass media. In: Crothers L, Lockhart C (eds) Culture and politics: a reader. Palgrave Macmillan, New York, pp 150–174

Ungku F (2018) Singapore DJ files court challenge against gay sex ban after India ruling. Reuters, 12 September

Vanita R (2013) Queering India: same-sex love and eroticism in Indian culture and society. Routledge, New York

Vanita R, Kidwai S (eds) (2008) Same-sex love in India: a literary history. Penguin Books, Delhi

Vitiello G (2011) The libertine's friend: homosexuality and masculinity in late imperial China. University of Chicago Press, Chicago

Wade M (2017) Swiping left to sexual racism in Australia's gay community. Star Observer, 10 April

Wah-Shan C (2001) Homosexuality and the cultural politics of Tongzhi in Chinese societies. J Homosex 40(3–4):27–46

Waites M (2010) Human rights, sexual orientation and the generation of childhoods: analysing the partial decriminalisation of 'unnatural offences' in India. Int J Hum Rights 14(6):971–993

Wei W (2007) 'Wandering men' no longer wander around: the production and transformation of local homosexual identities in contemporary Chengdu, China. Inter-Asia Cult Stud 8(4):572–588

Wong D (2010) Hybridization and the emergence of "gay" identities in Hong Kong and in China. Vis Anthropol 24(1–2):152–170

Wu J (2003) From "long yang" and "dui shi" to tongzhi: homosexuality in China. J Gay Lesbian Psychother 7(1–2):117–143

Yip AKT (2008) Researching lesbian, gay and bisexual Christians and Muslims: some thematic reflections. Sociol Res Online 13(1):1–14
Yongcharoenchai C (2013) The two faces of Thai tolerance. Bangkok Post, 8 September
Yue A, Zubillaga-Pow J (eds) (2012) Queer Singapore: illiberal citizenship and mediated cultures, vol 1. Hong Kong University Press, Hong Kong
Zhou YR (2006) Homosexuality, seropositivity, and family obligations: perspectives of HIV-infected men who have sex with men in China. Cult Health Sex 8(6):487–500

Migration and Managing Manhood: Congolese Migrant Men in South Africa

58

Joseph Rudigi Rukema and Beatrice Umubyeyi

Contents

Introduction	1112
The Concept of Migration	1112
The Need for Migration	1113
Consequences of Migration	1114
Migration Around the World	1115
Migration and the Economy	1116
Migration and Gender	1118
The Migrant Man	1119
Migration, Manhood, and Masculinity	1120
Methodology	1122
Results	1123
Education and Understanding of Manhood Among Congolese Migrant	1123
Work and Manhood Among Congolese Migrant Living in South Africa	1124
Understanding Manhood in Country of Origin	1124
Migration, Manhood Among Congolese Migrant in Durban, South Africa	1125
Conclusion	1126
References	1126

Abstract

The aim of this chapter is to explore and examine the management of manhood in the context of migration with a particular focus to Congolese men migrants living in Durban, Republic of South Africa. Human migration stands out to be one of the

---

J. R. Rukema (✉)
School of Social Sciences, University of KwaZulu-Natal, Durban, South Africa
e-mail: josephr1@ukzn.ac.za; jrukema@yahoo.com

B. Umubyeyi
School of Built and Environmental Studies, University of KwaZulu-Natal, Durban, South Africa
e-mail: umubyeyib@ukzn.ac.za; beatriceumubyeyi@yahoo.com

© The Author(s), under exclusive license to Springer Nature Singapore Pte Ltd. 2019
S. Ratuva (ed.), *The Palgrave Handbook of Ethnicity*,
https://doi.org/10.1007/978-981-13-2898-5_65

most important aspects of social science. From time immemorial, migration has been common feature in human society. It has managed to maintain a close relation with mankind from its earliest stage. Interdisciplinary approach to migration has significantly scholars in different fields such as geography, sociology, demography, economics, and other related disciplines. As a result of the complexity of human life and fast-changing socioeconomic conditions, human migration seems to gain importance.

Keywords

Migration · Manhood · Managing · Congolese · Forced migration

Introduction

Carletto et al. (2014) asserts that basic factors that have influenced the mobility of man to move from one region to another were uneven distribution of population and resources. Further, unbalanced utilization of resources and variation in economic and cultural developments is also another important factor that should not be taken for granted. Certain areas have been identified and they were marked as "centers of habitation." In these places, people were attracted from various regions, countries, and continents. It has also been established that different parts of the world on the whole have different types of mobility caused by various socioeconomic conditions. Consequently, this mobility of man has either favorably or adversely influenced the socioeconomic conditions of that area. It is therefore worth noting that, scholars have tried to study the phenomenon of migration from various angles. For instance, the current study focuses on migration and managing manhood with specific focus on Congolese migrant men in South Africa. As such, this section provides a comprehensive review of literature in order to achieve a succinctly articulated literature.

The Concept of Migration

Migration is a complex phenomenon that constitutes structural transformation in developing countries. People, especially in the developing world, are forced to leave their countries of origin in order to seek green pastures in the developed world. Migration patterns significantly vary across regions and countries, and it is also imperative to understand that flows have changed considerably over time. In many households, migration is considered as a strategy aimed at improving their livelihood, minimize their risks, and diversify their income sources (Carletto et al. 2014). Further, it is of paramount importance to note that Africa has a long history of internal and international migration where migrants move within and beyond the continent. In the year 2015, the United Nations Department of Economic and Social Affairs (UNDESA) estimated that 14% of international migrants in the world originated from the continent.

The Need for Migration

Common accounts of African migration in Africa are characterized by either ignorance or a weak theorization of the role of African states in migration processes. This reflects a comprehensive receiving country bias in migration research, and this bias obscures the role of origin states in a significant way (Vezzoli et al. 2014). Furthermore, it is important to note that the same bias ignores the fact that poor countries are destination countries too. Increasing immigration restrictions and border controls affected by Europeans have received wide recognition and attention; the role of postcolonial African states in shaping migration processes is poorly understood. The poor understanding of the process brings about a major research gap. This is in the sense that colonial occupation and associated practices of the slave trade and the systematic application of forced labor and recruitment have shaped contemporary migration patterns within and from the continent (Cohen 2007). During the colonial period, millions of people fled conflicts with colonial powers reluctant to relinquish control or with white settler groups determined to cling to their privileges; this was seen in countries like Zimbabwe and South Africa (Castles et al. 2014). However, the defeat of the old system of colonialism and the establishment of independent states did not necessarily mean a return to peaceful conditions (De Haas and Villares-Varela 2014). When the Cold War was underway, East and West fought proxy wars in Africa while backing undemocratic regimes such as Mobutu Sese Seko in the DRC and also they supported the toppling of democratic governments.

Political and economic pressures, the supply of arms, mercenaries, and direct military intervention were factors that contributed to new conflicts or the continuation of old ones (Zolberg et al. 1989). A good example of this is found in the struggles for domination in Angola, Mozambique, and Ethiopia which involved massive external involvement, with massive human costs for local populations (Castles et al. 2014). Decolonization also indicated a phase of state formation whereby newly established African states have endeavored to inculcate a sense of national unity in ethnically diverse societies. This often resulted in considerable internal tensions and has regularly erupted in violent conflicts (Castle et al. 2014). The state formation processes have theoretically uncertain effects on population mobility, which are poorly understood. Furthermore, instability and conflict may provide incentives for people to leave. It also provides incentives for people to stay in order to provide protection for their families. In the same vein, people living under authoritarian regimes may more often wish to migrate, but authoritarian states usually have a higher willingness and capacity to control and restrict emigration.

De Haas (2010) further proclaims that this explains the analysis of global migrant stock data found a robustly positive relationship between the level of political freedom and emigration. Even though the formation of nation states can go along with increasing migration either through conflict, infrastructure, or policies that encourage emigration, the same state formation processes have also compelled several African governments such as Algeria, Egypt, and Côte d'Ivoire to discourage the emigration of their own populations. This was done to control emigration or out of the fear of a "brain drain" and to restrict the immigration of foreigners (Natter

2014; Zohry and Harrell-Bond 2003). Particularly socialist and/or nationalist governments have traditionally been anti-emigration. The processes of state formation may also have increased the urge among leaders of newly established states to assert national sovereignty. This was done through the introduction of immigration restrictions and border controls and to portray immigrants as a threat to sovereignty, security, and ethnic homogeneity or stability in a bid to rally political support. In this scenario, African governments have frequently resorted to deportations and a good example is presented by Adepoju (2001) who counted 23 mass expulsions of migrants conducted by 16 different African states between 1958 and 1996.

Consequences of Migration

Migration has numerous consequences in both the receiving country and country of origin. Political tensions and military conflicts pushed many countries to attempt to seal off their mutual borders. This has largely been seen between the Frontline States in Southern Africa with South Africa as part of the anti-Apartheid struggle. Particularly, socialist states such as Algeria and Egypt saw large-scale emigration as a source of brain drain and a threat to sovereignty, and as such tried to curb emigration (Collyer 2003; Fargues 2004; Natter 2014). This shows that states can both facilitate and constrain migration in various direct and indirect ways, and that this relation needs an in-depth empirical inquiry to be better understood.

An analysis of the historical background of developing or developed parts of the world would present an unbalanced utilization of resources which ultimately lead to an unbalanced distribution of the population (Natter 2014). Because of peoples shift from an underdeveloped region to a developed region, their places of origin, as well as a destination, have been adversely affected (Castles et al. 2014). When people migrate from a particular underdeveloped country to a developed or developing country, their place of origin undergoes numerous positive as well as negative effects. Bakewell and Bonfiglio (2013) are of the view that positive effects may include an increase of the share of land holdings, improvement in the economic condition and living condition by the construction of good house among other issues. At the same time, the social status of the family improves because of education and better social contacts. However, the region which donates migrants experiences some setbacks that are a shortage of labor is experienced; sometimes movement of young or working force restricts the proper growth of the region. It has been observed mostly that people receive their basic education at the place of their origin but they rarely serve the place of their origin.

Different scholars have made numerous efforts in defining the concept of migration distinctly because of their different approaches (Schoumaker et al. 2015). While geographers have put more emphasis on the time and space significance of mobility, sociologists have stressed on social consequences of mobility whereas importance to the economic aspect of migration has been given by the economists (Bakewell and Bonfiglio 2013). The literal meaning of migration is shifting of people or an individual or group of individuals from one cultural area to another. The shift may be permanent or temporary. It can also be defined as an act of moving from one area to another in search of work. According to many scholars, the simplest meaning of the word migration can be a simple shift in the physical space. However, it would be interesting to note that the meaning of migration is changing simultaneously with the passage of time. Nowadays, both the scope and definition of migration have become more complicated that is only mobility in the physical state cannot define the concept of migration.

Migration Around the World

Notwithstanding the increasing accessibility of survey and interview-based data on African migration, data availability remains largely patchy and is generally focused on migration to Europe from a limited number of better-researched African countries, such as Morocco, Senegal, Ghana, and South Africa (Clemens 2014). It is apparent that what has been particularly lacking is macrodata that allows mapping the overall evolution of the migration patterns to and within Africa over the past decades. This is not only imperative to gain a more fundamental understanding into the factual evolution of African migration and to verify the validity of collective perception of massive and increasing African migration, but it also allows to contribute to the scholarly debate on the determinants of migration. On the one hand, this pertains to the debate pertaining to how development affects human mobility in which scholars have challenged conventional push-pull models by arguing that, predominantly in poor societies, development increases rather than decreases migration levels (Skeldon 1997; Clemens 2014; De Haas 2010). On the other hand, conventional accounts of African migration tend to ignore the role of African states in the shaping of migration. As a result, this reflects the more general Eurocentric focus of migration research.

Scholars fuel the image of a rising tide of poverty-driven African emigration. For instance, Myers (2005) argued that the current flow of "environmental refugees" from Africa to Europe will come to be regarded as a trickle when compared with the floods that are imminent in decades ahead. This feeds into more general ideas conveyed by Collier (2013), and there is a veritable South–North "exodus" that is driven by poverty and income gaps which threaten to spin out of control unless rights of immigrants are curtailed. A broader tendency is reflected in the research literature to cast "South–North" migration as a symptom of development failure (Bakewell 2008). Based on the common perception that poverty and income gaps between poor and rich countries are the "root causes" of migration, the frequently proposed long-term "solution" to this phenomenon is to stimulate development in countries of origin through aid, trade, or remittances (De Haas 2007).

Paradoxically, scholars argue that the most obvious problem is that, such ideas are based on assumption, selective observation, or journalistic impressions rather than on sound empirical evidence. There have been numerous reports on irregular migration, smuggling, trafficking, and the high death toll among trans-Mediterranean "boat migrants" which reinforce the impression that African migration is essentially directed towards Europe and it is driven by despair. Since the year 2000, there has been a recent surge in a survey or interview-based studies on contemporary African migrations (Berriane and De Haas 2012; De Bruijn et al. 2001). These studies have provided light on the diversity of African migration. Several studies have shown that most African migration activities are not directed towards Europe, rather towards other African countries where there are better opportunities such as South Africa (Schoumaker et al. 2015). Also, those moving out of Africa do not only move to Europe but also to the Gulf countries and the Americas too.

Contrary to the general assumptions that African emigration is essentially about irregular movement, previous research suggests that most Africans migrate out of the continent in possession of valid passports, visas, and other travel documentation. More generally, recent scholarship in the field of migration has started to question the implicit assumption that African migration is remarkable and different from migration elsewhere. More narratives indicate that most Africans migrate for family, work, or study (Schoumaker et al. 2015). In a study on the Great Lakes region, Bakewell and Bonfiglio (2013) argued that although it would be impossible to deny the importance of conflict as a cause of migration usually forced migration in particular in the region, it would be wrong to neglect the ongoing social processes that drive mobility, such as the search for an education, a spouse, or a better life in the city (Bakewell and Bonfiglio 2013).

Refugees and people in refugee situations represented 2.4 million or 14% of international migrants in Africa. Although this proportion is higher than in other regions, this implies that about 80% of international migration within Africa is not primarily related to the conflict. This is not only important to gain a more fundamental insight into the factual evolution of African migration and to verify the validity of common perception of massive and increasing African migration, rather it would as well allow to contribute to the scholarly debate on the determinants of migration. This pertains to the debate regarding how development affects human mobility in which scholars have challenged conventional push-pull models by arguing that, particularly in poor societies, development increases rather than decreases levels of migration (Clemens 2014). On the other hand, it has also been argued by scholars that conventional accounts of African migration tend to ignore the role of African states in shaping migration.

Migration and the Economy

It has been widely debated that migration is largely a result of economic challenges and the search for greener pastures. In the history of economic thinking on why people migrate, a variety of approaches have been developed (De Haas 2010). Neoclassical macroeconomic and microeconomic theories make a considerable attempt in explaining inter alia the mechanism of labor migration. The first framework that is neoclassical macroeconomic indicates that migration happens due to issues pertaining to economic development and wage differences. According to this theory, individuals try to maximize their income, and in so doing, they migrate to regions with higher wages (Clemens 2014). In the process, the country of origin equally enjoys benefits. This happens in two important ways: firstly, migrants reduce the ratio of labor to capital and secondly, migrants make up for their absence by sending remittances to their home country.

Furthermore, in the long run, the decline in the labor-capital ratio would remove the incentives for migration. The neoclassical microeconomic theory assumes that labor migration happens not only because of wage differences but also because migrants take a rational cost-benefit decision (De Haas 2010). This cost-benefit estimation relates to the personal intention and personal characteristics such as age, gender, etc. Other aspects relate to deciding whether to migrate or not as well as the choice of alternative destinations. Apart from wage differences and employment opportunities, it is of paramount importance to note that migration behavior also includes financial costs such as travel cost, the period of unemployment in the destination country, and psychological costs likely attached to leaving family and friends behind. Thus, the greater the differences in expected returns to migration between the country of origin and the country of destination, the larger the dimension of migration flows will be.

Further, one can also argue that mass migration not only occurs as a result of wage differences, as neoclassical economists tend to believe. Push factors, such as natural disasters, civil wars, and conflict have forced millions of people to move from their country of origin to other countries. Pull factors include higher standards of living, better employment opportunities, and a better educational system all of which attract people from their country of origin to the host country. This model has become the dominant model in the migration literature, because it incorporates not only the important factors that have any impact on migration decision-making but is also able to integrate other theoretical insights (De Haas 2010). However, there are particular migration issues that the theory cannot explain; for example, why some regions produce more migrants than others as well as why the direction of migration flows is often inconclusive (De Bruijn et al. 2001).

The new economics of migration theory indicates that migration is a family-based decision, and people migrate not only to maximize their income but also to minimize their migration risks. Consequently, unlike individuals, families are in a position to control the risk inside their households by diversifying the allocation of household resources. A good example is a scenario whereby a family sends the physically able members of their family abroad for work and invests in the higher education of the others. Some scholars argue that if the higher education inside the country does not pay off, they can rely on the remittances from the others who are working abroad. As a result, families in developing and less developed countries tend to be large, due to the fact that they are able to manage their risks by having many children. Moreover, in contrast to the neoclassical theory of migration where return migration is considered as a "failure" factor, in the new economics of migration theory the returnees are considered a success factor, because those who achieved a maximum benefit from his/her migration behavior return home with accumulated savings or knowledge.

Migration and Gender

Gender has always been a topical issue in international migration. Many studies have been conducted on how women or men are affected or how they benefit in the process of migration. Research has found that the proportion of women who are involved in international migration has increased rapidly. According to the United Nations, female migration represents 50% of the migrant population, and in some countries, it accounts for more than 70–80% of the total. Nonetheless, in some countries, little is known about the determinants of female migration and the factors that have contributed to the increase (United Nations 1995). In countries such as the USA and Canada, female migrants actually outnumber male migrants (Boyd 1992). Studies on gender and migration increased in the 1990s and these revealed gender selectivity for migration (Curran 1996). For example, research done in Asia and in the Philippines showed that most female migrants were relatively young.

Furthermore, found the same pattern in Zimbabwe where most of the migrants in this country were in the 16–19 year, 20–29 year, and 30–39 year age groups. Baker (2010) found that the decision to leave parents and seek employment in the city constituted a challenge to traditional expectations. Young women are seen as timid and reserved in front of men, confined to either the household or the village, and receiving financial assistance from their parents or husband. Hence, women in this category view migration as temporary, because their aim was to send remittances home to support the family (United Nations 1995).

It has also been noted that feminist analyses of migration revealed that gender relations are crucial in understanding both migrations flows as well as women's experiences of them, and that there are fundamental differences in the migration of men and women (United Nations 1995). When married women migrate on their own, it is more likely that women in this category assume the responsibility of breadwinner. The role of a breadwinner is assumed because the women may be forced to forge independent existences and raise children alone, as a result of a lack of support from absent partners. The implications for such movements are that, after migration, women gain independence in decision-making, control their resources, manage childrearing responsibilities, and enhance their economic status. The current migration research has shed light on questions such as what are the causes of female or male migration. What are their experiences in the migration process? What are the consequences of their migration? At the end of the day, both male and female migrants experience a strikingly similar form of challenges as a result of migration.

Studies of international migration have shown that the principal motivating factors for migration are socioeconomic and sociocultural in nature. Boyd (1992) is of the opinion that female and male migrations are different, because women have different social, cultural, and economic roles in their homes and in the economy. Women's opportunities and roles in the economic sphere are largely shaped by the interplay of cultural and historical forces. Women migrate for both economic and affiliational, that is family-related, reasons. A survey on both internal and international migration by Rose (2016) found that 50% of female migrants reported economic motivations as primary, whereas 35% cited marriage or accompaniment of husbands or other family members as the main reasons for their migration. In some instances, women migrated to run away from parental pressures. A good example emerges in Nigeria where women migrated to escape the pressures of entering unwanted marriages or the pressures of returning to intolerable marriages.

The Migrant Man

Smith based his concept of migration on the change in physical space and his definition of migration poses some problems when one looks at various types of cyclical migration that is the movement of people from villages to urban areas for the duration of their active life. The argument was that migration is a change of residence and need not necessarily involve any change of occupation, but it is closely associated with occupational shifts of one kind or another. Men as breadwinners are usually victims of migration since they are faced with various responsibilities of taking care of the family in difficult situations as economic hardships and wars. In some instances, they migrate with their families and at times alone. In the event that they migrate without their families, there are certain challenges that they face which require them to develop a mechanism of dealing with migration.

The principal directions of migration among men are illustrated by more or less continuous movements from rural areas towards the city, from areas of the stable population towards centers of industrial or commercial opportunity and from densely settled countries to less densely settled countries. Eisenstadt (2017) looks at migration as the physical transition of an individual or a group from one society to another. This transition usually involves abandoning one social setting and entering another and permanent one. As compared to the above-mentioned definitions of migration, migration as suggested by Weinberg appears relatively flexible because he considered human migration as the change of place permanently or temporarily for a particular duration of time as in the case of seasonal workers, and in most cases, these sessional workers are men.

If people maintain numerous residences in a city, town, and village, then their frequency of movement will help in deciding their status as a migrant. This is despite the fact that numerous social scientists came forward to discuss and define the concept of migration, and in the process, some of them have complicated its definition. However, according to Baker (2010), migration is the process of moving from one spatial unit to the other. A broad area has been touched by this definition and also it covers a large number of branches of naturalists, social scientists, and others. It is also worth noting that the center of gravity, for example, recreational and shopping movements may remain the same, while there will be a change in interurban movement. Rose (2016) also provides a considerable definition of migration. To him, migration does not add or subtract from the total population of the world, but it can have hand effect on the total population by involving the movement of people from areas where they are likely to reproduce less to areas they are likely to reproduce more.

The number of African migrants in the world increased by 46% up to a total of 32 million people. Roughly half of them (16 million) remained within the continent, corresponding to 80% of all African migrants in 2015. The data shows the importance of the Africa-to-Africa migration corridor, which is the fifth largest in the world. However, despite the growth of migratory flows in the continent and the increased political relevance, information on flows, and particularly on internal migration, is limited, albeit being the most dominant flow. It is of significant importance that socioeconomic conditions associated with migration in rural and urban areas are connected to adequate breakdown by age, sex, and origin of emigrants FAO (2016).

From the interdisciplinary approach viewpoint, very little work has been done on this aspect of social science. An attempt has been made in the field of human migration and interplay of demographic, economic, social, medical, and biological and many other factors to suggest a solution of this burning problem (Schoumaker et al. 2015). As per assumptions or beliefs, it is an uneven distribution of population and resources that has led to rapid growth of rural-urban migration. Other factors that contributed to this field were industrial growth, development of new territories, social change, and so forth that has led to the forcible migration of people from the places of their birth to different directions. Because of this displacement, people of different cultures have different social life (Bakewell and Jónsson 2011).

Furthermore, on contrary debates that African emigration is essentially about irregular movement, previous research suggests that most Africans migrate out of the continent in possession of valid passports and other relevant travel documentation (Bakewell and Bonfiglio 2013). Importantly, recent scholarship has ignited the question of the implicit assumption that African migration is "exceptional" and essentially different from migration elsewhere around the world. More and more micro-evidence emerges indicating that most Africans migrate for family, work, or study (Schoumaker et al. 2015), as is the case in other world regions. In a study on the Great Lakes region, Bakewell and Bonfiglio (2013) argued that although it would be impossible to deny the importance of conflict as a cause of migration in the region, that it would be equally wrong to neglect the ongoing social processes that drive mobility, such as the search for education, a spouse, or a better life in the city. According to Flahaux and De Haas Comparative Migration Studies (2016) to official data, refugees and "people in refugee situations" represented 2.4 million or 14% of international migrants in Africa. However, Africa has a considerably higher proportion than other regions. This implies that about 80% of international migration within Africa is not primarily related to the conflict.

Migration, Manhood, and Masculinity

In the modern world, migration process as articulated in the early stages of this review depends on various specifics as the socioeconomic status, educational backgrounds, nationality, religion, as well as gender or sexual identity of individuals. As a result, a combination of different intersectional identities makes any individual more or less likely to migrate such that gender identity is one of the most influential ones (Boehm 2008). Usually, individuals enter a new gender system through migration where they often discover their new roles radically different from what they have expected (Charsley 2005). However, it is worth noting that globally migration rate among women and men does not differ much. Men generally carry the pressure of expectation to support the family because of existing patriarchal social structure throughout the world. Almost every men living in human societies are to some extent confined within the hypothetical construction of ideal masculinity. Masculinity among men is not any construction that is unitary and immovable hence, they also differ in different contexts.

Studies of migration usually skip men as gendered constructs. This is because men are widely considered to belong at the hierarchical level of power structures and that creates barriers to judge the actual situation of men as gendered beings (Näre 2010). In that regard, scholars often emphasize public exposure of men as more important than their inner feelings of gender. Mckay (2007) asserts that the traditional concept of masculinity does not let men be dependent on female members of the family. As a result, being a man involves taking on the role of provider to the family. Migration is therefore considered to be a tool of reconfiguring one's masculinity by supporting or obstructing an individual's ability to provide his family (Hoang and Yeoh 2011). Some scholars believe that in today's societies, migration is not limited to enacting masculinities for men rather it also works to the assertion of their manhood. As in most source countries, destination countries are portrayed as a utopia of all modern facilities and prosperity, migration increases peoples' expectation to accumulate a fortune from the destination country after migration.

Boehm (2008) argues that for a majority of men in developing regions, the creation of masculinity is attached to migration, and that their mobility is a primary stage on which expressions of male subjectivities are performed. Through migration for work, men demonstrate the courage to take risk across borders. They have the ability to endure loneliness, and they also possess the capacity to provide for their family through hard work (Broughton 2008). Migration is largely considered to be a path to respectable manhood for men and that creates tension for men who stay. It also paves way to questions of how migrant men face and overcome their often less than desirable life circumstances after migration. Walter et al. (2004) reveals how undocumented and unemployed Mexican male immigrants in the USA cultivate a hyper-male identity that outwardly embraces an image of responsible strong or aggressive masculine pride in response to their precarious economic conditions and illegality.

Furthermore, Näre (2010) put forward that Sri Lankan male domestic workers in Italy negotiate their masculinity in a job that is considered feminine. They do this by distancing themselves from the daily tasks of the job and by focusing on the projects at home that they have succeeded in accomplishing through earnings from migrant work. Also, Sarti (2010) is of the view that male migrant domestic and elderly care workers in Europe believe that working in a feminine sector is a threat to their masculinity. They also overcome their gender identity crises through the emphasis of the lack of alternatives for migrants in the destination labor market. In such instances, they hide through arguments like their real identities are strategically positioned at home. Sarti further asserts that migrant men defend their engagement in what they consider as "women's work" by "re-masculinizing" domestic work. Scholars studying how migration shapes masculinity within the familial context paint a complex picture. Also financially, the earnings through migrant work usually help men strengthen their breadwinner roles and authority at home. At the same time, stay-behind husbands in migrant families are often propelled by social pressure to rework their gender identities after their wives have migrated (Boehm 2008).

Nevertheless, some studies reveal that, for fear that it may further erode their masculine identities, men who stay behind refuse to step into the care gap created by the migration of their wives. Concurrently, other studies suggest that stay-behind husbands do take care of the children when their wives migrate. However, the fact that whether stay-behind husbands adjust their practices to take up tasks formerly performed by their wives after their spouses migrate depends on local gender norms and the premigration gender division of labor within the household (Hoang and Yeoh 2011).

Boehm (2008) posits that men who migrate to join their wives or migrate with their wives face yet another set of challenges to their masculinity. In a study of Pakistani men migrating to Britain to join their wives after marriage, Charsley (2005) revealed how these migrant husbands struggle to cope with downward mobility and a transformed familial context in their destination country. Moreover, in another study of Mexican migrant families in the USA, Boehm (2008) shows that the traditional gender division of labor and male dominance are often reestablished in Mexican migrant families in the USA. This is despite the fact that women in these families continue to challenge male dominance and numerous privileges attached to them at home.

Methodology

This is a qualitative study, employing an interpretive approach. The key focus of qualitative approach was employed in data collection and analysis. The target group for this study is married men, divorced, or separated from Congolese migrant community living in Durban. The participants in this study have been selected because men generally carry the pressure of expectation to support the family because of existing patriarchal social structure throughout the world. This study use purposive sampling method for data collection.

In this study, face-to-face in-depth interviews involved eight men, married, divorced, or separated from Congolese migrant families, were undertaken. Respondents in this study were identified through two Churches. These Churches were selected because of the large number of Congolese men among the congregants. As participation was voluntary, the number of participants from each Church was determined by the availability and willingness of the participant. Open face-to-face interview was used to gain detailed picture of participants' beliefs, attitudes, perceptions, or accounts of the issue. Open questions gave the participants the opportunity to introduce all issues thought about the research topic.

This research conducted face-to-face interviews at the places and times convenient to the participants. Audio recorder was used to conduct interviews. It is important to note that before recording during the interview, the researcher presented the informed consent forms and explained to the participants the importance of research recording for the purposes of transcription.

Results

This section provides the findings to Congolese men's experiences and how migration has shaped men's understanding of being a man in the mist of migration. In order to understand Congolese men understanding and interpretation of manhood in the context of migration, it was important first to understand what manhood meant in the country of origin and how migration has reshaped this understanding. Although the objective of this study were not to explore the level of education and economic conditions of Congolese migrants men living in Durban, the researchers felt that education and economic situation of Congolese migrants to be important as these can determine how both can affect one's understanding of self.

Education and Understanding of Manhood Among Congolese Migrant

Education plays an important role in influencing how culture and self is constructed. During the interviews, researcher was interested in the level of education of participants and how this influences their understanding. Among eight participants, six had tertiary education, one with high school education, and one primary education. In response of how participants interpreter manhood, the finding showed that there were similarities in responses. The common response was based on man being the head of the household, not matter where can he be, in country of origin and in a foreign country. This has shown that education has little bearing on how Congolese interpret manhood. Analysis responses it was evident that culture is more powerful than education. There are many reasons to believe that culture among Congolese like any other African society has a very important space. Statements below illustrate responses of participants from two category groups:

> Man is a man everywhere. The level of education cannot define you who you are as man or a woman. In our culture you can be educated or not, but your parents are the one to tell you how to behave as man or a woman. This western education is contributing nothing. (Respondent man with tertiary education, 2018)

> You see, this Western Education will tell you that man and woman are equal. Not, even the Bible was written by western men, woman and man are not equal, so this education does not reflect who I m and does not help me understand who I'm as a man. Only my culture can tell me of what is expected of me. (Respondent man with High school education, 2018)

It is worth noting that education plays lesser role in influencing how Congolese migrant men living in Durban interpret their understanding of manhood. However, the culture that they have from the early age still influences their understanding.

Work and Manhood Among Congolese Migrant Living in South Africa

Self-employment remains the key to the economic survival of Congolese migrant men living in Durban, South Africa. Due to their political situation, unemployment among Congolese migrant remains high. This is well documented. As indicated above by participants in this study, self-employment remains the key survival among Congolese migrant men living in Durban. During the personal interviews, the researcher wanted to explore the nature of self-employment and employment among Congolese migrants' men in Durban. The findings show that the majority of Congolese men who are self-employed work as hair dressers, street vendors, and other forms of informal trading. Those who are formally employed are mainly in low paying jobs, such as security guards and car guards. The type of work that Congolese men have to undertake seems to be conflicting of their beliefs on the kind of jobs that man has to perform. Most of jobs undertaken by men are believed to be that of women in the country of origin. For instance, street vending and hair dressing are commonly performed by women. The following statement reads:

> You know, we do everything. We do women's work. In fact here in South Africa you cannot tell what job belongs to a man or a woman. In my county Congo, it is a shame to see a man sitting around the street selling. Hair is the job of women. Men's hair job in my country is to cut other men's hairs not cutting women, but here you dress hair of men as well as women. What can we do? We have to live. We swallow our pride and do everything in order to feed our children. (Participant no1, man, 2018)

Understanding Manhood in Country of Origin

Examining participants understanding of manhood in country of origin, the findings have demonstrated that the majority of participants had common understanding on what it means to be a man. One of the common understandings is that man is believed to be the head of the household and therefore is responsible in giving direction and controlling what has to happen at household level and well as at individual level of each member of the family. In addition, being a man is understood as being the breadwinner. This means, despite woman being employed and providing for their families, all these man is still under the control of man and is responsible in deciding on what to happen when it comes to finance even though woman is the one working.

Furthermore, the meaning of a man was seen in the context of the kind of work man has to undertake. This means that in the country of origin, there are kind of work that cannot be performed by men which are reserved for women. In this context, the type of work and economic condition can define how being man is interpreted among Congolese migrant in Durban, South Africa. This is illustrated in the following statements.

> In my country if you are a man, it means that you are in control of everything in your family. Even your wife. Yes, you can discuss with your wife and find a common understanding of how to manage the household, but as a man, you still responsible of everything. In addition, there are kind of work that man can do and cannot do. There are some jobs that are very shaming. Other people can laugh and can say that what kind of a man are you if you do that Job. (Participant no3, man, 2018)

Migration, Manhood Among Congolese Migrant in Durban, South Africa

During personal interviews, participants revealed the meaning of the family is reconstructed and reshaped due to migration. Participants believed that due to difficult economic conditions, most migrant families opted to have fewer children as a way to cope with their economic condition. While children are considered as assets in country of origin, in foreign country, due to economic hardship, children are considered as burdens rather than assets. As argued by Braithwaite and Baxter, interpretation of one's reality can be influenced by interaction between interconnected forces which are in nature economic, political, social, and environmental. Man being at the center of this interconnectedness becomes a major player in shaping and reshaping such reality and interprets it through various meanings and symbols. The reduction in number of children among Congolese migrants' men living in Durban should be regarded as a coping mechanism.

One statement reads:

> It is very hard to have many children under this condition we living. How can you have many children you cannot support and no one to assist you to take care of them? Back home, when you have many children, you do not worry how they will grow. If you have nothing to give them, you can send some to their grandmother and relatives, but here, it just you and your GOD. (Respondent four, 2018)

In response to the issue of change. There was also the issue of change in traditional gender roles. Where the participants indicated that in the country of origin, men occupied a traditional role of breadwinner and enjoyed its related status as head of the household within a traditional hierarchical family structure. Therefore, due to changes experienced in the country of migration such as changes in gender roles, unemployment, or alternatively. The participants indicated that when women work outside the home or migrant women work two jobs, their employment status causes their absence from home. In cases where their husbands hold a part-time job or are unemployed, men are expected to share household responsibility such as cooking. Change in gender roles participation increases the burden on both women and men. Until both find new ways of dealing with such a burden, the power relationship within the marriage will necessarily be affected. Men will try to maintain their position of authority and control over women; however, social and economic conditions under which Congolese men find themselves make it difficult for them to maintain the original meaning of being a man.

Conclusion

The aim of this chapter was to explore and examine the management of manhood in the context of migration with a particular focus to Congolese men migrants living in Durban, South Africa. Central to this chapter was to investigate factors affecting the meaning of manhood and its understanding. Several factors came into play. One of the major factors was the economic status that Congolese men enjoy in South Africa. It was found that the majority of Congolese in Durban, South Africa, are unemployed and have to rely of self-employment which also remain difficult to secure a decent living. Economic conditions of Congolese men makes it difficult for them to remain on control of the household has the culture dictates from the country of origin. In addition, the lack of social support experienced by Congolese men makes it difficult to maintain the meaning of being a man.

References

Adepoju A (2001) Regional integration, continuity and changing patterns of intra-regional migration in Sub-Saharan Africa. In: Siddique MAB (ed) International migration into the 21st century. Edward Elgar, Cheltenham/Northampton

Baker LM (2010) Migration and remittance nexus: A focus on Migration in Africa. Int J Migr 19(4):89–98

Bakewell O (2008) 'Keeping Them in Their Place': the ambivalent relationship between development and migration in Africa. Third World Q 29(7):1341–1358

Bakewell O, Bonfiglio A (2013) Moving beyond conflict: re-framing mobility in the African Great Lakes region. Working paper for the African Great Lakes Mobility Project (Vol. IMI working paper 71). International Migration Institutes, University of Oxford, Oxford

Bakewell O, Jónsson G (2011) Migration, mobility and the African city. International Migration Institute, Oxford

Berriane M, De Haas H (2012) African migrations research: innovative methods and methodologies. Africa World Press, Trenton

Boehm DA (2008) "Now I am a man and a woman!" Gendered moves and migrations in a transnational mexican community. Lat Am Perspect 35(1):16–30

Boyd M (1992) Gender issues in immigration and language fluency. In: Chiswick B (ed) Immigration, language and ethnicity. AEI Press, Washington, DC

Broughton C (2008) Migration as Engendered Practice: Mexican Men, Masculinity and Northward Migration. Gend Soc 22(5):568–589

Carletto C, Larisson J, Özden C (2014) Informing migration policies: a data primer. World Bank, Washington, DC

Castles S, De Haas H, Miller MJ (2014) The age of migration: international population movements in the modern world. Palgrave Macmillan Higher Education, Basingstoke

Charsley K (2005) Unhappy husbands: masculinity and migration in transnational Pakistani marriages. J R Anthropol Inst 11(1):85–105

Clemens MA (2014) Does development reduce migration? Center for Global Development, Washington, DC

Cohen R (2007) The new helots: migrants in the international division of labour. Oxford University Press and Oxford Publishing Services, Oxford

Collier P (2013) Exodus: how migration is changing our world. Oxford University Press, Oxford

Collyer M (2003) Explaining change in established migration systems: the movement of algerians to france and the UK. In: Migration working paper; 16. University of Sussex, Sussex Centre for Migration Research, Sussex

Curran SR (1996) Household resources and opportunities: The distribution of education and migration in rural Thailand. University of North Carolina

De Bruijn M, Van Dijk R, Foeken D (2001) Mobile Africa: changing patterns of movement in Africa and beyond. Brill, Leiden/Boston

De Haas H (2007) Turning the tide? Why development will not stop migration. Dev Chang 38(5):819–841

De Haas H (2010) Migration transitions: a theoretical and empirical inquiry into the developmental drivers of international migration, DEMIG, Working Paper No. 24. International Migration Institute, University of Oxford

De Haas H, Villares-Varela M (2014) The evolution of bilateral visa policies 1973–2014: new evidence from the DEMIG VISA database, DEMIG working paper. International Migration Institute, University of Oxford

Eisenstadt H (2017) International migration in the 21st century. J Soc Sci 19(6):159–168

FAO (2016) Migration, agriculture and rural development. Addressing the root causes of migration and harnessing its potential for development, Rome. Available at http://www.fao.org/3/a-i6064e.pdf

Fargues P (2004) Arab Migration to Europe: Trends and Policies. Int Migr Rev 38(4):1348–1371

Hoang LA, Yeoh BS (2011) Breadwinning wives and 'Left-Behind' husbands: men and masculinities in the vietnamese transnational family. Gend Soc 25(6):717–739

McKay SC (2007) Filipino sea men: constructing masculinities in an ethnic labour niche. J Ethn Migr Stud 33(4):617–633

Myers N (2005) Environmental refugees: an emergent security issue. Organisation for Security and Cooperation in Europe. http://www.osce.org/eea/14851

Näre L (2010) Sri Lankan men working as cleaners and carers: negotiating masculinity in Naples. Men Masculinities 13(1):65–86

Natter K (2014) Fifty years of Maghreb emigration: How states shaped Algerian, Moroccan and Tunisian emigration, Working Paper, DEMIG No. 21. International Migration Institute, University of Oxford. http://www.imi.ox.ac.uk/pdfs/wp/wp-95-14.pdf

Rose GH (2016) Understanding Migration. Oxford University Press, Oxford/New York

Sarti R (2010) Fighting for masculinity: male domestic workers, gender, and migration in Italy from the late nineteenth century to the present. Men Masculinities 13(1):16–43

Schoumaker B, Flahaux ML, Schans D, Beauchemin C, Mazzucato V, Sakho P (2015) Changing patterns of African Migration: A Comparative Analysis. In: Beauchemin C (ed) Migration between Africa and Europe: trends, factors and effects. Springer & INED Population Studies Series, New-York

Skeldon R (1997) Migration and development: a global perspective. Longman, Essex

United Nations (1995) International migration policies and the status of female migrants. United Nations, New York

Vezzoli S, Villares-Varela M, De Haas H (2014) Uncovering international migration flow data: insights from the DEMIG databases, DEMIG Working paper no. 17. International Migration Institute, University of Oxford. http://www.imi.ox.ac.uk/pdfs/wp/wp-88-14.pdf

Walter N, Philippe B, Margarita L (2004) Masculinity and undocumented labor migration: injured latino day laborers in San Francisco. Soc Sci Med 59(6):1159–1168

Zohry A, Harrell-Bond B (2003) Contemporary egyptian migration: an overview of voluntary and forced migration, Working paper C3. Development Research Centre on Migration, Globalisation and Poverty, University of Sussex. http://www.migrationdrc.org/publications/working_papers/WP-C3.pdf

Zolberg AR, Suhrke A, Aguayo S (1989) Escape from violence. Oxford University Press, Oxford/New York

Race and Sexuality: Colonial Ghosts and Contemporary Orientalisms

59

Monique Mulholland

Contents

Introduction	1130
Empire, Race, and Sexuality	1132
Young People, Race, and Sexualized Media	1134
Intergenerational Conflict, Sexuality, and Migrant Families	1139
Conclusion	1143
References	1144

Abstract

This chapter takes pause to reflect on what is meant by race and ethnicity and asks: How do historical meanings and discourses about race and ethnicity shape the present? And by extension, where and when did the idea of race and ethnicity emerge, and with what effects? It is vital to interrogate terms and how we use them because constructions of race and ethnicity are intimacy connected to history and power – as long argued by postcolonial and critical race scholars, the social constructions of race and ethnicity are intimately connected to colonial and orientalist discourses which "fixed" and homogenized the cultures of "others." As such, contemporary studies of race and ethnicity are haunted by "colonial ghosts" which orientate how we understand the present. As a way to explore these colonial ghosts, this chapter draws on current research about gender, sexuality, and race in Australia which have international relevance for the ways in which "raced others" negotiate sexuality in contexts of migration. In the first part of the chapter, I explore the connections between colonial discourses and constructions of sexuality. I then unpack two case studies which provide a fascinating set of reflections from participants about the ubiquitous

---

M. Mulholland (✉)
College of Humanities, Arts and Social Sciences, The Flinders University of South Australia, Adelaide, Australia
e-mail: monique.mulholland@flinders.edu.au

© The Author(s), under exclusive license to Springer Nature Singapore Pte Ltd. 2019
S. Ratuva (ed.), *The Palgrave Handbook of Ethnicity*,
https://doi.org/10.1007/978-981-13-2898-5_59

presence of colonial ghosts in their everyday lives. Most importantly, they provide a powerful set of reflections and responses from those cast as "other" in Australia, responses which work to "unfix" colonial alterities.

Keywords
Race · Orientalism · Colonial discourse · Sexuality

Introduction

This chapter begins by asking readers to take pause and reflect for a moment on the aims of this book. These volumes address a troubling erasure – issues of race and ethnicity are too often overlooked in favor of economic and political analyses of contemporary global developments. As such, they provide important accounts of the relationship between ethnicity and globalization, as well as the complex identifications and transnational identities that emerge in a globalized world. However, this chapter takes further pause to ask another critical question: How do historical meanings and discourses about race shape the present? And, by extension, where and when did the idea of race emerge, and with what effects? It is vital to interrogate terms and how we use them because constructions of race and ethnicity are intimacy connected to history and power – who decides what counts as ethnicity and what counts as "race" and "culture"? How do we border and characterize "race" and "ethnic" differences? Who does the bordering? And how do we position ourselves as researchers in this border-making?

This chapter draws inspiration from the insights of postcolonial and critical race theory to think through "when and where" race and ethnicity "came to mean as something tangible," as artefacts of discourse that "defines and produces the objects of our knowledge..." (Hall 1997, p. 44). As long argued by scholars of colonial history, race and ethnicity are social constructions – during the eighteenth century, earlier rudimentary classifications of racial types became increasingly systematized and fixed to biological scripts in the emergent field of race science (McConnochie et al. 1988; Hall 1997). (There is not the space, and nor is it the aim of this chapter, to explore the differences in the terms "race" and "ethnicity." For an excellent overview, see Ashcroft et al. (2006) *The Post-colonial Studies Reader* and Ashcroft et al. (1998) *Key Concepts in Post-colonial Studies*.) At the same time, theories about a "Great Chain of Being" established powerful schemas connecting biological race to questions of character – white Europeans sat firmly atop a hierarchical scale from the most to least civilized. In a similar vein, Social Darwinism applied evolutionary theories to powerful and weak socialities, in which primitive "races" would inevitably "die out" as a law of nature (Hollingsworth 2006; Reynolds 1987). As a result, powerful dualisms framed the Enlightenment, colonial project: civility/incivility, nature/culture, primitive/modern, refined/barbaric. These dualisms are most famously articulated in the work of Edward Said – orientalist discourses produced permanent and enduring tropes of otherness, fixed and homogenized through abject representations which worked to construct the

West as the epitome of human progress. As stated by Said, discourses of orientalism which established the West as the yardstick of comparison for culture, race, and civility had "less to do with the Orient than it does with 'our' world" (Said [1978] 1995, p. 12).

The upshot is that race and ethnicity have become tangible constructs – something we can touch, feel, and describe. They are places to begin, an identity marker, an axis of scholarly and social analysis. Most importantly, they are constructs that "fix" – "fix" cultural characteristics and worldviews to particular groups and identities in homogenizing and reductive ways. As this chapter will argue, it is important to reflect on the ways in which contemporary studies of race and ethnicity are tangled up in these colonial meanings, in these histories of "fixing." Indeed, while current language may differ in form and shape from early colonial history, colonial reproductions are alive and well. One example is clearly evident in a topic close to the heart of this book – colonial and orientalist dualisms continue to structure representations of development, modernization, and globalization: "First" World/"Third" World, Developed/Underdeveloped, Modernized/Traditional (Escobar 1995). Another example pervades contemporary representations of the poor Third World subject in charity discourses (Mulholland 1998).

Indeed, colonial continuities such as these are explored in Ann Stoler's recent book *Duress*, in which she asks: "How do colonial histories matter in the word today?...Those connectivities are not always readily available for easy grasp...colonial entailments may lose their visible and identifiable presence in vocabulary, conceptual grammar and idioms of contemporary concerns" (Stoler 2016, p. 1). Sara Ahmed similarly attends to colonial entailments in her cogent reflection on orientation and orientalism in *Queer Phemomenology*, arguing that "racism is an on-going and unfinished history, which orientates bodies in specific directions, affecting how they take up space" (Ahmed 2006, p. 111). She goes on to state that:

> the Orient provides the object, as well as the instrument, that allows the Occident to take shape, to become a subject, as that which "we" are around. The Occident would be what we are orientated around. Or we could even say that "the world" comes to be orientated "around" the Occident, through the very orientation of the gaze toward the Orient, the East, as the exotic other that can be seen just beyond the horizon. (Ahmed 2006, p. 116)

In these reflections, Ahmed reminds us that colonial representations orient bodies and meanings in particular ways, representations which organize how, where, and what we see. As terms which are intimacy connected to Empire, this chapter argues that contemporary understandings of race and ethnicity are haunted by colonial ghosts which orientate how we understand the present. My employment of the term "colonial ghost" is inspired by Clifton Crais and Pamela Scully's use of Ghost Story to title and animate their wonderful biography of Sara Baartman and the Hottentot Venus (2009). Indeed, as argued in the book, "ghosts haunt these pages," contemporary pages that are ridden with colonial discourses that fix and fasten race and ethnicity to a set of stereotypes and assumptions – and as argued by Ponzanesi (2005, p. 185) "grasping how the elaboration of contemporary racial stereotypes depends upon the past ingrained legacies is overdue."

As a way to explore these "colonial ghosts," this chapter draws on my current research about gender, sexuality, and race in Australia. In particular, I offer reflections on two case studies which reveal how colonial histories interrupt, circle, and orientate the present. I call these cases studies "contemporary orientalisms," and while they occur in Australia, they have international relevance for the ways in which "raced others" negotiate sexuality in contexts of migration. The first case draws from a study with young refugee people from a variety of cultural backgrounds: Ghana, Somalia, Palestine, Kenya, China, Vietnam, Liberia, and Nepal. Undertaken in South Australia, the project was a collaborative venture with a South Australian Multi-Cultural Sexuality and Health Service based on a series of focus groups designed to elucidate how these young people – often overlooked in academic studies and popular debates – perceived "sexy," "pornified," and "sexualized" media (Mulholland 2018, b). The second case study was also undertaken with the same service, exploring intergenerational conflicts about sex and sexuality which occur in migrant families. In this study, we also ran focus groups, this time with mothers, fathers, and young people from various African countries. In Australia, the cultural backgrounds that form the basis of this research are set up as "others" to the normative white Australian citizen (Sonia Magdalena Tascón 2008) – and as such, they provide a fascinating set of reflections on how those cast as "raced others" negotiate discourses of sexuality.

In the first part of the chapter, I draw on postcolonial, critical race theory and the work of feminist historians to examine the connections between colonial discourses and constructions of sexuality. I then move on to the case studies which provide a fascinating set of reflections from participants about the ubiquitous presence of colonial ghosts in their everyday lives. Most importantly, they provide a powerful set of reflections and responses from those cast as "other," responses which work to unfix the fixities of colonial mentalities. As will be argued throughout, the participants urgently reveal frustrations about how they are viewed by the "white" Anglo mainstream, and in particular, these indignities allow for:

> a better understanding of the political grammar of colonialism's durable presence, the dispositions it fosters, the indignities it nourishes, the indignities that are responses to those effects. (Stoler 2017, p. 9)

Empire, Race, and Sexuality

Colonial and orientalist discourses are powerful for the ways they set up privilege and marginality, along with "ways of seeing" that are stable and enduring. Of particular relevance for this chapter and the cases presented here are the connections between race, colonialism, and sexuality. As argued by Hall (1992, p. 210):

> Sexuality thus became a powerful element in the fantasy which the West constructed, and the ideas of sexual innocence and experience, sexual domination and submissiveness, play out in the complex dance in the discourses of "The West and the Rest."

Here Hall captures Stoler's now famous argument that discourses of empire were fundamentally connected to sexuality – the logic of empire gained authority through pervasive constructions of colonial "others" as uncivilized and sexually closer to nature. Indeed, as feminist historians and postcolonial and critical race scholars have long established, the sexualities of colonial subjects were viewed in axiomatical terms to those of the new middle classes in industrial capitalist modernity (Skeggs 1997). Bourgeois sexualities were cast as pure, disciplined, civilized, restrained, and "above nature." In contrast, black bodies and sexualities were viewed as uncontrolled, uncivilized, lascivious, and dangerous. In addition, scholars of feminist race history (Crais and Scully 2009; McClintock 1995; Lewis 2004; Levine 2008; Ponzanesi 2005) maintain that gendered discourses of empire established a hierarchy of femininity: the sexualities of white bourgeois femininity were set apart from black women, as well as those of the working classes.

In short, race was a powerful mechanism which established white "Western" sexualities as the yardstick of comparison, based on orientalist discourses of the abject sexualities of colonial subjects (Stoler 1995; Said [1978]1995). More recently, whiteness and critical race scholars contend that orientalist histories continue to establish white Western subjects at the normative center (Hage 2012; Moreton-Robinson 2000; Frankenberg 1993), retaining its surreptitious privilege to tell a single story of the other (Adichie 2009). In the Australian context, Sino Konishi presents a powerful and compelling case, revealing the ways in which colonial tropes of Aboriginal masculinity as violent, misogynistic, destructive, and dysfunctional were revitalized by John Howard's conservative Liberal government – as she argues, these representations are still "ubiquitous today" and can be "traced back to initial encounters between Europeans and Indigenous men" (Konishi 2011, p. 164). Indeed, black bodies are persistently constructed through colonial tropes across the globe as the "Spectacle of the Other" (Hall 2001) – fetishized and exoticized (Nash 2014; Miller-Young 2014; Ponzanesi 2005), dangerous and oppressed (Razack 2007; Abu-Lughod 2015; Imtoual 2009; Hussein 2009), and "other" to the West through tropes of the Third World women (Mohanty 1988; Narayan 1997). In addition, issues which concern white, middle-class women continue to dominate the feminist agenda (Moreton-Robinson 2000). The upshot of these "colonial recursions" (Stoler 2016) is to "fix" colonial sexualities – long viewed as dehistorized and homogenous, the views, attitudes, and identities of colonial others continue to be viewed in reductive terms. Indeed, to return to the work on Konishi as a consummate example, Indigenous men in the Australian context are fixed to the features of ethnicity:

> Aboriginal male violence is seen purely as a problem of ethnicity, for Aboriginal men are almost exclusively discussed in the context of Indigenous society and culture, and not in relations to other men. (Konishi 2011, p. 172)

This fixing leaves no room to imagine sexualities as hybrid (Bhabha 1994), multiple, mixed, and intersectional. As argued by Ahmed, colonizing discourses close down accounts that might reorientate race and ethnicity as a "genealogy of being mixed" (Ahmed 2006, p. 154). In the face of this, the participants in my studies present a fascinating set of reflections about the ubiquity of colonial discourse and make room for the complex mixings that make up their lives. They reveal how colonial ghosts shape how they are "read through difference" in their country of migration, ghosts which influence the assumptions held by normatively centered "white" Australian about their views and attitudes about sexuality. In addition, colonial ghosts shape and constrain the conditions on which they can negotiate issues of sex and sexuality in a culture that marks them as "other" through the "internal cycle" of difference (Fanon [1968]1970).

Young People, Race, and Sexualized Media

The first case study arose from a study undertaken in South Australia with a group of "culturally diverse" young people in collaboration with a South Australian Multi-Cultural Sexuality and Health Service. This organization provides counselling and community education programs on issues of sexual mental health and works with young people made up of refugee and voluntary (newly arrived and longer-term migrants to Australia), as well as international students from various countries in the region. They were interested to explore how sexualized popular media was being understood by the young people they work with, as well as the influence of "sexy" media on gender and sexuality identity formation. To achieve these aims, we ran three focus groups and organized discussion-based activities titled "Good and Bad Sexy." These discussions were open-ended and canvassed their respective views of "sexy" celebrities and the forms of sexy styling on offer in the mainstream media. These discussions allowed participants to explore their thoughts and attitudes on acceptable versus inappropriate forms of sexy expression and articulate the terms on which these distinctions were made.

As indicated above, it is vitally important to interrogate what is meant by "race" and "culture," as well as the powerful position held by researchers to define the limits of race and ethnicity in research projects (Haggis and Mulholland 2014). As I have argued elsewhere, the enduring power of orientalist and colonial discourses to fix and authorize the difference of others fails to account for the "deterritorialization of identity formation such that entanglement and connectedness become the motif of twenty-first-century subjectivity" (Haggis and Mulholland 2014, p. 57). In addition, as a normatively centered "white" researcher, I hold enormous privilege in a system that centralizes Western epistemologies and thus necessitates "an earthwide network of connections, including the ability partially to translate knowledge among very different – and power-differentiated – communities" (Haraway 1988, p. 580). As such, we wanted to design a study that tried to avoid overdetermining cultural difference or define its limits from the outset. Indeed, it was common for me to receive comments that sought to capture and constrain attitudes as fixed and immutable: "Muslim girls won't want to talk about sexy porno culture!," "Won't conversations like that be uncomfortable for 'them'?," and "A lot of the Muslim girls you talk to won't like Lady Gaga!". In order to address the problematics of difference represented in comments such as these, we did not ask participants to talk about "cultural backgrounds" or answer questions like "how does your cultural background influence your views of sex and sexuality?" Alternatively, we were interested to explore if "race" emerged from the discussion as part of the discussion (if at all) and on what terms.

Across the discussions, "race" and "culture" did emerge – however, rather than reflect cultural views of sexuality, the young people talked about how they were "read through difference" by their white, Anglo counterparts. Of course, much of the discussion involved views and attitudes about "Good and Bad Sexy" (for further elaboration, see Mulholland 2018, b). However, just as often, the discussion reversed the gaze to explore "how they were read by others." They urgently articulated concerns that their "views of sexuality" were misread through a persistent and relentless set of assumptions. As one young man states, their cultures and identities are seen as "little stereotypes," and as a result, they are "put into little boxes":

> Kg: So I think based on that they could almost put us in a little box based on what sexy means so for the Black man sexy probably means twerking
> *All laughing*
> Me: Exactly!
> Tahereh: So you have all these things and little stereotypes
> Kg: Yeah stereotypes

One pervasive "little box" was fiercely articulated by the Muslim young women in the focus groups. They were particularly exasperated by predetermined ideas about Islam and how these shaped how they were viewed – as stated by Ianna, they are tired of "the whole Muslim thing":

> When a Muslim Woman says she's a feminist they say "Well, arent you oppressed?" (Ianna)

They felt instantly typecast as oppressed and incapable of articulating a feminist position from "inside the veil" (Abu Lughod 2015; Imtoual 2009; Hussein 2009), which as argued by Imtoual is an enduring trope of colonialism in which Australia's Christian foundations scaffold the "secular" present. Ayana goes on to talk about the ways in which her Muslim identity and feminist politics were twisted by her tutor. In the following encounter, Ayana's agency was reconfigured back into the logics of orientalist discourses, captured by tropes of otherness that crystallize "the Rest" as idealized and homogenous (Spurr 1993):

> Ayana: You know it's quite funny actually when I was doing gender and popular culture as an elective, I would have loved the subject, but I was turned off by my tutorial teacher.
> Me: Really?

> Ayana: Yes, cause when I walked into that class she actually treated me as a victim, you know what I mean?...because of the whole Muslim thing...She would even go, "Ayana, do you even identify yourself as a feminist?" It was just terrible. And then me and her, we would just get into an argument, you know what I mean? And then at the end she turned into this... "Ayana you're not the same, Ayana you're different ... You know you grew up here."
> Serwa: Do you know how much I hate that!
> Ayana: Like my tutor jumping to this conclusion once she got to know me. She's like "Ayana you're different". I'm like – "hang on how do you know most Muslim women do not think the same way I do?" She just made me the minority within my own culture. "Your different, you've been influenced by popular culture." I'm like, "no I wasn't". These are actually my values and beliefs.

Here Ayana elucidates an enduring colonial ghost and represents a kind of productive indignity to colonialism's durable presence suggested by Ann Stoler (2017). When colonial subjects are seen as "successful," this success is attributed to living in the "West" – and by extension, attaining modern, progressive views from the West. Indeed, in many instances, the young people named moments when their "progressive" views were put down to the fact they had moved to Australia, not because they or their families were capable of forming their own views and opinions:

> Serwa: You're opinionated, your outspokenness is attributed to fact that you grew up here, not because of who you are!
> Ayana: Yes!

This inability to form independent views can best be understood in the context of colonialist linearity – as argued by Hall (1997), because success and civility is constructed in linear terms, the West is seen as the only end point. This is poignantly captured by Fanon:

> The colonized is elevated above his jungle status in proportion to his adoption of the mother country's cultural standards. (Fanon [1968]1970, p. 14)

This "end point" can only be viewed in stark contrast to the backwardness of colonial subjects – eternally framed by "black skin," this skin is scrutinized in opposition to modernity and in opposition to "the myths of progress, civilisation, liberalism, education, enlightenment and refinement" (Fanon [1968]1970, p. 138). Indeed, as argued by Said ([1978]1995, p. 108):

> a white middle-class Westerner believes it his human prerogative not only to manage the nonwhite world but also to own it, just because by definition "it" is not quite as human as "we" are. There is no purer example than this of dehumanized thought.

However, as noted by participants, the so-called success they achieve from "living in the West" is only a partial. The participants spoke of another "little box," a box that had the effect of putting them back "into place," a place marked out by colonial discourses of the "West" and the "Rest." At many points, they referred to relentless questions about "where are you from" – and while the following except elicited much laughter, this humor indicates a serious and pervasive intrusion in their lives:

> Kumal: What I've done is...many times people ask me..."Where are you from?" I answer "I am from China you know."
> *(All laugh)*

Here again, the following encounter is in part viewed with amusement, most particularly as their birth countries were colonized by Britain and English is their first or second language – nonetheless these everyday encounters represent the ubiquitous presence of colonial ghosts:

> Anu: Do people still ask you how did you learn English?
> Ayana: Mm Hmm. I knew English when I came here!
> Ianna: "Oh my god your English is so good!" It's like… (rolls eyes)…um. "I went to school!"
> Anu: You should probably say "I know! I speak another five languages!"
> *(All laugh)*

These moments are indicative of the impossible position set up by colonial ghosts. Questions such as "where are you from" set them outside or at the very best at margins. On the one hand, they are viewed as "making it" (through understanding pop culture, claiming a feminist politics, overcoming "piety" because you are "different"). However, on the other hand, their difference is constantly noted and thus made conspicuous. As argued above, the civilizing mission which underpins colonialism requires the other to achieve civility (and assumes they wish to do so) – however, it never confers these achievements (Schech and Haggis 2000). As argued by Fanon, success is always partial for colonized subjects:

> When people like me, they like me "in spite of my color." When they dislike me; they point out that it isn't because of my color. Either way, I am locked into the infernal circle. (Fanon [1968]1970)

In addition to the "whole Muslim thing" and "where are you from," participants also focused on the kinds of "sexy" they saw in the media. In this case, colonial ghosts made themselves felt in and through media representations of "sexiness." Time and time again, they noted that media in "the West" does not present a range or diversity of sexualities – and if present, the sexualities of "others" are fetishized and eroticized. Rather, these normative forms of sexiness that parade popular culture are given a name by the participants – "Western sexy": "dressing without a lot of clothes" (Lan), "English phrases" (Lan), "skinny" (Tahereh). By naming this style as "Western sexy," they expose the normalizing and naturalizing effects of discourse and identify the narrow range of sexualities on offer. Indeed, in the act of naming "Western sexy," they reveal the erasure of difference and diverse forms. As noted by one young woman:

Anu: Can I give an example? So in Nepal, women wear Sari, and it's quite revealing, and it's a sexy dress. So we come to a country like Australia, and obviously we won't be wearing Sari every day. And there are girls in the community who get into and are inspired by the "Western sexy" image (makes quote marks with hand movements). And they start dressing up in short skirts, and just like revealing clothes. And you know you have the Nepali sexy image, but they don't want that because that's not the form of sexy that's defined by the media. So they want to look "Western sexy."

The participants also noted how representations of "Western sexy" are imbued with colonial construction of the "West as Best," constructions which produce a fraught relationship with popular media culture. Across the discussion, participants reflected on the process of negotiating sexuality in the face of media that valorized and normalized particular images of "sexy" – as argued by Constance, there was always a tension between valuing her culture and viewing the West as the epitome of success and progress:

Constance: For me it's the way Western style is constructed as "better." In Kenya, the more European you are, it's a status thing. It stems from colonialism – white Western being better. People are still dealing with the colonial mentality. Of the West being better because they have better roads, better schools, etc....

Finally, in this study, the young people expressed a desire to tell similar stories. While seemingly well-intentioned, this narrow reading of their lives and identities has the effect of putting those marked as other "back in place." This strategy of "place-making" is acutely expressed by Ayana – as a youth leader in her community, she is frequently invited to speak at public events. However, she and the other participants are often made uncomfortable by this singular reading of their experience in which those asking to "hear" invoke colonial mentalities in the moment of asking. The stories "they" ask for are experiences of difference, of struggle, and of difficulty through migration – but most importantly, these requests show up the "instability of 'race' as a classifying device" (Zambelli 2018, p. 167):

Ayana: Cause lately in the last two years, people are like Ayana can you speak here, can you speak here, can you speak here...And this last month I was speaking at three different places, and often one thing I find interesting is how people expect you to tell "your" story. Ayana can you tell me "your story"?
Serwa: Yeah. Excuse me! What story!!??
Ayana: Yeah, what story!! And the story that I often tell is of my transition from high school, to university, to the workplace, and people are like...that's the same are ours! And I'm like, what do you want me to say? I was a refugee, I was this, I was that...

In the discussion that ensued, Ayana and others urgently displayed a desire to tell stories that represented the complex mixings of their lives. Rather than be captured by a "single story" (Adichie 2009), the participants wished to be viewed as "citizens of the word," as living "in a globalized world":

Ayana: I'm the only one in my family who is not a citizen. My family became citizen five years ago. And I'm like "I'm not gonna be a citizen." You know! The reason is I'm actually not a citizen of anywhere in the world. I was born on the border between Somalia and Kenya.

And I'm like my reasoning for not wanting to be a citizen is regardless even if you are a citizen of Australia because everyone asks you. "Where you from? What country are you from?"

I argue this desire to "not be a citizen" in favor of an implied transnational identity represents a powerful challenge to the colonial ghosts circulating their lives and ideas. As argued by Aihwa Ong, the experience of migration produces new forms of "flexible citizenry" which can be theorized as "new modes of subject making and new kinds of valorised subjectivity" (Ong 1999, pp. 17–18) – this flexible citizenry disrupts the oppositional or fixed views of culture produced by colonial discourses and mentalities. Indeed, Haggis and Schech's articulation of "transnational moves" (2010) reveals the ways in which colonial subjects speak back to bounded notions of the "West and the Rest" by making a claim to transnational citizenship – rather than reproduce "universalist and particularist" views of culture, they use transnational to make a claim *against* the universalizing language of colonialism:

A kind of counter-discourse, or resistant subjectivity, runs through these stories when taken together; a stubborn refusal to see themselves as anything other than fully part of humanity; a condition based on their rights – rights to inclusion, to be heard, and to social agency. (Haggis and Schech 2010, p. 377)

Intergenerational Conflict, Sexuality, and Migrant Families

The next case draws on another study undertaken with the same South Australian Multi-Cultural Sexuality and Health Service. In this study, the organization was interested to explore the intergenerational conflicts that emerge about issue of gender, sex, and sexuality in migrant families. Across their counselling and community education work, there was growing concern about a range of negative sexual health outcomes which resulted from these tensions: underuse of sexual health support services; poor sexual health knowledge; mixed messages about sexual health from community, peers, and broader society; stigma and cultural shame; risky sexual practices due to "secrecy"; fears about queer sexual identity; and fears about "coming out" (Dean et al. 2017).

Based on this urgent need for evidence-based research and resources, we designed a series of focus groups with fathers, mothers, and young people from the African community in South Australia. The participants were drawn from a wide range of African nations, such as Ghana, Tanzania, Kenya, Somalia, and South Sudan – all families had been living in Australia for longer or shorter terms over the past 15 years, and the young people were 16 years and above. Across the focus groups, we employed a range of open-ended questions designed to explore the tensions and misunderstanding that emerged in families about issues of sex and sexuality. In addition, we were also interested to explore how the tensions were negotiated and managed, in order to map community-based solutions to help resolve the conflicts. Building on these insights, the study has produced a video resource, co-designed with communities for use by sexual health practitioners and communities.

Across the focus groups, participants revealed a wide range of tensions: competing norms about sex before marriage and partner choice, fears about "what was being taught at school," the desire to live up the parent expectations while forging independent paths, and the vital necessity for trust and compromise. However, similar to the first case, participants also presented a powerful set of insights about colonial ghosts – in and through the discussions, reference was made to how they were "read through difference" by mainstream Australian society and how this affected tensions about sex. Indeed, in many cases, conflicts resulted from the complex pressures of migration, rather than "cultural attitudes" and cultural "taboos." This presents a challenge to the ways in which colonial discourses construct cultural attitudes in bound and fixed terms, as if these attitudes "come from the inside" – however, as argued by Peltola et al. (2017, p. 535), "Negotiations concerning sexuality, including conflicts, should not be examined as disconnected from the wider discourses..."

One of the most tangible "pressures" was an unequivocal desire to make the most of the opportunities offered in Australia. Indeed, in all of the focus groups, participants explained what this linear path to success looked like – secondary education, university, master's degree, then marriage, then children. As noted by one mother, in a humorous but highly serious account, children are expected to follow a set of milestones:

> Mother 3: May I just, may I just quickly add onto that about do well, as I joke with my children I tell them, I want you to go to school and then after they'd finish school go to Uni-
> Mother 2: Uni
> (All laughing)
> Mother 3: Go to Uni, finish Uni, go for Master's degree
> Q: Geez no pressure.
> (All laughing)
> Mother 3: Get a boyfriend and then after that get married.
> Mother 2: Get married.
> Mother 3: And then get children-
> Mother 2: Children.
> Mother 3: And then I tell them, "In that order."
> Mother 2: In that order-
> (All laughing)

However, while "making the most of opportunities" was desired in its own right, the participants simultaneously revealed how this pressure to succeed was exacerbated by a need to counter the negative stereotypes about "Africans" circulating Australian media (Nolan et al. 2011). Indeed, one recent example of this negative press has emerged in problematic and inaccurate representations of "African crime gangs" in Melbourne which disproportionately reduce the case of crime to "African youth" (Budarick 2018). As one father states:

Father 3: There's not a frame of reference here and also I sometimes feel like there's also an amount of race involved, there's a higher expectation on us as Africans...

This "need to excel" was also noted by another father, who names the extra pressure placed on "others" to make it – as noted in the above case, discourses of the "West" and the "Rest" require others to achieve the successes of the West, but this success is judged more harshly within "a racialized gaze." Here again, we are reminded of Fanon's "infernal cycle of difference" (Fanon [1968]1970), where color becomes the relentless focus of scrutiny:

Father 2: Black people need to excel, so you can't do anything that is going to compromise that success.

At other times, participants reflected on the overt racism that circulates their lives – in this case, racism did not occur as a "ghost" but as a visceral and visible set of insults that shape fears and cautions about how their culture – and by extension their sexualities – is viewed.

Young woman 8: Yes, exactly and all that thing and like I said in primary school I was really really cautious because I don't know if you all went to public schools, but kids that were my age back then were nasty, they were nasty.
Young woman 8: Yeah, it was traumatising.
Young woman 9: Kids are nasty, kids are.

In the face of negative stereotypes and racism, the participants presented a powerful challenge to the colonial imperative that fixes and binds culture as a "neat and tidy" package. In stark contrast, across the focus groups discussions, the participants revealed how race is fluid and mixed, constantly changing shape through the experiences of migration. As noted by one young woman, she sees herself as operating in a third culture, resonant of Bhabha's notion of a "third space" (Bhabha 1994):

Young woman 4: Yeah, I think that's hard because like I say with younger people when we come here I feel as though we create this third culture where we take the best bits that we like about our previous culture and the society that we live in and we create our own culture.

Indeed, the participants often mentioned how their views of sexuality are shaped by the mixings of culture that result from migration. In one discussion, one mother notes that even though it is difficult when children form different norms and attitudes about sex, it is important to remember that values and attitudes shift and change:

Mother 1: You see I don't know about everybody else, I've been here a bit more than 10 years I have evolved really well. And one thing I have recognised is living in Australia there are certain things that I can't, in my ... it's accepted in Australia. But am I living in Australia or I'm living in Ghana? So I raise my children according to the way of life here, so I make it very open. We have, every night we have dinner at the table we have open discussions.

This "shifting" was noted in another discussion, in which one young person names the complex mixings and disruptions that occur in migrations, disruptions that produce the "freedom illusion":

> Young woman 3: No, here it starts debate because of their freedom illusion. Because back home it's a collective, your neighbours know each other, even the neighbour dog will follow you ... there's that connection, so parents can-
> Young woman 4: The neighbour dog knows your name.
> Q: What's that?
> Young woman 4: I said the neighbour dog even knows your name.
> (Laughing)
> Young woman 4: It knows your boyfriend's name.
> Young woman 3: Yes!! (All laughing)
> Young woman 3: But here parents fear the freedom, the freedom of information.

What this "freedom illusion" points to are the interactions that construct the lives and identities of the participants – and as such, intergenerational tensions about sexuality cannot be reduced to "internal" or fixed cultural ideas. As long argued by theorists of intersectionality, a range of factors across class, race, gender, age, and ability shape tensions about sexuality (Peltola et al. 2017). In this study, many factors affected the tensions which occurred in families: working double jobs, low-paid work, single-parent families, lack of funding for migrant communities, and "mainstream" attitudes that misunderstand the needs of migrant families. As stated by one young man, there is often no time to "connect" or discuss issues because parents are struggling with work pressures:

> Young man 2: Well, to me because the reason why there's not a better connection between the African parent and their kid is because when we came here many of our parents are busy working, because they were working, working, working so much because they want to put their kid into a private school so they can get better education, so they don't spend too much quality time; you can only see your Mum like let me say it, five minutes in the morning before you go to school and then you come back and see your Mum like for ten minutes and then you go to bed. So because that time is not there and because of the culture...-
> Q: They're struggling too.
> Young man 2: They be like okay, I want my kid to have the best, so for them to do that I have to do double job.

An intersectional approach also reveals how colonial ghosts make themselves felt through the ways in which migrant family tensions are singled out as particular and problematic in popular and academic accounts of intergenerational tensions (Peltola et al. 2017; Foner and Dreby 2011) – and as argued throughout, any approach which "binds up" culture as fixed and immutable overlooks how "cultural difference" itself is not at issue. Rather, tensions about sexuality are produced in and through discursive constructions of race in the country of settlement. Paying attention to intersections is vital in order to challenge the ubiquity of colonial ghosts that miss out how gender, race, class, ability, and religion *work together* to lead to tensions and misunderstandings. In this way, as I have argued elsewhere, it is useful to think about migration and diasporas as "fluid, performative, and relational rather than fixed entities emanating from transnational movements across space" (Creese 2014, p. 5).

Conclusion

By way of conclusion, I revisit the questions raised out at the outset of this chapter: How do historical meanings and discourses about race shape the present? Studies that reflect on the role of race, culture, and ethnicity in a globalized world are vitally important – however, as I have argued throughout, it is equally important to reflect on what we mean by race and ethnicity. In short, ignoring colonial histories risks overlooking the annals of race and power that shape meanings and analyses of "ethnicity" in the present – as argued by Ahmed, colonial orientations are "lines given in advance":

> collectives come to have "lines" in the sense of being modes of following: to inhabit a collective might be to follow a line, a line that is already given in advance. (Ahmed 2006, p. 119)

Across the case studies, colonial meanings and "lines given in advance" made themselves felt in visceral ways – in the first case, they constrained what could be said by "others," they twisted how the views and attitudes of "others" were understood, and they limited what stories could be told and on what terms. In the second case, colonial ghosts shaped the pressures placed on migrant families to succeed and excel – most importantly, the experiences of migrant families challenged colonial ideas about "fixed and bound" culture.

However, attending to colonial ghosts tells only part of the story – more importantly, reflecting on "lines given on advance" allows us to imagine new forms of global connectivity, identity formation, and affinity which challenge reductive, fixed notions of race and ethnicity. As argued by Ahmed (2006, p. 156):

> what shape such a world might take, or what mixtures might be possible, when we no longer reproduce the lines we follow?

For the participants in this study, I wonder what "shape their world might take" if difference and identity (and by extension sexuality) was marked in decolonizing ways. For example, what if the young people heard questions like "where do you live" rather than "where are you from?" Would this allow conversations about place, identity, home, and belonging which avoided the trappings of the "West and the Rest"? Would it "reorientate" the question from abject difference to "mixed genealogy"? Or, what if they were asked to tell the stories of their lives on their own terms – to tell a broad range of stories, to tell stories of difference and similarity, rather than a "single story" (Adichie 2009)? And what if migrant families saw a complex range of representations about "Africans in Australia" in place of dehumanizing negative stereotypes?

Indeed, research on race and ethnicity must centralize "the questions we ask" – the questions we ask and the assumptions we make have the potential to "unfix" culture and open up the possibility to listen differently to the colonial ghosts which shape our lives.

References

Abu-Lughod L (2015) Do Muslim women need saving? Harvard University Press, London
Adichie CN (2009) The Danger of a single story. https://www.ted.com/talks/chimamanda_adichie_the_danger_of_a_single_story?language=en. Accessed 14 Dec 2015
Ahmed S (2006) Queer phenomenology: orientations, objects, others. Duke University Press, Durham
Ashcroft B, Griffiths G, Tiffin H (1998) Key concepts in post-colonial studies. Routldge, London
Ashcroft B, Griffiths G, Tiffin H (eds) (2006) The post-colonial studies reader. Routledge, London
Bhabha H (1994) Locations of culture. Routledge, London
Budarick J (2018) Why the media are to blame for racialising Melbourne's 'African gang' problem. The Conversation. August 1. Accessed 8 October. https://theconversation.com/why-the-media-are-to-blame-for-racialising-melbournes-african-gang-problem-100761
Crais C, Scully P (2009) Sara Baartman and the Hottentot Venus: a ghost story and a biography. Princeton University Press, Princeton
Creese G (2014) Gender, generation and identities in Vancouver's African diaspora. Afr Diaspora 6(2):155–178
Dean J, Mitchell M, Stewart D, Debattista J (2017) Intergenerational variation in sexual health attitudes and beliefs among Sudanese refugee communities in Australia. Cult Health Sex 19(1):17–31
Escobar A (1995) Encountering development: the making and unmaking of the third world. Princeton University Press, Princeton
Fanon F ([1968]1970) Black skins/White masks. Paladin, Frogmore
Foner N, Dreby J (2011) Relations between the generations in immigrants' families. Annu Rev Sociol 37:545–564
Frankenburg R (1993) White women, race matters: the social construction of whiteness. Routledge, London
Hage G (2012) White nation: fantasies of white supremacy in a multicultural society. Routledge, London
Haggis J, Mulholland M (2014) Rethinking difference and sex education: from cultural inclusivity to normative diversity. Sex Education 14(1):57–66
Hall S (1992) The West and the rest: discourse and power. In: Hall S, Gieben B (eds) Formations of modernity. Polity Press and The Open University, Cambridge, pp 184–227
Hall S (1997) Representation: cultural representation and signifying practices. London: Sage
Hall S (2001) The spectacle of the other. In: Wetherall M, Taykor S, Yates S (eds) Discourse theory and practice: a reader. Sage, London, pp 324–344
Haraway D (1988) Situated knowledges: the science question in feminism and the privilege of partial perspective. Fem Stud 14(3):575–599
Hollingsworth D (2006) The construction of Australian racism 1770–1920. In: Hollinsworth D (ed) Race and racism in Australia, 3rd edn. Thomson/Social Science Press, South Melbourne, pp 66–104
Hussein S (2009) Looking in or looking out? Stories on the multiple meanings of veiling. In: Dreher T, Ho L (eds) Beyond the hijab debates: new beyond the hijab debates: new conversations on gender, race and religion. Newcastle, Cambridge
Imtoual A (2009) 'Taking things personally': young Muslim women in South Australia discuss identity, religious racism and media representations. PhD thesis, University of Adelaide

Konishi S (2011) Representing aboriginal masculinity in Howard's Australia. In: Jackson RL, Balaji M (eds) Global masculinities and manhood. University of Urbana, Illinois Press, Urbana, pp 161–185

Levine P (2008) States of undress: nakedness and the colonial imagination. Vic Stud 50(2):189–219

Lewis R (2004) Rethinking orientalism: women, travel and the ottoman harem. Rutgers University Press, New Brunswick

Magdalena Tascón S (2008) Narratives of race and nation: everyday whiteness in Australia. Soc Identities 14(2):253–274

McClintock A (1995) Imperial leather: race, gender and sexuality in the colonial contest. Routledge, New York

McConnochie K, Hollinsworth D, Pettman J (1988) The meaning of 'race'. In: McConnochie K, Hollinsworth D, Pettman J (eds) Race and racism in Australia. Social Science Press, Wentworth Falls, pp 3–18

Miller-Young M (2014) A taste for brown sugar: black women, sex work and pornography. Duke University Press, London

Mohanty C (1988) Under Western eyes: feminist scholarship and colonial discourses. Fem Rev 30:61–88

Moreton-Robinson A (2000) Talkin' up to the white woman: aboriginal women and feminism. St. Lucia, University of Queensland Press

Mulholland, M (1998) Deconstructing development education: the politics of representation and Western activisim. Honors Doctoral dissertation, Flinders University of South Australia

Mulholland M (2017b) 'When difference gets in the way': young people, whiteness and sexualisation. Sex Cult 21(2):593–612

Mulholland M (2018) "Western sexy?": the West, the rest and sexualised media. Fem Media Stud 18(6):1102–1116

Narayan U (1997) Death by culture': thinking about dowry-murders in India and domestic-violence murders in the United States. In: Narayan U (ed) Dislocating cultures: identities, traditions and Third World feminisms. Taylor & Francis, London

Nash J (2014) The black body in ecstasy: reading race, reading pornography. Duke University Press, Durham

Nolan D, Farquharson K, Politoff V, Marjoribanks T (2011) Mediated multiculturalism: newspaper representations of Sudanese migrants in Australia. J Intercult Stud 32(6):655–671

Ong A (1999) Flexible citizenship: the cultural logics of transnationality. Duke University Press, Durham

Peltola M, Keskinen S, Honkasalo V, Honkatukia P (2017) Intergenerational negotiations on (hetero) sexuality and romantic relationships–views of young people and parents in multi-ethnic contexts. J Youth Stud 20(5):533–548

Ponzanesi S (2005) Beyond the black Venus: colonial sexual politics and contemporary visual practices In: Amkpa A and Toscano EM (eds) ReSignification – European Blackamoors, Africana Readings. Postcart, Rome, pp 137–147

Razack S (2007) Casting out: the eviction of Muslims from Western law and politics. University of Toronto Press, London

Reynolds H (1987) Frontier: aborigines, settlers and land. Allen & Unwin Australia Pty Limited, Sydney

Said E ([1978]1995) Orientalism. Penguin, London

Schech S, Haggis J (2000) Culture and Development. Oxford: Blackwell

Skeggs B (1997) Formations of class and gender: becoming respectable. Sage, London

Spurr D (1993) The rhetoric of empire: colonial discourse in journalism, travel writing, and imperial administration. Duke University Press, Durham

Stoler A (1995) Race and the education of desire. Duke University Press, Durham

Stoler A (2016) Duress. Duke University Press, Durham

Zambelli E (2018) Between a curse and a resource: the meanings of women's racialised sexuality in contemporary Italy. Mod Italy 23(2):159–172

Part VI

Globalization and Diaspora

Part Introduction

This part discusses and advances cutting-edge analyses of ethnicity, globalization, and diaspora through diverse multidisciplinary lenses and provides perspectives from anthropology, sociology, development, Pacific studies, education, psychology, political, and behavioural sciences, and how these fields inform current and, equally important, future developments in the ethnicity field.

All the chapters in this part are poignant examples of how globalization has enveloped and transformed diasporic societies through economic and financial integration, social media networks, knowledge transfer, transnationalism, technology, and education. But the new knowledge, insights, and perspectives they offer document critical ethnic, cultural, and intergenerational experiences which speak to the heart of diasporic and transnational worldviews, their perceptions of each other, and the centrality of relationships and issues of identity. Thus of significance here is, how these expose the deeper layers of realities, perceptions, and meanings of social change as they try to survive in ever-changing worlds. The chapters in this part thus provide a platform for inter-, cross-, and multidisciplinary dialogue across a myriad of perspectives.

There are eight chapter contributions in this part highlighting research across three major intersecting themes: diaspora, transnational ethnicities, and intergenerational perspectives. Three chapters are on the Indian diaspora. These are Kataoka (Indian diaspora – globalization allowing this group to retain ethnic bonds, regardless of state borders), Nachowitz (Indians in New Zealand – traces settlement from 1861 to 2018 and concluding that early settlers were entrepreneurs and professionals rather than scrub cutters and market gardeners), and Premdas (Indians and Africans in Guyana – challenges to overcome their bipolar positioning due to new petroleum resources wealth). One chapter by Zhang (Filipino and Chinese diaspora in Singapore and Macau) is on casino workers and their resistance to negative stereotyping. The European diaspora is covered in two chapters–Fanany and Avgoulas (Greeks in Australia – transnational identities being fuelled by Australian-born generations through internet and travel to homeland) and Luconi (Italians in the United States – US-born second generation reforming an Italian identity). There is one chapter on diaspora groups in Europe by P.E. and F.J. Villegas (North America and Europe – focuses on migrant illegitimization and how migrants are counteracting this and constructing safer contexts or reception). There is one chapter on the Pacific diaspora by Anae which focuses on transnational Samoan chiefs – pioneer and first-generation NZ/US/Australian-born chiefs in the diaspora and transformations of service to families and homeland as a new development strategy.

Melani Anae

Diaspora as Transnational Actors: Globalization and the Role of Ethnic Memory

60

Masaki Kataoka

Contents

Introduction	1150
Theoretical Explanations of the Diaspora	1151
Globalization and Diaspora's Transnational Power	1153
Controversies Under Globalization	1153
Growing Influence of Diaspora	1155
The Role of Ethnic Memory	1156
Collective Memory	1156
Collective Memory and Social Identity	1158
Social Networks and Ethnic Memory	1159
The Case of the Indian Diaspora	1161
Conclusion	1164
Cross-References	1164
References	1165

Abstract

Diaspora is a group of people who have dispersed from their homeland country to other parts of the world. Although they may have lived away from their homeland for several generations, they maintain a collective attachment to it. In addition, diaspora groups construct networks of people of the same ethnic origin, share an ethnic identity, and act transnationally. This collectiveness is strengthened by globalization and through the development of communication and transportation technologies that can assist a diaspora group with retaining ethnic bonds, regardless of state borders. This chapter focuses on the role of ethnic memory that

---

M. Kataoka (✉)
University of Canterbury, Christchurch, New Zealand

Institute of Developing Economies, Japan External Trade Organization, Chiba, Japan
e-mail: masaki.kataoka@pg.canterbury.ac.nz; Masaki_Kataoka@ide.go.jp

© The Author(s), under exclusive license to Springer Nature Singapore Pte Ltd. 2019
S. Ratuva (ed.), *The Palgrave Handbook of Ethnicity*,
https://doi.org/10.1007/978-981-13-2898-5_81

allows diaspora to retain their ethnic identity on a transnational level. The theory of collective memory argues that socially constructed collective memory compels people to retain a shared identity with people who share their collective memory. In the case of the diaspora, many believe that they or their ancestors experienced traumatic events or suffering when they dispersed from their homeland or settled in a host country. These negative memories strengthen ethnic bonds and construct and maintain the ethnic identity of the homeland among people of the same ethnic group who are settled in different countries. Then, the latter part of the chapter introduces the case of the Indian diaspora as an example of this theory in application.

Keywords

Diaspora · Globalization · Transnationalism · Collective memory · Ethnic memory

Introduction

Recently, the term "diaspora" has been used frequently in social media, newspapers, books, and blogs. However, it is doubtful that writers using the term correctly understand its meaning. In some cases, this term has been used to describe the people who live in a country where they were not born or brought up. Based on this understanding, people who go abroad for business or education for a short period may be included in the diaspora, which, theoretically speaking, is incorrect. This misunderstanding of the definition of diaspora has been caused by a rapidly growing globalized world. As explained in the following sections, when considering the diaspora, we need to focus on their transnational character and continuous links with homeland and ethnic peers scattered around the world. This chapter aims to provide readers with the characteristics of the diaspora, which should be clarified to separate diasporic individuals from mere migrants. To understand the differences between individuals in a diaspora and migrants is also helpful to understand the growing influence of the diaspora, which is affecting the political decision-making in many countries. Transnational economic activities by diaspora groups also have an impact on national economic policies. In the globalized world, the role of the diaspora has become salient; therefore, to grasp such impacts of the diaspora is necessary for scholars and university students who focus on international relations, immigration studies, globalization, and many other disciplines within the social sciences.

First, this chapter reviews the theoretical explanations of diaspora groups. Second, the chapter observes the impact and meaning of globalization, and third, it focuses on the role of ethnic memory in order to explain how diaspora groups maintain a strong connection with their homeland while they are abroad. Finally, this chapter discusses the Indian diaspora within the context of these theories, which shows the complexity of diaspora in a globalized world and the transnational features of diaspora groups who are navigating globalization.

Theoretical Explanations of the Diaspora

The term diaspora is derived from Greek and means scattering, which came to be used to refer to the dispersion of a population. Although the concept of diaspora is not a new phenomenon, many scholars began to pay attention to diaspora groups in the late twentieth century, because their unique natures had become prominent, and diaspora groups had begun to have a strong influence on states as international actors under globalization. Safran (1991), one of the leading diaspora thinkers, summarizes the diaspora with the following six characteristics:

- Dispersal from a homeland to two or more destinations
- Retention of collective memories, visions, and myths about the homeland
- The belief that they are not accepted by the society of their host countries and are marginalized
- The belief that their homeland is ideal and that they or their descendants should return to the homeland
- The belief that they should commit to maintaining and revitalizing the prosperity and safety of their homeland
- Maintenance of strong ethnic bonds based on continuous relationships with their homeland

According to this summary, a diaspora is not a group of people who moved from one country to another. As implied by the original meaning of the Greek words, it means a group of people dispersed to many parts of the world. It is noteworthy, then, that diaspora groups idealize their homeland and retain a collective, emotional, and continuous attachment to the homeland. For this reason, diaspora groups are willing to act for their homeland or ethnic peers who remained in their homeland.

The classical usage of this term applied to the people who were forcefully dispersed from their indigenous lands to other parts of the world. In the classical meaning, they are recognized as victims, as they experienced traumatic events that caused their dispersion. Examples include the Jewish diaspora whose history is filled with persecution, Africans who were forcefully removed from the African continent and sold as slaves, Armenians who experienced genocide in the late nineteenth and early twentieth centuries, and Palestinians who were forced to leave their homeland when the state of Israel was established.

Although victimization is an important feature of diaspora groups, however, Cohen (1997) adds several more categories, which include labor, trade, and imperial diaspora groups. Cohen suggests that people who voluntarily leave their homeland are also part of the diaspora. For example, if people who move to a foreign country for business and settle for a long period meet diasporic conditions, such as the maintenance of a collective attachment to their homeland, they can also be part of a diaspora. With the Indian diaspora, who dispersed to many parts of the world as indentured labor, their living conditions were poor, and many faced antagonism from their local societies. These experiences have accumulated in the Indian diasporic memory, and the collective memory plays a pivotal role in maintaining and strengthening the bonds with their homeland. Therefore, according to Cohen's classification, even though they voluntarily left India for economic reasons, Indian indentured labor is part of the diaspora.

However, it is not realistic to believe that perfect classification of the diaspora based on the categories introduced by Cohen is possible. For example, although the Jewish diaspora is representative of a victimized diaspora, some Jewish groups moved to take advantage of trade opportunities. Bearing these complexities and Safran's list of characteristics of the diaspora in mind, Cohen reorganizes the common characteristics of the diaspora as follows:

- Dispersal from a homeland to more than two destinations, and many experience traumatic events.
- Voluntary dispersal for business, trade, or colonial ambitions, if they did not experience a traumatic event.
- Sharing of collective memory and myth, which may include sites, histories, suffering, and achievements.
- Idealizing the homeland whether it is real or imagined and collectively dedicating to its maintenance, restoration, safety, and prosperity.
- Frequent movement to return their homeland, even though many are satisfied with imagined relationship with homeland or intermittent visit to homeland.
- Awareness of belonging to an ethnic group, and strong ethnic bonds are retained for a long time based on a sense of distinguishing feature, common history, inheritance of shared cultural and religious heritage, and belief of common destiny.
- Face troubles with their host societies that may cause another tragic event.
- Retain a common responsibility to people of the same ethnic origin living in different host countries.
- It is possible for them to enjoy a creative and prosperous life, if the host country tolerates a multicultural society.

These characteristics do not all have to be met for groups to be classified as diasporic; this is a general list of common features of diaspora groups, and it can be used to compile a description of the main components of the diaspora.

With regard to Cohen's list, it is important to maintain an awareness of the emphasis on diaspora groups' construction of extensive networks with people of the same ethnic group living in different countries and their actions as a collective for the benefit of their homeland. This indicates that diaspora groups have a transnational character. In studies on the nation-state or nationalism, political scientists apply theories such as Anderson's "imagined community" (1991), to observe the processes of unification and connection that construct identity. Similarly, Sökefeld (2006) suggests that researchers studying the diaspora focus on "imagined transnational communities" and the literature on the diaspora has revealed that "transnational imagination" plays a pivotal role in connecting diaspora communities with their homelands (Burla 2015). Transnational ethnic bonds are not well-explained by the traditional nation-state model of international relations. Diaspora groups act across state borders, and their identity is not confined within state borders. In short, they achieve a deterritorialization, and the "deterritorialized imagined communities" allow members of the diaspora to share "a collective past and common destiny" (Werbner 2002) with other members of the diaspora around the world. Therefore, diaspora groups should be treated as transnational actors.

It is notable that diaspora groups retain these transnational ethnic links with both the homeland and other members of the same diaspora group in different host countries for a long period of time. The maintenance of collectivity as an ethnic group is a key precondition for constructing and maintaining ethnic identity at a transnational level. The collectivity can continue for a long time, as diaspora members recognize that they are members of the diaspora group and they recognize the differences between their own ethnic group and other groups. The recognition of suffering, for example, a tragic experience that causes dispersal or unequal treatment in a host country, strengthens the sense of being different from other ethnic groups living in the same society. In order to escape from the suffering and improve their living conditions, they place their hope in their homeland and desire to become reconnected with people of the same ethnic group who have also suffered from traumatic events or difficulties in their host countries. For this reason, Safran and Cohen add antagonism from a host society as one of the diasporic features, because this creates a conscious idea among diaspora groups that they are more connected to ethnic peers living in other host countries than other ethnic groups living in their own host country. Therefore, they consciously attempt to stay connected with their ethnic peers and homeland rather than assimilate into their host society. This allows diaspora groups to maintain the ethnic identity of their homeland for a long period of time.

Globalization and Diaspora's Transnational Power

Controversies Under Globalization

The traditional approach to immigration studies utilizes analytical perspectives on assimilationism and nationalism. This approach applies the premise that emigration results in cutting off links with the homeland and that immigrants eventually assimilate into their host societies. Transnational approaches to studying diaspora groups, however, do not adopt this condition (Brubaker 2005). With transnationalism, immigration does not break the connection with a homeland; instead, a network or homeland culture continues to exist and is an important factor (Lie 1995). Therefore, diaspora research requires scholars to understand a variety of actors, including people who remain in the homeland country, people of the same ethnic origin in different host countries, and the relationships with other ethnic groups in the host country.

The development of the theoretical arguments above has been caused by globalization. When globalization was not very significant, most immigrants were not seen as diaspora groups, and they were expected to assimilate into the host country and relinquish their attachment to their homeland. However, through globalization and the development of transportation and communication technologies, it is now much easier to settle in foreign countries and retain a connection with one's homeland country. Globalization has significantly altered immigration, and the lifestyles of emigrants have become more diverse. For example, being involved in political or social affairs of a homeland country, the extent to which people are assimilated into a host society, whether they retain the identity of their homeland country or share the identity of their host country, or practice both, all depend on the varying circumstances of individuals.

Against this backdrop, some scholars argue that immigrants, who did not become part of diaspora groups decades ago, now satisfy some of the diasporic characteristics (Clifford 1994). The impact of globalization has led scholars to reconsider the diasporic frameworks and expand the definition and scope of the diaspora. Some researchers have reevaluated the theoretical framework and the classification of the diaspora developed by Safran and Cohen, because the diversified nature of immigrants makes it difficult to develop a common pattern for the diaspora. Diversity within a diaspora group is also important, because depending on social status, gender, generation, social class, occupation, and educational background, individuals demonstrate their own unique attachment to their homeland. In some cases, the differences within a diaspora group are as prominent as the differences of other ethnic groups (Anthias 1998). Accordingly, some scholars criticize Safran or Cohen's theoretical framework, because the frameworks contain fixed assumptions that diaspora groups are bound to their homeland. Some scholars argue that the framework is primordial and ignores the diversity of current diaspora groups amidst globalization (see, e.g., Clifford 1994; Anthias 1998). Hall (2003) argues that:

> The diaspora experience... is defined, not by essence or purity, but by the recognition of a necessary heterogeneity and diversity; by a conception of "identity" which lives with and through, not despite, difference; by *hybridity*. Diaspora identities are those which are constantly producing and reproducing themselves anew, through transformation and difference.

However, this transnationalism approach has caused side effects. As it encourages scholars to focus on the diversified and heterogeneous nature of immigrants, they tend to expand the definition of the diaspora. This type of broad definition has also faced criticism, because if all groups of immigrants are classified as diaspora, this term cannot distinguish diaspora groups from other groups of people. The inclusion of all types of immigrant groups into the term diaspora reduces the notable characteristics of diaspora groups. It is ironic that by expanding the definition of diaspora groups, the characteristics of the diaspora are reduced (see, e.g., Tölölyan 1996; Vertovec 1997; Brubaker 2005).

Despite such controversies, it seems that diaspora experts can agree with the following three features of diaspora groups (Butler 2001; Brubaker 2005). First, diaspora groups disperse from their homelands to at least two destinations. Diaspora groups do not just move from one place to the other. Without networks of people of the same ethnic origin around the world, the group of people cannot be seen as diaspora. Even though a group of people may have a strong connection with people of the same ethnic origin, if they all live in the homeland country, they are not a diaspora group, as this is a single linear connection. A web of network among people of the same ethnic group living around the world is required, with the homeland as an epicenter of their ethnic bonds. Second, they collectively maintain a strong attachment to their homeland and retain a relationship with their homeland. Although transnationalism may argue that this tendency weakened with globalization, without the strong collective attachment to and relationship with the homeland, it is not possible to transnationally maintain ethnic identity. Third, they intentionally draw a clear line between their own ethnic group and other groups in their host countries. This clear consciousness allows those in the diaspora group to recognize themselves as members of an ethnic group, and this recognition can last over generations. In short, diaspora groups consciously recognize themselves as members of an ethnonationalistic group of people who originated in a homeland, and they act based on this diasporic ethnic identity at the transnational level. This summary may still be subject to criticism from transnationalism. While diaspora groups should intentionally clarify a border between their diaspora group and other groups, the importance of the border is weakened according to the transnational approach, and this is the core of the controversy (Brubaker 2005).

Growing Influence of Diaspora

Traditionally, scholars on immigration have focused on the immigrant policies set by host countries. Conversely, however, diaspora scholars focus on policies set by homeland countries. As diaspora groups share the interests of the homeland, they may be able to act on behalf of the homeland (see, e.g., Sheffer 1986; Shain and Barth 2003). Subsequently, homeland countries are now aware of the importance of the diaspora. That is why the ethnic diaspora and its influence have recently been recognized as an important factor in studying globalization, immigration, and international relations.

One of the main benefits for homeland countries is diaspora groups lobbying the governments of host countries. Many countries currently evaluate the lobbying activities of the diaspora as an important diplomatic resource. Korean diaspora groups living in the USA, for example, have lobbied local governments in the USA regarding the sex slave or "comfort women" issue during the Japanese colonial era. They have drawn attention to the cruel atrocities of Japanese colonizers and soldiers toward Korean women and have criticized the Japanese government for not addressing the issue. They have built statues of comfort women in various places in the USA in order to draw international public attention to the issue. The formation of international public opinion is an important diplomatic achievement for the South Korean government who has been requesting action from the government of Japan on this issue.

In addition, economic benefits from the diaspora are an expectation of homeland countries. Traditionally, remittance was the main economic benefit for homeland, but their economic role has grown. In some cases, they engage in global supply chains and are the main consumers of certain products made in the homeland country. Some diaspora groups launch businesses in their host countries, and through their kinship networks, they cooperate and trade with business counterparts in their homeland countries. Additionally, migrants can be major investors in homeland countries, and if they return to their homeland after acquiring advanced business skills or completing higher education, they become valuable human resources for their homeland economy (Leblang 2017).

Many governments now recognize that these benefits are worthwhile, and they have developed policies to support the diaspora and to keep them connected to homeland countries (Ragazzi 2014). This newly developed government support for the diaspora includes consul support, health and welfare services, and cultural and religious development. Some countries dispatch experts on homeland culture or ethnic language in order to provide the diaspora with educational opportunities or establish cultural centers to disseminate information related to the homeland. Some diaspora groups are entitled to special rights, such as dual citizenship. Since these policies for diaspora assistance are implemented cross-sectionally, some governments have established a specific government office to coordinate diaspora assistance activities. Approximately 40% of United Nations member states have a specific institution for the diaspora (Gamlen 2014). For example, Armenia established the Ministry of Diaspora in 2008 in order to develop its policies to support diaspora groups and coordinate activities by various state bodies.

These policies are notable, because governments expand the influence of domestic policies to people living abroad who are from the same ethnic origin, but many of whom are not citizens of the homeland country. This is a challenge to the Westphalian regime, whose principal aim is territorial jurisdiction over the citizens of a state (Délano and Gamlen 2014). While diaspora groups are not new to the twenty-first century, the ways in which diaspora groups interact with their homeland countries have been affected by globalization. Subsequently, the role and definition of the diaspora has changed, and this has spurred academic research in this area.

The Role of Ethnic Memory

Collective Memory

The question here is "Through what mechanisms do people of the diaspora share, maintain, and strengthen the identity of their homeland while they are separated from their homeland?" To answer this question, this chapter reviews the role of ethnic memory. According to Maurice Halbwachs (1952), who developed the theory of collective memory, without a society, individuals cannot recall their past. To recall a past they experienced directly, individuals need to have the language and concepts provided by the society to which they belong. For a society's past that many individuals did not experience directly, such as a war, they learned their national history through newspapers, schools, museums, and messages from national leaders.

Most importantly, it is the society that determines history. Individual memory is established as the result of one's reaction to current social needs, interests, and ideas. As individuals are inclined to match themselves to society, they choose, delete, or adjust their memories in order to remain consistent with society's ideas. In this sense, collective memory is a product that is socially constructed to correspond to our current social, psychological, and political needs (Gibson 2004). Therefore, collective memory is not static but flexible, as social needs and interests change over time. Collective memory functions to change the interpretation of the past depending on the political situation, economic development, relationships with other social groups or foreign countries, and demographic changes. Thus, Friedman (1992) argues that "history is an imprinting of the present onto the past."

There are many tools that assist a society in storing past events as collective memory. One example is artificial objects, such as monuments, statues, and historical buildings. The previous section raised an example about the statues of comfort women built in the USA by members of the Korean diaspora. The Korean diaspora attaches specific meanings to the statues, such as the cruel nature of Japanese soldiers, Korean women as victims, and messages that the government of Japan has not yet atoned for its past wrongdoings and has neglected its responsibility to restore the dignity of the victims. Once such objects become the symbol of a social group, members of the group sanctify the objects (Irwin-Zarecka 1994), and for them, the meaning attached to the symbol becomes the absolute truth of what happened to the group in the past. In this situation, groups tend to exclude external factors, which may affect their collective memory.

Public and social commemoration is also important in the construction of collective memory (Gershoni and Jankowski 2004). Participating in a commemoration or ceremony serves not only to regularly recall a particular past event and prevent from forgetting the past but also to revise the memory in order to match it to the current social needs and interests. Zerubavel (1995) argues that commemoration adjusts the collective memory between the historical record and the current social and political agenda. It implies that the meaning of commemoration, whether through ritual or artifacts, is not fixed, but changeable. Although monuments stand still on a site without any change in their shape, and rituals seem to be successively practiced every year, details of contents and meaning attached to the commemoration vary depending on the mood and needs of the current society (Gershoni and Jankowski 2004). This change requires a society to change how they represent the past event. Therefore, investigating a changing history of contents, forms, and messages of commemoration is a useful method for understanding how collective memory develops and changes in society.

Collective Memory and Social Identity

Litvak (2009) argues that identity shared by group members cannot exist without memory, because continuity from the past is necessary to identify the uniqueness of a group, and therefore remembering the past is a necessary factor. Litvak also emphasizes the reciprocal relationship between memory and identity. A group develops its own unique memory about the past and emphasizes the differences between its identity and the identity of others in order to develop its own identity. In addition, as Ignatieff (1996) pointed out, "What you believe to be true depends...on who you believe yourself to be." This argument implies that, on the one hand, collective identity is an important factor in deciding what memories the group should maintain, and, on the other hand, collective memory assists in the formation of group identity. This interactive relation between memory and identity is important when studying collective memory and collective identity.

Individuals cannot represent themselves without society, and, in order to define ourselves, individuals depend on society. An individual's sense of belonging to a community is established when the individual places him- or herself into the community's past events (Hobsbawm 1972); to become a member of that society means to experience its history as if it had been their own (Zerubavel 1996). As a result, individuals have a sense of a pride, pain, and shame related to the history experienced by the community (Olick and Robbins 1998).

If the past memory is morally negative and traumatic, such as a massacre, a civil war, or serious discrimination, and these past memories are widely shared in the society, the group's solidarity is likely to be strengthened. Traumatic events that threaten their ethnic existence are a powerful catalyst for inducing people to form a group identity. Renan (1990) argues that:

> suffering in common unifies more than joy does. Where national memories are concerned, griefs are of more value than triumphs, for they impose duties, and require a common effort.

In short, the more traumatic the shared memory is, the more the bonds are strengthened; this is especially true of ethnic bonds among diaspora groups.

However, certain events may not be automatically traumatic, but they can be construed as being traumatic through society's mediation (Alexander 2004). Whether an event becomes traumatic depends on the social situation at the time. The speed of an event becoming traumatic also varies. Some events become traumatic as the event is occurring, while some events are seen as traumatic only after many years have passed since the end of the event. Even if no event occurred, a story of a traumatic event may be created. Whether the traumatic event actually occurred does not matter, but what is important is that people in the society believe that the traumatic event did occur.

How do socially constructed collective memories, whether real or imagined, permeate a group of people? To answer this question, we need to understand how collective memory is represented. Collective memory produces social narratives that represent the group memory and help spread it across society. In addition, the construction of history involves adding particular meaning to the past, and the narratives that convey the meaning demonstrate the codes of conduct that individuals are encouraged to obey. For example, nationalists may utilize a particular person as an exemplar – a hero or a tragic heroine – which demonstrates how members of the society should behave in that society. What we must bear in mind is that a social group emphasizes aspects of suffering in past events. The narratives of suffering reiterate moral responsibility toward the past, and the sense of victimhood urges members of the group to react to overcome the past tragedy or recover dignity. Therefore, in many cases, tragic elements are included in a meaning attached to social symbols and commemorations. The meaning attached to the statues of comfort women erected by the Korean diaspora in the USA emphasizes the tragedy of Korean women, and the symbol urges the Korean diaspora to keep taking social and political action to recover the victims' dignity. This socially constructed moral responsibility plays a pivotal role in deciding where the society is heading, and this is a basis for constructing group identity (Somers 1994). The decisive role of collective memory with a recognition of the tragic past can apply to diasporas, as in many cases diaspora members believe that they and their ancestors experienced traumatic events in the past.

Societies may adjust the story of the past developed by social narratives in order to fit it into their current social situation or, conversely, may reinterpret the current situation to match the story. This is a process of developing and stabilizing collective memory in a society, and the historical memory developed through this process stimulates their group identity. In this theoretical argument, Eyerman (2004) detailed constructing the process of African American identity in the USA. According to Eyerman, black Americans have repeatedly altered their collective memory about what happened to their ancestors as slaves and have reinterpreted the meaning of their history to apply it to today's society. African American identity was formed when slavery was already a past event. In addition, whether their own ancestors were slaves or not did not matter in the formation of black American identity. Speeches, poems, artworks, and other cultural products by black Americans represented the memory of slaves and conveyed that collective memory to all black Americans over generations, which became the basis for African American identity as a whole. The same can be said for other types of diasporas. Migrants who believe that their ancestors experienced traumatic events in their homeland, causing their dispersion to many parts of the world – and that their descendants, including themselves, have been suffering from alienated social conditions – carry the collective memory of the tragedy to future generations of the diaspora and help maintain diasporic identity for a long period over many generations.

Social Networks and Ethnic Memory

Baines (2007) explains that a particular memory becomes dominant after conflicting with other interpretations of past events. The dominant memories determine not only what the members of the society remember but also which memories they forget.

This is because a single narrative does not construct social memory, and many narratives exist in society and contest with one another (Olick and Robbins 1998). Many narratives are contested, and which narratives become dominant depends on the generation, social class, occupation, and gender of those who disseminate the narrative. Groups' interests, needs, and beliefs are key factors that determine where these contestations are represented in society. Memory and identity are constructed through such processes.

Among the many societal circumstances affecting memory construction, ethnicity is one of the most powerful determinant factors. Rydgren et al. (2017) conducted a quantitative survey in two cities in northern Iraq. One is Kirkuk, where the society is ethnically divided and ethnic violence is intense; the other is Erbil, which is also ethnically divided, but ethnicity-based violence is not as severe there compared to that in the ethnically polarized Kirkuk. The results reveal that memories about past events tend to be structured along ethnic lines in a multiethnic society. Especially when ethnic tension is intense, this tendency becomes clearer. According to the survey, social networks among ethnic groups are a central determinant of whether an ethnically divided society becomes more conflict-ridden or friendlier. Rydgren, Sofi, and Hällsten argue:

> Ethnically homogeneous friendship networks seemed to reinforce group-specific uniformities in memories and beliefs about the past, whereas ethnically heterogeneous networks worked in the opposite direction....Having a high proportion of friends belonging to a particular outgroup is often associated with sharing beliefs about the past that are more similar to the memories of that outgroup than to those of the ingroup.

Empirical study shows that when social networks develop between different ethnic groups, people can exchange beliefs of past memories with the other groups, which helps build understanding with other ethnic groups. Under such circumstances, reconciliation between conflicting groups is more likely to be achieved than in a society without multiethnic networks. Conversely, when the society encounters serious ethnic conflict and inter-ethnic relations are weakened, a group does not have opportunities to understand other ethnic groups. Without multiethnic social networks, people are inclined to share beliefs of past events within the boundary of their ethnic group. Under these circumstances, they clearly differentiate between "us" and "others," resulting in making group members exclude other ethnic groups.

Moral responsibility, derived from the tragic memory that social narratives provide, urges members of the group to maintain the memory for a long period. In addition, as people tend to have a positive perspective on the group to which they belong, they selectively memorize the past, which justifies themselves. That is why there are many cases in which the memory of past events by a group of victims differs from that of perpetrators. When victims see perpetrators trying to justify their wrongdoing, the trust between victims and perpetrators collapses. This results in the society losing a chance to develop multiethnic social networks – something that is likely to happen in ethnically divided societies. Literature on ethnic conflict points out that, in some cases, a clear boundary between victims and perpetrators was drawn before ethnic conflict occurred (see, e.g., Horowitz 1985).

The same can be said in the case of diasporas. Often, diaspora members view themselves as victims, and if the host society fails to construct multiethnic networks inclusive of their diaspora, members of the diaspora draw a clear line between the diaspora (as victims) and "others" (as perpetrators) in their host societies. For diaspora members, their ethnic peers, who dispersed from the same homeland country and live in other host countries, are in the same circle of the diasporic ethnic group. As a consequence, they can develop and share ethnic identity with diaspora groups scattered around the world. Even when diaspora groups are not marginalized in their host society, if groups of people in their homeland country who caused the dispersion deny their responsibility for the wrongdoing toward the diaspora groups, people in the diaspora may develop a sense of victimhood and may share it with their ethnic peers around the world. In sum, whether a group of people becomes diasporic or not depends on both social situations and external relations, such as how much they are discriminated against in a host society, the friendliness of the relationship they constructed with other ethnic groups in their homeland countries, how much the government of the homeland country tries to maintain the connection with the diaspora groups, how much of an ethnic network they have developed with their ethnic peers in other countries, and so on.

The Case of the Indian Diaspora

By focusing on globalization and the role of ethnic memory, the previous sections of this chapter explain the characteristics of diaspora groups. The rest of this chapter explores these characteristics by scrutinizing the identities of the Indian diaspora around the world.

One of the labor diaspora groups from Cohen's categorization is the Indian diaspora that was engaged as an indentured labor force, working on plantations during the colonial era. Although many other ethnic groups were dispersed around the world because of labor, the Indian diaspora is a strong example of the labor diaspora, because dispersed Indians are inclined to retain traditional Indian culture and maintain connections with their homeland.

The working conditions of Indian indentured laborers were extremely severe, to the extent that it could nearly have been considered slavery. In addition, they encountered negative confrontations with local communities and indigenous societies, and these experiences were stored in their ethnic collective memory. This strengthened their ethnic consciousness and motivated them to maintain Indian culture and religious norms. Consequently, they refused to assimilate into host societies and instead established a local Indian community with clear differences from the other groups in their host countries. They often believed that Indian indentured laborers living in other host countries were more connected to each other than to other ethnic people living in their host country.

After they were liberated from indentured labor, many remained in their host countries and started local businesses to improve their living conditions. Following the expansion of their economic activities, they spread to urban areas of the host countries (Helweg 1986). Though the Indian diaspora retained Indian culture, traditional norms, and religious beliefs while living in these new conditions, some Indian communities developed a unique culture by adapting to the life of their host societies (Pande 2011). However, there is no doubt that their culture originated in India, and for the Indian diaspora in some countries, this does not lead to a reduction in their closeness to India. The Indian diaspora recognize themselves as having an Indian origin, and that is why they actively connect with the homeland, for example, by reading Indian newspapers, going to Indian schools, and holding religious festivals, such as Holi.

The Indian government recently implemented new government programs to connect with the Indian diaspora scattered around the world, as it recognizes the importance and benefit of Indian diaspora. For example, the Indian government established the Ministry of Overseas Indian Affairs in 2004, which merged with the Ministry of External Affairs in 2016, for planning and implementing government diaspora policies, developing networks, and maintaining relationships between India and the Indian diaspora. Pravasi Bharatiya Divas, an event that celebrates the contribution of the overseas Indian community in the development of India, is held every year, which helps the Indian diaspora understand Indian policies and provides dialogue on the issues that the Indian diaspora around the world is encountering in their respective host countries. The "Know India Programme" (KIP) was also established to invite the Indian diaspora, especially young people, to India to deepen their understanding of India. One of the characteristics of KIP is that its main target comprises those who have not visited India in their lifetime, which indicates that the Indian government wants to strengthen ethnic connections with people in the diaspora who tend to have a weak relationship with India. India also implements other diaspora policies, including a scholarship program designed for the diaspora.

Another example of India's efforts to maintain a connection with its diaspora can be observed in Indian aid policies. For example, the Indian government has recently increased aid program to Fiji, where many of the Indian diaspora live. Much of India's aid to Pacific Island countries are directed to Fiji and Papua New Guinea. While it is clear that the government of India intends to acquire natural resources through the aid program to Papua New Guinea, the aim of the increased aid to Fiji is simply to strengthen the relationship with the Indian diaspora (Zhang and Shivakumar 2017). Unlike Chinese assistance, which mainly focuses on infrastructure development through concessional loans, India's aid to Fiji is characteristic in that it supports capacity building, assistance for information technology, industrial development, and assistance for climate change issues through grants and scholarship programs.

To further understand a diaspora's transnational character, this section focuses on the Indian diaspora in Fiji. Fiji is a multiethnic country where indigenous Fijians and members of the Indian diaspora, or Indo-Fijians, are the majority ethnic groups. According to the 2007 census, the Fijian population was comprised of 56.8%

indigenous Fijians and 37.5% Indian descendants (Fiji Islands Bureau of Statistics 2008). The population of the Indian descendants exceeded the population of indigenous Fijian at some historical point, and this Fijian demography is one of the root causes of political and social instability in Fiji.

As with other Indian diaspora groups around the world, Indian indentured laborers in Fiji suffered from severe working conditions and social inequality. In addition, as indigenous Fijians have sought political paramountcy over Indo-Fijians, Indo-Fijians have been politically discriminated against and have become the target of political violence at various points in its history. Coups are especially important political events when considering Indo-Fijians' victimization and the formation of their identity. There were four coups that occurred in Fiji in its history: two in 1987, one in 2000, and one in 2006. The first three coups were rooted in ethnic confrontation and originated from an Indo-Fijian political party winning the general election. Some indigenous Fijian nationalists felt this was a crisis, as it could have led to Indo-Fijian control over Fiji, and this prompted the forceful removal of the Indo-Fijian-led government.

As a result, many Indo-Fijians have left the country and have emigrated to Australia, New Zealand, the UK, or the USA, seeking a better and fairer place to live. These groups are labeled "twice migrants," a term that describes people who left their homeland country and settled in a host country, and then, after years or generations, they or their descendants left the first host country and settled in other places as a second host country. They maintain the culture and identity of their homeland but also retain emotional bonds with their first host country.

The twice-migrant Indo-Fijians moving to neighboring countries requested that the Indian government interfere to resolve the issues in Fiji, as the Indian diaspora suffered from political violence and social inequality. However, the Indian government did not actively engage in Fijian issues. Then, the twice-migrant Indo-Fijians started to support their ethnic peers still living in Fiji (Leckie 2015). For example, some politicians and activists who moved to New Zealand after the 1987 coup established a local branch of the Coalition for Democracy in Fiji to lobby for the return to power of the removed Indo-Fijian-led government and the restoration of democracy. After the 2000 coup, more Indo-Fijians moved to New Zealand, and there was an increase in aggressive lobbying activities. They held a peace gathering in Auckland to ask the New Zealand government to take direct action to intervene in the Fijian coup to solve the political turmoil (The *Fiji Times* 22 May 2000).

The twice-migrant Indo-Fijians retained ethnic bonds with India, where their ancestors originated, and with Fiji, which they previously recognized as a host country for the Indian diaspora but was now the origin of their identity. In other words, both India and Fiji are their homeland countries. It was possible for them to retain these multiethnic identities because they have a shared ethnic memory developed from the suffering of their ancestors when they settled in Fiji as indentured laborers and because of the political violence and social inequality that Indo-Fijians have experienced since then. These experiences of suffering were then stored in their collective memory, leading them to believe that Indo-Fijians were victims throughout Fijian history. The shared recognition of the past, accumulated in the

Indo-Fijians' minds, firmly unites Indo-Fijians along ethnic lines. Therefore, the sense of victimization and their ethnic collective memory motivate twice-migrant Indo-Fijians to help Indo-Fijians still living in Fiji, because for twice-migrant Indo-Fijians, Indo-Fijians in Fiji are still their ethnic peers.

Conclusion

This chapter reviewed the theoretical features of the diaspora, with a particular focus on their transnational character in a globalized era, which creates a more influential diaspora in both the homeland and host countries. This chapter examined the role of ethnic memory and its political and social effects to explain how diaspora groups play a pivotal role in the international arena as transnational actors. Shared ethnic memory leads to consolidated ethnic bonds among ethnic peers around the world. Because of the development of communication and transportation technologies, it is much easier for people to retain their ethnic identity wherever they live.

One of the distinctive features of the diaspora is that many of them believe that traumatic events caused the diasporic dispersion and create a miserable life in the host country. The negative perception of the past is reflected in the social narrative of diaspora groups, which is collectively shared among diaspora members as a powerful memory, and this collective memory constructs diasporic identity. In addition, narrative plays a central role in mediating the shared suffering of the society and distinguishes "us" as victims from "others" as the perpetrators. Diaspora recognizes that other diaspora members living in other host countries are in the same boat, making them feel a closeness to ethnic peers living in other countries and resulting in the sharing of diasporic ethnic identity with them.

The transnational ethnic bonds that diaspora groups hold must be reevaluated, as they provide us with a new understanding of the diaspora, an emerging concept in international relations. Their influence has already affected governmental policies, and many international actors have begun to recognize their importance. Diaspora groups are occasionally viewed as valuable, but often they are viewed as unpredictable. This trend is likely to continue. Instead of the traditional framework of the nation-state, which cannot sufficiently explain the characteristics of diaspora groups, further academic research is necessary to understand the future role of diaspora groups.

Cross-References

- ▶ Ethnic Migrants and Casinos in Singapore and Macau
- ▶ Ethnic Minorities and Criminalization of Immigration Policies in the United States
- ▶ Ethno-cultural Symbolism and Group Identity
- ▶ Global Chinese Diaspora
- ▶ Greek Identity in Australia
- ▶ Historical Memory and Ethnic Myths

▶ Indian Diaspora in New Zealand
▶ Indian Indentured Laborers in the Caribbean
▶ Italian Identity in the United States
▶ Migrant Illegalization and Minoritized Populations
▶ Museums and Identity: Celebrating Diversity in an Ethnically Diverse World

References

Alexander JC (2004) Toward a theory of cultural trauma. In: Alexander JC, Eyerman R, Giesen B, Smelser NJ, Sztompka P (eds) Cultural trauma and collective identity. University of California Press, Berkeley/Los Angeles/London, pp 1–30

Anderson B (1991) Imagined communities. Verso, London

Anthias F (1998) Evaluating 'Diaspora': beyond ethnicity. Sociology 32(3):557–572

Baines G (2007) The politics of public history in post-apartheid South Africa. In: Stolten HE (ed) History making and present day politics: the meaning of collective memory in South Africa. Nordiska Afrikaninstitutet, Uppsala, pp 167–182

Brubaker R (2005) The 'Diaspora' Diaspora. Ethn and Racia Stud 28(1):1–19

Burla S (2015) The Diaspora and the homeland: political goals in the construction of Israeli narratives to the Diaspora. Isr Aff 21(4):602–619

Butler KD (2001) Defining Diaspora, refining a discourse. Diaspora 10(2):189–219

Clifford J (1994) Diasporas. Cult Anthropol 9(3):302–338

Cohen R (1997) Global Diaspora: an introduction. University of Washington Press, Seattle

Délano A, Gamlen A (2014) Comparing and theorizing state – Diaspora relations. Polit Geogr 41:43–53

Eyerman R (2004) Cultural trauma: slavery and the formation of African American identity. In: Alexander JC, Eyerman R, Giesen B, Smelser NJ, Sztompka P (eds) Cultural trauma and collective identity. University of California Press, Berkeley/Los Angeles/London, pp 60–111

Friedman J (1992) The past in the future: history and the politics of identity. Am Anthropol 94(4):837–859

Gamlen A (2014) Diaspora institutions and Diaspora governance. Int Migr Rev 48(1):180–217

Gershoni I, Jankowski J (2004) Commemorating the nation: collective memory, public commemoration, and national identity in twentieth-century Egypt. Middle East Documentation Center, Chicago

Gibson JL (2004) Overcoming apartheid: can truth reconcile a divided nation? Russell Saga Foundation, New York

Halbwachs M (1952) Les Cadres Sociaux de la Mémoire. Presses Universitaires de France, Paris. English edition: Halbwachs M (1992) The social framework of memory (trans: Coser LA). In: Coser LA (ed) On collective memory. The University of Chicago Press, Chicago

Hall S (2003) Cultural identity and Diaspora. In: Braziel JE, Mannur A (eds) Theorizing Diaspora: a reader. Blackwell Publishing, Malden, pp 233–246

Helweg AW (1986) The Indian Diaspora: influence on international relations. In: Sheffer G (ed) Modern Diasporas in international politics. Croom Helm, Kent, pp 103–129

Hobsbawm EJ (1972) The social function of the past: some questions. Past Present Soc 55:3–17

Horowitz DL (1985) Ethnic groups in conflict. University of California Press, Berkeley/Los Angeles/London

Ignatieff M (1996) Articles of faith. Index Censorsh 5:110–122

Irwin-Zarecka I (1994) Frames of remembrance: the dynamics of collective memory. Transaction Publishers, New Brunswick

Leblang D (2017) Harnessing the Diaspora: dual citizenship, migrant return remittances. Comp Pol Stud 50(1):75–101

Lie J (1995) From international migration to transnational Diaspora. Contemp Sociol 24(4): 303–306
Litvak M (2009) Introduction: collective memory and the Palestinian experience. In: Litvak M (ed) Palestinian collective memory and national identity. Palgrave Macmillan, New York, pp 1–26
Olick JK, Robbins J (1998) Social memory studies: from "collective memory" to the historical sociology of mnemonic practices. Annu Rev Sociol 24:105–140
Pande A (2011) India and its Diaspora in Fiji. Diaspora Stud 4(2):125–138
Ragazzi F (2014) A comparative analysis of Diaspora policies. Polit Geogr 41:74–89
Renan E (1990) What is a nation? In: Bhabha HK (ed) Nation and narration. Routledge, Oxon
Rydgren J, Sofi D, Hällsten M (2017) Divided by memories? Beliefs about the past, ethnic boundaries, and trust in Northern Iraq. Geopolit Hist Int Relat 9(1):128–175
Safran W (1991) Diasporas in modern societies: myths of homeland and return. Diaspora 1(1):83–99
Shain Y, Barth A (2003) Diasporas and international relations theory. Int Organ 57(3):449–479
Sheffer G (1986) A new field of study: modern Diasporas in international politics. In: Sheffer G (ed) Modern Diasporas in international politics. Croom Helm, Kent, pp 1–15
Sökefeld M (2006) Mobilizing in transnational space: a social movement approach to the formation of Diaspora. Global Netw 6(3):265–284
Somers MR (1994) The narrative constitution of identity: a relational and network approach. Theory Soc 23(5):605–649
Tölölyan K (1996) Rethinking Diaspora(s): stateless power in the transnational moment. Diaspora 5(1):3–36
Vertovec S (1997) Three meanings of "Diaspora," exemplified among South Asian religions. Diaspora 6(3):277–299
Werbner P (2002) The place which is Diaspora: citizenship, religion and gender in the making of chaordic transnationalism. J Ethn Migr Stud 28(1):119–133
Zerubavel Y (1995) Recovered roots: collective memory and the making of Israeli national tradition. The University of Chicago Press, Chicago
Zerubavel E (1996) Social memories: steps to a sociology of the past. Qual Sociol 19(3):283–299
Zhang D, Shivakumar H (2017) Dragon versus elephant: a comparative study of Chinese and Indian aid in the Pacific. Asia Pac Policy Stud 4(2):260–271

Website

Fiji Bureau of Statistics (2008) Census 2007 results: population size growth, structure and distribution. Statistical News. 45. https://unstats.un.org/unsd/demographic-social/census/documents/fiji/fiji.pdf. Accessed 10 Aug 2018
Leckie J (2015) Fijians. In: Te Ara: the encyclopedia of New Zealand. https://teara.govt.nz/en/fijians. Accessed 29 May 2018

Newspaper

The Fiji Times (2000) NZ rules out intervention, 22 May 2000

Global Chinese Diaspora

Zhifang Song

Contents

Introduction 1168
Maritime Trade and the Chinese in Colonial Southeast Asia 1169
Decolonization and the Chinese in Southeast Asia 1171
Surviving Exclusion in White Settler Societies 1173
Negotiating a Niche in Multicultural Societies 1173
The Chinese in Other Societies 1175
From *Huaqiao* to *Huayi*: Constructing Chineseness Outside China 1177
Transnational Network, Globalization, and the Chinese Diaspora 1179
Conclusion and Prospects 1180
References 1181

Abstract

The Chinese living outside Mainland China, Taiwan, Hong Kong, and Macau form one of the biggest diasporic populations in the world. With more than 40 million people of diverse backgrounds distributed all over the world, the Chinese diaspora challenges any efforts of generalization and essentialization. This chapter starts with a brief overview of major theoretical themes in researches on the Chinese diaspora, followed by examinations of historical transformations of overseas Chinese communities in various parts of the world. The focuses are placed on Southeast Asia and North America, which claim the largest shares of diasporic Chinese population. It then goes to address two most important issues that define Chinese diaspora: Chineseness and transnationalism. The chapter concludes by suggesting some potential areas that call for more attention in future researches.

Z. Song (✉)
University of Canterbury, Canterbury, New Zealand
e-mail: zhifang.song@canterbury.ac.nz

© The Author(s), under exclusive license to Springer Nature Singapore Pte Ltd. 2019
S. Ratuva (ed.), *The Palgrave Handbook of Ethnicity*,
https://doi.org/10.1007/978-981-13-2898-5_82

Keywords

Southeast Asia · Settler societies · Chinese exclusion · Multiculturalism · Chineseness · Transnationalism

Introduction

Chinese people have a long history of emigration, and today overseas Chinese form one of the largest diasporic populations in the world. According to the most recent data, there are about 43 million people of Chinese ancestry living outside Mainland China, Taiwan, Hong Kong, and Macau in 2011, distributed in 148 countries (Poston and Wong 2016, p. 362). But this diasporic population is not evenly distributed, with Asia, especially Southeast Asia, claiming the largest share (73.3%) and America, especially North America, the second largest share (Poston and Wong 2016, p. 362). Today, the United States, Canada, Australia, and New Zealand are the four main host countries for new Chinese emigrants (Poston and Wong 2016, p. 369), while a significant increase of Chinese population has also been seen in nontraditional destinations for Chinese emigrants, including Africa (Poston and Wong 2016, p. 369).

Having emigrated during different historical periods, for different reasons, and living in countries of diverse social and political systems, the overseas Chinese form a diaspora that is highly heterogeneous and challenges any effort of generalization and essentialization (Thunø 2007). Through decades, scholars from different disciplines have proposed many theoretical frameworks to understand the diverse diasporic experience. Early researches adopted an assimilationist perspective toward immigration, emphasizing the sojourning nature of Chinese migrants that sets them apart from emigrants from other nations, but this exceptionalism of Chinese emigrants has been challenged by recent scholars (Thunø 2007, p. 45). Gungwu Wang (1991, pp. 3–21) tried to capture this diversity from a historical perspective and proposed four patterns of Chinese emigration: the trader pattern (*huashang*), the coolie patter (*huagong*), the sojourner pattern (*huaqiao*), and the remigrant pattern (*huayi*) (Wang 1991, pp. 3–21). But as McKeown has pointed out, it is not clear whether these patterns refer to "social structures or the orientation of individuals" (McKeown 1999, p. 313). In addition, these words, especially *huaqiao* and *huayi* in their Chinese versions, are very easy to be confused with their everyday usage that might have different connotations in different contexts.

The identity of overseas Chinese was the core of academic attention from the 1980s to the turn of the century. Wang points out that overseas Chinese have multiple identities that overlap and change through time and across contexts (Wang 1988). Tu (1994) proposed a model of cultural China consisting of three symbolic universes: the societies populated predominantly by ethnic Chinese, the Chinese who live as minorities in societies of their residence, and the community of scholars, journalists, teachers, etc., who try to understand Chinese culture.

Since the late 1990s, a diasporic perspective toward overseas Chinese has got the momentum. Rather than seeing overseas Chinese communities as isolated and immigration as a unidirectional process in which migrants are uprooted and transplanted to another society, this new perspective emphasizes transnationalism and deterritorialization in the migrating process and the global networks formed by diasporic Chinese (McKeown 1999). In examining the transnationality of Chinese diaspora, Aihwa Ong (1999) highlights the flexibility of Chinese subjects in practices, strategies, and disciplines in navigating the global system of capitalism, whereby flexible citizenship and identity are constituted by three interrelated regimes: the nation state, the market, and the family.

As the Chinese diaspora has caught more scholarly attention, a broad range of aspects of this diasporic experience has been brought under academic scrutiny. Women's experience in early and contemporary immigration history, interactions between Chinese immigrants and the colonized minorities, and literature as well as other forms of representation in identity construction are only a few of the numerous perspectives that have been added to the field in recent decades.

Due to the heterogeneity of the Chinese diaspora and numerous researches that have been conducted, this essay does not aspire to be a thorough coverage of the field. It will give more weight to the history and transformation of Chinese communities in Southeast Asia, North America, and Australasia, which have larger shares of the overseas Chinese population. It will also cover some thematic issues that are relevant to all diasporic Chinese communities.

Maritime Trade and the Chinese in Colonial Southeast Asia

European colonial expansion to Southeast Asia in the sixteenth century expanded maritime trade across the South China Sea. Chinese traders, especially the Hokkien (people from southern Fujian province), took advantage of this commercial expansion. Chinese communities sprang at colonial trading ports such as Manila, Batavia, and Malacca, as well as port cities of Siam, West Java, and Cambodia not yet controlled by Europeans (Lockard 2013, pp. 768–769). The Chinese were needed by Europeans as middlemen in "trading with China, extracting wealth from the natives, and servicing the colonial cities," but were not fully trusted by Europeans, who never hesitated in using violence to bring the Chinese under control (Kuhn 2008, pp. 62–64).

As few of these Chinese brought women with them, it was common for them to marry local women. Under colonial legal and political systems, descendants of Chinese men and local women formed communities distinct from both newcomers from China and native populations: the Mestizos in the Spanish colony of the Philippines, the Peranakans in the Dutch Java, and the Babas in the British Strait colonies (Skinner 2001, pp. 51–59). They spoke creole languages that were mixtures of Minnan and indigenous languages, and their clothing, cuisine, and kinship system showed a mixture of Chinese traditions and indigenous features (Skinner 2001, pp. 59–64). Before the massive migration from China in the second half of the nineteenth century, these creolized Chinese were dominant both in size and power in the Chinese population in European colonies in Southeast Asia (Skinner 2001, pp. 55–58).

Not all Chinese came to Southeast Asia as traders. In West Borneo, the Hakka Chinese miners gradually dominated the mining industry from the mid-eighteenth century. They organized their communities and mining businesses in the form of *kongsi*, an organization based on partnership and shares (Heidhues 1993, p. 68). Some of the *kongsi* confederated into larger political and economic systems (Heidhues 1993, p. 71). Such *kongsi* kept their relative autonomy for quite a long time, until the second half of the nineteenth century (Heidhues 1993, pp. 70–73).

The defeat of the Qing Empire by the British at Opium Wars initiated 100 years of massive Chinese emigration. From the 1850s to the 1950s, Southeast Asia saw increasing expansion of Chinese population. Massive emigration also diversified the Chinese communities in Southeast Asia. Among the migrants were not only Hokkien, but also Cantonese, Teochew, Hakka, and Hainanese (Yen 2014, p. 24). Different Chinese organizations sprang, and among them three types were important: dialect associations, clan (surname) associations, and secret societies (Yen 2014, p. 25).

These five dialect groups formed the major dialect associations, often called *bang*. Under these large dialect groups, there were also associations whose membership covered smaller regions in China. Each of these dialect and regional groups had its own temple, which housed Chinese deities for members to worship and served as the meeting place for the association (Yen 2014, p. 25). These associations also provided welfares to their members. In French Indochina, they were more institutionalized and were legally recognized as quasi-governments to help the colonial administration to rule the Chinese (Barrett 2012).

There are two types of clan associations: localized and non-localized (Yen 2014, pp. 26–30). The former was based on proved kinship connections, while the latter was based on sharing the same surname or several surnames considered related in ancient past.

Secret societies were usually known as brotherhood, *hui* or *kongsi*. In Southeast Asia, secret societies were not necessarily anti-society organizations. They might represent a political order that competed with the colonial regimes for authority among the Chinese (DeBernardi 1993, p. 230).

Chinese migrants also brought with them their religions. *Guanyin* and *Tianhou* were popular deities worshipped by the Chinese in Southeast Asia (Yen 2014, p. 37). Many religious sects found their places among the Chinese in Southeast Asia, but polytheism was one of the most important features of Chinese religious life there (Yen 2014, pp. 37–38). It was common to see Buddhist and Taoist deities, as well as immortals of folk religions, share the same temple.

Together with the population expansion was the cultural development within the Chinese communities in the first half of the twentieth century. Modern Chinese education began to develop (Wang 1991, p. 276). In Malaysia, the first modern Chinese school was founded in 1904 in Penang. This happened in all the important Chinese communities in Southeast Asia between the two world wars (Yen 2014, pp. 40–41). This helped to cultivate a consciousness of Chineseness and boosted the Chinese nationalism among the Southeast Asian Chinese.

One of the most important features of Southeast Asian Chinese was their economic success. There were many Chinese starting from very poor background and rising to owners of big businesses. During colonial time, ethnic Chinese businesses played an important role in the economies in Southeast Asia (Yen 2014). But rich tycoons were still few in number. Many Chinese were owners of family-based small businesses.

Decolonization and the Chinese in Southeast Asia

After WWII, the colonies in Southeast Asia won their independence one after another. As part of the colonial legacy, they all had non-native populations of diverse ethnic and cultural backgrounds within their boundaries. Defining citizenship rights was an important aspect of the nation building process. The citizen status of the Chinese posed a challenge to the new nation states. China's citizenship law had always been based on the principle of *jus sanguinis*, recognizing all the Chinese living abroad as Chinese citizens, and thus most of the Chinese living in these new states had Chinese citizenship by default (Suryadinata 2007, pp. 89–108). Due to the *jus soli* principle adopted by colonial authorities, many Chinese were also subjects of the colonial powers, particularly in Dutch and British colonies. When these colonies won their independence, such a tie to China was seen as a potential threat to the sovereignty of the new nations and thus was a problem to be solved. In 1955, Indonesia and China reached an agreement and signed a treaty, requiring the local-born Chinese to make a choice between the Indonesian and Chinese citizenships (Willmott 2009, pp. 63–88). That means, the Chinese who were born overseas could no longer claim Chinese citizenship by default. This was a policy that China has followed ever since and has been incorporated into subsequent citizenship laws (Suryadinata 2007, pp. 95–98). This treaty set precedence for other countries to deal with the dual citizenship status of residents of Chinese descent within their boundaries and also played a role in encouraging the Chinese born and living overseas to take the citizenship of their country of residence.

The experience of obtaining local citizenship varied from country to country. In Indonesia, the political turmoil in the 1960s created many difficulties for the Chinese to get their citizen rights despite the treaty signed with China (Tan 1997, pp. 35–38). The Philippines denied citizen rights to most Chinese residents until the 1970s (Suryadinata 2007). Situations in Vietnam were complicated by the postcolonial political chaos, the subsequent Vietnam War, and the changing international relations with Taiwan and Mainland China. Although the Chinese in Vietnam were unwilling to give up their Chinese citizenship, they were not given much choice before or after 1975. In Thailand, local-born Chinese had been seen as legitimate citizens of Thailand from the early twentieth century. Chinese in Cambodia were granted citizen rights in the 1950s, thanks to the good relationship between Cambodia and China. It was also relatively easy for the Chinese to get Malaysian citizenship (Suryadinata 2007).

Even after obtaining local citizenship, the Chinese soon found that their rights and interests were compromised by laws, government policies, and bureaucratic practices prioritizing the interests of the natives. As Suryadinata points out,

Southeast Asian countries are indigenous state-nations, in which "the nation is defined in indigenous group terms" (Suryadinata 1997, pp. 5–6). The concepts of *pribumi* in Indonesia and *bumiputra* in Malaysia both refer to indigenous groups, who are seen as the basis of the new nations and thus enjoy more rights than nonindigenous groups, such as the Chinese. In Indonesia, the Chinese were denied political participation for a long time and had to confine themselves within the economic domain. In Malaysia, the New Economic Policy adopted in 1970 institutionalized the privileges that were granted to the Malays (Yow 2017, pp. 281–282). Malays and other indigenous groups enjoy better business opportunities, job opportunities, educational opportunities, etc.

Most Southeast Asian countries see the indigenous cultures as their national cultures, taking various discriminatory policies toward the Chinese culture (Suryadinata 1997, pp. 11–13). For a long time, Indonesia, Thailand, and the Philippines adopted assimilationist policies, trying to reduce the ethnic cultural characteristics of the Chinese population. Chinese schools, Chinese media, and Chinese organizations, three pillars of overseas Chinese culture, were either been closed or reduced to the minimum. Malaysia has adopted an accommodationist policy, recognizing cultural rights of the Chinese, but they were not treated equally as their indigenous counterparts.

It needs to be pointed out that policies on Chinese cultures have always been changing in these countries, due to changes in the domestic and international politics. For example, Indonesia changed from a liberal policy in the 1950s to a harsh policy in the 1960s. In recent decades, a more liberal policy has been adopted, and many Chinese cultures have been resumed to a certain extent. This has happened in many of these countries.

The economic disparities between the Chinese and the indigenous populations became a political issue in most Southeast Asian countries after their independence. Many introduced policies to curtail the economic advantages of the Chinese. In the 1950s, the Soekarno government introduced the Benteng program which required importing companies to have 70% of their shares owned by the *pribumi*, the indigenous people (Suryadinata 2007, p. 231). In the subsequent decades, different policies and programs were introduced, encouraging joint ventures between the indigenous people and the Chinese and requiring the indigenous people to own at least 50% of the shares (Suryadinata 2007, pp. 232–233). Ironically, such policies enhanced rather than weakened the economic power of the Chinese. By collaborating with powerful figures, the Chinese businessmen turned the policies to their own advantage (Suryadinata 2007, p. 233).

In Malaysia, the government introduced the New Economic Policy in 1971. One of its two goals was to redress the economic imbalance between the indigenous Malays and the ethnic Chinese (Woon 2012). As a race-based program, it did give indigenous people advantage and helped to create a middle class of the indigenous people. While the Chinese were kept out of state-dominated sectors, they still prospered in the manufacturing sector (Lee 2012, pp. 52–56).

Surviving Exclusion in White Settler Societies

The United States, Canada, Australia, and New Zealand were all previous British colonies, populated by immigrants from Europe and their descendants, with indigenous people marginalized both in power and population size. The historical and contemporary experience of Chinese immigrants was quite different from what their peers have had in Southeast Asia.

The first sizable Chinese immigration was part of the mass emigration out of China after the 1840s. When news of gold rushes in California (from 1851), Australia (from 1854), British Columbia (1860), and New Zealand (1865) reached China, many people from Pearl River Delta of Guangdong Province exited via colonial ports of Hong Kong and Macao to seek fortune in these foreign lands (Kuhn 2008).

After gold mines were depleted, many returned to China, but some did stay. In Australia and New Zealand, the Chinese became self-employed or were employed by their countrymen in farming, shopkeeping, and hawking (Chan 2001; Boileau 2017). In American West, railroad construction employed many Chinese and attracted more immigrants from China. In the 1880s, Chinese laborers formed 25% of the labor force of California (Kuhn 2008, p. 205). In 1881, there were estimated 38,533 Chinese living in Australia (Chan 2001, p. 69).

As Chinese population increased, anti-Chinese sensation grew in these societies. The physical and behavioral differences of the Chinese reinforced the already existing cultural prejudices against the Chinese. The ticket-credit form of immigration arrangement was often mistakenly perceived as a kind of slavery. The media often emphasized prostitution and gambling in the Chinese communities as morally threatening to the American society. In the United States, all these factors, intertwined in a complex ways, contributed to the development of an anti-Chinese sensation from a regional phenomenon to a nationwide political movement, with the Chinese Exclusion Act passed in 1882 (Gyory 1998). Australia, New Zealand, and Canada all have head taxes imposed on Chinese immigrants and took legislative measures to restrict Chinese immigration.

All these legislative and bureaucratic measures had similar impacts on Chinese immigrants. These facts have been well known in works on Chinese American history: it was difficult for the Chinese to bring their women over, and most people were males in the Chinese communities; many occupations were closed to them, confining them to a limited number of trades such as laundry and Chinese restaurants; legislative and social discrimination confined their residence to racially segregated Chinatowns (Zhao 2010). In Australia and New Zealand, many Chinese were employed in market gardening and shopkeeping (Chan 2001; Boileau 2017).

Negotiating a Niche in Multicultural Societies

After WWII, all the four countries gradually changed their racially discriminatory immigration policy. The United States gradually removed discriminatory policies toward Chinese immigrants and implemented an immigration reform in the 1960s

(Zhou 2009). Canada introduced a points system that was race-neutral, giving priority to those with the skills, educational background, and other qualities that the country desired (Hawkins 1991). Similar policies were later adopted by Australia (1989) and New Zealand (1991). These reforms removed the barriers for Chinese immigration, and all four societies saw dramatic increase of Chinese population subsequently. In the United States, the population of Chinese Americans doubled every 10 years, reaching 2.9 million at the turn of the century and 3.5 million in 2006 (Zhou 2009, p. 46).

The change of immigration policies brought about diversity among Chinese immigrants (Zhou 2009, pp. 46–51). New immigrants after WWII have come from many different places, including Hong Kong, Taiwan, Mainland China, and Southeast Asia. Among them were students, entrepreneurs, refugees, illegal immigrants, and many more. Some of them were wealthy and brought with them abundant capital, while others had already obtained their college or even advanced degrees before they moved.

Such demographic changes have also led to different spatial distributions of the Chinese. In the United States, although some traditional Chinatowns are still prosperous Chinese neighborhoods, most new immigrants prefer to live in suburbs of major metropolitan areas. The concept of "ethnoburb" has been proposed by geographer Li Wei to theorize this new trend (Li 2009). An excellent example of "ethnoburb" was Monterey Park and other small suburban cities in San Gabriel Valley east of downtown Los Angeles. Since the 1970s, this area has been transformed from dominantly white communities into multiethnic communities with high percentage of Chinese population (Li 2009). Different from traditional Chinatowns that were self-contained, racially segregated, economically disadvantaged, and densely populated, these ethnoburbs are suburban communities of low population density, with a thriving ethnic economy that is not only closely connected to the mainstream economy but is also part of the transnational network that facilitates the global flow of capital, commodities, and personnel (Li 2009, pp. 45–47). Such ethnoburbs provide job opportunities for both high-skilled and low-skilled new immigrants who might be disadvantaged on the mainstream job market. They also serve as niches for Chinese immigrant entrepreneurs to develop their own businesses, tapping skills and talents within the community (Li 2009).

The socioeconomic status of the Chinese in these countries has greatly improved after WWII. For example, the data of 2010 American census show that over half (50.3%) of American Chinese (excluding Taiwanese) ages 25 and over has at least a bachelor's degree, much higher than the national level (27.8%) (APIAHF 2011). The Chinese (excluding Taiwanese) have an average median household income of $68,420 compared to the national average median household income of $51,369 (APIAHF 2011). Taiwanese had even higher figures. Many factors might have contributed to these achievements, but the selective immigration policy and the domestic and international factors behind it have helped the United States to attract immigrants from greater China with good educational background and the skills needed. This is a key factor behind the transition of the Chinese from the "yellow peril" to a "model minority" in the mainstream discourse.

Behind the positive figures of education attainment and economic achievements, class distinctions and poverty exist among the Chinese in these societies (Zhao 2010). While many well-educated professionals hold high-paying jobs, there are also many Chinese unskilled immigrants toiling in sweat factories and earning meager wages. The undocumented immigrants are vulnerable and often subjective to excessive exploitation by ethnic businesses. The life and experience of these disadvantaged Chinese Americans are overshadowed by the hegemonic discourse of a model minority, which deprived them of their right for social support.

Since the 1960s, seeing Asian Americans, including Chinese Americans, as a "model minority" has become a popular discourse in American media and the mainstream society, and has also been accepted in Canada and Australasia (Ip and Pang 2005; Chow and Feagin 2016). The rise of this discourse in the 1960s was not coincidental. As many scholars have pointed out, portraying Chinese Americans as industrial, disciplined, and docile, this discourse was a political weapon that the white adopted to counterattack the African Americans and Latinos' protests against discrimination in the civil rights movement (Chow and Feagin 2016). It is a stereotype imposed on the Asians not necessary to their benefit, as it assumes an illusionary homogeneity of Chinese Americans, ignoring the diversity among them and leaving the needs of disadvantaged Chinese Americans unheeded by the government and the society.

Currently these societies all claim to uphold the ideal of multiculturalism (in New Zealand's case, a biculturalism that recognizes the rights of the indeginous Maori people in a society that has been dominated by Pakeha, descendants of white immigrants from Europe). But how to carve a comfortable niche within the racial and cultural landscape in these societies is still a challenge to the Chinese. In all these societies, the Chinese are caught between the mainstream white population and the disadvantaged minorities. "Yellow peril" or "model minority," these imposed stereotypes all convey the sense of "otherness," although in different ways. Although statistics might look good, in-depth analysis shows that the Chinese still earn less than white people with the same qualifications and experience (Zhao 2010). That means glass ceilings still need to be broken for the Chinese.

The Chinese in Other Societies

The massive emigration starting from the 1850s to the 1950s also brought the Chinese to other parts of the world. Coolies were transported from Pearl River Delta to Latin America and the Caribbean to meet the labor shortage caused by the abolition of slavery in the second half of the nineteenth century (Lai and Tan 2010). Gold miners and coolies went to South Africa to work at the mines there (Zhou 2017). Chinese seamen came to port cities of Europe very early, and peddlers from Qingtian and Wenzhou of Zhejiang province traveled along the trans-Siberia railway all the way to many parts of Europe in the early twentieth century (Benton and Pieke 1998). During WWI, many Chinese were recruited to work in France and Russia. Most of the Chinese in Europe eventually returned to China. Thus the number of Chinese there was small before WWII. But Chinese communities developed in many countries of

Latin America and the Caribbean before WWII century (Lai and Tan 2010). South Africa also saw a small Chinese community there (Zhou 2017).

After 1949, China closed its door for lawful emigration. Immigration from China to South Africa, Latin America, and the Caribbean was cut short, and for a time few new immigrants arrived. In Europe, Chinese residents began to grow after WWII, as the first wave of postwar Chinese immigrants moved from Asian colonies to colonial metro centers in Europe. Rural residents from New Territories of Hong Kong came to the United Kingdom and developed the Chinese catering industry (Benton and Gomez 2007). Early Chinese immigrants from Indochina and Dutch East Indies to France and the Netherlands were generally well educated and thus were able to enter mainstream occupations and businesses (Benton and Pieke 1998).

In the 1970s, the economic boom in Taiwan, Hong Kong, and Southeast Asia sent another wave of Chinese immigrants to Europe, South Africa, and Latin America and the Caribbean (Benton and Pieke 1998; Lai and Tan 2010; Zhou 2017). They were well educated, and some were well funded and thus were able to enter mainstream occupations in the host countries. In South Africa, these new immigrants played an important role in securing an unofficial "honorable white" status for the Chinese (Zhou 2017).

Vietnam War refugees further expanded Chinese communities in Western Europe (Benton and Pieke 1998). France, due to its connections with Indochina, received a significant share. These refugees generally lacked education and skills. Their socioeconomic status still lags behind even today.

After China reopened its door for emigration, new immigrants expanded existing Chinese communities in all these places and established new communities in new locations (Zhou 2017). In South Africa, new immigrants significantly increased the Chinese population. In Spain and Italy, Chinese communities have been dominated by new immigrants from Qingtian and Wenzhou since the 1980s (Thunø 2007; Zhou 2017). These new immigrants came through chain immigration based on kinship and family ties. In Italy, the Chinese were initially mainly engaged in the fashion manufacturing industry, but now have shifted to commercial businesses selling imported goods from China (Thunø 2007). In Spain, retail and wholesale businesses selling imported Chinese goods have been the main Chinese economic activity (Zhou 2017). In Russia and other East European countries, most Chinese there have come after the collapse of the communist regimes (Nyiri 2007). Initially these Chinese came from North and Northeastern China as traders selling Chinese goods. They soon established a niche in the transition economies as cheap goods from China met the needs of the local market. In Latin America and the Caribbean, many Chinese came through kinship or other ties (Lai and Tan 2010).

In recent decades, the increasing investments from government-owned and privately owned Chinese businesses have brought many Chinese to Africa (Zhou 2017). Individual migrants looking for economic gains have followed their steps. Many of these Chinese stay there for profits, without a plan to stay long, although some of them do bring their families over. In this sense, they are similar to early Chinese traders going to Southeast Asia. As in many places of Africa, sizable Chinese populations appeared just in the last decade, they have not been integrated into the local societies and also lack communality among themselves (Zhou 2017). They are just foreigners from the perspectives of the local people. It is still too early to predict what will happen to them and how Chinese communities in Africa will develop in the future.

New immigrants after the 1980s have also dramatically expanded Chinese communities in South Korea and Japan. Currently, there are about one million Chinese nationals living in South Korea, forming three distinct groups: old *Huaqiao*, *Chaoxianzu* (ethnic Korean Chinese), and *Xin Yimin* (*han* Chinese new immigrants) (Zhou 2017). Both the latter two groups arrived after the 1980s. *Chaoxianzu* enjoy some legal advantages due to South Korean policy toward overseas ethnic Koreans. But like *han* Chinese new immigrants, they are also faced with discrimination from the mainstream society.

The community of Chinese immigrants in Japan has grown from a small size in the 1970s to 694,974 people in 2014 (Zhou 2017). Most of these people have moved to Japan after the 1980s. Compared with old immigrants who mainly lived in Chinatowns and worked as cooks, hairdressers, and tailors, these new immigrants are more diverse in occupations, with a significant percentage of them employed as professionals. As Japan has become more open to foreign immigrants, many of these Chinese immigrants have obtained their permanent residency, and some have already been naturalized. Visible and invisible barriers still exist in workplace. Chinese students and trainees are vulnerable groups that remain at the bottom of the society.

From *Huaqiao* to *Huayi*: Constructing Chineseness Outside China

Apparently, there is a great diversity in the historical and contemporary experiences of the Chinese living in different countries. Even in the same country, those coming during different time periods and from different places might show significant cultural and language differences. The colonial history of Hong Kong and the political separation between Mainland China and Taiwan have added another dimension of complexity to the already complicated landscape of identity construction. To what extent and in which ways does such a large population of diverse experience and backgrounds identify as Chinese? How has this Chineseness changed through history?

Early Chinese emigrants might have had what Gungwu Wang termed a historical identity of Chineseness (1988, p. 2). But in everyday life, they often identified more with their own regional and kinship groups. The boundaries between them and local populations were not fixed. Thus, the diasporic Chinese at that time lacked a conscious awareness of a unitary identity, and their identity was in a state of multi-strandedness with shifting boundaries (Duara 1997, p. 41).

The consciousness of a unitary Chinese identity among the overseas Chinese was produced by political developments both inside and outside China in the late nineteenth century and the first half of the twentieth century. The Qing state initiated a change in its policy toward Chinese overseas. The ban on emigration was lifted in 1893 (Duara 1997, p. 43; Kuhn 2008, pp. 240–241). A citizenship policy based on the principle of *jus sanguinis* was adopted, seeing all Chinese living overseas, whether born in China or overseas, as citizens whose loyalty should be cultivated.

The Qing state also extended its cultural and political influence to overseas Chinese communities, establishing consulate overseas, granting imperial titles, sponsoring the Confucian revival movement among the Chinese, and helping overseas Chinese consolidate their organizations divided by dialects and places of origin into ones incorporating all Chinese. As Duara points out, "the Qing effort to install a gentry model of Chinese community amounted to an effort to construct a Confucian nationalism" (Duara 1997, p. 45).

At the same time, the political mobilizations of revolutionaries led by Sun Yat-sen and reformists such as Kang Youwei and Liang Qichao played an important role in cultivating a modern nationalism among the overseas Chinese and turning the cultural China into a nation state that deserved loyalty from its citizens overseas (Kuhn 2008, pp. 239–282). An identity of *huaqiao*, unified by Chinese nationalism and loyalty to China, was created out of the otherwise apolitical *huashang* (Chinese traders) and *huagong* (Chinese coolies) (Wang 1991, pp. 6–8).

The political development in the first half of the twentieth century further consolidated the Chinese community overseas. After the Sino-Japanese war broke out in 1937, relief fund associations were organized in overseas Chinese communities throughout the world within months, raising funds to support the Chinese war efforts (Kuhn 2008, pp. 239–282). Such mobilization efforts required close cooperation among overseas Chinese, with dialect or class boundaries transcended. A unitary identity of *huaqiao* was constructed on the global landscape, holding together all who were willing to accept this discourse.

This identity based on political loyalty to China became a problem when new nation states arose in Southeast Asia after WWII (Wang 1988, pp. 2–3). The agreement the communist China signed with Indonesia in 1955 symbolized a major shift of Chinese policy toward overseas Chinese, who were encouraged to take the citizenship of their countries of residence. In subsequent decades, most Chinese living in Southeast Asia became citizens of their countries of residence. In the white settler societies, many Chinese were also allowed to be naturalized. Now, the majority of the overseas Chinese is no longer *huaqiao*, but has become *huayi* (foreigners of Chinese ancestry).

This change does not mean the complete loss of the Chineseness among diasporic Chinese. Just as the identity of *huaqiao* was a product of particular historical contexts, the postcolonial politics in Southeast Asia and multiculturalism in Western societies have created new contexts in which the identities of overseas Chinese are reconstructed. As Gungwu Wang (Wang 1991, pp. 198–221) has pointed out, overseas Chinese all have multiple identities that are highlighted in different contexts for different purposes. They are culturally and ethnically Chinese, but are also nationals of their own countries.

As Stuart Hall has pointed out, "identities are the names we give to the different ways we are positioned by, and position ourselves within, the narratives of the past" (Hall 1990, p. 225). The different historical and contemporary social contexts in which the Chinese live have created different senses of Chineseness between the Chinese living in white settler societies and those in Southeast Asian countries.

In Indonesia, an assimilationist policy once tried to suppress anything symbolic of Chineseness (Suryadinata 1997, pp. 11–13). In Malaysia the accommodationist policy put the Chinese and their culture in a subordinate position (Suryadinata 1997, pp. 13–14). In face of suspicion, harassment, and violence, the Chinese living in these countries are sharply conscious of their ethnic Chinese identity (Armstrong and Armstrong 2001, p. 4).

In white settler societies, Chineseness was once symbolic of "the other" that needed to be excluded. Although the ideal of multiculturalism has made these societies more culturally inclusive, this "otherness" is still something the Chinese need to overcome. The image of a "model minority" is an identity imposed on the Chinese by the mainstream discourse in the past decades, against which the Chinese have an ambivalent attitude. The Chinese are also active agents in constructing their identities out of their cultural heritage. Chinese language schools, Chinese newspapers and magazines, and Chinese cultural events are all efforts of the Chinese to retain their Chineseness in multicultural societies. Chinese food and restaurants have also become an important aspect of the Chinese identity (Mendelson 2016). Literary works, both in Chinese and in English, music, dance, art, and popular culture, have also become arenas where the Chinese fight to define their own cultural and ethnic identities (Zheng 2011; Fusco 2016).

At the same time, we should also recognize the "critical points of deep and significant difference" behind the Chineseness (Hall 1990, p. 225). Even in the same society, different background might produce different positioning toward their Chinese heritage. The Chineseness might mean different things to different people, particularly when political factors are involved. An immigrant from Taiwan might emphasize his/her identity as Taiwanese while downplaying or even denying their Chinese identity (Williams 2003). Recent achievements of China has cultivated a sense of pride among new immigrants from China and has contributed to the rise of a new Chinese nationalism in Chinese diaspora (Liu 2005). For many people, Chineseness is more cultural than territorial. Although it means different things to different people in different contexts, this Chineseness in its cultural sense is something that helps to define the Chinese diaspora.

Transnational Network, Globalization, and the Chinese Diaspora

One of the most important changes in the postwar global economy was the economic boom in Asia, in which Taiwan, Hong Kong, and Singapore played important roles. Mainland China began to catch up after the 1980s and has now become the second largest economy in the world. International investments and transfer of technology from developed countries played an important role in the success of these economies. Overseas Chinese with their connections to both sides were important players in the process. Thus, the Chinese diaspora has been an important part of the network through which capital, technology, commodity, and population flow transnationally.

With the rise of these economies, business firms of ethnic Chinese, with their personal and business connections, are playing a more and more important role in the global economy (Yen 2014). Traditional connections such as kinship ties and regional and language associations can all be mobilized for business purposes. Businessmen are behind many regular international conferences of ethnic Chinese associations, which provide platforms for building business networks. With Mainland China becoming a new player in international investment, the ethnic Chinese become precious assets that the Chinese capitalism can use, and this Chinese capitalism can also provide opportunities for the ethnic Chinese (Santasombat 2018). But whether the ethnic Chinese identity and Chinese cultural values have played an important role in the success of ethnic Chinese businesses has also been debated by scholars (Gomez and Hsiao 2013).

Transnationalism is not limited to cross-border business connections. In fact, it has become an important feature of population flow and kinship ties in the past decades. For many Chinese immigrants, immigration is not a unidirectional movement to new homes but an ongoing multidirectional process. Facilitated by modern transportation, a transnational Chinese might do business at home, leaving family overseas for educational opportunities of kids. Obtaining the citizenship of a host country is not necessarily out of political loyalty but in most cases out of business or family needs. "Flexible citizenship" has become an important feature for many Chinese immigrants (Ong 1999).

Cultural transnationalism has also been an important aspect of Chinese diaspora. Chinese religions might have been pioneers of cultural transnationality. From in the early twentieth century, Chinese Buddhist institutions actively sought cross-border connections, creating transnational network of clergies and devotees. Such transnational networks helped to get Buddhism established in Southeast Asia and North America and have also played an important part in the revival of Buddhism in twenty-first-century China (Ashiwa and Wank 2005). In recent decades, Buddhist institutions in Taiwan have been active in building transnational networks of temples, clergies, and devotees.

The rise of Sinophone studies in recent years provides a new perspective of this cultural transnationalism (Shih 2011). Bringing Chinese diaspora from the margin of the Chinese culture to the core, such studies examine cultural products of Chinese diaspora in both local and global contexts. Although cultural products such as films, literary works, and arts created in Chinese diaspora are not necessarily intended for the whole Chinese diaspora, Sinophone studies do help to paint them with a brush of transnationalism.

Conclusion and Prospects

Since the 1990s, there have been numerous researches published on Chinese diaspora, covering many different aspects of diasporic experience of overseas Chinese. The last two decades has also been a period that sees dramatic changes in China and Chinese diaspora. As a result, there are many new aspects of Chinese diasporic experience that are not yet or not sufficiently examined.

Although the heterogeneity of Chinese diaspora is a well-known fact, some aspects of this heterogeneity have not been thoroughly researched. The political heterogeneity within the Chinese diaspora is especially a field that calls for further research. Chinese Americans, for example, consist of many groups: descendants of old immigrants, immigrants from Taiwan, immigrants from Mainland China, and immigrants from Southeast Asia. Although we might label all of them as Chinese Americans, there are significant differences among them. The recent rise of Taiwanese nationalism has prompted some immigrants from Taiwan to distance themselves from the ethnic Chinese identity. Immigrants from Southeast Asia are also differently positioned in their relationship with China and the Chinese identity. How do these different groups compete and cooperate in the political and social contexts of the host societies need to be examined.

The rise of China in the last couple of decades and its impact on Chinese diaspora began to catch scholarly attention. But so far, there are still few researches conducted in this area. The growing cultural conservatism in Western countries increasingly sees the rise of China and the expansion of Chinese diaspora as a threat. This is not only reflected in the current politics of the United States, but is also explicitly or inexplicitly expressed in politics of Australia and New Zealand. What impact this will have on Chinese diaspora? Will this Sinophobia turn Chinese in these countries into the "yellow peril" again? How shall the Chinese position themselves in the politics of these societies and fight for their own political interests?

Another area that needs more research is the emerging Chinese communities in nontraditional destinations of Chinese emigration. For example, Chinese investments have brought many Chinese to Africa in recent decades. How will Chinese communities thus created develop in the future? What kind of ethnic relations these Chinese forge with the local populations is also yet to see.

References

APIAHF (2011) Demographic and socioeconomic profiles of Asian Americans, Native Hawaiians, and Pacific Islanders in the United States. Asian & Pacific Islander Health Forum: Oakland, CA

Armstrong MJ, Armstrong RW (2001) Introduction: Chinese population of Southeast Asia. In: Armstrong MJ, Armstrong RW, Mulliner K (eds) Chinese populations in contemporary southeast Asian societies: identities, interdependence and international influence. Curzon, Richmond/Surrey, pp 1–17

Ashiwa Y, Wank DL (2005) The globalization of Chinese Buddhism: clergy and devotee networks in the twentieth century. Int J Asian Stud 2:217–237

Barrett TC (2012) Chinese diaspora in South-East Asia: the overseas Chinese in IndoChina. I.B. Tauris, London

Benton G, Gomez ET (2007) The Chinese in Britain, 1800-present: economy, transnationalism, identity. Springer, New York

Benton G, Pieke FN (eds) (1998) The Chinese in Europe. Macmillan Press, London

Boileau J (2017) Chinese market gardening in Australia and New Zealand: gardens of prosperity. Springer, New York

Chan H (2001) Government control of Chinese immigration to Australia, 1855–1975. In: Chan H, Curthoys A, Chiang N (eds) The overseas Chinese in Australasia: history, settlement and interactions: proceedings. Interdisciplinary Group for Australian Studies (IGAS), National Taiwan University/Centre for the Study of the Chinese Southern Diaspora, Australian National University, Taipei, pp 69–81

Chow RS, Feagin JR (2016) Myth of the model minority: Asian Americans facing racism, 2nd edn. Routledge, New York

DeBernardi J (1993) Epilogue: ritual process reconsidered. In: Ownby D, Heidhues MFS (eds) Secret societies reconsidered: perspectives on the social history of early modern South China and Southeast Asia, 1st edn. Routledge, Armonk, pp 212–233

Duara P (1997) Nationalists among transnationals: overseas Chinese and the idea of China, 1900–1911. In: Ong A, Nonini D (eds) Ungrounded empires: the cultural politics of modern Chinese transnationalism. Routledge, New York, pp 39–60

Fusco S (2016) Incorporations of Chineseness: hybridity, bodies, and Chinese American literature. Cambridge Scholarly Publishing, Newcastle upon Tyne

Gomez ET, Hsiao H-HM (eds) (2013) Chinese business in Southeast Asia: contesting cultural explanations, researching entrepreneurship. Routledge, New York

Gyory A (1998) Closing the gate: race, politics, and the Chinese exclusion act. The University of North Carolina Press, Chapel Hill

Hall S (1990) Cultural identity and diaspora. In: Rutherford J (ed) Identity: community, culture, difference. Lawrence & Wishart, London, pp 222–237

Hawkins F (1991) Critical years in immigration: Canada and Australia compared, 2nd edn. McGill-Queen's Press – MQUP, Kingston

Heidhues MS (1993) Chinese organizations in West Borneo and Bangka: Kongsi and Hui. ME Sharpe, Armonk

Ip M, Pang D (2005) New Zealand Chinese identity: Sojourners, model minority and multiple identities. In: Liu JH, McCreanor T, McIntosh T, Teaiwa T (eds) New Zealand identities: departures and destinations. Victoria University Press, Wellington, pp 174–190

Kuhn PA (2008) Chinese among others: emigration in modern times. Rowman & Littlefield, Lanham

Lai WL, Tan CB (eds) (2010) The Chinese in Latin America and the Caribbean. BRILL, Boston

Lee KH (2012) QUO VADIS: the Chinese in Malaysia. In: Lee HG, Suryadinata L (eds) Malaysian Chinese: recent developments and prospects. Institute of Southeast Asian Studies, Singapore, pp 45–69

Li W (2009) Ethnoburb: the new ethnic community in urban America. University of Hawai'i Press, Honolulu

Liu H (2005) New migrants and the revival of overseas Chinese nationalism. J Contemp China 14:291–316. https://doi.org/10.1080/10670560500065611

Lockard CA (2013) Chinese migration and settlement in Southeast Asia before 1850: making fields from the sea. Hist Compass 11:765–781. https://doi.org/10.1111/hic3.12079

McKeown A (1999) Conceptualizing Chinese diasporas, 1842 to 1949. J Asian Stud 58:306–337. https://doi.org/10.2307/2659399

Mendelson A (2016) Chow chop suey: food and the Chinese American journey. Columbia University Press, New York

Nyiri P (2007) Chinese in Eastern Europe and Russia: a middleman minority in a transnational era. Routledge, New York

Ong A (1999) Flexible citizenship: the cultural logics of transnationality. Duke University Press, Durham

Poston DL, Wong JH (2016) The Chinese diaspora: the current distribution of the overseas Chinese population. Chin J Sociol 2:348–373. https://doi.org/10.1177/2057150X16655077

Santasombat Y (2018) The sociology of Chinese capitalism in Southeast Asia: challenges and prospects. Palgrave Macmillan, Singapore

Shih S (2011) The concept of the Sinophone. PMLA 126:709–718. https://doi.org/10.1632/pmla.2011.126.3.709

Skinner GW (2001) Creolized Chinese societies in Southeast Asia. In: Reid A (ed) Sojourners and settlers: histories of Southeast Asia and the Chinese. University of Hawai'i Press, Honolulu, pp 51–93

Suryadinata L (1997) Ethnic Chinese in Southeast Asia: overseas Chinese, Chinese overseas or southeast Asians? In: Suryadinata L (ed) Ethnic Chinese as southeast Asians. Palgrave Macmillan, New York, pp 1–24

Suryadinata L (2007) Understanding the ethnic Chinese in Southeast Asia. Institute of Southeast Asian Studies, Singapore

Tan MG (1997) The ethnic Chinese in Indonesia: issues of identity. In: Suryadinata L (ed) Ethnic Chinese as southeast Asians. Palgrave Macmillan, New York, pp 33–65

Thunø M (ed) (2007) Beyond Chinatown: new Chinese migration and the global expansion of China. NIAS Press, Copenhagen

Tu W (1994) Cultural China: the periphery as the center. In: Tu W (ed) The living tree: the changing meaning of being Chinese today. Stanford University Press, Stanford, pp 1–34

Wang G (1988) The study of Chinese identities in Southeast Asia. In: Cushman JW, Gungwu W (eds) Changing identities of the southeast Asian Chinese since world war II. Hong Kong University Press, Hong Kong, pp 1–21

Wang G (1991) China and the Chinese overseas. Times Academic, Singapore

Williams JF (2003) Who are the Taiwanese? Taiwan in the Chinese diaspora. In: Ma LJC, Cartier C (eds) The Chinese diaspora: space, place, mobility, and identity. Rowman & Littlefield, Lanham, pp 163–189

Willmott DE (2009) The National Status of the Chinese in Indonesia 1900–1958. Equinox Publishing, Jakarta/Kuala Lumpur

Woon TK (2012) The new Malaysian economic agenda: some preliminary observations. In: Lee HG, Suryadinata L (eds) Malaysian Chinese: recent developments and prospects. Institute of Southeast Asian Studies, Singapore, pp 125–143

Yen C-H (2014) Ethnic Chinese business in Asia: history, culture and business enterprise. World Scientific Publishing Company, Singapore

Yow CH (2017) Ethnic Chinese in Malaysian citizenship: gridlocked in historical formation and political hierarchy. Asian Ethn 18:277–295. https://doi.org/10.1080/14631369.2016.1155044

Zhao X (2010) The new Chinese America: class, economy, and social hierarchy. Rutgers University Press, New Brunswick

Zheng S (2011) Claiming diaspora: music, transnationalism, and cultural politics in Asian/Chinese America. Oxford University Press, Oxford

Zhou M (2009) Contemporary Chinese America immigration, ethnicity, and community transformation. Temple University Press, Philadelphia

Zhou M (ed) (2017) Contemporary Chinese diasporas. Springer, Singapore

Greek Identity in Australia

62

Rebecca Fanany and Maria-Irini Avgoulas

Contents

Introduction	1186
History of the Greek Diaspora in Australia	1186
The Meaning of Greek Identity	1188
Change in the Australian Greek Community	1193
Greek Identity in the Future	1196
Conclusion: Australian Greekness – The Formation of a New Cultural Identity	1197
References	1199

Abstract

The Greek diaspora community is well-established in Australia. While arrivals from Greece began in the nineteenth century and continued through the twentieth, peak migration occurred in the years following World War II and the Greek Civil War. Today people of Greek background are highly integrated into the mainstream of Australian society and culture. Nonetheless, the characteristics that are most closely associated with cultural identity, specifically the Greek language, membership in the Greek Orthodox Church, and a Greek lifestyle, are still prominent among members and tend to be viewed as extremely important, even by younger individuals. Older members of the community experienced considerable racism and exclusion, but this has now faded, and younger people tend to see themselves as possessing a dual identity as Greek and also fully Australian.

R. Fanany (✉)
School of Health, Medical and Applied Sciences, Central Queensland University, Melbourne, VIC, Australia
e-mail: r.fanany@cqu.edu.au

M.-I. Avgoulas
School of Psychology and Public Health, College of Science, Health and Engineering, La Trobe University, Bundoora, VIC, Australia
e-mail: m.avgoulas@latrobe.edu.au

© The Author(s), under exclusive license to Springer Nature Singapore Pte Ltd. 2019
S. Ratuva (ed.), *The Palgrave Handbook of Ethnicity*,
https://doi.org/10.1007/978-981-13-2898-5_83

As the Australian-born generations come to dominate the Greek community, an increasing shift from Greek to English has been observed, with many younger people lacking the fluency their parents (the transitional generation) usually possess. This, along with an attitude of pride and acceptance of their cultural heritage, is helping to create a new Greek identity that derives not just from individuals' own experiences in Australia but also from travel to Greece and interaction on the Internet with members of other diaspora communities elsewhere in the world as well as with people in Greece. The result is a conceptualization of Greek identity that is both more transnational in nature but also more characteristically Australian, reflecting the established nature of people of Greek background within the English-speaking Australian mainstream.

Keywords

Greek culture · Diaspora · Heritage · Greek language · Greek Orthodox · Dual identity

Introduction

As a people, the Greeks have a long and influential history, beginning in their region of origin in Europe and, in modern times, extending far beyond the borders of the ancient world. Migration and settlement in increasingly varied and dispersed regions have been characteristic of this long history beginning in the eighth century BC and continuing up to the present time (Testskhladze 2008). Today there are significant communities of people of Greek descent in other parts of Europe as well as in the United States, Canada, and Australia, whose members are generally well integrated into population and, in the second and third generation, have moved into a range of fields and professions across economic sectors (Glytsos and Katseli 2005).

History of the Greek Diaspora in Australia

While Greek migration to Australia occurred during the nineteenth and early twentieth centuries, the numbers of migrants arriving from Greece increased greatly in the period between the World Wars, reaching an estimated 15,000 individuals by 1940. Many of these migrants eventually settled in rural and remote areas because of the difficulty of finding employment and were often unable to maintain contact with family and countrymen because of the distances involved and limitations on communications technology (Tamis 2009b). The right to work in certain settings was reserved for British subjects at this time, and many of the Greek migrants experienced the impacts of negative stereotypes and a lack of tolerance for those whose language and customs were different than the English mainstream (Tamis 2000). Despite the difficulties experienced by Greek migrants to Australia, which were reported in the newspapers in Greece and were widely known to friends and family members of those who had gone, migration was often influenced by family ties and bonds of loyalty and kinship. In addition to a strong expectation that migrants would help their family members both in Greece and in Australia, the community, as well as individuals, placed a strong emphasis on marrying within the group, maintaining the Greek language in their new land, and continuing to respect and practice the customs and values of their region of origin (Tamis 2009b).

By the end of World War II, chain migration from Greece, where individuals often decided to come to Australia because another family member was already there and could potentially assist the migrant who would contribute to the household of the more established earlier migrants, was replaced by mass migration from Greece as well as from other parts of Eastern and Southern Europe. In 1949, following the Greek Civil War, about 270,000 people of Greek origin entered Australia (Tamis 2009a). At this time, the Australian government was recruiting immigrants from all over Europe in order to boost the postwar economy and maintain the security of the nation (Ongley and Pearson 1995). A baseline of 1% population increase through immigration annually was established in 1945 and remained in place until the early 1970s (Hawkins 1989). At this time, the Labour government rejected the concept of population growth through the acceptance of foreign nationals as a result of pressure on public resources and the resulting disapproval of the public (Price 1982). Immigration peaked at 185,000 people in 1969–1970, but, by 1976, the net population increase due to immigration had fallen to a negative level for the first time in three decades (Ongley and Pearson 1995).

Today's Greek diaspora in Australia was shaped by the postwar migration policies of several successive governments and, by the mid-1970s, had grown to the point where newcomers could settle within an established community where their language was used, and their cultures represented a local norm. In fact, however, even when the population of Greek origin had been much smaller, its members went to some lengths to establish cultural, religious, and educational organizations based on those they had known in Europe. Greek Orthodox churches were established early in the development of Australian Greek communities, initially under the Patriarchate of Jerusalem and then as part of the Church of Greece. Despite internal differences, most Greek immigrants respected the church as a central institution in the community and have remained loyal to their traditional faith. Similarly, ensuring that younger members of the community, especially those born in Australia, were able to speak Greek was extremely important to the community from its inception. As a result, Greek language classes, often held in churches or at the premises of businesses owned by members of the community, were established wherever people of Greek background were living, and parents were often adamant that their children attend (Tamis 2009b). A Greek language newspaper was established in 1898. Coffee shops (καφενείο) were opened and became gathering places and information hubs for the men of the community. Corner stores, known as "milk bars" in Australia, were features of residential neighborhoods across Australia (Alexakis and Janiszewski 2016). Mutual aid societies, based on region of origin in Greece (αλληλοβοήθεια), had been operating since 1912 and numbered more than 100 by 1945 and 1000 in 1995 (Allimonos 2002).

The majority of Greeks who made the decision to emigrate to Australia were young, unskilled, and possessed little formal education or capital. Most had sold their possessions and borrowed money from family to finance their trip. Many were traumatized as a result of the experiences of World War II and the Civil War that followed soon after. Nonetheless, they were overwhelmingly determined to succeed and also to maintain their Greek culture and way of life to the extent possible in the English-speaking context in which they were living (Tsounis 1975a). It also became increasingly apparent to many members of the Australian diaspora, whose largest communities grew up in Melbourne, Sydney, and Adelaide, that their residence in Australia would be permanent. It is this realization that supported the widespread commitment to and support for Greek cultural institutions intended to maintain the language and culture of their homeland, even though lack of facility in English was a serious barrier to employment and integration for the original migrants, most of whom were employed in factory settings that did not require much linguistic interaction (Tait and Gibson 1987).

As was the case in Greek communities elsewhere in the world, the majority of these immigrants (96%) eventually became Australian citizens (Tamis 2005). Their children, the first Australian generation, moved rapidly into the professions and politics. Despite the legacy of wariness and discrimination toward non-English-speaking communities, these individuals were products of Australian education and had the same cultural exposures as other Australians, which eased their integration into the mainstream. At the same time, they often faced pressure from parents and older relatives to maintain their Greekness and were pushed to marry within the community (Tsolidis 1995). The second generation of individuals of Greek origin born in Australia are even more a part of the larger Australian social and cultural environment. It has been noted that young adults of Greek background are the second largest cultural group to attend universities (Tamis 2005). As native speakers of English (often with limited in Greek) and fully integrated into Australian social and cultural life, this generation is represented in all fields and professions, and its members have become full participants in the Australian mainstream.

The Meaning of Greek Identity

The history of Greek people in Australia served to emphasize certain elements of the collective experience of the community and also reinforced natural divisions that, in some cases, led to internal differences among its members. Passing time and the change of generation has, to some extent, muted some of these conflicts, especially those whose roots were in Greece, but other elements widely viewed by members of the diaspora as fundamental to Greek identity have remained strong, even among members of the second and third Australian-born generations.

Among the earliest Greek immigrants to Australia, region of origin was one of the most significant elements of identity, with individuals identifying strongly with a specific village, island, or town where their family resided (Tamis 2005). This was perhaps not surprising as the practice of chain migration meant that newcomers would live with family members upon their arrival and would then assist other family members to come to Australia when they could. When it was not possible to join family members, many of these early migrants lived with others from their village who were already established (Burnley 1976). This practice solidified ties of origin and meant that people from a specific location tended to settle in the same general area. In the early years of Greek settlement in Australia, there was a significant gender imbalance with as men greatly outnumbering women (Tamis 2005). Many of these men eventually brought a wife from their own village, further strengthening the bond to their region of origin. In fact, it has been noted that among this original generation of migrants, Greeks tended to marry within the group and to prefer a spouse from the same region (Price 1982). Even among the first Australian generation, in-group marriage remained higher for people of Greek origin as compared to other groups, averaging 55–60% (Giorgas and Jones 2002).

The importance of geographic origin in the Greek community has remained high, even as subsequent generations became more integrated into the Australian mainstream (see Afentoulis and Cleland, 2015). The durability of this aspect of identity has been noted, even in the longest established communities, such as those from Castellorizo (Καστελλόριζο) in Perth and from Kythera (Κύθηρα) in Sydney. Tastsoglou (2009) finds that this regional identity is still strong today in the Castellorizian community that began to be established in the 1890s as well as in the Kytherian community which is even older and can be traced back to the 1870s. At present, and especially for those individuals of Greek descent who were born in Australia, the identification with a specific village or region is often most apparent within the community in the form of sporting, cultural, or social groups that align with family origin in Greece. Nonetheless, Greek Australians tend to see themselves as belonging to the wider Australian and Greek populations, suggesting that regional identification is a less immediate aspect of personal identity in the context of diaspora in an English-speaking country (see Chryssanthopoulou 2009). Younger Australians of Greek descent tend to view themselves as part of a larger Greek community in which regional original is less important than their specific cultural background relative to people of other cultures, rather than being a Greek from a specific village or island. This is a reflection of their integration into the Australian context and also of the fact that, even if they have visited Greece, they may never have seen the location their grandparents or other ancestors came from.

The second of the most important markers of Greek identity in Australia is language. The ability to understand and speak Greek has been a sign of community belonging from the Greeks' earliest presence in Australia and was viewed as being of paramount importance by most migrants, especially in terms of the education and upbringing of children and grandchildren (Tamis 2005). The 2016 Australian Census of Population and Housing reports that people of Greek descent make up 1.8% of the Australian population. Greek is spoken at home by 1.2% of the population, making it the sixth most widely used language in Australia. Even among people born in Australia, Greek is reported to be the home language of 0.8% of the population, reflecting language maintenance especially in the first Australian-born generation. The figures for cities with the largest Greek communities are even higher, with 1.5%

of the population of Australia's capital cities speaking Greek, as compared to 1.0% of the population of the nation as a whole. Unlike many of the heritage languages used by various cultural communities in Australia, however, the use of Greek is falling, which, along with Italian, showed a significant drop in users between 2011 and 2016 (id Community 2017).

Throughout their existence and up to the present time, Greek communities around Australia have maintained Greek language schools that were intended to support the maintenance of heritage language and culture by supplementing the English language education of regular schools. These Greek schools have historically been the responsibility of the Greek Orthodox communities, which represent an important structure in the cultural environment. Tsounis (1975b) reports that, by the 1970s, running the Greek schools was the main activity of some of these religious jurisdictions and a number of private Greek schools had come into existence as well in cities with larger populations of Greek origin. At present, Greek is one of Australia's community languages that is associated with a significant cultural group. In the interest of preserving heritage languages and supporting cultural maintenance, funding from state governments is available for such language schools that are also eligible to use government school premises and are represented by Community Languages Australia as well as various state-based organizations of a similar nature. The aims of Community Languages Australia are to raise awareness of the cultural, historical, and linguistic resources of various groups that make up modern multicultural Australia as well as to provide support for the maintenance of linguistic and culture heritage (Community Languages Australia 2018). As is the case with a number of community languages, Greek is generally not available as part of the regular school curriculum but can be counted toward high school graduation and university entrance through the examinations offered by state and territory departments of education that parallel those for the languages taught in regular schools (see, e.g., NSW Education Standards Authority 2018; Victorian Curriculum and Assessment Authority 2018).

Despite the emphasis on language maintenance within the Greek community itself, there is evidence that facility in Greek is declining and many younger individuals do not have the fluency their elders hope for. Members of the first Australian-born generation of Greeks in Australia often developed near native or bilingual ability in Greek because their parents (the original immigrants) spoke little English and needed the assistance of the fluent English-speaking children to interact in English-speaking contexts. This pattern is especially noticeable as the immigrant generation has aged and has needed more healthcare, for example (Avgoulas 2016). Adult children with bilingual ability often need to act as intermediaries for older parents and other relatives who do not have the ability to discuss complex health needs and treatment options in English. While often preferable to the older people involved, problems with this practice have been noted in the context of serious illness as family members tend to present medical information in a form that they feel is easier on the individual who is ill but that does not reflect the full content or its seriousness (see Goldstein et al. 2002). For members of the second and third Australian generation, English tends to be their main language and the one with which they are most comfortable. In practice, this means that their Greek may be limited to some understanding along with use of specific expressions, terms of address, and phrases in communication that takes place primarily in English (Pauwels 2005). Nonetheless, this cultural use of Greek remains an important behavior that identifies the speaker as a member of Greek community and is often central to the individual's sense of identity.

While there is notable shift in the size and nature of the role played by the Greek language in personal and community identity in Australia, religion, specifically membership in the Greek Orthodox church, is more constant. As has been noted in other parts of the world, participation in the faith is for Greek Australians an important element of group identity despite the weakening of the role of religion generally in day-to-day life and a continuing trend toward secularization (Safran 2008). In fact, the Greek Orthodox Church is the largest of the Eastern Orthodox churches in Australia with a membership that rose sharply through the 1950s and 1960s along with the rise in immigration from Greece. At present, 5.5% of the population of Melbourne, which has the largest Greek community in Australia, identifies themselves as belonging to the religion; the comparable figure for Sydney, with the second largest Greek community, is 4.2%. Of the religion community nationwide, 67.3% were born in Europe, North America, or New Zealand; 38.5% were born in Australia with one or both parents born overseas; 16.7% were born in Australia as were both parents; 3.4% were born in Asia or the Middle East; 1.7% were born elsewhere; and 2.3% were born in an unknown or unspecified location (Hughes et al. 2012). These figures correspond roughly to the demographic breakdown of the community, with the proportion of the religious community that was born in Europe representing the immigrant generation that may also be more observant and less affected by broader social change that can impact religious identification. The 38.5% of the religious community that was born in Australia but had one or two parents who were born overseas includes the first Australian generation, many of whom are now middle aged with adolescent or young adult children of their own. Many of these young people are represented in the 16.7% of the religious community, both of whose parents were born in Australia.

The experience of new arrivals in the years of heavy migration from Greece often centered on the church, which was the center of the Greek cultural community. The role of the church in supporting the integration of newcomers into the local environment has been noted in Greek diaspora communities in various parts of the English-speaking world, including in Australia (see Park 1994). While subsequent generations of Greek Australians have tended to attend church less than the immigrant generation, membership in the church has remained important in their personal conceptualization of identity (Watson 2009). It is especially notable that the Greek Orthodox Church in Australia has remained faithful to the practices established in Greece and that have been resilient despite relocation to Australia (Bouma 2006). Even as the language of some churches has begun to shift from Greek to English to accommodate younger members of the congregation, the religious rituals and teachings remain distinctly Greek in nature. This continuity of tradition and practice is important to members of community, and the distinct elements of Orthodox

Christianity that distinguish it from the western church, such as the celebration of Easter based on the Julian rather than Gregorian calendar, is an important identity characteristic among Australians of Greek background.

In many ways, the Greek community in Australia has shown a high level of acculturation and adaptation to the Australian context and now is fully integrated into the English-speaking mainstream (Murray 2018). Nonetheless, many individuals display certain behaviors and activities that they view as deriving from their Greek heritage and that set them apart from Australians of other backgrounds. While some of these practices derive from religion as noted above, others relate more to more commonplace elements of lifestyle, such as food preferences and diet as well as leisure activities.

A typically Greek diet is often integral in the lives of community members. While for the immigrant generation this often related originally to preferences developed early in life, broader potential health benefits of a "Mediterranean diet" have now been widely recognized, and, for this reason, the dietary practices of the Greek community have attracted some attention, based on the observation that life expectancy of Greek immigrants is greater than for most other groups, largely because of a lowered risk of cardiovascular disease (Kouri-Blazos 2002). Interestingly, it has been observed that consumption of a traditional diet is more likely among older members of the community who have less knowledge of medical views of disease prevention (Pillen et al. 2017). This suggests the connection between a Greek diet and identity as a member of the cultural community; by contrast, greater acceptance of the mainstream perspective on health, for this segment of the community at least, has been associated with dietary change and potentially a weakening of Greek identity. Similarly, younger members of the community who were born in Australia often state that they prefer a Greek diet that they feel is healthier than possible alternatives. They identify this view as having been learned from grandparents and older relatives and see it as an integral aspect of their Greek identity (Avgoulas and Fanany 2015). At present, many elements of Greek cuisine and cooking, as well as specific dishes, are fairly well-known in Australia, both because of the presence of sizeable Greek communities and also because of the popularizing effect of the food and cooking industry. However, many of these items and dishes are referred to in Greek by Australians of Greek background, even if they primarily speak English and are not fluent users of Greek (Avgoulas and Fanany 2016). Overall, the link between food, language, and Greek identity is very strong, even among the youngest members of the community, many of whom take great pride in eating a Greek diet (at least some of the time) and are convinced of the superiority of Greek food over other choices.

The desire to maintain a traditional diet to the extent possible in Australia is closely related to gardening as a leisure activity among members of the Greek community. Australia's comparatively mild, temperate climate makes it possible to grow many of the herbs, fruits, and vegetables familiar in Greece, and the idea that fresh food produced oneself is better and healthier than the same items from stores is very strong, especially among older Greek Australians (Pillen et al. 2017). Again, this idea is prevalent among members of the Australian-born generations as well as among older people and is recognized as being based on the views of grandparents that were formed in Greece (Avgoulas and Fanany 2018). The popularity of gardening among Greek communities in various parts of the English-speaking world has been noted and is often seen by the individuals involved as a typically Greek pastime (see, e.g., Trichopoulou et al. 1995; Aptekar 2015; Gerodetti and Foster 2015). Recently, there have been efforts to transmit the importance of the home garden to younger members of the Greek Australian community as well as to young people more generally. An example of this is a Greek-Mediterranean garden in Melbourne created by its owner to reflect his upbringing in Cyprus (Κύπρος) and serve as a teaching milieu for both adults and children (see Harrison 2015).

Participation in cultural or leisure activities that are seen as Greek or exist within the Greek community is also strongly associated with identity as a Greek Australian. The importance of sports as part of the acculturation process for immigrants to Australia has been noted (Lock et al. 2008), and soccer teams in particular have historically been linked with specific national origins. This has on occasion resulted in clashes among fans that were triggered by world events, such as conflict between their nations of origin (Skinner et al. 2008). At present, men's and women's Greek Australian soccer teams at the junior and senior levels still compete in the Hellenic Cup that was established in the 1960s in response to the interest among the growing population of Greek immigrants (see Hellenic Cup 2018). Many of the participating teams have a historic connection to various regions in Greece through the origin of their founding members. Other pastimes, such as traditional dancing, are also popular among members of the Australian Greek community. While individuals of all ages often take part in this activity, folk dancing tends to be seen by younger members of the community as a way of expressing their Greek identity and engaging in an activity that is important to their older relatives because it continues a tradition brought from Greece (Gardner et al. 2008). For many members of the first and subsequent Australian generations, participation in Greek dancing, along with eating a Greek diet, using Greek, and carrying out the rituals of the Orthodox Church, creates a self-perception of bicultural identity that gives validity to their experience as part of the Australian mainstream alongside their participation in an Australian shaping of Greek culture and traditions.

Change in the Australian Greek Community

The experience of the Greek community in Australia has been marked by acculturation, and the rapid movement of individuals of Greek background into the professions and all sectors of the economy has been marked (Tamis 2009b). At the same time, this adaptation to the English-speaking environment has not resulted in a loss of Greekness in the perception of the majority of the community, as demonstrated in the continued importance of family origin in Greece, religious affiliation and observance, maintenance of the Greek language, and lifestyle characteristics associated with their heritage. However, it has been observed that many Greek Australians are similar in much of their behavior to the English-speaking population but tend to differ in terms of values. The collectivist orientation of the Greek family remains strong in the Australian diaspora (Rosenthal et al. 1989), with young people expressing attachment to the views and perceptions of parents and grandparents because they see them as representing the Greek way (Avgoulas and Fanany 2015, 2018). In terms of behavioral norms, though, members of the Greek community tend to be similar to their counterparts from an English-speaking background, suggesting that acculturation has been more associated with behavior, while a characteristic Greek identity might be more associated with values (Rosenthal et al. 1989). Certainly, especially among younger members of the community, this appears to be the case, with the exception of a comparatively small number of activities specifically associated with being Greek. Typically, individuals who were born in Australia feel themselves to be Greek in certain largely intangible ways that relate to feelings, perceptions, attitudes, and choices that they connect to their heritage and that were learned from older relatives based on these relatives' experience and interpretation of life in Greece as well as the migrant experience. This distinctive position of belonging to two separate cultures with certain overlapping domains is very much characteristic of members of the Australian Greek community, but there is some indication that there has been a shift down the generations from the predominance of Greek identity to a self-conception among younger people that they are Australian of Greek descent (see Avgoulas and Fanany 2015, 2018). This situation has been viewed as an example of "social incorporation" attesting to the success of Australian multiculturalism, at least in the case of the Greek community (Dimitreas 1998).

The shift in identity perception among Greek Australians is especially observable in terms of language use and linguistic behavior more broadly. The migrant generation arrived in Australia speaking only or mostly Greek. The differences between Greek and English, in a linguistic sense, as well as the migrants' educational level, employment status, and a range of other personal and group factors made it difficult for many of these now older adults to master English to a high level. In the years prior to World War II, segregation in employment and living arrangements as well as the need to both offer support and accept it from others solidified links of heritage and origin that also worked to maintain language use in the immigrant community. However, increasing integration manifested by geographic and social movement in the Australian-born generations has resulted in an increasing rate of language shift from Greek to English, even though it has been suggested that Greek has the highest degree of intergenerational loyalty among Australia's community languages (Tamis 2009a). There is also some evidence that Greeks have long been aware of the connection between language and cultural identity and that language functions as a social marker in this context (Tsounis 1975a). On the one hand, domains of experience that are closely associated with the perception of cultural identity, such as family and the Greek Orthodox religion, are extremely important to the Australian Greek community and may serve to preserve the language alongside English (Tamis et al. 1993; Kipp and Clyne 2003). On the other, each generation born in Australia shows a growing decline in ability to speak Greek that corresponds to an increasing use of English, consistent with rising participation in mainstream Australian society (Clyne and Kipp 2002).

For young adults, who are typically members of the second or third Australian-born generations, Greek usage may be limited to a set of terms that relate to family (such as terms of address, names of relationships, such as γιαγιά "grandmother," παππού "grandfather"), religion (Ευχέλαιο "Holy Unction," Πάτερ Ημών "Lord's Prayer"), or food (σέλινο "celery," ρίγανη "oregano," χαμομήλι "chamomile tea"). Individuals in this age group often express a strong desire to "be Greek" but do not share the emotional attachment to the Greek language that their grandparents and other members of the immigrant generation express. Much of their knowledge about Greece and Greek culture is superficial because they have grown up in Australia and have gained much of their understanding through the medium of English. If they have visited Greece, it was as a tourist, often in the company of parents and other family members. They also differ from their own parents, in that they do not have the ambivalence that has characterized the experience of the first Australian-born generation whose members occupied a transitional status between the Greekness of their often non-English-speaking parents and their own desire to be accepted as part of Australian society. Younger individuals also tend to be proud of and willing to publicly acknowledge their Greek heritage, albeit in a form that is highly contextualized to the Australian social environment and conceptualized primarily in English (Avgoulas 2016). Interestingly, many of these younger Greek Australians share the view of their elders that mastery of Greek is an important aspect of cultural identity in Australia and hope that the language will be maintained. Nonetheless, this may be increasingly difficult as the original immigrant generation is gradually replaced by their children who tend to view themselves as primarily English speakers and, in fact, mostly use English in their daily lives (see Avgoulas and Fanany 2016).

By contrast, affiliation with the Greek Orthodox Church remains a very significant element in the lives of many younger Greek Australians. Despite a national trend away from organized religion in this age group overall as well as a shrinking number of Australians who identify themselves as Greek Orthodox (Bouma and Halahoff 2017), young Greek Australians tend to believe that their religion is very important, even if they do not attend church on a regular basis and do not practice their faith in the same way their parents and grandparents did (Avgoulas and Fanany 2015). This situation is especially interesting as it has been noted that the importance of religion to younger people has been declining in Greece itself. A recent Pew Research Report found that differences in generational views on the importance of being Christian in the context of national identity were largest in Greece, where 65% of older individuals agreed that affiliation with the Church was integral to national identity, while only 39% of younger people held a similar view. In Australia, only 13% of the public feels that it is necessary to be Christian to be Australian (Stokes 2017). This underscores the importance of the Greek Orthodox faith in the conceptualization of personal identity among Greek Australians because it is associated with their cultural and heritage identity, not with their position in the public or national context. It is not surprising, then, that religion serves as an important source of resilience for many Greek Australians of all generations and supplies both practices and strategies for coping with adversity (Avgoulas and Fanany 2015; Avgoulas 2016).

Greek Identity in the Future

There can be no doubt that Australian Greekness is developing and will likely change greatly in the future. One important factor in this is the inevitable change of generation. Most of the members of the large waves of immigrants who came to Australia before and in the decades following World War II are now elderly. Their children, who are well-established in the Australian mainstream, are increasingly taking over the social roles their parents have played as elders in the community. Their own children, the second Australian generation, are Australian in behavior, attitudes and language use to a degree that far surpasses that of their older relatives and also tend to view themselves as Australians of Greek descent, rather than as Greeks living in Australia as their grandparents did. While there is evidence that these younger Greek Australians share many of the values of their parents and grandparents (see Rosenthal et al. 1989), their understanding of life in Greece, the most significant elements of Greek culture, and what it means to be Greek in the day-to-day context derives largely from the memories and impressions of their grandparents, rather than from personal experience or observations in Greece. This maintenance of traditions but also elements of daily life by members of the immigrant generation through transmission to their children and grandchildren has resulted in very specific conceptualizations of identity that are increasingly filtered through the lens of life in Australia (see Cleland 2013). This identity has been characterized as "hybrid," assigning equivalent status to being Greek and being Australian, despite the fact "Greekness," however conceptualized, dominates the self-conceptualization of Greek Australians of all generations (Kefallinos 2012).

Cohen (1997: 180) identified a set of characteristics common to the experience of diaspora, namely, dispersal from an original homeland, which may have resulted from negative events or may have been triggered by a search for employment, opportunity, or to satisfy colonial ambitions; a collective memory embodying a group view about the region of origin; an idealized conceptualization of the ancestral home; a return movement; a strong group consciousness based on shared cultural characteristics and maintained over time; a problematic position in the host society; solidarity with other members of the cultural group in other countries; and the possibility of a satisfying experience fostering well-being in the host country. Many of these characteristics have been observed to apply to the Greek community in Australia as has the durability of language, religion, and family values and relationships in marking identity in the cultural community (Tsolidis 2003). The result is the situation often mentioned by individuals of Greek background who were born in Australia; they feel Greek in Australia where the distinctively Greek elements of their identity stand out in contrast to the English-background mainstream, but they feel Australian in Greece where the aspects of their perceptions, attitudes, and behavior that correspond to Australian norms are more visible (see Kefallinos 2012; Avgoulas and Fanany 2015, 2018).

This is an especially illuminating aspect of the Australian Greek identity that directly parallels the experience of people of Greek origin in other locations, such as the United States, Canada, or various European countries (see, e.g., Christou 2006;

King and Christou 2014). The existence of two separate identities is a characterizing feature of the experience of individuals of Greek background living in numerous diaspora locations, including Australia. The Greek component of personal identity often seems very marked against the Australian mainstream culture because it appears to differ considerably in a number of important domains that signify Greekness, including language, religion, food culture, and family structure. Nonetheless, for Greek Australians, as has been observed in other diaspora locations as well, a visit to Greece tends to emphasize the fact that they are also characteristically Australian in outlook, attitudes, and behavior. Just as their Greek identity is most apparent in comparison to other Australians of different background, their Australian identity is distinctive in the Greek context which is, to all Greek Australians except the now elderly migrant generation, a foreign culture. While Greek Australians commonly note the importance of the views and experiences of older relatives in shaping their knowledge of Greece and Greek ways, it is often not until they experience the modern culture of Greece firsthand that they realize that their Greekness incorporates a strong cultural memory that has evolved in diaspora and reflects, not only the experiences of older relatives in Greece but also their subsequent lives in Australia. At the same time, younger people especially are often unaware of the importance of Australian behaviors and attitudes in their own day-to-day life and the degree to which their experience has shaped the behaviors and perceptions they associate with being Greek. In this, the fact that they are largely English speaking is also significant, as the primary language of use determines many aspects of cognition, including the intangible concept of "worldview" that reflects the social environment in which a person lives (see Koltko-Rivera 2004, for discussion of this).

Conclusion: Australian Greekness – The Formation of a New Cultural Identity

At the present time, almost 50 years since the peak in migration, what it means to be Greek in Australia has changed significantly. The original immigrants saw themselves as Greek people who were living in a society that used a different language and that had many customs and practices that were different and strange, compared to those they were used to in their homeland. Nonetheless, these original migrants settled and succeeded across Australia and especially in its cities and larger towns. Their children, who were born in Australia, were compelled by necessity to bridge the gap between their immigrant parents and the larger Australian society of which they were a part by virtue of their education and life experiences. This generation suffered greatly from a sense of separateness and bias against individuals from non-English-speaking communities. Even so, they continued to move into the Australian mainstream, experiencing remarkable success as measured by integration, acculturation, and professional standing. Their children, in many cases second generation Australians, are, in many ways, more Australian than they are Greek, if their parents and grandparents are used as the standard. They remain characteristically and distinctively Greek, however, in terms of their affinity for the Greek language, their adherence to the religious faith of their ancestors and to the Greek way of life, as it has been translated to the Australian context, as well as in many of their values and attitudes.

These younger individuals, many of whom are now adolescents or young adults, will be the drivers of the continuation of a specific Australian Greek identity in the future and will shape what it means to be Greek based on their generation's experiences. This identity will develop alongside a feeling of full membership in the Australian mainstream that was not enjoyed by their parents and grandparents. It has been noted, for example, that some younger Greek Australians have adopted the term "wog," widely used in Australia in the 1970s and 1980s to denote members of migrant cultures especially from Southern Europe and the Near East, to refer to their own group. Rather than representing the racism the term might have suggested to their parents, it seems to connote a sense of solidarity and outsider status that has been aligned with similar ironic terms used by young people from other groups, such as American Blacks (Tsolidis and Pollard 2009). This same stance has been seen in a number of works of popular culture, such as the play, *Wogs Out of Work*, which was extremely successful and toured for several years beginning in 1987; the television sitcom, *Acropolis Now*, that ran from 1989 to 1992 on the Australian Seven Network; and the comedy film, *The Wog Boy*, that appeared in 2000.

As deeply ingrained as the specific Australian conceptualization of Greekness is in younger members of the community, it is interesting to note that members of the second Australian generation are increasingly turning back to Greece for insight and understanding of their own background. This is occurring as a result of technological development that makes it possible for people anywhere in the world to participate in virtual communities on the Internet. Many younger Australians of Greek background are using the Internet to participate in forums that center on the interests of members of diaspora communities around the world, such as Greek cooking, traditional dancing and folklore, history, cultural events, and politics and current issues in the Greek world. By contrast, older members of the community, often because of limitations in language, tend to watch Greek programming on television and radio through the SBS (Special Broadcasting Service, a public channel that broadcasts non-English language programming) and use the Internet (often tutored by children and grandchildren) to stay in contact with friends and family (Avgoulas 2016). YouTube is also a popular platform among younger users that allows them to view videos on numerous aspects of Greek culture and that also can provide exposure to language use. Social media and Internet sites may serve to reinforce ties to a particular region of Greece as well (Afentoulis and Clelland 2015).

The use of the Internet to create a hybrid identity has been noted in many locations and contexts (see, e.g., Androutsopoulos 2006; Brinkerhoff 2009). It serves this function for many second-generation Greek Australians who are trying to understand their own sense of dual identity by supplementing and building on their cultural knowledge through their own explorations of the virtual environment. Much of this includes interaction with members of other English-speaking Greek diaspora communities in the United States, Canada, and elsewhere (see, e.g., Panagakos 2003) and reflects the increasing tendency for younger people to elaborate their Greek cultural identity in English, the language they are most comfortable with. This, in itself, represents an important change in the components of Greek identity in Australia, where there are indications that facility in the Greek language may be decreasing in significance as an identity marker. This trend is likely to continue in the future, especially as intermarriage with people of other cultural backgrounds is prevalent in the Greek community in Australia. Some estimates suggest that two thirds of individuals marry out by the third generation. By comparison, only 12% of the immigrant generation married people of non-Greek origin (Khoo et al. 2009). This is likely a reflection of the level of integration of people of Greek background into the Australian mainstream, including in terms of language, and the fact that the other characteristics that are indicative of Greek identity are viewed by both Greeks and non-Greeks as compatible in the context of Australian multiculturism.

The future of Greek Australian identity then might be expected to be based on a Greek way of life, as developed and understood in the Australian context, and especially the associated food culture which has become more mainstream in recent years because of the interest in the Mediterranean diet as a preventive for chronic disease; membership in the Greek Orthodox Church, even as participation in organized religious practice is declining overall in Australia; and increasing use of English as the mediating language, associated with the linguistic practices of the younger generations born and brought up in Australia. At the same time, it might be expected that the Greek Australian identity will continue to be enriched by an increasingly eclectic mixture of cultural influences collected by individuals through social media and Internet exploration of their heritage as well as personal experiences, often in relation to other diaspora communities as well as with Greece itself. In this, the Australian conceptualization of Greekness seems to be taking on a more transnational veneer but is, at the same time, increasingly Australian in character because of its context and the unique manner in which it has come into existence.

References

Afentoulis M, Cleland A (2015) Diaspora at the crossroads: the future of Greek communities in Australia – a case study of two regional migrant communities. In: Miletic N, Vekemans T (eds) Discovering diaspora – a multidisciplinary approach. Inter-Disciplinary Press, Oxford, UK, pp 37–48

Alexakis E, Janiszweski L (2016) Greek cafes and milk bars of Australia. Halstead Press, Ultimo

Allimonos C (2002) Pre-World War II Greek community organizations in Australia. Unpublished thesis. La Trobe University, Melbourne

Androutsopoulos J (2006) Multilingualism, diaspora, and the Internet: codes and identities on German-based diaspora websites. J Socioling 10:520–547

Aptekar S (2015) Visions of public space: reproducing and resisting social hierarchies in a community garden. Sociol Forum 30:209–227

Avgoulas M-I (2016) Health beliefs and practices in three generations of Greek Australian women in Melbourne. Unpublished thesis. Deakin University, Melbourne

Avgoulas M-I, Fanany R (2015) The Greek diaspora of Melbourne, Australia, through the eyes of second generation Greek Australians. Athens J Soc Sci 2:99–108

Avgoulas M-I, Fanany R (2016) Greek as a marker of identity in Melbourne, Australia. In: Gavriilidou S, Gkaintartzi A, Markou E, Tsokalidou R (eds) 3rd crossroads of languages and cultures: issues of bi-/multilingualism, translanguaging, and language policies in education. Aristotle University of Thessaloniki/Polydromo, Athens, pp 4–10

Avgoulas M-I, Fanany R (2018) Conflicted identity across the generations of Greek-Australian women: the Greek diaspora in Melbourne, Australia. Athens J Soc Sci 5:79–95

Bouma G (2006) Australian soul: spirituality in the twenty-first century. Cambridge University Press, Melbourne

Bouma G, Halahoff A (2017) Australia's changing religious profile – rising nones and Pentacostals, declining British Protestants in superdiversity: views from the 2016 census. J Acad Stud Relig 30:129–143

Brinkerhoff J (2009) Digital diasporas: identity and transnational engagement. Cambridge University Press, New York

Burnley IH (1976) Greek settlement in Sydney 1947–1971. Aust Geogr 13:200–214

Christou A (2006) Deciphering diaspora – translating transnationalism: family dynamics, identity constructions and the legacy of 'home' in second-generation Greek-American return migration. Ethn Racial Stud 29:1040–1056

Chryssanthopoulou V (2009) Gender and ethno-regional identity among Greek Australians: intersections. In: Tastsoglou E (ed) Labor, community and identity in Greek migrations. Lexington Books, Lanham, pp 135–152

Cleland A (2013) The pear tree: a study of Greek-Australian families 50 years after migration. In: Tsianikas M, Maadad N, Couvalis G, Palaktsoglou M (eds) Greek research in Australia: proceedings of the biennial international conference of Greek studies, Flinders University June 2011. Flinders University Department of Language Studies – Modern Greek, Adelaide, pp 478–489

Clyne M, Kipp S (2002) Australia's changing language demography. People Place 10:29–35

Cohen R (1997) Global Diasporas: An Introduction, UCL Press, London.

Community Languages Australia (2018) About us. Available from: Community Languages Australia. http://www.communitylanguagesaustralia.org.au/aboutus/. Accessed 22 Aug 2018

Dimitreas YE (1998) Transplanting the agora: Hellenic settlement in Australia. Allen & Unwin, St Leonards

Gardner SM, Komesaroff P, Fensham R (2008) Dancing beyond exercise: young people's experiences in dance classes. J Youth Stud 11:701–709

Gerodetti N, Foster S (2015) "Growing food from home": food production, migrants and the changing cultural landscape of gardens and allotments. Landsc Res 41:808–819

Giorgas D, Jones FL (2002) Intermarriage patterns and social cohesion among first, second and later generation Australians. J Popul Res 19:47–64

Glytsos NP, Katseli LT (2005) Greek migration: the two faces of Janus. In: Zimmermann KS (ed) European migration: what do we know? Oxford University Press, Oxford, pp 337–388

Goldstein D, Thewes B, Butow P (2002) Communicating in a multicultural society II: Greek community attitudes toward cancer in Australia. Intern Med J 32:289–296

Harrison F (2015) Garden as education: learning the 'old ways' of traditional Mediterranean food practices. Landsc Rev 16:74–76

Hawkins F (1989) Critical years in immigration: Canada and Australia compared. New South Wales University Press, Kensington

Hellenic Cup (2018) Hellenic Cup history. Available from Hellenic Cup. http://www.helleniccup.com.au/08/08comp/history.html. Accessed 23 Aug 2018

Hughes PJ, Fraser M, Reid SB (2012) Australia's religious communities: facts and figures from the 2011 Australian census and other sources. Christian Research Association, Melbourne

Id Community (2017) Australia: language spoken at home. Available from id Community Demographic Resources. https://profile.id.com.au/australia/language. Accessed 20 Aug 2018

Kefallinos E (2012) Multiple intergenerational identities: Greek-Australian women across generations. Modern Greek Stud (Australia and New Zealand) Special Issue 173–193

Khoo S-E, Birrell B, Heard G (2009) Intermarriage by birthplace and ancestry in Australia. People Place 17:15–28

King R, Christou A (2014) Second generation "return" to Greece: new dynamics of transnationalism and return. Int Migr 52:85–99

Kipp S, Clyne M (2003) Trends in the shift from community languages: insights from the 2001 census. People Place 11:33–41

Koltko-Rivera ME (2004) The psychology of worldviews. Rev Gen Psychol 8:3–58

Kouris-Blazos A (2002) Morbidity mortality paradox of 1st generation Greek Australians. Asia Pac J Clin Nutr 11:S569–S575

Lock D, Taylor T, Darcy S (2008) Soccer and social transition in Australia: social networks in transition. In: Nicholson M, Hoye R (eds) Sport and social capital. Butterworth-Heinemann, Oxford, UK/Burlington, pp 317–338

Murray JC (2018) "You speak Greek well... (for an Australian)": homeland visits and diaspora identity. Diaspora 20:65–86

NSW Education Standards Authority (2018) Languages stage 6. Available from New South Wales Education Standards Authority. http://educationstandards.nsw.edu.au/wps/portal/nesa/11-12/stage-6-learning-areas/stage-6-languages. Accessed 20 Aug 2018

Ongley P, Pearson D (1995) Post-1945 international migration: New Zealand, Australia and Canada compared. Int Migr Rev 29:765–793

Panagakos A (2003) Downloading new identities: ethnicity, technology and media in the global Greek village. Identities: Glob Stud Cult Power 10:201–219

Park C (1994) Sacred worlds: an introduction to geography and religion. Routledge, London

Pauwels A (2005) Maintaining the community language in Australia: challenges and roles for families. Int J Biling Educ Biling 8:142–131

Pillen H, Tsourtos G, Coveney J, Thodis A, Itsiopoulos C, Kouris-Blazos A (2017) Retaining traditional Greek dietary practices among Greek immigrants to Australia: the role of ethnic identity. Ecol Food Nutr 56:312–328

Price CA (1982) International migration: contribution to growth and distribution of Australian population. In Population of Australia volume 1. ESCAP country monogram series 9. United Nations, New York, pp 46–70

Rosenthal DA, Bell R, Demetriou A, Efklides A (1989) From collectivism to individualism: the acculturation of Greek immigrants in Australia. Int J Psychol 24:51–71

Safran W (2008) Language, ethnicity and religion: a persistent link. Nations Nationalism 14:171–190

Skinner J, Zakus DH, Edwards A (2008) Coming in from the margins: ethnicity, community support and the rebranding of Australian soccer. Soccer Soc 9:394–404

Stokes B (2017) Religion and national belonging: do you have to be Christian to be "one of us"? Religion and the Public Sphere 29 March. Blog

Tait D, Gibson K (1987) Economic and ethnic restructuring: an analysis of migrant labour in Sydney. J Intercult Stud 8:1–26

Tamis AM (2000) The history of Greeks in Australia (1958–1975), vol II. Ellikon Press, Melbourne

Tamis AM (2005) The greeks in Australia, Cambridge University Press, New York.

Tamis AM (2009a) The Greek language in contact with English in Australia. Etudes Helleniques 17:20–42

Tamis AM (2009b) The Greeks in Australia. Cambridge University Press, Cambridge, MA

Tamis AM, Gauntlett S, Petrou S (1993) Unlocking Australia's language potential: Profiles of 9 key languages in Australia. Vol. 8: Modern Greek. National Languages and Literacy Institute of Australia, Canberra

Tastsoglou E (2009) Women, gender and diasporic lives: labor, community and identity in Greek migrations. Lexington Books, Lanham

Testskhladze GR (2008) Greek colonisation: an account of Greek colonies and other settlements overseas. Brill, Leiden/Boston

Trichopoulou A, Kouris-Blazos A, Wahlqvist ML, Gnardelis C et al (1995) Diet and overall survival in elderly people. BMJ 311:1457–1460

Tsolidis G (1995) Greek-Australian families. In: Hartley R (ed) Families and cultural diversity in Australia. Allen and Unwin/AIFS, St Leonards, pp 121–143

Tsolidis G (2003) Mothers, memories and cultural imaginings. Επιθεώρηση Κοινωνικών Ερευνών 110:141–163

Tsolidis G, Pollard V (2009) Being a 'wog' in Melbourne – young people's self-fashioning through discourses of racism. Discourse: Stud Cult Polit Educ 30:427–442

Tsounis MP (1975a) Greek communities in Australia. In: Price C (ed) Greeks in Australia. Australian National University Press, Canberra, pp 18–71

Tsounis MP (1975b) Greek ethnic schools in Australia. Int Migr Rev 9:345–359

Victorian Curriculum and Assessment Authority (2018) Victorian certificate of education (VCE): list of studies – languages. Available from Victorian Curriculum and Assessment Authority. https://www.vcaa.vic.edu.au/Pages/vce/studies/lote/lotelistindex.aspx. Accessed 20 Aug 2018

Watson S (2009) Performing religion: migrants, the church and belonging in Marrickville, Sydney. Cult Relig: Interdiscip J 10:317–338

Italian Identity in the United States

63

Stefano Luconi

Contents

Introduction	1204
The Identity of the *Risorgimento* Émigrés	1205
Campanilismo on the Other Shore of the Atlantic	1206
Anti-Italian Prejudice and the Reshaping of Ethnic Identity	1208
The Making of Italianness	1210
The Retention of the Italian Identity at Wartime	1212
The Decline of the Italian Identity	1214
Post-Ethnic Identity	1217
Conclusion	1218
Cross-References	1219
References	1219

Abstract

Italy's belated completion of political unification in 1861 let the Italian people long retain a regional, provincial, and even local identity. Likewise, the newcomers who arrived in the United States from different places in Italy between the late 1870s and the closing of mass immigration in the mid-1920s found it difficult to perceive themselves as members of the same ethnic minority and shied away from one another not only in areas of residence but also in social and religious life at the beginning of their stay in America. By the late 1930s, however, the emergence and consolidation of nationalistic feelings, following both Italy's entry into World War I and Fascist aggressive foreign policy, immigration restriction, the appearance of a US-born second generation with loose ties to the forebears' land, and, primarily, the experience of anti-Italian intolerance and discrimination in the United States made people of Italian descent aware of their common national ancestry and helped them develop an Italian identity that they or their

S. Luconi (✉)
Department of Education (DISFOR), University of Genoa, Genoa, Italy
e-mail: Stefano.Luconi@unige.it

parents had lacked upon settling in the United States. Racial tensions and the backlash at blacks' supposed encroachments in the postwar decades encouraged many Italian Americans to join forces with other immigrant groups of European origin from which they had previously distanced themselves. They, therefore, acquired a racial sense of belonging as white Europeans and nowadays retain an Italian identity only at a symbolic level, almost exclusively in leisure time activities.

Keywords

Campanilismo · Ethnic defensiveness · Immigration · Italian Americans · Racial unrest · Symbolic ethnicity · Whiteness

Introduction

In Austrian Chancellor Klemens von Metternich's notorious phrase, in the mid-nineteenth century, Italy was a mere "geographical expression." The peninsula and its islands had been divided among foreign possessions, regional states, and the papal sovereignty for centuries. Consequently, nobody was able to claim loyalty to such a nonexistent entity and Italians could not be regarded as a people. The establishment of the Reign of Italy in 1861 – at the end of the first phase of the *Risorgimento*, the struggle for the consolidation of the Italian regions into a single state – did not produce a major change to the self-perception of the bulk of the population living in the recently created kingdom. According to nationalist statesman Massimo D'Azeglio, the political unification of the country "made Italy," but it failed to "make Italians." In this view, the prolonged partition of the Italian territory into separate states still let most inhabitants of the new realm hang on to a regional, provincial, and even local sense of belonging in the second half of the nineteenth century (Griffin 1997, 139).

The term *campanilismo* (after *campanile*, the Italian word for bell tower) aptly expressed such a parochial identity and implied that people's allegiance hardly went beyond the earshot of the bells of their respective home villages (Manconi 2003). US sociologist Edward C. Banfield (1958) reported that, as late as the mid-1950s, especially in the southern regions of the country, a district that coincided with the major areas of emigration, the average Italian was unable to conceive any interest or affiliation transcending the nuclear family or the fellow villagers' narrow circle.

This same attitude at first shaped the identity of the members of the Italian diaspora in the United States at the time of the mass exodus across the Atlantic between the late 1870s and the mid-1920s. In those decades more than four million people resettled from Italy to the United States. At the beginning of their stay in the host society – unlike their predecessors who had moved to America mainly as political émigrés in the wake of the initially unsuccessful outcome of the *Risorgimento* – few of these newcomers for primarily economic reasons thought of themselves as Italians. Instead, a large majority revealed an attachment based on the respective local extractions in the native country. In due time, however, as a reaction to hostile and nativistic feelings by individuals who were unable to appreciate the immigrants' diverse regional roots and in response to the spread of patriotic sentiments arising from their former homeland in the years between World War I and World War II, the Italians and their children in the United States eventually developed an ethnic identity founded on their common national origins.

In the following decades, however, the renegotiation of Italian Americans' attachment underwent additional transformations. Most notably, the backlash at African Americans' alleged encroachments caused the immigrants' descendants to regard themselves as white Europeans and to close ranks with members of other ethnic minorities from European backgrounds. Nonetheless, the Italian identity did not disappear completely. It is nowadays relegated mainly to a symbolic dimension influencing leisure time activities and consumer choices rather than significant decisions in life.

The Identity of the *Risorgimento* Émigrés

The United States was not a major destination for the Italian diaspora until the late 1870s. From 1820 to 1870 as few as roughly 25,000 immigrants arrived from Italy out of the overall inflow tide of almost 7,400,000 newcomers to the United States. Many of these newcomers were refugees and exiles who had fled their native land or had been deported from it in the aftermath of the early defeats in the political initiatives, military campaigns, and popular insurrections by the various movements that planned to end foreign rule and to consolidate the indigenous entities ruling the Italian peninsula and its islands into a single national state.

Such émigrés – who briefly included Giuseppe Garibaldi, the gallant albeit unsuccessful defender of the Roman Republic in 1849, after a momentarily overthrow of the papal power, and the subsequent conqueror of Sicily and Naples on behalf of the first king of modern Italy in 1860 – were fully aware of their Italianness (Doyle 2017). Their patriotic commitment to Italy's independence and unification was the reason for their forced or voluntary banishment to the United States. Moreover, even after landing in the host country, they continued to promote the formation of a single Italian state. They wrote articles and made speeches to enhance the cause of the *Risorgimento* not only among fellow Italian immigrants who had chosen America to pursue better economic opportunities but also within the US political establishment and intellectual circles. They also raised money to fund upheavals and military operations aiming at Italy's political unification. In particular, as the northeastern regions were under the government of Vienna, they endeavored to fuel the flames of anti-Austrian feelings in the United States. Specifically, several exiles who taught Italian language and literature to earn a living abroad made a point of inserting patriot and dramatist Silvio Pellico's *Le mie prigioni* into Italy's literary canon. Despite its poor aesthetical value, this book – published in Italian in 1832 and translated into English as *My imprisonment* for Harper the following year – was an emotional account of the atrocious sufferings its author had undertaken during his detention in the Spielberg fortress and, therefore, seemed a proper means to stir the hostility of the US public opinion against the Austrian empire with regard to the latter's mistreatment of Italian patriots. The fact that, when political conditions looked favorable, some of these refugees did not hesitate to return to Italy and to participate again in the struggle for their native land's unity and self-determination offered further evidence of their vibrant Italian consciousness.

Campanilismo on the Other Shore of the Atlantic

The *Risorgimento* exiles' strong Italian identity was an exception. As the diaspora from Italy gained momentum in the last quarter of the nineteenth century and such a mass tide brought primarily economic immigrants to the United States, these people's sense of ethnicity revealed a significant lack of national self-perception and fell within the realm of *campanilismo*. Most newcomers defined themselves by their association with their native hamlet rather than with their country of origin. Remarkably, at the turn of the twentieth century, a native of Campania observed that "for me, as for the others, Italy is the little village where I was raised" (Williams 1938, 17).

In addition, disparate dialects and traditions, along with local antipathies and rivalries, separated immigrants who were born in different places in Italy. Author Joseph Napoli's recollections about his mother, a newcomer from the province of Messina, is a case in point for the hostility and misrepresentations that split the newcomers along lines of local origins. In his son's words, Ms Napoli despised fellow Sicilians from other areas of this island and even abhorred people from different regions of the country. As he put it, "Her special detestation was reserved for the Neapolitans. [...] She hated them openly. [...] With the index and little finger of her left hand she threw 'corni' – horns – at their home or when she saw them in the distance. She crossed the street to avoid walking near the house or near them, thus eluding their malice and their own potent evil eye. She hoped the horns would cause the malefactors to be stricken with indescribable diseases, the unmarried daughters to be impregnated by devils, and the family reduced to beggary" (Napoli 1986, 58–59).

It was primarily the Italian people's northern-southern divide that underwent a replica across the Atlantic in the United States. To Amalia Santacaterina, a woman from Veneto, in the country's northern district, newcomers from Calabria, in the nation's South, were so backward that they "even lower[ed] themselves as to go to pick up coal with the buckets" (Serra 2007, 125). Writer Marion Benasutti (1966, 3), the American-born daughter of a couple of Italians, aptly pointed out that northerner and southerner immigrants were "practically enemy aliens" to one another in their adoptive land.

Chain migration contributed to keeping local allegiances alive and sometimes even strengthened them. The Italian diaspora reached the United States mainly by means of chain migration through family and village connections. The pioneers in each settlement on American soil sent for relatives and acquaintances, who were usually from the same native places of their predecessors, and provided the newcomers with accommodation either in their own homes or within the same neighborhood. There the immigrants could continue to speak their dialect and to interact with individuals they were familiar with. Consequently, people from the same villages tended to band together and to reproduce the same social milieu they had come from. As sociologist Caroline F. Ware (1935, 155) has stressed, in Italian districts, such as New York City's Greenwich Village, "informal social relations [...] were almost wholly restricted to people from the same town or province." Therefore, instead of cohesive Little Italies, people from the Italian peninsula gave birth to patchworks of colonies mirroring the local divisions in the land of their origin. Referring to New York City a few years before World War I, the Italian vice-consul Luigi Villari (1912, 216) noted that "some neighborhoods are inhabited exclusively by newcomers from a given region; we can find only Sicilians in a street, only people from Calabria in another street, and immigrants from Abruzzi in a third one." A number of provincial and local enclaves could be identified even within the regional settlements. For example, Chicago's ethnic district of Little Sicily had a concentration of immigrants from the village of Altavilla along Larraba Street, natives of Bagheria in Townsend Street, and individuals from Sambuca-Zabat in Milton Street. Whole villages were sometimes transplanted to the United States. This was the case of Lapio, a small center in the province of Avellino, whose residents moved to a single district in Boston's North End. Likewise, Roseto, Pennsylvania, was home almost entirely to immigrants from the village of Roseto Valforte in Puglia. The residents' sense of community was so circumscribed in Roseto that, since they were often short and usually had light brown skin, they regarded individuals from Veneto who had moved to nearby townships in Pennsylvania as members of a different ethnic group made up of tall, blue-eyed, and fair-haired people.

Separation along lines of local descent extended to religious life. The great bulk of Italian immigrants were Catholics. But residual paganism and absence of formal observance contrasted the practices of southern Italians with the more orthodox rites of their northerner fellow citizens. As a result, the former and the latter shied away from each other so as they could stick to their own traditions. For example, New York City's churchgoers from northerner backgrounds in Italy did not want to attend services with Italians from the South. A cleavage between these two groups characterized Philadelphia, too. St. Mary Magdalen de Pazzi's, which had been established primarily for Genoese immigrants in 1853, retained a disproportionate number of parishioners from Liguria and Piedmont into the early twentieth century and forced southern newcomers to turn to the church of Our Lady of Good Counsel, as the latter began to arrive en masse in Philadelphia. Likewise, in Providence, Rhode Island, southern Italian-American Catholics made a point of having pastors from their own area in their native country and rejected ministers from the North.

Such divisions affected social life, too. The earliest Italian-American associations, which the nationalist exiles of the *Risorgimento* set up in the mid-nineteenth century, were all-inclusive clubs that did not discriminate against their prospective members on the basis of local extraction in the native land. This was the case of the Società di Unione e Benevolenza Italiana, created in 1825, whose purpose was "to keep alive a true feeling of nationality" among Italian expatriates in New York (Marraro 1945, 291). In this city Felice Foresti also formed an organization called Congrega Centrale della Giovine Italia (central gathering of Young Italy) in 1841 to support Giuseppe Mazzini's Young Italy movement for the unification of Italy under republican institutions. Nonetheless, admission rules began to change after such patriotic associations – which aimed primarily at backing the political unification of the peninsula from the United States – began to yield to mutual-aid societies that intended to take care of the primary needs of the unskilled workers bulking large within the massive tide of Italian immigrants at the end of the century.

Founded in 1905, the Order Sons of Italy in America, the largest and most influential Italian-American ethnic organization nationwide, accepted any person of Italian heritage regardless of their, or their parents', place of origin in the fatherland. But, despite this case and a few other exceptions, most Italian fraternal organizations admitted only those immigrants who had come from a specific region, province, or even village, while barring the natives of other Italian areas and their offspring. In Cleveland, for instance, the doors of the Sicilian Fraternal Society, which was created in 1896, were open to newcomers from this island only. By the same token, La Calabrese, which was formed 5 years later, allowed only people from Calabria to join its ranks. Affiliation was sometimes restricted to single hamlets. These clubs were often US branches of parent organizations created in the native towns in Italy. By conducting business in dialect and celebrating local festivities, these ethnic associations contributed to the survival of their members' subnational sense of belonging. In 1910 New York City was home to as many as 338 Italian-American organizations. Their denominations referred to specific villages or to their respective patron saints, which offered evidence for the social fragmentation of the Little Italy in the major US metropolis (Anonymous 1912, 31–36). The Caroline Brotherhood, for example, was a club exclusively for newcomers from Carloforte, a village in Sardinia whose inhabitants thought of other Sardinians as people different from themselves. Similarly, in Port Chester, in Westchester County, New York State, eligibility for the San Fele Society was limited to newcomers from San Fele and their offspring, while only people from Avigliano and their progeny could adhere to the Aviglianese Mutual Aid Society. Yet, fewer than 20 miles separated the town of Avigliano from the village of San Fele within the province of Potenza in Basilicata.

Anti-Italian Prejudice and the Reshaping of Ethnic Identity

With reference to a hypothetical turn-of-the-twentieth-century male immigrant from the Sicilian hamlet of Milocca, scholar Charlotte G. Chapman (1971, 27) has stressed that "in America he will be an Italian to all members of other nationalities, a Sicilian to all Italians, and a Milocchese to all Sicilians." Indeed, coeval American observers and individuals belonging to other ethnic groups were quite often unable to distinguish among people from diverse Italian places. The adoptive society usually regarded all newcomers from Italy as being alike. Such generalizations shaped especially prejudices and bigotry. Consequently, Italian immigrants faced a common experience of discrimination, regardless of their geographical background in the native country. In the eyes of both other minorities and Americans of Anglo-Saxon heritage, newcomers from Italy were Dagoes, Guineas, and Wops (all derogatory terms by which Italians were often addressed) whatever their places of origin were in their native country. To the former, Italian immigrants were competitors for jobs, cheap housing, as well as control of labor unions. To the latter, they were inassimilable and undesirable aliens who belonged to an inferior people by Wasp parameters. Political philosopher Max Ascoli (1942, 46), an Italian expatriate himself, explained that newcomers from Italy ended up being "unified into a 'national' block by the other Americans with whom they came to live and who called all of them Italians – or rather 'Wops.'"

Disparities in physical traits with the population of Anglo-Saxon ancestry seemed to corroborate the pseudo-scientific conclusion of eugenics, according to which southern Italians were inferior to northern Europeans because they belonged to a "Mediterranean race" that had been subjected to African contamination for centuries. Allegedly, these influences also enhanced emotional behavior, laziness, disregard for personal hygiene, as well as proclivity to violence and crime, all characteristics that turned Italian newcomers into social outcasts. These supposedly southern features, however, were applied to all individuals from Italy. Reformer Jacob Riis (1890, 48) contended that the average Italian "reproduces conditions of destitution and disorder which, set in the frame-work of Mediterranean exuberance, are the delight of the artist, but in a matter-of-fact American community become its danger and reproach."

To early twentieth-century US journalists, irrespective of whether the immigrant was a northerner or a southerner, the Italian newcomer was "a dirty, undersized individual, who engages in degrading labor shunned by Americans, and who is often a member of the Mafia, and as such likely at any moment to draw a knife and stab you in the back" (Meade 1905, 218). In other words, although the Mafia was a Sicilian criminal organization that made a point of excluding potential racketeers from other regions, any Italian immigrant was a potential member of this group of gangsters in the eyes of American reporters. Notwithstanding the evident northern-southern divide in the religious experience, even the Irish prelates who dominated the Catholic hierarchy in the United States considered parishioners from different regional backgrounds in Italy as members of a single ethnic group when priests stigmatized their Italian flock's superstition-prone faith, manifestations of popular piety, and reluctance to support the parishes financially. Consequently, Italian congregations were often forced to worship in the basements of churches. The humiliations people from Italy had to withstand because of their common national descent included informal segregation in movie houses and exclusion from upscale social clubs.

Anti-Italian bigotry spread a homogenizing perception of the newcomers that contributed to making the immigrants and their children realize that they shared the same national background and that they had to overcome both the legacy of *campanilismo* and the ensuing rivalries if they intended to assert their rights and to consolidate their standing in the host society. As a result, ethnic defensiveness played a key role in the development of an Italian identity that the immigrants had lacked upon disembarking at US ports. For example, an advocate of the merger of Philadelphia's various localistic societies into a single Italian association argued in the early 1930s, by resorting to a metaphorical language, that "single flowers do not make up a wreath and isolated soldiers cannot win a battle. Only by getting together [...] can soldiers be strong, fight, and protect themselves" (Saracco n.d., 19).

The Making of Italianness

The re-elaboration of Italian Americans' identity occurred primarily in the interwar period. These roughly two decades saw the appearance of a US-born second generation of individuals who had loose ties to the land of their parents and could hardly understand the local divisions and petty rivalries that had theretofore separated their fathers and mothers. The immigrants' American-raised progeny was more tolerant of regional diversities and more inclined to join forces with fellow Italians than their parents had been. Furthermore, the end of the mass influx from Italy by the mid-1920s discontinued the newcomers' tides that had until then helped fan the flames of subnational divisions among people from diverse Italian backgrounds. This major change occurred in the wake of the passing of the Quota Acts of 1921 and 1924, which severely restricted the arrival of Italian citizens, on the grounds that they were inassimilable and thereby undesirable in the United States, as well as in the aftermath of the enforcement of the 1927 Fascist anti-emigration policies in the native country. Italian Americans' mobilization to prevent the passing of the US restrictive legislation, though unsuccessful, strengthened their awareness of being a victimized minority and, thus, their Italian identity out of ethnic self-defense.

The emergence of nationalistic feelings following the outbreak of World War I and the rise of Fascism to power in Italy also contributed to the development of a sense of Italianness among the immigrants and their offspring. The ethnic leaders and press that celebrated Italy's 1915 declaration of war on the Austrian-Hungarian empire persuaded Italian Americans that they shared something despite their different places of origin in the ancestral land. Moreover, after enduring prejudice and discrimination because of their national extraction for decades, the newcomers and their descendants became aware of the fact that their Italian origin was no longer a stigma they had to feel ashamed of as soon as the United States entered World War I at the side of their native country. Significantly, with reference to his own fellow countrymen in America, Giuseppe Scandella, the editor of New Haven's Italian-language newspaper *Il Corriere del Connecticut* (the courier of Connecticut), remarked that at wartime "more than ever, we feel proud to be Italians" (Sterba 2003, 137). Notwithstanding its unsuccessful outcome, Italian Americans' mass campaign to support Italy's jingoistic claims over the Croatian port of Fiume after the end of the military conflict at the Paris Peace Conference, which eventually rejected Rome's demands, offered an insightful example of how Italianness had made inroads into the ranks of the US population of Italian extraction by the end of World War I.

Likewise, Italian Americans gained in self-respect, thanks to the alleged accomplishments of their fatherland during the Fascist rule. The prominent international status that their ancestral country achieved under dictator Benito Mussolini, who came to power in 1922, and the *Duce*'s aggressive foreign policy for the supposed defense of Italian prestige abroad made immigrants in the United States and their children proud of their national roots. Even anti-Fascists acknowledged that Mussolini "enabled four million Italians in America to hold up their heads [...]. If you had been branded as undesirable by a quota law you would understand how much that means" (Schonbach 1985, 92). Prior to 1922 many Italians expatriated in part following the disregard of the liberal governments for rank-and-file peasants, artisans, laborers, and industrial workers. In the eyes of all these categories, before the establishment of the Fascist regime, the Italian state was usually a hostile entity that confined itself almost exclusively to levying taxes and drafting young males into the army when their families needed them as breadwinners. This negative perception discouraged most individuals from identifying themselves with the institutions of the Reign of Italy and, therefore, from developing a sense of affiliation based on their common national roots. As an immigrant complained, the *patria* – namely the native country – "has never done anything for us" because it "belongs to the masters! The poor people's *patria* does not exist" (Margariti 1994, 40, 55).

Mussolini turned the previous approach upside down. Fascism took care of the expatriates by ensuring material assistance, promoting Italian culture, teaching the Italian language as opposed to local dialects, and fighting against anti-Italian stereotypes. The regime carried out these policies for propaganda purposes in order to build up consensus among Italians abroad. Yet, such campaigns helped migrants reconcile themselves with their native state and, thereby, solidify their Italian identity while they basked in the supposed glory of their motherland under the *Duce*'s dictatorship.

The popularity of Fascism with Italian Americans and the latter's ensuing sense of national pride reached a climax when Italy invaded Ethiopia on 3 October 1935 and established her own colonial empire in eastern Africa on 9 May 1936. At that time, many residents of the Little Italies endeavored to challenge the sanctions of the League of Nations against the Mussolini's regime. During the 7 months of the Italo-Ethiopian War, they raised money and donated gold objects, including wedding rings, to fund the Fascist venture. They also successfully lobbied Congress against the passing of measures restricting such US exports to Italy as oil, trucks, and scrap iron that were key to the *Duce*'s troops in the military campaign in eastern Africa. On that occasion, ethnic identity overcame Italian Americans' class consciousness and sense of allegiance to the labor movement. US unions unanimously condemned the Fascist unprovoked attack on Ethiopia, but most workers of Italian extraction criticized the stand of their leadership. One of them, for instance, argued that "wishing Italy's defeat to displace Mussolini" was "ridiculous" and that he would continue to collect money for his ancestral country's army (Farina 1936).

The transformation of Italian Americans' social institution reflected the reshaping of their identity in the interwar years. In the 1930s the Order Sons of Italy in America incorporated as new lodges a number of Italian-American ethnic associations with local denomination and helped their affiliates realize their common national ancestry. By the outbreak of World War II, for instance, 13 out of Newark's 22 Italian-American associations had become part of the Order Sons of Italy in America. Amendments to the membership requirements of many other ethnic organizations provided further evidence for the broadening of their associates' sense of belonging. Most of these associations opened their doors to individuals from anywhere in Italy. The newsletter of one of these clubs in Chicago stressed its members' recently achieved national ethnic consciousness by declaring that they had become Italians and were "no longer Tuscans, Lombardos, Sicilians, Emilians, Abruzians, Sardinians, Calabrians, etc." (Guglielmo 2003, 115).

Yet, at the same time, the widening of Italian Americans' identity did not extend beyond the borders of the ancestral country. The newcomers' progeny cherished *campanilismo* no more, but it perceived Italian Americans as an ethnic minority of their own that was different from other immigrant groups of European extraction. The 1930s marked the intensification of strife and conflicts with other white nationalities such as the Irish Americans and the Polish Americans, as all these minorities struggled with one another over cheap housing and shrinking job opportunities in the aftermath of the economic depression. The Italo-Ethiopian War could have been regarded as a conflict between white and black peoples. This interpretation, however, was not the case for most Italian Americans. It is hardly by a chance that, against the backdrop of Mussolini's colonial military campaign, pro-Fascist ethnic newspapers in the United States, such as New York City's *Il Progresso Italo-Americano* (the Italian-American progress), referred to an "Italian race" as opposed to other Caucasian minorities (Bencivenni 2011, 216). The dissemination of this concept was linked to the *Duce*'s regime. For instance, Philadelphia's *L'Opinione* (the opinion) contended that, as a "moral force," Fascism would enhance the standing of the "Italian race" (Diggins 1972, 82). The spread of anti-Semitism and the subsequent adoption of a racialized language in the Little Italies following the enactment of the 1938 Fascist anti-Jewish legislation further consolidated such a concept and the related Italian identity. Indeed, the premise of Mussolini's anti-Semitic provisions was the existence of an allegedly "Italian race" of "Aryan origin" to which Jews supposedly did not belong (Klein 2018, 87). In other words, the "Italian blood" made all those who had it running in their veins a group of their own that was separated from other white minorities.

The Retention of the Italian Identity at Wartime

Italy's declaration of war on the United States on 11 December 1941, after the Japanese attack against Pearl Harbor 4 days earlier, hardly weakened Italian Americans' recently acquired national ethnic identity. As the prewar pro-Fascism feelings in the Little Italies had resulted primarily from a sense of pride and from defensiveness within an anti-Italian hostile environment, the military conflict between their ancestral and adoptive countries turned attachment to Mussolini's government from an asset into a liability. Most Italian Americans were sincere in their disavowal of the Fascist regime, albeit at the eleventh hour, and in their display of loyalty toward the United States. An estimated half a million to a million and a half Italian Americans, out of a total population of roughly five million US citizens of Italian extraction, enlisted in the US army, navy, or air force, cooperated with Washington's intelligence, and did not even hesitate to take arms against their ancestral country (LaGumina 2016; Pretelli and Fusi 2018). Moreover, Italian Americans bought federal war bonds for the amount of millions of dollars to finance the US military machinery against the Axis powers. Nevertheless, to many of them, the conflict between Washington and Rome was an awesome scenario because they had relatives and friends who still lived in their motherland. Against their backdrop, Italian Americans conceived their commitment to Washington's victory as a contribution not to a war against Italy but to the liberation of the Italian population from the Nazi-Fascist rule. The identification with their forebears' nation and the sentimental ties to its people were so strong that, as sociologist Joseph S. Roucek (1945, 468) remarked at that time, "most American Italians looked for a mirage: American victory without Italian defeat."

Actually, many naturalized immigrants and their children continued to regard themselves as being US nationals of Italian descent. Consequently, they claimed their right to back Washington's military efforts by joining the US armed forces or raising funds not as mere Americans but as Italian Americans. After all, ethnic associations such as the Order Sons of Italy in America launched the major drives to stimulate the purchase of war bonds within the Little Italies and usually did it on the occasion of traditional Italian-American ethnic festivities such as Columbus Day that were not discontinued at wartime. The federal government itself played on Christopher Columbus and other Italy-related ethnic symbols to encourage the cohesiveness of this immigrant minority in the common struggle of all US nationals against Nazi Fascism. Specifically, Alan Cranston, the head of the Foreign Language Branch of the Office of War Information, turned the 1942 Columbus Day into an opportunity to celebrate anti-Fascism in Italian-American communities throughout the United States (Pozzetta and Mormino 1998). The Italian-language press also made a point of publishing reportages that celebrated the US servicemen of Italian origin who had been awarded military decorations. This was the case of John Basilone, the marine sergeant killed during the battle of Iwo Jima, who received both the Medal of Honor and the Navy Cross. Such articles stressed that Italianness did not equal disloyalty toward Washington. They, thereby, helped make Italian-American readers aware of the contribution of their own minority to the fight against the Axis powers and prevented them from disavowing their ethnicity based on their ancestral roots. The very motivations for Basilone's extolment within the Little Italies pointed to the survival of a sense of Italian identity among their members. Paul Pisicano, a New Yorker of Italian descent, explained that Basilone "was our hero. He did the right things, but he did them in the Pacific. He was shooting gooks, so that's okay. It would be very painful to see the same act of courage demonstrated against Italians. Even if he did it, he would have been forgotten about" (Terkel 1984, 141).

Furthermore, undaunted by fears of appearing a foreign lobby, Italian Americans and their ethnic organizations mobilized in the effort to win benefits and concessions from the US government to the advantage of Italy and her population in the regions occupied by the Anglo-American troops when the Fascist regime fell on 25 July 1943. These endeavors gained momentum as soon as the new Italian government not only announced its surrender to the Allies in 8 September but it also declared war on Nazi Germany, Italy's onetime Axis partner, on 13 October. After their ancestral country had switched sides, Italian Americans even lobbied Congress – albeit in vain – for the recognition of their fatherland as an ally, instead of a mere cobelligerent, of the United States. Such campaigns continued into the early postwar years. Specifically, Italian Americans fruitlessly called for a lenient peace treaty with Rome, but they managed to have Italy included among the nations that benefited from US economic aid for postwar reconstruction under the aegis of the 1948 Marshall Plan. They were also successful in gaining Italy's partial reinstatement to the prewar status of a Mediterranean medium power after their ancestral country was allowed to join the North Atlantic Treaty Organization in 1949, was admitted to the United Nations 6 years later, and secured a UN trusteeship over Somaliland – one of Rome's pre-Fascist colonies – from 1950 to 1960.

In any case, World War II played a significant role in removing all the surviving remnants of local, provincial, and regional identities among Italian Americans. In the aftermath of Pearl Harbor, unnaturalized Italian immigrants were designated as "enemy aliens," the Federal Bureau of Investigation interned some of them because of their alleged connections to the Fascist regime, and additional Italian citizens were forcefully relocated from the Pacific coast so that they could not cooperate with Tokyo's army in case of a Japanese invasion of the United States (Chopas 2017). People of Italian descent faced discrimination in employment and relief programs in everyday life because their allegiance to the United States was questioned. Even children became targets of their schoolmates' taunts on the grounds of their ancestry. Within this context, the wartime resurgence of ethnically motivated bigotry one more time reminded the immigrants and their progeny of their common national extraction and further contributed both to turning individuals from different geographical backgrounds into a more cohesive group and to strengthening its members' Italian identity.

The Decline of the Italian Identity

World War II per se was unable to make Italian Americans go beyond a concept of identity based on their national origin. Yet, other wartime events began to stimulate the reformulation of their self-perception and to instill the view that their Caucasian heritage was their defining feature. While African Americans moved to northern cities to take jobs with expanding war industries or to replace workers of European ancestry who were serving in the armed forces, the ensuing tensions between the black newcomers and the white residents let a racial consciousness start to make inroads among Italian Americans. When it came to take side along the color line, the children of the Italian immigrants discovered their own whiteness. After all, Pisicano's previously mentioned resort to such a racist epithet as "gooks" with reference to the Japanese disclosed the incorporation of whites' anti-Asian stereotypes and, therefore, implied a latent Caucasian self-image. However, Italian Americans' whiteness commenced surfacing in confrontation with blacks.

In Detroit, a magnet for African-American domestic migrants at wartime, as denizens from primarily Polish and Italian backgrounds endeavored unsuccessfully to prevent black tenants from moving to the Sojourner Truth federal housing project in 1942, Catholic priest Giuseppe Ciarrocchi, editor of the Italian-language weekly *La Voce del Popolo* (the voice of the people), complained that the arrival of black people was "a disgrace" for the neighborhood. In 21 June of the following year, after Joseph De Horatiis, a physician of Italian descent on a house call in an African-American district, had been beaten to death by an angry mob, many of his fellow ethnics participated in a racial riot that pitted white Detroiters against black Detroiters for a day and a half and eventually claimed 34 lives. Most casualties were African Americans, which led *La Voce del Popolo* to remark in racist overtones that "even if one wanted to blame Negroes for conduct unbecoming a civilized people, we think that the number of their dead is such to make them reflect and correct their faults" (Venturini 1997–1998, 86, 89). Two years later, when Oakwood was chosen for another black housing project in Detroit, Henry P. Fandanelli, the Italian-American pastor of Our Lady of Mount Carmel Church, voiced his concern over the consequences of racial mixing for his own white parishioners of Italian, Hungarian, and Polish extractions. He argued that "one can love both dogs and cats, but no sane person would throw a number of both into the same cage and pretend that they will get along." Other Italian Americans such as Louis J. Borolo, president of the Oakwood Blue Jackets Athletic Club, and Orville Tenaglia, chairperson of the Southwest Detroit Improvement League, were also active in the city's various protective associations that tried to keep designated white urban districts free of undesirable African Americans (Sugrue 1996, 77–85).

Anti-black feelings affected New Yorkers of Italian descent as well. In particular, Paul Pisicano recalled that the adoption of racist attitudes was a sort of rite of passage for Italian Americans' whitening: "There were riots in Harlem in '43. I remember standing on a corner, a guy would throw the door open and say, 'Come on down.' They were goin' to Harlem to get in the riot. They'd say, 'Let's beat up some niggers.' It was wonderful. It was new. The Italo-Americans stopped being Italo and started becoming Americans. We joined the group. Now we're like you guys, right?" (Terkel 1984, 141–142).

In the postwar years, the anti-black sentiments that people of Italian origin shared with fellow Americans of other European extractions contributed to making them drop their sense of affiliation based on their ancestral country and to elaborating an identity that drew upon their whiteness. With very few exceptions, Italian Americans, Irish Americans, Polish Americans, and Jews – who had lived in their urban "ghettos" upon arriving in the United States and had even appreciated residential segregation along ethnic lines – were unsympathetic toward African Americans' claims for racial integration and found a common purpose in opposing such demands. This trend gained momentum in the 1960s and 1970s. In these decades, Italian Americans put aside their previous ethnic rivalries with Irish Americans, Jews, and other immigrant groups of European extraction in order to join a common fight against affirmative action, busing for racial balance in public schools, and the integration of their neighborhoods in such major cities as Boston and New York (Formisano 2004; Rieder 1985). They, therefore, acquired a racial identity as white Europeans. In that period, for instance, Italian Americans in the Monte Carmelo district of New York City's Bronx welcomed immigrants from Albania and Yugoslavia, because these groups were Caucasians, but they antagonized the African Americans and Puerto Ricans who had begun to move into their neighborhood. Their task was to prevent the area from becoming "black" (LaRuffa 1988, 19–20).

Electoral behavior offered additional clues for Italian Americans' renegotiation of their identity and the increasing significance of a racial self-perception. While casting ballots, some of them began to give in to white supremacists' appeals. In the 1968 presidential race, for instance, George Wallace won the support of roughly 10% of Italian-American voters nationwide with a peak of 29% in Cleveland, a city that had been the setting of racial unrest the previous July with lootings, arsons, and a shootout between African Americans and police officers (Levy and Kramer 1972, 173–74). Italian Americans also formed political coalitions with other cohorts of the electorate of European extraction to back Caucasian candidates facing African-American challengers in local contests for public offices. In Chicago's 1983 mayoral race, for example, voters of Italian, German, Polish, and Irish descent united in the fruitless effort to prevent the election of black Democratic US Representative Harold Washington to City Hall. After a campaign that deeply polarized Chicago along racial lines, as much as 90.4% of the Italian-American voters cast their ballots for Bernard Epton, Washington's white Republican opponent, even if he was not from Italian background (Kleppner 1985, 219). Likewise, most New Yorkers of Italian, Jewish, and Irish origins bolted mayor John Lindsay in 1969 because they perceived him as a supporter of African-American aspirations and claims to the detriment of whites' expectations.

The case of Philadelphia further highlights the prevalence of a racial self-perception, i.e., whiteness, over an ethnic identity, namely, Italianness, with respect to the determinants of Italian Americans' vote in the postwar decades. In this city, antagonism with blacks caused low middle-class Jews, middle-class Irish, as well as working-class Italian Americans and Polish Americans to bridge what had once been considerable ethnic and class cleavages in the voting booth. They elected Frank Rizzo twice to City Hall, in 1971 and in 1975. Rizzo was a former police commissioner of Italian extraction who had won a nationwide reputation for his strong-arm methods against the Black Panther Party and other groups of African-American activists. However, Italian Americans regarded him as a white candidate rather than as a member of their own ethnic minority. When Rizzo urged his supporters to "vote white" in a 1978 referendum that aimed at amending the city charter and would have enabled him to serve more than two consecutive terms, 85% of the Italian-American electorate endorsed the change although the proposal was rejected at the polls. Moreover, over 90% of Italian-American voters cast their ballots for Rizzo in his additional – albeit unsuccessful – bids for mayor against an African-American candidate, W. Wilson Goode, in 1983 and 1987. Conversely, when Rizzo ran again for City Hall in 1991 against two white contenders in the Republican primaries, his following among Italian Americans fell to 62.5% only (Paolantonio 1993).

Post-Ethnic Identity

The 1965 repeal of the national origins system, which had restricted immigration from southern and eastern Europe since the enforcement of the 1921 and 1924 Quota Acts, failed to revitalize an Italian identity in the last third of the twentieth century. Not many Italians took advantage of the new provisions and moved to the United States. Indeed, the number of newcomers from Italy dropped from over 25,000 in 1966 to fewer than 7,500 in 1978, when they made only 1.2% of the total inflow as opposed to 7.8% 15 years earlier (Seggar 1985). The so-called economic boom, which turned Italy from a rural country into an industrial power between 1958 and 1963, supplied plenty of job opportunities in northern plants for southerner migrants, sparing the latter the necessity of making their way across the Atlantic in the hope of escaping poverty and improving living conditions. Moreover, for those who intended to leave the country anyway, Italy had signed several treaties with western European states, from Belgium in 1946 to the Federal Republic of Germany in 1955, to offer its nationals alternative positions in mines and factories in the Old World. Therefore, except for an increase in family reunions, no significant migration tide from Italy reached again the American shores and, thereby, there was no major stimulus contributing to invert the decline of Italianness by means of an injection of new Italian blood.

Italian Americans were not impervious to the ethnic revival of the late 1960s and the 1970s. But they experienced the identity related to their ancestral country especially in terms of what sociologist Herbert J. Gans (1979) has called symbolic ethnicity. They felt Italians when it came to consumer choices and leisure time activities as for the purchase of food, the preferences in fashion, and the selection of places where they wished to spend their holidays. Conversely, Italianness did not affect pivotal life decisions.

Ethnic organizations underwent a steady decline. The Order Sons of Italy in America, for instance, reached a peak of about 300,000 affiliates in the interwar years, but its membership decreased to only 75,000 regular dues-paying associates at the turn of the new millennium, when the number of its lodges nationwide shrank to roughly 700 from more than 2,700 in the 1970s (Massaro 2006). Language was another identifier for the erosion of the ethnic sense of belonging. Indeed, 95% of the people of Italian descent born between 1976 and 1985 did not speak their ancestral tongue at home (Alba and Nee 2003, 74). Therefore, Italian Americans were hardly subjected to the resurfacing of the native language that is usually part of the attempts by third and later immigrant generations to keep their own ethnic affiliation alive.

Marriage patterns offered additional evidence for the decay in the sense of Italianness to the benefit of a racialized self-perception. Endogamy prevailed in the Little Italies in the interwar years even in multiethnic New York City. Conversely, almost three quarters of the Italian Americans aged between 25 and

34 were of mixed ethnic heritage in 1990, as opposed to about one quarter entering adulthood before World War II. Moreover, roughly 80% of Italian Americans born in the 1980s declared a second ethnic ancestry. However, with a few exceptions, exogamy hardly crossed the racial divide and people of Italian extraction tended to have Caucasian spouses instead of marrying blacks or Asian Americans (Alba and Nee 2003, 91–94).

Italian-American communities also began to disappear as physical spaces. Most residents of the ethnic neighborhoods moved to the suburbs in the postwar decades, while advancing from blue-collar jobs and working-class communities to white-collar occupations and upper-level residential districts, following a pattern of - dispersal that was typical for many other European immigrant minorities. Furthermore, some Little Italies in Newark, St. Louis, and San Diego were destroyed by the implementation of urban renewal projects. Others, such as Boston's North End and Philadelphia's Bella Vista, underwent gentrification and lost in part their ethnic connotations because of the arrival of new upper-middle-class homeowners and the subsequent displacement of the native residents who could not afford the significant growth in rents and cost of living. If some inner-city blocks in New York City's Mulberry Street, South Philadelphia, and Providence's Federal Hill still retained some Italian flavor and characteristics, such features were mostly artificial. Indeed, former ethnic ghettos were preserved less as neighborhoods for their dwellers than as tourist attractions for visitors. As sociologist Jerome Krase (1999, 163–165) suggested some 20 years ago, such areas survived primarily as "Pompeian-like ruins" or "ethnic Disneylands" and "theme parks" in metropolitan environments that endeavored to capitalize on urban consumers' growing interest in ethnic foodways, shopping, and emotions, regardless of these people's specific ancestry.

Italian Americans' lobbying activities in behalf of their ancestral country underwent a demise, too. For instance, in 1997, in spite of the endorsement of the National Italian American Foundation, an ethnic organization that placed advancing US-Italian political relations among its leading goals, no more than 50,000 voters of Italian extraction nationwide pressured President Bill Clinton into letting Italy gain a permanent seat on the United Nations Security Council within a short-lived reform proposal for the expansion of membership in this body (Menzione 2017).

Conclusion

The 2008 economic recession and the subsequent steep increase in unemployment in Italy turned again North America into an attractive land for the Italian diaspora at the dawn of the new millennium (Fiore 2017). Actually, the United States fluctuated between the fifth and the sixth worldwide destination as well as between the first and the second transatlantic one in terms of the number of Italian migrants in the second decade of the twenty-first century. However, the inflow did not surpass the threshold of 6,000 per year and, therefore, was one more time quantitatively unable to give new life to Italian Americans' ethnic identity. On the one hand, these newcomers – who are primarily professionals, academicians, students, and highly skilled workers – have hardly ever intermingled with the previous immigrants and the latter's progeny. On the other, they have developed a cosmopolitan self-perception that has significantly undermined their own identification with Italy. The migrants' political behavior offers an illuminating example for the lack of transnational ties to the native country after leaving it. Although Italian citizens residing in the United States were granted external voting rights and were allowed to cast their ballots by mail in Italy's Parliamentary elections in 2001, turnout was rather low at the very beginning and has even undergone a further decline in the subsequent years. Specifically, it fell from 30.7% in 2006 to 26.1% in 2018 (Ministero dell'Interno 2018).

Attachment to Italy was no stronger among the offspring of the turn-of-the-twentieth-century newcomers. The number of US residents claiming Italian roots increased in the last few federal censuses, rising from about 15 million in 1990 to almost 16 million in 2000 and to over 17 million in 2010. Yet, these reports list national ancestries. They do not record ethnic self-images. In other words, the census data provide quantitative information about the background of the American population. But they do not offer insights as for to what extent the lives of such people are Italian-American or are perceived as such. After all, when the members of the Italian diaspora had the opportunity to demonstrate their identification with their ancestral country by means of practical actions, very few seized it. Indeed, between 1998 and 2007, only 16,500 US nationals of Italian descent reclaimed their forebears' citizenship, out of nearly 770,000 applicants worldwide, after the Italian Parliament had granted the expatriates' progeny such a right (Tintori 2009, 39).

Studies of present-day Italian Americans under the age of 35 reveal that most of them either are disconnected from their ancestral heritage or reveal it primarily in familial settings as symbolic ethnicity (Melone 2016; Serra 2017). This trend stresses one more time both the progressive erosion of the ancestral roots and the latter's optional character for the young generations, further pointing to a post-ethnic identity for Italian Americans.

Cross-References

▶ Ethnic Minorities and Criminalization of Immigration Policies in the United States
▶ Media and Stereotypes

References

Alba RD, Nee V (2003) Remaking the American mainstream. Assimilation and contemporary immigration. Harvard University Press, Cambridge, MA
Anonymous (1912) Elenco delle società italiane esistenti negli Stati Uniti alla fine del 1910. Bollettino dell'Emigrazione 3(4):19–54

Ascoli M (1942) On the Italian Americans. Common Ground 2(2):45–49
Banfield EC (1958) The moral basis of a backward society. Free Press, Glencoe
Benasutti M (1966) No steady job for papa. Vanguard Press, New York
Bencivenni M (2011) Italian immigrant radical culture: the idealism of the sovversivi in the United States, 1980–1940. New York University Press, New York
Chapman CG (1971) Milocca, a Sicilian village. Schenkman, Cambridge, MA
Chopas MEB (2017) Searching for subversives: the story of Italian internment in wartime America. University of North Carolina Press, Chapel Hill
Diggins JP (1972) Mussolini and fascism: the view from America. Princeton University Press, Princeton
Doyle DH (2017) America's Garibaldi: The United States and Italian unification. In: Connell WJ, Pugliese SG (eds) The Routledge history of Italian Americans. Routledge, New York, pp 69–90
Farina S (1936) Letter to the editor. La Stampa Libera 14 May:6
Fiore T (2017) Migration Italian style: charting the contemporary US-bound exodus (1990–2013). In: Ruberto LE, Sciorra J (eds) New Italian migrations to the United States: art and culture since 1945. University of Illinois Press, Urbana, pp 167–192
Formisano RP (2004) Boston against busing: race, class, and ethnicity in the 1960s and 1970s. University of North Carolina Press, Chapel Hill
Gans HJ (1979) Symbolic ethnicity: the future of ethnic groups and cultures in America. Ethn Racial Stud 2(1):1–20
Griffin R (1997) Italy. In: Eatwell G (ed) European political cultures: conflict or convergence? Routledge, New York, pp 139–156
Guglielmo T (2003) White on arrival: Italians, race, color, and power in Chicago, 1890–1945. Oxford University Press, New York
Klein S (2018) Italy's Jews from emancipation to Fascism. Cambridge University Press, New York
Kleppner P (1985) Chicago divided: the making of a Black mayor. Northern Illinois University Press, DeKalb
Krase J (1999) New York City's Little Italies yesterday, today, and tomorrow. In: Cannistraro PV (ed) The Italians of New York: five centuries of struggles and achievement. New York Historical Society/John D. Calandra Italian American Institute, New York, pp 155–166
LaGumina SJ (2016) The Office of Strategic Services and Italian Americans: the untold story. Palgrave Macmillan, New York
LaRuffa AL (1988) Monte Carmelo: an Italian-American community in the Bronx. Gordon and Breach, New York
Levy ML, Kramer MS (1972) The ethnic factor: how America's minorities decide elections. Simon and Schuster, New York
Manconi L (2003) Campanilismo. In: Calcagno G (ed) Bianco, rosso e verde: L'identità degli italiani. Laterza, Rome/Bari, pp 36–42
Margariti A (1994) America! America! Galzerano, Salerno
Marraro HR (1945) Italians in New York during the first half of the nineteenth century. New York Hist 26(3):278–306
Massaro DR (2006) The background, founding, evolution, and social relevance of the Order Sons of Italy in America. Ital Am 24(1):20–34
Meade EF (1905) Italian immigration into the South. South Atl Q 4(3):217–223
Melone P (2016) Emigrazione italiana e identità a New York: Una ricerca sui giovani italoamericani. Franco Cesati, Florence
Menzione E (2017) La sfida di New York: L'Italia e la riforma del Consiglio di Sicurezza dell'Onu. Rubbettino, Soveria Mannelli
Ministero dell'Interno (2018) Archivio storico delle elezioni. Rome. http://elezionistorico.interno.gov.it/. Accessed 14 Aug 2018
Napoli J (1986) A dying cadence: memoirs of a sicilian childhood. Marna, Bethesda
Paolantonio SA (1993) Frank Rizzo. The last big man in big city America. Camino Books, Philadelphia

Pozzetta GE, Mormino GR (1998) The politics of Christopher Columbus and World War II. Altreitalie 10(17):6–15

Pretelli M, Fusi F (2018) Fighting alongside the Allies in Italy: the war of soldiers of Italian descent against the land of their ancestors. In: Sica E, Carrier R (eds) Italy and the Second World War: alternative perspectives. Brill, Leiden, pp 299–324

Rieder J (1985) Canarsie: the Jews and Italians of Brooklyn against liberalism. Harvard University Press, Cambridge, MA

Riis J (1890) How the other half lives: studies among the tenements of New York. Charles Scribner's Sons, New York

Roucek JS (1945) Italo-Americans and World War II. Sociol Soc Res 29(6):465–471

Saracco F (n.d.) Unpublished and undated journals. Francesco Saracco papers, Historical Society of Pennsylvania, Philadelphia

Schonbach M (1985) Native American fascism during the 1930s and 1940s: a study of its roots, its growth, and its decline. Garland, New York

Seggar J (1985) Italian migration to the United States, 1966–1978: the transition period and a decade beyond public law (89–236). In: Tomasi LF (ed) Italian Americans: new perspectives in Italian immigration and ethnicity. Center for Migration Studies, New York, pp 32–56

Serra I (2007) The value of worthless lives: writing Italian American immigrant autobiographies. Fordham University Press, New York

Serra R (2017) Il senso delle origini: Indagine sui giovani italoamericani di New York. Franco Angeli, Milan

Sterba CM (2003) Good Americans: Italian and Jewish immigrants during the First World War I. Oxford University Press, New York

Sugrue TJ (1996) The origins of the urban crisis: race and inequality in postwar Detroit. Princeton University Press, Princeton

Terkel S (1984) "The good war": an oral history of World War II. Pantheon, New York

Tintori G (2009) Fardelli d'Italia: Conseguenze nazionali e transnazionali delle politiche di cittadinanza italiane. Carocci, Rome

Venturini N (1997–1998) African-American riots during World War II: reactions in the Italian-American communist press. Ital Am Rev 6(1):80–97

Villari L (1912) Gli italiani negli Stati Uniti d'America e l'emigrazione italiana. Treves, Milan

Ware CF (1935) Greenwich Village, 1920–1930. Houghton Mifflin, Boston

Williams P (1938) South Italian folkways in Europe and America. Yale University Press, New Haven

Faamatai: A Globalized Pacific Identity

64

Melani Anae

Contents

Introduction	1224
Pacific Transnationalism	1225
Transnationalism and Development	1225
"Tautua" Findings from Marsden Project Survey	1227
Samoan Transnationalism	1228
Faamatai	1229
Demographics from Marsden Project Survey	1230
O le ala i le pule o le tautua: Ethnographic Data	1234
Knowledge of Faamatai	1234
"The Reluctant Matai" Findings from Marsden Project Survey	1235
Tautua	1236
Intergenerational Challenges	1237
Transformations	1237
Women as Matai	1238
New Forms: The Atoalii in Hawaii	1239
The Future of Faamatai	1239
The "Future of Faamatai" Survey Findings	1240
Conclusion	1242
Cross-References	1244
References	1244

Abstract

Many social scientists – anthropologists, sociolinguists, economists, historians, and social theorists – view transnationalism and globalization as the movement or flow of people, goods, services, and ideas between nation-states or countries, as well as the complex connections between all of these

M. Anae (✉)
Pacific Studies|School of Māori Studies and Pacific Studies, Te Wānanga o Waipapa, University of Auckland, Auckland, New Zealand
e-mail: m.anae@auckland.ac.nz

© The Author(s), under exclusive license to Springer Nature Singapore Pte Ltd. 2019
S. Ratuva (ed.), *The Palgrave Handbook of Ethnicity*,
https://doi.org/10.1007/978-981-13-2898-5_85

(Appadurai (1996); Bauman (2001); Blommaert (2010); Brettell (2003); Castells (1996); Giddens (1999); Harvey (2005); Hobsbawm (1992); Marcus (1995); Stiglitz (2006); Tsuda (2003); Wallerstein (2004). This chapter is about how transnationality – the condition of cultural connectedness and mobility across space – which has been intensified by late capitalism and transnationalism is used to refer to the cultural specificities of global processes, by tracing the multiplicity of the uses and conception of "culture" (Ong (1999:4). Are Pacific nation-states being transformed by globalization into a single globalized economy? How are global cultural forces impacting on Pacific peoples, cultures, and identities? These questions will be explored with a focus on the links between cultural logics of human action and on economic and political processes within the Pacific, based on my Marsden research – a longitudinal study examining experiences of global Samoan matai (chiefs) and the Samoan transnational chiefly system (faamatai). Refuting claims about the end of traditional faamatai and the nation-state, what follows is an account of the cultural logics of globalization and development and an incisive contribution to the study of Pacific modernity and its links to global social change.

Keywords

Pacific transnationalism · Globalization from below · Comparative advantage · Faamatai: Samoan chiefly system · Transnational reincorporation

Introduction

This chapter explores the sacred tenet of Samoan faamatai leadership – O le ala i le pule o le tautua (the way to power is through serving) by emplacing pule (power) and tautua (serving) within a transnational framework – migration as development without return and as transnational expansion of leadership through "transnational reincorporation" (Levitt and de la Dehesa 2003: 588; Mahler 1998). In their leadership of their families and communities across the globe, transnational matai and their families have intensified travel, communications, repeat visits, and remittances to the homeland. This process creates economic, political, and social mechanisms that enable transnational Samoans to participate in Samoa's development process over the long term and from afar (Mangnall 2004: 14). In doing so, it is argued that previous studies have mistakenly viewed transnational faamatai as necessarily detrimental to the Samoan culture and the nation-state of Samoa and have ignored transnational matai agency in developing Samoa through the large-scale flow of people, images, and cultural and economic forces across borders and back to the nation-state. Homeland individual/family decisions to migrate and global markets have induced transnational matai to blend strategies of migration and of capital accumulation, and these transnational subjects have come to symbolize both the fluidity of capital and the tension between national and personal identities.

Pacific Transnationalism

Transnationalism is the wave of future studies in population movement and mobility in the Pacific and offers a meeting point between a shrinking world, facilitated by infrastructures that enable space-time compression and an expansionist globalization (Lee and Francis 2009). In this regard, the study of ethnicity is critical in delving deeper into people's worldviews, perceptions of each other, relationships, and sense of identification to help us uncover some of the deeper perceptions and meanings of social change as seen and shared by cultural groups as they adapt to the fast-changing world. To better inform ourselves of the complexities of ethnicity and relationship to contemporary global developments and challenges, an approach which is people-centered, balanced, comprehensive, and research-based is timely.

Migration and Transnationalism: Pacific Perspectives (Lee and Francis 2009) is the first edited volume to link a wider literature on transnational studies to specific cases in the Pacific and illustrates that rather than focusing on migration alone, Pacific transnationalism views migration in the broader context of indigenous movement and mobility. This perspective emphasizes kin-based agency in the negotiations and meanings and arrangements in diasporic settings. My work extends kin-based or aiga (family)-based agency to the focus on matai – family heads – as the leaders of aiga and their agency in which migration, remittances, and their experiences can now be viewed as extensions of local faamatai traditions as much as they are a result of the incorporation of Pacific communities into a global economy. That is, we can now view the home society and host society as a part of a single social field with families through the faamatai using indigenous conceptions of appropriate behavior to mediate new situations (ibid.; Small 1997: 193).

As Nahkid states "Pacific transnationalism is a way of life." (2009: 215). However, while there are other features of transnationalism, we cannot understate the value of remittances. Our interest in, attention to, and sustainability of remittances based on *why* billions of dollars are remitted to Samoa on an annual basis and *why* transnationals and their family leaders persist in maintaining a set of multi-related social relations that bind them and connect them and link their countries of origin with their countries of transnational settlement (Schiller et al. 1995), is crucial in understanding how and why Pacific transnationalism is indeed a way of life. The "myth of return" (Walton-Roberts 2004: 80. 92) provides the affective tie when transnationals balance the desire to return with the reality of settled life and fuels transnationals, especially matai to meet their cultural roles and responsibilities as aiga heads and leaders to meet social, cultural, and financial obligations in the homeland.

Transnationalism and Development

The relationship between transnationalism and development – and how best to study it – is emerging as a major international policy concern. Recently, transnational theory and research has stressed that the networks of socioeconomic relations of individuals and groups which embrace migrants' country of origin and destination are of paramount importance in the study of migration and return (Mangnall 2004; Byron and Condon 1996: 102; Nyberg-Sorensen et al. 2002: 18; Transrede 2001: 5). These studies also suggest that "people connected by transnational networks" is the most important resource for developing countries (Mangnall 2004: 8; Nyberg-Sorensen et al. 2002: 24).

Mangnall states that the advantage of transnationalism as a framework is that it recognizes that "neither return nor integration is the whole story for the study of international migration and development" (ibid.). Rather than doing one or the other, many migrants prefer to develop transnational lifestyles "between" or "across" two countries, economies, cultures, and lifestyles (Transrede 2002).

International migration has been shown to be a similarly "highly diverse and flexible phenomenon," with outcomes ranging from permanent settlement abroad to sporadic or regular returns to home for longer or shorter periods to permanent return (Gustafson 2001: 374 cited in Mangnall 2004: 9). So transnationalism is ideally suited to the study of faamatai, and transnational matai as heads of the corporations of kin, and their impact on development processes.

Mobility is at the heart of transnationalism literature. High rates of return and repeat visiting are considered a hallmark of mature transnational communities (Bedford 1997; Bertram and Watters 1985; Faist 2000: 13). Despite this, the scale and nature of the different types of transnational mobility remain largely unexamined, along with the importance of their contribution to transnational ties, identities, and development compared with other exchanges such as phone calls, goods, and remittances.

Faist's (1997) framework for such research is based on two premises. Firstly, international migration and return cannot be adequately described by focusing solely on countries of origin and destination. Instead, they must be studied as unfolding in "transnational spaces" within which flows of people, goods, capital, and services cut across the borders of nation-states (ibid:206). Secondly, return must be regarded as a factor of the strength of social ties and social capital within transnational spaces, as well as a strategy for social capital's transfer. The skills, knowledge, and contacts gained in the process of forming and expanding these social ties can be used to transfer human, financial, cultural, and other kinds of capital and, in the process, develop transnational identities and loyalties (Mangnall 2004: 8; Ammassari and Black 2001: 30; Faist 1997: 204, 2000; Levitt 2001: 202–203).

The creation and maintenance of these transnational ties and identities depends upon the interaction of physical and metaphoric return. Metaphoric return – or the "myth of return" – is the talking and thinking about return to their country of origin undertaken by those transnational migrants who decide to settle in the host country. At a personal level, the act of migrants talking and thinking about return can "create stable moorings" by bringing past and present, home and host countries, closer together. Metaphoric return can also lead to physical returns – resettlement and visiting (Mangnall 2004: 9). It also plays an important role in encouraging activities which keep ties to the homeland – teaching children their culture and language, joining cultural groups, remitting money and goods, exchanging letters and phone calls, fund-raising for home village development projects, and taking on matai titles and leadership roles in the host community. These activities of "tautua" reinforce the transnational ties of reciprocity and loyalty or affective ties which are essential for return visits on a wide scale.

"Tautua" Findings from Marsden Project Survey

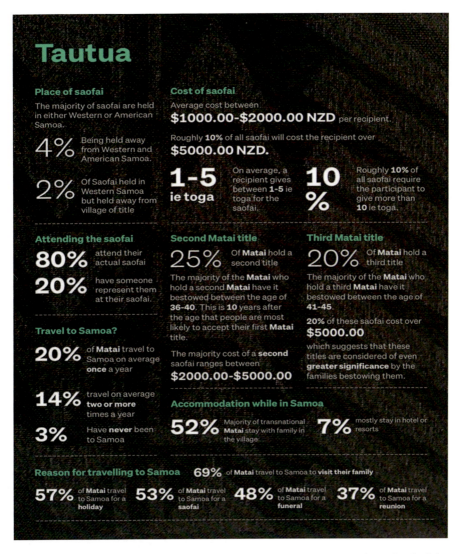

In the transnational view migration, host settlement and repeat homeland visits have two main development impacts. First it has created a "continuous socio-economic field" (Mangnall 2004: 22) flowing between Samoan communities in modern nation-states, the "traditional" families, villages, and bureaucratic sector in

Samoa, and ultimately capitalist metropoles. Within this transnational field, the benefits of migration are evidenced by the circulation of people, remittances, and goods within the aiga and faamatai networks. My Marsden research project "Samoan transnational matai: ancestor god 'avatars' or merely title-holders?" is a longitudinal project which examines intergenerational experiences of transnational faamatai across three nodes of meta-Samoa (Australia, Hawaii, San Diego). Findings reveal that key indicators of the stability of this socioeconomic field are the four directional flows of remittances as tautua: cash to families and villages; cash to families, villages, and Samoa through saofai (matai installations); cash to Samoa via tourist dollars; and cash to families and villages and Samoa via family reunions and funerals. These four cash flows are evidenced by high levels of repeat visits to Samoa, including malaga-transnational funding for community projects (Lilomaiava-Doktor 2004; Franco 1991) and au-malaga (visiting families as tourist visits).

Secondly, migration has led to an increase in the total Samoa population within that transnational field documented as approximately 200,000 in Samoa and a conservative 420,000 in the western metropoles of New Zealand, Australia, and the United States alone. Considering the fact that over a half of all Samoans now live overseas, the faamatai has clearly become transnational in scope.

Samoan Transnationalism

Governments of Pacific nations now recognize the influence that globalization is now having on their countries. Since 1970s they have been influenced by a set of economic drivers known as economic rationalism or neoliberalism. Leading known players influencing government policies such as the International Monetary Fund (IMF), the World Bank, and the Asian Development Bank (ADB), and blatant increasing role of China in the Pacific, all ascribe to this theory (Gough 2006: 83). How then have Samoans risen to this challenge? Through faamatai, Samoan individuals and families have responded strategically to both the challenges and opportunities impacting on them. Samoans are recognized for their adaptation to new circumstances, for striving to take from the new what suits them without relinquishing what is of great importance. They have demonstrated a tireless ability to survive through great change, such as the three Cs – colonialism, Christianity, and capitalism (Macpherson and Macpherson (2009). Their response to the current globalization era is no different: they have carved out their market niche and adjusted to new circumstances. They are part of a group of new transnational Pacific communities that are experiencing migration as a process of empowerment, a process referred to as "globalization from below" (Kennedy and Roudomet of 2003:6 cited in Gough 2006: 83).

Gough (2006: 84) refers to the period 1850s to 1914 – the opening up of Samoa by whalers, the first missionaries, foreign shipping companies, and "commercialism" – as the "first period of globalization" as Samoa's economy commenced integration into the global economy. This period of the three Cs was articulated by Samoans as occasions of "opposition" (Anae 2002: 163). Such occasions have fueled an enduring and persistent Samoan identity both in Samoa and among its transnational communities (Anae 1998). It is this enduring sense of Samoanness and adhesion to the ancient centrality of the well-being of the family through faamatai that has sustained Samoa and Samoans through many eras of transformation, including finding their niche in a neoliberal globalized world.

Faamatai

Today, Samoa is a nation governed by matai – titled family heads. The role and responsibilities of the matai in Samoa is to ensure the well-being of his/her family both domiciled in the village and in transnational spaces. The role and responsibilities of transnational matai domiciled out of Samoa is the well-being of both his/her family in the host country and the family in Samoa as well as other transnational spaces. In 2016, 70,000 registered matai and 146,481 matai titles accounted for 37% of the population in Samoa (Meleisea 2016). Only matai can be elected to Parliament, and a universal suffrage introduced in 1991 to replace the former electoral system that had restricted the right to vote to matai only has enabled all Samoans aged 21 and over the right to vote in elections. Prior to 1991, a crisis arose in Samoa precisely because only matai could vote or hold elected office. In order to increase the numbers of their voters, senior chiefs began to split lower matai titles among several holders or created new titles. This inflationary practice became so common that Samoans referred derisively to these new voters as matai palota (ballot chiefs) (Chappell 1999: 287).

This reform movement drew criticism from some scholars. Meleisea states that "Western notions of individual rights and freedoms have been promoted by mass education and emigration" (Meleisea and Schoeffel 1983: 111). The matai system, including splitting titles and creating new ones, had been exported overseas in diaspora to New Zealand, Australia, and the United States. Western-educated Samoans are earning better incomes, acquire palota titles, and enter politics. "The foremost source of change in Samoa today is from New Zealand," Meleseia says. "There is hardly a family in Samoa without relatives here, and there are few Samoans in New Zealand who do not maintain a relationship with their homeland" (Meleisea 1992: 63–64).

It is a well-known fact that Samoans in New Zealand are the powerhouse of faamatai in Samoa and in transnational spaces (see Demographics chart where of 550 responses, 58% matai survey responses came from New Zealand compared to 31% from Australia and 7% from the United States). Kane (1995) also states that economic indicators of remittance/cash flows are mainly coming from New Zealand.

Demographics from Marsden Project Survey

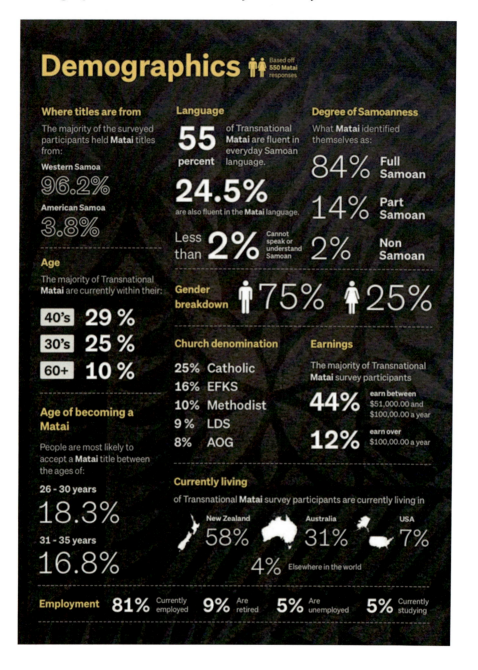

An examination of the 41 books of the Matai registers held in the Samoa Land and Titles Court in 2016 revealed that there was a total of 70,000 registered matai (Meleisea 2016) and 146,481 registered titles (Potogi 2016: 126).

On further examination of the matai registers in September 2018, I can now reveal that of the 70,000 registered matai, 2083 of them were born out of Samoa (born i fafo). This number is a very conservative number which does not take account of all registered matai born in Samoa and domiciled i fafo given that the Samoan population in Samoa is approximately 200,000, while the Samoan population overseas numbers approximately 420,000. Of the registered matai born i fafo, 83.5% were born in New Zealand, 6.6% born in Australia, 6.3% born in the United States, and 3.6% born elsewhere in the world.

Add to this NZ-born cohort – the 50% Samoan-born transnational matai domiciled in New Zealand respondents from the transnational matai survey – the math produces some strong trends. While we cannot be certain that these samples are representative of the entire population of Samoan matai, these results suggest that a very substantial proportion of transnational Samoan matai live in New Zealand (of the 420,000 Samoans who live outside of Samoa, over a quarter of them live in New Zealand); the Samoan population in New Zealand according to the 2013 census was 144,138, with projected population as 160,000 in 2018 (see Tables 1 and 2).

Such concerns are echoed by others. The Macphersons (2009) in their sociological study of the impact of globalization on a Samoan village presaged the role of globalizing forces on the shift from chiefly and religious authority to a questioning democracy in Samoa when they wrote that migration has created new, dispersed multi-nodal forms of the Samoan family and village that have become more dispersed and more complex than ever before and that the capacity of traditional faamatai in Samoa to manage change in religious and secular spheres is being challenged by transnational faamatai "because the criteria for membership in these elites have shifted over time, membership of family and village elites is no longer homogeneous as it once was" (p. 191) (Table 2).

Findings from my Marsden project (Anae et al. 2017) and Gough (2006, 2009) provide an important counterclaim to this assertion: a counterclaim which marks these shifts among transnational faamatai as Samoa's comparative advantage in a globalizing world. These shifts are occurring on the edges, Samoa i fafo (Lilomaiava-Doktor 2004). After all, Samoa cultural evolution is not merely a growth in complexity. It will involve stronger political controls, more exploitative relationships, more violence, more conflict, more risk taking, and greater general insecurity as transnational matai negotiate the edges of the transnational spaces. At the same time though, we observed the growth of skills of transnational Samoan skills in all fields – sports, academia, the arts, music, politics, and

Table 1 Samoan population in Samoa and i fafo 2000–2018

Year	Samoa[a]	NZ[b]	Australia[c]	Hawaii[d]	Mainland United States[e]
1990s–2000	162,866				
2000	174,610				
2001		115,000			
2002					
2003					
2004					
2005	179,929				
2006		131,103	15,244		
2007					
2008					
2009					
2010	186,205			184,440	
2011			55,843		
2012					180,000 (2010 census)
2013		144,138			
2014					
2015	193,759				
2016	195,125		75,755		
2017	196,440				
2018	197,695	160,000[f]			

[a]http://www.worldmeters.info/world-population/samoa-population/
[b]http://teara.govt.nz/en/interactive/l566/samoan-population-in-new-zealand-1961-2013
[c]http://culturalatlas.sbs.com.au/samoan-culture/samoans-in-australia http://en.wikipedia.org/wiki/SamoanAustralians
[d]http://www.census.gov/newsroom/releases/archives/native hawaiian/cb12-83.html
[e]https://en.wikipedia.org/wiki/SamoanAmericans
[f]Estimate

in the arts of poetry and filmmaking. Transnational matai, especially in New Zealand, are playing a prominent part in promoting their comparative advantage in a globalizing world, the precursor of high space-age progress (Anae 2006).

Journalist Gilbert Wong sums up Pacific Islanders' achievements in New Zealand:

> All that first-generational migrant drive for children to make the most of education has resulted in the police officers, nurses, teachers, bank managers, lawyers and doctors...Some have attained the higher reaches of society... professional associations have sprung up... a critical mass of Pacific people forming a new identity a few hours by 747 from their home islands. New Zealand is close enough to the springs of Pacific culture for those living here to be refreshed and constantly renewed, whatever they choose to call themselves. And wherever, in terms of class, they end up. (2002)

Table 2 Matai registrations of matai born out of Samoa (i fafo)

No.	District	Born in NZ	Born in Australia	Born in the United States	Born elsewhere	Total
1.	Vaimauga Sasae	70	4	2	1	77
2.	Vaimauga Sisifo	59	5	6	6	76
3.	Faleata Sasae	7	0	0	0	7
4.	Faleata Sisifo	18	2	2	0	22
5.	Sagaga le Falefa	54	1	10	4	69
6.	Sagaga le Usoga	66	3	8	3	80
7.	Aana Alofi Nu.1	59	1	3	2	65
8.	Aana Alofa Nu.2	8	0	0	0	8
9.	Aana Alofa Nu.3	80	9	1	3	93
10.	Aiga i le Tai	73	7	4	2	86
11.	Falelatai and Samatau	34	5	5	1	45
12.	Lefaga and Faleaseela	91	6	2	5	105
13.	Safata	66	1	2	0	69
14.	Siumu	33	1	2	2	38
15.	Falealili	43	0	2	1	46
16.	Lotofaga	10	1	1	0	12
17.	Lepa	10	1	1	2	14
18.	Aleipata Itupa i Luga	4	0	3	0	7
19.	Aleipata Itupa i Lalo	26	2	0	2	30
20.	Vaa o Fonoti	20	0	2	4	26
21.	Anoamaa Sasae	43	1	3	1	48
22.	Anoamaa Sisifo	16	0	2	2	20
23.	Faasaleleaga Nu.1	171	17	10	6	204
24.	Faasaleleaga Nu.2	92	2	12	4	110
25.	Faasaleleaga Nu.3	24	1	4	0	29
26.	Faasaleleaga Nu.4	22	5	4	2	33
27.	Gagaemauga Nu.1	44	2	5	3	54
28.	Gagaemauga Nu.2	63	7	2	2	73
29	Gagaemauga Nu.3	30	19	0	0	49
30.	Gagaifomauga Nu.1	22	1	2	0	25
31.	Gagaifomauga Nu.2	29	2	0	2	33
32.	Gagaifomauga Nu.3	6	2	0	2	10
33.	Vaisigano Nu.1	12	1	3	1	17
34.	Vaisigano Nu.2	16	1	1	2	20
35.	Falealupo	12	2	1	2	17
36.	Alataua Sisifo	116	10	11	0	137
37.	Salega	45	4	3	1	53
38.	Palauli Sisifo	36	4	9	0	49
39.	Satupaitea	33	2	0	1	36
40.	Palauli Sasae	53	4	5	6	68
41.	Palauli le Falefa	30	2	0	1	33
	TOTAL	1736	138	133	76	2083

In this context, transnational Samoan matai must create challenges in the religious and secular spheres and not accept meekly the increased pressure of adhering to arbitrary authority. At the same time though, this comparative advantage is driven by their commitment to achieve peace and harmony, not only for their families in transnational spaces but also for a transnational tenet of faamatai expressed by research participants as "to be lima malosi and loto alofa" (to have strong hands and a loving heart) which delineate the effective and affective ties to being a matai and the faamatai practised in transnational spaces (Anae et al. 2016). In these illustrative injunctions, we see the emergence and resurgence of a moral and ancient ethical code – o le ala I le pule o le tautua. This research shows that major cultural fundamental changes resulting from the impact of globalization are still anchored in the intensification of traditional widespread Samoan faamatai practices, which enables transnational matai to develop Samoa from afar.

O le ala i le pule o le tautua: Ethnographic Data

Based on ethnographic data from my Marsden Research Project (Anae et al. 2017) and findings based on a survey of faamatai experiences completed by 550 transnational matai, the sacred tenet of Samoan faamatai leadership – O le ala i le pule o le tautua – will now be discussed. Transnational faamatai experiences/ meanings and attitudes are important indicators of the sustainability of faamatai and faasamoa (Samoan culture) in transnational spaces and ultimately in Samoa and should be acknowledged.

The literal translation of o le ala i le pule o le tautua is "the way to power is through service." Pule infers secular authority and economic strength (malosi) and is the effective tie; tautua is to serve with reverence and dignity (mamalu) and is the affective tie.

Knowledge of Faamatai

The title only has meaning if the family is together. . .otherwise it's an empty symbol.

A strong theme emanating from the data is that of "the reluctant matai." Most matai preferred to stay at the back "cooking the pig" – the work of untitled men of the village – rather than take on a matai title. Many hesitated and procrastinated about this important decision before deciding to take on matai titles. Almost all matai participants recalled this "reluctancy" but still decided to accept the call from aiga in Samoa.

"The Reluctant Matai" Findings from Marsden Project Survey

The Reluctant Matai

Qualities of a Matai

According to **Matai**, the top five qualities of being a matai are:

Being **respectful**	88.6%
Being **understanding**	86.6%
Being **Humble**	86.1%
Being a good **decision maker**	85.2%
Being strong to **lead with love**	84.9%

The bottom five qualities of being a **Matai** are:

Being **rich**	7.3%
Being raised in **the village**	20.4%
Having status in **the church**	20.4%
Having status in **the community**	31.1%
Being good with **money**	37.5%
Speaking **fluent Samoan**	60%

Reasons for becoming a Matai

74.5% Family wanted them to become one

20% Of Matai wanted to become one

65.5% Wanting to serve one's Family

Understanding Faamatai

A majority of **Matai** believe that the faamatai is about **serving** their family

85.6%

This is followed closely by **serving your village**

76.9%

Being a good Matai

62%	7%	31%
Believe they're good	Don't think they are	Are not sure if they are

Reasons for NOT being a good Matai

Of those who considered themselves as NOT being a good **Matai**, half said it was because they don't attend family events and gatherings.

Just under half **46%** said it was because they can't speak Samoan and don't participate in family faalavelave.

Are you respected as a female Matai

👤 **84%** Believe they are   👤 **16%** Believe they aren't

What makes a good Matai

92.5% They have **respect** for their family

88% They **listen** to their family

78.4% They **contribute** to family faalavelave

Being fluent in the Samoan language and having oratory skills are much lower reasons for being a good matai with 51% and 33% respectively.

Are you respected as a Matai I fafo?

63% of **Matai I fafo** believe they are respected.

82.6% believe they are respected because they respect their families back

72.6% believe they are because they listen to their families.

Most feel no respect due to **not attending family events**, **contributing to faalavelave** as well as **not being able to speak Samoan**.

Reasons for accepting their matai titles varied, but all participants had a strong sense of their service to the village, family, church, and the Samoan community where they lived and in Samoa. Many expressed that their reason for accepting titles was for love of mother or father. Other common reasons for accepting were because the title acknowledged their service and support for faasamoa, to honor a parent's wish to take on a title, and to help their family. Some saw being a matai as exciting, a blessing from God, or a chance to use leadership skills from careers in the military or public service. Many resisted initially but changed their minds because of family wishes, the death of a parent, or the need to help in a family emergency like the 2009 tsunami.

Growing up, all the men knew about faasamoa and faamatai, was the work - the umu (oven), killing the pig, and other feau (work). For most, their first real education was serving a matai, usually their father. Service was "being a good son," learning by watching and doing rather than talking. The women usually learned from a parent, especially if their mother was a matai, but also from taking on leadership in their communities overseas, especially teaching the Samoan language and customs.

Being a good matai was seen as "taking care of your family so they're happy" rather than exercising power. For another "the power of the matai [is to] develop your family." It was also important for matai overseas to tautua mamao (provide service from afar) to be "loved" when they return to Samoa. A transnational matai also needed to understand and combine faasamoa and democracy. The women also stressed the need to understand "path of the matai" – having the right attitude, ethics, language, and respect.

Tautua

Tautua or service was seen as the most important requirement of a transnational matai. One young matai described it as the "best part" of Samoan culture. A pioneer matai agreed but lamented that "money carries more weight" than actual physical service.

For the pioneer generation, tautua embraced a range of community and church activities – organizing flag days and other anniversary celebrations; setting up cultural and language programs, radio and TV programs; hosting official delegations from Samoa; and raising help for villages. For the younger matai, showing respect for elders was important. Those born overseas tended to focus their tautua around the church. Their lack of confidence with the language and lack of extended family nearby were cited as reasons for them being less involved as matai at family occasions.

Support for family and villages in Samoa and elsewhere was an important part of tautua for all the matai. Tautua included leading the extended aiga monotaga (traditional contributions to the village or to family social obligations) and faalavelave (service in terms of money, time, hosting, and visiting during ritual occasions) for weddings, funerals, and "Church things."

Faalavelave at a distance from family and villages in Samoa caused misgivings for many overseas-born and raised matai. For some, it was a "burden," with relatives in the islands making excessive demands for excessive spending on funerals or not being honest about what the money was spent on. But one young matai felt those who complained did not understand faalavelave was reciprocal and a way to "work together so then the work load is easier and lighter."

Intergenerational Challenges

Loss of Knowledge of Faasamoa and Faamatai
This was identified as the most important challenge by both older pioneer (original migrant generation) and younger matai. Incompetency in tautala faasamoa, Samoan language, was seen as the biggest problem for a matai raised or born overseas. One pioneer matai felt "kids are hesitant" because they did not know the correct "respectful language" required by matai when speaking and by others when talking to them. A younger matai admitted he hesitated over accepting a title because of the injunction to "educate your mouth first before becoming a chief."

Younger matai gained confidence from speaking at church, learning from elders and at family faalavelave. Some enrolled in Samoan language classes or memorized from books. The absence of village meetings outside Samoa also contributed to the lack of understanding about the faamatai. Classes were a poor substitute for learning "from observing, on top of service."

As a result, young Samoans overseas felt "being a matai brings hardship." Many were turning their backs on faasamoa and faamatai because these were perceived as being just about faalavelave and giving money.

More Alii Titles
A trend identified by some participants was for transnational matai and women matai to be given alii (sacred chief) titles rather than tulafale (orator chief) or speaking titles. It was seen as further constraining young matai whose "faasamoa is weak" from taking part in discussions and decisions. Some female matai suggested it reflected views that women needed to be protected from potential political conflicts as tulafale or that the faamatai was the domain of men.

Transformations

The Church
For countries overseas there are no villages, so the church is the village.

As substitute villages, the churches were seen by the pioneer generation as the "the backbone" for maintaining the faasamoa and faamatai and passing them on to younger generations. There was a symbiotic relationship between pioneer matai and faifeau (Church ministers) of the various denominations. However, younger matai had concerns. Although the churches were "the primary school where you'll be educated and advised ... how to speak formally," if they did speak, they risked public criticism for their lack of Samoan language and knowledge of the faasamoa. Misgivings were also expressed about the churches' influence over faasamoa and faamatai and the lack of coherence with practices in Samoa. One younger matai felt the villages and the chiefs "don't really have a say anymore because priorities are firstly given to the leaders of denominations...they act as if they're chiefs in the village."

Women as Matai

The women matai expressed strong views about difficulties being recognized as "real" matai.

They themselves believed their titles reflected "ability" and "because the elders have faith in me." The main obstacles were from male matai who were "ignorant" about why female matai existed and from those who did not believe female matai should exist at all. Living overseas had provided ways to challenge such attitudes that would perhaps be unavailable in Samoa. In Hawaii, for example, a female matai used her Samoan radio program to challenge a male matai who had told a female tulafale she could not speak at a wedding.

Some of the women matai were acknowledged by their male counterparts for their leadership and strong service, particularly for promoting Samoan language and customs. A pioneer matai said opponents of female matai would do well to remember Salamasina, "one of the greatest traditional leaders in Pacific history," whose era marked "a moment of peace [and] the flowering of our race in voyaging and building fales (houses) and all of the art forms and the medicine."

Fiti-Sinclair et al. report the presence of cultural obstacles to women's political participation in villages (Meleisea et al. 2015). This found that although most villages in Samoa do not formally or overtly discriminate against women matai, there are barriers of Samoan "custom and usage" to women's participation in village government.

Few women matai sit in the village council (fono), but those who do so have a better chance to make themselves known as decision-makers in the community. In some villages there is an unspoken convention that male matai are the decision-makers, so women who want to take a public role in politics (compared to advising their menfolk privately) need to be quite courageous in taking their places and speaking in the councils (ibid.: 48).

Some also referred to the importance of holding a title of high rank and seniority as a consideration for a person aspiring to become an MP. This is because a senior, high-ranking title carries more prestige than a more minor matai title and can be more influential, they said. The issue of seniority was alluded to by one of the candidates, who said that while she attended the village council, she did not speak, in deference to a senior holder of the same title as her own who had that prerogative. These cultural considerations are very important in the Samoan system of politics and governance.

The women matai participant narratives argue that being overseas has opened up new opportunities for women matai not available in Samoa. For women matai in Sydney, Hawaii, and San Diego, one of these opportunities is the overt exertion of her pule (secular authority), malosi (economic strength), mana (spiritual power), and mamalu (reverence, dignity, and social power) in the absence of a traditional "village" and thus male-dominated village councils and suffocation of the dominance of churches and faifeau (Anae et al. 2016). In essence the transnational space away from Samoa provides the opportunity for the revitalizing of Samoan women matai as leaders of Samoan transnational communities (Anae 2017).

New Forms: The Atoalii in Hawaii

A unique development of the faamatai in Hawaii is the Atoalii, formed in the early years of Samoan settlement there and whose members act in similar ways to village matai in Samoa. Initially the council was instrumental in organizing faalavelave, annual flag days, hosting visiting Samoan groups, and working with social agencies to help with Samoan youth. But the Atoalii's prominence has faded in later years amid disagreements over the acceptance of government money to run flag days and the Atoalii bestowing some matai titles on members.

The Future of Faamatai

Some participants were pessimistic. One younger matai feared the faamatai was "tottering on the edge" because of arrogance by some matai. One pioneer matai suggested faasamoa would be overwhelmed by "the American life," and "after the old generation is gone, the children will not have anyone to listen to." But most believed the faasamoa and faamatai would survive outside Samoa, because "we are the faasamoa... that's part of who we are." One younger matai felt it would survive but "require much more to maintain it... financially."

Reinforcing that the faamatai could not be separated from duties to Samoa was important for some pioneer matai. It was essential to maintain Samoa as the "sacred place," the spiritual source that would sustain faasamoa "wherever we go and no matter how many generations we move." Among the younger matai, there was more emphasis on the need to respect elders in the aiga and church, and to know that despite hardships – the constant demands on money, time and services, this was the path of a chief. Most felt giving was central to maintaining faamatai overseas and "if you don't give, then you won't get blessings... matai i fafo need to realize this."

Some pioneer matai suggested changes to the way transnational matai were chosen and trained. Aiga should define the qualities needed to be a good alii or tulafale, then identify a young person, and "shape and mold" them for the role instead of "conferring to somebody in his eighties and then you know five years later...it's all over." It should also be the "best Samoan not the best male Samoan ...gender is irrelevant." As well, young overseas matai or matai-in-waiting could be sent back to Samoa "to do the village life, to learn."

The best way forward agreed by all participants was to teach younger generations born overseas about Samoan aganuu (customs) and language and, especially, the faamatai – to "implement the power of the matai, that's the power of the matai [to] develop your family." The need to teach Samoan language from preschool age to university level was stressed by several matai, as was the need for parents to "force" their children to speak Samoan.

The "Future of Faamatai" Survey Findings

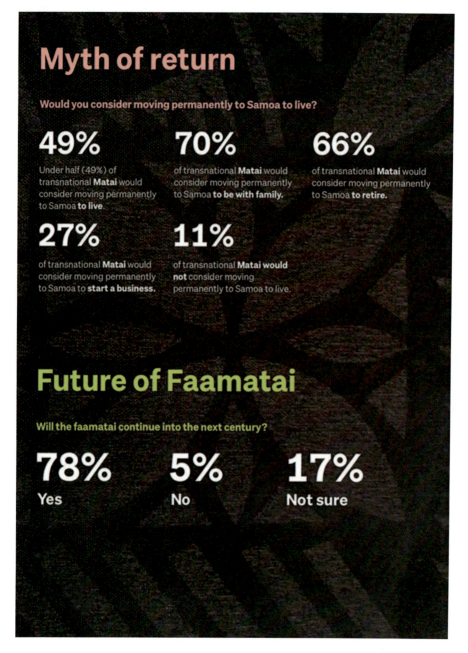

Criticism of matai outside Samoa for eroding faasamoa and not practicing "real" faamatai drew differing responses. One younger matai recounted shaking with anger on overhearing criticism from matai in Samoa, which he put down to them being "jealous because we were able to sustain the culture outside of Samoa." One pioneer matai observed he had seen "more erosion in Samoa than I saw outside of Samoa ... so I see more integrity trying to preserve our faasamoa [overseas]."

This a very salient observation given that the *Samoan observer* has been documenting crucial attacks on the faamatai in Samoa propelled by global pressures, sociopolitical upheavals through legislation, the Lands and Titles Court, and research directly impacting sa'o (paramount chiefs), monotaga (contributions to village of title), tautua, and Samoan custom. In 2015, the customary institution of matai sa'o was investigated by enquiries by the government of Samoa through its Law Reform Commission into the viability of the status of matai sa'o. Traditionally a matai sa'o was the sole head of an extended family owning common property, possessing authority over its members including holders of other matai titles belonging to that family. Meleisea suggests that the government's interest is very likely to be related to legislation passed subsequent to the Land Titles Registration Act 2008, such as the Customary Land Advisory Commission Act (CLACA) 2013, which makes it easier for customary lands to be leased (Meleisea 2017). This legislation suggests that a matai sa'o may authorize a lease on a portion of customary land appurtenant to his/her title on behalf of the extended family. This complicates the current situation whereby multiple holders of senior titles that have the status of matai sa'o are living in the village to which the title is associated, or in other places in Samoa, or in transnational spaces, and the issues in defining Samoan custom (ibid.).

Transnational matai experiences of faamatai, development, and the transnational framework are particularly useful as it allows for an integrated analysis of the relationship between social and symbolic ties, physical, metaphoric return, and repeat returns and the transfer of people, goods, and money between transnational corporations of kin, matai, and Samoa. The transnational framework (Faist 1997, 2000 cited in Mangnall 2004) proposes that a migrant's choices of physical or metaphoric return – whether to stay, return, or visit – are conditioned by their symbolic and social ties to host and origin countries. At the same time, those transnational and local social ties can be used to transfer human, financial, cultural, and other kinds of capital to the origin country through physical and metaphoric and real return via repeat visits.

All the key elements for the transnational framework – physical and metaphoric return, social and symbolic ties, various kinds of capital – are to be found in the participant narratives and survey responses presented above. They describe many kinds of physical return between Samoa and their host societies, including sporadic and regular visits, and more importantly reasons why the faamatai and matai identity is important to them. As leaders of families in the transnational space, this makes them doubly responsible for personal as well as familial tautua to their families in Samoa and across the globe. Their leadership roles are more significant among women matai. The narratives describe metaphoric return activities designed to keep ties to the homeland and maintain Samoan culture and identity through education programs, language preschools, church services, community groups, phone calls, and letters. Local and transnational social ties are forged by matai participants including spouses, children and grandchildren, individuals, and groups in the community such as churches, social, and sports groups.

Samoans and matai across the diaspora still express their migration in terms of tautua – an obligation to aiga – everywhere. Aiga encapsulates migrant identity and facilitates a wide range of overt functions, such as raising money, providing housing and employment, coping with life crises, and giving its members the security of living in a traditional, secure, well-loved group (Pitt and Macpherson 1974). Gough makes the point that not only is commitment to the traditional institution of aiga one of the major motivations behind migration but also that its replication across the diaspora is also one of the key reasons Samoans have been able to establish such successful diasporic communities and, ultimately, why these communities flourish. Samoans both personally and as part of a kin group led by their matai represent Samoa's comparative advantage; Samoans engaged successfully in the world economy in unique ways while retaining faithful links to traditional practices. Cultural practices based in a tradition have provided the framework for their engagement, enabling the comparative advantage that Samoa needs in order to ensure a sustainable future in a globalizing world.

Gough points out that Samoa's engagement in the globalized world, no matter how seemingly successful to date, is not without risks. Continued engagement is dependent on market opportunities and favorable migration policies of labor-importing countries; moreover the lives of transnational Samoans are now entrenched in the diaspora (2006: 91). Globally, they are considered "labor migrants," and the remittances they send home form part of the estimated $65 billion per annum that is returned to labor-exporting economies (Kane 1995). In the case of Samoa, between 30% and 50% of the GDP of the country, more than all the exports and aid, is remitted each year. Opportunities to participate in the global labor market have boosted per capita GNP and, as a result, assisted development in Samoa. Community services and opportunities, like access to health services and education, have broadened significantly.

There are costs however, like changing consumption patterns. When people favor imported food over local produce, this threatens to undermine local market opportunities. Moreover there are "long-term social and cultural implications" which need to be balanced against the benefits. There is also a strong argument too that emigration hinders development because of brain drain and skill export (Ahlburg and Levin 1990 cited in Connell 2003). There are pressing issues concerned with modernity on Samoan society, such as social disturbances, alcoholism, physical/sexual abuse, rise in crime, "unrest" among the youth, and suicide.

Conclusion

In their effort to negotiate the global economy through aiga links and transnational corporations of kin, Samoans have created a meta-Samoa with links across a well-established diaspora. Their competitive edge is founded on three key aspects of Samoan life: firstly, the acculturation of mobility; secondly, the remaining true to one of the key tenets of faasamoa, the welfare of the collective (Gough 2006:39); and thirdly, a leadership/faamatai, which intent is on attaining and maintaining peace and harmony for aiga and for Samoa. By participating in Samoan life across the diaspora, Samoans reinforce their relationships and fulfill their obligations and commitment to extended family and village. At the same time that they are becoming socioeconomically and politically successful in their countries of birth – the western metropoles – they are reproducing the social relations that ensure the reproduction of faasamoa. By doing this, they are demonstrating their comparative advantage in a neoliberal world.

Of course there are limitations. A strong remittance economy is a fragile economic MIRAB strategy (Bertram and Watters 1985, Bertram 1998) which depends on positive market forces and friendly migration policies and relies on an ongoing ability to balance the dialectical relationship between western acculturation aspects of the individualism associated with participating in a neo-liberalized world and the collectivism of the faasamoa. But more importantly the most crucial limitation is that diasporic Samoans are severely constricted in their practice of the faasamoa in terms of deep interaction with the homeland. Their faasinonomaga (identity) has been compromised by their contexts and for some may only exist in remittances to Samoa. Nevertheless they still see themselves as "Samoan" and identify strongly with the faasamoa, thus creating transnational nodes of this meta-Samoa. However, homeland Samoans may not see them as such. Despite diasporic remittances and the tourism dollar being a large part of Samoa's economic albeit fragile sustainability, "real" Samoans for them will always be those who are born in Samoa and who are rooted in their faasinomaga and who are physically "seen" to be serving their aiga, villages, and country in Samoa. Thus it depends on the ability of the Samoan diaspora to face these challenges with strategic foresight.

By emplacing pule and tautua within a transnational framework, migration as development with repeat returns and as transnational expansion of leadership through "transnational reincorporation" economic, political, and social mechanisms has been created which enables transnational matai to participate in Samoa's development process over the long term and from afar. Transnational faamatai experiences/meanings and attitudes encapsulated in the research findings and data are important indicators of the sustainability of faamatai and faasamoa in transnational spaces and ultimately in Samoa and should be acknowledged.

Having no control of erosion some say corruption of faamatai customary practices happening in Samoa, transnational matai are nevertheless continuing to value and act on their tautua to their diasporic Samoan communities, their families, and Samoa through their loto alofa ma lima malosi affective ties. Affective ties are much more than merely emotional ties. They are ties which produce effective action through remittances of comprehensive cash flows which are driving Samoa's development. Aiga cash remittances, "tourist" dollars and visits, saofai contributions, aiga reunion, and funeral contributions are providing the bulk of Samoa's development capital. Despite complaints of transnational Samoans and matai reading articles in *Samoa Observer* about challenges to faamatai from the Government and Land and Titles Court in Samoa, very few transnational matai have totally departed from its practices. It is an integral part of their lives despite its alleged faults and ambiguities, and Samoa's sustainable future depends on it.

Soifua.

Cross-References

▶ Ethnic Migrants and Casinos in Singapore and Macau
▶ Ethnic Minorities and Criminalization of Immigration Policies in the United States
▶ Ethno-cultural Symbolism and Group Identity
▶ Greek Identity in Australia
▶ Historical Memory and Ethnic Myths
▶ Indian Diaspora in New Zealand
▶ Indian Indentured Laborers in the Caribbean
▶ Italian Identity in the United States
▶ Migrant Illegalization and Minoritized Populations
▶ Museums and Identity: Celebrating Diversity in an Ethnically Diverse World
▶ Romanian Identity and Immigration in Europe

Acknowledgment The author, Lupematasila Misatauveve Dr Melani Anae wishes to thank the Marsden Fund, Royal Society of New Zealand, for their assistance, without which my team (Seulupe Dr Falaniko Tominiko, Muliagatele Vavao Fetui, Malepeai Dr Ieti Lima) would not have been able to conduct our Marsden Project research. We also wish to thank our matai research participants who kindly agreed to be interviewed by the team, the 550 transnational matai who completed our online survey, and Pacific Studies, Te Wānanga o Waipapa, University of Auckland, for supporting this research project. A big thank you to Emmet Hawe who provided the Marsden Survey findings info-graphs.

References

Ammassari S, Black R (2001) Harnessing the potential of migration and return to promote development: applying concepts to West Africa. IOM Migration Research Series No. 5 Geneva: International Organization for Migration

Anae M (1998) Fofoa-i-vao-ese: the identity journeys of NZ-born Samoans. Unpublished PhD thesis. Department of Anthropology, University of Auckland

Anae M (2002) Papalagi redefined: toward a New Zealand-born Samoan identity. In: Spickard P, Rondilla JL, Wright DH (eds) Pacific diaspora: island peoples in the United States and across the Pacific. University of Hawaii Press, Honolulu, pp 150–168

Anae M (2006) 'Samoans' in settler and migrant peoples of New Zealand. David Bateman Ltd, Albany, pp 230–235. Published with the assistance of the Ministry for Culture and Heritage Te Manatu Taonga, 230–235

Anae M (2017) Tama'ita'i toa: Samoan womanist agency and reflections on Nafanua. New Horizons in Samoan Faamatai (chiefly System) in the 21st Century Symposium, University of Auckland, 23–24 November 2017

Anae M, Tominiko F, Fetui V, Lima I (2016) Faavae o matai: transnational women matai voices. Measina a Samoa Conf Proc 7:185–204

Anae M, Tominiko F, Lima I, Fetui L (2017) Transnational Samoan chiefs: views of the faamatai (chiefly system). J Samoan Stud 7:38–50

Appadurai A (1996) Modernity at large: cultural dimensions of globalization. University of Minnesota Press, Minneapolis

Bauman Z (2001) Community: seeking safety in an insecure world. Polity, Cambridge, UK

Bedford R (1997) Migration in Oceania: reflections on contemporary theoretical debates. N Z Popul Rev 23:45–64

Bertram G (1998) The MIRAB model twelve years on. Contemp Pac 11(1):105–138

Bertram G, Watters R (1985) The MIRAB Economy in South Pacific Microstates. Pacific Viewpoint 26(3):497–519, September 1985

Blommaert J (2001) Investigating narrative inequality: African asylum seekers' stories in Belgium. Discourse Soc 12:413–449

Blommaert J (2010) The Sociolinguistics of Globalization. London: Cambridge University Press

Brettell C (2003) Anthropology and migration: essays on transnationalism, ethnicity, and identity. Altamira Press, Walnut Creek

Byron M, Condon S (1996) A comparative study of Caribbean return migration from Britain and France: towards a context-dependent explanation. Trans Inst Br Geogr 21:91–104.102

Castells M (1996) The rise of the network society. Blackwell Publishers, Cambridge, MA

Chappell DA (1999) Transnationalism in central oceanian politics: a dialectic of diasporas and nationhood? J Polynesian Soc 108(3):277–304

Connell J (2003) In: Iredale R, Hawesly C, Castles S (eds) An ocean of discontent? contemporary migration and deprivation in the South Pacific. Migration in the Asia Pacific. Edward Elgar, Cheltenham/Northampton, pp 55–77

Faist T (1997) The crucial meso-level. In: Hammar T, Brochmann G, Tamas K, Faist T (eds) International migration, immobility and development: multidisciplinary perspectives. Berg, Oxford, pp 187–217

Faist T (2000) The volume and dynamics of international migration and transnational social spaces. Clarendon Press, Oxford

Firth S (2000) The Pacific Islands and the Globalization Agenda. The Contemporary Pacific (TCP), 12, 1, 2000

Fiti-Sinclair R, Schoeffel P, Meleisea M (2017) Women and political participation: the 2016 election in Samoa. National University of Samoa, Apia

Franco B (1991) Samoan perceptions of work: moving up and moving around. AMS Press, New York

Giddens A (1999) Runaway world: how globalisation is reshaping our lives. Profile, London

Gough D (2006) Mobility, tradition and adaptation: Samoa's comparative advantage in the global market place. Grad J Asia Pac Stud 4(1):31–43

Gustafson P (2001) Retirement migration and transnational lifestyles. Ageing Soc 21:371–394

Harvey D (2005) A brief history of neoliberalism. Oxford University Press, Oxford

Hobsbawm E (1992) Nations and nationalism since 1780: programme, myth, reality, 2nd edn. Cambridge University Press, Cambridge, UK

Kane H (1995) Worldwatch paper #125: the hour of departure: forces that create refugees and migrants. World Watch Institute. World Watch Institute, Washington, DC. 2005

Lee H, Francis ST (2009) Migration and transnationalism: Pacific perspectives. ANU Press, Canberra, p 2009

Levitt P (2001) The Transnational Villagers. Berkley: University of California Press

Levitt P, de la Dehesa R (2003) Transnational migration and the redefinition of the state: variations and explanations. Ethn Racial Stud 26(4):587–611

Lilomaiava-Doktor S (2004) Fa'a-samoa and population movement from the inside-out: the case of Salelologa, Savaii. PhD thesis in Geography. University of Hawaii, Manoa

Macpherson C, Macpherson L (2009) The warm winds of change: globalisation and contemporary Samoa. Auckland University Press, Auckland

Mahler S (1998) Theoretical and empirical contributions towards a research agenda for transnationalism. In: Smith MP, Guarnizo LE (eds) Transnationalism from below. Comparative Urban and Community Research, vol 6. Transaction Publishers, New Brunswick, pp 64–100

Mangnall K (2004) Retiring to Niue. MA thesis in Pacific Studies, University of Auckland

Marcus G (1995) Ethnography in/of the world system: the emergence of multi-sited ethnography. Annu Rev Anthropol 24:95–117

Mata'afa MF (2015) Au-malaga: Samoans in New Zealand as VFR (Visiting Friends and Relatives) travellers, the hidden riches. MA thesis in Pacific Studies, University of Auckland

Meleisea M (1992) Change and adaptation in Western Samoa. Macmillan Brown Centre, Christchurch

Meleisea LM, Meredith M, Chan Mow MI, Schoffel P, Lauano SA, Sasa H, Boodoosingh R, Sahib M (2015) Political Representation and women's empowerment in Samoa. Centre for Samoan Studies, National University of Samoa, Apia, Samoa

Meleisea M (2016) Afterword. In: Potogi TTKK (ed) Aganu'u ma Agai'fanua o Suafa Matai ma Fanua Samoa: the cost of the silence of the land and titles court's practices relating to matai titles and customary land. University of the South Pacific (USP) Press, Suva

Meleisea M (2017) Authority of the matai sa'o in contemporary Samoa. Paper delivered at the transnational Fa'amatai symposium. University of Auckland, Fale Pasifika, 23–24 November 2017

Meleisea M, Schoeffel P (1983) Western Samoa: "Like a slippery fish". J Polit Polynesia 1983:81–112

Nahkid C (2009) Conclusion: the concept and circumstances of Pacific migration. In: Lee H, Francis ST (eds) Migration and transnationalism: Pacific perspectives. ANU Press, Canberra

Nyberg-Sorensen N, Van Hear N, Endberg-Pedersen P (2002) The migration-development Nexus: evidence and policy options. IOM Migration Research Series No. 8. International Organisation for Migration, Geneva. Available at http://www.iom.int

Ong A (1997) Flexible citizenship: the cultural logics of transnationality. Duke University Press, Durham NC

Pitt D, Macpherson C (1974) Emerging pluralism: the Samoan community in New Zealand. Auckland: Longman Paul

Potogi TTKT (2016) Aganu'u ma Agai'fanua o Suafa Matai ma Fanua Samoa: the cost of the silence of the land and titles court's practices relating to matai titles and customary land. USP Press, Suva

Schiller NG, Basch L, Blanc CS (1995) From Immigrant to Transmigrant: Theorizing Transnational Migration. Anthropological Quarterly 68(1)

Shankman P (2011) Review of migration and transnationalism: Pacific perspectives by Helen Lee, Steve Tupai Francis. Australia National University (ANU) Press, Canberra. 2009. Pacific Affairs, University of British Columbia, 84(2):407–409, June 2011

Small C (1997) Voyages: from Tongan villages to American suburbs. Cornell University Press, New York

Stiglitz J (2006) Making globalization work. W.W.Norton & Company, New York

Transrede (2001) Migration, return and development in West Africa. Report of a Workshop at the University of Sussex. Available at http://www.geog.sussex.ac.uk/transrede

Transrede (2002) Harnessing migration potential for development: examples from West Africa. Sussex Centre for Migration Research, University of Sussex

Tsuda T (2003) Strangers in the ethnic homeland: Japanese Brazilian return migration in transnational perspective. Columbia University Press, New York

Wallerstein I (2004) World-systems analysis: an introduction. Duke University Press, Durham

Walton-Roberts M (2004) Transnational migration theory in population geography: gendered practices in networks linking Canada and India. Population, Space and Place 10:361–373

Wong G (2002) Pride of the Pacific. Metro 256:106–107

Migrant Illegalization and Minoritized Populations

65

Paloma E. Villegas and Francisco J. Villegas

Contents

Introduction	1248
Of Binaries and Multiplicities	1248
Race, Gender, Class, and Illegalization	1252
Borders	1254
Support for Undocumented Migrants and Practices of Resistance	1258
Conclusion	1259
Cross-References	1261
References	1261

Abstract

This chapter reviews literature on the production of migrant illegalization – the identification of immigrants/migrants and those imagined as immigrant/migrant as not belonging and a threat to the nation – and the ways it affects minoritized populations. It employs an intersectional framework to connect the ways immigration status, race, gender, and class converge to define specific populations as "other" and illegalized. It also proposes moving away from binary framings of immigration status, given the multiplication of temporary and precarious statuses globally that produce temporally and spatially specific contexts of precarity. Although socially produced, migrant illegalization has material effects that define individuals as disposable through forced removal or the creation of internal borders that "deter" or produce inhospitable migration contexts. Therefore, migrant illegalization contributes to the local (internal) and transnational

---

P. E. Villegas (✉)
Sociology, California State University, San Bernardino, CA, USA
e-mail: paloma.villegas@csusb.edu

F. J. Villegas
Department of Anthropology and Sociology, Kalamazoo College, Kalamazoo, MI, USA
e-mail: francisco.villegas@kzoo.edu

© The Author(s), under exclusive license to Springer Nature Singapore Pte Ltd. 2019
S. Ratuva (ed.), *The Palgrave Handbook of Ethnicity*,
https://doi.org/10.1007/978-981-13-2898-5_87

development of borders. Finally, the chapter highlights the ways migrants and their allies mobilize to counteract illegalization and construct safer contexts of reception.

Keywords
Borders · Precarious immigration status · Citizenship · Deportability · Deservingness

Introduction

Migrant illegalization involves a set of processes and projects that identify particular individuals as not belonging to a nation-space because of their real or presumed immigration status. These categorizations facilitate the deportability of migrants (the ever-present possibility of deportation) (De Genova 2005; De Genova and Peutz 2010) as well as their exclusion from social goods (Goldring et al. 2009). While it is mainly discussed in relation to juridical status and the law, the complexities and consequences of migrant illegalization are far-reaching and involve discursive and affective circulations in which differently situated actors participate to enforce social exclusion. For instance, individuals, through their implicit and explicit deputization, can contact immigration enforcement. They can also act as gatekeepers and participate in the enforcement of categories of belonging. These bordering practices uphold the external and internal boundaries of the sovereign state and categorize those deemed to belong or merit recognition. In this way, the space of illegalization is any location that dictates differential membership given the population's immigration status. However, illegalized migrants and their allies negotiate and challenge migrant illegalization, albeit in limited ways. This chapter focuses on the ways migrant illegalization is produced in specific contexts (primarily North American and Europe) and how racialized and minoritized migrants experience its effects.

Of Binaries and Multiplicities

Migrant illegalization is socially produced and embedded in the lives of migrants, their communities, popular discourse, the law, and media representations (De Genova 2005; De Genova and Peutz 2010; Goldring et al. 2009; Menjívar 2006; Gonzalez and Sigona 2017). It is an active process rationalized through the acceptance of sovereignty and nation-state borders as natural and commonsensical despite the fact that nation-states and borders are not natural entities; they are produced through conflict, dispossession, and negotiation. This essentializing of sovereignty and borders allows nation-states to determine rules for membership including who can enter, the conditions for entry, and when someone must leave. As a result, migrants are imagined to have contravened nation-states' sovereignty when they do not have the appropriate documents to reside or work in a country. As discussed below, this process is influenced by forms of racialization and other interlocking forms of oppression.

The pejorative term "illegal immigrant" is often a starting point to think through the social production of migrant illegalization. Its use contributes to the circulation of criminalizing discourses, about immigrants/migrants and those identified as immigrants/migrants, through narrow conceptions of membership as well as stereotypes and profiling practices. Examples range from slogans about immigrants/migrants taking citizens' jobs, health care, and other services to their presumed inherent criminality and lack of morality (Cacho 2012; Chavez 2008). While research consistently shows that noncitizens generally engage in less criminal activity than their citizen counterparts (Light and Miller 2018), the conflation of undocumented with "criminal" or "immoral" persists and works to legitimize the exclusion, exploitation, and deportation of migrants. These processes of criminalization therefore align with the reality that the end goal for nation-states is not to exclude everyone. Instead, states seek to manage docile migrants and funnel them to labor demands. Illegalization works to control the ways such migrants negotiate their rights and ability to complain about exploitation. And, immigration authorities can make an example of some migrants by vilifying and deporting them when their laboring bodies are no longer needed or when aiming to curry political goodwill.

The media is an important institution for disseminating ideas about immigrant/migrants (Santa Ana 2002; Nevins 2002; Chavez 2008; Goldring et al. 2009). Often depicted as neutral and objective, media editors make decisions about terminology and reproduce state and popular categorizations of migrants, e.g., the "illegal immigrant." Such coded language is often deployed as a means of signaling specific emotions about migrants including their construction as "threats" to be feared or exploited and pitied. Stories repeat "official discourse" and circulate ideas of "illegal" migrants engaging in "criminal" activity, "stealing" citizen jobs, or "floods" and "waves" of immigrants/migrants "threatening" the nation's border. Alternatively, stories of suffering migrants toiling long hours produce images of pity and abject existence. And, depictions of youth with exponential potential facing the "burden" of having migrated with their parents seek to depict precarious status migrants as exceptional and valuable to the nation. However, while these discourses seek to provide alternative representations, they reinforce migrant illegalization and one-dimensional representations. For instance, not all migrants can fulfill the ideals of the young *dreamer* given the various borders experienced in their daily lives.

Illegalizing terminology is often contrasted to the citizen or permanent resident, producing a binary understanding of citizenship and non-citizenship (Goldring et al. 2009; Menjívar 2006; Gonzalez and Sigona 2017). Examples of binary framings include "illegal"/"legal," legal/extralegal, citizen/alien, status/non-status, regular/irregular, authorized/unauthorized, and documented/undocumented. While these categories are useful to examine the production and development of juridical statuses as well as those constructed through anti-immigrant and pro-immigrant discourses, the reality of immigration status is more complex.

Significant variability exists in the ways migrants are illegalized across the globe; however, the law is a fundamental aspect of the process. The law, like nation-states, is not inherent; it changes over time and produces new or different legal categories that illegalize people. As a result, illegalization is not only reserved for the undocumented; some people are not citizens or permanent residents but are also not fully "undocumented." Illegalization can also affect permanent residents and citizens (Coutin 2007; Zedner 2016).

Instead of a binary relationship to status, migrant illegalization signals a spectrum of "less than full" immigration status or non-citizenship (Goldring et al. 2009; Goldring and Landolt 2013). Migrants can experience "partial or incomplete forms of status" (Gonzales and Sigona 2017), "liminal legalities" (Menjívar 2006), semi-legality (Kubal 2013), precarious immigration status, or precarious legal status (Goldring et al. 2009; Goldring and Landolt 2013). These conceptualizations point to the variability and multiplication of status categories and how they influence a person's relationship to the state, its legal institutions, labor markers, social services, and communities. In fact, "citizenship and alienage may be best understood as two key figures of a spectrum of bordered identities – categorical distinctions among different sorts of people configured in relation to territorially defined states by the differences in space produced by borders" (Gonzales and Sigona 2017, p. 11).

Several pertinent categories merit further discussion. First, the term undocumented is often used to refer to individuals who cross borders undetected and/or live in a country without legal rights to stay, work, and access social goods. A dominant example is Mexican migration to the USA, which is imagined to occur through land borders. However, undocumented migrants can arrive with temporary legal status (e.g., a visa) and then lose that status, meaning that some undocumented migrants are not lacking in documents but instead have lost legal rights due to a shift in status. Sometimes undocumented migrants are referred to as non-status, irregular, or extralegal although the categories can be taken up differently depending on the geographic and social context.

The second category involves asylum seekers or refugee claimants who seek protection due to varied types of persecution and displacement. Their status is often organized through international bodies like the UNHCR or national asylum systems. However, asylum seekers/refugee claimants often find difficulty having institutional systems understand their experiences *as* persecution, often a state strategy to restrict refugee flows and "send a message" to potential claimants to not follow suit. Asylum seekers/refugee claimants are often depicted by politicians and the media as "frauds" seeking to take advantage of nation-state services. This manifests through the language of "bogus" claimants (Zetter 2007). They also often face carceral systems in camps or detention centers while their cases are being heard resulting in additional forms of violence and temporal limbo (Vaughan-Williams 2015; Chak 2014). If their claims are refused, they can also become undocumented and deportable.

The third category includes temporary migrant workers who are "invited" to work in a country for set amounts of time and with set restrictions, often also referred to as "guest workers" or circular migration (Castles and Derya 2014). Because of their immigration status, which is often tied to their employment, they often cannot access the same rights and entitlements as citizens. If they lose work eligibility or stay beyond their permitted time, they can become undocumented (Calavita 2005).

Temporary permits are often organized under "skilled" and "unskilled" categories. The former provides more rights and the possibility of access to permanent residence (see, for instance, H1B visa in the USA or Temporary Foreign Worker Program in Canada). Under class-based, gendered, and/or race-based rationales, the latter often prevents access to permanent residence and promotes the production of a revolving door of global disposable migrant workers.

Binary framings of status fail to capture these realities. They also do not illustrate the ways migrants can shift immigration status categories across space and time, what Goldring and Landolt (2013) refer to as legal status transitions. In fact, Goldring and Landolt (2013) conceptualize these "legal status transitions" through the concept of "chutes and ladders." Alluding to the children's game, they illustrate the upward and downward trajectories possible for migrants and the rewards and punishments associated with each, also pointing to the fact that reaching secure status is a time-consuming, expensive, and intensive process for many, producing a long-term liminality or temporariness (Vosko et al. 2014). Common examples include transitioning to undocumented or no status, a downward trajectory in terms of protection from deportation and access to certain social goods. For instance, a temporary migrant worker may lose their status and become undocumented. Or, a refugee claimant may receive a negative decision, face deportation, and make the difficult decision to stay in the country undocumented. Alternatively, moving to a more secure status may involve significant bureaucratic knowledge to navigate governmental red tape (Calavita 2005), financial investment, and often luck. A commonality among these legal status categories is the possibility of deportation. And, the multiplication of illegalizing categories and migrants' legal status transitioning also produce new opportunities for nation-states and other intermediaries to attempt to remove migrants who may have had secure status, including recent trends to deport permanent residents and citizens (Coutin 2007; Zedner 2016).

While some statuses provide temporary protection from deportation (for instance, Temporary Protected Status and Deferred Action for Childhood Arrivals in the USA), the possibility of deportation is ever present and menacing for illegalized migrants. Furthermore, deportation can also work to discipline them (De Genova and Peutz 2010), making them less likely to demand employment rights and social services to which they are eligible and control their day-to-day interactions. Deportability occurs through the public performance or spectacle of deportation: through media coverage, conversations of punitive raids, and arrests. Furthermore, an infrastructure to detain and manage deportable migrants has been produced through the growth in the immigration industrial complex and crimmigration, which seek to link the criminal justice system and local policing authorities with immigration enforcement, often also linked to private for-profit policing enterprises (Stumpf 2006).

Deportability also depends on the concept of conditionality. As Goldring and Landolt (2013) note:

> Conditionality has two dimensions. It refers to the insecurity and contingency surrounding an individual's ongoing presence, and includes the formal and practical conditions that must

be met in order to retain some form of legal status and/or remain present in a jurisdiction. It also refers to the uncertainty of access: to the multi-actor negotiations required to secure resources or public goods, whether these are formally defined as a right of the precarious non-citizen or not. (pp. 3–4)

The conditions that must be met depend on a person's specific immigration status category. For instance, a temporary migrant worker must keep her work permit valid to continue to have her (precarious) legal status. This often makes her presence and status contingent not only on the immigration system but on her employer. Someone seeking a spousal sponsorship is dependent on the spouse agreeing to fulfill the application as well as the immigration system and the possibility of eligibility requirements changing. Access to social goods can be dependent on gatekeepers and allies, as discussed below in reference to internal borders.

Race, Gender, Class, and Illegalization

Illegalization is affected by power structures and intersecting social locations. To be identified as other involves a process that outlines the parameters of belonging and non-belonging. In the context of migration, the intersections of race, gender, and class connect in ways that situate particular bodies as outside the national character, depicting them as inherent threats, as antithetical to the nation, or as a potential "burden/charge." There is a long history of theorizations and legislation sensationalizing the movement of non-dominant bodies in the Global North bolstered by eugenics, deficiency theories, and ideas about such bodies carrying a culture of poverty (Ngai 2004). Resulting representations become the justification for increased bordering and illegalizing practices as well as draconian measures to "deter" migration, often by redirecting migrants into crossing locations that can endanger their lives such as deserts and the open sea.

Migrant illegalization is inherently racialized. It is a process whereby the category of migrant is automatically imagined as racialized body in a Global North context (Dei 1996; Li 2001). Stephen Castles (2010) notes that there is a significant difference between the act of migration and the ability to engage in mobility. In large part, the latter refers to collective human movement imagined as skilled and desirable and the former as the flows of "unskilled" racialized laborers. Migration also takes a geopolitical and spatial character as it often involves movement from South to North, whereas mobility often relates to the ability to cross borders when privileged by the power of citizenship and cosmopolitanism in a northern nation. Castles' conceptualization of migration is key to analyzing the types of anxieties present in discourse in the Global North regarding the movement of poor and racialized peoples across its borders. This can include discourses regarding Mexicans and Central Americans in the USA, Syrians and Turks in Germany, Jamaicans in Canada, and North African migrants from previous colonial territories in England and France. It also affects the racialization of refugee claimants, who often come from Global South countries. Finally, temporary migrant worker programs are often rationalized through the logic of supporting the development of poor Global South nations by recruiting workers to the Global North.

The fear of the "browning of the nation" (Santa Ana 2002) also manifests through vigilantes along the border and other overt white supremacist mobilizations, demands to remove birthright citizenship, calls to build physical obstacles across borders, and the denial of social services for migrants already in the country. While the use of pejorative discourses such as the "anchor baby," "birth" and "health tourist," and "bogus refugee" and depictions of abusive and violent migrants may not reference a clearly defined racial category, they inherently carry a racialized understanding of migrant bodies as constituting a threat to the national well-being.

The configuration of the "other" is also linked to colonial expansion projects and their justifications for genocide, chattel slavery, and displacement (Goldberg 2004). These processes are not only features of the past; they carry contemporary reverberations. For example, in the context of North America, they manifested in the ways colonial logic categorized Black and Indigenous peoples as subhuman. They are also present in the development of laws banning the migration of particular peoples in North America such as Chinese Exclusion Acts and Gentlemen's Agreements and continuous raids to remove Latinx migrants and citizens from the USA, including the *braceros* between 1940 and 1960 through campaigns like Operation Wetback (Ngai 2004). Through these moves, the state identified particular communities as a threat to the nation and mobilized race to inform these practices.

One lens to think through the co-constitution of racialization and illegalization involves racial capitalism. Racial capitalism is a theoretical analytic used to explore the accumulation of capital as inherently linked to processes of racialization and racial exploitation (Robinson 1983). While capitalism has used the language of liberalism and democracy to produce a seemingly raceless process of capital circulation and accumulation, race has been and remains fundamental to its workings, from the inception of European colonialism to contemporary neoliberalism (Melamed 2015). Migrant illegalization is linked to racial capitalism through the subordination of transnational migrant labor to global capital. While offshoring has led industries to operate and exploit Global South contexts, some labor needs cannot be removed from localized Global North contexts, including the rise in service industries and creative classes in global cities. This produces seeming contradictions vis-à-vis border enforcement and labor protections. As mentioned above, border enforcement cannot be absolute given labor needs across class categories. At the same time, labor protections are limited or not granted to some migrants because they are seen to be contravening immigration law. Given Global North states' support of racial nationalism and their reluctance to invest in the social reproduction of migrants, they prioritize temporary, precarious, regulated migration (e.g., temporary migrant worker programs) that increases risk and deportability for workers and provides employers and governments more power and control.

Gender is another important factor that influences migrant illegalization (Abrego 2014; Hondagneu-Sotelo 2007). Gender influences the recruitment of temporary migrant workers, the perception of refugee claimants/asylum seekers, and the representation of undocumented migrants. Oftentimes men are depicted as more adept for arduous physical labor (e.g., construction), while women are seen as more likely to engage in service and domestic/reproductive work (paid and unpaid) (Hondagneu-Sotelo 2007). In fact, scholars refer to the feminization of migration, which involves not only increased numbers of women migrating on their own or as part of families but also the ways these migrations influence the treatment and understanding of migrants. When migrant illegalization is also accounted for, the feminization of migrant illegalization emerges. For instance, women migrants are often represented as "dependent," "overusing" state services, and critiqued for their reproductive decisions. Gender intersects with race to inform ideas of abuse and violence, often depicting racialized immigrant/migrant women as "victims" and men as sexually aggressive, "macho," and abusers. In terms of reproduction, discourses circulate about women utilizing their children to gain citizenship in places where birthright citizenship exists (Chavez 2008). This situates racialized migrant women as a "threat" to racial purity through discourses of racial nationalism. Furthermore, regardless of citizenship policy, anxieties about racialized immigrant/migrant women persist because they are seen as physical and social reproductive agents that birth and raise racialized children and pass down their culture, which is often imagined as "deficient." These discourses contribute to the practice of migrant illegalization.

Borders

Borders are fundamental to the study of migration and illegalization. They designate not only the boundaries of sovereign space but also function as a filter delineating who belongs in the imagined community. McLaughlin (2010) states, "the idea of the border can be extended to include the lines that delineate movement and membership both between and within nations" (p. 81). Through iterations of nation-building projects, borders become naturalized and cross-border movement considered a transgression against the nation.

The border is also imagined as playing an important insulating capacity that "protects" those who have been categorized as belonging, what Anderson (2013) calls the "community of value," from a dangerous "other." The sensationalized fears of the migrant, driven by the aforementioned intersections of race, gender, and class, facilitate a demand for more stringent border control as a mechanism to protect "citizens" from "dangerous migrants." In relation to the USA, DeChaine (2012) states that:

> public attitudes regarding migrants, border inhabitants, and other border-crossing subjects are conditioned by prevalent narratives and imagery that depict the US-Mexico border as a badlands that is out of control—an unruly space in dire need of containment from the ravages of criminals, illegal aliens, terrorists and other undesirable threats to the national body. (p. 8)

In this way, the border is socially constructed as needing constant vigilance and enhancement and serves a rhetorical purpose as the distinguishing factor between several Manichean constructs: rule of law and chaos, violence and safety, and the sovereign and the illegitimate.

For example, technologies such as walls, checkpoints, and identification documents are used to legitimate the sovereignty of the national space as well as monitor the movement of goods and people. The use of passports and other technologies of documentation emerged more consistently in the early 1900s to monitor and control the movement of individuals more extensively given increased access to travel (Torpey 2000). Such technologies of documentation have intensified in the ensuing decades, particularly due to discourses of national security. In this context, the border becomes imagined as a protective apparatus that provides safety from the "other" (DeChaine 2012). Implementing such a border requires the law to outline crossing requirements, a police force to implement them, and a citizenry to endorse it. The discourses produced at geographic and external borders are mobile and can "travel" beyond their initial application. Put differently, borders can also become externalized and internalized. For the former, borders extend beyond the geographic delimiting of nation-states through processes of interdiction and externalization (Casas-Cortes et al. 2011). These processes seek international or transnational cooperation among states to interdict migration through the implementation of buffer zones. They may engage third parties to practice border enforcement including airport officials. For example, the Canadian border is present in ports of entry within and outside the nation, including international airports (Pratt 2005). Similarly, many governments have placed penalties on airlines that transport individuals who are rejected at the port of entry, forcing the airline to fly pay for their return flights (Salter 2007).

In comparison, internal borders are those that operate through the policing of migrants, the gatekeeping of important services, and the control of migrants' mobility on the basis of their immigration status (Willen 2007; Mutsaers 2014; Villegas 2018). Mutsaers (2014) identifies two types of internal border controls: "practices intended to trace, apprehend and deport migrants from state territories...[and] aims to exclude migrants from societal institutions and public provision" (p. 6). In terms of the former, policing bodies are increasingly incorporated into the work of immigration enforcement through municipal deputizing in the USA (such as the 287g program in the USA), the use of transit officials to identify undocumented migrants, and the extension of ties between police and border/immigration officials (including the renting of beds in county jails and the holding of uncharged individuals at the behest of immigration enforcement). Some police departments and municipalities have refused to participate in this process, for instance, through the passing of sanctuary policies or revoking prior agreements with immigration enforcement. Other stakeholders cooperate with immigration officials, for instance, through the building of detention centers in marginalized rural places or the passing of punitive municipal policies (Longazel 2016).

The exclusion of undocumented or precariously documented migrants from public institutions also creates boundaries of belonging. Often these services and protections are collectively understood as essential to people's well-being, such as health care, housing, and schooling, but remain beyond the reach of illegalized communities. Rhetoric regarding the need to protect social institutions like welfare and community housing defines the undocumented as likely to abuse such systems. Thus, the dangers placed on the border can also be recycled and reattached to local institutions. Often, exclusions do not explicitly outline their ineligibility but rather demand normalized documents, unavailable to them, to receive a social good. For instance, state-issued ID cards can be demanded in locations where undocumented migrants are barred from receiving them, making it difficult to enroll children in school, pick up medication, turn on utilities, or forward one's mail (Villegas et al. 2017). The normalization of identification serves to illegalize a significant portion of that population, not because they are legally ineligible to receive the service but because the process demands the display of such unattainable documents. In this sense, illegalization is also a process of rendering the undocumented abnormal and removing them from the space of community. Refugee claimants/asylum seekers may require evidence of an ongoing claim to access services to which they are eligible. Finally, temporary migrant workers might be eligible for state-sponsored benefits but may face difficulties obtaining them.

Formal education and health care are imagined as central features of a productive society. Schooling, often described as the great equalizer and the space where individuals may find social mobility, is a hotly contested area. Although the UN Convention on the Rights of the Child dictates the availability of K-12 schooling as a fundamental right to all children and many nations imagine it as a foundational space to society, this is far from an assured reality. In Canada, access to K-12 schooling for undocumented students remains an uneven terrain where individuals can be excluded based on their immigration status (Villegas 2018). There is significant variability across the European Union where banning of undocumented children has gained considerable traction and where institutional procedures can make it very difficult to enroll undocumented youth (Dorling 2013). And, efforts to ensure access can be met with limited implementation and an unwillingness to advocate on behalf of precariously documented students.

Higher education, now considered fundamental to receive a good job, also largely remains inaccessible to undocumented students without access policies. In the USA, while the availability of K-12 schooling is ensured by Plyler v. Doe, higher education is a difficult terrain to navigate as states can develop their own policies and these range from the availability to pay resident tuition and receive financial aid, to only being able to pay resident tuition, to outright exclusion (Gonzales 2016). Similar variability exists in Canada and Europe, where some migrants, like refugee claimants/asylum seekers, might receive access, while non-status migrants might continue to be excluded. Furthermore, access policies do not always attenuate financial need or responsibilities, particularly because precariously documented migrants often experience precarious working conditions as discussed below.

Another common site of exclusion is access to health care, which affects migrants' experiences of physical and mental well-being (Cuadra 2012). This is particularly the case in states with thick social welfare benefits because citizens feel compelled to "protect" those services for those deemed "deserving," i.e., citizens and long-term residents (Willen 2012). Access is often denied, ad hoc, or negotiated by migrants and gatekeepers who evaluate eligibility on the basis of specific status as well as race, gender, age, and length of residence (Villegas 2013). Children are often depicted as more deserving given their age and assumed innocence, although race and gender often temper those categorizations. Those with chronic illnesses, pregnant women, and the elderly are often marked as less deserving because the assumption is that they will take up more resources than citizens or require long-term social reproduction from the state for their children. Long-term residents are also often depicted as more deserving than the newly arrived, particularly those who have visitor/tourist status, often referred to as "medical tourists." Racial stereotypes, which already influence the medical field, also influence the quality of care precarious status migrant patients receive. Examples include lower-quality care, refusal of care, and use of criminalizing and vilifying stereotypes. Finally, cost also becomes an issue, especially if costs are unregulated for precarious status clients or if treatment requires hospital stays, expensive medicine, or exams. One outcome is that vulnerable, deportable precarious status migrants will delay accessing healthcare services, often waiting until it becomes an emergency. This waiting turns treatable, preventable illnesses into more serious ones, something that increases costs for both patients and the health-care systems who treat them.

Workplaces also serve as bordered locations (De Genova 2005). One example is that nation-states require workers provide eligibility documents, such as a social security card in the USA and a social insurance card in Canada, to procure work. Like passports, the availability of a social security number at birth for US citizens is a relatively new process and is now normalized. Furthermore, the use of technologies has evolved from the issuing of employment eligibility documents to the availability of online databases validating a person's ability to work in the country through programs like "e-verify" in the USA. Despite the law, there are many sectors of the labor market dependent on migrant labor, including undocumented workers. Agriculture, construction, domestic and care work, and landscaping often operate through the employment of racialized precarious status migrants. As discussed above, jobs are often also gendered, with more women in care and domestic work and more men in construction and landscaping. Migrants with other skills and qualifications, either from their countries of origin or obtained through post-secondary access policies, face deskilling unless they can access programs that provide a reprieve for deportation, like Deferred Action for Childhood Arrivals, leading to a loss of human capital.

While some precarious status migrants, including temporary migrant workers, have access to employment eligibility, they often face similar instances of vulnerability as their undocumented or non-status counterparts. And, sometimes, migrant workers with work permits face difficulties their undocumented counterparts may not face like the freedom to change employers (Mclaughlin 2010). Finally, work permits expire and require effort, time, and money to renew, which can lead some migrant workers to fall out of status and face the possibility of not having their permits renewed (Calavita 2005).

Furthermore, as discussed above, the threat of deportability is not meant to bring about the removal of all migrants but instead serves as simultaneous spectacle of a country doing something about immigration enforcement and the disciplining undocumented migrants. In relation to the latter, the threat of deportation facilitates the streaming of undocumented migrants into workplaces that hire individuals who cannot furnish the necessary documentation.

The jobs which precariously documented migrants can access are often precarious. Precarious employment refers to insecure, casual, temporary, and/or dangerous work with few benefits. Precarious jobs are often referred to as 3D jobs: dirty, difficult, and dangerous. Often imagined as doing "the jobs citizens won't do," precarious status migrant workers are fundamental to the maintenance of local economies while also reflecting the unwillingness of employers to provide living wages in jobs often characterized as "unskilled" (although "high-skill" employment can also be precarious when seasonal or contract-based). While it is clear that not all workers engaging in precarious employment are undocumented or have precarious immigration status, there is a high likelihood that said individuals are forcibly relegated to this labor sector given their inability to provide labor permits. Often this work is done under the table and includes being paid in cash and below the minimum wage. Thus, an important consequence of precarious immigration status is the relative unavailability of secure labor and the high possibility of exploitation.

Precarity is a direct result of the understanding of an abundant labor force, the construction of workers as disposable, and in the case of precarious status migrants, including the undocumented, legal limitations placed on workers due to their immigration status. Such workers also have a higher likelihood of experiencing wage theft (manifesting through no pay, less pay than agreed to, pay cuts, or fees charged to employees), unsafe conditions, and other forms of exploitation due to their immigration status and the fact that making complaints can lead to deportation. Similarly, immigration status places women and sexual minorities at an increased risk of sexual violence and harassment in the workforce (among other contexts). Finally, in addition to the relegation to precarious employment, precarious status migrant workers may not be eligible to safety nets available to citizens in welfare states such as unemployment benefits and disability protections.

Support for Undocumented Migrants and Practices of Resistance

Illegalization is not always an overt process. It often includes coded language that appears positive on the surface. This can consist of humanitarian language that aims to "save" migrants. For example, politicians and other stakeholders often use benevolent rhetoric when they claim to act on undocumented migrants' behalf while criminalizing businesses, institutions, and strategies developed to survive lack of access to essential services (Menjívar and Kil 2002). Other examples include the circulation of a deservingness discourse that proclaims subsections of undocumented or precarious status migrants as the "good migrants" and by extension defines those outside such parameters as "bad migrants" (Anderson 2013; Willen 2012). These discursive tools uphold the boundaries of belonging and carry an important material consequence when they become the basis for action for politicians and officials to pass punitive legislation, develop physical boundaries at the border space, carry out immigration raids, and separate families and communities.

While these multiple and assembled mechanisms illegalize migrants, they are not without agency. Migrants consistently engage in individual and collective practices of resistance. Individuals may negotiate their experiences of illegalization by avoiding certain public places and workplaces, speaking out against punitive practices, developing community ties with migrants and nonmigrants, and interacting with government representatives. They may also pressure or collaborate with governmental entities to enact policy changes and develop alternate structures to safeguard communities. These processes illustrate migrants' "embodied experiences of being-in-the-world," an important correction to focusing on migrant illegalization exclusively from a legal lens (Willen 2007). They also illustrate how migrants can participate in citizenship practices even when they do not have formal citizenship status (Coll 2010).

Scaling up from individuals, groups may engage in public workshops, demonstrations, and other manifestations of dissent alongside other stakeholders including allies and politicians. While developing spaces of absolute safety from immigration enforcement can only come through comprehensive immigration reform and the dismantling of borders, communities endeavor to create a patchwork of relative safety and access through the development of spaces of non-compliance with immigration authorities and rapid response teams. For example, campuses, municipalities, and other governments may pass welcoming policies (e.g., sanctuary cities). While these processes to negotiate illegalization may not bring about secure legal status, they demonstrate how migrants are not abject victims of global structural processes. Instead, they negotiate, to the best of their abilities, their experiences and strategize options for becoming more secure. This raises an important point about the ways migrant illegalization is experienced temporally. Scholars refer to long-term experiences of insecure or precarious status, for instance, undocumented migrants or temporary migrant workers without avenues for permanent residence, through the language of temporariness (Vosko et al. 2014). This liminal or limbo status makes it difficult for migrants to make plans for the future. Despite experiencing deportability, precarious status migrants engage in the making of short- and long-term plans, understanding that those plans are contingent on immigration applications, evading immigration enforcement, and often luck (Villegas 2014).

Conclusion

Migrant illegalization is a lens through which to understand the intersection between migration, legalities, and other forms of oppression. It is context specific, relying on legal precedents, discursive and affective circulations about migrants, and nation-state requirements for precarious laboring bodies, among other factors. The implication is a hierarchy of formal citizenship categorizations. These categorizations demonstrate the multiplication of precarious statuses as well as how migrants experience and transition across them while often resisting the limitations placed around their access to social goods, mobility, security, and decent work.

Further research is needed in four research strands. First is the connection between migrant illegalization and affect (the social circulation of emotions). This research will expand work on migrant deservingness as well as provide a link between cultural studies of emotions and studies of migration/migrant illegalization, which have had limited conversations thus far. One example involves how migration is interpreted by citizens and lawmakers through the circulation of affect, that is, national sentiments can often drive policy responses. This is particularly important as law is a reactive institution, and ideas of deviance shift across time and space. Additional nuance in the ways collective responses to migration are defined, mobilized, and socially expressed can provide insights into policy creation and implementation. This will provide avenues to understand the creation of punitive legislation as well as social movements to facilitate access to formal citizenship. In this way, affect is integral to a better conceptualization of the drawing and redrawing of the boundaries of belonging.

Second, further research is needed on how other forms of oppression (besides race, class, and gender) affect specific instances of illegalization as well as its multiplicative consequences when analyzed through an intersectional lens. For instance, Queer, Trans, and LGBT studies provide important concepts to further refine framings of immigrant/migrant criminality at the border and within nation-states. They also refine discussions of how documents police and surveil what are framed as nonnormative bodies. Another example involves conversations with critical disability and crip studies and how framings of deservingness and medical admissibility also influence debates on migrant illegalization.

Third, more research is needed on the links between colonial practices and migrant illegalization. One strand of this research involves historicizing migratory trajectories given colonial and imperialist relationships. However, a second less studied process is how migrants relate to Indigenous communities in their spaces of residence. For instance, in settler colonial states, more research is needed in the sometimes contradictory ways in which migrants align themselves or challenge colonial practices of dispossession.

Finally, as described in the last section of this chapter, because of national governments increasing the punitive consequences of living with precarious immigration status, migrants and their allies have mobilized to develop spaces of relative safety. These moves include the use of local governmental structures to pass ordinances making their daily context safer: sanctuary policies, access without fear policies, resolutions prohibiting immigration holds in local jails, and the development of municipal and county IDs. Furthermore, mobilizations have targeted single institutions such as schooling, policing, health care, and housing to become spaces of non-compliance with immigration enforcement. While these moves do not remove the possibility of detention and deportation, they display migrant agency in reconstructing spaces. Specifically, although a school or health clinic may prohibit immigration enforcement from entering their grounds or accessing migrants' records, individuals liable for deportation remain vulnerable in other social spaces.

In this way, the development of safer spaces, through sanctuary policies or other strategies, is valuable to the community in question but is limited by state powers. The literature on resistance has primarily focused on the development of strategies within community-based organizations and large-scale protests to change federal policy. Additional work in this area will provide insight into the variance between local and national politics and the power and utility of smaller-scale community-building. It will also facilitate a more nuanced understanding of local spaces and their potential to have relative degrees of autonomy from national governments, rather than imagining politics at this broader level as concrete.

Cross-References

▶ Ethnic Minorities and Criminalization of Immigration Policies in the United States
▶ Ethnicity and Class Nexus: A Philosophical Approach
▶ Media and Stereotypes
▶ Policing Ethnic Minorities: Disentangling a Landscape of Conceptual and Practice Tensions
▶ Racism and Stereotypes

References

Abrego LJ (2014) Sacrificing families: navigating laws, labor, and love across borders. Stanford University Press, Stanford

Anderson B (2013) Us and them? The dangerous politics of immigration control. Oxford University Press, Oxford

Cacho LM (2012) Social death: racialized rightlessness and the criminalization of the unprotected. Nation of newcomers: immigrant history as American history. New York University Press, New York

Calavita K (2005) Immigrants at the margins: law, race, and exclusion in Southern Europe. Cambridge University Press, Cambridge, UK

Casas-Cortes M, Cobarrubias S, Pickles J (2011) Stretching borders beyond sovereign territories? Mapping EU and Spain's border externalization policies. Geopolitica(s) Rev Estud Sobre Espacio Poder 2(1):71–90

Castles S (2010) Understanding global migration: a social transformation perspective. J Ethn Migr Stud 36(10):1565–1586

Castles S, Derya O (2014) Circular migration: triple win, or a new label for temporary migration? In: Battistella G (ed) Global and Asian perspectives on international migration. Springer, Cham, pp 27–49

Chak T (2014) Undocumented: the architecture of migrant detention. Sections, The Architecture Observer, Montreal

Chavez LR (2008) The Latino threat: constructing immigrants, citizens, and the nation. Stanford University Press, Stanford

Coll KM (2010) Remaking citizenship: Latina immigrants and new American politics. Stanford University Press, Stanford

Coutin SB (2007) Nations of emigrants: shifting boundaries of citizenship in El Salvador and the United States. Cornell University Press, Ithaca

Cuadra CB (2012) Right of access to health care for undocumented migrants in EU: a comparative study of national policies. Eur J Pub Health 22(2):267–271

De Genova N (2005) Working the boundaries: race, space, and "illegality" in Mexican Chicago. Duke University Press, Durham

De Genova N, Peutz NM (2010) The deportation regime: sovereignty, space, and the freedom of movement. Duke University Press, Durham

DeChaine DR (2012) Introduction: for rhetorical border studies. In: DeChaine DR (ed) Border rhetorics: citizenship and identity on the US-Mexico frontier. University of Alabama, Tuscaloosa, pp 1–15

Dei GJS (1996) Anti-racism education: theory and practice. Fernwood, Halifax

Dorling K (2013) Growing up in a hostile environment: the rights of undocumented migrant children in the UK. Migrant Children's Project, Colchester

Goldberg DT (2004) The end(s) of race. Postcolonial Stud 7(2):211–230

Goldring L, Landolt P (2013) The conditionality of legal rights and status: conceptualizing precarious non-citizenship. In: Goldring L, Landolt P (eds) Producing and negotiating non-citizenship: precarious legal status in Canada. University of Toronto Press, Toronto, pp 3–27

Goldring L, Berinstein C, Bernhard J (2009) Institutionalizing precarious migratory status in Canada. Citizenship Stud 13(3):239–265

Gonzales RG (2016) Lives in limbo: undocumented and coming of age in America. University of California Press, Oakland

Gonzales RG, Sigona N (2017) Mapping the soft borders of citizenship: an introduction. In: Gonzales RG, Sigona N (eds) Within and beyond citizenship: borders, membership and belonging. Routledge, New York, pp 1–16

Hondagneu-Sotelo P (2007) Domestica: immigrant workers cleaning and caring in the shadows of affluence. University of California Press, Berkeley

Kubal A (2013) Conceptualizing semi-legality in migration research. Law Soc Rev 47(3):555–587

Li PS (2001) The racial subtext in Canada's immigration discourse. J Int Migr Integr 2(1):77–97

Light MT, Miller T (2018) Does undocumented immigration status increase violent crime? Criminology 56(2):370–401

Longazel J (2016) Undocumented fears: immigration and the politics of divide and conquer in Hazleton, Pennsylvania. Temple University Press, Philadelphia

McLaughlin J (2010) Classifying the "ideal migrant worker": Mexican and Jamaican transnational farmworkers in Canada. Focaal J Glob Hist Anthropol 57:79–94

Melamed J (2015) Racial capitalism. Crit Ethn Stud 1(1):76–85

Menjívar C (2006) Liminal legality: Salvadoran and Guatemalan immigrants' lives in the United States. Am J Sociol 111(4):999–1037

Menjívar C, Kil SH (2002) For their own good: benevolent rhetoric and exclusionary language in public officials' discourse on immigrant-related issues. Soc Justice 29(1/2):160–176

Mutsaers P (2014) An ethnographic study of the policing of internal borders of the Netherlands. Br J Criminol 54(5):831–848

Nevins J (2002) Operation gatekeeper: the rise of the "illegal alien" and the making of the U.S.-Mexico boundary. Routledge, New York

Ngai MM (2004) Impossible subjects: illegal aliens and the making of modern America. Princeton University Press, Princeton

Pratt A (2005) Securing borders: detention and deportation in Canada. UBC Press, Vancouver

Robinson CJ (1983) Black Marxism: the making of the black radical tradition. University of North Carolina Press, North Carolina

Salter MB (2007) Governmentalities of an airport: heterotopia and confession. Int Political Sociol 1(1):49–66

Santa Ana O (2002) Brown tide rising: metaphors of Latinos in contemporary American public discourse. University of Texas Press, Austin

Stumpf JAUR (2006) The crimmigration crisis: immigrants, crime, and sovereign power. Am Univ Law Rev 56:367–419

Torpey JC (2000) The invention of the passport: surveillance, citizenship, and the state. Cambridge University Press, Cambridge, MA

Vaughan-Williams N (2015) "We are not animals!" Humanitarian border security and zoopolitical spaces in Europe Political Geography. Polit Geogr 45:1–10

Villegas PE (2013) Negotiating the boundaries of membership: health care providers, access to social goods and immigration status. In: Goldring L, Landolt P (eds) Producing and negotiating non-citizenship: precarious legal status in Canada. University of Toronto Press, Toronto

Villegas PE (2014) "I can't even buy a bed because I don't know if I'll have to leave tomorrow:" temporal orientations among Mexican precarious status migrants in Toronto. Citizenship Stud 18(3–4):277–291

Villegas FJ (2018) "Don't Ask, Don't Tell": examining the illegalization of undocumented students in Toronto, Canada. Br J Sociol Educ 39(8):1111–1125

Villegas JF, Morales A, Munoz E, Brown S, Butler M, Chung P, Lal N, Williams K (2017) The Kalamazoo county ID: recognizing a need and addressing the barriers. Kalamazoo County ID Taskforce, Kalamazoo, pp 1–33. https://reason.kzoo.edu/csjl/assets/Kalamazoo_County_ID_Report.pdf

Vosko LF, Preston V, Latham R (2014) Liberating temporariness?: Migration, work, and citizenship in an age of insecurity. McGill-Queen's Press, Montreal

Willen SS (2007) Toward a critical phenomenology of "illegality": state power, criminalization, and abjectivity among undocumented migrant workers in Tel Aviv, Israel. Int Migr 45(3):8–38

Willen SS (2012) Migration, "illegality," and health: mapping embodied vulnerability and debating health-related deservingness. Soc Sci Med 74:805–811

Zedner L (2016) Citizenship deprivation, security and human rights. Eur J Migr Law 18(2):222–242

Zetter R (2007) More labels, fewer refugees: remaking the refugee label in an era of globalization. J Refug Stud 20(2):172–192

Indian Diaspora in New Zealand

66

Todd Nachowitz

Contents

Introduction	1266
Existing Myths	1267
Background	1269
Earliest Indian Presence, 1769–1782	1273
Timber and Sealing Voyages, 1783–1808	1276
Earliest Indian Settlement, 1809–1850	1280
Indian Settlement from 1851	1282
Indians in the New Zealand Census, Phase I: 1851–1911	1283
Indians in the New Zealand Census, Phase II: 1916–1981	1291
Indians in the New Zealand Census, Phase III: 1986–Present	1302
Conclusion	1306
Cross-References	1307
References	1307

Abstract

This chapter surveys the Indian diaspora in New Zealand through both the earliest historical presence of Indians in Aotearoa and through the lens of Indian settlement as recorded in the New Zealand Census. The earliest Indian presence is summarized through a previously unused historical source, the ships logs and muster rolls of the very earliest European vessels of exploration and exploitation to New Zealand. It places Indians in Aotearoa at the very instance of Māori-European first contact on land in 1769, 70 years earlier than previously recorded. Indian settlement, viewed through a more complete review of the New Zealand Census than previously reported, also places the first instance of Indians in the New Zealand Census 20 years earlier than previously reported, back to 1861. The chapter also charts the historical growth of the Indian population, ranging from

---

T. Nachowitz (✉)
University of Waikato, Hamilton, New Zealand
e-mail: todd@earthdiverse.org.nz; toddnach@gmail.com

© The Author(s), under exclusive license to Springer Nature Singapore Pte Ltd. 2019
S. Ratuva (ed.), *The Palgrave Handbook of Ethnicity*,
https://doi.org/10.1007/978-981-13-2898-5_90

their first appearance in the 1861 Census through to the 2018 Census. It also discounts the previous belief that early Indian settlers were predominantly scrub cutters, hawkers, bottle collectors, and market gardeners, showing instead that early Indian settlement consisted of entrepreneurs, teachers, and skilled professionals as well. The chapter concludes with a brief look at Indian accomplishments in terms of their political participation, and their greater inclusion in modern New Zealand society, as compared with the invisibility that characterizes their earliest presence and settlement.

Keywords

Indian diaspora · New Zealand · History · Earliest arrival · First contact · Indian presence · Indian settlement · Census · Ethnicity · Migration · Demography

Introduction

New Zealand's Indian population, as one of many possible minority ethnic communities to examine, makes an ideal case study due to a number of historical processes and unique conditions. These include (1) the early and wide dispersal of Indian populations globally (Clarke et al. 1990; Parekh 1993; Peach 1994; Lal 2006); (2) the resultant geographic range of birth countries from which they have emigrated to New Zealand (Kadekar 2005; Didham 2010), considering that most other migrant communities tend to have a higher degree of sociocultural and linguistic homogeneity and generally arrive from a single country or region of the world; (3) the direct immigration from India to New Zealand (Tiwari 1980; Zodgekar 1980; Leckie 2007); and (4) the extensive range of cultural, ethnic, social, caste, religious, and linguistic variation in the Indian population (Zodgekar 2010; Nachowitz 2015) not evident in other migrant communities in New Zealand. The long history of the Indian diaspora in New Zealand, beginning with its earliest sojourners in the late eighteenth century, continuing with Indian settlement in the 19th and 20th centuries, and comprised of both a well-established domestically-born minority and recent overseas-born migrants who hail from a wide variety of sending nations (Leckie 2010; Friesen and Kearns 2008; Bandyopadhyay 2010; Nachowitz 2015), should allow Indians to claim an equitable position in New Zealand's settlement narrative. Yet inclusion of non-Māori non-*Pākehā* minority communities in Aotearoa's earliest history has remained elusive.

Historically, South Asian sojourners first appear in Aotearoa along with the very first European ships of exploration and exploitation in the late eighteenth century (Nachowitz 2018). Indian settlement in New Zealand began in the mid-nineteenth century and consisted of mostly small populations of Punjabi and Gujarati settlers (McGee 1962, 1993; Tiwari 1980; McLeod 1980, 1986; McLeod and Bhullar 1992; Leckie 1995, 1998, 2007). Since reform introduced by the 1986 Immigration Policy Review and implemented following the Immigration Act 1987, the constitution of migrant populations underwent rapid transformation, significantly altering New Zealand's demographic composition (McMillan 2006;

Bedford and Ho 2008). The 1986 Census reported 15,810 ethnic Indians before immigration reform, while the 2013 Census recorded 156,567 ethnic Indians, an increase of 890.3% growth over the 27 intercensal years from 1986 to 2013. Those of Indian ethnicity in today's New Zealand are no longer just Gujaratis and Punjabis. There is a deeper heterogeneity in existence that is not evident in the publicly released statistics that hides a complex assemblage of Indian subethnicities that renders them virtually invisible through compacting differentiation into the single category "Indian." While the New Zealand census lumps Indians into the "Asian" category, most merely see "Indian" without ascertaining the myriad underlying differences of ancestry, regional geography, linguistic variation, religious affiliation, caste, country of birth, and national identity that more accurately define "Indian." This differentiation underscores the importance of a proper understanding of the concept of ethnicity and the significance of the invisibility of subethnicities. Although census figures are one indicator of population growth and demographic dispersion, they do not portray the dramatic internal changes within minority communities such as the Indian diaspora in New Zealand.

This chapter will briefly explore the circumstances surrounding the earliest Indian presence in Aotearoa, the period of permanent settlement which follows, and the demographic history of the population as reported in the Census statistics. A critical look at historic accounts of the earliest Indian arrivals in Aotearoa may reveal different interpretations of known history relevant to Māori-European first encounter. Indeed, the possibility of the involvement of non-Māori non-European others in the exploration and early settlement of Aotearoa has previously been poorly considered by historians. Being aware of their involvement in the early history of nation-building may help advance Indian objectives of inclusion in a shared national identity. Such an awareness of participation may further the aspirations of other minority communities in New Zealand which may help move Aotearoa New Zealand from its multidecade focus on biculturalism towards today's more modern notion that New Zealand is a multicultural state comprised of multiple ethnicities and subethnicities. Likewise, a brief examination of the census history of Indian settlement, as well as an examination of their early occupations, will reveal the extent and nature of their dispersal, as well as deflect a few well-known myths about the earliest Indian settlement in New Zealand. Finally, I will present more recent statistics of the Indian population in New Zealand and briefly report on Indian political representation in the New Zealand Parliament. The most recently available census statistics are currently from the 2013 Census. The online version of this chapter will be updated with the 2018 Census statistics when they are released publicly in 2019, in order to give a more complete snapshot of the Indian population in New Zealand today.

Existing Myths

There are a few existing myths in New Zealand's settlement narrative that can serve as a point of departure. The first myth is that of the general order of human settlement, which generally proceeds as follows: Māori were the first arrivals (as *tangata whenua*), followed by Europeans, then Asians, and finally Pasifika populations. This narrative holds that Māori, arriving from their homeland of *Hawaiki*, were the first humans to settle Aotearoa. Europeans are believed to have followed many centuries after Māori settlement. The first European to sight Aotearoa was Able Tasman, who arrived in 1642 but did not come ashore. This was followed well over a century later by the very first European landings in 1769 by ships captained by James Cook (October 1769) and Jean-François-Marie de Surville (December 1769). Numerous other European vessels of exploration and exploitation followed in the wake of Cook's and Surville's initial visits. Nearly a hundred years later (1860s), this would be followed by the very first Asian arrivals, consisting of predominately Chinese miners who came to work the gold fields of central Otago on the South Island. Small numbers of Indians were also said to have arrived at this time. These early Asian settlers were then followed a century later (1970s) by Pasifika populations who settled in New Zealand in large numbers. Major immigration reform in 1986–1987 brought about new waves of migration, particularly from Asia, which helped nudge New Zealand further away from its bicultural roots. This story is therefore the dominant settlement narrative of Aotearoa New Zealand and represents the most commonly held belief. The narrative tells of Māori arrival and settlement, multiple centuries of developing a unique Māori culture and history (distinct from other Polynesian peoples throughout the South Pacific), then shifts into a bicultural narrative with the arrival of Europeans and their subsequent domination of Māori throughout the colonial period. Although Asian and Polynesian peoples are believed to have settled here from around the mid-1860s on, it is not until major immigration reform (the Immigration Act of 1986) that helps move New Zealand from a bicultural to a multicultural society. The Māori→European→Asian/Pacific settlement narrative mirrors this general monocultural→bicultural→multicultural shift. Multiculturalism, after over a century of bicultural discourse, is now seen as the dominant social form evident today. Indeed, New Zealand has maintained the unique nature of its bicultural discourse until very recently, when large numbers of migrants, from Asia and other parts of the world, helped changed the nature of the narrative from a bicultural focus (Māori and Europeans) to one of ethnic pluralism (Singham 2006; Sibley and Ward 2013). While parts of this narrative are true, the serial nature of movement into Aotearoa is less than accurate and includes the mistaken understanding that Asian populations arrived much later than Europeans. Also, the narrative shift towards multiculturalism is still a work in progress, while many still maintain the belief that biculturalism is still the dominant societal form.

A second myth holds that Chinese and Indian arrival generally began with the discovery of gold in Central Otago (1860s). While permanent Asian settlement generally begins around this time, Asian arrival, and Indian presence in particular, begins with the very first Europeans to Aotearoan shores. A third myth categorically states that "No one knows who was the first Indian to enter New Zealand" (McLeod 1986, p. 51). While McLeod and other historians and academics working on the Indian diaspora in New Zealand have contributed much scholarship, many missed the more obscure sources, inadvertently perpetuating the myth of more recent Asian arrival to New Zealand. Unfortunately, this misnomer has prevailed throughout much of the research regarding the Indian diaspora in New Zealand and needs rectification (e.g., "The first Indian ever to set foot on New Zealand soil was a Bengali. We do not know his name, but he was a sailor who jumped ship in 1809 and was living with a local Māori") (Bandyopadhyay 2006, p. 125). We do indeed know the names of the very earliest Indian arrivals, their ports of origin, and when, how, and under what circumstances they arrived on Aotearoan shores.

Background

This chapter briefly summarizes the hidden history of the very earliest Indian arrival and presence in Aotearoa. More detailed accounts can be found in earlier publications (Nachowitz 2015, 2018), but these are summarized here in an attempt to provide key details of the history of Indian arrival and settlement in Aotearoa New Zealand. The fact that this knowledge still remains obscure underlies the invisibility that early non-Māori non-Pākehā minorities still have in becoming part of a shared national identity within the still currently dominant bicultural Māori-European narrative. Making these stories more visible to students and teachers of New Zealand history, and those interested in ethnic pluralism and cultural diversity, is a primary objective. Members of ethnic minorities in New Zealand today are largely unaware of the importance of their ancestral contributions to the settlement of New Zealand, and wider awareness of such a past could help minorities reclaim a much-needed voice in the current debate over multiculturalism and within the wider context of the debate over immigration. As an example, Indians can now argue that since they were present at the very onset of Māori-European encounter, they have as much right to settle in New Zealand as do Europeans.

The historical invisibility of minority others supports the existing dominant bicultural settlement narrative and undermines minority inclusion in the history of the modern nation state. Such a retelling of events, which includes Indian presence at the time of Māori-Pākehā first encounter, may assist in the formation and strengthening of a shared national identity, allowing the knowledge of early participation in critical historical events to more deeply effect what it means to be a New Zealander of Indian ethnicity. A shared national identity would, therefore, build upon the necessary foundations of biculturalism that exclude the participation of non-Māori minority others in the historical narrative of Aotearoa's founding. Unpacking erased histories in this way may increase minority and majority awareness of greater minority participation in its history, and knowledge of presence at initial Māori-European contact may help relevant minorities reclaim association in a newly formed shared national identity that has the potential to strengthen social cohesion and inclusion.

Of particular note is the distinguishing nature of early Indian migration to and settlement in New Zealand. What differentiates Indian arrival in Aotearoa from the other destinations of Indian émigrés during this period is that these voyages were predominantly voluntary, as opposed to the indentured servitude of the *girmitiya* that characterized the overwhelming majority of Indian dispersal from South Asia through to the mid-1800s (see Lal 2006). While use of the term "voluntary" to refer to the earliest Indian migration to Aotearoa may be problematic, it is decidedly of a different nature than the early Indian emigration that occurred elsewhere (e.g., to countries of the British colonies under the Indian indenture system, such as Mauritius, Trinidad and Tobago, Guyana, Suriname, the Caribbean, Fiji, Malaysia, Singapore, and East Africa).

The earliest Indian arrivals and migrants can be depicted as reaching Aotearoan shores in three distinct waves. The very earliest Indian "sojourners" to Aotearoa were hired as ship labor on European vessels of exploration and exploitation and represent the first "presence" of South Asians in Aotearoa, their appearance brief and transitory, yet nonetheless, demonstrable and evident. These initial sojourners were later followed by sporadic "ship-jumpers," Indian sailors who chose to remain and settle while their ships were temporarily anchored offshore. A possible reason to abandon crew mates and settle among Māori may have been the unsatisfactory shipboard conditions and the deplorable treatment that the Indian crew may have received while under European power and authority. The lure of the unfamiliar would have been an appealing incentive when compared with the tribulations of the voyage. These "ship-jumpers" may be considered the first Indian "settlers," as some documentation exists attesting to their settlement among Māori and of their assistance to Māori as intermediaries with regard to European encounter. Documentation for these first two groups is poorly known and what evidence that has been uncovered to date has already been presented (Leckie 2007; Nachowitz 2015). The third group would be considered de facto settlers, either coming of their own accord (e.g., to mine gold, escape unfavorable conditions in India, or to farm) or arriving while under the employment, as *naukar* (household servants), of former British officers of the Rāj who were often granted land in New Zealand upon the successful completion of their tours of military duty in India. This group has been well documented in the existing literature. The following section, therefore, summarizes the very earliest Indian presence and arrival in Aotearoa.

Although there is still debate surrounding the actual date of the first human arrival and settlement, there is general agreement that Māori arrival is estimated to have occurred during the thirteenth century, and recent evidence shows that this settlement occurred more recently than was previously thought (McGlone 1989; Howe 2008; Moon 2013). As a way of providing important context, the first European explorer to the region, the Dutchman Abel Tasman, transited the islands in the summer of 1642–1643, although it was not until James Cook's and Jean François Marie de Surville's visits in 1769–1770, more than 126 years later, that Europeans began to become aware of the land "down under." Cook was the first to extensively map the newly "discovered" territory and report back to Europe its resource largesse – its flax, timber, seals, and whales, which were, no doubt, of tremendous importance to his benefactors. Cook made two subsequent visits to New Zealand (1773–1774 and 1777), and his initial reports later led to the first European settlers. The first to arrive were timber merchants, sealers, whalers, and traders in the late 1700s, followed by missionaries in the early 1800s, with European settlers arriving in large numbers from the late 1830s onwards (Graham 1992; King 2003). In the 1840 Treaty of Waitangi, Māori chiefs ceded "sovereignty" or "governance" to the British Queen, in exchange for which the chiefs and tribes retained their "full exclusive and undisturbed possession of their lands and estates, forests, fisheries and other properties" (Owens 1992, p. 51), along with granting to Māori their rights and privileges as British subjects. Although the meaning and intent of the treaty is disputable due to the nature of its poor translation and misrepresentations, it, nonetheless, secured British rule over Aotearoa, marked the genesis of the modern nation state, and provided Māori with a tangible base for the settlement of later historic grievances against the Crown.

The reports of initial European visits led to a rising awareness in Europe of the Antipodes and of the great store of natural resources available for exploitation. Anne Salmond (1991, 1997) provides detailed historical accounts of first contact between indigenous Māori and European explorers and settlers between the years 1642 and 1815. The early settlements of European sealers, whalers, and missionaries soon gave way to more permanent settlements throughout Aotearoa, bringing further migration from Europe, the Americas, and Australia. That small numbers of Indians were among the earliest post-Māori sojourners to Aotearoa is not well known.

The very earliest Indian presence in Aotearoa has remained obscure, hidden in old ship logs from captains on early sealing and timber voyages. Previous research on the history of Indian migration and settlement pegged the first known record of an Indian in Aotearoa to a Bengali who jumped ship in 1809 or 1810 to marry a Māori woman, although Leckie (2007, p. 21, 2010, p. 48) mentions earlier Indian visits without providing details. The exact date is unclear, as some cite 1809 (Salmond 1997, pp. 373–377; Entwisle 2005, pp. 103–106; Leckie 2006, p. 389, 2007, p. 21; Didham 2010, p. 4), while others 1810 (Friesen 2008, p. 47; Pio 2012, p. 2; Swarbrick 2015). Bandyopadhyay (2006, p. 125) states, "The first Indian ever to set foot on New Zealand soil was a Bengali. We do not know his name, but he was a sailor who jumped ship in 1809 and was living with local Māori." These sources all appear to be based on the 3 May 1820 entry in the journal of Richard Cruise (1824), an English army officer on a 10-month visit to New Zealand. Referring to a man of Indian descent, he writes:

> This man had left an East Indiaman that touched at the Bay of Islands ten years before, and married a woman of the tribe subject to Tekokee, whom he considered his chief. Though quite a New Zealander in his dress and habits, his diminutive person and dark complexion made him appear to great disadvantage among the handsome and athletic people among whom he had settled. (Cruise 1824, p. 315)

This would account for various claims of 1809 or 1810 as the first known recorded account of Indian presence. Complicating matters, Murphy (2007, p. 2) states that "the first known Indian person to come to New Zealand was Bir Singh Gill, an itinerant Sikh herbalist who arrived in 1890." The murkiness and details surrounding the first known Indian presence in Aotearoa are complicated by both conflicting sources and researchers inability to pursue possible earlier and more obscure materials. Earlier accounts of Indian sojourns to Aotearoa can be culled from ship logs and muster rolls from the earliest European voyages of exploration, including the earliest sealing and timber ventures to Aotearoan shores.

What is certain, however, is that Indian presence in Aotearoa is recorded along with the very earliest European explorers, an occurrence that is little known and absent from official histories which have generally neglected early Asian appearance and settlement prior to the arrival of Chinese goldseekers in the 1860s. Of the general invisibility of the Chinese from official history, Murphy (2003, p. 282) writes: "Chinese New Zealand history has rated barely a mention. Many earlier works compounded the neglect with a dismissive racism that reflects the attitude to Chinese New Zealanders at the time." The same is true of general immigration histories to New Zealand, which equally ignore the earliest Asian appearance (Taher 1970, p. 38; Borrie 1991; Greif 1995) – Borrie's history, for instance, begins with Chinese arrival in 1870. While Māori arrival and settlement, followed by European exploration, exploitation, missionization, and colonization, are both well documented, little or no mention is made of the earliest Asian contributions, even though Indian presence is recorded on the first visits of European vessels to the southern oceans from 1769. It is only recently that histories of early Chinese and Indian presence have begun to contribute to a wider, more inclusive, retelling of *tauiwi* arrival and settlement in Aotearoa (McLeod 1986; Ng 2003; Ip 2003; Leckie 2007; McCarthy 2009), yet these stories are poorly known – excluded from general texts of New Zealand history – and all of them disregard the earliest Asian presence.

Such easy dismissal of the very earliest Asian contributions prior to the Chinese gold rush is further reflected in the state reporting of minorities in such official documents as the national census (see Nachowitz 2015, Chap. 6). As early Asian sojourners are markedly absent from such histories (see Murphy 2009 for a discussion of Chinese exclusion), their appearance is insufficiently recognized in official documentation. While not totally absent, pre-1860s Asian presence in New Zealand is certainly difficult to discern. While newer ethnic histories are becoming increasingly accessible, the earliest accounts still remain concealed. It is unfortunate that we have few surviving records that can be directly attributed to our earliest Asian sojourners. We are, regrettably, forced to shape our understanding of their presence through the only means available to us – the eyes of those Europeans who accompanied them. While once removed, they nevertheless give us some insight as to how the early *tauiwi* may have lived and provide records of encounters for which there are no other extant sources. In examining the earliest stories of Indian encounters with both European and Māori, the historical misconception that there were only a handful of known Indians prior to the 1860s is rectified, and their presence affirmed with the earliest accounts of Māori–European encounter. There were hundreds of nameless and unknown South Asians who accompanied Europeans on the earliest voyages of exploration and exploitation to Aotearoa. Such a re-examination would thus revise existing scholarship on Indian history in the Antipodes and alter the majority narrative that characterizes *tauiwi* arrival and settlement as being a much later occurrence.

Earliest Indian Presence, 1769–1782

The first known record of Māori–European encounter was the visit of Dutchman Abel Tasman in December 1642. Although Tasman never came ashore, four members of his crew were lost in a watery skirmish after an initial misreading of first contact at Taitapu (Golden Bay, north-eastern corner of the South Island). One hundred and twenty-seven years would pass before the next known European visits to Aotearoa by Cook and Surville in 1769. These initial visits were followed by two subsequent Cook expeditions (1773–1774 and 1777) and numerous additional voyages by other Europeans in the late 1700s, all well documented (Tapp 1958; Beaglehole 1968; Richards 2010).

After Tasman's 1642 voyage, Māori–European encounter next occurred during Cook's visit to Tūranganui (Poverty Bay, near Gisborne, east coast of the North Island) between 6 and 11 October 1769, marking the first known European landing and presence ashore, followed by subsequent encounters during Cook's first voyage through 31 March 1770 on the *Endeavour*. Most of the vessels of European exploration in the South Pacific were of the British East India Company traveling from India on their way to deliver convicts and supplies to the recently established settlements at Botany Bay in Australia and Norfolk Island. The British East India Company had played a key role in bringing Europeans to Aotearoan shores with regular sailings between India and Port Jackson, Australia. The French India Company, engaged in a commercial war with the British for power and control of the East, was also pursuing its interests in the South Pacific. Indian sojourners arriving on these trips were the first documented South Asians to set foot on Aotearoan soil.

Cook's first visit to Aotearoa on the *Endeavour*, having sailed from Plymouth, England in August 1768, was unlikely to have had any Indian sailors aboard. The story of Indian sojourns to Aotearoa therefore begins in 1769 with the sailing of the third European ship to visit Aotearoan waters, the French ship *Saint Jean Baptiste* under the command of its captain, Jean François Marie de Surville. Surville had been in India looking for trade opportunities between French colonies in India and China. He set sail from the French colony of Pondicherry, India, on 2 June 1769 on a voyage of combined exploration and trade to the central Pacific. He arrived off the coast of Hokianga (south of Ninety Mile Beach, near the tip of the North Island) on 12 December 1769 – just 2 months after Cook entered Aotearoan waters on the *Endeavour* – and looking for suitable anchorage, set off around North Cape, eventually stopping for 2 weeks between 18 and 31 December in Doubtless Bay (at present day Whatuwhiwhi on the eastern side of the northern tip of the North Island). Surville's crew suffered severely from the effects of scurvy, and he had taken them ashore multiple times to collect water and greens that helped restore the crew's health (Dunmore 1969). Dunmore's translation (1981, pp. 273–287) of the ship's muster roll of the crew reports a total of 53 Indian lascars from a crew of 232, making up 22.8% of the entire crew. These are recorded as: three Indian warrant officers, 47 Indian sailors, and three other Indians. Some of the lascars are named, and some of their deaths recorded in the ship's log. The three Indian warrant officers are recorded

(Dunmore 1981, p. 283) as an unnamed *serang* (chief lascar, or boatswain's mate) recorded as having "died at sea, date unknown"; "Taudel [?]," although this probably refers to the *serang*'s assistant, which is usually rendered in English as a *tindal* or gang boss (see Fisher 2006), recorded as dying at sea on 29 October 1769; and the third as "Kasap," a deck supervisor and lamp attendant, dying at sea on 10 November 1769. Of the remaining 50 lascars, the roll records three as dying in October, with 44 dying in November 1769, just prior to reaching Aotearoan waters in December 1769. Of the remaining three lascars, one is recorded as the chaplain's servant, a Bengali named "Nicolas," who died of scurvy on 29 November 1769. Of the total 53 lascars aboard the *Saint Jean Baptiste*, it would appear that only two survived to reach Aotearoa. The first is recorded as "Mamouth Cassem" in the ship's log, whose real name was probably Mahmud Qāsim, born in Pondicherry about 1755. The second is listed as a Bengali named "Nasrin," aged about 16 or 17 years, on the muster roll. Given their names, it can be assumed that both were Muslims. Both are recorded as dying in Peru on 14 April 1770, where the ship sailed after leaving Aotearoa under duress. Dunmore's earlier work (1969, pp. 113–114), however, mentions a Bengali lascar dying during the night of 7 March 1770, and two additional lascars (the first another Bengali lascar, the second a "Bengali servant boy, aged twelve or thirteen") as having died on 30 March 1770. This means that these additional Indians would have also survived the Aotearoan excursion in December 1769, bringing the total number of lascars surviving the Aotearoan excursion to five. Given their recorded survival, we can be certain that these men would have gone ashore along with the other sick crew members of the *Saint Jean Baptiste* during their 2-week stay from 18 to 31 December 1769 and their subsequent departure for South America. While numerous log entries attest to the crew's excursions on land, none of the landing parties are named, although it is known that Surville was quite concerned for their health and took sick crewmen ashore for short periods of time during their stay.

> Sickness and death which appear indistinguishable among our crew have caused me to reflect seriously, to see if I could not find a solution more certain than that of following the course, planned from the start, which I am now keeping, and go, if I can, to New Zealand, and seek there a place of refuge where we can rest awhile. After considering the position, I believe that anything we could attempt elsewhere would be far less certain than this New Zealand suggestion, and that, anyhow, we have no alternative in the state in which we are. (Surville's log entry, 23 November, translated by Dunmore 1981, p. 126)

The journals of both Surville and his second, Guillame Labé, record daily entries between 18 and 31 December in which sick crew members were taken ashore for fresh air, water, and greens to help combat the ill effects of scurvy from which the crew greatly suffered. Since arriving,

> our crew has been attacked by scurvy. Only 7 or 8 men are fit. I hope that this call will restore them by staying a whole month and putting them ashore. If not, we would be in a nasty situation. (Labé's log, 18 December 1769, translated by Dunmore 1981, p. 245)

Both Surville's and Labé's logs discuss the daily excursions ashore for the sick to recuperate and collect fresh water and greens. Although it is not recorded which sailors went ashore on which days, it is apparent, from both logs, that the sick were rotated, giving the ill a chance to rest and recover ashore for the day, returning to the ship by nightfall. It is clear that the landings were of immense value to the infirm and would have enabled the remaining lascars to survive their Aotearoan excursion. Due to misunderstandings and skirmishes with the local Māori, the crew was forced to leave and set sail for South America.

While there is no written record confirming lascar presence ashore in Aotearoa, their mere survival attests to the fact that they would have been included in the sick crew's landings and recuperated sufficiently to continue their journey to Peru. Of the remaining lascars that survived, three apparently died while traversing the Pacific, while the remaining two lascars died shortly after reaching Peru (Dunmore 1969, p. 113, 1981, p. 287). These two would have been Mahmud Qāsim of Pondicherry and the Bengali lascar Nasreen, both mentioned in the original muster roll, as both are recorded as dying on 14 April 1770. The manner of their deaths is unrecorded, though presumably from scurvy. On the basis of their being alive during the Aotearoan landings, we can be certain that Qāsim and Nasreen, along with the unnamed three lascars who died during the trans-Pacific journey, were the first South Asians to set foot in Aotearoa. The landings of these Indian lascars at Doubtless Bay would have occurred, perhaps multiple times, during the 2-week period of 18–31 December 1769. There is a plaque mounted at the site near today's settlement at Whatuwhiwhi (Karikari Peninsula), but it does not mention that Indian lascars were a part of the landing parties.

Monument and commemorative plaque marking the anchorage of the *St. Jean Baptiste* at Pātia Head, Whatuwhiwhi, Doubtless Bay

The next European ship to visit was the voyage of Marion du Fresne to the Bay of Islands, April–July 1772. Although the muster rolls of those departing on the two ships of this expedition, the *Mascarin* and the *Marquis de Castries*, are known (Kelly 1951, p. 18), only the officers aboard are named. As the ships departed from the French colony in Mauritius and called in at Cape Town, South Africa, before reaching Aotearoa's west coast at Taranaki, it is unlikely that lascars were aboard. Although a shore station was established to help the sick recuperate from scurvy

(Salmond 1991, p. 393) and to repair their ships (Kelly 1951, p. 29), there is no mention of an Indian crew. The four small straw huts that the crew built to remain ashore for several days and the repair camps they established at various anchorages during their 4-month stay might be regarded as the first known residence of Europeans in Aotearoa. Grant (2015) erroneously identifies the first European "residents" as a group of sealers dropped off at Tamatea in 1792 (with the uncertainty of a ship's return many months later), having spent months ashore and providing for themselves while awaiting passage on a returning ship.

No lascars are known to have been aboard either Cook's second expedition to Aotearoa on the *Resolution*, which he commanded, and the *Adventure*, captained by Furneaux, which sailed from England on 13 July 1772, nor on his third expedition on the *Resolution*, accompanied by the *Discovery*, which left Plymouth, England, on 12 July 1776 and reached Aotearoa in February 1777. Neither expedition is likely to have had any Indian crewmen. Cook's voyages were considered to be largely exploratory and scientific in nature, and British engagement in the South Pacific only began in earnest as it subsequently solidified its trade interests in India and China.

Timber and Sealing Voyages, 1783–1808

The story of British engagement and sustained lascar involvement in Aotearoa began in 1783, when one of James Cook's former companions, James Matra, first suggested establishing a permanent British settlement in Aotearoa in order to supply settlers in New South Wales with valuable flax and timber (Tapp 1958, p. 3). At the time, British East India Company (Salmond 1997, p. 235) ships were plying the waters between England, South Africa, India, Australia, and China engaging in trade. Many such voyages also brought convicts to Australia. The first named Indian on British ships plying these routes was the Indian Muslim convict, Zimran Wriam, on the *Atlantic* in 1791 on route to the convict settlement in Port Jackson (Akbarzadeh and Saeed 2001, p. 14). Establishing a British colony in Aotearoa to support the nascent Port Jackson settlement and to provide timber would become a priority.

In November 1792, John Thomson wrote to Henry Dundas, the British secretary of state at Botany Bay, suggesting that a British colony be established in Aotearoa. Thompson first suggested that a colonizing party from British India consisting of "fifty sober men; one hundred sepoys, & 100 convicts" might be sent to Aotearoa along with military supplies and stores necessary for 1 year. According to Thompson, the people in India were "just in that state of civilization proper to be made useful" (Salmond 1997, p. 234). Many of the ships that plied the route between India and Australia between the years 1794 and 1801 – in what Salmond calls "the timber voyages" (1997, p. 234) – were crewed by Indian lascars and *sepoys*. These ships most often sailed between India and China by way of Australia and Aotearoa. There are a number of records in the ships' logs and passenger manifests documenting Indian crews and landfall in Aotearoa, with a few records of "ship-jumpers" while transiting, and other records recounting landfall and work ashore (Furber 1970; Leckie 2007, p. 21; Kolig 2010, p. 22).

One of the first timber voyages to be recorded making landfall in Aotearoa was the *Fancy*, commanded by Edgar Dell, charged with delivering provisions from India to Port Jackson, and procuring the necessary timber and spars for delivery to India, which were desperately needed to repair British ships. The *Fancy*, along with an unknown number of Indian lascars and sepoys, departed from Mumbai in May 1794, arriving in Port Jackson 2 months later. After delivering its cargo, the *Fancy* set sail on 29 September 1794. Dell arrived in Aotearoa in November 1794 at Tokerau. The search for suitable timber led Dell to take the *Fancy* into the same waters that Cook had taken the *Endeavour* in 1769, inland, along the Waihou River (near present-day Thames in the Hauraki Gulf). Dell's diary records:

> At 4:00 am on 23 November, the brig's boats were lowered, and at ten o'clock [we] went off in the longboat accompanied by six Europeans, two Lascars and five Sepoys; and the third officer Alms was in the jolly boat with two Europeans and two Lascars, to take soundings of the river. (Dell 1795, in Salmond 1997, p. 245)

Dell's account records Indian crew in nearly equal numbers as Europeans. It is only the second known European visit to the Waihou River after Cook's initial shore party in 1769. Yet, while both accounts are known, the fact that the second visit was accompanied by so many Indian sailors is not.

Dell recounts his visit ashore, numerous encounters with Māori, and the procurement of the necessary timber to transport back to India. Another log entry, from 3 December 1794, records "Denniston and Alms went with the carpenter, the sawyer, six Lascars and two Sepoys in the longboat to begin felling trees" (Dell 1795 in Salmond 1997, p. 248). The log entry for 5 December records Dell taking "a party of nine Europeans, a Sepoy and four Lascars up the river, where they cut down two tall trees, and four more at another place where trees had already been felled" (Dell 1795 in Salmond 1997, p. 249). These three references in Dell's journal mark the second instance of documented Indian presence ashore in Aotearoa, after Surville's 1769 visit. Regarding additional British visits, a total of "seven vessels had arrived in Port Jackson before 1795 with timber from New Zealand" (Tapp 1958, p. 51), and it is likely that many of these would have been carrying Indian crew and convicts on their journeys between India and Australia.

In addition to the timber voyages, ships were also outfitted for sealing and lascars served on these. Although Cook first visited Tamatea (Dusky Sound in Fiordland, South Island) in 1773 on the *Resolution*, and his sailors are reported to have killed a number of seals for food, the first known sealing expeditions to the South Island were not organized until 1791–1793. Sealing began in earnest in October 1792 with the arrival of the *Britannia* in Tamatea. The *Britannia* had earlier left England with the task of delivering convicts to the penal colony at Botany Bay, subsequently sailing to Aotearoa to procure seal skins for the Chinese market. Under the command of William Raven, the *Britannia* had left behind a gang of 11 sealers. This was not an unusual practice, as many sealing gangs were left ashore to exploit the rookeries until their ships returned (Richards 2010, p. 165). When the *Britannia* did not return as scheduled, the sealing gang had abandoned hope and had begun constructing a schooner of about 60 tons, made entirely from Aotearoan timber. This half-constructed boat was left behind when the *Britannia* and *Francis* finally arrived 10 months later to pick up the sealing party in September 1793 (Richards 2010, p. 174). As most of these ships also plied the waters between Port Jackson and India and stopped in Aotearoa to fetch sealskins, it is likely that lascars were aboard these ships.

News of the partly built boat that had been left behind by the *Britannia* party attracted the next visitors to Tamatea in September 1795, when two ships, the East Indiamen sealing supply ship *Endeavour* and the small brig *Fancy*, arrived to collect sealskins, oil, and meat, all of which would have fetched profits in European and Chinese markets. This visit records that "244 people had arrived in the Sound, including European ex-convicts, escapees, deserters, passengers, officers, and sailors," and "also carried Lascars and Sepoys," and the ship's extensive log records the movements of these men while on the coast, sealing and cutting timber to repair their boats (McNab 1914, pp. 518–534; Richards 2010, p. 174). The *Endeavour* made it into harbor after crossing the Tasman Sea in a raging storm, but it was badly damaged upon arrival in Tamatea and had to be left behind. This ship is the first Aotearoan shipwreck recorded by Europeans (Hutching 2006). Good timber that could be salvaged from the *Endeavour* was added to finish the construction of a new boat that was built from the half-constructed ship that the previous party had left behind. This newly constructed boat was named *Providence* (Richards 2010, p. 174), the first ship to be built mostly of Aotearoan timber. In January 1796, after four "settled" months of sealing and building boats, the *Fancy* and the *Providence* set sail for Norfolk Island. Not all of the original crew from the *Endeavour* and *Fancy* were allowed to board, and 35 men, including several Indian seamen, were forced to stay behind, "their dependence for provisions being chiefly on the seals and birds which they might kill" (Collins 1798, Vol. II, p. 460; Richards 2010, p. 174). This pathetic company of castaways, including lascars, was, in effect, the second sealing gang to be "stationed" in Aotearoa. Upon arrival of the two ships in Norfolk Island, supplies were loaded and "several Lascars and Portuguese seaman, and forty-eight half-starved passengers" were put ashore before carrying on to China to sell their cargo (Collins 1798, Vol. I, pp. 460–461; McNab 1914, Vol. II, p. 553). An American boat, *Mercury*, was later dispatched to Fiordland in 1797 to pick up "thirty-five half-starved survivors, finally landing them in Norfolk after a stay of more than eighteen months on their own in the Sound" (Collins 1798, Vol. II, p. 48).

These tales tell of the hardships experienced by the very earliest of the sealing gangs left behind in Fiordland between the years 1791 and 1797. While it is commonly believed that these parties consisted of only Europeans, it is evident from the information earlier that Indian lascars were also present and that not only did they serve as sailors aboard the vessels that plied these waters, but they also worked ashore as an integral part of the sealing and boat-building crews. While it has not been possible to confirm Indian presence on earlier sealing visits from 1791 to 1793, it is clear that Indian lascars were present in Tamatea from 1795 to 1797.

Sealing did not last very long, as the rookeries were soon depleted and the value of the procured skins had diminished. Richards (2010, p. 183) records the startling brevity of the sealing heyday which had collapsed by 1809. This helped focus the attention of European merchant ships back to the lucrative timber trade.

There were four subsequent visits by European ships to collect timber in the years since the 1794 sailing of the *Fancy*. These occurred between the years 1798–1800, and some of these would have had lascars aboard. The *Hunter* is recorded as sailing from Calcutta to Port Jackson and, under the command of Captain William Hingston, is known to have sailed from Port Jackson to the Waihou in Hauraki in October 1799 to collect timber and then return to Calcutta to deliver it (Salmond 1997, p. 525). Confirmation of lascar presence re-emerges in the 1801 crew manifest of the *Royal Admiral*, which was on its way from London to China via Port Jackson and sailed into the Hauraki Gulf on 20 April 1801, "heavily armed and manned by a crew of eighty-three European sailors and fifteen lascars" to obtain timber to sell in China. Captain William Wilson gives lengthy accounts of more crewmen going ashore to collect timber (Salmond 1997, p. 256). After the arrival of the *Royal Admiral* in 1801, there are over 50 European vessels recorded reaching Aotearoa between 1801 and 1809 (Salmond 1997, pp. 525–530), when our Bengali lascar who "jumped ship" in 1809 first appears, the same lascar who was previously believed to have been the first Indian in Aotearoa. It should be clear that many of these ships would have had lascars aboard, many of whom would have gone ashore with the ships' officers to fell timber and transport it back to the ship to use as spars for ships needing repair or for the lucrative markets in China. Additional research should uncover the extent of Indian presence in Aotearoa during this period.

Overall, the presence of Indian lascars with Europeans on the very earliest voyages of exploration in 1769 and on subsequent sealing and timber ships to Aotearoa is poorly recorded and not well known. It is certain, however, that Indian sailors were there at the dawn of European arrival in Aotearoa and are equally entitled to claim their place in the history of first encounter and the exploration and settlement of New Zealand. What we have instead is a dominant discourse of a sequence of events that begins with Māori arrival and settlement, followed by European arrival and colonization, and later by Asian and Pacific migration and settlement, with New Zealand moving from a bicultural to a multicultural state with more recent immigration reform in 1987. This discourse is misinformed and largely a result of European control of historical narrative. Aotearoa, *from the very earliest appearances of Europeans ashore*, was markedly multiethnic in nature. Indian lascars aboard early European sealing and timber vessels may have been more numerous than suggested here and, in some instances, may have outnumbered their European crew. It should be clear, however, that Indian lascars made up significant portions of the crew aboard many of the earliest ships to visit Aotearoa. European retelling of events often reported and named only European officers serving aboard or going ashore. There are numerous references to named Europeans ashore retrieving timber or seals, and any accompanying Indians, if documented, were only mentioned in passing. As unnamed participants, they remain mostly invisible and, hence, absent from the earliest history of European exploration, exploitation, and settlement in Aotearoa.

Earliest Indian Settlement, 1809–1850

As the presumptive "first Indian" on Aotearoan soil, it is important to recount the incident and embed it within its broader historical context. Although hundreds of South Asians may have left footprints prior to this event, it nonetheless remains significant as the first well-documented symbol of Indian settlement. Entwisle (2005, pp. 103–106) records an Indian of Bengali descent deserting the ship, *City of Edinburgh*, in 1809 in the Bay of Islands to live with his Māori wife. Salmond (1997, pp. 373–377) records in great detail the ship's visit in March–May 1809. In 1809, Captain Alexander Berry sailed from Australia to Aotearoa with the intent to repatriate two Ngāti Manu chiefs to the Bay of Islands and with the hope of procuring much needed timber for spars (Perry 1966; Swords 1978). While under the protection of the two Māori chiefs in the Bay of Islands, Berry (1912) records an accompanying Bengali servant. It is certain that this servant is the same one recorded as deserting ship to marry and settle with a Māori woman. While certainly not the first record of Indian presence, this Bengali is evidently the first known reference to a prolonged Indian settlement as opposed to being put ashore with a sealing crew or landing for a few nights to procure timber. Although there may be earlier instances yet to uncover, this defiant act records the first currently known intended Indian settlement in Aotearoa and suggests that our Bengali preferred the company of the Māori ashore to that of shipboard life with British colonials. Hence, it becomes significant as a first recorded instance of Māori-Indian intermarriage and potential offspring.

The 1809 visit of the *City of Edinburgh* is also noteworthy, as it records the presence of an Indian-Portuguese servant, and both a Chinese blacksmith and a Chinese carpenter aboard ship (Salmond 1997, p. 379), which dates Chinese presence in Aotearoa much earlier than the currently believed year of 1842 (Ng 1993). Ships that sailed between Europe and its colonies not only carried Indian seamen, but also others of Asian and African ancestry. Since many of these sailed for the British East India Company and often made China a port of call for trade, small numbers of Chinese would also have served aboard European vessels.

Another significant account records the Macquarie Island shipwreck of the *Campbell Macquarie*, built and registered at Calcutta and under the command of Richard Siddons. While searching for new sealing sites south of Aotearoa, the ship ran aground on 10 June 1812 and was destroyed.

> Her crew of 12 Europeans and 30 lascars were all got ashore. She had nearly three suits of sails, and when the weather cleared up the crew succeeded in getting these ashore, where they were stored in a hut, which was afterwards accidentally destroyed by fire. All her stores were lost, independently of which she had on board 2,000 prime skins, 36 tons of salt, and 118 tons of coal taken in lieu of ballast. Captain Siddons, Mr. Kelly, chief mate, and the

crew remained ashore from 10th June to 11th October, when they were taken off by the *Perseverance* and given passages to Sydney, where they arrived on 30th October at Broken Bay. While on the island four of the lascars died, also a seaman of the *Mary and Sally* named Thomas McGowen. (McNab 1907, p. 185)

This incident is noteworthy in that its British crew were considerably outnumbered by Indians, and it records unknown lascars who perished on the island. It is ironic that while the names of the Europeans are well documented and recorded, early mariner historians did not deem the reportage of the names of the Indian sailors necessary, giving some indication of British regard for the lascars. Their historic invisibility is palpable, given that this account records the death of the Indian crew in the southern oceans, not unlike lascars aboard Surville's 1769 visit on the *Saint Jean Baptiste*.

Further incidents of Indo-Māori engagement have been recorded. Otakou (an early Māori settlement on the Otago Peninsula, near present-day Dunedin) was also visited by occasional ships during this period, most probably searching for seal rookeries. One such visit involving lascars was that of Captain Fowler and the Matilda in August 1813 (McNab 1907, p. 216). He had entered Otago Bay "in some trepidation since his crew of lascars were emaciated by fatigue, being for a length of time without vegetables or fresh provisions and with only a few gallons of water left" (Richards 2010, p. 193). Fowler recalls an incident in which he lost

14 of his men on the coast of New Zealand, together with three of his boats. One was stolen by the natives, another was carried off by six of his crew of lascars. The third was sent with his chief officer (Brown), two Europeans and five lascars, all of whom are supposed to have foundered as no tidings were got of either boat or crew. (Carrick 1903, p. 172; McNab 1907, p. 115)

Entwisle (2005, pp. 103–106) and Leckie (2007, p. 21) record this anecdote in which six Indian sailors deserted the *Matilda*, making off with one of its boats.

Three were reportedly killed by Maori but three survived, probably settling near Whareakeake in Otago until 1823. This means they were some of the earliest long-term non-Maori residents of the Dunedin area. During this time, they assisted Ngai Tahu with strategies for attacking European ships. (Leckie 2007, p. 21, citing Bishop Selwyn's notes in Howard 1940, p. 379)

These passages are noteworthy, for they record the first instance of the theft of British property by Indian sailors, possibly lending support to the theory that lascars were not particularly well looked after. While their European crew may have labeled them as deserters and sent others for their capture (those sent to retrieve both the boat and the "thieves" also never returned), it is possible that the Indians, desiring change, left with whatever means they had at their disposal. McNab offers additional details:

Later on evidence was discovered of the fate of the men. De Blosseville ascertained in Sydney, in 1823, that of the six lascars in the second boat, three were killed by the natives and the others were kept alive and taught the natives how to dive and cut the ship's cables during the night and how to reduce the efficiency of firearms by attacking in wet weather. Mr. Kelly was told by one of the surviving lascars of the Matilda that Mr. Brown, with six men, had been killed and eaten by the natives. (McNab 1907, p. 217)

It is evident, however, that some survived, and those who did aided local Māori in managing European presence in Otakou. Living under Māori *kaitiakitanga* (guardianship) may have been what the Indian "thieves" had intended.

There are further isolated incidents of Indians being left behind. McNab (1914, p. 202) records four lascars left under the charge of the missionaries at the Bay of Islands in 1814, while the Europeans amongst them proceeded to Tahiti. After the visits of the *Matilda* and subsequent incidents, there are few detailed accounts of Indian sailors ashore. There are, however, literally hundreds of newspaper accounts recording the comings and goings of ships in the various ports and settlements from the early 1800s onwards, and these warrant further research. Newspapers such as the *Sydney Gazette* regularly reported the movements of European vessels along with their ports of call, including destinations, cargo, and passenger lists. Accounts of crew movement were likewise considered important news. Many of these describe the numbers of Indian sailors arriving or departing, with names withheld, and little is known of their activities. They remain innumerable yet invisible.

Indian Settlement from 1851

What follows begins a more formal period of early Indian settlement in which many are named or enumerated. The first Indian to achieve fame was an Anglo-Indian from Goa who arrived in 1853, having previously worked at the California gold fields. Edward Peter, later known as "Black Peter," was a farm laborer and gold prospector. Although the Australian Gabriel Read is credited with discovering gold at Tuapeka in Otago, it was Peter who told him where to find it (McLintock 1966; Leckie 2007, p. 21, 2010, p. 48, 2011, p. 54; McLeod 1986, p. 51), leading to the first workable gold claim at Glenore, Otago (Ip and Leckie 2011, p. 162). His gold prospecting in Central Otago brought about the gold rush upon which much of Otago's wealth was built, but Peter received very little attention (Leckie 1998, p. 163). What little is known of Peter comes predominantly from a few main sources (Mayhew 1949; McLeod 1986, p. 51; Dwyer 1990; Williams 2009). Instead, historians focused on honoring the European Read as the discoverer of Otago gold (Leckie 1998, p. 163), furthering notions of historical minority invisibility and the dominant colonial discourse, obscured by a European history dedicated to retelling its revisionist tale. *Te Ara*, the official online encyclopedia of New Zealand, states that "Otago's first gold rush was in 1861, after Gabriel Read found gold in what would be called Gabriel's Gully. Thousands of diggers, later including men from China, went there to make their fortune" (Walrond 2006). Even though Peter had discovered gold at Otago, Read was the one to remain historically visible, while the Indian Peter is relegated to a historical footnote. Through peopling the historical record with what European history has expunged, a contrasting narrative emerges.

Reinserting Asian presence into an overwhelmingly European history produces a more thorough and inclusive account. The first step towards righting this historical inaccuracy was the publishing of William's book (2009) and the erecting of an interpretive monument to Edward Peter's discovery of gold in Otago (Phillips 2009).

The advent of the gold rush coincides with the first visible Indian settler to be named (McLeod 1986, p. 51), and details of his doings can be found in the historical record. Bishop Selwyn (Howard 1940; Leckie 2010, p. 48) mentions another Indian who settled with Otago Māori, took *moko* (tattoo), and was renamed Te Anu. As his Indian name is lost to history, his region of birth in India and his religion will also remain obscure. These incidents mark the end of the earliest "settlement" narrative, as it transitions from a period of early sojourner to that of the more visible early Indian settler. The history of Indian settlement that follows is exceptionally well documented by Leckie and others (McGee 1960, 1962, 1993; McLeod 1980, 1984, 1986; Tiwari 1980; Zodgekar 1980, 2010; McLeod and Bhullar 1992; Leckie 1998, 2006, 2007, 2011; Kolig 2010; Ip and Leckie 2011; Bola 2014).

Indians in the New Zealand Census, Phase I: 1851–1911

The previous sections revealed that accounts of early Asian presence in Aotearoa have been largely ignored by currently accepted histories, and reset the date of earliest known Indian presence from 1809 (Bandyopadhyay 2006, p. 125; Leckie 2007) back to 1769, 40 years early than previously thought. This places Indians in Aotearoa at the precise point of Māori-European encounter. The only difference being that Europeans were present in larger numbers than Indians during the early period of contact and held the balance of power in their colonial relationship. The implementation of census enumeration is symbolic as it marks the move from Indian presence to permanent Indian settlement, as initial records of domicile appear. Yet, like historical accounts of early presence, census records also obscured early Asian settlement. This section also reveals earlier evidence of Indians in the census then previously known, as notations were often relegated to insignificant footnotes or concealed in ambiguous census categories that obfuscated the tabulation of Indian ethnicity. Examining these categories provides insight into early state reportage of Asian presence in New Zealand, as much of what is presented is as relevant for early Chinese settlement as it is for Indian.

While early censuses record Indian ethnicity, these are just as inaccessible as the historical anecdotes presented earlier. Early European censuses constructed a past in which minorities are thoroughly absent, reaffirming a predominantly colonial narrative. As examples, Māori are not included in the official New Zealand Census until 1951, and formal recording of Indian ethnicity did not occur until 1916. This section therefore reviews historical census records of Indian settlement from the first national census in 1851, picking up where the earlier "presence" narrative roughly ends. Statistics detailed here continue through to the most recently available Census Statistics from the 2013 Census. A more details analysis of Indians in the New Zealand census can be found in Nachowitz (2015). More recent Census figures on the Indian population from the March 2018 Census will be publicly released in 2019. This chapter will be updated once these figures become available.

This section summarizes three distinct periods of Indian demography as evident in the New Zealand Census. The first period of census reporting begins with the original national Census of 1851 through to the 15th Census of 1911. The earliest references to Indian ethnicities or religions in the 1851–1911 censuses are reported in Table 1. This phase ends with the 1911 Census as censuses from 1916 had standardized ethnicity reporting, and the enumeration of Indian ethnicity was clearly and continually reported. The religious affiliation of census respondents has been recorded from the very first census and continues today. It is in these records of religious affiliation that the very first references to those of Indian ethnicity appear. This is probably why other researchers, examining census records for those of Indian ethnicity, overlooked footnotes to religious affiliation tables and pegged

Table 1 Indians in the New Zealand Census, Phase I: 1851–1911

Year	Total population				Indians		
	Total European	Māori (estimates)	Total stating an ethnicity	Total people	Number of Indians	% of total people stating an ethnicity	% of total people
1851	28,865	–	–	28,865	–	–	–
1858	61,294	56,049	117,343	117,343	–	–	–
1861	106,315	56,336	162,651	165,651	14	0.009	0.008
1864	172,158	–	172,158	172,158	–	–	–
1867	218,668	38,540	257,208	257,208	–	–	–
1871	256,398	37,502	293,895	295,350	–	–	–
1874	294,698	45,470	344,984	344,984	9	0.003	0.003
1878	409,979	43,595	458,007	458,007	–	–	–
1881	484,923	44,097	534,030	534,030	6	0.001	0.001
1886	573,940	41,969	620,451	620,451	–	–	–
1891	622,214	41,953	668,651	668,651	–	–	–
1896	699,603	39,834	743,214	743,214	46	0.006	0.006
1901	769,838	43,112	815,862	815,862	24	0.003	0.003
1906	886,002	47,701	948,649	948,649	11	0.001	0.001
1911	1,005,823	49,829	1,070,910	1,070,910	15	0.001	0.001

Sources: Censuses from 1851 to 1911, Nachowitz 2015, Appendix A. The numbers of Indians in the years 1861 and 1874 are found in the Religious Affiliation tables in their respective Censuses and are listed as "Hindoos."

Note: European figures in the Census years 1851, 1858, 1861, and 1871 include figures reported in an "Other" category, which includes "Military and their families." There were no Māori estimates for 1851 and 1864. Total of those Stating an Ethnicity for the 1874–1886 Censuses included those of Chinese ethnicity. Total of those Stating an Ethnicity for the 1891–1901 Censuses included those of Chinese ethnicity as well as those that stated their ethnicity as "Moriori at Chatham Islands." Total of those Stating an Ethnicity for the 1906 and 1911 Censuses included those of Chinese ethnicity, those that stated their ethnicity as "Moriori at Chatham Islands," and those that stated at Pacific Islands ethnicity.

Indian enumeration to later dates. Early census reporting of minority populations was tenuous at best, and there was considerable blurring of census categories. Table 1 presents actual population numbers, as gleaned from different sections in the Census reports, e.g., religious affiliation, birthplace, and race are combined to create a true representation of the actual numbers of Indians reported in the Census statistics. For example, no Indian *ethnicities* are reported in 1861, yet 14 "Hindoos" are reported in a footnote for the "Other" category for religious affiliation; hence, Table 1 reports 14 Indians in the 1861 Census, where previous research recorded no Indians. This is only done in years where no ethnic Indians have been reported, so as to make certain that no duplications occur. In *no* years have numbers of Indian ethnicity been combined with numbers of Hindus or Muslims, as some overlap may occur. As a result, the statistics presented here may not correspond with official Census statistics for *ethnicity*, nor will they reflect previously presented statistics on the Indian diaspora in New Zealand. Instead, they present a more accurate rendition of the population that appears by scrutinizing in the various sections on religious affiliation, birthplace, and ethnicity in the published Census tables. Since ethnicity reporting becomes standardized from the 1916 Census onward, the numbers presented from 1916 represent the actual reported "ethnicity" figures for the Indian diaspora. Table 1, however, does present compiled numbers from 1851 to 1911 from the various ethnicity, birthplace, and religious affiliation tables where there is certainty that no duplication has occurred.

Although Indian sojourners have been recorded entering and leaving Aotearoa since 1769, it was not until the third national Census of 1861, that their official enumeration began. New Zealand's first national population census took place in 1851, although smaller regional official enumeration goes as far back as 1842. Many of the Indians present in Aotearoa between 1769 and 1861 had either come for a brief period lasting days or months (i.e., the fleeting visits of Indian lascars on European ships, or the more prolonged stays of European sealing parties ashore), or while transiting on ships that plied the international trade routes between Europe, India, Australia and China. The majority of Indians present during these years would have been considered sojourners, not settlers. Although there were instances of Indians jumping ship, settling under Māori protection, marrying into Māori tribes, and others who came to prospect for gold, only a few of these early sojourners and settlers were recorded in early New Zealand censuses.

While the comings and goings of ships' crews are well recorded in the arrival and departure records of main ports or in ship captain's logs, it is unclear how many Indians may have arrived, however briefly, during the period 1769–1861. Old newspaper accounts of arrivals and departures of Indian lascars on transiting ships suggests the possibility that dozens of Indian sailors were domiciled in New Zealand before they begin to appear in the census. Since these are "newsworthy" stories, many refer to extraordinary situations (e.g., lascars arriving in ports in emaciated states, ill treatment at the behest of European superiors, or having been left ashore in sealing parties) or antisocial behavior, while others refer to specific crimes committed by both Europeans and Indians, or lascars remanded to jail.

Early censuses recorded predominantly European Christian adherents and great detail was paid to the particular denominations to which respondents belonged. Like practices in other national censuses based on race (e.g., "white" and "non-white"), early religious affiliation in New Zealand was described solely in terms of "Christian" or "non-Christian" dichotomies. The first national Census of 1851 records the only non-Christians as "Jews," along with those recorded as "Non Sectarian, professing to belong to no Sect, or neglecting or refusing to state their adherence to any." If ethnic Indians were enumerated in 1851, they would have been included in this category. In that year, 97.8% of the population were recorded as "Christian," tabulated under entries denoting their particular denominations. The second national census of 1858 recorded similar categories of Christian denominations, and as with the first national census, only European populations appear to have been tabulated, although separate estimates of the Māori population were appended.

In subsequent censuses, the categorization of religious affiliation grew more complex. The third national Census of 1861 is important to historians of religious diversity as it includes the first genuine tabulation of those with "Other" religious persuasions, referring to non-Christian or non-Jewish Europeans. This census is significant as it records a total of fourteen "Hindoos," four "Mahometans," and three "Buddhists" in a footnote to the "Other" category that appears in the original tables in the 1861 census documents. Knowledge of this footnote has not previously been identified by researchers of the Indian diaspora in New Zealand, and this mention uncovers an earlier appearance of Indians in the New Zealand Census than previously known. It is likely that these 14 "Hindoos" are Indians recorded in the religious affiliation tables who were not elsewhere classified, as ethnicity was not formally recorded in the Census until 1916. Many of the early censuses record ethnic Indians in the religious affiliation tables, but these, curiously, were subsumed in the European category before the section on "Race Aliens" was introduced in the 1916, and subsequent, censuses. This meant that "Hindoos" were enumerated and categorized as Europeans. The four "Mahometans" recorded in this census would be more difficult to place. It is likely, however, that they were brought here on European ships, making it possible that some originated on the Indian subcontinent as lascars, or were Chinese Muslims coming to work the Otago goldfields. It is not possible to state with any certainty based solely on available data presented in the census record. If "Hindoos" are to be considered ethnic Indians, then presence in the 1861 Census has not been previously uncovered by other researchers of the history of religious diversity or of the Indian diaspora in New Zealand, and the reporting here represents the earliest known or published citation of their presence in a census. Taher (1965, p. 44), McLeod (1984, 1986, p. 52), and McLeod and Bhullar (1992, p. 5) all mention that the first Indians to appear in census returns were six recorded in the 1881 Census, and Taher categorically states that "statistics showing arrivals of Indians before 1897 are not available" (Taher 1970, p. 39). The 1881 citation probably references the "Birthplace" tables from the 1881 Census that record the numbers of both "European" and "Asiatic" populations born in India. There are six "Asiatics" recorded as being born in India in the 1881 Census. Leckie

(2007, p. 22, 2010, p. 48), possibly following earlier references from Taher and McLeod, also makes reference to the three Indian males noted as living in Canterbury on the Census of 1881 as being the first, but prior to this no other earlier citation of Indian presence on the census exists. This reference therefore places the earliest Indian appearance in the New Zealand Census back 20 years from when previously thought, from 1881 to the 1861 Census.

After an absence in the censuses of 1864, 1867, and 1871, Muslims and Hindus next appear in the 1874 Census; and Buddhists, who also first appear in the 1861 Census, do not specifically reappear as "Buddhists" in the religious affiliation section until the 1896 Census, although ethnic Chinese first appear in the Census of 1874, and in all successive census records. Chinese, however, do appear in the religious affiliation tables in the 1867 Census. It is unclear if the early reference to three "Buddhists" in the 1861 Census actually refers to Buddhism as a religious affiliation, as the category "Buddhist," used as a proxy for race or nationality similar to "Hindoo," cannot be easily discounted. Thus, it is possible that this 1861 reference represents the earliest appearance of Chinese in the national census.

Indian presence in the fourth Census of 1864 is wholly absent. While Indians were recorded in the 1861 census, their nonappearance here is likely due to inconsistent application of census categories, census enumerator inexperience, their disappearance into Māori communities, or the possibility that none were present during enumeration. The 1916 Census attempts to correct the record with a full accounting going back over 50 years and states that early Indian appearance was underreported in the very earliest censuses. The fifth 1867 Census marks the beginning of measuring racial fractions, as "Half-castes" are included for the first time in the European totals. This Census is also the first to mention "Other Foreign Countries" in more detail, and records 2,448 persons born in either Europe, North America, New Zealand, Australia, "Other British Dominions," "At sea," or "China," so it is possible that of these 2,448 individuals, some may have originated in South Asia and appeared in the "Other British Dominions" category. In this census, it is impossible to determine if all of those born in "Other British Dominions" are European, as it has been previously shown (Nachowitz 2015) that some of these numbers referred to enumerated "Hindoos" and "Mahometans." The 1871 Census introduces a new category enumerating the Chinese. Porous boundaries and inconsistent use of terms also prevail in the 1871 Census, and "Birthplace" tables, inconsistently used as a proxy for ethnicity where non-Europeans were included, largely reflected colonial attitudes of the time as these consisted mostly of British citizens born in overseas colonies.

> In considering the tables of birthplaces, it should be borne in mind that the numbers given as born in any country are not necessarily natives of that country, the children born of British parents being included. (1871 Census, p. 10)

The use of "not necessarily natives" in the 1871 Census demonstrates the ambiguity of the Birthplace tables as being unreliable markers for ethnicity. "Other British Possessions" lists 713 persons as born in India, although many (or most) of these were of European ethnicity.

In the absence of any formal ethnic categorization, the religious affiliation tables in the 1874 Census again provide the best evidence of non-European non-Māori populations. Nine "Hindoos" appear in the religious affiliation tables, 13 years after the first known appearance of Indians in the 1861 Census and 7 years before the previous earliest-known reference in the 1881 Census. This would account for two earlier confirmed citations (the 14 "Hindoos" referred to in 1861 Census, and the nine recorded in 1874) than those referred to by others (Taher 1965, p. 44, 1970, p. 39; Shepard 1980, p. 150, 2002, p. 234; McLeod 1984, 1986, p. 52; McLeod and Bhullar 1992, p. 5; Drury 2000, 2006; Leckie 2007, p. 22, 2010, p. 48; Kolig 2010, p. 21; Pratt 2010, 2011) as being the first known census record.

Regarding birthplace, the 1878 Census lists 905 people as born in India, but presumably these are of European ethnicity rather than ethnic Indians, although this is impossible to verify. Table IV (1878 Census, p. 230) includes "Birthplace Unspecified" which has two distinct subcategories entitled "British Names" (686 individuals), and "Foreign Names," which accounts for 26 persons (19 males and seven females) living in New Zealand in 1878 with non-British names. This would presumably include non-Māori and non-Chinese names as well. These 26 are distributed through the colony as five (four males and one female) in Wellington, 11 (six males and five females) living in Nelson, three males in Canterbury, and seven (six males and one female) in Otago. It is possible that this earlier record of three males with foreign names living in Canterbury is the same referred to in the 1881 Census (McLeod 1986; Leckie 2007, p. 21, 2010, p. 48; Beattie 2011, p. 142) as the servants of Sir Johan Cracoft Wilson, a retired magistrate from the British Civil Service in India, who settled in New Zealand after his years of service to British India along with his Indian servants. It is likely that their ethnicity became obscured by census enumerators in 1878. If these are indeed the same Indians, it would uncover an earlier reference for birthplace (i.e., those of Indian ancestry or ethnicity) than that of the 1881 citation.

Ethnic Indians receive no mention in the religion tables in the 1881 Census, but there is a solitary reference in the "Birthplace" Tables (1881 Census, Table IV, p. 192) that separates the 1,106 Europeans from the six "Asiatics" born in India. This listing confirms that six Indian males are included in the European ethnicity totals, as they are not elsewhere accounted for. This would appear to be the first confirmed reference to Indian ethnicity in the census, although not the first reference for Indian religious affiliation. Indian presence in the 1881 Census is corroborated by McLeod (1986, p. 51) and Leckie (2007, p. 22, 2010, p. 48), who make reference to a retinue of 17 Indian servants eventually brought to Canterbury by Sir Wilson. This small enclave that served under Wilson is perhaps the first known settled Indian community in New Zealand.

> Several of the Wilson retinue deserted their master when they discovered that they could earn better wages elsewhere. Most of them, the loyal and the deserters alike, are said to have married Māori wives. If indeed they can be regarded as a community it was a transient one, obscure while it existed and eventually merging in the society which surrounded it. (McLeod 1986, pp. 51–52)

Leckie (2007, pp. 21–22, 2010, p. 48) records some of the original Indian settlers that arrived with Wilson, and their descendants, as the Sohman and Bussawan families, who have subsequently married into both Māori and Pākehā families, taking on new identities. There is, however, a claim that the six Indians mentioned in this census were independent Punjabi settlers rather than in Wilson's service:

> According to an old Indian resident of Pukekohe, the six Indians recorded in the 1881 census were Punjabis and North Indians who, destined for Fiji, had stayed here instead, for a few years. (Taher 1965, p. 44)

McLeod (1986, p. 52) states that this is unlikely to be true. Gillion (1977, p. 131) records that the first free Punjabi immigrants reached Fiji in 1904, which would render Taher's citation incorrect, leaving McLeod's and Leckie's accounts more likely to be accurate.

The religious affiliation and birthplace tables of the 1886 Census make no separate reference to ethnic Indians or the religious affiliations of Hindus or Muslims, although it can be stated that if these did exist, they would either be listed as "Other denominations-Pagans," which recorded a total of 4,472 individuals (4,466 males and six females), or as "Other denominations-others (variously returned)," which recorded a total of 179 individuals (111 males and 68 females). As the Chinese population is not elsewhere included in the religious affiliation tables this year, it is likely that the majority of those returned as "Pagans" are ethnic Chinese, although some of the remainder, and those returned as "others (variously returned)," are likely to be ethnic Indians. The "Birthplace" category makes the explicit mention that those included in the tables are those with "British names" only, so ethnic Indians can be discounted as having been included in the birthplace tables this year. The same convention for birthplace and religious affiliation continued in the 1886 Census, so no ethnic Indians or revealing religious affiliations can be ascertained from the tables and no further footnotes mention either.

The 1896 Census records 46 Indian males, 43 of whom are listed as "Mahometans" while three are listed as "Hindoos." These appear in Table VI of the Census of 1896 (p. 124), which lists 1,192 Europeans (664 males and 528 females) and 46 "Asiatics" (all male), as being born in India. It is assumed that all 46 males would be of Indian ethnicity. Leckie corroborates:

> Religious returns indicated that most of these were Muslims. Only three people in New Zealand that year declared themselves as 'Hindoos'. (Leckie 2007, p. 22)

The religious affiliation tables of the 1901 Census list two male "Brahmins," 41 male "Mahometans," and three "Zoroastrians." The two male "Brahmins" would certainly be Indian Hindus, although it is unclear which countries the 41 Muslims are from. This reference is the first to conflate Indian caste affiliation with ethnicity. The three "Zoroastrians" listed in the religious affiliation tables are enumerated as two "Zoroastrians" and one "Parsee," which would indicate that the Zoroastrians were probably of Persian descent, and, as Zoroastrian Indians are generally known as "Parsis" (or "Parsees"), the sole "Parsee" listed in the 1901 Census would most certainly represent the first confirmed Indian Zoroastrian. In addition to the entries in the religious affiliation tables, the birthplace tables list a total of 24 Indian "Asiatics." Of these 24, two would be male "Brahmins," one "Parsee," and the remainder presumably Indian Muslims.

Birthplace and Religious Affiliation tables in the 1906 Census continue to serve as proxies for ethnicity. This year records six India-born male "Asiatics" along with 1,224 India-born Europeans (695 males and 529 females). In the religious affiliation tables, ten Hindus are described, consisting of nine "Brahmins" and one "Hindoo," all of whom are certain to be ethnic Indians. There are also 17 Muslims described, 16 as "Mahometans" and one returning as "Islam." A single "Zoroastrian" is also enumerated. These tables record two "Vedantists," but it cannot be said with any certainty that these are ethnic Indians, as ethnic Indians were unlikely to report a Hindu religious affiliation as "Vedantist," although Vedanta philosophy had become fashionable in European circles due to the writings of Thoreau, Emerson, Blavatsky, and others. It is unclear why only six ethnic Indians are enumerated in the birthplace tables as "Asiatics" while ten Hindus are mentioned in the religion tables, so it is likely that the actual number of ethnic Indians recorded in the 1906 Census is slightly greater than six. These examples underscore the great number of inconsistencies throughout this census phase. It also demonstrates the difficulty early census enumerators experienced in recording ethnicity in the field, as the concept was poorly described by census bureaucrats to insufficiently trained enumerators. Instead, religious affiliation, birthplace, race, or skin color often substituted for ethnicity.

The 1911 Birthplace tables record 15 India-born male "Asiatics" along with 1,191 India-born Europeans (677 males, 514 females), so at least 15 ethnic Indians were recorded this year. The religious affiliation tables record two male "Hindoos," 12 male "Mahometans," and two male "Zoroastrians." The first "Sikh" in New Zealand is also recorded, unsurprisingly categorized under "No Religion," which explains why it was previously overlooked by other researchers. McLeod (1980, p. 115, 1986, p. 53) correctly states that the very first known Punjabi immigrants, two brothers, Phuman and Bir Singh, most likely came to New Zealand in the early 1890s, with the first census record of an Indian domiciled here in 1881 (1986, p. 52), which is incorrect. The first census record of Indian presence would be the 1861 reference mentioned earlier, with this 1911 census citation being the first of a Punjabi Sikh in the New Zealand census. While the Bir brothers, of whom much is already known (McLeod 1980, 1986; McLeod and Bhullar 1992; Leckie 2007), may have arrived circa 1890, it does not necessarily mean that they were the first Punjabis to reach New Zealand nor the first Punjabi settlers, as others could have arrived earlier and were unreported. However, this 1911 Census citation is the first to record a Punjabi Sikh in New Zealand, and, following McLeod, it is entirely possible that they may have arrived, and appeared on a census, long before this, although such references would not be distinguishable from other ethnic Indians enumerated in earlier census years.

In sum, this census period is marked by inconsistencies in race and religion reporting, and the relative invisibility of non-European populations. While exclusionary legislation prevented Asian populations from immigrating, and ideologues campaigned to keep New Zealand racially white, the low numbers of Indians and Chinese reported appear out of proportion to the exaggerated emotions stirred by fervent anti-immigration campaigners (see Leckie 1985). As a result, this period was mostly characterized by ideological concerns at play by both political actors in the legislative realm and those charged with the collection and presentation of census statistics designed to reflect such principles.

Indians in the New Zealand Census, Phase II: 1916–1981

Ethnicity, as a distinct table, did not appear in a national census until 1916, which saw the introduction of a novel section entitled "Race Aliens." The use of this term to refer to racialized ethnic "others" categorizes non-European non-Māori populations as "alien," i.e., without "race." This confirms their ambiguous status as neither belonging nor welcomed and elevates those *with* "race" (Europeans), as racially superior to others *alien to* "race." The 1916 Census, therefore, marks the beginning of a distinct phase of minority statistical reporting that, over a period of 65 years, saw the ideologically driven elements of the first phase give way to a more embedded racialization in the second (Table 2).

Regarding the first appearance of ethnic Indians, Vasil and Yoon (1996, p. 2) state "It was only with the 1916 Census that Indians began to be listed separately as a distinct ethnic segment." While technically correct, earlier references to religious affiliation, the 14 "Hindoos" in the 1861 Census, which Vasil and Yoon (1996) missed, cannot be so easily dismissed. Prior to 1916, Indians were not officially enumerated as

Table 2 Indians in the New Zealand Census, Phase II: 1916–1981

Year	Total population	Indians Number	% of total population	Intercensal increase Number	Percent
1916	1,162,022	181	0.016	166	1,106.7
1921	1,321,216	671	0.051	490	270.7
1926	1,463,264	987	0.067	316	47.1
1936	1,647,278	1,200	0.073	213	21.6
1945	1,790,256	1,554	0.087	354	29.5
1951	1,939,472	2,425	0.125	871	56.0
1956	2,174,062	3,151	0.145	726	29.9
1961	2,414,984	4,179	0.173	1,028	32.6
1966	2,676,919	6,843	0.256	2,664	63.7
1971	2,862,631	7,807	0.273	964	14.1
1976	3,129,383	9,247	0.295	1,440	18.4
1981	3,175,737	11,244	0.354	1,997	21.6

a distinct ethnic category, although earlier censuses list the numbers of Chinese, Māori, Chatham Islands Moriori, and Pacific populations over which New Zealand had dominion. Although Indians do indeed appear in earlier censuses, they regularly appear in the "Race Alien" tables begun in 1916. The "Race Aliens" section also included minority breakdowns of religious affiliation for the very first time:

> The principal religions of the Hindus were: Hindu, 53; Mohammedan, 25; Vishna, 22; Sikh, 15; Brahmin, 12; while 20 returned themselves as belonging to the Church of England. (1916 Census, pp. 143–144)

The first instance of "Hindu" used in the above quote refers to those of Indian ethnicity and the second to religion. The Census of 1921 was also the last to refer to ethnic Indians as "Hindoos" or "Hindus," and from 1926 on, those returning a Hindu religious affiliation were identified as such and appropriately distinguished from Indians of other religious affiliations. "Vishna" [sic], instead of the correct "Vishnu" or "Vaishnavite," is how it appears in the Census. It is unclear why "Vishna" and "Brahmin," both of which should clearly fall under the religious use of the term "Hindu," are listed separately. This is most likely due to census enumerator error or ignorance, or perhaps they were instructed to record exactly what respondents returned when questioned. The above quote also indicates that by 1916, over half (25 individuals) of the 47 Muslims enumerated in the religious affiliations tables were Indian Muslims. This provides insight into earlier enumerations, which record the total number of Muslims, but provide no ethnicities or birthplaces. Extrapolating backwards, this reference provides further evidence that the known Indian Muslim population in earlier census years may have been underreported, with the balance being ethnic Chinese. Earlier censuses record the total Muslim population as follows: 1861 (4 Muslims), 1874 (17 Muslims), 1878 (39 Muslims), 1881 (7 Muslims), 1896 (43 Muslims), 1901 (41 Muslims), 1906 (16 Muslims), and 1911 Censuses (12 Muslims).

The 1916 Census also marks the first appearance of a distinct subcategory of the "Occupations" section that records the various trades in which 167 male and 14 female "Hindus" (following earlier practice, the use of "Hindus" here refers to those of Indian ethnicity) were engaged in at the time. Table 3 is remarkable for what it reveals. Of the 167 Indian males "38 were engaged in dealing in food, &c, 26 in pastoral and 24 in agricultural pursuits" (1916 Census, p. 146).

Another Table (1916 Census, p. 147) details the specific occupations of selected "Race Aliens" (i.e., "Chinese, Hindus, Syrians, and Others"). It provides insights into the working lives of the Indian population in 1916. Summarizing, the largest number worked in agricultural or pastoral pursuits (27.6%), followed by those selling food and drinks (21.0%), followed by those dependent on natural guardians (7.7%), and those engaged in domestic service (7.2%). The table provides earlier and more detailed employment records than has been previously published in academic accounts of the earliest Indian settlers (Taher 1970; Palakshapa 1973; Tiwari 1980; McLeod 1986). McGee (1962, p. 215) and Zodgekar (1980, pp. 195–196) provide similar tables, but only beginning with the 1921 Census, and Leckie (1998, pp. 169–170, 2007, pp. 36–65) discusses the diversification of the employment of early

Table 3 Occupations of 181 ethnic Indians recorded in the 1916 Census

Occupations	Males	Females	Total	Percent
Employer	6	0	6	3.3
Self-employed	49	0	49	27.1
Relative assisting	4	0	4	2.2
Wage earner	99	6	105	58.0
Wage earner unemployed	0	0	0	0.0
Not applicable	9	8	17	9.4
Not stated	0	0	0	0.0
Totals:	**167**	**14**	**181**	**100.0**

Table 4 Length of residence of the Indian population, 1916 Census

	Full-blooded			Half-caste		
Length of residence, in years	Male	Female	Total	Male	Female	Total
Under 1	31	–	31	1	–	1
1 and under 2	3	–	3	–	2	2
2 and under 3	16	1	17	2	1	3
3 and under 4	42	–	42	–	1	1
4 and under 5	21	1	22	–	–	–
5 and under 6	7	–	7	1	–	1
6 and under 7	–	–	–	–	–	–
7 and under 8	2	–	2	1	–	1
8 and under 9	1	–	1	–	–	–
9 and under 10	1	–	1	1	–	1
10 and under 15	4	–	4	–	–	–
15 and under 20	3	1	4	–	–	–
20 and under 30	8	–	8	–	–	–
30 and under 40	3	–	3	–	–	–
40 and under 50	3	–	3	–	–	–
50 and over	–	–	–	–	–	–
Not stated	11	–	11	–	2	2
Born in New Zealand	4	2	6	1	3	4
Totals:	**160**	**5**	**165**	**7**	**9**	**16**

Source: "Table showing the number of Hindus in New Zealand classified according to Length of Residence in the Dominion, Census". (1916 Census, p. 149)

Gujarati and Punjabi settlers during this period and beyond in great detail, based on her ethnographic research.

Table 4 specifically details the number of years that 181 Indians have lived in New Zealand. Of these, 165 are recorded as "Full-blooded" and 16 as "Half-castes." The number of "half-castes" recorded provides early evidence of Indian intermarriage with European and Māori populations, as the second parent's ethnicity is unclear. This Table provides evidence of settlement 40–50 years prior to 1916, that three males were settled as far back as 1876–1886.

> It will be noted that of 145 full-blooded male Hindus born abroad whose length of residence is known, 113 had been under five years in the country; and of 6 half-caste males 3 had been under three years in the country, 4 under six, 5 under eight, and all under ten. These figures clearly show the increase in the number of persons of this race in the Dominion. It will also be noted that 6 full-blood and 4 half-caste Hindus have been born in the country. The table affords good evidence that until recent years at least a large proportion of Hindu arrivals in the country merely stayed here a few weeks in transit to, or from, the Pacific Islands. A comparison of the arrivals of Hindus during each of the 10 years ended 1916 with the approximate year of arrival of those included in the above table gives the following results (1916 Census, pp.148–149).

Table 5 provides evidence that the majority of the early Indian arrivals recorded in the 10 years before the 1916 Census were transient, for instance, of the 325 ethnic Indians that arrived in New Zealand in 1912, only 22 were still recorded as domiciled in New Zealand in 1916. If cross-referencing the list of Punjabi immigrants provided by McLeod (1984) with the years of arrival above, it might be possible to put names to many of the numbers referenced above.

Note the discrepancy between the numbers of Hindus recorded in the religious affiliation tables in 1916 (88 individuals), versus the number of "Hindu" (i.e., Indian) "Race Aliens" (181 individuals). This means that only 48.6% of the ethnic Indians recorded in 1916 were Hindu, with the remainder most likely being Muslims or Christians. Of the 181 ethnic Indians recorded, 165 were full ethnic Indians and 16 were children of mixed marriages, 4 of whom were New Zealand-born, 10 born overseas (possibly the progeny of European-Indian marriages born in India), and 2 unknown (see 1916 Census, p. 139).

Zodgekar (1980, p. 183) records that "Indians have largely arrived since the suspension of the indentured system in 1917 and its abolition in 1920" and notes

Table 5 Indian arrivals in the Colony, 1907–1916

Year	Arrivals during the year	Number in Dominion in 1916 who arrived in same year
1907	20	2
1908	24	1
1909	157	3
1910	80	0
1911	190	8
1912	325	22
1913	133	43
1914	257	20
1915	13	5
1916	92	32

Source: extracted from the 1916 Census, p. 139

that many of the early arrivals came from Fiji as a result of the end of the indenture system. Historical evidence, however, suggests that the increase in arrivals of Indians in New Zealand may be more due to the increasing awareness of impending immigration restrictions in New Zealand rather than the end of the indenture system in Fiji. Leckie (1998, 2007) also considers that increased chain migration from Gujarat and Punjab to New Zealand were important factors. This is corroborated by Kondapi (1951) and was the major source of the dramatic increase in ethnic Indians in the 1921 Census. This year saw an increase from the 181 individuals noted in the 1916 census to 671 individuals in the 1921 Census. Although Zodgekar notes the presence of ethnic Indians based on census figures from 1916 onwards, he does not record any earlier Indian presence in census records before 1916.

The 1921 Census continues the "Race Alien" section begun in 1916:

> Third in numerical importance (behind the Chinese and Syrians) among the race-alien communities are the Indians. The Indians arriving in New Zealand are British subjects, and in that respect differ from the bulk of other race-alien immigrants. Until very recent years there was scarcely a handful of Indians resident in the Dominion. (1921 Census, p. 118)

New Zealand had difficulty classifying Indian arrivals during this period as Britain governed colonial India until 1947 and Indians under the British Rāj in India were considered British citizens. This created conflict for anti-Asian immigrationists in enacting suitable legislation upholding a white New Zealand policy that prevented further Indian and Chinese immigration (see Murphy 2007 and 2008 for the legislative differences between the Indian and Chinese populations, respectively). This exemplified the rather ambiguous positioning of Indian immigrants at the time, as their status as British subjects did not translate into a more favorable immigration status (see Murphy 2007).

Table 6 clearly shows that Indians who do not appear in earlier censuses, were indeed present and recorded, most probably as "Others." This table confirms the first recorded instance of ethnic Indians present, although not separately enumerated, in earlier censuses, even though it remained unrecorded until 1921.

Table 6 Summary of Indians noted in previous Census years (1921 Census, p. 118)

Census year	Males	Females	Total
1881	6	–	6
1886	–	–	–
1891	–	–	–
1896	46	–	46
1901	–	–	–
1906	6	–	6
1911	15	–	15
1916	167	14	181
1921	622	49	671

The intercensal increase between 1916 and 1921 was 409, or 270 percent. It is however, believed that the number in 1916 was slightly understated owing to the method of inquiry presenting a possible defect, remedied in 1921. (1921 Census, Race Aliens, p. 118)

The religious affiliation of "Race Aliens" are also described in the 1921 Census, as follows:

> Speaking generally, non-Europeans are comparatively illiterate, and this fact combined with language difficulties and customs foreign to New Zealand practice tends towards a reduction in the degree of accuracy in census statistics. It seems probable that statistics of religions are among those more affected. A large number—2113—of the race aliens was recorded as Christian, comprising 24 percent of the males of full blood and 76 percent of the females. Half-castes were almost all (males, 92 percent; females, 97 percent) described as Christians. The various churches with their adherents are briefly tabulated. (1921 Census, p. 121)

This table confirms that the majority of ethnic Chinese that came to work the Otago goldfields in the late 1860s were largely recorded as Confucian (63.7%, or 2,081 Confucians recorded from 3,266 ethnic Chinese). It is unclear, however, if these are indeed Confucians or a proxy for Chinese ethnicity, as in the use of the word "Hindoo." The 371 Hindus recorded in the above table account for 55.3% of the 671 ethnic Indians recorded in the "Race Alien" table, which would mean that of the remaining 300 ethnic Indians, the majority would have been Muslims, with a smaller number of Christians (Table 7).

There are 386 "Hindus" listed in the religious affiliation Tables (1921 Census, p. 125) for all respondents (371 of whom are Hindus accounted for in the religious affiliations of the "Race Aliens" table above). However, a closer inspection under the section "Non-Christian Religions" in the general tables for all respondents (not just

Table 7 Religious affiliation for "Race Aliens," 1921 Census

Religious affiliation	Number
Church of England	703
Presbyterian	198
Roman Catholic	756
Methodist	112
Baptist	117
Other Christian churches	227
Confucianism	2,081
Hinduism	371
Buddhism	36
Others	837
Total:	5,438

Only about one-sixth of the Chinese are Christians, belonging principally to the Church of England, Presbyterian, and Baptist Churches. The great majority were returned simply as followers of Confucius. Syrians, who were almost all Christians, are chiefly adherents of the Roman Catholic Church. Such few of the Indians as claimed Christianity were mainly attached to the Church of England. The great bulk were Hindus or Mohammedans. (1921 Census, p. 121) for "Race Aliens") reveals further breakdowns into Muslims, Buddhists, and Hindus: "Mohammedans, Buddhists, and followers of one or other of the group of religions associated under the generic name of 'Hindu' compose the greater part of the remainder." Note that the conflation of "Hindu" with ethnic "Indian" continues in the 1921 census. Those labeled "Hindu" in the religion section are those of Indian ethnicity answering the religion question and include Muslims and Buddhists. As Muslims are not specifically mentioned, there is no way to confirm the numbers present in 1921, although the figure of 837 "Others" provides some insight.

The "Industrial Distributions" of "Race Aliens" are given in great detail in the 1921 Census. Table 8 represents the 671 ethnic Indians recorded this year. In order to simplify the table, the Chinese data has been removed and a percentages column of the total population added.

Chinamen are comprised very largely of market-gardeners, laundrymen, and fruiterers. Industries followed by Indians are very much more varied and of considerably different character. (1921 Census, p. 121)

The various "Grades of Occupation" of those of Indian ethnicity from the 1921 Census given in Table 9 represent the 671 ethnic Indians recorded this year.

The 1926 "Race-Aliens" section is quite extensive. It records 987 ethnic Indians, and the first children of Indian-Māori marriages ("half-castes"). This Census lists a total of nine "Indian-Māori," enumerated in the Race Alien tables. Table 10 lists the various religious affiliations of all 987 ethnic Indians and continues to highlight the preoccupation with reporting mixed races. This table shows that 35.7% of ethnic Indians in 1926 recorded a Hindu religious affiliation (this consists of the 34.3% who returned "Hindu" plus the 1.1% that returned "Brahman"), 32.4% Christian, 9.9% Sikh, 5.5% Muslims, with 9.7% objecting to answer the question. However, while 338 "Hindus" returned as ethnic Indians under "Race Aliens," an additional 21 ethnic Indians (15 "Brahmins," one "Rajput," one returning as "Temple of India,"

Table 8 Industrial distribution of ethnic Indians, 1921 Census

Type of employment	Number	Percent
Sale of vegetables and fruit	102	15.20%
Staff of licensed hotels	42	6.26%
Dependent on hosts or natural guardians	41	6.11%
Brick and tile making	42	6.26%
Dairy-farming	36	5.37%
Hawking	32	4.77%
Land-drainage	31	4.62%
Dealing in scrap metal, used bottles, &c.	30	4.47%
Shipping	28	4.17%
General farming	27	4.02%
Others	260	38.75%
Totals:	**671**	**100%**

Source: 1921 Census, p. 121

Table 9 Grade of Occupation of "Race Aliens" described in the 1921 Census

Grade of occupation	Indians Number	Percent
Employer	21	3.1
Working on own account	187	27.9
Relative assisting	12	1.8
Wage-earner	363	54.1
Wage earner, but unemployed	24	3.6
Not applicable	64	9.5
Unspecified	0	0.0
Totals:	**671**	**100.0**

Source: 1921 Census, p. 122

Table 10 Indian religious affiliation, 1926 Census

Religion	Males Full-blood	Mixed	Females Full-blood	Mixed	Total Number	Percent
Church of England	10	57	2	45	114	11.55%
Roman Catholic	12	13	6	25	56	5.67%
Presbyterian	2	34	3	45	84	8.51%
Methodist	7	8	5	9	29	2.94%
Baptist		2			2	0.20%
Salvation Army	3	6		13	22	2.23%
Missions	1				1	0.10%
Latter-day Saints	1	3			4	0.41%
Protestant, *nfd*	1				1	0.10%
Bretheren	1	1			2	0.20%
Christian, *nfd*		1			1	0.10%
Christian, other	3			1	4	0.41%
Hindu	333	2	3		338	34.25%
Buddhist	4	1			5	0.51%
Sikh	90	1	7		98	9.93%
Mohammedan	49	5			54	5.47%
Brahman	11				11	1.11%
Theosophist	4			1	5	0.51%
Other non-Christian	11				11	1.11%
No religion	1	1			2	0.20%
Other beliefs	10	1	3	2	16	1.62%
Object to state	78	12	1	5	96	9.73%
Not specified	29	1		1	31	3.14%
Totals:	**661**	**149**	**30**	**147**	**987**	**100%**

Source: Census of 1926, Vol. 6 – Race Alien Population, Tables 12 and 13, pp. 26–27
Note: *nfd* not further defined

and four stating their religious affiliation as "Vedic") would bring the total to 359. Also of note is the large increase in the Sikh population (98 individuals) up from a population of 18 recorded in 1916, and the first Indian "Jain" appears in 1926. It is evident from the overall number of Muslims in the 1926 Census (76 "Mahometans" and four "Sufis" recorded in the general religious affiliation tables), that 54 were of Indian ethnicity with 22 originating in other countries, possibly China.

The 1926 Census also reports in detail the number of male and female Indians engaged in different industries. These tables reveal a far wider set of occupational skills than has previously been recorded for the Indian population. For example, Leckie states: "Most Indian pioneers worked long hours, in hard work, and travelled widely as hawkers, rural labourers or as domestic workers. These men were part of New Zealand's working class" (Leckie 2010, p. 51). Others scholars described this early period of Indian settlement, approximately 1910–1930, in this way:

> The majority of Indians intended to take up farming and a few of the artisans hoped to continue with their trades such as shoemaking. But as land was too expensive to buy, they were forced into rural labouring jobs such as road-building, or rural industries such as brick and tile making. The artisans found their intentions frustrated by the trade unions. The Indians in the urban areas were forced into the hawking of fruits and vegetables, bottles and rags. Here, at least, hard work and long hours could yield some return. Others became servants or washerman. Everywhere the Indians met with occupational prejudice and were forced to take jobs which limited the form of their contact with the host society. (McGee 1962, p. 214)

> The history of Indians in New Zealand has been closely bound up with the dairy and market-gardening industries but at the early stages of their immigration they sought employment as flax workers, bottle-collectors, drain diggers and scrub cutters. (Tiwari 1980, p. 7)

These statements are not necessarily true, and were probably based on anecdotal or interview evidence, rather than statistical data. Table 11 demonstrates a broader degree of expertise noted by the higher percentage of skilled jobs (e.g., administrators, shop owners, teachers, lawyers) that Indians were employed in 1926, and many of these might have been civil servants in the British Rāj (i.e., telegraph operators, government service) prior to emigration.

Based on an analysis of Table 11, only 16% of the total Indian population in 1926 was involved in agricultural and pastoral industries, 2.2% involved in clearing bush (forestry), 0.3% in the mining and quarrying industry, 4.2% in milling flax, 2.2% in land drainage, 1.9% in scrap metal and bottle collecting, 2.5% in hawking and street selling, for a total of 29.4% of the population involved in menial labor. A considerable percentage (21.9%) were dependent on their "natural guardians," demonstrating the increasing numbers of children of Indian migrants, or recently arrived Indian wives not otherwise employed, while 1.3% of the total population were either in hospitals, wards, mental institutions, or jail. A further 0.3% of the population was retired. This accounts for a total of 52.9% of the total population. An additional 7.0% of the population is not specified. The remainder (40.1%), forming the majority, were involved in other manufacturing and industrial pursuits; the building and

Table 11 Industries of the ethnic Indian population, 1926 Census (main sectors only)

Industry	Gender Males	Females	Total Number	Percent
Agricultural and pastoral:	158	0	158	16.0
Forestry:	22	0	22	2.2
Mining and quarrying:	3	0	3	0.3
Manufactures and industrial:	66	5	71	7.2
Building and construction:	30	0	30	3.0
Transport and communication:	49	0	49	5.0
Commerce and finance:	223	2	225	22.8
Public administration and professional:	10	9	19	1.9
Recreation:	3	0	3	0.3
Personal and domestic service:	78	28	106	10.7
Other industry, or not specified:	168	133	301	30.5
Totals:	**810**	**100**	**987**	**100.0**

Source: This table is based on a more complete Table that appears in the 1926 Census, Vol. VI "Race Aliens," pp. 28–29. The original Table contains the subcategories while the above Table contains only the main headings. Percentages and totals for each sector have been added for easier comparison

construction, and the transport and communication sector; commerce and finance; public administration and professional employment; recreation; and personal and domestic services. In sum, approximately 30% held low-waged menial jobs, approximately 30% employed in other services, while approximately 40% were involved in more settled, higher-waged positions.

Many of the early Indian and Chinese settlers are often portrayed as market gardeners in the 1920s, and the difficulties they faced in making ends meet were emphasized (Tiwari 1980, pp. 7–9; Leckie 1985, 2007). However, Table 11 reveals that only six ethnic Indians were recorded as market gardeners in 1926, while 1,144 ethnic Chinese held the same occupation (1921 Census, p. 28). Many more Indians at the time were engaged in mixed farming practices, or in bush- and scrub-cutting, trades or commercial occupations.

Table 12 records the "Occupations" of ethnic Indians in the 1926 census. These are only presented once, in the detail in which they appear in the census, in order to reveal and substantiate the wide range of economic activities in which the Indian population was engaged at the time. A thorough accounting of the breath of occupations has not previously been presented outside of the original census.

The wide array of skills and occupations, including a doctor, and shopkeepers is evident (see the original Table in the 1926 Census, Vol. VI "Race Aliens," pp. 30–32). This information shows that the early Indian settlers of this period were a mix of highly skilled and unskilled laborers, and not just flax and scrub cutters, hawkers, market gardeners, or bottle collectors as is often portrayed in histories of the Indian diaspora in New Zealand. Many held reputable positions, owned shops, had employees, taught school, drove trains, and were cooks. This data further supports the emergence of an Indian entrepreneurial class as early as 1916. Additionally, as three (2 males, 1 female)

Table 12 Reported occupations of the ethnic Indian population, 1926 Census

Occupations	Indians Males	Indians Females	Total Number	Total Percent
Agricultural and pastoral:	132	0	132	13.4
Forestry:	58	0	58	5.9
Miners and quarrymen:	2	0	2	0.2
Nonprecious metal workers, electrical fittings, &c.	5	0	5	0.5
Workers in fibrous materials other than clothing:	17	0	17	1.7
Workers in clothing and dress:	7	4	11	1.1
Workers in food, drink, and tobacco:	3	0	3	0.3
Workers in wood:	11	0	11	1.1
Workers in building and construction, *nei*:	35	0	35	3.5
Workers in transport and communication:	44	0	44	4.5
Commercial occupations:	211	2	213	21.6
Public administration:	1	4	5	0.5
Clerical and professional occupations:	7	5	12	1.2
Occupations connected with sport and recreation:	2	0	2	0.2
Personal and domestic occupations:	84	29	113	11.4
Other ill-defined occupations:	92	2	94	9.5
Persons not actively employed in gainful occupation:	99	131	230	23.3
Totals:	**810**	**177**	**987**	**100.0**

Source: The complete Table, along with the various sub-categories, can be found in the 1926 Census, Vol. VI "Race Aliens," pp. 30–32. Only the main categories are included here. The percentages column, with sector totals, has been added for easy comparison
Notes: *nei* not elsewhere identifiable

are listed as students, this may be the first reference to Indians attending public school, demonstrating sustained Indian settlement.

From 1926, enumeration of ethnic Indians continued in this fashion, so further descriptions are unnecessary, as subsequent history is well described (Leckie 2007). Indian presence in the census continued to increase throughout this period, and a greater transparency is evident in improved, more consistent, ethnic reporting. The eventual inclusion of Māori in the 1951 Census marks an important turning point roughly halfway through this phase and provides an example of the increasing participation of minority populations in the national arena, although the inclination to maintain racial purity remained a primary concern of the majority. This second phase is bounded by the historical significance of allowing individuals to report multiple ethnicities for the first time in the 1986 Census, largely brought about by significant sociopolitical changes occurring in New Zealand society leading up to the transition. Such macro-political factors (e.g., significant changes in immigration policy, rapid demographic change, increased bicultural discourse, Māori cultural resurgence and the beginnings of Treaty of Waitangi claims) neutralized the need for the continuation of "Race Alien" reporting and categories that identified and highlighted miscegenation.

Indians in the New Zealand Census, Phase III: 1986–Present

The third census phase is marked by the emergence of ethnicity as the central concept for minority reporting in the national census. The 1986 Census is a critical starting point for this transition as it marks the move away from the previous preoccupation with blood quantum and "race alien" reporting to that of self-identification with the particular ethnicities of one's choice. The first appearance of the ability to tick affiliation with more than one ethnicity is one of this phase's chief characteristics. This adaptation parallels the corresponding transformations that were occurring in immigration reform at the time, which ceased to rely on the traditional source countries of Western Europe (and more recently, the Pacific Islands), and opened up migration from nontraditional sources, including Asia. The focus on ethnicity, rather than physical characteristics, replaced the nomenclature of race, but the classifications and categories continued to conflate birthplace, ancestry, nationality, and culture. Ethnic self-identification coincided with general improvements of minority performance in a variety of socioeconomic indicators (Callister 2007; Poata-Smith 2013), the emergence of political representation (Banducci et al. 2004; Park 2010; Sullivan 2010), and the commencement of inclusion in a common national identity (Greif 1995; Ip 2003; Ip and Pang 2005; Bandyopadhyay 2006; Dobson 2011). Such recognition allowed advancement of both government and minority interest in improving inequality and in better addressing minority aspirations (Park 2010, Kukutai 2012:28).

These changes brought about, or are a result of, identity politics based on increasing minority recognition, as this period witnesses the substantial growth of minority communities. Demographic change can best be observed in the increases in intercensal growth in minority populations during this phase. The growth in the Indian population is highlighted in Table 13, which grew 1,292% between 1981 and 2013, i.e., since just prior to when immigration reform began in 1987. While intercensal growth reached its zenith of 93.6% in the 1986–1991 period, in the wake of the passing of the 1987 Immigration Act, the Indian population continued to increase. The 2006 Census identified an Indian population growing at a faster rate

Table 13 Indians in the New Zealand Census, Phase III: 1986–2018

Year	Total population	Indians Number	% of total population	Intercensal increase Number	Percent	Change since 1981 (%)
1986	3,307,086	15,810	0.48	4,566	40.6	40.6
1991	3,373,962	30,606	0.91	14,796	93.6	172.2
1996	3,618,303	42,408	1.17	11,802	38.6	277.2
2001	3,737,346	61,803	1.65	19,395	45.7	449.7
2006	4,027,947	104,625	2.60	42,822	69.3	830.5
2013	4,242,051	156,567	3.69	51,942	49.6	1,292.4
2018						

Note: 2018 statistics will be released in 2019

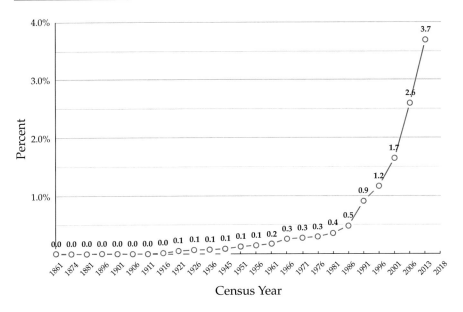

Fig. 1 Indians as a percentage of the total New Zealand Population, 1861–2018

than the Chinese for the first time, and this trend was confirmed by the 2013 statistics.

Figure 1 displays the Indian population as a percentage of the Total New Zealand population historically, including all years in which Indians were present in the Census. It shows the tremendous growth of the Indian diaspora in New Zealand, especially in the aftermath of recent immigration reform.

Along with rapid and consistent population growth came an increased need for Indian sociocultural groups, as a larger population brought about a communal shift away from primary economic pursuits and the business of survival, evident in the first two phases, towards a greater enjoyment and celebration of one's heritage and cultural roots, which became important in the third phase. Greater political organization and representation also emerged during this period. Rapid population growth mirrored significant changes in the number and extent of organizations and associations that cater to the thriving Indian population today. Prior to 1986, there were only a handful of organizations and associations that represented the needs of the Indian community. The first to form was the New Zealand Indian Central Association.

> Ironically, it was the vehement opposition to their settlement in New Zealand that induced Indians to form a national association in 1926 that would long outlive the White New Zealand League. (Leckie 2007, p. 140)

The early formation and expansion of such cultural, religious, and political networks, along with the growth of an increasingly expressive Indian identity, is well chronicled by Leckie (2007, pp. 140–168). Today, there are hundreds of Indian organizations and associations that represent the needs and aspirations of the various regional, cultural, religious, linguistic, sporting, women's, professional groups and trade organizations that now operate in New Zealand (see a list of Indian organizations and associations in Nachowitz 2015, Appendix K). This list, however, does not represent the continued growth and influence of Indian enterprise in the economic sector and the steady drive towards a New Zealand-India free trade agreement, currently underway.

Whereas there was scant political representation of the Indian community in New Zealand, there have been a number of key representatives and elected officials at local, regional, and national levels, including two mayors and several MPs, since the beginning of the third census phase. These changes all represent minority aspiration and affirmation for greater political voice in the national arena that is a defining characteristic. Figure 2 demonstrates that the proportion of the Indian community to the total New Zealand population stating an ethnicity (solid line) is in close approximation to the proportional representation of Indian MPs elected to the New Zealand Parliament (dotted line). The first South Asian elected to Parliament was Dr. Ashraf Choudhary in 2002, at which point the total Indian population represented 1.7% of the total New Zealand population. As the only

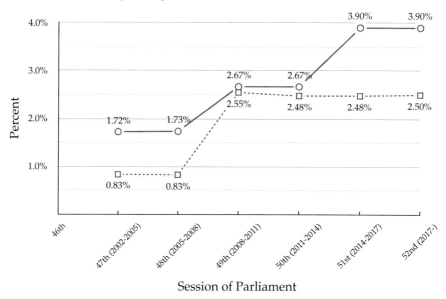

Fig. 2 Indian representation in New Zealand's Parliament. (Note: The figures for 47th and 48th Parliaments are based on statistics from the 2001 Census, the figures for the 49th and 50th Parliaments are based on statistics from the 2006 Census, and the figures from the 51st and 52nd Parliaments are based on statistics from the 2013 Census)

elected South Asian member in the 47th Session of Parliament, his representation amounted to 1 of 120 seats, or a proportion of 0.8%, less than half of what proportional representation should account for, and well below parity. This scenario was repeated in Parliament's 48th session, which had 121 members. Near parity was reached in the 49th and 50th Parliaments, both of which saw a total of three South Asians MPs.

In the 2013 Census, the Indian population reached 3.9% of the total New Zealand population stating an ethnicity. Due to the dramatic rise in the Indian population in the 2013 Census data, and the fact that only three Indian MPs were elected to Parliament in the September 2013 elections, the 51st Session again fell below parity. This trend continued in the 52nd Parliament, which currently continues to have three elected members of Indian ethnicity. It should be noted, however, that each of the South Asians that made their way into Parliament were List MPs and not Electorate MPs, i.e., they were not elected by the constituency of their electorate. This allowed, for example, New Zealand First MP Mahesh Bindra (ranked 11th on the New Zealand First party list) to be awarded a seat in the 51st Parliament on the coattails of New Zealand First's party vote, even though he received a total of only 717 votes of the 34,097 received in his Mount Roskill electorate (2.1% of the total number of votes cast in his electorate), losing to Phil Goff, who received 18,637 votes (or 54.7% of the total votes cast in the electorate). The differential between the two lines in Fig. 2 reached its largest gap in the 51st and 52nd Parliaments (a difference of 1.4%, compared with the lowest, achieved in the 49th Session, of 0.1%), since South Asians first appeared in the New Zealand Parliament during its 47th Session. This would be due to the increase in the Indian population without a concomitant rise in the number of Indian MPs entering Parliament in October 2014. It will be interesting to continue tracking proportional representation in Parliament in this way as minority populations continue to increase. What remains then would be for Indian political representation to achieve or exceed parity in proportion with the percentage of Indians in the total New Zealand population.

Table 14 includes a list of South Asians elected to the New Zealand Parliament, along with their political party, country of birth, respective religions, and the years each served in Parliament. Other politicians of note include one of the earliest elected

Table 14 South Asian representation in New Zealand Parliament

Name	Party	Dates served	Religion	Electorate or list MP	Country of birth
Dr Ashraf Choudhary	Labour	2002–2011	Muslim	List MP	Pakistan
Dr Rajen Prasad	Labour	2008–2014	Hindu	List MP	Fiji
Kanwaljit Singh Bakshi	National	2008–	Sikh	List MP	India
Mahesh Bindra	NZ first	2014–2017	Hindu	List MP	India
Dr Parmjeet Parmar	National	2014–	Sikh	List MP	India
Priyanca Radhakrishnan	Labour	2017–	Hindu	List MP	India

officials of South Asian descent in New Zealand, Dame Sukhinder (Sukhi) Kaur Gill Turner, who served as the Mayor of Dunedin from 1995 to 2004, serving a full three terms. Turner was born in Ludhiana, Punjab, educated in the USA, and became a New Zealand citizen in August 1973 (Kumar and Jacob 2004). She is a Sikh, married to the New Zealand cricketer Glenn Turner. In 2004, Turner received a *Pravasi Bharatiya Samman* award, presented by the Indian government to honor those making significant contributions in the countries of their residence. She has also been twice awarded in New Zealand, in 2002 Queen's Birthday Honours as Distinguished Companion of the New Zealand Order of Merit (*New Zealand Gazette* 2002, issue 57), and again in 2009 as a Dame Companion of the New Zealand Order of Merit (*New Zealand Gazette* 2009, issue 118).

Another statesman of merit is The Right Honourable Sir Anand Satyanand, who served as the 19th Governor-General of New Zealand from 2006 to 2011. Satyanand, born in raised in an Indo-Fijian family in Auckland, became a lawyer, graduating from the University of Auckland in 1970, later becoming a Judge of the District Court of New Zealand in 1982. Appointed by Prime Minister Helen Clark, he became the first Governor-General of Indian descent. In 2009, he became a Knight Grand Companion of the New Zealand Order of Merit (GNZM). He also served as Chair of the Commonwealth Foundation from 2012 to 2016. A full biography of Satyanand appears in Leckie (2018). Another Indian politician, K (Guru) Gurunathan, was elected as the Mayor of the Kapiti Coast in 2016. Gurunathan, a Malaysian-born Indian, former journalist and City Councillor, became the first ever non-European elected to office in his district.

Conclusion

This chapter refashions minority history in New Zealand and establishes early Indian presence at the time of initial Māori-European first contact, and Indian settlement according to the Census, long prior to dates originally reported. Indians are not just recent migrants pinching Pākehā jobs, but are, more appropriately, a population that played a vital role in the very foundations of New Zealand history alongside indigenous Māori and their European colonizers. That Indians have a claim, however small, to Aotearoan history and early Māori-European encounter has significant implications for both how majorities perceive minorities and how minorities perceive themselves in relation to majority society. *Tauiwi* need no longer consider themselves recent arrivals or as outsiders needing to be integrated into society, but rather as having just as much a right as Europeans to live and fully engage in a plural, deeply diverse, New Zealand society.

Demographically, the Indian population in New Zealand is expected to continue to grow and flourish. New Zealanders of Indian origin are expected to continue to engage in all sectors of society, have attained notable achievements, and made significant contributions in the Arts and Entertainment industry, media, business, politics, and sports.

Cross-References

▶ Indian Identity in South Africa
▶ Indian Indentured Laborers in the Caribbean
▶ The Legacy of Indentured Labor

References

Akbarzadeh S, Saeed A (2001) Muslim communities in Australia. University of New South Wales Press, Sydney
Banducci S, Donovan T, Karp J (2004) Minority representation, empowerment and participation in the US and New Zealand. J Polit 66(2):534–556
Bandyopadhyay S (2006) Reinventing Indian identity in multicultural New Zealand. In: Johnson H, Moloughney B (eds) Asia in the making of New Zealand. Auckland University Press, Auckland
Bandyopadhyay S (2010) India in New Zealand: local identities, global relations. Otago University Press, Dunedin
Beaglehole JC (1968) The journals of captain James cook on his voyages of discovery, volume one: the voyage of the endeavor, 1768–1771. Cambridge University Press for the Hakluyt Society, Cambridge
Beattie JJ (2011) Making home, making identity: Asian garden making in New Zealand, 1850s–1930s. Stud Hist Gdn Des Landsc 31(2):139–159
Bedford R, Ho E (2008) Asians in New Zealand: implications of a changing demography. Asia New Zealand Foundation, Wellington. http://www.asianz.org.nz/reports/report/asians-in-new-zealand/asians-in-new-zealand. Accessed 8 Oct 2018
Berry A (1912) Reminiscences. Angus & Robertson, Sydney
Bola MK (2014) The legacy: the life of Baram (Waryam) Singh Ark, 1883–7th June 1950. Polygraphia, Auckland
Borrie WD (1991) Immigration to New Zealand, 1854–1938. Australian National University, Canberra
Callister P (2007) Special measures to reduce ethnic disadvantage in New Zealand: an examination of their role. Institute of Policy Study, Wellington
Carrick RO (1903) Historical records of New Zealand south prior to 1840. The Otago Daily Times and Witness Newspapers Company, Dunedin
Clarke C, Peach C, Vertovec S (1990) South Asians overseas: migration and ethnicity. Cambridge University Press, Cambridge, MA
Collins D (1798) An account of the English colony in New South Wales, with remarks on the dispositions, customs, manners &c. of the native inhabitants of that country, vols. I and II. Cadell, Jun and Davies, London
Cruise R (1824) Journal of ten months' residence in New Zealand, 1820. Capper, republished in 1957 by Pegasus Press, Christchurch
Didham R (2010) Future potential and the invisible diaspora: New Zealand and South Asia diasporas. Outlook edition 12. Asia New Zealand Foundation, Auckland. http://www.asianz.org.nz/reports/report/future-potential-and-the-invisible-diaspora/future-potential-and-the-invisible-diaspora>. Accessed 8 Oct 2018
Dobson S (2011) Asian Muslim women negotiating identity in New Zealand. In: Voci P, Leckie J (eds) Localizing Asia in Aotearoa. Dunmore Publishing, Wellington
Drury A (2000) A short history of Ponsonby Mosque, New Zealand in Al-Nahdah 19(3):36–38
Drury A (2006) Islam in New Zealand: the first mosque. Xpress Printing, Christchurch
Dunmore J (1969) The fateful voyage of the St. Jean Baptiste. Pegasus, Christchurch
Dunmore J (1981) The expedition of the St. Jean-Baptiste to the Pacific, 1769–1770: from journals of Jean de Surville and Guillaume Labé. Hakluyt Society, London

Dwyer D (1990) Tuapeka's obscure prospector. Otago Daily Times, November 6, p 18

Entwisle P (2005) Taka: a vignette life of William Tucker 1784–1817: convict, sealer, trader in human heads, Otago settler, New Zealand's first art dealer. Port Daniel Press, Dunedin

Fisher MH (2006) Working across the seas: Indian maritime labourers in India, Britain, and in between, 1600–1857. Int Rev Soc Hist 51(Supplement S14):21–45

Friesen W (2008) The evolution of 'Indian' identity and transnationalism in New Zealand. Aust Geogr 39(1):45–61

Friesen W, Kearns R (2008) Indian diaspora in New Zealand: history, identity and cultural landscapes. In: Raghuram P, Sahoo AK, Maharaj B, Sangha D (eds) Tracing an Indian diaspora: contexts, memories, representations. Sage, New Delhi

Furber H (1970) John company at work: a study of European expansion in India in the late eighteenth century. Octagon Books, New York

Gillion KL (1977) The Fiji Indians: challenge to European dominance, 1920–1946. Australian National University Press, Canberra

Graham J (1992) Settler society. In: Rice GW (ed) The Oxford history of New Zealand. Oxford University Press, Auckland

Grant D (2015) Southland places: Fiordland's coast. In: Te Ara: the encyclopedia of New Zealand. https://teara.govt.nz/en/southland-places/page-10. Accessed 8 Oct 2018

Greif SW (1995) Immigration and national identity in New Zealand: one people, two peoples, many peoples. Dunmore Press, Palmerston North

Howard B (1940) Rakiura: a history of Stewart Island, New Zealand. AH & AW Reed, Dunedin

Howe KR (2008) The quest for origins: who first discovered and settled New Zealand and the Pacific islands? Revised edition. Penguin New Zealand, Auckland

Hutching G (2006) Shipwrecks: perils of the sea: 19th century. In: Te Ara: the encyclopedia of New Zealand. https://teara.govt.nz/en/shipwrecks/page-2. Accessed 8 Oct 2018

Ip M (2003) Unfolding history, evolving identity: the Chinese in New Zealand. Auckland University Press, Auckland

Ip M, Leckie J (2011) 'Chinamen' and 'Hindoos': beyond stereotypes to Kiwi Asians. In: Voci P, Leckie L (eds) Localizing Asia in Aotearoa. Dunmore Publishing, Wellington

Ip M, Pang D (2005) New Zealand Chinese identity: sojourners, model minority and multiple identities. In: Liu J, McCreanor T, McIntosh T, Teaiwa T (eds) New Zealand identities: departures and destinations. Victoria University Press, Wellington

Kadekar LN (2005) Global Indian diaspora: an overview. Department of Sociology, University of Hyderabad, Hyderabad

Kelly LG (1951) Marion Dufresne at the Bay of Islands. AH. & AW Reed, Wellington

King M (2003) The penguin history of New Zealand. Penguin Books, Auckland

Kolig E (2010) New Zealand's Muslims and multiculturalism. Brill Publishers, Boston

Kondapi C (1951) Indians overseas 1838–1949. Indian Council of World Affairs, New Delhi

Kukutai T (2012) Quantum Māori, Māori quantum: state constructions of Māori identities in the census, 1857/8–2006. In: McClean R, Patterson B, Swain D (eds) Counting stories, moving ethnicities: studies from Aotearoa New Zealand. University of Waikato/Faculty of Arts and Social Sciences, Hamilton

Kumar R, Jacob J (2004) Bowling 'em over: such turner. India Empire, October issue. http://www.indiaempire.com/v2/magazine/2004/Oct/sukhi-turner.html. Accessed 8 Oct 2018

Lal B (2006) The encyclopedia of the Indian diaspora. University of Hawai'i Press, Honolulu

Leckie J (1985) In defence of race and empire: the white New Zealand league at Pukekohe. N Z J Hist 19(2):103–129

Leckie J (1995) South Asians: old and new migrants. In: Greif S (ed) Immigration and national identity in New Zealand: one people, two peoples, many peoples? Dunmore Press, Palmerston North

Leckie J (1998) The southernmost Indian diaspora: from Gujarat to Aotearoa. South Asia 21(1):161–180

Leckie J (2006) New Zealand. In: Lal B (ed) The encyclopedia of the Indian diaspora. University of Hawai'i Press, Honolulu

Leckie J (2007) Indian settlers: the story of a New Zealand south Asian community. Otago University Press, Dunedin
Leckie J (2010) A long diaspora: Indian settlement. In: Bandyopadhyay S (ed) India in New Zealand: local identities, global relations. Otago University Press, Dunedin
Leckie J (2011) Indians in the South Pacific: recentred diasporas. In: Edmond J, Johnson H, Leckie J (eds) Recentring Asia: histories, encounters and identities. Global Oriental, Boston
Leckie J (2018) A rich tapestry: the life and heritage of sir Anand Satyanand. In: Bandyopadhyay S, Buckingham J (eds) Indians and the antipodes: networks, boundaries, and circulation. Oxford University Press, New Delhi
Mayhew WR (1949) Tuapeka, the land and the people: a social history of the borough of Lawrence and its surrounding districts. Whitcombe and Tombs, Dunedin
McCarthy A (2009) Migration and ethnic identities in the nineteenth century. In: Byrnes G (ed) The new Oxford history of New Zealand. Oxford University Press, Auckland
McGee TG (1960) The Indian community in Wellington city: a geographical contribution to the study of assimilation. MA thesis, Victoria University, Wellington
McGee TG (1962) Indian settlement in New Zealand: 1900–1956. N Z Geogr 18(2):205–223
McGee TG (1993) Indians in New Zealand. In: Motwani JK, Gosine M, Barot-Motwani J (eds) Global Indian diaspora: yesterday, today and tomorrow. Global Organization of People of Indian Origin, New Delhi
McGlone MS (1989) The Polynesian settlement of New Zealand in relation to environmental and biotic changes. N Z J Ecol 12(Supplement):115–129
McLeod WH (1980) The Punjabi community in New Zealand. In: Tiwari KN (ed) Indians in New Zealand: studies of a sub-culture. Price Milburn, Wellington
McLeod WH (1984) A list of Punjabi immigrants in New Zealand 1890–1939. New Zealand Central Indian Association-Country Section, Hamilton
McLeod WH (1986) Punjabis in New Zealand: a history of Punjabi migration 1890–1940. Guru Nanak Dev University, Amritsar
McLeod WH, Bhullar SS (1992) Punjab to Aotearoa: migration and settlement of Punjabis in New Zealand, 1890–1990. The New Zealand Indian Association, Taumaranui
McLintock AH (1966) An encyclopedia of New Zealand, vol 1. RE Owen, Wellington
McMillan K (2006) Immigration policy. In: Miller R (ed) New Zealand government and politics, 4th edn. Oxford University Press, Auckland
McNab R (1907) Murihiku: a history of the South Island of New Zealand and the islands adjacent and lying to the south, from 1642 to 1835. Whitcombe & Tombs, Wellington
McNab R (1914) From Tasman to Marsden: a history of northern New Zealand from 1642 to 1818. J Wilke, Dunedin
Moon P (2013) Encounters: the creation of New Zealand: a history. Penguin Books, Auckland
Murphy N (2003) Present archival and library resources on the study of the Chinese in New Zealand, including recent Asian immigrants. In: Ip M (ed) Unfolding history, evolving identity: the Chinese in New Zealand. Auckland University Press, Auckland
Murphy N (2007) Report on Indian New Zealand community grievances. Private report commissioned by the New Zealand Indian Central Association
Murphy N (2008) Guide to laws and policies relating to the Chinese in New Zealand 1871–1997. New Zealand Chinese Association, Auckland
Murphy N (2009) 'Māoriland' and 'yellow peril' discourses of Māori and Chinese in the formation of New Zealand's national identity. In: Ip M (ed) The dragon and the taniwha: Māori and Chinese in New Zealand. Auckland University Press, Auckland, pp 1890–1914
Nachowitz T (2015) Towards a framework of deep diversity: identity and invisibility in the Indian diaspora in New Zealand. PhD thesis, University of Waikato. http://hdl.handle.net/10289/9442. Accessed 8 Oct 2018
Nachowitz T (2018) Identity and invisibility: early Indian presence in Aotearoa New Zealand. In: Bandyopadhyay S, Buckingham J (eds) Indians and the antipodes: networks, boundaries, and circulation. Oxford University Press, New Delhi, pp 1769–1850

Ng J (1993) Windows on a Chinese past, vol 1. Otago Heritage Books, Dunedin

Ng J (2003) The sojourner experience: the Cantonese goldseekers in New Zealand. In: Ip M (ed) Unfolding history, evolving identity: the Chinese in New Zealand. Auckland University Press, Auckland, pp 1865–1901

Owens JMR (1992) New Zealand before annexation. In: Rice G (ed) The Oxford history of New Zealand, 2nd edn. Oxford University Press, Auckland

Palakshapa TC (1973) Indian immigrants in Waikato: a study in dynamics of institutions. Working paper, Department of Sociology, no. 8, University of Waikato, Hamilton

Parekh B (1993) The Indian diaspora. In: Motwani J, Gosine M, Barot-Motwani J (eds) Global Indian diaspora: yesterday, today and tomorrow. Global Organisation of People of Indian Origin, New Delhi

Park SJ (2010) Asian participation. In: Miller R (ed) New Zealand government & politics, 5th edn. Oxford University Press, Auckland

Peach C (1994) Three phases of south Asian emigration. In: Brown J, Foot R (eds) Migration: the Asian experience. St Martin's Press, Oxford

Perry TM (1966) Berry, Alexander (1781–1873). In: Australian dictionary of biography, vol 1. National Centre of Biography, Australian National University. http://adb.anu.edu.au/biography/berry-alexander-1773/text1987. Accessed 8 Oct 2018

Phillips J (2009) Hoisting history on their backs. In: Te Ara signposts: a blog about the encyclopedia of New Zealand. http://blog.teara.govt.nz/2009/02/10/hoisting-history-on-their-backs/. Accessed 8 Oct 2018

Pio E (2012) Caste away? Unfolding the Māori Indian. Office of Ethnic Affairs, Wellington

Poata-Smith ETA (2013) Inequality and Māori. In: Rashbrooke M (ed) Inequality: a New Zealand crisis. Bridget Williams Books, Wellington

Pratt D (2010) Antipodean angst: encountering Islam in New Zealand. Islam Christ Muslim Relat 21(4):397–407

Pratt D (2011) Antipodean ummah: Islam and Muslims in Australia and New Zealand. Relig Compass 5(12):743–752

Richards R (2010) Sealing in the southern oceans 1788–1833. Paremata Press, Wellington

Salmond A (1991) Two worlds: first meetings between Maori and Europeans 1642–1772. Viking, Auckland

Salmond A (1997) Between worlds: early exchanges between Maori and Europeans 1773–1815. Viking, Auckland

Shepard W (1980) The Muslim community in New Zealand: studies in Islamic religion and institution. In: Tiwari K (ed) Indians in New Zealand: studies of a sub-culture. Price Milburn and Company, Wellington

Shepard W (2002) Muslims in New Zealand. In: Hadad Y, Smith J (eds) Muslim minorities in the west: visible and invisible. Altamira Press, Walnut Creek

Sibley CG, Ward C (2013) Measuring the preconditions for a successful multicultural society: a barometer test of New Zealand. Int J Intercult Relat 37(6):700–713

Singham M (2006) Multiculturalism in New Zealand – the need for anew paradigm. Aotearoa Ethnic Netw J 1(1):33–37. http://www.aen.org.nz/journal/1/1/AENJ.1.1.Singham.pdf. Accessed 8 Oct 2018

Sullivan A (2010) Māori participation. In: Miller R (ed) New Zealand government & politics, 5th edn. Oxford University Press, Auckland

Swarbrick N (2015) Indians – early immigration. In: Te Ara – the Encyclopedia of New Zealand. http://www.TeAra.govt.nz/en/indians/page-2. Accessed 8 Oct 2018

Swords M (1978) Alexander Berry and Elizabeth Wollstonecraft. Wentworth Press for North Shore Historical Society, Sydney

Taher M (1965) Asians in New Zealand: a geographical review and interpretation. PhD thesis, Geography, University of Auckland, Auckland

Taher M (1970) The Asians. In: Thomson KW, Trlin AD (eds) Immigrants in New Zealand. Massey University, Palmerston North

Tapp EJ (1958) Early New Zealand: a dependency of New South Wales 1788–1841. Melbourne University Press, Melbourne

Tiwari KN (1980) The Indian community in New Zealand. In: Tiwari KN (ed) Indians in New Zealand: studies of a sub-culture. Price Milburn, Wellington

Vasil R, Yoon H (1996) New Zealanders of Asian origin. Institute of Policy Studies, Victoria University, Wellington

Walrond C (2006) Gold and gold mining – Otago. In: Te Ara–the encyclopedia of New Zealand. https://teara.govt.nz/en/gold-and-gold-mining. Accessed 8 Oct 2018

Williams A (2009) Edward Peters (black Peter): the discoverer of the first workable goldfield in Otago. Clutha Print, Clutha

Zodgekar A (1980) Demographic aspects of Indians in New Zealand. In: Tiwari KN (ed) Indians in New Zealand: studies of a sub-culture. Price Milburn, Wellington

Zodgekar A (2010) Indian presence: a demographic profile. In: Bandyopadhyay S (ed) India in New Zealand: local identities, global relations. Otago University Press, Dunedin

Ethnic Migrants and Casinos in Singapore and Macau

67

Juan Zhang

Contents

Introduction	1314
Ethnic Migrants and Complex Inequalities	1316
Research and Methods	1318
The Asian Casino Economy	1319
The Perfect Worker? Ethnicity as Soft Skills	1321
Local Workers as the Other	1325
Concluding Remarks	1327
References	1328

Abstract

This chapter offers an empirical account on migrant workers, their identities, and their embodied experiences of labor hierarchy along ethnic lines in mega-casino resorts in Asia. As casino resorts become opportunities for fast-track economic development and urban renewal in the region since 2010, the Asian gaming sector has become a major industry relying heavily on rural-urban, inter-regional, and international migrant labor. With a focus on Filipino and Chinese casino workers in Singapore and Macau, this chapter explores complex inequalities experienced by migrants in a highly cosmopolitan and highly competitive work environment. Job hierarchies are often established based on cultural assumptions of particular characteristics and competencies attributed to different groups, consolidating classed and gendered stereotypes in the workplace. Although migrant workers in casinos try to resist negative ethnic stereotyping by emphasizing on their credentials and professionalism, they continue to perform the identity of

J. Zhang (✉)
Department of Anthropology and Archaeology, University of Bristol, Bristol, UK
e-mail: juan.zhang@bristol.ac.uk

© The Author(s), under exclusive license to Springer Nature Singapore Pte Ltd. 2019
S. Ratuva (ed.), *The Palgrave Handbook of Ethnicity*,
https://doi.org/10.1007/978-981-13-2898-5_91

the "perfect worker" with an "Asian-style" of conformity, self-discipline, and flexibility.

Keywords

Ethnic subjectivity · Casino · Complex inequalities · Transnational migration · Singapore · Macau

Introduction

Workers in Southeast Asia are on the move. The World Bank (2017) estimates that countries of the Association of Southeast Asian Nations (ASEAN) now supply 8% of the world's migrants, who cross various national, cultural, and politicoeconomic boundaries in search of better economic opportunities. Intraregional migration has grown significantly over the past decades, with Malaysia, Singapore, and Thailand as regional migration destinations. Around 6.5 million migrants now reside and work in these most desirable destinations, taking up a range of employment in agriculture, manufacturing, construction, health care, domestic work, hospitality, and service sectors (United Nations 2015).

As millions cross borders in Southeast Asia, migrants constitute a mobile workforce that continues to provide inexpensive, flexible, and often times disposable labor that supports the region's rapid economic growth and integration. Perceived by many as "a necessary cog in the machinery of capital accumulation" (Terry 2014: 79), most migrant workers are seen as to be "naturally suited" for low-end, low-skilled, and undesirable jobs that somehow match their "cultural traits" or various "innate characteristics." Such imaginations of migrant "natural dispositions" justify inequalities in wage levels, labor rights, and welfare processes across borders. They also consolidate the hierarchical formation of stratified work relations along racial, ethnic, gender, and class lines (Leitner 2000; Pratt 1997; Waldinger and Lichter 2003). Construction workers from Thailand and Myanmar are often described as "hardworking" and "diligent," who rarely complain about the "bare life" they live in the host society (Kitiarsa 2014). Filipino workers, on the other hand, are seen as "naturally caring" and "cheerful" (e.g., Chin 2008; Guevarra 2014), and are therefore "perfectly suited" to work in care work and service-oriented industries. Prevailing stereotypes that certain kinds of jobs are best performed by certain groups normalize the discursive framing of labor identity, denying migrant workers the ability to access a higher degree of entitlement, acknowledgement, and upward social mobility in host societies (see Kelly 2012; Mullings 2012).

This chapter contributes to the debate on the production of multiple and complex inequalities in the cosmopolitan workplace, where ethnicity, gender, and class continue to bear significance on laboring subjectivities. Locating Southeast Asian migrants in an exceptional and truly globalized industry of casino gaming and entertainment in two holiday destinations in the region – Singapore and Macau, this chapter aims to show how migrant subject formation and social relations are produced through intersectionality. In particular, ethnicity, gender, and class shape the ways in which migrant "self-fashioning" takes place in cosmopolitan casino resorts, where schemes of discipline and regulation reinforce hegemonic ideas of skill, competency, and professionalism. Ethnicity in this case is theorized as a purposefully constructed and carefully maintained *awareness of difference* that produces a set of categorizing practices to formalize and normalize unequal positions of power (Louie 2014; Wallman 1996). In the cosmopolitan workplace, a worker's ethnicity is both ascribed as a pre-given social identity (i.e., often one and the same as one's nationality) and as a set of "soft skills" that indicates this person's "natural disposition," communicational competencies, and labor market desirability (Friberg and Midtboen 2018). Rather than showing something "innate" and "unchanging" about an individual, ethnicity makes sense only in social situations where "us" and "them" need some degree of differentiation. As Wallman (1996: 2) argues eloquently, "it is not possible for me to be 'ethnic' by myself, or even in the company of others of my own ethnic kind. Each of us needs a 'them' to make us feel like part of an 'us'." The production of difference in the globalized workplace becomes extremely useful when laboring subject are "interpellated" into working beings with appropriate appearances, proper conducts, and the right kind of attitudes (Gill 2008; McDowell et al. 2007). Along this theoretical line, this chapter examines not the "ethnicity" of transnational casino workers per se but the specific social relations and power locations where workers' ethnicity can be used as a productive marker of difference and hierarchy.

Mega casino resorts provide an interesting case for analysis because of their "exceptionality" (Zhang and Yeoh 2016). On one hand, these resorts are the cosmopolitan workplace par excellence where employees from diverse cultural and national backgrounds come together and work under one roof in the global gaming industry that is deeply rooted in the speculative logic of neoliberal capitalism (Vlcek 2015). On the other hand, casino resorts often require a more fundamental separation between "us" and "them" in the Asian contexts, when the moral economy of gambling produces sharply differentiated subjects associated with notions of productivity and risk (Zhang 2019). Chinese and Indian nationals of a lower socioeconomic status (often loosely defined, as these two categories can include a much wider group of individuals with East Asian and South Asian features), for example, are often believed to face a "higher risk" of gambling addiction and are in need of "regulation" and "protection"; whereas Western (i.e., white) patrons and employees are believed to be "low risk" individuals who are capable of working and having a good time at the casino. This form of "typecasting" of different groups at casino resorts shows the intersectionality of power, when one's appearance and skin color are tied to economic status, class positions, self-conduct, gender identities, and social relations. Ethnic typecasting also implicates the wider perceptions on work competency, professionalism, and performance as it influences silently the ways in which individual ranks, wage levels, and career development are determined in the cosmopolitan workplace.

This chapter begins with a theoretical engagement of ethnicity and its embodied complex inequalities in the context of labor migration in Southeast Asia. Following a brief discussion of research methods, this chapter introduces the

Asian casino economy and its rapid development in the past few years, with Singapore and Macau as examples of success. Next, discussions on ethnicity as a skill in the casino will show how one's ethnic identity becomes an indicator of a set of informal skills. In this process, certain ethnic migrant groups "fashion" a particular professional identity that fits and conforms to the dominant perception of the "ideal worker" in the casino. This "fashioning" in turn consolidates the cultural association of ethnicity and "soft skills." Lastly, this chapter examines the politics of differentiation through the making of "strategic alterity" (Kingsolver 2007). The chapter concludes by drawing attention to migrant strategies of building a transnational "portfolio career" that plays up on what they believe as positive ethnic stereotyping. In doing so, they also downplay negative stereotyping that trivializes their professional contribution and identity in the workplace. Ethnicity in this case can be performed strategically as migrant workers actively promote an "Asian-style" of conformity, self-discipline, and flexibility that may potentially enhance their desirability in the neoliberal labor market.

Ethnic Migrants and Complex Inequalities

Ethnicity has been an enduring concept in the social sciences and continues to be a focus of theoretical debate. Earlier studies on race and ethnicity focus primarily on the power relations between groups that are categorized as "us" and those deemed as the "Other" (e.g., Bhabha 1983; Briggs 2003). Such a focus shows the intellectual tradition of colonial and imperial projects, where racial and ethnic classifications have been used as a powerful tool to serve the management of Empire (e.g., Stoler 2010). Classic works such as Fabian (1983), McClintock (1995), Loomba (2005), and Eriksen (2002) show the persistence of the politics of making difference through colonial, imperial, and nationalist projects, where groups are classed and categorized by a set of selected cultural, social, and biological traits regarded as "natural" and "inherited characteristics" of these individuals. Critical race and ethnic studies have since moved the debate forward to highlight the specific conditions of power where one group is able to exercise dominance over others based on ideologies of ethnic differentiation (Sonenshein 1993; Yelvington 1995).

Feminist scholars point to the interrelationships between race, ethnicity, gender and class, and call for a stronger analytical attention on questions of power and multiple forms of social inequalities through an examination of intersectionality (Valentine 2005; Yuval-Davis 2006). Scholars also suggest racial performativity as a key analytical lens to unmask the ways in which identities are socially constructed and contested (Muñoz 2006; Veninga 2009). Classrooms and workplaces are particular social sites where "bodies do race" (Veninga 2009: 107), as individuals perform their identities in the normalized context of discipline, surveillance, and self-regulation (Crang 1994; McDowell 2009). It has been noted that many forms of work involve specific "performances" of certain laboring subjectivities. Low-skilled service sectors, for example, rely heavily on feminized labor to perform domestic and care work (see England 2005; Parreñas 2015). Merchant seafaring, on the other hand, has become a male-dominated ethnic niche industry staffed primarily by Fipilino maritime workers (McKay 2007).

Domestic and care work, commercial seafaring, health and hospitality (Batnitzky and McDowell 2013), call centers (Shome 2006) – these sectors are among the emerging and globalizing "ethnic labor market" that relies on the racialization and the specific "sorting" of different immigrant groups into different lines of work. The reproduction of a niche industry is maintained through a continuation of ethnic and gendered "typecasting" which determines who gets what jobs. Ethnic migrants are allocated into different types of work because "each group is perceived to posit a unique set of informal qualifications or 'soft skills'" (Friberg and Midtboen 2018: 1464). It is not uncommon to hear employers in different trades comment that migrant workers are more "hardworking" (McLaughlin 2010: 79), willing to "go the extra mile" (Friberg and Midtboen 2018: 1472), and more "service-oriented" (Chin 2008: 12). Southeast Asian migrant workers in particular embody the "naturalness" of good service work, as Chin (2008: 12) cites a cruise line management staff who claims that: "they seem to have been born with a wonderful service culture. They always greet the guests and always smile. And they do it so naturally." As Mullings (2012: 414) notes, "performances of deference, docility, aggression, or care can be crucial to the way that individual bodies are recruited, assessed, or advanced within work systems." The ascription of "service orientation" to Southeast Asian migrant workers effectively places them on the global labor market hierarchy where they are seen as "naturally suited" to be "servants of globalization" (Parreñas 2015) from various social and economic positions.

Once such stereotypical cultural representations are firmly established in the global labor market, migrant workers often find it difficult to shake off biased images and perceptions. With the rapid expansion of neoliberal industries on a global scale, a process of "strategic alterity" (Kingsolver 2007) produces different categories of laboring subjects. Using tobacco farmers and farmworkers as examples, Kingsolver (2007: 89) shows how American farm owners are valued as "independent" and "free-trading citizens of the market," whereas low-wage and non-wage farmworkers (mostly migrants) are no more than being part of the "globalized labor force" supplementary to the tobacco industry. Migrant workers therefore are denied any claim of ownership or recognition of their contribution to the multi-million dollar industry, as they are "othered" as strategic alters and enslaved labor in neoliberal capitalism. McKay's (2007) study shows a similar "othering" process on commercial ships where Asian workers constitute nearly 70% of the seafaring labor force onboard yet remain devalued as cheap maritime workers who can be easily replaced. Filipino seamen have learned to "fashion themselves as masculine exemplars" (McKay 2007: 626) to resist and go beyond ethnic stereotyping to defend their status on and off the ship, at work, and in their home communities.

In a truly cosmopolitan workplace like the mega casino resort, categorical associations between ethnicity, gender, and occupational "sorting" remain stubbornly consistent. Similar to McDowell et al.'s (2007: 3) description of Bellman International (pseudonym of an international hotel chain in London), within the casino resorts "a set of often-stereotypical assumptions about embodied social attributes influences employers' and managers' judgments about the acceptability of particular workplace presences and performances." There have been studies on the gendered, and often sexualized identities of female casino workers (de Volo 2003; Jones and Chandler 2007), and the hegemonic control of labor practices in the United States and South Africa (Sallaz 2009). Zhang et al. (2017) use "self-fashioning" to describe the embodied experiences of flexibility and discipline in Singapore's casinos. As casino workers perform professionalism, many strive to become "exceptional workers" (Zhang et al. 2017: 4) who are highly employable in the transnational labor market. What remains missing in these discussions is an examination of how ethnicity and class also play into the construction of a working identity in global casino establishments. This chapter aims to fill this gap and provide a preliminary account on cultural representations, class, and labor subjectivation in Asia's thriving casino economy.

Research and Methods

This chapter is based on two years of research (2013–2015) in Singapore and Macau's mega casino resorts. Data used in this chapter were collected in two projects, the first on the expanding casino industry in Singapore and its associated labor and consumer mobilities, and the second on the development of the Asian casino economy with a focus on Macau. Fieldwork included semi-structured interviews with local and migrant workers in the casino resorts in these two destinations, and employees in hotel and hospitality, entertainment, and retail as part of the lager casino resort establishments.

This chapter draws insight from interviews and interactions with 40 casino employees in Singapore and Macau. One third of the interviews were with Singapore and Macau local workers, and the rest come from the Philippines, Malaysia, China, Taiwan, and Japan. Most of the migrant workers in Singapore's casino resorts are hired as skilled or semiskilled employees with either an Employment Pass or an S Pass under the country's "highly stratified system of work visas (Wise 2016: 2289)." With the ASEAN agreement on visa exemption, Malaysia and Philippine nationals can enter Singapore without a visa for 14 days. A number of Malaysian and Filipino employees are able to find work in Singapore's casino resorts within the 14-day period and convert to work visas subsequently. In recent years, however, it has become increasingly difficult to gain employment this way as Singapore tightens its immigration regulations. Migrant workers now have to either go through labor agencies or apply for vacancies via online job search engines (e.g., JobStreet.com or JobsDB.com). Interviews by skype are common. Internal referrals within multiple casino establishments are widely practiced.

In Macau, most Southeast Asians can enter and stay as a visitor for 30 days without a visa. This longer time frame allowed more migrant workers from, for instance, Indonesia and the Philippines to go to Macau without a job offer in hand. Once arrived, they often stay with friends or acquaintances and start actively looking for work. Migrant workers obtained nonresident work visas in order to be legally employed in the cosmopolitan resorts. As casinos and tourism are the main industries in Macau, and due to Macau's local labor protectionism (Choi 2016), available jobs to migrants are mainly in the low-paying service sectors with limited long-term employment prospect. Workers from Southeast Asia constantly rely on co-ethnic networks for work-related introductions and referrals. They also use employment agencies if they are close to the end of the visitor's visa. At the time of research, most of the workers interviewed had been working in the casino resorts in a range of services for as little as six months to as long as about 3 years. By the time of writing, some have left the casinos for a better job and others are actively looking for new positions. Most of the employees working on the main casino floors had to sign a confidentiality agreement as part of the contract, which prohibited them from sharing any specific information concerning the day to day operations within the casino establishment. To respect the confidentiality agreement, interviews centered mainly on casino employees' professional experiences, migration trajectories, and personal views on their lives and employment in a foreign country. Informant identities and their specific occupations are deliberately kept vague, and pseudonyms are used throughout this chapter.

The Asian Casino Economy

In the past decade, a "casino fever" took over Asia (New York Times 2014) where luxurious mega casino resorts became spectacles of economic growth and urban development. PricewaterhouseCoopers projected in 2015 that casino revenues throughout the Asia Pacific region grew by 18.3% per annum on average (PwC 2015) led by the exceptional performances in Singapore and Macau. The *New York Times* reported that within 2 years of the opening of Singapore's two casino resorts, or Integrated Resorts (IR) – Marina Bay Sands and Resorts World Sentosa – visitor arrivals increased by 50% and tourism revenue reached $18 billion (New York Times 2014). The IR business success helped to fashion a new "Singapore model" in leisure gaming with a highly regulated approach (Zhang 2017). After Macau, Singapore has become the second best grossing leisure and gambling destination in the region, cashing in billions in not only gaming but also hospitality, retail, and entertainment.

Macau's status as the most established gambling hub in Asia has also elevated to being an Asian metropolis during the past decade (Simpson 2014) and a consumption heaven frequented by the increasingly affluent Asian visitors. As a Special Administrative Region (SAR) of China, Macau is home to over 40 casino resorts with major international casino operators including Wynn, Sands, Galaxy Entertainment, SJM Holdings, MGM Holdings, and Melco Crown. In 2013, Macau's leisure and gaming revenue grossed US$45 billion, surpassing the total revenue generated on the entire Las Vegas Strip by seven times (Simpson 2018: 75). Although the gaming industry in Macau and Singapore took a massive hit in 2014 with China's economic slowdown, and especially when Beijing launched a series of anti-corruption crackdown that targeted overseas VIP casino gambling, in 2016 the industry saw a turnaround. The Global Betting and Gaming Consultants (GBGC, an international gaming consultancy company) estimated that the global gambling revenue achieved US$435 billion in 2017, with Asia being the largest gambling region, taking up 31.3% of the market (GBGC 2018).

Such success stories inspired other Asian cities to follow suit. In the less developed parts of Asia, mega casino resorts are seen as opportunities "for fast-track economic accumulation and infrastructural development," and for "drawing in foreign direct investment, contributing to state tax revenue, and creating local jobs (Zhang 2017: 651)." In countries like the Philippines, Laos, Cambodia, and Vietnam, large-scale international casino resorts were built and in operation, contributing to the booming gambling industry across Asia. As of 2017, at least 17 new IRs are being planned in the region. South Korea opened the "first Korean-style integrated resort" Paradise City in 2017. Japan's parliament passed a bill of casino legalization. Taiwan is going through rounds of referendums on casino legalization as well. These projects, backed by strong market and states' political interests, promote different versions of Asian "casino urbanism." As Zhang (2017: 666) notes, "China's growing wealth and Asia's rise in power and influence stimulate imaginations of a profitable future made possible by the recent casino fever."

In both Singapore and Macau, the mega-casinos and associated leisure and entertainment industries make significant contribution to the national economies and labor force participation. S. Iswaran (2012), a Singaporean minister in the Prime Minister's Office and second minister for Home Affairs and Trade and Industry in 2012, noted that Singapore's two IRs contributed between 1.5% and 2% of the nation's GDP and employed nearly 2% of Singapore's total labor force. The gaming industry in Macau contributed to 47% of the GDP in 2016 and provided over 92,000 jobs, accounting for 23.8% of Macau's total employment (Sheng and Gu 2018: 76).

In order to support the operation and expansion of the gaming industry, large numbers of imported workers are recruited from the region, mostly in China, Malaysia, the Philippines, Indonesia, Taiwan, and Hong Kong. In Macau, migrant workers are barred from taking up the higher-end occupations in the gaming industry, such as croupiers and pit supervisors (Sheng and Gu 2018: 74). In Singapore, although there is no specific regulatory order that prohibits foreign workers from taking up certain types of jobs in the casino industry, the Ministry of Manpower (MOM) maintains a strict "foreign worker quota" system that sets a limit on the number of Work Permit and S Pass holders the industry can hire. (See https://www.mom.gov.sg/passes-and-permits/s-pass/quota-and-levy/levy-and-quota-requirements. The current cap for hiring S Pass holders is 15% of the company's total workforce in the service sector. Employers are also required to pay a "foreign worker levy" for S Pass holders. In the service sector, the monthly levy rates for one worker are tiered at SG$330 and SG$650.)

There is no official statistics on the exact number of migrant workers hired in the casino industry in Singapore and Macau. Interviews with several Human Resource (HR) staff members in the industry yielded vague answers. Foreign workers remain a sensitive issue and processes of hiring are confidential information in both countries. It is clear, however, that the casino sectors cannot function properly without migrant workers, and business operators are constantly battling with hiring restrictions and quota systems because, as one HR manager has implied, they prefer foreign workers over local workers if given a choice. One Singaporean HR staff made a comment off the record that the casinos would have to hire local workers just to have more quotas for foreign workers. With restrictive labor regulations, migrant labor become invisible in official statistics and are treated as secondary to local residents and citizens. While they make significant contribution to the economic success of the industry and the national economies, they remain "an indentured, invisible majority" and "immediately deportable noncitizens," just like the disenfranchised migrant workers in Dubai (Davis 2006: 64).

The Perfect Worker? Ethnicity as Soft Skills

As a multi-billion dollar industry and as new icons of Asia's tourism destinations, mega casino resorts in recent years have become a highly desirable place for work in the region. The cultural fascination with glamourous casinos (usually fuelled by images and imaginations of Las Vegas or Monaco portrayed in Hollywood blockbusters), the cosmopolitan lure of working in a world-class facility, working among international colleagues, and attractive salary packages (compared to other available jobs to transnational workers) give casino work a particular kind of appeal that is beyond just an ordinary "service job." Zhang et al. (2017: 10) have shown how working in Singapore's casinos is associated with not only "gaining relevant skills and qualifications" but also "gaining status, recognition and possibly prestige" in the globalizing labor market within the service and hospitality sectors. In their 2007 study of employment in an international hotel in London, McDowell et al. (2007: 8) note the increasing presence of migrant labor in London's hospitality sectors due to their low labor cost and the possibility of making flexible employment contracts. Citing a survey of UK employers, they show that foreign workers not only "filled technical skill gaps" but also embodying work attitudes as "being more appropriate for the hospitality sector." In fact, one of the key reasons for the employment of migrant workers was their "capacity for hard work" (McDowell et al. 2007: 8).

In Asia's casino resorts, similar views and perceptions of migrant "work attitudes" and "capacities" are also strong, as employers rely on a flexible migrant labor force to keep their businesses functional and profitable. Asian employees are particularly welcome as they fit in different types of jobs that require different kinds of skills and knowledge. Employees from mainland China, Hong Kong, and Taiwan usually work in front office, customer relations, and VIP services. Most of them are female, embodying a specific kind of femininity for appropriate "emotional labor" (Hochschild 1983). The main reasons for Chinese and Taiwanese employees to work directly with resort guests are their perceived "cultural affinity" to Chinese gamblers and their ability to speak fluent mandarin Chinese and Cantonese. These front-office employees are selected based not only on their ability to "understand our valued guests better" (according to a casino management staff member in Macau) but also on their "pleasant appearances and personalities." In Singapore's resorts, the management places a strong emphasis on diversity and the importance of having a multinational team of workers in the establishment to service international guests. Employees' ability to communicate in English and to provide "professional services" (e.g., servility, deference, effective communication) is considered more important than individual appearances. By simply having a "Chinese" face is usually enough, and the ability to understand and speak Chinese is a plus.

In Macau, however, things work out differently. Because the majority of the clientele come from mainland China and Hong Kong, specific requirements on the cultural and image presentations in the casinos become a must. Young female workers who are employed as receptionists, front-desk staff, and VIP lounge staff usually come from the northern parts of China, who are believed to be taller, "in shape" (*shencai hao*), "more beautiful" with "a fairer skin tone" (compared to Chinese originally from southern provinces who are believed to be shorter and have darker skin tones). There are also fairly open criteria for body height and weight. One of the front-desk employees explained that although it was never stated in the hiring conditions, everyone knew that one's appearance was extremely important for female job applicants. "The taller and the slimmer the better of course," she explained matter-of-factly, "and image management is key. If we are not careful and have gained weight while on the job, we will be removed from front-line services." A male guest relations employee originally from Shandong province in northern China commented that "the employer wants everyone on the front line to look like models." Although male workers are subjected to less scrutiny with regard to their appearances, they are expected to be "well groomed" in general – i.e., dressing sharply, doing up their hair in style, and keeping fit.

In both Singapore and Macau, many mainland Chinese employees are aware that they are hired not because of their professional qualifications but simply because they are Chinese. Their supposed cultural knowledge of what mainland Chinese casino guests need and desire for is considered an important part of their employment. A Chinese employee in one of Singapore's casino resorts who called himself Jim explained that it was not just simply about understanding the Chinese language. "Singaporean Chinese or Malaysian Chinese can understand and speak Chinese well, but they may not understand what a mainland Chinese guest really likes or dislikes." Some mainland Chinese gamblers believe that the likelihood of losing is greater if they gamble within the same casino resort where they stay. Some guests believe that by consuming free drinks and free meals within the same casino where they gamble, their luck is likely to run out because they have taken advantage of casino "freebies." In these instances, Jim explained, it would be important to not promote in-house gambling packages or give free gifts or drinks so as to avoid offending these Chinese guests. But such "taboos" may not apply to all Chinese guests, as ethnic Chinese from Malaysia or Indonesia usually enjoy free gifts and packaged deals very much. A nuanced understanding of the different cultural preferences among guests of different Chinese backgrounds therefore is key to the delivery of satisfactory services. There are also occasions when problems take place in the guest's hotel room where housekeeping staff may have accidently moved the arrangements of the guests' personal items during cleaning (e.g., the orientation of shoes and bags, or the specific positioning of lucky charms that are supposed to enhance the guest's winning chance), guest relations staff like Jim need to come in to act as a cultural mediator and to resolve potential conflicts. In this sense, being mainland Chinese itself is seen as a kind of skill in guest relations and guest services that comes with the familiarity of certain cultural notions and practices.

Away from the front line of casino work, in switchboard and in a range of other VIP services, for example, Taiwanese employees are seen as perfect for the job because they are more soft spoken, more gentle, and polite in comparison to mainland Chinese employees (who are often stereotyped as being loud and lacking a "soft touch"). In the more hidden lines of work, gentle voices, patience, and a pleasant demeanour are regarded as more important than the guest's first impression of striking beauty or physical attractiveness. This is especially the case when VIP services involve taking care of the VIP gambler's family members (usually the wife and children who do not gamble). Taiwanese employees are seen as gentle, detailed, and caring. Female employees are not required to look like "models," as they project a professional image of being friendly and approachable, suitable to work with the entire family. Their line of service is still heavily feminized, but intentionally de-sexualized so it is seen as less aggressive and more care-oriented.

In food and beverage, housekeeping, and concierge, Southeast Asian employees become the dominant group. The stereotypical portrayal that Southeast Asians are diligent, hard-working workers who rarely complain persists. These jobs and positions are key to the successful operation of casino resorts, yet they are often located further away from direct interaction with casino guests. Kitchen work and housekeeping in particular provide backstage functions in all casino resorts. This line of work is strenuous and highly labor intensive, and it is something local workers are reluctant to take up. Filipino, Malaysian, and Indonesian workers with restaurant and hotel experiences usually fill up these positions. Mainland Chinese workers who are hired through transnational employment agencies also take up these jobs with lower visibility and lower status. They are often older and do not possess the physical attractiveness to work in the front line. One Filipino supervisor in the housekeeping sector of one casino resort in Singapore made clear that "Asian people are the best labour." He said:

> Compared to the Europeans, Americans, and the Western side, Asians are the best. Hardworking, best in service, good recall, patience, everything. Mostly patience, mostly Southeast Asian people. Pinoys, Indonesians...Indonesians are quite good. It's the way we Filipinos work and Indonesians work, almost the same. But if you see someone, oh, from China, (big sigh and laugh), we are not being racist! We are not being racist. We just know. It comes from experience.

Apart from making cultural differentiations between Asian and non-Asian workers in the back stage operations of the casino resort, there is also an internal ethnic hierarchy between different groups of Asian workers. Mainland Chinese, in this instance, are often seen as less capable and less international compared to the more seasoned employees from the Philippines. Filipino supervisor Neal who managed a team of 23 staff members in the concierge services of one casino resort in Singapore shared the difficulties of working with mainland Chinese colleagues in his day to day experience. In the interview Neal said:

> Neal: To be honest, because of the communication, it is not that easy. Because there is a (language) barrier. I don't blame them because they are from China, so they have a different attitude, you know. Maybe it's their culture or whatever. Okay, so for them it is like "okay this is my job". They don't go the extra mile. I think because of the government that they have over in China, they just follow orders, you know. They have to be told what to do, and nothing more. If their daily work is this, even though they see something else, they will not touch it.
> Interviewer: But are the Malaysians or Filipinos in your team different? Are they more willing ... (interrupted)?
> Neal: Yes, especially Filipinos. I am not saying this because I am a Filipino. But you know Filipinos are actually, they are just automatic. Yeah, automatic. They have the pride.
> Interviewer: Pride?
> Neal: About their jobs. Meaning, if this work is assigned to me, nothing problematic will happen. A sense of ownership is there.

In Neal's view, mainland Chinese workers are more difficult to work with and they deliver less satisfactory job performances because of their "culture" and "attitude," which have stopped them from becoming competent employees in the cosmopolitan casino resort. In contrast, Filipino workers are "automatic" who have a strong sense of pride and responsibility in their job, which enables them to uphold a professional identity as the "perfect worker" (Terry 2014: 76) in a globalized work environment.

The contrasting constructions of laboring identities and the ethnic hierarchies based on notions of work-related "soft skills" and competencies consolidate the categorical inequalities within the stratified arrangement of casino work. Just as Friberg and Midtboen describe:

> Such soft skills may also be related to the social and communication competencies needed to interact with co-workers, employers and customers, or to more intangible personal traits, such as sociability, pleasantness, or discreetness – whatever makes someone "fit in" in a particular workplace and in particular positions. In the end of the day, subtle traits such as, demeanour, accent, style, and physical appearance, will often influence employer's gut feelings about which worker "looks and sounds right" for a particular job. (Friberg and Midtboen 2018: 1465)

For mainland Chinese workers who have specific cultural knowledge, stronger communicational skills, and a more attractive appearance, they are able to occupy the much desired front line work that enjoys higher visibility and better employment benefits (e.g., opportunities to receive gifts and cash tips from guests and promotions if they receive compliments). Other Southeast Asian workers will have less access to these positions. Within the back stage operations of the casino business, less attractive and less qualified Chinese workers are perceived as professionally inferior to other Asian workers who embody more desirable traits and attitudes. In the cosmopolitan workplace, what Chinese, other Asian, and non-Asian employees can and cannot do often boils down to a specific understanding of culture and ethnicity masked as "skills." Such perceptions of "skills" in return reinforce persistent stereotypes of labor and the hierarchical formations of recognition and reward in the global labor market.

Local Workers as the Other

The politics of ethnic differentiation play out not only between different groups of migrant employees in the casinos; they are also salient in the ways in which local workers are differentiated from those with transnational experiences. Quite different from studies that demonstrate workplace ethnic hierarchies where local workers are usually the valued labor force whereas migrant workers tend to occupy lower places of marginalization (e.g., Harris and Valentine 2016; Lee 2018), in the casino resorts, such hierarchies are often actively resisted and on occasions reverted. Given the casino's cosmopolitan image and reputation, local workers with little or no overseas experience are regarded as less qualified, less competent, and less competitive. Migrant employees complain that locals remain employed in casino resorts simply because of their citizenship status and the local workforce protective measure that governments have enforced. In this regard, many believe that local employees in Singapore and Macau do not possess the competitive edge if they are placed in the global labor market. When migrant employees talk about their local colleagues, a common impression has it that locals are spoiled, too "fragile" as they lack a sense of self-direction and work responsibility.

The Filipino supervisor Neal in one of Singapore's casinos described the problem with manpower he had to deal with in the workplace. In concierge services where he managed over 20 employees, most came from China, Malaysia, and the Philippines. There were a few local Singaporean employees from time to time, but Neal professed that these local workers often gave him various issues. Singaporeans did not really want to work in the service industry, he explained, and they certainly did not want to work under a Filipino. Employees from other countries worked with him collegially because they respected his extensive overseas experience working in international hotel chains and resorts elsewhere. But local Singaporeans would always see him as "just a Filipino," he complained.

In Macau's casinos, high-earning jobs such as croupiers (or card dealers) are reserved only for local residents. Local dealers as young as 18 years of age can already apply for entry level positions in the casino establishments. Shi and Liu (2014) have made a clear case that young people in Macau often quit schooling to work for a casino for immediate economic gains. "Because the gambling sector does not require a college education to work in the casino and because the job market has been dominated by the sector and offers little opportunity for non-gambling professionals, education is never seen as necessary to get a 'good' job" (Shi and Liu 2014: 938).

In contrast, most of the migrant workers in Macau's casinos have received tertiary education or specific vocational training (e.g., in tourism or hospitality sectors) in their home countries before getting employed. Many have had extensive work experiences in the service industry. Migrant employees therefore like to see themselves as more mature, more experienced, and more qualified than local workers.

In interviews, Filipino and Chinese employees often highlight their training and professionalism, and complain that their local co-workers perform poorly yet receive high salaries and bonuses. A Chinese mid-level management employee Leo said that of all the 50 plus staff members he was in charge of, the locals could not meet the same standards set by his migrant employees. "I wouldn't see anyone (local workers) who would work voluntarily overtime; but we (foreign workers) can extend working hours without payment. I can see the difference in the amount of passion for work." What Leo's words reveal is quite a troubling perception that the willingness to perform overtime work (without pay) is equated to a strong passion for work. Just as Friberg and Midtboen (2018: 1465) argue, this kind of willingness is interpreted as a skill or "work ethic" that ethnic migrant workers possess, which also shows the level of exploitation they are willing to endure just to be perceived favorably in the workplace. Employers are likely to see this "willingness" as a plus, and local workers in comparison offer "no value added."

In the casino workplace, local workers are thus constructed as the "other" who make little actual contribution but continue to occupy favorable positions simply because of their resident status. In the migrant discursive construction of the local-foreign divide, local employees are strategically undervalued as the "other" to the more diligent, competent, and competitive migrant professionals. In doing so, a process of "strategic alterity" (Kingsolver 2007) takes place in the casinos where the assertion of local workers as "the other" establishes a sense of pride and superiority among transnational workers who see themselves as capable individuals in the neoliberal labor market. The Filipino housekeeping supervisor in Singapore indeed described local employees who worked under him as almost a "burden" – "even though I see that local staff are not at the standard that I want, I cannot kick them out." Because of the labor quota system in Singapore, he explained:

> Manpower is a problem. Local can decide, "Eh, I go to another company tomorrow", and it's quite difficult for the company because we have to fight to get another local staff to fill (the gap). So you have to manage them (local employees). If he has one year (contract), you have to live with him. Especially right now MOM doesn't give us any quota (for foreign workers). Our quota is closed and of course we have to work on the budget. At the moment, the quota for PRC (mainland Chinese workers) is closed for the rest of the year. MOM is encouraging the company to hire more Singaporeans, which is difficult for us. No Singaporeans want to do work (in housekeeping). There are some, but the age is … (long pause) quite mature (laughing). We have local staff like over 60 years old. You can't scold these aunties or uncles, or tell them how to do their job.

A Filipino guest services manager Adam who works in the same resort in Singapore believed that foreign employees like him and his colleagues are far more exceptional than their local colleagues. "They (Singaporeans) somehow think that the government took foreigners in and that's why we are losing our jobs. But on the other hand, the reason why the government actually took foreigners in is that ... their locals cannot do the work!" These discursive constructions that foreign workers can do the job better than locals reflect a strategic process of elevating migrants' social and professional status in the workplace. Datta and Brickell (2009: 459) in their study of Polish builders on London's building sites show a similar strategy where Polish builder construct themselves as "artistic, versatile, professional, cultured, and hence 'superior' workers to English builders." In this way, Polish builders are able to "stress a Polish work ethic" and "negotiate their place in the London labor market and the social hierarchies of the building site." Polish workers thus claim that "we have a little bit more finesse as a nation" to deflect detrimental stereotypes that run along ethnic and class lines. In a similar fashion, in Singapore and Macau's casino resorts, migrant employees also highlight professional differences between themselves and local workers. In doing so, they may be able to counter certain cultural stereotypes and fashion themselves as high skilled and highly valuable employees in the neoliberal labor market (see Zhang et al. 2017).

Concluding Remarks

This chapter brings to light the intersectionality of ethnicity, gender, and class in identity politics and labor hierarchies in a cosmopolitan workplace like the mega casino resorts in Singapore and Macau. Focusing on migrant workers' experiences, this chapter shows how migrant subject formation and social relations are shaped by various notions of skill, competency, and attitude that play along ethnic and class-based assumptions about "culture" and "nature." With a focus on Filipino and Chinese casino workers in Singapore and Macau's mega resorts, this chapter shows how "Asian" workers turn themselves into "perfect employees" in global casino resorts, capable of demonstrating the right kind of professionalism, self-responsibility, and self-discipline as the ideal "neoliberal worker" (Waite 2009). Their desirability is further contrasted in the casino space against other low-wage South Asian migrant workers who patronize casinos as gamblers, who are seen as lacking self-control and easily fall into "debt traps" and develop "addictions" (e.g., Ang 2010; Kok and Lin 2010; Lee and Kor 2017). The juxtaposition of the ideal "Asian professionals" in the cosmopolitan resorts and the vulnerable low-skilled migrant workers in construction sites reflects the socially constituted meanings of ethnicity and class in migrant recipient countries.

In the casino workplace, an implicit labor hierarchy is in place based on the logic of labor racialization. Workers' racialized identities often "dictate the sorting of different immigrant groups into particular kinds of work" (Kelly 2012: 438), reinforcing stereotypical perceptions of which group is suited to perform what kinds of tasks. In the casino resorts, Asian and non-Asian migrant workers occupy different positions of recognition and reward, with Chinese workers performing front line services due to imagined cultural affinity to Chinese gamblers, and Southeast Asian workers performing behind the scene tasks of cooking, cleaning, serving, and other types of care giving. Within the broader classification of "Asian workers," more subtle differentiations persist to separate the more "qualified Asians" who enjoy higher social and economic status in the workplace, and the less qualified Asians who are rendered more or less powerless in their social relations. Qualification in this sense is akin to "skill" and remains a vague and often arbitrary marker (Friberg and Midtboen 2018: 1465) that serves to differentiate rather to define. It can be about the migrant worker's education, work experience, background, or simply about one's language proficiency, cultural knowledge, and physical appearance. These different aspects are often folded into unquestioned ideas of ethnic identities and national characteristics, where some Asians are perceived as more competent and more desirable than other Asians in the labor market.

This chapter also argues that in the casino workplace migrant workers often place a strong emphasis on their transnational competencies, professionalism, and flexibility to resist being identified as the inferior "Other." Many build successful "portfolio careers" (Power et al. 2013; Waite 2009) in different sectors and in different locations with the hope that their transnational work experiences would downplay their ethnic identity and its associated presumptions, and highlight their professional identity as highly desirable in a global market. In this sense, ethnic characteristics and differences are minimized where necessary when migrant workers need to project a more "cosmopolitan" identity that embodies the neutral corporate professionalism in the workplace. Their "ethnic characteristics" and cultural knowledge can also be activated strategically when these workers need to bank in on their social capital and "soft skills" when it comes to securing an employment or demonstrating better competent work performance. The production of cultural differences in and around the casinos reinforces different positions of power, naturalizing regulatory structures that serve the neoliberal workplace.

References

Ang B (2010) Too many foreign workers in casino? The New Paper. http://www.asiaone.com/News/The%2BNew%2BPaper/Story/A1Story20100222-200207.html. Accessed 22 Aug 2018

Batnitzky A, McDowell L (2013) The emergence of an 'ethnic economy'? The spatial relationships of migrant workers in London's health and hospitality sectors. Ethn Racial Stud 36(12):1997–2015

Bhabha HK (1983) The other question. Screen 24(6):18–36

Briggs L (2003) Reproducing empire. University of California Press, Berkeley

Chin CBN (2008) Labour flexibilization at sea. Int Fem J Polit 10(1):1–18

Choi AH (2016) The politics of consent in the casino economy: negotiations and contests of the migrant worker system in Macau. Asian Educ Dev Stud 5(4):408–422

Crang P (1994) It's showtime: on the workplace geographies of display in a restaurant in Southeast England. Environ Plan D 12(6):675–704

Datta A, Brickell K (2009) "We have a little bit more finesse, as a nation": constructing the polish worker in London's building sites. Antipode 413:439–464

Davis M (2006) Fear and money in Dubai. New Left Rev 41:47–68

de Volo LB (2003) Service and surveillance: infrapolitics at work among casino cocktail waitresses. Soc Polit 10(3):346–376

England K (ed) (2005) Who will mind the baby? Geographies of child care and working mothers. Routledge, London
Eriksen TH (2002) Ethnicity and nationalism, 2nd edn. Pluto, London
Fabian J (1983) Time and the other: how anthropology makes its object. Columbia University Press, New York
Friberg JH, Midtboen AH (2018) Ethnicity as skill: immigrant employment hierarchies in Norwegian low-wage labour markest. J Ethn Migr Stud 44(9):1463–1478
GBGC (2018) Global gambling report 13th edition 2018. Global Betting & Gaming Consultants. https://www.gbgc.com/news/global-gambling-report-2018. Accessed 29 Aug 2018
Gill R (2008) Culture and subjectivity in neoliberal and postfeminist Times. Subjectivity 25(1):432–445
Guevarra AR (2014) Supermaids: the cacial branding of global Filipino care labour. In: Anderson B, Shutes I (eds) Migration and care labour. Palgrave Macmillan, London, pp 130–150
Harris C, Valentine G (2016) Encountering difference in the workplace: superficial contact, underlying tensions and group rights. Tijdschr Econ Soc Geogr 107(5):582–595
Hochschild A (1983) The managed heart. University of California Press, Berkeley
Iswaran S (2012) The Casino Control (Amendment) Bill. Casino Regulatory Authority Singapore. http://www.cra.gov.sg/cra/the-casino-control-amendment-bill.aspx. Accessed 22 Aug 2018
Jones JB, Chandler S (2007) Surveillance and regulation: control of women casino Workers' bodies. Affilia 22(2):150–162
Kelly PF (2012) Labor, movement: migration, mobility and geographies of work. In: Barnes TJ, Peck J, Sheppard E (eds) The Wiley-Blackwell companion to economic geography. Wiley-Blackwell, Chichester, pp 431–443
Kingsolver AE (2007) Farmers and farmworkers: two centuries of strategic alterity in Kentucky's tobacco fields. Crit Anthropol 27(1):87–102
Kitiarsa P (2014) The "bare life" of Thai migrant workmen in Singapore. Silkworm Books, Chiang Mai
Kok M, Lin TJ (2010) It's off to the gambling tables on their days off. Straits Times. http://eresources.nlb.gov.sg/newspapers/digitised/issue/straitstimes20101106-1. Accessed 22 Aug 2018
Lee S (2018) Encounters in the workplace: everyday diversity in a multinational professional firm. Soc Cult Geogr. https://doi.org/10.1080/14649365.2018.1499040
Lee P, Kor J (2017) The migrant workers falling into debt traps in Singapore's casinos. South China Morning Post. https://www.scmp.com/week-asia/society/article/2118342/migrant-workers-falling-debt-traps-singapores-casinos. Accessed 22 Aug 2018
Leitner H (2000) The political economy of international labor migration. In: Sheppard E, Barnes TJ (eds) A companion to economic geography. Blackwell, Oxford, pp 450–467
Loomba A (2005) Colonialism/Postcolonialism, 2nd edn. Routledge, Abingdon
Louie V (2014) Ethnicity everywhere and nowhere: a critical approach towards parsing ethnic and non-ethnic processes. Ethn Racial Stud 37(5):820–828
McClintock A (1995) Imperial leather. Routledge, New York
McDowell L (2009) Working bodies: interactive service employment and workplace identities. Wiley-Blackwell, Oxford
McDowell L, Batnitzky A, Dyer S (2007) Division, segmentation, and interpellation: the embodied labors of migrant workers in a greater London hotel. Econ Geogr 83(1):1–25
McKay SC (2007) Filipino Sea men: constructing masculinities in an ethnic labour niche. J Ethn Migr Stud 33(4):617–633
McLaughlin J (2010) Classifying the "ideal migrant worker". Focaal 57:79–94
Mullings B (2012) Economic geographies of race and ethnicity: explorations in continuity and change. In: Barnes TJ, Peck J, Sheppard E (eds) The Wiley-Blackwell companion to economic geography. Wiley-Blackwell, Chichester, pp 407–419
Muñoz JE (2006) Feeling Brown, feeling down: Latina affect, the performativity of race, and the depressive position. Signs 31(3):675–688
New York Times (2014) Casino fever in Asia. https://www.nytimes.com/2014/01/24/opinion/casino-fever-in-asia.html. Accessed 2 Sept 2018

Parreñas RS (2015) Servants of globalization, 2nd edn. Stanford University Press, Stanford

Power S, Brown P, Allouch A, Tholen G (2013) Self, career and nationhood: the contrasting aspirations of British and French elite graduates. Br J Sociol 64(4):578–596

Pratt G (1997) Stereotypes and ambivalence: the construction of domestic workers in Vancouver, British Columbia. Gend Place Cult 4(2):159–178

PwC (2015) Global gaming industry regulatory frameworks. PricewaterhouseCoopers. https://recursos.pwc.mx/landing.asp?pagina=global-gaming-industry-regulatory-frameworks. Accessed 25 Aug 2018

Sallaz JJ (2009) The labor of luck: casino capitalism in the United States and South Africa. University of California Press, Berkeley

Sheng M, Gu C (2018) Economic growth and development in Macau (1999–2016): the role of thebooming gaming industry. Cities 75:72–80

Shi W, Liu S-D (2014) Living with casinos: the experience of young dealers in Macau. J Youth Stud 17(7):930–947

Shome R (2006) Thinking through the diaspora: call centers, India, and a new politics of hybridity. Int J Cult Stud 9(1):105–124

Simpson T (2014) Macau Metropolis and mental life: interior urbanism and the Chinese imaginary. Int J Urban Reg Res 38(3):823–842

Simpson T (2018) Neoliberal exception? The liberalization of Macau's casino gaming monopoly and the genealogy of the post-socialist Chinese subject. Plan Theory 17(1):74–95

Sonenshein RJ (1993) Politics in black and white. Princeton University Press, Princeton

Stoler AL (2010) Carnal knowledge and imperial power, 2nd edn. University of California Press, Berkeley

Terry WC (2014) The perfect worker: discursive makings of Filipinos in the workplace hierarchy of the globalized cruise industry. Soc Cult Geogr 15(1):73–93

United Nations (2015) Trends in international migrant stock: the 2015 revision. http://www.un.org/en/development/desa/population/migration/data/estimates2/docs/MigrationStockDocumentation_2015.pdf. Accessed 3 Sept 2018

Valentine G (2005) Theorizing and researching intersectionality: a challenge for feminist geography. Prof Geogr 59(1):10–21

Veninga C (2009) Fitting in: the embodied politics of race in Seattle's desegregated schools. Soc Cult Geogr 10(2):107–129

Vlcek W (2015) Taking other people's money: development and the political economy of Asian casinos. Pac Rev 28(3):323–345

Waite L (2009) A place and space for a critical geography of precarity? Geogr Compass 3(1):412–433

Waldinger R, Lichter MI (2003) How the other half works: immigration and the social organization of labor. University of California Press, Berkeley

Wallman S (1996) Ethnicity, work and localism: narratives of difference in London and Kampala. Ethn Racial Stud 19(1):1–28

Wise A (2016) Becoming cosmopolitan: encountering difference in a city of mobile labour. J Ethn Migr Stud 42(14):2289–2308

World Bank (2017) Migrating to opportunity: overcoming barriers to labor mibility in Southeast Asia. https://openknowledge.worldbank.org/handle/10986/28342. Accessed 3 Sept 2018

Yelvington K (1995) Producing power. Temple University Press, Philadelphia

Yuval-Davis N (2006) Intersectionality and feminist politics. Eur J Women's Stud 13(3):193–209

Zhang J (2017) Introduction: integrated mega-casinos and speculative urbanism in Southeast Asia. Pac Aff 90(4):651–674

Zhang J (2019) The moral economy of casino work in Singapore. In: Hoang LA, Alipio C (eds) Money and moralities in contemporary Asia. Amsterdam University Press, Amsterdam

Zhang J, Yeoh BSA (2016) Harnessing exception: mobilities, credibility, and the casino. Environ Plan A 48(6):1064–1081

Zhang J, Yeoh BSA, Ramdas K (2017) Self-fashioning exceptionality: flexible workers in Singapore's casino resorts. Asian Anthropol 16(1):4–19

Ethnic Minorities and Criminalization of Immigration Policies in the United States

68

Felicia Arriaga

Contents

Racialization and Racialized Immigrant Groups	1332
Becoming White and Free from Criminalization	1332
Asians	1335
Latinos	1336
Criminalization Processes	1337
Criminalization Pre-civil Rights	1337
Criminalization Post-civil Rights	1337
Crimmigration	1338
Crimmigration After 9/11	1339
Changes Under the 45th Presidential Administration	1340
Border and Internal Enforcement	1343
Border Enforcement	1343
Internal Enforcement	1343
Surveillance Techniques	1344
Mexico's Internal Deterrence Policies	1345
Direct Threats and Resistance (A Case Study)	1345
Conclusion	1346
Cross-References	1347
References	1347

Abstract

Immigration policies in the United States not only describe the inclusive and exclusive nature of citizenship but also define that very citizenship through various arenas of law, namely, immigration and criminal law. Some ethnic groups are able to "become white" through legal definitions of citizenship, while others – racialized immigrants – remain as "second-class citizens" subject to criminalization and perceived criminality. It is only by considering how criminalization processes target

F. Arriaga (✉)
Sociology Department, Appalachian State University, Boone, NC, USA
e-mail: arriagafa@appstate.edu; felicia.arriaga@gmail.com; felicia.arriaga@duke.edu

other racial groups that one can construct how the criminalization of immigration policies serves to maintain a system of domination. The racialization process of certain immigrant groups has occurred through relational race making, whereby ethnic immigrants and the immigration policies pertaining to these groups also serve to criminalize them vis-à-vis other racial or racialized immigrant groups.

Keywords

Criminalization · Racialized immigrants · Crimmigration · Immigration enforcement

Racialization and Racialized Immigrant Groups

In *Race and Races: Cases and Resources for a Diverse America*, the authors:

> Define an **ethnic** group as a group of people larger than an extended family whose boundaries are marked by a social practice or experience perceived as distinct: a history or a religion; customs or traditions; a language or alphabet; perhaps even a geography. An ethnic group, in other words, is defined by the perception of a unique culture.

Whereas, **race** has been defined in a variety of ways:

- The nineteenth century – defined in quasi-biological terms as a group of humans with common biological ancestors who share certain physical characteristics, especially skin color and lip and eye shape (Perea et al. 2006).
- Racial ascriptions (initially) are imposed externally to justify the collective exploitation of a people and are maintained to preserve status differences (Bonilla-Silva 1997).

And for the purposes of this chapter, the term **racialized immigrants** (Sáenz and Douglas 2015) is also used to indicate the racialization of ethnic immigrants. **Racialization** has a variety of meanings from the application of racial categories to individuals from colonized nations based on biological differences (Banton 1977) to signifying the extension of racial meaning to a previously racially unclassified relationship, social practice, or group (Omi and Winant 1986), to a definition not dependent on phenotype but used to demarcate difference based on ideological or cultural traits (Miles 1993). This racialization process has occurred through relational race making, whereby ethnic immigrants and the immigration policies pertaining to these groups also serve to criminalize them vis-à-vis other racial or racialized immigrant groups. In this section, three broad groups are highlighted, whites, Asians, and Latinos.

Becoming White and Free from Criminalization

It is very rare to hear a news story about a white immigrant facing deportation proceedings. But was that always the case? The 1790 Naturalization Act began to construct the legal definition of white by the common understanding and/or through biology (Haney Lopez 2006). Furthermore:

> Many new immigrants learned to deploy and manipulate white supremacist images from vaudeville stage and the screens of Hollywood film where they saw "their own kind" stepping out of conventional racial and gender roles through blackface and other forms of cross-dress. (Perea et al. 2006)

In the late nineteenth century, Karen Brodkin Sacks (1994) suggests all southern and eastern European immigrants were subjects of racism like Asian immigrants and were therefore subject to similar exclusionary immigration policies in the 1920s. After 1880, 23 million European immigrants came to work in the United States, and some of these individuals were targeted in a conflation of anti-communism and anti-immigrant sentiment in 1919 during the Red Scare. Theodore Roosevelt also insisted that these groups were inferior individuals, so by the 1920s, "scientific racism sanctified the notion that real Americans were white and came from northwest Europe" (Perea et al. 2006: 519). Furthermore, this notion of eugenics stemming from the European model, namely, that proposed by Cesare Lombroso in *The Born Criminal*, proposed that criminality was a function of various physical abnormalities. Also influential in this area was Madison Grant (1916) who wrote *Passing of the Great Race*, which claimed that southern and eastern races were inferior. This extended into "intelligence tests," which grouped together southeastern European immigrants, African-Americans, American Indians, and Mexicans as "feebleminded" (Perea et al. 2006: 518; Painter 2010).

Irish

Between 1845 and 1855, 2 million Irish migrated to the United States pushed by the Great Famine, which meant they arrived with limited resources. The Irish were often the target of more racial differentiation than some of their European immigrant counterparts. The development of the term "Irishism" – an alleged condition of depravity and degradation habitual to immigrants and maybe even their children exemplifies this:

> Negative assessments of Irishism or Celtism as a fixed set of inherited traits thus became linked at mid-century to a fixed set of observable physical characteristics, such as skin and hair color, facial type, and physique. (Jacobson 1998: 48)

At points in history, the census bureau gave this group their own racial category, separate from other foreign populations, yet the Irish were often compared to African-Americans for the following reasons:

- They often lived side by side in American cities in the 1830s.
- They both worked in domestic service and the transportation industry.
- Both were poor and often vilified.
- Both had experienced oppression and wrenched from a homeland (Roediger 2007: 134). Although many Irish in Ireland were against slavery, this did not

necessarily transfer when many emigrated as a result of famine after 1845 and Roediger suggests the Irish became white through a two-sided process. They won acceptance among the larger population, and second they embraced their own whiteness driven by "the particular 'public and psychological wages' whiteness offered to a desperate rural and often preindustrial Irish population coming to labor in industrializing American cities" (Roediger 2007: 137). Democrats also capitalized on recruiting the Irish to their party during a time of conflict with Mexico, a rise of Chinese immigrants, and continued disenfranchisement of blacks.

Jews

Although Jews were the first to enter colleges, Protestants did not praise this entrance into higher education, and some individuals were openly opposed to Jews at Harvard but still used the opportunity to block both black students and Jewish instructors (Graham Synott 1986). Elite schools utilized psychological tests and other quotas to try to keep Jews out but Jewish social mobility but Stephen Steinberg (1989) suggests, "Jewish success in America was a matter of historical timing." They came from urban, commercial, craft, and manufacturing backgrounds and were able to became the:

> first of the new European immigrants to create a middle class of small businesspersons early in the 20th century...Compared with other immigrants, Jews were upwardly mobile. But compared with that of nonimmigrant whites, their mobility was limited and circumscribed. Anti-immigrant racist and anti-Semitic barriers kept the Jewish middle class confined to a small number of occupations. (Perea et al. 2006: 521)

For Jews, class differences persisted, while simultaneously fascism in Europe probably contributed to confronting anti-Semitism at home.

Italians

At first, Italians were considered "the Chinese of Europe" and were associated with the US black population During the Louisiana state constitutional convention of 1898 when the "white man's government" was being disputed, Italians were considered "as black as the blackest negro in existence" (Cunningham 1965). More specifically, Italians were scrutinized for their possible connection to Moorish or African blood. Two years after the Louisiana state constitutional convention, a murder trial showcased "a popular understanding of Italians' innate criminality," which resulted in the lynching of 11 immigrants accused of conspiring to murder the police chief of New Orleans. Furthermore:

> So fused in popular perception were the issues of Mafia conduct and Italian racial character that, in editorials about the affair, the *Times* would cast Italian immigrants' behavior as racially determined and question their fitness for citizenship. "These sneaking and cowardly Sicilians," pronounced one editorial, "who have transplanted to this country the lawless passions, the cutthroat practices, and the oath bound societies of their native country, are to us a pet without mitigation. Our own rattlesnakes are as good as they get. (Jacobson 1998: 56)

Similar efforts across the country focused on an Italian immigrant connection to the Mafia and suggested this type of violence would continue without proper migration control. A 1925 study of immigrants and the justice system concluded that "Italians are by nature emotional and demonstrative, and should not be allowed to drive into racial communities [ghettos], forming habits of thought..that are limited and warped" (Jacobson 1998: 62).

Asians

Chinese

Chinese immigrants first began to migrate to the United States as sojourners in 1849/1850 when about 400,000 came to California in the gold rush. In the 1850s and 1860s, various restrictions existed delegating who could and could not give testimony in court against a white man, which included in writing black, mulatto, or Indian person but in the broader sense was determined to mean any nonwhite person to include the Chinese in this group, effectively excluding them from providing testimony and from "becoming white with all its privileges (Perea et al. 2006: 401). The California Constitution of 1879 targeted immigrants but Chinese immigrants specifically and labeled them as criminals in a variety of ways (Elmer Sandmeyer 1991):

- Section 1 sought to protect the state "from the burdens and evils arising from the presence of aliens, who are or may become vagrants, paupers, mendicants, criminals or invalids afflicted with contagious or infectious diseases...provide the means and mode of their removal from the state."
- Section 2 sought to implement employer sanctions for hiring Chinese or Mongolians.
- Section 3 restricted any employment "except in punishment for crime."

The first act excluding one country was the Chinese Exclusion Act in 1882, which suspended the use of Chinese laborers, charged those with facilitating their migration with a misdemeanor. The Geary Act, passed in 1892, imprisoned Chinese immigrants not lawfully entitled to be in the country before removal and required any legally residing Chinese laborers to obtain a certificate of residence or face deportation.

Japanese

Japanese immigrants began coming to the United States in 1885. Early restrictions focused on land claims in the Alien Land Laws. Under Executive Order 9066, then President Franklin D. Roosevelt created internment camps for Japanese immigrants prohibited from becoming citizens. Many stayed in these camps from 1942 to 1944. These camps were proposed as a means to provide security against sabotage and espionage. No acts were committed by these individuals during this time period, and similar internment were not directed at ethnic whites like the Germans and Italians whose "countrymen" were also participating on the opposite side of the war (Perea et al. 2006: 436).

Latinos

Mexicans
Although a relationship between the United States and Mexico existed prior to the Treaty of Guadalupe Hidalgo in 1848, this treaty solidified the territory lines between the two countries. According to Article VIII of this treaty, Mexican nationals could remain on their lands in US territory and become citizens or return to Mexico. At the time, Mexico did not have formal racial restrictions on who could be full citizens like the United States did, and many Mexicans applying for US citizenship were forced to assert their Spanish ancestry even though this would still not guarantee that legislatures would not discriminate against someone's phenotype (Menchaca 1993). After this, Mexican resistance to conquest took the form of border warfare, social banditry, community upheavals, long-term skirmishes, and coordinate rebellions (Perea et al. 2006). From this point forward, Massey et al. (2002) describe five periods of Mexico-US migration.

1. Enganche (1900–1929) characterized by restrictive immigration policies for other countries, namely, the Chinese and Japanese, resulting in a labor shortage for the United States that needed to be filled.
2. Era of Deportations (1929–1941) coinciding with the Great Depression in the United States, and Mexican laborers became scapegoats.
3. Bracero Era (1924–1964) created by Theodore Roosevelt to work during war years. But in 1954 Operation Wetback also resulted in the apprehension of one million Mexican migrants, while visas for braceros doubled.
4. Era of Undocumented Migration (1965–1985) began once the bracero program was ended, but the labor demand still existed.
5. Great Divide (1986–2000) characterized by the passing of Immigration Reform and Control Act (IRCA) of 1986 which included employer sanctions for hiring undocumented workers among other provisions. The creation of the North Atlantic Free Trade Agreement in 1994 also highlights the desire to "export goods and not people."

Central Americans
The Central American Free Trade Agreement, impacts of Hurricane Mitch in 1998, and political uncertainty have encouraged increased migration from Central America, namely, from the countries in the Northern Triangle formed by El Salvador, Guatemala, and Honduras (Menjivar and Abrego 2012; Lesser and Batalova 2017). More recently, unaccompanied children from these areas have arrived in the United States – forcing some changes in family detention centers with the United States. Many of these children can remain in the country for a limited amount of time, but recent incidents also demonstrate that both the 44th and 45th

presidential administrations took a strong stance to quickly deport newcomers to the United States of any age (Johnson 2014). From 1980 to 2015, the Central American population residing in the United States grew from approximately 354,000 to 3,385,000. In 2015, 40% of that population was from El Salvador, 27.4% from Guatemala, and 17.7% from Honduras. Unfortunately, the current presidential administration often conflates migration from these countries with gang violence and activity, some of which originated in the United States. For example, MS-13 or the Mara Salvatrucha originated in Los Angeles during the 1980s by El Salvadorians fleeing the country's civil war. In the 1990s, the United States conducted anti-gang crackdowns and deported members of the gang, and now the gang has more members outside the United States (BBC News 2017; Wolf 2010).

Criminalization Processes

Criminologists define **criminalization** as the process whereby criminal law is selectively applied to social behavior through a threefold process involving (1) the enactment of legislation that outlaws certain types of behavior, (2) the surveillance and policing of that behavior, and (3), if detected, the punishment of that behavior (Beirne and Messerschmidt 2014: 19). Yet, the criminalization of certain groups, namely, ethnic minorities, racial groups, and racialized immigrants, extends beyond this definition, particularly because these groups are perceived, judged, and policed by the overextension of criminal law. In the section that follows, I trace both the criminalization of these groups and the convergence of criminal and civil law procedures and practices. The latter phenomenon is called **crimmigration** or the criminalization of immigration law and procedure (Stumpf 2006). These changes in both criminal and immigration law focus on individual migrants while simultaneously broadening penalties to those facilitating their presence within the country.

Criminalization Pre-civil Rights

Not only were immigrant groups undergoing the process of racialization (previously outlined) vis- à-vis the law subject to criminalization practices through immigration laws, but so too were any individuals who previously committed crimes. The Page Act of 1875 included a prohibition against the entry of convicted felons (Garcia Hernandez 2013). The 1882 Chinese Exclusion Act not only barred Chinese from entering the country but also added criminal penalties for those helping them migrate.

Criminalization Post-civil Rights

During this time period, it was no longer acceptable to base immigration policies solely on overtly racial terms. Cesar Cuauhtemoc Garcia Hernandez (2013: 1485–1487) describes this shift:

> Cultural and legal shifts in race relations spurred by the civil rights movements of the mid-twentieth century constrained reliance on overt racism. In place of openly racist rhetoric and de jure racism, policymakers adopted facially neutral legal regimes in criminal law and procedure and immigration law and procedure that proved anything but racially neutral in practice. Crucially, lawmakers concerned about the civil rights era's elimination of cultural and legal mechanisms used to subordinate entire racial groups turned to the government's criminal law power to stigmatize and punish. With the legitimacy of ostensibly race-neutral criminal law and procedure, lawmakers reproduced the racial hierarchies of decades past...
> Civil rights era legislative successes did not assure the end of deeply ingrained racial biases that dominated the United States' history. Instead, individuals who in the past had openly championed explicitly racialized methods of subjugating people of color set their sights on discrimination packaged in a race-neutral veneer. They found their answer in crime. A "law and order" discourse that had existed in limited fashion prior to the demise of Jim Crow quickly gained ground as the new paradigm of choice for governing social relations.

During this time, the Hart Cellar Act or the Immigration Act of 1965 repealed national origins quotas, which would impost uniform immigration rules. Particularly for those migrants from Mexico – coming to the United States for economic purposes – these changes shifted a long-standing relationship with the United States, whereby Mexicans "became illegal." As Massey et al. (2002) describe, prior to the 1965 Act, the relationship between the United States and Mexico was characterized by the Bracero Era, spanning from 1924 to 1964. This program created in 1924 continued until the Immigration Act followed the liberalization of the Civil Rights Act that created formal equality. Unfortunately, this did not account for the long-standing relationship between the two countries nor the dependence on Mexican labor. Like most immigration policies, considerations for other country's economic situation were not taken into account. On the other hand, migrants from Asian countries were able to immediately benefit from lifted quota restrictions. This shift also framed migration as a moral issue:

> By framing its formal equality regarding the number of people from a given country who could lawfully immigrate each year as a gesture of fairness, immigration law pinned the onus of unauthorized immigration on the migrants themselves.

In some ways, crime became a proxy for race in the post-civil rights period foreshadowing the disproportionate impacts of the convergence between criminal sanctions and migration flows.

Crimmigration

The term **crimmigration** or the criminalization of immigration law and procedure emerged in the past three decades and is distinct from both criminal and immigration law. Criminal law meant to punish social harms to individuals, whereas immigration law focuses on who may or may not cross our borders. Both areas of law "regulate the relationship between the state and the individual" and are "systems of inclusion and exclusion" (Stumpf 2006). Juliet Stumpf further describes this merger has taken place in three arenas:

1. The substance of immigration law and criminal law increasingly overlaps.
2. Immigration enforcement has come to resemble criminal law enforcement.
3. The procedural aspects of prosecuting immigration violations have taken on many of the earmarks of criminal procedure (381).

First, a series of acts showcase Stumpf's first point. The 1986 Immigration Reform and Control Act created a variety of penalties for those hiring unauthorized workers, for bringing someone into the country, and for possession or use of false documents (Garcia Hernandez 2013). In addition, the Immigration Marriage Fraud Amendments Act created a penalty for knowingly committing marriage fraud by marrying an unauthorized immigrant in order to avoid immigration laws. In 1988, the Congress raised the maximum term of imprisonment to 15 years for those immigrant previously convicted of an aggravated felony.

Second, although most criminal law enforcement agents carry firearms, not until 1990 did representatives from the precursor to ICE, Immigration and Naturalization Services (INS) begin to do so. In 1952, Border Patrol agents were able to make immigration arrests. In the mid-1980s, INS officers also began to participate in drug-related enforcement activities.

Crimmigration After 9/11

In a recent Breitbart interview with Kris Kobach, Kobach reiterates his stance which would guide him to create the template for a variety of statewide anti-immigrant legislation across the country.

> All Americans should be aware of that. We had the opportunity to stop the 9/11 hijackers, but because state and local police didn't have the information they needed, it didn't happen. (Kobach 2005; Binder 2018)

The turn toward interior enforcement is described further on this chapter, but other notable changes are described by Juliet Stumpf (2006: 286):

> As examples, soon after September 11, 2001 the Department of Justice initiated the National Security Entry-Exit Registration System ("NSEERS") that required noncitizen men from certain Muslim and Arab countries to register with the INS. The DHS Absconder Apprehension Initiative targeted for detention and deportation noncitizen men of Muslim faith and Arab ethnicity who had criminal convictions or immigration violations, regardless of whether the crimes or violations related to terrorism. The USA PATRIOT Act of 2001 has resulted in detentions of noncitizens without charge for an undefined "reasonable period of time" under extraordinary circumstances. All of these examples permit the government to employ immigration rules to detain or deport noncitizens suspected of terrorist tendencies without resort to the criminal justice system.

Other scholars particularly note the both the racialized and gendered aspects of those impacted by immigration enforcement. Tanya Golash-Boza and Pierrette Hondagneu-Sotelo (2013) describe this new course after 9/11 as a gendered and racial removal project. They find most deportees are working-class Latino men. They further comment (2013: 273):

> that the institutionalized criminalization and surveillance of men of color in urban streets-heightened in the post-9/11 climate of Islamaphobia and male joblessness exacerbated by global financial crisis and economic restructuring–have created the context for this shift.

After 9/11, the majority of individuals removed are of Mexican origin. In FY2016 and FY2017, this was still the case where 146,821 Mexican nationals were removed and 128,765 were removed, respectively (ICE FY2017 Report). Furthermore, 61% of the total people removed were Mexican nationals in FY2016 and 57% of the total removed in FY2017. The remaining top five countries of removals by country of citizenship were Guatemala, Honduras, El Salvador, and Haiti. Although the number of removals declined for most of those countries, those removed from Haiti increased from 310 in FY2016 to 5578 in FY2017 (ICE FY2017 Report). Although these numbers come directly from ICE Enforcement and Removal Operations, the Transactional Records Access Clearinghouse (TRAC) at Syracuse University also requests case-by-case deportation records from ICE but frequently runs into challenges obtaining sufficient amounts of data (TRAC 2014). In 2012 and 2013, they found that Mexican nationals were the largest group of those deported, that the typical median age for these individuals was 30, and that 9/10 were identified as male.

Changes Under the 45th Presidential Administration

It is important to note that many of the efforts to criminalize migration behaviors stem from **moral panics** whereby the mass media channels viewer attention toward particular events in an episodic fashion (Stanley Cohen 2002). One example is the story of Mollie Tibbetts, who was killed by a native of Mexico (Peters 2018). This story has now become a rallying cry for the conservative media and Republicans to continue pushing forward anti-immigrant legislation and enforcement practices both within the country and in immigration policies more generally. The current administration has ceased opportunities like this and capitalized on issues of immigration to push forward a series of changes relatively unique in the history of the criminalization of immigration policies in the United States. Some of these are described below.

Executive Orders: Border and Internal Enforcement

On January 25, 2017, the 45th President of the United States issued two Executive Orders to expand border and interior immigration enforcement. The Border Security and Immigration Enforcement Improvements Executive Order (Executive Order 2017b) included:

- Authorization to construct a more fortified wall at the southern border with Mexico and expedited decisions for those crossing the border.
- Resources to construct and operate more detention facilities along the southern border.
- A change from the catch and release policy previously implemented and forcing individuals to be detained.
- The hiring of 5000 additional Border Patrol agents.
- More enforcement of paroles and asylum seeker processes.
- And, encroaching on tribal sovereignty to allow for officials to enter federal lands to enforce these laws (Levin 2017).

That same day, the Enhancing Public Safety in the Interior of the United States Executive Order was also signed, which focuses more on internal enforcement (Executive Order 2017a). This order included the following:

- Targeting of **sanctuary cities** and localities by threatening to withhold federal funding from these places. Following this, many states also began to consider copycat legislation that would also limit state funding like North Carolina House Bills 100 and 318.
- Broadening the scope of who is deportable. On November 20, 2014, then Department of Homeland Security Secretary Jeh Johnson announced a new set of priorities for deportation known as the **Priority Enforcement Program (PEP)**. Under this Executive Order, PEP was terminated and **Secure Communities (S-Comm)** was reinstated and allows immigration officers to prioritize for removal those that "In the judgment of an immigration officer, otherwise pose a risk to public safety or national security."
- Proposes the payment of fines for those living in the country without legal status.
- Hiring of 10,000 new immigration officers and increased resources to see the prosecution of criminal immigration crimes.
- Proposed expansion of 287(g) programs and most striking was the recent effort in 2017 where 18 law enforcement agencies adopted these programs along the border and proudly announced this at a joint press conference (ICE News Release 2017).
- Public lists of criminal actions committed by those without legal status.
- Restricting Privacy Act to no longer apply to those who are not lawful citizens or permanent residents. Collection of the immigration status of those currently in a variety of federal, state, and local prisons and/or detention centers.

Executive Order: Muslim Ban

Two days later, on January 27, 2017, the "Muslim Ban" or the Executive Order 13769: Protecting the Nation from Foreign Terrorist Entry into the United States was signed. This ban restricted immigrants and those with immigrant visas from majority-Muslim countries (initially Iraq, Iran, Libya, Somalia, Sudan, Syria, and Yemen) from entering the United States for 90 days, builiding upon a racialized history of this group (Selod and Embrick 2013). It also barred refugees for 120 days and an indefinite ban on those from Syria. Protests erupted across the country in response, and many states began to file lawsuits to block the executive order. The order was revised in March and a partial travel ban would go into effect in June (McGraw 2017). The full ban has been in effect from January 2018 to the present, and North Korea and Venezuela were added (Parlapiano 2018).

Ending Temporary Protected Status (TPS)

Temporary protected status is one type of humanitarian program that attempts to protect migrants seeking refuge from a variety of conditions in their homeland. According to the US Citizenship and Immigration Services (USCIS) website, the Secretary of Homeland Security may designate a country for TPS due to the following conditions in a country:

- Ongoing armed conflict (such as civil war)
- An environmental disaster (such as earthquake or hurricane) or an epidemic
- Other extraordinary and temporary conditions

Although the USCIS website currently lists the following countries designated for TPS(USCIS 2018) – El Salvador, Haiti, Honduras, Nepal, Nicaragua, Somalia, Sudan, South Sudan, Syria, and Yemen – in 2017 and 2018, announcements to strip individuals from the following countries were announced, Haiti (set to terminate on July 22, 2019), El Salvador (set to terminate on September 9, 2019), Nepal (June 24, 2019), Honduras (set to terminate on January 5, 2020), and Nicaragua (set to terminate on January 5, 2019). These would force individuals, many of whom have lived in the country for more than 20 years, to return to countries where the conditions listed above have not changed or become part of the roughly 12 million people living in the United States without legal authorization.

Department of Justice Guidelines and Public Shame Lists

In 2017, Attorney General Jeff Sessions announced that the Department of Justice (DOJ) would award extra points to those agencies willing to comply with ICE. Moreover, these grants require applicants to certify that (1) if the applicant operates a detention facility, the applicant must provide DHS access to their detention facility and (2) the applicant must provide advance notice as early as practicable (at least 48 hours, where possible) to DHS of an unauthorized immigrant's release date and time (DOJ Press Release 2017). Similar language was included in the 2018–2019 grants. In 2017, DHS also began to publish list of jurisdictions that rejected immigrant detainer requests as another incentive for localities to comply and communicate with ICE. This practice eventually failed as jurisdictions disputed finding themselves on the list, showcasing the disorganization of the agency (Gonzales 2017).

Border and Internal Enforcement

Border Enforcement

In 1924 the Border Patrol was created by the Labor Appropriation Act and in 1925; it was expanded to patrol the seacoast (Border Patrol History 2018). It was mainly constructed in response to the 18th Amendment, which prohibits "the importation, transport, manufacture, or sale of alcoholic beverages" and the Immigration Acts of 1921 and 1924 (Border Patrol History 2018). The Border Patrol initially functioned under two directors – one for the Mexican border and one for the Canadian border. At that time, the majority of the Border Patrol was placed at the northern border. In 1952, the Border Patrol was able to begin arresting individuals entering into the country illegally. In 1986 the Immigration Reform and Control Act (IRCA) increased allocations for border security. In 1990, more Border Patrol officers were hired through the Immigration and Nation Act and in 1996 IRAIRA provided even more funding for military equipment and additional officers (Massey et al. 2016).

In 2003, the Department of Homeland Security was established, which now houses a variety of agencies including the US Customs and Border Protection and US Immigration and Customs Enforcement. In 2004, the National Intelligence Reform and Terrorism Protection Act included funding for equipment, aircraft, agents, immigration investigators, and detention centers (Massey et al. 2016: 1569). The 2006 Secure Fence Act allowed the agency to fortify fences, satellites, and unmanned drones among other things.

Internal Enforcement

Large-scale studies focus on the implementation of immigration policies across the country and at the state level instead of focusing on the site specificity or the "local migration state" (Coleman 2012). This omission neglects to provide a thorough understanding of the devolution of immigration federalism which allows the criminalization of immigrants to occur within the interior of the United States, where local law enforcement is taking on more immigration policing responsibilities. Furthermore, the implementation of state and national policies are not implemented similarly across localities, particularly when it comes to immigration enforcement practices.

Immigration enforcement programs, like 287(g) and Secure Communities introduced in the late 1990s and early 2000s, were amended to the 1996 Illegal Immigration Reform and Immigrant Responsibility Act. Initially, few localities showed interest in 287(g) programs until after 9/11. Prior to Obama's Executive Order in November of 2015 which formally did away with Secure Communities and replaced with the Priority Enforcement Program (PEP) but did not do away with the technology and biometric data sharing, every local law enforcement agency in the country participated in the program, giving local law enforcement officers the ability to run arrestee prints through an FBI criminal database and the IDENT database. These fingerprints are then routed to ICE officials, who can determine whether to initiate removal proceedings. 287(g) programs, on the other hand, authorize local law officers to detect, detain, and deport unauthorized immigrants through an agreement with ICE (Nguyen and Gill 2010). These fingerprints were then routed to ICE officials, who could determine whether to initiate removal proceedings, a technological process which Juan Pedroza (2013) refers to as "removal roulette." Coleman and Kocher (2011) also highlight de facto immigration enforcement that may result from the collaboration between Secure Communities and a 287(g) partnership, and Menjivar (2014) shows how enforcement at various levels of government work together to compound the effects of federal policies. Menjivar (2014, p. 1806) describes this multilayered enforcement regime as "the federal, state, and local level laws and ordinances and the various enforcement strategies, acting all at once and often in highly articulated fashion, exacerbating the effects of each layer on the everyday lives of immigrants." Under the current presidential administration, Secure Communities has been reinstated.

Surveillance Techniques

Database Expansion

Fueled by efforts to create systems within the interior of the country after 9/11, biometric screening became central in migration control within the United States (Activated Jurisdictions 2013).

> As part of the Secure Communities strategy, ICE is levering a federal biometric information sharing capability to quickly and accurately identify aliens in law enforcement custody.

This technology activation began in 2008, and by 2013, 100% of 3181 jurisdictions were activated. Early adopters of this tool – where at least one county began adopting in 2008 – were Arizona, Maine, Massachusetts, North Carolina, Pennsylvania, and Texas.

Facebook Monitoring

In 2017, ICE officials began searching for data/text mining tools to comb Facebook, Twitter, and the broader Internet for their "Extreme Vetting Initiative" (Harwell and Miroff 2018). Those opposing such a move considered this to be a "digital Muslim ban." Earlier this year, ICE backtracked taking this route and opted for enhancements in staff training for about 180 people to monitor social media posts among other things, although ICE's Counterterrorism and Criminal Exploitation Unit spokeswoman Carissa Cutrell stated:

> an automated system would provide a more effective way to continuously monitor the 10,000 people determined to be the greatest potential risk to national security and public safety...that system could provide nonstop tracking of social-media behavior for "derogatory" information that could weigh against their applications, including radical or extremist views.

Ankle Bracelets and Electronic Monitoring

Prior to the 45th presidential administration, ICE implemented the Intensive Supervision Alternative Program (ISAP), a GPS ankle monitoring program. This program is run by a subsidiary of the GEO Group and allows case workers and immigration officers to track immigrants with GPS ankle monitors linked to a cell phone application (Fernandez Campbell 2018). This program led to a 99.6% compliance rate for court appearances, saw a lower rate for deportation orders, and is considered less costly than indefinite detention – the current administration's most recent focus.

Mexico's Internal Deterrence Policies

Increasingly migrants from Central American countries are crossing through Mexico to welcoming states within the country or to continue on to the United States. As an extension of United States border enforcement and migrant control, Mexico does the following to deter migrants throughout the country:

- Limited funding for migrant shelters throughout the country.
- Participates in the Southern Border Plan – funded by the United States. "Rather than amazing troops on its border with Guatemala, Mexico stations migration agents, local and federal police, soldiers and marines to create a kind of containment zone in Chiapas state. With roving checkpoints and raids, Mexican migration agents have formed a formidable deportation force" (Fredrick 2018).
- Seizing "La Bestia" from private control in order to, "patrol the train lines with extra guards, cameras, motion detectors, geolocation devices, and even drones" (Campoy 2016).
- Participates in the Merida security assistance program launched by President George W. Bush in 2008 where information gathered from individuals in Mexican custody is forwarded to DHS and other US law enforcement databases (Partlow and Miroff 2018).

Direct Threats and Resistance (A Case Study)

Sheriff elections in 2018 are forcing ICE to also make distinctions among its programs, particularly in localities where candidates include noncompliance with ICE as part of their platform to counter the criminalization of immigrants. Unfortunately, ICE has also taken this opportunity to further threaten and demonize the Latino community. This is characteristic of four recent responses by ICE officials – mainly from the Southeast Communications Director, Bryan Cox – justifying an increase in local ICE raids if these localities ended local partnerships and communication with ICE. These threats throughout the state began in March of 2018 in Western, NC, which experienced increased ICE arrests prior to Henderson County's annual 287(g) Steering Committee meeting. Community members with a local organization – Companeros Inmigrantes de las Montanas en Accion (CIMA) – followed ICE around Western, NC, for 3 days during these arrests and then turned their attention to encouraging community members to show up to the annual steering committee meeting in an effort to question ICE about the recent raids. During that steering committee meeting – ICE officials made it clear that ending the 287(g) program in that county would increase the likelihood that more arrests where ICE officials were out in the community would occur. Moreover, they emphasized the possibility of "collateral" arrests – whereby community members could be arrested even if they were not on a specific list but were encountered by ICE officials out in the field (DeGrave 2018; Feldblum 2018).

During this time, the 287(g) program and detainer usage became front and center in the Mecklenburg County Sheriff's race. Two of the three Democratic candidates agreed to end the 287(g) program, while the third, the incumbent maintained his desire to keep the program. Sheriff Carmichael echoed the warnings made by ICE officials in the 287(g) Steering Committee in Henderson County. A small community group – Comunidad Colectiva – put pressure on all these candidates to discuss the program during a variety of public events and led the local campaign against the 287(g) program that deported 15,000 immigrants over a 10-year period. Immediately after Carmichael lost (Terry 2018) to Gary McFadden, ICE put out a statement again warning how the end of the program would impact ICE operations locally.

Two hours away, although with no 287(g) program, detainer usage became an important issue in the Durham County Sheriff's race. After years of questioning the incumbent, Mike Andrews, about his collaboration with ICE, a challenger promised a different way forward – both more transparent and willing to end collaboration with ICE. Clarence Birkhead overwhelmingly won the election – provoking a response from ICE officials (Blythe 2018).

Prior to these 2018 Sheriff races, only three Sheriffs claimed to not honor detainer requests from ICE, yet ICE did not make direct statements against this new policy. That is until July 23, 2018 when ICE officials made comments to *The Herald Sun* about the Orange County Sheriff's Office's decision to release an undocumented man without first notifying ICE (Lamb 2018). Orange County ended that policy in 2017. In this instance, ICE focused on the individual's previous offense, "What is not in dispute is the sheriff's major failed to contact ICE to let us know he had an egregious criminal offender he was about to return to community." This statement further iterates how racialized immigrants in particular are viewed by ICE – the individuals who upload immigration policies throughout the United States.

Conclusion

The criminalization of immigration policies clearly shifts under each presidential administration in response to economic, social, political, and relational race dynamics. Yet, it is still unclear who is ultimately responsible in what some call a **deportation continuum** (Kalir and Wissink 2016), **deportation regime** (Golash-Boza and Hondagneu-Sotelo 2013), or the **immigration industrial complex**

(Trujillo-Pagan 2013). The first term alludes the variety of actors and ways that civil society and NGOs participate in the deportation process. This chapter mainly focuses on those entities who enforce immigration and criminal justice policies, but a more thorough study would consider the ways in which other actors within society participate in the criminalization of racialized immigrants. Furthermore this criminalization does not simply take place in the legal sense, but is expanded to a sense of perceived illegality (Garcia 2017), which equates to perceived criminality or criminalization.

Cross-References

▶ Policing Ethnic Minorities: Disentangling a Landscape of Conceptual and Practice Tensions

References

Banton M (1977) The idea of race. Tavistock, London

BBC News (2017) MS-13 gang: the story behind one of the world's most brutal street gangs. https://www.bbc.com/news/world-us-canada-39645640. Accessed 15 Sept 2018

Beirne P, Messerschmidt JW (2014) Criminology: a sociological approach. Oxford University Press, New York

Binder J (2018) Exclusive-Kris Kobach: three 9/11 planes could have been stopped by immigration enforcement. https://www.breitbart.com/big-government/2018/09/11/exclusive-kris-kobach-three-9-11-planes-could-have-been-stopped-by-immigration-enforcement/. Accessed 15 Sept 2018

Blythe A (2018) ICE picks up Durham man days before hearing on legality of 48-hour hold. https://www.newsobserver.com/news/local/article211996234.html. Accessed 15 Sept 2018

Bonilla-Silva E (1997) Rethinking racism: toward a structural interpretation. Am Sociol Rev 62(3):465

Campoy A (2016) Mexico has its own version of Donald Trump's border wall and it's just as controversial. https://qz.com/778314/mexico-wants-to-stop-central-american-immigrants-from-boarding-la-bestia-train/. Accessed 15 Sept 2018

Cohen S (2002) Folk devils and moral panics : the creation of the Mods and Rockers. London ; New York: Routledge, 2002

Coleman M, Kocher A (2011) Deportation and civic stratification in the U.S., post-9/11. Geogr J 177:228–237

Coleman M (2012) The "Local" Migration State: The Site-Specific Devolution of Immigration Enforcement in the U.S. South. Law & Policy, 34(2):159–190. https://doi.org/10.1111/j.1467-9930.2011.00358.x

Cunningham G (1965) The Italian: a hindrance to white solidarity in Louisiana, 1890–1898. J Negro Hist 50(34):22–26

DeGrave S (2018) ICE challenged at public meeting over 287(g), no supporters speak out among crowd of 40. https://www.citizen-times.com/story/news/local/2018/04/25/ice-challenged-public-meeting-over-287-g-no-supporters-speak-out-among-crowd-40/545741002/. Accessed 15 Sept 2018

Elmer Sandmeyre C (1991) The anti-Chinese movement in California. University of Illinois Press, Urbana

Feldblum S (2018) ICE raids shine spotlight on Henderson County's 287(g) program. https://mountainx.com/news/ice-raids-shine-spotlight-on-henderson-countys-287g-program/. Accessed 15 Sept 2018

Fernandez Campbell A (2018) Trump doesn't need to put families in detention centers to enforce his immigration policy. There are better options. https://www.vox.com/2018/6/22/17483230/family-separation-immigration-alternatives-immigrant-detention-centers. Accessed 15 Sept 2018

Fredrick J (2018) Mexico deploys a formidable deportation force near its own Southern border. https://www.npr.org/sections/parallels/2018/05/07/607700928/mexico-deploys-a-formidable-deportation-force-near-its-own-southern-border. Accessed 15 Sept 2018

García SJ (2017) Racializing 'illegality': an intersectional approach to understanding how Mexican-origin women navigate an anti-immigrant climate. Sociol Race Ethn 3(4):474–490

Garcia Hernandez CC (2013) Creating crimmigration. Bringham Young Univ Law Rev 6:1457–1515

Golash-Boza T, Hondagneu-Sotelo P (2013) Latino immigrant men and the deportation crisis: a gendered racial removal program. Lat Stud 11(2013):271–292

Gonzales R (2017) DHS publishes list of jurisdictions that rejected immigrant detainer requests. https://www.npr.org/sections/thetwo-way/2017/03/20/520851267/dhs-publishes-list-of-jurisdictions-that-rejected-immigrant-detainer-requests. Accessed 15 Sept 2018

Graham Synott M (1986) Anti-semitism and American universities: did quotas follow Jews? In: Gerber D (ed) Anti-semitism in American history. Illinois Press, Urbana, pp 233, 238–239, 249–250

Haney-López I (2006) White by law. [electronic eresource]: the legal construction of race. New York University Press, New York [c2006]

Harwell D, Miroff N (2018) ICE just abandoned its dream of 'extreme vetting' software that could predict whether a foreign visitor would become a terrorist. https://www.washingtonpost.com/news/the-switch/wp/2018/05/17/ice-just-abandoned-its-dream-of-extreme-vetting-software-that-could-predict-whether-a-foreign-visitor-would-become-a-terrorist/?utm_term=.1d1d94bc019c. Accessed 15 Sept 2018

ICE (2017) ICE announces 18 new 287(g) agreements in Texas. https://www.ice.gov/news/releases/ice-announces-18-new-287g-agreements-texas. Accessed 15 Sept 2018

ICE (2018) Fiscal year 2017 ICE enforcement and removal operations report. https://www.ice.gov/sites/default/files/documents/Report/2017/iceEndOfYearFY2017.pdf. Accessed 15 Sept 2018

Jacobson MF (1998) Whiteness of a different color: European immigrants and the alchemy of race. Harvard University Press, Cambridge

Kalir B, Wissink L (2016) The deportation continuum: convergences between state-agents and NGO-workers in the Dutch deportation field. Citizsh Stud 20(1):34–49

Kobach KW (2005) The quintessential force multiplier: the inherent authority of local police to make immigration arrests. Albany Law Rev 69(1):179–235

Lamb A (2018) Orange sheriff, ICE square off over release of inmates in US illegally. https://www.wral.com/orange-sheriff-ice-square-off-over-release-of-inmates-in-us-illegally/17724377/. Accessed 15 Sept 2018

Lesser G, Batalova J (2017) Central American immigrants in the United States. Migration Policy Institute https://www.migrationpolicy.org/article/central-american-immigrants-united-states. Accessed 15 Sept 2018

Levin S (2017) Over my dead body': tribe aims to block Trump's border wall on Arizona land. https://www.theguardian.com/us-news/2017/jan/26/donald-trump-border-wall-tohono-oodham-arizona-tribe. Accessed 15 Sept 2018

Massey DS, Malone NJ, Durand J (2002) Beyond smoke and mirrors: Mexican immigration in an era of economic integration. Russell Sage Foundation, New York

Massey DS, Durand J, Pren KA (2016) Why border enforcement backfired. Am J Sociol 121(5):1557–1600

McGraw M (2017) A timeline of Trump's immigration executive order and legal challenges. https://abcnews.go.com/Politics/timeline-president-trumps-immigration-executive-order-legal-challenges/story?id=45332741. Accessed 15 Sept 2018

Menchaca M (1993) Chicano Indianism: a historical account of racial repression in the United States. Am Ethnol 20:583–584

Menjivar C (2014) The "Poli-Migra": multilayered legislation, enforcement practices, and what we can learn about and from today's approaches. Am Behav Sci 58(13):1805–1819

Menjivar C, Abrego LJ (2012) Legal violence: immigration law and the lives of Central American immigrants. Am J Sociol 117(5):1380–1421

Miles R (1993) Racisms after 'race relations. Routledge, London

Nguyen M, Gill H (2010) The 287 (g) program: the cost and consequences of local immigration enforcement in North Carolina communities. The Latino Migration Project. http://cgi.unc.edu/uploads/media_items/287g-report-final.original.pdf. Accessed 15 Sept 2018

Omi M, Winant H (1986) Racial formation in the United States: from the 1960s to the 1980s. Routledge, New York City

Painter NI (2010) The history of white people. W.W. Norton, London

Parlapiano A (2018) The travel ban has been upheld. Here are some of its effects so far. https://www.nytimes.com/interactive/2018/06/27/us/politics/trump-travel-ban-effects.html. Accessed 15 Sept 2018

Partlow J, Miroff N (2018) U.S. gathers data on migrants deep in Mexico, a sensitive program Trump's rhetoric could put at risk. The Washington Post. https://www.washingtonpost.com/world/national-security/us-gathers-data-on-migrants-deep-in-mexico-a-sensitive-program-trumps-rhetoric-could-put-at-risk/2018/04/06/31a8605a-38f3-11e8-b57c-9445cc4dfa5e_story.html?utm_term=.483c864d4f9d. Accessed 15 Sept 2018

Pedroza J (2013) Removal roulette: secure communities and immigration enforcement in the United States (2008–2012). In: Brothrton D, Stageman D, Leyro S (eds) Outside justice: immigration and the criminalizing impact of changing policy and practice. Springer, New York, pp 45–65

Perea J, Delgado R, Harris A, Stefancic J, Wildman S (2006) Race and races: cases and resources for a diverse America. West, St. Paul

Peters J (2018) How politics took over the killing of Mollie Tibbetts. https://www.nytimes.com/2018/08/23/us/politics/mollie-tibbetts-republicans-immigration-trump.html. Accessed 15 Sept 2018

Roediger D (2007) The wages of whiteness: race and the making of the American working class. Verso, London

Sacks KB (1994) How did Jews become white folks? In: Gregory S, Sanjek R (ed) Race. Rutgers University Press, New Brunswick, p 78–99

Sáenz R, Douglas KM (2015) A call for the racialization of immigration studies: on the transition of ethnic immigrants to racialized immigrants. Sociol Race Ethn 1(1):168–180

Selod S, Embrick DG (2013) Racialization and muslims: situating the muslim experience in race scholarship. Sociol Compass 7(8):644–655

Steinberg S (1989) The ethnic myth: race, ethnicity, and class in America. Beacon, Boston

Stumpf J (2006) The crimmigration crisis: immigrants, crime, and sovereign power. Am Univ Law Rev 56(2):367–420

Terry T (2018). https://www.wsoctv.com/746653691?ecmp=wsoctv_social_facebook_2014_sfp. Accessed 15 Sept 2018

TRAC (2014) ICE deportations: gender, age, and country of citizenship. http://trac.syr.edu/immigration/reports/350/#f1. Accessed 15 Sept 2018

Trujillo-Pagan N (2013) Emphasizing the 'complex' in the 'immigration industrial complex. Crit Sociol 40(1):29–46

U.S. Customs and Border Protection (2018) Border patrol history. https://www.cbp.gov/border-security/along-us-borders/history. Accessed 15 Sept 2018

USCIS (2018) Temporary protected status. https://www.uscis.gov/humanitarian/temporary-protected-status. Accessed 15 Sept 2018

Whitehouse (2017a) Executive order: enhancing public safety in the interior of the United States. https://www.whitehouse.gov/presidential-actions/executive-order-enhancing-public-safety-interior-united-states/. Accessed 15 Sept 2018

Whitehouse (2017b) Executive order: border security and immigration enforcement improvements. https://www.whitehouse.gov/presidential-actions/executive-order-border-security-immigration-enforcement-improvements/. Accessed 15 Sept 2018

Wolf S (2010) Maras transnacionales: origins and transformations of Central American street gangs. Lat Am Res Rev 45(1):256

Diaspora and Ethnic Contestation in Guyana

69

Ralph Premdas and Bishnu Ragoonath

Contents

Introduction	1352
The Making of a Multiethnic State	1352
Decolonization and Ethnic Mass Politics	1354
Seizure of Power and Ethnic Domination by the PNC	1356
Conclusion	1359
The Future Trajectory? Some Concluding Remarks	1360
References	1362

Abstract

Guyana, an ethnically bipolar state has suffered immense developmental damage as a consequence of competitive partisan elections based on communal mobilization. After colonial control was relinquished, the country fell into two and half decades of corrupt authoritarian ethnocratic rule. In 1992, free and fair elections were restored, but in succeeding general elections, the pattern of ethnic preference persisted. The discovery of immense petroleum resources in 2016 is about to confer unprecedented wealth on this small country of about 800,000 people. The problem now consists in the challenge to overcome the bipolar ethnic antagonism between Indians and Africans even as the new wealth itself threatens to unleash its own form of curse.

The original version of this chapter was revised: the co-author name has been corrected now. The correction to this chapter is available at https://doi.org/10.1007/978-981-13-2898-5_171

R. Premdas (✉)
University of the West Indies, St. Augustine, Trinidad and Tobago
e-mail: ralphpremdas@hotmail.com

B. Ragoonath
Department of Political Science, University of the West Indies Trinidad, St. Augustine, Trinidad and Tobago
e-mail: bishnu.ragoonath@sta.uwi.edu

© The Author(s), under exclusive license to Springer Nature Singapore Pte Ltd. 2019
S. Ratuva (ed.), *The Palgrave Handbook of Ethnicity*,
https://doi.org/10.1007/978-981-13-2898-5_45

Keywords

Ethnic bipolarity · Communal elections · Authoritarian rule · Walter Rodney · Cheddi Jagan · Forbes Burnham · Cooperative republic · ExxonMobil · Resource curse

Introduction

Situated on the northeast shoulder of South America, Guyana with only about 746,955 people is the only English-speaking state in South America. A former British colony independent since May 1966, Guyana's peoples are a multiethnic polyglot (Table 1) derived mainly from Africa and Asia; they are embroiled in persistent ethnic inter-communal strife that has left the country deeply divided and chronically unstable resulting in as many Guyanese living within the country as outside (Despres 1967; Premdas 1995; Spinner 1984; Williams 1991; Morrison 1998). From its colonial history, a society of ethno-cultural compartments has emerged with various forms of inter-communal antagonisms of which the African-Indian dichotomy dominates all dimensions of daily life. Its multiethnicity has been created mainly by the importation of immigrants from other countries to meet the colonial demands for labor on plantations (Smith 1962).

The majority of the population are diaspora, as shown in the 2012 census figures below.

The Making of a Multiethnic State

In the seventeenth century, the Dutch were the first European settlers; they established plantation production of coffee, cotton, and sugar which required massive amounts of cheap labor. After the Amerindians and "Poor Whites" were experimented with, massive numbers of African slaves were imported. The Dutch were evicted by the British in 1803, and in 1807, the British slave trade with Africa was halted, and in 1833 slavery was abolished. The anticipated dearth of labor after the freeing of the slaves prompted the planters to recruit, between 1835 and 1840, small batches of German, Portuguese, Irish, English, Indian, and Maltese laborers. In

Table 1 Ethnic distribution of the Guyanese population

Ethnic group	Percent and total
Indians	39.8 (297,493)
Africans	29.2 (218,483)
Mixed Races	19.9 (148,532)
Portuguese and Europeans	0.26 (1910)
Chinese	0.8 (1377)
Amerindians	10.5 (78,492)

Source: Ministry of Information: 2012 Census

the end, Asian Indians proved most adaptable, economical, and available. They came, under 5-year contract indentures (Nath 1950). The first batch of Indians (396) arrived in the colony during May, 1838. With the exception of a brief interruption in the early 1840s, Indian immigration continued until the indentureship system was abolished in 1917 (Nath 1950). Between 1838 and 1917, approximately 238,960 Indian laborers arrived in Guyana. An additional 707 Indians were imported as free settlers between 1917 and 1926. At the expiration of their indentures, nearly two-thirds opted to remain as permanent residents.

After the abolition of slavery, few Africans returned to the sugar plantations, for their place was taken gradually by the arrival of indentured laborers. Employment in urban centers attracted many Africans; migration to the cities proceeded apace so that by 1891, Africans constituted about 47.19% of the colony's urban population. Between 1900 and 1965, this figure stabilized at roughly 50%. Africans who have remained in villages constitute about 20% of the total village population; most live predominantly in African villages. Paralleling their concentration in urban centers, Africans increasingly provided the staff for government service so that by 1950, Africans dominated every department of the civil service. In 1960, some 73.5% of the security forces, 53.05% of the civil service, 62.29% of the government agencies, and 58.87% of teachers in primary education were Africans.

Many Indians acquired farmland contiguous to the estates in exchange for giving up their contractual right to return to India. Gradually, however, many Indians moved away from the sugar estates, turning completely to peasant farming. A series of Indian villages sprang up, mainly within a radius of 10 to 15 miles of plantation lands. In the 1960s, 25.5% of the Indian population was on the sugar plantations, 13.4% in urban centers, with the remaining 61.1% found in villages. Guyana's Indians are therefore predominantly rural dwellers, living mainly in Indian villages and on land adjacent to the sugar plantations. Indians, known for their thrift, invested their savings in small businesses and in the education of their children. Increasingly after the World War I, they began to compete for places in the civil service and the teaching profession, but prior to World War II, Indian participation in the governmental bureaucracies was negligible. According to the 1931 census, Indians constituted 8.08% of all persons in the public service, and nearly half of them were in the lower grades such as messengers. Out of 1,397 teachers, only 100 were Indians. By 1964, when Indians constituted slightly over half the country's population, their social, political, and economic condition had improved so dramatically that they constituted 33.16% of the civil service, 27.17% of government agencies and undertakings, and 41.49% of teachers in primary education. Indians not only regard themselves as a separate community in Guyana but are perceived by other Guyanese as a distinct entity.

Portuguese also were imported as indentured laborers to serve on plantations. Between 1834 and 1890, the period of Portuguese immigration, over 32,000 Portuguese from Madeira arrived in Guyana. Many Portuguese returned home with savings after serving their indentures, but most stayed in the colony. Those who remained immediately abandoned the estates and entered the retail trades. Chinese were the last of the indentured laborers brought to Guyana (Fried 1956). The first

Chinese immigrants landed in 1853; by 1880, a total of only 13,533 had arrived. The Amerindians, who also preceded the arrival of Africans, are the descendants of the original people of Guyana (Saunders 1987). When the first colonist arrived, there were 19 tribes with about 700,000 Amerindians. This number had diminished significantly so that by 1969, the Amerindian Lands Commission estimated the number of Amerindians as 32,203 living in 138 communities.

Thus then would a multiethnic plural society be formed constituted of East Indians, Africans, Amerindians, "Coloreds" (Mixed Races), Portuguese, Europeans, and Chinese. Slavery and indenture were the twin bases on which successful colonization occurred. A work force of culturally divergent immigrants was recruited to labor on plantations in the New World. The different patterns of residence, occupation, and political orientations by the imported groups reinforced the original differences of the settlers laying from the inception of colonization the foundations of Guyana's multiethnic politics. By the beginning of the twentieth century, certain features were clearly embedded in the social system. A communally oriented, multiethnic society was being fashioned and institutionalized. Several layers of cleavage appeared and reinforced each other. Hence, separating East Indians and Africans were religion, race, culture, residence, and occupation. Multiple coinciding divergences deepened the divisions without the benefit of a sufficiently strong set of countervailing integrative forces. To be sure, most immigrants participated in varying degrees in a commonly shared school system, national laws, color-class stratification system, and experiences in suffering. At an elementary level, there was even a measure of shared cross-communal class unity at places where Indians and Africans worked such as certain factories or labor gangs. But these were few and far between.

Decolonization and Ethnic Mass Politics

The twentieth century would witness the unleashing of new forces which would eliminate the seemingly permanently set colonial structures of dominance in Guyana. Against the trajectory of a divided society consigned to perpetual internal strife dominated by a manipulative colonizer, a new tidal force of unity was unleashed in an independence movement. A common enemy in colonialism impelled the emergence of cross-communal leadership which mobilized non-white workers and others to challenge the plantocracy, the color-class value system, the unjust distribution of jobs and privileges, and all the other iniquitous aspects of the multiethnic immigrant society. A multiethnic independence movement called the People's Progressive Party (PPP) was formed under the leadership of two charismatic sectional leaders, one an African (Forbes Burnham) and the other, an Indian (Cheddi Jagan). They successfully won the first elections but almost immediately after victory engaged in a rivalry over sole leadership of the PPP. In the end, this led to a fatal split in the independence movement along ethnic lines. The two leaders parted company and formed their own party, and thereafter Guyana was transposed into a territory riven by deep and destructive ethnic and racial politics (Premdas 1996). A new type of party emerged constructed on the discrete ethnic fragments into which the old unified party had broken. Following the historic split of the national independence party, the PPP, two new factional parties emerged around the leadership of Dr. Jagan and Mr. Burnham. After the 1955 split, a general scramble commenced between the Jaganite and Burnhamite factions to ensure that Indians and Africans respectively stayed with their ethnic leaders. Sectional identification with the two major parties emerged as a fundamental fact of Guyanese politics. *Apanjaat*, the local colloquial term for "vote for your own kind," was the dominant factor which governed the political choices of nearly all Guyanese. Everyone expected an Indian to support and vote for the PPP and an African for the PNC.

The spiral of intensifying ethnic conflict slowly but inexorably exacerbated by the way the political parties organized the lives of their constituents, the manner in which election campaigns were waged, and the method by which voluntary associations were enlisted in the struggle for communal ascendancy, led almost inevitably to cataclysmic inter-ethnic confrontation and civil war. Between 1961 and 1965, the screws of communal conflict were slowly tightened so that few persons could escape being a coopted participant in a system of mutual communal hate. Inter-ethnic relations especially between Africans and Indians were increasingly marked by covert contempt and deceptive distrust. The elements of an impending explosion were registered first in the fear of ethnic domination of Indians by Africans and of Africans by Indians. A new drama was unfolding in which the main motif was a struggle for ethnic ascendancy compounded by a politically instigated terror of internal communal colonization. Introduced mass politics was betrayed by sectional leaders jockeying for power. A moment of opportunity for reconciliation and reconstruction was squandered, and the innocence of legitimate inter-ethnic suspicion was nurtured into a monster obsessed with the fear of communal dominance. One cleavage after another that separated the ethnic segments – race, traditional values, religion, residence, and occupation – was reinforced by a mode of modern mass ethno-nationalist politics that drove the society to the brink of self-destruction.

After the 1961 elections, in the aftermath of an intensively organized ethicized election campaign and with the promise of independence soon thereafter, the victory by Cheddi Jagan's Indian-based PPP posed a fundamental threat to the survival of Africans, Mixed Races, Europeans, Amerindians, Chinese, and Portuguese. The system of electoral politics enabled the victor in a zero-sum game of competition to assume complete control of the resources of the government. In the multilayered communal order established by the colonial power, an interdependent economy of specialized parts, each part dominated by one ethnic group, was institutionalized. No ethnic group could live without the other.

The impending ethnic catastrophe in Guyana following the 1961 elections was compounded by a second factor apart from the inter-communal conflict and the attendant fear of ethnic domination. Ideology assumed a salient role, for Dr. Jagan's PPP unabashedly espoused a Moscow-oriented socialist policy for the transformation of colonial Guyana (Jagan 1966). More specifically, Guyana under the avowed Marxist-Leninist Cheddi Jagan sought a new radical direction at the inopportune time that Cuba under Castro had become an acutely uncomfortable thorn in the side of the United States. After the Bay of Pigs fiasco, President Kennedy had firmly decided that there would not be another Cuba in the Western Hemisphere (Schlesinger 1965). Defiantly, Dr. Jagan had declared unreserved support for Fidel Castro calling him the greatest liberator of the twentieth century. Guyana was still a colony at the time. Hence, the PPP government posed a triple threat to various opponents, both internal and external. First, the Burnham-led PNC representing mainly the African section saw Jagan's PPP as a communal threat in the possibility of permanent ethnic domination. Second, the laissez-faire capitalist-oriented United Force (headed by Portuguese businessman Peter D'Aguiar), representing for the most part the well-off non-African non-Indian sections of the Guyana population, feared the PPP because of the communist threat to private property. Third, the Kennedy regime feared the PPP because of its threat to the geopolitical security interests of the United States in the Western Hemisphere in the context of Cold War politics (Sheehan 1967).

Seizure of Power and Ethnic Domination by the PNC

After the historic 1964 elections which witnessed the defeat of Jagan's PPP, the new coalition of Forbes Burnham and Peter D'Aguiar acceded to power. Subsequently, disenchantment between the UF and PNC grew to intense proportions destroying the coalition. About 6 months before the elections, party crossings in parliament, giving the PNC a majority, allowed the party to evict the UF from the coalition government. The PNC reconstituted the Electoral Commission, staffing it with its own sympathizers and changing the procedures of administering the elections. In the 1968 elections, in what would be established incontrovertibly as rigged elections, involving tens of thousands of fictitious votes, an astounded UF and PPP witnessed a PNC "victory" at the polls (Guyana 1984). We refer to the 1968 elections as "a seizure of power." By declaring Guyana a republic, Burnham thwarted legal challenges to the election results that would have led to adjudication by the Privy Council of England (Burnham 1970).

From mid-1968 onward, Burnham would preside over a minority government kept in office by repeated electoral fraudulence and a politicized and ethnically sanitized army and police. The "seizure of power" in 1968 was a watershed in ethnic relations in Guyana. In a multiethnic society, the PNC representing a minority African group (32%) grabbed the government. To avert internal disruption, the PNC government embarked on purging the critical pillars of its power – the coercive forces and the civil service – of most of its non-African elements. Where communal malcontents did not strike and demonstrate, many migrated to Europe and North America. Especially this became the case of the Europeans, Chinese, and Portuguese. The massive migration of this group from Guyana left a society predominantly polarized between Africans and Indians.

Toward the end of 1969, then, the PNC regime proclaimed a socialist framework for Guyana's reconstruction. In 1970, Guyana was declared a "cooperative republic." From private enterprise, the economy was to be founded on cooperatives as the main instrument of production, distribution, and consumption. But crises continued to bedevil the regime. The government ran a gauntlet besieged by high unemployment (30%), underemployment (36–40%), double-digit inflation, demonstrations, boycotts, strikes, and, later on as a result of the Arab-Israeli war, prohibitive fuel costs. A vicious cycle of poverty was created by a pattern of polarized and unstable ethnic politics intermixed with the salve of socialist rhetoric and programmatic justifications.

Between 1971 and 1976, the government nationalized nearly all foreign firms bringing 80% of the economy under state control (Thomas 1983). These public agencies were staffed overwhelmingly by the regime's communal supporters. The police, security, and armed forces, in particular, were expanded to protect the besieged PNC government (Hintzen and Premdas 1982). The judiciary also came under the PNC's regime's direct influence. The appointment of judges and magistrates was routinely based on party loyalty (Premdas 2017). The polarization of the two main ethnic races was probably attributable as much to ethnic chauvinism among PNC activists as to PPP boycotts and strikes against the government. The economic situation had deteriorated so badly that toward the end of the 1970s, the impact reverberated adversely on everyone alike, regardless of ethnic membership. Strikes and demonstrations and other challenges to Burnham's power increasingly came from all ethnic segments including Africans. The arsenal of coercive powers previously used against Indians was now used against African dissidents also. Among the victims of the purge was famed scholar Walter Rodney (Rodney 1980).

Since 1968 when the PNC first rigged the elections, and repeated fraudulence in 1975, 1980, and 1985, systematically cutting down all its opponents in the process, the ruling regime retained power from external Western support because of its anticommunist stand. In 1992, however, in, the wake of the disappearance of the Cold War, the United States and the West abandoned their support of anticommunist authoritarian regimes and actively embarked on sponsoring democratic governments based on free and fair elections and respect for individual human rights. It was this external factor above all else that led to the first free and fair elections, which were actively promoted by the Atlanta-based *Carter* Center, which had overseen similar elections in Nicaragua, Panama, Haiti, and Zambia. The repressive PNC government was thereby shorn of its Cold War shield of protection and compelled in a new international order of human rights and democracy to submit itself to the voice of the electorate.

In the watershed elections of 1992, Guyana witnessed the ousting of the People's National Congress (PNC) regime from power (Premdas 1993). Led by Dr. Cheddi Jagan, the old sell-styled Marxist-Leninist who in the Cold War setting of the 1960s was maneuvered out of power by covert US-British interference, the People's Progressive Party (PPP) was voted back to power in free and fair elections. Central to the October 5, 1992 elections was the electoral machine itself, the procedure by which political power is legitimized in democratic settings. The words "free," "fair," and "transparent" became the defining terms and the substantive feature of the elections. The elections were about the elections – its authenticity and its honesty.

After nearly three decades of exclusion, the PPP regained power in 1992 as well as in the successive elections of 1997 and 2001. In 1996, Cheddi Jagan died in office, and his wife, Janet Jagan, succeeded to the Presidency. During its new tenure, the PPP restored much health to the economy but failed in forming a government of national unity across the ethnic divide that separated Indians from Africans. The PPP had promised to form a government of national unity during its successful campaign to oust the PNC from power. It failed to follow through in sharing office not only with the African-based PNC but with a number of smaller multiethnic parties which were its electoral allies. In addition, the PPP dragged its feet in reforming the old "imperial constitution" against which it inveighed while it was out of power.

The neglect of the political aspects of power in the reconciliation of PPP and PNC followers came back to haunt it in the subsequent elections of 1997 and 2001. While the PPP had benefited from a demographic shift in favor of an Indian majority, the PNC faced a permanent minority condition in a society that was deeply polarized and in which ethnic identity determined voter preference. In the 1997 elections, the PPP won but the PNC was unwilling to accept defeat. Its supporters practically seized Georgetown, the capital city which was its stronghold, claiming that the elections were rigged. Independent recounts showed that the PNC supporters were wrong; the PNC did lose. But, what was at stake was not merely an arithmetic count of ballots but the fate of a communal section who felt that they were doomed to permanent domination under the governance of another community. The facts of the PPP term in office suggested that on balance, the PPP did not overly discriminate against Afro-Guyanese. The facts were irrelevant however with the PNC portraying the PPP regime as racist and communalist. Controlling Georgetown and the loyalty of the public service and the coercive forces which were predominantly staffed by Afro-Guyanese, the PNC was in a position to nullify in practice the election victory of the PPP through persistent demonstrations and riots. Accompanying the PNC intransigence was widespread communal violence reminiscent of the 1963–1964 period when similar strife wreaked havoc on the country's social fabric leaving deep scars and memories of hurt. The PNC riots and demonstrations came to an end in a political compromise which abbreviated the PPP's 5-year tenure by 2 years. Mrs. Jagan, the European widow of the deceased PPP leader Cheddi Jagan, hounded by the PNC, stepped down as President of Guyana ostensibly for reasons of health and was succeeded by an Indian, Bharrat Jagdeo. Meanwhile, as part of the PPP-PNC agreement, a new constitution was supposed to be negotiated incorporating elements of power sharing. New elections came again in 2001, and again in a familiar cycle of a PPP victory, the PNC argued that the elections were rigged and mounted protracted demonstrations and strikes that brought the government to a standstill leading eventually to a political compromise. The PPP under President Jagdeo remained in power but agreed to the establishment of a number of bipartisan committees which made policy recommendations on a wide variety of subjects expected to be implemented by the government. Even this very limited cooperation floundered with the PNC withdrawing from the committees as well as the national parliament threatening more street demonstrations. The stalemate was broken taking a turn for the better after the death of the Opposition PNC Leader, Desmond Hoyte and the accession of Robert Corbin as the new party leader in late 2002. Not only have the bipartisan committees been resurrected but also the Opposition PNM has returned to the parliament. Even an Ethnic Relations Commission has been established. While these arrangements manifested a tenor of power sharing, it has failed to make much of an impact on the ethnically divided population, deeply suspicious of each other, in reconciliation or healing.

The PPP would win the next elections again in 2011, but it would lose power in 2015 to a multiethnic coalition of parties called APNU led by the African-based PNC. An analysis of these election results showed that ethnic partisan pattern persisted. Dramatic events would intervene in 2016 with the discovery of huge oil deposits off the coast of Guyana in an event that would challenge the leaders of the ethnically based parties to overcome their primordial loyalties for a wider unity that transcends ethnic preference in voting and policy behavior. Fears abound that the old pattern of ethnically bipolar politics would prevail against all reasons.

Conclusion

Essential to the analysis of Guyana's communal strife is the creation of an "ethnic state," a concept that alludes to the descensus in the social demographic structure created by colonialism. The multiethnic state in Guyana, as in many parts of the Third World, was a colonial artifact. State and nation were not co-terminus entities; rather, the colonial state deliberately spawned an ethnically segmented social and cultural fabric. The role of the state in the creation of the underlying conditions of communal conflict is therefore critical to an understanding of Guyana's difficulties. In looking at the state, attention is focused not only the policies related to the formation of a multiethnic society but also on the political institutional apparatus through which state power is contested. Specifically, this refers to the competitive parliamentary system that was engrafted onto Guyana as part of the state apparatus and that engaged parties in zero-sum struggles for power. When Guyana obtained independence, the state apparatus that was bequeathed to the local rulers was the most highly articulated and developed set of institutions in the entire society. However, it was trammeled by an institutional political apparatus that tended to accentuate the ethnic segmentation in the society. A particular variant of the imported parliamentary system fashioned on the zero-sum electoral and party system in Britain played a major role in structuring and institutionalizing ethnic conflict and competition in the state. The rival parties, linked to discrete ethnic clusters, confronted each other in a manner similar to military warfare over fundamental issues on the form of the society, economy, and polity. The salient issue was that the mode of conflict resolution in collective decision-making that was adopted tended to encourage the formation of ethnic groupings which in turn competed for outright control of all the values of the state. Zero-sum parliamentary contests do not encourage sharing or fixed proportions. This meant that the stakes were high in the contest for political power and victory viewed as conquest. A system of pre-arranged results with guaranteed minimum rewards would have tended to depoliticize the intensity and stakes in the contests enabling the defeated a share in the polity and society (Lijphart 1977). This is particularly important in a setting where the constituent elements in the population are cultural communities which share few overarching traditions and institutions.

The logic of the communal society implanted in Guyana pointed to a future of inevitable sectional strife (Despres and Premdas 1996). Not only were many layers of fairly distinct communal divisions erected, but in the absence of equally strong rival overarching integrative institutions, the immigrant groups viewed each other from the perspective of their respective compartments with misinformed fear and much hostility. The colonial pie was small, most of it allocated to the governing European colonizer element occupying the top echelon of the color-class stratified system. Of the remaining jobs and other opportunities, the non-white segments fought among themselves for a share. African-Indian rivalry for the few scarce values of the colonial order would feature as a fundamental source of inter-communal conflict from the outset of the creation of the multi-tiered communal society. It would be sustained by a deliberate policy of divide and rule but would be mitigated by the urban-rural pattern of residence especially of Africans and Indians, respectively. What had evolved assuming the pretensions of a society was an order based on sustained and manipulated communal conflict without any prospect of overcoming these basic divisions in the foreseeable future. Institutionalized division and embedded conflict were the defining features of the system in perpetuity. Or so it seemed even at the end of the nineteenth century.

The Future Trajectory? Some Concluding Remarks

The trajectory of Guyana's pattern of ethnic politics will soon be challenged by the arrival of new wealth anticipated in 2020 when ExxonMobil will commence oil production. This is expected to provide unsurpassed revenues for Guyana and raises fundamental issues regarding the future of the country. It is important to explore what this could conceivably mean in this concluding section of the essay. With the sugar industry becoming unprofitable, petroleum will constitute the main pillar of Guyana's economy. Without a government of national unity that brings Indians and Africans together, chances are that the spoils of petroleum will become a curse stemming from the anticipated ethnic rivalry that will be enacted in the familiar pattern. Apart from the threat of a new oil-based ethnic conflict, Guyana faces a serious border problem with its militarily superior neighbor, Venezuela. Guyana's territorial boundaries are contested by Venezuela on the West claiming about 130,000 km^2 or 60% of the entire country and Suriname on the east claiming another significant segment, about 6,000 km^2. Guyana's oil-rich region which is about 50 miles off shore from its northern coast has now been claimed by Venezuela. In making the deal with ExxonMobil for the exploitation of the oil in contested territory, the United States has declared that it does not accept Venezuela's claims. In the absence of a credible Venezuelan threat, clearly, this implies that Guyana will have to manage its massive new revenues within the context of its pattern of ethnic competition.

The literature on oil and gas (and other resources) exploitation following major discoveries that has witnessed a pattern of boom and bust describes the experience as "a resource curse" (Acar 2017; Sachs et al. 2007). According to its chief proponents (Sachs and Warner 2001; Auty 2001), this adverse consequence is empirically based on patterns found between 1970 and 1990 in nearly all of 95 cases examined (except Malaysia and Mauritius). Apart from the argument that the sudden booms in wealth and revenues tend to lead to distortion in the development of the economy labelled the "Dutch disease," there are also negative social and political consequences that have a direct bearing on Guyana. Specifically, a distributive crisis may occur as partisan and factional conflicts arise when different interests compete for "a fair share" or control over the wealth. This distributive crisis is likely, in the case of Guyana to take on an ethnic form. Inequalities are also likely to become wider and insidious, both between sectors and individual workers' wages, where the rewards of workers in the boom sector are privileged, provoking unrest and organized discontent that may spillover into disorder and systemic instability. The wealth may also attract external bidders triggering another conflict as exemplified by the claims of Venezuela. Thus, conflicts both internal and external may eventuate destabilizing the country suddenly blessed with oil or mineral wealth. The resource curse argument points also to the creation of weak governments stemming from these conflicts, and further the additional wealth tends to create the conditions for corruption. In this vein, it is also argued that when domestic decision-makers discover that they are not accountable to the general population for the wealth, they in turn become unresponsive to popular will, and thus this undermines democracy and promotes authoritarianism.

The "resource curse" thesis is however hotly contested by other researchers who empirically examined a different set of countries like Chile, Botswana, Canada, Finland, the United States, and Sweden and came to the opposite conclusion (Maddison 1994; Maxwell 2001). They have argued that there was nothing inevitable about the decline of economic growth and the instigation of political conflict and instability when the economies of these oil/mineral-rich states are properly managed. In effect, part of the resource curse is traced to financial mismanagement and inappropriate economic planning and shortsighted strategy. Thus, in challenging the resource curse hypothesis, they point to other causes of decline in governance and rise of social and political tensions in those developing countries which have been blessed by sudden oil/mineral wealth. They suggest institutional and structural factors that account for the collapse and crisis following the boom. All of this points to the role of the ethnic bipolarity in Guyanese social structure as a likely institutional factor in determining the impact of the upcoming oil boom.

References

Acar S (2017) The curse of natural resources. Palgrave M, London
Auty R (2001) The Political Economy of Resource Abundant States. In: Auty R (ed) Resource Abundance and Economic Development. Oxford University Press. pp 126–144
Burnham LFS (1970) A destiny to mould. Longman Caribbean, London
Despres LA (1967) Cultural pluralism and nationalist politics in British Guiana. Rand McNally, Chicago
Despres L, Premdas R (1996) Ethnicity, the state and economic development. In: Premdas R (ed) Identity, ethnicity, and culture in the Caribbean. School of Continuing Studies, University of the West Indies, Trinidad
Fried M (1956) Some observations on the Chinese in British Guiana. Soc Econ Stud 9:57
Guyana: Fraudulent Revolution (1984) Latin American Bureau, London, pp 75–76
Guyana Ministry of Information (2012) National Census. Guyana Ministry of Information, Georgetown
Hintzen P, Premdas R (1982) Guyana: coercion and control in political change. J Inter-Am Stud World Affairs 24(3)
Jagan C (1966) The west on trial. Michael Joseph, London
Lijphart A (1977) Democracy in plural societies. Yale University Press, New Haven
Maddison A (1994) Explaining the economic performance of nations. In: Baumol W, Nelson R, Wolff E (eds) Convergence of productivity. Oxford, Oxford University Press.
Maxwell (2001) The political economy of resource abundant states. In: Auty AM (ed) Resource abundance and economic development, Oxford, Oxford University Press. pp 126–144
Morrison A (1998) Justice: the struggle for democracy in Guyana 1952–1992. Red Thread Women's Press, Georgetown
Nath D (1950) A history of Indians in British Guiana. Thomas Nelson, London, pp 179–180
Premdas R (1993) The 1992 critical elections in Guyana. Caribbean Affairs, 2:1 (pp.1–30)
Premdas R (1995) Ethnicity and development: the case of Guyana. Avebury Press, Ashgate
Premdas R (1996) Race and ethnic relations in Burnhamite Guyana. In: Dabydeen D, Samaroo B (eds) Across the dark waters: ethnicity and Indian identity in the Caribbean. Macmillan, London
Premdas R (2017) The Fascistization of the state under Burnham. CLR James J 22(12):243–254
Sachs JD, Warner AM (2001) Natural resource and economic development: the curse of natural resources. Eur Econ Rev 45:827–839
Sachs J, Humphries M, Stiglitz (2007) Escaping the resource curse. Columbia University Press, New York
Saunders A (1987) The powerless people. Macmillan Caribbean, London
Schlesinger AJ (1965) A thousand days. Houghton Mifflin Co, Boston
Sheehan N (1967) C.I.A. men aided strikes in Guiana against Dr. Jagan. New York Times, February 22
Smith RT (1962) British Guiana. Oxford University Press, London
Spinner T Jr (1984) A political and social history of Guyana, 1945–1983. Westview Press, Boulder
The Rodney Affair: Assassination or Accident? (1980) 5:4, p 5. Caribbean Contact, June
Thomas C (1983) State capitalism in Guyana. In: Ambursley F, Cohen R (eds) Crisis in the Caribbean. Monthly Review Press, New York
Williams BF (1991) Stains on my name, war in my veins: Guyana and the politics of struggle. Duke University Press, Durham